P9-EKC-814

Social Work Diagnosis in Contemporary Practice

SOCIAL WORK DIAGNOSIS IN CONTEMPORARY PRACTICE

Edited by

Francis J. Turner

New York   Oxford
OXFORD UNIVERSITY PRESS
2005

OXFORD
UNIVERSITY PRESS

Oxford University Press, Inc., publishes works that further
Oxford University's objective of excellence
in research, scholarship, and education.

Oxford   New York
Auckland   Cape Town   Dar es Salaam   Hong Kong   Karachi
Kuala Lumpur   Madrid   Melbourne   Mexico City   Nairobi
New Delhi   Shanghai   Taipei   Toronto

With offices in
Argentina   Austria   Brazil   Chile   Czech Republic   France   Greece
Guatemala   Hungary   Italy   Japan   Poland   Portugal   Singapore
South Korea   Switzerland   Thailand   Turkey   Ukraine   Vietnam

Copyright © 2005 by Oxford University Press, Inc.

Published by Oxford University Press, Inc.
198 Madison Avenue, New York, New York 10016
www.oup.com

Oxford is a registered trademark of Oxford University Press

All rights reserved. No part of this publication may be reproduced,
stored in a retrieval system, or transmitted, in any form or by any means,
electronic, mechanical, photocopying, recording, or otherwise,
without the prior permission of Oxford University Press.

Library of Congress Cataloging-in-Publication Data
Social work diagnosis in contemporary practice / edited by Francis J. Turner
      p.   cm.
   Includes bibliographical references and index.
   ISBN-13   978-0-19-516878-5
   ISBN 0-19-516878-X
   1. Social service.   2. Social case work.   3. Counselor and client.   4. Psychiatric social
 work   5. Medical social work.   I. Turner, Francis J. (Francis Joseph)

HV40.S6178   2005
361.3'2—dc22   2004061706

9 8 7 6 5 4 3 2 1
Printed in the United States of America
on acid free paper

To Mary (June 20, 1925–June 5, 2001)

Sister, religious, teacher, scholar, and advocate for social justice.

Beatae pacifici.

Foreword

For those reading the work of Francis J. Turner for the first time, the title *Social Work Diagnosis in Contemporary Practice* may be intriguing. Isn't juxtaposition of the words "diagnosis" and "contemporary" an oxymoron, given the preference of many social workers in the twenty-first century for the word "assessment" to denote the practice behavior of gathering and interpreting information we need to be helpful to clients?

At the beginning of his introduction, Dr. Turner addresses this question by explaining what he means by the term "diagnosis"—not a labeling of problems, not a search for pathology, and not skill in using the *DSM* (*Diagnostic and Statistical Manual of Mental Disorders*), but rather a "conscious and concise statement of the spectrum of judgments we make . . . that serve as the basis on which we decide to engage or not engage in particular activities with the client." The book's premise is that to offer the best possible help to clients, making informed judgments about the specific strengths and problems inherent in each situation is critical. Judgment—forming ideas about the nature of the client's needs and practitioner responses most likely to help meet those needs—must be distinguished from being judgmental, a cognitive and emotional evaluation of goodness versus badness. Good judgment is always tempered by humility and uncertainty, in contrast to the arrogance of certainty inherent in judgmentalism.

Once we have arrived at a reasoned judgment of strengths and problems, we still must access knowledge about interventions that can utilize the strengths we have identified to address the problems that bring the client to services. Only when we have done our own "homework" can we engage in a collaborative process with the client, guided by the client's preferences and based on the expectation that together we will search for solutions drawing on the client's expertise in conjunction with our own expertise.

Dr. Turner notes that practitioners today are faced with major challenges in arriving at accurate judgments. Informed judgment requires accountability to a knowledge base that has become daunting in its size and scope. In order to use current knowledge to help the real people whom we're committed to serve, at least three practice activities are needed. These activities must be contemporaneous, not serial, because information gained from each enhances the information from the others.

First, we need to identify strengths and problems in the client's situation. We begin by drawing on our own experience and practice wisdom to do this. A second activity, searching electronic databases using keywords relevant to particular client situations, gives us access to research-based knowledge. This information can illuminate the first activity (identifying strengths and problems) by deepening our knowledge about aspects of individual client characteristics and the environmental factors impacting them—that is, in Dr. Turner's words, it can enhance diagnostic acuity. It can inform us about the likelihood of effectiveness of a range of interventions to enhance those strengths and diminish those problems. Database searching is necessary to go beyond random reading of literature (where typically we find one or two relevant writings), because it allows systematic review of a large number of current sources. If we limit ourselves to spotting relevant articles in a haphazard fashion, we are likely to miss really important material.

The third activity involves scanning published material to familiarize ourselves with the many choices the field offers as possible avenues of client help. For this activity, books like the present volume are invaluable—entries in scientific databases cannot encompass anything so broad and diverse as the material in this book.

Dr. Turner's volume enhances database searches by giving us ideas about possible avenues to pursue. He has combed current literature, a task too vast for most busy practitioners; culled articles representing a broad spectrum of subject areas and practice philosophies and approaches; and then made these writings available in a one-stop source. A major strength of *Social Work Diagnosis in Contemporary Practice*, in my opinion, is that it allows us to survey the terrain of social work practice and appreciate the enormity of our profession's contributions to the quality of life of our service consumers.

Dr. Turner has chosen and compiled 80 articles from a pool of 2,500 listed in Social Work Abstracts since the beginning of the new millennium. These articles, taken as a whole, introduce us to contemporary practice issues inherent in many different fields of practice (such as mental health, child welfare, gerontology, substance abuse, and domestic violence), phases of life (infancy and childhood, adolescence, early and late adulthood), diversity (race, ethnicity, gender, sexual orientation, ability), and practice philosophies and approaches that engage social work practice today (such as ecological, empirical, neurobiological, cognitive-behavioral, psychodynamic, and postmodern).

The range of perspectives in this book is so great that it's unlikely any reader will agree with all the points of view represented in the articles. Practitioners with psychodynamic or postmodern perspectives will probably prefer a different set of readings from those who espouse empirical and cognitive-behavioral approaches. This range of ideologies and related practice strategies characterizes the field of social work today. The book intends to offer, and I believe succeeds in offering, a smorgasbord of rich and varied fare to be sampled or devoured, depending on the reader's appetite.

A second important contribution is the inclusion of articles reporting innovative approaches—strategies and interventions that have recently been implemented but don't form part of the typical repertoire of social work interventions. Examples in this anthology are plentiful. Derezotes (chapter 78) reports a training program in yoga and meditation with 14 adolescent male sex abusers. The boys expressed positive feelings about the program, enjoyed the relaxed feeling they had after classes, felt they had gained a sense of mastery and control over urges to abuse, and reported using yoga techniques on their own. Noble, Perkins, and Fatout (chapter 77) report the application of a model from athletics training, called strengths coaching, to work with families in the child welfare system. Racine and Sévigny (chapter 61) describe the use of a board game as a vehicle for participant narratives among women in a homeless shelter. Northcut (chapter 57) describes how she integrates spirituality into psychodynamic counseling. Ebenstein and Wortham (chapter 73) review the many benefits of pet companionship to elderly clients and show us ways that the pet-owner bond can be sustained. Gordon (chapter 76) explains how interactive videodisk technology has been used to disseminate a behaviorally oriented family-based substance abuse prevention program via a three-hour CD-ROM.

I found these and other offerings from Dr. Turner's book engrossing to read and also highly instructive. I commend it to social work practitioners, scholars, and students as an important source of ideas and as a panorama of rich social work practice today.

Harriette C. Johnson, MSW, Ph.D.
Professor, University of Connecticut
School of Social Work
West Hartford, Connecticut
August 9, 2004

Preface

Snoopy, my long-time hero in the late Charles Shultz's comic strip *Peanuts*, always opened each of his new books with the words "It was a dark and stormy night." Somehow this does not seem appropriate for a book focusing on social work practice. Hence, we will begin with another, less prosaic dictum, one that has been reflected in my teaching, writing, and practice over the decades. It is that "the essence of effective and accountable practice is diagnosis."

Let me pause here immediately and examine for a moment what I mean by diagnosis in general and social work diagnosis in particular. This is best done by focusing first on what is not meant by diagnosis, regardless of the profession to which we are referring. It is not the labeling of problems, it is not a search for pathology, it is not the assigning of labels, it is clearly not a one-time-only process, although all of these processes may be a part of the diagnostic activity. From the perspective of social work it is not skill in the use of *DSM* in whatever of its editions is current. Rather, a social work diagnosis is a conscious and concise statement of the spectrum of judgments we make on first meeting a client and expand and modify throughout our contact with him or her. These judgments serve as the basis on which we decide to engage or not engage in particular activities with the client, activities for which we are prepared to accept professional responsibility.

This perception of diagnosis is neither an emphasis on the client's strengths only, nor is it a focus on problem areas only, but a balance of the two. Clearly, we need to make judgments of a client's strengths and resources. But of equal importance, we need to assess and come to conclusions about any limitations or problems in the clients' biopsychosocial profile that may be relevant to the situation at hand and that may influence what actions I take or not take with them and for them.

For a variety of reasons, social workers have not liked the word *judgment* and have tended to avoid it. It seems to sound too much like the word *judgmental*, one that everyone, from a first-year student onward, knows is a word and concept that is to be eschewed. But just as adamantly as we stress the avoidance of being judgmental, we state and emphasize in our teaching and practice that we must be accountable. Thus we must build our practice on the ever-expanding body of knowledge and skills that has emerged as we now move into our third century of existence. To be accountable we must make decisions about our clients, decisions that move, develop, clarify, and change through the life of a case. And decisions about who is the client are based on the judgments we have made and continue to make about him or her and the situation.

As we begin this process of decision making about our clients, a process that starts in the very first instances in which we are in contact, we are attempting to come to a series of conclusions about the presenting person's situation as quickly as possible. We are asking ourselves and attempting to answer Who is this person? What does this person want and need? What can I, or others, responsibly do with and for this person? What can this person do for himself or herself? As we seek to answer this cluster of questions we base our judgment-making process on a triad of further questions: How is this client like all human persons I have met? How is this client like some other persons I have met? And how is this person like no other person I have met?

In answering these questions as responsible practitioners we of course draw on the body of knowledge acquired in our training and career and, as far as possible, on the broader body of knowledge acquired and developed by the profession to which we have access. I am aware that in a profession such as ours, which encompasses the vast spectrum of the human condition and societal realities, it is impossible to know all there is to know about all of the situations with which we are faced.

Yet we must act, frequently with a level of uncertainty. Hence, one of our most important ethical responsibilities in today's professional world is to develop a process whereby we can have at least some way of keeping in touch with current thinking in the areas of practice for which we are held responsible by society.

Of course, one of the exciting realities of today's world is not a lack of relevant material for a particular area of practice. This might have been so in earlier times. Rather, our current challenge is how to access material in this age of information overload. It has been exciting for me as a teacher to watch the development of printed material in our field now available to practitioners. When I first started to teach in the mid-1960s, there were some forty social work journals in existence; there are now at least two hundred such journals. The same is true of the expansion of textbooks. A glance at our daily mail or a half hour spent at the book display section of one of our conferences quickly reminds us of the dramatic expansion of new books in the field. As well, the resources of technology and the ever-present Web are a daily reminder of the expansion of our knowledge base.

The challenge for the busy practitioner, then, is not wondering if knowledge exists but how to tap into this wealth of new material in a way that is opportune. Hence the rationale for a volume such as this, which seeks to accomplish what the busy practitioner cannot. Its goal is to comb the extant contemporary literature and organize a selection of articles that are deemed to be of use for colleagues wishing to access a broad spectrum of today's practice wisdom to enhance their diagnostic acuity. That is, it seeks to present to students and practitioners a spectrum of contemporary practice-based articles from the wealth of current literature in a format that aims at assisting in the ongoing enhancement of our diagnostic skills. It does so by focusing on the second question of our diagnostic triad: How is this client like some other clients we meet in practice?

One of the skills we bring to our practice is the knowledge we have of the human condition in its many facets. This helps us to understand in an empathic and facilitating way new situations with which we are faced and quickly to engage in a process that can be helpful. We do this by drawing on our acquired knowledge from the past of similar situations. As well, we draw from the accumulated wisdom of our colleagues who have dealt with similar situations and who have shared this wisdom with us through the discipline of the refereed journals and texts to which we have access. But we need always

to remember that as we draw on the knowledge of others about a particular facet of the human condition to help us understand this client we need to keep very much in mind the third question of our triad; how is this client different? This, of course, is the way we can draw on the tremendous power of classifications yet in a manner that keeps us from falling into the traps of inflexible "labeling."

To this end, we used as our base the hundred-plus journals abstracted in *Social Work Abstracts* and searched for articles we judged to be of particular use for practitioners to give them up-to-date viewpoints and information about specific aspects of practice. This entailed the review of some 2,500 articles. These articles were selected under four headings that comprise critical components of the diagnostic profile of judgments. Thus, we looked for (1) articles that address aspects of the developmental stages in our existential journey through life; (2) articles that deal with diversity in its many forms, a topic so critical to current practice; (3) articles that targeted a range of problems met in practice and (4) articles that address various developments in technique and strategies of intervention. I comment further on the rationale for these four areas in the introduction to each section.

Unlike earlier works of a similar nature, in this instance I have focused solely on the prior three years of publications. I did this for two reasons: I wanted to mark this historic moment in our profession where we have moved into a new millennium as one of the major players in the group of the human service professions; I wanted to demonstrate just how rapidly our body of knowledge is developing. In earlier similar books, to get an adequate profile of articles in particular areas of practice it was necessary to go back thirty or forty years. In this instance the problem was not locating suitable articles for each section; rather, it was the reverse. Toward the goal of keeping to a manageable size for a volume such as this, my challenge was reducing the selections from about four hundred that had survived the first cut to the necessary amount.

This proved to be one of the most satisfying, albeit difficult processes in which I have been involved as an editor. Satisfying because it demonstrated clearly the extent to which our body of knowledge has developed and expanded to create the present richness of our accumulated wisdom and tested data. This richness enables us to more effectively respond to the psychosocial realties of "person in situation." Challenging, in that I was amazed at the range and quality of the literature in these past three years. In fact, it would have been possible to prepare volumes that dealt with each of the four areas separately. Perhaps that is a topic for another day. In this instance I wanted to present these four aspects of the diagnostic and interventive process as a group because in my perception, they better present the interventive process in a holistic way, which separate collections would not.

There was one final challenge following the selection of the articles, and that was how to order them. The initial section, of ages and stages, was relatively easy. However, the other three presented a much greater challenge that I have not fully an-

swered. This is especially true for the section on problems, as the range and type of problems met in practice is wide and rich. I will continue to ponder this issue for future ventures but for the present go ahead with this collection and the order in which it is presented in the hopes that it will assist the reader to bring more precision and effectiveness to practice based on the accumulated wisdom of our colleagues and the requisite skill in social work diagnosis.

Toronto, December 2003

Acknowledgments

In completing this work I am, as always, conscious of the many persons who contributed to it, both directly and indirectly. I am most appreciative of the work of two social work doctoral students at the University of Toronto, Susan Preston and Michael Woodford, who assisted greatly in the prodigious search of all the journals. As well, I want to thank my research assistant, Carlos Pereira, for keeping the process on track and in a most efficient manner. Working with Oxford University Press was a delight, and I am grateful for the initial inspiration of Joan Bossert.

The cooperation of the various publishers of the selected articles was most helpful and essential to the book. Two distinct groups of authors were essential to the process. The first, of course, were those colleagues who wrote the articles that were finally selected. They are indeed the essence of the finished project. However, I need also mention the authors of the many articles that were not selected. These colleagues contributed to this project as well as they assisted in the process of selection and aided greatly in helping me clarify my thinking about the parameters I developed that led to the final selec-tion. The process of selection was difficult, and frequently I had seven or eight excellent articles covering the same topic.

Last I am particularly appreciative of the interest and support of Joanne.

A Postscript

Just today I finished the proofreading of this volume's manuscript. One of the final articles was written by Dr. Herb Strean, a long-time friend and colleague. Just a few weeks ago I learned of his recent death and want to here acknowledge this and his special contributions to our profession's literature.

Throughout his career he was without doubt the most prodigious writer in our field; writings that will endure as major contributions to the clinical literature. Over the years he and I collaborated on several projects and I am honored that his article in this collection will stand as one of his last, among many, important contributions to social work.

Contents

PART II: THE PROBLEM AS A COMPONENT OF DIAGNOSIS

A. Problems with a Mental Illness Basis

B. Problems of a Psychosocial Nature

PART III: ELEMENTS OF DIVERSITY TO BE ADDRESSED IN OUR DIAGNOSIS

A. Specific Components of Diversity

Social Work Diagnosis in Contemporary Practice

PART I

WHO IS THE CLIENT FROM A DEVELOPMENTAL PERSPECTIVE?

Diagnosis has always been an essential component of responsible social work practice. However, the term itself, not the process, has suffered considerably by being allotted a series of pejorative mismeanings, which then was thought to justify its rejection. Whatever it was called, the need to understand who the client is so that we may respond effectively and accountably in his or her and our conjoint quest for enhanced psychosocial being has remained constant.

A critical facet of this understanding has always been based on the awareness that persons do not come into this world as fully developed and functioning human beings. Rather, each of us develops and matures through a series of ages and stages, by which and through which we achieve our full flowering and potential as a human being. Over the centuries, through the long process of the development of human thought, considerable attention has been given by all manner of disciplines to the process of human development, to the identification of patterns of commonality and difference, to factors that influences either positively or negatively the process of development, and to ways to enhance the human potential in a predictable way.

Social work, too, began with this assumption, which held that to intervene responsibly in the human condition one needed to understand who the person is and where he or she is on the road to development. Hence, curricula of all schools of social work in all parts of the world contain some component of study that focuses on this effort to identify, classify, and understand the stages of human development. But encompassed in this commitment lies considerable diversity of content as knowledge expands, as various theories of personality, psychology, pedagogy, and indeed ideology take and lose precedence in and among the family of human professions.

If there has been any pattern to the development of this critical component of diagnosis in social work it appears to fall into three developmental stages of its own. In the beginning, our body of knowledge of this area of practice was predominantly intrapsychic in nature. This was probably due to the extremely strong influence of the emerging theories of personality, especially those with a psychodynamic base. This stage was closely followed by a period when the influence of social and environmental factors was beginning to be given proper attention. Out of this development emerged the term *psychosocial*. Once viewed as a descriptor of a unique approach to practice in social work, this term then became a generic descriptor of all social work practice and has now become a pan-professional concept used by a coterie of professions. In very quick succession, as all professions have become much more holistic in their purviews, the descriptor *biopsychosocial* became the term that best generalizes social work's base in seeking to understand the process of human development.

But this in no way suggests that a degree of conceptual consensus exists in the profession. Rather, as our knowledge expands, so too does the diversity that accompanies it, a diversity decried by many who seek the apparent certitudes that doctrine brings, but applauded by most, who understand that this is the reality in which we practice. This especially as we become more responsive to this diversity among the human family.

The articles selected for this section of the book reflect this diversity and reflect as well a comfort in the aforementioned spinoff of complexity. It is clear that we moved far beyond an era when we viewed each segment of the human life journey as a distinct unidimensional process. More and more, as the critical and differential impact of diverse societal systems on us all is appreciated, we are aware that from the very moment of existence, indeed even prior to birth, each of us develops in a unique manner, and that to understand oneself and others we must understand this uniqueness. Some question whether this uniqueness is so vast that there is no point in attempting to generalize this process into a body of knowledge. What is exciting in this quest for human knowledge is that there are clear and distinct patterns to this diversity. Even though there are more and more factors that influence our development than we have previously considered, there are patterns within each factor. Hence, if we enhance our understanding of each factor in general, we enhance our understanding of each factor in this particular human being with whom I am interacting professionally and whom I am seeking to understand.

In our professional writing on life stages, we have focused on the more specific aspects of the human journey, some that apply to all of us and others that apply only to some. In seeking to examine and understand each aspect of the developmental journey, we learn about that facet of life that applies to some persons we will meet in practice. But, in an even more important way, we learn about other aspects of life as well and other situations, as we now have new searchlights to bring to bear on new phenomena.

Earlier descriptions of a comprehensive social security system referred to "womb-to-tomb" coverage. As the selected articles for this section manifest, we are using this concept in our professional writing in a much richer way than in an earlier day. We are much more aware of prenatal factors that effect our later development and understand that these are indeed biopsychosocial in nature. At the other end of the life spectrum, we find a much greater comfort in talking about the joys and challenges of old age, including death, a topic rarely considered in earlier literature. We are also much more comfortable viewing other life aspects as parts of developmental history. For example, it is important that we are beginning to view adoption and foster care as a critical variable in the developmental history of many of our clients and to see

these phenomena as distinct phases with commonalities that help us understand individual situations.

As well, we are increasingly able to view homosexuality as an important component of life for many of our clients, a reality that, when fully understood, aids us in the understanding of all of us. Another area where we have enriched our ages and stage knowledge relates to a richer appreciation of the roles of both mothers and fathers and expanding this knowledge far beyond our earlier psychodynamic position to the complex societal, systemic, overlapping, interchangeable roles of both parents.

These recent developmental stage articles further reflect two additional developmental facets of our current professional writing: not all of them are written by social workers, and most of them have an overt or implied research base. The first facet reflects our own developmental step. We seem clearly to have moved beyond deeming articles written by social workers as having less value than those written by someone outside the profession. We then moved to a point where, if an article was not written by a social worker, it was to be ignored. This from a perspective that we needed to stand on our own two feet. In our new stage of maturity, we seem be comfortable seeking knowledge wherever it is to be found: the utility of an article for theory and practice is to be the measuring stick, rather than an author's professional credentials.

The matter of a much greater research base is also to be signaled. In an earlier day, much of our developmental literature was written from practice wisdom or practice authority bases rather than from the analysis of data. This latter development of a richer research commitment increased the possibility of further questions being asked from data and speculating on alternative explanations and conclusions, as befits all dissemination of knowledge.

Another aspect of this selection of ages and stages articles related to the ongoing maturation of our professional writing is that the articles selected for this section presume two things. The first is the reader's rich body of knowledge: these materials are written from the perspective that the reader is very knowledgeable about the general aspects of whatever stage or facet of development is being discussed and so focus on some specific aspect of it. The other presumption is that stages of human development are growth stages, not problem stages. Much of our earlier human growth and development material was written from an at least implied "problem perspective"; that is, the age itself was a problem-laden one which had to be endured to move on in the maturation odyssey. But one never got there, for the final years, instead of being the full flowering of our maturation were viewed as being so problem-laden that we rarely wrote or talked about them. Indeed, just living seemed to be viewed as a problem. Fortunately, we have moved beyond this and now are focusing much more on seeking to understand the strengths, potentials, and satisfactions of each of life's milestones in order to develop rich views of our clients' potentials, strengths, and resources.

Knowing and seeking to know where each of our clients is along his or her life's journey is a critical part of our diagnostic process. It is not a seeking for problem areas, although of course these are not to be overlooked and need to be understood. Rather, it is a process whereby we seek with the client to understand who and where the client is along the developmental odyssey to help provide a base of strengths and limitations for the establishment of the therapeutic alliance.

SANDRA J. WEISS
MARY ST. JONN SEED

1

Precursors of Mental Health Problems for Low Birth Weight Children: The Salience of Family Environment during the First Year of Life

Substantial numbers of low birth weight (LBW) children are being diagnosed with moderate to severe emotional and behavior problems,[1-3] which in turn are forecasting later mental disorders.[4-7] But there are conflicting views regarding the source of these problems, fueled by the traditional nature versus nurture controversy. Many clinicians are convinced that the biological limitations posed by low birth weight have a strong negative impact on early interactive capacity as well as overall intellectual and social competence during the first year of life. All of these infant characteristics are thought to influence the development of behavioral and emotional problems for the child. Other clinicians speak to the importance of the child's environment as a central foundation for the LBW child's later emotional and behavioral well-being. However, little research exists to substantiate either perspective. A few studies have addressed risk factors for mental health problems of LBW children but much of what is hypothesized has been borrowed from studies of infants who were born with normative weight. The purpose of this study was to build upon extant literature regarding potentially important risk factors and to determine their contributions to the emotional and behavioral problems of LBW children at age 2.

Infant Characteristics

Evidence does suggest that certain characteristics of the infant may be related to a greater likelihood of emotional-behavioral problems. The degree of perinatal morbidity is one important factor. The cumulative effect of many neonatal medical problems appears to play a role.[8,9] In particular, extremely immature infants born after only 23–26 weeks gestation have a higher incidence of behavioral disorders that are associated with neurological abnormalities and other medical problems.[10-12] Infants with more medical problems also have longer hospitalizations, which may compromise their later behavior.

Smaller birth weight itself has been linked to problem development.[13-15] There are also data pointing to the infant's early interactive capacity as a predictor of later problems.[16] An infant's capacity for responsiveness to parents seems particularly important because it contributes to parent attitudes and interactions that may affect infants' perceptions of self and others as they mature.[17]

An infant's emerging social skills have also been implicated in later mental health problems. They have been associated with conduct disorders,[18] attention deficit hyperactivity disorder,[19] as well as both aggression and withdrawal in peer relationships.[20] Communication difficulties and trouble socializing have been identified as social antecedents of special importance to the development of emotional and behavioral disorders.[21,22] Last, cognitive ability (especially early language competence) has been related to behavioral outcomes for children, including those of low birth weight.[23-27]

Family Environment

Previous research also supports the view that factors in the family environment have a potential relationship to child mental health. These factors cluster into two major domains: variables specific to the maternal caregiving environment, and others related to the immediate context surrounding caregiving.

The Maternal Caregiving Environment

A mother's own mental health status appears to have significant implications for her child's development of problems. Maternal depression has received the most study, with results indicating that it is one of the greatest risk factors for emotional and behavioral problems among preschool children[28–30] as well as in later childhood.[26,31,32] Much of the impact of maternal psychopathology appears to be its ongoing effect on the quality of the mother-infant interaction.[33] Studies find mothers with mental health problems to be less responsive, more disengaged, more negative, harsh, and angry toward the child, less affectionate, and to provide less overall stimulation.[34–39]

Regardless of the mother's mental health status, the quality of her caregiving has been associated with child mental health problems. Children with emotional and behavioral problems have been found to receive less maternal sensitivity, responsiveness, and support as well as more negativity.[40,41] Maternal hostility and rejection of the child seem particularly important, with strong relationships of criticism and harsh discipline to both internalizing and externalizing disorders.[42–46]

The attachment relationship is a central component of this caregiving environment. But there have been contradictory findings regarding the role of attachment as a precursor to later mental health or psychopathology. Some studies have found no clear association between attachment and later behavior problems.[47,48] However, a substantial body of research has found strong relationships between early insecure attachment and the development of later problems, both internalizing and externalizing disorders.[26,49–51]

The Context of Caregiving

A number of contextual variables within the family may play a role as risk or protective factors for child mental health. The functioning of the family unit is especially noteworthy, specifically the quality of the interactions among members of the family, including hostility, cohesion, supportiveness, and flexibility. Family climate during the infant's first years of life has been associated with the probability of psychiatric symptoms for children when they are 2 to 3 1/2 years of age.[52,53] The specific quality of the relationship between the child's parents during year one has been found to predict the frequency and impact of preschool behavior problems for preterm, LBW children.[54,55] When the quality of the mother-infant relationship places the child at risk, the overall cohesiveness and adaptability of the family can be a critical factor in protection of children from development of mental health problems.[37]

A closely related variable is the presence of the child's father in the home. Father co-residence has been among the strongest predictors of child outcomes.[56] Studies suggest that mothers who live with a partner provide better caregiving environments for their children. Irrespective of the quality of the father's involvement, these mothers appear to be more emotionally and verbally responsive, use more positive parenting practices (including less punishment), and provide more learning opportunities for the child.[57–59] Similarly, infants with fathers in the home smile, vocalize, and explore more readily.[60] Even the presence of a nonpaternal father figure has been associated with fewer child behavior problems.[61] Studies show consistent findings for older children as well, with boys in single-mother families being at especially great risk for development of problems.[62] Research specific to preterm LBW children has identified the father's presence as a major predictor of children's school outcomes at age 10.[63] This finding was particularly significant in light of the fact that these researchers also examined the effects of many medical variables which had almost no impact on outcome.

A third important contextual factor is the adequacy of the family's income. Lower socioeconomic status has been associated with greater risk of preschool behavior problems.[54,64] This same relationship has been noted at later ages as well, with poverty linked especially to more depression and anxiety in children.[33,65–67] The psychological distress from factors such as financial insecurity, lack of employment, and the cumulation of negative life events appears to severely tax the parents' emotional resources and their ability to cope when interacting with the infant.[68,69] Perhaps as a result of these constraints, poorer mothers have been found to have less optimal parenting behavior.[50,70]

Research Aims

The purpose of this study was to determine the degree to which infant characteristics and family environment during the first year of life contribute to the development of emotional and behavioral problems for LBW children at age 2. We examined five infant characteristics: birth weight, perinatal medical complications, interactive capacity, cognitive ability, and social competence. Four aspects of the maternal caregiving environment were assessed: a mother's mental health, the quality of her caregiving skills, her rejection of the child, and the attachment of infant to mother. Lastly, we examined three features of the family context: family functioning in terms of cohesion and adaptability, the presence of the child's father in the home, and the adequacy of the family's income.

Methods

Sample

The sample included 110 infants and their mothers who were recruited into the study during the infant's first two weeks of life and followed through their second birthday. Criteria for inclusion were infant weight below 2500 grams at birth, residence in the state, and the ability to read and speak either English or Spanish. We did not exclude infants on the basis of medical risk so that our sample would not be biased toward healthy subjects. However, if infants had not been discharged from the hospital by 3 months of corrected age (the point at which we made our first home visit), the family was not included in our final sample.

This convenience sample was ethnically diverse, including 46% Caucasian, 28% Hispanic, 19% African American, and 7% Asian or Native American babies. Forty-three percent of the babies were girls and 57% were boys. Their weight ranged from 650 grams to 2500 grams, with a mean birth weight of 1739 grams (SD = 522). Infants had a mean gestational age of 32 weeks. Their most typical medical problems as neonates were respiratory distress (experienced by 80% of the sample) and hyperbilirubinemia (75%). Sixty-six percent of the babies required mechanical ventilation during their first few weeks of life and 22% required surgery. Twenty-one percent were known to have been drug-exposed in utero.

Mothers had a mean age of 29 years (SD = 7), ranging from 16 to 44. They averaged 12.5 years of education (SD[=4), with a spread from 1 to 20

years. The infant's father was present in 83% of the families. Family income ranged from $7–10,000 per year to above $150,000 per year. Forty-five percent of the families were living below the poverty level. Sixty-one percent of the mothers were employed at least part time and 29% were the sole support for their family.

Procedures

All procedures were approved by the University Human Research Committee as well as the review boards of all participating hospitals. Families were recruited from the neonatal intensive care units of three major teaching hospitals. Once an informed consent was acquired, the mother was given a demographic questionnaire regarding both herself and her baby to complete. At this time, a research assistant did an initial mental health assessment of the mother, using the Global Assessment of Functioning from the *Diagnostic and Statistical Manual of Mental Disorders*. This same assessment occurred at each of three subsequent home visits during the infant's first year of life. Medical records were reviewed by a clinical specialist for birth weight and data related to complications surrounding the birth and during the neonatal period. These data were used to complete the Perinatal Complications Scale. The first home visit took place when the infant was 3 months old. Mother and infant were videotaped during an infant feeding. The mother-infant interaction on this videotape was analyzed at a later time using the Nursing Child Assessment Feeding Scales. Mothers also completed the Family Adaptability and Cohesion Scales. When the infant was 6 months old, the mother completed the Parental Acceptance and Rejection Questionnaire at a second visit. At the third, one-year home visit, the demographic questionnaire was again completed by the mother and the infant's security of attachment was ascertained with the Attachment Q-Set. In addition, a clinic visit was set up for the mother and child around this same time. This visit involved cognitive tests of the infant employing the Mullen Scales of Early Learning and a measure of infant social adaptation, the Vineland Adaptive Behavior Scales. When the infant was 2 years of age, a final home visit occurred to have the mother complete Achenbach's Child Behavior Checklist/2–3, a measure of emotional and behavioral problems.

Measures

Demographic Questionnaire The demographic questionnaire was completed by each mother when the child was born and again at 1 and 2 years of infant age to assure stability of the data. Both the presence of the father in the home and the adequacy of the family income were determined via this questionnaire. The item regarding presence of the father was a yes or no response to whether he lived in the home. Adequacy of income was measured by a score combining three items on the questionnaire. The first item asked the degree to which the family's income was enough to cover the family's needs. This item was a five-point scale including (5) not enough, (4) barely enough, (3) adequate but no extra to spend, (2) adequate with some extra to spend, and (1) more than adequate. The second and third items acquired a yes or no response as to whether the family (1) had an income below the poverty level (ranging from $12 to $16,000 per year) and (2) was homeless. The sum score for these three items was used as the final score for adequacy of income. It had a possible 7 points, with higher scores reflecting inadequate, poverty-level income. We specifically chose this approach to examining income because the actual amount of family income is somewhat meaningless in light of the number of independents in the household and other economic demands. Considering such variability, it seemed best to trust the family's judgment regarding adequacy of their funds. We did, however, identify a significant relationship between actual income level and perceived adequacy of income ($r = .74$, $p < .000$). In addition, families who were making less than $16,000 per year scored significantly lower on their adequacy of income ($M = 3.9$ or barely enough) than did families who were above the poverty threshold ($M = 2.3$, adequate with some extra to spend [$t = 9.67$, df = 108, $p < .000$]). The demographic questionnaire also provided other information about the families for descriptive purposes.

Perinatal Complications Scale   Degree of perinatal morbidity was determined by the Perinatal Complications Scale, developed by Parmelee.[71,72] The measure assesses maternal obstetrical history, pregnancy events, perinatal measures of the infant (e.g., gestational age and apgar), and hazardous postnatal events such as need for ventilatory assistance, metabolic abnormality, or surgery. A summary score is based on the number of risk factors incurred by a mother-infant pair, with higher scores indicating greater risk. Risk data were acquired primarily from chart review during the first month postnatal, with supplemental input from the infant's primary nurse. Reliability and validity have been demonstrated for the scale.[73,74] Although it

was developed in the 1970s, the scale's categories are still highly salient and broad enough for classification of medical problems encountered in contemporary clinical care.

The Global Assessment of Functioning   Mothers were assessed for their overall mental health status using the Global Assessment of Functioning (GAF) Scale from Axis V of the *Diagnostic and Statistical Manual of Mental Disorders-IV*.[75] An individual is rated on a mental health-illness continuum ranging from 1 to 100 with respect to psychological, social, and occupational functioning. The lowest level of functioning reflects persistent danger of severely hurting self or others, persistent inability to maintain minimal personal hygiene, or serious suicidal behavior with clear expectation of death. A score of 100 reflects superior functioning in a wide range of activities with no symptoms of psychiatric problems. This measure was developed and tested specifically for use by clinicians in predicting outcomes and measuring impact of treatment. Therefore, its clinical utility has been demonstrated as well as its predictive validity and interrater reliability.[76–78] The concurrent validity of the measure with mothers of LBW infants has been supported by its relationship to mothers' own ratings of their psychological symptoms on the Brief Symptom Inventory,[79] a measure of mental health symptoms of depression, anxiety, and other disorders.

The research assistant used the GAF to rate the mother at entry to the study and then after completion of home visits when the infant was 3, 6, and 12 months of age. The mean of all four GAF scores was used as the final measure of a mother's mental health functioning during the infant's first year of life.

The Nursing Child Assessment Feeding Scales   The NCAFS[80] was used to measure the nature of the videotaped maternal-child interaction: both an infant's interactive capacity with the mother and the mother's caregiving skills with the child. The two infant subscales measure clarity of cues and responsiveness to the mother and the four maternal subscales measure sensitivity to cues, responsiveness to distress, socioemotional growth fostering, and cognitive growth fostering. The subscales can be combined to yield a total infant interaction score and a total maternal interaction score. The measure was developed for use in both breast and bottle feeding, has established normative data, and has shown internal consistency, test-retest reliability, construct, concurrent, and predictive validity.[81] The subscales each consist of binary items which are summed. Higher scores indicate more optimal maternal caregiving or greater infant capacity for clear and responsive interaction.

An expert coder was trained and certified as reliable in use of the NCAFS by the University of Washington site where the scales were developed (i.e., met their criterion of at least 85% reliability on a series of standardized observational tests). This individual completed the coding for all infants based on review of the entire videotape of their feeding situation with the mother. The coder was blind to any other information about the mother-infant pairs.

Parenteral Acceptance-Rejection Questionnaire A mother's rejection of her infant was measured using the PARQ.[82] This measure is a self-report tool regarding the mother's specific behavior toward the infant. Sixty items provide a total composite score for degree of acceptance versus rejection on bipolar ends of a continuum where more overall rejection yields a higher score. There are four subscales contributing to the total rejection score: lack of warmth/affection, aggression/hostility, neglect/indifference, and undifferentiated rejection.

The reliability of the measure has been demonstrated,[82,83] with the internal consistency of the total scale having an alpha of .91. Subscales range from .86 to .95. Content, concurrent, convergent, and discriminant validity have also been established.[82,84,85] Response bias and social desirability have been tested, with no evidence of their effects. The measure shows substantial cross-cultural validity and utility.

The Attachment Q-Set Security of attachment was measured with the Attachment Q-Set.[86] This is a 90-item Q Sort using observations of secure-based behavior of infants and young children during their interactions with primary caregivers in the home. The items are sorted into nine categories in terms of whether they are characteristic or uncharacteristic of the child being described. All RAs who were assigned to follow various families longitudinally had been trained in the use of the Q-Set. Each RA completed the Q-Set for a particular child with whom they had worked for a full year prior to the Q-Set completion. Although RAs had not seen the mother and infant for six months when they administered the Q-Set, they were able to use previous home visits with each family as an additional source of input for sorting the statements.

Specific to the attachment Q-Set, the RA spent approximately three hours in the home shortly after the child's first birthday, observing the child and

mother during a playtime and a feeding. As part of our protocol for the observations, the mother was asked to leave the room at one point without telling the child where she was going or when she would return. After a period of observing the child's response, the RA offered the baby a new toy and initiated a play attempt. After about 3–5 minutes, the mother returned. During each of these separate periods of time, the RA observed the infant's level of distress specific to the brief separation and reunion, the various responses to mother and RA, and the interaction of mother and infant. While not attempting to replicate the carefully standardized features of the Strange Situation protocol, this semistructured aspect of the home observation did enhance the RA's ability to characterize the child on the attachment-related behaviors in the Q-Set. Finally, as an additional attempt to create a comprehensive and valid database from which to determine the child's characteristics, the RA interviewed the mother to acquire her input regarding the behaviors in the Q-Set. For this interview, the 90 statements were converted into a respondent-friendly interview format. Within 24 hours after this home observation and interview, the RA completed the Q-Set, integrating past experiences with the family, the three-hour home observation, and maternal interview data to make judgments regarding the relevance of each statement to the child. Waters and Deane's (1985) criterion set of items for secure attachment was used as the measure of security, with the percent of agreement for an infant's ranking on the criterion items being the final score for secure attachment.

Studies report interobserver reliability ranging from .72 to .95 for the Q-Set.[87–89] Content, construct, and predictive validity have been supported.[90–93] Concurrent validity is evidenced by the measure's ability to differentiate attachment classifications using the Strange Situation in several but not all studies.[87,94,95]

The Mullen Scales of Early Learning The MSEL were used as the measure of a child's cognitive competence. The MSEL is a standardized and norm-referenced measure with established internal consistency, test-retest reliability and interrater reliability, as well as concurrent and predictive validity.[96–98] It has scales for five areas of cognitive development: gross motor, visual receptive, visual expressive, receptive language, and expressive language. We used three scores as measures of cognitive competence: the gross motor scale score, the average of the two visual scale scores, and the average of the two language scale scores. A total score was also computed, representing the sum of all scales. The tests were administered to each infant at 1 year of age by a developmental psychologist who was expert in their use.

The Vineland Adaptive Behavior Scales These scales were employed as a measure of the child's social competence.[99] The items in the measure are each on a three-point scale and are divided into three separate domains: communication, daily living skills, and socialization. There is also a motor skills domain which was not used in this study. We used a composite of the three social adaptation subscales as a total social competence score. A child's placement on the items was based on interview with the mother when her child was 1 year of age. Split-half, test-retest, and interrater reliability have been established for the measure as well as concurrent and predictive validity.[100–102]

The Family Adaptability and Cohesion Scales The FACES-III measure of family functioning has 30 items, each on a five-point scale.[103] The adaptability subscale identifies the extent to which the family can flexibly change its patterns of leadership and role sharing in response to situational and developmental demands. The cohesion subscale measures the extent to which family members are emotionally bonded or connected with one another. There is documentation of the measure's reliability and validity as well as its cross-cultural appropriateness.[103–106]

The Child Behavior Checklist The Child Behavior Checklist/2–3 was used to assess the incidence of behavioral and emotional problems manifested by children at 2 years of age.[107] This questionnaire consists of 99 items describing potential problems that a child might experience, each on a three-point scale. The checklist provides a total problem score, scores for externalizing and internalizing behaviors, and six scales indicating specific syndromes, each with standardized comparison scores for a normative sample. Syndrome scores include social withdrawal, anxiety/depression, sleep disorders, somatic problems, aggression, and destructive behavior. Internalizing problems suggest that a child is attempting to deal with concerns or conflicts through internal mechanisms, including the syndrome scores for withdrawal and anxiety/depression. The externalizing score reflects the syndromes of aggression and destructive behavior, suggesting that the child is acting out or externalizing inner conflicts or concerns. We used the total score

as well as the scores for externalizing and internalizing disorders as the primary indices to determine emotional and behavioral problems because the reliability of these scores is the most robust and least subject to measurement error.

The questionnaire has been tested and normed with a broad cross-section of socioeconomic and cultural groups as well as children with varying degrees of perinatal risk. Its reliability and validity have been documented in numerous studies,[107–110] including internal consistency, stability, and discriminant and predictive validity.

Data Analysis

Pearson correlation coefficients were computed to determine preliminary relationships between children's emotional-behavioral problems and 10 of the independent variables. These independent variables were correlated with the total number of problems for children as well as with the subscales for internalizing and externalizing problems. In order to correct for the number of correlations tested, we made a Bonferroni adjustment to the probabilities. The correction indicated that a level of .001 would be necessary for each pairwise correlation to be considered significant. One of the family context variables (presence vs. absence of the father) was a discrete rather than continuous variable so t-tests were performed to identify any differences in children's emotional-behavioral problems for those with and without a father present. A significance level of .02 was set to correct for the multiple comparisons regarding father's presence or absence in the child's life.

Then, a stepwise multiple regression was computed to examine how all of the 11 child and family variables might work in concert with one another to contribute to the variance in child mental health problems. For this regression analysis, the child's total number of problems was used as the dependent variable. In addition, total scores for perinatal risk, interactive capacity, cognitive competence, and social competence were used as independent variables rather than the individual subscale scores. Similarly, total scores for maternal caregiving skill, rejection of the child, and family functioning were used in the regressions. Adequacy of income was entered in the first step to account for any of its variance prior to considering other child and family variables. All other independent variables were allowed to enter the equation at the second step based on the strength of their contributions to emotional-behavioral problems. Only variables significant at p < .01 were accepted into the model. After the variables in the model were identified, correlations were computed between these variables and the variables that had not entered the regression model in order to better understand the relationships among potential predictors. The Bonferroni correction indicated that p < .002 was necessary to establish a significant relationship between any of these variables.

Results

Relationships between Predictor Variables and Emotional-Behavioral Problems

None of the infant characteristics was related significantly to a child's incidence of emotional-behavioral problems. The correlations of language skill and visual organization showed trends towards a relationship with externalizing behavior and total problems, but they did not even reach p < .05. Perinatal morbidity showed no relationship at all to the incidence of behavior problems (r = .04).

As shown in Table 1.1, three of the variables related to a mother's caregiving were significant. The child's greater security of attachment and more optimal maternal mental health were both related inversely to the incidence of children's problems. Their correlations with internalizing problems were stronger than with the externalizing subscale. Mother's rejection of her infant was also positively associated with more emotional-behavioral problems, of both the internalizing and externalizing type.

All aspects of the family context were related significantly to children's problems. Both the family's cohesion and its adaptability scores were associated with problems, although cohesion showed

the strongest relationships to fewer problems (see Table 1.2). Family adaptability had a significant relationship to externalizing problems only. The inadequacy of a family's income was also related to problems for the child. Internalizing problems showed the highest correlations to inadequate income. t-tests to examine differences in children's problems based on fathers' presence in the home were significant for internalizing problems only (t = 2.61, df = 104, p < .01). Children without a father in the home (n = 19) had significantly more internalizing behaviors (M = 12.16) than children with a father (n = 91, M = 8.02). However, the difference in size of these two groups could have distorted this finding. There were no significant differences in the incidence of externalizing problems or in total problems for children with or without a father present.

The Integrated Contributions of Child and Family Factors

When all child and family variables were considered together, three of them entered the regression model for total child problems at p < .01. As shown in Table 1.3, the adequacy of the family income was responsible for 19% of the variance, with less adequate income related to more problems. After controlling for income, less optimal family functioning contributed to 16% of the variance in a child's incidence of emotional-behavioral problems. The security of a child's attachment to the mother contributed an additional 13% of the variance, with greater security associated with fewer problems. The total model explained 48% of the variance accounting for a child's development of emotional-behavioral problems by age 2.

Correlations of the remaining variables with those in the model produced four significant coefficients. Three of these were related to the infant's security of attachment to the mother. Infant social

Table 1.1 Correlations between the Maternal Caregiving Environment and Children's Emotional and Behavioral Problems

	Internalizing	Externalizing	Total Problems
Mothers' Mental Health	−.33*	−.28*	−.39*
Attachment Security	−.35*	−.30*	−.35*
Mothers' Caregiving Skills	−.05	−.02	−.04
Maternal Rejection	.33*	.33*	.36*

*p < .001.

Table 1.2 Correlations between Family Context and Children's Emotional and Behavioral Problems

	Internalizing	Externalizing	Total Problems
Family Functioning			
Cohesion	−.50*	−.41*	−.49*
Adaptability	−.22	−.29*	−.27*
Adequacy of Income	−.37*	−.29*	−.38*

*$p < .001$.

competence was associated positively with the child's security in the attachment relationship ($r = .28$, $p < .001$). This was the only infant characteristic related to any of the model's variables. Mothers' mental health was also significantly related to attachment security ($r = .34$, $p < .000$). Third, there was a significant difference in security of attachment for children who had a father in the home ($M = 77$) versus children who did not ($M = 63$ [$t = 4.05$, $df = 30$, $p < .000$]). The final relationship showing significance was a negative association between family functioning and maternal rejection of the infant ($r = −.29$, $p < .001$).

Discussion

The Child's Characteristics

Overall, results suggest that the family's environment is substantially more influential in a LBW child's risk of developing emotional or behavioral problems than either children's initial medical complications and interactive attributes or their emerging cognitive and social competence at age 1. Individual child characteristics did not even show a direct relationship to emotional and behavioral problems in the preliminary correlational analyses. It is especially noteworthy that birth weight itself showed no relationship to later emotional and behavioral problems because some studies have found a higher incidence of these problems for very low birth weight (VLBW) infants than for those above 1500 grams.[1,14] Although our results relate to the preschool period, they are congruent with others who have found that birth weight and perinatal complications have little correlation with school-age outcomes.[63,111] As a whole, research that is accumulating suggests that perinatal risk factors are not as critical as environmental influences in predicting behavioral and emotional outcomes.

Our findings that infant competence did not predict later behavioral problems parallel the results of other research involving infants of normative birth weight during their first year.[112] In addition, studies with children whose disabilities might be expected to have a potent impact on behavior have provided similar evidence. For children with Down Syndrome, family cohesion and the nature of the mother-child interaction were found to be much stronger influences on child behavior and adaptation than any of the child's characteristics.[113] Sameroff and Fiese[114] note that, when children are studied in the context of their environments, there is little evidence to support any relationship between a child's characteristics and mental health problems. Only when they are examined in isolation of environmental factors do a child's characteristics appear to influence problem development.

Table 1.3 Stepwise Regression Analysis for the Contribution of Infant Characteristics and Family Environment to Emotional and Behavioral Problems

	Beta at Final Step	SE	R^2
Adequacy of Income	−.23	1.78	.19
Family Functioning	−.42	.36	.35
Security of Attachment	−.37	14.12	.48

Note: Total Model ($F = 21.96$, $p < .000$, $R^2 = 48$).

It is important to note that we did find a relationship between infant social competence and a child's security of attachment. This finding could suggest that social competence and related variables such as temperament could have some indirect effect on behavioral and emotional problems through the attachment relationship. However, it is also possible that less secure attachments simply contribute to less social competence, independent of any effect on children's mental health problems.

The Caregiving Environment

Security of infant attachment was the one variable associated with the maternal caregiving environment that entered the regression model. Secure attachment may function as a protective factor for the LBW child while insecure attachment seems to place the child at risk for later problems. Attachment was significantly correlated with both internalizing and externalizing disorders, indicating its potential relationship to development of childhood depression, withdrawal, and anxiety as well as to aggressive and destructive behavior.

Correlations among potential predictors indicated that a mother's mental health was associated with the child's security of attachment. Initial correlations also suggested that mother's mental health is related to later child problems, but when all variables were considered together, attachment appeared to account for most of the variance contributed by a mother's mental health. The interrelationships among these variables have been highlighted by other studies.[38,115] Our findings reinforce the potential interaction among them. Although maternal rejection was associated with children's problems in the preliminary correlations, its relationship to family functioning may explain why it did not enter the regression model. It is not clear from the data whether a rejecting maternal style may carry over to the larger family climate, creating worse family functioning, or whether family dysfunction catalyzes maternal rejection of her infant. It is likely that there are bidirectional effects. Regardless, family functioning was the stronger of the two and accounted for any variance that rejection might have contributed to children's behavioral and emotional problems.

A mother's early caregiving skills (i.e., her sensitivity, responsiveness, and growth-fostering behavior) had no relationship to the child's later emotional-behavioral problems. This finding suggests that a mother's lack of awareness and/or use of these more optimal caregiving approaches may be less important to her child's development of later problems than her overt rejection of the child or her own mental health problems. In other words, the absence of "optimal" caregiving seems less important to the development of early child mental health problems than the presence of "detrimental" caregiving that is potentially neglectful or abusive. Our results also raise the possibility that rejection of the infant or a mother's psychopathology may not necessarily lead to problems for the child unless they foster an insecure attachment. The nature of these interactions warrants further study.

Family Context

The beta coefficients shown in Table 1.3 indicate that, of the three variables that entered the model, family functioning had the strongest relationship to emotional-behavioral problems. This finding supports the contention of Seifer and Dickstein[116] that family functioning is emerging as the single strongest predictor of child functioning. The initial correlation matrix showed evidence of a stronger association between a family's cohesion and a child's problems than between their adaptability and children's problems. This outcome implies that the closeness among family members may have a greater impact than how flexible a family is in making decisions or handling their responsibilities. A close-knit family may not only provide support to the mother to enhance her caregiving but also expose the child to other direct sources of love, guidance, and value formation. This input may be especially important if a mother's caregiving is ineffective or is in some way detrimental to the child's mental health.

Our results also indicate that a family's closeness and ability to adapt well to situations may be more important to the child's adjustment than the mere presence of the father in the home. Simply having a father around does not imply that the father is supportive of the mother's caregiving or that he is a source of positive parenting for the child. However, the regression analysis indicated that only when the variance from a family's functioning had been accounted for in the model did the presence or absence of the father become insignificant to the child's problems. In other words, family functioning accounted for much of the variance that might have been attributed to father coresidence. t-tests had shown a significant difference for internalizing problems of children with or without a father but not for total problems. Because we used the total problem score as the dependent variable in the regression equation, the effects of fathers' presence on a child's withdrawal or depression were diminished to some extent.

Inadequate family income contributed substantially to the child's risk of incurring emotional-behavioral problems. This finding supports previous research that has shown disadvantage to be associated with increased risk of mental health problems for children.[117,118] High levels of risk for mental health problems in preschool children are concentrated in low-income families, especially those who earn less than the poverty threshold.[119,120] It has been noted that poverty can increase parental stress and despair, augmenting the potential for inattentive or erratic parental care and abuse and neglect in the interactions between parents and children.[121-123] However, as presented in the results, we found no significant relationships between adequacy of income and measures of the caregiving environment. They seemed to reflect distinct contributions to children's problems.

Inadequate income is most likely a proxy for a larger constellation of factors that reflect a generally disadvantaged environment. For instance, studies have shown that poverty significantly heightens the infant's risk of exposure to violence, toxic substances, and malnutrition.[120,124] Half of disadvantaged children in the United States have young parents who have not completed high school and lack the most minimal personal and social resources to meet their child's needs.[125] Economic adversity has many faces, all of which could potentially contribute to mental health problems.

Summary

Factors within the family environment during the infant's first year of life explained 48% of the variance in the LBW emotional and behavioral problems at age 2. A family's lack of cohesion and adaptability, an insecure attachment of child to mother, and the family's economic disadvantage emerged as significant precursors to problem development. The presence of a father in the home did not enter the regression model but appeared to be an important aspect of family functioning that protected children from developing problems. Similarly, maternal mental health and degree of a mother's rejection of her child were related to problem development but did not enter the model.

Internalizing problems of withdrawal, depression, and anxiety had the strongest relationship to these family environment variables. This is noteworthy in that family dysfunction and economic adversity are often discussed as predictors of conduct disorder and other externalizing problems. However, our results imply that it may be particularly important to assess children for symptoms of potential depression and anxiety when they appear to be at risk because of their environmental context.

This study has examined the relationship of only certain variables to short-term outcomes for preterm, LBW children. Future research to determine whether our findings hold up in the longer term will be essential. Will these same variables predict mental health problems when the children are of school age and into adolescence? In addition, other variables need to be examined that were not addressed in this study. For example, infant temperament, chronic health problems, the presence of extended family, and number of siblings in the home could all be either risk or protective factors for LBW children.

Early problem behaviors have been linked quite clearly to later psychopathology,[126,127] so these findings reinforce the critical importance of early intervention programs for families of LBW children. Data indicate that a focus on the larger family context, not only the mother-child relationship, is essential. Helping the family to replace conflict with interpersonal support and closeness and to more flexibly share various family responsibilities may provide a more adaptive environment for mother and child that could foster child mental health. Results also emphasize the need for special attention to the attachment relationship between mother and child. Insecure attachments may be prevented if mothers are counseled about approaches that can engender their child's security and if the mother's own mental health problems are addressed. Last, findings speak to the importance of support for families who are living in poverty. For children who are at risk from high levels of family dysfunction or insecure attachment, poverty may exacerbate the risk and be the determining catalyst in a child's path toward mental illness.

Notes

This research was funded by the NIH, NINR, #R01 NR02698.

1. Bennett, F. The low birth weight, premature infant. *Helping Low Birth Weight, Premature Infants*, eds. R. Gross, D. Spiker, C. Haynes. Stanford: Stanford University Press. Ch. 1:3–16, 1997.

2. Hay, E., Sykes, D., Bill, J., et al. The social competence of very low birth weight children: Teachers, peer and self-perceptions. *Ab Child Psych* 20:123–150, 1992.

3. Hill, E. Behavioural problems in children who weigh 1000 grams or less at birth in four countries. *Lancet* 357:1641–1643, 2001.

4. Botting, N., Powls, A., Cooke, R., Marlow, N. Attention deficit hyperactivity disorders and other psychiatric outcomes in very low birth weight children. *J Child Psychol Psychiatry* 38(8):931–41, 1997.

5. Breslau, N., Chilcoat, H. Psychiatric sequelae of low birth weight at 11 years of age. *Biol Psychiatry* 47(11):1005–11, 2000.

6. Burd, L., Severud, R., Kerbeshian, J., Klug, M. Prenatal and perinatal risk factors for autism. *J Perinat Med* 27(6):441-450, 1999.

7. O'Callaghan, M., Harvey, J. Biological predictors and co-morbidity of attention deficit and hyperactivity disorder in extremely low birth weight infants at school. *J Ped Child Health* 33: 491–6, 1997.

8. Meceli, P., Goeke-Marey, M., Whitman, T., Kolberg, K., Miller-Loncar, F., White, R. Birth status, medical complications and social environment: Individual differences in development of preterm, very low birth weight infants. *J Pediatr Psychol* 25: 353–8, 2000.

9. Minde, K. Prematurity and serious medical conditions in infancy implications for development, behavior and intervention. *Handbook of Infant Mental Health*, ed. C. Zeanah, New York: Guilford Press, 2000.

10. Chapieski, M., Evankovich, K. Behavioral effects of prematurity. *Semin Perinatol* 21(3):221–39, 1997.

11. Lorenz, J., Woolierer, D., Jetton, J., Paneth, N. A quantitative review of mortality and developmental disability in extremely premature newborns. *Arch Pediatr Adolesc Med* 152, 425–35.

12. Whitaker, A., Van Rosen, R., Felman, J., Schonfeld, I., Pinto-Martin, J., Shaffer, C., Paneth, N. Psychiatric outcomes in low birth weight children at age of 6 years: Relation to neonatal cranial ultrasound abnormalities. *Arch Gen Psychiatry* 54:847–56, 1997.

13. McCormick, M., Gortmacker, S., Sobol, A. Very low birth weight children: Behavior problems and school difficulty in a national sample. *J Pediatr* 117(5):687–693, 1990.

14. Pharoah, P., Stevenson, C., Cooke, R., Stevenson, R. Prevalence of behavior disorders in low birth weight infants. *Arch Dis Child* 70:271–274, 1994.

15. Sykes, D., Hoy, E., Bill, J., Halliday, H., McClure, B., Reid, M. Behavior adjustment in school of very low birth weight children. *J Child Psychol Psychiatry* 38:315–26, 1997.

16. Van Beek, Y., Hopkins, B., Hoeksma, J. The development of communication in preterm infant-mother dyads. *Behavior* 12–9 (1–2):35–61, 1994.

17. Van den Boon, O. The influence of temperament and mother on attachment and exploration. *Child Dev* 65:1457–1477, 1994.

18. Webster-Stratton, C., Lindsey, D. School competence and conduct problems in young children: Issues in assessment. *J Clin Child Psychol* 28(1):25–43, 1999.

19. O'Callaghan, M., Harvey, J. Biological predictors and co-morbidity of attention deficit and hyperactivity disorder in extremely low birth weight infants at school. *J Ped Child Health* 33: 491–6, 1997.

20. Redmond, S., Rice, M. The socio-emotional behaviors of children with SLI: Social adaptation or social deviance. *J Speech and Hear Res* 41:688–700, 1998.

21. Hirshfeld, D., Rosembaum, J., Biederman, J., et al.: Stable behavioral inhibition and its association with anxiety disorder. *J Am Acad Child Adolesc Psychiatry* 31:103–111, 1992.

22. Prizant, B., Audet, L., Burke, G., Hummel, L., Maher, S., Theodore, G. Communication disorders and emotional/behavioral disorders in children. *J Speech and Hear Disorders* 55:179–192, 1990.

23. Cohen, N., Menna, R., Vallance, D., Barwik, M., Im, N., Horodezky, N. Language, social cognitive processing and behavioral characteristics of psychiatrically disturbed children with previously identified and unsuspected language impairments. *J Child Psychol Psychiatry* 39(6):853–64, 1998.

24. Harris, J. *Developmental Neuropsychiatry*. New York: Oxford University Press. 1998.

25. Liaw, F., Brooks-Gunn, J. Cumulative familial risk and low birth weight children's cognitive and behavioral development. *J Clin Child Psychol* 23(4):360–372, 1994.

26. Lyons-Ruth, K., Easterbrooks, M., Cibelli, C. Infant attachment strategies, infant mental lag, and maternal depressive symptoms: Predictors of internalizing and externalizing problems at age 7. *Dev Psychol* 33(4):681–692, 1997.

27. Prizant, B., Meyer, E. Socio-emotional aspects of language and social-communication disorders in young children. *Am J Speech-Lang Pathol* 56–81, 1993.

28. Alpern, L., Lyons-Ruth, K. Preschool children at social risk: Chronicity and timing of maternal depressive symptoms and child behavior problems at school and at home. *Dev Psychopathol* 5(3):371–387, 1993.

29. Cicchetti, D., Rogosch, F., Toth, S. Maternal depressive disorder and contextual risk: Contributions to the development of attachment insecurity and behavior problems in toddlerhood. *Dev Psychopathol* 10:283–300, 1998.

30. Weissman, M., Warner, V., Wichramaratne, P., Moreau, D., Olfson, M. Offspring of depressed parents: 10 years later. *Arch Gen Psychiatry* 54(10):932–940, 1997.

31. Beck, C. Maternal depression and child behavior problems: A meta-analysis. *J Adv Nurs* 29(3):623–629, 1998.

32. Downey, G., Coyne, J. Children of depressed parents. *Psychol Bull* 108:50–76, 1990.

33. Aber J.L., Jones, S., Cohen, J. The impact of poverty on the mental health and development of very young children. *Handbook of Infant Mental Health*, ed. C Zeanah. New York: Guilford Press. 113–128, 2000.

34. Cummings, E., Davies, P. Maternal depression and child development. *J Child Psychol Psychiatry* 35:73–112, 1994.

35. Goodman, S., Brumley, H. Schizophrenic and depressed mothers: Relational deficits in parenting. *Dev Psychol* 26:31–39, 1990.

36. Lyons-Ruth, K., Connell, D., Grunebaum, H., Botein, S. Infants at social risk: Maternal depression and family support services as mediators of infant development and security of attachment. *Child Dev* 61(1):85–98, 1990.

37. Seifer, R., Sameroff, A., Dickstein, S., Keitner, G., Miller, I., Rasmussen, S., Heyden, L. Parental psychopathology, multi-contextual risks and one year outcome in children. *J Clin Child Psychol* 25:423–435, 1996.

38. Teti, D., Gelfard, D., Messinger, D., Isabella, R. Maternal depression and the quality of early attachment: An examination of infants, preschoolers and their mothers. *Dev Psychol* 31:364–376, 1995.

39. Zahn-Waxler, C., Iianotti, S., Cummings, E., Denham, S. Antecedents of problem behaviors in children of depressed mothers. *Dev Psychopathol* 2:271–291, 1990.

40. Denham, S., Workman, E., Cole, P., Weissbrod, C., Kendziora, K., Zahn, C. Prediction of externalizing behavior problems from early to middle childhood: The role of parental socialization and emotion expression. *Dev Psychopathol* 12(1):23–45, 2000.

41. Keren, M., Feldman, R., Tyano, S. Diagnoses and interactive patterns of infants referred to a community based infant mental health clinic. *J Acad Child Adolesc Psychiatry* 40(1):27–35, 2001.

42. Asarnow, J., Tompson, M., Hamilton, E., Goldstein, M., Guthrie, D. Family expressed emotion, childhood onset depression, and childhood onset schizophrenia spectrum disorders: Is expressed emotion a nonspecific correlate of childhood psychopathology or a specific risk factor for depression? *J Abnorm Child Psychol* 22:129–146, 1994.

43. Eiden, R. Exposure to violence and behavior problems during childhood. *J Interpersonal Violence* 14(12):1299–1313, 1999.

44. Hirshfeld, D., Biederman, J., Brody, L., Faraone, S., Rosenbaum, J. Associations between expressed emotion and child behavioral inhibition and psychopathology. *J Am Acad Child Adolesc Psychiatry* 36(2):205–213, 1997.

45. Nix, R., Pinderhughes, E., Dodge, K., Bates, J., Pettit, G., McFadyen, S. The relation between mothers' hostile attribution tendencies and child externalizing behavior problems: The mediating roles of mothers' harsh discipline practices. *Child Dev* 70(4):896–909, 1999.

46. Stubbe, D., Zahner, G., Goldstein, M., Leckman, J. Diagnostic specificity of a brief measure of expressed emotion: A community study of children. *J Child Psychol Psychiatry* 34:139–154, 1993.

47. Fagot, B., Kavanagh, K. The prediction of anti-social behavior from avoidance attachment classifications. *Child Dev* 61:864–873, 1990.

48. Lyons-Ruth, K., Alpon, L., Repacholi, B. Disorganized infant attachment classification and maternal psychosocial problems as predictors of hostile-aggressive behavior in the preschool classroom. *Child Dev* 64(2):572–585, 1993.

49. Carlson, E., Sroufe, L. Contributions of attachment theory to developmental psychopathology. *Developmental Psychopathology*, eds. D. Cicchetti & D. Cohen. New York: Wiley. (1):581–617, 1995.

50. Shaw, D., Vondra, J. Infant attachment security and maternal predictors of early behavior problems: A longitudinal study of low-income families. *J Abnorm Child Psychol* 23:335–357, 1995.

51. Shaw, D., Owens, E., Vondra, J., Keenan, K., Winslow, E. Early risk factors and pathways in the development of early disruptive behavior problems. *Dev Psychopathol* 8:679–700, 1997.

52. Sanson, A., Oberklaid, F., Pedlow, R., Prior, M. Risk indicators: Assessment of infancy predictors of preschool behavioral maladjustment. *J Child Psych Psychiatry* 32:609–26, 1991.

53. Shaw, D., Winslow, E., Owens, E., Hood, N. Young children's adjustment to chronic family adversity: A longitudinal study of low income families. *J Am Acad Child Adol Psychiatry* 37:545–53, 1987.

54. Benzies, K., Harrison, M., Magill-Evans, J. Impact of marital quality and parent-infant interaction on preschool behavior problems. *Public Health Nurs* 15(1):35–43, 1998.

55. Katz, L., Gottman, J. Patterns of marital conflict predict children's internalizing and externalizing behaviors. *Dev Psychol* 29:940–950, 1993.

56. Wakschlag, L., Hans, S. Early parenthood in context: Implications for development and intervention. *Handbook of Infant Mental Health*, ed. C. Zeanah. New York: Guilford Press. 129–144, 2000.

57. Cole, R., Olds, D., Sidora, K. Family context as a moderator of program effects in prenatal and early childhood home visitation. *J Community Psychol* 26(1):37–48, 1998.

58. Fox, R., Platz, D., Bently, K. Maternal factors related to parenting practices, developmental expectations, and perceptions of child behavior problems. *J Genet Psychol* 156(4):431–441, 1995.

59. Shapiro, J., Mangelsdorf, S. The determinants of parenting competence in adolescent mothers. *J Youth Adolescence* 23:621–641, 1994.

60. Field, T., Widmayer, S., Adler, S., DeCubas, M. Teenage parenting in different cultures, family constellations and caregiving environments: Effects on infant development. *Infant Ment Health J* 11:158–174, 1990.

61. Coley, R. Children's socialization experiences and functioning in single-mother households: The importance of fathers and other men. *Child Dev* 69(1):219–230, 1998.

62. Florsheim, P., Tolan, P., Gorman-Smith, D. Family relationships, parenting practices, the availability of male family members, and the behavior of inner city boys in single mother and two parent families. *Child Dev* 69(5):1437–1447, 1998.

63. Gross, R., Mettelman, B., Dye, T., Slagle, T. Impact of family structure and stability on academic outcomes in preterm children at 10 years of age. *J Pediatr* 138:169–175, 2001.

64. Adams, C., Hillman, N., Gaydos, G. Behavioral difficulties in toddlers: Impact of sociocultural and biological risk factors. *J Clin Child Psychol* 23:373–381, 1994.

65. Buckner, J., Bassuk, E., Weinreb, L., Brooks, M. Homelessness and income relations to the mental health and behavior of low income school age children. *Dev Psychol* 35(1):246–257, 1999.

66. Korbin, J., Coulton, C., Chard, S., Platt-Houston, C., Su, M. Impoverishment and child maltreatment in African American and European American neighborhoods. *Dev Psychopathol* 10(2): 215–233, 1998.

67. Lynch, M., Ciccheti, D. An ecological-transactional analysis of children and contexts: The longitudinal interplay among child maltreatment, community violence, and children's symptomatology. *Dev Psychopathol* 10(2):235–257, 1998.

68. McLeod, J., Shananhan, M. Poverty, parenting and children's mental health. *Am Soc Review* 58(3):351–366, 1993.

69. Watson, J., Kirby, R., Kelleher, K., Bradley, R. Effects of poverty on home environment: An analysis of three-year outcome data for low birth weight premature infants. *J Pediatr Psychol* 21(3): 419–431, 1996.

70. Osofsky, J. The effects of violence exposure on young children. *Am Psychol* 50:782–788, 1995.

71. Littman, B., Parmelee, A. Medical correlates of infant development. *Pediatr* 61:470–4, 1978.

72. Parmelee, A., Kopp, C., Sigman, M. Selection of developmental assessment techniques for infants at risk. *Merrill-Palmer Quart* 22:177–99, 1976.

73. Francis, P., Self, L., Horowitz, F. The behavioral assessment of the neonate: An overview. *Handbook of Infant Development*, ed. D. Osofsky. New York: John Wiley. 1987.

74. Scott, D., Bauer, C., Draemer, H., Tyson, J. The Neonatal Health Index. *Helping Low Birth Weight Premature Babies*, eds. R. Gross, L. Spiker, C. Haynes. Stanford: Stanford University Press, 1997.

75. American Psychiatric Association: *Diagnostic and Statistical Manual of Mental Disorders* (4th edition). Washington, DC: American Psychiatric Press, 1994.

76. Endicott, J., Spitzer, R., Fleiss, J., Cohen, J. The global assessment scale: A procedure for measuring the overall severity of psychiatric disturbance. *Psychiatric Epidemiology: Assessment, Concepts and Methods*, ed. J. Mezzich, M. Jorge, I. Salloun. Baltimore, MD: Johns Hopkins University Press, 1994.

77. Patterson, D., Lee, M. Field trial of the Global Assessment of Functioning Scale–Modified. *Am J Psychiatry* 152(9):1386–1388, 1995.

78. Piersma, H., Boes, J. The GAF and psychiatric outcome: A descriptive report. *Community Ment Health J* 33(1):35–41, 1997.

79. Weiss, S., Chen, J. Factors influencing maternal mental health and family functioning during the low birth weight infant's first year of life. *J Ped Nurs* 17(2):114–125, 2002.

80. Barnard, K., Hammond, M., Booth, C., Bee, H., Mitchell, S., Spiker, S. Measurement and meaning of parent-infant interaction. *Applied Developmental Psychology*, eds. F. Morrision, C. Lord, D. Keating. New York: Academic Press. 1989.

81. Sumner, G., Spietz, A. *NCAST Caregiver/Parent-Child Interaction Feeding Manual*. Seattle: NCAST Publications, University of Washington, 1994.

82. Rohner, R. *Handbook for the Study of Parental Acceptance and Rejection: The Parental Acceptance-Rejection Test Manual*. Storrs: University of Connecticut Press. 1991.

83. McGuire, J., Carls, F. Exploring the reliability of measures of family relations, parental attitudes and parent-child relations in a disadvantaged minority population. *J Marriage and the Family* 55:1042–1046, 1993.

84. Gorman, J., Leifer, M., Grossman, G. Nonorganic failure to thrive: Maternal history and current maternal functioning. *J Clin Child Psychol* 22(3):327–336, 1993.

85. Myers, H., Alvy, K., Arrington, A., Richardson, M., Marigna, M., Huff, R., Main, M., Newcomb, M. The impact of a parent training program on inner city African American families. *J Comm Psychol* 20:132–147, 1992.

86. Waters, E., Deane, K. Defining and assessing individual differences in attachment relationships: Q methodology and the organization of behavior in infancy and early childhood. *Monogr Soc Res Child Dev* 50:41–65, 1985.

87. Belsky, J., Rovine, M. Q-Sort security and first-year non-maternal care. *New Dir Child Dev* 49:7–22, 1990.

88. Solomon, J., George, C. The measurement of attachment security in infancy and childhood. *Handbook of Attachment: Theory, Research and Clinical Applications*, eds. J. Cassidy & P. Shaver. New York: Guilford Press. 287–316, 1999.

89. Teti, D., McGourty, S. Using mothers versus trained observers in assessing children's secure base behavior: Theoretical and methodological considerations. *Child Dev* 67:597–605, 1996.

90. Kerns, K. A longitudinal examination of links between mother-child attachment and children's friendships in early childhood. *J Soc & Personal Relationships* 11:379–381, 1994.

91. La Freniere, P., Provost, M., Dubeau, D. From an insecure base: Parent-child relations and internalizing behavior in the preschool. *Early Development and Parenting* 1:137–148, 1992.

92. Posada, G., Waters, E., Crowell, J., Lay, K. Is it easier to use a secure mother as a secure base: Attachment Q-Sort correlates of the adult attachment interview. *Monogr Soc Res Child Dev* 60:133–145, 1995.

93. Strayer, F., Verissimo, M., Vaughn, B., Howes, C. A quantitative approach to the description and classification of primary social relationships: Caregiving, cultural and cognitive perspectives on secure base behavior and working models. *Monogr Soc Res Child Dev*, ed. E. Waters, B. Vaughn, G. Posada & K. Kondo-Ikemura 60:49–70, 1995.

94. Mangelsdorf, S., Plunkett, J., Dedrick, C., Berlin, M., Meisels, S., McHale, J., Dichtellmiller, M. Attachment security in very low birth weight babies. *Dev Psychol* 32:914–920, 1996.

95. Vaughn, B., Waters, E. Attachment behavior at home and in the laboratory: Q Sort observations and Strange Situation classifications of one year olds. *Child Dev* 61:1965–1973, 1990.

96. Gilliam, W., Mayes, L. Developmental assessment of infants and toddlers. *Handbook of Infant Mental Health*, ed. C. Zeanah. New York: Guilford Press. 236–248, 2000.

97. Mullen, E. *Mullen Scale of Early Learning*. Circle Pines, MN: American Guidance Services, 1995.

98. Mullen, E., Buka, S., Merenda, P., Vohr, B. Identifying specific learning profiles in young developmentally delayed children: Infant Mullen Scales of Early Learning. *Pediatr Res* 25:83–90, 1989.

99. Sparrow, S., Balla, D., Ciccetti, D. *The Vineland Adaptive Behavior Scales*. Circle Pines, MN: American Guidance Service. 1984.

100. Atkinson, L., Beve, I., Dickens, S., Lackwell, J. Concurrent validities of the Stanford-Binet, Leiter, and Vineland with developmentally delayed children. *J Sch Psychol* 30(2):165–173, 1992.

101. Middleton, H., Keene, R., Browne, G. Convergent and discriminant validities of the Scales of Independent Behavior and the Revised Vineland Adaptive Behavior Scales. *Am J Ment Retardation* 94:669–673, 1990.

102. Raggio, D., Massingale, T. Comparability of the Vineland Social Maturity Scale and the Vineland Adaptive Behavior Scale–survey form with infants evaluated for developmental delay. *Percept Mot Skills* 71:415–418, 1990.

103. Olson, D., McCubbin, H., Barnes, H., Larsen, A., Muxen, M., Wilson, M. *Family Inventories*. St Paul: University of Minnesota. 1985.

104. Edman, S., Cole, D., Howard, G. Convergent and discriminant validity of FACES-III: Family adaptability and cohesion. *Fam Process* 29(1):95–103, 1990.

105. Knight, G., Tein, J., Shell, R., Roosa, M. The cross-ethnic equivalence of parenting and family interaction measures among Hispanic and Anglo-American families. *Child Dev* 63(6):1392–1403, 1992.

106. Weiss, S., Goebel, P., Page, A., Wilson, P., Warda, M. The impact of cultural and familial context on behavioral and emotional problems of

preschool Latino children. *Child Psychiatry Hum Dev* 29(4):287–301, 1999.

107. Achenbach, T. *Manual for the Child Behavior Checklist (2–3) and 1992 Profile*. Burlington: University of Vermont Press. 1992.

108. Crawford, L., Lee, S. Test-retest reliability of the child behavior checklist ages 2–3. *Psychol Rep* 69:496–498, 1991.

109. Leadbeater, B., Bishop, S. Predictors of behavior problems in preschool children of inner-city Afro-American and Puerto Rican adolescent mothers. *Child Dev* 65:638–648, 1994.

110. Spiker, D., Kraemer, H., Constantine, N., Bryant, D. Reliability and validity of behavior problem checklists as measures of stable traits in low birth weight, premature preschoolers. *Child Dev* 63:1481–1496, 1992.

111. Taylor, H., Klein, N., Schatxchneider, C., Hack, M. Predictors of early school age outcomes in very low weight children. *J Dev Behav Pediatr* 19:235–243, 1998.

112. Sameroff, A., Bartko, W., Baldwin, A., Baldwin, C., Siefer, R. Family and social influences on the development of child competence. *Families, Risk and Competence*, ed. M. Lewis & C. Feiring. Mahwah, NJ: Erlbaum. 161–185, 1998.

113. Hauser-Cram, P., Warrfield, M., Shonkoff, J., Krauss, M., Upshur, C., Sayer, A. Family influences on adaptive development in young children with Down Syndome. *Child Dev* 70:979–989, 1999.

114. Sameroff, A., Fiese, B. Models of development and developmental risk. *Handbook of Infant Mental Health*, ed. C. Zeanah. New York: Guilford Press. 3–19, 2000.

115. Manassis, K., Bradley, S., Goldberg, S., Hood, J., Swinson, R. Attachment in mothers and anxiety disorder and their children. *J Am Acad Child Adolesc Psychiatry* 33:1106–1113, 1994.

116. Sefer, R., Dickstein, S. Parental mental illness and infant development. *Handbook of Infant Mental Health*, ed. C. Zeanah. New York: Guilford Press. 145–160, 2000.

117. Rutter, M. Resilience reconsidered: Conceptual considerations, empirical findings and pol-

icy implications. *Early Childhood Intervention*, ed. J. Shonkoff & S. Meisels. New York: Cambridge University Press, 2000.

118. Sampson, R., Laub, J. Urban poverty and the family context of delinquency: New look at structure and process in a classic study. *Child Dev* 65, 523–40, 1994.

119. Duncan, B., Brook-Gunn, J., Aber J. (eds). *Neighborhood Poverty: Context and Consequences for Child and Adolescent Development*. New York: Russell Sage, 1997.

120. Knitzer, J. Early childhood mental health services: A policy and systems development perspective. *Early Childhood Intervention*, ed. J. Shonkoff & S. Meisels. New York: Cambridge University Press, 2000.

121. Halpern, R. Poverty and infant development. *Infant Mental Health*, ed. C. Zeanah. New York: Guilford Press, 1993.

122. Hardin, B. Home visitation with psychologically vulnerable families and children. *Zero to Three Bulletin of the National Center for Infants, Toddlers and Families* 17(4), 1997.

123. Parker, F., Piotrkowski, C., Horn, C., Greene, S. The challenge for Head Start: Realizing its vision as a two-generation program. *Advances in Applied Development Psychology*, vol. 9, ed. I. Sigel & S. Smith. Norward, NJ: Ablex, 1995.

124. National Center for Children in Poverty: *Young Children in Poverty: A Statistical Update*. New York: Columbia School of Public Health. 1998.

125. Halpern, R. Early childhood intervention for low income children and families. *Early Childhood Intervention*, ed. J. Shonkoff & S. Meisels. New York: Cambridge University Press, 2000.

126. Caspi, A., Moffit, T., Newman, D., Silva, P. Behavioral observations at age 3 years predict adult psychiatric problems. *Arch Gen Psychiatry* 53:1033–1039, 1996.

127. Offord, D., Boyle, M., Racine, Y., Fleming, J., Cadman, D., Blume, H., et al.: Outcome, prognosis, and risk in a longitudinal follow up study. *J Am Acad Child Adolesc Psychiatry* 31: 916–923, 1992.

2

Resilient Children: What They Tell Us about Coping with Maltreatment

Introduction

The costs of child maltreatment to children, families, and society has been extensively documented for the past 30 years. In 1990, the magnitude of child maltreatment led the U.S. Advisory Board on Child Abuse and Neglect to declare the existence of a "national emergency" (Cicchetti, 1994). Particularly for children and adolescents, the costs are great and complex. They include the loss of self-esteem and a sense of identity, lack of trust and social skills, and a wide range of social, developmental, emotional, and intellectual problems (Farber and Egeland, 1987). These costs suggest the need for social policy and programs to deal with teen pregnancy, alcohol abuse, mental illness, and more serious delinquent behaviors. Maltreated adolescents have been reported to have more attentional problems, more stress, and lower family cohesion that younger maltreated children (Crittenden, Claussen, and Sugarman, 1994).

The effects of violence and inadequate child rearing on children's development, and overall adjustment has been studied within the context of a broad theoretical framework that considers the significance of developmental stages and environmental requirements. Despite the expanding knowledge of the impact of maltreatment, however, these phenomena have seldom been studied comprehensively and interactively in relation to adolescent adjustment (Wolfe and McGee, 1994).

Many researchers have looked at risk factors as to why children fail, become ill, or engage in delin-

quent behaviors as a result of adverse parenting and caretaking circumstances (Anthony, 1987; Baldwin, Baldwin, Kasser, Zax, Sameroff, and Seifer, 1993; Cicchetti, Rogosch, Lynch, and Holt, 1993; Conrad and Hammen, 1993; Egeland, Carlson, and Sroufe, 1993; Garmezy, Masten, and Tellegen, 1984; Radke-Yarrow and Brown, 1993; Spencer, Cole, DuPree, Glymph, and Pierre, 1993; Stouthamer-Loeber, Loeber, Farrington, Zhang, vanKammen, and Maguin, 1993; Werner and Smith, 1982).

Along with these researchers, others have also studied protective factors that buffer negative outcomes for maltreated children (Cicchetti and Toth, 1992; Compas, 1987; Manly, Cicchetti, and Barnett, 1994; Radke-Yarrow and Sherman, 1990; Werner and Smith, 1982; Wolin and Wolin, 1993). Both risk and protective factors are essential to understanding the concept of resilience.

Assessing and observing behavior from a resilience perspective is an alternative paradigm to the disease model of viewing behavior. Masten (1989) noted that successful adaptation had been ignored by students of psychopathology, dominated by the disease model, and was concerned with symptoms, classification, prognosis, treatments, and risk factors. The interest in resilience is a transformation in theoretical conceptualizations and approaches to understanding the development of psychopathology. It is a positive approach, identifying strengths in individuals and providing a basis for collaborative problem solving and empowerment of the individual.

Despite the fact that maltreatment exerts a deleterious impact on the developmental process, not all children are equally affected by their experience of maltreatment. Indeed, it would be surprising if all maltreated children displayed the same developmental profile. Baldwin et al. (1993) recognized that children develop in a dialectical process of meeting challenges, resolving them, and then meeting new ones. If the challenge is too severe, the developmental process breaks down. Resilience is a name for the capacity of the child to meet a challenge and use it for psychological growth.

Research Questions

The intent of this research was to explore how adolescents have adapted to adversity in the parent-child relationship and how they may have coped by perceiving either an external or internal locus of safety. If a perception of safety, either external (school, friend, relative), or internal (fantasy and/or creativity), has been achieved, then these individuals may have developed a useful coping strategy to the abuse. Would this sense of safety provide a protective factor to the maltreatment, resulting in less negative behaviors by the child, or would the resultant successful adaptation to the maltreatment encourage a more resilient developmental process?

Therefore, the questions of this research were: What are the perceptions of adolescents regarding safety in their home environment? What internal and external areas have these youth explored in response to the search for safety? Are there similarities and/or differences for these adolescents in terms of outcome?

Population

The context for this study was an independent living program, developed and serviced by a private child care residential facility, in south-central Pennsylvania. Adolescents are referred to the program through the courts, juvenile probation offices, and county child welfare agencies. Participants in the independent living program live in foster care placements and/or situations where they are involved in independent living activities. They might attend school, be employed full or part time, and are encouraged to volunteer at various community work sites. Teens participate in mandatory weekly meetings that include group activities, speakers, workshops, videos, and take-home assignments. They are required to demonstrate the ability to survive on their own to successfully complete program goals.

Professionals participating in the study were child welfare caseworkers, foster mothers, and child care workers. Their years of experience in working with children and adolescents in the child care system ranged from four to 25 years.

Research Methodology

The qualitative grounded theory method (Glaser and Strauss, 1967) was chosen for this study because the research questions focused on the exploration and explanation of adolescent perspectives of their coping methods to maltreatment based on their perceived areas of safety. While the relationship between familial conflict and child problems has been established, there has been an increasing need for process-oriented studies that specify the nature of this relationship. Therefore, the development of methodologies and approaches that go beyond the correlational and questionnaire-based clinical field methods is required in describing the effects of adults' angry behavior on children. Conceivably, in angry home environments, one might find qualitatively different relations between variables than are found in typical community samples (Cummings, Hennessy, Radideau, and Cicchetti, 1994).

Discovering the processes by which maltreated children develop adaptive personality organizations despite aversive family experiences has been a central challenge for understanding resilience in children's development. Exploring aspects of parent-child relationships and interactions may elucidate qualitative points of divergence in the experiences of maltreated children that may influence the course of their development (Cicchetti et al., 1993). Life stories inform about individual dispositions and protective mechanisms that transcend cultural boundaries and operate effectively in a variety of high-risk contexts (Werner, 1993).

Grounded theory research aims at understanding how a group of people interpret their reality. Theories are generated using the everyday behaviors and organizational patterns of group members employing an inductive, from-the-ground-up approach. It is predicated on the assumption that people make order and sense out of their environment although their world may appear disordered or nonsensical to others.

Participants were selected on the basis of theoretical sampling and participation was voluntary. Two groups chosen for the study were child care professionals who were experienced in the field of child abuse and adolescents who had experienced childhood maltreatment. A total of 13 participants (7 adolescents, 3 child welfare caseworkers, 1 residential caseworker [independent living coordinator], and 2 foster parents) were interviewed. Demographics included four female and three male adolescents ranging in age from 13 to 20, and all were Caucasian. The 20-year-old male was living independently and fully employed. The 13-year-old male lived in the home of one of the foster mothers being interviewed and demonstrated competency behaviors in coping with his earlier abusive experience.

Three of the adolescent females lived in foster homes and attended public school; one was a senior and would graduate; the others were sophomores. Each had part- or full-time jobs. The fourth had recently left foster care on turning 18 and was living with a boyfriend. She was employed and continued to participate in the independent living program. All adolescents had a history of physical, sexual, or emotional abuse, documented by self-report and corroborated by the child care professionals, as well as the case record review by the researcher.

Data were collected through three interviews (the first two in person, the third by telephone) with both the adolescents and the professionals, a review of case records, and attendance at meetings of the independent living program. Two formal, semistructured, open-ended interviews were conducted with each to gather data. The interviews consisted of both direct and indirect questions and averaged 45 to 90 minutes. During the first round of interviews, the professionals were asked their opinions of the adaptation and coping skills of the adolescents with which they have worked. Adolescents were asked to relate their experiences of maltreatment, their feelings of the abuse and the perpetrator, and their response to the abuse.

Interview questions moved from the general to the specific during the second round of interviews, based on formulated hypotheses from the first round of interviews. The specific aim was to clarify commonalities and similarities that emerged from the interviews with all groups. The third-round interviews were conducted for the purpose of obtaining participant input as to clarification or challenge to the findings from the first two interviews.

Management of the data (words) was done through content analysis of the field notes, audiotapes of the interviews, and records. Responses were categorized according to adaptation, coping, and competency patterns. These were then used in the final analysis to indicate the presence of resilience factors. These patterns were then categorized into working hypotheses and themes of the meaning of the results of this qualitative field study.

Results

Five major themes creating meaning for this grounded theory on resilience were revealed. They showed a developmental progression of the adolescents' perceptions of their skills in coping with the abusive environment. Each theme built on the other toward children finding a means to make sense of the abuse. The themes are: loyalty to parents, norming of the abusing environment, invisibility from the abuser, self-value, and future view of life.

Loyalty: the child's view of and feelings toward the abusing parent and their perception of the intentions and behaviors of their parents. Both child care professionals and adolescents identified an ongoing loyalty of the adolescents for their parents. This occurred in the form of a defensiveness of their parents' actions and acknowledgment of the belief that their parents still loved them and that they loved their parents.

> I never got to understand why he did the things he did and I never really had a dad and I wanted to get to know him, in spite of everything he did, because he was still my father. I needed a gentle hand to guide me, and I mean, they were just showing their love in a different way I guess. That is all I wanted was to be loved and they just had a different way of showing it.

Professionals described this loyalty.

> This father or mother or stepfather does other things for them besides hitting them. I mean they once in a while bring home a new pair of shoes and that kind of thing so that they have a loyalty to that kind of person.

Adaptive coping skills were indicated by the ability to separate the abusive behaviors of the parent from the good parent and eventually to see the abusive behaviors as unrelated to the actions of the child. They had the ability to see the abusing parent as both good and bad, categorizing them as the one who is hurtful and also the one who does fun and caring things with them. They evidenced a balancing of the parent-child relationship that provided a way for the children to maintain self without fear of annihilation:

> if he had a bad day or if she had a bad day, and that person was drunk or just the little things would set them off most of the time. He was very short-tempered.

Normalcy: the perception of the abusive home environments as "normal" family life. Six of the seven adolescents agreed that the ability to tolerate frequent abuse was tied to acceptance of the abuse as ordinary family living. While professionals tended to assume and expect that reactions to abuse would be negative, the adolescents viewed it as a common way of life.

> Being hit was normal, a way of life. But since it happened to me practically every day and I grew up with it, I thought it was just something normal that happened.

Professionals supported the perception that

> this is how my family is. I think it is something that maybe they get themselves into a routine

While being abused was by no means accepted, the presence of and expectation of being abuse resulted in a sense of normalcy—a way of life—about the abuse. The adaptiveness of this perception, based on an acceptance of the way things are, to cope with the abusive environment may have provided a protectiveness of not feeling trapped in this very frightening world. This theme of normalizing the environment appeared to be an adaptive use of denial, strengthening the child's sense of control in a maltreating environment. The perception that an abusive home environment was not out of the ordinary provided a protective factor for resilience.

Invisibility: both child care professionals and adolescents described behaviors indicative of the ability of the child to become "invisible" to avoid being a available to the abuser and to minimize the opportunities to be in harm's way. Invisibility was accomplished by not being present in the view of the abuser through either externalizing or internalizing actions. Externalizing actions included absenting the house, going to one's room, not talking to the abuser, or just "staying out of their way."

> I wouldn't go around them for a couple of days. I kept my distance. I spent the majority of the time in my bedroom. Whenever I was in my room and my dad didn't leave me alone, I went underneath the bed. I would go to my closet. I had to lie to stay out of trouble . . . when I was older, I ran away.

> I tried forgetting about things that happened at home when I was in school. I liked going to school so I could interact with people. . . . I liked

running, jogging, getting out and walking. After seven, I kind of moved out. I just was never home. I would always be out with my friends. I would stay at other people's houses.

Internalizing actions included daydreaming, play with various toys, writing, reading, and numerous artistic endeavors. They were described:

> I would draw, play with my sister or just read or something. Actually I couldn't read. I didn't know how. I would just look at the pictures. . . . I had a make believe friend named, Fred. He talked to me and was somebody to play with, somebody to help me out. I would daydream that just me and my brother and my mom, just us three in the house away from every thing. We would just be us and safe. I would draw. I would play with my toys. I had a bear for a make believe friend. I would talk to him, that he was the only one that really cared about me, the only one who is there, and who understands. He would just listen. I made little worlds with my Barbie dolls and had little hide away places with them, castles and unicorns and horses and flying horses. I had this really huge bear. . . . I used to sit on it to laugh and tell it stories when I was little. . . . I started writing in sixth grade when I got a diary from a friend. It helped me a little because to me, I didn't think that anybody would really listen and at least, I knew that I got it out of my system somehow.

The ability to avoid being in the presence of the abuser, or to stay out of view, a perception of invisibleness, became a means by which these children managed the ongoing possibility of being maltreated. From this data, it became apparent that the ability to avoid the abuse had become a skill. Each time abuse was avoided, the behavior was reinforced and became an action the children were able to use to attain a sense of control as to what might happen to them.

This sense of invisibility was also observed in those youth who by dissociation or dissociative-like behaviors took themselves elsewhere in thought while the abuse might have been occurring. In children who have experienced sexual abuse, this has already been established as an etiology of dissociative behaviors. It was also indicated by the adolescents in this study who had been physically abused. Similarities were observed between the child care professionals and adolescents in styles of coping with the abuse. The professionals also believed that children coped with abuse by engaging in distancing behaviors either by physical actions or mental actions.

> She would lose parts of conversations. She would shut down and go somewhere else. She wasn't aware of where she went. It was almost like a daydream state. They tend to be creative. They like to draw, they like to write poetry. They like to tell their story in a story form. They like to play control games, where they are the person in charge of the game and make the rules. They make their own little world. And that is their protection all day long . . . they close off and they think their own way. They make their own set of rules on how to do things. They seem to channel energy towards a safety zone and that could be just about anything—reading, drawing, playing sports, being out of the home. They pick a safe place. The real world as they want it to be . . . like a fantasy island.

This coping strategy of invisibility for children, when successful, providing a perception of safety that enabled them to feel some sense of being able to control what happened to them. The more successful, the more this sense of control was strengthened. By repeatedly creating a world of safety for themselves, they had power and control and believed that they were capable of protecting themselves from hurt.

From an adult perspective, the behaviors used by these children may appear maladaptive. While avoidance, manipulation, withdrawal, and dishonesty are generally viewed as inappropriate and maladaptive behaviors, for children, left to their own survival instincts or skills, they become behaviors to cope with danger and may become adaptive actions. They are protective factors because they are adaptive toward growth of the individual.

Self-value: the perception of being cared for, being valued, being "someone" and a positive attitude about self. This perception appeared to be predicated on the successful accomplishment of the first three themes. This theme emerged as a protective factor of resilience in how successful children were in establishing value about themselves. Being valued meant being loved, being respected, and belonging. Six of the seven adolescents had religious beliefs about God as a higher power who was loving and who watched over them.

> I still have lots of work to do, but now I am a loving, caring person. I feel better about myself because I know that all of the things that I have accomplished, things that have happened to me, and that I am not the only one that is out there who is like me. The abuse experience made me stronger . . . cause I have had to work for a lot of what I have. I am funny at times. I am loud, I can be obnoxious at times, but I do understand people. No matter whatever happens, I know God will always protect me from everything.

The ability to overcome negative thoughts about self was a contributory factor toward resilience. Professionals saw a "toughness" in children who make it successfully after experiencing an abusive home. By not showing weakness, children actually reinforced strengths within themselves. Knowing in themselves that they can be strong and withstand the abuse enhances the value placed on self and is a protective factor. The discussions by both professionals and adolescents followed a developmental pattern in how abused children viewed self-value over a period of time. What they may have believed as children, they no longer thought about themselves as adolescents.

> I was five and I wasn't big enough to make decisions. I was just a little girl. I realized later on that that is not how it was. Because I was just a little kid. When I was 12, I started looking at things differently. But then at that time I didn't think about it that much, because I was a little kid. Now that I think about it and I know more, he shouldn't have done it. When I was little, I thought it was my fault. When I was older, I realized it was the drugs and alcohol that made my father do things he wouldn't normally do. I did not feel safe as a child. Now I am not scared of him and have stood up to him.

One professional noted:

> I am excited in seeing change, to be able to see children grow into adolescence and to young adulthood. It is very gratifying for me to see children have come from an abusive situation and go through various different stages, trials and tribulations, growth experiences, try to find their potential, their successes.

The experience of these adolescents was that their parents did not listen to them, talk to them, or inquire about their feelings. Home life involved very little verbal interaction or communication among parents or children. The words that were heard were those of anger, threats, intimidation, and demeaning, accusatory phrases: "You're dumb, you're no good, you'll never amount to anything, you're so ugly, stupid." Children who achieve value about themselves have been able to confront these statements and acquire more positive descriptions about the value of self.

Future view of life: the ability to visualize how a future might be. The final theme predicting resilience emerged regarding adolescent awareness and actualization of future capabilities. A potential for success was evident in terms of the child care professionals' hopeful but cautious projection of future capabilities and the adolescents' optimism that they would be okay. If youth had inner strengths and knew at some level that they were survivors, they had more optimism that they were going to achieve goals. Many maintained part-time jobs, planned graduation from high school, and anticipated being parents themselves.

> I have been trying to be independent. Hope is for a better tomorrow. I have a job. Yes, I am going to graduate. No matter what, I am going to graduate and I am going to college if I can. I want my parents to know that I am happy with my life now. For one, I am going to show my dad that I am somebody.

Positive future expectations have been linked with resilient adaption (Wyman, Cowen, Work, and Kerley, 1993). When individuals believe events and outcomes can be controlled, learned helplessness is avoided (Luthar, 1993; Werner, 1993). Belief in the future also carries an attitude of hopefulness, a common theme of the adolescent group in this study and a concept found in the research of Werner (1982), Egeland et al. (1993), and Baldwin et al. (1993).

The processes by which maltreated children develop adaptive personalities and self-esteem is a challenge for understanding resilience in development (Cicchetti et al., 1993). The five themes that emerged from this research show a progression of children's skills in coping with an abusive caregiver. Each theme builds on the other toward children finding a means to adapt to the abuse or toward maladaptive behaviors. The successful progression through each of these themes results in a more resilient adolescent who demonstrates competency and mastery of adolescent tasks and is able to achieve independence.

Abuse and neglect literature has extensively discussed the impact of abuse on children. The betrayal of the parent-child relationship robs the child of the essential nurturing environment wherein safety is established for the child's optimum opportunity for growth. Deprived of this security, the child searches other sources to establish a support base for this basic need. If a trusting relationship with the parent is not accomplished, the child will go elsewhere for safety.

Several resilience clusters, identified by Wolin and Wolin (1993), corroborated the emerging themes of these findings. Insight, a sensing or intuition that family life is untrustworthy, provides the context of the abusive events as an ordinary way of life. Because of the stressfulness of any life event depends on a child's appraisal of it (Luthar and Ziglar, 1991), the abilities of the child to adjust to an abusive environment may depend on the ability to distinguish the abusing parent from the good parent. Abuse may be tolerated when it is balanced with times when the parent does caring and loving activities with a child.

In resilient children, initiative occurs when the children turn away from the frustration of their troubled parents and follow the call of their curiosity to go exploring. Creativity is a safe harbor of the imagination for refuge and rearranging life to one's pleasing (Wolin and Wolin, 1993). Adolescents in this study identified ways they were able to avoid the abuser and create their own world of safety from the abuse. Through play, reading, writing, creative activities, and involvement with other families, real or created, they established a world where they perceived that they could be safe and protected. As children the qualities of needed nurturing were assigned to transitional objects (bears, dolls, trucks).

If being valued is not provided by parents, resilient individuals are capable of attaining it through a received valuing by others, whether real or imagined. In reading, children can escape into worlds that adults may see as doomed childhood fantasy, but that provide assurance, methodical thinking, and optimism for the child (Wolin and Wolin, 1993). In their own created worlds, children can be in control and be loved and valued by those they choose to identify with until there is opportunity to receive this from an outside source.

Werner and Smith (1982) discussed children who kept the memories of childhood adversities at bay by being in the world, but not of it. Though not always real, the perception of invisibility was, when repeatedly successful for the child in avoiding abuse, adaptive and reinforced the continuation of these behaviors in the child. An internal locus of control, the belief that shaping one's life is within your control, was found in the protective processes (Luthar, 1993; Werner, 1993).

Implications for Social Work Practice

There are several implications from this study in the areas of research, child welfare practice, policy, and treatment modalities. While the intent of this study was to "hear it in the worlds of the children themselves," the sample size was very small. Larger sampling, a more diverse population regarding age, ethnicity, and geographic location would provide additional data. Future studies might be conducted with maltreated adolescents who may be receiving child welfare services but continue to live with an abusive caregiver. Additional research with children by developmental age categories could be conducted to compare the emerging themes of this study. At what ages do children begin to separate the good and hurtful parent, or to normalize the abuse family environment? Also, a nonresilient comparison group would provide additional data to confirm or refute these findings.

Similar studies might be conducted with other child care professionals to confirm the findings from this population of participants. Also, because this study population had only Caucasian adolescents, a similar study with children of minorities, African American and Hispanic, should be conducted to compare results.

The results of this study do, however, provide additional considerations to working with children who have been maltreated. The child protection field has not reached consensus on the most pertinent criteria for assessing the safety of children at risk of maltreatment, and no studies have examined the safety of maltreated children from a family preservation framework (DePanfilis and Scannapieco, 1994). The coping skills identified in this study should be viewed as strengths and skills to be built upon to assist children and their parents in providing in-home services. The use of play therapy can encourage a child to develop adaptive skills through play activities. It enhances coping strategies for children within the family when external supports cannot be provided to them to assure their safety. Invisibility activities can be developed or reinforced so that the child will have an internal support for coping. Children who are most vulnerable are those not expressing either external or internal protective factors. These children may benefit from short-term out of home care to establish a knowledge base of safety so they might begin to build resilience skills. Safety must be in place before adaptation and treatment can begin (James, 1994).

It is important to be cautious regarding the findings of this study in relation to policy development. If the indication is that children are resilient and, therefore, possibly self-correcting, some may advocate for fewer dollars and programs for the abused child. Although many children are resilient, we do not know the numbers. We do know, however, through extensive research, that many children are and will continue to be seriously abused. They need ongoing protection and advocacy for policies and programs that provide protection in terms of community services and treatment programs for maltreating families.

Finally, children give us the clues, through their behaviors, activities, and interests, as to how they may be coping with life events. We need to go there with them, in their play and activities, and listen to them. They are forgiving and willing to give parents numerous opportunities to "get it right." Treatment programs need to be family-centered, with support systems that understand and encourage the preservation of the parent-child relationship. Treatment based on the strengths and coping behaviors of children is potentially more beneficial for the growth of abused children.

There has been no intent to minimize the experience of abuse on individual. There is horror and fear of living with abuse, being hit by someone who is out of control. Rather, it is to say that many children are able to find the ability within themselves to be in control when another is out of control. These behaviors may look chaotic and nonsensical to others as they attempt to make sense out of their experience. What may appear to be maladaptive defense mechanisms for adults, may be in reality very adaptive to children attempting to cope with an adult abuser. Because this defies logic, the child's solution may also appear illogical. It is the child's strength and creative problem solving that assures resilience.

References

Anthony, J. (1987). Risk, vulnerability, and resilience: An overview. In E. J. Anthony & B. Cohler. (Eds.). *The Invulnerable Child* (pp. 3–48). New York: Guilford Press.

Baldwin, A., Baldwin, C., Kasser, T., Zax, M., Sameroff, A. & Seifer, R. (1993). Contextual risk and resiliency during late adolescence. *Development and Psychopathology, 5*, 741–761.

Cicchetti, D. (1994). Advances and challenges in the study of the sequelae of child maltreatment. *Development and Psychopathology, 6*, 1–3.

Cicchetti, D., Rogosch, F., Lynch, M. & Holt, K. (1993). Resilience in maltreated children:

Processes leading to adaptive outcome. *Development and Psychopathology, 5,* 629–647.

Cicchetti, D. & Toth, S. (1992). The role of developmental theory in prevention and intervention. *Development and Psychopathology, 4,* 489–493.

Compas, B. (1987). Coping with stress during childhood and adolescence. *Psychological Bulletin, 101*(3), 393–403.

Conrad, M. & Hammen, C. (1993). Protective and resource factors in high and low-risk children: A comparison of children with unipolar, bipolar, medically ill, and normal mothers. *Development and Psychopathology, 5,* 593–607.

Crittenden, P., Claussen, A. & Sugarman, D. (1994). Physical and psychological maltreatment in middle childhood and adolescence. *Development and Psychopathology, 6,* 145–164.

Cummings, E., Hennesy, K., Radideau, G. & Cicchetti, D. (1994). Responses of physically abused boys to interadult anger involving their mothers. *Development and Psychopathology, 6,* 31–41.

DePanfilis, D., & Scannapieco, M. (1994). Assessing the safety of children at risk of maltreatment: Decision-making models. *Child Welfare, 73*(3), 229–245.

Egeland, B., Carlson, E. & Sroufe, L. (1993). Resilience as process. *Development and Psychopathology, 5,* 517–528.

Farber, E. & Egeland, B. (1987). Invulnerability among abused and neglected children. In E. J. Anthony & B. Cohler. (Eds.). *The Vulnerable Child* (pp. 253–288). New York: Guilford Press.

Garmezy, N., Master, A. & Tellegen, A. (1984). The study of stress and competence in children: A building block for developmental psychopathology. *Child Development, 55,* 97–111.

Glaser, B.G. & Strauss, A.L. (1967). *The Discovery of Grounded Theory.* Chicago: Aldine Publishing.

James, B. (1994). *Handbook for Treatment of Attachment-Trauma Problems in Children.* New York: Free Press.

Luthar, S. (1993). Annotation: Methodology and conceptual issues in research on childhood resilience. *Journal of Child Psychology and Psychiatry, 34*(4), 441–453.

Luthar, S. & Zigler, E. (1991). Vulnerability and competence: A review of research on resilience in childhood. *American Journal of Orthopsychiatry, 6*(1), 6–22.

Manly, J., Cicchetti, D. & Barnett, D. (1994). The impact of subtype, frequency, chronicity, and severity of child maltreatment on social competence and behavior problems. *Development and Psychopathology, 6,* 121 143.

Maston, A. (1989). Resilience in development: Implications of the study of successful adaptation for developmental psychopathology. In D. Cicchetti (Ed.). *The Emergence of a Discipline: Rochester Symposium on Developmental Psychopathology* (pp. 261–294). Hillsdale, NJ: Lawrence Erlbaum Publishers.

Radke-Yarrow, M. & Brown, E. (1993). Resilience and vulnerability in children of multiple-risk families. *Development and Psychopathology, 5,* 581–592.

Radke-Yarrow, M. & Sherman, T. (1990). Hard growing: Children who survive. In J. Rolf, A.S. Masten, D. Cicchetti, K. Nuechterlein, & T.S. Weintraub (Eds.). *Risk and Protective Factors in the Development of Psychopathology* (pp. 97–120). London: Cambridge University Press.

Spencer, M., Cole, S., DuPree, D., Glymph, A. & Pierre, P. (1993). Self-efficacy among urban African-American early adolescents: Exploring issues of risk, vulnerability, and resilience. *Development and Psychopathology, 5,* 719–739.

Stouthamer-Loeber, M., Loeber, R., Farrington, D., Zhang, Q., vanKammen, W. & Maguin, E. (1993). The double edge of protective and risk factors for delinquency: Interrelations and developmental patterns. *Development and Psychopathology, 5,* 683–701.

Werner, E. (1993). Risk, resilience, and recovery. Perspectives from the Kauai Longitudinal Study. *Development and Psychopathology, 5,* 503–515.

Werner, E. & Smith, R. (1982). *Vulnerable but Invincible.* New York: Adams, Bannister & Cox.

Wolfe, D. & McGee, R. (1994). Dimensions of child maltreatment and their relationship to adolescent adjustment. *Development and Psychopathology, 6,* 165–181.

Wolin, S. & Wolin, S. (1993). *The Resilient Self: How Survivors of Troubled Families Rise above Adversity.* New York: Random House.

Wyman, P., Cowen, E., Work, W. & Kerley, J. (1993). The role of children's future expectations in self-system functioning and adjustment of life stress: A prospective study of urban at-risk children. *Development and Psychopathology, 5,* 649–661.

LAUREE C. TILTON-WEAVER
ERIN T. VITUNSKI
NANCY L. GALAMBOS

3

Five Images of Maturity in Adolescence: What Does "Grown Up" Mean?

Introduction

A cornerstone of developmental research in childhood and adolescence is the search for a deeper understanding of the processes by which a child grows into maturity. Scholars of adolescence worldwide have long recognized that maturity is a multifaceted concept incorporating physical, social, psychological, emotional, and behavioral elements (Hurrelmann and Engel, 1989; Coleman and Hendry, 1990; Peterson, 1996; Galambos et al., 1999). Recently, researchers have begun to focus on the subjective meanings of maturity in adolescents and young adults in a quest to ascertain what features of maturity are commonly recognized, understood, and respected by young people. Notably missing, however, are qualitative studies examining maturity vis-à-vis adolescents' own experiences. Through understanding adolescents' conceptions of maturity, we will learn more about the subjective representations that draw adolescents ever closer to adulthood. With this goal in mind, the current study triangulates qualitative and quantitative methods of analysis to examine the images of maturity seen by young adolescents.

Psychosocial Maturity

There is certainly some consensus in the literature about what it means to be mature. Greenberger and her colleagues (Greenberger et al., 1975; Greenberger and Sorenson, 1974), for instance, developed an integrative model of psychosocial maturity that originally consisted of three domains: autonomy (functioning independently), interpersonal adequacy (communicating and interacting with others effectively), and social responsibility (contributing to the well-being of society). The first domain, autonomy, is embodied in individuals who have well-defined, cohesive identities, who are self-reliant, have goals, and are willing to work to meet them. Interpersonal adequacy, according to the model, is exemplified by strong communication skills (including being able to send and receive messages and to empathize with others), a balanced trust in others (neither afraid of others nor gullible), and working knowledge of social roles (including knowledge of appropriate behavior and ability to manage conflict). Although this dimension was later dropped from the model due to difficulties in measurement, the construct may still have relevance for understanding adolescents' progress toward maturity. Given the importance that peers play in the development of adolescents, it is difficult to imagine that being able to communicate and relate to others effectively is not important to the establishment and maintenance of peer relationships. The last domain, social adequacy, is seen in individuals who are committed to social goals, open to sociopolitical change, and tolerant of differences in others. As adolescents develop, they move progressively closer to this ideal of maturity typically associated with adulthood.

Pseudomaturity

A number of forces act upon adolescents, sometimes pushing them toward greater maturity, sometimes impeding their progress. Some of these forces are external (e.g., pressure from parents, teachers, other adults, and peers to "act like an adult"), whereas others are internal to the adolescent (e.g., physiological and emotional pressures, such as looking more mature, but fearing the responsibility associated with growing up). For some adolescents, these forces "push" individuals toward greater maturity than they might prefer. For other adolescents, these forces can hinder attempts to gain the independence that is perceived as legitimately theirs (Eccles et al., 1993; Hendry et al., 1993). In other words, social relationships and experiences may lead to delays in some areas of maturity or to premature entry into more mature behavior and activities. Adolescents' paid employment may be one example of experiences that lead, for some, to what may be a premature entry into adult behaviors.

In contrast to psychosocial maturity, Greenberger and Steinberg (1986) observed "pseudomaturity" among some adolescents who were engaged in paid work. Contrary to expectations that regular employment would lead adolescents to more responsible (and presumably, more mature) behavior, many working adolescents in their sample learned unethical business practices (e.g., stealing from employers) and increased their engagement in problem behaviors (e.g., smoking, drinking). Greenberger and Steinberg coined the term "adultoid" to describe adolescents who engage in activities, often "risky" activities, that symbolize adult status (e.g., smoking, drinking, staying out late, having sex). Although adultoid adolescents engage in "adult-like" behaviors, they do so without having the "underlying perceptions, beliefs, or understanding that a person who is psychologically adult would bring to a similar situation" (p. 174). Hence, they evidence pseudomaturity rather than genuine maturity.

Other researchers (e.g., Newcomb and Bentler, 1988; Coleman and Hendry, 1990; Hendry et al., 1993), too, have referred to adolescents gaining a sense of maturity through engaging in behaviors that are considered normatively acceptable activities for adults. Coleman and Hendry point out, for example, that drinking alcohol and taking drugs may be part of adolescents' attempts to act "like adults" while trying to develop and establish their identity. In a focus group of South African adolescent males, researchers found that boys reported benefits of drinking alcohol, including having status more like an adult (Ziervogel et al., 1997–98). Moreover, the boys also attributed negative characteristics to adolescents who either did not drink (e.g., immature and conservative) or overindulged (e.g., lack of self-control and self-respect), whereas they attributed positive characteristics to those who drank in moderation (e.g., mature and socially adept).

One of the strongest correlates of adolescents' problem behaviors is association with deviant peers (Ketterlinus and Lamb, 1994; Jessor, 1998). That is, problem behaviors take place, more often than not, in the company of peers. Some problem behaviors, then, may not only take place in the company of peers, but may be for the benefit of peers—attempts to fit in with, be accepted by, or gain status among peers. Moffitt (1993) argued that such desires for more mature status may be the motivational force behind most adolescents' engagement in problem behaviors—a motivational drive that is more normative than not.

The Adultoid Adolescent

In a recent study aimed at identifying the precise profile of characteristics that define pseudomaturity, Galambos and Tilton-Weaver (2000) submitted measures of adolescents' problem behavior, subjective age (i.e., how old one feels relative to chronological age), and psychosocial maturity (i.e., identity, self-reliance, and work orientation) to a cluster analysis. They specified, a priori, three constellations of adolescents who would differ in their patterns of scores on problem behavior, subjective age, and psychosocial maturity. These three types of adolescents were labeled as genuinely mature, immature, and pseudomature (or adultoid) adolescents. Indeed, empirical support was found for the existence of these three groups. The genuinely mature adolescents had a profile suggestive of developmentally appropriate maturity: they reported low levels of problem behavior, felt slightly older than their chronological age, and had the highest levels of psychosocial maturity. The immature group's profile suggested inexperience: they engaged in relatively low levels of problem behavior, felt relatively young, and were psychosocially immature. The adultoids, on the other hand, displayed a mixed bag of maturity: they reported the highest levels of problem behavior, felt notably older than their peers, and scored below the ample mean on all three indices psychosocial maturity. Further probing painted a remarkable picture of adultoids—adolescents who appear to be growing up "too fast" without really growing up at all. In contrast to mature and immature adolescents, adultoids appeared older (i.e., taller and more physically mature), wanted to be even older, and were more peer-involved. In contrast to mature adolescents, adultoid adolescents were less industrious. The adultoids also expected to have privileges (such as going to mixed-gender parties and going away with friends for a few days without an adult) earlier than did their mature and immature counterparts. Although this research clearly pointed to different manifestations of maturity in adolescents, we do not know whether the images of maturity seen by researchers converge with the images of maturity experienced by adolescents.

The Transition to Adulthood

Studies of individuals' subjective experiences of the transition to adulthood provide some insight into the characteristics that adolescents might construe as indicative of maturity. Several studies suggest that in Western society the timing and manner in which adolescents make the transition to adulthood vary substantially among individuals and are subjectively cued by intangible, often ambiguous markers (e.g., "being responsible" or "being independent") (Arnett and Tabor, 1994; Scheer and Palkovitz, 1994; Switzman et al., 1998). However, these studies also suggest a convergence in the characteristics most often associated with genuine adult status. In a study asking individuals how they knew they had or had not attained "adult status," college students cited feelings of intrapersonal agency (e.g., "I make my own decisions," "I organize my life by myself and make all the choices I want," "I figure things out for myself") more frequently than either discrete social events (e.g., attaining legal age, graduating from school) or elements of interpersonal relationships (e.g., "I am still very dependent on my parents") (Switzman et al., 1998). Arnett (1994) also found that college students were more likely to endorse criteria for adulthood that reflect independence and self-sufficiency. This research demonstrates concordance in the way that young adults and researchers, at least in North America, view being "grown up" or genuinely mature.

Research examining the transition to adulthood in other countries has found that rapid social and economic changes have impacted this transition, making the passage to adult status longer and more unpredictable for some youth. For example, in the U.K., social and economic changes have led to higher youth unemployment and a greater dependency on family for some youth, when independence and self-reliance are stressed as developmentally appropriate. Coleman and Hendry (1999) have argued that the economic and social ambiguity that delayed entry into adult roles leads some youth to develop a "hedonism for hard times" (p. 171). This hedonism, or escape from the harsh realities of their lives, is manifested in risky behaviors such as increased alcohol and drug use. For some youth, then, risky behavior may represent an alternative and compelling route into adulthood.

Given the importance of understanding the paths that adolescents take on the road to adulthood, it is surprising that there are few studies examining adolescents' subjective perceptions of maturity. A notable exception is a study contrasting adolescents' and young adults' descriptions of the characteristics that distinguish adults from nonadults. Greene et al. (1992) asked twelfth-graders and college students to describe the characteristics and/or experiences that make a person an adult. A content analysis of their responses displays a litany of criteria that could be subsumed under Greenberger's model of psychosocial maturity—"autonomous decision making," "responsibility," "self-understanding," "emotional maturity," "financial independence," "well-educated," "commitment potential," "altruism," and "adaptability." Moreover, four of these criteria showed age-related differences: financial independence, autonomous decision making, commitment potential, and education were more frequently listed by college students than by high school students. Still notably missing, however, in the examination of adolescents' images of maturity are the perspectives of younger adolescents, who are only beginning the journey to adulthood. We do not yet know how maturity is viewed by young adolescents. Do adolescents view being more "grown up" as synonymous with being responsible and productive? Do they also see their peers' adultoid activities as indicating more "grown up" status? What other characteristics do they describe as "grown up"? These questions guided the present study.

This Study

The goal of this study was to describe from adolescents' perspectives, the characteristics that are associated with being "grown up." Although Galambos and Tilton-Weaver (2000) clearly demonstrated that there are at least two representations or "images" of maturity (i.e., genuine and pseudomature), these presentations have not been documented from the perspective of adolescents. To accomplish this, a qualitative analysis was conducted of adolescents' descriptions of what it means to be "grown up." We hoped to provide, from adolescents' experiences and in their own voice, a picture of their "images" of maturity. We expected, a priori, to find images that would include elements of genuine maturity (such as self-reliance and respect for others) and indicators of pseudomaturity (such as engaging in problem behaviors). We were open, however, to the idea that adolescents would have experienced other aspects of maturity and were particularly interested in what these might be. Self-reports of what "grown up" means were provided by adolescents in the sixth and ninth grades. This allowed for the investigation of age (grade) differences in adolescents' conceptions of maturity. The extent to which young people in early and middle adolescence view maturity similarly is an interesting issue, considering that adolescents may focus on different developmental issues depending on their age (Coleman, 1979). Gender differences in conceptions of "grown up" were also examined.

Method

Sample

Participants for the qualitative study were drawn from a larger study of a school-based community sample of adolescents ($n = 452$), who were primarily Caucasian (15% were visible minorities). Individuals who provided information about their perceptions of maturity were selected, resulting in a subsample of 345 adolescents. These participants were 155 sixth-graders (89 girls, 66 boys) and 190 ninth-graders (100 girls, 90 boys) who lived in a medium-sized Canadian city. Within this subsample, the mean age of the sixth-graders was 11 years and 11 months (S.D. = 0.31 years) and the mean age of the ninth-graders was 15 years and 0 months (S.D. = 0.40 years). Sixty-four percent lived with both biological parents, 12% lived with a parent and a stepparent, 20% lived with a single parent, and the remaining 5% lived in other situations (joint custody, foster family, grandparent or other relative, nonrelative). All but about 5% of the mothers (or the female parent with whom the adolescent lived) had earned a high school degree (30% had received a high school diploma or its equivalent); an additional 20% obtained a vocational or technical degree, and 45% completed university. With respect to fathers (or the male parent with

whom the adolescent lived), 4% had not completed high school, 26% had a high school education, an additional 19% completed a vocational or technical degree, and 43% obtained a university degree. According to the adolescents' reports, fathers had a mean score of 45.67 (S.D. = 15.07) on the Blishen and McRoberts (1976) socioeconomic status SES index; employed mothers had a mean score of 43.52 (S.D. = 13.75). Examples of occupations and their SES scores are dental assistant, 45.02; bookkeeper, 40.28; and engineer, 70.27. The SES scores indicated that the participants were primarily from working- and middle-class families. These demographic characteristics are similar to those found in regionwide studies of the area of Canada from which the sample was drawn (McCreary Centre Society, 2000).

Student's t-tests and chi-squares, used to examine differences between those who provided a response and those who did not, revealed that nonrespondents were more likely to be younger, $t(1,443) = -2.43$; less independent $t(1,443) = -2.24$; with mothers and fathers and fathers that were less educated, $t(1,430) = -3.08$ and $t(1,406) = -2.38$ (respectively). Nonrespondents were more likely than respondents to be boys, $\chi^2 (1,452) = 17.30$, $p < 0.001$. The nonrespondents did not differ, however, in terms of their reported subjective age (i.e., how old they feel relative to their age-mates), problem behavior, or their parents' SES scores.

Procedure

Participants were drawn from the Victoria Adolescence Project, a longitudinal study of psychosocial maturity. The study was conducted in eight elementary schools (from which the sixth-graders were drawn) and three secondary schools (from which the ninth-graders were drawn). In all but two schools, passive consent procedures were used (parents received letter of information and were asked to respond only if they did not wish their adolescents to participate). Questionnaires were administered in testing sessions in school by members of the research team. School personnel were rarely present during the testing sessions. For each adolescent who participated, $5 (Canadian) was paid to school or class funds. Out of 345 students who provided some response, 236 provided descriptions that could be coded. The remaining 109 students either indicated that they did not know a peer who seemed more grown up (e.g., "I can't think of anyone") or gave a response that was not codable (e.g., "I don't think this question is important," or "bubba, cheese, czechechaza, papu"). Student t-tests were conducted to determine if important differences existed between those whose responses were codable and those whose responses were not. Results indicated that respondents were not different from nonrespondents in terms of their parents' education level, parents' socioeconomic status, or family structure. Nor did they differ in terms of their age, level of independence, subjective age, or problem behaviors. Chi-square results however, showed that the codable responses were more likely to be from girls than boys $\chi^2(1,345) = 6.21$, $p < 0.05$.

Measures

Descriptions of "Grown up"   To gather information about adolescents' conceptions of what it means to be grown up, they were asked: "Please think of *someone your age* who seems more 'grown up' than most other kids (do not name him or her). What are some words that describe the ways in which this person seems grown up?" Ample space was left in the questionnaire so that adolescents could write down as many characteristics as they wished. Following this question, adolescents were also asked "Is this person a girl or boy?" and "Would you like to hang out with this person?" (no; maybe; yes).

Results

Qualitative Analysis

The descriptions provided by the adolescents were explored using content analysis. Two of the authors independently examined the descriptions (which included up to seven different descriptors or statements), looking for thematic concepts of maturity. We looked first for similarities in descriptions, noting when adolescents were describing characteristics that were essentially the same (e.g., "confident" and "self-assured"). We noted when these descriptions suggested broader themes. For example, descriptions such as "not a procrastinator," "hard worker," "gets her school work done right away," and "commits to something he enjoys and works well at it" are all describing positive aspects of work orientation.

By reading through the descriptions multiple times, we independently identified four hallmarks. These hallmarks reflect variations in the extent to which the descriptions focused on one or more aspects of independence, responsibility, privilege, or power. The first hallmark, which we recognized as genuine maturity by North American cultural standards, was described by the adolescents as responsibly independent behavior and through (e.g., "a girl in my grade, she has her own thoughts and follows them, she does not let other people tell her what's right and wrong for her"; "he makes a lot of mature decisions, he usually knows what's always right and wrong, he doesn't conform to people's decisions just to be cool").

The second hallmark identified was a variation suggesting a large degree of independence, but also a higher degree of engagement in problem or risky behavior (e.g., "has a girlfriend, goes far distances without guardian, curses at home, watches R-rated movies"; "almost every weekend she will drink and do drugs, she will stay out really late and break her curfew"; or "he drinks beer, smokes pot, steals stuff with his friends, acts older, controls his parents, talks about and wants sex"). The independence described in these cases seemed to focus primarily on privileges (described by some adolescents as "getting to do things" and "say[ing][to the adolescent about himself or herself] that I'm a grown up and have the right to do anything"), with occasional additional remarks that suggest poorer judgments or negative evaluations by the adolescent providing the description (e.g., "wears clothes *way too big* for them, talks in *bad* language, wears *no helmet* when riding"; "swearing, likes *trouble*, says *inappropriate* things"; or "puts on *too much* make-up, swears a lot, talks about boys *too much*, she says she smokes" [emphasis added]). More important, we found descriptions of mature adolescents whose maturity, in part, depended on refraining from problem behaviors or acknowledging the inherent risk associated with problem behaviors (e.g., "doesn't go about looking for trouble, doesn't let anger get in the way of good judgment"; "if someone wants to fight him, he just walks away," "doesn't become outrageously drunk, is the one who says what not to do"). This suggests that these are divergent images—one genuine, the other pseudomature.

We also found descriptions of adolescents who had assumed a level of responsibility that their peers seemed to feel was beyond their years ("*too* serious, doesn't have fun"; "*only* thinks about working, talks to adults *all* the time"; "doesn't really like having fun, *only* thinks about working, not much fun" [emphasis added]). This we felt, was the hallmark of another, yet unnamed image. Finally, we found characterizations of bossy adolescents. These adolescents were described by their peers in terms that reflected having taken on a position of power that their peers seemed to resent ("thinks she is the leader of everyone, she is bossy")—and could be considered inappropriate by the adolescents' standards. Moreover, we found descriptions of other adolescents whose maturity was marked by refraining from bossy and controlling behavior (e.g., "doesn't push you round" and "when she wants something, she makes sure she gets it without being pushy"). Thus, the bossy image seemed to be another form of maturity, divergent from the descriptions of genuine maturity.

Although these hallmarks indicated various types of maturity to us, we recognized that the adolescents had provided greater detail and integrated additional dimensions into their descriptions. Using these four hallmarks as guidelines, then, we re-examined the data to see what additional kinds of characteristics were associated with these hallmarks. Through this kind of immersion in the data, four pictures of maturity emerged. We then formulated an exhaustive description of each image based on the adolescents' own words. These descriptions (see the first four descriptions below) included defining characteristics grounded in the data. Examples were taken directly from the data to illustrate the essence of each image (see Table 3.1).

Initially, we used these four images as categories for coding the data and discovered that there were some data that could not be utilized. These responses, when reviewed further, revealed a fifth image emphasizing physical aspects of maturity. A description of this image was derived from the data, providing us with a data-grounded picture of five different maturities, as experienced by the adolescents.

Image 1: balanced, genuinely mature. Adolescents' descriptions of individuals who we refer to as *genuinely mature* would fit well into Greenberger's framework of psychosocial maturity. The adolescents indicated that these peers exhibit a good deal of autonomy, interpersonal adequacy, and social integration. Their autonomy is evident in descriptions of these individuals as independent and self-reliant ("he doesn't conform to people's decisions just to be cool," "confident, calm, secure, happy")—they seem to know who they are and what they want. They are also described as responsible ("he makes a lot of mature decisions," "serious when need be," "more accepting of responsibility"), setting and working toward goals ("knows her life goals," "does all her work," "completes important tasks"). Interpersonally, they appear to be adept: they are capable of controlling and expressing their emotions ("they are very calm, are helpful, do not get agitated easily," "can con-

trol and explain his feelings," "he talks about feelings instead of hiding them"), communicating their needs without being overbearing ("doesn't have to be pushy"), and able to settle disputes ("she is very calm when people are fighting, she tries to break it up or get them back together"), and seem to be accepted by their peers. Socially, they are caring and tolerant individuals, who may be described as nonjudgmental and accepting of others ("respects others' feelings, opinions, decisions, character," "the person doesn't judge people by what they look like, which I think is good"). As responsible as these individuals seem to be, they are able to maintain a developmentally appropriate balance of work and fun ("very responsible, knows all the time what's right and wrong, but always knows how to have a good time").

Image 2: focus on privileges. Adolescents with the image that focused on privileges reportedly engage in behaviors that create a façade of maturity. These individuals engage in a variety of problem behaviors to varying degrees, for example, "almost every weekend she will drink and do drugs she will stay out really late and break her curfew"; "gets in trouble by the police"; "fights." Interpersonally, they may get along with others, but appear to have a preference for older peers ("hangs around older kids," "doesn't talk to anyone her age only older people, thinks of us as immature and childish"). Many are also described as having an older "serious" boyfriend or girlfriend. There is also an emphasis on appearance, which may help them create a mature façade. For example, they may be described as "dressing older" or "dresses revealingly," wearing makeup ("wears a lot of make-up which makes her look 18"), and generally looking older ("they try to dress more 'grown up,' uses too much perfume"). There may also be a consumer orientation, with focus on shopping, buying the latest or most expensive fashion ("must wear the most expensive shoes," "buying clothing that is Levi's, Fruit of the Loom, etc."). These individuals probably lack true psychosocial maturity but are nevertheless looked up to and respected by many adolescents, who see them as being "cool" or "wicked." Other descriptions, however, suggest resentment toward these individuals (e.g., thinks that everyone else is too immature, shows off, looks down on others, drinks every weekend"; "I know some girls who try to act like they are grown up, but they are not, they're so immature most of the time, they think they're 'all that' when they're together, they try to dress more 'grown up' but people just end up calling them nasty names!"). The descriptions of individuals do not convey a sense

Table 3.1 Examples of the Five Images of Maturity in Adolescents' Own Words

Image of maturity	Frequency	%
Genuinely mature	115	48.7
"He thinks ahead of time and sacrifices, plans for something that is more beneficial in the long run, commits to something that he enjoys and works well at it, knows what is appropriate to do in the circumstances."		
"Doesn't let anger get in the way of good judgement, acts more mature, doesn't go about looking for trouble, enjoys sports but isn't overly rough helps people when they need it."		
"She knows her life goals and can look at things in a big picture, she's very open minded and outspoken, when she wants something she makes sure she gets it without being pushy."		
"This person is not self conscious, he likes his own life without people telling him how to act, he watches cartoons and does not rush to be older, but he does not whine when work is too hard."		
Focus on privileges	59	25.0
"He drinks beer, smokes pot, steals stuff with his friends, acts older, controls his parents, talks about and wants sex."		
"Wears too much make-up, thinks she's so great, swears too much, drinks and smokes and her parents don't care, talks about boys too much."		
"She wears older girls' clothes, she thinks too much of having a boyfriend, she smokes, she brags about wearing a bra."		
"He wears all this stuff that is way too big and he watches all the rated R movies and doesn't have to go to bed until he wants to. He has every video game and computer game you could think of."		
Focus on power and status	29	12.3
"Nagging, respectful, not rowdy, calm, thinks she is the leader of everyone, she is bossy."		
"Everything done perfectly, controlling."		
"Kinda snotty, not altogether that nice, 'know-it-all.' "		
"He acts stronger than his age and bosses me around."		
Focus on responsibilities	18	7.6
"She does not know how to have fun, she would never do something that made her look slightly foolish, quiet, never amused."		
"Only thinks about working, talks to other adults all the time."		
"Doesn't really like having fun, only thinks about working, not much fun."		
"Responsible, boring, 'perfect,' wears less colour."		
Focus on physical development	15	6.4
"This person is more physically mature."		
"His size, he's got to be 6′3″ "		
"He is mature, tall, looks old, big (strong)."		
"She is much, much taller than me."		
Total	236	100

of responsibility or orientation toward the future. Rather, the impression left by the descriptions is one of irresponsibility and living for the moment.

Image 3: focus on power and status. The image of maturity that focused on power and status described an adolescent who seems to have usurped or assumed a mature status, rather than being granted this status by socializing others (e.g., "thinks she's better than the average person," or "she thinks she is the leader of everyone"). They are generally described as being pushy and overbearing ("she is bossy," "nagging," "controlling"). They may have genuinely mature characteristics, such as being responsible or autonomous, but seem to have difficulty negotiating relationships in a socially inappropriate manner. For example, they may appear dictatorial, arrogant, or rigid ("everything done perfectly, controlling"), and may be seen in a somewhat negative light by their peers ("he is very selfish, thinks he's hot shit") Packer and Scott (1991) described similar qualities in a case study of a young girl who was largely rejected by her peers.

Image 4: focus on responsibilities. Those adolescents who fit the image focused on responsibilities are described as having assumed a level of responsibility and solemnity that may be beyond their years ("being *much too* serious," "she is *so* responsible" [emphasis added]). The evaluation of these adolescents is somewhat negative, in that other adolescents realize that these individuals may be unable to enjoy themselves ("doesn't really like having fun, only thinks about working, not much fun"), and, at the same time, positive in that these individuals may be perceived as responsible and intelligent. It seems that although they may be accepted by their peers, the responsibility-focused adolescents do not quite fit in. For example, their social life is described as being spent with adults or engaging in work rather than fun ("*only* thinks about working [emphasis added]," "talks to other adults all the time," or "doesn't know how to have fun," "not fun-loving, quite, not outgoing"). It is the perceived *inappropriate degree* of responsibility and seriousness and the perceived inability to have fun that distinguish them from the genuinely mature adolescents.

Image 5: focus on physical development. Those adolescents who fit this image are described as being more developed physically. Their maturity status is essentially based on nearly unidimensional description of their physical appearance, most often on their size and strength. No reference is made to behavior or personality characteristics that would place them in one of the other four categories. These peers were described as physically bigger (e.g., "bigger," "tall," "6'3''") or stronger (e.g., "more athletic," "can run fast," "is stronger").

These individuals do not necessarily lack the characteristics of any of the other four images, as they could very well fit into any of the groups. Rather, the descriptions of their focus solely on physical appearance. It may be that these individuals are more pubertal advanced than their peers.

These descriptions were used to code each adolescents' response into one of five categories. Questionable responses were brought to all three authors for discussion and consensus vote. To establish reliability of coding, the first 20 responses (approximately 10% the total) were coded by one of the authors and an independent rater. With adequate reliability established (94% agreement) and clarifications made, the rest of the description were coded by the independent rater. For a final reliability check, 40 of the responses were coded by one of the authors and the independent rater, resulting in 88% agreement (kappa = 0.84).

Quantitative Analyses

The frequencies of the categorical coding (see Table 3.1) reveal that the images that emphasize genuine maturity and focus on privileges are described most frequently, followed in succession by the images focusing on power and status, responsibility and physical development. Girls most frequently described a female peer (92.5%) and boys most frequently described a male peer (77.9%).

Gender and age differences in the frequency of maturity descriptions were examined using chi-square analysis (see Table 3.2). Although boys and girls both described genuinely mature most often, there was a difference in which image was described with the next highest frequency: girls described peers focusing on privileges, and boys described physically mature peers, χ^2 (4, n = 236) = 18.48,

Table 3.2 Gender and Grade Differences in the Images of Maturity

| Category | Cell count and percentage within category | | | | | | |
	Genuinely mature	Focus on privileges	Focus on physical	Focus on responsibilities	Focus on power/status	df/n	χ^n
Gender							
Female	65(46.4%)	45(32.1%)	9(6.4%)	13(9.3%)	8(5.7%)	4,236	18.48*
Male	50(52.1%)	14(14.6%)	20(20.8%)	5(5.2%)	7(7.3%)		
Grade							
6th	35(34.3%)	36(35.3%)	13(12.7%)	9(8.8%)	9(8.8%)		
9th	80(59.7%)	23(17.2%)	16(11.9%)	9(6.7%)	6(4.5%)	4,236	17.36*

*$p < 0.005$.

p < 0.005. A chi-square revealed grade differences in frequencies as well: sixth-graders described genuinely mature and privilege-focused peers at about the same rate, but ninth-graders described genuinely mature peers nearly four times as often as they described privilege-focused peers: χ^2 (4, n = 236) = 17.36, p < 0.005.

Next, a chi-square analysis was conducted to examine differences in descriptions based on whether the adolescent respondent wanted to "hang out" with the peer described (see Table 3.3). Due to small cell sizes for power/status-focused, responsibility-focused, and physically mature images, only the genuine mature and privilege-focused images were included in the analysis. Those adolescents who described genuinely mature peers overwhelmingly indicated that they would like to spend time with these peers, whereas adolescents describing privilege-focused peers were more mixed in their response, χ^2 (2, n = 168) = 33.24, p < 0.001. Specifically, more than two-thirds of adolescents describing mature peers wanted to spend time with them (i.e., answered "yes" to the question about whether they wanted to hang out with this peer), and among the remaining third, 22% indicated they might like to spend time with the mature peer (i.e., they answered "maybe"). In contrast, less than a third of those adolescents describing privilege-focused peers indicated they would, without qualification (i.e., they answered "yes"), like to spend time with the peer described. Slightly over one-third responded with an unqualified "no" and more than a third responded with an equivocal "maybe."

DISCUSSION

What does "grown up" mean to adolescents? These results suggest that most adolescents view maturity in much the same way as adults, focusing primarily on the hallmarks of genuine maturity. That is, in order to be considered mature, an individual must demonstrate competence on individual, interpersonal, and societal levels. These are the qualities of psychosocial maturity that are consistent with the values of Western society.

A smaller percentage of adolescents focused on other aspects of maturity. Adulthood in our society is achieved in part by physical maturation and brings with it power, privilege, and responsibility. Each of these elements is captured in one or more of the images of maturity. The images found have revealed portraits of maturity that may be understudied. Perhaps the most valuable information to be derived from this study is the descriptions of the power status- or responsibility-focused behaviors might be worthy of more attention. After all, power/status- and responsibility-focused images described by 12% and 8% of adolescents, respectively. If the adolescents' descriptions reflect reality, adolescents who could be described as having power/status- and responsibility-focused adolescents could conceivably suffer because of their apparent lack of connection to their peers.

We also discovered elements of pseudomaturity in the descriptions of privilege-focused images, cited by one-fourth of the sample. These descriptions reinforce suggestions by other scholars, for example, that consumerism, smoking, drinking alcohol, and other adult-like behaviors, appear to be driven by the desire to create and sustain an image of maturity. Finally, the least frequent image portrayed, physical maturity, demonstrated that physical markers were important to boys in particular.

A general theme that emerged from the adolescents' descriptions was the importance on balance. For example, adolescents' descriptions suggested that balancing elements of maturity was important. Some descriptions of maturity, such as the images focusing on responsibilities, privileges, or power and status, suggest that overemphasizing one aspect or maturity might result from or lead to short-

Table 3.3 Frequency of Adolescents' Desire to Hang out with Genuinely Mature and Privilege-Focused Peers

| Image | Cell count and percentage within category | | | df/n | χ^2 |
	Yes	Maybe	No		
Genuinely mature	80(70.8%)	25(22.1%)	8(7.1%)		
Focus on privileges	15(27.3%)	21(38.2%)	19(34.5%)	2,168	33.24*

*p < 0.001.

comings in interpersonal adequacy. For example, genuinely mature adolescents were often described as able to handle their emotions, express their emotions in respectful ways, convey their needs and desires without impinging on the rights of others, interact pleasantly with peers, and resolve interpersonal conflict. In contrast, the adolescents who seemed to be focusing on power and status were described as pushy and dictatorial, indicating a lack of interpersonal adequacy. These adolescents, judging from the tone of the adolescents' descriptions, may have been more likely to create interpersonal conflict than to resolve it.

Emphasis on balance was echoed in the adolescents' descriptions of mature adolescents who could balance work and fun. For example, not being able to balance work and fun was the hallmark of the image focused on responsibilities—being too invested in responsibilities to be able to enjoy being with and acting like an adolescent. Most of the adolescents seem to recognize the importance of not "growing up too fast"—relating through their descriptions that they are not wholly enamored with their peers whose maturity was focused on privilege, power, or responsibility, without being tempered by a balanced emphasis on getting along well with others and behaving responsibly, while still having fun.

The quantitative phase of this study revealed gender and grade differences in the images described, highlighting potentially interesting interindividual and developmental differences. Although boys and girls both described a genuinely mature peer most frequently, the second most frequently described image for boys and girls differed. Boys described the physical characteristics of a peer, while girls described a peer who was privilege-focused. Perhaps for boys, the schema of physical use is important because being larger is associated with masculinity. For girls, their greater pubertal maturity (relative to boys) might draw them into the kinds of behavior associated with the privilege-focused image.

With respect to the grade difference, sixth-graders describe the privilege-focused image of maturity almost four times as often as ninth-grades. Perhaps younger adolescents, who are just beginning to explore what becoming an adult means, find the image of maturity represented by the privilege-focused peers, with its apparent emphasis on instant gratification, more appealing than genuine maturity's delay of gratification in service of future goals. Greene's (1986) review of the relevant literature suggests that older adolescents, when compared to younger adolescents and children, have more complex future orientations and are more purposeful and organized about their future aspirations. This orientation may make mature, future-oriented peers more salient or desirable to older adolescents.

Another explanation for the grade difference stems from the increased importance of peer relations in early adolescence (Savin-Williams and Berndt, 1990). For younger adolescents, associating with "adultoids" and engaging in risky behavior with them may be viewed as a means of gaining peer acceptance. Maggs et al. (1995) found that those adolescents who engaged in more frequent risk-taking activities reported more peer involvement. Also, those who increasingly took more risks between the ages of 12 and 14 years experienced increased peer acceptance. For the younger adolescent, taking increased risk may be perceived as a viable and legitimate way to facilitate desired peer involvement.

With regard to the question of whether or not the adolescents wanted to spend time with the peer they described, interestingly, it was found that the majority of adolescents who described mature peers also wanted to spend time with them. In comparison, adolescents who described privilege-focused peers seemed more ambivalent toward them. Those that indicated that they would like to spend time with their privilege-focused peers may perceive the privilege-focused peers as "cool" and desire similar attention. Moffitt (1993) argues that problem behaviors serve to raise adolescents' peer status and that the attention that such status draws is justification enough for some to engage in deviant behavior. In comparison, those who responded "maybe" to spending time with the privilege-focused peers, while being drawn to the attention and status, may find the lure of problem behaviors too risky for their tastes. Alternatively, given that adolescents vary considerably in their evaluation of the benefits (e.g., relieving boredom, having fun, being accepted by peers) and risks (e.g., disappointing parents, getting addicted to drugs, being called a "goody-goody") of problem behaviors (Furby and Beyth-Maron, 1992; Maggs et al., 1995), perhaps those adolescents who expressed a desire to associate with privilege-focused peers have different evaluative processes than those adolescents who were more cautious.

The adolescents who want to spend time with their privilege-focused peers may be attracted to the "living for the moment" attitude, similar to the adolescents in Europe who seem to be engaging in "hedonism for hard times" (Coleman and Hendry, 1999). This route to maturity might be more compelling to these adolescents, especially if these adolescents perceive that what others consider more "normative" or "legitimate" routes to maturity are not amenable to them.

A limitation of this study is the homogeneity of the sample, which was made up primarily of individuals of European descent. It may be that adolescents from cultures that are less individualistic and more commonly oriented (e.g., some Asian cultures) may provide interesting variants of the images in this sample. For example, instead of emphasizing self-reliance and independent thinking, adolescents from other cultures might describe some as more grown up when they focus on responsibility to family and respect for elders. There is also a self-selection bias inherent in the way the information was collected. That is, not all adolescents responded to the open-ended questions. Examination differences between those who responded with information about their experiences and those who did not showed that those who responded were more likely to be girls, older, more independent, with better-educated parents. Perhaps these individuals are more likely to respond because of perceived expectations (e.g., expected to complete all the questions wanted to appear helpful to the researchers or the school staff), or because they felt comfortable in responding (e.g., more open to revealing personal information). Perhaps those who did not respond could not be bothered. Some caution then, is needed in generalizing the results.

Although other coding systems might have coded the data differently (e.g., descriptive categories such as those utilized by Arnett, 1994), the vivid, multidimensional pictures that were provided by this analytic strategy would probably not have merged. The strength of qualitative analysis is that it allows for rich thematic portrayals to be drawn from the data. Additionally, reframing the question we used might yield variations on these themes. For example, if adolescents were asked to describe someone who seems like an adult, the response might paint yet another picture.

This study's portrayals stemming from adolescents' subjective experiences echoed what other researchers have suggested—that attending to adolescents' understandings their experiences allows us to gain a deeper understanding of what is important in their lives and to their development (Shucksmith and Hendry, 1998). It is good news, to hear from adolescents, that they are fully cognizant of what it means to be truly mature—being self-reliant, responsible, and concerned about the well-being of others as well as oneself. Perhaps it is not surprising, though, that for many adolescents the lure of adulthood may be in the privileges that it

represents, and not on the assumption of responsibilities and behaviors associated with psychosocial maturity. We would not expect young adolescents to have either a truly adult understanding of maturity or to act, think, and feel like genuinely mature adults. In one phase of our study, we asked their parents to write down the way they help their adolescents mature. One mother noted: "Engage her in different conversations about growing up and what is expected of her *at this age* and what *will* be expected *as she grows up and matures* [emphasis added]." This mother recognizes that the development of psychosocial maturity is a process that continues well into adulthood.

This work was funded by the Social Sciences and Humanities Research Council of Canada to N. Galambos. N. Galambos and E. Vitunski are at the University of Victoria, B.C., Canada. We would like to thank the Greater Victoria District staff, students, and parents who made this research possible.

References

Arnett, J. J. (1994). Are college students adults? Their conceptions of the transition to adulthood. *Journal of Adult Development, 1,* 213–224.

Arnett, J. J. and Tabor, S. (1994). Adolescence terminable or interminable: When does adolescence end? *Journal of Youth & Adolescence, 23,* 517–537.

Blishen, B. R. and McRoberts, H. A. (1976). A revised socio-economic index for occupations in Canada. *Canadian Review of Sociology & Anthropology, 13,* 71–79.

Coleman, J. C. (1979). *The School Years.* London: Methuen.

Coleman, J. C. and Hendry, L. (1990). *The Nature of Adolescence* (2nd edition). London: Routledge.

Coleman, J. C. and Hendry, L. (1999). *The Nature of Adolescence* (3rd edition). London: Routledge.

Eccles, J. S., Midgley, C., Wigfield, A., Buchanan, C. M., Reuman, D., Flanagan, C. and MacIver, D. (1993). Development during adolescence: The impact of stage-environment fit on young adolescents' experiences in schools and in families. *American Psychologist, 48,* 90–101.

Furby, L. and Beyth-Maron, R. (1992). Risk taking in adolescence: A decision-making perspective. *Developmental Review, 12,* 1–44.

Galambos, N. L., Kolaric, G. C., Sears, H. A. and Maggs, J. L. (1999). Adolescents' subjective age: An indicator of perceived maturity. *Journal of Research on Adolescence, 9*, 309–338.

Galambos, N. L. and Tilton-Weaver, L. C. (2000). Adolescents' psychosocial maturity, problem behavior and subjective age: In search of the adultoid. *Applied Developmental Science, 4*, 178–192.

Greenberger, E., Josselson, R., Knerr, C. and Knerr, B. (1975). The measurement and structure of psychosocial maturity. *Journal of Youth and Adolescence, 4*, 127–143.

Greenberger, E. and Sorensen, A. B. (1974). Toward a concept of psychosocial maturity. *Journal of Youth and Adolescence, 3*, 329–358.

Greenberger, E. and Steinberg, L. (1986). *When Teenagers Work: The Psychological and Social Costs of Adolescent Employment.* New York: Basic Books.

Greene, A. L. (1986). Future-time perspective in adolescence: The present of things future revisited. *Journal of Youth & Adolescence, 15*, 99–113.

Greene, A. L., Wheatley, S. M. and Aldava, J. F., IV. (1992). Stages on life's way: Adolescents' implicit theories on the life course. *Journal of Adolescent Research, 7*, 364–381.

Hendry, L. B. (1983). *Growing up and Going out.* Aberdeen: Aberdeen University Press.

Hendry, L. B., Shucksmith, J., Love, J. G. and Glendinning, A. (1993). *Young People's Leisure and Lifestyles.* London: Routledge.

Hurrelmann, K. and Engel, U. (1989). *The Social World of Adolescents: International Perspectives.* Berlin: W. de. Gruyter.

Jessor, R. (1998). *New Perspectives on Adolescent Risk Behavior.* New York: Cambridge University Press.

Ketterlinus, R. D. and Lamb, M. E. (1994). *Adolescent Problem Behaviors: Issues and Research.* Hillsdale, NJ: Lawrence Erlbaum.

Lerner, R. M. and Galambos, N. L. (1998). Adolescent development: Challenges and opportunities for research, programs, and policies. *Annual Review of Psychology, 49*, 413–446.

Maggs, J. L., Almeida, D. M. and Galambos, N. L. (1995). Risky business: The paradoxical meaning of problem behavior for young adolescents. *Journal of Early Adolescence, 15*, 344–362.

McCreary Centre Society (2000). *Listening to BC Youth: Capital Region.* Burnaby, BC: McCreary Centre Society.

Moffitt, T. E. (1993). Adolescence-limited and life-course-persistent antisocial behavior: A developmental taxonomy. *Psychological Review, 100*, 674–701.

Newcomb, M. D. and Bentler, P. M. (1988). *Consequences of Adolescents Drug Use: Impact on the Lives of Young Adults.* Newbury Park, CA: Sage.

Packer, M. J. and Scott, B. (1991). The hermeneutic investigation of peer relations. In *Children's Development within Social Context, Vol. 1: Metatheory and Theory*, L. Winegar and V. Valsiner (Eds.) (pp. 75–111). Hillsdale, NJ: Lawrence Erlbaum.

Peterson, C. (1996). *Looking Forward through the Lifespan: Developmental Psychology* 3rd edition. Sydney, Australia: Prentice-Hall.

Savin-Williams, R. C. and Berndt, T. J. (1990). Friendship and peer relations. In *At the Threshold: the Developing Adolescent*, S. S. Feldman and G. R. Elliott (Eds.) (pp. 277–307). Cambridge, MA: Harvard University Press.

Scheer, S. D. and Palkovitz, R. P. (1994). Adolescent-to-adult transitions: Social status and cognitive factors. *Sociological Studies of Children, 6*, 125–140.

Shucksmith, J. and Hendry, I. (1998). *Health Issues and Adolescents.* London: Routledge.

Switzman, S., Marshall, S., Tilton-Weaver, L. and Adams, G. R. (1998). *Are We There Yet? Subjective Experiences of the Transition to Adulthood.* Paper presented at the biennial meeting of the Society for Research on Adolescence, San Diego, CA.

Ziervogel, C. F., Ahmed, N., Flisher, A. J. and Robertson, B. A. (1997–98). Alcohol misuse in South African male adolescents: A qualitative investigation. *International Quarterly of Community Health Education, 17*(1), 25–41.

JAMES G. BARBER
FLOYD BOLITHO
LORNE BERTRAND

4

Parent-Child Synchrony and Adolescent Adjustment

Introduction

Although the notion of interactional synchrony has received a great deal of attention in the developmental literature (Chu and Powers, 1995), most of the interest has centered on infants and their caregivers, particularly mothers. Synchrony has been variously defined depending on the context and intent of the research but all definitions share an emphasis on patterns of reciprocation or "give-and-take" between two interacting parties. More specifically, the available evidence suggests that successful parenting is associated with the caregiver's capacity to see the world through the child's eyes. Brazelton, Yogman, Als, and Tronick (1979), for example, have described synchrony as comprised of behavioral, affective, and cognitive signals that structure communication within a "mutually regulated feedback system" (p. 30). In most studies, operational definitions have involved monitoring levels of harmonious responsiveness (Brown and Avstreith, 1989) and, most commonly, accurate interpretation of infant signals (Ainsworth, 1973; Bowlby, 1982; Isabella and Belsky, 1991). There is now firm evidence from this work that synchronous parent-child interactions confer substantial advantages in the areas of cognitive and social development. Signal responsiveness, for example, has been associated with secure attachment during infancy itself (Ainsworth, 1973, 1989; Isabella and Belsky, 1991), as well as with social competence and various other measures of social adjustment many years later (Rice, 1990; McGee and Williams, 1991).

Efforts to extend the concept of synchrony beyond infancy have been relatively rare, but what work has been done supports the proposition that parent-child synchrony remains developmentally significant at least into adolescence. Papini and Micka (1991), for example, have shown that congruence between parents' and adolescents' ratings of adolescent pubertal maturity is associated with positive family functioning, leading the authors to conclude that parent-adolescent relationships are influenced by the degree to which the parties have shared (synchronous) evaluations of adolescent maturity. Similarly, Eccles et al. (1993) and Chu and Powers (1995) have proposed stage-environment fit models that are built on the idea that adolescent adjustment is strongly influenced by the synchronicity of adolescent-parent interactions and expectations. Such work supports Eleanor Maccoby's (1992) claim that the field of adolescent development has been moving away from the idea that parenting is something adults do to children, toward the view that adults and children are partners in the child's development; that what matters most is the parent-child *relationship*, characterized by reciprocity of influence and mutual responsiveness, and empathy.

By contrast, Forehand et al. (1997) found parental limit-setting and monitoring to be much more important than parent-child communication in accounting for deviant behavior among African American and Hispanic adolescents. In this study, the authors surveyed almost 1,000 adolescents and their mothers across three communities and found that higher levels of monitoring, but not parent-adolescent communication, predicted lower levels of adolescent deviance in each community and in both ethnic groups. Similarly, Deslandes and Royer (1997) administered a questionnaire measuring family predictors of school disciplinary events to around 250 first-year high school students and found that parental supervision and limit-setting were negatively correlated with school disciplinary events. What the work of Forehand et al. (1997) and Deslandes and Royer (1997) have in common is their use of antisocial behavior as the operational definition of adjustment. Thus, it may be that parenting practices, particularly limit-setting, are important in the prevention of behavior problems among adolescents, but that parent-child synchrony exerts greater influence on adolescent emotional adjustment.

As a mean of addressing this possibility directly, the present study compared parenting behavior with measures of relationship synchronicity in accounting for adolescent adjustment. Based on the foregoing literature, it was expected that parent-child synchrony would account for more of the variance in adolescent emotional adjustment, while parental limit-setting and involvement would account for more of the variance in conduct disorder. For the purposes of this study, parent-child synchronicity was operationally defined as the degree of concordance between parent reports and child reports of the family environment and of the adolescent's emotional and behavioral state. Thus, our fundamental predictions were that higher psychological adjustment would be found among adolescents when adolescents and their parents shared similar views of the family environment and the adolescent's psychological adjustment, but that lower conduct disorder scores would be more strongly associated with parental involvement and limit-setting.

Method

Respondents

The sample comprised 984 junior and senior high school students and their parents drawn from 95 schools in the Canadian province of Alberta. Parents and children completed separate questionnaires containing overlapping content. Respondents were drawn from schools that were randomly selected from each of the nine school districts in the province. Within these schools individual stu-

dents were selected by stratified random sampling according to age group from 12 through 18 years. In this way, the proportion of students within each age group from the total population within school districts was reflected in the final sample. Individual school districts were responsible for drawing the sample of students based on a required sample size. In a few cases where individual sampling was not possible, a classroom sampling method was adopted. In these cases, one or more classes that were mandatory for all students within the schools were randomly selected for participation in the study, thereby enhancing the representativeness of the sample. The 1,942 pupils who agreed to participate represent 72.5% of the children selected by the sampling strategy. After completing their own questionnaires, these children brought home a questionnaire and a reply-paid envelope for their parents. Nine hundred and eighty-four parents returned usable questionnaires. This figure represents 51% of the parents of children who participated. A demographic profile of participating parents and their children appears in Table 4.1.

Measures

The adolescent questionnaire comprised four sections: (1) questions relating to parenting practices, family background and demographic characteristics; (2) measures of behavior, psychological adjustment and relationship difficulties; (3) a measure of family environment, questions about the school environment and respondents' social lives; and (4) questions about respondents' experiences with cigarettes, alcohol, and other drugs. The parent questionnaire contained the same four sections as the adolescent questionnaire, although parents completed sections 2–4 in relation to the child.

In this report we focus on the correlates of child self-reported behavior and psychological adjustment. A more detailed description of the relevant measures follows.

Family Environment   Both the adolescent and parent questionnaires contained the 12-item summary scale of the Family Assessment Device (FAD) developed by Epstein, Baldwin, and Bishop (1983). The FAD measures the respondent's perception of how the family unit works together on essential tasks. Sample items from the FAD include: "In times of crisis we can turn to each other for support," "There are lots of bad feelings in our family," "I respect my parents' opinions on most things," and "Planning family activities is often dif-

Table 4.1 Demographic Characteristics of Respondents Broken Down by Gender

Variable	Males (n = 484)		Females (n = 500)		Total (n = 984)	
Age of Adolescent						
Mean	(15.01)		14.81		14.91	
(SE)	(7.61)		(7.24)		(5.25)	
	n	Percent	n	Percent	n	Percent
Performance in School						
90–100%	18	3.7	16	3.2	34	3.5
80–89%	119	24.6	128	25.6	247	25.1
70–79%	138	28.5	172	34.4	310	31.5
60–69%	134	27.7	128	25.6	262	26.6
50–59%	48	9.9	38	7.6	86	8.7
Below 50%	15	3.1	8	1.6	23	2.3
Father's Education						
Grade 9 or less	24	5	46	9.2	70	7.1
Some high school	67	13.8	53	10.6	120	12.2
Completed high school	90	18.6	104	20.8	194	19.7
Some col. or univ.	93	19.2	75	15.0	168	17.1
Completed col. or univ.	163	33.7	164	32.8	327	33.2
Don't know	47	9.7	58	11.6	105	10.7
Mother's Education						
Grade 9 or less	15	3.1	21	4.2	36	3.7
Some high school	44	9.1	60	12.0	104	10.6
Completed high school	153	31.6	178	35.6	331	33.6
Some col. or univ.	103	21.3	84	16.8	187	19.0
Completed col. or univ.	156	32.2	145	29.0	301	30.6
Don't know	13	2.7	12	2.4	25	2.5
Family Composition						
Mother & Father	377	78.0	393	78.6	770	78.3
Other arrangement	107	22.0	107	21.4	214	21.7
Religion						
Catholic	207	42.8	220	44.0	428	43.5
Protestant	112	23.1	112	22.4	224	22.8
Other	58	12.0	54	10.8	111	11.3
None	107	22.1	114	22.8	221	22.4
Location of Home						
Urban	341	70.5	341	68.2	682	69.3
Rural	143	29.5	159	31.8	302	30.7

ficult because we misunderstand each other." The 12-item summary scale produces a global assessment of family functioning, with higher FAD scores indicating poorer family functioning. Byles, Byrne, Boyle, and Offord (1988) have reported that this summary scale possesses an acceptable level of internal consistency ($\alpha = 0.86$).

Conduct Disorder   Adolescent conduct disorder was assessed using the adolescent's responses to the 15 items of the conduct disorder subscale from Boyle et al.'s (1987) Child Behavior Checklist (CBC). The CBC contains four subscales measuring somatization disorder, emotional disorder, hyperactivity, and conduct disorder. Subscale items were selected to operationalize DSM-III criteria for each disorder. Under the definition, conduct disorder refers to a "persistent pattern of physical violence against persons or property and/or severe violation of social norms" (Boyle et al., 1987, p. 826). Responses to each item are scored on 3-point scales from "0. Never or not true," "1. Sometimes true," "2. Often or very true."

Thus, total scores on the conduct disorder subscale could range from 0 to 30. Sample items include, "I am mean to animals," "I disobey at school," "I get in many fights," and "I cheat and lie."

Emotional Adjustment   The adolescents' emotional adjustment was measured using their own responses to the remaining subscales of the CBC: somatization disorder, emotional disorder, and hyperactivity. These subscales comprise 11, 13, and 6 items, respectively, and all are score in the same fashion as the conduct disorder subscale described above, meaning that scores could range from 0 to 22, 26, and 12, respectively. Somatization disorder refers to "current somatic symptoms without organic cause (Boyle et al., 1987, p. 826), emotional disorder items reflect high levels of anxiety, affective disorder, and obsessive-compulsiveness; and items on the hyperactivity subscale measure inattention, impulsivity, and hyperactive behavior. Sample items from the emotional disorder subscale include: "I can't get my mind off certain thoughts," "I cry a lot," and "I am not as happy as other children." Hyperactivity items include: "I act without stopping to think," "I have trouble sitting still," and "I am easily distracted, have difficulty sticking to any activity." Somatization items include: "I feel dizzy," "I have aches and pains," and "I worry a lot about my health."

After establishing threshold scores for clinically significant levels of each disorder (including conduct disorder), Boyle et al. (1987) assessed the concurrent validity of all subscales by comparing them to psychiatrists' diagnoses. This procedure resulted in very high levels of agreement (87% overall). Subscale test-retest reliabilities were high over a six- to nine-month separation. Internal consistency for each subscale was assessed using our own sample and all coefficients were acceptable: for somatization $\alpha = .80$, emotional disorder $\alpha = .82$, hyperactivity $\alpha = .70$, and for conduct disorder $\alpha = .86$.

Based on the current data set, correlations between CBC subscales were moderate to weak, ranging from $r = .42$ between hyperactivity and conduct disorder to $r = .29$ between somatization and conduct disorder.

Parental Behavior   Parenting items included 17 items measuring parental involvement extracted from the Canadian "Monitoring the Future Project" (Johnston, O'Malley, and Bachman, 1989). The parental involvement items asked respondents to indicate which of a list of 17 activities they engaged in with their children at least once per week. Sample items include: "Go to a video arcade or pool hall," "Go shopping," and "Church activi-

ties." Respondents scored 1 for each item checked. The internal consistency of the scale, calculated for the present sample, was $\alpha = 0.75$.

Parental limit-setting was measured on five separate 4-point scales in which parents indicated how often they: (1) checked on their child's homework, (2) helped the child with homework, (3) required the child to perform home chores, (4) limited the amount of time spent watching television, and (5) limited the time spent outside the home with friends on school nights. Scores on these items ranged from "1. Never" to "4. Often."

Procedure

Following identification of the students selected for the study, mailing labels containing parents' names and addresses were prepared by each school district. Each of these parents was dispatched a letter describing the study and indicating that their child had been selected to participate. The letter explained the content and purpose of the questionnaire in general terms and that participation was voluntary. If a parent or child refused permission, that child was removed from the list. A final list of participating students was then compiled and a convenient time for in-school administration of the questionnaire was determined with each school. After completing their own questionnaires, children were given another letter containing a parent questionnaire and a reply-paid envelope. A covering letter invited the parent to complete and return the questionnaire.

Results

Table 4.2 presents adolescent mean scores for each subscale of the CBC together with parent and adolescent FAD scores. The mean number of activities parents reported engaging in with their children (parental involvement) has also been presented in Table 4.2, along with means for each limit-setting items. Table 4.2 also records parent-child discrepancy scores. Discrepancy scores measure the difference between parent and child scores on the three psychological adjustment subscales of the CBC combined, the FAD, and parental limit-setting and involvement scores. In all cases, discrepancy scores were standardized and the sign was ignored so as to express the magnitude of the difference between parents and children, irrespective of direction. In the case of CBC discrepancy scores, each subscale was standardized before calculating total discrepancy scores expressed in the same fashion. Table 4.2 indicates that there was marginally more parental involve-

Table 4.2 Means and Standard Deviations (in parentheses) of Selected Variables

Variable	Males (n = 484)	Females (n = 500)	Total (n = 984)
Emotional Disorder[a]	6.41	8.91	7.68
	(4.05)	(4.71)	(4.57)
Somatization Disorder	4.80	6.93	5.88
	(3.44)	(4.07)	(3.92)
Hyperactivity Disorder	4.12	4.19	4.16
	(2.34)	(2.22)	(2.28)
Conduct Disorder	3.83	2.82	3.32
	(3.83)	(3.04)	(3.56)
Parental Involvement	4.58	4.22*	4.40
(Parent report)	(2.88)	(2.66)	(2.78)
Family Environment	35.02	34.74	34.88
(Child report)	(5.71)	(7.26)	(6.54)
Parent Limit-setting Items			
(Parent report)			
1. Checks Homework	3.19	3.01**	3.10
	(.88)	(.92)	(.90)
2. Has Home Duties	3.54	3.54	3.54
	(.64)	(.60)	(.62)
3. Limits TV Time	2.70	2.50***	2.59
	(.96)	(.98)	(.97)
4. Limits Time with	3.15	3.16	3.15
Friends	(.93)	(.92)	(.92)
CBC Discrepancy Score	.66	.75*	.80
	(.75)	(.66)	(.60)
FAD Discrepancy Score	.74	.80	.70
	(.60)	(.66)	(.71)

*p < .05; **p < .01; ***p < .001.
[a]Disorder scores calculated from child responses.

ment and limit-setting in the case of boys than girls. There was also a tendency for greater psychological discrepancy between girls and their parents than between boys and parents.

The variables appearing in Table 4.2 together with selected parent background variables from Table 4.2 were used as predictors in multiple regression analyses for conduct disorder and emotional adjustment. For the purposes of this analysis, emotional adjustment scores were a composite of scores from the hyperactivity, emotionality, and somatization subscales of the CBC. Results of the multiple regression have been summarized in Table 4.3, which presents standardized beta coefficients separately for boys and girls for each of the predictor variables in the model.

As Table 4.3 indicates, only two variables accounted for significant amounts of variance in dependent measures across adolescence: the child's assessment of family environment and the difference between adolescent and parent scores on the CBC.

With regard to the first of these variables, results indicate that higher levels of perceived family pathology were associated with more conduct disorder and poorer emotional adjustment. And with regard to CBC discrepancy scores, results indicate that the greater the discrepancy between parents and their children in their assessment of the child's conduct disorder and emotional adjustment, the greater was the level of disturbance in the child. Just as important as the significant results is the fact that the parenting variables accounted for so little of the variance in the adolescent's conduct or adjustment scores. Only limiting the time spent with friends was significantly associated with conduct disorder, and then only in girls, and even in their case, the effect was weak.

Discussion

Contrary to expectations, adolescent conduct disorder and psychological adjustment were not associ-

Table 4.3 Standardized Beta Coefficients of Predictor Variables with Adolescent Behavior and Adjustment Measures Controlling for Gender of Child

	Conduct Disorder		Emotional Adjustment	
	Male	Female	Male	Female
Child's Age	−.09*	.00	.06	.11**
Family Background Variables				
• Father's Education	−.09*	.03	−.10	.00
• Mother's Education	.02	−.04	.06	−.02
Family Environment (Child report)	−.32****	−.37****	−.35****	−.34****
Parental Involvement	−.06	−.04	.03	.02
Limit-Setting Variables				
• Checks homework	−.03	.06	−.05	.05
• Assigns home duties	.03	−.02	.01	−.03
• Limits TV time	.00	.00	.00	.02
• Limits time with friends	.06	.11**	.00	−.02
CBC Discrepancy Score	.44****	.32****	.26****	.31****
FAD Discrepancy Score	−.05	.03	.01	.02
F	23.8****	19.4****	12.5****	15.8****
R^2	.40	.34	.26	.30
Adjusted R^2	.38	.32	.24	.28
SE	3.13	2.50	1.95	2.11
N	483	499	483	498

*$p < .05$; **$p < .01$, ***$p < .001$, ****$p < .000$.

ated with different characteristics of the parent-child relationship. Of particular interest was the absence of associations between parenting practices and conduct disorder scores. By contrast, family environment and parent-child synchrony were strongly predictive of emotional adjustment and conduct disorder. From one point of view, these are encouraging results because they imply that, during adolescence at least, children may be capable of adapting to considerable variation in parenting practices, particularly in relation to limit-setting and parental involvement. What really does seem to matter to adolescents, however, is their subjective experience of the family environment and the extent to which their parents are attuned to their (the adolescents') psychological state. In other words, a warm, supportive family environment, together with the presence of at least one parent capable of taking the child's perspective, are the factors most likely to optimize adolescent development generally.

In arriving at these conclusions, it is acknowledged that the study itself contains two important limitations. The first of these concerns the study sample. Although the level of agreement to participate in the study was quite good at 72.5%, only 51% of the parents who agreed actually returned their questionnaires. As a result, the representativeness of the sample is uncertain. A second limitation of the study concerns the scope of the measure of parent-child synchrony, which was operationalized as the level of agreement between parents and their children in their appraisal of the family environment and the child's level of adjustment. While this is clearly a valid indicator of synchrony, it is also a limited one. In keeping with the infant-parent literature, it would be preferable to obtain more direct measures of the parent's accuracy in interpreting the child's verbal and nonverbal behavior, as well as of the parent's responsiveness to these signals. If these same measures were also obtained of the adolescent child's accuracy and responsiveness in relation to his or her parent, it would be possible to derive an index of the degree of mutuality in the parent-child relationship.

Notwithstanding these limitations, results of this study have potentially important implications for social work practice. The emphasis in numerous popular parenting programs is that specific practices (particularly limit-setting and parental involvement) are associated with optimal developmental outcomes and that parents should be trained in these behaviors. Such thinking is built on a 'top-down' view of parenting. The assumption is that if parents act on their children correctly, the children will be formed appropriately and in accordance with the parents' aspirations for the child. In contrast to this view, the findings of this study imply that no one set of parenting practices is likely to be right for all adolescents. Rather, clinical social work with adolescents and their parents needs to focus on the promotion of family harmony and parental empathy. No doubt these qualities of family life are influenced by parenting practices. However, the point is that it is the relationship—not the parenting practices—that is paramount, so whatever parenting strategies are promoted, the ultimate measure of success should be relationship synchrony, not compliance with a set of prescriptions about parental behavior.

References

Ainsworth, M. D. S. (1973). The development of infant-mother attachment. In B.M. Caldwell & H.N. Ricciuti (Eds.), *Review of Child Development Research* (*Vol. 3*). Chicago: University of Chicago Press.

Ainsworth, M. D. S. (1989). Attachments beyond infancy. *American Psychologist, 44,* 709–716.

Amato, P. R. (1984). *The Piers-Harris Children's Self Concept Scale: An Evaluation of Its Use on an Australian Population.* Melbourne: Australian Institute of Family Studies Working Paper No. 6.

Bernieri, F. J., Reznick, J. S. & Rosenthal, R. (1988). Synchrony, pseudosynchrony, and dissynchrony: Measuring the entrainment process in mother-infant interactions. *Journal of Personality and Social Psychology, 54,* 243–253.

Bertrand, L. D., Smith, R. B., Bolitho, F. H. & Hornick, J. P. (1994). *Substance Use among Alberta Adolescents: Prevalence and Related Factors.* Edmonton, Alberta: Premier's Council in Support of Alberta Families.

Bowlby, J. (1982). *Attachment and Loss, Vol. 1: Attachment.* New York: Basic Books.

Boyle, M. H., Offord, D. T., Catlin, G. P., Byles, J. A., Cadman, J., Crawford, W., Links, P. S., Rae-Grant, N. I. & Szatmari, P. (1987). Ontario Child Health Study: I. Methodology. *Archives of General Psychiatry, 44,* 826–831.

Brazelton, T. B., Yogman, M. W., Als, H. & Tronick, E. (1979). The infant as a focus for family reciprocity. In M. Lewis & L. Rosenblum (Eds.), *The Child and Its Family.* New York: Plenum Press.

Brown, J. J. & Avstreith, Z. A. (1989). On synchrony. *Arts in Psychotherapy, 16,* 157–162.

Byles, J., Byrne, C. M., Boyle, M. H. & Offord, D. R. (1988). Ontario Child Health Study: Reliability and validity of the general functioning subscale of the McMaster Family Reliability and validity of the general functioning subscale of the McMaster Family Assessment Device. *Family Process, 27,* 97–103.

Chomsky, N. (1959). Review of verbal behavior, by B.F. Skinner. *Language, 35,* 26–58.

Chu, L. & Powers, P. A. (1995). Synchrony in adolescence. *Adolescence, 30,* 453–461.

Clark, R. D. & Shields, G. (1997). Family communication and delinquency. *Adolescence, 32,* 81–92.

Deslandes, R. & Royer, E. (1997). Family-related and school disciplinary events at the secondary level. *Behavioral Disorders, 23,* 18–28.

Eccles, J. S., Midgley, C., Wigfield, A., Buchanan, C. M., Reuman, D., Flanagan, C. & Iver, D. M. (1993). Development during adolescence: The impact of stage-environment fit on young adolescents' experiences in schools and families. *American Psychologist, 48,* 90–101.

Epstein, N. B., Baldwin, L. M. & Bishop, D. S. (1983). The McMaster Family Assessment Device. *Journal of Marital and Family Therapy, 9,* 171–180.

Forehand, R., Miller, K. S., Durta, R. & Chance, M. W. (1997). Role of parenting in adolescent deviant behavior: Replication across and within two ethnic groups. *Journal of Consulting and Clinical Psychology, 65,* 1036–1041.

Hartup, W. W. (1989). Social relationships and their developmental significance. *American Psychologist, 44,* 120–126.

Isabella, R. A. & Belsky, J. (1991). Interactional synchrony and the origins of infant-mother attachment: A replication study. *Child Development, 62,* 373–384.

Kochanska, G. (1992). Children's interpersonal influence with mothers and peers. *Developmental Psychology, 28,* 491–499.

Lewis, C. C. (1981). The effects of parental firm control: A reinterpretation of findings. *Psychological Bulletin, 90,* 547–563.

Maccoby, E. E. (1992). The role of parents in the socialization of children: An historical overview. *Developmental Psychology, 28,* 1006–1017.

Marta, E. (1997). Parent-adolescent interactions and psychosocial risk in adolescents: An analysis of communication, support and gender. *Journal of Adolescence, 20,* 473–487.

McGee, R. & Williams, S. (1991). Social competence in adolescence: Preliminary findings for a longitudinal study of a New Zealand 15-year old. *Psychiatry, 17,* 493–514.

Noller, P. & Callan, V. J. (1990). Adolescents' perceptions of the nature of their communication with parents. *Journal of Youth and Adolescence, 19,* 349–362.

Papini, D. R. & Micka, J. C. (1991). Synchronization in ratings of pubertal maturity and faulty beliefs about family relationships. *New Directions for Child Development, 51,* 33–49.

Piers, E. V. & Harris, D. B. (1969). *Manual for the Piers-Harris Children's Self Concept Scale.* Nashville, Tenn.: Counselor Recordings and Tests.

Piers, E. V. & Harris, D. B. (1977). *The Piers-Harris Children's Self Concept Scale. Research Monograph No. 1.* Nashville, Tenn.: Counselor Recordings and Tests.

Rice, K. G. (1990). Attachment in adolescence: A narrative and meta-analytic review. *Journal of Youth and Adolescence, 19,* 511–538.

Russell, A., Pettit, G. & Mize, J. (in press). Horizontal qualities in parent-child relationships: Parallels with and possible consequences for children's peer relationships. *Developmental Review.*

Scott, W. A. & Scott, R. (1989). Family correlates of high-school student adjustment: A cross-cultural study. *Australian Journal of Psychology, 41,* 269–284.

Scott, W. A., Scott, R. & McCabe, M. (1991). Family relationships and children's personality: A cross-cultural, cross source comparison. *British Journal of Social Psychology, 30,* 21–35.

Shek, D. T. L. (1997a). The relation of parent-adolescent conflict to adolescent psychological well-being, school adjustment, and problem behavior. *Social Behavior and Personality, 25,* 277–290.

Shek, D. T. L. (1997b). Family environment and adolescent psychological well-being, school adjustment, and problem behavior: A pioneer study in a Chinese context. *Journal of Genetic Psychology, 158,* 113–128.

Shek, D. T. L. (1998). A longitudinal study of the relations between parent-adolescent conflict and adolescent psychological well-being. *Journal of Genetic Psychology, 159,* 53–67.

Steinberg, L. (1987). Recent research on the family at adolescence: The extent and nature of sex differences. *Journal of Youth and Adolescence, 16,* 191–197.

Steinberg, L. (1990). Autonomy, conflict, and harmony in the family relationship. In S.S. Feldman & G.R. Elliot (Eds.). *At the Threshold: The developing Adolescent.* Cambridge, Mass.: Harvard University Press.

GREER LITTON FOX
CAROL BRUCE
TERRI COMBS-ORME

5

Parenting Expectations and Concerns of Fathers and Mothers of Newborn Infants

As reflected in the small but rapidly growing professional literature on fathers' roles in early infant development, recognition of the potential importance of fathers in caring for newborns is itself in its infancy. The nature of father involvement and its impact on child outcomes have dominated the attention of researchers (Lamb, 1997a). There is less evidence of focus on the motivations, values, and beliefs that lead men to construct their father role in various ways. Role theory would suggest that the expectations of significant others are of great importance in shaping the enactment of one's role (LaRossa & Reitzes, 1993a).

Changes cultural definitions of the role of father, including changing expectations of the nature and extent of his involvement and intended impact on his offspring, have been traced over more than two centuries of American history by several researchers (Coltrane, 1995; Griswold, 1993; LaRossa, 1988; LaRossa, Gordon, Wilson, Bairan, & Jaret, 1991; LaRossa & Reitzes, 1993b; Pleck & Pleck, 1997). Currently, the good father is defined as a coparent who is expected to share the roles of provider, protector, and caregiver with the mother (Furstenberg, 1988; Marsiglio, 1995; Pleck & Pleck, 1997). Some contest whether this set of cultural expectations is shared equally across race and social class lines and whether these expectations are reflected in men's behavior (Furstenberg, 1995; Griswold, 1993). Recent survey evidence points to a gap between such participatory expectations and men's behavior in the home; even so, it is the care of children that the highest rates of

men's domestic participation are seen (Acock & Demo, 1994; Goldscheider & Waite, 1991).

The popular literature and media reflect the current definition of the good father as coparent, with special media features routinely focused on the new "nurturant father." It is not unreasonable to expect that at least some of the attention in the popular media to new styles of fathering may be reflected in a changed set of normative expectations for whether and how fathers are to be involved with their infant children. However, little is known about the schedule of expectations parents may actually have of the father's participation in caring for a new baby or for his provision of financial, material, and emotional support to the mother. This paper provides an overview of such expectations on the part of fathers of newborns, with paired comparisons to those of mothers. That is, we ask what fathers of newborns expect of themselves and what their baby's mother expects of them as well.

A second issue explored in this paper is the expression of concerns and worries that mothers and fathers have about taking care of their infant, including concerns about potential maltreatment. Some who have studied parents of newborns have discovered them anxious to discuss their fears and concerns (Cowan & Cowan, 1990). However, little empirical research has specifically addressed fathers' concerns about aspects of caring for their children. In particular, there is no research that addresses fathers' and mothers' concerns about the potential for abusing or neglecting their children

(Egeland, 1991), and there are no reports of child abuse prevention programs directly asking either mothers or fathers about these concerns. It is reasonable that knowledge about the concerns parents voice about parenting, in general, could provide important and useful information for designing family life education and preventive interventions for both mothers and fathers of newborns. Thus, a second purpose of this paper is to describe the concerns of fathers and mothers about caring for their new child.

A third issue explored here is the relationship between the consistency of a couple's expectations of paternal support and involvement with the newborn and the level of concern each parent expresses about taking care of his or her infant. We suggest, following the work of Kelley and Thiebaut (1978), that expectations are not only useful indicators of a person's location in "cultural space," but they also are powerful shapers of one's evaluations of experience. Previous research, drawing on violated expectations theory, has suggested that primiparous mothers' unmet expectations for help following childbirth were associated with greater dissatisfaction with mothering and a more difficult transition into the parent role six months postpartum (Kalmuss, Davidson, & Cushman, 1992). We extend this idea to couples, exploring whether associations exist between partners' expectations for father's involvement in parenting and levels of mother's and father's concerns about caring for their child. Following violated expectations theory, we reason that inconsistency across the parents in their expectations for the father's assistance with the baby will be an additional stressor in their transition to parenting. If we are correct in our reasoning, we would expect this additional stress to be reflected in the expression of a greater number and higher levels of concerns about caring for the child on the part of both the father and mother. Additionally, given that the study of Kalmuss et al. focused on the experiences of primiparous mothers, we explore whether the relationship between unmatched parental expectations for paternal participation and concerns about child care might vary with the mother's or father's previous parenting experience.

Each of these issues is investigated with interview data from a study of mothers of newborns and their partners. The remainder of the paper is structured as follows: a description of study methods and sample characteristics is provided, along with a detailed description of measures. Then fathers' and mother' expectations for father participation are examined and compared, followed by a description and comparison of fathers' and mothers' concerns and worries about parenting their child. Next, couples are characterized by the match of their expectations about the father's participation: the relationship between the level of consistency in their expectations and their expressions of concern about parenting is then explored. We conclude with a discussion of implications of our findings for further research and for those who work with expectant parents and parents of newborns.

Methods

Sample

Mothers Over consecutive seven-day periods in different weeks, we interviewed newly delivered mothers with surviving, well infants in two large Tennessee hospitals. One was an urban, university-affiliated hospital in a metropolitan area of moderate size, and the other was a nonuniversity hospital located in a smaller, regional city. Both hospitals served not only their base urban populations, but provided services for rural and small-town residents in outlying areas. Private interviews with mothers took place in the mothers' room, after they were moved from Labor and Delivery to the postpartum units and were comfortable and free of anesthetic. Mothers with uncomplicated vaginal deliveries are discharged approximately 24 hours after delivery, and those with uncomplicated Caesarean sections are discharged 48 hours after delivery, so our interviews took place from 12 to 48 hours following delivery. Of the total 93 delivering women we approached in the two sites during the sample period, we collected usable data from 88 (94.5%). This sample of 88 women is reasonably representative of the population, with the exception of a slight underrepresentation of very young mothers. Our overall refusal rate for mothers was 4.5% in the metropolitan site and 6.1% in the regional city site.

Recruitment of Fathers At the end of their interview, mothers were asked for permission to interview their partner; only after receiving the mother's permission were partners recruited for the study. Of the 88 women, 75 agreed to our interviewing their partner and provided contact information. We were able to interview 54 of the partners (72%). Comparisons of the sociodemographic characteristics of mothers with interviewed partners and mothers whose partners were not interviewed revealed no significant differences (χ^2 tests) between the mothers by age, race, education, relationship status, or parenting experience.

Fathers were successfully recruited in conjunction with a hospital visit to the mother prior to discharge. Extensive effort was made to reach fathers not available in the hospital for a telephone interview, but these efforts (just over 150 telephone calls) netted only four additional interviews. The four fathers who were interviewed by telephone were interviewed within two weeks of their child's birth. With one exception, there were no differences of expectations or concerns between these fathers and those interviewed face-to-face. The fathers who were interviewed after the child returned home reported significantly higher expectations for providing emotional support to their partners when compared to those who were interviewed in the hospital (t = -3.560, p = .011). This fact is taken into account for analyses including this variable.

Interviews were completed with 66% of the partners of White women and 61% of African American women. As might be expected, relationship status was selective of men's participation: 70% of married, residential fathers participated;

48% of father living with but not married to their partner participated; and 40% of nonresidential fathers participated. Fathers were interviewed apart from mothers, generally in an available office or other hospital room where privacy could be assured. As was also true of mothers, fathers who completed interviews were given $10 gift certificates to a discount chain store.

Couple Characteristics As Table 5.1 shows, the sample of couples obtained at the two sites was diverse in terms of age, race, education, income, relationship status, and parenting experience. Although the paired sample was predominantly in their twenties, both teenage and older parents were represented (mean age = 27.6 (fathers), 26.2 (mothers); SD = 6.2 (fathers), 6.2 (mothers)). Approximately one-fourth (n = 11) of the couples were Black, 3 were biracial, 1 was Asian, and the remainder were White. The majority of both mothers and fathers in this sample achieved a high school diploma or beyond; incomes varied substantially, with a slight overrepresentation of couples in higher income categories (the median household income for the state in 1994–96 was $30,327; Pollard &

Table 5.1 Sociodemographic Characteristics of Fathers and Mothers (N = 54)

Variable		Fathers N	Fathers %	Mothers N	Mothers %
Age	<20	4	7.5	8	14.9
	20–30	30	54.6	31	57.3
	>30	20	37.7	15	27.8
Race	White	39	73.6	41	75.9
	Black	13	24.5	12	22.2
	Other	1	1.9	1	1.9
Education	Less than high school	7	16.7	15	27.7
	High school diploma or GED	31	57.4	18	33.3
	Post high school training	7	13.0	12	22.4
	College 4 years or more	7	13.0	9	16.7
Total Annual Income	$ <5,000	3	5.6	—	—
	$ 5K–15K	6	11.1	—	—
	$15K–25K	13	24.1	—	—
	$25K–35K	8	14.8	—	—
	$35K–60K	16	29.6	—	—
	$ 60K +	8	14.9	—	—
Relationship Status	Married, coresident	37	68.5	36	66.7
	Married, not coresident	0	—	1	1.9
	Unmarried, coresident	12	22.2	11	20.4
	Unmarried, not coresident	5	9.3	6	11.1
Previous Parenting Experience	None	21	38.9	23	42.6
	Some	33	61.1	31	57.4

Crews, 1998). In terms of marital or relationship status, two-thirds were married and living together, just over one-fifth were coresidential unmarried partners, and the remaining couples were nonresidential unmarried partners. (Four couples had discrepant reports of their marital or residential status.) To assess previous parenting experience, respondents were asked, "In the past year, how many children (your own or other children you had responsibility for) were living with you?" As shown in Table 5.1, over one-half of the fathers and mothers reported living with children for whom they were responsible in the past year. Comparisons across sites showed more Black couples in the smaller regional city site ($\chi^2 = 3.14$, p = .076), but no significant differences in respondents by other sociodemographic indicators, including income and education.

Measures

The interviews required about 20 minutes and included standard sociodemographic items, an assessment of expectations for paternal assistance, concerns about parenting, and several other attitudinal scales not included in the present analyses. Because several measures were new to this study, we paid particular attention to their psychometric properties.

Help Expectations   The assessment of expectations for paternal assistance was developed for this study based on a measure used by Kalmuss et al. (1992). In order to facilitate comparability, and despite its construction of the father as "mother's helper," we retained the wording of the question stem used in the original source. The series of questions was introduced as follows: "Some men help out a lot after a baby is born; other men don't. How much help do you expect [your baby's father] to be . . . " Then both mothers and fathers were asked to respond, using a 7-point helpfulness rating scale (1 = not at all helpful; 7 = a very great help), to a general "overall helpfulness" question and five domain-specific questions, including basic economic support; monetary support specifically for baby items such as diapers and formula; direct baby care such as feeding, and diapering, and bathing; housework such as laundry and meal preparation; and providing emotional support for the partner. The individual items were designed to tap both traditional male gender role domains (resource provision) as well as more contemporary constructions of father-partner participation (baby care, house-

work, and emotional support of the partner). Although exploratory factor analysis for the mothers' responses showed that the items comprised a single dimension of helpfulness, this was not the case for the fathers' responses. Given this finding and our interest in domain-specific expectations, the Help Expectation items were used singly in the analyses.

Parenting Concerns   Parenting concerns is a new measure. It contains 14 items for mothers and 16 items for fathers and is designed to be used with parents of newborns, regardless of previous parenting experience, for assessing a range of potential concerns about caring for their new infant. The problematic nature of definitions and assessments of child maltreatment has long been recognized in the literature (Garbarino, 1989; Sedlack & Broadhurst, 1996; Zuravin, 1991). In constructing this scale we took care to include a few items that could be indicative of parents' fears about their potential for maltreatment through neglect or abuse, with items roughly paralleling some of the kinds of behaviors that have been used as indicators of maltreatment (Sedlack & Broadhurst, 1996). For each item of concern, parents were first asked if the item (e.g., "That you will have enough food to feed your baby") was of concern to them. Parents who responded affirmatively were then asked to rate their level of concern on a scale of 1 (not much concern) to 10 (a very great deal). The format of this scale was taken from the divorce concerns scale, a similarly structured sale that assesses men's concerns about the potential impact of divorce parenting (Fox & Bruce, 1999). Exploratory factor analyses indicated that the concerns items could be used as a unidimensional scale (Total Concerns: alpha = .91 for mothers; alpha = .90 for fathers), or that we could derive three factors with items including Physical Care (6 items, alpha = .85 for mothers, alpha = .88 for fathers), Parenting (5 items, alpha = .59 for mothers, alpha = .63 for fathers), and Maltreatment (2 items, alpha = .97 for mothers, alpha = .93 for fathers).

Results

Help Expectations

The first two columns of Table 5.2 show, respectively, the expectations (means and standard deviations) of fathers' helpfulness across different domains for fathers (Dads) and their partners (Moms). Al-

TABLE 5.2 Help Expectations for Fathers (Dads), Paired Mothers (Moms), and Mothers with Partners Not Interviewed (PNI Moms)

Helpfulness Domain	1		2		3		4		5	
	Dads (n = 54)		Moms (n = 54)		PNI Moms (n = 34)		Dads and Moms Comparison		Moms and PNI Moms	
"How helpful do you expect [the baby's father] to be . . . "	Mean	SD	Mean	SD	Mean	SD	t	p	t	p
Overall help	6.52	1.21	6.15	1.23	5.09	2.04	1.937	0.58	−3.044	.003
Providing money for basic needs	6.87	0.52	6.65	1.17	5.41	2.41	1.244	.219	−3.220	.002
Providing money for baby's needs	6.70	0.74	6.65	1.07	5.94	2.01	0.312	.756	−2.149	.034
Baby care tasks	5.89	1.49	5.61	1.55	4.24	2.40	1.054	.297	−3.273	.002
Housework tasks	6.11	1.30	5.65	1.80	4.12	2.52	1.914	.061	−3.318	.001
Emotional support of baby's mother	4.50	2.42	6.20	1.48	5.12	2.47	−4.207	.000	−2.579	.012

though this is a study of couples, a third group—mothers whose partners were not interviewed (PNI Moms)—was included for comparative purposes in the examination of help expectations. Having found no sociodemographic differences between the women, we were curious as to whether the partner expectations held by the two groups of women would be similar as well. The fourth column shows the results of paired t-tests and resulting significance levels for the help expectations of Dads and Moms, and the fifth column shows results of independent t-tests and resulting significance levels for Moms and PNI Moms.

Looking first at the expectations of the fathers, it is notable that the levels of expected helpfulness were uniformly high (6.11 or above on a 1–7 point scale) across all but two domains: physical care of the baby and emotional support of the partner. The average father expected to be quite involved in supporting his family. It is also notable that the two areas in which men expect to be most helpful were the gender role traditional provider functions: providing money for running the household and providing money for "things the baby needs." In analyses not shown, paired comparisons of the fathers' responses across each of the five specific help domains showed that fathers held significantly higher expectations for their help as economic provider than for being helpful in the remaining domains (baby care; t = 4.77, p = 0.000; housework, t = 4.19, p = .000; and emotional support, t = 7.15, p = .000).

The mothers' expectations for help from the fathers (column 2) showed overall expectations for the same high levels of father involvement as was seen among the fathers; all means are 5.6 or above

on the 1–7 scale. As with the fathers themselves, mothers expected their partners to be of greatest help in the economic provider functions (paired t's were nonsignificant on these items). In contrast to the fathers' expectations, mothers expected their partner to be less helpful in providing direct physical care for the baby and in helping with housework, although these differences are not significant. The largest discrepancy in partners' expectations for the fathers' helpfulness was found in the mothers' expectations of emotional support, an expectation not reciprocated by the Dads (t = −4.207; p = .000).

In analyses not shown, we examined the impact of previous experience with children on expectations of helpfulness from fathers. It is not unreasonable to expect that previous parental experience would lead to a different schedule of expectations of one's own or one's partner's performance as a father than found among first-time parents. For fathers, previous parental experience was not a significant factor in the levels of help they expected to provide. Mothers with previous parental experience reported significantly lower expectations in two areas: maternal assistance (t = 2.26, p = .030) and assistance with infant care (t = 2.50, p = .016), and marginally lower expectations for assistance with domestic tasks (t = 1.83, p = .074).

We also examined the relationship between three sociodemographic variables (education, income, and race) and help expectations for fathers and mothers separately. In a multiple regression model containing the three variables simultaneously, none predicted mothers' expectations for helpfulness. For fathers, race was significant for three of the six help expectations: Black fathers had significantly higher expectations for baby care and housework helpfulness (B = −.334, p = .024, B = −.310, p = .034); and they had lower expectations for provision of emotional support than nonBlack fathers (B = .348, p = .020). To control for the possible impact of the larger number of Black respondents at one site, a variable for hospital site was entered into the regressions for mothers' and fathers' helpfulness expectations. The results for the mothers were unchanged. But the effects for race on fathers' expectations for helpfulness were almost completely mediated by the site variable, and no longer significant.

The expectations of partner support from women whose partners were not interviewed (column 3) offer additional insight into the nature of expectations for father involvement after the birth of his child. Immediately noticeable is the lower level of average expectations for help among the PNI Moms as compared to the mothers whose partners we interviewed: all of the pairwise differences are significant (column 5). It is also notable that the order of expected help across domains is similar for both sets of mothers; that is, after expecting their partner to provide economic support for the baby and secondarily for the home, the mothers expected their partner to be most helpful in providing them with emotional support. Recall that there were no significant differences between the Moms and the PNI Moms on sociodemographic indicators, including relationship status. The distinction between these two sets of mothers lies in our not reaching the fathers for the study. The fathers' inaccessibility to us during the study (caused primarily by their not visiting the hospital during the hours of our data collection and not responding to our attempts to reach them by telephone) is matched by their seeming remoteness from the mother of their new baby, at least as measured in terms of her low expectations for his involvement in helping to care for his new child.

Parenting Concerns of Fathers and Mothers

The Concerns measure elicited at least some response of concern or worry from nearly all of the fathers, and from two-thirds of the mothers. Among the 54 parental pairs, only 4 fathers (7%) and 18 mothers (33%) expressed no concerns from our list. As Table 5.3 shows, the concerns voiced by the greatest number of fathers related to his ability to "take good enough care" of his child (61%)

and his ability to "keep your kids safe" (52%). Among mothers, concerns about safety (31%) and finding child care (31%) predominated. The items that asked specifically about fears of maltreatment yielded substantially different patterns between Dads and Moms. Not only did more fathers of newborns indicate some concern about their potential to harm their child, but their level of concern was significantly higher than that of the mothers, as shown in the paired t-tests. Moreover, more fathers than mothers were concerned that the mother might potentially harm their child. (Mothers inadvertently were not asked a comparable concerns question bout the child's father's potential to harm.)

A notable pattern in the responses of fathers to this list of concerns was the number of fathers worried about their ability to perform adequately in the provider role: the ability to provide food, a place to live, safety, someone to care for the child, and general provisions. The levels of worry about these concerns were among the highest in the list, and as shown in the results of the paired t-tests in column 3, Dads were significantly more concerned about their ability to provide than were Moms. Taken in conjunction with the high levels of expectation on both the mothers' and the fathers' parts about the fathers' helpfulness in the economic provider role (see Table 5.2), these results suggest that fathers of newborns may feel especially burdened by performance expectations in precisely the area in which their performance is most taken for granted.

Two other items differentiate fathers from mothers in terms of the number and level of concern. More men than women fear losing their children (18% vs. 4%), and their level of concern is significantly higher (t = 2.309, p = .025). This may say less about fear of child welfare agency personnel than it does about the men's recognition of the precarious linkage of young fathers to their children. Men, more than women, are likely to lose ready access to children when custody becomes an issue (Fox & Kelly, 1995). We suspect that for many of the men in these couples, especially those who are unmarried fathers, the fear that "your kids might be taken away from you" is more than a hypothetical concern (Fox & Bruce, 1999; Hetherington & Stanley-Hagan, 1997).

Significantly, more fathers than mothers (28% vs. 4%) expressed concern that "your kids tie you down too much" (t = 3.607, p = .001). The expression of reluctance to take on the father role immediately and completely is not uncommon among younger fathers (Christman, 1990; Fox, Sayers, & Bruce, 1998; Marsiglio, 1991). Given the burden

Table 5.3 Parent Concerns for Dads and Moms

Concern	Dads			Moms			Dads and Comparison**	
"Please tell me whether this is a concern to you . . . "	% with Concern	Mean*	SD	% with Concern	Mean*	SD	t	p
Physical Care Concerns								
Have enough food for baby	26	8.29	2.87	13	6.86	2.85	2.375	.021
Able to provide place to live	37	7.25	3.43	18	5.50	2.95	2.930	.005
Able to keep kids safe	52	6.79	3.00	31	6.82	2.75	1.091	.280
Able to find child care	37	6.05	3.35	31	7.00	2.89	0.050	.961
Able to provide for child	30	7.38	3.52	11	7.00	3.69	2.522	.015
Able to get baby to doctor when sick	18	5.67	4.15	13	6.86	3.80	0.117	.907
Able to pay for medicine when baby is sick	22	5.50	3.47	15	6.13	3.52	0.243	.809
Parenting Concerns								
Child could be taken away	17	6.78	3.90	4	4.00	1.41	2.309	.025
Child will tie you down	28	7.20	3.28	4	4.50	0.71	3.607	.001
Able to control child	18	4.40	2.50	22	4.33	3.14	−.0366	.716
Able to give enough attention	26	6.57	3.39	20	4.18	1.72	1.648	.105
Able to take good enough care	61	6.59	1.56	18	5.30	2.87	4.778	.000
That you will know how to take care of a baby	19	4.92	3.26	—	—	—	—	—
Maltreatment Concerns								
Could be tired enough to hurt baby	20	5.27	4.03	4	4.50	3.54	2.224	.030
Child could be so bad that you could hurt child	17	6.67	4.03	2	5.00	—	2.439	.018
That mother would hurt baby	15	4.88	4.00	—	—	—	—	—

*Means were calculated including only those with concern, range = 1–10.
**Paired t tests of means calculated for all responses, range = 0–10.

of expectations of providing and their concerns about meeting those expectations satisfactorily, it is not surprising that some of these fathers of newborns expressed worry about becoming locked into the father role.

As we did with the help expectations variables, we looked for an effect of previous parenting experience with children on the expression of concerns of fathers and mothers, respectively. Contrary to our expectations, this factor failed to differentiate among levels of expressed concern for either fathers or mothers. In further exploration, a multiple regression of concerns onto three sociodemographic factors (education, income, and race) indicated that these factors were significant predictors only for concerns associated with Physical Care. Among fathers, Physical Care concerns were predicted by income (B = −.421, p = .013), such that fathers with more income expressed fewer concerns in this area. Among mothers, race and income were significantly associated with Physical Care Con-

cerns (B = .376, p = .011; B = −.434, p = .011), such that White mothers and mothers with more income reported fewer concerns in this area. Notably, none of the sociodemographic variables were significantly correlated with the Parenting or Maltreatment Concerns subscales for either parent. As we did with the help expectations, we also reran the regressions including a dummy variable for hospital site; the addition of this variable did not alter the results for concerns for either the mothers or fathers.

Expectation Consistency and Parental Concerns

Recall that based on violated expectations theory we had suggested that discrepant expectations across partners would be associated with higher Concerns scores. Table 5.4 shows results of our examination of the relationship between the consistency of help expectations a couple has and their

Table 5.4 Regression of Mothers' Concerns Subscales on
Couple Discrepancies in Expectations for Help

Concerns Subscale	B	t	p
Overall Help Expectations[a]			
Physical Care Concerns	.045	0.32	.754
Parenting Concerns	−.300	−2.27	.027
Maltreatment Concerns	−.058	−0.41	.686
Domestic Help Expectations[a]			
Physical Care Concerns	−.279	−2.04	.047
Parenting Concerns	−.300	−2.27	.028
Maltreatment Concerns	−.132	−0.93	.357
Emotional Support Expectations[a]			
Physical Care Concerns	.108	0.76	.451
Parenting Concerns	.427	3.40	.001
Maltreatment Concerns	.205	1.47	.149

Discrepancy Score = Dad's Expectations − Mom's Expectations: higher de-
screpancy scores indicate that the father's expectations for helpfulness exceeded
the mother's.

level of expressed concern about caring for their child. Consistency in help expectations was measured by creating a differential expectations variable, computed by subtracting the score for the mother's expectations from the father's. Low scores on the resulting variable indicated that within the couple, the mother's expectations for assistance exceeded the father's, and high scores indicated that the father's expectations for providing help exceeded the mother's expectations for receiving help. A series of simple regression analyses were performed to test the influence of differential expectations on each of the three types of concerns. None of the analyses of the fathers' Concerns subscales was significant and are not shown. Table 5.4, which provides the analysis of the mothers' Concerns subscales, shows that the level of mothers' concerns about parenting is affected by discrepancies in a couples' expectations for help with housework and emotional support, as well as their expectations for overall helpfulness. When the mother's expectations for overall helpfulness exceeded the father's expectations, the mother reported higher Parenting Concerns. When the mother's expectations for help with domestic tasks exceeded the father's expectations, the mother reported higher Parenting and Physical Care Concerns. Finally, when the father's expectations for providing emotional support to the mother exceeded her expectations, the mother reported higher Parenting Concerns.

Although having had previous experience with children did not predict the level of concerns expressed by mothers, concerns or helpfulness expectations of fathers, and significantly predicted lower expectations of helpfulness for the mothers in only two areas, we decided to examine whether the relationships between helpfulness expectation differentials and expressed concerns might vary depending on the mother's previous parenting experience. The significance and directions of the reported relationships were not altered by the addition of the interaction between expectation differential and previous parenting experience. Similarly, the addition of interaction terms for race with expectation differential and for location with expectation differential did not alter the pattern of results reported in Table 5.4.

Discussion

Help Expectations

In general, the results show a high level of expectation on the part of fathers of newborns for participation in and support of their new family member. In this sense, the fathers in this study reflect the predominant cultural construction of the "nurturant father." Although our measuring instrument implies a "father as helper" construction, which relegates the father role to one that is subordinate to the mother role, nevertheless most of these fathers expected to be highly involved in the care of their newborn. At the same time, there was a clear differentiation in the arenas in which the fathers expected to participate and to provide assistance.

The provider role continues to dominate their expectations of "helpfulness," thus pointing to the continuing importance of the economic provider function to men's understanding of what it means to be a father.

It is of interest that, prior to taking hospital location into account, race was the only one of the three sociodemographic factors that differentiated among help expectations of fathers in the simultaneous regression models. The finding of Black fathers' higher levels of help expectations in baby care and chores around the home is consistent with the more egalitarian patterns of domestic task sharing some have found among Black couples (Acock & Demo, 1994; McAdoo, 1993). Black fathers were also significantly less likely to expect to provide emotional support to their baby's mother. This item taps into a domain of nurturance that could be considered central to the new "sensitive, nurturant" model of manhood and fatherhood. Some commentators have expressed concern that the "new man/father" model fosters cleavages among social classes, in part because the accessibility of real-time caregiving participation on the part of men may be a function of having sufficient resources and leisure time to enact this model (Fox & Bruce, 1996), and in part because knowing the "correct" social conventions (such as portrayal of self in interview settings) is a function of education and social class. In this way the "new man/father" model serves as a cultural icon that fosters and perpetuates social class distinctions in men's constructions of their husband and fathering roles (Griswold, 1993). Our finding from the multivariate regression that it was Black fathers who were less likely to expect to provide emotional support to the baby's mother lends only partial support to this argument, because both income and education were held constant in the analysis. At the same time, the fact that the effect of race was mediated or channeled through the hospital location variable suggests that the diffusion of cultural innovations may occur at different paces, not just along sociodemographic lines. It suggests that, despite the tendency of the mass media to push toward cultural homogeneity, change may occur more slowly in areas out of the mainstream. This pattern of effects may point to possible cultural particularities and cleavages in fathers' construction of the partnered parent role.

Of greater significance, however, is the potential impact of differential expectations for the father's support (regardless of the particular support domain) on the couple's interactions and relationship quality, and the subsequent quality of parental care that is provided to the couple's infant. Although we posited that discrepant expectations are likely experienced as stressful and thus would feed into higher levels of parental Concerns, we emphasize that stress in this model is an unmeasured, hypothesized intervening variable. Other pathways (e.g., role strain) also provide reasonable hypothesized linkages. It is also plausible that women minimize their expectations as a way of avoiding disappointment and conflict (Komter, 1989). The positive relationship between quality of marital (or coparental) interaction and parenting quality is one of the most consistent findings in the child and family development literature (excellent reviews are provided in Cummings & Davies, 1993; Cummings & O'Reilly, 1997; Lamb, 1997b). Unfortunately, given the nature of our data, we cannot demonstrate empirically a causal connection between our measures of couples' expectations of help from the father, their likely interaction patterns, the care they provide to their infant, and child outcomes. Our findings that the level of the mother's concerns about her parenting is associated with discrepancies in the mother's and father's expectations of his overall helpfulness and with housework and emotional nurturance are consistent with such a causal chain. The findings of Kalmuss et al. (1992) are pertinent here as well. They suggest that when mothers' expectations for help from their partner are violated, the potential for negative marital interactions, difficult transitions to parenthood, and less positive child outcomes is more likely.

Because the expectations of others are powerful shapers of behavior, partner expectations are salient to parenting in yet another way. In general, according to symbolic interaction theory, people seek to conform to the expectations that others have of their behavior, especially if the other person is significant or valued in some way by the actor (Klein & White, 1996). This implies that the expectations that mothers express for their partner's helpfulness can shape the level of involvement that men feel called on to provide. The finding that mothers generally expected lower levels of help than the fathers expected to provide is instructive because it could portend a lower level of actual participation than that preferred by the fathers of newborns. Ethnographic research among fathers has shown that sometimes new fathers have feelings of being pushed aside or discounted as caregivers by their partners in the first months of new parenthood (Fox & Bruce, 1996; Furstenberg, 1995; Heimer & Staffen, 1995). More attention to the subtle ways that men are shifted into lower levels of involvement or out of the father role altogether is warranted (Allen & Hawkins, 1999).

Parent Concerns

In general, the parents in this study expressed a high degree of confidence in their ability to care for their newborns. Mothers were significantly less likely than fathers to express high levels of concern. Two of our findings merit special attention. First, the fathers' expression of concern with fulfilling the provider functions of the father role suggest that this is a domain of potentially high role strain for fathers. Historically, the provider role has been the one consistent component in the construction of broad cultural models of the "good father" (Amato, 1998; LaRossa et al., 1991; Pleck & Pleck, 1997). It may well be that this is one element in male parenting that cannot be compensated for by more active participation in other domains of the parent role. Failure to meet expectations in the provider function of the father role has been blamed for the disengagement of men from their families, most especially among younger, lower-income, and inner-city families (Furstenberg, 1995; Liebow, 1967; Marsiglio, 1995). Our data suggest no diminution in the potency of provider role expectations in engendering concern on the part of the fathers.

Second, the expression of concern by fathers about their own and their partner's potential to harm their children is of considerable significance. Our findings that fathers of newborns, when given the opportunity, will voice concerns about behaving in potentially abusive ways toward their infant provides an important tool for accessing and short-circuiting the hidden family processes that result in child maltreatment. Our findings bear replication with a larger sample of couples who are parents of newborns, and one that does not have the regional limitations of the present data set. Although we looked for correlates of expressions of parent concerns, recall that none of the multivariate relationships was significant in identifying sociodemographic factors associated with maltreatment concerns for either fathers or mothers. A larger sample size would provide not only more power to detect small but significant relationships but also could accommodate the analyses necessary for more complete understanding of parenting concerns.

We are gratified that our new measure of parent concerns was able to elicit from parents a sense of the risks they feel they will face in caring for their children, especially concerns about maltreatment. This becomes important in light of the fact that research on parental behaviors indicative of child maltreatment is fraught with difficulties, ranging from legal requirements to report suspicion of parental maltreatment, to selectivity in respondent loss from study samples, to social desirability biases in reporting socially stigmatized and legally proscribed behavior. It should be noted that we found the total parent concerns measure to be almost as reliable as the more narrow maltreatment subscale. The total measure would incur less stigma than a measure specifically about abuse and neglect and could also be used to identify fathers and mothers and with other significant concerns about caring for their child. Further research is needed to refine this measure and to determine how it might be useful for identifying parents who need support and services to prevent early maltreatment. These findings are particularly noteworthy for settings where a primary prevention approach is desired, but where the routine administration of a child abuse screening measure may be unacceptable or impractical, that is, where there is access to a general population such as during prenatal care and in delivery settings.

Pregnancy has been called a "window of opportunity" to change parental behavior because of parents' high motivation at this time (Helfer, 1987); for example, drug-abusing parents frequently are able to stop or reduce consumption with the aid of such motivation (Chavkin, Allen, & Oberman, 1991). The delivery setting may provide strong motivation for men and women who have concerns about parenting, including reasons to fear their potential for hurting their children. Parents of newborns are usually enthralled by their infant, desirous of being good parents, and yet anxious about the task ahead of them (Cowan & Cowan, 1990; Lamb, 1997b). Moreover, most new parents are receptive to advice about parenting difficulties (Schmitt, 1987). Such circumstances may provide the optimal opportunity for identifying those at risk of partner misunderstandings, miscues, mismatched expectations, and parental maltreatment through the use of measures such as the Help Expectations and Parental Concerns measures with separate and conjoint discussions about identified problems. Indeed, we would reiterate the recommendation of Daro (1988) that pediatricians, nurses, social workers, and family life educators within the existing health care delivery system might use the postpartum period as an opportunity to inquire about parents' concerns. For service providers, the postpartum setting does not suffer from the selectivity bias of prenatal care settings, especially important for working with parents for whom prenatal care is obtained only late in pregnancy or not at all.

We emphasize that several of our findings have specific import for family life educators, in health care settings. First, our findings would support broadening the content of postpartum education services beyond family planning and immediate health care concerns to family life, parenting, and couple issues such as those reported here.

Second, we note the importance of making contact with experienced parents as well as those entering parenthood for the first time. The expectations and concerns voiced by experienced parents in this study were not simply hypothetical but were based on the realities of their previous experiences with children. The fact that the experienced mothers and fathers were virtually indistinguishable on our measures from their new parent counterparts underlines the importance of broad-based service provisions as opposed to approaches that triage recipients and reserve preventive education services for those presumed most needy. At the same time, we caution that while our measures were designed to be useful with both experienced and new parents for assessing a range of potential expectations and concerns about caring for their new infant, the scale items do not specifically include matters that could be expected to be of concern only to parents with additional children at home, such as incorporating the newborn into the household or establishing good sibling relationships. We acknowledge the suggestions of the associate editor and an anonymous reviewer of *Family Relations* who pointed out the incomplete nature of the concerns scale for experienced parents and who suggested that the inclusion of additional items of salience to experienced parents would alter our results and conclusions.

Finally, our comparison of two sets of mothers—those whose partner was and those whose partner was not interviewed—underlines the importance of bringing the male partner into the service setting. It is possible to overinterpret a father's absence from the birth of a child, in the same way that we may err to assume that men who display attentiveness in public settings, such as health care facilities, ae equally supportive to their partner and newborn in private. Nonetheless, the PNI mothers were not an insignificant group; they accounted for more than one-third of the women in the study. The dynamics of parenting by mothers of newborns with nonsupportive or noninvolved father/partner need exploration. How to respond to and provide family life educational services to couples with nonparticipatory father/partner is a special challenge.

Conclusion

The results support the contention that vital information can be obtained by asking fathers and mothers of newborns about their parenting expectations and concerns during the immediate perinatal period in health care settings. The fathers and mothers of newborns appear to have a sense and range of potentially serious problems. The timing and setting might make such information from parents useful for the effective design and delivery of family life and parenting education, including child abuse prevention services.

Funding for this research was provided by a grant from the National Institute of Mental Health (NIH R24 MH53623, "Children's Mental Health Services Research Center"). Charles Glisson, Principal Investigator. The authors thank the Mother Baby Unit staffs at the University of Tennessee, Knoxville and Jackson-Madison County General Hospital for their assistance in collecting these data.

REFERENCES

Acock, A., & Demo, D. (1994) *Family diversity and well being.* Thousand Oaks, CA: Sage.

Allen, S. M., & Hawkins, A. J. (1999) Maternal gatekeeping: Mothers' beliefs and behaviors that inhibit greater father involvement in family work. *Journal of Marriage and the Family, 61,* 199–212.

Amato, P. R. (1998) More than money? Men's contributions to their children's lives. In A. Booth & A.C. Crouter (Eds.), *Men in families—when do they get involved? What difference does it make?* (pp. 241–278). Mahwah, NJ: Erlbaum.

Chavkin, W., Allen, M. H., & Oberman, M. (1991) Drug use and pregnancy: Some questions on public policy, clinical management, and maternal and fetal rights. *Birth, 18,* 107–112.

Christmon, K. (1990) Parental responsibility and self-image of African-American fathers. *Families in Society: The Journal of Contemporary Human Services, 12,* 563–567.

Coltrane, S. (1995) The future of fatherhood: Social, demographic, and economic influences on men's family involvement. In W. Marsiglio (Ed.). *Fatherhood:*

Contemporary theory, research, and social policy (pp. 255–274). Thousand Oaks, CA: Sage.

Cowan, P. A., & Cowan, C. P. (1990) Becoming a family: Research and intervention. In I. E. Sigel & G. H. Brody (Eds.). *Methods of family research: Biographies of research projects. Volume I: Normal families* (pp. 1–52). Hillsdale, NJ: Erlbaum.

Cummings, E. M., & Davies, P. (1993) *Children and marital conflict: The impact of family dispute and resolution.* New York: Guilford.

Cummings, E. M., & O'Reilly, A. W. (1997) Fathers in family context: Effects of marital quality on child adjustment. In M.E. Lamb (Ed.). *The role of the father in child development* (pp. 49–65). New York: Wiley.

Daro, D. (1988) *Intervening with the new parents: An effective way to prevent child abuse.* Chicago: National Committee to Prevent Child Abuse.

Egeland, B. (1991) A longitudinal study of high-risk families: Issues and findings. In R. H. Starr, Jr. & D. Wolfe (Eds.). *The effects of child abuse and neglect: Issues and research* (pp. 33–56). New York: Guilford.

Fox, G. L., & Bruce, C. (1996) Development and validation of measures of parenting for low-income, high-risk men. In A. Acock (Ed.). *Proceedings of the NCFR theory construction and research methods workshop* (pp. 221–232), Minneapolis. National Council on Family Relations.

Fox, G. L., & Bruce, C. (1999) The anticipation of single parenthood: A profile of men's concerns. *Journal of Family Issues, 20,* 485–506.

Fox, G. L., & Kelly, R. F. (1995) Determinants of child custody arrangements at divorce. *Journal of Marriage and the Family, 57,* 693–708.

Fox, G. L., Sayers, J., & Bruce, C. (1998, March). *Beyond bravado: Self-appraisals in the fathering accounts of men who batter.* Paper presented at the meetings of the Southern Sociological Society, Atlanta, GA.

Furstenberg, F. F., Jr. (1988) Good dads—bad dads: Two faces of fatherhood. In A. J. Cherlin (Ed.). *The changing American family and public policy* (pp. 193–218). Washington, DC: Urban Institute.

Furstenberg, F. F., Jr. (1995) Fathering in the inner-city: Paternal participation an public policy. In W. Marsiglio (Ed.), *Fatherhood: Contemporary theory, research, and social policy* (pp. 119–147). Thousand Oaks, CA: Sage.

Garbarino, J. (1989) The incidence and prevalence of child maltreatment. In L. Ohlin

& M. Tonry (Eds.). *Family violence* (pp. 219–262). Chicago: University of Chicago Press.

Goldscheider, F. K., & Waite, L. J. (1991) *New families, no families? The transformation of the American home.* Berkeley: University of California Press.

Griswold, R.L. (1993) *Fatherhood in America: A history.* New York: Basic.

Heimer, C. A., & Staffen, L. R. (1995) Interdependence and reintegrative social control: Labeling and reforming "inappropriate" parents in neonatal intensive care units. *American Sociological Review, 60, 635–654.*

Helfer, R. (1987) The perinatal period, a window of opportunity for enhancing parent-infant communication: An approach to prevention. *Child Abuse & Neglect, 11, 565–579.*

Hetherington, E. M., & Stanley-Hagan, M. M. (1997) The effects of divorce on fathers and their children. In M. E. Lamb (Ed.). *The role of the father in child development* (pp. 191–211). New York: Wiley.

Kalmuss, D., Davidson, A., & Cushman, L. (1992) Parenting expectations, experiences, and adjustment to parenthood: A test of the violated expectations framework. *Journal of Marriage and the Family, 54,* 516–526.

Kelley, H., & Theibaut, J. (1978) *Interpersonal relations: A theory of independence.* New York: Wiley.

Klein, D. M., & White, J. M. (1996) *Family theories: An introduction.* Thousand Oaks, CA: Sage.

Komter, A. (1989) Hidden power in marriage. *Gender and Society, 3,* 187–216.

Lamb, M. E. (1997a) Fathers and child development: An introductory overview and guide. In M. E. Lamb (Ed.). *The role of the father in child development* (pp. 1–19). New York: Wiley.

Lamb, M. E. (1997b) The development of father-infant relationships. In M. E. Lamb (Ed.). *The role of the father in child development* (pp. 104–120). New York: Wiley.

LaRossa, R. (1988) Fatherhood and social change. *Family Relations, 37,* 451–458.

LaRossa, R., Gordon, B. A., Wilson, R. J., Bairan, A., & Jarét, C. (1991) The fluctuating image of the 20th century American father. *Journal of Marriage and the Family, 53,* 987–997.

LaRossa, R., & LaRossa, M. (1991) *Transition to parenthood: How infants change families.* Beverly Hills, CA: Sage.

LaRossa, R., & Reitzes, D. C. (1993a) Symbolic interactionism and family studies. In P. G. Boss, W. J. Doherty, R. LaRossa, W. R.

Schumm, & S. K. Steinmetz (Eds.). *Sourcebook of family theories and methods: A contextual approach* (pp. 135–162). New York: Plenum.

LaRossa, R., & Reitzes, D. C. (1993b) Continuity and change in middle class fatherhood, 1925–1939: The culture-conduct connection. *Journal of Marriage and the Family, 55,* 455–468.

Liebow, E. (1967) *Tally's corner.* Boston: Little, Brown.

Marsiglio, W. (1991) Male procreative consciousness and responsibility. *Journal of Family Issues, 12,* 268–290.

Marsiglio, W. (1995) Fathers' diverse life course patterns and roles—theory and social interventions. In W. Marsiglio (Ed.), *Fatherhood: Contemporary theory, research, and social policy* (pp. 78–101). Thousand Oaks, CA: Sage.

McAdoo, J. L. (1993) Decision making and marital satisfaction in African American marriages. In H.P. McAdoo (Ed.). *Family ethnicity: Strength in diversity* (pp. 109–119). Newbury Park, CA: Sage.

Pleck, E. H., & Pleck, J. H. (1997) Fatherhood ideals in the United States: Historical dimensions. In M. E. Lamb (Ed.). *The role of the father in child development* (pp. 33–48). New York: Wiley.

Pollard, K. M., & Crews, C.A. (1998) *1998 United States population data sheet.* Washington, DC: Population Reference Bureau.

Schmitt, B. D. (1987) Seven deadly sins of childhood: Advising parents about difficult developmental phases. *Child Abuse & Neglect, 11,* 421–432.

Sedlack, A. J., & Broadhurst, D. D. (1996) *Third national incidence study of child abuse and neglect. Final report.* U.S. Department of Health and Human Services National Center on Child Abuse and Neglect. Washington. DC: U.S. Government Printing Office.

Zuravin, S. J. (1991) Research definitions of child physical abuse and neglect: Current problems. In R. H. Starr, Jr. & D. A. Wolfe, (Eds.), *The effects of child abuse and neglect: Issues and research* (pp. 100–128). New York: Guilford.

J. MORGAN
D. ROBINSON
J. ALDRIDGE

6

Parenting Stress and Externalizing Child Behavior

Introduction

This paper reviews the literature on the relationship between parenting stress and children with externalizing behavior. Following an introduction to parenting stress and externalizing behavior, research that has investigated the predictors of parenting stress is reviewed. The third section addresses the consequences of high levels of parenting stress.

Children perceived as having externalizing behaviors, characterized by problems such as inattention, defiance, impulsivity, and aggression, account for a significant proportion of referrals to child and adolescent clinic psychology services. Conduct disorder has been identified in 8.3% of referred children age 4–11, and in 14% of referred children age 12–16 (Offord 1987), and attention deficit hyperactivity disorder (ADHD) in 16% of referred children (Taylor et al. 1996). Childhood externalizing behaviors also increase the risk of poor outcomes later in life, including criminality, mental, and physical health difficulties, and occupational, social, and marital adjustment difficulties (Farrington 1995; Kazdin 1995). Consequently, the identification of factors associated with increased risk for such behavioral problems in children and adolescents has been a major focus of developmental research (Spencer & McLloyd 1990; Johnston 1996). However, research in this area has typically focused on the behavioral characteristics of children and tended to neglect psychosocial and family environment (Schachar 1991; Cantwell

1996). In more recent research there has been an increasing recognition of the stressors faced by parents of children with behavior problems and how these stressors can affect parent-child relationships, for example, parents' ability to manage child behavior effectively and appropriately (Anastopoulos et al. 1992).

Although a number of different definitions of parenting stress have been used in the literature, there is a general consensus that it involves a mismatch between perceived resources (e.g., knowledge and self-efficacy beliefs) and the actual demands of the parenting role (Goldstein 1995; Deater-Deckard & Scarr 1996). It has been suggested that this mismatch and the subsequent stress is "experienced as negative feelings towards the self and towards the child or children, and by definition these negative feelings are directly attributable to the demands of parenthood" (Deater-Deckard 1998, p. 315). One of the most influential models of parenting stress has been developed by Abidin (1976, *A Model of Parenting Stress*, unpublished manuscript, University of Virginia, Charlottesville). The model proposes that the total stress a parent experiences is a function of certain salient parent characteristics (e.g., depression, sense of competence, health, attachment relationship with child, relationship with spouse, perceived role restrictions) and child characteristics (e.g., adaptability, acceptability, demandingness, mood, hyperactivity, reinforcement of the parent). Abidin proposes that these parent and child characteristics, together with external situational variables, such as life stresses (e.g., divorce, bereavement, career difficulties), lead to an increased risk of dysfunctional parenting. Abidin's model was subsequently used to guide the construction of the Parenting Stress Index (PSI) (Abidin 1995). This is a self-report instrument comprising three main subscales measuring stress in the Parent Domain and the Child Domain and Life Stress. The PSI has been used as a clinical screening tool (p. 2), to allow early identification of parent-child systems under excessive stress, and to improve the efficacy of interventions aimed at helping parents manage their child's behavior more appropriately and effectively (Kazdin 1995).

Predictors of Parenting Stress

Although all parents experience parenting stress to some degree (Crnic & Greenberg 1990), parents of children with externalizing behaviors report significantly higher levels of parenting stress than parents of nonexternalizing children (Gillberg et al. 1983; Mash & Johnson 1983a; Barkley et al. 1988; Webster-Stratton 1988; Beck et al. 1990; Eyberg et al. 1992; Ross et al. 1998). Parents of externalizing children typically perceive themselves as having less parenting knowledge, less parental competence, and fewer emotional and instrumental supports than parents of nonexternalizing children (Mash & Johnson 1990). The variables identified as being related to levels of parenting stress include child characteristics (e.g., behavior, age, birth order, number of siblings), parent characteristics (e.g., psychological well-being), and negative life events.

Child Variables

Child behavior problems, as measured by parental reports (e.g., using the Child Behavior Checklist, Achenbach & Edelbrock 1983), have been found to be predictive of parenting stress (Anastopoulos et al. 1992; Baker 1994). Mash and Johnston (1983b), in a study investigating parents of children diagnosed with ADHD, reported higher levels of parenting stress among parents of younger children. Higher levels of parenting stress have also been observed among parents of first-born externalizing children (Mash & Johnston 1990) and in families where more siblings are present (Mash & Johnston 1983b). The child's health status has also been proposed as a potential influence on parenting stress; some studies have found that raising a child with health difficulties is associated with higher levels of parenting stress (e.g., Bendell et al. 1986). This is important since children with exter-

nalizing behaviors tend to experience higher incidences of health problems than nonexternalizing children (Hartsough & Lambert, 1985).

Parent and Family Characteristics

Research has attempt to identify those characteristics of parents and family structure which are predictive of parenting stress. Although it is generally recognized that the experiences of coping with a family environment that includes a child displaying externalizing behavior may be different for mothers and fathers, the majority of research has neglected fathers and focused on mothers (Phares 1995, 1996, 1999). The few studies that have compared mothers' and fathers' parenting stress have produced conflicting evidence. Some researchers have found little difference between mothers and fathers in terms of their mean levels of stress and anxiety in the parenting role (Krauss 1993; Deater-Deckard et al. 1994; Creasey and Reese 1996). Others have argued that mothers experience higher levels of parenting stress than fathers (Webster-Stratton 1988; Baker 1994). A number of different explanations have been proposed to account for these conflicting findings. Stoneman et al. (1989) suggest that mothers' parenting stress may be more strongly related to attributes of the child, whereas fathers' parenting stress may be most strongly related to satisfaction in the marital relationship. On the other hand, Deater-Deckard (1998) argues that gender differences in the levels of parenting stress may emerge only within certain family contexts, for example, where there are high levels of marital discord. Other researchers (e.g., Barnett and Baruch 1987) have turned to social role theory, which argues that gender differences are due to socialization pressures which are present from an early age. Within this framework it is argued that the extent to which mothers and fathers experience different levels of parenting stress is dependent on how they perceive family roles such as household tasks, caregiving, and employment. The more similar their perceptions of these roles, the more likely they are to report similar levels of parenting stress, and vice versa. However, empirical research in this area is rather sparse.

Despite the fact that the majority of research has focused on mothers, there is a paucity of studies that include single mothers as a separate group. Studies that have looked at the experiences of single mothers in general suggest that they experience more stress than women living with partners (Weinraub & Wolf 1983; Forgatch et al. 1988). In families with one or more children with some form of externalizing behavior there is evidence that single mothers fare less well than women living with a partner. Single mothers perceive themselves as being significantly more stressed, reported more child behavior problems, and were observed to have more critical and controlling behaviors than mothers who reported themselves as being either martially distressed or supported by their spouses. Children of these single mothers were also observed to exhibit more deviant and noncompliant behaviors than the children of either martially distressed mothers or supported mothers (Webster-Stratton 1989). More recently, Melzter et al. (2000) have argued that children living with a stepfather or a single parent are approximately twice as likely to be identified as having externalized behavior problems than those living with both biological parents. However, it is important to point out that this relationship is not simply cause and effect. There are a number of factors, including the complexity of the stepfamily, length of time within the stepfamily, and age of the child or children, which can act as moderators (Fine & Schwebel 1991). Nevertheless this evidence does suggest that single mothers of children exhibiting externalizing behavior may be particularly vulnerable to high levels of parenting stress.

Life Events

Abidin (1995) argues that life events occurring outside the parent-child system have their effect by depleting parents' emotional resources and perceived ability to cope with their parenting role. There is a considerable amount of research that suggests that stressful life events (e.g., housing problems, death of a relative, loss of employment) are associated with the levels of parenting stress experienced by parents of children with externalizing behavior (e.g., Gaines et al. 1978; Patterson 1983; Wahler & Dumas 1984; Adamakos et al. 1986; Forgatch et al. 1988; Webster-Stratton 1988; Campbell & Ewing 1990; R. Taylor et al. 1997).

Although some researchers have found that socioeconomic status (SES) does not significantly predict parenting stress (Anastopoulos et al. 1992), others have found it to be significantly predictive of high level of such stress (Mash & Johnston 1990; Baker 1994). The nature of the relationship between SES and parenting stress is by no means clear. Baker's findings suggest that higher SES is associated with higher levels of parenting stress, whereas Mash & Johnston found the opposite: lower SES was associated with high levels of parenting stress. In an attempt to explain these contradictory findings, Baker suggests that both high and low SES have their own "particular set of stressors that limit parent coping or resources in such a way as to heighten parent-child interactive stress" (p. 50). However, the extent to which SES is predictive of parenting stress in parents of children exhibiting externalizing behavior remains unclear.

Consequences of Parenting Stress

A number of studies have set out to explore the hypothesis that increased parenting stress is associated with dysfunctional parenting. The concept of dysfunctional parenting is based on two main assumptions which are generally accepted within clinical psychological settings. The first assumption is that it is possible to identify different parenting styles. The second is that some styles are more likely to be beneficial for children's development than others. Although the concept of dysfunctional parenting and the way it is operationalized in research varies, nevertheless the research presented in this section highlights important issues that are relevant to practitioners working with children and families. The link between high levels of parenting stress and negative parental behavior is well established in the literature. For example, Ethier, Lacharite, and Couture (1993, *Childhood Adversity, Parental Stress and Depression of Negligent Mothers*, unpublished manuscript, University of Quebec, Trois Rivieres, Canada) found higher levels of parenting stress associated with mothers whose parenting style was classified as negligent. MacInnis (1984) found that mothers reporting high levels of parenting stress also tended to report high levels of irrational beliefs about parenting behavior. Mothers categorized as physically abusive have also been found to have significantly higher levels of parenting stress than non-physically abusive mothers (Mash et al. 1983).

Having established that there is an association between parenting stress and dysfunctional presenting, more recently the aim of research has been to identify factors that mediate this relationship. Spencer and McLloyd (1990) argue that parenting stress does not inevitably lead to dysfunctional parenting, and the vast majority of parents, even in difficult situations, do manage a competent level of parenting. This implies that there are other factors that may act as a "buffer," reducing the detrimental impact of such stresses on parenting behavior. Johnston (1996) suggests that parental perceptions of child behavior mediate the relationship between parent stress and parent behavior. According to Johnston, parents' perceptions of child behavior are highly influenced by their expectancies of child behavior, which are general and stable beliefs about how their child will behave. For example, parents who hold the belief that sugar ingestion causes their child's externalizing behavior have been found to rate their child's behavior more negatively and be more critical and directive in their interaction with their child when informed that their child had recently received sugar, regardless of whether this was actually true or not (Hoover & Milich 1994). This suggests that parental expectancies not only influence parental perceptions of child behavior, but also influence parent behavior. Fischer (1990) suggests that a mechanism for the relationship between parenting stress and dysfunctional parenting behavior may include:

> (a) selective attention to negative aspects of past and current child behavior (Jouriles et al. 1989), (b) increased likelihood of making negative attributions about the behavior (Patterson 1982), and (c) lowering of parental threshold for aversive child behavior (Lahey et al. 1984; Schaughency & Lahey 1985), all of which may result in increased negative responses to the child. (p. 344)

This framework has obvious clinical and practical implications. Given that the initial request for referral usually comes from the parents, it is reasonable to assume that they already perceive their child as behaving in some kind of undesirable way and have begun to develop a cognitive set of expectancies of their child's behavior. Importantly, the process of requesting a referral to a child and family service may itself act to strengthen these expectancies. If parents respond to their children on the basis of these expectancies, rather than on actual behavior, as already described, then they may continue to request help, despite the initial behavior ceasing or becoming less of a problem. However, as Reid et al. (1987) rightly state, given the relationship between parents' expectancies and parenting behavior, the accuracy of parents' perceptions is not as important as realizing that if "an involved adult reports that there is a problem with a child, whether this represents perceived or actual difficulties, there is in fact a problem" (p. 458).

One of the problems faced by researchers investigating the relationship between parent stress and externalizing child behavior is identifying the direction of any causal relationships between parenting stress, perceptions of child behavior, parenting behavior, and child/parent factors such as age and SES. The directional nature of such relationships has been the subject of disagreement within the literature. For example, researchers such as Johnston (1996) and Fischer (1990) suggest a unidirectional relationship between parent stress, parental perceptions of child behavior, and parent behavior. That is, child behavioral disturbance may be the effect, rather than the cause, of preexisting parenting stress. Conversely, researchers such as Anastopoulos et al. (1992) suggest that it is child behavior, and the increased caretaking demands that externalizing children impose on their parents, that results in, at least to some extent, increased parent stress, and therefore dysfunctional parenting. Supportive evidence comes from studies in which parent-child interactions were examined as a function of whether ADHD children were on or off stimulant medications. Such studies have consistently shown that, as the child's ADHD symptoms improve while on medication, there are accompanying changes in parent behavior. In particular, parents give fewer commands, express less criticism, engage in more nondirective interactions, and express more warmth (Schachar et al. 1987; Barkley 1989). These changes in parenting style, following improvements in child behavior, presumably reflect decreased stress in the parenting role, although it is likely that the relationship between these factors is bidirectional (Johnston 1996).

Concluding Comments

This paper has reviewed the literature concerning the parenting stress of parents of externalizing children. Parenting stress has been defined in several different ways; however, there is a consensus that it involves the extent to which parents perceive themselves as having access to the resources required to carry out the parenting role.

It is not only parental perceptions of the availability of resources that are important; their perceptions of their child's behavior also play a crucial role in determining behavior. These perceptions of child behavior are influenced by parental characteristics such as affective distress and situational factors such as high levels of marital discord. It is likely that as levels of parenting stress increase, perceptions of current child behavior diminish in accuracy and parents are more likely to be influenced by their long-term beliefs about the behavior of their child. In addition, parents experiencing high levels of parenting stress are also more likely to focus on negative aspects of their child's behavior and attribute that behavior to the child rather than to the situation. Together with a lowered threshold for the tolerance of behavioral problems these factors increase the likelihood of dysfunctional parenting behavior.

Parents of externalizing children tend to report significantly higher levels of parenting stress than parents of nonexternalizing children. Developing a greater understanding of parenting stress and its associated factors is important, since it has been found to be predictive (to a greater or lesser degree, depending on various mediating factors) of dysfunctional parenting behavior, which in turn is associated with problem child behavior.

The experience of fathers has been generally neglected in parent-child research. Phares (1995, 1996, 1999) suggests that developmental research has traditionally used sexist theories to inform its methodologies. Dating back to Freud (1955), Bowlby (1951), and Harlow (1958), mothers have been directly implicated in children's development, while fathers have not. In particular, there has been a major focus on maternal culpability in relation to children's abnormal development, while paternal factors and roles have been ignored. These sexist assumptions have been unquestionably integrated into contemporary research and have contributed to the development of incomplete models thought to reflect parental influences on child disorders (Caplan & Hall-Mc-Corquodale 1985). A comprehensive understanding of parenting stress of fathers of externalizing children is limited, because research of this kind has tended to focus on the female experience or has used this as a benchmark against which to consider the male experience. Given that the limited research that has included fathers seems to suggest that fathers' experiences of parenting stress may be different from mothers', one of the challenges for research in this area is to further elucidate the parenting stress experiences of fathers of externalizing children.

There is also an issue concerning the generalizability of research findings on parenting stress. The vast majority of the research reviewed in this paper is based on North American samples who have presented to clinical services. In order to generalize the finding to parents of externalizing children living in different cultures there is a need for research to be carried out within a range of cultural settings.

We thank Dr Christine Horrocks for her helpful comments on earlier drafts of this paper.

References

Abidin, R. R. (1995) *Parenting Stress Index: Professional Manual*, 3rd edn. Psychological Assessment Resources Inc., New York.

Achenbach, T. M. & Edelbrock, C. (1983) *Manual for the Child Behaviour Checklist and Revised Child Behaviour Profile*. University of Vermont, Burlington, VT.

Adamakos, H. Ryan, K. & Ullman, D. (1986) Maternal social support as a predictor of mother-child stress and stimulation. *Child Abuse and Neglect: The International Journal*, 10, 463–470.

Anastopoulos, A. D., Guevremont, D. C., Shelton, T. L. & DuPaul, G. J. (1992) Parenting stress among families of children with attention deficit hyperactivity disorder. *Journal of Abnormal Child Psychology*, 20, 503–520.

Baker, D. B. (1994) Parenting stress and ADHD: A comparison of mothers and fathers. *Journal of Emotional and Behavioral Disorders*, 2, 46–50.

Barkley, R. A. (1989) Hyperactive girls and boys: Stimulant drug effects on mother-child interactions. *Journal of Child Psychology and Psychiatry*, 30, 379–390.

Barkley, R. A., Fischer, M., Newby, R. F. & Breen, M. J. (1988) Development of a multimethod clinical protocol for assessing stimulant drug response in children with attention deficit disorder. *Journal of Clinical Child Psychology*, 17, 14–24.

Barnett, R. C. & Baruch, G. K. (1987). Social roles, gender, and psychological distress. In: *Gender and Stress* (eds R. Barnett, L. Biener & G. Baruch), pp. 13–38. Free Press, New York.

Beck, S. J., Young, G. H. & Tarnowski, K. J. (1990) Maternal characteristics and perceptions of pervasive and situational hyperactivities and normal controls. *Journal of the American Academy of Child and Adolescent Psychiatry*, 29, 558–565.

Bendell, R., Culbertson, J., Shelton, T. & Carter, B. (1986) Interrupted infantile apnea: Impact on early development, temperament, and maternal stress. *Journal of Clinical Child Psychology*, 15, 304–310.

Bowlby, J. (1951) *Maternal Care and Mental Health*. World Health Organization, Geneva.

Campbell, S. B. & Ewing, L. J. (1990) Follow-up of hard-to-manage pre-schoolers: Adjustment at age 9 and predictors of continuing symptoms. *Journal of Child Psychology and Psychiatry, 31,* 871–889.

Cantwell, D. P. (1996) Attention-deficit disorder: A review of the past 10 years. *Journal of American Academy of Child Adolescent Psychiatry, 35,* 978–987.

Caplan, P. J. & Hall-McCorquodale, I. (1985) Mother-blaming in major clinical journals. *American Journal of Orthopsychiatry, 55,* 345–353.

Creasey, G. & Reese, M. (1996) Mothers' and fathers' perceptions of parenting hassles: Associations with psychological symptoms, nonparenting hassles and child behaviour problems. *Journal of Applied Developmental Psychology, 17,* 393–406.

Crnic, K. & Greenberg, M. (1990) Minor parenting stress with young children. *Child Development, 54,* 209–217.

Deater-Deckard, K. (1998) Parenting stress and child adjustment: Some old hypotheses and new questions. *Clinical Psychology—Science and Practice, 5,* 314–332.

Deater-Deckard, K. & Scarr, S. (1996) Parenting stress among dual-earner mothers and fathers: Are there gender differences? *Journal of Family Psychology, 10,* 45–59.

Deater-Deckard, K., Scarr, S., McCartney, K. & Eisenberg, M. (1994) Paternal separation anxiety: Relationships with parenting stress, child rearing attitudes, and maternal anxieties. *Psychological Science, 5,* 341–346.

Eyberg, S. M., Boggs, S. R. & Rodriguez, C. M. (1992) Relationships between maternal parenting stress and child disruptive behaviour. *Child and Family Behaviour Therapy, 14,* 1–9.

Farrington, D. (1995) The development of offending and antisocial behaviour from childhood: Key findings of the Cambridge Study of Delinquent Development (The Twelfth Jack Tizzard Memorial Lecture). *Journal of Child Psychology and Psychiatry, 36,* 929–964.

Fine, M. A. & Schwebel, A. I. (1991). Step-parent stress: A cognitive perspective. *Journal of Divorce and Remarriage, 17,* 1–15.

Fischer, M. (1990) Parenting stress and the child with attention deficit hyperactivity disorder. *Journal of Clinical Child Psychology, 19,* 337–346.

Forgatch, M. S., Patterson, G. R. & Skinner, M. (1998) A mediational model for the effect of divorce in antisocial behavior in boys. In: *Impact of Divorce, Single Parenting, and Step-parenting on Children* (eds. E. M. Hetherington & J. D. Arasteh), pp. 135–154. Lawrence Erlbaum Associates, Hillsdale, NJ.

Freud, S. (1955) *The Complete Psychological Works of Sigmond Freud.* Hogarth Press, London.

Gaines, R., Sandgrund, A., Green, A. H. & Power, E. (1978) Etiological factors in child maltreatment: A multivariate study of abusing, neglecting and normal mothers. *Journal of Abnormal Psychology, 87,* 531–540.

Gillberg, C., Carlstrom, G. & Rasmussen, P. (1983) Hyperkinetic disorders in seven year old children with perceptual, motor and attentional deficits. *Journal of Child Psychology and Psychiatry, 24,* 233–246.

Goldstein, D. S. (1995) Stress as a scientific idea: A homeostatic theory of stress and distress. *Homeostasis in Health and Disease, 36,* 177–215.

Harlow, H. F. (1958) The nature of love. *American Psychologist, 13,* 673–685.

Hartsough, C. S. & Lambert, N. M. (1985) Medical factors in hyperactive and normal children: Prenatal, developmental, and health history findings. *American Journal of Orthopsychiatry, 55,* 190–210.

Hoover, D. W. & Milich, R. (1994) Effects of sugar ingestion expectancies on mother-child interactions. *Journal of Abnormal Child Psychology, 2,* 501–515.

Johnston, C. (1996) Addressing parent cognitions in interventions with families of disruptive children. In: *Advances in Cognitive-Behavioural Therapy* (eds. K. S. Dobson & K. D. Craig), pp. 193–209. Sage, London.

Jouriles, E. N., Murphy, C. M. & O'Leary, K. D. (1989) Effects of maternal mood on mother-son interaction patterns. *Journal of Abnormal Child Psychology, 17,* 513–525.

Kazdin, A. (1995) Child, parent and family dysfunction as predictors of outcome in cognitive-behavior treatment of antisocial children. *Behaviour Research and Therapy, 33,* 271–281.

Krauss, M. W. (1993) Child-related and parenting stress: Similarities and differences between mothers and fathers of children with disabilities. *American Journal on Maternal Retardation, 97,* 393–404.

Lahey, B. B., Conger, R., Atkeson, B. M. & Treiber, F. A. (1984) Parenting behavior and emotional status of physically abusive mothers. *Journal of Consulting and Clinical Psychology, 52,* 252–256.

MacInnis, S. (1984) *The relationship between maternal beliefs about childrearing and maternal discipline/annoyance: Implications for physical child abuse.* MSc thesis, University of Calgary, Alberta, Canada.

Mash, E. J. & Johnston, C. (1983a) Sibling interactions of hyperactive and normal children and their relationship to reports of maternal stress and self-esteem. *Journal of Clinical Child Psychology, 12*, 91–99.

Mash, E. J. & Johnston, C. (1983b) Parents' perceptions of child behaviour problems, parenting self-esteem, and mothers' reported stress in younger and older hyperactive and normal children. *Journal of Consulting and Clinical Psychology, 51*, 86–99.

Mash, E. J. & Johnston, C. (1990) Determinants of parenting stress: Illustrations from families of hyperactive children and families of physically abused children. *Journal of Clinical Child Psychology, 19*, 313–338.

Mash, E. J., Johnston, C. & Kovitz, K. (1983) A comparison of the mother-child interactions of physically abused and non-abused children during play and task situations. *Journal of Clinical Child Psychology, 12*, 337–346.

Melzter, H., Gatward, R., Goodman, R. & Ford, T. (2000) *Mental Health of Children and Adolescents in Great Britain*. A Publication of the Government Statistical Service. The Stationary Office, London.

Offord, D. R. (1987) Prevention of behavioral and emotional disorders in children. *Journal of Child Psychology and Psychiatry, 28*, 9–19.

Patterson, G. R. (1982) *Coercive Family Process*. Castalia, Eugene, OR.

Patterson, G. R. (1983) Stress: A change agent for family process. In: *Stress, Coping and Development in Children* (eds. N. Garmezy & M. Rutter), pp. 235–264. McGraw-Hill, New York.

Phares, V. (1995) Fathers' and mothers' participation in research. *Adolescence, 30*, 593–602.

Phares, V. (1996) Conducting nonsexist research, prevention, and treatment with fathers and mothers: A call for a change. *Psychology of Women Quarterly, 20*, 55–77.

Phares, V. (1999) *Poppa Psychology: The Role of Fathers in Children's Mental Well-being*. Praeger Publishers, New York.

Reid, J. B., Kavanagh, K. & Baldwin, D. V. (1987) Abusive parents' perceptions of child problem behaviors: An example of parental bias. *Journal of Abnormal Child Psychology, 15*, 457–466.

Ross, C. N., Blanc, H. M. & McNeil, C. B. (1998) Parenting stress in mothers of young children with oppositional defiant disorder and other severe behaviour problems. *Child Study Journal, 28*, 93–110.

Schachar, R. (1991) Child hyperactivity. *Journal of Child Psychology, 32*, 155–191.

Schachar, R., Taylor, E., Wieselberg, M., Thorley, G. & Rutter, M. (1987) Changes in family function and relationships in children who respond to methylophenidate. *Journal of the American Academy of Child and Adolescent Psychiatry, 26*, 728–732.

Schaugheney, E. A. & Lahey, B. B. (1985) Mothers' and fathers' perceptions of child deviance: Roles of child behaviour, parental depression, and marital satisfaction. *Journal of Consulting and Clinical Psychology, 53*, 718–723.

Spencer, M. B. & McLloyd, V. C. (eds.) (1990) Minority children (Special Issue). *Child Development, 36*, 263–589.

Stoneman, Z., Brody, G. & Burke, M. (1989) Marital quality, depression, and inconsistent parenting: Relationship with observed mother-child conflict. *American Journal of Orthopsychiatry, 59*, 105–117.

Taylor, F., Chadwick, O., Heptinstall, E. & Danckaerts, M. (1996) Hyperactivity and conduct problems as risk factors for adolescent development. *Journal of the American Academy of Child and Adolescent Psychiatry, 35*, 1213–1226.

Taylor, R. D., Roberts, D. & Jacobson, L. (1997) Stressful life events, psychological wellbeing and parenting in African-American mothers. *Journal of Family Psychology, 11*, 436–446.

Wahler, R. G. & Dumas, J. E. (1984) Changing the observational coping styles of insular and non-insular mothers: A step toward maintenance of parent training effects. In: *Parent Training: Foundation of Research and Practice* (eds. R. F. Dangel & R. A. Polster), pp. 379–416. Guilford, New York.

Webster-Stratton, C. (1988) Mothers' and fathers' perceptions of child deviance: Roles of parent and child behaviours and parent adjustment. *Journal of Consulting and clinical Psychology, 56*, 909–915.

Webster-Stratton, C. (1989) The relationship of marital support, conflict, and divorce to parent perceptions, behaviors and parent adjustment. *Journal of Marriage and the Family, 51*, 417–430.

Weinraub, M. & Wolf, B. (1983) Effects of stress and social supports on mother-infant interactions in single and two parent families. *Child Development, 54*, 1297–1311.

SHMUEL SHULMAN
MIRI SCHARF
DANIEL LUMER
OFFER MAURER

7

Parental Divorce and Young Adult Children's Romantic Relationships: Resolution of the Divorce Experience

Research during the past decade has started to deal with the long-term impact of childhood family disruption on young adults' adjustment. Demographic surveys have shown that young adults who experienced parental divorce during childhood or adolescence had fewer years of education, earned less money, and were more likely to be unemployed (Amato, 1999). In addition, they were likely to have more sexual partners (Garbardi & Rosen, 1991) and to marry and bear children earlier than were young adults from non divorced families (McLanahan & Bumpass, 1988). Data are accumulating that show higher rates of divorce among adult offspring of divorce than among those with no history of parental divorce (Amato, 1999).

This higher incidence of troubled marriages and divorce among this population has been attributed (Amato, 1999, 2000) to poorer parental models of interpersonal behavior, which may lead to difficulties in forming stable, satisfying, intimate, and trusting relationships with a spouse. Based on her seminal work, Wallerstein (Wallerstein & Corbin, 1999) observed that when her sample of children whose parents had divorced reached adulthood, many wondered about their own chances for love and commitment and their ability to make a decision about marriage. Also, many were fearful of disappointment, betrayal, and abandonment. These children's stories over the years suggested that the internal developmental tasks of establishing intimacy with the opposite sex were burdened to some

extent by the template of failed male-female relationships they carried with them (p. 84).

However, the research also suggested (Wallerstein & Blakeslee, 1989) that experience of their parents' divorce may lead some children to be more sensitive to problems in relationships and to make a greater commitment to solving them. Moreover, Wallerstein and Lewis (1998) reported that while some children of divorce struggle with the fear that their relationships will fail, as did their parents', many overcame their dread of betrayal to find loving partners and become successful, protective parents. Conceptually, it could be argued that some young people carry forward the less-than-optimal relationship template to which they were exposed in their family of origin, while others build their own more adaptive codes of relationships. How may the different outcomes be explained?

Differential reactions to and varying effects of past experiences can be elucidated through attachment theory. More specifically, a study of adults' attachment representation by Main, Kaplan, and Cassidy (1985) found that adults' reflections and evaluations regarding their childhood experiences, rather than the content of the experiences per se, affected their emotional bonds with their own children. People with highly unfavorable attachment-related experiences, who worked through them and could discuss them coherently ("earned-secure" people), have been found (Pearson, Cohn, Cowan, & Cowan, 1994) to be as sensitive and responsive to their children as have their counterparts with more favorable experiences, even when parenting under stressful conditions.

Resolution of negative past experiences is characterized by coherent speech when talking about the unfavorable experience (Main & Hesse, 1990), recognition of change since the event was experienced, and, above all, ability to understand the complexity of past events. Such resolution means that negative past experiences are less likely to color current perception of self and relationships adversely, and more likely to contribute to current understanding of relationships. Lack of such resolution is characterized by incoherent speech, insistence on inability to recall the events, or excessive preoccupation with them. This suggests that the negative experiences are still emotionally laden and therefore interfere with current functioning (Pianta, Marvin, Britner, & Borowitz, 1996).

From this, it may be inferred that in parental divorce, it is not just the actual loss or trauma that affects an individual's subsequent behavior, but also how that individual currently appraises and represents that loss or trauma. If the sense of loss attributed to divorce is addressed and resolved, individuals should be more psychologically free to pursue their goals.

Although cumulative evidence suggests that parental divorce is related to the quality of adult children's romantic relationships and marital stability, it appears that no previous research has examined the extent to which adult children resolve the experience of parental divorce. The study reported here, therefore, examined the role played by resolution of the divorce experience in mediating the effects of that experience. It focused on how organizational aspects of the divorce experience, plus the extent to which the experience was resolved, were related to the quality of the relationships young adults established with their romantic partners, after controlling for such demographic variables as age at the time of divorce, gender, and level of parental conflict (Amato, 1999). It was hypothesized that a more integrated and resolved pattern of appraising parental divorce would be related to more adaptive romantic relationships in young adulthood.

Method

Participants

Data were collected from 51 Israeli college students (30 females and 21 males) whose parents were divorced. Purposive sampling techniques were used, and the research team posted notices throughout two universities in the center of Israel. Since more women than men responded, additional notices were posted so as to achieve a total of 21 male subjects.

None of the participants was married, but all had a romantic partner in a relationship that had lasted more than three months. Current age was 19–29 years (M = 23.9), while mean age at time of parental divorce was 11.8 years, and mean duration of the romantic relationship was 23.4 months (SD = 18.4). Of their divorced parents, 23% of mothers and 63% of fathers had remarried. Most participants (72.5%) had been raised by their mother, and a few were in either their father's or joint custody. The divorce rate in Israel during the past decade has reached 35–50% in nonreligious sectors (about 60%) of the population, bringing its social acceptability closer to that of other industrialized countries.

Procedure and Measures

Two modes were used to collect data for the study: interviews that were later transcribed and rated, and questionnaires.

Interviews   Interviews were held individually with each subject at their home or in a laboratory. During the first part of the interview, participants were asked to speak for five minutes about their romantic partner, telling "What kind of person your partner is, and how you get along together." The sessions were tape-recorded, transcribed, then rated independently by two raters on five scales adapted from Feeney and Noller (1991). The five-point rating scales were: Idealization (the extent to which the relationship was described as special or unique), Friendship, Enjoyment, Relationship Problems, and Trust. Agreement between raters ranged from .68 to .89; all disagreements were discussed until consensus was reached.

During the second part of the interview, participants were asked to respond to the following questions about their parents' divorce: "Please describe your parents' divorce: what you remember from that time, any specific memories" "What is the meaning of the divorce to you?" "What do you think about it today?" Their replies were tape-recorded, transcribed, then rated independently by two raters on five scales developed by the authors in line with the salient topics found in the transcripts and with the study's hypothesis, the latter suggesting an examination of ability to resolve the loss inflicted by the divorce and to perceive the divorce in a comprehensive manner.

The five-point rating scales were as follows: Integrative Perception of the Divorce (the degree to which the subject is aware of its complexity; is able to understand it from mother's, father's, and children's perspective; and has a coherent view of the divorce); Sense of Loss in the Past; Sense of Current Loss; Anger; and Lack of Memory (the extent to which the subject is unable to remember details from the time of the divorce). Agreement between raters ranged from .67 to .84. All disagreements were discussed until consensus was reached.

Survey   Subjects also completed, in a single session, two questionnaires, one assessing their relationship with the romantic partner, the other the intensity of parental conflict during and after the divorce.

The first, the Triangular Theory of Love Scale (TTLS) (Sternberg, 1998), is a 45-item self-report measuring three components (15 items on each) of love: intimacy in emotion, passion in physical relations, and commitment in cognition. Participants were asked to rate each item on a nine-point Likert-type scale. Cronbach alpha coefficients for the three scales were above .90.

Items on the second scale, Parental Conflict, were adapted from the Interparental Conflict Questionnaire (ICQ) (Forehand & McCombs, 1989) to assess frequency of parental conflict (quarrels, arguments, "heated arguments," etc.) at two points of time: during the divorce period and three years after divorce. Subjects were asked to indicate, on a scale of 1–7, the frequency or intensity of the various indices of conflict. Cronbach alpha of the inventory at the two points of time was .81 and .64, respectively.

Results

Prior to the analysis of the study's main question—the influence of the resolution of the divorce experience on the romantic relationship—analyses were conducted to determine the role of demographic variables and parental conflict in those relationships.

Variables

Demographic   A set of t-tests was conducted to examine gender differences on the five indices adapted from Feeney and Noller (1991) of perception of the relationship with the romantic partner. A second set examined gender differences on the TTLS ratings. No significant gender differences were found in any of the eight items.

Pearson correlations between age of child at divorce and current perception of romantic relationships were computed. No significant correlations were found. Age of child at divorce was not found to be related to quality of romantic relationships in young adulthood.

A set of t-tests was conducted to compare quality of romantic relationships of young adults whose mothers stayed single with that of those whose mothers had remarried. The latter were found to enjoy their romantic relationships more than the former, $t = 2.45$, $p < .05$; M = 4.55 (SD = 0.08) and M = 3.85 (SD = 0.10), respectively. In addition, young adults whose mothers had not remarried described more problems in their romantic relationships than did those whose mothers had remarried; $t = 2.21$, $p < .05$; M = 2.51 (SD = 0.11) and M = 1.70 (SD = 0.09), respectively. No association between current paternal marital status (remarried versus not remarried) and young adults' quality of romantic relationships was found.

Parental Conflict   Significant correlations were found between level of parental conflict during divorce, as reported on the adapted ICQ, and two aspects of current romantic relationships, as reported on the TTLS: a higher level of conflict during divorce was related to higher levels of intimacy and passion with the romantic partner: $r = .28$ ($p < .05$) for both.

Current Perception of Parental Divorce   Pearson correlations between current perception of divorce and quality of relationships with romantic partner were computed. As can be seen in Table 7.1, a more integrative perception of the divorce was related on the indices adapted from the Feeney and Noller (1991) scale to higher levels of friendship, enjoyment, and trust in the romantic relationships, and to a lower level of relationship problems. Conversely, difficulties in remembering details of the divorce were related to less trust in the romantic partner. No significant associations were found between current perception of the divorce and the three aspects of love—intimacy, passion, commitment—on the TTLS.

To control for the possible contribution of other variables to the quality of romantic relationships among young adults, a hierarchical regression was performed. First, demographic variables (gender, age at the time of divorce, and current maternal and paternal marital status) and the two measures

Table 7.1 Pearson Correlations: Perception of Parental Divorce and Quality of Relationship with Romantic Partner

Relation. Factor	Integrative Perception	Past Loss	Current Loss	Anger	Lack of Memory
Idealization	0.16	0.13	0.03	0.03	0.15
Friendship	0.32*	0.02	−0.07	0.06	−0.26
Enjoyment	0.48*	−0.11	−0.07	−0.28	−0.12
Problems	−0.30*	−0.02	0.08	−0.01	−0.07
Trust	0.40*	−0.11	−0.22	−0.15	−0.30*

*p < .05; **p < .01.

of parental conflict (during the divorce and three years after divorce) were inserted prior to the insertion of level of integrative perception of the divorce. Results indicated that, even after controlling for these variables, the description of an integrative perception of the divorce was related to greater friendship ($\beta = .34$, p < .05) and enjoyment ($\beta = .51$, p < .01) and to fewer problems ($\beta = .42$, p < .01) in the romantic relationship. Integrative perception of the divorce explained 9–13% of the quality of the relationship with a romantic partner.

Additional hierarchical regressions were conducted to learn whether integrative perception of divorce explained the three young adult love types on the TTLS after controlling for the demographic variables and the two indices of conflict. Results showed that the description of an integrative perception of the divorce explained 9% of intimacy with the romantic partner ($\beta = .35$, p < .05).

Discussion

Unexpectedly, the results of this study showed that sense of loss or anger associated with parental divorce was not related to the quality of offspring's romantic relationships during young adulthood (see Table 7.1).

As hypothesized, an integrative perception of divorce was found to be related to higher levels of friendship, enjoyment, and intimacy and to fewer problems in young adults' romantic relationships. The appraisal of the events is probably more important that their mere occurrence (Kurdek, 1993). When reexamining stressful events, individuals may focus not only on painful feelings in the past, but also on the future and its possibilities. Such an attitude facilitates the search for new perspectives and acknowledgment of change, without denying reality. This is consistent with ideas found in attachment theory suggesting that representations of former experiences are governed by organizational principles that may be helpful in dealing with past trauma (Main & Hesse, 1990; Main et al., 1985). In contrast, people who refrain from dealing with the past trauma tend to exhibit problems later: the results of the present study showed that difficulties in remembering details of the divorce were related to less trust toward the romantic partner.

Painful feelings, then, are not necessarily associated with pathology (Emery & Forehand, 1996). Arditti and Prouty (1999) showed that divorce can also offer new alternatives for family members and may thus be related to renewal, as well as loss. Similarly, divorce has been conceptualized as a transformation in family relations that should not be perceived only in terms of deficit (Stewart, Copeland, Chester, Malley, & Barenbaum, 1997).

Another factor that contributed to a higher quality of the participants' romantic relationships was their mother's marital status. Maternal remarriage was related to young adults' higher levels of friendship, enjoyment, intimacy, and passion and fewer problems in their romantic relationships. Previous studies on the role of remarriage of custodial parents in children's life have produced mixed findings. In his study on the impact of remarriage on young adult children, Aquilino (1998) found no difference in quality of relationships reported by children in single-mother and custodial remarried-mother families. However, mothers' remarriage was related to a significant decrease in frequency of contact with adult children. As already noted, the event per se is likely to be less important than its meaning. When a mother has remarried, her young adult child may understand that divorce is not only a loss but carries new possibilities for marital life as well. Under these circumstances, negative expectations and attitudes about marriage may change—a speculation that awaits examination in further research.

Results showed that several indices on the quality of romantic relationships measure were related to level of integrative perception of divorce. However, trust and commitment between romantic partners were not explained by such a perception. It would be reasonable to assume that an integrative approach facilitates interaction between partners so that they enjoy the relationship more and experience fewer problems. Trust and commitment, however, are probably more difficult to achieve. Of young adults whose parents had divorced, 82% indicated that they did not fully trust their dating partner and feared to commit themselves to a serious relationship (Duran-Aydintug, 1997).

Because of its design, the study's findings did not tell us what factors contribute to the development of an integrative perception of divorce. No association was evident between level of integrative perception of divorce and child's age at divorce, child's gender, current parental status, or even parental conflict. From a social constructionist approach, it is probable that as children grow older they are more capable of interpreting and reconstructing their personal experience of parental divorce, as well as of understanding the meaning of divorce in society (Arditti & Prouty, 1999; Kurdek, 1993), but this assumption needs to be tested in further research.

The results of this study did not point to a major role for parental conflict in young adults' romantic relationships. Moreover, the two significant findings showed that a higher level of parental conflict during divorce was related to higher levels of intimacy and passion with a romantic partner in young adulthood. This finding is counterintuitive. However, it is possible that a high level of friction in parental divorce gives impetus to leaving the family and trying to establish a different relationship with a romantic partner. Current study results cannot tell us whether the higher intimacy and passion with a romantic partner reflected a mature relationship or dependency on the partner.

An important limitation of this study must be considered. Participants were young adults involved in a romantic relationship. Consequently, the role of an integrative perception of divorce among young adults without a romantic relationship, or whose relationship lasted less than three months, remains unknown. Results can be generalized only to young adult children of divorce who have been able to establish a romantic relationship lasting at least three months.

Implications for Practice

There is a vast literature on intervention methods with families of divorce during and after divorce. Less attention has been paid to the needs of young adult children of divorce, and intervention methods with them have emerged mainly from a deficit model. For example, Hage and Nosanow (2000) presented a psychoeducational group intervention whose goals include reducing isolation, establishing connectedness, and teaching communication skills and assertiveness. Results of the study reported here suggest that it is important to work with young adults on how they perceive parental divorce, cope with the sense of loss, and arrive at a new and comprehensive understanding of the divorce and its role in their lives. Overcoming the sense of trauma can offer renewal in life and increased sense of agency.

References

Amato, P. R. (1999). Children of divorced parents as young adults. In E. M. Hetherington (Ed.), *Coping with divorce, single parenting, and marriage: A risk and resiliency perspective* (pp. 147–163). Mahwah, NJ: Lawrence Erlbaum.

Amato, P. R. (2000). The consequences of divorce for adults and children. *Journal of Marriage and the Family, 62*, 1269–1287.

Aquilino, W. S. (1998). Impact of childhood family disruption on young adults' relationships. *Journal of Marriage and the Family, 60*, 295–313.

Arditti, J. A., & Prouty, A. M. (1999). Change, disengagement, and renewal: Relationship dynamics between young adults and their fathers after divorce. *Journal of Marital and Family Therapy, 25*, 61–81.

Duran-Aydintug, C. (1997). Adult children of divorce revisited: When they speak up. *Journal of Divorce and Remarriage, 27*, 71–83.

Emery, R. E., & Forehand, R. (1996). Parental divorce and children's well-being: A focus on resilience. In R. J. Haggerty, L. R. Sherrod, N. Garmezy, & M. Rutter (Eds.), *Stress, risk, and resilience in children and adolescents: Processes, mechanisms, and interventions* (pp. 64–99). New York: Cambridge University Press.

Feeney, J. A., & Noller, P. (1991). Attachment style and verbal descriptions of romantic partners. *Journal of Social and Personal Relationships 8*, 187–215.

Forehand, R., & McCombs, A. (1989). The nature of interparental conflict of married and divorced parents: Implications for young adolescents. *Journal of Abnormal Child Psychology, 17*, 235–249.

Garbardi, L., & Rosen, I. A. (1991). Differences between college students from divorced and intact families. *Journal of Divorce and Remarriage, 15*, 175–191.

Hage, S. M., & Nosanow, M. (2000). Becoming stronger at broken places: A model for group work with young adults from divorced families. *Journal for Specialties in Group Work, 25*, 50–66.

Kurdek, L. A. (1993). Predicting marital dissolution: A 5-year prospective longitudinal study of newlywed couples. *Journal of Personality and Social Psychology, 64*, 221–242.

Main, M., & Hesse, E. (1990). Parents' unresolved traumatic experiences are related to infant disorganized attachment status: Is frightened and/or frightening parental behavior the linking mechanism? In M. T. Greenberg & D. Cicchetti, (Eds.), *Attachment in the preschool years: Theory, research, and intervention* (pp. 161–182). Chicago: University of Chicago Press.

Main, M., Kaplan, N., & Cassidy, J. (1985). Security in infancy, childhood, and adulthood: A move to the level of representation. In I. Bretherton & E. Waters (Eds.), *Growing points of attachment theory and research. Monograph of the Society for Research in Child Development, 50*, (1–2, Serial no. 209), 66–104.

McLanahan, S. S., & Bumpass, L. (1988). Intergenerational consequences of family disruption. *American Journal of Sociology, 94*, 130–152.

Pearson, J. L., Cohn, D. A., Cowan, P. A., & Cowan, C. P. (1994). Earned- and continuous-security in adult attachment: Relation to depressive symptomatology and parenting style. *Development and Psychopathology, 6*, 359–373.

Pianta, R. C., Marvin, R. S., Britner, P. A., & Borowitz, K. C. (1996). Mothers' resolution of their children's diagnosis: Organized patterns of caregiving representations. *Infant Mental Health Journal, 17*, 239–256.

Sternberg, R. J. (1998). *Love is a story: A new theory of relationships*. New York: Oxford University Press.

Stewart, A. J., Copeland, A. P., Chester, N. L., Malley, J. E., & Barenbaum, N.B. (1997). *Separating together: How divorce transforms families*. New York: Guilford Press.

Wallerstein, J., & Blakeslee, S. (1989). *Second chances: Men, women and children a decade after divorce*. New York: Ticknor & Fields.

Wallerstein, J., & Corbin, S. B. (1999). The child and the vicissitudes of divorce. In R. M. Galatzer-Levy & L. Kraus (Ed.), *The scientific basis of child custody decisions* (pp. 73–95). New York: Wiley.

Wallerstein, J. S., & Lewis, J. (1998). The long-term impact of divorce on children: A first report from a 25-year study. *Family and Conciliation Courts Review, 36*, 363–383.

WILLIAM MARSIGLIO
SALLY HUTCHINSON
MARK COHAN

8

Envisioning Fatherhood: A Social Psychological Perspective on Young Men without Kids

Interest in the social psychology of fatherhood has grown significantly in recent years (Marsiglio, 1998). Much of the scholarship in this area focuses on how individuals construct meaning in relation to paternity, fathering, and the negotiation of family roles. Research on men's evolving identities as fathers, and their commitments to their children, is critical for understanding these social processes and the microlevel dimensions to the fatherhood terrain. This work is particularly vital when considering the diverse paths men take on their way to acknowledging and embracing their fecundity, paternity, and father roles, respectively.

While much of the research germane to this area focuses on men who have already become fathers, we extend this literature by studying young single men's subjective experiences who have not yet, to their knowledge, sired a child or, in the case of most of our participants, impregnated a woman. Our analyses build on earlier work with these data that focused on how males become aware of their perceived fecundity, experience themselves as procreative beings once they become aware, and view responsibility issues while orienting themselves toward their sexual and potential paternal roles (Marsiglio, Hutchinson, & Cohan, in press). We now focus on several issues that relate more directly to the social psychology of fatherhood. In particular, we highlight two main interrelated dimensions associated with men's efforts to envision aspects of fatherhood: sense of readiness for becoming fathers (*fatherhood readiness*) and views about the ideal fathering experience, images of the good or ideal father, and visions of future fathering experiences (*fathering visions*). In a more limited fashion, we discuss men's fantasies about what their children might be like and the comparative appraisals they use to organize their thinking about fatherhood.

Throughout our discussion, we also emphasize how gender and relationship commitments can influence the way some men perceive specific issues. Because paternity, and in many instances social fatherhood, can be viewed as joint accomplishments involving a man and woman, we explore how men's orientation to prospective fatherhood is sometimes influenced by their involvement with particular romantic partners. We examine young men's thoughts about the prospects of fatherhood independent of specific romantic relationships as well.

Consistent with our grounded theory perspective, we have read our data with an eye toward capturing distinctive features of the way men express their thoughts about procreation, social fathering, and children. Our analyses revealed, for example, several preliminary themes that appear to cut across the dimensions listed above that characterize men's efforts to envision fatherhood. We introduce and define these themes when we analyse men's sense of being "ready" for fatherhood. These themes provide an explicit organizational structure for this section. Further, because we suspect that men's sense of readiness is linked to their image of what represents a good or ideal father, we then selectively use three of these themes to illuminate men's views about fathering in general, and more specifically, their visions about how they themselves plan to act as fathers. In this context, we consider the significance and symbolic meaning underlying men's desire to father their own biological child someday, and discuss men's perceptions of their own father. Finally, we comment briefly on the nature of men's visions of their hypothetical children.

Our research with men who are not yet fathers is warranted because many men who eventually do become fathers begin to develop their paternal identity prior to their child's birth, and for some, even before their child is conceived. This study is also consistent with recent initiatives to incorporate males into important policy debates and program interventions that address sex, pregnancy, paternity, and social fatherhood issues (Federal Interagency Forum on Child and Family Statistics, 1998; Levine & Pitt, 1995; Marsiglio, 1998; Moore, Driscoll, & Ooms, 1997; Sonenstein, Stewart, Lindberg, Pernas, & Williams, 1997). These efforts embrace broader schemes for conceptualizing and promoting responsible fatherhood, especially among teens and young adults. Thus, our study generates insights relevant to both theory and program development.

Background

Though our study used grounded theory methodology (Glaser, 1978, 1992; Strauss, 1987), our analysis of young men's subjective lives as persons capable of procreating and assuming father roles is informed by the symbolic interactionist (Mead, 1934) and life course perspectives (Marsiglio, 1995). The former directs our attention to how men construct and interpret their perceptions about their potential experiences as fathers, and the latter reminds us that men's views about the timing of fatherhood are shaped by their ideas about how they would like to sequence and time other critical life course events, including education, work, and relationships (marriage in particular). From an interactionist perspective, we are interested in the meanings men assign to situations, events, acts, others, and themselves as they relate to aspects of fatherhood and the social psychological processes by which this occurs. These processes include both the identity work men do by themselves as they attempt to define what they value for themselves and others, and the interactions they share with partners (and others) as they coconstruct their views about fathering and children.

Using samples of men, most of whom are not fathers, researchers have studied different facets of young men's perceptions regarding sexual and contraceptive responsibility, as well as pregnancy resolution (see Marsiglio, 1998, for review). Additionally, some research has attempted to unravel how men of varying ages think and feel during their partner's pregnancy and the transitional period to first-time fatherhood (Herzog, 1982; LaRossa & LaRossa, 1989; May, 1980; Sherwen, 1987; Soule, Stanley, & Copans, 1979; Zayas, 1988). These types of analyses are grounded on men's lived experiences with the pregnancy and childbirth processes. Much less is known about how young men who have not yet become fathers envision fatherhood and children (Gohel, Diamond, & Chambers, 1997). Thus, the bulk of what we know about young men's sense of the meanings and responsibilities of fatherhood comes from studies of acknowledged fathers and their partners (Allen & Doherty, 1996; Furstenberg, 1995).

Because of the stigma associated with teen pregnancy and unplanned paternity, many young men are hesitant to establish legal paternity or even report informally that they have fathered a child; others may not be aware that they have sired a child. Consequently, information regarding young fathers comes only from those who acknowledge their paternity, a subset of the larger population that may have special characteristics. This potential bias in the data gathered from fathers further emphasizes the need to explore young men's perceptions about fatherhood and children before they experience paternity.

Insights gleaned from surveys of social service providers who have developed male involvement and pregnancy prevention programs throughout the United States are also relevant to our study (Levine & Pitt, 1995; Sonenstein et al., 1997). While it is beyond our purposes here to present Sonenstein et al.'s full summary of the practical advice and program philosophies of these programs, it is useful to repeat their observation that

> these programs try to change males' attitudes toward themselves, their relationships with women, and their futures. Most focus on comprehensive life issues—improving self-esteem, relationship skills, and employment skills—to give young men the tools they will need to take control in multiple areas of their lives, to exercise responsibility, and to give them hope for positive futures. (p. 143)

Most of the program insights have emerged out of interventions in low-income, inner-city areas, but some can and should be adapted to teenage and young adult men in more advantaged neighborhoods as well as other groups (e.g., military and prison populations).

Methods

Sample

The purposive sample we used for this analysis is part of a larger ongoing project in which we secured interviews with single men ages 16–30 who had dated at least one woman in the past three years (or had been married). These men fit one of five primary procreative experience profiles: (1) "procreative novices," no pregnancy or fertility experience; (2) "abortion veterans," responsible for a pregnancy that was aborted within the previous 12 month period; (3) "fathers-in-waiting," partner is currently pregnant with their first child; (4) "new fathers," those whose child is 6–12 weeks old; and (5) fathers. For this paper, we restricted our focus to those 32 men who had not yet fathered a child (we included the six participants who were involved with their pregnant partner at the time of our initial interview with them).

We conducted 17 interviews with procreative novices, 11 with abortion veterans, 6 with fathers-in-waiting, and 2 miscarriage veterans (a few men are categorized in more than one category). We used these experience profiles to broaden the range of data available to us as we examined men's views on fathering, rather than as a basis for examining differences and commonalities among the different categories of participants. We use pseudonyms throughout the text to refer to all participants, and we abbreviate quoted excerpts to eliminate redundancies (e.g., "then, then I knew") and extraneous utterances (e.g., "you know," "uhm").

Our recruitment strategy sought to enhance diversity by taking into account men's procreative life experiences mentioned above as well as their age, race/ethnicity, education, financial status, and relationship status. Of the 32 participating men, 19 were White, 10 were African American (one biracial), 2 were Hispanic, and 1 was Native American Indian. The mean age of the sample was 21.6 years, with seven being younger than 19 and seven others being 26 or older. Three of our participants were still in high school, another seven had no college experience (one of these men had not completed high school), 21 had some college experience (one of these men had not completed high school), and 1 was a college graduate. Three participants were either separated or divorced.

We recruited participants in a number of ways. Screening interviewers arranged 16 interviews with men who were visiting a local Department of Motor Vehicles' office, and we identified the remaining participants through abortion clinics, a prenatal clinic, a prepared child birth class, a local employment agency, homeless shelter, personal contacts, and word of mouth.

Interviews

Our semistructured, audiotaped face-to-face interviews lasted between 60 and 90 minutes and took place in on-campus offices, public libraries, and other locations convenient to the participants. Four interviewers—two White males, an African American male, and a White female, age 30, 40, 45, and 55, respectively—conducted the interviews. With an eye toward the past, present, and future, we encouraged our participants to talk about their perceptions and experiences involving paternity, social fatherhood, children, and relationships. We focused extensively on their current relationship, if they had one. Men had the opportunity to discuss moments and events that shaped the level and type of awareness they currently had of themselves as procreative beings and potential fathers. Our analyses for this article were informed by interview questions that dealt primarily with the following: (1) instances where they thought they might have impregnated someone; (2) instances where they talked to someone about impregnating a girl/woman or becoming a father; (3) talk about situations or events that happened to them that changed how they thought about impregnating someone; (4) the importance for them to father their own biological child; (5) relationships in which they thought about what it would be like to have a child with a particular partner; (6) whether or not they saw kids in their future; and (7) imagery they had about their possible children and of themselves as fathers.

While interviewing, we were aware that interviewees could respond to our sensitive and sometimes personal questions with idealized responses, telling us what they thought we wanted to hear. To minimize "correct answers" we attempted to portray a nonjudgmental attitude while emphasizing the importance and value of their feelings, beliefs, and experiences for our understanding.

Sensitivity to temporal issues implicit in our interview questions was also important. Our questions about procreative events often prompted men to reference different time frames as they discussed their views and experiences. Thus, they sometimes described their experiences by moving back and forth in the narrative between their past, present, and future selves.

Data Analysis

Data were subjected to the methods of grounded theory analysis (Glaser, 1978, 1992; Strauss, 1987), including substantive and theoretical coding, memoing (the writing of theoretical notes), and theoretical sampling. The constant comparative method facilitated the comparisons of incident with incident and incidents with the developing codes. Data collection and analysis occurred simultaneously, permitting the data analysis to inform data collection by suggesting the importance of a particular code and/or the need to obtain more data on a particular code. Memoing helped in the identification of relationships among codes. As a technique to enhance dependability, the first two authors of this paper coded each interview separately and then together (Lincoln & Guba, 1985). As we analyzed our data, we attempted to differentiate between the narratives men used to depict their orientation to procreative issues independent of the interview context and questions per se, and those responses that were more clearly constructed for the first time in direct response to an interviewer's questioning. Our analyses were designed to expand and enrich theoretical concepts rather than identify factors that reliably predict or shape whether individuals think about fatherhood or think about it in particular ways.

Envisioning Fatherhood

Because our sample included participants ranging in age from 16 to 30, it is not surprising that most had given at least passing thought to their ability to impregnate a sex partner. All of our participants recognized the connection between sexual intercourse and conception. While we interviewed a few notable exceptions, those participants who were older and more experienced in having relationships, negotiating sex, contraception, and in some instances resolving a pregnancy, typically had given more thought to being a father. However, some men, despite being sexually active, had not thought about the prospects of fatherhood or imagined what it would be like to some day be a father. While it is noteworthy that these latter participants did not think about fatherhood, our analyses focused primarily on those men who had reflected on this topic.

As we listened to participants discuss their images and concerns about fatherhood and children, several interrelated themes emerged from the data. The present analyses examine these themes, among a sample of nonfathers, in order to better understand what being "ready" for fatherhood means, how men perceive ideal fathering, and how they envision fathering for themselves. We have labeled the more prominent themes: degree and form of collaboration, focus of attention (relational and substantive), temporal orientation, experience (source and intensity), and degree of clarity. Again, we use each of these themes to organize our analysis of fatherhood readiness while incorporating three themes (focus of attention, temporal orientation, and degree of clarity) into our subsequent analysis of fathering visions. In both analysis sections, we highlight, where possible, how the relevant themes intersect with one another.

Fatherhood Readiness

Many participants commented on the nature of their preparedness to become fathers and assumed the responsibilities associated with social fathering. Their remarks underscored the connection, as well as the subtle distinction, between men's desires to become a father now or in the future, and their sense of being ready to do so at this point in their lives. Some men were receptive to the idea of paternity or fathering a child in an abstract sense, but they realized that they were currently not inclined or prepared to embrace all aspects of being a father. Desmond, a 30-year-old African American, remarked:

> I do not mind being [becoming] a father . . . if I had a child, I could be ready to be a father. What I do not want to give up is the time. I'd like my son, well let's just say son, may not be a son, might be a daughter, but I'd like my child to be very well educated, to have good advantages, to do well in life, to be all it can be, and I would support it as best I could. But, I wish there was a way to do that without, right now, without giving up the time.

In this excerpt, Desmond talks about his fatherhood readiness in terms of a contradiction: he has high aspirations for this hypothetical (male) child, and is willing to commit to supporting these aspirations, but he is not currently willing to make the time commitment he associates with fatherhood. Considered at the present time, fatherhood holds seemingly irreconcilable positives and negatives: helping a child "be all it can be" versus time demands.

Degree and Form of Collaboration   We found that men were attentive to their sense of readiness by reflecting on it alone and/or when they discussed it with others. Patterns of private reflection and more collaborative experiences had distinctive features, yet were likely to reinforce one another over time. Both may also be relevant intermittently to men's sense of readiness as it varied over time within and between relationships. While a few men recalled instances where they had acknowledged their sense of readiness without discussing it with someone, most men reported having at least meeting conversations with others about their own sense of readiness. Most of these conversations did not include truly collaborative exchanges where men were constructing and negotiating their sense of readiness with others; rather, they tended to serve as reinforcement for the orientations men had developed previously.

Seeing pregnant teenagers and young parents out in public triggered some men to reflect privately about how ill-prepared they were to become a father at the time. Thus, some men, like Arthur, a 21-year-old man raised in a rural area, attended to their sense of readiness privately when they reflected on how others (e.g., family, friends, individuals in school or in public, persons on TV talk shows) were affected by off-time parental responsibilities. In Arthur's case, he based his sense of readiness and explicit preference to delay fatherhood until he was about 28 on his desire to improve on the meager material life his father provided for him when he was a child:

When I grew up my dad, he didn't have nothin'. They [parents] had me when they were like eighteen, and they pretty much didn't have anything. We drove ol' beat up cars, lived in an old mobile home, and I just don't want to be like that for the rest of my life.

Arthur was also quick to add his personal conviction: "I want to be sure it's [having child] with the person I'm going to be with for the rest of my life. Not just go and make a buncha kids." Although it does not appear that Arthur spent much time thinking about these issues in private, our reading of Arthur's interview suggests that he had given some thought to these issues, away from his family and partner. In other portions of his interview, he did

make it clear that he had also talked explicitly to his partner, mother, and grandmother about wanting to wait to have children until he was in his late twenties.

Marcus, a 19-year-old biracial participant, provided a specific example of a collaborative process when he recalled his conversation with one of his girlfriends: "And then we just talked about, she was like, I can't have no kids right now. I'm like, you? I can't have none neither. Too damn young." While this excerpt illustrates a rather superficial type of exchange, talk of this variety can be important if it activates the men's sense of procreative responsibility and provides them with an opportunity to establish or reassert their own views about their fatherhood readiness.

Desmond offered another colorful example of a form of collaboration men can experience as they fashion their sense of readiness. During his interview, he reenacted for the interviewer a conversation he had in which a friend shared with him some folk wisdom about girlfriends and father readiness. Desmond had said to his friend, "You know, I could have a baby from this girl. I'd like to give this girl a baby." His friend responded, "Well, you don't know that yet, until [you], look in her eyes." To which Desmond asked, "Why?" The friend replied: "If you can look in her eyes and, when you look at her, see your children in her eyes, then that's when you know." Desmond went on to tell the interviewer how he attempted to put his friend's advice into practice: "I tried to do that, and it kind of, I kind of saw what they [the friend and other friends] were talking about."

Focus of Attention   When men talked about their degree of readiness they varied in their focus of attention. Our data showed that this focus involved both a relational object (self, partner, child) as well as substantive features (e.g., financial and occupational stability, educational attainment, emotional well-being, time). Most men focused primarily or exclusively on their own well-being or personal development. Typically they reported fears about not being able to complete their education or career plans, and/or having their mobility or leisure activities unduly restricted. For example, Alex, 18 years old and White, asserted: "There's a lot I want to do, a lot of things I want to see. A lot of things I want to accomplish before I want to settle down and have a family.

A more dramatic and unique example was provided by Kyle, a White, 21-year-old devout Christian. Following on the heels of his comments about how little he has thought about girls and pregnancy, Kyle remarked:

> I need to know what a husband and father needs to be and start working towards that. As I started realizing the character qualities that need to be there, and I realize I'm not anywhere near that and how much work is gonna need to be done on myself to prepare myself for that, the list keep[s] on getting longer, and I'm tackling them one at a time or whatever ones I can handle at each moment, but I think by just having them in my thoughts, maybe it's just like a physical maturing now. . . . I want to be a good husband, I want to be a good father—I don't have any concept of what a husband or a good father is but, the Bible does. . . . I have notes of character qualities and then verse after verse that talks about it.

While Kyle hadn't thought about impregnating a girl, this passage clearly reveals that he had thought extensively about his degree of fatherhood readiness. Kyle was unique in our sample, and uncharacteristic of the more general population, because of the commitment and effort he has made to prepare himself for fatherhood, even before becoming sexually active. Another way Kyle was unique was that his preparation for becoming a good father focused primarily on his personal and moral development. Instead of being worried about how fatherhood would thwart his personal life or development, as we saw with Alex above, Kyle drew attention to how his current stage of personal and moral development would restrict his ability to be a good Christian father. He clearly felt he was ill-prepared to be a good father at this point in his life.

Kyle's orientation to self was also instructive because it illustrated how some men in our sample portrayed aspects of their personal character and then linked them to their degree of readiness for fatherhood. These types of portrayals required men to have a degree of self-awareness, the ability to articulate it, and an understanding of how it may influence their preparedness for being a father.

A smaller number of men voiced their concern about how an unplanned pregnancy and birth would affect their child's well-being. These comments tended to emphasize the financial aspects of providing for children. Reflecting on the financial struggles his single mother grappled with as she tried to raise three kids, Jerry, a White 19-year-old, said:

> She always did what she had to do to get us what we wanted and what we needed, even if it was sacrificing stuff she needed at the time, but she couldn't get. She just wanted to make sure we had everything. Like come Christmas time she'd do whatever she could to give us presents and stuff, but then you see some people where their parents don't have enough money to even buy them things, and so lot of things like that makes you want to, like makes you think that you need to have the money, and definitely want to be able to take care of your kids as well as you can.

Though it was not common, a few participants explicitly mentioned or hinted at how their sense of readiness was, or would be, tied to their partner's circumstances. Not surprisingly, men voiced their concerns for their partner in conjunction with their concerns about their own well-being, sometimes mentioning, for example, that they were both still in school. After stating that he wanted kids someday, and then being asked the ideal age at which this might occur, Jerry said: "When I'm through with college, and when I have a job, and my life's steady, and if I'm with someone that her life's steady, and just when we know the time's right, when you have the money that you're going to be able to take care of it and stuff."

In addition to associating their degree of readiness to their concerns about either their partner, child, themselves, or some combination, our participants' views often implicated specific substantive concerns. In light of prevailing gendered beliefs about fathering and breadwinning in the United States, it was not surprising to find that financial considerations were by far the most consistently mentioned concern. As Desmond's earlier remarks indicate, some men identified the loss of time as a nonfinancial worry affecting their sense of fatherhood readiness. Furthermore, Tom, a Native American 22-year-old, responded to a question about what being ready to have a child means to him:

> Steadiness, cause right now I've got a lifestyle that's like, I'll go work in a place for a while, and get set up. And get as much money saved up and then try to go off and move somewhere else a little better. I just haven't really found a place yet that I'm comfortable with staying.

Our data consistently show, either implicitly or explicitly, that most men's focus of attention was multifaceted and not limited to just relational or substantive concerns. Kyle's earlier comments implicitly suggested, for instance, that while his focus of attention is self-oriented, he believes his child and partner would suffer because he has not yet developed the traits that would allow him to express himself as a Christian father. Moreover, his comments reveal that he combines his explicit relational focus on self with his substantive interests regarding Christian fatherhood.

Temporal Orientation   When men were asked to reflect on their perceptions about being ready to become a father, they organized their replies by introducing a temporal orientation to the way they both conceptualized their readiness and depicted it in their narratives. In various ways, men's description of their sense of readiness was framed by their tendency to contrast perceptions, experiences, and desires they associated with different time periods. We saw this, for example, with Arthur, who linked fatherhood readiness with improving on the financial circumstances he experienced as a child. Thus, men sometimes drew on their previous familial or personal experiences to mold a message for themselves about their readiness to be a father. In other words, men assessed what they had witnessed in the past (e.g., living in poverty) and then speculated on how assuming or postponing father roles would influence them now and/or in the future.

Men sometimes characterized transformations over time that they had personally experienced in terms of their readiness to have children. Miller, a White 28-year-old, recalled that he "never even really gave much thought to it [having children]. You know, I like to travel. I like to work and take my time off and go and see and do. I never really made place in that life for a, for a kid." He then added, "I'm getting to almost to the point where I should start settling down a little bit and actually, possibly looking for a house to live in and a job that I work at for more than a year or so." Here, Miller juxtaposes his previous and perhaps fading lifestyle with his emerging thoughts about a "nesting" strategy that would foster a more stable lifestyle, one that apparently would be more conducive to fathering a child. The narrative device he uses reveals his slowly evolving shift in identity while highlighting the more continuous features of his procreative consciousness and sense of readiness to be a father.

In other instances, men privileged their current experience and did their best to avoid other time references. Marcus, for example, noted that he and his partner "wouldn't really talk about what if we have a kid because we were scared to talk about like, I didn't even want to look . . . at that. I just wanted to talk about things right now, didn't want to talk about the future."

Men commonly compared, either implicitly or explicitly, their current situation with what they projected for themselves in the future. One 17-year-old Hispanic participant, Reynaldo, provided a useful example:

> I'm hoping to at least be out of college, have a steady job, be financially stable and be mature about things, and hopefully be married. And then I can think about being a father. But, right now I don't really think about myself being a father, it's just in the distant future. Like when I'm 26, 27 around there. But, I'm picturing myself being a good father.

Reynaldo, like some of our other participants, was able to visualize relatively long-term goals that he wanted to accomplish prior to becoming a father.

Experience (Source and Intensity)   We earmarked men's firsthand experiences with aspects of the reproductive realm and child care because some men viewed these experiences as salient to their father readiness. They also warranted attention, given men's limited exposure to certain types of experiences that result from the gendered nature of the reproductive realm and child care. Several men's sense of readiness was affected by their fertility-related experiences. Indeed, some men found that being confronted with the prospect of becoming a father to an unplanned child acted as a wake-up call for them to think about fatherhood issues more seriously. When asked if his abortion experience affected the way he thought about kids, Austin, 21 years of age and White explained, "It's definitely reminded me that I'm definitely not ready for that kind of responsibility. I knew that I wasn't before this happened, but if anything it reminded me that I wasn't ready for that at all." In Tom's case, on the other hand, his miscarriage experience deflated his desire and sense of readiness to have another child.

> Before the miscarriage I was more "amped" to have a child, I guess you could say and more willing. And nowadays I'm going to be very selective, it's going to be a while till I have another, try to have another kid.

Tom's description not only identifies miscarriage as the source of his experiential connection to his sense of readiness, but his use of the word "amped" reveals that the miscarriage must have been an intense experience to transform his earlier readiness to have a child.

Nonfertility experiences can also act as turning points in men's lives by affecting the way they think about fatherhood. In his response to a question about whether he sees kids in his future, Marcus conveyed how his sense of fatherhood readiness had been shaped by his frequent interaction with his niece. After describing his niece as "the cutest thing on earth to me right now," he provided a detailed account of a day of babysitting her as a way of explaining why he is not ready to be a father:

> I picked her up at twelve thirty, and I was with her from . . . twelve thirty to like seven. . . . And just being around her from twelve thirty to seven thirty and just constantly having to like give her bottles . . . and changing the diaper, and when I put her down, she cries, she wants to hold me, she wants me to walk around the house with her. She doesn't want to be put down. I can't watch TV, I mean I can watch TV but I have to keep an eye on her. It's just things like that, that right there's being responsible. . . . I have a lot of other things in my life right now to take care of before I have children. So that's why I say that she makes me want to have one [a child] . . . and, then again, she doesn't.

As Marcus observed, his exposure to the moral labor of child care offered him a dose of reality that convinced him that he's not quite ready to be a hands-on father, despite the possible appeal of having his own child. However, similar types of moral labor experiences may encourage other men to decide that they are actually ready for fatherhood. Likewise, opportunities to be involved in the more playful aspects of spending time with children may encourage men to embrace the idea of fatherhood and increase their sense of readiness. The following three excerpts capture a sentiment that was shared by a number of the men:

> I've always liked kids, like my cousin had a little kid a couple of years ago and I just like messing, playing with them and stuff. (Cal, 16, White)

> Eventually I'd love to be a father, I mean I love kids. I love playing with them. (Alex, 18, White)

> I've always liked kids. You know, I have like nieces and nephews I love, I want to have me a kid, you know. (Harper, 29, African American)

While the attraction to the playful aspects of spending time with kids may have enhanced Cal's and Alex's fatherhood readiness, this does not necessarily mean that they will challenge prevailing gendered patterns of parental involvement once they become fathers. In other words, their sense of readiness may actually hinge on their willingness to express more traditional forms of father involvement that center on play, rather than attending to their children's everyday needs (Lamb, 1997).

Degree of Clarity   Many of the excerpts we have presented thus far illustrate men's level of clarity about their perceived fatherhood readiness. Given the age range of our sample, it is not surprising that most participants were relatively clear about not being ready to have a child. However, as we just saw with Marcus, some men expressed a degree of ambivalence about the prospects of fatherhood, and others, like Desmond, indicated a considerable amount of clarity that they have been ready at various times in their lives to have a child. Desmond shared his thoughts about the possibility of having children with two recent partners:

> It was all positive, just thinking about raising a child. Because, really, the last two, I probably could have married them in the wink of an eye. So I thought about how we would look in a house, raising a family, with a child, being accepted, being loved, nurtured, cared for, and all of those things.

Desmond reveals his clarity about being ready for fatherhood in these relationships by contrasting his recent orientation with the way he responded during his early twenties to a pregnancy scare. His narrative construction about his evolving fatherhood readiness over time is consistent with the "doubling of self" technique involving identity work (Denzin, 1987). Those who use this technique explicitly construct and present their current identity by contrasting it to an identity they had previously expressed. Commenting on his reaction to his partner's possible pregnancy, Desmond said: "I immediately tried to distance myself from it or, it was just, I wasn't ready to deal with that. When I look back at it, that was not fair to her because I probably hurt her feelings at the time. When you're young and immature, sometimes you're not in control of your feelings." In addition to highlighting how some men used a "doubling of self" technique to make sense of changes in their procreative identity, Desmond's narrative is instructive because it illustrates how an understanding of men's subjective experiences is fostered by attending to the intersection of multiple themes, such as the focus of attention, temporal orientation, and degree of clarity.

Fathering Visions

Since our earlier analysis implied that men's sense of readiness is related to their expectations of how fathers should ideally express themselves as fathers, we now address men's views of the ideal fathering experience, the good or ideal father, and their visions of how they expect to act as fathers toward their future children. While some had given considerable thought to these matters, others had not. In this section, we selectively emphasize several of the themes we introduced previously while broadening our analysis to highlight men's penchant for biological fatherhood, their thoughts about their own father, and their ideas about what their children might be like.

When asked about the importance of fathering their own biological children, most men were quick to point out that being genetically related to children they might "father" in the future was an important feature of what they would consider to be their ideal fathering experience. Marcus, for example, indicated that biological paternity was important to him, "Cuz it's gonna be my seed. It's gonna be me. I made that being, that human being, that person. And I'm going to father it jis like my father fathered me." Meanwhile, Justin stressed his affinity for the intergenerational connection by first commenting on how proud his parents were when he graduated high school, and then noted:

> I see children as, it's like you're passing on your genes, you're passing on your hereditary information. . . . it's like you get to a certain point in your life where you're not going to achieve much more. You're just at a standstill and you can bring up a child who can achieve great things and continue on the family.

In Justin's everyday words, he associates his desire for biological paternity and social fathering with what theorists of adult development refer to as generativity—the need to nurture and guide younger generations (Hawkins & Dollahite, 1997). While most participants focused, as Justin did, on the relationship between themselves as a father and their potential children when evaluating the importance of biological paternity, Jerry accentuated

the shared experience among prospective parents that can accompany a pregnancy.

> Just the whole thing that you and your wife will go through. Just her becoming pregnant, going to the doctors with her, and when she has her checkups, and just the whole experience pretty much. Going to the hospital with her and, being there in the delivery.

Jerry's comments reflect his appreciation for a type of collaborative approach to the prebirth process that he associates with the ideal fatherhood experience; fathering is made special by sharing the gestation process with the prospective mother.

Consistent with research that has sampled fathers (Allen & Doherty, 1996; Daly, 1993), our sample of men reported several key features of good fathering and indicated that men's own fathers can serve as positive or negative role models. While economic provisioning was mentioned by a number of men, participants were quick to stress the importance of fathers spending time with their kids and their desire to be actively involved in their own children's lives. Responding to what being a father meant to him, Antoine, a 19-year-old African American, offered a reply that reflects the sentiments of a number of participants:

> Always there, no matter what you do, right or wrong, thick and thin, whatever. Somebody that's not just a provider, not just put a roof over you head, but taking care of you, gives you advice. Just your mentor and everything, friend, best friend.

Using glowing language, Reynaldo reinforced Antoine's comment by noting how his father can be a good father even while he is unemployed:

> My dad is a real man right now cause he can support us even though he's unemployed right now, but you know, whenever he had a job, he was doing good. And he supported us and right now he is showing how he can get us through tough times right now.

Thus, for many in our sample, the essence of being a good father involved being present, approachable, a friend, and a dispenser of measured discipline.

During the course of the interviews, this general conception of the "good father" appeared to be closely related to how participants assessed their own father. Whether they described their father as a positive or negative role model, the benchmark against which they articulated their assessments amounted to a fairly consistent ideal. Typically, their father's contributions as disciplinarian and provider were appreciated, but the men wanted these necessary roles balanced with direct involvement and emotional concern. Not surprisingly, those facets in which particular men found their own father lacking were the ones they seemed most eager to improve on when they become fathers, and those qualities that the men most appreciated were the ones they hoped to emulate. At one extreme, men who felt their father was absent physically vowed not to leave their children fatherless. The comments of Warren, a 23-year-old African American, were representative of this small but important group:

> I was just thinking that I didn't want to have children in X number of cities and also have a wife who wasn't the mother of those children [pause] cause that's pretty much how, what it was with my father. . . . I never felt cheated out of a father, cause I think my life turned out a little better, but at the same time I would have liked to [have] known him.

At the other end of the spectrum, some men praised their father for developing a strong emotional connection with them or knowing how to provide just the right amount of discipline and supervision:

> I'd be a very loving father like my father was. And I would try to model myself as he raised me . . . I'd be firm but I'd never hit the child. I'd be very loving and supportive no matter what. Just be his best friend. [Mitchel, White, 22 years old]

> Like my father is good, so I'm gonna pretty much be the same way that he is to me. You know, not strict but having a level head and keeping me down and not letting me get out of control really. Giving me a little bit of line but not too much. [Reynaldo, Hispanic, 17 years old]

Men whose experiences fell somewhere in between these two poles presented a similar dynamic. For instance, David, who is 28 years old and White, praised his father's achievement of the provider ideal, but sees himself being emotionally closer to his children:

Well he was a good provider. You know, he worked full time and he brought home the money, paid the bills but he wasn't like real affectionate. It didn't seem like he made an effort to like go out of his way to do things with his kids. . . . I think I would be a lot closer to my kids than he was.

Talking about their fathers, then, became an opportunity for these men to refine their visions of themselves as future fathers by reflecting on what they valued or missed in their experience of being fathered.

Focus of Attention, Degree of Clarity, and Temporal Orientation   Of the five themes we discussed in connection with fatherhood readiness, the focus of attention, degree of clarity, and temporal orientation themes were the most relevant to how participants attempted to bridge the conceptual divide between the father ideal and how they expected to be with their children. As they contemplated their future fathering behavior, men's focus of attention typically involved their child(ren) as well as the dynamic relationship between them and their child(ren). For a few men, their focus of attention evolved around some type of child development and/or family process philosophy. Miller, for instance, forcefully concluded that

> kids are spastic. What are you going to do? . . . I hate that, when you constantly see parents who are like, "Don't do that. No, don't touch that. No don't do that. No don't do this." I mean, for Christ's sake: Just buy a leash, put the kid on the leash, and deal with it that way, if you're going to be that neurotic about it.

With this philosophy as a backdrop, Miller asserted: "My kids are going to experience and go out and do and see the stuff. Because that's how life should be." These excerpts demonstrate Miller's degree of clarity about children's personalities in general, and his future role as a laid-back father. He has a definite belief about children's temperament and how a parent (father) should treat them.

Warren's comments provide us with another angle for thinking about the degree of clarity theme. This 23-year-old African American presented his vision of himself as a father someday in the context of a story that emphasizes the pitfalls of parenting. He recalled that his mother once "beat" both him and his sister because his sister did something wrong but would not "fess up." While Warren clearly disliked that experience as a child, he now anticipates that as a father he cannot guarantee that such situations will never arise, any more than his mother could. Consequently, he resigns himself to the ideal that fathering will be a "learning experience," noting: "I can have a blueprint set up right now and then when you have children, who's to say that that blueprint is going to work." Ironically, then, Warren asserted his clarity about fathering by emphasizing what he perceived to be the uncertainty associated with parenting. Notice, too, that he did so by first assuming a temporal orientation directed toward the past as he drew a lesson from his mother's actions when he was a child.

In most cases, men's visions of themselves as fathers carried with them implicit or explicit visions of the children they would father. As earlier analyses with these data revealed, men emphasized gender, personality, and physical features in addition to imagining doing specific activities with their children (Marsiglio, Hutchinson, & Cohan, in press). Moreover, some men tended to focus on these hypothetical children as small children, whereas others referenced their children's development through the years. Justin, a White 18-year-old, acknowledged trying to imagine his and his partner's children, "but at most they're just like infants, really young children." In contrast, Tom admitted to thinking about the differences in raising a girl or a boy. From his perspective, gender differences do not become relevant to parenting until the children reach puberty. At that point, he anticipates that if he had a daughter he would be uncomfortable with her emerging sexuality:

> Like girls would start getting interested in boys and start looking at them. Uhm, I don't think I'd be as comfortable taking them to like baseball games and stuff. [Interviewer: Why not?] Uhm. I don't know. I've seen a lot of like young girls out there . . . hollering at the guys. I don't know. I wouldn't even want to think that my daughter's got that part where the rear-ends gets her excited.

These men differ not only in how far into the future they "forecast" the lives of their hypothetical children, but they also focus their attention differently in this regard. While Justin's child visions were linked with a specific partner, Tom's thoughts at least gave the impression of being independent of a particular relationship.

Program Implications

We have organized our analysis of how men envision fatherhood around two key interrelated substantive dimensions: fatherhood readiness and fathering visions. Both of these dimensions are relevant to the expanding number of male involvement and pregnancy prevention programs in the United States and, taken together, provide a substantive foundation for these types of interventions. Likewise, the five theoretical themes (degree and form of collaboration, focus of attention, temporal orientation, experience, and degree of clarity) that emerged from our data are instructive because they provide insights for strengthening these types of programs. These themes supplement the practical advice Sonenstein and her colleagues (1997) offered based on their review of model programs, and are also relevant to programs suitable for high schools, colleges, the military, and prisons. Our purpose in this section, then, is to show briefly how the two substantive dimensions and five interrelated theoretical themes can inform efforts designed to heighten young men's procreative responsibility and encourage them to consider their long-term visions for fathering prior to impregnating a partner. More specifically, we recommend that programs develop opportunities for men to address at least the following five areas: (1) self-knowledge, appraisals, and aspirations; (2) relationship issues with partners; (3) past experiences with fathers (painful and valued); (4) current paternal role models; and (5) philosophies of fathering and child visions.

Consistent with Sonenstein et al.'s (1997) stated goal of encouraging men to respect themselves, we add that it is critical for young men to "know" themselves. Efforts to enhance men's self-awareness should not only encourage men to identify their self-perceptions about a range of personal attributes (character portrayals) and long-term aspirations, but men should also be prompted to identify the sources that have affected their perceptions about these matters. Men should be prompted to ask themselves what they value and how they came to feel that way. What are their long-term aspirations in terms of education, employment, finances, and family? How important do they feel it is to travel, be independent, spend time with friends, and nurture others? Much of this self-knowledge may have little, if anything to do directly with their views of fathering, children, and family. However, men's values and perceptions about human capital issues are likely to be related indirectly to their future approach to family-related matters, and opportunities should be created for men to discover these connections.

Part of men's self-knowledge involves understanding how their identities as men are affected by their perceptions of their romantic partner(s) and/or women in general. What are the qualities they would like in a partner? What are the qualities they desire in the mother of their child? What does a "good" relationship look like? Encouraging men to think about these issues should, in many instances, lead men to become introspective and evaluate themselves, partners, family, and friends. In addition, these questions may assist men in considering alternative definitions of masculinity. Thus, programs should help men expand their self-knowledge by enlightening them about the competing images of masculinity, and how these images implicate different ways to relate to one's female partner. Depending on the nature of the program, a range of ideological perspectives on gender relations from pro-feminism to religious conservatism could be presented and debated.

Our data showed that men's interactions with their female partners contributed to the diverse criteria men use to evaluate their sense of being ready for fatherhood. Efforts to raise young men's level of procreative consciousness should therefore encourage men to recognize how their sense of readiness may be related to their partner's perceptions and experiences. By alerting men explicitly to the three primary foci of attention (self, partner, and child), programs could help young men recognize that their procreative abilities can have diverse consequences, not only for them, but for others as well. Developing men's gender/partner sensitivity and child sensitivity is important. For example, assisting men to forecast the short- and long-term outcomes of a birth for their partner and for the unintended child may promote a revisioning of that scenario. Such discussions could also sensitize men to a range of possible situations they or others might encounter. For example, they might be apprised that those men who perceive themselves to be in love with their partner may be more likely than those in casual dating relationships to recognize the possible negative consequences an unplanned pregnancy and birth may have for their partner. Or, men could be reminded that their affection for their partner may in some instances obscure their ability to see beyond the idealized image of creating a child (and family) with their beloved. Messages such as these can sharpen men's understanding of the tacit and explicit collaboration that can take place between partners as men develop their sense of readiness for fatherhood.

As is commonly shown in fatherhood research, men's relationship with their father played a significant role in shaping our participants' views about the ideal father and the visions they had for fathering their own children. Our data showed that, when given a chance, men often linked their visions about their future experiences as a father with their positive and negative experiences with their own father. Programs therefore should be designed to provide young men focused opportunities to think systematically about the connections they make between their childhood experiences and their fathering visions.

In addition to having men identify their personal visions of fathering, programs can encourage men to consider how they perceive children in general and whether they have given thought to what their own children might be like. A number of men in our study remarked that they "loved" or "really liked" children and enjoyed "playing" with them. While a few mentioned how their firsthand experiences with the everyday care of children made them question whether they were ready for fatherhood, many men had a limited understanding of the demands of full-time parenting. Thus, whenever possible, programs should provide men supervised chances to develop firsthand experience with child care responsibilities so that they are better informed about what active father involvement entails.

Two main assumptions guiding our previous suggestions are that it is worthwhile to target young men, and it is possible to reach them prior to their involvement in an unplanned pregnancy that they may be ill-prepared to handle. While designing programs that are sensitive to the various developmental stages for teenage and young adult males is a challenging task, we found that males of varying ages are eager to talk about fatherhood and related issues. Getting men to not only understand the full significance of paternity and social fatherhood, but also make sexual and contraceptive decisions that reflect that understanding should be a critical goal for those who work with young men in schools, social service agencies, the military, prisons, and the health care arena. Based on this research we advocate programs that promote introspection, evaluation, and a temporal orientation that assists men in a "doubling of self" to examine their past and present in order to project their future. Programs may be most effective in this regard when they provide an organizational context, a structured format, and an appropriate set of concepts (e.g., fatherhood readiness, father visions, child visions) that allow men to construct and share narratives about their procreative selves in the presence of their peers.

Conclusion

By using the grounded theory method and in-depth interviews with a sample of young men who have not yet fathered a child, we have been able to offer fresh theoretical insights about the way men envision aspects of fatherhood. Although our sample may not be suitable for generalizing to specific groups, it permitted us to conceptualize and explore sensitizing concepts, including the two substantive dimensions to the process of envisioning fatherhood (fatherhood readiness, father visions) and the five theoretical themes (degree of collaboration, focus of attention, temporal orientation, experience, and degree of clarity). These concepts advance the social psychology of fatherhood by emphasizing aspects of prospective fatherhood and can be incorporated into other studies of fatherhood with different samples of men.

Our study serves the dual purpose of informing both theory and program development. With additional work, researchers can tease out the dimensions, phases, contexts, degrees, contingencies, types, and other theoretical codes that permit further expansion, integration, and grounding of the concepts, thus moving toward theory generation. This theoretical work can promote effective program development by attending to young men's voices (i.e., their subjective perspectives about envisioning fatherhood).

While we studied a diverse sample of young men with varied educational, economic, and ethnic backgrounds, our sample was small, and the number of men who represented any category was even smaller. In the future, we will expand and diversify our sample and examine both within and between group data, concentrating on the similarities and differences of, for example, the father visions of specific groups such as young inner-city Black males, rural males, males with varying degrees of experience with sex and pregnancy, and the like. We will also augment our theoretical sampling by obtaining more data on the interrelationships of the substantive dimensions and the theoretical themes. These additional data will provide the foundation for developing and enhancing more client-specific programs. In addition, the generated concepts can be useful in evaluating existing programs and, with further refinement, the conceptualization of outcome variables for intervention studies.

This research was sponsored by a University of Florida Opportunity Fund Grant (UPN#98041676).

The authors would like to thank Dan Duarte for conducting a subset of the interviews for this study. We also acknowledge the research assistance of Dana Bagwell, Chris Carlin, Nikki Cline, Laurie Dennison, Tricia Duthiers, Tara Hatch, Brian Lapinski, Jenny Miles, Angela Sheffler, Brad Tripp, Gustavo Vargas, and Amanda Welton; and Mr. Marvin Dukes's assistance in recruiting at the Department of Motor Vehicles, Alachua County, Florida.

References

Allen, D. A., & Doherty, W. J. (1996) The responsibilities of fatherhood as perceived by African American teenage fathers. *Families in Society: The Journal of Contemporary Human Services, March,* 142–155.

Daly, K. (1993) Reshaping fatherhood: Finding the models. *Journal of Family Issues, 14,* 510–530.

Denzin, N. K. (1987) *The recovering alcoholic.* Thousand Oaks, CA: Sage.

Federal Interagency Forum on Child and Family Statistics (1998) *Nurturing fatherhood: Improving data and research on male fertility, family formation, and fatherhood.* Washington, DC.

Furstenberg, F. F., Jr. (1995) Fathering in the inner city: Paternal participation and public policy. In W. Marsiglio (Ed.), *Fatherhood: Contemporary theory, research, and social policy* (pp. 119–147). Thousand Oaks, CA: Sage.

Glaser, B. (1978) *Theoretical sensitivity.* Mill Valley, CA: Sociology Press.

Glaser, B. (1992) *Basics of grounded theory analysis.* Mill Valley, CA: Sociology Press.

Gobel, M., Diamond J. J., Chambers C. V. (1997) Attitudes toward sexual responsibility and parenting: An exploratory study of young urban males. *Family Planning Perspectives, 29,* 280–283.

Hawkins, A. J., & Dollahite, D. (1997) *Generative fathering: Beyond deficit perspectives.* Thousand Oaks, CA: Sage.

Herzog, J. M. (1982) Patterns of expectant fatherhood: A study of fathers of premature infants. In S. H. Cath, A. R. Gurwitt, & J. M. Ross (Eds.). *Father and child: Development and clinical perspectives* (pp. 301–314). Boston: Little, Brown.

Lamb, M. E. (1997) *The role of the father in child development* (3rd edition). New York: Wiley.

LaRossa, R., & LaRossa, M. M. (1989) Babe care: Fathers vs. mothers. In B. J. Risman & P. Schwartz (Eds.). *Gender in intimate* relationships. *A microstructural approach.* Belmont, CA: Wadsworth.

Levine, J. A., & Pitt, E. W. (1995) *New expectations: Community strategies for responsible fatherhood.* New York: Families and Work Institute.

Lincoln, Y., and Guba, E. (1985) *Naturalistic inquiry.* Beverly Hills, CA: Sage.

Marsiglio, W. (1998) *Procreative man.* New York: New York University Press.

Marsiglio, W. (1995) Fathers' diverse life course patterns and roles: Theory and social interventions. In W. Marsiglio (Ed.). *Fatherhood: Contemporary theory, research, and social policy* (pp. 78–101). Thousand Oaks, CA: Sage.

Marsiglio, W., Hutchinson, S., & Cohan, M. (in press). Young men's procreative identity. Becoming aware, being aware, and being responsible. *Journal of Marriage and the Family.*

May, K. A. (1980) A typology of detachment/involvement styles adopted during pregnancy by first-time fathers. *Western Journal of Nursing Research, 2,* 445–453.

Mead, G. H. (1934). *Mind, self, and society: From the standpoint of a social behaviorist.* Chicago: University of Chicago Press.

Moore, K. A., Driscoll, A. K., & Ooms, T. (1997) *Not just for girls: The roles of boys and men in teen pregnancy prevention.* Washington, DC: National Campaign to Prevent Teen Pregnancy.

Sherwen, L. N. (1987) The pregnant man. In L. N. Sherwen (Ed.). *Psychosocial dimensions of the pregnant family* (pp. 157–176). New York: Springer.

Sonenstein, F. I., Stewart, K., Lindberg, D. L., Pernas, M., & Williams, S. (1997) *Involving males in preventing teen pregnancy: A guide for program planners.* The California Wellness Foundation: The Urban Institute.

Soule, B., Stanley, K., & Copans, S. (1979) Father identity. *Psychiatry, 42,* 255–263.

Strauss, A. (1987) *Qualitative analysis for social scientists.* New York: Cambridge University Press.

Zayas, L. H. (1988) Thematic features in the manifest dreams of expectant fathers. *Clinical Social Work Journal, 16,* 282–296.

9

The Function of Fathers: What Poor Men Say about Fatherhood

The incidence of nonmarital parenting and divorce and their relationship to child poverty has brought renewed attention to the influence of fathers in the acquisition of skills and access to resources by their children (Duncan, Hill, & Yeung, 1996; Perloff & Buckner, 1996). While it is beyond the scope of this paper to detail the evolution of the paternal identity with its multiple functions and the subsequent growth of female-headed families, this paper addresses recent work on paternal identity and its implications for social policies affecting fathers. This research uses information obtained from interviews with poor young men who used General Assistance (GA), a cash assistance program primarily for single adults and childless couples. The perceived influence fathers had on their sons' decisions to use welfare and seek employment is discussed in an earlier work (Kost, 1997a). The present work examines the relationship respondents had with their fathers. For those young men who are themselves fathers, it also explores how those relationships influenced their own paternal identity and the relationships they have with their children.

This paper is divided into five sections. The first section briefly discusses the theories and the tasks thought to be necessary for a fully functioning paternal identity. The second examines the absence of support for these tasks in current social and economic policy. The third section details the methods used to gather the sample; this is followed by an examination of the findings. The last section explores the implications this study has for social work practice and makes recommendations for future research.

The Construction of Fatherhood

Historical evidence suggests that the identity of a man as a father, the importance placed on this role, and its function in the family has undergone several permutations (Demos, 1982; Lamb, 1986; Radin, 1981; Vinovskis, 1986). A key element in these changes is the adaptation of understanding and acceptance of the diverse meanings of this role for the individual and society over time. As Berger and Luckmann (1966) note, to learn a role effectively the individual must not only acquire the knowledge and routines that are associated with it, but also internalize the role's "socially agreed-upon meanings" (p. 82). In Berger and Luckmann's view, roles in the family such as father and mother are constructed by society. Consequently, these "agreed-upon meanings" would change over time. Individual behaviors and routines associated with the role would adapt in response to these different meanings. Likewise, the function or purpose of a role, in this case that of "father," would also change over time. For while a man may be a father, his paternal conduct "provides insight into the meaning that he attaches to that role." (Ihinger-Tallman, Pasley, & Buehler, 1995, p. 63). Therefore, it is important to distinguish between the role of father and the identity one may develop as a father.

Paternal Identity

The theoretical framework for this discussion of paternal identity comes out of work on the theories of social exchange and identity. Each of these theories suggests a dimension needed for parenting. The moral norm of univocal reciprocity is the ability to engage in social exchanges without expecting reciprocation (Ekeh, 1977). Generativity, on the other hand, is a developmental task of the parental identity in which one learns to care for another without regard to self-interest (Erikson, 1980). In general, men are less likely to be exposed to activities that encourage the development of these behaviors (Chodorow, 1978; Dinnerstein, 1976).

Within the context of paternal identity, univocal reciprocity represents the ability to provide for another without the expectation of return. The stereotypical way a father would engage in univocal reciprocity is through the economic arena in his role as breadwinner, an enduring facet of the early construction of the father's identity. For example, fathers have historically been responsible for the financial well-being of their wife and children. In the past, fathers controlled the resources of the family (Flax, 1982; Lamb, 1986).

Apart from the economic sphere, the univocal reciprocity practiced by parents can best be understood as an investment in a child's well-being. This investment may be in the form of time spent reading and listening to the child and/or allowing the child access to activities that enhance his or her skills, such as music, dance, or sports-related lessons or taking the child to libraries, museums, the theater, or concerts. While some of these activities carry a financial cost, others, such as being a coach or a volunteer in the child's school, do not. Parents participate in these activities without the expectation that this investment of time will be returned by the child. Thus univocal reciprocity differs from mutual reciprocity in that reciprocation for this investment may come from someone other than the child (Scanzoni & Marsiglio, 1993).

Similar to univocal reciprocity, generativity involves being other-directed, that is, caring for a child to the extent that the child's needs have priority over the parent's (e.g., losing sleep while caring for a sick child). In his theory of the development of identity over the life course, Erikson (1980) notes that it is through this caregiving activity that an adult develops the need to be needed, and without which one is prone to narcissistic self-indulgence. Erikson considers generativity essential to the successful performance of parental tasks needed for the caring of and commitment to children.

Ihinger-Tallman and others (1995) argue that in order for a man to develop and maintain an identity as a father, four conditions must be present. The paternal role must first have saliency or meaning to him. In their view, when a man's identity as a father is connected to other roles, such as baseball coach, breadwinner, husband, and scout leader, it is likely to have "high salience" (p. 69). The degree to which this identity has meaning will, in turn, influence a man's commitment to the second component, fulfilling the basic socially prescribed duties of the paternal role. The authors then posit that this identity must be fostered by a community which reinforces the fulfillment of the prescribed duties associated with the role of father. The expectations of this community, manifesting through policies and programs, influence a father's ability to respond to and maintain contact with his children over time, particularly during periods of financial or emotional distress and separation. Finally, a man's peers within the community reinforce and support these socially prescribed paternal behaviors by modeling interaction and activity with children. Thus the construction of a paternal identity is a societal as well as an individual psychosocial endeavor.

The Paternal Role in Social Policy

Society prescribes its expectations of parents to their children through legislation and policies. Public policies in the social and economic arenas detail the duties and responsibilities of a father, further reinforcing his commitment to this identity. These policies may influence paternal behavior directly, as in the case of child protection and child support policies, or indirectly, as in the availability of paternal leave and tax deductions for child care. Another example is policy mandating the economic support of children by the noncustodial parent, who is usually the father. Establishment of paternity and payment of child support are the cornerstones of this policy.

Within the child welfare system, unwed, noncustodial fathers are rarely considered when social workers develop plans for protection of children. Workers usually consider grandparents or even neighbors for kinship care placements before attempting to locate or involve fathers. These practitioners assume that the father is uninvolved in his child's life or unconcerned about the child's welfare because he does not live with the child or pay child support (Kadushin, 1980).

Child support policy does not allow fathers to substitute the provision of in-kind services when circumstances prevent their economic support. For example, absent, unemployed fathers are not permitted to provide child care that might allow the mother to continue working and reduce the cost of such care to her in place of their child support payment. This type of in-kind support has the potential to enhance a man's development of univocal reciprocity and generativity. Currently, fathers face incarceration when they do not keep their payments up to date, and may abandon their children rather than risk being jailed (Waller & Plotnick, 2000). The potential use and effect of alternative forms of support by the absent parent is unknown.

This emphasis on an economically based paternal identity, to the near exclusion of others, is central to the welfare reform legislation within the Personal Responsibility and Work Opportunity Reconciliation Act of 1996 (PRWORA). The Temporary Assistance to Needy Families (TANF) Block Grant, which eliminated entitlement to cash assistance for poor families in PRWORA, is premised on the concept that marriage is essential to the foundation of a successful society. While the legislation mandates the establishment of paternity and the enforcement of child support, it is silent on the need for services that might encourage or support a psychological commitment to children by fathers. Instead, mothers must identify the father of the child and tell authorities where he can be located or lose their benefits under TANF. Rather than have children lose cash assistance, poor fathers may disappear. Thus this welfare policy further attenuates the emotional connection these fathers may have with their children (Roy, 1999; Waller & Plotnick, 2000).

In general, fathers are not expected to need assistance in fulfilling their financial responsibility. Until the initiation of the Parent's Fair Share Demonstration Project in 1992, the need for employment assistance for the fathers of children born outside of marriage was largely ignored (Blank, 1995). This project, existing in only seven sites, was created to examine and provide services to noncustodial parents (NCPs), most of who are fathers. The emphasis in this project is on increasing the NCP's ability to pay child support (Johnson & Doolittle, 1996). There is little or no attempt to improve a father's relationship with or emotional commitment to his child. The project was not designed to integrate the role of breadwinner with other paternal roles or tasks identified earlier as contributing to the high salience of the paternal identity.

In the context of adolescent pregnancy, federal funding is restricted to abstinence-based programs. The political debate surrounding this funding is filled with moral overtones about the influence funds have on adolescent sexual behavior and whether funding services for adolescent parents encourages adolescents to become parents in order to receive assistance. What little money there is for parenting programs and services targets mothers and children, who are seen as more worthy and in need of services than fathers (Vinovskis, 1992). As a consequence, there is little attention paid to the development of parenting skills by males (Klinman, 1986; Leitch, Gonzalez, & Ooms, 1993).

Finally, recent economic policy changes to the Earned Income Tax Credit (EITC), the minimum wage, child health care coverage through Medicaid, and child care assistance provide important market incentives that could influence a father's ability to provide financial support. Largely absent from this economic policy are initiatives to increase attachment to the labor market by low-skilled men that would assist them in fulfilling their role as a breadwinner. Absent as well are economic incentives that would increase a father's commitment to his child (Blank, 1995; Blank & London, 1995). For example, men may receive time off from work if they take a paternal leave to care for their child; however, the costs to their career may be so great they cannot afford to do so. Given that this parental leave is unpaid, few low-income fathers use it. These fathers define their identity in terms of their ability to contribute financially. The value of their interaction with their children is linked to their income (Furstenberg, 1995; Sullivan, 1989) with child-rearing activities considered the exclusive responsibility of mothers (Biller, 1981; Sullivan, 1994).

Thus, the role of breadwinner is the most visible socially prescribed duty of the paternal role in the American construction of fatherhood. While its successful performance is critical to the economic well-being of children, its primacy depends to relegate fathers to a unidimensional and potentially peripheral function in their child's development.

Methods

This research utilizes a sample of young men, many of whom are the fathers of children of poor, unwed mothers. Semistructured, open-ended interviews were conducted with 20 men at two neighborhood centers in Madison, Wisconsin, between September 1993 and June 1994. Although the sample is small, this qualitative approach provided a unique opportunity to study the personal circumstances that influenced a young man's decisions about welfare, work, and family. By allowing the respondent to describe his life history in his own words, each man was able to express opinions about the meaning of events and what influenced him. In particular, the reflective opportunities of this narrative research provided crucial information for capturing the perceived effects of paternal influence, often unmeasured when using other methods.

The primary question of this research was why a young, able-bodied man would use welfare when he could earn much more money working part time at a minimum-wage job. Participants had to meet the following three criteria: (1) be men between the ages of 18 and 30; (2) have received General Assistance at least once; and (3) be considered able-bodied, that is, not eligible for Supplemental Security Income (SSI) at the time of their initial receipt. Participants were recruited through the use of informational flyers and informal contacts from neighborhood center staff and social workers that thought they would meet the criteria for inclusion in the study. In addition to these sampling strategies, snowballing was also used; that is, respondents were asked to tell other eligible men about the study. Men agreed to participate in this study, sign a statement of informed consent, and have their interview tape-recorded. All interviews were conducted by the author and lasted approximately 90 minutes.

Each participant was asked to describe his life, including his education, family structure and support system, and criminal, employment and welfare histories. They were also asked to describe the informal and formal support they received during their lives, particularly from their family, with specific probes regarding their perception of the influence of their father on their own employment and paternal decisions.

Bias was introduced in the selection of this sample from at least three sources. Two were through the use of neighborhood centers as distribution points for the flyers. First, not all men who use General Assistance utilize the services and/or resources of neighborhood centers; these may include free meals, food pantries, free clothing, and support services. Thus, only those men who used or knew someone who used these services learned about the survey. Second, these neighborhood centers were located in areas with little ethnic diversity. Respondents were obtained from only two of the seven centers that agreed to participate. The majority of the respondents were African American; there was only one Hispanic respondent and there were no Asian respondents. The third source of selection bias was introduced because a $20 stipend was offered to each participant. Further, respondents were self-selected: they needed to contact the researcher and set up an appointment. Thus, men in this sample may differ in unmeasured ways from others that receive General Assistance.

Results

Men in this sample varied in their experiences with their fathers and their perception of the importance of his contribution to their development of a paternal identity. Respondents ranged in age from 18 to 30; 17 of the 20 respondents were minorities. Thirteen of these men were fathers and five others acted as surrogate fathers (see Table 9.1). Most re-

Table 9.1 Demographic Characteristics of General Assistance Recipients

Average Age	26 years
Ethnicity	
African American	15
Caucasian	3
Hispanic	1
Native American	1
Own marital status	
Never-married	17
Married	1
Divorced/separated	2
Paternity	
No children	7
1 child	6
2 children	6
> 2 children	1
Number of GA spells	
1	11
2	6
3–4	3
Education	
≤ 8 years	1
9–11 years	5
HS diploma or GED	8
12 years	6
Parental marital status	
Never-married	3
Married	8
Divorced/separated	8
Widowed	1
Ever in jail	14
Ever homeless	11
Parental use of welfare	9
Average GA spell	7.5 months

Note: $N = 20$

ported sporadic work histories and limited academic achievement; few were working at the time of the interview. Those who were working worked predominately in the low-wage service sector as janitors, dishwashers, and manual laborers (Kost, 1997a).

The majority of respondents knew little about their father's childhood and few had met their paternal grandparents. While the majority of these young men had maintained a close relationship with their mother into adulthood, very few characterized their current relationship with their father as close and supportive. It is important to note that two men refused to talk about their father, simply stating that they did not know where he was and did not want to answer questions about him. More than half of the 20 respondents reported spending at least some time in a single-parent home. One man reported being in foster care as a child after the death of his father.

Only three men were raised in families that were free from violence and poverty. All the men in this study had witnessed violence at some point in their lives and either personally experienced or had a family member who had experienced violence, including the murder of siblings. Many told stories of physical, emotional, and substance abuse by their father as well as by paternal surrogates. Eleven men reported that they had been homeless, some as children, for more than a week—a majority of them more than once.

Fourteen respondents had spent time in a juvenile detention center, jail, or prison. Sentences ranged from one day to seven years; offenses ranged in seriousness from disorderly conduct and shoplifting to auto theft, carrying a concealed weapon, and attempted murder. For a majority of the men, time in an institution had been preceded by multiple police contacts.

These respondents had difficulty talking about the influence and modeling of their father or his surrogate when it was not positive. Sometimes their stories were punctuated with bravado; insisting that their negative experiences with their father did not matter because they had their mothers. At other times questions were met with silence or a shake of their head. As one 29-year-old man stated, "Growing up was hard." Another 24-year-old man explained:

I didn't have much of a relationship with my father. He came. He was violent towards my mother. She got beat up a lot. I saw a lot of it. My other brothers and sisters saw it.

Another 24-year-old man described the relationship with his father this way:

Me and my dad can never talk. It was always at the start of the talk, "Here, get an attitude." I get an attitude. Then it turns into an argument, fight, cussing each other out. Feelings getting hurt.

Many of the respondents reported that their father "hung out" with a rough crowd, was in prison, or had a criminal history. One 28-year-old with a criminal history described the influence of his older sibling who had assumed the role of father, noting, "My brother was like a leader to me when I was growing. He did a lot of bad things. Some of it sort of rubbed off on me." Other young men expressed anger about the lack of guidance, nurturing, and support they received from their father or his surrogate. They expressed frustration and disappointment over the lack of appropriate modeling and direction they received.

My father was an abusive alcoholic. He drank a lot of alcohol. My mother is never blessed with nothing. As far as my knowledge, she never messed with anything. She has been a church lady all her life; she still is a church lady. . . . My father was a real strict man on his kids. I was not allowed to leave my yard. I was not allowed to participate at no times in school activities at night because of the battle that was going on. . . . Even my father—I mean he never took time to educate us on drugs or nothing. (28-year-old)

Men whose father had left while they were children had conflicted feelings about their father. While these respondents missed their father and what they thought he might have been able to give them, they were angry because he had not lived up to their expectations. They felt that being a father meant having a commitment to one's child and protecting the child and family when there was a crisis. They found that their lives changed profoundly when their father left, as one 25-year-old man reported:

It really started when my father left. Things got hectic. . . . I was 13. The child had to go to work and help the mother, or whatever. [Where we were living] it was really dangerous. . . . [My father left because] he was just stressed out. I guess he wanted to better things for himself. For us—I guess he figured he couldn't do it. So he had to leave. . . . I always wanted to see him. There are a lot of things I didn't know about women and everything else that I think a father should have been there for me. I always despised [him] because he left.

Another 25-year-old man adamantly expressing his disapproval stated:

I am never going to walk out on my family. They got a problem—I am going to talk to them and work it out. That is something I never hear. . . . I used to have problems when I was a child, and I wouldn't even tell my mother because I didn't want to add to her worries. It was so strange. I didn't understand why we had to live like that.

Those few men who felt a close bond with their father or father surrogate generally spoke about his positive influence on their lives and the importance of his modeling appropriate behavior. While these men described the problems they encountered in meeting their father's expectations, they also noted the emotional support they received from him when they tried to meet these expectations.

Basically, I spoke to my father a lot, too. He helped me out a lot. As far as gangs, they tried to initiate me like they try to initiate everyone. I was in a gang for a little while, but I felt that it was wrong. I went to my father. . . . I got away from it. (30-year-old)

Similarly,

My daddy was my idol even though he was a drinker. But everything I know today from growing up as a kid—I can still recall everything he ever told me. And everything he told me never was bad—it was always good. If it wasn't for them—my mother and father—I would probably be dead somewhere today. (28-year-old)

In most cases this modeling of appropriate behavior took the form of fulfilling one's responsibility and conforming to appropriate social norms that meant supporting the family.

I mean I did work odds and ends with my father and he paid me out of his pocket. Basically, I got all my training and experience from him. He does a lot of stuff. . . . And the skills that I have that he rubbed off on me, maybe I can try

to pick them up over there, so I can go a little further. Because some of the things I know how to do. I just need more training on other skills. (23-year-old)

And

I never wanted to be on welfare either because when I was growing up also, I had a lot of part-time jobs. So I basically learned how to support myself. My father always taught me to support yourself, and my mother always taught me to support yourself. (30-year-old)

The level of education among a majority of respondents was low, and for those who knew something about their father's history, their education level appears similar to that of their father. For example, several men spoke about their father being illiterate. Six of the 20 respondents had neither a high school diploma nor a General Educational Development (GED) diploma; eight had a high school or GED diploma, but three of these eight men had completed their high school education while in prison or in a juvenile detention center. Of those men who had more than 12 years of education, only one had graduated from college. The fathers in this sample shortened their education as a result of the birth of their child. Even though this decision limited their potential employment opportunities and ability to support a child, respondents identified fulfillment of their economic responsibilities as important.

I graduated from high school. I had a year at circle campus. I started working, had kids, et cetera. I had the wife and the baby. My father told me, "You gotta work now. You got kids." So school was out. I just started working. (30-year-old)

When fathers could not be relied upon, some men reported the presence of other important persons who acted in their place, giving them the time and nurturing they needed. For example, when asked whether he missed not having his father around when he young, one 18-year-old man responded:

No big deal because my mom acted like a father, too. Plus I got a stepfather up here, and he is more than a father. He is a person you can communicate with and talk to in a time that you need someone to talk to.

Another 29-year-old man noted that his grandparents took on the duties of child rearing that his parents were unable to perform

> because my mother and father were alcoholics, but my grandmother took us, and she made us go to church; she taught us "thank you" and "no, thank you," and that's basically how it was with me, but I have always had the working attitude. I have always had it because my grandfather always said, "Anything worth having is worth waiting for, and if it is worth waiting for, it is worth working for. And a man that don't work ain't no man." I had that to motivate me and move me on.

Many of these respondents admitted that even when their father's influence was positive, life on the street was more powerful. Neither their environment nor the community reinforced or supported positive behavior. One 28-year-old man who reported that his father was "a real nice role model" who always tried to teach him the right thing stated:

> There was a lot of gangs, drug dealing going around, fighting, violence, lot of robbing and stealing. . . . There were not too many role models around me when I grew up. Everybody had their own way of life. They believed in taking from someone instead of trying to achieve something out of life. So it was kind of miserable because every time you looked around, you'd hear police sirens, someone's going to jail, or someone is beating their girlfriend.

According to Ihinger-Tallman et al. (1995), a key factor supporting the identity of "father" is the assumption of its socially prescribed duties. While two men talked about their father as having a role beyond that of breadwinner, only one was a father himself. This 30-year-old noncustodial parent provided child care for the working mother of his child. A third man whose two children were born to different women who lived in different states talked about helping his surrogate children with homework. He also coached their sports teams. Although fathers in this study expressed strong feelings about the role a father should play in the life of a child, few lived with their children.

Thus, one of the concerns of the present research is whether respondents felt they had experienced an intergenerational transfer of norms about how one behaves as a father. This was a difficult issue

for these men to address. As a consequence, responses were more often related to specific skills they had learned from their father, such as those described above relating to employment or what their father had done that they would not repeat. In the latter instance, men reported that their father's abuse and/or abandonment had affected their sense of responsibility toward their own children.

> But, like I said, with my son, I don't want him to see that stuff and go through that stuff now. . . . That's why I like to go get him and be with him, because I don't think he needs to be around that kind of stuff. I know how it affected me. I don't want to do the same thing to him. I just don't want to do the same thing to him. I just don't like it. If a kid is here, he needs both his parents, because like I said, life is already hard enough. . . . My mother raised me by herself. Mothers always mean well, but like I said, daddies need to be there too. They need both parents. Even if they are not together, he needs to see your face and know that you care about him and that somebody is there for him. (24-year-old)

However, these men lacked the resources to maintain contact their children when the mother moved to another city or state. One 24-year-old father who had not seen his son in several months because the mother had moved to Illinois expressed frustration with his limited income and sorrow over not having his son in his life:

> I am at that stage where I want to be around my son, and I am not able to be with him [because the mother of the child relocated]. I go get him and bring him up here sometimes. But it is hard because I don't know anybody who can really watch him, and paying child care is almost like paying rent. That's the problem I have with being up here because I really miss my son. I really like to show him everything, because, like I said, when I was growing up, I didn't have a man around who wanted to be with me, and I want to be with my son and show him things he needs to know to grow, the guidelines that young men need to know. For a while he was up here with me—it was everyday, and he was like—when I came home, he was there. We would go home and we would just do father-son things. We'd play and talk. He'd laugh.

The children of respondents ranged in age from 1 month to approximately 12 years. None of these children was the result of a planned pregnancy. Few men spoke of having a positive relationship with the mother of their child. Those fathers who had been abandoned by their own father appear to be repeating this behavior with their children. In some cases, this was due to a relocation, either their own or that of the mother. In other cases the mother would not allow them visitation because of the father's lack of financial support, or the men themselves felt that their loss of income hampered their ability to act like a father. Given the fact that few of these men had regular and routine contact with their children, opportunities to practice paternal conduct were limited. Although the meaning of the paternal role for these men appears to have had a strong influence on their expressed concern for the level of their involvement and responsibility for their children, the degree to which they acted in response to their concern is unknown. Thus, it is uncertain whether the salience of the paternal identity, as demonstrated by the level of their involvement with their children, will be greater than that modeled by their own father.

Discussion

Few of these men described a childhood where univocal reciprocity and generativity were consistently demonstrated. A majority of men in this sample grew up in poverty and experienced many of its associated social conditions, including violence, substance abuse, adolescent paternity, limited educational achievement, incarceration, and limited employment experience; only three men described their family as middle class.

All of the fathers in this study expressed aspects of generativity, in that they felt needed by their child and observed their own growth from interacting with their child. However, the saliency of their identity as a father does not appear high, nor do these men place much value on the emotional contributions they made to their children. For example, although they felt they had gained something from the interaction with their child they discounted the effect their interaction had for the child.

This was in sharp contrast to their expressions of both a need for and appreciation of the nurturing and support they received from their father or his surrogate. For example, despite the lack of attention they may have received, men reported that the bond they felt with their father or father surrogate was more influential than the poverty, homelessness, or violence they experienced. While he was not always present or positive, these men said their father had an important influence on their ability to mediate with the external world. Many felt that contact with their father or his surrogate provided a level of confidence and certainty that helped them survive their bad decisions, such as getting drunk or high rather than going to work. They spoke of remembering their father's advice and his warnings of support. These men admitted that even though these bad decisions limited their ability to provide economic support to their children, they were committed to helping their children as best as they could.

Despite this expressed commitment, the young men in this study appear to have adapted their fathering behavior in response to their own father or a father surrogate and to their relationship with the child's mother, and not in response to their child. For example, they spoke about "what fathers should do" rather than what their son or daughter needed. When the mother relocated, they made little attempt to maintain contact with the child. When she refused visitation because she had not received the child support payment, they withdrew rather than pay it. In some cases men who were unable to pay their child support regularly stopped seeing their own children and had become surrogate fathers to children in another family.

Findings from this research support recommendations (Furstenberg, 1995; Hawkins, Christensen, Sargent, & Hill, 1995; Marsiglio, 1995) that socially appropriate mechanisms and policies must be created to assist men in the development of caregiving skills. Policy initiatives that neglect the importance of the social norms and tasks necessary for the paternal role may have unintended negative consequences and be unsuccessful in solving the problems faced by poor children (Furstenberg, 1995). The exclusion of noneconomic activities in public policies pertaining to fatherhood may undermine the commitment of fathers to their children (Roy, 1999). Moreover, the underlying message that noncustodial parents, a majority of whom are men, can fulfill their responsibility to children simply by paying their child support on time misrepresents the intention of these policies (Garfinkel & McLanahan, 1995). The men in this study agreed; in their view, a financial commitment is not enough.

While it is true that one cannot legislate concern for another or for family involvement, there is nothing biological about child rearing, as opposed to childbearing. One appropriate mechanism may be the implementation, in public schools through course work and afterschool programs, of the early development of skills needed to care for, nurture, and socialize children. For example, many schools and neighborhood center programs teach children how to negotiate and resolve conflict. By including activities associated with generativity and reciprocity, social work practitioners could foster the development of these attributes. In the same way, practitioners could advocate for programs in community colleges that increase opportunities for fathers to participate in activities with their children. By providing support for parents within educational settings, the saliency of the paternal identity would increase as men increased their labor market potential (Hochschild, 1983; Kost, 1997b).

The implications of this research for practice clearly suggest that child welfare practitioners should consider placing children with their father in the case of foster care and in permanency planning. As Erikson (1980) argues, one must have access to opportunities to practice paternal skills if they are to be integrated into one's identity as a parent.

Future research should be done with a more representative sample of fathers, including a broader range of ages, economic circumstances, and entry patterns into paternity. While men in this sample varied on the age they became fathers, only one of the 13 men who were fathers in this sample married the mother of his child. Likewise, research should be conducted using a sample of fathers and their sons in order to explore the perceived intergenerational effects of paternal influence. Discovering patterns of paternal behavior and influence could assist both practitioners and policymakers in developing programs that strengthen the connection and commitment of fathers to their children.

This research was supported in part by a grant from the Society for the Psychological Study of Social Issues, the Rand Corporation, and the Institute for Research on Poverty, University of Wisconsin-Madison. Any opinions expressed are those of the author and not of any sponsoring institution.

References

Berger, P. L., & Luckmann, T. (1966). *The social construction of reality.* New York: Anchor Books.

Blank, R. M. (1995). Outlook for the U.S. labor market and prospects for low-wage entry jobs. In D. S. Nightingale, & R. H. Haveman (Eds.), *The work alternative* (pp. 33–69). Washington, DC: Urban Institute Press.

Blank, R. M., & London, R. A. (1995). Trends in the working poor: The impact of economy, family and public policy. In T. R. Schwartz & K. M. Weigert (Eds.), *America's working poor* (pp. 86–122). South Bend, IN: University of Notre Dame Press.

Chodorow, N. (1978). *The reproduction of mothering: Psychoanalysis and the sociology of gender.* Berkeley: University of California Press.

Demos, J. (1982). The changing faces of fatherhood: A new exploration in American family history. In S. H. Cath, A. R. Gurwitt, & J. M. Ross (Eds.), *Father and child: Developmental and clinical perspectives* (pp. 425–445). Boston: Little, Brown.

Dinnerstein, D. (1976). *The mermaid and the minotaur.* New York: Harper & Row.

Duncan, G. J., Hill, M., & Yeung, J. (1996). *Father's activities and children's attainments.* Institute for Policy Research Working Papers, WP-96-25. Chicago: Northwestern University.

Ekeh, P. (1974). *Social exchange theory.* Cambridge, MA: Harvard University Press.

Erikson, E. H. (1980). *Identity and the life cycle.* New York: Norton.

Flax, J. (1982). The family in contemporary feminist thought: A critical review. In J. B. Elshtain (Ed.), *The family in political thought* (pp. 223–253). Amherst: University of Massachusetts Press.

Furstenberg, Jr., F. F. (1995). Fathering in the inner city: Paternal participation and public policy. In W. Marsiglio (Ed.), *Fatherhood: Contemporary theories, research, and social policy* (pp. 119–147). Thousand Oaks, CA: Sage.

Garfinkel, I. & McLanahan, S. (1995). The effects of child support reform on child well-being. In P. L. Chase-Lansdale & J. Brooks-Gunn (Eds.), *Escape from poverty: What makes a difference for children?* (pp. 211–240). Cambridge, England: Cambridge University Press.

Hawkins, A. J., Christensen, S. L., Sargent, K. P., & Hill, E. J. (1995). Rethinking father's involvement in child care: A developmental perspective. In W. Marsiglio (Ed.), *Fatherhood, Contemporary theories, research, and social policy* (pp. 41–56). Thousand Oaks, CA: Sage.

Hochschild, A. R. (1983). *The managed heart: Commercialization of human feeling.* Berkeley: University of California Press.

Ihinger-Tallman, M., Pasley, K., & Buehler, C. (1995). Developing a middle range theory of father involvement postdivorce. In W. Marsiglio (Ed.), *Fatherhood: Contemporary theories, research, and social policy* (pp. 57–77). Thousand Oaks, CA: Sage.

Johnson, E. S., & Doolittle, F. (1996). *Low income parents and the parents' fair share demonstration: An early qualitative look at low income noncustodial parents (NCPs) and how one policy initiative has attempted to improve their ability to pay child support.* MDRC Working Papers. Manpower Demonstration Research Corporation.

Kadushin, A. (1980). *Child welfare services.* New York: Macmillan.

Klinman, D. G. (1986). Fathers and the educational system. In M. E. Lamb (Ed.), *The father's role: Applied perspectives* (pp. 413–428). New York: Wiley.

Kost, K. A. (1997a). A man without a job is a dead man: The meaning of work and welfare in the lives of young men. *Journal of Sociology and Social Welfare, 26*(2), 91–112.

Kost, K. A. (1997b). The effects of support on the economic well-being of young fathers. *Families in Society, 78*(4), 370–382.

Lamb, M. E. (1986). The changing roles of fathers. In M. E. Lamb (Ed.), *The father's role: Applied perspectives* (pp. 3–27). New York: Wiley.

Leitch, M. L., Gonzalez, A. M., & Ooms, T. J. (1993). Involving unwed fathers in adoption counseling and teen pregnancy programs. In R. I. Lerman & T. J. Ooms (Eds.), *Young unwed fathers* (pp. 267–287). Philadelphia: Temple University Press.

Marsiglio, W. (1995). Fathers' diverse life course patterns and roles: Theory and social interventions. In W. Marsiglio (Ed.), *Fatherhood: Contemporary theories, research, and social policy* (pp. 78–101). Thousand Oaks, CA: Sage.

Perloff, J. N., & Buckner, J. C. (1996). Fathers of children on welfare: Their impact on child well-being. *American Journal of Orthopsychiatry, 66*(4), 557–571.

Radin, N. (1981). The role of the father in cognitive, academic, and intellectual development. In M. E. Lamb (Ed.), *The role of the father in child development* (pp. 379–427). New York: Wiley.

Roy, K. (1999). Low-income single fathers in an African American community and the requirements of welfare reform. *Journal of Family Issues, 20*(4), 432–457.

Scanzoni, J. & Marsiglio, W. (1993). New action theory and contemporary families. *Journal of Family Issues, 14*(1), 105–132.

Sullivan, M. L. (1989). Absent fathers in the inner city. In W. J. Wilson (Ed.), *The ghetto underclass: Social science perspectives. Annals of the American Academy of Political and Social Science, 501,* 48–58.

Sullivan, M. L. (1994). Young fathers and parenting in two inner-city neighborhoods. In R. I. Lerman & T. J. Ooms (Eds.), *Young unwed fathers* (pp. 52–73). Philadelphia: Temple University Press.

Vinovskis, M. A. (1986). Young fathers and their children: Some historical and policy perspectives. In A. B. Elster & M. E. Lamb. (Eds.), *Adolescent fatherhood* (pp. 171–192). Hillsdale, NJ: Erlbaum.

Vinovskis, M. A. (1992). Historical perspectives on adolescent pregnancy. In M. K. Rosenheim & M. F. Testa (Eds.), *Early parenthood and coming of age in the 1990s* (pp. 136–149). New Brunswick, NJ: Rutgers University Press.

Waller, M., & Plotnick, R. (2000). A failed relationship? Low-income families and the child support enforcement system. *Focus, 21*(2), 12–17.

DEBORAH RUTMAN
SUSAN STREGA
MARILYN CALLAHAN
LENA DOMINELLI

10

"Undeserving" Mothers? Practitioners' Experiences Working with Young Mothers in/from Care

Introduction

This paper has emerged from a Canadian research project focused on young women who have children while in the care of government (see note 1). Our research focused on three questions: first, how do young mothers in/from government care experience their lives in care; second, how do social workers and other youth-serving practitioners perceive their practice with young women and their children; and finally, what policies and practices are most essential to shaping these young people's lives and how might they be strengthened or changed? This paper reports on our findings in regard to the second of these questions.

Adolescent pregnancies are increasing in Canada (Wadhera 1996 in Horton 1997), and the teen pregnancy rate is higher in British Columbia (BC) than the Canadian average. In examining the literature on teen pregnancies, it is apparent that a central focus concerns the ways adolescent mothering has been identified as a social problem (Fraser & Gordon 1994; Appell 1998). The problem is often framed as a moral one, reflecting moral decay and the laxity of social mores within Western society. However, the problem is also ascribed to have significant social and economic ramifications, as young, poor, single mothers are viewed by many as a serious drain on state resources. Consequently, numerous authors have noted that young single mothers are increasingly being pilloried within the media and public policy discourse (Lawson & Rhode 1993; Sidel 1996; Harris 1997; Appell 1998; Flanagan 1998). Several authors have also noted that the construction of adolescent pregnancy as inherently "bad," with negative consequences for both mother and child, comes from predominantly white, middle-class definitions of what is acceptable mothering which ignore the positive functions of adolescent pregnancy and mothering in marginalized racial, class, and ethnic communities (Phoenix et al., 1991; Lawson & Rhode 1993; Jacobs 1994).

Although adolescent pregnancy and mothering has received considerable attention from researchers within the past 10 years (Phoenix 1991; Lawson & Rhode 1993; Jacobs 1994; Horowitz 1995; Allen & Bourke-Dowling 1998; Appell 1998; Flanagan 1998), there is a near complete absence of information about the particular experiences of young women who become mothers while in government care. Similarly, the growing literature focusing on the experiences of youth in and from care is conspicuously silent on the topic of mothering while in care (Raychaba 1993; Martin & Palmer 1997). This research and knowledge gap is all the more surprising given recent indications that a disproportionate number of Canadian adolescents who become pregnant are young women in/from care (Martin 1996); recent British research echoes these trends and indicates a comparable gap in knowledge (Mullins & McCluskey 1999).

A particular focus on the experiences of young mothers in care and on the practitioners who work with them is warranted for several reasons. Most notably, there has been a significant restructuring in North America of social programs for low-income mothers, such as young mothers in care, that has reduced both eligibility and entitlements (Baker & Tippin 1999). In addition, Canadian child welfare practice is undergoing substantial shifts as a result of the meteoric rise in influence of risk assessment protocols; consequently, families are able to access supportive services only if their situation is assessed as a child protection risk. Arguably, young mothers in/from care are likely to bear the brunt of these, and other, major neoliberal social welfare initiatives. These women's experiences, as well as those of the frontline practitioners who work most closely with them, need to be voiced and taken into consideration in all ensuing policy debates around issues of youth pregnancy.

In an earlier publication, we reported on the experiences and perceptions of young mothers in care, using grounded theory approaches to analyze our data (Callahan et al. 2002). We determined that the social process of mothering while in/from care could be conceptualized as "prevailing on the edge on my own." In developing our explanatory variables and grounded theory regarding the variability in women's experiences of mothering in care and their interactions with the child welfare system, we were struck by the importance of Ministry for Child and Family Development (MCFD) social workers' perspectives and experiences working with these young women (see note 2). This paper thus describes the experiences of Ministry-based practitioners who work with young women who become mothers while in care. Practitioners' perspectives on the challenges and policy barriers to engaging in supportive practice, as well as their analysis of what is needed to change to better support young mothers in/from care, are also discussed.

Research Process

In order to address our second research question (How do social workers perceive their practice with young women and their children?), we conducted three focus groups, involving 20 Ministry workers attached to youth and/or guardianship teams. These focus groups were carried out as guided conversation and focused on practitioners' experiences of working with young mothers, what enabled and what were barriers to supportive practice, and what needed to change in policy and practice to better

support these young women. The focus groups were audiotaped and transcribed verbatim. All members of the research team then engaged in a thematic data analysis of the transcripts. Transcripts were initially read several times in order to get a sense of the whole. We then returned to the transcripts to identify preliminary themes, guided by the precept borrowed from grounded theory that we must look for "what the participants anguish the most over" (Keddy et al. 1996). We clustered these themes into related categories of meaning, and also related them to the results of our grounded theory study of young mothers' experiences.

We used several means to ensure the rigor of our research process and hence the validity of our data. The research team engaged in memo writing (presenting and critiquing one another's emerging reflections, insights, and ideas about the data) and examined the findings within the context of our extensive review of the research literature. We also shared our findings on an ongoing basis with an advisory committee composed of young mothers from care, social workers, policy analysts, and community-based service providers, and at a Policy and Practice Forum convened through the project partly as a means to test out our findings with young mothers, practitioners, and policymakers. At all of these report-back sessions, it was evident that our analyses resonated with participants' experiences and perspectives. Finally, the composition of our research team, which included a former youth in care, a former child welfare worker, and a researcher who had been engaged in a community-based project working with youth in transition from care, provided a unique contribution to considerations of rigor and validity.

While this study, given its small sample and exploratory nature, does not attempt to claim generalizability to all other jurisdictions, we believe it accurately depicts the experience and situation for young mothers and workers within our region, and that it would also resonate elsewhere. The study also provides a basis for formulating questions and hypotheses for further exploration regarding the interactions and negotiations between young mothers in/from care and their social workers.

Findings

Workers' Experiences Serving Young Mothers in/from Care

Workers' stories of their practice with young mothers contained rich descriptions not only of what it was like and how it felt to work with the young women, but also of workers' values and attitudes about this population or client group. Workers' stories also revealed that their values profoundly influenced the lens through which they constructed their notion of "deserving' mothers and perceived the adequacy of their clients' parenting. The social workers who took part in the focus groups held middle-class values that were deeply entrenched, and the state's child welfare apparatus that social workers served and represented was similarly rooted in middle-class norms. Although workers made many very direct statements indicating that their ideas and practice reflected middle-class values, it must be noted that the class and racial bias of ideas about adolescent pregnancy and mothering are largely implicit. Several authors have noted the "moral embeddedness" of social services for teen mothers (Horowitz 1995) in which concerns about the wrong women giving birth in the wrong circumstances have to do with implicit racial and class dimensions in how mothering is valued (Phoenix et al. 1991).

Based on our research, we argue that workers' middle-class values gave rise to a number of interrelated assumptions about young mothers in/from care; foremost among these was an expectation that these young women were almost always bound to repeat "the cycle" of "parenting failure" and thus of state intervention. At the same time, social workers experienced their practice with young mothers as very challenging and psychologically taxing, due at least in part to the tensions inherent in attempting to reconcile the fundamentally opposing roles that they were expected to play (e.g., worker-as-state-parent and worker-as-parenting-cop). Workers also recognized that current child welfare policies—informed by middle-class values and globalizing tendencies that enjoin to reinforce residualist approaches—hindered supportive practice with young mothers in/from care, in particular: the requirement that supportive resources including respite can be accessed only if a child is deemed to be at risk for protection; the dual strongholds of risk assessment/management and pressures for worker accountability, necessitating that workers "parent" their wards while simultaneously scrutinizing their wards' parenting, all the while being subject to scrutiny themselves and having less and less time to spend in relationships with clients because of mounting paperwork requirements; and finally, the significant underresourcing of young mothers in/from care, whose poverty almost certainly guarantees their being targets for child projection investigation and state intervention. These themes are explored in greater detail below.

We Have Middle-class Values   Many participants expressed the view that "We're a middle-class organization." Some workers also acknowledged that many, if not most, of their clients were not middle class, which sometimes resulted in value clashes, conflicts between workers and clients, or workers' pronouncements of their clients' poor decision making or judgment:

> We have middle-class values that we're trying to impose on clients who may or may not have middle-class values."

One core middle-class value influencing practice, held by many workers, is that teenagers should not become pregnant. Almost universally, workers were unable to conceive of an adolescent pregnancy as a positive, welcome, or normative event. Indeed, getting pregnant as a teenager was generally seen as confirmation that a young woman was repeating or bound to repeat "the cycle" (i.e., these young women were behaving much like their own mothers), and also reinforced stereotypes of "this class/race" of women. Sometimes, workers even questioned whether "these women" deserved to be mothers:

> "I'm very fond of her, but certainly for the child's sake, she should not have had any [children], in my opinion. She should not have access to that child."

When pregnancy happened, substitute parents embodied by state social workers sometimes became "saddened":

> "She got pregnant in a foster home . . . so yeah, I was kind of saddened by that. Cause I thought that maybe she was, I was feeling hopeful for her. Now I'm not feeling quite so hopeful anymore for her."

Implied here is that this worker had been "feeling hopeful" that the young woman would escape the cycle; however, the girl's pregnancy reinforced the worker's belief in its inevitability.

The Inevitability of the Cycle

> "You know, these kids have never been parented, and so they're not going to be parents. So it kind of becomes a vicious circle."

Workers voiced their belief that although many young mothers from care were determined to be different from their own mothers, the cycle of poor parenting was all but inevitable. Workers' comments indicated that their notion of the cycle included being a teenage mother; being a welfare mother; being a poor mother; and thus being an inadequate mother:

"And this one girl, I was really happy or heartened that she would say to me and her foster mother, after years of chaotic abusive history, that she didn't want to repeat the cycle. That she wanted to get on with her life, she wanted to be more of a success than her peers. . . . *She wanted to take the example of what's happened to her and break the cycle. . . . And then she went and got pregnant. And of course the child was apprehended and now she's pregnant again.*" (emphasis added)

In viewing the multigenerational cycle, some workers also tended to pathologize the individuals involved, without considering how structural factors such as chronic poverty, marginalization, and racism may come into play:

"I think that's the issue with parents: the grandparents, and the great grandparents, are all dysfunctional. They have no sense of relationships with anyone, so this pattern continues."

Linked to their beliefs about the inevitability of the cycle was workers' adherence to the view that "inadequate" parenting in the formative years had lifelong negative effects which a person would have tremendous difficulty in ever surmounting:

"I think when the bonding process between mother and child is disrupted, that child is probably going to be into a lifetime of uncertainty and chaos. . . . If that doesn't happen, you know, you're sunk. We have a lot of kids who have never bonded with anyone, and probably won't. Those formative years are so important."

Implicit in workers' comments with regard to young mothers from care was that these women's traumatic childhood experiences would prevent them from establishing healthy relationships; hence, they would be unable to adequately parent their own children. Workers thus indicated that their beliefs about the inevitability of the cycle influenced their "worries" or beliefs about risk:

"They have a lot of history that just can't be ignored. There's some good things, but there's some flags. And especially if you've been working for the family over a period of generations—I mean there's some very key points there, you know: mental health issues, drug and alcohol issues, and things like that, abuse. You worry."

It was also evident that much of workers' practice with young mothers involved their attempts to connect the women with community-based support services. In large measure, this aspect of practice stemmed from social workers' class-based belief that young mothers needed to acknowledge their own parenting limitations and accept the parenting support and resources that the Ministry offered. Workers wanted young mothers to "cooperate" and be appreciative of existing parenting-related resources. Moreover, young mothers' refusal of support often signaled a child protection risk in the minds of workers—and sometimes triggered child protection investigation procedures—since workers did not have confidence that the women possessed the necessary skills and resources to care for their child on their own:

"And in her first pregnancy she wouldn't accept anything, not anything. 'I can do this, you know. Fuck off, who do you think you are, telling me.' I mean that's the reason that the kid got removed, cause she was so out to lunch around the issue that it just made everybody terrified. . . . The child was born, apprehended, removed. Now she's pregnant again and she's going to [a parenting program]. [She's] really, really cooperative with her child protection worker. Well, she is a different person. . . . Anyway, the point is, she got the message, and so her current position is . . . 'Now I got a second chance and this time I'm going to do it right.' "

Finally, although many workers were appreciative of the young women's poverty and financial need, the kinds of supports offered to them tended to focus on resources aiming to develop or enhance parenting skills even though the women themselves typically voiced the need for material goods. This mismatch in the young women's expressed needs versus the resources suggested by workers may have contributed to the young women's ambivalence regarding the use of community resources, and, in turn, tensions with workers around the women's apparent noncompliance or refusal of support. For workers, these tensions contributed to their experience of their practice with young mothers in/from care as highly exacting, and to their questioning of their adequacy and efficacy as a substitute parent.

Feeling Like an Inadequate Parent   In many ways, and under a variety of circumstances, workers described feeling like an inadequate parent in their practice with young mothers. For the most part, workers reflected that recent shifts in child welfare policy, as identified above, coupled with chronic underfunding of the system, were at the heart of these practice/parenting failures. At the same time, the yardsticks for adequate parenting were also influenced by workers' middle-class norms. For example, since a primary goal of their practice with young women was to help prevent pregnancy, when it occurred some workers tended to feel as though they had failed in their surrogate parent role:

"Our job is to see that they don't get pregnant if we can, which is impossible."

"We work against them being young moms, so that when they do become young moms, I think some [workers]—well, me for example—see it as a failure. That's a terrible thing to say, but it's true."

Interestingly, young mothers most often spoke of their pregnancy as a positive turning point in their lives, and as an opportunity that they seized to quite drinking, drug taking, and other self-destructive behaviors. For many of the young women, pregnancy filled them with hope. And some workers did appreciate this:

"I've had some kids, some youths who've led a pretty wild lifestyle become pregnant and actually see that as a catalyst to settling in and going forward."

"I'd had one mom who had a child. She was working the streets, she was involved with cocaine and drugs, and she became pregnant as a result of working the streets. But when she became pregnant she totally turned her life around."

Some workers also commented on their experience of parenting at a distance and across the "revolving door" of multiple placements. Workers recognized their physical and emotional separation from young women, and that their practice typically entailed providing or facilitating instrumental/practical assistance rather than emotional support. The focus of their work was to help youth become independent, in line with societal (and workers' own) values and pressures to get youth—particularly marginalized youth—to stand on their own two feet, thereby avoiding state dependency:

"We're their guardian or take the role of the parent, but we're sitting in an office. We're not out there. We pay somebody else to look after them."

"But I haven't really gone through that emotional state with her because we're still trying to get them independent. We don't talk about what their aspirations are."

At the same time, many workers appreciated that this parenting style was inadequate, all the more so for young people who had a troubled or traumatic childhood and great instability in their life. That is, workers plainly articulated, not without irony, the importance of sustained relationships for these youth; yet, prevailing policies placed significant time and resource constraints on workers, preventing them from engaging in ongoing relationships with youth in transition from care:

"What kind of parenting do we model, when the average kid in our system, for any period of time, goes between 12 and 14 different placements? And you know, what kind of modelling is that for parenting? It's a revolving door."

Dual Roles, Conflicted Loyalties

"And me as their guardian: which am I, 'we' or 'they'?"

In discussing their experience of their practice working with young mothers in/from care, workers' use of war-related metaphors to describe their dual role as parent/guardian of the young women and agent of the child protection ministry was extremely powerful. Practitioners walked in "no man's land" and traversed through "minefields," struggling to bridge the gulf between their role as parent/guardian/helper and their responsibilities to child protection. Workers' distress about their dual roles was clearly evident from their discourse:

"The part that's difficult for these kids, I suspect, is that not only am I their guardian, and the protection has got their child, but I'm also an agent of the Ministry. So I'm also a child protection kind of person. So I can't be like other parents, guardians who say, 'Well, those big bad guys. They shouldn't have taken away your child' and 'Let's dig in and let's take them on.' And so I become kind of in no man's land . . . and I try to be as neutral as I can—as their guardian—but a lot of times the protection people have expectations for me to be on board, which of course I need to be because that's my mandate. So that always becomes a bit of a minefield for me."

Being and Feeling Scrutinized and Under Surveillance as a Worker   Workers also described being under an increasing degree of scrutiny in their day-to-day practice. There were more eyes on them than before, from more sources, both within the Ministry and outside (e.g., the media, the BC Children's Commission, the BC Child, Youth and Family Advocate's Office), and much of this scrutiny appeared to be part of ongoing shifts in policy:

> "We have a lot more people looking over our shoulder now than we did before too. . . . And you know you get three and four of them coming at you at the same time on any given issue. We have to satisfy a lot more accountability issues. So this takes up a lot of time."

Workers' feelings of being under surveillance paralleled those of the young mothers, and many workers recognized the similarities in experience. Workers were also troubled by the amount of time that they needed to spend attending to this scrutiny, as it necessarily usurped time away from relationships and interactions with clients.

Finally, a number of workers said they found working with young mothers was very challenging and psychologically taxing. In part, this was due to worker-client conflicts over the use (or refusal) of community resources. Probably it was also partly due to the tensions inherent in attempting to reconcile their fundamentally opposing multiple roles. In addition, many of the workers' comments revealed their deep frustration with existing policy and resource limitations that placed significant constraints on what they were able to offer to the young women. Workers generally appreciated that there was an ever-widening gap between these women's resource needs and what government as parent was currently sanctioned to provide.

Workers' Perspectives on Policy (Barriers) for Young Mothers in/from Care

Our focus groups revealed that workers were currently experiencing a confluence of several major forces relating to policy, including existing policies that do not support young mothers; a vacuum in relation to supportive policies for young mothers;

and Ministry leadership priorities that felt out of synch with the lived realities of frontline practitioners. Perhaps most important, and at the broadest level, however, workers maintained that current allocations of government resources were plainly insufficient to address the basic human needs of young mothers in and from care. A brief discussion of these policy issues and barriers follows, beginning with examination of current policies that do not serve the needs of young mothers.

Only Way to Access Services is via Child Protection

> "We don't do family support anymore. It's all protection."

Workers felt very strongly that the Ministry's current focus on child protection—and, consequently, its shift away from family support—was a significant barrier to supportive practice with young mothers. More specifically, workers were highly critical of policies that made child protection the only possible means to access supportive services. Young mothers' needs for respite, day care subsidies, teaching homemakers, and so forth needed to be legitimized and viewed as positive supports that would strengthen families. Thus, there needed to be avenues to offer these resources as a first rather than last resort, removed from the veil of child protection:

> "But we don't fix families, we break them apart."

> "There are some supports that I feel we should be able to provide to our young moms from our office that are more routinely offered from child protection offices. I feel like I would like to be able to have those services amongst our toolbox. So that we don't have to refer [to child protection] in order to access that service.' "

Predominance of Risk Assessment Model   Coupled with the state's current child protection focus was its preoccupation with standardized risk assessment procedures and instruments as its means to identify those in need of protection (and thus those eligible for assistance and resources). Workers expressed concern that a large component of the risk assessment framework focused on historical issues in a person's life that couldn't be changed, such as childhood abuse or neglect. In doing so, the risk assessment instrument effectively earmarked and penalized all young mothers from care, who would obviously enter into an assessment process with their past serving as a strike against them, and their current skills, capabilities, circumstances, and qualities as a parent having to offset their history. Some workers also commented that the Ministry's focus on documentation and standardized assessments, while serving the administration's demand for accountability, took precious time away from their face-to-face practice with families and children, and as such, contributed to workers' sense of inadequacy as state/substitute parents. In addition, risk assessment processes exacerbated workers' sense of having dual roles and divided loyalties:

> "We've developed really good tools for sniffing out risk. You know, we're like pigs sniffing out truffles in terms of the risks. But what happens once you establish risk? What do you do? Do you have the ability to take the chance and look at supporting the family, or does it direct you towards the legislated resolution to this? And the answer, sadly, is that . . . you [are pushed] towards the Court System."

> "Somebody makes a determination based on a risk assessment. . . . If the major issues are somewhat historical on the parents' part, that can't be changed. You can educate them. You can do some things. But those issues still remain."

State as Circumscribed, Time-limited Parent and Absentee Grandparent   Workers identified other child welfare policies that were indicative of the state's shortcomings as a substitute parent. For example, despite Canadian census data showing that young adults are continuing to live at home and receive parental support well into their twenties, all youth in government care are required to exit upon reaching age of majority (19 in BC) and give up their foster placement and accompanying supports, regardless of their personal circumstances or degree of readiness. Workers recognized that the transition to adulthood was a process rather than an event triggered by a person's nineteenth birthday. They were therefore quite saddened and frustrated by existing policy that abruptly "turfed' young people out, especially in situations where the support provided through a foster parent's guidance enabled a young mother to successfully care for her child, and then when the dismantling of that support precipitated instability, crisis and ultimately the child's removal from the home:

> "My own kids are 25 and 23—they need $100 for the rent, they need some help with their tuition, you do it. But what do we do: 'Sorry, 19'.

> . . . I would like to see some availability to continue to work with these kids other than just the personal relationship you do have with them."

> "One of the issues that I think is probably the most frustrating or saddest that I had, I had a 15-year-old who became pregnant, we placed her in a foster home. She, by the age of 19, was a good mother in that home. . . . But when that magic number 19 came she went out on her own, and of course she floundered. That's a real frustration. I almost, I almost feel like we set her up. She did her very, very best and she basically was a good parent within that foster home while someone was fostering and taking care of her, but once she had to stand on her own two feet, umm, it wasn't great, it wasn't great. . . . I felt I let her down."

As another example of the incongruities of the state as parent, several workers pointed out the paradox of acting as parent to a youth in care but not being able to assume the role of grandparent (and to provide resources accordingly) to that young person's child, unless the child came into care. For workers, this policy disjunction was unnatural and discordant. It also served, potentially, to break families apart further, as it suggested that families' most probable means of tapping into supports came if or when the child came into the Ministry's care:

> "Our job is to work with the young person and not with their infant necessarily."

> "We have the ability to tap in sometimes for extra funds for our child in care, but it's much more difficult if not impossible to tap into funds for the child who is not in care."

Policy Vacuum and Leadership's Misplaced Priorities   In keeping with some of the young women's comments regarding the absence of policies that focus on mothering while in care, several workers observed that there was considerable murkiness when it came to questions of policy versus practice in relation to issues concerning parenting youth. This policy vacuum was experienced by some workers as a barrier to supportive practice with young mothers.

> "It's not really written in policy, it's inferred. But it's essentially a decision that middle management makes and there are exceptions."

Along similar lines, workers expressed frustration about policy fragmentation both within the

MCFD (e.g., between child protection and family support, to the degree that the latter still existed) and between ministries and levels of government (e.g., MCFD and the Ministry of Human Resources, the ministry governing income assistance rates, affordable/subsidized housing availability, child care support, etc.).

"I think there's a real need for a youth policy, in general, not just parenting teens. There needs to be some integrated policies with [MHR], us, and community agencies. There's a real need because again we're trying to turn a Roberts screw with a Philips screwdriver. It's just not working."

In addition, a number of workers expressed tremendous frustration about the apparent disconnection between leaders' emphasis on Ministry "reorgs" and the real issues facing families and field-based workers. Workers believed that the energy and funds expended as a result of these reorganizations and their associated communications activities could be far better used to address families' needs directly, and that by choosing to allocate funds to reorgs rather than families or the front line, leadership was demonstrating its lack of understanding of families' and workers' lived experience. At a broader level, workers' comments suggested that they felt marginalized and unsupported by Ministry leadership:

"All Ministry employees received a message from the deputy minister the other day that talked about the remaining of some of the divisions and appointing people to different levels, and it was just of no interest to anybody who works in the field. . . . Can you get down here, Deputy Minister, and talk to us about the real issues? The clients and all that kind of stuff. . . . Folks in Headquarters are, frankly, quite removed from us."

"The reality is young moms are having difficulty raising their kids cause we don't fund them, we don't support them. We can't fund them like we want. Yet you can create new divisions and appoint new people and spend millions on revamping the Ministry and appoint new ministers every six weeks."

Income Support Provided to Young Mothers Is Insufficient   Finally, as an overarching theme again reflecting how current policies rendered government

a poor parent, many workers spoke passionately about the state's inadequate funding for young parents in care. Workers knew that it was almost impossible to find adequate housing given current housing allowances. Workers also knew that without safe, decent housing—or adequate food and clothing—young parents would be subjected to the Ministry's scrutiny and possible child protection investigation, and that this scrutiny was all the more exacting when money was spent on items other than immediate survival needs. Thus, legislated poverty set young parents up for failure, and workers, as parents/guardians, were embarrassed and often outraged to be complicit actors in this state-sanctioned negligence:

"I'm appalled that we allow our children in care to live under the poverty line. I think that the government is just disgusting, and it's just appalling to me that these people who we're supposed to be guardians of we're allowing to live in poverty and deprivation. And it's been going on for the 20 years that I've been working in this Ministry. And it's said, it's absolutely sad."

"You know, when I look at our kids, most of their money goes into having a decent place to live, and if you don't have a decent place to live then your kid comes to our attention."

In summing up workers' perspectives on the policy related issues and barriers associated with practice with young mothers from care, workers' twin concerns regarding the Ministry's shift toward being a child protection ministry first and the inadequacy of the income support provided to families were paramount. While workers held strong values and beliefs regarding the inevitability of the cycle of poor parenting and children's entry into care, many also fundamentally understood the relationship between a young mother's poverty and the likelihood of her surveillance by the child protection arm of the Ministry:

"I don't know of any one of the kids that I've worked with . . . who didn't really believe that they were going to break the chain—that they were going to treat their child differently than they were. But they forget that at 2:00 in the morning the baby wakes up and needs changing his diapers. And if you don't have the money for diapers, what do you do? Or you don't have food in the fridge to feed it?"

Discussion

Workers, as embodiments of state parents, reflect and reinforce prevailing middle-class values, including norms about "good" and "bad" parenting (Boxill 1987; Swift 1995; Appell 1998). In our project, one of the most significant ramifications of workers' middle-class values and norms was their belief about the inevitability of the cycle (of children in care begetting children who were destined to come into care, i.e., of "parenting failures"). Ironically, though workers and young mothers were both preoccupied by the concept of the cycle and each were determined to break it, the two groups had very different ideas about what the cycle was all about, what perpetuated or contributed to it, and what served to sever it.

From the workers' point of view, the cycle was primarily about young wards bearing children of their own. Moreover, from the workers' class-informed perspective, mothering while in care most often posed significant child protection risks, and the ills associated with wards' inevitably inadequate or risky parenting were rectified only, or in nearly all cases, by the state's apprehension of the baby.

From the young mothers' perspective, by contrast, the cycle of an unhealthy, high-risk lifestyle was broken through their pregnancy, the birth of their baby, and the resulting change in their life circumstances. For them, as for other groups of marginalized women engaged in parenting, having a baby and having to assume responsibility for another human being gave them a new sense of direction and purpose (Bruce & Williams 1994; Flanagan 1998; Mullins & McCluskey 1999; Rutman et al. 2000). Nevertheless, from the young mothers' standpoint, the cycle of a traumatic childhood leading to a high-risk lifestyle could be perpetuated all too easily by their baby's removal by the state and its entry into government care.

While some workers in our study did recognize that pregnancy had a positive impact on the lives of these young women, workers appeared not to appreciate that they and the young mothers operated from such contrasting viewpoints about the cycle. Arguably, workers' belief in the probability of the cycle and their goal of breaking it informed their practice and the focus of their work with young mothers in care. Unfortunately, the disjuncture in workers' and young women's views about the cycle, along with major recent shifts in the direction of child welfare policy and practice and related constraints in the resources at workers' disposal, conjoined to create barriers to what workers and young women both recognized as supportive practice with youth in care. These factors also contributed to frontline workers' subjective experience of their practice with young mothers as being quite demanding and stressful.

Stemming from concerns about accountability and productivity, there have been major shifts in child welfare policies over the past 20 years (Wharf 1993; Trocmé et al. 1995). For workers whose practice involves young mothers in/from care, there are several key policy areas that, particularly in combination, serve to effectively sabotage best or supportive practice. These include having child protection act as the entry point to accessing supportive services, and the current focus on risk assessment/management within child welfare policy and practice.

Currently in British Columbia, supportive services can be accessed only if the situation is deemed at risk by the child protection arm of the Ministry. Clearly the stipulation that services and supports be available only in cases designated at risk of requiring child protection–related intervention substantially limits what social workers are able to offer the children, youth, and families in their care. As workers in this study related, these policies serve to diminish both the nature of the tools and the size of the toolbox they have at their disposal in the interest of helping to support children and families and/or keep them together. Instead, the Ministry's current child protection mandate effectively serves to break families apart. Perhaps more important, having child protection as the only means to access support reinforces workers' dual role as parent/guardian and parenting police (Wharf 1993). This crazy-making approach takes its toll on both workers and young people and runs fully counter to best/supportive practice principles (Callahan et al. 1998).

In a similar vein, recent policy shifts have resulted in Ministry social workers' practice becoming increasingly circumscribed in terms of the nature of the supportive relationships that they are able to offer to children and youth. As state parents their role now typically focuses on doling out dollars, setting spending limits, and trying to arrange for services that most often are geared to promoting the young person's independence. Workers' large caseloads and other documentation-related duties generally prevent them becoming involved in young people's emotional concerns; indeed, workers often see their wards as little as once a month or less, which in itself constrains the degree to which they can be present in the emotional life of a child or youth. In terms of role or function, Ministry social workers thus act much like stereotypical father figures: they are remote, distant, and sometimes punitive. As a result of the restructuring of the social service system, the crucial "mothering" work of building intimate relationships with children/youth and of maintaining those relationships—the work that youth state they value and crave the most—is now typically assumed by contracted agency workers and/or foster parents, to the extent that it takes place at all. Ironically, these service providers, while often providing excellent support to youth, are also constrained by their dual role as support people/child protection watchdogs, as prescribed by their contractual relationship with the Ministry.

In addition to the above, the current focus on risk assessment/management in child welfare policy and practice hampers supportive practice with families, including young mothers in/from care (Callahan 1993). The primacy of risk management as the current centerpiece of child welfare/protection practice stems from political and bureaucratic pressures for standardization, accountability, and auditability (Dawson & Callahan 2001). Not surprisingly, however, risk assessment protocols and tools reflect middle-class biases which are calibrated to be triggered by those living on the margins (Ferguson 1997; Krane & Davies 2000; Swift, 1995), including—and perhaps in particular—young mothers from care. While risk assessment processes contribute to the Ministry's stigmatization and (hyper)scrutiny of young mothers in care, these processes do not necessarily result in young mothers gaining access to the services and assistance that they say they need in order to have support in caring for their child. Moreover, as workers in our study and others (e.g., Krane & Davies 2000; Swift, unpublished) pointed out, when practice is consumed by standardized assessment protocols and paperwork put in place to satisfy audit/accountability demands, then traditional facets of good social work practice (e.g., face-to-face, relationship-orientated social work) get sidelined and suffer.

As a backdrop—but intricately connected—to all else is the state's insufficient resourcing of the children, youth, and young parents in its care. In our research, workers appreciated that the state was not providing adequately for young mothers in/from care, and that state-induced poverty further contributed to the young women's vulnerability to state scrutiny. The cycle, already so intractable from the workers' perspective, was that much harder to break given that young mothers in/from care do not have sufficient means to provide for their child safely and adequately. Inadequate or poor parenting is inextricably linked to parenting in poverty.

In sum, our findings, as well as other research, reveal that policy and practice informed by middle-class values serves to punish those who are not white and middle class, as evidenced by disproportionate rates of child investigation and removal (e.g., Swift 1995, unpublished; Ferguson 1997; Krane & Davies 2000; Scourfield 2000; Strega et al. 2002). Thus, young mothers in/from care face stigma and bias as a result of their age, class, race, and family history. This stigmatization segues into systematic and often relentless scrutiny and surveillance, oftentimes by the very state parents whose job it is to raise and support them in their transition to adulthood.

Clearly, changes in policy and practice in relation to young mothers in/from care are needed. Foremost among these is a rethinking of the middle-class construction of "breaking the cycle" and the ways to do it; the system's current response to the cycle has proved futile and unproductive, arguably because it lacks an appreciation of young mothers' lived experience. The voices of young mothers and frontline social workers, such as has been highlighted in this study, need to inform this crucial work. Recasting this construction of the cycle would require practitioners to take time to critically examine and reflect on their own values and assumptions, and policymakers to reconsider the basis on which they support young mothers and social work practitioners. Moreover, such a reconsideration would include explicit acknowledgment of the link between poverty and removal of children by the state, recognition of the value of mothering work, and thus political commitment, and interdepartmental coordination to bring young mothers out of poverty.

Notes

1. This project was carried out through the Research Initiatives for Social Change (RISC) unit within the School of Social Work, University of Victoria, and was funded by the Social Science and Humanities Research Council (SSHRC).

2. In British Columbia, the Ministry for Child and Family Development is the government department that oversees child welfare services, including child protection investigations and the removal of children, and adoption and guardianship services to children and youth who come into the temporary or permanent care of the state. Since 1996, as a result of a major public inquiry by Jus-

tice Thomas Gove regarding the death of 5-year-old Matthew Vaudreuil, there have been considerable shifts and upheaval in BC child welfare policy and practice. The Gove inquiry resulted in the "paramountcy" of a child protection focus within the Ministry, accompanied by reduced resources for family-focused supports. Ministry leadership and direction continues to be in flux, as there have been six ministers in as many years.

References

Allen, I. & Bourke-Dowling, S. (1998) *Teenage Mothers: Decisions and Outcomes*. Policy Studies Institute, London.

Appell, A. (1998) On fixing "bad" mothers and saving their children. In: *"Bad" Mothers: The Politics of Blame in Twentieth-century America* (eds. M. Ladd-Taylor & L. Umansky), pp. 356–380. New York University Press, New York.

Baker, M. & Tippin, D. (1999) *Poverty, Social Assistance and the Employability of Mothers*. University of Toronto Press, Toronto.

Boxill, N. (1987) How Would You Feel. . . . *Journal of Child and Youth Services, 8*, 35–48.

Bruce, L. & Williams, K. (1994) Drug abuse in pregnancy. *Journal of the Society of Obstetricians and Gynaecologists of Canada, 24*, 1469–1476.

Callahan, M. (1993) Feminists recreate child welfare. In: *Rethinking Child Welfare in Canada* (ed. B. Wharf), pp. 172–209. McClelland and Stewart, Toronto.

Callahan, M., Field, B., Hubberstey, C., & Wharf, B. (1998) *Best Practice in Child Welfare*. University of Victoria, Victoria.

Callahan, M., Rutman, D., Strega, S. & Dominelli, L. (2002) *The Experiences of Young Mothers in/from Care*. Child Welfare League of Canada, Ottawa.

Dawson, R. & Callahan, M. (2001) Risk assessment in child protection services: Yes or No? *Canadian Social Work Review, 18*, 155–164.

Ferguson, H. (1997) Protecting children in new times: Child protection and the risk society. *Child and Family Social Work, 2*, 221–234.

Flanagan, P. (1998) Teen mothers: Countering the myths of dysfunction and developmental disruption. In: *Mothering against the Odds: Diverse Voices of Contemporary Mothers* (eds. C. Coll, J. Surrey & K. Weingarten), pp. 238–254. Guilford Press, New York.

Fraser, N. & Gordon, L. (1994) A genealogy of *dependency*: Tracing a keyword of the U.S. welfare state. *Signs: Journal of Women in Culture and Society, 19*, 309–336.

Harris, K. (1997) *Teen Mothers and the Revolving Welfare Door*. Temple University Press, Philadelphia.

Horowitz, R. (1995) *Teen Mothers: Citizens or Dependents?* University of Chicago Press, Chicago.

Horton, J. (1997) Adolescent pregnancy and young women in care. *Canada's Children . . . Les Enfants du Canada, 4*, 35–36.

Jacobs, J. (1994) Gender, race, class and the trend toward early motherhood. *Journal of Contemporary Ethnography, 22*, 442–462.

Keddy, B., Sims, S. & Noerager Stern, P. (1996) Grounded theory as feminist research methodology. *Journal of Advanced Nursing, 23*, 446–453.

Krane, J. & Davies, L. (2000) Mothering and risk protection practice: Rethinking risk assessment. *Child and Family Social Work, 5*, 35–45.

Lawson, A. & Rhode, D. (eds.) (1993) *The Politics of Pregnancy: Adolescent Sexuality and Public Policy*. Yale University Press, New Haven.

Martin, F. (1996) Tales of transition: Leaving public care. In: *Youth in Transition: Perspectives on Research and Policy* (eds. B. Galaway & J. Hudson), pp. 145–159. Thompson Educational Publishing, Toronto.

Martin, F. (1996) Tales of transition: Leaving public care. In: *Youth in Transition: Perspectives on Research and Policy* (eds. B. Galaway & J. Hudson), pp. 145–159. Thompson Educational Publishing, Toronto.

Martin, F. & Palmer, T. (1997) *Transitions to Adulthood: A Child Welfare Youth Perspective*. Unpublished report of the Youth-in-Care. Successful Transitions to Adulthood Project. Child Welfare League of Canada, Ottawa.

Mullins, A. & McCluskey, J. (1999) *Teenage Mothers Speak for Themselves*. Public Policy Unit, London.

Phoenix, A. (1991) Motherhood: Social construction, politics and psychology. In: *Motherhood: Meanings, Practices and Ideologies* (eds. A. Phoenix, A. Woollett & E. Lloyd), pp. 13–27. Sage, London.

Phoenix, A., Woollett, A. & Lloyd, E. (eds.) (1991) *Motherhood: Meanings, Practices and Ideologies*. Sage, London.

Raychaba, B. (1993) *Pain . . . Lots of Pain: Family Violence and Abuse in the Lives of Young People in Care*. National Youth in Care Network, Ottawa.

Rutman, D., Callahan, M., Lundquist, A., Jackson, S. & Field, B. (2000) *Substance Use and Pregnancy: Conceiving Women in the*

Policy Making Process. Status of Women Canada, Ottawa.

Scourfield, J. (2000) The rediscovery of child neglect. *Sociological Review, 48,* 365–382.

Sidel, R. (1996) *Keeping Women and Children Last*. Penguin Books, New York.

Strega, S., Callahan, M., Rutman, D. & Dominelli, L. (2002) Undeserving mothers: An historical analysis of social policy and disadvantaged mothers. *Canadian Review of Social Policy*.

Swift, K. (1995) *Manufacturing "Bad" Mothers*. University of Toronto Press, Toronto.

Trocmé, N., Tam, K. & McPhee, D. (1995) Correlates of substantiation of maltreatment in child welfare investigations. In: *Child Welfare in Canada: Policy and Practice Implications* (eds. J. Hudson & B. Galaway), pp. 20–40. Thompson Education Publishing, Toronto.

Wharf, B. (1993) *Rethinking Child Welfare in Canada*. McClelland and Stewart, Toronto.

11

Redefining Motherhood: Adaptation to Role Change for Women with AIDS

The unique experiences of women with human immunodeficiency virus (HIV) illness have been the focus of recent research efforts. Psychosocial concerns, including finances, housing, isolation and stigma, sexuality, health issues, death and dying, and concern for their partners and children with HIV, were identified in early studies of women with AIDS (Buckingham & Rehm, 1987; Chung & Magraw, 1992; Kaspar, 1989; Ybarra, 1991; Zuckerman & Gordon, 1988). More recently, researchers have begun to detail processes of disclosure of HIV and AIDS status (Marcenko & Samost, 1999; Moneyham et al., 1996; Pliskin, Farrel, Crandles, & DeHovitz, 1993; Regan-Kubinski & Sharts-Hopko, 1995; Walker, 1998) and adaptation (DeMarco, Miller, Patsdaughter, Chisholm, & Grindel, 1998; Guillory, Sowell, Moneyham, & Seals, 1997; Nannis, Patterson, & Semple, 1997; van Servellen, Sarna, & Jablonski, 1998) and to point to benefits women find in the experience of HIV illness (Dunbar, Mueller, Medina, & Wolf, 1998). This article extends those research efforts by describing the ways mothers with AIDS understand and fulfill their parental responsibilities. Specifically, it addresses their definition of motherhood, the benefits they receive from being mothers, and their efforts to maintain this important role as illness challenges both the definition and performance of the role of mother. In addition, two unresolved issues for mothers with AIDS are identified: reunion with children previously placed out of the home or removed by child welfare authorities and conflictive relationships with children.

Mothers with AIDS in the United States

Women represented more than 16% of all adult AIDS cases (or 114,621 of 702,748) in the United States through June 1999 (Centers for Disease Control [CDC], 1999b), and the incidence of AIDS among women is increasing at a faster rate than that among men (CDC, 1998). African American and Hispanic women constitute 57% and 20% of cases of AIDS among women, respectively, although together they represent only a quarter of the female population in the United States (CDC, 1999a). Twenty-one percent of women are in their twenties, 43% are in their thirties, and 21% are in their forties at age of diagnosis (CDC, 1999b). Forty-two percent of women contracted HIV through injecting drugs and 40% through heterosexual contact. For 15% of women, no risk factor was initially reported (CDC, 1999b), but follow-up studies found that heterosexual contact is the mode of transmission for two-thirds (CDC, 1999a). Little direct information about the economic status of women with AIDS is available, but commentators describe this group as poor (American Association for World Health, 1997). In an 11-state study of persons with AIDS, 50% of women had less than a high school education, 90% were unemployed, and 77% had annual household incomes of less than $10,000 (Diaz et al., 1994).

Although not all women with HIV or AIDS are mothers, it appears that the vast majority are. In one study of patients in an HIV clinic, 75% of female patients were parents, while only 22% of the male patients were (Niebuhr, Hughes, & Pollard, 1994). Projections of "AIDS orphans" gives further evidence of the number of mothers with AIDS, by estimating the number of children whose mother dies of AIDS. One model estimated that this number would exceed 80,000 by the year 2000 (Michaels & Levine, 1992), while another predicted a range of 93,000 to 112,000 between the years 1992 and 2000 (Levine, 1994). Data from years subsequent to its development have been used to update the former model; results suggest that initial projections underestimated the number of children who would lose their mother to AIDS (Federation of Protestant Welfare Agencies, 1996). Although new and more effective treatments have decreased death rates among women, this might mean that more children will live with mothers who are living with HIV illness.

Psychosocial research on mothers with HIV illness has focused on four areas: psychosocial challenges and concerns about children which are raised by the illness; disclosure of HIV or AIDS status to others, including children; benefits mothers with AIDS receive from their children; and adaptation to the illness.

Mothers with AIDS face a number of psychosocial concerns, including finances, housing, health issues, death and dying, and concern for their children with HIV (Gillman & Newman, 1996). Their children's future (Chung & Magraw, 1992; Florence, Lützén, & Alexius, 1994; Gillman & Newman, 1996; Hackl, Somlai, Kelly, & Kalichman, 1997), child-care arrangements when sick (Chung & Magraw, 1992), guilt and self-blame for their inability to care for children (Gillman & Newman, 1996), and protecting children from crises and stigma (Hackl et al., 1997) are additional concerns for these mothers.

Mothers' disclosure of HIV or AIDS status to children has been examined in studies (Moneyham et al., 1996; Pliskin et al., 1993; Regan-Kubinski & Sharts-Hopko, 1995) that have focused primarily on factors involved in mothers' decisions to disclose, rather than the impact on the mother-child relationship. Mothers who disclose their status do so because of their opposition to family secrets, wish to prepare children, wish for greater intimacy, and desire to prevent children from finding out from other sources. Mothers who had lost an immediate family member to AIDS are twice as likely to disclose their status to their children. Factors preventing disclosure include fear of psychological harm to children, concern that children might tell others, belief that children would be incapable of understanding, and fear of rejection by their chil-

dren (Pliskin et al., 1993). Mothers who are HIV-positive who were interviewed about children's reactions to disclosure report responses including fear, anger, distancing, and caretaking to their mothers (Marcenko & Samost, 1999; Walker, 1998). Mothers also report distress around the ways children handle this news (Regan-Kubinski & Sharts-Hopko, 1995).

Mothers with HIV illness receive many benefits from their children. Children are seen as the most important factor influencing their response to the illness motivating women to make changes in their lives such as finding decent housing or recovering from drug abuse (Gillman & Newman, 1996; Regan-Kubinski & Sharts-Hopko, 1995). Children provide support, comfort, and assistance (Gillman & Newman, 1996; Walker, 1998) and, in some cases, a child becomes the mother's caregiver (Florence et al. 1994). Dunbar and associates (1998) comment on the paradoxical effect of children for mothers living with HIV: children are a reason to live but are also sources of stress. Similarly, van Servellen, Sarna, and Jablonski (1998) report that the presence of children contributes to both women's "best days" and "worst days."

A number of factors promote women's adaptation to HIV illness, including appraisals of the illness as a challenge, active coping responses, social support, and spirituality. Women who see HIV illness as something requiring action change their lifestyles: they enter recovery, seek out resources, and resolve relationship problems (Regan-Kubinski & Sharts-Hopko, 1995). Conversely, women who see the illness as a threat report higher levels of emotional distress (Moneyham et al., 1997). A "fighting spirit" style of coping, as opposed to "helpless/hopeless" or "stoic" styles, is associated with fewer symptoms of emotional distress (Nannis et al., 1997). The importance of social support from peers and professionals can spur women to move from the gender-normative behavior of "silencing the self" to action and self-advocacy, resulting in self-care and efforts at resolving problems and conflicts (DeMarco et al., 1998). Many women consider spiritual practices, such as prayer, an integral part of coping and link their self-worth to their relationship with God (Guillory et al., 1997; Regan-Kubinski & Sharts-Hopko, 1995; van Servellen et al., 1998). Dunbar and associates (1998) describe a process of psychological and spiritual growth that allows women with HIV illness to find unexpected positive benefits in the experience; this process includes reckoning with death, affirming the will to live, creating meaning, affirming oneself, and redefining relationships.

The literature points to a number of psychosocial issues facing women with HIV illness and describes a variety of strategies they use in coping. In particular, the complex relationships mothers with HIV illness have with their children is highlighted: children are motivators and supporters of their mother but also sources of stress and worry. Less attention, however, has been given to the ways mothers with HIV illness carry out their day-to-day responsibilities toward their children and their perceptions of themselves as mothers. The present study addresses this gap in the literature by focusing on four areas: (1) the definition of motherhood held by women with AIDS; (2) the ways AIDS changes mothering; (3) the functions children serve for mothers with AIDS; and (4) strategies used by women with AIDS to maintain the role of mother, even as illness forces changes in the way they perform the role. In addition, unresolved issues for mothers with AIDS, particularly those with drug-use histories, are identified. These include reunion with children who had been placed out of the home years earlier and conflictive relationships with adult children who lived with them during their years of drug use.

Method

The research reported here is part of a larger exploratory study of coping and adaptation in women with AIDS (Van Loon, 1996). Grounded theory methods (Charmaz, 1990; Strauss & Corbin, 1990) were used to guide data collection and analysis. Two semistructured interviews (60 to 75 minutes each) were conducted by the researcher with each participant in participants' home after written informed consent was obtained. The researcher developed an interview schedule that included questions on a broad range of topics, including history of the illness, understanding of HIV and AIDS, psychosocial concerns raised by the illness, the participants' ways of dealing with those concerns and their self-evaluations of coping and adaptation. All interviews were audiotaped and transcribed by the researcher, and participants were compensated $45 for their time.

In accordance with grounded theory procedures (Charmaz, 1990), data analysis proceeded concurrently with data collection, allowing the researcher to revise the interview schedule to focus on topics salient to participants. Transcribed interviews were loaded into HyperQual2, a Macintosh program for qualitative data analysis, and were initially coded for content areas and themes. The resulting codes were organized into categories, and the dimensions and properties of each category were described, as were connections among them. Focused coding followed, as the data were resifted in light of categories already identified, resulting in their modification. These categories formed the basis for the findings that are presented here. Quotations from the interviews are provided as illustrations.

Flyers advertising the study were circulated to staff and clients of Chicago-area community-based AIDS service organizations. Women who responded were included in the study if they had been diagnosed with AIDS for at least three months. The final sample included 12 women. One woman had no children, so she is not included in the results presented here.

Sample Characteristics

The majority of participants were in their twenties and thirties and members of varied racial and ethnic groups, primarily African American. Most did not have partners, although one woman lived with her common-law husband and two lived with boyfriends. One woman held full-time employment and two worked part time; the rest were unemployed. The majority were dependent on Social Security Disability, Supplemental Security Income, or Aid to Families with Dependent Children (AFDC) benefits, or a combination of these, to support themselves and their families; their low-income status is reflected in Table 11.1.

All participants had been living with AIDS for a significant length of time, with a third surviving beyond three years, as indicated in Table 11.2.

Health status varied within the sample. Although all reported having symptoms, with tiredness and fatigue being the most common, five women said they currently had no major medical problems or had conditions that were amenable to treatment. five others reported serious chronic or life-threatening conditions, including cancers and liver failure. While all were able to attend to their personal care needs without assistance and none were housebound, seven needed help with household chores.

The number of children among women in the sample ranged from one to nine, with a mean of 3.5. Only one mother had a child with AIDS. Examination of household arrangements revealed three patterns. Four mothers lived with all their minor children, three mothers lived with none, and four mothers lived with some of the minor children. Except for one woman who lived with her common-law husband, all were single mothers. This included one woman who lived with the fa-

Table 11.1 Sociodemographic Characteristics of Participants (n = 11)

Age (mean = 34.7 years)	
20–29	2 (18%)
30–39	7 (64%)
40–49	2 (18%)
Race/ethnicity	
African American	5 (45%)
White	3 (27%)
Latina	1 (9%)
French-speaking Caribbean	1 (9%)
Other	1 (9%)
Relationship status	
Married	0
Common-law marriage	1 (9%)
Divorced	3 (27%)
Widowed	2 (18%)
Single	5 (45%)
Education	
Less than high school graduate	5 (45%)
High school graduate	2 (18%)
Post high school	4 (36%)
Employment	
Full time	1 (9%)
Part time	2 (18%)
Unemployed	8 (73%)
Income (per month)	
Less than $750	7 (64%)
$750 to $1,100	3 (27%)
$1,100 to $2,000	1 (9%)

ther of her youngest child; she considered herself single because she did "the most for [her] kids," acting as both "the mom and the dad."

Participants reported that drug use, not HIV or AIDS, was the primary determinant of household arrangements. Only one mother reported that having AIDS was a factor in her child's residing elsewhere. Five mothers reported that arrangements involving placement of children out of the home predated their diagnosis of HIV or AIDS and were the result of their drug use. Most of these children were in the care of family members, with the mothers having some contact with them. Only one mother in this group had children removed by child welfare authorities. One mother had a child residing in a juvenile facility, and in part attributed this to the child's difficulties growing up with a mother who used drugs.

Findings

All but one of the women interviewed reported that motherhood was their most important role. While they recognized difficulties in child rearing and relationships with their children due to HIV or AIDS, mothers focused greater attention on the benefits of having children and the supportive functions served by their children.

Despite changes in physical status due to AIDS, most mothers continued acting as caregivers to their children. When physical decline limited their ability to perform certain functions associated with motherhood, or when their children no longer lived with them, these women redefined the role of mother. By altering the meaning of motherhood, they were able to retain the role and the status and satisfaction it provided.

Definition of Motherhood

The women defined the role of mother broadly to include education, emotional support, discipline, physical care, involvement in the children's activities, and financial responsibility. Education consisted of teaching skills and appropriate behavior and instilling values. Emotional support was defined as "being there" when a child needed his or her mother, and being "giving and understanding." As one mother stated, "I'm able to be there and encourage them and give them support. Discipline included recognizing when a child was behaving improperly and correcting the situation. For some mothers, this included physical punishment. Meeting a child's day-to-day needs constituted physical care. Being able to participate in school and recreational events constituted being involved in children's activities.

Ways AIDS Changes Mothering

Mothering was affected by both changes in health status and issues unique to AIDS. Changing health status made some tasks associated with motherhood more difficult to perform, particularly those involving physical exertion. Mothers also had to

Table 11.2 HIV and AIDS Status of Participants

Mode of transmission	
Heterosexual contact	5 (45%)
Injected drug use	3 (17%)
Multiple-risk behaviors	2 (18%)
Unknown	1 (9%)
Survival time since diagnosis of AIDS (in months)	
Less than 18	4 (36%)
18 to 36	3 (27%)
More than 36	4 (36%)

negotiate special concerns associated with AIDS, such as stigma and isolation, ways their illness might affect their children's well-being, and the impact of widespread loss in the family's social network.

Health Status   Changing health status affected performance of the tasks associated with motherhood. This was particularly evident in the areas of discipline, physical care, involvement in children's activities, and financial support. Discipline, physical care, and being involved in children's activities took more energy than many mothers had at times. One mother said about discipline, "And I try not to whoop them because I don't . . . I kind of need the energy so that's a lot of energy wasted." Reflecting on her ability to meet her children's day-to-day needs, another mother said she found herself "hollering at them and screaming. . . . And the only reason I do is because I don't feel good and can't deal with them. Fix me this, get me that, do this." Another described the change in her level of participation with her children:

> The really only bad thing is that 'cause of having AIDS, it puts me harder to go places, but I can't go as many places, 'cause I used to go on all the field trips the kids went, they were younger, I used to go on all of the field trips, and now it's not that easy. I can imagine me walking around Science and Industry Museum for like three hours. I don't know if I would be able to handle it. It would be kind of hard for me.

Finances were affected by AIDS, as illness had forced several women to stop working. Income received from entitlements was considered inadequate, as one woman explained: "It's real hard when a person, you know, when you have a disease and then you have to live month to month financially . . . 'cause our check is only one a month and our bills . . . " Another mother's financial contributions to a son who lived with family members had decreased since she became disabled. She stated, "Sometimes I say well, if there wasn't that disease, I could do more for him."

AIDS-Related Issues   Concerns unique to HIV illness also affected parenting. For example, the women were well aware that their children could be affected by the stigma associated with HIV and AIDS and made efforts to protect them. One mother worried that her children would be ostracized if others knew "their mommy's got AIDS." Another mother, active as a public speaker for

AIDS organizations, had discussed this with her daughter:

> We had to sit down and explain to her that if she told people about HIV disease, they may not like her. And well, why? You know, well, people are scared of it and it's . . . she knows, you know, I would never stop her from telling friends, but she knows that they may not like her if she tells them. Or their mommies may not let them play with her.

Mothers recognized, too, that the isolation they experienced could extend to their children and they tried to prevent that. One woman who virtually shut herself into her home during an episode of depression associated with her diagnosis of AIDS eventually recognized the effect this had on her daughter: "All she did was go to school and come home and go to school and come home." This realization prompted her to seek help.

The women also knew that living with a "sick" mother could be emotionally troubling for children. Several reported that their children became fearful during episodes of acute illness. One mother stated that her children were educated about AIDS but that "they jump to conclusions. . . . If I've got a cold or I'm going into the hospital or something, then they think that, you know, it's a death . . . I'm going to die and never come back." Another mother said about her son: "When I get real sick he becomes a behavior problem. And it's only for fear." She recognized this as his way of eliciting reassurance:

> We're real real close and, um, when I lay around, he gets real worried so he, the only way he counteracts that is to react bad so that he can misbehave so that I can constantly be on him. So that he be secured.

The effect of widespread loss due to AIDS was another concern for these mothers. More than half of the women had husbands or partners who had died of or were living with AIDS. In addition, most had social networks that included many persons with HIV and AIDS, including two who stated that all their friends had AIDS. Loss due to death was one result, but children often experienced other losses due to AIDS, as this mother described:

> The one thing . . . that I've learned as an HIV-positive mother, who has been since her child's first year of life, and who has been going to groups, surrounded by people with HIV disease,

[my daughter] was very much affected by that . . . her friends were children of HIV-positive people. And if their mothers died, well [she] knew via mommy and mommy's talking with friends that so-and-so was sick, and we were concerned. Then all of a sudden, so-and-so passed away. . . . And while we're mourning so-and-so's passing . . . it's not dawning on anyone's mind that this child has just lost its friends 'cause the friends went with the aunt, the uncle, the grandma, and this child has thing going on in her mind, like what happened to them? Their mommy's died, they're gone.

Children's Supportive Functions

As described above, the women reported frustrations and difficulties in dealing with their children. However, the benefits of motherhood clearly outweighed the burdens. Mothers looked to their children for practical help, emotional support, and, most important, motivation. While the women valued their children's help, they also struggled with the ways this might adversely affect their children's well-being or development.

Practical Help   Practical help from children included caregiving to sick mothers and helping with household chores. Mothers relied on children to help with such household tasks as washing dishes, sweeping, emptying garbage, and cleaning the bathroom. One mother stated,

I try to get them to help. because, you know, my, you know they're getting older and they can help around the house. . . . They all try to help, you know . . . even my little six-year-old tries to help. They're my little workers in my life.

Caregiving tasks children performed included providing personal care, such as help with bathing; this was particularly evident during episodes of illness.

Mothers had concerns about relying on children for practical help. One mother reported that her expectations for helping around the house were age-appropriate for her 9-year-old daughter, and stated that she would teach her to perform tasks such as dishwashing at this age regardless of her health status. On the other hand, another mother remarked that her "children are still children, too," and that she hated "to put a lot of pressure on [her] kids" to help.

Emotional Support   While many mothers said they received emotional support from their children in a general way, a few mothers reported that a child served as a confidant. These were generally eldest children in a family. One mother stated that she wrote letters to her 17-year-old son who lived in a juvenile detention facility: "I sort of turn to him, my oldest son. You know, of course, he can't, he isn't here to give me advice, but at least I have somebody to tell how I'm feeling." Another mother explained that her 13-year-old daughter was the only one of her three children who knew of her illness. She said:

I feel comfortable around her reading my Test Positive Aware magazine or my AIDS-related . . . sometimes I'm able to read with her the different, you know, things that's going on, and I feel comfortable with her know[ing], you know.

Motivation   Motivation was the most important function children served. Children were a motivating force in many ways. They prompted their mothers to be active, get involved in AIDS causes, recover from episodes of illness, and survive. They also influenced their mothers' drug use.

Children pushed mothers to stay active, even when this was a struggle. One mother reported "making" herself do things with her children even when she felt tired: "Now I get where I'm too tired to even take them out to the park or something like that, you know I do it but I do it once in a while." Another explained, "If it's yourself, you don't want to do something you don't have to," but that "you've got to get up and do something" when children are involved.

For a few mothers, being active included being involved in AIDS causes. One mother described how her daughter was a motivating force in this process:

And what happened was I kept thinking to myself, my God, my beautiful daughter, you know, someday she's going to want to have a relationship, and she'll be at higher risk of contracting HIV then than I was in my time, if the scientists don't come up with a cure, if the epidemic continues to grow. I said this is appalling and this is scary for me. And I'll be dead. How will I be able to help her? I need to begin this process of helping her now. So I started going out and speaking to people about what I had learned.

Children also provided motivation for recovery from episodes of illness and for survival. The mother described earlier, who experienced depression and isolation, attributed her recovery from this episode to concern for her daughter's well-being. Responsibility for children also prompted efforts toward survival. One mother said that even when she was most depressed she had never considered suicide: "I've got kids to raise . . . they keep me going." Another commented, "I'm a strong lady . . . because I have a daughter that I have to be . . . with." Wanting to see their children grow up also provided motivation for survival. One mother said she wanted "to live long enough to raise" her daughter, "not where I'm going to have to give her to some strange people." Another's wish was "to live long enough to see a grandbaby or two." For another mother, survival was connected to her children, but for less specific reasons. She simply said, "I don't know what I would do if they weren't here."

Children of drug-using mothers also affected their efforts at recovery. Mothers often attributed their entry into drug rehabilitation programs to their children. One mother entered treatment when her infant child seroconverted; she realized this child would grow up and would need his mother's care. Another's recognition that she needed treatment came on a day that she spent with her two children, an unusual occurrence during her drug-using days. She recalled:

> The day I decided to go into recovery . . . I shot some drugs and a light switch went on. What the hell are you doing? . . . I had the children for the day. . . . And I looked at each one of them and I says, "My God, look at what I'm doing." And just the switch went on.

One mother's three older children had been removed by child welfare authorities because of her drug use. She was not enrolled in a methadone maintenance program. Although she still used illegal drugs at times, her efforts at recovery were prompted by the two children she had at home: "I believe it too if I was still using every single day I would probably lose the kids. And I said, 'I'm not going to let that happen with these two.' "

Maintaining the Role of Mother

Health problems and the possibility of death constituted threats to the role of mother. Changing health status limited role performance for some mothers and had already resulted in placement of their children for others. All were acutely aware that others would need to assume responsibility for

their children if they died and had thought about plans for their children's future. Most had plans in progress, either making if normal arrangements with relatives or working with agencies to formalize future adoptions.

To retain the role in the face of these threats, the women negotiated a new definition for motherhood. Two themes can be seen in this redefinition. Mothers emphasized tasks associated with the existing definition that could be maintained despite changing health status, and when even those tasks could no longer be performed, they reframed the role as one of oversight of their children's well-being.

Mothers emphasized the importance of the education and emotional support functions of mothering when physical limitations prevented them from fulfilling other functions of the role. One mother could no longer go out with her children but said, "I still you know . . . if they ask me to, I'll read them a story at night." Another said she could still teach her child appropriate behaviors, and was considered a good mother by her community for having "instilled in [her] son principles and values."

When mothers could not perform even these kinds of tasks, as was the case when they were no longer a custodial parent, they still felt responsible for their children's welfare and stressed supervisory functions. One mother explained that being a good mother to her son, who lived with his grandmother, meant making sure he went to a good school. Another mother arranged for her children's adoption so that they could move to a better neighborhood and attend better schools. Another said, "I have to make sure that my daughter is . . . taken care of" and did this by keeping in touch with her sister, who was the girl's legal guardian.

Unresolved Issues for Mothers with AIDS

Some mothers, particularly those who had been drug abusers, reported two additional unresolved issues: reunion with children previously removed or placed out of the home, and troubled relationships with adult children.

Women struggled to define relationships with children who had been placed out of the home. Two women had placed infant children with sisters to raise as their own. When AIDS was diagnosed or their conditions worsened, these children were told of their mother's true identity. This resulted in uncertainty and confusion for mother and child. One woman reported that her 12-year-old son "took it real bad. . . . He loves me, but it's not like that motherly love. . . . It's hard. . . . He doesn't call me 'mom.' He calls me 'auntie.' " The other mother stated that her son had tried living with her once he knew she was his mother, but that they did not get along. She commented about this child and the three others who had been placed out of the home:

> I love him, you know. I don't love him the same as I love [the daughter who lived with her]. I can say that. I learned that the hard way. But I love him . . . the only thing I can say to myself is that I love them and maybe someday they'll understand, you know, that their mommy was all f—ed up and that she made mistakes. . . . I can't take that back.

One woman placed her infant daughter with her own mother to raise. Years later, she tried to raise the girl herself, but "couldn't handle it" and returned her to her mother. She noted, "I don't really have a mother relationship. I don't even know what my relationship is with my daughter." Another woman, whose three oldest children were in foster or relative care, saw these children regularly but said she was not working on having them return to her home: "They're doing really good where they're at."

Mothers reported troubled relationships with adult children. This was particularly true for women with drug-use histories whose children had been neglected in some way earlier in their lives, but it was also true for other women who were emotionally closer to younger children because of the constraints of their illness. One mother who had used drugs said her two oldest daughters had animosity and anger. "They thought I only loved [her youngest child], 'cause I only kept him." She said it took a lot of work to repair the mother-daughter relationships. Another mother said:

> My oldest son, you know, he hasn't got the opportunity to really be around me now that I'm clean, 'cause it . . . I took him through a lot of stuff, a lot of stuff, and I just want to show him that I'm not that person anymore. . . . That's one of the things I definitely need to accomplish. And I just pray the Lord will give me that chance.

A third woman said her adult children were jealous of her youngest child: "They get angry sometimes, 'Well, mom, you never used to take us to piano and take us to clay class.' " She had tried to make them understand the differences in the situations, but the difficult feelings continued to surface.

Limitations of the Study

The usefulness of this study may be limited by sample characteristics and its cross-sectional design. Additional research with minority women and women currently using drugs is needed to determine transferability of these findings to those groups. Longitudinal studies may contribute to a fuller understanding of the changing experiences and perceptions of motherhood among mothers with AIDS.

Implications for Social Work Practice

This study confirms findings previously reported, but provides new information for social workers serving mothers with AIDS. The centrality of the role of mother is highlighted, as well as specific ways AIDS challenges its performance. Unresolved issues in relationships between mothers with drug-use histories and their children and unanticipated negative consequences of reunions between mothers and children who had been placed out of the home are identified as areas for social work intervention.

As others have found, the mothers with AIDS in this study relied on their children for both practical and emotional support, and in some cases, children took on the role of confidant for mothers. This phenomenon is not atypical in single-parent families (Nestmann & Niepel, 1994). In addition, single mothers, whether ill or not, worry about the effects of this on their children. This family pattern is in part the result of the social isolation these families experience. Social workers can intervene by helping mothers clarify developmentally appropriate expectations of their children and making sure that they have access to practical help for personal care, household chores, and counseling services, particularly peer support.

The social networks of families affected by AIDS have been depleted. Children not only lose parents, they often lose other family members. The need for grief counseling services for these children has been documented elsewhere (Gruendel & Anderson, 1995). In addition, these mothers and their children lose friends to both death and relocation. Social workers need to be aware of the pervasive loss these families experience, so that they can educate mothers about the ways children express grief and help them minimize loss by finding ways to maintain connections to friends who have moved away.

The literature about families affected by AIDS has highlighted the need for planning for children's placement (Draimin, 1995; Marcenko & Samost, 1999). This is an essential task for social workers. However, the centrality of motherhood for these women suggests that helping them refashion and retain this role is equally important. Social workers can be instrumental in helping mothers with AIDS discover new ways to perform parenting functions, particularly alternative discipline methods, so that they can remain effective parents as long as possible. The significance of the oversight function of the role of mother can be highlighted for women who have placed their children. Social workers can also help this latter group of women develop ways of maintaining meaningful contact with their children.

Women with drug-use histories typically have unresolved issues about children neglected, voluntarily placed out of the home, or removed by authorities during that time in their lives. Social workers should be prepared to offer counseling directed at repairing the disrupted relationships between mothers and children or resolving guilt and other feelings associated with children who are no longer part of the family. Although reunions with these children may seem desirable, the mothers in this study who were reunited with children previously placed out of the home had difficulties redefining these relationships. Social workers serving mothers seeking reunions should help them consider potential positive and negative outcomes and explore the meaning and boundaries of a new or different relationship with their child, so as to prevent the kind of confusion and hurt that mothers in this study and their children experienced.

References

American Association for World Health. (1997). *Give children hope in a world with AIDS.* Washington, DC: Author.

Buckingham, S. L., & Rehm, S. J. (1987). AIDS and women at risk. *Health & Social Work, 12,* 5–11.

Centers for Disease Control. (1998). *HIV/AIDS surveillance report 10*(1). Atlanta: Author.

Centers for Disease Control. (1999a). *HIV/AIDS among U.S. women: Minority and young women at continuing risk.* Atlanta: Author.

Centers for Disease Control. (1999b). *HIV/AIDS surveillance report 11*(1). Atlanta: Author.

Charmaz, K. (1990). "Discovering" chronic illness: Using grounded theory. *Social Science in Medicine, 30,* 1161–1172.

Chung, J. Y., & Magraw, M. M. (1992). A group approach to psychosocial issues faced by HIV-positive women. *Hospital and Community Psychiatry, 43,* 891–894.

DeMarco, R. F., Miller, K. H., Patsdaughter, C. A., Chisholm, M., & Grindel, C. G. (1998). From silencing the self to action: Experiences of women living with HIV/AIDS. *Health Care for Women International, 19,* 539–552.

Diaz, T., Chu, S. Y., Buehler, J. W., Boyd, D., Checko, P. J., Conti, L., Davidson, A. J., Hermann, P., Herr, M., Levy, A., Shields, A., Sorvillo, F., Mokotoff, E., Whyte, B., & Hersch, B. S. (1994). Socioeconomic differences among people with AIDS: Results from a multistate surveillance project. *American Journal of Preventive Medicine, 10,* 217–222.

Draimin, B. (1995). A second family? Placement and custody decisions. In S. Geballe, J. Gruendel, & W. Andiman (Eds.), *Forgotten children of the AIDS epidemic* (pp. 125–139). New Haven: Yale University Press.

Dunbar, H. T., Mueller, C. W., Medina, C., & Wolf, T. (1998). Psychological and spiritual growth in women living with HIV. *Social Work, 43,* 144–154.

Federation of Protestant Welfare Agencies. (1996). *Families in crisis: Report of the Working Committee on HIV, Children, and Families.* New York: Author.

Florence, M. E., Lützén, K., & Alexius, B. (1994). Adaptation of heterosexually infected HIV-positive women: A Swedish pilot study. *Health Care for Women International, 15,* 265–273.

Gillman, R. R., & Newman, B. S. (1996). Psychosocial concerns and strengths of women with HIV infection: An empirical study. *Families in Society, 77,* 131–141.

Gruendel, J. M., & Anderson, G. R. (1995). Building child- and family-responsive support systems. In S. Geballe, J. Gruendel, & W. Andiman (Eds.), *Forgotten children of the AIDS epidemic* (pp. 165–189). New Haven: Yale University Press.

Guillory, J. A., Sowell, R., Moneyham, I., & Seals, B. (1997). An exploration of the meaning and use of spirituality among women with HIV/AIDS. *Alternative Therapies, 3,* 55–60.

Hackl, K. L., Somlai, A. M., Kelly, J. A., & Kalichman, S. C. (1997). Women living with

HIV/AIDS: The dual challenge of being a patient and caregiver. *Health & Social Work, 22,* 53–62.

Kaspar, B. (1989). Women and AIDS: A psychosocial perspective. *Affilia, 4,* 7–22.

Levine, C. (1994). The new orphans and grieving in the time of AIDS. In B. O. Dane & C. Levine (Eds.), *AIDS and the new orphans* (pp. 1–11). Westport, CT: Auburn House.

Marcenko, M. O., & Samost, L. (1999). Living with HIV/AIDS: The voices of HIV-positive mothers. *Social Work, 44,* 36–45.

Michaels, D., & Levine, C. (1992). Estimates of the number of motherless youth orphaned by AIDS in the United States. *Journal of the American Medical Association, 268,* 3456–3461.

Moneyham, L., Seals, B., Demi, A., Sowell, R., Cohen, L., & Guillory, J. (1996). Experiences of disclosure in women infected with HIV. *Health Care for Women International, 17,* 209–221.

Moneyham, L., Seals, B., Sowell, R., Hennessy, M., Demi, A., & Brake, S. (1997). The impact of HIV on emotional distress of infected women: Cognitive appraisals and coping as mediators. *Scholarly Inquiry for Nursing Practice, 11,* 125–145.

Nannis, E. D., Patterson, T. L., & Semple, S. J. (1997). Coping with HIV disease among seropositive women: Psychosocial concerns. *Women & Health, 25,* 1–22.

Nestmann, F., & Niepel, G. (1994). Social support in single parent families: Children as sources of support. In F. Nestmann & K. Hurrelmann (Eds.), *Social networks and social support in childhood and adolescence* (pp. 321–345). Berlin: Gruyter.

Niebuhr, V. N., Hughes, J. R., & Pollad, R. B. (1994). Parents with human immunodeficiency virus infection: Perceptions of their children's emotional needs. *Pediatrics, 93,* 421–426.

Pliskin, M., Farrel, K., Crandles, S., & DeHovitz, J. (1993). *Factors influencing HIV positive mothers' disclosure to their non-infected children* [Abstract no. PO-D22-4081]. *9th International Conference on AIDS, 9,* 898.

Regan-Kubinski, M. J., & Sharts-Hopko, N. (1995). Illness cognitions of HIV-infected mothers. *Issues in Mental Health Nursing, 16,* 327–344.

Strauss, A., & Corbin, J. (1990). *Basics of qualitative research.* Newbury Park, CA: Sage Publications.

Van Loon, R. A. (1996). *Coping and adaptation in women with AIDS.* Unpublished doctoral dissertation, University of Chicago.

van Servellen, G., Sarna, L., & Jablonski, K. J. (1998). Women with HIV: Living with symptoms. *Western Journal of Nursing Research, 20,* 448–464.

Walker, S. E. (1998). *Women with AIDS and their children.* New York: Garland.

Ybarra, S. (1991). Women and AIDS: Implications for counseling. *Journal of Counseling & Development, 69,* 285–287.

Zuckerman, C., & Gordon, L. (1988). Meeting the psychosocial and legal needs of women wit AIDS and their families. *New York Journal of Medicine, 88,* 619–620.

DAVID HOWE

JULIA FEAST

12

The Long-term Outcome of Reunions between Adult Adopted People and Their Birth Mothers

Although there is an established literature on adopted people who search for their birth relatives, little is known about the actual experience of contact and reunion. When the long-term view is taken of people's reunion experiences, even less is understood. The subject matter is not only of practical interest to adopted people and those who counsel them on the search process; it also taps into deeper themes to do with biology and upbringing, nature and nurture, identity and belonging, connectedness and family relationships. What is the nature and origin of filial relationships? Are the ties of blood stronger and more compelling than the social bonds formed during childhood?

A number of recent studies have followed adopted people's experiences of searching and reunion beyond the initial contact. It is clear from these investigations that there is no one postreunion pathway, although most adopted people report that the reunion experience, whatever its outcome, was positive, satisfying, and worthwhile (Sorosky et al., 1974; Depp, 1982; Bertocci and Schechter, 1987; Campbell et al., 1991; Boult, 1992; Pacheco and Eme, 1993; March, 1995; Cowell et al., 1996; Howe and Feast, 2000). Most people report feeling more "complete" as a result of the search, contact and reunion experience. Gonyo and Watson (1988), and Pacheco and Eme (1993) explored what happens over the first year or so after a reunion. They describe an initial intense phase of getting to know the birth relative, followed by a stage in which the adopted person begins to accommodate the relative into his or her everyday network

of family and social relationships. Contact becomes less frequent. In some cases, the adopted person and birth relative drift apart and contact ceases (Gonyo and Watson, 1988; Sachdev, 1992). Class and cultural differences between the adopted person and the birth relative can also be experienced as too great and as a result the relationship struggles or ends (for example, see Parish and Cotton, 1989).

Over the longer term, researchers have recognized that reunions have as much to do with people's search for identity and the resolution of experiences of loss as a desire for new family relationships (McMillan and Irving, 1994; Iredale, 1997; Feast et al., 1998). Lifton (1983) describes the search and reunion experience as one that helps heal the trauma of the initial rejection. In all these accounts, the reunion is seen as the starting point of a long process of readjustment. There is growing recognition that one of the major benefits of a reunion is that the adopted person feels more in control of their personal life, they experience fewer autobiographical gaps, and they have more information and a greater understanding of their origins and background (Lifton, 1983).

Auth and Zaret (1986) identify five possible search and reunion outcomes: (1) failure to find the birth relative; (2) the birth relative rejects the adopted person; (3) a satisfying one-time meeting; (4) the adopted person remains in contact with the birth family but maintains a primary relationship with the adoptive family; and (5) the adopted person develops a primary relationship with the birth family, perhaps with some continued contact with the adoptive family. In his study of 124 adopted people who had reunions with their birth mother, Sachdev (1992) found that 50% saw their birth mother "regularly," about 20% saw her "occasionally," and 17% reported that they had stopped seeing her after the first contact. Howe and Feast (2000) found that of the 215 people (including 17 people who were refused contact and were rejected outright) who had traced their birth mother, 85% were still in contact with her after the first year, and 63% were still in contact five years postreunion.

In their analysis of 67 interviews with voluntary and self-selected adopted adults who had a reunion with a birth relative, Gladstone and Westhues (1998) identified seven types of postreunion relationship:

1. *No contact* (6%).
2. Still *searching* for a stronger relationship with their birth relative with whom they have moderate to frequent contact (8%).
3. *Ambivalent* relationship with their birth relative with only limited current contact (14%).
4. *Tense* relationship with the birth relative with only limited or moderate contact (6%).
5. *Distant* but satisfactory relationship with the birth relative with only limited or moderate contact (22%).
6. *Close, but not too close* relationship with the birth relative with moderate contact (10%).
7. *Close* relationship and frequent contact with the birth relative (35%).

All but three people had their first reunion meeting at least three years prior to the research interview. The authors also identify a number of mediating factors that affect the development of these postreunion relationships, including structural factors (for example, time, distance, and transport); interactive factors (for example, amount of support from the adoptive family, perceived nonresponsiveness of the birth relative); and motivating factors in maintaining contact (for example, a sense of involvement, pleasure, obligation, ambivalence, guilt, or sexual attraction). In their discussion, Gladstone and Westhues provide some useful reminders that contact and reunion experiences are both complex and varied. Developing the work of Sachdev (1992), they propose that postreunion experiences might be distinguished on the basis of frequency of contact, the level of satisfaction with the contact, and the degree to which feelings of emotional closeness are experienced.

The more recent studies by Auth and Zaret (1986), Sachdev (1992), and Gladstone and Westhues (1998) follow the postreunion story beyond the first encounter. They recognize that although people's feelings and experiences vary a great deal, nevertheless there appear to be a limited and recognizable number of postreunion pathways that people follow. Explanations for these different outcomes have sought to combine structural and psychological factors as a way of understanding what happens as the relationship between the adopted person and the birth relative evolves over time. The interest in pursuing further research in this field is not only to help refine the classification of these postreunion relationships but also to see what light they might shed on the quality, character, and sustainability of filial relationships across the life span.

Method

The present study formed part of a larger project that set out to compare a group of adult adopted people who initiated a search for one or more of their birth relatives (searchers) with those who did not (nonsearchers) (Howe and Feast, 2000). As an extension of the main project, the long-term outcome of adopted people who had searched for and had contact with their birth relative was investigated.

Data were gathered using a postal questionnaire sent to all adopted people who had received direct information, advice, and counseling (the searchers) from the Children's Society (London) between 1988 (the first year when a full, recorded service began) and 1997 (the last completed year of service provision prior to the study). Searchers were asked 90 primary questions, with many broken down into a series of secondary and subgroup questions. Information was sought about people's biographical characteristics, their experience of being adopted, reasons for searching, and their experiences of the search and reunion process. At the time of the survey adopted people were at different stages of the search and reunion process. In total, 451 people who had actively searched for a birth relative received the questionnaire and 394 completed and returned it, giving a high response rate of 87%. Qualitative interviews were also carried out with a subsample of 60 searchers who had also completed the questionnaire. The current paper does not present a qualitative analysis of these interviews, but it does use brief extracts to illustrate the quantitative findings.

Comparisons between adopted people who search for a birth relative and those who do not are reported in Howe and Feast (2000). The present paper investigates the outcome experiences of a particular subgroup of 48 searchers who had first *met and had contact with* their birth mother *at least eight years* prior to receipt of the questionnaire. This group provides a view of the postreunion experience over the medium to long term. The analysis does not include adopted people who located their birth mother but who were refused contact by her and in effect suffered an outright rejection (n = 17). Although it is also possible to identify subgroups of adopted people who first had contact with their birth fathers (n = 28) or birth siblings (n = 32) eight years or more previously, the numbers are relatively small even for modest statistical purposes. There is some overlap between those who had contact with their birth mothers, birth fathers, and/or birth siblings. For example, 24 people had had a reunion with both their birth mother and birth siblings. The analysis in this paper concentrates solely on those who had had a reunion with their birth mother on the grounds that their numbers are reasonably large; for most adopted people this contact was emotionally the most important in terms of issues of loss, identity, and background information; and by concentrating on one group of birth relatives, the number of variables and other complex intervening factors is kept to manageable proportions.

Results

All Searchers

The number of years since this long-term group of adopted people first had contact and reunion with their birth mothers had a mean of 10.6 (SD = 3.33). The mean age at which people first formally began their search was 27.4 years (SD = 8.5 years), the youngest being 17 and the oldest being 50 years. Sixty-three percent of searchers were women and 37% men, a ratio in line with most other surveys in this field. Adopted people's mean age at which they were placed with their adoptive parents was 9 months. Eighty-three percent were placed before the age of 12 months. Eight percent were placed after their second birthday. Eight percent of adopted people were of mixed ethnicity and placed transracially, the remaining 92% being raised in matched white same-race placements. Seventy-seven percent of people said they had "always

known" or had been told from a very young age that they were adopted. The remaining 23% remembered being told of their adoption sometime between the age of 6 and 10 years.

Although not necessarily carrying a negative connotation, 68% of people said that they "felt different" to their adoptive family when growing up. Fifty-seven percent of searchers felt that they "belonged" in their adoptive families during their childhood. In answer to the question "Did you love your adoptive mother when growing up," 80% said yes. Seventy-three percent said that they felt "loved by their adoptive mother" as a child. Fifty-six percent of adopted people reported that they agreed that they felt happy about being adopted, leaving 18% feeling "uncertain," and 26% disagreeing. When asked to evaluate their adoption overall, 54% assessed their experience positively, 34% had mixed feelings and 12% felt negative.

At the time of the survey, 63% of adopted people were still in some form of contact with their birth mother. This left 37% whose contact with their birth mother had stopped (these figures exclude three people who had located their birth mother more than eight years previously but had been refused contact and therefore they had never met).

Comparisons between Adopted People Still in Contact and Those No Longer in Contact with Their Birth Mothers Eight Years Postreunion

There were a number of trends (although only three reached statistical significance at the 5% level) suggesting possible differences between the continued contact and ceased contact groups. For example:

- Women (71%) were more likely to remain in contact than men (50%) (NS).
- The mean age of first contact was younger for the continued contact group (26.8 years, SD = 8.1) than the ceased contact group (29.3 years, SD = 9.4) (NS).
- Adopted people who said they felt different to their adoptive family when growing up (77%) were significantly more likely to remain in contact than those who said that they did not feel different (39%) (p < 0.05).
- Adopted people who said that they felt they did not belong or were uncertain that they belonged in their adoptive family when growing up (68%) were slightly more likely to remain

in contact than those who said they felt they did belong (56%) (NS).

- Adopted people who felt uncertain or disagreed that they loved their adoptive mother as a child (67%) were more likely than those who agreed that they loved their adoptive mother (60%) to remain in contact with their birth mother (NS).
- Adopted people who felt uncertain or disagreed that their adoptive mother loved them as a child (77%) were more likely than those who said they did love their adoptive mother (56%) to remain in contact with their birth mother (NS).
- Adopted people who felt uncertain or disagreed that they felt happy about being adopted (77%) were significantly more likely than those who said they did feel happy about being adopted (39%) to remain in contact with their birth mother ($p = 0.05$).
- Adopted people who evaluated their overall experience of adoption with either mixed or negative feelings (77%) were significantly more likely than those who evaluated their adoptions positively (39%) to remain in contact with their birth mother ($p = 0.05$).

The above list suggests that a number of minor differences in terms of evaluating their adoption experience did exist between those who were still in contact and those who had ceased contact with their birth mother. However, this evidence cannot be used as a single or simple explanation of who does and does not continue to see their birth mother. For example, although people who ceased

contact were more likely to have evaluated their adoption positively than negatively, those who remained in contact were as likely to describe their adoption experience positively as they were to describe it with mixed feelings or negatively. Figure 12.1 identifies four broad postreunion outcomes in terms of adoption experience and contact status with the birth mother eight years postreunion: (1) continued contact/positive adoption evaluation; (2) ceased contact/positive adoption evaluation; (3) continued contact/mixed or negative adoption evaluation; and (4) ceased contact/mixed or negative adoption evaluation.

As might be expected, there is also a rough correspondence between people evaluating their adoptions either positively or negatively, and whether or not they felt they belonged or felt happy about being adopted. We can therefore model four types of postreunion position along the lines defined by Figure 12.1 (the general distribution of these four types using the present survey results is indicated as a percentage):

1. Continued contact *and* positive evaluation/felt they belonged in adoptive family/feel happy about being adopted (30%).
2. Ceased contact *and* positive evaluation/felt they belonged in adoptive family/feel happy about being adopted (30%).
3. Continued contact *and* mixed or negative evaluation/feelings about belonging in adoptive family uncertain or negative/feelings of happiness about being adopted uncertain or negative (30%).

contact status with birth mother:

		continued contact	ceased contact
	positive	1. contact + positive adoption experience n = 13	2. ceased contact + positive adoption experience n = 12
Evaluation of adoption experience	mixed/ negative	3. contact + mixed/negative adoption experience n = 16	4. ceased contact + mixed/ negative adoption experience n = 6

Figure 12.1 Evaluation of adoption experience and contact status with birth mother (where still alive) eight years postreunion

4. Ceased contact *and* mixed or negative evaluation/feelings about belonging in adoptive family uncertain or negative/feelings of happiness about being adopted uncertain or negative (10%).

This distribution shows that, overall, people who evaluated their adoptions with mixed or negative feelings were more likely to stay in contact (Type 3 [30%]) than to cease contact (Type 4 [10%]). In contrast, those who evaluated their adoptions positively were as likely to remain in contact (Type 1 [30%]) as to cease contact (Type 2 [30%]). Negative evaluations therefore have some predictive power about whether or not adopted people are likely to remain in contact; positive evaluations do not.

Evaluating the Reunion Experience

Whether or not they were still in contact with their birth mother, most searchers felt that the contact had been worthwhile. Eighty-four percent of adopted people said the reunion had helped answer important questions about themselves and their adoption. As an overall experience, 88% of adopted people rated the contact with their birth mother as positive.

However, not surprisingly, adopted people who were still in contact with their birth mother eight years or more after their reunion reported higher rates of feeling more positive toward their birth family. For example, 54% of the continued contact group said that their birth relatives were "just like me" compared to 33% of the "ceased contact" group. Those still in contact were more likely than those who had stopped seeing their birth mother to say that they felt "a conflict of loyalties" between their adoptive and birth families (44% vs. 15%). Eighty-five percent of those who had ceased contact said they "felt more at home with their adoptive family" compared to 44% of adopted people who were still seeing their birth mother. Both groups were equally likely to say that they had learned to appreciate their adoptive family more since the reunion (54% of the continued contact group and 59% of the ceased contact group).

Frequency of Contact with Adoptive and Birth Mothers

Seven adopted people reported that at the time of the survey their adoptive mother was dead. Five of this group were still in contact with their birth mother. One adopted person's birth mother had died since her first contact. She was still in contact with her adoptive mother. This left 40 cases in which people's adoptive and birth mothers were still alive. Patterns of contact with adoptive and birth mothers (where both were still alive) are described in Table 12.1.

Table 12.1 shows that in cases where both the adoptive and birth mother are alive eight years or more after the initial reunion, more adopted people are still in some form of contact with their adoptive mother (80%, n = 32) than with their birth mother (63%, n = 25). This difference is more pronounced when we consider only face-to-face contact. Whereas 60% of adopted people said they saw their adoptive mother at least once a week, only 3% said they had face-to-face contact with their birth mother at least once a week.

Adapting Auth and Zaret's (1986) helpful categorizations, we can identify six outcomes based on levels of contact that adopted persons have with their adoptive and birth mother eight years postreunion (see Figures 12.2 and 12.3).

Figures 12.2 and 12.3 shows that eight years postreunion the majority of adopted people had either an exclusive or primary relationship with their adoptive mother (55%, n = 22). Levels of contact between the two mothers was equal in a fifth of

Table 12.1 Frequency of Adopted People's Contact (letter/telephone/face-to-face) with Their Adoptive and Birth Mothers (in cases where adoptive and birth mother are both alive)

Contact	Percentage	Number
No contact with either adoptive or birth mother	13	5
Contact with adoptive mother but not with birth mother	25	10
Contact with birth mother but not adoptive mother	8	3
Contact with both adoptive and birth mother	55	22
	5	2
All searchers	100	40

Balance of
contact
with adoptive
mother
compared to
birth mother

exclusive	higher	equal	lower	ceased	ceased
exclusive relationship with adoptive mother n = 10	primary relationship with adoptive mother n = 12	equal relationship with both, adoptive and birth mother n = 8	primary relationship with birth mother n = 2	exclusive relationship with birth mother n = 3	contact ceased with both adoptive or birth mother n = 5
ceased	lower	equal	higher	exclusive	ceased

Balance of
contact with
birth mother
compared to
adoptive
mother

Figure 12.2 Balance of contact between adoptive and birth mothers eight years postreunion where both mothers are still alive

cases (20%, n = 8). A minority of adopted people had either an exclusive or primary relationship with their birth mother (13%, n = 5). Five people (13%) had ceased contact with both their adoptive and birth mothers. (See Table 12.2 for brief case illustrations drawn from the qualitative interviews. Because only one in six people in the survey were followed up with an in-depth interview, it was not possible to cover all possible contact combinations. No one was interviewed who had either a primary relationship with their birth mother or had ceased contact with both their adoptive and birth mother.)

In short, eight years postreunion, adopted people are more likely to remain in contact with their adoptive mother than their birth mother (80% vs. 63%), *and* in those cases where there is contact

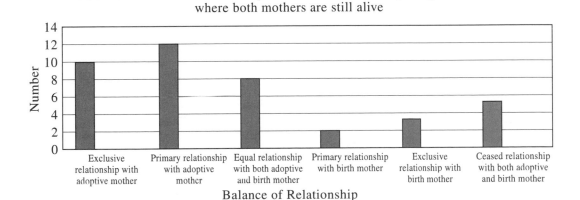

Balance of contact between adoptive and birth mother 8 years post reunion where both mothers are still alive

Figure 12.3 Balance of contact between adoptive and birth mothers eight years postreunion where both mothers are still alive

Table 12.2 Balance of Contact between Adoptive and Birth Mothers Eight Years Postreunion

Relationship	Case example
Exclusive relationship with adoptive mother	(1) All my birth mother wanted to do was make me feel negative about life. It got to me so bad. I just couldn't handle her attitude towards me . . . my sister and I wrote saying that we didn't want to have any more contact with her. . . . As I got older I started to get a better relationship with my [adoptive mum]. (2) She [birth mother] cancelled after the third meeting—a headache or something . . . then she didn't reply to any of my letters . . . I wrote and told her I was getting married—no response, so I think she doesn't want to know. . . . My [adoptive] parents are quite old-fashioned. They are lovely, lovely people but they are not the huggy, kissy type. I still feel uncomfortable when my mum tries to talk about anything "close."
Primary relationship with adoptive mother	(1) The closeness for my adoptive family has come since having my son. I feel closer to my adoptive family than I do my natural family. I want to be close to my mother who brought me up. I'm not incredibly close to my birth mother. I speak to her more on the phone now. (2) It has got to the stage now where I feel completely comfortable ringing her [birth mother] up and we see each other fairly regularly and I really enjoy seeing her . . . we have so much in common, it's unbelievable, we just get on very well. I see her now as a friend. I still don't see her as my mum—she will never be my mum. Because I don't have any real history with them, it's difficult to see them as a family. My family is my adoptive family . . . my birth family is like an extended family.
Equally balanced relationship between adoptive and birth mother	(1) My "two mums" eventually spoke on the phone and that was quite emotional for both, I think. I think mum was sort of thanking her for me and she was thanking mum for looking after me and bringing me up! My kids have sort of got three grandmas. . . . My relationship with them both is equally real. I suppose in lots of ways I can confide more, probably ask more questions with my natural mother, but that said there's a lot more I can say now to my [adoptive] mum. (2) My adoptive parents have never been particularly supportive. . . . But whatever my feelings for my adoptive parents, I don't think I'd ever be able to love my real, my birth parents in the same way, even though I like my birth parents a lot more than my adoptive parents. . . . My birth mother only lives down the road, which is really strange. I think in some ways she's a bit like me, that I'm a bit like her. She let me down a couple of times, though, so our relationship now is kind of laissez-faire.
Primary relationship with birth mother	(No examples available from interview sample)
Exclusive relationship with birth mother	My adoptive father died when I was five or six . . . and my adoptive mother was having an affair pre his death . . . and subsequently had a baby . . . the boyfriend wouldn't marry my adoptive mother because of me. I was a spanner in the works of their nice little ideal family unit, so I spent most of my adoptive childhood having a pretty rough time. . . . I have no contact now with my adoptive mother. . . . If you'd asked me a few years ago, I would say it's like me having a good friend [with birth mother], but the last few years it seems a bit more strained and more emotional for me
Contact ceased with both adoptive and birth mother	(No examples available from the interview sample)

with both parents, the frequency of contact (particularly face-to-face contact) is likely to be higher with adoptive mothers than birth mothers.

Evaluation of the Adoption Experience and Levels of Contact with Adoptive and Birth Mothers

It is possible to compare adopted people's experience of being adopted and the levels of contact they have with their adoptive and birth mothers eight years postreunion. Table 12.3 compares the adoption experience of adopted people who have either an exclusive or primary adoption relationship with their adoptive mother, and adopted people who have either an exclusive or primary relationship with their birth mother.

The numbers in Table 12.3 are far too small for statistical purposes, but the trends are all in the same direction, and to that extent they are at least suggestive—that those who form an exclusive or primary relationship with their birth mother eight years postreunion are more likely than those who form an exclusive or primary relationship with their adoptive mother to evaluate key aspects of their adoption experience negatively.

Again, with the same caveat about the small numbers involved, those who have equal and relatively frequent contact with both their adoptive and birth mothers are more likely to evaluate their adoption experience positively than those who have equal but relatively infrequent contact (or indeed have ceased contact altogether) with both their adoptive and birth mothers.

Discussion

The findings confirm and extend the results of previous studies. Whatever the outcome of adopted people's reunion with their birth relative, most said the search and contact experience had been satisfying and worthwhile. It helped answer questions about origins, background, and the reasons for being placed. Meeting face-to-face meant that the adopted persons could see someone to whom they were biologically related and who might well look like them.

The long-term view that is emerging is one that reveals a number of postreunion pathways and outcomes. Eight years or more after their first reunion, 63% of adopted people who had actually met their birth mother were still in some form of contact with her (this figure excludes a small number of cases in which the adopted person had located the birth mother but she refused to have any contact). Therefore, what the present study and others appear to be showing is that although year on year a steady number of adopted people cease contact with their birth mother, the rate of attrition is sufficiently low to result in over half of searchers remaining in touch eight years or more after their first reunion. In cases where the adoptive mother was alive, 80% of adopted people were still in contact with her eight years postreunion.

When the adopted person was in touch with both adoptive and birth mother, the frequency and quality of contact with each parent varied widely. Auth and Zaret's (1986) useful distinction between primary relationships being with either the adop-

Table 12.3 Comparisons of People's Adoption Experience and Levels of Contact with Adoptive and Birth Mothers

Adoption experience	Positive/ negative reaction	Exclusive/primary relationship with adoptive mother (%)	Exclusive/primary relationship with birth mother (%)
Felt different to adoptive family when growing up	yes	67	80
	no	33	20
Felt I belonged in my adoptive family when growing up	agree	59	40
	uncertain/disagree	41	60
Feel happy about being adopted	agree	59	20
	uncertain/disagree	41	60
Evaluation of being adopted	positive	64	20
	mixed feelings/negative	36	80

Exclusive/primary relationship with adoptive mother n = 22
Exclusive relationship with birth mother n = 5

tive or birth family receives further refinement in this study. Six postreunion categories are recognized: (1) exclusive relationship with the adoptive mother; (2) a primary relationship with the adoptive mother; (3) an equal relationship with both mothers (split into high-frequency contact with both, and low-frequency contact with both); (4) a primary relationship with the birth mother; (5) an exclusive relationship with the birth mother; and (6) no contact with either adoptive or birth mother. The distribution of cases allocated to these six categories is weighted toward primary and exclusive relationships being with the adoptive mother. Put another way, not only are adopted persons more likely to remain in contact with their adoptive mother than their birth mother, the frequency of contact with the adoptive mother is likely to be greater than that for the birth mother. These results complement those of Gladstone and Westhues (1998), who weave a qualitative thread into their seven types of adopted person–birth relative relationship. This allows the authors to speak of relationships that are either close, tense, ambivalent, or distant.

Gladstone and Westhues (1998) go on to examine how structural, interactive, and motivating factors might affect the quality and quantity of the postreunion relationship between adopted person and birth relative. The present study also looks at the durability and intensity of the postreunion relationship but uses adopted people's evaluation of their adoption as a factor that might influence long-term outcomes. It was found that a negative evaluation of the experience of being adopted made it more likely that individuals would remain in contact with their birth mother. However, a positive evaluation of the adoption experience had no discernible effect—the adopted person was as likely to remain in contact as not. Therefore, on its own, a negative evaluation of the adoption experience is not sufficient to predict who is likely to remain in contact over the long term. About a third of the sample in the present study evaluated their adoption positively and were still in contact with their birth mother eight years or more after the initial reunion.

The identification of multiple postreunion pathways suggests that a number of factors are likely to be present and that these factors probably interact in ways that are highly complex. There is good empirical evidence that issues around identity and self-worth are present in the lives of most adopted people (for example, see Grotevant, 1997). Gaps in one's biography and feelings of unresolved loss mean that questions such as Who am I? and

Why was I rejected and placed for adoption? remain important. The wish to have these questions answered explains why so many adopted people feel the need to search for and have contact with their birth mother. She is the person best placed to answer questions about origins and background (Who am I?) and self-worth (Why was I rejected?). These needs propel people into a relationship with their birth mother. It is at this point that other factors come into play that influence the direction and character of the relationship.

Adopted people with happy, positive adoption experiences may simply be looking for information about their background and not another family relationship. However, when they meet their birth mother, they may discover that they have a lot in common (temperament, looks, interests, humor) and that they get on well together (the "interactive" factors described by Gladstone and Westhues, 1998). The success of the relationship with the birth mother neither devalues the positive adoption experience nor affects the strength of the adopted person's ties with his or her adoptive family.

On the other hand, if adopted persons meet a birth mother with whom they do not get on or who does not get on with them (different social and cultural backgrounds, a birth mother who makes heavy emotional demands on her birth son or daughter, clash of personality, a lack of a shared history), the contact is likely to cease. The reunion is evaluated as worthwhile and satisfying because it has met its primary purpose of answering questions of identity and self-worth. The adopted persons did not set out to establish a new or alternative filial relationship. Feeling positive about both their adoption and their adoptive parents, and having gained information that helps them "complete the jigsaw," the overall feeling is one of satisfaction, whatever the outcome.

In contrast, adopted people who evaluate their adoption experience more negatively might approach their search with a double agenda: the need for background information *and* a desire for another filial or family relationship with their birth mother and her family. Their motivation to establish a long-term relationship is likely to be higher than it is for those who had a positive adoption experience. This might explain in part why more adopted people who evaluated their adoption with either mixed or negative feelings were still in contact with their birth mother eight or more years after their initial reunion.

Nevertheless, a small number of adopted people who evaluated their adoption experience with mixed or negative feelings did cease contact with their birth mother. Again, the reasons for not getting on with her, or their birth mother not getting on with them, might well involve clashes of personality, lack of a shared history, and gross mismatches in social and cultural backgrounds. This group of people is most vulnerable to losing touch with both the adoptive and birth mother. It is also the group most likely to evaluate the reunion experience as less than satisfactory. Although the contact helps answer questions of identity and possibly those of self-worth, it does not fulfill the desire for a new or alternative filial or family relationship. Indeed, we might speculate that in a few cases, the combination of a negative adoption experience and a (second) failed relationship with or rejection by one's birth mother is likely to exacerbate existing anxieties about feelings of self-worth and acceptability.

In general, however, eight years or more postreunion, the majority of those surveyed said that their primary relationship was still with their adoptive mother, even in those cases where a long-term relationship had been established with their birth mother. This finding suggests that parent-child relationships established during childhood have an enduring quality. Children's experiences of being nurtured by caregivers create strong socioemotional bonds that continue into adulthood. Children raised continuously by their parents also have a shared history, class, and culture. These elements favor the continuation of a long-term relationship and go some way toward explaining the postreunion bias toward maintaining a primary relationship with one's adoptive family.

Arguments in favor of nurture are not necessarily incompatible with those that recognize the role that nature might play in people's reunion experiences. The need to have a sense of genealogical and genetic connectedness appears strong. It is part of the drive that motivates people to search. Who do I look like? Where do I come from? Who am I like in terms of temperament and interests, skills and outlook? But, although these needs trigger people to search and seek contact, they do not necessarily imply the desire for a relationship. They are information-led; they are designed to meet autobiographical and identity needs.

However, once the birth relative is met, nature may bring other factors into play. If the adopted person looks like the birth relative or shares a number of emotional, intellectual, and temperamental interests, there may well be a strong mutual attraction (including sexual attraction, in some cases) (for example, see Goldstein and Rosenfield, 1969; Leonard, 1975; Bentler and Newcomb, 1978; Fein-

gold, 1988). Child and birth parent may find that they get on well together. This provides the possible basis for a long-term relationship. The restored relationship does not necessarily invalidate or dilute the affectional bonds formed with the adoptive parents. This might explain why more than half of adopted people eight years or more after their initial reunion were still in touch with both their adoptive and birth mothers. On the other hand, if the adoption experience has been poor and there is a desire for another filial relationship, feelings of attraction and relatedness between birth parent and child, whether physical or psychological, are likely to increase the chances of the relationship surviving over the long term.

Finally, in those cases where there are no strong feelings of attraction and closeness or a desire for another filial relationship, contact with the birth mother typically peters out. The reunion has helped the adopted person meet identity needs but once they have been met, there is nothing, other than the blood tie to sustain the relationship. Thus, although genetic similarities might produce psychologically similar people who find that they get on, it is not the genetic link itself (the tie of blood) that sustains the relationship but the two personalities involved, each the result of a complex interplay between the individual's genes and psychosocial history (Plomin, 1994). It is personalities that get on, clash, or fail to ignite, not genes. Genes and their contributory effect on personality simply increase the likelihood of two genetically related people having personality traits in common which might, in some cases, increase their chances of forming and sustaining a relationship (Loehlin, 1992; Plomin et al., 1997).

The findings of the present study add weight to the mounting evidence that the affectional bonds formed in childhood (nurture) are strong and long-lasting, that most adopted people have a need to feel a sense of genetic/genealogical connectedness that of itself does not imply a desire for another filial relationship, and that these two observations are neither incompatible nor pull the adopted individual in different directions in terms of filial ties. These findings suggest that nature and nurture are probably interacting in ways that are more complex than implied by many evolutionary psychologists. They argue that parents who are genetically related to their offspring are likely to have a greater interest in their children's development and survival than those who are genetically unrelated. For example, Cronin and Curry (2000, p. 12) write, "A wealth of evidence shows that, on average, stepparents and children view the relationship as less loving and less dependable emotionally and materially. A step-parent in the home is the single most powerful risk factor for severe child maltreatment. They add, "To the blind forces of natural selection, altruism towards kin is just one way of replicating genes: help those who share your genes and you help the genes." Or turned around, stepparents are less likely to invest emotional and psychological resources in the upbringing of their stepchildren (Daly and Wilson, 1998).

Adoption and its well-documented outcome successes, particularly baby adoptions, do not square easily with these ideas. The robust and enduring quality of the relationship between adopted children and adoptive parents compared to birth parents and adopted children on the face of it appears to run counter to those who argue that the more powerful socioemotional investments and ties are between those who are genetically related.

However, there need not be a disagreement between the two positions. Affectional bonds formed in childhood, themselves the product of evolutionary-based reflex behaviors, result in children forming strong attachments with their primary caregivers that increase their protection and chances of survival (Bowlby, 1969; Cassidy, 1999). Our arguments favor a more dynamic, interactive relationship between genes and environment, nature and nurture, biology and culture (also see Howe, 1998). We feel that a genetic, evolutionary perspective is a powerful one in all adoption studies, but that adoption outcomes also help us understand the vital, albeit complex and subtle role that environmental and caregiving experiences play in behavior and development.

The study was supported by a grant from The Nuffield Foundation. We are extremely grateful for the time and commitment of our colleagues at The Children's Society Post Adoption and Care Team, Peckham, London, who helped in both the collection of data and its interpretation. And finally we should like to thank the many hundreds of adopted people who participated in the study and allowed us an insight into their lives and experiences.

References

Auth, P. J. and Zaret, S. (1986) The search in adoption: A service and a process. *A Social Casework, 67,* pp. 560–8.

Bentler, P. M. and Newcomb, M. D. (1978) Longitudinal study of marital success and failure. *Journal of Consulting and Clinical Psychology, 46,* pp. 1053–70.

Bertocci, D. and Schechter, M. D. (1991) Adopted adults perception of their need to search: Implications for clinical practice. *Smith Collection of Studies of Social Work,* 61(2), pp. 179–96.

Boult, B. (1992) The complexity of adult adoptees' needs to search for their origins: Research finding. *Social work, 28*(1), pp. 13–18.

Bowlby, J. (1969) *Attachment.* London, Hogarth Press.

Campbell, L., Silverman, P., and Patti, P. (1991) Reunions between adoptees and birth parents: The adoptees' experience. *Social Work, 3,* pp. 26–33.

Cassidy, J. (1999) The nature of the child's ties, in Cassidy, J. and Shaver, P. (eds.), *Handbook of Attachment.* New York, Guilford Press.

Cowell, J., Crow, K. and Wilson, A. (1996) *Understanding Reunion: Connection and Complexity.* New South Wales, Post Adoption Resource Centre.

Cronin, H. and Curry, O. (2000) Pity poor men. *Guardian, 5* February, p. 12.

Daly, M. and Wilson, M. (1998) *The Truth about Cinderella: A Darwinian View of Parental Love.* London, Weidenfeld and Nicolson.

Depp, C. H. (1982) After reunion: Perceptions of adult adoptees, adoptive parents and birth parents. *Child Welfare, 61,* pp. 115–19.

Feast, J., Marwood, M., Seabrook, S. and Webb, E. (1998) *Preparing for Reunion: Experiences from the Adoption Circle.* London, The Children's Society.

Feingold, A. (1988) Matching for attractiveness in romantic partners and same-sex friends: A metanalysis and theoretical critique. *Psychological Bulletin, 104,* pp. 226–35.

Gladstone, J. and Westhues, A. (1998) Adoption reunions: A new side to intergenerational family relationships. *Family Relations, 47,* pp. 177–84.

Goldstein, J. W. and Rosenfield, H. M. (1969) Insecurity and preference for persons similar to oneself. *Journal of Personality, 37,* pp. 253–68.

Gonyo, B. and Watson, K. W. (1988) Searching in adoption. *Public Welfare,* Winter, pp. 14–22.

Grotevant, H. (1997) Coming to terms with adoption: The construction of identity from adolescence into adulthood. *Adoption Quarterly, 1,*(1), pp. 3–27.

Howe, D. (1998) *Patterns of Adoption: Nature, Nurture and Psychosocial Development.* Oxford, Blackwell Science.

Howe, D. and Feast, J. (2000) *Adoption, Search and Reunion: The Long Term Experience of*

Adopted Adults. London, The Children's Society.

Iredale, S. (1997) *Reunions: True Stories of Adoptees' Meetings with Their Birth Parents*. London, The Stationery Office.

Leonard, R. L. (1975) Self-concept and attraction for similar and dissimilar others. *Journal of Personality and Social Psychology, 31*, pp. 926–29.

Lifton, B. J. (1983) *Journey of the Adopted Person*. Oxford, Basic Books.

Loehlin, J. (1992) *Genes and Environment in Personality Development*. Newbury Park, CA, Sage.

March, K. (1995) Perception of adoption as a social stigma: Motivation for search and reunion. *Journal of Marriage and the Family, 57*, pp. 653–60.

McMillan, R. and Irving, G. (1994) *Heart of Reunion: Some Experiences of Reunion in Scotland*. Essex, Barnado's.

Pacheco, F. and Eme, R. (1993) An outcome study of the reunion between adoptees and biological parents. *Child Welfare, 72*, pp. 53–64.

Parish, A. and Cotton, P. (1989) *Original Thoughts: The View of Adult Adoptees and Birth Families Following Renewed Contact*. Essex, Barnado's.

Plomin, R. (1994) *Genetics and Experience: The Interplay between Nature and Nurture*. Newbury Park, CA, Sage.

Plomin, R., DeFries, J., McClearn, G. and Rutter, M. (eds.) (1997) *Behavioral Genetics*. New York, W.H. Freeman.

Sachdev, P. (1992) Adoption reunion and after: A study of the search process and experience of adoptees. *Child Welfare, 71*, pp. 53–68.

Sorosky, A., Baran, A. and Pannor, R. (1974) The reunion of adoptees and birth relatives. *Journal of Youth and Adolescence, 3*(3), pp. 195–206.

KAREN MARCH
CHARLENE MIALL

13

Adoption as a Family Form

Adoption creates a family that, in important ways, differs from the traditional biologically related nuclear family. As a family form, adoption, according to Bartholet (1993), "creates a family that is *connected* to another family, the birth family, and often to different cultures and to different racial, ethnic, and national groups as well" (p. 186). Adoption as a family form is also an institution in transition. The trend toward more openness in adoption, the increase in international, interracial, and special needs adoption, and the rising number of stepparent, single parent, and gay-lesbian adoptive families has generated an awareness that current perspectives on how adoption is conceptualized and how adoption practice is approached need to be reexamined. Although we have come a long way since Kirk's (1964) groundbreaking study of adoptive parenting and his "acknowledge of difference" paradigm, we still place adoptive families within the purview of welfare services, designating this family type as a special case in need of *rehabilitation* and *social reform*. This placement is generated, to some extent, by the needs of adoptive family members themselves as they respond to the special conditions involved in constructing their families. It is also maintained, in our opinion, by a cultural bias toward the primacy of the blood bond and the predominance of blood ties as the basis for family formation. From this perspective, our involvement with adoptive families has tended to inadvertently stigmatize them as a problematic family form in need of specialized intervention. In this special edition of *Family Relations*, we examine these assumptions and approach adoption as a family form that is neither better than the biologically based family nor inherently inferior. To do so, we employ an interdisciplinary perspective, drawing on research from the disciplines of anthropology, psychology, social policy, social work, and sociology.

Many of the issues discussed in the October 2000 issue center on topics such as child development, family cohesion, parent-child relationships, and emotional stability in families. These topics are relevant to all types of families in our society, not just those involved in the adoption process. Thus, Priel et al.'s examination of self-reflectiveness among adoptive mothers and how it impacts on their assessments of their children is also relevant to non-adoptive mothers. Glidden's identification of factors that contribute to successful long-term placement of children with disabilities can assist practitioners who work with biologically based families dealing with the same issues. On the other hand, we cannot ignore the unique aspects of adoption. Such consideration requires a fine balancing act that acknowledges the inherently positive aspects of adoption as a family form yet attempts to identify how intervention can take place effectively if and when problems arise. This balancing act, which is maintained by viewing the adoptive family as one particular family form among many, serves as a guide toward a stronger understanding of family issues and family practice in general, while at the same time increasing our particular knowledge of adoption.

Content and Organization of the Issue

This issue is divided into four major topic areas which consider (1) the social context of adoption,

(2) adjustment and adoption outcome, (3) openness in adoption, and (4) transitions in adoption services. The headings have been chosen to reflect the more salient themes in the adoption research, practitioner, and social policy literature, but the topics presented in each section overlap considerably. For example, although the article by Fravel and her coresearchers examines the impact of openness for birth mothers, it also discusses adoptive family relationships, adoptive identity, and social agency. Similarly, the Borders et al. article on the current functioning of adult adoptees considers social work agency contact and adoptees' perceptions of community acceptance. To further this understanding of the overlap and continuity of themes presented in this special edition, we provide a summary of the four topic sections below.

The Social Context of Adoption

Traditionally in North American culture, the blood bond has served as the basis for the creation and continuation of family kinship systems. Consequently, there has been a tendency in the clinical, research, and social policy literature to view adoption as pathological by starting with the assumption that adoptive family ties are "second best" and adoptive children are "second choice" (Bartholet, 1993; Kirk, 1964, 1981; Miall, 1996, 1989; Model, 1994). Both adoptive parents (Miall, 1987, 1989) and adult adoptees (March, 1995) have revealed their sense of being socially stigmatized by others who question the strength of their adoptive family ties. Birth parents have also experienced considerable self-doubt and personal loss for placing their children for adoption with nonrelatives (March, 1997; Weinberg & Murphy, 1988). Any journal edition focusing on adoption as family form must, therefore, consider the symbolic meaning of "blood" as a way of assessing family structure, family membership, and personal identity. Although we cannot resolve the question of what should constitute kinship in one or two articles, this topic is central to understanding the future of adoption practice and our continued support of adoption triad members.

Thus, the articles presented in this section highlight the pervasive impact of the cultural distinction between biological and adoptive kinship. The first article by Wegar describes how community attitudes toward adoption, illegitimacy, and infertility have been integrated as part of social policy, adoption research, and social work practice. She counsels us to recognize how our own focus on "negative" versus "positive" adoption outcomes contributes to the sense of social stigma experienced by adoptive families, who must continually confront their secondary status as nonbiologically related family members. Offering alternate visions of family relations taken from other cultures, Wegar's analysis sensitizes us to our own personal and professional biases in approaching adoption as inherently problematic and leads us into a discussion of how we can assist adoptive families in meeting cultural challenges to their family form.

Lebner's article on adoption and the biomedical boom discusses how an increasing emphasis on *geneticization*, that is, the determination of genetic antecedents to illness, disease, and behavior, create further problems for how adoptive families view themselves in a cultural context. Lebner identifies concerns adoptive parents have about the unknown genetic/medical histories of their internationally adopted children. In particular, she documents their sense of being incomplete parents because they cannot safeguard their children's future health with genetic knowledge. While acknowledging the potential usefulness of genetic technology, Lebner challenges the "inevitability" of genetic inheritance independent of environmental considerations, and directs practitioners to understand and address these limitations as part of the support functions offered adoptive families with limited genetic information on their children.

Grotevant and his coresearchers consider this theme further in their analysis of adoptive identity in adolescents. The authors isolate three different contexts affecting identity development: the intrapsychic, the family environment, and the external social environment, which includes friends, community connections, and culture. Their examination reveals a noticeable variation in adolescent responses to adoption that fall along a continuum ranging from an obsession with achieving birth family contact to little or no interest at all in the subject. None of these responses is considered pathological. Rather, the authors argue that each represents a possible way of integrating adoption as a part of identity. Adopted individuals possess a wide spectrum of personality traits and social characteristics that influence their perception of adoption. For this reason, Grotevant et al. caution us to avoid a uniform approach to adoptive families and urge us to keep these contexts in mind when developing intervention strategies, designing programs, and creating social policy.

Adjustment and Adoption Outcome

The authors in this section build on the theme of social context in their focus on adjustment and adoption outcome. What similarities and differences exist between adoptive and biological families? Does the lack of a biological connection affect family functioning, parent-child bonding, and psychosocial adjustment? If so, what special needs do these adoptive families have and how can we, as practitioners, provide them with adequate and timely assistance? What background characteristics create an effective match? How might we avoid the possibility of a future family breakdown? Answering such questions is crucial, given our inordinate responsibility for placing the children under our care in safe family environments. In the process, the authors in this section direct our attention, not only to potential difficulties within adoptive families, but to the resiliency such families exhibit.

Priel and her coauthors begin the process of investigating these factors in their study of the role that maternal self-reflectiveness plays in adjustment among adopted children in Israel. Contrasting adoptive and nonadoptive mothers' reports on their children's behavior and their responses to a Parental Awareness Assessment interview, these authors reveal a pattern in which adoptive mothers in their study were likely to assess their children's adjustment more positively but their own mothering more negatively than were nonadoptive mothers. Noting society's stigmatizing attitude toward adoption and adoptive parenthood as a possible source of the difficulties that these women experienced in accepting themselves as mothers, Priel et al. recommend making adoptive parents more aware of how this social context may affect their assessments of themselves as parents.

Glidden examines the special case of adopting children with developmental disabilities and also bases her assessment of long-term adjustment and adoption outcome on mothers' perception of children's behavior. Like Priel et al., she finds these mothers report high rates of satisfaction with their decision to adopt and with their children's developmental progress. However, Glidden also notes that these adoptive families draw on a variety of parenting skills, interpersonal abilities, and social characteristics to cope with the difficulties involved in raising a developmentally disabled child. The only predictive factors for poor adjustment are single parenting, mother's initial depression at the time of adoption, and the child's level of functioning. Although cautioning us to watch for these factors, Glidden recommends taking a more flexible attitude in the implementation of policy and placement decisions for these adoptive families. Her recommendations include the consideration of a wider range of potential adoptive family types, and a pos-

sible regard for placing multiple children with disabilities in the same family environment, if its unique characteristics suggest it.

Borders and her coresearchers contribute to our knowledge of adoption outcome by comparing the current functioning and psychosocial well-being of adult adoptees in midlife and their friends. The results of this study suggest that, while adoptees at midlife may face the additional challenges created by a lack of biological kinship ties (e.g., missing medical background), their overall adjustment is similar to that reported by their friends of a comparable age. Notably, the data in this study reveal a greater distinction within the group of adopted respondents than between adoptees and nonadoptees. Search status accounts for much of this variability. Searchers tend to demonstrate lower self-esteem scores, higher rates of depression, and less marital and friendship satisfaction than nonsearchers. Furthermore, those adoptees desiring more biological background information express stronger emotions of anger, frustration, and a sense of powerlessness over their lack of access to this key aspect of self. Borders and her colleagues speculate that these differences between adopted adults may be affected more by seachers' inability to reconnect with their biological ties than adoption outcome per se.

Openness in Adoption

More than anything else, the issue of adoptee–birth family contact has had a consequential impact on the changing face of adoption today. By challenging the previous practice of closure, searching adoptees have increased our understanding of the social construction of identity and altered our view of the significance of genetic and genealogical background for perception of self (March, 1995; Pacheco & Eme, 1993; Sachdev, 1989, 1992; Wegar, 1997). This understanding has led to the development of more open adoption arrangements involving some type of contact between adoptive and birth family members (Berry, 1991, 1993; Daly & Sobol, 1993; Grotevant & McRoy, 1998). Moreover, the topic of adoptee–birth family contact captures many of the implicit issues involved in the biological/social construction of family. As such, open adoptions present a significant area of interest for educators, adoption researchers, family practitioners, and social policy makers.

Sobol, Daly, and Kelloway summarize the research literature on openness in the first article in this section which examines paths to the facilitation of open adoption. They also report on their own study of practitioner attitudes toward contact between adoptive and birth family members. The results of their study provide support for a model in which practitioners are viewed as playing a major role in facilitating contact decisions. Specifically, the less rigid social workers are toward considering placement with particular types of adoptive parents and the more accepting they are of the birth mothers' right to be involved in the adoption decision-making process, the more likely they are to effect open adoption arrangements. These findings are significant in light of our new knowledge about the positive effects for many of birth family contact on adoptive identity and adoptive family relationships (Berry, 1991; Grotevant & McCroy, 1998). As mediators in the adoption process, we should be aware that our own perspectives on openness can impact, perhaps inappropriately, the kinds of decisions potential adoptive parents make about the form their family should take. Limiting options provided to birth parents and adoptive parents may, in fact, hinder open adoption arrangements that might work effectively and successfully for the parents and children involved.

The movement toward more openness has created another developmental task for adoptive parents, birth parents, and adoptees, who must clarify their respective family roles, rights, and responsibilities. Drawing from a sample of 163 birth mothers, Fravel and her coresearchers explore the concept of positive or negative psychological presence, that is, how and to what extent adopted children remain in their birth mother's consciousness, when the adoption engaged in is confidential, mediated, or fully disclosed. The authors conclude that a more positive psychological presence of the child occurs for birth mothers in fully disclosed adoptions. However, it is not markedly negative in other levels of openness. Further, the authors note that, regardless of type of placement, birth mothers do not appear to forget their adopted children. In this respect, Fravel and her colleagues advise practitioners working with these women to help them acknowledge their thoughts about the adopted child as normal and appropriate, and not a sign of some inherent "failure" to adjust to the placement of their children.

Notably, this study highlights the boundary ambiguity existing for birth mothers engaged in some type of contact arrangement. There is no socially institutionalized role for the birth mother in the adopted child's life and no guidance as to how the two should interact. Consequently, the birth mothers in this study express considerable self-doubt and confusion over how they should respond to the adopted child, the child's adoptive parents, or others who might question their contact arrangements. Social workers, adoption professionals, and family educators can address these complexities by helping adoption triad members to establish more effective contact roles which do not depend on biological assumptions about the nature of "real" families and "real" parents.

The issue of openness is further examined by Frasch and her colleagues who present a long-term follow-up study of foster family adoption. Specifically, the authors examine adoptive mothers' assessments of contact between their adopted children and their birth families. Significantly, in this sample the strongest predictor of contact continuation is the type of contact decision made at the beginning of placement. Adoptive mothers who hesitate over birth family contact still maintain their commitment to this relationship, while adoptive mothers who had originally decided on non-contact rarely establish it at a later date. Not surprisingly, contact between biological siblings and other birth relatives tends to occur more often than with biological parents who may have played a major role in the child's foster placement. These findings may reassure adoptive parents and birth parents that their original contact agreements are likely to be maintained. However, they also indicate a stronger need for preadoption counseling highlighting all contact options. Provided with this information, potential adopters and birth family members can make a more informed choice about what option may be best for them both presently and in the future.

Transitions in Adoption Services

Traditionally, adoption was conceptualized as the placement of healthy, White infants with middle-class, infertile couples. Yet social services agencies are placing increasing numbers of older children, mixed-race children, sibling groups, and children with a wide range of physical, emotional, and social needs (Avery, 1997; Groze, 1996; Kramer & Houston, 1998). These placements have altered the profile of potential adoptive families such that single parents, older couples, families with biological children, and former foster parents are now considered. Traditional helping strategies may no longer address the realities of these "nontraditional" adoptive families who may need more postadoption services than before, and for different reasons. Moreover, the decline in the number of "adoptable" infants has increased the demand for more transracial and intercountry adoptions

(Bagley, Young, & Scully, 1993; Westhues & Cohen, 1995). In this section, three articles address these transitions in policy and practice through a focus on postadoption services, social policy barriers to international adoption, and the recruitment of gay and lesbian couples as potential adoptive parents.

Barth and Miller, in their evaluation of current postadoption services, note that the majority of adopters rarely return for assistance. The authors identify, however, three basic categories of postadoption requests that do arise when adopters seek support: (1) educational and informational, (2) clinical, and (3) material aid. Those families with special needs children, transracial, and intercountry adopted children frequently ask for more complex, long-term support than "traditional" adoptive families. Thus, Barth and Miller believe that the dominance of attachment theory as an approach for guiding postadoption services no longer applies. The multiplicity of factors involved in the construction of adoptive families demands consideration of other issues such as the adoptive parents' access to preadoption information, the prenatal alcohol exposure of children, previous foster care placement, length of time of adoption, and the child's age when first presenting symptoms. Such issues, these authors argue, are addressed more effectively through multisystemic family therapy approaches and assertive community treatments that view adoptions in a family context, refrain from blaming adoptive parents, consider child development issues, and honor the child's past.

McGuinness and Pallansch address some of the issues identified by Barth and Miller as impacting on postadoption services. Based on the reports of mothers who had adopted children from the former Soviet Union, the authors use a multiple regression model to examine child competence. That model reveals length of time spent in an orphanage as the factor having the strongest negative impact on adopted children's competence. However, low birth weight and the presence of fetal alcohol effects also appear as significant risk factors. In contrast, the authors note that the adoptive family environments were generally positive and accepting. These mothers did not have excessive expectations of their children, often perceiving their developmental difficulties and negative behavior as a result of preadoption factors rather than poor adoption outcome. McGuinness and Pallansch draw attention to the future challenges emerging for these types of families and the need for greater preparation for adoptive families beforehand and more education on the potential problems for children adopted from the former Soviet Union.

Many of us have identified similar risks with international adoption as those outlined by McGuinness and Pallansch in our own practice and clinical experience. This recognition has produced considerable controversy over whether we should become involved in creating this family form. Hayes addresses one effect of this controversy in his article on barriers to intercountry adoption in Britain. Some social work agencies in that country are delaying the preadoption assessment process as a way of discouraging what they perceive to be problematic intercountry adoptions. Potential adopters are therefore seeking alternative, unauthorized ways of bringing children into the country. Hayes explores the structural and ideological components giving rise to unauthorized international adoption and proposes changes in social work attitudes and social policy procedures for international adoption in general. As such, he reminds us of how our own attitudes may affect our ultimate goal of helping all types of family members who come to us for assistance.

Conclusion

We have attempted, through this special edition on adoption, to draw attention to the traditional assumptions that have shaped our understanding of adoption and to provide information on the transitions in adoption that are challenging these assumptions. As part of this provision of information, various authors have directed clinicians and researchers to consider their own preconceptions and how these shape policy, practice, and the assessments made about adoptive family forms. Thus, various articles have considered how the social context impacts adoptive families, how social work preconceptions shape the kinds of open adoption alternatives offered to potential clients, how post-adoption services are structured, and how potential adoptive parents are evaluated. Assessments of adjustment to adoption have been made with adoptive mothers, birth mothers, adoptees in midlife, and internationally adopted children. In addition, other authors have examined alternative adoptive family forms, focusing on international adoption, adoption of children with long-term disabilities, foster parent adoption, and open adoption arrangements.

According to Bartholet (1993) adoption, in many if not most cases, arises out of loss which, like all tragedies, holds "the potential for transformation and rebirth" (pp. 44–45). Yet a focus on the potential negatives of adoption, based on preconceptions about the importance of the biological tie, has cast adoption as a problematic family form rather than the successful alternative family form that it is. The limiting of adoption in terms of its openness because of preconceptions about how adoptive families should be and the exclusion of individuals because of social attributes deemed personally to be undesirable may ultimately work against the best interest of the children in our care, who, more than anything, need stable, loving, committed parent(s) regardless of the form their families take.

As a parenting option, adoption separates the biological from the social nurturing part of parenting. As such, it shares features with stepparent families formed through divorce and remarriage and same-sex couples where one parent may be biologically related to the children. In particular, families formed through reproductive technologies involving donors share many features with adoptive families. The continued strength and viability of the adoptive family, particularly as it moves away from a proprietary focus on the ownership of children and the secrecy that accompanies it, offers us a prototype for establishing effective intervention and support for these other contractual family forms, if and when the need arises.

To conclude as we began, adoption creates a family that, in important ways, differs from the traditional biologically related nuclear family. As a family form, adoption "creates a family that is *connected* to another family, the birth family, and often to different cultures and to different racial, ethnic, and national groups as well. Adoptive families might teach us something about the value for families of connection with the larger community" (Bartholet, 1993, p. 186).

References

Avery, R. (1997). *Adoption policy and special needs children.* Newport: Auburn House.

Bagey, C., Young, L., & Scully, A. (1993). *International and transracial adoptions: A mental health perspective.* Aldershot, U.K.: Avebury.

Bartholet, E. (1993). *Family bonds: Adoption and the practice of parenting.* New York: Houghton Mifflin.

Berry, M. (1991). The effects of open adoption on biological and adoptive parents and the children: The arguments and the evidence. *Child Welfare, 70,* 637–651.

Berry, M. (1993). Adoptive parents' perceptions of, and comfort with, open adoption. *Child Welfare, 72,* 321–353.

Daly, K., & Sobol, M. (1993). *Adoption in Canada.* Guelph: University of Guelph Press.

Grotevant, H. D., & McRoy, R. G. (1998). *Openness in adoption: Exploring family connections.* Thousand Oaks, CA: Sage.

Groze, V. (1996). *Successful adoptive families.* Westport, CT: Praeger.

Kirk, D. (1964). *Shared fate: A theory and method of adoptive relationships.* Washington: Ben-Simon Publications.

Kirk, D. (1981). *Adoptive kinship.* Toronto: Butterworths.

Kramer, L., & Houston, D. (1998). Supporting families as they adopt children with special needs. *Family Relations, 47,* 423–432.

March, K. (1995). *The stranger who bore me: Adoptee-birth mother relationships.* Toronto: University of Toronto Press.

March, K. (1997). The dilemma of adoption reunion: Establishing open communication between adoptees and their birth mothers. *Family Relations, 46,* 99–105.

Miall, C. (1986). The stigma of involuntary childlessness. *Social Problems, 33,* 268–282.

Miall, C. (1987). The stigma of adoptive parent status: Perceptions of community attitudes toward adoption and the experience of informal sanctioning. *Family Relations 36,* 34–39.

Miall, C. (1989). Authenticity and the disclosure of the information preserve: The case of adoptive parenthood. *Qualitative Sociology 12,* 279–302.

Miall, C. (1996). The social construction of adoption: Clinical and community perspectives. *Family Relations, 45,* 309–317.

Modell, J. S. (1994). *Kinship with strangers: Adoption and interpretations of kinship in American culture.* Berkeley: University of California Press.

Pacheco, F., & Eme, R. (1993). An outcome study of the reunion between adoptees and biological parents. *Child Welfare, 72,* 53–64.

Sachdev, P. (1989). *Unlocking the adoption files.* Toronto: Lexington Books.

Sachdev, P. (1992). Adoption reunion and after: A study of the search process and experience of adoptees. *Child Welfare, 71,* 53–68.

Wegar, K. (1997). *Adoption, identity and Kinship: The debate over sealed birth records.* New Haven: Yale University Press.

Weinreb, M., & Murphy, B. (1988). The birth mother: A feminist perspective for the helping professional. *Women and Therapy, 7,* 23–36.

Westhues, A., & Cohen, J. (1995). Intercountry adoption in Canada: Predictors of well-being. Pp. 266–279 in J. Hudson, & Galaway (Eds.), *Child welfare in Canada: Research and policy implications.* Toronto: Thompson Educational Publishing.

KATE WILSON
IAN SINCLAIR
IAN GIBBS

14

The Trouble with Foster Care: The Impact of Stressful "Events" on Foster Carers

At any one time, around 6 out of 10 of the children looked after by local authorities are placed with foster carers (Department of Health, 1997). Although the number of foster children (currently around 33,000) has remained fairly constant (Berridge, 1997), they constitute a proportion of those in the care system that has roughly doubled since the 1970s. So it seems likely that foster carers are having to cope with more troubled and more challenging children (Warren, 1997), at the same time as they negotiate the treacherous waters between the Scylla of family needs and rights and the Charybdis of child protection. Such strains may lead foster carers to leave fostering or to switch from caring for a local authority to the allegedly better supported independent foster care sector (James, 1995).

Despite its growth and the strains upon it, fostering remains a cheap service in comparison with residential care and one that has received comparatively little research attention. Generally, the service is seen as low status and undertrained, and there has been concern about the effects on foster carers of fostering breakdowns and allegations of sexual abuse (see summaries in Sellick and Thoburn, 1996; Berridge, 1997). There is, however, a lack of large-scale, recent studies of these strains. The purpose of this article is to report some findings from the first stags of a longitudinal study involving a large sample of foster carers—the linchpin on which the service depends—and, in particular, to consider the difficult experiences they encounter in the course of fostering, and the rela-

tionship between these and the carers' mental health and intentions to continue fostering. These questions are obviously preliminary to exploring the vital issue of how it is that so many foster carers are able to survive such stresses and what kind of support enables them to do so. We will report findings on these issues separately. In the meantime, we think it important to document the importance and apparent impact of one set of stresses to which foster carers are exposed.

The difficult experiences, or "events," we have in mind are those such as allegations of abuse or fostering disruptions which constitute a definite and serious episode in a carer's fostering career. Most of these build up over a period so that the word "event" is not intended to imply too rigid a boundary in time. Moreover, events are clearly not the sole causes of stress in foster care. Daily "hassles"— the unfriendly comments of neighbors, the problems of transporting different children to different places, the need to provide reports—and numerous other undramatic but wearing experiences may also place a strain on the foster carer. Nevertheless, there are a number of more clear-cut events or episodes that might be expected to have a considerable impact. So it is important to explore how common they are, what they mean to foster carers, and what their consequences seem to be.

Our research covered six events in particular. The events were selected on the basis of the existing literature, which has highlighted certain kinds of difficulties as having a notably discouraging impact on the foster carers who experience them. The literature is particularly concerned with disruptions and allegations, and hence with the relationship between foster carer and child. However, relationships between the foster carer and the social services department, those within the foster family, and those between the foster family and the birth family are also important (see Sellick and Thoburn, 1996; Berridge, 1997). We therefore included events that would be likely to affect all these relationships and that might for this reason have an impact on the foster carer's mental health (by which we mean, sense of well-being rather than psychiatric status) and attitude to fostering. We list the six events below, together with the reasons for selecting them.

Breakdowns or disruption: These were defined by Berridge and Cleaver (1987) as "a placement ending that was not included in the social work plan either in the ending itself or the timing of the termination." A major concern about foster care has been the instability of many of the placements. Qualitative work by Aldgate and Hawley (1986) suggests that these are often highly stressful.

Allegations: The National Foster Care Association (NFCA) suggests that roughly one in six foster carers will experience a complaint or an allegation in the course of their fostering career (Wheal, 1995). There is evidence that the incidence of complaints is growing (Coffin, 1993), and the greater public awareness of child abuse and, arguably, the greater attention to what parents and children are saying would seem to increase the likelihood of allegations being made. There is evidence that foster carers find the experience and the accompanying investigations highly distressing (Hicks and Nixon, 1989).

Relationship with birth parents: Early research suggested that foster carers often had little contact with birth parents and that such contacts as they had were rarely sources of difficulty to them (Rowe et al., 1984; Berridge and Cleaver, 1987). Indeed, concern about the lack of involvement and contact between birth parents and their "looked after" children contributed to many reforms in the Children Act 1989, and to the emphasis on working in partnership in the guidance accompanying the legislation (Department of Health, 1991b) and in *Working Together* (Department of Health, 1991a). We do not know the extent to which the situation has changed since the implementation of the Act (although it is reasonable to suppose that contact may have increased), nor the extent of the difficulties that may ensue if there is greater involvement. There is evidence from Scotland (Triseliotis, personal communication) that, in a significant minority of cases, foster carers are finding contacts with birth parents difficult. This may in some cases reflect the foster carers' own attitudes toward contacts, which are known to vary (Triseliotis, 1989).

Family tensions: The extent and persistence of difficult behavior among foster children, and the adverse effects that fostering may in consequence have on foster families, have been described in a number of studies (Aldgate and Hawley, 1986; Baxter, 1989). One of the recurring and best validated findings of foster care research is that break down is more likely where the foster carers are looking after their own children as well as foster children (see, for example, Thoburn, 1996; Berridge, 1997). It seems likely that the reason has to do with family tensions and conceivable that these may also involve spouses. Thoburn and her colleagues (1986) list a strong marriage or partnership as a factor leading to successful foster care.

"Tug of love" cases: Disagreements with social services departments over where children should live make the headlines in national newspapers but have not been the subject of research. They can be seen, perhaps, as the most dramatic example of the tensions that arise between the expectations of social services that foster carers do not compete with birth parents when the latter wish to resume care, and the feeling that foster carers may naturally have for the children. As such, they are likely to be highly stressful.

Other disagreements with social services: It seems reasonable to suppose that as the task of fostering becomes more complex and more fraught (a likely result of the changes introduced by the Children Act, 1989) the relationships between foster carers and social workers will become even more vital to the process, but also more prone to tension and disagreement. Social services may disagree with foster carers over a wide range of issues, for example, over the way the carers discipline or bring up the foster child. Such disagreements may involve matters that are central to the foster carers' definition of themselves as caring and competent people, and, potentially, might be seen as highly stressful. Again, they do not seem to have been the subject of research.

As will be seen from the above, varying amounts are known about these various events, and that which is known may or may not now apply as the legislation and guidance have moved things on. The immediate objectives of this paper are to address this problem in three ways. First, we describe the frequency with which a large sample of foster carers have experienced these problems in the course of their fostering career and, as a subsidiary objective, the degree to which this frequency varies with length of time fostering and type of foster care provided. Second, we try to say something about the nature of these experiences by describing them in the foster carers' own words. Third, we examine their impact by looking at their association with a measure of strain, with the foster carers' satisfaction with fostering, and with their intention to carry on with fostering.

Method

The Study

The data have been taken from an ongoing study of the support given to foster carers and its effects on them and on the outcomes for foster children. The study is funded by the Department of Health.

The Authorities

The study is being carried out in seven authorities selected to provide social and organizational diversity and to be reasonably accessible to the research team. Two are London boroughs (one inner, one outer), two are urban unitary authorities, one is a metropolitan borough with a rural hinterland, and the remaining two are large and diverse shire counties. Three of the authorities have sizable ethnic minority populations, a fact that is reflected in the ethnic composition of their foster carers.

The Sample

The sample consisted of all those foster carers registered with the seven authorities, with two exceptions: child minders who had been registered as foster carers only so that they could look after the children overnight if necessary were excluded, as were a small number of foster carers where the local authority had requested us to do so because it was taking disciplinary proceedings against them. The potential sample after these exclusions was 1,528.

Response Rate

The overall response rate was 61%. This is respectable by the standards of postal questionnaires but is less important in itself than whether the sample is biased, in the sense that some carers are more likely to respond than others. The authorities completed a brief pro forma on each carer in the sam-

ple, covering the factors we thought likely to influence response. The main variables that were related to response were: local authority (from a low 35% in a London borough to a high of 71% in a shire county), whether the carer was active (65% as against 45% where the carer was not fostering or not expected to do so again), age of eldest foster child (from 75% where the child was aged under 2 to 58% where the young person was 16 or more), and whether the carer had other paid work (58% where this was so, to 65% where it was not). In addition, carers who were said to describe themselves as not of British origin were significantly less likely to respond (44% against 65%). This association was partly, but not wholly, explained by the fact that the majority of these carers were in the London boroughs, where the response rate was relatively low among all respondents.

We discuss the potential impact of these biases in our conclusion, although there seems no a priori reason why they should unduly affect the results. As can be seen from the totals, response rates varied slightly by question. The data were analyzed on a mainframe computer using SPSS for Unix, release 6.2 (see SPSS Inc., 1988).

Results

How Many Foster Carers Had Experienced an "Event"?

The foster carers were asked whether they had experienced a number of "special difficulties" since they began fostering. Table 14.1 gives the proportion who responded in each category.

As can be seen, the most common event (experienced by nearly half the carers) was a breakdown or disruption. In addition, nearly a third said they had experienced severe family tensions because of a difficult foster placement, and nearly a quarter said that they had had severe difficulties with birth parents. At the other end of the scale, removal of a foster child against their strong advice was reported by less than one in seven.

The likelihood of an event naturally increases with the number of foster placements and the length of time during which a respondent has been fostering. The relevant data are set out in Table 14.2.

It is striking that almost exactly a third of those who had been fostering for a year or less had already experienced at least one event. The likelihood that those who have not previously experienced an event will experience one in a subsequent year must be somewhat less than this (otherwise, at least 80%

Table 14.1 Proportion of Foster Carers Reporting "Events"

Have Previously Experienced	n	% of total
Removal of foster child against your strong advice	125	13
Allegation by child (e.g., of abuse)	149	16
Other strong disagreement with social services over plans for child	182	19
Severe difficulties with birth parents	229	24
Severe family tensions because of difficult foster placement	290	31
Breakdown or disruption of placement	439	47
At least one of above	617	65
Total	944	

Note: As some foster carers had experienced more than one event, the total is greater than 100%.

would have experienced an event within four years). Nevertheless, more than three-quarters of foster carers with five or more years experience had had at least one of these upsetting events. In a similar way the likelihood that a foster carer would experience at least one event increased from 42% among those who had fostered no more than four children to 82% among those who had fostered 15 or more.

As can be seen from Tables 14.3 and 14.4, the likelihood that a foster carer would have experienced an event varied with the type of foster care provided.

Although these differences are highly significant, a number of them were explained by association between the type of foster cae and the length of time for which the foster carer had been caring and the number of foster children they had taken. Relatives, for example, had typically been caring for a shorter time and taken fewer children than other foster carers. We tested the relevant associations in two ways, looking first at whether the carer had experienced an event using logistic regression, and

then at the mean number of events per event category using multiple regression. Both analyses were consistent in showing that only the age of the oldest first child was significantly associated with our dependent variable after the number of previous foster children had been taken into account ($p = .05$ and $p < .0001$), a fact that adds weight to the generally held view that older foster children are more difficult than younger ones.

The Meaning of Events

We placed these events in context by asking the foster carers to comment on their experience of them. We first "trawled" all the questionnaires where an event was ticked in order to gain an understanding of what was involved, identified the main themes, and selected quotations that seemed to represent them. The replies made it clear that one event often involved others. For example, a difficult foster child might lead both to family tensions and to a disruption. The multifaceted nature of many events is brought out by the quotations given below. In

Table 14.2 Foster Carers Reporting at Least One "Event" by Time Fostering

Time Fostering	Percentage Reporting at Least One Event Row Total	
	n	%
Less than 1 year	114	30
1–2 years	101	47
3–5 years	203	72
6–11 years	264	74
12 years and more	188	81
Total	870	66

Chi square for Mantel-Haenszel test for linear association $\chi^2 = 112.24$, df = 1, p < .00001

Table 14.3 Mainstream, Relative, and Respite Carers by Experience of "Events"

	Row total	No event (%)	At least One Event (%)
Relative carer only	59	66	34
Respite carer only	290	41	59
Both relative and respite carer	13	62	38
Neither relative nor respite carer	589	28	72

$\chi^2 = 45.66$, df = 3, p < .00001

grouping the quotations, we have followed the classification which the carers implied by their ticks on our questionnaire (e.g., if they ticked "disruption" but included a description of family tensions we have reported this under the head of disruption).

The comments on *placement breakdown* support Aldgate and Hawley's study (1986) in suggesting that the impact is both distressing to the carer in itself and also because it is often the culmination of a long series of stressful events. An experienced carer from one of the unitary authorities who had suffered four of these disruptions described her sense of failure thus:

Hate breakdowns. I feel a failure. Could I have offered more?

This may be compounded by a sense of isolation from other sources of support or ameliorated by their presence. The carer just quoted had experienced both:

We had a girl who just kept packing and finally ran off. We felt we did not have any support from social services until afterwards. Our link worker did come out straight away to reassure us as it comes as a shock.

Many of the comments convey the severity of the difficulties before the disruption and the feelings on the part of the carers of being stretched to breaking point before they have given up:

I have had two boys who had behavioural difficulties which affected our own grandchildren. We stood it all we could before we made the hard choice of having them removed.

Daily reports were given via telephone. One child became uncontrollable, verbally aggressive, not returning home and eventually I was kicked and punched in the face, this caused final breakdown.

Understandably, *severe family tensions* often led to the final breakdown of the placement. An experienced foster carer from one of the shire counties felt that her family had suffered as a result of the inappropriate placing with them of two very difficult children:

We had a troubled placement with two siblings who had been sexually abused. They were seriously disturbed and disruptive and badly affected our own children. We were not warned of any

Table 14.4 Age of Oldest Foster Child by Experience of "Event"

Age of Oldest Foster Child	Row Total	No 'Event' (%)	At Least One 'Event' (%)
Under 5	107	50	50
5–10	205	42	58
11 and over	455	27	73
Total	767	34	66

$\chi^2 = 29.32$, df = 2, p < .00001

history of abuse or of the children's behaviour. It was a great strain on our family and we asked to have the children moved after 4 weeks.

The family tensions that may arise in dealing with a difficult foster placement are clearly considerable and the comments offered described a whole range of such stresses. In one case, for example, it seems as if the carer chose fostering over her marriage:

> Fostering contributed to the breakdown of my marriage because fostering has become a way of life.

Other problems reflect the wear and tear of dealing with difficult foster children or the distress felt by other members of the family at the effect on the main foster carer:

> Tension caused mainly by lack of sleep and screaming of child.

> Sometimes my son and daughter get annoyed at the way the [foster children] treat me. This causes difficulty.

Although placements with relatives are often sought because they may be less disruptive for the child—a view supported by research (Rowe et al., 1984; Berridge and Cleaver, 1987) and guidance (Department of Health, 1991b)—some comments show that they are not immune to difficulties and may carry some particular stresses:

> I feel under lots of pressure because of the girls' parents. Basically because they are my family and it's hard to tell them how they make me feel.

> When my cousin whose children I'm fostering started making things difficult by being abusive the social worker did everything in resolving the problem by finding another contact place.

Difficulties with birth parents are obviously not confined to fostering by relatives, and, as we have seen, roughly a quarter reported them. Some of these difficulties had to do with handling aggressive or violent birth parents:

> Mother and current boy friend attended contact. Boy friend always drunk. Mother argumentative/aggressive, threatening.

> We have experienced threats of serious physical violence against us and this child from natural parents with previous convictions of serious violence including murder . . . In these circumstances where it is known that there is past serious violence we don't think it appropriate for natural families to know the name or address of the people caring for the child.

Such experiences could lead placements to disrupt:

> I have had four children removed for the same reason—violence [of birth parents] towards us.

A second common cause of complaint arose from the impact of the birth parents on the child:

> Two years ago we had a problem with a third foster child (boy). He was 12 years and had been with us two years. In that time we found because of very little access to his birth parents he was settled and happy. Until the SSD decided to allow him access to his parents' own home without our knowledge. He became aggressive and abusive towards myself and our other foster child.

Many of the children are far more disruptive after contact with birth parents. Sometimes the birth parents were seen as deliberately working against the foster carer:

> Brain washing the child that we are bad foster parents.

> Encouraged child to be naughty.

And there were complaints that social services gave precedence to the needs of the parents over those of the child:

> It seems that contact is agreed at weekends too readily and can be very disruptive to the child because they feel left out of things and it can stop certain things for the family.

> Social services are biased in favour of natural parents, however much damage they do their own children.

As indicated in our introduction, earlier research has demonstrated that allegations of abuse are not an uncommon experience for foster carers. The approximate numbers in our sample (138 or 16% of the total) were in keeping with the experience of the NFCA, but were heavily concentrated on allegations of physical abuse. It is unlikely that the only allegations were of this nature, and foster carers, even when exonerated, may have felt inhibited about describing allegations of sexual abuse:

> I was accused of hitting a child which later at a meeting she confessed that she was lying. I felt that I did not get hardly any support.

> Alleged to have smacked the younger child age 2. The three year old reported it. It was found untrue. Luckily I had taken them to the doctor's and he knew about the bruises so he could say I had not done it.

The overwhelming impression from the comments is that it was not so much the allegation itself, or the fact that social services had to investigate it, that was the worst aspect of the experience. Rather, it was the lack of information and exclusion from the proceedings and poor feedback concerning the conclusion that really seemed to rankle. Obviously, it is extremely difficult to make such enquiries sensitively, and, even if foster carers are kept informed, they may not find the situation very much more tolerable. Nevertheless, carers in our study felt that the pain could be reduced. One single female carer described her feelings about the way the allegation was handled thus:

> An allegation of physical abuse was made against me by a so-called professional. The allegation was totally unfounded and was probably self-inflicted by the child itself. I cannot describe the effect that such an allegation had on myself and my daughter. Whilst I accept that allegations must be taken seriously, I feel that official procedures were not followed in my case and I was left in the dark as to what was happening. No support was offered at all.

We also asked about times when a foster child had to be *moved against the carer's strong advice*. Such events were clearly a source of distress. The foster carers commented that plans for rehabilitation were adhered to, come what may, that children were returned to environments that had caused the trouble in the first place, and that their judgment had been vindicated by subsequent events:

> Father's behaviour was wrong with children and myself and social worker wanted children to stay in care but they still went home.

> On advice of guardian ad litem, girls were placed with aunty to live, hence in my opinion back in family unit whence they had been taken because of problems.

> Foster children went back to their natural parents. Within six weeks they were both back in care. We strongly disagreed with the social workers and said the placement would break down which it did and the children lost a placement with us.

Sometimes the removal was designed to relieve the pressure on the foster carer. One, for example, was given another placement because of the foster carer's serious illness. Nonetheless, the foster carer felt that the child's need for a stable placement should have been given greater weight. She commented that her own children had remained with her and went on.

> The middle child was placed in another foster home against our wishes and against advice. He eventually returned but he had learned a whole new way of life and I don't think he ever recovered.

A number of these conflicts seemed to involve issues around race. One white carer from one of the unitary authorities commented:

> One child we had was a quarter Asian and her mother wanted her to be placed with a white family. After six months with us it was decided she should go to a half Asian family. We were not at all happy with this as the child was very settled.

Another carer, also white, and this time from one of the London boroughs, also felt that issues of race had taken undue precedence over consideration of the child's other needs:

> Black child moved to black placement. No consideration given to child's feeling when he wanted to stay.

Finally, we asked parents about *other strong disagreements with social services*. The replies sometimes conveyed a feeling that they were not given appropriate status:

> Foster carers are second class citizens.

Foster carers are unimportant and their views are ignored.

Other comments focused more specifically on the way decisions were taken:

> After a placement breakdown, foster carers are shut out of planning.

> Continually upset by the children's social workers. Plans do not accord with day-to-day experience of actual child.

A number of comments focused on resources supplementary to the placement (e.g., psychiatric resources) or to lack of appropriate placements so that children had to stay longer than originally agreed or go to an inappropriate placement:

> Any difficulties we have experienced have usually arisen because child's social worker has tried to pressure us into extending placement after the agreed terms, even when the placement has been less than ideal match.

Carers' Feelings about Themselves and about Fostering

Given the traumatic nature of some of the events described above, it seemed important to see whether they were associated with a measure of strain exhibited by the carers and with their attitude to continuing fostering.

Foster carers were asked to complete a shortened (12-item) version of the General Health Questionnaire (GHQ) as a measure of sense of well-being. This was devised as a screening device identifying those who, on further investigation by a psychiatrist, would have a high probability of receiving a psychiatric diagnosis. The questionnaire included some "positive" questions—for example, "Have you recently felt you were playing a useful part in things?"—and also "negative" ones—for example, "Have you recently lost much sleep over worry?" Two methods of scoring are available. One counts the number of times a respondent says "less or much less than usual" for the positive questions and "more or much more than usual" for the negative questions. The other method scores the positive questions in the same way but counts "same as usual" as well as "more or much more than usual" for the negative ones. The second gives a more normal distribution, and we preferred it for this reason (see Golderg and Williams, 1988; Bowl-

ing, 1991). For ease of presentation we have divided the scores into three roughly equal groups.

We examined whether those who had experienced the events discussed above were more likely to show signs of being under strain than those who had not. Table 14.5 sets out the results. Two events (allegations and experience of removal) were not significantly associated with strain as tested by analysis of variance and reported in Table 14.5. However, they were significantly associated with it if a rather more sensitive analysis was used to compare the average score for those with an event with the average score for those without one (allegations, $t = 1.99$, df = 942, $p = .047$; contested removal (unequal variances), $t = 2.14$, df = 152.74, $p = .034$). The remaining events were all associated with strain at a high level of significance.

We next examined the association between events and attitudes to fostering. We asked foster carers to say how far they agreed with the statement that "we get a lot of satisfaction out of fostering." Foster carers responded less positively to this question if they had experienced an event and, in particular, if they had experienced a negative impact on their family or a disruption. We also asked them how often they had considered giving up fostering in the past. As can be seen (Table 14.6), all events except for the removal of a child against advice were significantly associated with the frequency with which a carer had thought of doing so. Taken together, the results for this question suggest that about 60% of our respondents had considered giving up fostering at some time in the past, a finding broadly in line with Gorin's (1997) recent study.

Finally, we asked them whether they intended to give up fostering in the future. Future intentions were less closely associated with the existence of events, and only in the case of family tensions was the association significant. One reason for this may have been the fact that many of the events had taken place at some time in the past. Among those who had started fostering in the past eighteen months, experience of an event was strongly associated with intentions to give up.

Before concluding, we should note some differences between foster carers from minority ethnic groups and the remainder. Ethnic minority foster carers (mainly black and Asian) did not differ from the others in the average length of time for which they had fostered or in the average number of events they experienced. They were, however, significantly less likely to report an event that affected family relationships. Their mental health as they reported it was also significantly better than that of

Table 14.5 Experience of "Events" and Symptoms of Strain

	Row Total	Low Strain (%)	Medium Strain (%)	High Strain (%)	Probability of difference
Severe difficulties with birth parents					
Yes	229	20	32	48	$\chi^2 = 15.49$
No	715	28	39	32	df = 1
					p = .00008
Severe family tensions					
Yes	290	18	37	46	$\chi^2 = 23.33$
No	654	30	38	32	df = 1
					p < .00001
Removal of foster child against strong advice					
Yes	125	22	33	45	$\chi^2 = 3.74$
No	819	27	38	35	df = 1
					p .053
Other strong disagreement with social services over plans					
Yes	182	15	37	47	$\chi^2 = 17.91$
No	762	29	38	34	df = 1
					p .0002
Disruption					
Yes	439	23	36	41	$\chi^2 = 9.57$
No	505	30	39	32	df = 1
					p .002
Allegation					
Yes	149	27	37	36	$\chi^2 = 201$
No	795	22	39	40	df = 1
					p .1559

Chi square for Mantel-Haenszel test for linear association.

the majority community, but this seemed to be a reflection of the rather lower number of events they reported: the difference was no longer significant when this number was taken into account. There was no difference between ethnic minority carers and others in the proportion saying that they had ever thought of giving up fostering. There was, however, some slight evidence that events had had a greater effect on the attitude toward fostering among the majority community carers than they had on that of ethnic minority carers, although this interaction was only just significant ($p = .04$). Taken as a whole, then, these findings give little ground for thinking that carers from ethnic minority communities are any less in need of support than others.

Conclusion

This article has concentrated on the negative events that may be experienced by foster carers. It would be wrong if, as a result, it gave an unbalanced impression of the joys and pains of fostering. Over-all, the foster carers were strongly positive about what they were doing. Forty-five percent strongly agreed, and a further 51% agreed, with the statement "We get a lot of satisfaction from fostering." Only 7% said they definitely intended to give up fostering in the next two years and, where they proposed to do so, this was not necessarily because they were dissatisfied with fostering. Only 18% of carers (fewer than one in five) said that fostering affected their current sense of well-being as we had tried to measure it, albeit they were much more likely than others to have experienced events. These positive findings parallel those of Dando and Minty (1987), who reported that three-quarters of their sample of foster carers felt that fostering had had a positive effect on their family.

That much acknowledged, it remains true that fostering is a job that intrudes into family life and that can produce acute distress. The events we have described can simultaneously assault carers' picture of themselves as a caring and effective person, destroy their sense of being supported by people they may have seen as colleagues in social services, and produce acute tensions among family members. In

Table 14.6 "Events" and an Intention of Giving Up Fostering in Next Two Years

Have You Ever Felt You Would Like to Give Up Fostering?

	Hardly Ever/Never (%)	Sometimes (%)	Very Often/Often (%)	Probability of Difference
Severe difficulties with birth parents				
Yes	41	40	19	$\chi^2 = 18.23$
No	53	37	9	df = 1
				p = .00002
Severe family tensions				
Yes	32	46	23	$\chi^2 = 74.07$
No	58	35	7	df = 1
				p < .00001
Removal of foster child against strong advice				
Yes	45	40	15	$\chi^2 = 2.25$
No	51	38	11	df = 1
				p = .1333
Other strong disagreement with social services over plans				
Yes	41	42	16	$\chi^2 = 8.59$
No	52	37	11	df = 1
				p = .0033
Disruption				
Yes	38	45	17	$\chi^2 = 49.77$
No	61	32	7	df = 1
				p < .00001
Allegation				
Yes	41	39	20	$\chi^2 = 10.92$
No	52	38	10	df = 1
				p = .0001

Chi square for Mantel-Haenszel test for linear association.

some cases, foster carers may feel they have a choice between damaging their own families and failing their foster children. And there are further difficulties which we have not discussed, problems with neighbors or tensions produced by the length of time courts take to come to a decision, to name but two. In such circumstances, the provision of effective support becomes a moral imperative, irrespective of any effect it may have on the recruitment, effectiveness, and retention of foster carers.

In analyzing these issues, this article provides support for a number of pervious findings. The distressing nature of disruptions has been documented by Aldgate and Hawley (1986) and Berridge and Cleaver (1987). Hicks and Nixon (1989) have already discussed the impact of allegations on foster carers and the way this can be exacerbated by social work practice. Other events have been less commonly discussed, and we hope it is useful to have evidence of their frequency and their apparent impact on mental health and attitude to fostering. We say "apparent impact" because causation may not be all one way: strain may lead to less skillful fos-

tering and so to events, as well as events leading to strain. Each of these events was experienced by a sizable minority of foster carers, and a third of those who had been fostering for less than a year had experienced at least one of them. So, too, had two-thirds of the whole sample.

In general, our analysis will have given a misleadingly low impression of the frequency of the events. Those experiencing these events would probably be more likely to stop fostering. They would thus be less likely to be identified in a study such as ours which looked at foster carers at a particular point in time and would be less likely to pick up foster carers who gave up quickly. It is likely that many people give up fostering after an allegation, even if exonerated. Moreover, the likelihood of responding to the questionnaire was related to the age of the eldest child fostered (the older the child, the less likely the response). As carers fostering older children are more likely to experience events, we may have slightly underestimated the number likely to do so. The other respects in which the sample was known to be biased—type of local authority, ethnicity of carer, other paid work, dormant or active carer—were not associated with the number of events experienced, after allowing for time fostering and number of children fostered.

In one respect, our findings seem somewhat at odd with earlier research. There has been little reported contact between birth parents and foster carers and little reported trouble either. In this regard, matters may have changed since the Children Act. As we have seen, a quarter of the foster carers reported that they had had difficulties in their relationship with birth families. They also frequently thought that the greater weight given to the views of birth parents or their involvement in the placement was responsible for the removal of children against foster carers' own strong advice, placement disruption, and, to a lesser extent, disagreements with social services over plans. We cannot comment on the wisdom or otherwise of these decisions. What is clear from the study is that close involvement with birth parents may expose foster carers to situations in which they feel physically threatened, and where they may believe that the best interests of the child are being sacrificed to what some perceive as dogma. Such a demanding professional role for foster carers carries with it implications for support, remuneration, the provision of information, and care in making practical arrangements (e.g., over where, in certain circumstances, foster children and birth parents should meet).

In conclusion, there is a wide spectrum of difficult experiences that may trouble foster carers. There is a need to look in detail at these events, to tease out what bothers various parties, and to consider ways in which good practice might address these difficulties—matters that we hope to explore in later stages of our research.

Thanks are due to our colleague, Dr. Nigel Rice, for reading and commencing on the statistics in this paper.

References

Aldgate, J. and Hawley, D. (1986) *Foster Home Breakdown*, London, British Agencies for Adoption and Fostering.

Baxter, S. (1989). *Fostering Breakdown: An Internal Study*, Belfast, Department of Health and Social Security (Northern Ireland).

Berridge, D. (1997). *Foster Care: A Research Review*, London, Stationery Office.

Berridge, D. and Cleaver, H. (1987) *Foster Home Breakdown*, Oxford, Blackwell.

Bowling, A. (1991) *Measuring Health: A Review of Quality of Life Measurement Scales*, Buckingham, Open University Press.

Coffin, G. (1993) *Changing Child Care: The Children Act 1989 and the Management of Change*, London, National Children's Bureau.

Dando, I. and Minty, B. (1987) What makes good foster parents? *British Journal of Social Work*, 17, pp. 383–400.

Department of Health (1991a) *Working Together under the Children Act 1989: A Guide to Arrangements for Inter Agency Co-operation for the Protection of Children Against Abuse*, London, HMSO.

Department of Health (1991b) *The Children Act 1989. Guidance and Regulations: Volume 3—Family Placements*, London, HMSO.

Department of Health (1997) *Children Looked After by Local Authorities. Year Ending March 31 1996*, London, Department of Health.

Goldberg, D. P. and Williams, P. (1988) *A User's Guide to the General Health Questionnaire*, Windsor, National Foundation for Educational Research.

Gorin, S. (1997). *Time to Listen? Views and Experiences of Family Placement*. Report No. 36. Portsmouth, Social Services Research and Information Unit, University of Portsmouth.

Hicks, C. and Nixon, S. (1989) Allegations of child abuse: Foster Carers as victims, *Foster Care*, 58, pp. 14–15.

James, G. (1995) *Independent Fostering Agencies Study*, London, Department of Health Social Services Inspectorate.

Rowe, J., Caine, M., Hamilton, M. and Keane, A. (1984) *Long Term Foster Care*, London, Batsford.

Sellick, C. and Thoburn, J. (1996) *What Works in Family Placement?* Ilford, Barnardos.

SPSS Inc. (1988) *SPSS-X User's Guide*, 3rd edition, Chicago.

Thoburn, J. (1996) Psychological parenting and child placement, in Howe, D. (ed.), *Attachment and Loss in Child and Family Social Work*, Aldershot, Avebury.

Thoburn, J., Murdoch, A. and O'Brien, A. (1986) *Permanence in Child Care*, Oxford, Blackwell.

Triseliotis, J. (1989) Foster care outcomes: A review of key research findings, *Adoption and Fostering*, 13, pp. 5–17.

Warren, D. (1997) *Foster Care in Crisis*, London, National Foster Care Association.

Wheal, A. (1995). *The Foster Carer's Handbook*, London, National Foster Care Association.

15

The Importance of Partners to Lesbians' Intergenerational Relationships

In describing family relationships, Bowenian theory delineates the need for balance between the life forces of individuality and togetherness (Kerr & Bowen, 1988). Practitioners of Bowenian family therapy use the term differentiation of self to describe how an individual establishes autonomy from his or her family members while also maintaining meaningful connections with them (Bowen, 1978). Problems arise when family members sublimate their own needs to avoid conflict, or distance themselves by emotionally cutting off from one another. In turn, unresolved emotional issues from problematic, family-of-origin relationships are often projected onto spouses, resulting in marital strain (Kerr & Bowen, 1988).

The available research sheds some light on the connection between intergenerational relationships and heterosexual marriage. Good relationships with parents (Lewis, 1989) as well as frequent intergenerational contact (Burger & Milardo, 1995) have been found to be associated with harmonious marital relations. On the other hand, parental disapproval may be associated with being distrustful, critical, and negative toward one's spouse (Driscoll, Davis, & Lipetz, 1972), can influence mate choice (Jedlicka, 1984), and may impede the progression of a relationship from dating to marriage (Leigh, 1982). Compared with those who had maintained relationships with their parents, adult children who were emotionally cut off from their parents were found to be less satisfied with their marriage (Dillard & Protinsky, 1985).

Some have postulated that coming out may be an important component of the differentiation pro-cess for lesbians (Iasenza, Colucci, & Rothberg, 1996; LaSala, 2000). Nevertheless, in applying Bowen theory and the aforementioned findings to the families of lesbians, one must consider how parents feel about their daughter's sexual orientation. On coming out, lesbians have been known to face parental reactions from guilt and disappointment to rejection, verbal threats, and even physical violence (D'Augelli, Hershberger, & Pilkington, 1998; "Results of Poll," 1989; Warshow, 1991). Whereas parent-child relationships have been found to improve with time following the initial disclosure, parental disapproval often persists (Beeler & DiProva, 1999; Ben-Ari, 1995; Bernstein, 1990; Cramer & Roach, 1988; Muller, 1987; Warshow, 1991). These findings suggest that parental attitudes toward a daughter's lesbianism are complex and warrant further study.

Not surprisingly, parental feelings may affect lesbians and their unions. For young lesbians, self-esteem and comfort with being gay have been found to be correlated with maternal acceptance (Floyd, Stein, Harter, Allison, & Nye, 1999; Savin-Williams, 1989a, 1989b). Among a sample of 124 coupled lesbians, relationship quality was found to be significantly associated with parental acceptance (Caron & Ulin, 1997). Conversely, parental negativity can have adverse affects on gay women and their relationships. Among a sample of 1,925 lesbians, Bradford, Ryan, and Rothblum (1994) discovered that difficulties with family was one of the top five problems listed by their respondents and the second most common reason for seeking mental health services. In a sample of 706 lesbian couples, women listed problems with relatives as the third greatest challenge to their relationships (Bryant & Demian, 1994). In a qualitative study of 20 partnered lesbians, 20% reported that their parents' disapproval adversely affected their relationships (Murphy, 1989).

The available clinical and empirical literature begins to explain the variety of ways coupled lesbians might cope with parental disapproval. From a Bowenian perspective, family therapists have described how some lesbians might react to parental disapproval by sublimating their own independence needs and prioritizing their relationship with their parents, resulting in conflict with their partner (Iasenza et al., 1996; Krestan & Bepko, 1980). Parental hostility also might lead lesbians to distance themselves from their family, which in turn could result in couple difficulties, as unsettled intergenerational problems get projected onto partners (LaSala, 2000). Kurdek and Schmitt (1987) compared samples of 79 heterosexual, 50 gay male, and 56 lesbian couples and discovered that, in contrast to heterosexuals, gay and lesbian couples were less likely to list family members as major sources of support. In a follow-up study, Kurdek (1988) found that emotional support from friends was more important than that of family to the relationship satisfaction and psychological well-being of gays and lesbians. These findings suggest that lesbians (and gay men) cope with family disapproval by finding alternative sources of support. However, it is also possible that they are disavowing the importance of family. Although it may be possible to compensate for a lack of closeness to one's family by cultivating supportive friendships, Bowenian theory would suggest that those who distance themselves from their parents and deny the importance of parental relationships may be prone to dysfunctional interactions with partners or friends who restimulate unresolved issues with parents (Kerr & Bowen, 1988). Most likely, it is desirable to have a network of good relationships that includes not only friends, but also family. Clearly, more research is needed to better understand how gay women cope with parental attitudes toward their lesbianism and relationships.

The purpose of this exploratory research was to develop new understandings that would add to the knowledge describing the intergenerational dynamics of coupled lesbians. More specific research questions included: How do coupled lesbians perceive their parents' feelings and opinions about their lesbianism? How do coupled lesbians respond to or cope with their parents' attitudes? What, if anything, helps lesbians and their parents maintain relationships that are meaningful and developmentally appropriate? I anticipated that the results of this study could suggest how to intervene with lesbians and their families sensitively and effectively.

Method

To obtain "thick descriptions" of lesbians' family dynamics in all of their complexity (Lincoln & Guba, 1985), qualitative methods were used.

Participants

The sample consisted of 40 self-identified lesbians in 20 couples. All of the women lived in the New York City metropolitan area; 17 couples resided in central and northern New Jersey; one couple lived in Brooklyn, another on Staten Island, and a third on Long Island. Thirty-five of the 40 women were non-Hispanic white, three were African American, and two were Latina. Household incomes ranged from $12,000 to $240,000 with a median of $80,000. The age range of the respondents was 26 to 49 years with a mean of 37 (SD = 5.10). The lengths of time couples were together ranged from one to 22 years with a mean of 6.5 (SD = 3.65). For the purpose of this study, *coming out* to parents was defined as explicitly telling a parent she was gay, and by this definition all but one woman had come out to at least one of her parents. The intervals from the coming-out disclosure to the time of the interview ranged from two to 27 years with a mean of 11 years (SD = 6.17).

Criteria

To be included in this study, both members of each couple had to agree to participate. The respondents needed to be living together and to have been in their relationship for at least one year. In addition, at the time of the interview both members of the couple needed to have at least one living parent.

Data Collection

A convenience sample was gathered (Fortune & Reid, 1998). Researchers have recommended that those who study lesbians recruit respondents from multiple sources to maximize the potential diversity of their samples (Institute of Medicine, 1999). An advertisement for this study was placed in a newsletter received by members of a gay/lesbian community center that serves central New Jersey. In addition, flyers were distributed at a dance for lesbians sponsored by this community center. This advertisement also was posted on a listserv subscribed to by lesbian and gay male graduate students, faculty, and alumni of a large public university in central New Jersey. To attract respondents who did not own computers, were not members of a gay organization, and were not affiliated with the university, an announcement was posted in restaurants and coffee shops in central New Jersey and New York City.

Potential participants contacted the interviewer by telephone or e-mail, at which time they were screened to determine if they met the study criteria. The primary reason for a couple not meeting the criteria was that one or both women's parents were deceased. Potential participants were told that their identities and responses would be kept confidential. In addition, each respondent was informed that she would be paid $20 for participating.

Only one couple canceled a scheduled interview appointment, stating that they did not have the time to participate. All others who scheduled an interview completed the study.

My assistant, a lesbian and first-year MSW student, and I, a gay man, collected data over a five-month period. I developed a standardized interview protocol of open-ended questions (Patton, 1990). Women were asked their perceptions of their parents' attitudes about their lesbianism, how their parents and in-laws felt about their partner relationships, and how their parents' and partner's parents' opinions affected their relationships. We took thorough notes during the interviews, which also were audiotaped.

I anticipated that members of a couple might disagree about the intergenerational effects on their relationship and that a participant might censor certain responses in the presence of her partner. Therefore, partners were interviewed privately in separate rooms of each couple's home.

Data Analysis

Coding of Data   Once we collected all the data, I read the quoted responses to a related set of questions. After reviewing the answers of eight to 10 interviewees, I was able to establish initial codes. Examples of these preliminary codes were as follows: parental shame, parental fear, parental guilt, parental support, assertive coping, partner encouraging, parental contact, partner acting as buffer, and partner helping to set boundaries. I sorted

quoted responses by code using word processing software. As coding of responses within and across targeted areas continued, it became apparent that several codes could be combined to form secondary or axial codes (Glaser, 1978). For example, partner encouraging contact and partner acting as a buffer could be combined into a broader code called partner facilitation.

Glaser (1978) defined memos as "the theorizing write-up of ideas about codes and their relationships as they strike the analyst while coding" (pp. 83–84). Toward the end of the coding process, I wrote memos to identify and elaborate emerging themes, such as the role of the partner in parental relationships. Memos also served as drafts of the Results section of this article.

Reliability   Several authors have described the benefits to data collection and analysis if the researchers and respondents share demographic and social similarities (Lofland & Lofland, 1984; Martin & Knox, 2000). Because we had common experiences and could speak the language of the gay culture, it was relatively easy to establish the necessary rapport to encourage participants to discuss these potentially painful areas of their lives. However, we ran the risk of allowing our views of gay life to bias our perceptions. To minimize this possibility, coded segments of the interview transcripts were reviewed regularly with gay and heterosexual clinical and research colleagues throughout data collection and analysis. As a result of these reviews, I revised several codes. For example, after some preliminary coding, I was alerted that I might have been bringing a bias to my analysis that might have led me to judge parents too dichotomously, categorizing them as either disapproving or supportive. I was advised to more thoroughly review the segments of the transcripts describing perceived parental reactions and, in doing so, I became aware of how most of the respondents saw their parents as having a complicated mix of feelings about their lesbianism.

The research assistant independently sorted written and tape-recorded data into key codes that emerged during the data analysis. Although codes were not changed as a result of these reliability checks, there were a few incidents when our sorting choices for a particular response did not agree. At these times we both reread entire transcripts of the interview in question and then discussed the responses. As a result several responses were recoded. The final overall agreement between her codes and mine was 92.3% with a range of 8 to 97% across key codes.

Findings

Shift in Parental Reactions

On coming out, lesbians are almost certain to face parental and in-law antipathy. This has been reported in earlier research (D'Augelli et al., 1989; "Results of Poll," 1989) and by the women of this study. Thirty-four of the women encountered disapproval on coming out to their parents, with 23 women experiencing hostile or rejecting reactions. However, as time passed, their parents' attitudes seemed to improve. Most of the respondents indicated that their parents' feelings at the time of the interviews were a blend of support and disapproval. When parents were negative, it was because they felt guilty, embarrassed, or ashamed of their daughter's lesbianism. Furthermore, participants reported that parents worried for their daughter's well-being, fearing that the respondents would grow old alone or that they would experience discrimination. Nevertheless, respondents stated that their parents like their partner and supported their relationship. As a matter of fact, besides feeling relieved about not having to hide their lesbianism, these women reported that the support and validation offered by their parents was a primary benefit of being out to them.

As stated by a 31-year-old respondent who had been out to her parents and also with her partner for five years: "They would say they like her but they'd rather me be married with children. My mother would say she's embarrassed. She's said this."

However, she reported that her parents included her partner in family events and that this benefited her relationship with her partner. Another respondent, who was 37, out to her parents for eight years, and currently in a three-year relationship, reported:

> My mother claims she is embarrassed in her natural surroundings. They're [mother and father] only open in her immediate family. . . . They're afraid of what others would think.

Nevertheless, this same respondent described how her father bought her a plane ticket so she could relocate to be with her lover. Also, she reported that her mother allowed her teenage sister to visit the couple overnight and she perceived this to be evidence that her parents had accepted her lesbianism. A 33-year-old respondent who had been out to her parents for nine years and was currently in a two-year relationship noticed that neither her mother nor her mother-in-law had told their extended families about their daughter's lesbianism. She believed this to mean they both were ashamed. Still, both sets of parents included both partners in family events. She reported: "Family is important to me, and being accepted as a couple helps by knowing we have our family to support us." Thus, although most of the women perceived their parents to be embarrassed about their lesbianism or worried for their well-being, their parents also demonstrated support for their relationships, and this support benefited their unions.

Parental Disapproval and Boundary Setting

The majority of women indicated that parental disapproval did not substantially affect their relationships. In all but two couples, there was at least one member who described how she protected the relationship from parental or in-law disapproval. In response to a minor incident, such as if a parent said something insensitive, couple members might ignore it or discuss it among themselves. However, when parents were perceived to be invalidating the relationship, the women responded assertively. For example, one respondent's mother wanted to visit her for an extended stay but requested that her daughter and her partner sleep separately for the duration of the visit. The interviewee adamantly refused, telling her mother, "This is our house and we'll do it by my rules."

Several women mentioned that a partner's assertively affirming the couple's relationship to her parents was seen as a sign of her love and commitment: "The fact that she took that stand with her parents showed me how much she cared for me."

For many of these women, their relationship with their partner catalyzed the developmentally appropriate restructuring of their intergenerational relationships. The following woman, who had been out for four years and with her current partner for one year, stated,

> They used to have expectations of me. They would expect I would stay with them on vacations and to come stay with them. Ever since I was with Fran, I don't do that anymore. They've adjusted to it. They accept I can't spend a lot of time with them.

After being out and with her partner for 13 years, this woman described what appeared to be a developmentally appropriate change in her relationship with her parents:

> It's become stronger. I'm not so much their "daughter" anymore as much as their adult friend. This is due to me being happy with Cheryl.

Some of the women gave examples of how their partners actively encouraged or helped them to set boundaries with their parents. A 41-year-old graduate student who had two children from her heterosexual marriage, and who was currently in a four-year relationship, recounted:

> Mom took pictures and made an album with no pictures of Marie. Marie and I talked about it and decided how we would deal with her. I wrote her a letter and told her I was offended.

In speaking of her parents' and her partner's parents' disapproval, she stated, "Our relationship is sealed against outside influences. Our primary commitment is absolutely to each other, and nobody fucks with that. If anybody tries . . . we deal with it." Early in their relationship, the following couple had argued because one of the women's parents insisted that the couple spend all of the holidays at their home. As stated by one of the women: "If we were a straight couple, her [partner's] family wouldn't mind her splitting the holidays with her in-laws."

At her urging, her partner asserted herself to her parents: "As I got older and when I realized Lisa was the one, I made it clear to them. That changed me. I will not allow anything to cause us problems."

Partner Facilitates Parental Relationships

The positive influence of partners went beyond merely providing a reason to set boundaries with parents. Anger or guilt in response to parental disapproval could potentially lead a gay woman to excessively distance and even cut off from her family of origin. However, 27 of the women reported that their relationship with their parents had improved since they had been with their partner, and 35 of the women described specific ways their partner facilitated parental relationships. This facilitation could simply be urging the partner to contact her parents: "She thinks I should go see my mother more than I do."

In addition, partners often acted in ways to buffer the problematic parental relationship. The following 33-year-old respondent pushed her partner of two years to "lighten up" on her own mother: "I am more tolerant of her mother. I feel she is very short with her at times. I have told her." In speaking about her relationship with her father, whom she described as homophobic, this 29-year-old woman stated:

> My father and I had a terrible relationship when I was a teenager. It's evolved since then because my father has worked really hard on it. Toni is a good buffer between us . . . she puts up with his irritability and temperament. She's very calm and patient with him and tries to get special things for him; bake him things. . . . [As a result] he's always asked about her feelings. He's including her in family finances. Now my relationship with him is good, loving, and supportive.

Another woman talked about how she convinced her partner to soften her position regarding her own mother:

> When Kathy and her mother and her sister have conflict, I try to explain Mom's point of view. I remind Kathy her mother is mourning [her heterosexual image of] her daughter, and I tell her to be more patient as she mourns.

She went on to say: "It makes me feel good that I can act as a buffer between Kathy and her mother."

For a 45-year-old respondent, her relationship with her partner helped her work through her anger at her mother for not protecting her from childhood sexual abuse perpetrated by her stepfather. For years, she and her mother were unable to speak without arguing about her childhood. When asked how her relationship with her parents had changed since she had been with her partner, she replied, "In a positive way. I am not as furious with her [mother]. Marge and I had a daddy-girl relationship, and I worked through my dad issues."

At times, a partner's actions could create some mild conflict, as it did for the following couple. One partner reported, "I keep telling her not to shout at her mother." And this was echoed in the responses of her partner who said, "If I say something nasty to my mother, she says: 'You can't say that to your mother!' I do the same." Even though she sometimes got slightly annoyed at her partner for seeming to take her mother's side, she conceded:

"I like the fact that my partner respects my mother."

Thus, on the basis of the reports of these respondents, it seems that a partner's encouragement and coaching might have prevented the distancing that would be expected between disapproving parents and their lesbian daughters.

Couple and Family-of-Origin Discord

Sometimes the partner's involvement resulted in conflict, particularly when parents were strongly disapproving of their daughter's lesbianism. In couples in which one woman had a profoundly negative relationship with her parents, pushing the partner to have more contact or to improve her relationship with her parents resulted in conflict. One respondent described how her partner urged her to have contact with her rejecting mother and how this created tension between them: "We argue weekly, she wants me to call my mother. I'll say no, and we go back and forth with that." Another described her partner's mother as very hostile, yet she implored her partner to call her mother:

> I think Julie's missing a lot, and I would like her to make an attempt [to contact her disapproving mother]. On Mother's Day I bug her all day to call her mother, and by the afternoon she does it. By the end of the call she is so upset, and she's saying, "Why do I subject myself to this?"

Thus, although pushing for contact and intergenerational harmony benefited most of the couples in this study, for women with the most negative parents, this action could strain the couple's relationship.

Discussion

According to Bowen (1978), individuals in functional families are intimately connected yet allow each other the autonomy to define or differentiate themselves and develop relationships with significant others. Because they are able to distinguish between thoughts and feelings, differentiated family members are able to disagree without letting their emotions interfere with their ability to negotiate and compromise. As a result, differing points of view can be tolerated without threatening family relationships (Kerr & Bowen, 1988).

Conversely, *fusion* describes the inability to separate thinking from feeling (Kerr & Bowen, 1988). The fused person is immersed in emotionality, as are her or his relationships, and is unable to understand accurately or tolerate the discomfort that arises when family members disagree. Attempting to control others through destructive arguments, distancing, or sublimating one's needs for the sake of harmony are ways family members undermine their own and each other's independence and maintain a fused homeostasis. Conceptually, fusion as defined by Bowen is not to be confused with the high levels of intimacy found in many lesbian relationships (Green, Bettinger, & Zacks, 1996). Fusion actually impedes intimacy; people struggling with fusion are so overwhelmed with their own anxiety and dependency needs that they are unable to recognize and attend to the needs of their partners.

Bowen (1978) and Kerr and Bowen (1988) believed that even the healthiest family's differentiation levels could diminish in a crisis, and the profoundly negative parental reactions experienced by the respondents on coming out suggest that such a regression may have occurred. However, despite their ongoing shame and worry about their daughter's lesbianism, many parents' attitudes improved to the extent that they were able to support their daughter's relationship. Maintaining connections despite differing points of view, as these parents did, is a hallmark of differentiation. In a related manner, lesbians who come out could be seeking to differentiate themselves because they are defining who they are and risking parental disapproval in the hopes of eventually establishing a more honest closeness. Asserting oneself when necessary, as did the women in this study, could be seen as one way a lesbian avoids the pitfalls of fusion and maintains appropriate intergenerational boundaries.

Boszorymenyi-Nagy and Spark (1973) claimed that for marriages to flourish individuals must place their relationship with their spouse ahead of that with their parents. However, it is reasonable to imagine that in the face of parental disapproval, gay women might hide or minimize the importance of their long-term partner relationship to maintain intergenerational peace. Such prioritization of parents would, in turn, be expected to lead to conflict in the partner relationship. However, for the women in this study, parental disapproval did not affect their relationship, thanks to their own boundary-setting behavior. In addition, the respondents' partners seemed to facilitate functional intergenerational relationships by helping the interviewees affirm appropriate intergenerational boundaries when parental hostility threatened to interfere with the partner relationship.

Furthermore, partners pushed respondents to maintain contact with family when, presumably, they perceived too much strain or distance between generations. For some women, their partner helped them see their parents in a more objective way. Thus, partners may have functioned in ways to minimize the potential for fusion and encourage healthy, intergenerational relating. According to Bowen (1978), *differentiation* describes an appropriate balance between connection and autonomy among family members, and the partner's support of not only protective intergenerational boundaries but also harmonious parental connections could be interpreted as efforts to help the respondents establish or maintain appropriate levels of differentiation.

The emergence of the women's partner as an important resource in the respondents' parental relationship was somewhat surprising considering that the literature on coming out to parents generally does not address how partners can help or hinder intergenerational relationships. In addition, according to Bowenian theory, a person's differentiation level is a product of past family relationships (Bowen, 1978; Kerr & Bowen, 19988). The findings from this study raise the possibility that a strong partner relationship might increase the basic level of differentiation and improve an individual's relationship with her parents. Certainly, this is an important topic for future research.

Fusion was evident in some of the respondents' parental and partner relationships. It seemed that parents who were continuously antagonistic were unable to put aside their own feelings to have a meaningful relationship with their daughter, and this suggests a lack of differentiation. Several of the women with hostile parents were emotionally distant or cut off from their families. However, their partner pushed them to relate to their parents, even when this seemed to hurt their relationship with each other. Bowen (1978) believed that fusion was transmitted across generations by the tendency of people to marry others whose low differentiation level matched their own. Some of the women from troubled families may have pushed their partner to the point of conflict because they were projecting their own unresolved issues with their parents onto their partner and in-laws. In addition, putting herself between her partner and her partner's hostile parents by arguing the parents' viewpoint could have given the troubled partner an outlet to express her anger without threatening the homeostasis of the problematic intergenerational relationship. In these circumstances, partner encouragement did not help parental relationships and actually strained partner relationships.

Additional research is needed to determine the relationships between parental disapproval, intergenerational discord, and relationship satisfaction for lesbian couples. In the meantime, social workers and other clinicians helping lesbians heal their relationship with their parents need to understand that whereas parental feelings and opinions about a daughter's lesbianism may improve from the initial disclosure, parental shame and worry can persist. Even if her parents never fully accept her sexual orientation, helping a lesbian client set intergenerational boundaries can assist her in maintaining healthy relationships with her parents and her partner. In addition, the often helpful but at times problematic role of the partner in encouraging intergenerational relationships found in this study suggests that social workers and family therapists need to assess carefully the partner's potential as a resource for their lesbian clients' parental relationships.

Caution should be taken in generalizing the findings from this small, mostly white sample. The family dynamics of lesbians of color may differ from those of their white counterparts. For example, Greene and Boyd-Franklin (1996) pointed out that for African Americans, the family serves an important protective function by buffering its members against the economic and psychological burdens of racism. As a result, an African American lesbian might be less willing to risk the family rejection that can occur if she chooses to live outside the closet. An African American respondent from this study decided to terminate her relationship in the face of intergenerational pressure, and perhaps her fear of losing this special, protective family support contributed to her decision.

Research findings suggest that Latinos, African Americans, and Asian Americans may be more reluctant to come out to their parents, fearing that the antigay sentiment in their cultures makes parental rejection likely (Chan, 1989; Merighi & Grimes, 2000; Tremble, Schneider, & Appathurai, 1989). Clearly, more information is needed regarding family issues that are unique to lesbians of various races and ethnicities.

These findings support and in some ways add to those of earlier studies (Ben-Ari, 1995; D'Augelli et al., 1998) that found that parental attitudes toward their daughter's lesbianism that were initially very negative seemed to improve as time passed from the initial disclosure. However, the qualitative methods used in this study helped add to this information by identifying the blend of perceived parental feelings that included shame, fear, and support. It should be noted that this was a study not of actual parents' attitudes but of their daughter's perceptions of those attitudes. Interviews with parents could better elicit their feelings and opinions about their gay daughter. The qualitative approach also was used in identifying what may be the important facilitative role of the partner in improving relationships with parents.

Researchers who study the issues and concerns of lesbians have called for more investigation of the effects of family relationships on lesbians' well-being (Institute of Medicine, 1999). Clearly, more quantitative and qualitative examination of how lesbians negotiate intergenerational family dynamics is needed to inform family scholars about this variant family form and to help social workers and other mental health professionals understand the distinct clinical needs of this understudied population.

References

Beeler, J., & DiProva, V. (1999). Family adjustment following disclosure of homosexuality by a member: Themes discerned in narrative accounts. *Journal of Marital and Family Therapy, 25,* 443–459.

Ben-Ari, A. (1995). The discovery that an offspring is gay: Parents', gay men's and lesbians' perspectives. *Journal of Homosexuality, 30,* 89–112.

Bernstein, B. (1990). Attitudes and issues of parents, gay men and lesbians and implications for therapy. *Journal of Gay & Lesbian Psychotherapy, 1,* 37–53.

Boszorymenyi-Nagy, I., & Spark, G. (1973). *Invisible loyalties: Reciprocity in intergenerational family therapy.* New York: Harper & Row.

Bowen, M. (1978). *Family therapy in clinical practice.* New York: Aronson.

Bradford, J., Ryan, C., & Rothblum, E. (1994). National lesbian health care survey: Implications for mental health care. *Journal of Consulting and Clinical Psychology, 62,* 228–242.

Bryant, A. S., & Demian. (1994). Relationship characteristics of American gays and lesbians: Findings from a national survey. *Journal of Gay & Lesbian Social Services, 1,* 101–117.

Burger, E., & Milardo, R. (1995). Marital interdependence and social networks. *Journal of Social and Personal Relationships, 12,* 403–415.

Caron, S. L., & Ulin, M. (1997). Closeting and the quality of lesbian relationships. *Families in Society, 78,* 413–419.

Chan, C. (1989). Issues of identity development among Asian-American lesbians and gay men. *Journal of Counseling and Development, 68,* 16–20.

Cramer, D., & Roach, A. (1988). Coming out to mom and dad: A study of gay males and their relationships with their parents. *Journal of Homosexuality, 15,* 79–91.

D'Augelli, A. R., Hershberger, S. L., & Pilkington, N. W. (1998). Lesbian, gay, and bisexual youth and their families: Disclosure of sexual orientation and its consequences. *American Journal of Orthopsychiatry, 68,* 361–371.

Dillard, C., & Protinsky, H. (1985). Emotional cutoff: A comparative analysis of clinical versus nonclinical populations. *International Journal of Family Psychiatry, 6,* 339–349.

Driscoll, R., Davis, K., & Lipetz, M. (1972). Parental interference and romantic love: The Romeo and Juliet effect. *Journal of Personality and Social Psychology, 24,* 1–10.

Floyd, F., Stein, T., Harter, T., Allison, A., & Nye, C. (1999). Gay, lesbian, and bisexual youths: Separation-individuation, parental attitudes, identity consolidation, and well-being. *Journal of Youth and Adolescence, 28,* 719–736.

Fortune, A. E., & Reid, W. J. (1998). *Research in social work* (3rd ed.). New York: Columbia University Press.

Glaser, B. G. (1978). *Theoretical sensitivity: Advances in the methodology of grounded theory.* Mill Valley, CA: Sociology Press.

Green, R. J., Bettinger, M., & Zacks, E. (1996). Are lesbian couples fused and gay male couples disengaged? Questioning gender stereotypes. In J. Laird & R. J. Green (Eds.), *Lesbians and gays in families: A handbook for therapists* (pp. 185–230). San Francisco: Jossey-Bass.

Greene, B., & Boyd-Franklin, N. (1996). African American lesbians: Issues in couples therapy. In J. Laird & R. J. Green (Eds.), *Lesbians and gays in families: A handbook for therapists* (pp. 251–271). San Francisco: Jossey-Bass.

Iasenza, P., Colucci, P., & Rothberg, B. (1996). Coming out and the mother-daughter bond: Two case examples. In J. Laird & R. J. Green (Eds.), *Lesbians and gays in families: A handbook for therapists* (pp. 123–136). San Francisco: Jossey-Bass.

Institute of Medicine. (1999). *Lesbian health: Current assessment and directions for the future.* Washington, DC: National Academy Press.

Jedlicka, D. (1984). Indirect parental influence on mate choice: A test of psychoanalytic theory. *Journal of Marriage and the Family, 46,* 65–70.

Kerr, M., & Bowen, M. (1988). *Family evaluation: An approach based on Bowen theory.* New York: Norton.

Krestan, J., & Bepko, C. (1980). The problem of fusion in the lesbian relationship. *Family Process, 19,* 277–289.

Kurdek, L. A. (1988). Perceived social support in gays and lesbians in cohabitating relationships. *Journal of Personality and Social Psychology, 54,* 504–509.

Kurdek, L. A., & Schmitt, J. P. (1987). Perceived emotional support from family and friends in members of homosexual, married and heterosexual cohabitating couples. *Journal of Homosexuality, 14,* 57–68.

LaSala, M. C. (2000). Lesbians, gay men and their parents: Family therapy for the coming-out crisis. *Family Process, 39,* 67–81.

Leigh, G. (1982). Kinship interaction over the family life span. *Journal of Marriage and the Family, 44,* 197–208.

Lewis, J. (1989). *The birth of the family: An empirical inquiry.* New York: Brunner/Mazel.

Lincoln, Y. S., & Guba, E. G. (1985). *Naturalistic inquiry.* Beverly Hills, CA: Sage Publications.

Lofland, J., & Lofland, L. (1984). *Analyzing social settings: A guide to qualitative observation and analysis.* Belmont, CA: Wadsworth.

Martin, J. I., & Knox, J. (2000). Methodological and ethical issues in research on lesbians and gay men. *Social Work Research, 24,* 51–59.

Merighi, J. R., & Grimes, M. D. (2000). Coming out to families in a multicultural context. *Families in Society, 81,* 32–41.

Muller, A. (1987). *Parents matter: Parents' relationships with lesbian daughters and gay sons.* Tallahassee, FL: Naiad Press.

Murphy, B. C. (1989). Lesbian couples and their parents: The effects of perceived parental attitudes on the couple. *Journal of Counseling & Development, 68,* 46–51.

Patton, M. Q. (1990). *Qualitative evaluation and research methods* (2nd ed.). Newbury Park, CA: Sage Publications.

Results of poll. (1989, June 6). *San Francisco Examiner,* p. A19.

Savin-Williams, R. (1989a). Coming out to parents and self-esteem among gay and lesbian youths. *Journal of Homosexuality, 18,* 1–35.

Savin-Williams, R. (1989b). Parental influences on the self-esteem of gay and lesbian youths: A reflected appraisals model. *Journal of Homosexuality, 17,* 93–109.

Tremble, B., Schneider, M., & Appathurai, C. (1989). Growing up gay or lesbian in a multicultural context. *Journal of Homosexuality, 17,* 253–267.

Warshow, J. (1991). How lesbian identity affects the mother/daughter relationship. In B. Sang, J. Warshow, & D. Smith (Eds.), *Lesbians at midlife: The creative transition* (pp. 81–83). San Francisco: Spinster Books.

16

The Evolution of Homoerotic Behavior in Humans

Evolutionary psychology is a fascinating new field. The evolutionary model has proven to be rich in heuristic value and has generated a wealth of academic dialogue (Buss, Haselton, Shackelford, Bleske, & Wakefield, 1998). The evolutionary explanation focuses on why a behavior exists. Contemporary advantages and disadvantages are considered largely irrelevant to the larger evolutionary question (Buss et al., 1998). Cosmides, Tooby, and Barkow (1992) have indicated that the examination of psychological mechanisms (e.g., homoeroticism) can be used to investigate the possibilities of adaptive function. A behavior may be considered adaptive if it can be demonstrated that during evolution the behavior may have solved an adaptive problem by contributing to reproduction either directly or indirectly (Buss et al., 1998; Tooby & Cosmides, 1992).

The most widely recognized evolutionary theory of homosexuality is that of E. O. Wilson (1975, 1978). The theory holds that homosexual individuals in early human societies may have helped close family members, either directly or indirectly, to reproduce more successfully. Thus, genes for homosexuality would have been passed on indirectly through relatives. The theory does not posit any direct or indirect adaptive value for homosexual behavior itself. Wilson's theory is based on a number of false assumptions (Dickemann, 1995), and there is no evidence to support it. Consequently, it has been largely rejected as an explanatory model (Muscarella, 1999).

Overall, the consensus within the field of evolutionary psychology is that homosexual behavior does not have adaptive value and consequently did not evolve (Archer, 1996; Buss, 1994; Futuyma & Risch, 1984; Gallup & Suarez, 1983; Margulis & Sagan, 1991; McKnight, 1997; Posner, 1992; Ridley, 1993; Seaborg, 1984; Stevens & Price, 1996; Symons, 1979; Thiessen, 1996; Wright, 1994). I have argued that this interpretation may be due to several factors: the negativity with which homosexuality is viewed, a false dichotomization of human sexuality (heterosexual and reproductive; homosexual and nonreproductive), and the use of unreliable terms like "gay" and "homosexual" in scientific writing (Muscarella, 1999). Moreover, an analysis of the evolutionary origins of any behavior is complex and requires consideration of a number of competing explanations (see Buss et al., 1998).

Based on earlier theorizing (Muscarella, 1999), and in sharp contrast to the traditional approach, this paper examines same-sex sexual behavior irrespective of sexual orientation and uses the term "homoerotic" to describe it. Homoerotic behavior is defined as same-sex sexual behavior involving genital contact that is experienced as pleasurable. The motivation of the behavior (e.g., sexual orientation, exploration, lack of opposite-sex partners) is not taken into account. The relation of behavior to sexual orientation will be discussed later in the paper. The term homosexual is used when the operational definition of homoerotic cannot be applied and when it is awkward to apply the term homoerotic to other writers' descriptions of same-sex sexual behavior.

It is assumed that human sexuality is not dichotomous. Thus, for most of the species for most of its evolutionary history, individuals would have exhibited both heteroerotic and homoerotic behavior, a characteristic seen in closely related non-human primates. In the remainder of the paper I will attempt to demonstrate how homoerotic behavior may have solved an adaptive problem during the course of human evolution.

The Proposed Model

It is posited that a specieswide disposition for homoerotic behavior in humans has evolved through natural selection because it had adaptive value. Specifically, it is speculated that hominid adolescents and young adults may have gone through a period of sex-segregated social and physical peripheralization similar to that found among many primates. A disposition to engage in homoerotic behavior may have served as a mechanism of affiliation which reinforced and strengthened the relationships among same-sex peripheralized hominids themselves and with higher-status conspecifics. The social assistance of peers and higher-status companions may have increased the likelihood of access to resources and may have provided allies to help ward off attacks from other conspecifics.

Consequently, a disposition to engage in homoerotic behavior, which is assumed to exist concurrently with a disposition for heteroerotic behavior, can be seen as having had direct effects upon survival and indirect effects upon reproductive success. Same-sex friendships, reinforced by erotic behavior, may have helped individuals of both sexes to attain personal survival. Further, the long-term social alliances formed in this way may have facilitated males' abilities to mate with females likely to conceive and females' abilities to successfully raise their offspring. The evolutionary hypothesis presented incorporates evidence from current evolutionary theory, primatology, cultural anthropology, and history.

The Adaptive Value and Evolution of Homoerotic Behavior

Human sexual behavior is considered to be the most complex and highly evolved of any animal species (Bancroft, 1989). It has been argued that among humans sexual behavior evolved primarily to promote bonding between males and females, which was secondarily related to reproductive success (Fisher, 1992; Lovejoy, 1981). Diamond (1992) writes, "In no species besides humans has the purpose of copulation become so unrelated to conception" (p. 78). It is speculated that complex and frequent sexual behavior promoted strong male-female bonds. When pregnancy did occur, the presence of a bonded parental pair increased the likelihood of the offspring's viability and the ultimate propagation of the parents' own genes. Because complex heterosexual behavior ultimately led to reproductive success, it was adaptive. De Waal (1987) argues that through the course of human evolution affiliative behavior between adult males and females may have increased the reproductive success for both, and that homosexual behavior then evolved from heterosexual behavior. However, it has also been argued that affiliative behaviors may have also been adaptive for other social units independent of mating units (Kinzey, 1987).

Hominid Life and the Adaptive Value of Homoerotic Behavior

The behavior of hominid ancestors is unknown, but the social behavior of other primates, particularly common chimpanzees (chimpanzees) and pygmy chimpanzees (bonobos) is often used as a model (e.g., Diamond, 1992; de Waal, 1996). It is speculated that early hominid ancestors lived in loosely affiliated groups of 50–60 individuals that included males, females, and their offspring. They may have survived by gathering plant stuffs, scavenging, and engaging in some cooperative hunting (Campbell, 1985; Wilson, 1975). Hominid ancestors lived in a threatening and dangerous world. They were probably more often prey than hunters (Susman, 1987) and probably engaged in frequent and fatal intergroup aggression (Diamond, 1992; van der Dennen, 1995; Wrangham 1987; Wrangham & Peterson, 1996).

In this threatening context, adolescence may have been a particularly dangerous age for hominids because adolescent primates tend to become socially and physically peripheralized. This leaves them in a highly vulnerable position, with an increased chance of mortality and limited reproductive opportunities (Pusey & Packer, 1987; Sapolsky, 1993). Peripheralization occurs among a number of nonhuman primate species (Pusey & Packer, 1987). These include rhesus macaques (Boelkins & Wilson, 1972) and baboons (Hall,

1965) as well as gorillas (Fossey, 1983), chimpanzees (de Waal, 1982; Tutin, 1979), and bonobos (Kuroda, 1979). The peripheralized adolescents and young adults no longer have the close attention and protection of their mothers, and they lack the maturity and social status to help ensure their own survival and reproduction. Depending upon the species, adolescents tend to be pushed to life on the periphery of their own natal group or that a foreign group to which they may have immigrated.

In view of the cross-species evidence, it is likely that adolescent hominids endured a period of peripheralization. Sexually maturing adolescent and young adult hominids must have been faced with two powerful selective pressures: basic physical survival and successful reproduction. Isolated and vulnerable adolescent hominids with restricted access to the opposite sex may would have benefited from the ability to affiliate with the same-sex conspecifics. The same-sex partners of both male and female hominid adolescents may have helped them to survive by providing access to food and protection from aggression. Further, the social alliances formed and reinforced through homoerotic behavior may have offered advantages for the particular and unique reproductive needs of each sex. The alliances of males may have helped them to move up the male social hierarchy and ultimately obtain mates. Females may have gained entry to the middle of the social group where the relative stability and assistance from female friends would have increased the chances of their offspring surviving. In the following sections, corroborating data from the areas of primatology, anthropology, and history are presented.

Nonhuman Primate Homosexual Behavior

Homosexual behavior in nonhuman primates has been inadequately studied, and its causes and functions are poorly understood (Hambright, 1995). Further, only some homosexual behavior can be accurately described as erotic. Consequently, its implications for homosexual behavior in humans remain unclear at this time (Hambright, 1995; Nadler, 1990; Wallen & Parsons, 1997). However, evidence of commonalities in the behavior of closely related species can give some insight into broad evolutionary trends (Hambright, 1995).

Vasey (1995) speculated that some aspects of primate homosexual behavior may have developed as an exaptation. That is, the behavior is not a di-

rect product of natural selection. Rather, it may have originated as a neutral variation which then demonstrated some fitness-enhancing quality. Consequently, there was selection for the behavior because of this quality which ultimately enhanced reproductive success. Vasey has suggested that natural selection may have begun to act upon homosexual behavior because it served a number of sociosexual roles that might have incidently increased reproductive success.

It is recognized that sexual behavior among nonhuman primates, as among humans, can serve functions other than direct reproduction (Hambright, 1995). One function may be related to the development and maintenance of affiliative bonds between the participants (Hambright, 1995; Nadler, 1990; Parish, 1994; Wallen & Parsons, 1997; Yamagiwa, 1978). In some cases it has been suggested that the homosexual behavior reinforces relationships which may contribute to individual survival and ultimate reproductive success (e.g., Akers & Conaway, 1979; Small, 1993; Vasey, 1995; Wrangham, 1976 cited in Crook, 1980; Yamagiwa, 1987) although this hypothesis has not been carefully and systematically studied (Hambright, 1995; Vasey, 1995; Weinrich, 1980). Nonetheless, there is ample evidence that nonhuman primates engage in homosexual behavior (some of which is clearly erotic) which coexists with heterosexual behavior and does not preclude reproduction (Akers & Conaway, 1979; Boelkins & Wilson, 1972; Carpenter, 1942; de Waal & Lansing, 1997; Ford & Beach, 1951; Fossey, 1983; Hall, 1965; Hambright, 1995; Harcourt, Stewart, & Fosey, 1981; Hess, 1973; Mori, 1979; Nadler, 1990; Small, 1993; Vasey, 1995; Wallen & Parsons, 1997; Wolfe, 1979, 1986; Yamagiwa, 1987).

Monkeys

Male homosexual behavior is particularly well-documented among baboons and rhesus monkeys. Baboon and rhesus groups contain a central core of dominant males surrounded by females. Subadult males are pushed to the outside of the group and are considered peripheralized (Mori, 1979; Pusey & Packer, 1987). Sexual behavior is very common among these peripheralized males and is not limited to dominance-submission displays (Hall, 1965; Mori, 1979; Wrangham, 1976 cited in Crook, 1980). Peripheralized baboon males form "friendships" which are characterized by mutual embracing, grooming, penis display and touching, masturbation, oral stimulation, and mounting

(Ford & Beach, 1951; Wrangham, 1976 cited in Crook, 1980). When there is a significant age difference between the two partners, the older partner may also provide the younger partner with social protection. It has been speculated that sexual activity among the peripheralized males may also indirectly contribute to reproductive success. The sexual activity may stimulate the production of testosterone and lead to collaborative male-male alliances, both of which increase the likelihood of gaining a harem (Wrangham, 1976 cited in Crook, 1980). Homosexual behavior among rhesus males occurs commonly (Carpenter, 19742; Ford & Beach, 1951; Goldfoot, Wallen, Neff, McBrair, & Goy, 1984; Southwick, Beg, & Siddiqui, 1965). Maturing young males change group membership, and they enter into new groups by forming an apparently affectional relationship with an established male who offers access to resources and social protection (Boelkins & Wilson, 1972).

Female-female sexual behavior has also been well-documented for rhesus monkeys and is considered an essential component of their complex social behavior (Akers & Conaway, 1979; Carpenter, 1942; Harlow, 1965). Akers and Conaway noted that females appeared to establish very strong and enduring affectional bonds of which the sexual behavior was only a part. The females sometimes formed consort pairs. Membership in such a pair, either homosexual or heterosexual, appeared to temporarily raise the dominance status of the subordinate animal, and the partner was often an ally in aggressive confrontations against other troop members (Akers & Conaway, 1979). It is recognized that female-female sexual behavior and consortships are also an integral part of the sexual repertoire of the Japanese macaque (Hanby, Robertson, & Phoenix, 1971; Wolfe, 1979, 1986).

The Great Apes

The great apes share a high degree of genetic relatedness to humans (Diamond, 1992), and their sociosexual behavior may provide especially important insights into the origins and functions of human sexual behavior (Graham, 1981). Same-sex sexual behavior has been documented among both captive and feral gorillas of both sexes. Hess (1973) reported male-male mounting in the presence of receptive females among captive gorillas. Yamagiwa (1987) reported a high level of male-male sexual behavior with ejaculation among a group of feral unrelated males. Further, he reported that this sexual behavior appeared to contribute to the high level of cohesiveness among group members and

that group living was advantageous to the younger males because it may have protected them from the dangers found within bisexual groups and traveling alone. Fossey (1983) reported that in the highly unusual case of a young blackback male immigrating to a new group, the resident silverback copulated with him frequently; meanwhile, he mated with the silverback's harem in his absence. Genital exploration and stimulation has been observed among both captive (Hess, 1973) and feral (Nadler, 1986) juvenile female gorillas as well as among adult feral females (Harcourt, Stewart, & Fossey, 1981).

Both chimpanzees and bonobos exhibit same-sex behavior, although it appears to be more developed and complex in the bonobos (Savage-Rumbaugh & Wilkerson, 1978). Grooming behavior, particularly in the anogenital areas, frequently causes erections in chimpanzee males of all ages (Taub, 1990). Adult male chimpanzees demonstrate the highest frequency of grooming among all age-sex classes (Simpson, 1973; Sugiyama, 1969), and grooming and appeasement frequently involve the fondling of the dominant male's scrotum by the subordinate male (de Waal, 1982; Goodall, 1965; Sugiyama, 1973). It has been theorized that the frequent and intense grooming that occurs between male chimpanzees reinforces their social bonds (de Wall, 1982) and that male coalitional alliances are associated with reproductive success (van der Dennen, 1995). Male-male sexual behavior among bonobos has been observed in all age combinations. It includes French kissing, oral-genital contact, genital massaging, dorso-ventral mounting, ventroventral mounting with penis rubbing, and rump-rump rubbing (de Waal, 1987, 1990; de Waal & Lansing, 1997; Kuroda, 1980; Linden, 1992; Savage-Rumbaugh & Wilkerson, 1978; Small, 1992; Thompson-Handler, Malenky, & Badrian, 1984).

Female bonobos frequently engage in genito-genital (GG) rubbing. This reinforces the social and coalitional bonds between them and results in increased social status (Parish, 1994). In some instances females have been observed to prefer GG rubbing to copulation with a willing male (Small, 1992). Adolescent females transfer out of their natal group at maturity and immigrate to groups where they have no social contacts. These young females quickly identify the most dominant females and initiate sexual contact with them. In this manner, they form "friendships" and alliances with established females that allow them to become integrated into the group and, more importantly, allow the access to food resources (de Waal & Lansing, 1997; Small, 1993).

Homoerotic Behavior among Humans

Among humans, homoerotic behavior exists concurrently with heteroerotic behavior, and exclusive homoerotic behavior is rare (Ford & Beach, 1951; Greenberg, 1988; Kinsey, Pomeroy, & Martin, 1948; Kinsey, Pomeroy, Martin, & Gebhard, 1953; McKnight, 1997; Posner, 1992). However, humans appear to be the only primates who exhibit exclusive homoerotic behavior (Hambright, 1995; Vasey, 1995). Homoerotic behavior in various forms has been recorded among a large number of the world's historical and contemporary peoples (e.g., Herdt, 1997; Ford & Beach, 1951; Greenberg, 1988), and its *absence* in a culture rather than its presence appears to be unusual. In a classic study, Ford and Beach found that some homoerotic behavior was accepted in 64% of the 76 cultures studied. However, this may actually be an underestimate. There has been much criticism of the anthropological study of homosexuality in the past, which was seen to be biased, uninspired, and plagued with theoretical and methodological problems (Blackwood, 1986a; Greenberg, 1988; Herdt, 1988, 1997; Williams, 1986).

Male Homoerotic Behavior

Vasey (1995) indicated that some hominid or protohominid individuals appear to have evolved the behavioral capacity to engage in excusive homosexual behavior and consort bonding by the late Miocene–early Pliocene era. There is evidence that human male homoerotic behavior has existed since prehistory (Taylor, 1996). There are extant paleolithic cave paintings dating back 17,000 years of men with erections and lines connecting them (Ross, 1973) which have been interpreted as representing men engaging in sexual behavior (Boswell, 1980; Greenberg, 1988). The culture of a group of Melanesians who practice ritualized homosexuality has been traced back 10,000 years (Herdt, 1981). Some Australian aborigines practice institutionalized homosexuality (Adam, 1986; Greenberg, 1988), and they are believed to be descended from a group of people who migrated to Australia 116,000 years ago (Fullagar, Price, & Head, 1996).

The world appears to have a long history of institutionalized homosexuality between higher-status and lower-status males, which usually, but not always, involves a significant age difference (Greenberg, 1988; Rind, 1998). Mackey (1990) presented data suggesting that humans evolved a mechanism of attraction between adolescents and same-sex adults. He states that among males this may serve the function of incorporating young males into all-male groups, which contributes to the survival of the group as well as the individual. These relationships tend to socialize the youths into the adult male role, nurture and protect the youths, and provide the basis for life-long friendships, social alliances, and consequent social status (Adam, 1986). Some authors have posited that erotic behavior (which may but does not necessarily include consummated sexual acts) is an important psychological factor in contemporary societies for bonding, alliance formation, and maintenance of dominance hierarchies in sports (Guttman, 1996), the military (Henningsen, 1961; Poundstone, 1993; Shilts, 1993), and fraternities (Wingate, 1994). It may be a vestige of the social use of direct sexual expression seen among early humans (cf. Rawson, 1973).

The degree of reproductive advantage associated with dominance status is being reevaluated for many species with advances in research technology (C. Hughes, 1998). However, L. Ellis (1995) reviewed the literature on dominance and reproductive success and found that among nonhuman primates higher-ranking males tend to have a slight but consistent lifetime reproductive advantage over the lowest-ranking males. The reproductive advantages of dominance status for male chimpanzees have been actively debated, but the advantages do appear to be significant in small groups (Nishida & Hiraiwa-Hasegawa, 1987). De Waal (1982) reported that among the chimpanzees he studied, dominant males did the majority of mating with the females most likely to conceive.

Social status, a reflection of political strength and alliances, appears to have played a large role in the evolutionary history of human male reproductive success. Wolpoff (1976) suggests that early hominid males were twice as large as females. Such sexual dimorphism in size suggests that early hominids were polygamous and that there was much intramale competition. It has been speculated that during the early period of human evolution males' sexual access to females was probably indirectly resolved through fighting for social rank (Fox, 1971; Zillman, 1984), which may account for prominent sexual dimorphism in facial hair and baldness among humans (Muscarella & Cunningham, 1996). Among human males, social status is a primary determinant of perceived attractiveness as a potential mate and is often associated with increased reproductive success because of more mating opportunities (Boone, 1986, 1988; Buss, 1989,

1992, 1994; B. Ellis, 1992; Hill, Nocks, & Gardner, 1987; Mealey, 1985; Symons, 1979).

Homoerotic behavior may have reinforced relationships that helped socially peripheralized lower-status hominid males climb the social hierarchy and ultimately increase their reproductive success. Van der Dennen (1995) suggests that human males, like chimpanzee males, evolved a coalitional reproductive strategy. Male chimpanzee coalitions are reinforced by grooming (de Waal, 1982), which is often sexually arousing (de Waal, 1982; Taub, 1990). Dominant male chimpanzees sometimes allow their closest allies (those who groom them the most) copulations with estrus females that are denied other males, and this has been interpreted as "sexual bargaining" (de Waal 1982). Considering that the average female chimpanzee produces only five viable offspring in her lifetime (Tutin, 1979), any behavior that increases a male chimpanzee's chance of fathering an infant can be interpreted as contributing to his fitness. It is speculated that hominid females, like human females throughout most of their history, had a reproductive rate similar to that of chimpanzees (Symons, 1979). Thus, the behavioral flexibility to engage in same sex sexual behavior, in the service of alliance formation and sexual bargaining, may have had the same adaptive value for male hominids that it appears to have for chimpanzees.

Churchill (1967) has argued that patterns of sexual behavior in nonhuman primates that lead only to arousal (e.g., that associated with grooming in chimpanzees) could be expected to lead to a consummated act in humans (and by implications close human ancestors) because of the increased complexity of their sociosexual behavior. Thus, an argument could be made that the sociosexual behavior associated with grooming, appeasement, and sexual bargaining was a preadaptation for a greater range of homoerotic behavior in hominids.

It has been suggested that there is a long history of human males seducing each other for both sexual pleasure and social gain (Boswell, 1980; Hinsch, 1990). Boswell states that historically, contrary to contemporary attitudes, younger, subordinate males as well as females have been acceptable objects of sexual interest for older, dominant males. History reveals that in a number of cultures the relationships between the older and younger males provided not only sexual pleasure but clear social advantages for the younger partners. The relationships often increased their social status, which allowed them to attract high-status mates for themselves and their relatives. Such was the case among the Chinese (Hinsch, 1990), Japanese (Hinsch,

1990; Ihara, 1972), Romans (Boswell, 1980, 1994), and Greeks (Cantarella, 1992; Dover, 1978). It has been suggested that Augustus Caesar as well as many other Roman and Byzantine emperors may have gained access to the throne partly through sexual relationships with their predecessors (Boswell, 1980, 1994).

The direct reproductive advantages of homoeroticism for males is described in one of the earliest works in Western literature, *The Iliad*, through the relationship of Achilles and Patroclus, which was commonly understood as being sexual in nature (Boswell, 1980). Patroclus is a low-status male who is peripheralized in a foreign group after fleeing his natal group to avoid punishment for a murder he committed. He enters into a high level of the social hierarchy as a result of his relationship with Achilles, one of the dominant males of the society. Secondarily, Patroclus has a large number of reproductive opportunities because Achilles gives him access to many of the female captives he himself is accorded due to his own high status.

In a number of societies the homoerotic relationships developed among socially peripheralized males who banded together for survival are evocative of the strategies hominid ancestors may have relied on themselves. Burg (1984) reports that transgenerational homosexuality was an essential part of the all-male society of pirates in past centuries, and the relationships and social alliances benefited both partners. Rocke (1996) indicates that in Renaissance Florence many of the powerful guilds and gangs to which lower-class men belonged appear to have derived their strength from the homoerotically reinforced relationships among the members. R. Hughes (1987) indicates that much sexual behavior and mutual support occurred between socially peripheralized and vulnerable British men sent to Australia as punishment for crimes. The survival and ultimate reproductive benefits of homoerotically reinforced alliances between socially peripheralized males and males with higher social status are also evidenced in reports of working-class England at the turn of the century (Gardiner, 1992), Australian Aborigines (Adam, 1986), tribes in Melanesia and Papua, New Guinea (Herdt, 1984; Schiefenhovel, 1990), and contemporary Thailand (Allyn, 1991).

Female Homoerotic Behavior

Homoerotic behavior among human females has been documented among both historical and contemporary peoples (Greenberg, 1988). These include the ancient Greeks and Romans (Cantarella,

1992), early Europeans (Boswell, 1980), the ancient Chinese (Hinsch, 1990), and numerous others (Blackwood, 1986b; Ford & Beach, 1951; Greenberg, 1988). Female-female sexual behavior among humans is considered less frequent than male-male sexual behavior (Kinsey et al., 1953; McKnight, 1997; Posner, 1992), but the true incidence is unknown and may be underestimated because of methodological and theoretical problems with anthropological research (Blackwood, 1986a; Greenberg, 1988). The historical incidence is also unknown because of the lack of literature and poetry addressing the issue secondary to the nearly universal lack of access that women had to these vehicles of communication in the past (Boswell, 1980).

Traditionally, in scenarios of human evolution, much emphasis has been given to increased heterosexual pairbonding, which has theoretically allowed and coevolved with increased intelligence and infant dependence (Campbell, 1985). However, there seems to be little published speculation regarding the female hominid strategy for successfully rearing offspring before the advent of reliance on the biological father. Theoretically, most hominid fathers would have been concurrently pursuing a number of other mating opportunities (cf. Symons, 1979), leaving limited time and assistance for any one female and their offspring.

Among chimpanzees and bonobos the biological father appears to play no direct role in raising offspring. Fisher (1992) states that even among humans, males and females have a tendency to want to remain pairbonded for only 3–4 years. This time period allows a human child to develop enough so that the mother alone can care for it. Historically and cross-culturally, the fact that many heterosexual couples remain together for life is partly an artifact of culture as a function of local social, political, and economic pressures (Boswell, 1980; Faderman, 1981; Hinsch, 1990). Relationship longevity is not a reliable measure of the couple's happiness and desire to remain together. Furthermore, even when culture encourages life-long heterosexual pairbonds, severe economic and political situations appear more likely to result in fathers abandoning their children than mothers (Benson, 1968; Dudley, 1991; Gerson, 1991). This phenomenon is partly reflected in the significant number of adult and adolescent males in contemporary societies who do not take responsibility for the children they have fathered. Given the history of problems with human fathers, the role played by hominid fathers remains unclear.

Current evolutionary theory implies that during the early period of human evolution hominid females confronted a number of simultaneously occurring phenomena: increasing infant dependence, increasing but still unreliable assistance from the biological fathers, and coexistence with a number of other unrelated females in the same territory because of male polygyny and female exogamy (Campbell, 1985; Fox, 1971; Morris, 1967; Symons, 1979; van der Dennen, 1995; Wilson, 1975; Wolpoff, 1976; Wrangham & Peterson, 1996; Zillman, 1984). These interacting factors suggest that alternative strategies to reliance on the biological father would have been adaptive. For example, there may have been an increased likelihood and necessity of strong relationships between unrelated females. It is reasonable to speculate that homoerotic behavior would have been adaptive for reinforcing the female-female relationships and alliances, as it is among bonobos (cf. Parish, 1994). Interestingly, Bohan (1996) reports that same-sex relationships are common among cowives in polygynous societies in Africa. The relationships are not viewed as definitive of the women's sexuality or an obstacle to their heterosexuality.

During the course of evolution, homoerotically reinforced alliances and friendships may have allowed young females to move toward the more stable and life-preserving core of the group. They may have also allowed females to unite against attacks against themselves and their offspring and to assist in the feeding and protection from predators of their offspring. Consequently, there may have been strong selection pressures for females to exhibit homoerotic behavior because it worked in the service of their own survival and ultimate reproductive success.

Selection pressures to exhibit homoerotic behavior may have been exerted on both male and female hominids. The observed sex difference in this behavior among humans may be explained in at least two ways. First, the selection pressures among hominids may have been greater for males than females because of the close association between dominance status and reproductive success for males. In fact, there may have been a selection against males who could not express homoerotic behavior to reinforce alliances or engage in sexual bargaining. Second, human females may not exhibit the full range of their disposition toward homoerotic behavior as they often do not with heteroerotic behavior. Kaplan (1974) states that males have a more compelling sex drive than females, suggesting a greater tendency to act on sexual desires. Furthermore, historically, all female behavior has tended to be closely regulated by males (Faderman,

1981), and their sexual behavior is sometimes brutally controlled, as demonstrated by the historically long custom of female genital mutilation (Lightfoot-Klein, 1989a, 1989b, 1993).

There is some agreement that the incidence of human female homoerotic behavior increases concomitantly with women's economic and social power and the consequent freeing of their sexual behavior from the control of men (cf. Faderman, 1981). Sankar (1986) describes the homoerotic relationships that developed among Chinese women who were able to resist marriage and live without husbands because of the opportunity to work in factories. The Mombasa women of Kenya are unique among Muslim women for their system of open social networks and homoerotic relationships between older wealthier women and poorer younger women (Greenberg, 1988). Hinsch (1990) reports that there are records of female-female marriages in China, particularly in Guangzhou. He states that the female couples could adopt female children, and the marriages were a manifestation of a wider range of female homoerotic practices.

The homoerotic relationships between some human females, in environments that may have been quite similar to those of hominids, allow a cooperative, supportive social unit that could be interpreted as increasing one or both women's chances of survival and successfully raising her offspring. Gay (1986) describes the "mummy-baby" relationships that exist among Lesotho women in Africa. These women live in an economically depressed area where the men are forced to leave as migrant labor. The women rely on themselves and each other for support in living and raising their children. Older and younger women form homoerotic relationships which help the younger partner to learn about sex and child care. These women often form life-long bonds and share food and provide assistance to each other. Wekker (1993) has described the institution of mati-ism among the women of Surinam, where many people are the descendants of slaves and where the cultural institution of marriage was weak. Mati are women who have homoerotic relationships with other women as well as relationships with men, and who usually have children. The women often set up households together and give each other mutual support and assistance. In the past, mati-ism was common among women of all social backgrounds, but in contemporary Surinam it appears to be more common among working-class women than among upper-class women.

For both female and male hominids homoerotic behavior may have been a part of a greater range of social manipulation used for alliance building among individuals of all status levels. The elaborate sexual behavior of bonobos appears to be closely related to social manipulation (Nishida & Hiraiwa-Hasegawa, 1987). It has been speculated that a capacity for social manipulation, particularly among males, was selected for during human evolution (Western & Strum, 1983). Social manipulation is an important part of creating and maintaining alliances (de Waal, 1982), which may have been critical for hominid male reproductive success (van der Dennen, 1995). Its role in powerful female alliances is clearly seen in bonobos (Parish, 1994). The higher-status partners in homoerotically reinforced relationships may have benefited indirectly from increased social alliances. A higher-status adult hominid with long-term standing in a group would have had the opportunity to befriend a number of peripheralized individuals. Theoretically, this would provide the opportunity for a network of alliances through both the protégés who reached adulthood and also through their kin.

Limitations of the Proposed Model

I have conceptualized a disposition for homoerotic behavior as having evolved because it can be seen as having had adaptive value during the course of human evolution. There are several limitations to the proposed model. It has the weaknesses inherent in all evolutionary models based on inference, although such models may prove rich in heuristic value. Cross-species comparisons of behavior may not always be reliable indicators of evolutionary trends; however, such comparisons form the basis of many evolutionary hypotheses regarding human behavior (e.g., de Waal, 1982; Diamond, 1992). The current analysis presents evidence that homoerotic behavior, particularly the transgenerational type, has been a persistent feature of the human species since recorded history. However, it does not prove that such a behavioral disposition evolved through natural selection. Evidence of recurring behavior among different groups of people is traditionally used in conjunction with cross-species evidence to infer specieswide behavioral dispositions in humans (Tooby & Cosmides, 1992). There are no alternative methods. There are a variety of expressions (e.g., Blackwood, 1986b) as well as suppression of homoerotic behavior among human groups. These patterns can be expected to express the effects of particular ecological and social contexts on the manifestation of an evolved behavioral disposition (cf. Tooby & Cosmides, 1992).

The relationship between homoerotic behavior and sexual orientation is not fully explained by this model. However, it is not the intent of this paper to do so. Sexual orientation is a complex construct, the definition of which lacks consensus among those who research it (Bohan, 1996; Diamant & McAnulty, 1995; Gonsiorek & Weinrich, 1991; Greenberg, 1988; Herdt, 1997; Shively, Jones & De Cecco, 1984) despite continued attempts to explain its development (Bem, 1996; Money, 1986). Further, much homoerotic behavior among humans occurs independently of the concept of a homosexual orientation (Bohan, 1996; De Cecco & Parker, 1995; Diamant & McAnulty, 1995). However, it is generally agreed among sexologists that sexual orientation appears to result from an interaction between genetic, cultural, and personal historical factors (Bohan, 1996; De Cecco & Elia, 1993; De Cecco & Parker, 1995; Greenberg, 1988; Herdt, 1988; McWhirter, Sanders, & Reinisch, 1990; Money, 1986; Weinrich, 1987). The theory presented here attempts to explain the evolution of a disposition to engage in homoerotic behavior, a component of sexual orientation, and presupposes a genetic component that can be expected to vary among individuals.

Implications for Future Study

A change in paradigm that allows homoerotic behavior to be viewed as having had adaptive value during human evolution may lead to new perspectives of the behavior and generate some new hypotheses for testing. For example, an increase in homoerotic behavior in single-sex groups is often attributed to lack of opposite-sex partners. Using the new model, it may be understood as a type of behavioral scaling. That is, homoerotic behavior may be evoked as a normal response to placement in an environment that closely resembles the environment in which it evolved and was adaptive in the evolutionary past. Homoerotic behavior has been described as nearly universal among human male adolescents (McKnight, 1997). This may reflect a developmentally linked predisposition for the behavior consistent with the behavior's speculated evolutionary history. Studies could be constructed to ascertain the incidence of homoerotic behavior in various sex-segregated settings, hypothesizing a greater incidence in environments believed to be

more similar to the speculated environmental conditions of hominids.

Other studies could be designed to try to predict sex differences in the manifestation of homoerotic behavior as a function of the types of coalitional strategies used by human males and females. For example, in chimpanzees and bonobos the sex that demonstrates the greatest same-sex coalitional strength appears to exhibit the most frequent and intense sociosexual behavior with same-sex allies (cf. de Waal, 1982; Parish, 1994). Application of the model to studies of self-identified lesbian, gay, and bisexual populations may generate some testable hypotheses about the nature of the relationships and patterns of sexual behavior. For example, McWhirter and Mattison (1984) reported that in male couples most likely to remain together there was an age difference of at least five years. Perhaps this reflects a difference in age-related dominance status which may be necessary for the maintenance of a long-term same-sex mating pair. Also, the current model may prove to be more helpful than others in attempts to explain the historical shift in the predominant expression of homoerotic behavior from the transgenerational type to the adult-peer type (cf. Rind, 1998).

Conclusions

A new model for the evolution of the homoerotic behavior in humans has been presented. It has the weaknesses inherent in all inferentially derived models, but such models can provide significant heuristic value. The current model has a number of advantages over other contemporary models. It is comprehensive and integrates data from a number of important and related disciplines. It clearly distinguishes between homoerotic behavior and culture-bound definitions of homosexual behavior and can contribute to theories of the development of sexual orientation. It also addresses the adaptive value of homoerotic behavior among hominids. The current model allows new interpretations of same-sex behavior among humans and can generate testable hypotheses about homoerotic behavior. In turn, the results of such tests can be used to demonstrate the usefulness, or lack thereof, of the model. Finally, the application of the evolutionary model to homoerotic behavior may prove to be heuristically rich and generate new thinking about homoerotic behavior in humans.

The author is grateful to Michael R. Cunningham, Douglas J. Garber, James Gregg, Linda M. Peterson, Christopher Starratt, and Lenore T. Szuchman for valuable comments on the manuscript.

References

Adam, B. D. (1986). Age, structure, and sexuality: Reflections on the anthropological evidence on homosexual relations. In E. Blackwood (Ed.), *The many faces of homosexuality* (pp. 19–33). New York: Harrington Park Press.

Akers, J., & Conaway, C. (1979). Female homosexual behavior. *Macaca mulatta. Archives of Sexual Behavior, 8,* 63–80.

Allyn, E. (1991). *Trees in the same forest: Thailand's culture and gay subculture.* San Francisco: Bua Luang.

Archer, J. (1996). Attitudes toward homosexuals: An alternative Darwinian view. *Ethology and Sociobiology, 17,* 281–284.

Bancroft, J. (1989). *Human sexuality and its problems* (2nd ed.). New York: Churchill Livingstone.

Bem, D. J. (1996). Exotic becomes erotic: A developmental theory of sexual orientation. *Psychological Review, 103,* 320–335.

Benson, L. (1968). *Fatherhood: A sociological perspective.* New York: Random House.

Blackwood, E. (1986a). Breaking the mirror: The construction of lesbianism and the anthropological discourse on homosexuality. In E. Blackwood (Ed.), *The many faces of homosexuality* (pp. 1–17). New York: Harrington Park Press.

Blackwood, E. (Ed.). (1986b). *The many faces of homosexuality.* New York: Harrington Park Press.

Boelkins, R. C., & Wilson, R. P. (1972). Intergroup social dynamics of the Cayo Santiago rhesus (*Macaca mulatta*) with special reference to changes in group membership by males. *Primates, 13,* 125–140.

Bohan, J. S. (1996). *Psychology and sexual orientation: Coming to terms.* New York: Routledge.

Boone, J. L. (1986). Parental investment and elite family structure in preindustrial states: A case study of late medieval–early modern Portuguese genealogies. *American Anthropologist, 88,* 859–878.

Boone, J. L. (1988). Parental investment, social subordination, and population processes among the 15th and 16th century Portuguese nobility. In L. Betzig, M. B. Mulder, & P. Turke (Eds.), *Human reproductive behavior: A Darwinian perspective* (pp. 201–219). Cambridge, MA: Cambridge University Press.

Boswell, J. (1980). *Christianity, social tolerance, and homosexuality.* Chicago: University of Chicago Press.

Boswell, J. (1994). *Same-sex unions in premodern Europe.* New York: Villard Books.

Burg, B. R. (1984). *Sodomy and the pirate tradition.* New York: New York University Press.

Buss, D. M. (1989). Sex differences in human mate preferences: Evolutionary hypotheses tested in 37 cultures. *Behavioral and Brain Sciences, 12,* 1–49.

Buss, D. M. (1992). Mate preference mechanisms: Consequences for partner choice and intrasexual competition. In J. H. Barkow, L. Cosmides, & J. Tooby (Eds.), *The adapted mind: Evolutionary psychology and the generation of culture* (pp. 249–266). New York: Oxford University Press.

Buss, D. M. (1994). *The evolution of desire: Strategies of human mating.* New York: Basic Books.

Buss, D. M., Haselton, M. G., Shackelford, T. K., Bleske, A. L., & Wakefield, J. C. (1998). Adaptations, exaptations, and spandrels. *American Psychologist, 53*(5), 533–548.

Campbell, B. (1985). *Human evolution* (3rd ed.). New York: Aldine.

Cantarella, E. (1992). *Bisexuality in the ancient world.* New Haven: Yale University Press.

Carpenter, C. R. (1942). Sexual behavior of free ranging rhesus monkeys (*Macaca mulatta*). *Journal of Comparative Psychology, 33,* 113–142.

Churchill, W. (1967). *Homosexual behavior among males.* New York: Hawthorn.

Cosmides, L., Tooby, J., & Barkow, J. H. (1992). Introduction: Evolutionary psychology and conceptual integration. In J. H. Barkow, L. Cosmides, & J. Tooby (Eds.), *The adapted mind: Evolutionary psychology and the generation of culture.* New York: Oxford University Press.

Crook, J. H. (1980). *The evolution of human consciousness.* Oxford: Clarendon Press.

De Cecco, J. P., & Elia, J. P. (1993). A critique and synthesis of biological essentialism and social constructionist views of sexuality and gender. *Journal of Homosexuality, 24* (3/4), 1–26.

De Cecco, J. P., & Parker D. A. (Eds.). (1995). *Sex, cells, and same-sex desire: The biology of sexual preference.* New York: Haworth Press.

de Waal, F. (1982). *Chimpanzee politics: Power and sex among apes.* New York: Harper & Row.

de Waal, F. (1987). Tension regulation and nonreproductive functions of sex in captive bonobos (*Pan paniscus*). *National Geographic Research, 3,* 318–335.

de Waal, F. (1990). Sociosexual behavior used for tension regulation in all age and sex combinations among bonobos. In J. R. Feierman (Ed.), *Pedophilia: Biosocial dimensions* (pp. 378–393). New York: Springer-Verlag.

de Waal, F. (1996). *Good natured: The origins of right and wrong in humans and other animals.* Cambridge, MA: Harvard University Press.

de Waal, F., & Lansing, F. (1997). *Bonobo: The forgotten ape.* Berkeley: University of California Press.

Diamant, L., & McAnulty, R. D. (Eds.). (1995). *The psychology of sexual orientation, behavior, and identity: A handbook.* Westport, CT: Greenwood Press.

Diamond, J. (1992). *The third chimpanzee.* New York: Harper-Collins.

Dickemann, M. (1995). Wilson's panchreston: The inclusive fitness hypothesis of sociobiology re-examined. In J. P. De Cecco & D. A. Parker (Eds.), *Sex, cells, and same-sex desire: The biology of sexual preference* (pp. 147–183). New York: Haworth Press.

Dover, K. J. (1978). *Greek homosexuality.* Cambridge, MA: Harvard University Press.

Dudley, J. R. (1991). Fathers who have infrequent contact with their children. *Family Relations, 40,* 279–285.

Ellis, B. J. (1992). The evolution of sexual attraction: Evaluative mechanisms in women. In J. H. Barkow, L. Cosmides, & J. Tooby (Eds.), *The adapted mind: Evolutionary psychology and the generation of culture* (pp. 267–288). New York: Oxford University Press.

Ellis, L. (1995). Dominance and reproductive success among nonhuman animals: A cross-species comparison. *Ethology and Sociobiology, 16,* 257–333.

Faderman, L. (1981). *Surpassing the love of men.* New York: Quill William Morrow.

Fisher, H. E. (1992). *Anatomy of love.* New York: Norton.

Ford, C. S., & Beach, F. A. (1951). *Patterns of sexual behavior.* New York: Harper.

Fossey, D. (1983). *Gorillas in the mist.* Boston: Houghton Mifflin.

Fox, R. (1971). Sexual selection and human kinship systems. In B. Campbell (Ed.), *Sexual selection and the descent of man: 1871–1971* (pp. 282–331). Chicago: Aldine.

Fullagar, R. L. K., Price, D. M., & Head, L. M. (1996). Early human occupation of northern Australia: Archeology and thermoluminescence dating of Jinmium rock-shelter, Northern Territory. *Antiquity, 70*(270), 751–773.

Futuyma, D. J., & Risch, S. J. (1984). Sexual orientation, sociobiology, and evolution. *Journal of Homosexuality, 9,* 157–168.

Gallup, G. G., & Suarez, S. D. (1983). Homosexuality as a byproduct of selection for optimal heterosexual strategies. *Perspectives in Biology and Medicine, 26,* 315–321.

Gardiner, J. (1992). *A class apart: The private pictures of Montague Glover.* London: Serpent's Tail.

Gay, J. (1986). "Mummies and babies" and friends and lovers in Lesotho. In E. Blackwood (Ed.), *The many faces of homosexuality* (pp. 97–116). New York: Harrington Park Press.

Gerson, K. (1991). Choosing between privilege and sharing Men's responses to gender and family change. In A. Wolfe (Ed.), *America at century's end* (pp. 35–57). Berkeley: University of California Press.

Goldfoot, D. A., Wallen, K., Neff, D. A., McBrair, M. C., & Goy, R. W. (1984). Social influences on the display of sexually dimorphic behavior in rhesus monkeys: Isosexual rearing. *Archives of Sexual Behavior, 13* 395–412.

Gonsiorek, J. C., & Weinrich, J. D. (1991). The definition and scope of sexual orientation. In J. C. Gonsiorek & J. D. Weinrich (Eds.), *Homosexuality: Research implications for public policy.* Newbury Park, CA: Sage.

Goodall, J. (1965). Chimpanzees of the Gombe Stream Reserve. In I. DeVore (Ed.), *Primate behavior: Field studies of monkeys and apes* (pp. 425–473). New York: Holt, Rinehart, & Winston.

Graham, C. E. (1981). Great apes as models in reproductive biology. In C. E. Graham (Ed.), *Reproductive biology of the great apes: Comparative and biomedical perspectives* (pp. 407–427). New York: Academic Press.

Greenberg, D. F. (1988). *The construction of homosexuality.* Chicago: University of Chicago Press.

Guttman, A. (1996). *The erotic in sports.* New York: Columbia University Press.

Hall, K. R. L. (1965). Baboon social behavior. In I. DeVore (Ed.), *Primate behavior: Field studies of monkeys and apes* (pp. 53–110). New York: Holt, Rinehart & Winston.

Hambright, K. (1995). Sexual orientation: What have we learned from primate research? In L. Diamant & R. D. McAnulty (Eds.), *The psychology of sexual orientation, behavior, and identity: A handbook* (pp. 136–161). Westport, CT: Greenwood Press.

Hanby, J. P., Robertson, L. T., & Phoenix, C. H. (1971). The sexual behavior of a confined troop of Japanese macaques. *Folia Primatologica, 16,* 123–143.

Harcourt, A. H., Stewart, K. J., & Fossey, D. (1981). Gorilla reproduction in the wild. In C. E. Graham (Ed.), *Reproductive biology of the great apes: Comparative and biomedical perspectives* (pp. 265–279). New York: Academic Press.

Harlow, H. F. (1965). Sexual behavior in the rhesus monkey. In F. A. Beach (Ed.) *Sex and behavior* (pp. 234–265). New York: Wiley.

Henningsen, H. (1961). *Crossing the equator: Sailor's baptism and other initiation rites.* Copenhagen: Munksgaard.

Herdt, G. H. (1981). *Guardians of the flutes.* New York: McGraw-Hill.

Herdt, G. H. (1984). A comment on cultural attributes and fluidity of bisexuality. *Journal of Homosexuality, 10,* 53–61.

Herdt, G. (1988). Cross-cultural forms of homosexuality and the concept "gay." *Psychiatric Annals, 18*(1), 37–39.

Herdt, G. (1997). *Same sex different cultures: Exploring gay and lesbian lives.* Boulder, CO: Westview Press.

Hess, J. P. (1973). Some observations on the sexual behavior of captive lowland gorillas, *Gorilla g. gorilla.* In R. P. Michael & J. H. Crook (Eds.), *Comparative ecology and behavior of primates* (pp. 507–581). London: Academic Press.

Hill, E. M., Nocks, E. S., & Gardner, L. (1987). Physical attractiveness: Manipulation by physique and status displays. *Ethology and Sociobiology, 8,* 143–154.

Hinsch, B. (1990). *Passions of the cut sleeve: The male homosexual tradition in China.* Berkeley: University of California Press.

Hughes, C. (1988). Integrating molecular techniques with field methods in studies of social behavior: A revolution results. *Ecology, 79,* 383–399.

Hughes, R. (1987). *The fatal shore: The epic of Australia's founding.* New York: Knopf.

Ihara, S. (1972). *Comrade loves of the Samurai* (E. P. Mathers, Trans.), Rutland, VT: Tuttle.

Kaplan, H. S. (1974). *The new sex therapy: Active treatment of sexual dysfunctions.* New York: Times Books.

Kinsey, A. C., Pomeroy, W. B., & Martin, C. E. (1948). *Sexual behavior in the human male.* Philadelphia: Saunders.

Kinsey, A. C., Pomeroy, W. B., Martin, C. E., & Gebhard, P. H. (1953). *Sexual behavior in the human female.* Philadelphia: Saunders.

Kinzey, W. G. (1987). A primate model for human mating systems. In W. G. Kinzey (Ed.), *The evolution of human behavior: Primate models* (pp. 105–114). Albany: State University of New York Press.

Kuroda, S. (1979). Grouping of the pygmy chimpanzees. *Primates, 20,* 161–183.

Kuroda, S. (1980). Social behavior of the pygmy chimpanzees. *Primates 21,* 181–197.

Lightfoot-Klein, H. (1989a). Rites of purification and their effects: Some psychological aspects of female genital circumcision and infibulation (Pharaonic circumcision) in an Afro-Arab Islamic society (Sudan). *Journal of Psychology and Human Sexuality, 2*(2), 79–91.

Lightfoot-Klein, H. (1989b). The sexual experience and marital adjustment of genitally circumcised and infibulated females in the Sudan. *Journal of Sex Research, 26*(3), 375–392.

Lightfoot-Klein, H. (1993). Disability in female immigrants with ritually inflicted genital mutilation. *Women & Therapy, 14*(3/4), 187–194.

Linden, E. (1992, March). Chimpanzees with a difference: Bonobos. *National Geographic, 181,* 46–53.

Lovejoy, C. O. (1981). The origin of man. *Science, 211,* 341–350.

Mackey, W. C. (1990). Adult-male/juvenile association as a species-characteristic human trait: A comparative field approach. In J. R. Feierman (Ed.), *Pedophilia: Biosocial dimensions* (pp. 299–323). New York: Springer-Verlag.

Margulis, L., & Sagan, D. (1991). *Mystery dance: On the evolution of human sexuality.* New York: Summit Books.

McKnight, J. (1997). *Straight science? Homosexuality, evolution and adaptation.* New York: Routledge.

McWhirter, D. P., & Mattison, A. M. (1984). *The male couple: How relationships develop.* Englewood Cliffs, NJ: Prentice Hall.

McWhirter, D. P., Sanders, S. A., & Reinisch, J. M. (Eds.). (1990). Homosexuality/ Heterosexuality: Concepts of sexual orientation. New York: Oxford University Press.

Mealey, L. (1985). The relationship between social status and biological success: A case study of the Mormon religious hierarchy. *Ethology and Sociobiology, 6,* 249–257.

Money, J. (1986). *Lovemaps: Clinical concepts of sexual/erotic health and pathology, paraphilia, and gender transposition in childhood, adolescence, and maturity.* New York: Irvington.

Mori, U. (1979). Development of sociability and social status. In M. Kawai (Ed.), *Ecological and sociological studies of gelada baboons* (pp. 125–154). Tokyo: Kodansha-Karger.

Morris, D. (1967). *The naked ape.* London: Cape.

Muscarella, F. (1999). The homoerotic behavior that never evolved. *Journal of Homosexuality, 37*(3), 1–18.

Muscarella, F., & Cunningham, M. R. (1996). The evolutionary significance and social perception of male pattern baldness and facial hair. *Ethology and Sociobiology, 17,* 99–117.

Nadler, R. D. (1986). Sex-related behavior of immature wild mountain gorillas. *Developmental Psychobiology, 19,* 125–137.

Nadler, R. D. (1990). Homosexual behavior in nonhuman primates. In D. P. McWhirter, S. A. Sanders, & J. M. Reinisch (Eds.), *Homosexuality/heterosexuality: Concepts of sexual orientation* (pp. 138–170). New York: Oxford University Press.

Nishida, T., & Hiraiwa-Hasegawa, M. (1987). Chimpanzees and bonobos: Cooperative relationships among males. In B. B. Smuts, D. L. Cheney, R. M. Seyfarth, R. W. Wrangham, & T. T. Struhsaker (Eds.), *Primate societies* (pp. 165–177). Chicago: University of Chicago Press.

Parish, A. R. (1994). Sex and food control in the "uncommon chimpanzee": How bonobo females overcome a phylogenetic legacy of male dominance. *Ethology and Sociobiology, 15,* 157–194.

Posner, R. A. (1992). *Sex and reason.* Cambridge, MA: Harvard University Press.

Poundstone, W. (1993). *Biggest secrets.* New York: William Morrow.

Pusey, A. E., & Packer, C. (1987). Dispersal and philopatry. In B. B. Smuts, D. L. Cheney, R. M. Seyfarth, R. W. Wrangham, & T. T. Struhsaker (Eds.), *Primate societies* (pp. 250–266). Chicago: University of Chicago Press.

Rawson, P. (1973). Early history of sexual art. In P. Rawson (Ed.), *Primitive erotic art* (1–76). New York: G. P. Putnam's Sons.

Ridley, M. (1993). *The red queen: Sex and the evolution of human nature.* New York: Penguin Books.

Rind, B. (1998). Biased use of cross-cultural and historical perspectives on male homosexuality in human sexuality textbooks. *Journal of Sex Research, 35,* 397–407.

Rocke, M. (1996). *Forbidden friendships: Homosexuality and male culture in Renaissance Florence.* New York: Oxford.

Ross, A. (1973). Celtic and northern art. In P. Rawson (Ed.), *Primitive erotic art* (pp. 77–106). New York: G. P. Putnam & Sons.

Sankar, A. (1986). Sisters and brothers, lovers and enemies: Marriage resistance in southern Kwangtung. In E. Blackwood (Ed.). *The many faces of homosexuality* (pp. 69–81). New York: Harrington Park Press.

Sapolsky, R. (1993, March). The young and the reckless. *Discover,* 58–64.

Savage-Rumbaugh, E. S., & Wilkerson, B. J. (1978). Socio-sexual behavior in *Pan paniscus* and *Pan troglodytes*: A comparative study. *Journal of Human Evolution, 7,* 327–344.

Schiefenhovel, W. (1990). Ritualized adult-male/adolescent male sexual behavior in Melanesia: An anthropological and ethological perspective. In J. R. Feierman (Ed.), *Pedophilia: Biosocial dimensions* (pp. 394–421). New York: Springer-Verlag.

Seaborg, D. M. (1984). Sexual orientation, behavioral plasticity, and evolution. *Journal of Homosexuality, 10,* 153–158.

Shilts, R. (1993). *Conduct unbecoming: Gays and lesbians in the U.S. military.* New York: St. Martin's Press.

Shively, M. G., Jones, C., & De Cecco, J. P. (1984). Research on sexual orientation: Definitions and methods. *Journal of Homosexuality, 9,* 127–136.

Simpson, M. J. A. (1973). The social grooming of male chimpanzees. In R. P. Michael & J. H. Crook (Eds.), *Comparative ecology and behavior of primates* (pp. 411–505). New York: Academic Press.

Small, M. F. (1992, June). What's love got to do with it? *Discover,* 46–51.

Small, M. F. (1993). *Female choices: Sexual behavior of female primates.* Ithaca, NY: Cornell University Press.

Southwick, C. H., Beg, M. A., & Siddiqui, M. R. (1965). Rhesus monkeys in North India. In I. Devore (Ed.), *Primate behavior: Field studies of monkeys and apes* (pp. 111–159). New York: Holt, Rinehart, & Winston.

Stevens, A., & Price, J. (1996). *Evolutionary psychiatry: A new beginning.* New York: Routledge.

Sugiyama, Y. (1969). Social behavior of chimpanzees in the Budongo Forest, Uganda. *Primates, 10,* 197–225.

Sugiyama, Y. (1973). The social structure of wild chimpanzees: A review of field studies. In R. P. Michael and J. H. Crook (Eds.), *Comparative ecology and behavior of primates* (pp. 375–410). New York: Academic Press.

Susman, R. L. (1987). Pygmy chimpanzees and common chimpanzees: Models for the behavioral ecology of the earliest hominids. In W. G. Kinzey (Ed.), *The evolution of human behavior: Primate models* (pp. 72–86). Albany: State University of New York Press.

Symons, D. (1979). *The evolution of human sexuality.* New York: Oxford University Press.

Taub, D. M. (1990). The functions of primate paternalism: A cross-species review. In J. R. Feierman (Ed.), *Pedophilia: Biosocial dimensions* (pp. 338–377). New York: Springer-Verlag.

Taylor, T. (1996). *The prehistory of sex: Four million years of human sexual culture*. New York: Bantam Books.

Thiessen, D. (1996). *Bitter-sweet destiny: The stormy evolution of human behavior*. New Brunswick, NJ: Transaction Press.

Thompson-Handler, N., Malenky, R. K., & Badrian, N. (1984). Sexual behavior of *Pan paniscus* under natural conditions in the Lomako Forest, Equateur, Zaire. In R. L. Susman (Ed.), *The pygmy chimpanzee* (pp. 347–368). New York: Plenum.

Tooby, J., & Cosmides, L. (1992). The psychological foundations of culture. In J. H. Barkow, L. Cosmides, & J. Tooby (Eds.), *The adapted mind: Evolutionary psychology and the generation of culture* (19–136). New York: Oxford University Press.

Tutin, C. E. G. (1979). Mating patterns and reproductive strategies in a community of wild chimpanzees (*Pan troglodytes schweinfurthii*). *Behavioral Ecology and Sociobiology, 6*, 29–38.

van der Dennen, J. M. G. (1995). *The origin of war: The evolution of a male-coalitional reproductive strategy*. Groningen, Netherlands: Origin Press.

Vasey, P. L. (1995). Homosexual behavior in primates: A review of evidence and theory. *International Journal of Primatology, 16*(2), 173–203.

Wallen, K., & Parsons, W. A. (1997). Sexual behavior in same-sexed nonhuman primates: Is it relevant to understanding human homosexuality? In R. C. Rosen, C. M. Davis, & H. J. Ruppel (Eds.), *The annual review of sex research: Vol. 8* (pp. 195–223). Mount Vernon, IA: Society for the Scientific Study of Sexuality.

Weinrich, J. D. (1980). Homosexual behavior in animals: A new review of observations from the wild and their relationship to human sexuality. In R. Forleo & W. Pasini (Eds.), *Medical sexology: The third international congress* (pp. 288–295). Littleton, MA: PSG Publishing.

Weinrich, J. D. (1987). *Sexual landscapes: Why we are what we are, why we love whom we love*. New York: Scribners.

Wekker, G. (1993). Mati-ism and black lesbianism: Two ideal typical expressions of female homosexuality in black communities of the diaspora. *Journal of Homosexuality, 24*, 145–158.

Western, J. D., & Strum, S. C. (1983). Sex, kinship, and the evolution of social manipulation. *Ethology and Sociobiology, 4*, 19–28.

Williams, W. L. (1986). *The spirit and the flesh*. Boston: Beacon.

Wilson, E. O. (1975). *Sociobiology: The new synthesis*, Cambridge, MA: Belknap.

Wilson, E. O. (1978). *On human nature*, Cambridge, MA: Harvard University Press.

Wingate, B. (Ed.). (1994). *Hazing: An anthology of true hazing tales*. New York: Outbound Press.

Wolfe, L. M. (1979). Behavioral patterns of estrous females of the Arashiyama West troop of Japanese macaques (*Macaca fuscata*). *Primates, 20*, 525–534.

Wolfe, L. M. (1986). Sexual strategies of female Japanese macaques (*Macaca fuscata*). *Human Evolution, 1*, 267–275.

Wolpoff, M. H. (1976). Primate models for Australopithecine sexual dimorphism. *American Journal of Physical Anthropology, 45*, 497–509.

Wrangham, R. W. (1987). The significance of African apes for reconstructing human social evolution. In W. G. Kinzey (Ed.), *The evolution of human behavior: Primate models* (pp. 51–71). Albany: State University of New York Press.

Wrangham, R., & Peterson, D. (1996). *Demonic males*. Boston: Houghton Mifflin.

Wright, R. (1994). *The moral animal: Why we are the way we are: The new science of evolutionary psychology*. New York: Pantheon Books.

Yamagiwa, J. (1987). Intra- and inter-group interactions of an all-male group of Virunga Mountain gorillas (*Gorilla gorilla beringei*). *Primates, 28*, 1–30.

Zillman, D. (1984). *Connections between sex and aggression*. Hillsdale, NJ: Lawrence Erlbaum.

PETER S. THEODORE
SUSAN A. BASOW

17

Heterosexual Masculinity and Homophobia: A Reaction to the Self?

Heterosexual masculinity (Herek, 1986) is the cultural ideology that extends the belief that masculinity and femininity consist of two bipolar sets of behaviors, traits, and social roles. Gender identity researchers have found that the polarization of masculinity and femininity begins at birth and continues throughout the life span (Greenwald & Banaji, 1995; Katz, 1986; Shively & De Cecco, 1993; Spence & Helmreich, 1978). With gender marking an important cue for both self-definition and societal reaction, boys and girls learn to value masculine attributes over feminine attributes as more socially effective and rewarding. For example, while independence, success, and achievement are part of society's construct of masculinity, these culturally valued qualities remain absent from the construct of femininity.

In addition to measuring masculinity through gender attributes, Herek (1986) asserts that contemporary society deems heterosexuality an essential condition of masculinity. Through its insistence that "true" men are heterosexual, heterosexual masculinity has been linked to homophobia. Due to the common belief that homosexuality is an aberrant "life style" that deviates from the bipolar view of masculinity and femininity, Herek argues that many individuals have come to view homosexuals as a threat to their self-identities as men or women. He proposes that the ideological belief in heterosexual masculinity causes heterosexuals, especially males, to internalize society's gender expectations and consequently develop anxiety over not fulfilling those expectations. This anxiety leads

many males to reject gay men as a means to reaffirming their sense of masculinity (Harry, 1990; Herek, 1987; 1988). Herek (1987) termed this the "defensive function" of homophobias. While the rejection can range anywhere from covert expressions of disgust and disapproval to overt forms of physical and verbal abuse, each form of homophobia "defines who one is by identifying gay people as a symbol of what one is not" (Herek, 1993, p. 98).

Empirical research investigating homophobia lends support to Herek's (1986) assertion that heterosexual masculinity engenders antigay prejudice (Black & Stevenson, 1984; Herek, 1987, 1988; Holzten & Agresti, 1990; Sinn, 1997; Wells, 1991). Black and Stevenson, and Herek (1988) both assessed the relationship between sex-role ideology and homophobia among college students. They found that males, especially those who view homosexuals as predominantly gay men (and not lesbians), rejected homosexuality significantly more than females. The most homophobic males had the strongest beliefs in traditional gender roles. Despite administering different measures of homophobia and gender ideology on separate samples, both sets of researchers suggest that the variance in homophobia among males may be due to differences in men's anxiety regarding their ability to behave within a perceptually stringent set of gender role expectations. This suggestion has not been fully tested. The goal of the present study, therefore, is to identify whether self-esteem, self-discrepancy regarding gender attributes, and gender attribute importance constitute a set of factors predictive of homophobia among male college students.

Self-esteem

Wills (1981) defines self-esteem as the self-evaluation of one's abilities and personal attributes in relation to those that are valued by the general population. The basic premise of Wills's downward comparison theory is that self-esteem can be enhanced and protected through direct comparison of oneself with a less fortunate other. The theory additionally posits that downward comparison will most likely occur when a person's self-esteem is low and his or her subjective well-being is threatened (Wills, 1991). Luhtanen and Crocker (1991) add that low self-esteem (LSE) individuals tend to compare downward by actively derogating threatening others, especially if the threatening other is a "safe target, . . . lower in status . . . whom the dominant culture considers relatively acceptable to derogate" (p. 213). According to this definition, homosexuals should constitute a "safe" population vulnerable to downward comparison by heterosexuals with LSE. Indeed, researchers have identified a significant correlation between low self-esteem and high levels of homophobia (Holzten & Agresti, 1990; Wells, 1991).

Research with LSE individuals suggests that they have inconsistent and unstable self-concepts which underlie their greater dependence on and susceptibility to external, self-relevant information (Campell, 1990). Such dependence may catalyze intergroup prejudice. As such, it appears theoretically consistent to predict that perceived risk of association with homosexuality may correlate with a less defined, uncertain heterosexual identity in LSE individuals.

Self-discrepancy

It is unlikely that all heterosexuals with LSE lack structurally defined heterosexual self-concepts. Thus, the present study addresses the possibility that ill-defined heterosexual self-concepts may stem from self-discrepant views of one's actual versus expected gender identity. Higgin's (1987) research on self-discrepancy theory has demonstrated the existence of six possible self-states. Each person has three domains of the self: the "actual," "ideal," and the "ought" selves. The actual self is the self that a person believes himself or herself to be, while the

ideal self is the person that he or she would like to become, and the ought self is the person the individual believes he or she should be. Furthermore, two standpoints exist within each self-domain, the other and the own. While each of the preceding domain reflects one's "own" standpoint, an example of an "other" standpoint (in this case, the ought/other standpoint) would be "the person an individual believes others expect him or her to be." Discrepant, incompatible self-views may occur between any two of the six possible self-states (e.g., actual/own versus ought/other).

Higgins, Klein, and Strauman (1985) found that the various types of self-discrepancies induce different types of psychological discomfort. The actual/own versus ought/other discrepancy, in particular, contributed uniquely and significantly to reactions of fear, agitation, panic, and threat. While Higgin's research has demonstrated that actual-ought discrepancies eliminate anxiety and threat, the present research sought to extend Higgin's findings by assessing whether actual-ought gender role discrepancies elicit homophobic anxiety and threat.

Gender Attribute Importance

Another facet of the self-discrepancy theory relates to the importance of various attributes to overall self-concept and the degree to which one possesses an actual-ideal discrepancy along those attributes. Pelham and Swann (1989) found that self-esteem was significantly correlated with the importance and certainty ratings of each attribute as well as the obtained self-ideal discrepancy score. Attribute importance was significantly related to self-esteem, especially among individuals with negative self-views. Due to the significance of both attribute importance and self-discrepancy in determining one's overall self-concept, the present study measures both gender-role discrepancy and attribute importance in assessing the relationship between self-views and homophobia.

Hypotheses and Predictions

Based on Herek's (1986) theory of heterosexual masculinity, Wills's (1981) downward comparison theory of self-esteem, and Higgins's (1987) self-discrepancy theory, the present study examines whether level of self-esteem, degree of self-discrepancy along gender attributes, and level of importance associated with these attributes contribute to the variance in homophobia among male college students. It was hypothesized that each of the three predictor variables would contribute significantly and uniquely to the variance in homophobia, with attribute importance accounting for most of the variance, followed by self-discrepancy, followed by self-esteem. With regard to attribute importance and self-discrepancy, it was predicted that the masculine-feminine bipolar attributes would account for most of the variance, followed by the masculine attributes and then the feminine attributes. Additionally, it was predicted that most variance would be accounted for along the Personal Anxiety subscale of the Attitudes Toward Homosexuality Scale (Black & Stevenson, 1984). It was also hypothesized that interactions among the predictor variables would account for a significant portion of variance above and beyond that of the unique predictors. In particular, it was predicted that the interaction between high attribute importance and high self-discrepancy would account for more variance than either of the two-way interactions with low self-esteem, while the three-way interaction would account for the least variance.

Method

Participants

Eight-five male undergraduates participated in this study, 85% of whom received extra credit in their psychology or statistics courses while 15% volunteered as pledges or brothers of various fraternities. Eleven participants were eliminated from analyses due to incomplete questionnaires. Of the final sample of men, 32% were Protestant, 28% were Catholic, 13% were Jewish, 13% considered themselves to belong to "other" religions, and 14% considered themselves to have no religion. Ethnically, 87% of the participants were Caucasian, 8% African American, Asian American, or Hispanic, and 5% comprised "other" ethnicities.

Materials

Personal Self-esteem Measure   The measure of personal self-esteem was Helmreich and Stapp's (1974) Texas Social Behavior Inventory (TSBI), Short Form A. Participants responded to 16 items along a five-point Likert scale ranging from (1) "not at all characteristic of me" to (5) "very much characteristic of me." The scale responses proved to be internally consistent (Cronbach of .82).

Self-discrepancy Measure   To measure the actual/own versus ought/other self-discrepancy scores, a modified version of the Self-Attribute Questionnaire (Pelham & Swann, 1989) was used (see Appendix A). This modified version, called the Ought Self Questionnaire (OSQ), was formed by replacing the 10 attributes from Pelham and Swann's original questionnaire with all of the attributes contained within the 24-Item Personal Attributes Questionnaire (PAQ), which measures perceived levels of masculinity and femininity (Spence & Helmreich, 1978). Some modification of PAQ items was needed. The PAQ items that contained a different attribute at each end of the scale were split into two separate OSQ items (e.g., the single PAQ item ranging from "very submissive" to "very dominant" was split into two OSQ Likert scales: one scale for "submissive" and one scale for "dominant"). Some minor rewording of two attributes was also needed.

On the OSQ, respondents assessed themselves relative to their ought selves, defined as "the person you would be if you were exactly as you think your peers expect you, as a male, ought to or should be." Respondents rated themselves along a nine-point Likert scale ranging from (1) "very different from how I think my peers expect I ought to or should be" to (9) "very much like how I think my peers expect I ought to or should be." Reverse scoring was used when entering the self-discrepancy data for analysis such that higher scores indicate greater self-discrepancies. Since the original PAQ has three subscales (masculine, feminine, and a bipolar masculine-feminine scale), the OSQ was similarly divided. The eight masculine attributes had a Cronbach of .75, the eight feminine attributes of .79, and the 10 masculine-feminine bipolar attributes of .56. Since a value of .56 reflects inconsistent responses along the bipolar attributes, the bipolar discrepancy scores were not used in the statistical analyses.

Attribute Importance Measure   The Attribute Importance Questionnaire (see Appendix B) was based on the Pelham and Swann (1989) study. Each of the attributes used on the OSQ was randomly reordered and mixed with seven filler attributes so as to minimize respondents' abilities to selectively rate the importance of attributes based on how they previously measured themselves along the attributes.

To complete the AIQ, each respondent was instructed to rate, on a nine-point Likert scale, the personal importance of each attribute to his own self-identity as a male. In doing so, a rating of 1 indicated "not at all important to my masculinity," whereas a rating of 9 indicated "extremely important to my masculinity." The same subscales used with the OSQ were examined, with the Cronbach values measuring .69 for the eight masculine attributes, .91 for the eight feminine attributes, and .59 for the 10 masculine-feminine bipolar attributes. Given the questionable reliability of the bipolar attributes subscale it was dropped from further analyses.

Homophobia Measure   The present study measured homophobia through the Political Ideology Survey, a disguised version of the Attitudes toward Homosexuality Scale (ATH) created by Milham, San Miguel, and Kellogg (1976). The twenty ATH statements used in this scale were taken directly from Black and Stevenson (1984), who adapted the original ATH by using the term homosexuals in place of lesbians and/or gay men and by changing the response format from agree/disagree to agree/uncertain/disagree. Black and Stevenson's adapted version minimized the risk of response bias as they rephrased the ATH statements to yield an equal number of positive and negative statements regarding homosexuals. The only additional adaptation in the present scale occurred in ATH statement number three. In the current study, the phrase "Homosexuals are sick" was replaced with "Homosexuality is sick." This altered statement fit better with the political context of the new scale.

The ATH scale yields a total score as well as three subscores: personal anxiety in the presence of homosexuals (HPA), ideas of moral reprobation (HMR), and the belief that homosexual behavior is dangerous and needs to be repressed (HRD). In the present study, the total scale and each subscale response proved to be internally consistent: the Cronbach values for the overall ATH, and the three homophobia subscales (HPA, HMR, and HRD) were .92, .88, .94, and .70, respectively.

The first page of the Political Ideology Survey, entitled Demographics, assessed participants' ethnic backgrounds, religious affiliations, and political affiliations. Participants were also asked to identify their political attitude as liberal, moderate, or conservative and to rate their level of political awareness (i.e., very informed, somewhat informed, not at all informed).

Procedure

A male experimenter introduced the investigation as a study assessing the influence of males' perceptions of themselves on their political beliefs. Within individual cubicles, participants completed the four questionnaires in the following sequence: the self-esteem questionnaire, the self-discrepancy questionnaire (OSQ), the attribute importance questionnaire (AIQ), and the Attitudes toward Homosexuality Scale (disguised as the Political Ideology Survey and assessing participant demographics). The study was structured such that each participant had possession of only one questionnaire at a time; every time a participant finished one questionnaire, the experimenter collected that questionnaire and handed out the next one.

A debriefing summary clarifying the true purpose of the investigation was distributed to each participant via campus mail once all the data had been collected and analyzed.

Results

Correlations among Measures

Table 17.1 displays the descriptive statistics of each predictor and criterion variable measured in this study. Deviations from normality (skewness) are most marked for HRD, the repression subscale (positive skew) and self-esteem (negative skew).

As shown in Table 17.2, homophobia scores measured by the entire ATH as well as by the moral reprobation (HMR), personal anxiety (HPA), and repression (HRD) subscales, correlated positively with masculine attribute importance (AIMASC), while the HPA and HMR subscales correlated negatively with feminine attribute importance (AIFEM). This indicates that the greater the importance of masculine traits, the greater all forms of homophobia; whereas, the less importance given to feminine traits, the greater one's score for homophobic anxiety and for the moral reprobation of homosexuality.

There also was a significant negative relationship between masculine tribute importance (AIMASC) and self-discrepancy along masculine traits (SDMASC) (r = −0.33). Similarly, a significant negative relationship was found between feminine attribute importance (AIFEM) and self-discrepancy along feminine traits (SDFEM) (r = −0.57). Higher attribute importance values were associated with lower discrepancy scores along those attributes.

Self-esteem scores did not have a significant relationship with the overall ATH scale nor with any of the three subscales, despite correlating with masculine attribute importance, AIMASC (r = 0.32) and self-discrepancy along the masculine attributes,

Table 17.1 Distribution of Scores among 74 Participants

Variable	Mean	St. Dev.	Minimum	Maximum	Kurtosis	Skewness
AIFEM	6.28	1.49	2.00	8.88	−0.11	−0.50
AIMASC	7.10	0.93	4.75	9.00	−0.34	−0.14
ATH	35.24	10.10	20.00	60.00	−0.96	0.24
HMR	15.13	5.86	8.00	24.00	−1.54	0.08
HPA	15.20	5.00	8.00	24.00	−1.27	0.01
HRD	12.70	3.39	8.00	24.00	0.38	0.73
SDFEM	4.50	1.55	1.25	8.00	−0.46	−0.10
SDMASC	3.87	1.33	1.88	7.25	−0.31	0.60
SE	60.20	7.98	36.00	74.00	0.25	−0.69

Note. AIFEM and AIMASC, attribute importance for feminine and masculine traits, respectively, could range from 1 to 9; ATH, the entire Attitudes toward Homosexuality scale, could range from 20 to 60; HMR (the homophobia subscale based on moral reprobation), HPA (the homophobia subscale based on personal anxiety), and HRD (the homophobia subscale based on the belief in a need for repression due to danger) could each range from 8 to 24; SDFEM and SDMASC, self-discrepancy along feminine and masculine traits, respectively, could both range from 1 to 9; and SE, self-esteem, could range from 16 to 80.

SDMASC (r = −0.47). High self-esteem is associated with high importance of masculine traits and low self-discrepancy along those traits.

Multiple Hierarchical Regressions

The null correlational findings between self-esteem and homophobia, coupled with the nonnormal distribution of self-esteem scores, led to the omission of self-esteem from the multiple regression analyses. With each of the remaining predictor variables, four stepwise multiple regression equations were computed. Each of these four equations predicted one of the four criterion variables: ATH, HMR, HPA, and HRD.

Unique Predictors of Homophobia   With respect to the first hypothesis, the first set of predictor variables entered into the stepwise regression were attribute importance along masculine traits, attribute importance along feminine traits, and self-discrep-

ancy along masculine traits. For the entire ATH scale, attribute importance across both masculine and feminine traits and self-discrepancy along the masculine attributes accounted for a significant portion (22%) of the population variance (see Table 17.3). As predicted, masculine attribute importance scores entered the regression equation during step one, self-discrepancy scores during step two, followed by the feminine attribute importance scores on step three. Men for whom masculine traits were important yet who had high self-discrepancy regarding those traits and who viewed feminine traits as unimportant had the highest scores on the global homophobia measure. Overall, attribute importance accounted for a significantly greater portion of the statistical variance than self-discrepancy.

In running the second, third, and fourth hierarchical regression equations using the three subscales of the ATH as criterion variables, similar results were obtained (see Table 17.3). While masculine

Table 17.2 Correlations among the Homophobia Scales and the Predictor Variables

Predictors	ATH Subscales						
	ATH	HMR	HPA	HRD	SE	AIFEM	AIMASC
AIFEM	−0.20	−0.22*	−0.22*	−0.04	0.05	—	0.11
AIMASC	−0.29**	0.26*	0.25*	0.28*	0.32**	0.11	—
SDFEM	0.13	0.17	0.16	−0.02	−0.02	−0.57***	−0.07
SDMASC	0.14	0.15	0.09	0.13	−0.47***	−0.06	−0.33**
SE	0.03	0.04	−0.00	0.06	—	0.05	0.32**

*p < .05, **p < .01, ***p < .001

Table 17.3 Summary of Unique Predictors of Homophobia as Identified through the Multiple Hierarchical Regression (N = 74)

| | ATH Subscales | | | | | | | |
| | ATH | | HMR | | HPA | | HRD | |
Variable	B	β	B	β	B	β	B	β
Entered								
Step 1								
AIMASC	4.80	0.44***	2.60	0.41***	1.73	0.33**	1.36	0.38**
Step 2								
SDMASC	2.13	0.28*	1.18	0.27*			0.66	0.26*
AIFEM					−0.91	−0.27*		
Step 3								
AIFEM	−1.74	−0.25*	−0.98	−0.25*				
	R^2	F	R^2	F	R^2	F	R^2	F
	0.22	6.86***	0.20	6.35***	0.15	6.39**	0.14	6.24**

Note. Variables are listed in decreasing order of their unique contribution to the corresponding homophobia scale/subscale. AIMASC stands for masculine attribute importance. AIFEM stands for feminine attribute importance, and SDMASC stands for self-discrepancy along masculine traits. For all βs and Fs, *p < .05, **p < .01, ***p < .001.

attribute importance was the strongest predictor for all three subscales, low feminine attribute importance predicted HMR and HPA but did not significantly predict HRD. Self-discrepancy along masculine traits significantly predicted HMR and HRD but not HPA.

Interactive Predictors of Homophobia For the second set of four hierarchical regression equations, the predictor variables were: AIMASC, AIFEM, SDMASC, AIMASC × AIFEM, AIMASC × SDMASC, AIFEM × SDMASC, and AIMASC × AIFEM × SDMASC. The three-way interaction among masculine attribute importance, feminine attribute importance, and self-discrepancy along masculine attributes did not contribute to the variance in homophobia scores (see Table 17.4). However, the two-way interactions between masculine attribute importance and self-discrepancy along masculine traits (AIMASC × SDMASC) and between feminine attribute importance and self-discrepancy along masculine traits (AIFEM × SD-MASC) did account for significant portions of homophobic variance above and beyond the unique predictors. While AIFEM × SDMASC contributed to the variance along the ATH, it did not affect the variance along any of the three subscales. On the other hand, AIMASC × SDMASC contributed to the variance along the HMR subscale in addition to the overall ATH. It did not, however, contrib-

ute toward the variance along the HPA and HRD subscales.

The interaction effects show that both low feminine and high masculine attribute importance are particularly predictive of homophobia among men who had greater self-discrepancies along masculine attributes, as measured by the entire ATH scale and the HMR (moral reprobation) subscale.

Other Variables

Four one-way ANOVAs were performed on the categorical variables of religion, political attitudes (conservative versus moderate versus liberal), political awareness (very informed versus somewhat informed versus not informed at all), and political affiliation (Democrat versus Republican versus neither), using each homophobia measure. No significant differences were found among the religious groups or the differing degrees of political awareness. However, with regard to political attitudes, liberals scored significantly less homophobic on the entire ATH ($F(2) = 6.48$; $p < .01$), the HPA ($F(2) = 4.71$; $p < .05$), and the HMR ($F(2) = 7.01$; $p < .01$) than moderates and conservatives. On the HRD, the liberals scored significantly less homophobic than only the conservatives ($F(2) = 3.78$; $p < .05$). For political affiliation, Republicans scored significantly more homophobic than both Democrats and the politically nonaffiliated on the total

Table 17.4 Summary of Interaction Effects between Predictors of Homophobia as Identified through the Multiple Hierarchical Regression (N = 74)

| | ATH subscales | | | | | | | |
| | ATH | | HMR | | HPA | | HRD | |
Variable	B	β	B	β	B	β	B	β
Entered								
Step 1								
AIMASC	Removed in step 4		1.94	0.31**	1.73	0.33**	1.37	0.38**
Step 2								
AIMASC × SDMASC	0.73			0.67***	0.16	0.25*		
AIFEM					−0.91		−0.27*	
SDMASC							0.67	0.26*
Step 3								
AIFEM × SDMASC	−0.53	−0.51**						
AIFEM			−0.96	−0.25*				
Step 4	AIMASC removed							
	R^2	F	R^2	F	R^2	F	R^2	F
	0.19	8.78***	0.20	6.38**	0.15	6.39**	0.14	6.24**

Note. Variables are listed in decreasing order of their unique contribution to the corresponding homophobia scale/subscale. AIMASC and AIFEM stand for masculine and feminine attribute importance, SDMASC stands for self-discrepancy along masculine traits, AIMASC × SDMASC stands for the interaction between high masculine attribute importance and high self-discrepancy along those traits, and AIFEM × SDMASC stands for the interaction between low feminine attribute importance and high self-discrepancy along masculine traits. For all βs and F's, *p < .05, **p < .01, ***p < .001

ATH ($F(2) = 5.40$; $p < .01$) and HMR ($F(2) = 6.79$; $p < .01$), while on the HPA ($F(2) = 3.48$; $p < .05$), Republicans scored significantly more homophobic than only those who were nonaffiliated. No significant differences were identified along the HRD subscale.

Discussion

The statistical results partially supported the first hypothesis and set of predictions: masculine attribute importance was the best and strongest predictor of homophobia, followed by self-discrepancy along masculine attributes, followed by feminine attribute importance. These results suggest that college-age males who not only are highly sensitive to gender stereotypes but who also evaluate themselves negatively based on a belief that they don't fulfill the masculine stereotypes are most likely to hold homophobic attitudes and beliefs.

The fact that attribute importance and self-discrepancy both significantly predicted homophobia supports Higgins's (1987) and Pelham and Swann's (1989) research on self-discrepancy. Possessing a discrepancy regarding one's own masculine qualities significantly predicted participants' overall levels of homophobia as well as homophobia specifically due to moral reprobation and due to the belief that homosexuality is dangerous and should therefore be repressed. The finding that highly discrepant males are more likely to fear that homosexuality is dangerous supports Higgins's research that ought-other discrepancies elicit fear, hostility, and threat. Furthermore, Strauman and Higgins (1987) found that persons with high ought-other discrepancies scored very high on several social anxiety scales, including the Fear of Negative Evaluation Scale. College-age males who believe they do not adequately match society's definition of masculinity may, therefore, feel increased distress about receiving negative evaluations from others, explaining why they would be more likely to fear and avoid circumstances that and people (i.e., homosexuals) who may lead others to question their masculinity.

These results also support Pelham and Swann's (1989) conclusion that the importance of people's beliefs about themselves should influence whether or not they evaluate others' judgments when making their own decisions. Males who believe strongly in the importance of possessing high levels of masculine attributes and low levels of feminine traits should be more easily persuaded by the cultural gender-role expectations inherent in heterosexual masculinity to make harsh judgments regarding homosexuals and homosexuality in general (Herek, 1986, 1993). The present study also found that the influence of one's perceived discrepancy along a specific attribute depends on how important that attribute is in defining the person's identity, supporting Pelham and Swann's finding of an interaction between attribute importance and self-discrepancy. Specifically, males who believed that the possession of stereotypically masculine attributes was important to their identities as men were significantly more homophobic only when they believed themselves to inadequately measure up to others' expectations regarding appropriate masculine behavior. These same males also tended to devalue the importance of feminine attributes to their identities as "men." As these findings demonstrate, gender is an extremely prominent cue for self-identification during late adolescence and early adulthood; it is during this period of development that adolescents learn to distinguish appropriate from inappropriate heterosexual behavior (Katz, 1986).

Despite general support for the first hypothesis, some anomalies arose regarding the specific predictions. Contrary to prediction, self-discrepancy along the masculine traits did not significantly predict variance in homophobia due to personal anxiety. This prediction was based on Strauman and Higgins's (1987) finding that ought-other discrepancies elicit anxiety as well as Black and Stevenson's (1984) finding that participants rejected homosexuals significantly more when they focused on their own personal anxiety. The conflict presented by the present study, however, may simply be due to the manner in which the ATH was scored. Homophobia is typically measured along the ATH by identifying two separate sets of scores, one indicating acceptance of homosexuality and one indicating a rejection of homosexuality (Black & Stevenson, 1984). The present study measured responses to ATH items along Likert scales, thereby achieving one as opposed to two measures of homophobia. Another reason why the prediction regarding homophobic anxiety may not have been supported relates to the present study's self-discrepancy measure, the OSQ. In accordance with Spence and Helmreich (1978), the masculine-feminine (MF) bipolar attributes (socially desirable in one gender while undesirable in the other) were expected to elicit high anxiety among participants who perceived themselves as highly discrepant on them. However, the bipolar OSQ scales had low reliability and could not be used. In the absence of

a reliable measure of participants' reactions regarding self-perceived discrepancies along the most highly gendered attributes, the current results may not reflect a strong test of the relationship between self-discrepancy and homophobic anxiety.

Also contrary to prediction was the lack of predictive ability for the self-esteem measure. This may be due to a ceiling effect created by the negatively skewed self-esteem scores of this sample. The overwhelming majority of male participants reported comparatively high self-esteem (average score of 60.2 compared to Spence and Helmreich's 1978 average TSBI score of 37.9 among college-aged males). On the other hand, although self-esteem was not significantly predictive of homophobia, it was significantly related, in the expected direction, to masculine attribute importance and self-discrepancy along masculine attributes. That is, males with high self-esteem also tended to have a strong belief in the importance of possessing masculine attributes and tended to have small discrepancies regarding their possession of such traits. Since both masculine attribute importance and self-discrepancy are predictors of homophobia, the present study suggests that, with greater variability, self-esteem may have influenced college-age males' levels of homophobia, especially as an interaction term. Previous research has demonstrated that homophobia and low self-esteem are related (Holzten & Agresti, 1990; Wells, 1991).

Limitations and Future Directions

Generalization from the current results should be made cautiously. The student body in question was very homogeneous in terms of age (predominantly 17–23), economic status (predominantly middle and upper-middle class), and political ideology (moderate to conservative). Furthermore, demand characteristics may have impacted responses on the homophobia scale and subscales.

Another limitation of the study relates to the fact that only about 20% of the variance in homophobia scores was accounted for by the self-variables utilized. Although this amount is significant, it is likely that other predictors of homophobia may be equally or more important than self-variables. Some of these variables include religiosity, political beliefs, belief in traditional family values, and belief in traditional gender roles (Herek, 1987, 1988; Holtzen & Agresti, 1990; Sinn, 1997). A study including all these major variables in one prediction equation would shed more light as to the relative importance of self-variables in predicting homophobia. Since this study also throws no light on negative attitudes toward lesbians, it would be interesting to examine if homophobia among females partly represents a reaction to self-variables as well.

In spite of its limitations, the present study provides evidence that self-discrepancy and gender attribute importance help to explain homophobia among college-age men. Perhaps the most interesting extension future researchers could make to the present study lies in assessing how the "undesired self," in addition to the "ought/other" self, relates to heterosexual masculinity and homophobia (Ogilvie, 1987). If homophobia does fulfill the role of a defense mechanism against objectionable gender characteristics in males who feel inadequate regarding their masculinity, research regarding the "undesired self" should pick this up.

In summary, the present study suggests that college-age men in their late adolescence and early adult years who define themselves and their masculinity according to societal standards are likely to hold homophobic attitudes toward gay men as a means toward reconciling their own feelings of gender inadequacy. These findings have implications for our understanding of antigay violence and victimization, since it is primarily males in their late adolescence and early adulthood with feelings of gender inadequacy who perpetrate gay-bashing and verbal assaults (Harry, 1990; Herek, 1993). Only by further exploring the interplay among gender identity, homophobia, and self-perception will society fully understand that homophobia may represent as much a reaction to the self as it does to gays, lesbians, and bisexuals.

The authors wish to thank April W. Gresham, Ph.D., for her assistance in conceptualizing the project.

References

Black, K. N., & Stevenson, M. R. (1984). The relationship of self reported sex-role characteristics and attitudes toward homosexuality. *Journal of Homosexuality, 10*, 83–93.

Campell, J. D. (1990). Self-esteem and clarity of the self-concept. *Journal of Personality and Social Psychology, 59*, 538–549.

Greenwald, A. G., & Banaji, M. R. (1995). Implicit social cognition: Attitudes, self-esteem, and stereotypes. *Psychological Review, 102*, 4–27.

Harry, J. (1990). Conceptualizing anti-gay violence. *Journal of Interpersonal Violence, 5*(3), 350–358.

Helmreich, R., & Stapp, J. (1974). Short forms of the Texas Social Behavior Inventory (TSBI), an objective measure of self-esteem. *Bulletin of Psychonomic Society, 4*, 473–475.

Herek, G. M. (1986). On heterosexual masculinity. *American Behavioral Scientist, 29*, 563–577.

Herek, G. M. (1987). Can functions be measured? A new perspective on the functional approach to attitudes and females. *Social Psychology Quarterly, 50*, 285–303.

Herek, G. M. (1988). Heterosexuals' attitudes toward lesbians and gay men: Correlates and gender differences. *Journal of Sex Research, 25*, 451–477.

Herek, G. M. (1993). The context of antigay violence: Notes on cultural psychological heterosexism. In L. D. Garnets & D. C. Kimmel (Eds.), *Psychological perspectives on lesbian and gay male experiences* (pp. 89–107). New York: Columbia University Press.

Higgins, E. T. (1987). Self-discrepancy: A theory relating self and affect. *Psychological Review, 94*, 319–340.

Higgins, E. T., Klein, R., & Strauman, T. (1985). Self-concept discrepancy theory: A psychological model for distinguishing among different aspects of depression and anxiety. *Social Cognition, 3*, 51–76.

Holtzen, D. W., & Agresti, A. A. (1990). Parental responses to gay and lesbian children: Differences in homophobia, self-esteem, and sex-role stereotyping. *Journal of Social and Clinical Psychology, 9*, 390–399.

Katz, P. A. (1986). Gender identity: Development and consequences. In R. D. Ashmore & F. K. Del Boca (Eds.), *The social psychology of female-male relations* (pp. 21–67). Orlando, FL: Academic Press.

Luhtanen, R., & Crocker, J. (1991). Self-esteem and intergroup comparisons: Toward a theory of collective self-esteem. In J. Suis & T. A. Wills (Eds.), *Social comparison: Contemporary theory and research* (pp. 211–234). Hillsdale, NJ: Erlbaum.

Millham, J., San Miguel, C., & Kellogg, R. A. (1976). Factor analytic conceptualization of attitudes toward male and female homosexuals. *Journal of Homosexuality, 2*, 3–10.

Ogilvie, D. M. (1987). The undesired self: A neglected variable in personality research. *Journal of Personality and Social Psychology, 52*, 379–385.

Pelham, B. W., & Swann, W. B., Jr. (1989). From self-conceptions to self-worth: On the sources and structure of global self-esteem. *Journal of Personality and Social Psychology, 57*, 672–680.

Shively, M. G. & De Cecco, J. P. (1993). Components of sexual identity. In L. D.

Garnets & D. C. Kimmel (Eds.),
*Psychological perspectives on lesbian and
gay male experiences* (pp. 80–88). New
York, NY: Columbia University Press.

Sinn, J. S. (1997). The predictive and
discriminant validity of masculinity ideology.
Journal of Research in Personality, 31(1),
117–135.

Spence, J. T., & Helmreich, R. L. (1978).
*Masculinity and femininity: Their
psychological dimensions, correlates, and
antecedents.* Austin: University of Texas
Press.

Strauman, T. J., & Higgins, E. T. (1987).
Vulnerability to specific kinds of chronic
emotional problems as a function of self-
discrepancies. Unpublished manuscript, New
York University.

Wells, J. W. (1991). What makes a difference?
Various teaching strategies to reduce
homophobia in university students. *Annuals
of Sex Research, 4,* 229–238.

Wills, T. A. (1981). Downward comparison
principles in social psychology. *Psychological
Bulletin, 90,* 245–271.

Wills, T. A. (1991). Similarity and self esteem in
downward comparison. In J. Suls & T. A.
Wills (Eds.), *Social comparison:
Contemporary theory and research* (pp.
51–78). Hillsdale, NJ: Erlbaum.

Appendix A
Ought Self Questionnaire

The items below inquire about what kind of person you think you are versus what type of person you think your peers expect you should or ought to be. In other words, after thinking about how each item relates to you, you are then to consider how your rating of yourself on each specific item compares to your *ought self*, or how you think your peers expect you, *as a male, should* or *ought* to measure along each item.

As an example, consider the item *artistic*:

Rate yourself relative to your *ought self*—the person you would be if you were exactly as artistic as you think your peers expect you, *as a male, ought to* or *should* be.

$$A \ldots B \ldots C \ldots D \ldots E \ldots F \ldots G \ldots H \ldots I$$

very different from how —I think my peers expect I *ought to* or *should* be.	somewhat like and unlike how—I think my peers expect I *ought to* or *should be.*	very much like how —I think my peers expect I *ought* *to* or *should* be

If you believed you had no artistic ability but think that your peers believe you should, as a male, be extremely artistic, then you would circle a letter close to A. If instead, you believed that you had no artistic ability and think that your peers believe you should, as a male, be somewhat artistic, then you would circle E. On the other hand, if you believed you had no artistic ability and thought that, according to your peers, you as a male, should not be very artistic anyway, you would circle a letter close to I.

Now, for the following 29 items follow the same procedure described in the example. Rate yourself relative to your *ought self*—the person you would be if you were exactly as you think your peers expect you, *as a male, ought to* or *should* be.

Attributes

 1. aggressive
 2. independent
 3. emotional
 4. dominant
 5. excitable in a MAJOR crisis
 6. active
 7. able to devote myself completely to others
 8. gentle
 9. helpful to others
10. competitive
11. worldly
12. kind
13. needful of others' approval
14. easily hurt (emotionally)
15. aware of others' feelings

16. decisive
17. persistent
18. likely to cry
19. self-confident
20. superior
21. understanding of others
22. warm (in relations with others)
23. needful of security
24. strong under pressure
25. submissive
26. passive
27. rough
28. home-oriented
29. inferior

Appendix B
Attribute Importance Scale

Please take a couple of minutes to indicate how important each of the following attributes is to your masculine identity. In other words, rate how important each of the following attribute domains is to determining your self-identity as male. There is no line as to how many attribute domains you can rate with the same degree of importance. Thus, as an extreme example, you can circle E for every single attribute if they are each somewhat important to you.

1. sense of humor

A ... B ... C ... D ... E ... F ... G ... H ... I

not at all	moderately	extremely
important to	important to	important to
my masculinity	my masculinity	my masculinity

2. submissiveness
3. emotionality
4. gentleness
5. likelihood to cry
6. cleanliness
7. aggressiveness
8. helpfulness
9. intellect
10. degree of activism
11. excitability in a MAJOR crisis
12. self-confidence
13. worldliness
14. competitiveness
15. artistic ability
16. degree of passivity
17. independence
18. kindness
19. degree of courage
20. ease with which your feelings become hurt
21. awareness of others' feelings
22. warmth in relations to others
23. decisiveness
24. persistence
25. sense of adventure
26. understanding of others
27. feelings of superiority
28. ability to devote myself completely to others
29. self-security

30. neatness
31. strength under pressure
32. dominance
33. roughness
34. feelings of inferiority
35. degree to which you are home-oriented
36. degree of need for others' approval

Deborah P. Waldrop
Joseph A. Weber

18

From Grandparent to Caregiver: The Stress and Satisfaction of Raising Grandchildren

American society has witnessed growing numbers of middle-aged and older adults who have assumed the primary responsibility for raising their grandchildren (Fuller-Thompson, Minkler, & Driver, 1997; Lugaila, 1998; Roe & Minkler, 1999). Grandparents take on the caregiver role following a traumatic event or as the result of long-term problems that render their adult child unable to function as a parent. Grandparents act as parents temporarily in some families and permanently in others. They face both challenges and opportunities during these difficult times.

Grandparents who are raising their grandchildren may have looked forward to middle and later adulthood as a relaxed period of time. However, this expectation is changed as grandparents step into a troubled situation and attempt to offer stability and security for their grandchildren. In so doing, grandparents manage the combined responsibilities of family caregivers and parental figures.

This paper discusses the current literature about the stressors of grandparents who are caregivers and examines the family, legal, and financial problems they face. It provides information about responses to caregiving, including situation-specific coping strategies and health changes that are developed by grandparent caregivers. Finally, the paper addresses the sources of satisfaction found by grandparents in this situation. Increased knowledge about grandparent caregivers' responses to stress is important for human service professionals who encounter the complex needs and problems of this emerging group in society.

The Transition from Grandparent to Caregiver

Grandparenthood represents a time of great joy and fulfillment for most people. The significant family ties, which develop as adult children marry and become parents, is referred to as family continuity (Hagestad, 1985). Involvement with younger family generations is important for healthy later-adult development and well-being (Kivnick, 1982) and are significant for all generations (Kornhaber, 1996; Waldrop, Weber, et al. 1999). Becoming a grandparent fulfills developmental expectations and can create meaning and satisfaction in the life of an older adult (Kivnick, 1982). The lengthening life span makes it possible for grandparenthood to last three or four decades of adult life and for individuals to occupy various grandparental roles over time (Kornhaber, 1996; Kornhaber & Woodward, 1981).

Disruptive family events such as an adult child's addiction, incarceration, or death cause family crises and become a catalyst for other difficult conflicts in these intergenerational households. Problems such as substance abuse or mental illness negatively influence parenting abilities and precipitate the need for substitute care of a child. If an adult child denies these problems and refuses to relinquish care, a grandparent may pursue legal custody (Jendrek, 1994a). Family distress is heightened by the financial and emotional burden of a custody battle. Intense emotion often accompanies both an adult child's problems and discussions about cus-

tody (Burton, 1992; Minkler & Roe, 1993). Once grandparents begin raising their grandchildren, they face a new set of needs and challenges. Grandparent caregivers deal with changed expectations for themselves and their families with this interruption of life cycle events.

Grandparent caregivers find themselves living a different lifestyle than expected at this time in life (Ehrle & Day, 1994; Jendrek, 1994b). Feelings of social isolation may occur because they have concerns and problems that are different from those of their peers. Grandparents may be uncertain about how to help a grandchild who has emotional outbursts or difficulty in school (Minkler, 1999). Feelings of loneliness and exhaustion stem from the combination of responsibilities and uncertainties that accompany grandparent caregiving (Minkler, 1999; Roe, Minkler, Saunders, & Thompson, 1996; Shor & Haslip, 1994).

Previous research indicates that grandparent caregivers have most often been female, African American, living in the inner city, and raising a daughter's children (Fuller-Thompson, 1997). Figures indicate that 4.1% of White children, 13.5% of African American children, and 6.5% of Hispanic children were being raised by grandparents in the late 1990s (Fuller-Thompson, 1997). The multiple complex and interrelated problems that are associated with grandparent caregiving may affect both mental and physical health (Burnette, 1997, 1999; Burton, 1992; Pruchno, 1999; Minkler & Roe, 1994; Whitley, White, Kelley, & Yorker, 1999). Additional information about the effects of these issues is important in clarifying the needs of grandparent-headed families (Jendrek, 1994a; Roe, Minkler, Saunders & Thompson, 1996; Strawbridge, Wallhagen, Shema & Kaplan, 1997).

Financial problems have been universally documented in studies with grandparents who are raising their grandchildren (Burton, 1992; Fuller-Thompson, Minkler & Driver, 1997; Jendrek, 1994a; Minkler, 1999). Financial burdens faced by grandparent caregivers include but are not limited to the following: strain from additional expenses, difficulty applying for governmental assistance, poverty, and underemployment (Jendrek, 1994a). Underemployment occurs when grandparents attempt to reenter the job market but are unable to earn sufficient income either because employers think they are too old for a job or their skills are not up to date. Grandparent caregivers may be both employed and married, but still burdened by the additional expenses of a dependent grandchild, or they may face the extra expenses of caring for more than one child on an income that is already stretched.

Grandparents who are raising their grandchildren are not automatically entitled to receive financial benefits and may have difficulty establishing eligibility for assistance (Flint & Perez-Porter, 1997). Ongoing financial problems create the feeling of living on the edge (Burnette, 1999; Burton, 1992; Minkler & Roe, 1993).

A grandparent's legal authority for a grandchild is often established after a period of conflict about who should have custody. Grandparents may watch their child's problems go from bad to worse for a long time before they begin caring for a grandchild. Voluntary legal custody, however, requires permission from a custodial parent, which can be difficult to obtain from a troubled adult child who refuses to consent (Jendrek, 1994a; Flint & Perez-Porter, 1997). Discussions about grandparental custody may intensify ongoing conflict with an adult child.

Grandparent caregivers often seek to establish formal parental authority so they can provide stability for their grandchildren. In most cases, grandparents do not have legal guardianship of the grandchild they are raising. Many grandparents apply for legal custody or guardianship and in some cases pursue adoption (Jendrek, 1994b). Legal custody provides decision-making capacity for the child's upbringing, education, medical care, and discipline. The courts can assign permanent legal guardianship in cases of child abuse and neglect (Jendrek, 1994a; Wagner, Weber, Hesser, & Cooper, 1995). Adoption requires termination of parental rights, which can occur either voluntarily or involuntarily in court. Each type of legal arrangement has different emotional and financial ramifications. The ongoing relationship between a grandparent and his or her children may become hostile or vindictive when parental rights are transferred to a grandparent. Simultaneously, grandparents experience feelings of sorrow and loss related to their child's inability to function adequately as a parent (Burton, 1992; Fuller-Thompson & Minkler, 2000; Minkler & Roe, 1993).

The purpose of this study was to explore the stressors that are present in grandparent caregiving. The study sought to examine caregivers' responses and coping strategies to these stressors, and to describe the satisfaction grandparents often gain from raising their grandchildren.

Methodology

This qualitative study involved semistructured, indepth interviews with grandparents who had the primary responsibility for raising one or more grandchildren. Primary responsibility was defined as the complete physical and financial responsibility for at least one grandchild who was under age 18 and lived in the grandparents' home. Children's parents were not living in the home and child custody had been entrusted to grandparents either legally or informally.

Sample

Fifty-four grandparents representing 38 family units participated in this research (37 grandmothers and 17 grandfathers). This sample was primarily Caucasian, with three African American and two Native American grandparents. Eighty-five percent were married. Interviews were conducted with both spouses in 16 families. The age of the grandparents in the study ranged from 41 to 79 with a mean age of 56.8 years. The age range for men was 48 to 79 with a mean age of 59.4 years, while the age range for women was 41 to 76 with a mean age of 56.4 years. All participants lived in suburban areas, small towns, or rural communities. Table 18.1 provides a profile of grandparent participants.

Participants' socioeconomic circumstances were determined by the discussion of financial status, which included prior economic situation, caregiving-related expenses, monetary support available for grandchildren as well as the household, and the additional expenses of raising children. Grandparents were asked if there was financial strain associated with raising grandchildren, and if so, what factors precipitated it. An assumption of this study was that there are factors other than income that exacerbate financial burden. For example, out-of-pocket payments on an adult child's hospital bills may diminish a substantial life savings or substantial monthly income.

Two conceptual hypotheses were developed to examine the relationships between stress, coping, and satisfaction in grandparent caregivers. Conceptual hypotheses can be formulated to test a theory about the relationships in exploratory research (Kerlinger, 1992). One hypothesis stipulated that a positive relationship exists between the quality of the parent/adult child relationship and the grandparent caregiver's satisfaction. That is, as the quality of the parent/adult child relationship improves, so do the caregiver's feelings of satisfaction. A second conceptual hypothesis stipulated that a negative relationship exists between the permanency of legal authority and the caregiver's feelings of stress. That is, the more permanent the grandparent's authority, the less stress for the grandparents.

Table 18.1 Profile of Grandparent Caregivers

Categories	Number	Percent
Individual Participants (N = 54)		
Gender		
Male	17	31
Female	37	69
Age		
40–50	11	20
50–60	24	44
60–70	11	20
70–80	8	15
Marital Status		
Widowed	5	9
Divorced	4	7
Married	46	85
Occupations		
Not employed outside the home	11	20
Retired	3	
Homemaker	7	
Disabled	1	
Employed full time	40	74
Professional	13	
Service	17	
Construction/manufacturing	10	
Full-time student	3	6
Family Units (N = 38)		
Family Type		
Original marriage	16	42
Second marriage	13	34
Single head of household		
Widowed	4	11
Divorced	5	13

Conceptual hypotheses were evaluated using negative case testing (Berg, 1995). Negative case testing involves sorting cases to determine the numbers that do and do not fit the hypothesized relationship. Negative case testing was used to increase rigor in qualitative research (Berg, 1995; Padgett, 1998). In this study, conceptual hypotheses were employed to begin generalizing about the relationship between grandparent caregiving, stress, and coping. Conceptual hypotheses were not tested quantitatively, but negative case testing was used to confirm or disconfirm the hypothesized relationship between concepts (Padgett, 1998).

Data Collection

Multiple methods were developed to locate grandparent caregivers during the planning phase of the study. First, grandparents who attended a statewide conference for caregivers were invited to participate. Grandparents who attended local support group were also contacted. A snowball effect was employed as these participants led the researcher to other grandparent caregivers. Interviews were scheduled at a location chosen by participants and preceded at a pace they established. Locations included participants' homes, restaurants, and places of employment. Married couples were interviewed either individually or jointly according to their preference.

An interview schedule, adapted from Minkler and Roe's (1993) initial study of grandmother caregivers, was used to guide grandparent participants. A series of essential topics related to caregiving stress and response were followed by probing questions designed to elicit more complete stories from participants (Berg, 1995; Padgett, 1998). The essential topics were physical and mental health, legal issues, emotional reactions, social support system, and family relationships. Participants often discussed the topics without the use of probing questions during the course of retelling their stories. The interview schedule is lengthy, so an abbreviated version is provided for illustration in Table 18.2. The full interview schedule is available from the authors.

Data Analysis

Fifty-one of the 54 interviews were audiotaped and transcribed. QSR NUD*IST software was used to sort and categorize transcript text. QSR NUD*IST

facilitates the organization of large amounts of textual data in two ways. First, the researcher creates an outline or a coding structure of fixed headings to which all participants' comments on the same topic are copied. These fixed headings, called index nodes, represent the essential topics in the interview schedule. The index nodes become an overall outline for coding and categorizing data. The researcher assigns codes to units of text and copies them under an established node or category.

Second, QSR NUD*IST allows the researcher to sort through textual data and establish new themes. "Free nodes" are flexible categories that can be used to temporarily store text units that are used to build emerging themes. Free nodes can later be moved or combined with others as analysis continues. For example, a free node was used to collect stories about the behavior changes that caregivers observed in their grandchildren after a visit or phone call from a parent. These observations contributed to the understanding of grandchildren's well-being as a primary stressor for grandparents once caregiving had begun. Free nodes become an important tool to facilitate learning from the experiences of participants in exploratory, qualitative research.

Finally, typologies or categories were created from participants' experiences within the combined text of all experiences with the same issues. Typologies represent the range of responses within this population of grandparent caregivers. Frequency counts were used to determine the rate of occurrence for each category.

Results and Analysis

In-depth interviews with grandparent caregivers yielded candid and detailed information about multiple family problems. The problems that precipitated grandparent caregiving in the study population included substance abuse, parental abandonment, divorce/breakup, teen pregnancy, mental health problems, or the death of the adult child. The frequencies of precipitating problems in this sample are found in Table 18.3. The percentages in each section represent the number of participants who discussed the topic. Participants often gave more than one answer to questions, so percentages do not total 100%.

Grandparent caregivers' problems were most often related to family conflicts, financial strain, and legal difficulties. Variations of these problems emerged from grandparents' stories about caregiving, and in many situations, the problems were interrelated. For illustration, a representative anec-

Table 18.2 Interview Schedule

Demographics
Family relationships
 Adult child whose children the grandparent is raising
 Other adult children
 Other grandchildren
 Marital relationship
 Extended family
Events that triggered caregiving
Physical and mental health
Legal issues
Emotional reactions
Social support system
Finances
Employment situation
Support group membership
Advice for grandparents about to assume responsibility
 for their grandchildren

Table 18.3 Problems That Precipitated Grandparent Caregiving

Preexisting Sources of Stress	Number of Families (N = 38)	Percent*
Drug/alcohol problems	25	66
Child abuse/neglect	17	39
Parental abandonment	15	39
Divorce/breakup	14	37
Teen pregnancy	10	26
Mental health problems	7	18
Death of adult child	3	8

*Participants commonly gave more than one answer; consequently, percentages do not add up to 100%.

dote is found at the end of each of the following sections. Anecdotes use grandparents' own words, but their names have been changed. Each illustrates more than one of the themes, underscoring the complexity of and interrelationships between the issues faced by grandparents who raise their grandchildren.

Family Stress

This section describes the family problems that precipitated the change in grandparents' roles from grandparent to caregiver. Family relationships were most often cited as the main source of long-term stress for grandparent caregivers and was related to ongoing concerns, such as a troubled adult child's unpredictable behavior, grandchildren's well-being, and marital strife. An adult child's precipitating problems often created a state of perpetual tension and conflict that altered relationships among all family members. Adult children's deviant lifestyle, criminal activities, and emotional manipulation created fear of harm.

Grandchildren's well-being caused ongoing worry for many grandparents. Grandparents explained that the children they were raising had been previously traumatized by their parents' behavior. In many situations, grandparents described children's problems that resulted directly from abuse or neglect. Participants also discussed apprehension about potential future problems such as the eventual incarceration or death of an adult child, and the potential impact on their grandchildren.

Marriages were changed by grandparent caregiving. Both men and women described marital problems they believe were exacerbated by stress. Thirty-nine percent of the family units in this study

involved original marriages and grandparents who were raising their own children's children. Thirty-seven percent of the family units involved second marriages. The dynamics in these stepfamilies became strained when blame for an adult child's problems was directed at his or her parent. Two couples separated for a period of time, when the stress became so intense they needed time to cool down. Grandparents who were widowed or divorced headed 24% or nine family units.

Work-family strain resulted from balancing the demands of job with the needs of a grandchild. Concerns about child care and dependent benefits were issues that some grandparents had not previously dealt with. Participants explained that they had planned to stop working at a particular age, but when they began raising grandchildren they were forced to reconsider employment options. In other situations, grandparents expressed frustration in dealing with their inability to find well-paying jobs. Some grandparents worked at part-time jobs and 13% became home day care providers so they could generate additional income by working at home. Participants' employment status is illustrated in Table 18.1.

Some of the family problems experienced by grandparent caregivers are illustrated in the following anecdote related by a 48-year-old grandmother who had established legal custody of her 7-year-old grandson.

Rachel [her daughter] has been using drugs since she was 11 years old. She has always been in trouble somehow, someway. She has always been a problem from the time that she was just a little bitty thing. She has been in and out of drug rehab. They would just clean her up, put her back on the street, and probably within hours she was high again. I have been through the years of calling child welfare begging them to do something. My concern was always about Andrew, being there for him, trying to keep him safe. She was using heavy-duty stuff—heroine and morphine, shooting up. All of these ins and outs she would leave Andrew with me and he grew accustomed to being here. There were so many times when she wasn't living with me that I would call him and he would say "Mom is asleep and I can't get her awake. I'm scared, Will you come?" I would just go get him—sometimes I would leave her a note and sometimes I wouldn't. Finally, I decided to apply for guardianship. She signed the papers because she was in trouble. If she hadn't, he would be in child welfare custody. Recently, she said she wanted him back. I said, "There is no need of talking with me about it because you are not ready. Whenever you are ready and you really are cleaned up and have a real job and a real home that will be fine with me. I won't fight you a bit, but until then you won't take him anywhere." So, she doesn't really talk to me about it, she just mentions it, but our relationship is strained. She has used me and abused me throughout her life, but that little boy deserves better. At least I can offer him a safe place to live, and food in his tummy.

Legal Problems

Grandparents' decision to pursue formal authority for their grandchildren generates legal problems. Grandparents are concerned about the type of authority to seek, when and how to pursue it, and about the amount of conflict to expect in the process. The type of legal authority grandparents pursued depended on family history, child welfare involvement, and the preexisting problems of the adult child. In this study, 17% of the children had been adopted by grandparents, 38% were under permanent legal guardianship, 13% were under temporary legal guardianship, and 33% lived with grandparents who did not have legal authority.

The decision to intervene in an adult child's life usually followed a long period of concern for grandparents who had observed a deteriorating situation. Speaking to an authority about an adult child's parental insufficiency was difficult for two reasons. First, acknowledging an adult child's failures or inadequacies to child welfare authorities can be emotionally devastating for a parent. Feelings of "turning on your own" carried a heavy emotional burden. Second, legally removing parental custody, even temporarily, requires thorough documentation of child abuse and neglect—not just hearsay. When concerned grandparents finally did take action, some were surprised that a judge did not automatically grant them custody. Many reported that their first encounter with the legal system served as a wake-up call and provided important information, which ultimately made a future attempt to establish grandparental custody successful.

The choice to pursue legal authority was followed by a grandparent's decision about how to proceed. Grandparents chose to contact (1) child welfare, (2) an attorney, or (3) a judge to begin the process. A judge ultimately decides legal guardianship, but the type of authority granted to grandparental caregivers was not always the same. Participants explained that legal decisions depended on a variety of factors that include the amount of documentation provided in court, the judge's views on family unity and removal of parental custody, as well as the current atmosphere in the county or city where the hearing took place.

Grandparents were sometimes awarded only temporary guardianship by a judge who stated the intent of helping a parent get his or her life back on track in a short period of time. Temporary guardianships make the relationship between grandparent caregivers and their grandchildren tenuous and insecure for both generations. Temporary legal authority was described as causing a phenomenon participants referred to as a "yo-yo" effect. Several grandparents used this term to describe the situation that occurs when children go back and forth between parents and grandparents. A child may be living with a grandparent temporarily when a parent takes the child but then only maintains this living arrangement until another crisis occurs. A grandparent then takes the child back and attempts to reestablish stability but lives with constant anticipation that the adult child will return and demand the child again. In these situations, children seem to represent someone over whom a parent can have control. Grandparents attempt to stabilize a volatile situation and help their grandchildren, but an adult child's erratic behavior keeps anxiety and uncertainty high. Judges who assign only temporary guardianship to a grandparent or do not rule for grandparental custody in volatile situations continue the yo-yo effect.

Grandparents without legal custody of their grandchildren described verbal agreements with their adult children about informal and temporary custody of a grandchild. These informal arrangements had been made between grandparents and their adult children without involving a lawyer. This group of grandparents agreed to raise their grandchildren for an indeterminate period of time. Only one grandparent with an informal arrangement for care in this study had power of attorney (POA) for emergency authority. Grandparents without a POA provided the day-to-day care and depended on the adult child to sign official documents for school or medical treatment. Some troubled adult children ultimately used the absence of a formal custody arrangement to intimidate their parents. For instance, adult children threatened to take the grandchild(ren) back if the grandparent refused to comply with their demands for money or other resources.

The following anecdote was told by the 67-year-old grandparents of 7-year old Megan, who was currently in their legal custody. The grandfather (Paul) was a semiretired attorney. Megan was the daughter of their son (Bob) and drug-addicted ex-daughter-in-law (Ann). This anecdote illustrates how legal issues overlap with financial and family problems.

> Ann had custody of the baby, but of course she had been leaving Megan here all the time because I was buying her clothes, paying for a place for her to live and keeping the baby while she tried to get her life in order. We treated Ann like a daughter, really. Bob's child support was paid in full. She filed a nonsupport document and two police officers carted our son off to jail. She parked down the street and watched. Meanwhile, she was selling drugs and had several boyfriends. Then one night, she called and asked, "Can you keep Megan for visitation this weekend—I wanted to make plans and my pipes are frozen and I don't have water." Well, she came to pick Megan up on Saturday night at midnight and Paul wouldn't let her have the baby because we didn't know if she had any water or heat and it was freezing. So, Monday morning, she came again with the police, but we still wouldn't let her have the baby because we wanted proof. After that we entered an all-out custody battle and we were allowed to keep Megan but Ann got visitation—supervised. This cost us over $20,000—a large chunk of what could have been college money to be sure.

Financial Burden

Financial burden in grandparent-headed families results from the combined effects of several factors, including the strain of providing for extra people in the household, the cost of legal intervention, and paying for an adult child's psychiatric care or drug treatment. In 24% of the situations, ongoing financial burden resulted when parents paid an adult child's living expenses. Although nearly half of the grandparent caregivers profiled by Fuller-Thompson (1997) lived below the poverty level, no grandparent caregivers in the study were living on public welfare assistance. Seventy-four percent of the participants were employed.

Custody battles, court appearances, and legal fees were the cause of difficult financial burdens for 22% of the families. Frequent trips to court or an attorney's office are very costly. Eighteen percent of the participants paid the cost of psychiatric hospitalization and drug rehabilitation for an adult

child out-of-pocket. These multithousand-dollar bills occurred when the young adult was not working and did not have health insurance coverage. Parents spared no expense in attempting to eliminate their adult child's problems.

Theft of property, money, or credit cards by an adult child had occurred in 18% of the families. These stories were told with sadness and disbelief. Money from the sale of personal property most often went toward the purchase of drugs. The use of a parent's credit card by a minor precipitated bankruptcy in one family.

The financial consequences of raising a grandchild are multifaceted. The following anecdote is from the 47-year-old stepgrandfather of a 4-year-old. His words describe both current and previous financial situations as well as the extra expenses.

> I'm making more money now than ever before in my life. And I'm scraping. There are times when my kids want to stop and get an ice cream cone, and I can't but it. I'll just tell you, I make about $70,000 a year, which I don't think is bad for a guy who has a bachelor's degree, you know. And I don't think I'm living beyond my means. We've spent about, probably about $8,000 this year, fighting this legal battle, and we went through long periods of time where Tommy wasn't covered on our insurance and so you take him to the doctor anyway, you know. A kid has an earache, a kid has an earache. You don't sit there and look at your checkbook balance and decide how bad his earache is. But then, no matter what we spend, his life will never be "normal," and that's what I want most for him.

Coping Strategies

Coping strategies are specific responses to stressful situations that are developed from personal and family resources. These strategies involve cognitive and behavioral attempts made to manage a stressful situation. Coping strategies diminish the effects of overwhelming anxiety and emotions. Grandparent participants described various ways they coped with different types of problems. A typology of coping strategies was created from the themes that emerged and appears in Table 18.4.

Taking Action   Assertive action was taken to stabilize situations that grandparents believed were out of control. Forty-one percent of the participants in

Table 18.4 Coping Mechanisms Used by Grandparent Caregivers

Coping Mechanisms	Number	Percent*
Take action	22	41
Talk about feelings	17	31
Spiritual faith	11	20
Work more	10	19
Focus on child	7	13
Outreach to others	7	13
Less desirable mechanisms	5	9

*Participants commonly gave more than one answer; consequently, percentages do not add up to 100%.

Note: N = 54

the study described actions such as hiring an attorney, learning legal definitions and policies, and taking an adult child to court. Other grandparents involved the Department of Human Services or documented child neglect and parental unfitness in their families. Those who feared the potential erratic or violent behavior of an adult child contacted law enforcement, purchased a gun, or installed a security system as a way of taking action.

Talking about Feelings   Myriad emotions accompanies grandparent caregiving, including unresolved feelings of guilt, shame, grief, fear, and anger. Thirty-one percent of the participants cited talking about their feelings as a way of coping with the intense emotions that accompany ongoing family problems or frustration from attempts to find resolution of financial and legal problems. Fears were expressed around the potential for harm or death of an adult child that could result from a drug habit or from retaliation by unsavory associates. Grandparents who described feeling anger explained that it was directed at adult children, the legal system, spouses, and the social service system. Feelings of grief were related to the loss of parents' hopes and dreams for an adult child. Grandparents talked about feelings with a friend, counselor, or minister, or in a support group. Grandparents were sometimes unable to resolve their feelings about a troubled adult child's lifestyle because there was continuous upheaval. Grandparents explained that there were times when they felt that no one understood their situation.

Religious Faith   Faith provided inner strength and direction in times of trouble. Faith was described as a way of coping by 20% of the participants. Many related that they turned to prayer and meditation to help them cope with daily uncertainty and anxiety.

Work   Working hard was described as a way to keep from dwelling on problems and to vent frustration. Work was a coping mechanism described by 19% of the grandparent participants. In some situations, grandparents explained that they sought extra paid work hours to alleviate some of the financial burdens.

Focusing on a Grandchild's Needs   New responsibilities helped create a positive focus for grandparents who had previously felt helpless to change their adult child's destructive lifestyle. Focus on a grandchild was expressed as a way of coping by 13% of the participants. It is important to note that participants also expressed unconditional parental love for troubled adult children despite ongoing problems. Many participants nurtured hope that their focus on grandchildren would provide the support an adult child needed to get his or her life straightened out.

Outreach to Others   Grandparents explained that reaching out to others through volunteer or self-help organizations helped them feel that they were making a positive contribution to society and made some good come from the difficulty in their lives. Outreach was a coping strategy described by 13% of the participants. Examples of this type of involvement included educational outreach about birth defects, teen pregnancy, or groups of troubled youth. Some participants explained that they were hopeful their efforts might help other families avoid having similar problems.

Less Desirable Coping Mechanisms   Grandparents related that at times they indulged in habits they knew were not good for them, but at least temporarily made them feel better. Nine percent of the participants described using less desirable ways of coping. Participants described using less desirable ways of coping. Participants described increased smoking, drinking coffee, overeating, or staying up too late as ways they coped with the difficult changes in their lifestyle. No grandparents reported using drugs or alcohol to alleviate stress.

The following anecdote is from a 50-year-old grandmother who was raising two grandchildren and a nephew. This anecdote represents her answer to the question, "How do you cope with the situation?"

I have faith. I have lots of faith. My family supports each other. People that I work with are wonderful. They are just marvelous. They work with me, they support me and say, "Sarah is there anything that I can do to help you, and stuff like that." It makes a difference—100% difference as opposed to people who won't work with ya. Ya know, that is my support. There were times when I worked full time at the hospital, part time at the nursing home, and then I squeezed in a part-time job one day per week at the shelter. I refused to get on welfare. I refused food stamps . . . I just worked my butt off.

Health

Changes in health status have previously been linked to the stress of grandparent caregiving (Joslin & Brouard, 1995; Minkler & Roe, 1993; Roe, Minkler, Saunders, & Thompson, 1996). Grandparents in this study were also asked about changes in their health status since they began raising grandchildren. Preexisting conditions such as diabetes, high blood pressure, or cardiac disease were exacerbated by stress for 30% of grandparent participants.

Some participants reported mental health problems such as depression resulting from caregiver stress. Grandparents explained the importance of counseling when they were having emotional problems. Five grandparents had begun taking medication for depression. Some participants noted increased frequency of colds, viruses, and digestive problems, and all discussed increased fatigue from caregiving responsibilities. It is important to note that 11% of the participants perceived that their lifestyle became more active and healthier as a result of raising grandchildren, and 13% indicated that grandparent caregiving had no effect on their health.

The following anecdote illustrates the complex interaction between health, stress, and work demands for grandparent caregivers. Mr. and Mrs. Snyder have been raising a 9-year-old with special needs since his birth.

Mrs. S. (age 52): There are days we feel like we're 70. I have high blood pressure, and stomach problems, and migraines, but not all of it is caused by my grandson, I've had a hard life, but now I have to give 150% to this child I don't have anything left. I'm exhausted.

Mr. S: I am 50 years old, I've had my career, I'm not in good health, as far as trying to stand on my feet or anything. I had an injury a few years ago and my spine, my right side, I fell down the stairs. DSS forces you to go to work in the work program now even in your 50s 'til you're 55. If you don't you'll get a letter they're gonna cut off your benefits until you have to go and get documentation why you don't go to work. So I have a job as a pizza delivery person at night.

Satisfaction in Grandparent Caregiving

Satisfaction and rewards from caregiving for grandchildren is an important outcome of grandparent caregiving (Minkler & Roe, 1993; Morrow-Kondos, Weber, & Cooper, 1997). In the midst of stress and family conflict, participants found meaning and satisfaction in being able to provide stability and security for their grandchildren. Participants often cited more than one source of satisfaction.

Joy from Sharing a Child's Life   Joy arose from the love children give freely and the feelings of delight one inevitably gets from being around them. This joy was described as intangible to others but an important source of satisfaction for 43% of the grandparent participants.

Joy from the Tasks of Child Rearing   Tangible evidence of a grandchild's growth, improved health, and feelings of security that demonstrated well-being helped grandparents feel that the decision to begin raising a grandchild had positive outcomes. Thirty-nine percent of the grandparent participants described satisfaction from involvement in child rearing.

Activities Shared with Grandchildren   Grandparents enjoyed participating in activities with their grandchildren. Coaching team sports, school involvement, and being scout leaders or chaperones were described by 13% of the participants. Meeting new people through their grandchildren's activities was enjoyable. Activities shared with grandchildren provided enjoyment and an opportunity to focus on having fun together.

A New Sense of Purpose and Direction for Life   Difficult experiences that precipitated the need to raise grandchildren also generated important meanings to the grandparents. Nine percent of the grandparent participants expressed feeling satisfaction about focusing on grandchildren.

Grandchildren's Accomplishments Helping grandchildren learn skills and show academic improvement was very satisfying for 7%. They explained that their grandchildren's accomplishments were visible proof that the decision to assume this responsibility had brought positive outcomes.

When asked if there are joys associated with raising his 10-year-old granddaughter, a 68-year-old grandfather responded by saying:

> Yes, to have her look up and say, "I love you." And she'll come around once in a while and she'll say, "I'm so glad. I'm so lucky I have you and grandma," she'll say. And I'll say, "Kellie, we're lucky we have each other. Yeah, we're lucky we have you." The fact that we almost lost her at birth and the thrill of her life, and the fact that her teachers and her peers and all my friends love her. One of my buddies that I ride bikes with had access to a Furby. Well, we couldn't have gotten one. He said, "If you want to buy it, I'll sell it to you at the regular cost." His lady friend, Sara, said, "Kellie is the coolest kid in town." I mean, that's the way she described her, and she is. Everybody loves her.

Relationship between Stress and Satisfaction

The interrelationship between stress, coping, and satisfaction are important for those who want to understand and help grandparent-headed families. The quality of the grandparent caregiver/adult child relationships was expected to be positively related to grandparent caregivers' satisfaction. Parents who had worked through difficulties and stabilized their relationship with an adult child were expected to express greater amounts of satisfaction. Descriptions of the relationship with an adult child were paired with the satisfaction participants expressed. Negative case testing was used to evaluate those situations that fit and did not fit the profile. Fifty-two caregivers described the relationship with their adult child as strained and tense. All 54 caregivers gave examples of satisfaction that were derived from a grandchild's well-being and stability. Relationships between parents and their adult children appear to have no effect on grandparents' abilities to find satisfaction in their caregiving role.

The permanence of the legal relationship between a grandparent caregiver and his or her grandchildren was expected to contribute negatively to the amount of stress experienced. Grandparents with more permanent legal custody were expected to feel less stress than those who had only a temporary arrangement. The responses of grandparent caregivers with permanent authority (55%) were compared with those who had only temporary authority (45%) on questions about the sources of stress. "Permanent authority" was defined as adoption or permanent legal guardianship. "Temporary authority" was defined as guardianship that was reviewed less than yearly or informal arrangements. The sources of stress were not different between groups. Grandparents with temporary authority expressed heightened anxiety about losing custody, and those with permanent authority explained that it provides a measure of security. However, grandparents with more permanent custody explained that permanent custody does not eliminate concern that an unstable parent will kidnap a child. The other sources of stress cited were the same regardless of the type of legal authority that had been established. Permanent legal authority appears to establish a feeling of increased security in grandparent-headed families, but does not diminish the overall amount of stress experienced.

Discussion and Implications

The transition from grandparent to caregiver is precipitated by difficult family crises and ongoing problems for which individuals develop situation-specific coping strategies. Understanding caregivers' responses to these problems is important for human service, health care, and legal professionals who may encounter troubled individuals from one or more generations in these families. Financial burdens are present in grandparent-headed families on all socioeconomic levels. Employment and savings accounts may place some grandparent-headed families in a higher income bracket, but when those resources are used for family emergencies, financial strain occurs. Public assistance is not always accessible for grandparents without formal custody of the grandchildren in their care, and they become frustrated by a system that appears insensitive to their needs. This study establishes the inherent stress of spending all the money available to take care of children and grandchildren, whether that income is far above or below the poverty line.

Grandparent caregivers remain a marginalized group in American society; their individual needs and stories can become lost in the complex systems with which they interact. One grandmother, a social worker, expressed frustrations with professionals who do not attemptr to understand the interrelationship between problems:

I would say the biggest problem is over-generalization—we're not all the same. This is a special child. This is a different situation. No two situations are going to be exactly alike, but they just generalize, and they just put us all in the same cattle chute. They don't make any exceptions for exceptional situations. I'm not saying we were any better or any more unique—every one of us is unique. But I'd know when the worker was sitting there looking at us, but all she had in mind was the next court date and what she had to write up for the court report. We were dealing with a daughter who's still out using drugs and stealing from us. We were dealing with my ex-husband's wife who wanted to take the baby away from us. We were dealing with trying to fight the DSS system to get the baby equipment that she needed. We were arguing with people at the hospital because they wouldn't treat her without DSS being involved, and we knew what she needed, and sometimes we couldn't get the tests that she needed done, because they didn't see it was necessary and she was in their custody. Grandparents need to just find an advocate in the system and hand on tight.

Grandparent caregivers' problems are largely unknown and misunderstood by professionals who work with intergenerational families in a variety of situations. Professionals who provide intervention must understand both the similarities and differences between diverse groups of caregivers and respect the chronic stress and uncertainty present within the grandparent caregiver population. Satisfaction, derived from stabilizing the life of a child, is always an important result to consider.

This research was supported in part by a dissertation grant from the Fahs-Beck Foundation, and by a John and Sue Taylor Research Grant at Oklahoma State University.

References

Berg, B. L. (1995). A dramaturgical look at interviewing (Ch. 3). *Qualitative research methods*. Boson: Allyn & Bacon.

Burnette, D. (1999). Custodial grandparents in Latino families: Patterns of service use and predictors of unmet needs. *Social Work, 44*(1), 22–34.

Burnette, D. (1997). Grandparents raising grandchildren in the inner city. *Families in Society, 78*, 489–499.

Burton, L. M. (1992). Black grandparents rearing children of drug-addicted parents: Stressors, outcomes, and social service needs. *The Gerontologist, 32*, 744–751.

Ehrle, G. M., & Day, H. D. (1994). Adjustment and family functioning of grandmothers rearing their grandchildren. *Contemporary Family Therapy, 16*, 67–82.

Flint M. M., & Perez-Porter, M. (1997). Grandparent caregivers: Legal and economic issues. *Journal of Gerontological Social Work, 28*, 1–2.

Fuller-Thompson, E. F., Minkler, M., & Driver, D. (1997). A profile of grandparents raising grandchildren in the United States. *The Gerontologist, 37*, 406–415.

Hagestad, G. O. (1985). Continuity and connectedness. In V. L. Bengtson & J. F. Robertson (Eds.). *Grandparenthood* (pp. 31–48). Beverly Hills: Sage.

Jendrek, M. P. (1994a). Grandparents who parent their grandchildren: Circumstances and decisions. *The Gerontologist, 34*, 613–622.

Jendrek, M. P. (1994b). Policy concerns of White grandparents who provide regular care to their grandchildren. *Journal of Gerontological Social Work, 23*(N 1–2), 175–200.

Joslin, D., & Brouard, A. (1995). The prevalence of grandmothers as primary caregivers in a poor pediatric population. *Journal of Community Health, 20*, 383–401.

Kerlinger, F. (1992). *Foundations of Behavioral Research*, 3rd edition. (pp. 15–21), Fort Worth, TX: Harcourt Brace College Publishers.

Kivnick, H. Q. (1982). Grandparenthood: An overview of meaning and mental health. *The Gerontologist, 22*, 59–65.

Kornhaber, A. (1996). *Contemporary grandparenting*. Thousand Oaks: Sage.

Kornhaber, A., & Woodward, K. L. (1981). *Grandparents/grandchildren: The vital connection*. Garden City, NY: Doubleday.

Lugaila, T. (1998). Marital status and living arrangements: March 1997 (Current Population Report Series, pp. 20–506). Suitland, MD: U.S. Bureau of the Census.

Minkler, M. (1999). Intergenerational families headed by grandparents: Contexts, realities and implications for policy. *Journal of Aging Studies*.

Minkler, M., & Roe, K. M. (1993). *Grandmothers as caregivers: Raising children of the crack cocaine epidemic*. Newbury Park: Sage.

Minkler, M. & Roe, K. (1999). Keeping the promise. *Generations* (winter, 1998–1999), 25–32.

Morrow-Kondos, D., Weber, J. A., Cooper, K. (1997). Becoming parents again:

Grandparents raising grandchildren. *Journal of Gerontological Social Work, 28,* 35–46.

Padgett, D. K. (1998). *Qualitative methods in social work research.* Thousand Oaks: Sage.

Pruchno, R. A. (1999). Raising grandchildren: The experiences of Black and White grandmothers. *The Gerontologist, 39,* 209–221.

Roe, K. M., & Minkler, M. (1999). Grandparents raising grandchildren: Challenges and responses. *Generations* (winter 1998–1999), 25–32.

Roe, K. M., Minkler, M., Saunders, F., & Thompson, G. E. (1996). Health of grandmothers raising children of the crack cocaine epidemic. *Medical Care, 34,* 1072–1084.

Shor, R. J., & Haslip, B. (1994). Custodial grandparenting: Implications for children's development. In A. E. Gottfried and A. W. Gottfried, (Eds.), *Redefining families: Implications for children's development* (pp. 171–217). New York: Plenum Press.

Strawbridge, W. J., Wallhagen, M. I., Shema, S. J., & Kaplan, G. A. (1997). New burdens or more of the same? Comparing grandparent, spouse, and adult-child caregivers. *The Gerontologist, 37,* 505–510.

Wagner, E. M., Weber, J. A., Hesser, J. & Cooper, K. (1995). Grandparents' visitation rights: Who decides? *Family Perspectives, 29,* 153–162.

Weber, J. A., & Waldrop, D. (2000). Grandparents raising grandchildren: Families in transition. *Journal of Gerontological Social Work, 33*(2), 27–46.

Waldrop, D., Weber, J. A., Herald, S. L., Pruett, J. Cooper, K., & Juopavicius, K. (1999). Wisdom and life experience: How grandfathers mentor their grandchildren. *Journal of Aging and Identity, 41*(1), 33–47.

Whitley, D. M., White, K. R., Kelley, S. J., & Yorker, B. (1999). Strengths-based case management: The application to grandparents raising grandchildren. *Families in Society, 80*(2), 110–119.

Joseph A. Weber
Deborah P. Waldrop

19

Grandparents Raising Grandchildren: Families in Transition

Nearly 4 million American children live in households headed by grandparents and the number continues to rise (Lugaila, 1999). The circumstances that cause grandparents to become responsible for their grandchildren are varied. Parental drug and alcohol abuse, child abuse and neglect, chronic unemployment and teenage pregnancy are some of the social and economic problems grandparents attempt to stabilize. These circumstances have an impact on all generations in a family. Grandparents are often the closest relatives asked to care for a child during difficult times. Grandparents assume parental responsibility at a time in their lives when retirement interests would normally occupy their attention. Grandparent caregivers accept new responsibilities and often become involved in uncertain situations.

Grandparents as Parents

Grandparents who function as parents for their grandchildren face financial, legal, and social issues and generate new concerns for social workers, social service agencies, and policymakers. The stress of these difficult issues can affect grandparents' mental and physical health (Greensburg, 1991; Minkler, Roe & Price, 1992; Pruchno, 1999). Previous studies have been conducted primarily with grandmother caregivers, but this growing population is diverse and includes men and women of all racial and socioeconomic groups (Burnette, 1999; Burton, 1992; Minkler & Roe, 1993; Thompson, Minkler, & Driver, 1997; Waldrop, Weber, Herald, Pruitt, Cooper & Juozapavicius, 1999).

Grandparent caregivers are motivated by commitment to the well-being of their grandchildren (Ehrle & Day, 1994; Jendrek, 1994a; Minkler & Roe, 1993). This commitment is not short term. Over half of the grandparents raising grandchildren provide this care for more than three years (Thompson et al., 1997). This commitment is also not made impulsively. Grandparents have often watched the effects of an adult child's problem behavior on their grandchildren for a long time. In these situations, the decision to assume parental responsibility is made when grandparents choose to focus on the grandchild's well-being rather than the adult child's problems (Morrow-Kondos, Weber & Cooper, 1997; Strawbridge, Wallhagen, Shema & Kaplan, 1997). Grandparent caregivers maintain hope that their adult children will be able to recreate a stable family environment in the future.

Grandparenthood, for many older adults, is a time of happiness and satisfaction. Grandparent-grandchild relationships represent an intergenerational bond that offers opportunities for a special kind of sharing (Kivnick, 1982; Kornhaber, 1996). Family continuity is established as individuals watch their adult children become parents. Individuals can now anticipate living long enough to watch their grandchildren reach adulthood. However, these intergenerational family relationships change when grandparents assume parental responsibility for their grandchildren.

Family caregiving by grandparents can be generated from two different scenarios. First, if grandparents become caregivers following the death of an adult child, a permanent custodial relationship can be created. Second, if grandparents assume responsibility as a result of the ongoing dysfunction of an adult child, the custodial relationship may be tenuous (Burnette, 1999; Minkler & Roe, 1993). This second situation may force the grandparent-grandchild dyad to manage a continually changing relationship with the adult child (Ehrle & Day, 1993; Jendrek, 1994a).

Grandparents can become caregivers as a result of their adult children's problems or death. In most situations these problems have continued for years. Statistics are becoming available that reflect the problems of specific racial and cultural groups of grandparent caregivers (Burnette, 1999; Burton, 1992; Jendrek 1994a; Joslin & Brouard, 1995; Minkler & Roe, 1993; Pruchno, 1999). The unique financial, legal, social, and emotional problems of these groups have become increasingly more apparent to social workers, social service agencies, and policymakers. Grandparent caregiving often leads to increased stress and burden for the caregiver.

The purpose of this study was to explore the family relationships that change when grandparents begin raising their grandchildren. Grandparent caregivers have needs and reactions to family problems that are different from other people in their age group. The focus was on the multigenerational family relationships in grandparent-headed households. The term grandparent-headed household will be used in this study to refer to families made up of grandparents and their grandchildren, with the parent being an entity outside of the family unit. Through in-depth interviews and the stories told by grandparents, this paper examines the ways that family relationships become different as grandparents become responsible for raising their grandchildren.

Methodology

The events that precipitate grandparent caregiving are emotionally charged and potentially difficult to understand. This study was exploratory in nature and involved qualitative research methods. Qualitative methods were used to encourage the meaningful expression of difficult and personal experiences by the participants.

Sample

This study involved a purposive sample that was generated from contacts made through the Grandparents as Second Parents Support Group and professional colleagues. The Oklahoma Department of

Aging Services also allowed recruitment of participants at the annual Grandparents Raising Grandchildren conference.

The sample population for this study was defined as families in which grandparents were primarily responsible for raising their children's children. Grandparent couples were sought whenever possible. The sample included 38 families: 14 stepfamilies, 15 couples still in original marriages, and 9 female single heads of households. In 16 families, both spouses agreed to be interviewed, which yielded important information about marital issues in grandparent-headed families. It is important to note that the sample for this study was primarily Caucasian and living in rural areas or small towns. This represents variation from the current national profile of grandparent caregivers (Thompson et al., 1997). Demographic information about this sample is summarized in Table 19.1.

Table 19.1 Demographic Characteristics of Sample

Categories	Number	Percent
Gender of Grandparents:		
Male	17	31
Female	37	69
Age of Grandparents:		
40–50	11	20
50–60	24	44
60–70	11	20
70–80	8	15
Race of Grandparents:		
Caucasian	49	90
African American	3	6
Native American	2	4
Current Family Type:		
Stepfamily	14	37
Single head of household	9	24
Original marriage	15	39
Age of Grandchildren:		
<1 year	1	2
1–5 years	19	30
6–10 years	25	40
11–15 years	8	13
>15 years	11	17
Length of Time Living with Grandparents:		
≤1 year	10	16
1–5 years	28	44
6–10 years	14	22
11–15 years	5	7
>15 years	7	11

Grandparents in this study had assumed primary responsibility for raising their grandchildren despite whatever ongoing contact there was with the child's parents. It is important to note that sudden death was the precipitating event in only one family in this sample. All other families dealt with long-term problems of a troubled adult child, which led to grandparent caregiving. In these situations, families managed multiple problems, which became more complex over time.

Data Collection

Semistructured, in-depth interviews were conducted at a time and place of the participants' choice. Sixteen married couples were interviewed: nine were interviewed jointly and individual interviews were conducted separately with each spouse in seven other families. During joint interviews, grandparents were asked for their individual responses to questions. Over half of the individuals interviewed spoke of the therapeutic value of being able to talk about their experiences and expressed thanks for being included in the study.

Instrumentation

The interview schedule was developed to guide discussion about family dynamics in grandparent families. Questions were adapted from the instrument used by Minkler and Roe (1993). Participants were asked a series of demographic questions (i.e., age, years of caregiving, and number of children) and a series of questions about the family events that precipitated their caregiving responsibilities. Grandparents were also asked about lifestyle changes and advice they would give to others facing a similar situation.

Data Analysis

Thirty-seven families allowed interviews to be audiotaped and transcribed. Transcription of couple interviews involved separating responses of individual participants for each question. Results were coded using QSR NUD*IST 4 (Non-numerical Unstructured Data Indexing Searching and Theory-building) software for quality analysis.

QSR NUD*IST software allowed exploration of the similarities and differences among participants' responses to the same questions. Coding was carried out in two ways. First, all answers were compiled for each question. Response categories were established within the answers for each question.

The second type of coding occurred as insights and new theories emerged. The software allowed the establishment of "free" or "new" themes that were not related to specific questions but came from interviews with people in similar life circumstances. Quotes and anecdotal information were then attached to these free themes creating typology of responses.

Results and Analysis

The results of this study suggested that there are three themes that came from exploring issues in families headed by grandparents. These themes are:

1. Blended grandparent-parent roles
2. Parent-child relationships
3. Collateral family relationships

Each of these themes was developed using the words and stories of grandparent caregivers. The names and identifying characteristics of participants were changed to protect confidentiality.

Blended Grandparent and Parent Roles

The first theme from the experiences of multigenerational factors is that which forces a blending of both grandparent and parents. The loss of a pure grandparent role and gain of parental responsibilities for young children were described by all participants. Some expressed feelings of loss associated with being unable to fulfill their dreams of being a grandparent who typically enforces fewer rules, acts as the wise historian, and has fun with grandchildren on a regular basis. Participants discussed the blended responsibilities of their new role as important and serious as follows:

I've never been able to be the grandparent with her. And I would like to be able to do that. So I'm ending up being her mother. I had to accept that and then to go ahead and grab hold of the reins and say okay, I'm going to take full responsibility as a mother figure. (a 52-year-old grandmother)

I'd planned on my grandchildren being in my life but not being my life. (a 41-year-old grandmother raising three grandchildren)

You know I'm certainly the family historian to her but I think what she doesn't get and can't get is kind of that unconditional acceptance for a few hours at a time that a grandmother can give. I mean as parents we are setting rules or enforcing rules and bedtime and this and that and that changes the relationship. (a 67-year-old grandmother)

Positive and negative feelings about raising young children were also expressed by all grandparent caregivers. They described a range of changes that this combined role brought to their lives. Parenting responsibilities were welcomed by some and accepted as necessary by others.

I loved it, I took care of them, I bottled them, I diapered them, I bathed them, we played, we did anything they wanted. I tried to see that they had what they wanted to play with. We'd take trips. We went to Carlsbad Caverns and places like that. We really enjoyed the children. (a 72-year-old grandmother who had been raising her grandchildren for 12 years)

Here I am getting a grouchy little kid out of bed in the morning, teaching prayers, brushing teeth, bandaging little what's its . . . How the heck did I get here? (a 54-year-old grandmother raising a 4-year-old granddaughter)

Grandparents related feelings of ambivalence about their new blended family role. They explained that they were sometimes confused in their simultaneous parental and grandparental roles. The uncertainty of this new family role is illustrated through the choice of names that grandparents are called by the grandchildren they are raising. Four distinct categories of titles were discovered. A majority of grandparent caregivers are called by clear grandparent titles, but many are called by either parental or mixed titles that changed from day to day. The four types of grandparent titles are:

Clear grandparent titles (i.e., Grandma, Grandpa, Nana, Paw Paw)
Clear parent titles (i.e., Mom, Dad, Mama, Papa)
Mixed grandparent-parent titles (i.e., Mom or Grandma at different times)
Grandparent's own name

Parent-Child Relationships

The second theme that emerged from exploration of the dynamics in grandparent-headed families is that of parent-child relationships. Regardless of the amount of strain, parents and children remain significant forces in each other's lives. These relationships continue to have primary importance whether the parent and child are living in close proximity or not.

Four sets of continuing parent-child relationships exist in families with grandparents raising grandchildren. These four ongoing parent-child relationships in multigenerational grandparent-headed families are:

1. Grandparent-grandchild relationships
2. Parent–adult child relationships
3. Adult child–grandchild relationships
4. Other parent-grandchild relationships

Grandparent-Grandchild Relationships The first parent-child relationship in multigenerational grandparent-headed families is that between grandparents and grandchildren who are living together as a nuclear family. Their relationship is based on care and security in the face of traumatic events, in most situations. Grandparents often assume care for children who have both emotional and physical needs. Most grandparents expressed reluctance about having to discipline their grandchildren as a parent would. Some grandparents dealt with extreme emotional reactions in their grandchildren following a traumatic event.

Behavior problems are associated with various aspects of grandparent-grandchild relationships in this situation. Some grandparents report that their grandchildren have behavioral problems which are directly associated with abuse and/or neglect. Other children in the study were described as having ADD or ADHD. Grandparents generally verbalized their understanding that children with ADD or ADHD developed symptoms as a direct result of having endured times when their physical and psychological needs were not met. Other grandparents related that behavior problems stem from medical problems that may have been induced by drug use during pregnancy. Many grandparents describe behavior changes after a child sees or has phone contact with a parent. These behavior changes are demonstrated with bouts of underlying anger, aggression, or anxiety (Table 19.2).

Most grandparents express very loving and positive feelings about their relationship with their grandchildren. Grandparents in this study expressed satisfaction about the difference they believe they are making in their grandchildren's lives and futures.

Table 19.2 Grandchildren's Problems Reported by Grandparent Caregivers

Problem	Number of Children	Percent
Medical problems	4	6
Positive drug screen at birth	2	3
Known drug use during pregnancy	23	36
Sexual abuse	7	11
Physical abuse	7	11
Neglect	17	27

Participants often gave more than one answer, consequently percentages do not add to 100%.
N = 64

The little girl is sunshine. We really think a lot of her. In fact I used to sing "You are my sunshine" to her when she was little. (a 54-year-old grandmother of a 14-year-old)

Watching her grow and develop, learn new things is really wonderful. I guess I was busier and not as involved with my own kids. The times that are stressful are getting less and less frequent. (a 68-year-old grandfather of a 7-year-old granddaughter)

Parent–Adult Child Relationships Adult children often continue a power struggle with their parents, which involves manipulation of resources, child custody arrangements, or emotional ties. Parents described many incidents in which an adult child stole money, credit cards, or other belongings from them. The emotional climate that results from these ongoing conflicts are expressed:

She's my daughter and I love her but she is not what I hoped for and certainly not what I know that she is capable of. It is really disappointing. She has lied to me, used and abused me. There have been times in my life that I did not think there was anything left by the time she got through. (a 53-year-old mother of a 26-year-old drug-addicted daughter)

Other parents express the feeling of being on an emotional roller coaster. A manipulative adult child may approach a parent with a conciliatory attitude but when the request is denied, begin screaming and raging.

Our relationship is volatile. She has decided that she loves me and she has forgiven me [for taking custody of her son] but she'll never trust me. (a 57-year-old mother of a 29-year-old recovering drug addict)

Parents became attuned to the emotional manipulation involved when adult children use the relationship to get what they want from their families. For example, after four episodes of abandonment, Roni's parents changed the locks on their house. When she called a week later, Roni told her parents, "I miss my babies and I miss the family. I know you love me and I want to come home." (Roni is 29 and her parents are 53 and 54 years old)

Another set of grandparents related that their son calls only when he needs something. When he recently asked if he could move back in with them, his father replied, "The revolving door is closed."

Many parents expressed frustration with their adult children who "never put their child's needs above their own." This lack of emotional commitment to a child caused broken relationships with their parents. Grandparent caregivers described this relationship damage as irreparable by these expressions:

I have a hard time forgiving her for what she has done. Ours is not a warm relationship.

I get so angry, it makes me crazy. I just avoid her.

Our relationship is very strained. We have little to say to each other.

Parents of troubled adult children related that they question their abilities as parents. Some parents expressed feelings of self-blame for their adult children's problems. Many made the statement, "I often wonder what I did wrong." They also related that they had learned they could no longer dwell on these issues, believing that they must conserve their physical and emotional energies for their grandchildren's needs.

Adult Child–Grandchild Relationships   The third parent-child relationship in multigenerational grandparent-headed families is the relationship between an adult child and his or her children. This relationship continues to be central in children's lives despite separate living situations. Children's reactions range from idealization of parents to disassociation from the parent. Some children express intense anger at their parents for abuse or neglect.

Katie has told her psychologist that she wishes she were dead so she would never have to see her mother again. (Katie is 10 years old)

Sean has gone so far as to tell other kids that his mother is dead. He tells me he never wants to have to see her again. (Sean is 7 years old)

Other children are described as being revived by contact with an absent parent even if he or she has historically paid minimal attention to the child's needs.

Ronnie just adores her. It's just like you've sprinkled some type of magic dust on him and he comes alive. (Ronnie is 71/2)

They adore their mommy, children always do. I just can't stand to see them hurt when she lets them down. (a 53-year-old grandfather of two, ages 5 and 6)

Some children have fantasies about reunification. Grandparents relate that these are generally grounded in reality, including promises that parents have made and later broken.

Robbie said that the last time she was here she told him she was going to get his two brothers and they would all live together. She hasn't called him or seen him in two years. (Robbie is the 10-year-old son of a 26-year-old alcoholic)

Other children have reversed roles with their parents and become parental in their interactions. These children and their grandparents seem to have created a set of rules, which surround interaction with the adult child-parent. Seven-year-old Jana

talks to her mother on the phone and has been overheard to ask her each time, "Do you have a job and a place to live yet? The judge said I can't live with you until you do."

The parent-child bond is likely to change with the individual growth and development over the years. Despite sporadic or infrequent contacts with a parent, the primary nature of this bond appears to remain significant. Ongoing relationships with noncustodial parents may potentially have "sleeper" effects. Sleeper effects occur when psychological or emotional issues that have remained dormant suddenly become relevant in a new developmental phase. Sleeper effects might transpire and first-time parenthood when the new parent was raised by a grandparent. This person may experience fear or doubt about whether he or she will succeed as a parent based on childhood experiences.

Relationships with the Other Parent   The fourth parent-child relationship in multigenerational grandparent-headed families is that between a child and the "other" parent. Custodial grandparents related stories about their grandchildren's interactions with the former spouse or partner of their adult child. In these situations the parents of the grandchildren were divorced or had broken off the relationship in all but two families. Contact between the "other" parent and child was sporadic in most situations, but the impact on the child was still described as meaningful.

I guess the first time we heard anything from the daughter-in-law was after court when she called on Cassie's birthday at about 10:30 at night. She'd been drinking and did speak to her but we didn't hear anything else from her until Thanksgiving, almost six months later and we found out she'd had three addresses since then. (a paternal grandfather with custody of a 10-year-old granddaughter)

Most grandparents explained that they realize that verbal discussion of the absent parent must be positive for the child's benefit, despite negative feelings they may personally have. Grandparents made conscious efforts not to show feelings about an adult child's former spouse or partner. In some situations, parents of a troubled adult child recognized that the former spouse had had many problems in life.

Several grandparents described the efforts they make at not talking about the absent parent in front of their grandchildren, mainly due to the respect they have for this child's need to form his or her own opinions. Noncustodial parents often lose touch with their children when a spouse's parents retain custody. It is unknown how much of the situation is related to choice or difficulty in the relationship.

Collateral Family Relationships

The third theme that emerged from exploring the dynamics in families headed by grandparents was of relationships other than parent-child bonds. These relationships are considerably changed by the onset of grandparent caregiving. The collateral relationships that were explored in this study were:

1. Other adult children
2. Other grandchildren
3. Marital relationships

Relationships among all family members are affected by events that precipitated grandparent caregiving. Grandparent caregivers may receive help and support or additional responsibility from other family members.

Other Adult Children   The first collateral relationship explored was that of a troubled adult and his or her siblings. Siblings often have strong feelings about the family events they have observed and sometimes participated in. These adult siblings had varying amounts of contact with each other. Parents describe the reactions of other adult children as ranging from those who "disowned" a sibling, to those who made a concerted effort to help. Adults who felt angry with their troubled sibling were described by their parents:

Her brother (my son) has disowned her. He feels his own daughter is getting shortchanged of both our time and money.

She's stressed out and bitter. We never knew how much they have struggled financially. They never told us because we had so much to do with our son.

Adult children who tried to be supportive of their parents are described in this way:

My daughter is glad because she knows it's good for Ryan but mad because she knows that this is the time in my life when I shouldn't have this type of responsibility.

She's a tremendous help. She's the only stable one. The judge asked her what she and the others felt about us getting custody. She spoke for all of them and said we all support it.

Parents related that their other adult children have become their greatest source of support. There were no sibling relationships described as unchanged by the events that preceded grandparent caregiving.

Other Grandchildren   The second collateral family relationship that was explored was the one between grandparent caregivers and grandchildren they are not raising. Grandchildren who are not being raised by a grandparent are keenly aware of the differences in the relationships their cousins have with shared grandparents.

Yea your grades are better than mine. If I lived with grandma and grandpa I'd have more time to study, too. (a 15-year-old cousin of a 17-year-old being raised by their grandparents)

Grandparents admitted that their relationship varies between different sets of grandchildren. They voice realization of their limited emotional and physical resources. One 59-year-old grandmother explained this by saying, "I know that I don't treat them all the same but I can't do anything about it."

Marital Relationships   The third changed collateral family relationship was the marital relationship. It is important to note that 76% of the individuals in this sample were married. The onset of grandparent caregiving had varying effects on the marital relationship. Some couples describe the changes as very damaging to their relationship. Others explained that raising grandchildren caused less strain than other family events such as retirement, death of a parent, or the ongoing problems of an adult child. Couples who describe the strain as devastating to their marriage illustrate:

Our marriage is horrible. But it's not just my granddaughter, it's really the marriage. She is just the focus of the problems we've had for 27 years. (a 54-year-old wife)

One couple described their daughter's attempts to openly drive a wedge between them. This is illustrated in the following dialogue:

Husband: It has affected our marriage in some harsh ways and some good ways. You know, we've learned to deal with a lot of problems together and probably learned to depend on each other more than we would have otherwise. We really cherish the few moments that we have together.

Wife: It's changed our relationship, we don't have the communication we did. We really appreciate it when we have a weekend together. We just have to get away from all the knocks on the door and the "Mom's!" and "Memaws!", etc.

Several married couples discussed communication problems. These people explained that the stress they lived with eroded that important component of their marriage. The continuing stress of an adult child's problems presented continuous obstacles to overcome. Several couples had sought marriage counseling. One couple had actually divorced, but at the time of the interview, they had been reunited for five years and planned to remarry.

Others related that they had grown together while raising grandchildren. Couples that had experienced growth expressed the belief that sharing the common goal of offering grandchildren security and love had helped them develop wisdom and understanding in their own relationship.

Discussion

Families adapt to stressful times and crises by drawing on individual strengths and developing new ways of coping with adversity. Grandparent-headed families experience long-term effects of the family crisis that precipitated the need for grandparent caregiving. Complex intergenerational family relationships are permanently changed by these traumatic events.

Grandparent-headed families deal with a variety of difficult social, financial, and legal problems. Families may be simultaneously handling multiple problems, which include a troubled adult child, behavioral issues of a grandchild who has been living in chaos, and the declining health of an older family member. The problem that is presented for social service help may be generated from any one of the generations but simultaneously affects each of them. For example, a child's behavior may provoke the need for counseling. In the process, professionals need to be aware of the interdependence found in multigenerational households. Further, clinicians should be aware of how a child's family history contributes to his or her behavior. Clinicians should also be aware of the difficulty an older

grandparent may have in handling a child's acting-out behaviors.

Grandparents experience loss of the hopes and dreams they had for an adult child and for this stage of their family's life. They also experience a sense of loss from missed opportunities for enjoying traditional roles with the grandchildren they are raising. The disciplinarian aspects of the parent role are especially difficult for grandparents to adopt. At the same time, grandparents have the opportunity to provide safety and security for their grandchildren during some of the most difficult times of their lives. They gain an important sense of satisfaction in this blended role.

There are several simultaneous parent-child relationships in grandparent-headed families. Parents and children rarely disassociate themselves from each other despite challenges and difficult problems. In some families, both grandparents and grandchildren deal with severed contact with an adult child on a long-term basis. In other families contact with the adult child is sporadic, erratic, and conflicted. In both situations parents experience sadness and grief about lost hopes and dreams.

Grandparents and the children they are raising have been called "skipped generation" families (Burnette, 1999; Minkler & Roe, 1993). These families actually remain multigenerational with a middle generation, which is physically absent but emotionally significant. The physical absence of the adult child generates difficult feelings of loss and abandonment, which appear to have long-lasting effects on both grandparents and grandchildren. Parent-child relationships in families continue to have an important emotional influence, even if it is negative, throughout the life cycle. Infrequent contacts with a troubled adult have as significant an emotional impact on both older and younger generations as frequent contacts do. The missing generation has a significant effect on family history and relationships even in their absence.

Implications for Social Work Practice

This research has documented that grandparents raising grandchildren face many complicated problems and circumstances. Social work can provide a needed service to grandparent caregivers by assisting and supporting this growing population. There are some specific services that social work can provide grandparent-headed families. This research suggests that social work can help grandparents develop:

- Coping strategies/mechanisms for multiple sources of stress related to family relationship issues, child circumstances, and institutional/organizational contacts.
- Stability by allowing grandparent-headed families to function as a family unit.
- Appropriate directions for fulfilling short- and long-term family goals.
- A meaningful view of life for the grandparent and the grandchild.

Implications for Further Research

Additional research is needed to further understand this unique grandparent population. The more social scientists understand the needs of this population, the better the services that can be provided. One particular area of study should focus on the great diversity that exists within this population. It is suggested that different populations of grandparents (i.e., culturally and ethnically diverse groups) be surveyed to gain an understanding of their specific needs and concerns.

Final Reflections

Families with an absent middle generation experience difficult transitions. Birthdays, anniversaries, and special events bring feelings of regret and loss to the surface. Children continue to fantasize about reunification with their parents. Family members live in a state of anticipation that the adult child will reappear. Practitioners are advised to consider the feelings that grandparents and grandchildren maintain about the absent member. Social workers must consider potential "sleeper effects" for children whose parents are unable to raise them and parents whose children are missing from the mainstream of the family.

Grandparents seek meaning in the traumatic experiences they have had as caregivers for their grandchildren. It is important to note that they spoke with deep feeling and passion about the importance of making a difference in their grandchildren's lives. Middle and later life development includes the knowledge and wisdom from lived experience. The ability to find inner meaning and growth through pain appears to be a significant factor in grandparents' adaptation to raising grandchildren. Grandparent caregivers must focus not only on the physical and concrete needs of their grandchildren, but also maintain concern for their emotional, psychological, and spiritual needs. Grandparents may need assistance in their attempts to help their grandchildren overcome and to prevent long-term emotional repercussions of traumatic events. Grandparents are concerned about the long-term impact of their caregiving decisions. Social workers in all types of agencies need to be able to help grandparent-headed families cope with the multiple issues they are facing.

References

Burnette, D. (1997). Grandparents raising grandchildren in the inner city. *Families in Society, 78,* 489–499.

Burnette, D. (1999). Custodial grandparents in Latino families: Patterns of service use and predictors of unmet needs. *Social Work, 44*(1), 22–34.

Burton, L. M. (1992). Black grandparents rearing children of drug-addicted parents: Stressors, outcomes, and social service needs. *The Gerontologist, 32,* 744–751.

Ehrle, G. M., & Day, H. D. (1994). Adjustment and family functioning of grandmothers rearing their grandchildren. *Contemporary Family Therapy, 16,* 67–82.

Greenberg, J. R. (1991). Problems in the lives of adult children: Their impact on aging parents. *Journal of Gerontological Social Work, 16,* 149–161.

Jendrek, M. P. (1994a). Grandparents who parent their grandchildren: Circumstances and decisions. *The Gerontologist, 34,* 613–622.

Jendrek, M. P. (1994b). Policy concerns of white grandparents who provide regular care to their grandchildren. *Journal of Gerontological Social Work, 23* (1/2), 175–200.

Joslin, D., & Brouard, A. (1995). The prevalence of grandmothers as primary caregivers in a poor pediatric population. *Journal of Community Health, 20,* 383–401.

Kivnick, H. Q. (1982). Grandparenthood: An overview of meaning and mental health. *The Gerontologist, 22,* 59–65.

Kornhaber, A. (1996). *Contemporary Grandparenting.* Thousand Oaks, CA: Sage.

Lugaila, T. (1998). *Marital status and living arrangements: March 1997* (Current Population Report Series, P20–506). Suitland, MD: U. S. Bureau of the Census.

Minkler, M., Driver, D., Roe, K. M., & Bedeian, K. (1993). Community interventions to support grandparent caregivers. *The Gerontologist, 33,* 807–811.

Minkler, M., & Roe, K. M. (1993). *Grandmothers as caregivers: Raising children of the crack cocaine epidemic.* Newbury Park, CA: Sage.

Minkler, M., Roe, K. M., & Price, M. (1992). The physical and emotional health of grandmothers raising grandchildren in the crack cocaine epidemic. *The Gerontologist, 32,* 752–761.

Morrow-Kondos, D., Weber, J. A., & Cooper, K. (1997). Becoming parents again: Grandparents raising grandchildren. *Journal of Gerontological Social Work, 28,* 35–46.

Pruchno, R. A. (1999). Raising grandchildren: The experiences of black and white grandmothers. *Gerontologist, 39,* 209–221.

Strawbridge, W. J., Wallhagen, M. I., Shema, S. J., & Kaplan, G. A. (1997). New burdens or more of the same? Comparing grandparent, spouse, and adult-child caregivers. *The Gerontologist, 37,* 505–510.

Waldrop, D., Weber, J. A., Herald, S., Pruett, J., Cooper, K. & Juozapavicius (1999). Wisdom and life experience: How grandfathers mentor their grandchildren. *Journal of Aging and Identity, 4*(1), 13–26.

CHERYL D. LEE
LOUANNE BAKK

20

Later-Life Transitions into Widowhood

Introduction

The loss of one's spouse can be described as the single most stressful life event. It is more stressful than a serious personal illness, separation, or divorce; being sentenced to prison; or living through the death of a parent or child (DiGiulio, 1989). In a pilot study of the social, emotional, service, and economic supports of widowed women, an assessment of 34 life events was included in the interview. Without exception, these widows, with a minimum of five years and a maximum of 10 years of widowhood, indicated that the loss of a spouse had affected them more than any other single life event (Matthews, 1991).

For women, widowhood in late life is a high-probability event (Bennett, 1997; Cox, 1996; Johnson & Barer, 1997; Matthews, 1991). At every age, male mortality exceeds female mortality (Cox, 1996). In 1990, 68% of the American population 80 years and older were women. As one advances in age, the differences between the number of men and women grow. At ages 65 to 69, women outnumber men 5 to 4; for those 75 years and over, women outnumber men 5 to 3. This difference further increases as a woman reaches age 85. For those age 85 years and older, women outnumber men 5 to 2 (U.S. Bureau of the Census, 1990).

A woman's transition into widowhood changes her identity and the way she views herself. It also has a significant impact on her social support systems, as well as her past and present roles. A transition is initiated when a person's current reality is disrupted. Its purpose is to build a bridge from the disrupted reality to one of the possible realities that

can be created (Steffl, 1995). For most widows, this devastating and lonely path often leads them to new and unexpected life satisfactions. Some, however, are not able to cope with this transition. They become depressed, develop poor health habits, and are at higher risk for residing in a nursing facility (Markson, 1984). This paper examines the psychological and social transitions a woman faces as the result of becoming a widow.

Initial Reactions and Transitions

Profound changes occur when a woman loses the partner with whom she has shared the ongoing process of defining herself and her surroundings. These changes involve a complete redefinition on the part of the widowed of who she is and how she views her world. This event causes a complete transition of her taken-for-granted reality. A woman's experience of becoming aware of her changing identity may begin immediately upon bereavement. This awareness gradually sets in more deeply as the widowed person goes about her daily life (Matthews, 1991). Within the first 12 to 18 months following the death of their spouse, most women claim that they can still feel the presence of their partner and go about their daily activities as if he were still present (DiGiulio, 1989).

A woman's personal identity becomes disoriented when she experiences the death of her spouse; part of her is perceived as being "lost" along with her spouse. At first, this disorientation is numbing and is similar to a shell shock experience. It later becomes more a question of "Who am I now that my spouse is dead?" Because women are more likely to have incorporated the marital relationship into their sense of themselves, they feel that they have lost not only a spouse but also a part of themselves (DiGiulio, 1989). One newly bereaved woman describes her initial reaction to the death of her husband:

> It seemed like hours before I could be persuaded to walk out of that room. When I did, I was conscious of my hands dangling uselessly by my sides. I was a person with no job to do, no place to fill, no function in life. The line had been drawn—the line between the world that contained someone who needed me and the world that had to somehow go on without him. (Matthews, 1991, p. 24)

Married men rarely describe themselves as "the husband of" their spouse. As a result, when their spouse dies, their identity remains intact. Women, on the other hand, have a tendency to describe themselves as part of their spouse and part of a family (DiGiulio, 1989). Therefore, a woman's identity is often defined through relationships and caring for others. When she loses a loved one, she also loses a sense of self, which intensifies grief and requires a new identity formation (Hurd, 1999). A husband's death leaves numerous voids in a woman's life; because her self-image was shaped by her identity as half of a couple, she must reexamine herself and move from a "we" to an "I" (Lieberman, 1996).

A New Sense of Self

The adverse effects of widowhood diminish with time (Lee & Willetts, 1998). Despite the initial psychological disruption of bereavement, many individuals experience widowhood as an opportunity for growth and independence (DiGiulio, 1989; Lieberman, 1996; Matthews, 1991). After the first difficult period following their husband's death, many women have found they have been able to advance and develop, establishing new and meaningful lives.

Morton Lieberman (1996), conducted a seven-year study of over 600 widows between the ages of 28 and 80. Eight out of 10 widows experience difficulty with at least one aspect of singleness after their husband's death. One year later, he found this number was significantly reduced. The majority of the women developed a greater ability to cope

with their problems. In addition, he found that they experienced significant improvements in their functioning abilities in both the world and their personal lives. These widows exhibited a greater sense of well-being, self-esteem, and life satisfaction. Most women adapt quite successfully to lives without husbands; some even discover that they enjoy and relish their freedom. For many, widowhood presents a time for meaningful life change (Lieberman, 1996; Walker, 1999).

In another study conducted with 26 widows in Guelph, Ontario, Canada, it was discovered that the majority of the women interviewed felt that they are now more thoughtful and appreciative than they had been in the past. They also felt that they are more decisive and independent than they were in their marriage (Matthews, 1991).

Some widows, after having time to reflect on their lives as married women, come to the conclusion that they were and are happier as single people (Hurd, 1999; Lieberman, 1996). Some reconnect with their past dreams and talents and rediscover a lost part of themselves. Others achieve dreams submerged during marriage when taking care of their husband and children; they develop their own sense of personal identity and begin to live full lives (DiGiulio, 1989; Lieberman, 1996). Frequently, parts of themselves that had seemed important, such as continuing their education or developing talents, were not pursued. Their husband, children, and home took priority. In some cases, husbands actively discouraged their wife's desires. Approximately one out of three widows studied felt they were stunted during their marriage, and one half had regrets about some aspects of their lives (Lieberman, 1996). In many cases, feeling stunted is what often led to their personal growth and development.

Widowed Women Who Transition Poorly

Some women, however, are unable to successfully recover and grow. They seem incapable of deriving pleasure from developing themselves or expressing previously unvoiced goals and desires. For the most part, they live their lives very much as they had prior to their husband's death. They are afraid of change and often cling to their husband's possessions for years after his death. In some cases, a husband's possessions become a shrine dedicated to his memory (DiGiulio, 1989; Matthews, 1991). Many of these widows suffer from anger at their husband for dying and guilt about thoughts unspoken, things left undone, and especially feelings that they had somehow let their husband down at the end of their lives. For these women, loneliness and sadness are severe problems which often lead to other health dilemmas (Lieberman, 1996).

Women in these more dependent marriages tend to describe their husband in almost mythical terms; their husband and marriage are idealized. When describing characteristics of these men, words such as intelligent, handsome, extremely kind, and generous are often used. There are no negative statements. They see their marriage as perfect and cannot consider anything that could have been different (DiGiulio, 1989; Matthews, 1991). Sanctification is a vital and necessary step in the bereavement process; it permits the widow's previously fused identity to become separated. This, however, should be a temporary phase. If sanctification is prolonged, it can become "canonization." If this occurs, the widow is immobilized and unable to move forward with personal identity reformulation. The majority of her energy is directed toward her deceased husband in an activity that can provide her with little ongoing fulfillment (DiGiulio, 1989).

Role Transitions

Role theory is the theoretical framework of several major studies of widowhood (Lopeta, 1979; Matthews, 1991). Roles have a profound effect on an individual's self-concept and sense of worth. Society fails to provide adequate role expectations or rewards for taking an old-person status; old age is a stage of life for which we are not properly socialized. This period represents a major loss of roles and is seen by the aged themselves as a negative experience that most would prefer to avoid (Brown, 1996; Cox, 1996; Dychwald & Flower, 1989).

For the majority of their lives, many widows think of themselves as housewives. With the death of their husband, these women's roles suddenly decline in importance and involve them in fewer community-related activities. They are left with no role expectations to perform and are no longer expected to participate in any of the activities typically related to the role of wife. Many widows consider the role of wife to have been a very important one, and the difficulties surrounding the loss of this identity are compounded by the fact that most widows lack an alternative major role to focus on. Disengagement and loss of life satisfaction often result

from the loss of this major life role that provided them with identity, purpose, and meaning in their lives (Brown, 1996; DiGiulio 1989; Hooyman & Kiyak, 1993; Matthews, 1991).

Widows who have several but not an overwhelming number of roles are more likely to successfully adapt after the death of their spouse. They are less likely to succumb to depression and illness than those whose sense of themselves is limited. The importance of having a role other than "wife" or "widow" is critical to their health and well-being. A widow who has not developed alternative roles is at a disadvantage. Developing relationships rooted in the present is essential to her recovery (DiGiulio, 1989).

Social Supports

In addition to providing emotional support, family members often provide significant practical support for the newly widowed. They can take on roles once occupied by the deceased person, such as managing finances or household maintenance. In examining the important health-promoting functions of support network members, many studies have focused specifically on the family as "one crucial form of social support" (Bohm & Rodin, 1985, p. 280; Matthews, 1991), particularly in relation to such age-related life events as bereavement. Family is frequently looked on as being a major and key source of strength during this difficult transition period (DiGiulio, 1989; Lieberman, 1996; Matthews, 1991).

The power and presence of this family support network should begin to recede after the first year (DiGiulio, 1989; Matthews, 1991). In some instances, they may interfere with a widow's recovery (Lieberman, 1996). Although children provide both socioeconomic support and assistance with tasks, this may not necessarily reduce their mother's loneliness. Interactions with an adult child are less reciprocal, while friends and neighbors are better suited for sharing leisure activities and providing companionship. This reciprocity tends to be associated with higher morale (Hooyman & Kiyak, 1993; Lee & Willetts, 1998). In fact, more widows prefer to be independent from their children (Johnson & Barer, 1997). Studies have shown that receiving considerable assistance from children can be depressing rather than supportive (Lee & Willetts, 1998).

Those widows in middle and later life almost universally feel alienated from married friends. The old "couples networks" that they previously relied on gradually begin to fade away (Lieberman,

1996). Many widows reported that they felt snubbed by people who were once their friends, especially those whose spouses were still alive (DiGiulio, 1989). When attending social functions, they began feeling like a fifth wheel. Widows commonly find that old friends are unable to provide them with the help they need; they no longer share commonalities. As a result, most develop new relationships, often with other widows who have similar experiences to share (DiGiulio, 1989; Lieberman, 1996). A 62-year-old widow of four months best illustrates this point by summarizing what she considers to be the source of her greatest help:

> While my neighbors and family were very helpful, only another widow can really know what you are going through. You don't have to wonder if they really understand you, you know they do. (Lieberman, 1996, p. 97)

Unfortunately, widows who do not develop social networks and relationships with their peers are at risk for alcohol addiction. It is estimated that as many as 10% of those age 60 or older have a problem with alcohol, and one-third of these older people first develop problems in later life, frequently after the death of a spouse. Socialization contributes significantly to lowering incidents of alcohol abuse and to increasing a widow's self-esteem and sense of well-being (Lachs & Boyer, 1999).

Many women tend to rely on a senior center as a social network that compensates for the loss of a husband and the accompanying social ties of marriage. Social interaction and physical activity are important aspects and give meaning to their lives. Peer group networks are an increasing pattern among the widowed. Social networks can become a source of new forms of self-esteem and self-worth (Brown, 1996; Hurd, 1999). Involvement in these networks often leads to a widow developing a sense of purpose. Her sense of worth, however, may not be apparent to an outsider. Following is an example illustrating this point:

> An elderly lady came to a senior center daily to do nothing but play Chinese checkers with a few choice friends. She very rarely missed a day. She lived alone and so, on the surface, it appeared that she came purely because she likes the game and to avoid being lonely. Her life seemed to have little or no purpose or worth. However, she related in an interview that, in fact, she was gaining a whole new sense of self-worth by coming to the center each day. She explained that the others with whom she played often told her that they were dependent upon her for their enjoyment of the day's activities. She had come to accept it as her duty to be there every day. (Brown, 1996, p. 72)

Widows with an abundance of social contacts enjoy better cognitive function than their more isolated peers (MacReady, 1999). Human contact is critical in counteracting loneliness, the most predictable consequence of widowhood. For these women, social supports, particularly close friends, confidants, and other widows, are essential to their physical and mental well-being, as well as their survival (DiGiulio, 1989; Hooyman & Kiyak, 1993; Lieberman, 1996; Matthews, 1991).

Sampling Procedure

This qualitative study was conducted at a senior center. Because of the nature of the facility, interviews were not audio recorded; however, notes were taken and transcribed immediately succeeding the interviews in order to preserve the accurateness of the information that was obtained. The sample consisted of eight widows who ranged from 74 to 86 years of age. All have children; the number of children ranged from two to eight. One individual has been married twice; the remainder of those interviewed were married once. The average length of marriage was 43 years. The number of years these women were widowed ranged from 5 years to 23 years. With the exception of one individual, all are residing alone.

The objectives of the interviews were: (1) to understand the significance of senior centers and social interaction with peers in the lives of widows who attend senior centers; (2) to determine whether new and/or additional roles are frequently undertaken after the death of a spouse; (3) to ascertain the role of family, the role of friends, and the role of other widows in the lives of widows; and (4) to investigate whether older widows are interested in romantic involvement after an extended period subsequent to their partner's death.

Results

All those interviewed attend the senior center at least three times per week, and when attending, stay an average of four hours. Three of the women stated that in addition to frequenting the senior center at which the study was conducted, they also visit a nearby center. All of the widows interviewed identified the facility as a major social system in their life. The social interaction, planned activities, and shared meals were unanimously defined by the group as being essential to their well-being and to counteracting loneliness. One respondent summarized her reasons for attending:

I just can't stand sitting in the house and watching TV. I know other widows who do that, but I don't associate with them. They're not happy. I got to get out and be with people. I look forward to coming here and seeing everyone. It feels like home to me.

In addition to attending the senior center, six of the eight women interviewed stated that they are active volunteers in this organization, and five of these individuals also volunteer in other groups and associations. The Air Force, choir, neighborhood association, arts and crafts guild, and golf clubs are just some of those mentioned. Four women stated that they became more involved in volunteer work and took on new roles since the death of their husband, and two stated that they had remained just as active as they had during their marriage. Seven of the eight interviewees stated that they had at least one other hobby or interest besides the senior center. The following is an excerpt from one widow who stated her motivation for remaining active and involved:

I just got to keep going. If I don't, I start to get tired and depressed. I start feeling sorry for myself. There are lots of things for me to do. When you're widowed, you just got to get involved and keep doing things.

Another widow was quoted as stating:

There's just not enough hours in the day—time goes so quickly. I'm always busy—I love it.

All of the widows interviewed were involved with their adult children in some way; however, the level of involvement varied. Over half had children living outside the state. Seven out of eight widows talk to at least one adult child each week, either by phone or in person. One woman reported living with her 62-year-old daughter, but as the following remarks illustrate, the relationship appears less than ideal:

She doesn't want to do anything—I can't stand it! All she does is sit in the house and watch TV: she never wants to go anywhere. We argue all the time about this [her lack of motivation].

Another widow stated that she has not talked to her adult son in over three months because of a disagreement. Contrary to these negative relationships, one woman stated that she is extremely close to her children and considers them to be a major source of strength. Despite the amount and type of contact with adult children, all those interviewed stated that they felt closest to other widows. The following statement identifies this apparent correlation:

They understand the best—what it's like. We just have a lot in common. Others [widows] know what I've been through. I think other widows are most supportive to me and understand better than anyone else.

Past couples networks that were a part of their previous social system have, for the most part, disappeared. There were numerous accounts of feeling like a fifth wheel and no longer socializing with married friends because of this discomfort. Two widows stated that female friends who still have their spouse appear threatened by their presence. One woman's account illustrates her encounters with a married female friend:

When I'm around, she [the married woman] pulls her husband in close to her, as if I'm going to steal him. This started happening shortly after my husband died—I couldn't believe it. She started thinking that I'm after him.

Six of the eight widows interviewed indicated that they would have an interest in becoming romantically involved again; however, as research and personal accounts indicate, there appears to be a lack of eligible widowers. As we discussed the availability of men, one interviewee jokingly remarked:

Look around [pointing around the senior center]—how many men do you see here?! And the ones that are here—let's just say they're not the ones I'm interested in!

One individual who has been widowed six years reported recently becoming involved in a relationship with a gentleman in her apartment building.

She described her feelings surrounding the relationship with this man:

> He's so kind—he sends me flowers once a week. When my husband died, I didn't think I'd ever want anyone [another man] again. It's nice to be cared about.

Alignment with Current Knowledge

Results of this study indicate that social supports and human contact, preferably with other widows who understand their situation, are essential to the physical and mental health and well-being of widows. All those interviewed had at least one social outlet, and half have taken on additional roles and pursued new activities since the death of their spouse. It appeared that those with numerous roles had successfully adapted to the transitions they experienced.

While children play a key role in providing practical support, peer relationships appear to take precedence. In two cases, assistance from adult children was found to be nonsupportive and depressing. However, contrary to the literature review, one widow reported having an extremely satisfying and close relationship with her adult children. As both research and personal accounts indicate, for the majority, connections with other widows are the prime source of fulfillment for these older women. The understanding nature of these relationships often furnishes widows with the emotional support and kindness they need. In opposition to these nurturing relationships, old couples networks provide little friendship for widows and often cause feelings of uneasiness, discomfort, and alienation.

Study Limitations

The small sample size and the fact that the study was conducted in senior centers are the two primary limitations of this study. Conducting the study in centers meant that we were not reaching socially isolated older widows. The women in our study were not isolated and had at least one social support, and it seems likely, therefore, that their transition to the role of widow was more successful than would be true of the socially isolated. If we were able to expand the sample size, including widows who do not attend senior centers

and replicate these findings in other diverse settings and geographic locations, better data could be obtained.

Implications for Social Work

Study findings indicate the importance of educating and preparing social work professionals in advance to be conscious of critical issues involving the female widowed aging population. When performing direct practice interventions with individuals, groups, and/or families, workers who possess an awareness of positive coping techniques will have the ability to enable this group to advance toward more successful transitions, as well as identify and differentiate between positive and negative coping styles. Another practice recommendation is that social workers meet with elderly widows in groups to facilitate discussion of stages in the grief process; personal growth issues; utilization of support from peers; and creation of opportunities for increased socialization. These findings also suggest the importance of encouraging policymakers to support services relevant to the needs of this growing population. Such services might include a more efficient transportation system so that widows can easily access activities in the community and allocation of funding for outreach by social workers in neighborhoods where there are likely to be senior widows. An objective of the outreach services would be to encourage widows' participation in a senior center or other interactive activities in the community.

References

Bennett, Kate Mary. (1997). Widowhood in elderly women: The medium- and long-term effects on mental and physical health. *Mortality, 7*(2), 137–149.

Bohm, L. C. & Rodin, J. (1985). *Health, illness and families: A life-span perspective.* New York: Wiley.

Brown, Arnold S. (1996). *The social process of aging and old age.* Prentice Hall.

Cox, Harold G. (1996). *Later life: The realities of aging.* Prentice Hall.

DiGiulio, Robert C. (1989). *Beyond widowhood.* New York: Free Press.

Hooyman, Nancy R. & Kiyak, H. Asuman. (1993). *Social gerontology.* Allyn and Bacon.

Hurd, Laura C. (1999). We're not old! Older women's negotiation of aging and oldness. *Journal of Aging Studies, 13*(4), 419–440.

Johnson, Colleen L. & Barer, Barbara M. (1997). *Life beyond 85 years: The aura of survivorship.* New York: Springer.

Lachs, Mark S. & Boyer, Pamela. (1999). Don't let alcohol get the upper hand. *Prevention, 51*(2), 142–145.

Lee, Gary R. & Willetts, Marion C. (1998). Widowhood and depression. *Research on Aging, 20*(5), 611–631.

Lieberman, Morton. (1996). *Doors close, doors open.* New York: G.P. Putnam's Sons.

Lopeta, H. Z. (1979). *Women as widows: Support systems.* New York: Elsevier.

MacReady, Norra. (1999). Cognitive function linked to social activity in elderly. *Lancet, 354* (9177), 491.

Markson, E. W. (1984). *Older women: Issues and prospects.* D.C. Heath.

Matthews, Anne M. (1991). *Widowhood in later life.* Toronto: Butterworths.

Steffl, Bernita M. (1995). *Women and aging in Arizona.* Arizona Women's Town Hall.

U.S. Bureau of the Census. (1990). *Census of population and housing.* Series CPH-L-74. Washington, D.C.: Government Printing Office.

Walker, Margaret Urban. (1999). *Mother time.* New York: Rowman & Littlefield.

21

Understanding the Ageing Process: A Developmental Perspective of the Psychosocial and Spiritual Dimensions

A Developmental Perspective of the Psychosocial and Spiritual Dimensions

It is often thought that the ageing process is all decline; this certainly appears to be the state from a physiological view. However, and perhaps fortunately, the contribution of the psychosocial and spiritual dimensions of life provides a very different picture of the ageing process. It is far from simple to separate out these two dimensions of ageing; however, it is important to distinguish between these two perspectives when considering the contribution of each to the understanding of the ageing process. This chapter will present a perspective of the ageing process, focusing mainly on spirituality in ageing.

"I'm not really religious." How many times have you heard that said? I asked the 83-year-old woman (I'll call her Eva) what she meant by "being religious"; her response was: "Well going to church and a 'do gooder' but you don't mean it."[1] Often, being religious is seen in a negative way that presents a restricted view of the capacity of the human spirit. This was the case for Eva, who, despite her claim not be "be religious," had developed a deep sense of spirituality. She had not attended church for many years; she lived alone, in fairly fragile health, surrounded by her cats, her garden, and lots of interesting books. She went to a contact center for older people each week. Eva had a sense of

peace and joy in her life. Eva had grappled with loss and adversity in her long life. She had been both mother and father to her children, as her husband had died while she was pregnant. Eva had never remarried. She had grown spiritually through all of this and continued to question life. Eva described herself as a First World War baby boomer. She said experience had made her question life and its meaning. She was a real survivor and displayed a deep wisdom in the way she spoke of the important things of life.

Some may wonder why I have chosen to use an example of a woman who is not actively involved in church activities to write of spirituality in ageing. She is one of many I could have chosen, and in a way she is not untypical of many of the older people we meet and care for or minister to in Western society of the early twenty-first century.

In my studies I would have classified Eva as having a sense of spiritual integrity, which I defined as:

> A state where an individual shows by their life example and attitudes, a sense of peace with themselves and others, and development of wholeness of being. The search for meaning and a degree of transcendence is evident.[2]

It seems that what Fowler is describing in his final stage of faith development is spiritual integrity.[3] Spiritual integrity must also be closely related to wisdom; Erikson would say that wisdom is an outcome of ego integrity in ageing.[4] These authors and others have recognized that psychosocial and faith development continues into old age. Indeed, it seems helpful to consider these dimensions from a developmental perspective.

Psychosocial Development and Ageing

No consideration of ageing and psychosocial development would be complete without reference to Erikson's eight stages of psychosocial development across the life span. Erikson described the final stage of psychosocial development that occurred in later life as integrity versus despair.[5] It is clear that this stage is not isolated from earlier stages, but is in a sense cumulative. It seems that the individual is able to revisit earlier stages of psychosocial development and attempt to see life experiences in a new way, to reframe what has gone before. There may be tension for elderly persons as they struggle to bring these experiences into a balance. The successful achievement of this leads to integrity, with an outcome of wisdom. However, wisdom itself should be seen as a cumulative process as the person continues to develop psychosocially. This development is frequently witnessed in older people in the naturally occurring process of reminiscence. It seems important in this final life stage to acknowledge recognition of the approaching end of the life span. A denial of the inevitability of approaching death may lead to a failure to effectively deal with this stage of psychosocial development.

Peck, recognizing the length and complexity of this final stage of psychosocial development, based on Erikson's work, suggested three developmental tasks during the ageing process.[6] Several decades on, these tasks now make even more sense in an ageing society, where people can expect to live for maybe 40–50 years labeled "old."

Peck called the first task ego differentiation versus work-role preoccupation. This stage involved the role changes, particularly in retirement, that require individuals to make crucial shifts in their personal value system to redefine their worth as older persons. Loss of meaning in life may be a critical factor for older men as they seek to find new meanings in life outside of their work-role identity. Rising rates of suicide among older men may be a sign of the difficulties that older men face as they age in current Western society and struggle to find meaning in later life.[7] This may also become a greater issue for women of the baby boomer generation, as workplace participation has been both

more frequent and longer term for many of these women.

Peck's second task is body transcendence versus body preoccupation. Here the individual has to come to terms with living in an ageing body, accepting that, and overcoming problems such as disability and pain that are not uncommonly encountered in chronic illnesses. Successful negotiation of this stage enables the person to transcend the physical decline of the body in ageing. Failure to come to terms with this stage leaves the person preoccupied with the difficulties of the body.

The third task is termed egotranscendence versus ego preoccupation. Peck saw this as the point of realization by persons that death would occur to them. Peck saw this task to be letting go of self-centeredness and transcending the self. From Fankl's perspective, this would be a self-forgetting.[8] These three tasks described by Peck, although described out of a psychosocial view, could quite legitimately be seen from a spiritual perspective, as they deal with issues of meaning in life and self-transcendence.

So What Is Spirituality?

Still following a developmental approach to understanding ageing, the work of Fowler and others since the early 1980s has added much to understanding faith development across the life-span.[9,10,11] Although Fowler has used the term "faith" rather than "spirituality," his use of the term is similar. Fowler sees faith as both *relational and as a way of knowing*. It is important to note that Fowler does not state a content of faith; rather, he describes a structure of faith development.

Fowler has argued that just as there are stages of psychosocial development across the life span, so there are stages of faith development. He describes faith as having seven possible stages (starting at stage 0), but not everyone will pass through each of these stages.

Older people seem more likely to be at one of the stages from 3 to 6. Stage 3 is called synthetic-conventional faith. This stage is described as everybody's faith, that is, conformist in nature. Although this stage is seen as occurring in late childhood, it can also become a terminal stage of faith development for some older adults. The holder of this type is tuned to the expectations and judgments of significant others and has not seen the need to construct his or her own faith stance. It is synthetic in that it lacks analysis and it is accepted without question.

The fourth stage of faith development is termed individuative-reflective faith: in this stage there is a relocation of authority in the self.[12] That is, the individual will be critical of the advice and knowledge of others. This stage is typical in early adulthood, but again, may be a final stage for some. The transition into this stage may occur at any time from young adulthood onward. Fowler's fifth stage is termed paradoxical-consolidative or conjunctive faith and it is described as a "balanced faith, inclusive faith, a both/and faith."[13] A marked feature of this stage is a "new openness to others and their world views, and a new ability to keep in tension the paradoxes and polarities of faith and life."[14] A new humility and recognition of interdependence is seen at this stage.

The final stage of faith development, called universalizing faith, is said to be rare and occurs only in later life. It has been described as a selfless faith; it involves a relinquishing and transcending of the self. Although Fowler's research indicated that few people reached this stage, I would question his findings here and suggest that further research with older adults may show otherwise. I refer particularly to numbers of residents of nursing homes who certainly demonstrate being in this stage of faith development.[15]

Of course, we could use the term spirituality rather than faith. I think the term spirituality is the more accessible term, at least in Australian society, where spirituality is in more common use in the wider community. The word spirituality is also more widely understood in the health and psychology literature, while it is also in common usage within the fields of pastoral theology and pastoral care.

How, Then, Is the Spiritual Dimension in Ageing to Be Understood?

For older people the real issues of the spiritual dimension may well include worship, but will also include issues of finding ultimate meaning in life, of coping with a failing body, of dealing with loss, and the need for forgiveness and reconciliation. These are all issues belonging to the spiritual domain of life. There is an overlap between psychological and spiritual dimensions, and it seems reasonable to acknowledge this. It may indeed be asked: How important is it to distinguish between psychosocial and spiritual needs? It is suggested that it is important to the extent that *spiritual* needs

assessed and diagnosed as *psychosocial* will not be met by appropriate strategies. However, it appears that there is still considerable confusion about what spirituality is both within the community and also among health professionals.

Spirituality in Frail Older People

I first started listening to the stories of frail older residents of nursing homes in 1992.[16,17] These early studies indicated a range of spiritual need and spiritual well-being among the residents. Some older people referred to the nursing home as "God's waiting room." Comments included: "Not even God could help me now I am in a nursing home"; "I would rather be dead than here"; "I would welcome death." Yet the faith of another older woman allowed her to accept being in a nursing home. These people were residents in well-appointed and well-maintained nursing homes. These were nursing homes that have prided themselves on the quality of care given to their residents. The context of these comments was a study done in conjunction with a course of continuing education for registered nurses at University of Canberra. One hundred and seventy-two nursing home residents were interviewed by registered nurses in an assessment of spiritual needs of older people. In this study the nurses reported that they benefited greatly from the experience of this study, one saying: "What an important area this is for registered nurses . . . we do not properly address this area." They were often surprised at how ready the residents were to share their concerns, and that for a number of residents, it was the first time they had felt free to talk about the deeper things of life. These nurses learned a lot about the people they had cared for for months, or years. These were things that led them to see nursing in a new way and to change the way they were giving care.

A Study of Spiritual Awareness of Registered Nurses Working in Nursing Homes

These same nurses initiated the request for a project to raise nurse awareness of the spiritual needs of older adult residents in nursing homes. This request coincided with my concerns at the lack of spiritual care residents in nursing homes were receiving. Thus, the project to raise nurse awareness of their own spirituality and assist them to recognize spiritual needs of their residents in six nursing homes (five in Canberra and one in New South Wales) was developed. The study consisted of a pretest that examined nurse understanding of the term spirituality and also asked them to identify a number of behaviors as being in the physical, psychosocial, or spiritual domains, or a combination of psychosocial and spiritual (see Table 21.1). The subsequent analysis, using SPSS, was set up to take account of moves from psychosocial to spiritual or the reverse.

A workshop followed, where nurses examined their individual spirituality and how this impacted on their own lives. Following this, basic strategies were outlined to enable the workshop participants to identify spiritual needs in residents and either meet these or refer residents to appropriate pastoral care providers. A posttest was administered after the workshops.

Comparison of the Pre- and Post-Continuing Education Surveys

Each item was compared before and after the session; the sample size for each item varied from 35 to 53.

The objective of analysis was to determine whether there was a change in the respondent's perceptions of the spiritual aspect of each activity on the inventory between the pre- and postsession surveys. All postsession surveys were completed less than two weeks after the education sessions. Follow-up of some respondents was difficult, due to people going on leave or being unobtainable for other reasons.

Significant changes in participant identification of the spiritual dimension were shown between the pre- and postsurveys (Table 21.2). In the presession inventory, the only items that were rated high as spiritual behaviors were those associated with worship or that contained the word "God" or "Bible." This is consistent with a common perception that religion and spirituality are synonymous, yet human spirituality is a much broader dimension than that. Comparing the pre- and postresponse, the change was for more respondents to identify the spiritual dimension either alone or with the psychosocial dimension.

These nurses subsequently identified the spiritual dimension more frequently in their work with older nursing home residents. In fact, one problem that emerged for me following this study was receiving more referrals from nursing staff for cases of spiritual distress/need than I could meet. Nurses who have completed studies in spirituality and nursing could address a number of these issues as part of their holistic nursing care.[18] It was evident that many of the nurses working in the nursing homes where these studies were conducted had no preparation in providing spiritual care and did not feel comfortable providing this care. While my sessions with them certainly increased their sensitivity to the spiritual needs of their residents, it did not provide them with strategies they felt comfortable to use.

An Understanding of Spirituality

For an adequate understanding of spirituality it is necessary to consider, first, the human need for ultimate meaning in each person, whether this is fulfilled through relationship with God, or some sense

Table 21.1 List of Spiritual Behaviors/Actions Developed for the Study

1. Praying with patient	13. Assisting an elderly person to worship according to his or her faith
2. Assisting a person to find meaning in suffering and death	14. Assisting an elderly person who is fearful of the future
3. Listening to a patient	15. Supporting a person in the feeling of being loved by others/God
4. Supporting a person in his or her hope of life after death	16. Assisting a person to deal with feelings of guilt
5. Developing a trusting relationship with patient	17. Caring for a person who feels hopeless
6. Reading the Bible or other religious material	18. Referral of a person who needs forgiveness
7. Calling the chaplain or minister	19. Facilitating reconciliation among family members
8. Facilitating reminiscence	20. Facilitating reconciliation with God
9. Assisting an elderly person to find meaning in life	21. Assisting a person to achieve a sense of self-acceptance
10. Caring with integrity for an elderly person	22. Honoring a person's integrity
11. Assisting a person in the process of dying	23. Assisting a person to deal with anger
12. Facilitating relationship with an elderly person	24. Assisting a person to deal with grief

Table 21.2 Using McNemar's Test, at the 95% Level of Significance, 10 Items Were Significant

Item	Behavior	Score
3	listening to a patient	6.23
8	facilitating reminiscence	4.76
11	assisting a person in the process of dying	6.00
14	assisting an elderly person who is fearful of the future	9.00
15	supporting a person in his or her feeling of being loved by others/God	4.50
16	assisting a person to deal with feelings of guilt	11.27
17	caring for a person who feels hopeless	4.45
19	facilitating reconciliation among family members	8.89
22	honoring a person's integrity	7.36
23	assisting a person to deal with anger	8.07

of "other"; or whether some other sense of meaning becomes the guiding force within the individual's life. Second, human spirituality involves relationship with others. Spirituality is a part of every human being. Once acknowledging the universal nature of human spirituality, there is a real need to have a definition of spirituality that is inclusive of all religious groups and of the secular.

It seems appropriate to consider spirituality as having two components: a broad, generic component and a specific component. The generic component is that which lies at the core of each human's being. It is that which searches and yearns for relationship in life and for meaning in existence. Individual humans may find this need addressed in all sorts of situations in life, in love, in joy, in suffering, and in pain and loss. Ashbrook says: "Beyond the self of culture lies the soul in God, the core of each person's being."[19] The specific component of spirituality is understood as the way individuals work out their spirituality in their lives. This may be in the practice of a particular religion, it may be through relationship with other people and in community, work, or through particular centers of meaning and interests in life.

A Definition of Spirituality

There are many definitions of spirituality. The operational definition used in my studies takes into account the main characteristics of the sample of older people interviewed. These were Christians and others who acknowledged no faith or denominational affiliation. This definition of spirituality was:

That which lies at the core of each person's being, an essential dimension which brings meaning to life. Constituted not only by religious practices, but understood more broadly, as relationship with God, however God or ultimate meaning is perceived by the person, and in relationship with other people.[20]

What Happens with Spirituality in the Ageing Process?

As the person reaches and passes middle age there is a tendency to become more introspective and to come to a new sense of time. Neugarten, taking a psychological perspective, sees this as a refocus from time yet to live, to time already lived.[21] Reminiscence becomes more important, and is now well recognized as a spiritual task of ageing. As individuals become more conscious of the approaching end of their lives the search for final meaning of life gains greater urgency. Questions such as "Why was I here?" "Has my life been worthwhile?" gain a new importance.

A number of authors have recognized changes that occur in the spiritual dimension in ageing. Clements writes of spiritual development being the developmental stage of the fourth quarter of life.[22] Fischer writes of the necessity of letting go to be able to move onward, viewing this as the ability to affirm life in the face of death.[23] Frankl wrote of the search for final meanings in life, as one grows older.[24] Kimble too writes of the search for meaning in later life and the spiritual nature of this search.[25]

The losses of loved ones and the losses of roles of middle life may lead to a new questioning of life and its meaning. In conjunction with this, the onset of chronic illnesses and disabilities and the physical decline so commonly encountered in ageing lead to a shift in focus from doing to being. This may be used as an opportunity to reflect and become more introspective, or it may become a time of struggle and tension in the process of wanting to hold onto a midlife focus of associating meaning in life through roles and activities in life. In a sense, there is an inextricable connection between physical decline and spiritual development. It seems that in ageing, as Paul wrote (2 Corinthians 4:16): "Even though our outer nature is wasting away, our inner nature is being renewed day by day." Transcendence and growing into a sense of integrity as well as coming to final meanings of life can be seen as critical tasks of ageing. There is the potential for spiritual development to continue to the point of death. In fact, it can be said that the process of dying itself is part of the spiritual journey.

Conclusion

This chapter has examined ageing taking a developmental perspective, considering this under two related aspects: psychosocial developmental processes and spiritual developmental processes. While there are close links and, in fact, interactions between the two aspects, there are also differences that are important to acknowledge. When the developmental aspects of ageing are too narrowly defined in terms of the psychosocial, one result is that access is denied to spiritual interventions of the sacraments and pastoral care. The risks of assigning all things to the spiritual domain has the disadvantage of denying access to the rich strategies of the psychosocial domain that are also valuable in assisting older people to continue to develop in these dimensions in later life. A better understanding of the spiritual dimension in ageing seems an important avenue to explore in examining the holistic role for nurses as well as the roles of other health professionals and clergy.

Notes

The second study was supported by the Anglican Diocesan Foundation, Diocese of Canberra and Goulburn and Anglican Retirement Community Services (ARCS) Canberra and Goulburn.

1. E. B. MacKinlay, "The Spiritual Dimension of Ageing: Meaning in Life, Response to Meaning, and Well Being in Ageing" (doctoral thesis, La-Trobe University, 1998).

2. Ibid., 292.

3. J. W. Fowler, *Stages of Faith: The Psychology of Human Development and the Quest for Meaning* (San Francisco: Harper, 1981).

4. E. H. Erikson, J. M. Erikson, and H. Q. Kivnick, *Vital Involvement in Old Age* (New York: Norton, 1986).

5. Ibid.

6. R. C. Peck, "Psychological development in the second half of life," in *Middle Age and Aging: A Reader in Social Psychology*, edited by B. L. Neugarten (Chicago: University of Chicago Press, 1968).

7. R. Hassan, *Suicide Explained: The Australian Experience* (Melbourne: Melbourne University Press, 1995).

8. V. E. Frankl, *Man's Search for Meaning* (New York: Washington Square Press, 1984).

9. Fowler, *Stages of Faith*.

10. J. W. Fowler, K. E. Nipkow, and F. Schweitzer, eds., *Stages of Faith and Religious Development: Implications for Church, Education, and Society* (London: SCM Press, 1992).

11. J. W. Fowler in *Faith Development and Fowler*, edited by C. Dykstra and S. Parks (Birmingham, Ala.: Religious Education Press, 1986).

12. Fowler, *Stages of Faith*, 179.

13. J. Astley and L. J. Francis, *Christian Perspectives on Faith Development* (Grand Rapids: Eerdmans, 1992), viii.

14. Ibid., xxii.

15. E. B. MacKinlay, data from study of elderly residents of nursing homes in Canberra, Australia (unpublished. Study completed 2000).

16. E. B. MacKinlay, "Spiritual Needs of the Elderly Residents of Nursing Homes" (unpublished report, submitted in part fulfillment of requirements for BTh at St Mark's National Theological Centre, Canberra, 1992).

17. E. B. MacKinlay, "Spirituality and Ageing: Bringing Meaning to Life," in *St Mark's Review*, Spring 155 (1993), 26–30.

18. E. B. MacKinlay, "Ageing, spirituality and the nursing role," in *Spirituality: The Heart of Nursing*, edited by S. Ronaldson (Melbourne: AUSMED Publications, 1997).

19. J. B. Ashbrook, *Minding the Soul: Pastoral Counseling as Remembering* (Minneapolis: Fortress Press, 1996), 74.

20. MacKinlay, "Spiritual Needs of the Elderly Residents."

21. B. L. Neugarten, "Adult Personality: Towards a Psychology of the Life Cycle," in *Middle*

Age and Aging: A Reader in Social Psychology, edited by B.L. Neugarten (Chicago: University of Chicago Press, 1968).

22. W. M. Clements, "Spiritual Development in the Fourth Quarter of Life," in *Spiritual Maturity in the Later Years*, edited by J. J. Seeber (New York: Haworth Press, 1990), 69.

23. K. Fischer, *Winter Grace: Spirituality for the Later Years* (New York: Paulist Press, 1985).

24. Frankl, *Man's Search for Meaning*.

25. M. A. Kimble, S. H. McFadden, J. W. Ellor, and J. J. Seeber, eds., *Aging, Spirituality, and Religion: A Handbook* (Minneapolis: Augsburg Fortress Press, 1995).

RONIT D. LEICHTENTRITT
KATHRYN D. RETTIG

22

Values Underlying End-of-Life Decisions: A Qualitative Approach

Awareness of death clarifies our values. As a result, death can give meaning to life.
—Koestenbaum, 1976

Human values play important roles in human behaviors because they influence perceptions, decisions, and actions and, as a result, affect the welfare of individuals, their family members, and the community. In view of the importance of values in guiding human judgments (Nenon, 1997), researchers and practitioners would benefit from explicit descriptions of the central values underlying the deliberations faced by people concerned with decisions to prolong or to end life (Brigham & Pfeifer, 1996).

The ethical challenges and moral issues of end-of-life decisions are recognized widely (President's Commission for the Study of Ethical Problems in Medicine and Biomedical and Behavioral Research, 1983), but the empirical understanding of these decisions is limited. Few studies have examined the perspectives of nonprofessional people toward the different acts of end of life, and even fewer have attempted to reach an understanding of the decision-making considerations (Roberto, 1999). The current study attempts to fill these gaps and explores, for the first time, the values that influence end-of-life decisions for Jewish Israeli elderly people (age 65 years and older) and their family members.

Literature Review

End-of-life decisions are practical problems. A *practical problem* is a value-based question about what should be done in a particular situation within a particular context (Brown, 1985). End-of-life decisions are practical problems because their solutions vary for particular people in their specific contexts (Lee, Kleinbach, Hu, & Chen, 1996), given their unique personal value priorities (Leichtentritt & Rettig, 1999a).

Values: Definitions and Categorizations

The term "value" is derived from the Latin word *valere*, meaning "to be strong, to prevail, or to be of worth" (Meinert, 1980, p. 5). Although the roots of the term are known, there are many variations in meanings of the term, and as a result, the word "value" is difficult to define. A review of social science publications revealed 180 different definitions for the term (Timms, 1983). These definitions provided only five features that were common to all. *Values* are concepts or beliefs about desirable end-states that transcend specific situations, guide selection or evaluation of behaviors and events, and are ordered by relative importance (Schwartz & Bilsky, 1987). These features describe the formal characteristics of human values and can be found in the work of Rokeach (1973), who defined *value* as "an enduring belief that a specific mode of conduct or end-state of existence is preferable to a converse mode of conduct or end-state of existence" (p. 3).

The theoretical classifications of values by Rokeach (1973) distinguished between terminal and instrumental values. Terminal values refer to desirable end-states of existence, whereas instrumental values are desirable modes of conduct. Terminal values may be society-centered or person-centered. Examples of society-centered terminal values include justice, national security, peace, and brotherhood. Person-centered terminal values include wisdom, inner harmony, and self-respect.

Instrumental values may be of intrapersonal or interpersonal focus and include competence and moral values (Rokeach, 1973). Instrumental competence values are person-centered (intrapersonal) and apply to behaviors that work toward individual competence, courage, independence, and honesty. Instrumental moral values are relationship-centered (interpersonal) and include love, loyalty, devotion, and compassion.

Values and Decision Making

Values play an integral part in shaping personal decisions because they influence all of the stages of choice (Paolucci, Hall, & Axinn, 1977). Theoreticians who described the varied roles of values in the decision-making process concluded that values influence the selection from available modes, means, and ends of action and therefore serve as criteria for ranking alternative goals in preferential order and for selecting the preferable goal. Values assist individuals in evaluating and judging others and ourselves and serve as standards of comparison when determining whether we are as moral or competent as others. Values provide the standards to determine which "beliefs, attitudes, values, and actions of others are worth challenging, protesting, and arguing about, or worth trying to influence or to change" (Rokeach, 1973, p. 13).

Values are also the standards that guide us in deciding how to rationalize beliefs and actions that are unacceptable, either personally or socially (Rokeach, 1973). These descriptions highlight the roles of values in reaching an ethical decision and draw attention to the interdependence of individuals and social environments in the decision-making process. The social environment for this study is Israeli society.

Israeli Social and Value Contexts

Scholars have previously drawn attention to the unique aspects of Israeli society in regard to end-of-life decisions. Some aspects include the strong influence of the Orthodox Jewish tradition (Leichtentritt & Rettig, 1999a); the recent (1996) recog-

nition of patients' rights at end of life; the lack of appropriate terminology referring to an individual's rights at end of life (Leichtentritt & Rettig, 1999a, 1999b); the social norms surrounding care for a dying parent (Freedman, 1996; Gross, 1999); and the discrepancies between regulations and practices in health care settings (Glick, 1997). Readers are encouraged to examine these works for an overview of the social context of this study.

Israeli legal and medical guidelines toward end-of-life acts have long been characterized by communitarian philosophical values (Glick, 1997). A *communitarian* framework refers to values that are embedded with a high degree of collective consciousness, solidarity, belonging, mutual concern, and interdependence. The communitarian philosophy tempers individual interests in favor of some collectively defined ideas or values (Glick, 1997). These collective values were generated in Israel partly by the influence of Jewish religious beliefs and partly by historical conditions, forced communal isolation, and anti-Semitism (Shuval, 1992). This collectivist worldview is often the overriding norm in Israel when addressing end-of-life decisions (Gross, 1999).

Method

The purpose of this study was to reveal the values that would receive attention from elderly Israelis and their family members when considering an end-of-life decision in four hypothetical scenarios. The study involved elderly people and their family members, because these are the most vulnerable people in regard to legitimizing and implementing end-of-life decisions (Leichtentritt & Rettig, 2000). The justification for the research is grounded in the understanding that encouraging individuals to engage in conversations about end-of-life decisions is a valuable experience that provides an opportunity for clarifying intentions (Roberto, 1999). The research provided the informants with the opportunity to examine their value conflicts and priorities toward a phenomenon rarely discussed in family settings (Leichtentritt & Rettig, 1999b).

Research Design

The hermeneutic phenomenological method (van Manen, 1990) was appropriate for the study because value analysis focuses on judgments and interpretations in the investigation (Nenon, 1997). The method also was found to be effective in studying health and health care practice (Benner, 1994).

Participants

Elderly participants were located through advertising and the snowball sampling technique. The snowball procedure involves a search for "information-rich cases" and asking participants to recommend others for interviewing (Patton, 1990, p. 169). The 19 elderly participants (11 women and eight men) were healthy individuals, ages 65 years and older, who were living independently in the community. They were asked about family members whose opinions are or will be important to them in considering an end-of-life choice. The elderly individuals identified family members, including spouse, child, grandchild, and sister. Family members were then contacted and 28 of them agreed to participate. The 47 participants represented 19 families (29 men and 18 women). They were 27 to 86 years of age, and most had at least a high school diploma. Elderly participants were identified in this study by the numbers from 1 to 19, and family members by the numbers from 101 to 128.

Interviews

The face-to-face individual interviews were conducted in Hebrew, took place at the participants' homes, and lasted from two to four hours. Before the interview, informant consent was discussed in detail with the participants, emphasizing confidentiality. Participants were given an explanation about the research intentions and potential risks and benefits of involvement in the project and were clearly told that they could withdraw from the project at any time. The active interview approach was used because it helps to activate the informants' different stocks of knowledge as the interviewer "intentionally, concertedly provokes responses by indicating narrative positions, resources, orientations, and precedents" (Holstein & Gubrium, 1995, p. 39).

The informants were presented with four case scenarios at the beginning of the interview. Recent studies have recommended the use of case studies as a starting point for discussing the moral issues of end-of-life decisions (Coppola et al., 1999; Roberto, 1999). The case examples also provided consistency across interviews, encouraged the participants' involvement in the issue, and assisted in overcoming the shortage of words in Hebrew referring to end-of-life decisions (Leichtentritt & Rettig, 1999b). The first two scenarios referred to passive acts of ending life, including avoidance of prolonging life by withholding and withdrawing

life-sustaining treatment. The third case scenario was an example of an active act to end life, and the last scenario portrayed physician-assisted death. The decisions were examined as a result of both voluntary acts, when the decision is implemented following the patient's request, as well as nonvoluntary decisions, when the act is based on the decision of others for a patient who can no longer make the request (Beauchamp & Childress, 1994).

> *Withholding Treatment.* A terminally ill cancer patient requested that her life not be prolonged by mechanical breathing machines because she wished for a natural death. The machines were not used, and the patient died a week later of lung failure.
> *Withdrawing Treatment.* A patient relied on an artificial kidney machine to stay alive. He was bedbound and in severe pain. The patient asked not be kept alive. The machine was stopped and he died.
> *Active Euthanasia.* A 70-year-old terminally ill patient had severe pain that was not treatable with pain drugs. At the patient's request the physician gave the patient a drug that would end her life. Shortly after taking the drug, the patient died.
> *Physician-Assisted Death.* A 70-year-old parent with terminal cancer suffered from severe pain that was not treatable with pain drugs. At the patient's request the physician supplied the patient with drugs. The patient took the drugs. Shortly after taking the drugs, the patient died.

Data Analysis

The analysis was performed at the individual level, and no attempts were made to identify shared values across family members or patterns of value priorities within families. The interpretive analysis began with each individual, then moved to the whole group of interviews. The next step involved returning to the individuals, thus completing one circle in an ongoing process. "The hermeneutic circle is a methodological device in which one considers the whole in relation to its parts and vice versa" (Schwandt, 1998, p. 227).

The analysis had four main phases. The first phase involved getting a sense of the whole, a feel for the data, by reading the transcripts to get an overview of the various thoughts, feelings, and reactions expressed by the participants (van Manen, 1990). Each interview was read several times, and each time questions, notes, and reflections were recorded until we established a global sense of the data. The second phase identified working segments or values and value statements that were established by using the selective, detailed, and holistic approaches (van Manen, 1990). The third phase of the analysis examined the value segments to recognize themes and to examine the text as a whole for additional concerns that may have been overlooked when working with the text in segments. This holistic inductive process identified consequences and fears raised by the informants while discussing end-of-life decisions.

The last phase of the analysis involved articulating the value units and themes that were influencing individuals' end-of-life choices, by presenting them in a visual format that conveys the essence of the experience (van Manen, 1990). The process of creating the visual format required consulting with the participants and returning several times to the transcripts to verify the interpretations.

Evaluating the Research Process and Results

The plausibility of an interpretive phenomenology method is based on its comprehensiveness and on the descriptive data being presented in a manner that illustrates understanding (Benner, 1994; van Manen, 1990). Several strategies were used to strengthen the plausibility of the results. First, our involvement—we have different academic and cultural backgrounds and are at different stages in our lives—provided a comprehensive perspective on the data during all phases of the research. Second, the circular manner of analysis forced the researchers to check consistently for coherence between their interpretations and the informants' narratives. Third, direct quotes are presented so that readers can examine them and question the connections made between participants' words and the conclusions that were drawn. Fourth, several participants and family members examined the results, which provided strong validation for the interpretations.

Findings

Participants in this study struggled with the value priorities in end-of-life decisions when considering acts of hastening and causing death and with the fears and consequences of the decisions. The four accomplishments of the analysis were to identify the (1) four themes referred to as life domains that

need to be taken into consideration in the valuing process when reaching an end-of-life decision; (2) unique values that were considered within each of the life domains; (3) three transcendent values that crossed all life domains; and (4) fears and consequences addressed by the informants in the decision-making process and after reaching a decision.

Holistic Perspective

Three main understandings were recognized in the initial phase of the data analysis. First, informants made no distinctions in their value considerations while discussing the different acts of end of life. Their attitudes changed, but the underlying values remained the same, although the priority of these values changed. The fact that the underlying values were consistent when the informants referred to different case scenarios strengthened the understanding that all of the examples fell within the boundaries of the phenomenon of an end-of-life decision.

Second, although no distinctions were made in the underlying values when referring to the different case examples, participants did make a separation between two forms of nonvoluntary end-of-life decisions on the basis of their role in the decision. Different value priorities guided the decisions made by self for another family member, compared with the decision made by another family member for the self. Therefore, a distinction is made between these two nonvoluntary scenarios. Third, no substantial differences in the underlying values were identified between elderly participants and younger family members, although the priority of the values was often different. Therefore, examples from both elderly individuals and their family members are presented interchangeably.

Unique Value Priorities in Different Life Domains

The value emphases were based on four life domains (themes), each representing a perspective that needs to be taken into account in end-of-life decisions. The domains were physical-biological, social-psychological, familial, and societal. The central values underlying each of the four life domains are competence, integrity, loyalty, and legacy (see figure 22.1).

Physical-Biological Life Domain   Participants talked about their biological self when referring to values of competence, strength, energy, endurance, health,

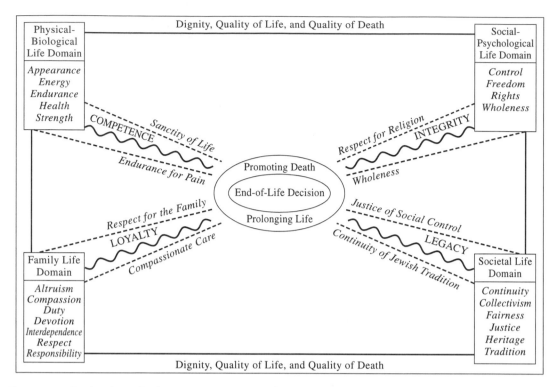

Figure 12.1 Evaluation of adoption experience and contact status with birth mother (where still alive) eight years postreunion

appearance, dignity, and quality of life and death. These values fit the theoretical description of instrumental competence values identified by Rokeach (1973). The value of competence was the main value underlying the personal focus of the human biological life domain.

> For some people what is frightening is being in a wheelchair, needing help, things like that. . . . I know these things used to bother my mother. She was less concerned about other issues that I was worried about. . . . She was very much focused on pain . . . on losing her competences (107). Even then, even when the person I do not know . . . even when you can no longer hear, speak, or walk, even then you are still a human being! (05) I came into this world as a human being, and I wish to leave this world in the same manner. Being able to walk, to communicate, to take care of my own needs, to think, to feel. . . . There is no need for me to reexperience the first few months of my life through my last months in this world (09). We all wish to die when we are strong and capable. We also wish to die at an elderly age—this is the irony, as these two wishes usually do not go together (101).

Social-Psychological Life Domain Participants talked about their social-psychological self by highlighting terminal personal values such as integrity, control, rights, wholeness, dignity, and quality of life and death. Integrity was the central value.

> This is who I am; this is how I live my life. I never had anything that came easily. I always had to fight for everything. Nothing comes easily and I learned to live with that. I learned not to give up, because if I had given up when things started to be difficult, then I would probably never have reached anything in my life. I had cancer a few years ago, went through a very difficult time, but never gave up! I always fought for life (02). This is not I, I am too chicken . . . you have to be strong to make these decisions and to implement them (109).

Family Life Domain Participants talked about family considerations at times of end of life, and those interpersonal considerations highlighted instrumental moral values such as loyalty, interdependence, devotion, altruism, compassion, duty, responsibility, respect, dignity, and quality of life and death. Loyalty was the main value underlying the family life domain, regardless of whether the decision was made by self for other family members or by other family members for self.

> It is not an easy decision to make. It is difficult to let a stranger die, let alone your own family members, but avoiding the decision, forcing them to live as incompetent human beings, that stands against everything they [husband and mother] ever fought for. Never mind how difficult the decision will be, I know this is what they believed in. . . . This is what I believe in. . . . It is going to be difficult living with such a decision, but living is going to be even more difficult knowing I am forcefully keeping them alive (117). One of the things you have to consider is how your decision [to end life] will affect your family members (08).

The value of respect was emphasized, along with the value of loyalty, when considering a nonvoluntary end-of-life decision that was reached for self by other family members.

> I wish my family member will respect my wishes, will recognize that this is not what I would have wanted: being kept alive while not being able to live. . . . People should learn when to "let go." It is much more respectful this way (09).

The value of devotion was dominant in the decision process, along with the value of loyalty, when referring to nonvoluntary end-of-life decisions made by the informants on behalf of an incompetent family member.

> I will not be able to help my parents in such a way. It is unfair after all they have done for me. . . . I do not think you can have a point when you decide your parents should no longer live (128). I will never let my parents end up in a nursing home. . . . My parents took care of my grandmother. . . . She died in their home, at this house. . . . Towards the end she could barely walk. My father used to carry her to the bathroom. I will not desert them. I will not let them be in an institution (109).

Societal Life Domain   When participants took the perspective of citizens in society, they emphasized terminal social values including legacy, heritage, continuity, collectivism, tradition, justice, fairness, dignity, and quality of life and death. Social values are society-centered and interpersonal in nature

(Rokeach, 1973). The value of legacy was the central value underlying the societal life domain.

> People as individuals can do whatever they want, but legitimizing those acts on a societal level—that would be a mistake. I believe they found a good and respectful compromise between Jewish traditions; what this place stands for; what Israel ought to symbolize to the Jewish people; and individual rights to seek death. Right now it is not a clear law. It requires going through hospital committees. The issue of death is dealt with by the patient, his physician, and his close family members. . . . This way the patients, as well as the Israeli state, are safe (03). I do not think it is fair to legalize these acts. . . . What does it say to a dying person? I believe it should be very clear to everyone—physicians as well as patients—that we are all committed to fight for saving life (111). I do not wish to be remembered as the one who committed suicide, as the one who gave up on life (07).

Transcendent Values

Participants talked about the four life domains, human-biological, social-psychological, familial, and societal, as connected to one another by three transcendent values: dignity, quality of life, and quality of death (figure 22.1).

Dignity   Dignity was identified as a central value, although what might be perceived as a dignified death in regard to one's own death could be perceived as undignified by the same informant when referring to the death of another. Dignity was addressed by the participants as a terminal value (a desirable end-state), an instrumental value (a desirable mode of conduct), and a value underlying all of the different forms of end-of-life decisions. The value of dignity crossed the theoretical categories of personal, social, competence, and moral values. It was used by the participants when addressing the human-biological dimension of their lives (that is, instrumental competence values), the social-psychological aspects of their life and death (that is, terminal personal values), the family domain (that is, instrumental moral values), and the societal influence (that is, terminal social values).

Quality of Life   The notion of quality of life was perceived as an overall value across the four domains, although the point where participants perceived life as not worth living differed by informants as they described an intolerable quality of life. Quality of life refers to the "good and satisfactory character of people's lives" (Szalai, 1980, p. 8) and was referred to as both an instrumental and terminal value in the participants' descriptions.

> The one thing I am not willing to live with is the loss of my mental capacities. Without the ability to think, I have nothing left [giggle]. Ask anyone who knows me. My whole life is surrounded by the fact that I am capable of thinking, I use my mind. I rarely use my heart. It is sad but true. Without my mental capacity, I definitely prefer to be dead, no doubts about that! (129).

Quality of Death   Quality of death was identified as the third transcendent value when considering an end-of-life decision and was perceived as a continuous and connected value to one's quality of life. Quality of death was a central concern when considering end-of-life scenarios for one's own death and for the death of a close family member.

> So now I might have to choose whether I would like to be hooked to machines to survive, or be hooked to machines so I can die. Ironic don't you think? What happened to people before medicines intervened so much in our natural course of life? I think they had a much more peaceful life, and a much more respectful death. They did not have a choice. It seems easier to accept the natural cycle of life this way. . . . I just want to die as a fully human being with no machines around (06).

Fears and Consequences

The value struggles of participants highlighted imagined fears and consequences resulting from the tentative value choices for end-of-life decisions. Fears and consequences are worries about values that might be threatened if the event (whether promoting death or prolonging life) would occur. The main fears and consequences of end-of-life decisions were centered on the four domains of life that formed the foci of the phenomenon. These fears are presented in figure 22.1 by dotted lines and are stated using a value language to highlight that fears are threats to a main value.

Physical-Biological Life Domain   Participants addressed the fears of threatening the sanctity of life that would result from acts of promoting death.

The values of comfort (a consequence of suffering) and endurance (a consequence of pain) would be threatened when referring to acts of prolonging life. Informants worried about loss of energy and strength to care for themselves sufficiently. The fear of loss of appearances or human image also was expressed.

> One thing that worries me the most is pain. . . . I still believe these people [refers to the case scenarios] reached the wrong decision and that they should not have received help for that. . . . Nevertheless, being under extreme pain is something I am worried about (10).

Social-Psychological Life Domain   The fears and consequences within the social-psychological domain for prolonging life were about loss of self and were centered on one's inability to function as a whole person because of mental incompetence, incontinence, dependence on machines, and lack of courage. The consequences of promoting death included violation of religious laws, loss of faith, and lack of obedience to social norms. Violations of the religious and social expectations were surrounded by the fear of nonconformity and the resulting religious implications.

> Never mind under how much pain I will have. I know I will not be able to do a thing to end my life. . . . It is not something I can explain in a rational way. . . . I was raised in a religious home; my parents closely followed the Jewish tradition, believing that acts of suicide are wrong, immoral, against God, unspeakable. . . . Something of all that must have stuck to me. I believe, no logic included, that there are going to be implications for such an act (105).

Family Life Domain   The fears and consequences when addressing the family domain were about being compassionate toward caretakers by not placing a burden on others resulting from one's wishes to prolong life. The wish to promote death brought fears that respect for the family would be diminished and family members would experience shame.

> I want to leave this world in a respectful way. I do not wish people to stand near the fresh, open grave gossiping. . . . A person who seeks death by jumping off a roof or by taking an overdose is a juicy gossip item. . . . I wish people to remember me for who I was, and not by the way I died, I want my family to be able to say what

happened. I do not want them to have to deal with covering things up. I do not want people to refer to them as the kids of the crazy woman who committed suicide (03). For the sake of others, I think it should be allowed . . . from experience I am telling you there are times when a dead relative is much better than a live one. . . . It is better this way for everyone—for the patient as well as his/her family. I have seen families who died in the process of caring for a dying family member (118).

Societal Life Domain   Participants talked about the social consequences of discontinuity when addressing acts of prolonging life. They feared losing Jewish traditions and important components of the Israeli culture. Anarchy was perceived as the consequence of allowing individuals in society to act toward promoting their own death or the death of incompetent or suffering family members. The participants expressed fears of chaos, loss of social control, and danger in misuse of social power.

We fought for the right to be a Jewish state. . . . Don't you think it will be a bit pretentious to, at the same time, allow these acts to be carried out here in Israel? [Pause] These things belong more to places like the Netherlands or to several of the Scandinavian states . . . it does not fall under the Israeli spirit (11). People around here tend to carry things to the extreme. There is hardly ever a middle ground. Legitimizing those actions, it is dangerous. . . . It will get to the extreme. People may misuse these opportunities. It will be a spin, that once started we will have no idea how to stop it (16).

Discussion

The results of the study highlight three main understandings. The first is that values that were emphasized by the informants in each life domain corresponded to the value conceptualization presented by Rokeach (1973). Second, multiple systems (individual, family, and social) need to be considered when reaching end-of-life decisions. The third is that it is not appropriate to separate an individual's quality of life and death.

Validation of a Value Classification

An unexpected result of the study was the finding that the set of value priorities emphasized in each

life domain corresponded similarly to the value conceptualization of Rokeach (1973). The physical domain emphasized instrumental intrapersonal values. The psychological domain called forth terminal personal values; the family domain led to emphasis on instrumental interpersonal values; and the societal domain emphasized terminal social values. There are very few studies that have supported the theoretical value conceptualization of Rokeach using an inductive research process with qualitative methods of data analysis (Leichtentritt & Rettig, 1999a). More studies are needed to explore Rokeach's (1973) and other values conceptual frameworks.

Importance of Participants' Contexts in the Decision-Making Process

Ecological theory acknowledges that an end-of-life decision is an individual, relational, and social-cultural phenomenon. Similarly, participants in the decision-making process took into consideration the social, community, and family contexts, giving attention to both past (heritage) and future (legacy) time perspectives.

Earlier research has addressed the social context by emphasizing this influence on individuals' perspectives toward ethical and moral issues (Hessing, Blad, & Pieterman, 1996; Lee et al., 1996). Similarly, in this study, the Israeli social context was identified as an important contributor in establishing individuals' values toward end-of-life decisions. Participants' perspectives were influenced by the Jewish and Israeli heritage, which emphasizes the value of life, the importance of a dignified death, the social and religious meanings of suicide, and the role of Israel as a Jewish state.

Discussions that have taken place in most Western countries have concluded that individuals tend to ignore the social consequences of their act by providing the explanation that "the society is only very marginally affected by how I live, or by whether I live or die" (Hardwig, 1997, p. 36). The uniqueness of the reciprocal perspectives of participants from the Israeli context may be attributed to the communitarian philosophical perspective that characterizes Israeli laws and norms surrounding death and dying (Gross, 1999). This perspective requires that individuals not only examine the social values, but also inquire into the social and community consequences of personal end-of-life decisions and actions.

Quality of Life and Quality of Death

The study results suggest a strong connection between the individual's current life quality and anticipated events, an understanding that often is missing in the quality-of-life literature (Keith, 1998). The fact that inevitable events of death and dying contribute to the individual's current life quality also has been supported in other studies (Leichtentritt & Rettig, 2000). Keith concluded that "because the literatures on views of life and death have developed along somewhat separate lines" (p. 165), these two concepts typically have been addressed separately. The process of making an end-of-life decision that gives the individual the right to choose some of the elements associated with his or her dying process made the connection between these concepts stronger. As a result, quality of life cannot be addressed separately from quality of death.

Implications

The results of the study suggest that individuals are capable of considering the different acts of end-of-life, because the informants involved themselves in a prolonged, thoughtful decision-making process. This empirical understanding stands against the concerns raised by policymakers claiming that legitimizing euthanasia will increase the risk of promoting an unethical, manipulative process by family members toward their elderly relatives (Emanuel, 1994).

It is of high priority, therefore, that social workers in health care settings facilitate communication between the health care team, patients, and families so that concerns about appropriate medical treatments may be addressed and resolved in a responsible manner. A responsible manner is one that provides individuals with quality in their living and dying processes; allows for protection of the central values of dignity, competence, integrity, loyalty, and legacy; and takes into consideration the consequences of decisions.

The results of this and other research demonstrate clearly that people have the capacity and are willing to address end-of-life issues while ill (Leichtentritt & Rettig, 1999a), as well as long before having to implement decisions (Roberto, 1999). This understanding also calls on social workers in the community to facilitate and encourage such dialogues among family members and patients. An advance discussion on the issues will enrich family members' knowledge about the wishes of elderly family members and provide an opportunity to address some of the fears and consequences associated with various choices.

This study is among the first to examine explicitly the values underlying end-of-life decisions. Future studies should examine more fully the differences between elderly and younger family members' value priorities, as well as the different value priorities of individuals, when discussing different end-of-life scenarios (passive versus active as well as voluntary versus nonvoluntary euthanasia). Furthermore, studies in less communitarian as well as more communitarian states should examine the values underlying end-of-life decisions, as well as the fears and consequences associated with these decisions. Such studies can provide meaningful information to social workers who assist individuals and their family members in considering end-of-life options.

References

Beauchamp, T. L., & Childress, J. F. (1994). *Principles of biomedical ethnics* (4th ed.). New York: Oxford University Press.

Benner, P. (1994). The tradition and skill of interpretive phenomenology in studying health, illness, and caring practices. In P. Benner (Ed.), *Interpretive phenomenology: Embodiment, caring, and ethics in health and illness* (pp. 99–127). Thousand Oaks, CA: Sage Publications.

Brigham, J. C., & Pfeifer, J. E. (1996). Euthanasia: An introduction. *Journal of Social Issues, 52*(2), 1–11.

Brown, M. M. (1985). *Philosophical studies of home economics in the United States: Our practical intellectual heritage* (Vol. II). East Lansing: Michigan State University, College of Human Ecology.

Coppola, K. M., Bookwala, J., Ditto, P. H., Lockhart, L. K., Danks, J. H., & Smucker, W. D. (1999). Elderly adults' preferences for life-sustaining treatment: The role of impairment, prognosis, and pain. *Death Studies, 23*, 617–634.

Emanuel, E. J. (1994). Euthanasia: Historical, ethical, and empiric perspectives. *Archives of Internal Medicine, 154*, 1890–1901.

Freedman, B. (1996). Respectful service and reverent obedience: A Jewish view of making decisions for incompetent parents. *Hastings Center Report, 26*(4), 31–37.

Glick, S. M. (1997). Unlimited human autonomy: A cultural bias? *New England Journal of Medicine, 336*, 954–956.

Gross, M. L. (1999). Autonomy and paternalism in communitrian society: Patient rights in Israel. *Hastings Center Report, 29*(4), 13–20.

Hardwig, J. (1997). Is there a duty to die? *Hastings Center Report, 27*(2), 34–42.

Hessing, D. J., Blad, J. R., & Pieterman, R. (1996). Practical reasons and reasonable practice: The case of euthanasia in the Netherlands. *Journal of Social Issues, 52*(2), 149–168.

Holstein, J. A., & Gubrium, J. F. (1995). *The active interview*. Thousand Oaks, CA: Sage Publications.

Keith, P. M. (1998). Investigation of a typology of life and death as an indicator of quality of life. *Omega, 37*, 151–165.

Koestenbaum, P. (1976). *Is there an answer to death?* Englewood Cliffs, NJ: Spectrum Books.

Lee, Y. T., Kleinbach, P. C., Hu, Z. Z. P., & Chen, X. Y. (1996). Cross-cultural research on euthanasia and abortion. *Journal of Social Issues, 52*(2), 131–148.

Leichtentritt, R. D., & Rettig, K. D. (1999a). My parents' death is different from mine: Moral problem solving regarding euthanasia. *Journal of Social and Personal Relationships, 16*, 385–406.

Leichtentritt, R. D., & Rettig, K. D. (1999b). Meanings and attitudes toward end-of-life preferences in Israel. *Death Studies, 23*, 323–358.

Leichtentritt, R. D., & Rettig, K. D. (2000). Elderly Israelis and their family members' meanings towards euthanasia. *Families, Systems and Health, 18*(1), 61–78.

Meinert, R. G. (1980). Values in social work called dysfunctional myth. *Journal of Social Welfare, 6*(3), 5–16.

Nenon, T. (1997). Values, reasons for actions, and reflexivity. In J. G. Hard & L. Embree (Eds.), *Phenomenology of values and valuing* (pp. 117–136). Dordrecht, Netherlands: Kluwer Academic.

Paolucci, B., Hall, O. A., & Axinn, N. (1977). *Family decision making: An ecosystem approach*. New York: Wiley.

Patton, M. (1990). *Qualitative evaluation and research methods*. Newbury Park, CA: Sage Publications.

President's Commission for the Study of Ethical Problems in Medical and Biomedical and Behavioral Research. (1983). *Making health care decisions: The ethical and legal implications of informed consent in the patient-practitioner relationship* (Vol. 3). Washington, DC: U.S. Government Printing Office.

Roberto, K. A. (1999). Making critical health care decisions for older adults: Consensus among family members. *Family Relations, 48*, 167–178.

Rokeach, M. (1973). *The nature of human values*. Glencoe, IL: Free Press.

Schwandt, T. A. (1998). Constructivist, interpretivist approaches to human inquiry. In N. K. Denzin & Y. S. Lincoln (Eds.), *The landscape of qualitative research: Theories and issues* (pp. 221–259). Thousand Oaks, CA: Sage Publications.

Schwartz, S. H., & Bilsky, W. (1987). Toward a universal psychological structure of human values. *Journal of Personality and Social Psychology, 53*, 550–562.

Shuval, J. T. (1992). *Social dimensions of health: The Israeli experience*. Westport, CT: Praeger.

Szalai, A. (1980). The meaning of comparative research on the quality of life. In A. Szalai & F. Andrews (Eds.), *The quality of life: Comparative studies* (pp. 7–32). Thousand Oaks, CA: Sage Publications.

Timms, N. (1983). *Social work values: An enquiry*. London: Routledge.

van Manen, M. (1990). *Researching lived experience*. London: University of Western Ontario.

PART II

THE PROBLEM AS A COMPONENT OF DIAGNOSIS

Client problems have of course been a high level focus of social work practice over the years. Indeed, at times, the problem has been seen as the primary target of practice, as reflected in some definitions of practice as a problem-solving process. The current interest in what is called generalist practice, although purporting to be responsive to all theories and perceptions of practice, includes a strong stress on problem solving, as does the recently adopted new definition of social work adopted by several international associations.

One of the challenges over our century-plus of development is to find ways of organizing and categorizing the types of problems addressed in our practice. A principal challenge to this from our profession's purview arises from the breadth of our practice, which from its biopsychosocial focus encompasses a very wide, complex, and ever expanding coterie of problems in the human condition to which we need to and are asked to respond. Some of the recent important work of Dr. James Karls and associates in the development and ongoing testing of Person In Environment (PIE) has made a critically important advance in identifying and organizing the range of problems met in practice. Because the problem is a critical component of practice, essential to the diagnostic role is to establish what, if any, problems in biopsychosocial functioning the client has and to which we need to respond both from the client's perspective, society's, and our own.

Critical as is the need to identify problems as a part of the diagnostic process, it is essential that we do not focus only on problems in our diagnostic activities. This we have frequently done in the past,

and I suggest at times we have been led astray in two ways. Our first error was the belief that the essence of diagnosis was to identify and describe problems of the client; our second, that there was a proper or correct way to treat each problem. Thus, over the decades we have seen a vast range of articles in our practice literature that dealt with the social work treatment of many different types of problems. These articles of course are not to be eschewed; they have played an important role in the development of our literature and our knowledge and in the accumulation of a practice-based, specifically focused body of knowledge. This in turn helps us to understand in a richer way the complexities of our clients' lives, hopes, and expectations for a therapeutic response to them and the need for a broad understanding of such problems.

I suggest that in our presentation of many of these treatment-focused writings we have minimized the need to more fully understand the problem itself from a biopsychosocial perspective, but as well its meaning to the client and its differential impact on the client. This personalizing of the problem is the essence of the diagnostic process. The better that we are, and become, able to understand problems in general terms, the better we will become in more sensitively perceiving the idiosyncratic implications of each problem for the client. This personalizing of the problem is, of course, the essence of sensitive practice and helps us to avoid our earlier temptation to presume that if we know the client's problem or problem cluster we will know what can be done about it from a social work perspective.

This focus on which interventions are required by which problem is one reason the concept of diagnosis took on a pejorative meaning. What we now understand about problems comes from the concept of "multifinality" from systems theory. This principle holds that there are many different ways of dealing with a similar situation to bring about a similar outcome; that is, different inputs can have similar outcomes. Thus, social workers A and B may agree completely on who the client is from a developmental perspective, what is or are the problems to be addressed, how the problems are viewed by the client and his or her significant others, yet take totally different, yet fully appropriate, approaches with similar outcomes.

It is the concept that knowledge of a client's problem leads to a "particular" type of social work intervention that we have now put behind us. Of course we need to understand as deeply and broadly as we can the kinds of problems met by our clients. But we also need to combine this knowledge and understanding with an equally strong stress on judging who the is client and how he or she reacts to and perceives the problem. It is this that helps us shape from our ever expanding coterie of knowledge, theories, strategies, and techniques a responsible and effective way of intervening.

Although at this point I do not think we have sufficient supporting evidence, probably as our knowledge accumulates there will emerge trends and clusters of intervention that are more efficacious in regard to particular problems. However, this in no way will be in the form of a prescription that this problem requires this profile of intervention. Perhaps as a first step in this direction we will find clusters of interventions that are counterindicated by particular types of problems rather than the reverse.

But of course we respond to clients more sensitively to the extent that we understand problems and problem areas in themselves and in their relationship to others. It is this that sharpens our diagnostic acumen. Thus, the search for categorization of problems is important. It pushes us to test the clarity of our knowledge and to seek for similarities and differences, which enhance our understanding.

The above comments may sound as if I am minimizing the importance of the problem as a part of the diagnostic process. This is certainly not my intention. What I am attempting to do is to move away from the position that implies that assessment of problems is the essence of diagnosis. Clearly we must understand who the client is from many perspectives. But just as important, we must understand the problems present in clients' lives that they wish to address and in what way. To help them in this regard it is essential that we have as rich an understanding of problems in all their detail and of the differential ways in which such problems have affected them and others. Thus, the ongoing study of problems will and must remain an essential component of our diagnostic responsibilities.

In gathering and selecting material for this volume we did not follow any particular classification system of problems. Rather, we selected a period of time, the first three years of this new millennium, to explore what kinds of problems were being addressed in the practice literature of our field. Two patterns emerged. The first, one that should not be of great surprise to us, is that there appear to be patterns in the kinds of clinical materials about which we are currently writing. That is, over the decades, different problems have a higher profile than others. This is partially due to the sociopolitical interest that gets focused on different problems at different times in history; understandably, we write about what is current. For example, in the range of journals we examined there was a strong prevalence of articles on abuse in general, with specific focus on sexual abuse of all kinds, elder abuse, and intrafamily violence.

In addition to topics receiving a high profile in professional circles, a second trend was topics being addressed that are new or hitherto neglected, either from a lack of interest in professional circles or perhaps a lack of sufficient professional knowledge. These are important articles, even if many are of a descriptive exploratory type; they ask more questions than are answered, for this type of article serves to reinforce the need for further professional discussion.

Although, as mentioned, we did not select articles to match any particular typology of problem, not surprisingly, the articles selected do appear to fall into three categories. Without allotting any category more importance than any other, the first category of problem about which we have been writing in recent years deals with the psychosocial implications of some type of physical condition or situation, such as a specific type of diabetes, or that discusses social work practice with oncology patients. This type of article, of which there have been many in the literature, demand detailed knowledge about the physical condition itself, as well as understanding of the patterns of impact of such conditions on people and their families and also the types of interventions on our part that can be of assistance to them. This type of article underscores the growing awareness of the social worker's need for a biological view of clients along with our psychosocial perspective.

The second group of topics included in our writings deal with issues of a psychological or psychiatric nature, requiring some degree of interprofessional collaboration as well as a high degree of mental health knowledge. Again, there is nothing new in our interest in this type of problem; what is new is a growing sophistication in our understanding of them. Unfortunately, many of our colleagues view social work diagnosis only as skill in the utilization of the *DSM*. Over the decades we have written much about our roles and interventions in this component of our practice. The number of articles in this area demonstrates that it is a component of our practice with which we are comfortable and competent, both in learning from and teaching other disciplines. It is that area of practice most significantly marked by interprofessional practice.

The third type of problem encompasses those aspects of the human condition best categorized as psychosocial, the area where we clearly and demonstrably have claimed our particular expertise. I am speaking here of those many types of problems met by our clients that are the effects of societal situations and the impact of these on clients. Such topics as homelessness, bullying, and stalking are examples of this cluster of problems in this collection. As practitioners, not only do we have to understand the causalities of the problem from a societal as well as a psychosocial perspective, but we must consider the range of impacts such problems have on individuals and groups and what patterns of intervention are helpful.

Of course, as in virtually all efforts at problem categorization in our discipline, there is and should be considerable overlap between and among the various problems we need in practice. In many ways, all human problems are biopsychosocial. Nevertheless, it is critical that we continue to examine all problems from all facets and clarify the interconnection between the many impinging factors that influence the human condition and response. This we must do always from the perspective of how this understanding helps us to help this client in this situation in this setting and with what degree of certainty and comfort.

A. Problems with a Mental Illness Basis

23

A New Understanding of Attention Deficit Hyperactivity Disorder: Alternate Concepts and Interventions

Contemporary research and theories on the etiology of attention deficit hyperactivity disorder (ADHD) are based on contrasting ideas and data. Some studies test for neurological causation, searching for proof that ADHD can be traced to abnormalities in brain chemistry or anatomy. However, there is currently no consensus that ADHD is based solely on a specific neurological dysfunction. In contrast, the behavioral symptoms of "inattention, impulsivity, and hyperactivity" are often interpreted as psychopathological (American Psychiatric Association, *DSM-IV*, 1994). When behavioral problems accompanying, and integral to, the diagnosis of ADHD are defined solely as psychopathology, the individual acquires a pejorative, stigmatizing label.

While current research continues the important search for an understanding of a biochemical and neuroanatomical basis for ADHD, emphasis needs to be directed to studying many of the daily coping difficulties of those who are diagnosed with ADHD. Therefore, we need to understand the common presence of the intrapsychic and interpersonal distress that brings people additional and profound struggles. These people do battle on a daily basis with difficulty staying on task, completing assignments, utilizing listening skills, and adhering to curriculum that is required but is often uncaptivating. And while staying on task, follow-through of task, and ability to concentrate are all important for one's scholastic and/or employment success, the key to more fully understanding and treating those di-

agnosed with ADHD may be a focus on the intense psychological and social despair that is experienced. This is magnified especially when failure is consistently experienced with intimate relationships and peer groups. Those with ADHD require patience and understanding not always available from the outside world. Individuals with ADHD experience their deepest struggles, not with inanimate objects and tasks, but with people.

It is the ever present reproaches and yelling by parents, teachers' criticisms and impatience, spouses and family members' dismay and confusion, and peer group rejection that probably is perceived as more agonizing than the inability to compute numbers or fulfill a written assignment. Contributing to self-image problems are evolving depression, life-threatening substance abuse, and conduct disorders (potentially leading to legal involvement). As mental health professionals, educators, parents, and caregivers, we often experience these mood, anxiety, and legal problems as going hand in hand with ADHD. The individual's perception and subsequent behaviors of being "out of it" psychologically, academically, and socially lead to the misperception that ADHD's basis is psychopathology.

Critical to this discussion on ADHD, and frequently reviewed in the literature, is the issue of comorbid conditions (Zametkin, 1995). In combination with ADHD, comorbid conditions refer to the presence of mood and/or anxiety disorders and/or substance abuse and/or conduct disorders. These comorbid conditions are assigned as distinct and additional diagnoses, and when present are currently acknowledged as indicators for difficult and poor treatment outcomes. I suggest that these comorbid conditions are not always separate diagnoses, but can be untreated, internalized affective responses that produce mood and anxiety symptoms. Here again is reason to provide emphasis on how one with ADHD attempts to mediate intra/interpersonal difficulties. If we continue to presume that the mood and anxiety symptoms we observe are distinct comorbid conditions we may be incorrectly assigning treatment plans and erroneously placing negative labels of psychopathology on the individual (and family members). Through further investigation these comorbid conditions can be revealed as the by-products of metabolizing one's interactions and reactions to continuous negative family, school, and social environments.

Fundamental to my discussion will be the incorporation of Russell A. Barkley's application of Bronowski's language theory. Along with Barkley, I believe that behaviors previously labeled as inattention, impulsivity, and hyperactivity are actually problems created by underinhibition of responses. Barkley (1993, 1994) relies on specific concepts of Bronowski's language theory to explain that the main symptom of ADHD is the inability to inhibit responses which impacts all spheres of one's life. The psychoanalytic theories of object relations and affect attunement will be explained and will be linked to underinhibition of responses via dynamic intra/interpersonal processes and the presenting psychological and social problems. Comorbidity that presents with ADHD will be considered and redefined as possible accompanying and maladaptive symptoms resulting from one's inability to master feelings of dissonance with the outside world. This is not to refute that, at times, comorbidity can be the presence of distinct and additional psychopathology. However, we do need to understand whether or not this is the case. This understanding is most meaningful in relation to considering specific treatment modalities, which may prevent further suffering and moreover can improve the quality of one's intra/interpersonal life.

Why Language Theory Is Important for Understanding ADHD

Bronowski's theory of "delayed responding and language" explains that humans are distinguished by a unique capacity to inhibit their behaviors in response to signals, messages, and events. Bronowski has identified four categories of cognitive processes that constitute his theory: *separation of affect, prolongation, internalization,* and *reconstitution.* These four cognitive processes appear to be directly impaired in cases of ADHD (the foundation of Barkley's thesis), which I believe helps to explain the intra/interpersonal difficulties seen in individuals with ADHD. Previous clinical understanding held that maintaining attention, impulse control, and hyperactivity were the significant developmental behavior problems evidenced with ADHD. Recent studies, however, depict underinhibition of responses (the inability to delay a response to a signal, message, or event) as the fundamental symptom of ADHD. I will examine the above-mentioned cognitive processes in direct association to underinhibition of responses. Implications for the individual with ADHD, for whom it is believed there is notable impairment in these four cognitive processes, will be explored (Barkley, 1994).

Separation of affect defines the cognitive ability to divide language signals into discrete components of affect and data. In the case of ADHD, where there is diminished ability to delay responses, Barkley proposes that there is likely impairment to separation of affect. When this occurs, it is possible that the distinction between the content and the emotion of a message become blurred. Thus, messages are likely to be received that are overloaded with fact, emotion, or both. These individuals experience messages and events less objectively, less rationally, and less logically. In addition, their responses tend to be less objective, less rational, and less logical. The implication for impaired functioning in this domain is profound: communication is received and sent with great potential for affective and factual distortions (Barkley, 1994).

Prolongation is Bronowski's term for the mental process that enables a message to be more solidly placed in one's mental fixing and stored for future expressions of language. The problem that can arise here with poor delay of responses, as seen with ADHD, is twofold. First, these individuals seem less able to learn from previous communication and/or events. Therefore, they appear unable to hold onto the message or event for enough time so that a mental reproduction can occur. Second, these individuals appear to display less concern for future events. This may happen because the individual has not been able to sustain a mental representation of the message or event and is thus unable to base future responses on an accurately fixed memory. There is diminished ability for these people to reference back, store information, and utilize this information to guide future behaviors. Put simply, those with ADHD often appear to "live in the moment" (Barkley, 1994).

Internalization as defined by Bronowski explains the delaying of signals and responses to messages and events, not only with others, but with oneself. Unique to the human species is our capacity, not only to communicate with others, but to maintain inner dialogues. These inner dialogues filter and metabolize outside data and control the delaying of responses until this inner dialogue has been conducted. Alternately termed "rule-governed behaviors," we sustain internalization of messages so that we can guide self/others' behaviors; impart our knowledge and learning to others; direct messages to the self, thereby controlling our own behavior (i.e., willpower, self-control); and recall known rules while formulating new rules. All of these are utilized and necessary for adaptive problem solving. For those with ADHD, underinhibition of responses means less control of language with others, as well as with oneself. Consequently, impairment of this domain will interfere with one's ability to set goals, conduct current and future planning, and adhere to established rules in addition to formulating new rules. Here we observe those with ADHD to respond immediately, without taking the time to consider inner messages that can more adaptively direct behaviors with regard to planning, goals, rules, and instructions (Barkley, 1994).

Reconstitution of language is Bronowski's term for the cognitive ability that guides the classification of experiences and messages into segments. Once the message or experience is taken in, the individual has the opportunity to creatively analyze and incorporate the information, ultimately distributing it into subcategories (e.g., objects, attributes, deeds). When reconstitution receives appropriate inhibition of responses, the individual can attend to many aspects of a message or event and analyze the information and emotions and plan a course of response. With underinhibition of responses, as is common with ADHD, the individual will not properly subclassify the many aspects of the message or event and therefore is likely to be careless in giving appropriate responses (Barkley, 1994).

In summary, Bronowski's language theory provides a solid foundation for understanding how underinhibition of responses negatively affects those with ADHD. All components of language in relation to inhibition of responses are integral aspects of our cognitive abilities to accurately receive and transmit information. If one cannot properly make the distinction between data and emotion, or subclassify aspects of messages for purposes of analyzing the message and planning a course for action, then it is unlikely that the individual will be able to maintain adaptive communication. Individuals who cannot properly learn from previous events or display appropriate concern for future events are often characterized as impaired morality and decision making. Individuals with ADHD often appear to "live for today," without showing adequate concern for the past, the future, or both.

The Intra/Interpersonal Significance of Underinhibition of Responses: Object Relations Theory and Affect Attunement

The psychoanalytic theories of object relations and affect attunement will be linked to underinhibition of responses via the intra/interpersonal distress that people with ADHD commonly experience. Because communication and interpretation of language and events usually occurs with people, I believe incorporating object relations and affect attunement theories can aid our understanding and help those with ADHD.

Object relations theory is a psychoanalytic concept that describes how our own perceptions and experiences of others are based on our consistent and repetitive patterns of relationships with significant others throughout the life cycle. Through a definitive psychological process, termed internalization (not to be confused with Bronowski's use of internalization), we take in from the outside, from our significant caretakers, certain components of their attributes and behaviors. It is with our ability to internalize aspects of significant others that we derive our motivation for relationships, develop intricate mental and social abilities from infancy into adulthood, and self-pattern specific types of relationships that make each of us unique relational beings. According to these concepts we are, by nature, social and interactional beings (Moore & Bernard 1990).

> Human beings did not evolve and then enter into social and cultural interactions; the human mind is in its very origins and nature, a social product. . . . Protohumans gradually became involved in social interchanges such as sharing, sensitivity, perhaps empathy. . . . These social skills provided a selective advantage which made larger brains more adaptive. (Mitchell, 1988)

With ADHD, an original message or event is often recast into a modified form of the original expression (due to underinhibition of responses). The ADHD individual is then predisposed to providing responses to the original message that are interpreted by the other participant as incongruent, nonfocused, confused, disoriented, and so on. In turn, the other (non-ADHD) need not (and usually does not) proceed with empathy or understanding or attempt to clarify the inconsistencies in communication. A slippery slope of communication results, with participants growing more and more dismayed as communication becomes increasingly difficulty to maintain. These obstacles in communication produce extraordinary anxiety and conflict. Thus, many of the intra/interpersonal difficulties evidenced in those with ADHD can be explained in association by object relations concepts. Those with ADHD commonly internalize aspects of significant others that are frustrated, confused, and angry. The self-patterning of behavior in these relationships consequently reflects the feeling states of frustration, confusion, and anger. Distress is the mediating emotion. If it were merely that the individual evolved in solitary existence, there would be no belief by self or others that one with ADHD cannot "get it." There would be no perception by those with ADHD, despite futile attempts to succeed, that due to some "behavioral" defect, they are unable to stay on task, absorb data, or fulfill assignments. The point is that we are social beings and that we desire relationships for nurturing, love, and positive reinforcement.

The concept of affect attunement as it is used by Stern (1985) can further advance our understanding and help those who struggle with ADHD. Stern refers to a resonating of emotional states between an infant and primary caretaker/s as affect attunement, commonly termed "mirroring" (Winnicott, 1971). According to Stern,

Affect attunement like empathy, starts with an emotional resonance and automatically recasts the interpersonal experience into another form of expression. Attunement thus need not proceed toward empathic knowledge or response. Attunement is a distinct form of affective transaction in its own right. . . . They give the impression that a kind of imitation has occurred. What is being matched is not the other person's behavior per se, but some aspect of the person's behavior that reflects a feeling state.

Affect attunement is an aspect of object relations that goes beyond one's internalizing aspects and

patterns of relationships; it explains the actual imitation of feeling states. Although Stern conceptualizes affect attunement as interactions that occur between infants and significant caretakers, I suggest that affect attunements are ongoing affective dynamics that continue to present in our interactions as we develop throughout life.

Affect attunements that result with ADHD are a very distinct form of emotional transaction that actually imitate the received frustration, confusion, criticism, and conflict. Further complicating the matter, it is well documented that "one in every four children diagnosed ADHD has a biological parent who is similarly affected" (Zametkin, 1995). When both parent and child struggle with ADHD, we can predict the negative manner in which these communications (affect attunements), proceed, that is, usually with tremendous escalation of confusion, frustration, and conflict. These affect attunements may play a large role in the formation of mood and anxiety disorders, substance abuse, and legal involvement. It is quite possible that what we currently diagnose as comorbidity is really the anger, frustration, and conflict that has been internalized, imitated, and left untreated.

A sole focus on theory will fail to improve our helping unless we translate the theory into practice. In the interest of providing improved helping for those with ADHD, language theory, underinhibition of responses, comorbidity, object relations, and affect attunement will provide the blueprints for all interventions. Ideally, we should address the intra/interpersonal distress before low self-esteem, substance abuse, and legal involvement becomes irreversible. Acknowledging the intra/interpersonal struggles that accompany ADHD does not preclude the fundamental need for professional/family emphasis on behavior management. Nor does this imply that once focused on, the intra/interpersonal dilemmas will be immediately alleviated. Difficulties arise in any situation where confusion, frustration, anger, and conflict mediate the relationship.

Interventions for ADHD: Anticipating Underinhibition of Responses and Intra/Interpersonal Difficulties

The following interventions are formulated to anticipate and address underinhibition of responses and the maladaptive intra/interpersonal behaviors that manifest with ADHD. The suggested interventions are predominantly behavioral and psychopharmacological, with a systems approach. Current research for more successful treatment outcomes with ADHD notes greater success with these modalities. Cognitive therapy is contraindicated for treating those with ADHD (Zametkin, 1995). Cognitive therapy requires transforming one's conceptualizations, thereby redefining one's moods and behaviors to associate with new and different perceptions (Beck, 1988). Clearly, cognitive therapy will prove unsuccessful for those with ADHD. It will exacerbate their struggles with communication because it focuses on the interpretation of messages and events (that which goes haywire for those with ADHD due to underinhibition of responses).

Interventions for ADHD

1. Anticipate and address the potential that individuals with ADHD experience "underinhibition of responses" with accompanying maladaptive intra/interpersonal functioning:

   • Assess all other family members to rule out the presence of ADHD. When ADHD is present in more than one family member, make those with ADHD the initial focus for interventions. It is likely that this family subsystem is experiencing significant intra/interpersonal difficulties and can be preventing the rest of the family from dealing with their own developmental needs. However, providing marital/family therapy is indicated irrespective of the presence of additional family members with ADHD.
   • Your assessment needs to apply multimodal treatment methods on a case-by-case basis. Include individual therapy, marital/family therapy, support groups, psychoeducation, outreach and multidisciplinary collaboration, social skills/extracurricular activities, special education and tutoring referrals, psychopharmacology as indicated, and behavior modification techniques. Combining behavior modification techniques and psychopharmacology is reported to provide greater success than either intervention by itself (Zametkin, 1995).

2. Develop specific behavioral techniques with individuals and families that highlight the negative impact of underinhibition of responses. These strategies need to utilize methods that will help people self-acknowledge underinhibition of responses; self-monitor interactions while emphasizing the individuals'

perceptions of the process in which these interactions evolve; and slow down their cognitive and behavioral responses. This can be accomplished by:

   • *Process illumination:* This is a method in which the therapist can assess and highlight the reasons for observed and reported intra/interpersonal difficulties. Communications in therapy can be used to illuminate how maladaptive interactions evolve. In this manner there is a diminished focus on the content of the communications, with increased focus on the dynamic processes that cause intra/interpersonal distress (Yalom, 1985). For example, the therapist can encourage family members to engage in discussions. The therapist then acknowledges the point when communication became frustrated, confusing, and/or conflictual, and illuminates (defines) the negative communication processes causing the difficulties. It is necessary to shift focus away from the cognitive areas that are most negatively impacted by underinhibition of responses (e.g., separation of affect, prolongation).
   • *A focus on underinhibition of responses:* The therapist needs to actually time the interval between individuals' receiving versus responding to a message or event. The therapist can identify the rapid manner in which the individual/s with ADHD respond, often without listening to/interpreting the message or event. Request that each individual increase the time it takes to respond to a message in one-minute increments, finding an amount of time in which satisfying communication can occur. Reinforce positive communication exchanges by explaining how and why this positive change has occurred.
   • Encourage members to chart their intra/interpersonal responses outside of therapy. This will provide a means for self-monitoring these new behavioral techniques, thereby continuing to reinforce more adaptive communication styles.

3. Helping those with ADHD needs to specifically include a focus on ruling out true comorbidity. The therapist needs to accurately diagnose mood and/or anxiety disorders, substance abuse, and legal involvement. Professional assessments can determine whether or not the comorbid symptoms are actually distinct diagnoses or a direct response to the individual's inability to adaptively cope with

ADHD. Some suggested methods for obtaining accurate diagnoses of comorbidity are:

- Measure increases, no change, or decreases in comorbid symptoms after beginning therapeutic modalities and/or psychopharmacology. Decreases in previously assumed comorbidity (depression, anxiety, substance abuse, and sociopathy), when correlated to increases in treatment modalities and/or psychopharmacology, are indications that individuals who were previously unable to experience satisfying intra/interpersonal functioning are now functioning more adaptively. Increases in comorbid behaviors can verify the presence of true comorbidity. This will necessitate a change in your treatment plan or is an indication that there needs to be a longer period of assessment. No change in comorbid behaviors should be carefully evaluated to determine the need for a longer period of assessment and for changes in your treatment plan.

4. Determine the extent to which intra/interpersonal difficulties are interfering with social, employment, and academic success. As emphasized throughout this paper, those with ADHD can be helped only if we intervene at the level where people can experience increased success intra/interpersonally. Social skills groups, by their nature, place people in a social arena and can help improve socializing in groups, performance at work, and functioning within the structure and demands of school. Social skills groups can be formed to address the following maladaptive behaviors: substance abuse, legal involvement, inability to cope with anger, inability to cope with aggression, social cues, low self-esteem, and social isolation/social anxiety.

Case Examples

Two case examples are presented that illustrate how the above-outlined theories and treatment techniques are used in actual practice. Conclusions regarding the correlation of variables and case outcomes are based on the therapist's experiences and observations with these cases and the collection of school data.

Both cases are of individuals participating in a school-based non-public agency program for teens titled *The Page Web Program* in the Simi Valley Unified School District, Simi Valley, California. *The Page Web Program* is a highly structured behavioral program which offers daily support (through therapeutic modalities and/or daily telephone contacts) and a daily system for earning privileges. Adolescents who are referred are diagnosed learning disabled or emotionally disabled (or both) and display behavioral problems. These students are extremely high risk for out-of-district placement. A systems approach to treatment is an inherent part of this program. *The Page Web Program* requires that each teen participate in two group sessions per week, two family sessions per month, and individual therapy as needed; therapist/school district/interdisciplinary meetings and contacts are conducted as needed on a monthly basis.

Case #1

M. is a 16-year-old, 10th-grade male student who was referred to *The Page Web Program* in September 1998. M.'s parents are divorced. He lives with his biological mother and an 18-year-old brother. Reasons for the referral were 53 school truancies (9/97–6/98), 36 class tardies (9/97–6/98), failing grades in all major subjects (9/97–6/98), and oppositional/defiant behaviors toward teachers and school staff (as defined by school personnel). For the time period 9/97–1/98 M. received nine school suspensions for "angry/oppositional outbursts" toward school personnel. M. was diagnosed ADHD, Predominantly Inattentive Type (grade 7) and Learning Disabled (processing deficits and visual motor perceptual skills) in 1995. At the time of diagnosis, ADHD was treated with Ritalin. M. and his mother report "a bad reaction" to the Ritalin. M. experienced headaches and feelings of extreme agitation. M. states that he refused to continue taking the Ritalin. A psychopharmacology referral was made in keeping with *The Page Web Program*'s structure, 10/98. M. is currently taking 50 mg. Wellbutrin a day, with no reported negative side effects. At the time of referral, M. appeared easily frustrated, he displayed a labile mood, he was unmotivated toward school and home responsibilities, and he was intolerant of ideas and opinions that differed from his. He denies substance abuse, which is confirmed by urine screenings. Clinical focus has carefully monitored for true comorbidity with ADHD, with the need to rule out oppositional-defiant disorder. The following process is an excerpt from a recent family session:

M.: (angry, yelling) She's a liar.

D.: (M.'s mother, yelled) I am not a liar.

M.: (yells louder) You are a liar.

Therapist: I need someone to talk about what happened. Why are you both yelling at each other?

M: (yells) She does this all the time, she's a liar.

D.: (yells) Don't you dare call me a liar, I am not a liar.

Therapist: Can someone explain what this is about?

M.: (At this point M. cut me off and yelled) I'm telling you she's a liar.

Therapist: I am requesting that all yelling stop. We cannot continue in this session with yelling. In order for us to work through this, you need to wait for me to finish speaking, and you need to slow down and really listen to what I am saying. You've been answering me before I'm finished speaking. I want us all to take a three-minute time-out so that the yelling can stop. During these next three minutes I would like you both to think about *how* you both got so worked up. (When M. displays an inability to inhibit his responses, as was the case here, I find it very useful to speak in a low monotone. It forces him to focus more acutely on what I am saying.)

M.: How will that change the fact that she's a liar?

Therapist: (Still speaking in a low monotone) We'll only be able to get somewhere if you, your mom, and I can speak about what happened and why you are both so upset.
(Both agreed to the three-minute time out.)

At this juncture M. is experiencing notable difficulty inhibiting his responses long enough to analyze and incorporate all the events and messages (both from the incident between him and his mother, and with the therapist). While I attempt to steer him away from the content of the communication and thereby examine how he and his mother became unable to communicate, M. is unable to shift his focus. He is stuck on the word "liar." As is indicated by the overload of emotion, M. experiences a message from his mother that becomes greatly distorted and laden with affect. His responses lack an adaptive level of objectivity and rationale necessary for effective self- and interpersonal communication. This illustrates notable impairment to the cognitive domain of *separation of affect* (Barkley, 1994). M. is also displaying impairment to *reconstitution* (Barkley, 1994). He demonstrates this in his inability to equilibrate the

many aspects of the messages and experiences, preventing subclassification so that he can respond appropriately and adaptively. He is careless in giving his response, which also serves to escalate the arguing between him and his mother.

Therapist: Three minutes are up. M., do you feel able to speak about how you got so worked up? D., do you feel that you can do the same? (Both said yes).

M.: She always disappoints me, she said she was going to take me for lunch, I'm starving, and on our way here she said that there was no time.

D.: That's because he was late in getting out of school, and I wasn't going to be late for this appointment.

M.: Well a promise is a promise.

Therapist: I want to compliment both of you on your ability to move away from arguing and giving us a chance to look at how you both got into such a heated argument. Can you both try to count to 10 before you answer each other?

M.: That's gay (colloquial for dumb. I took it as a yes, as it wasn't a no, a useful tactic when working with teens).

D.: O.K.

By complimenting M. and D., I grabbed their attention and averted the approaching argument, "A promise is a promise." They were able to slow down their responses to me, allowing them to take in my messages more carefully. Once they were able to communicate with me more slowly and carefully, they were able to use this more positive communication style with each other. Asking them to count to 10 before responding also helped them to inhibit their responses. The remainder of the session was spent focusing on M.'s need to be accountable for being on time for his therapy. Therefore, if M. wants lunch before his therapy appointment, he needs to leave school on time. D. was able to express her frustration which results from waiting for M. in front of school and going without her own lunch because M.'s therapy is during her lunch hour from work. D. also expressed how angry she feels when she is not able to budge M. from calling her names. The most positive gain for both M. and D. during this session was that they were able to "filter and metabolize" communication while at the same time delaying their responses to each other. Ultimately, M. and D. were able to demonstrate an improved capacity for *internalization*, thereby controlling their own behaviors while exerting the necessary willpower for problem solving (Barkley, 1994). Process illumination was utilized to provide M. and D. with an in-depth understanding of how and why their communication became angry and frustrated. They were both able to acknowledge the point at which each was unable to hear the other's explanation of feelings and circumstances prior to their arrival for therapy. M. and D. were able to recognize that they would have prevented escalation of conflict if they had been able to slow down their responses to each other. I asked them to continue using these techniques outside of therapy (i.e., process illumination and inhibition of responses).

Table 23.1 provides comparative data that show significant improvement in all but one area of M.'s school functioning. I have recently assessed that true comorbidity regarding oppositional-defiant disorder is not present. This is corroborated by an 89% improvement in school suspensions, a 48% improvement in school truancy, and 52% improvement in school tardies, and a 100% improvement in angry outbursts at school. M. displays decreased lability of moods with increased ability to inhibit his responses and more accurately and adaptively respond to communication and events (as noted in therapy, school, and home). M.'s attendance in therapy in excellent; he has missed two out of 45 appointments.

As stated earlier, process illumination, anticipating and addressing underinhibition of responses, multimodal treatment methods, a systems approach to treatment, and psychopharmacology all appear to be providing meaningful interventions and encouraging improvements in M.'s intra/interpersonal functioning. Therefore, social and intra/interpersonal stressors appear to be diminished. Future work will continue to focus on M.'s ability to delay responses and thereby promote intra/interpersonal accomplishments. An area that requires immediate therapeutic intervention is M.'s inability to acquire any academic credits for this semester. Academic stressors need to be identified and problem-solved. Collaboration with M.'s school and district personnel has been ongoing since *Page Web* services began, 9/98.

Case #2

C. is a male, 14-year-old, 8th-grade student. He lives with his biological parents, a 16-year-old brother, and an 18-year-old sister. C.'s father and sister are diagnosed ADHD, and both are treated with Ritalin. C. was referred to *the Page Web Program* November 1998. Reasons for the referral were inappropriate behaviors at school and home. School reports depict C. making odd sounds, annoying his peers during class and socializing, and low academic performance with gifted scholastic ability in the areas of verbal skills and reading. C.'s mother reports that C. makes odd, animal sounds at home. C. has not been observed with any tics or odd sounds while in session. As reported by C.'s parents, C. pulled out a patch of his hair approximately three inches in diameter last year. This behavior is reported to have ceased four months after its onset, and is currently not evident. There is serious therapeutic and parental concern regarding one episode, eight months ago, in which C. tried to hang himself. Suicidal ideation and attempts are denied prior and subsequent to this incident. C. was immediately evaluated by his treating psychiatrist, who diagnosed the suicide attempt to be a substance-induced psychotic disorder. C. was taking Zoloft and Ritalin at the time of the suicide attempt. C. was diagnosed with ADHD, Combined Type, in 1995. Currently, he is being treated with Ritalin and Tenex.

At the time of referral, C. became easily engaged in therapy and the structure of *The Page Web Pro-*

Table 23.1 Comparative Data for Targeted School Problems

Truancy	Suspensions	Tardy	Angry Outbursts	Academic Credits
9/98–1/99 = 11	9/98–1/99 = 1	9/98–1/99 = 28	On campus = 0 At home = 3	9/98–1/99 = 0
9/97–1/98 = 21	9/97–1/98 = 9	9/97–1/98 = 58	On campus = Many were reported At home = Many were reported	9/97–1/98 = 20

gram. C. has presented in therapy with loose associations and disorganized speech five times. C.'s family denies inordinate stressors or changes in C.'s prescription medication. C. does present with good reality testing; that is, he is always able to refocus his thoughts to associate appropriately when I prompt him to do so. C. denies substance abuse. Drug urine screenings test negative for illicit substances. Clinical focus continues to evaluate for true comorbidity in combination with ADHD. Immediate diagnoses need to rule out substance-induced psychotic disorder; schizophrenia: residual type; and Tourette's disorder. The following process is from an individual session, 1/99. This session was schedule on an "emergency basis" to address the reasons for the school suspension the day prior. C. was suspended for giving "pills" to three classmates. The pills were confirmed by the therapist and C.'s father to be the father's Ritalin; the pills seized on campus were equal in number and appearance to those missing from the father's prescription.

C.: I did not bring those pills from home. I found them in the planter and I gave them to those kids. I know that I should have brought them right to the office, but the kids asked me for them.

Therapist: Why didn't you bring them to the office when you found them?

C.: The kids were making fun of me. They told me to give them the pills.

Therapist: Did you take time to think about the consequences of giving the pills to those kids?

C.: No, I just wanted them to stop, and I really found them in the planter. I wanted the kids to stop making fun of me.

Therapist: I want to ask you to do something. I'd like you to close your eyes and try to be relaxed. I am going to time you for two minutes and I'll tell you when the time is up.

C. agreed to this intervention, which was designed to produce two desired outcomes. One was to chip away at C.'s denial and prevent him from merely focusing on the content of the allegations ("I found them in the planter. I did not bring them from home"). The second was to give C. time to conduct an "internal dialogue" with himself and thereby inhibit his responses to this incident. This was eliciting *internalization* of messages and events

(Barkley, 1994), thus providing a strategy for C. to improve his self-control.

Therapist: O.K., two minutes are up. You did a great job. What did you think about in the two minutes?

C.: I made a really bad choice.

Therapist: What was that?

C.: Giving those kids the pills.

Therapist: Why did you?

C.: I want more friends, everyone makes fun of me.

Therapist: What do they make fun of?

C.: My teeth, my clothes, that I'm dumb.

Therapist: That stinks. It must feel awful.

C.: I want them to stop doing this to me. So one of them asked me to bring some pills from home, and I did.

Therapist: What do you think you should do now?

C.: I have to tell my parents and the school that I brought the pills from home.

Therapist: That's a very responsible way to handle what you did. Do you want to talk to me about it some more, before we call your parents in? (We spent a few minutes discussing C.'s fears regarding punishments and his parents' and the school's responses to hearing the truth.)

It is important to note that C. did not display any loose associations, disorganized speech, or tics during this session. Clearly, the psychic stress imposed throughout this session could have easily fragmented tenuous ego processes. The two-minute time-out enabled C. to reflect on his behavior and the consequences of peer pressure. He was able to hold himself accountable for his behavior while displaying *prolongation* (Barkley, 1994). Defined earlier, *prolongation* allowed C. to hold onto the message/event for the requested two minutes and then mentally reproduce his perceived situation. He was then able to transfer this mental reproduction onto a fixed memory of the consequences for bringing pills to school. Ultimately, he was able to address the initial problem, peer pressure, as his reason for submitting to such a harmful decision.

We continued to work on C.'s need to conduct inner dialogues that will improve his ability to adhere to established rules and allow him to consider the consequences of his behavior. Evident from this school incident is C.'s inability to inhibit his responses to social cues that are dangerous and inappropriate. In addition, low self-esteem and social skills are target behaviors and are prioritized for current interventions. We continue work on C.'s perception of how he dresses, his teeth, and being placed in resource classes that address his learning needs. As is true for many children with learning disabilities, feeling "dumb" is a painful and unfortunate by-product.

Interventions with C. are being accomplished through individual therapy, family therapy, role-play, social skills activities, process illumination, forthcoming participation in a social skills group, and interdisciplinary collaboration. C.'s treating psychiatrist will medically supervise stopping all prescription drugs during a school vacation, so that a substance-induced psychotic disorder can be confirmed or ruled out. Pending that evaluation, and the presence or lack of continued thought disorder, further psychiatric evaluations will be done. Psychiatric and *Page Web* assessments will continue to screen for Tourette's disorder. Drug urine screenings will be continued. Pending the outcome of further evaluations, a diagnosis for true comorbidity will be determined. The moderate improvements academically, socially, and intra/interpersonally are correlated to C.'s newly acquired ability to monitor and inhibit his responses.

Summary

An accurate understanding of ADHD's etiology will help guide professionals, families, caretakers, and individuals into improved treatment modalities. Currently, there is growing consensus that ADHD is caused by neurological dysfunction, not psychopathology. Most profoundly, any disorder that is defined as psychopathological assigns a pejorative label to individuals and their family. If faulty brain chemistry is found to be the primary cause of ADHD, a medical definition will underlie the evidenced symptomology. A change in diagnosing will necessitate a change in our axis designation. While currently we assign our diagnosis as Axis I (psychopathological distinction), a neurological basis will require an Axis III diagnosis (medical distinction). If we can test positive for neurological causation, we will be removing ADHD's label of psychopathology, and we will be encouraging insurance reimbursements that claim medical diagnoses as opposed to less reimbursable claims of mental disorder. In addition, we will need to decipher (case by case) whether the comorbidity that we observe is really distinct or whether these comorbid diagnoses are in actuality mood and anxiety responses that are caused by untreated intra/interpersonal distress.

While it provides hope for all concerned to continue the search for ADHD's basis, we will fail to provide true helping unless we intervene with a focus on the quality of intra/interpersonal functioning. We can offer meaningful help by guiding future research to evaluate the maladaptive intra/interpersonal dynamics that are the outgrowth of ADHD. Explicit research and treatment studies can empirically determine the intra/interpersonal impact of underinhibition of responses as it is related to the sufferer's interpretation and expression of language and events. We will need to further understand how underinhibition of responses is directly correlated to particular patterning of relationships, and how it is that the repetitive frustration, anger, and conflict, once becoming insidious affect attunements, become one's expression of frustration, anger, and conflict. Focusing solely on research will not ease the burden imposed by ADHD. We will need to specifically address the manner in which ADHD interferes with one's ability to develop constructive and contented relationships with people.

The author thanks Phoebe Frank Ph.D., and Susan Wallace M.D., for their collaboration and editorial assistance. A special thank you to Professor Herb Schwarz, Adelphi University School of Social Work. Professor Schwarz's emphasis on the human element in providing social work services has always guided my work.

References

Barkley, Russell A. "A New Theory of ADHD." *ADHD Report. Vol. 1, No. 5*, October 1993: 1–12.

Barkley, Russell A. "More on the New Theory of ADHD." *ADHD Report. Vol. 2, No. 2*, April 1994: 1–12.

Beck, Aaron T. *Love Is Never Enough*. New York: Harper and Row, 1988.

Diagnostic Criteria from DSM-IV, 1994. Washington D.C.: American Psychiatric Association.

Mitchell, Steven A. *Relational Concepts in Psychoanalysis*. Cambridge, MA: Harvard University Press, 1988.

Moore, Burness, Fine, Bernard. *Psychoanalytic Terms and Concepts*. New Haven: American Psychoanalytic Association and Yale University Press, 1990.

Stern, Daniel N. *The Interpersonal World of the Infant*. New York: Basic Books, 1985.

Winnicott, D. W. *Playing and Reality*. New York: Routledge, 1971.

Yalom, Irvin D. *The Theory and Practice of Group Psychotherapy*. New York: Basic Books, 1985.

Zametkin, Alan J. "Attention-Deficit Disorder: Born to Be Hyperactive?" *Journal of the American Medical Association*. Vol. 273, no. 23, June 21, 1995: 1871–1874.

24

When She Was Bad: Borderline Personality Disorder in a Posttraumatic Age

Within the past decade, two syndromes—borderline personality disorder (BPD) and posttraumatic stress disorder (PTSD)—have quickly become "women's" diagnoses, each for its own reason. It has been suggested that the increase in the application of the borderline diagnosis to women owes much to the fact that, over the decades, its diagnostic criteria have been reshaped to resemble those of the affective disorders, such that these criteria have come less and less to represent the "border" between psychosis and neurosis from which the disorder takes its name (Kroll, 1988). In the case of PTSD, the scope of its application has broadened to include those individuals who suffer the psychological aftereffects of sexual or physical abuse, a large proportion of whom are women.

Designations of normality and pathology owe their origins not only to biological and psychological factors, but also to the sociocultural contexts in which individuals find themselves. The conceptualization of BPD embodied in the *DSM-IV* (American Psychiatric Association, 1994) continues to reflect a view of women's problems as inherently intrapsychically derived. Object relations theories concerning the origins of BPD that held sway for many years have very likely reinforced among clinicians the notion that, for the individual suffering symptoms designated "borderline," a problematic early mother-child relationship has resulted in developmental arrest and subsequent deformations of character. In contrast, PTSD is one of only a handful of diagnoses in the

DSM-IV whose symptoms can be said to stem from situational causes alone. This in itself has rendered PTSD particularly attractive to feminist therapists, who have found in this "nonblaming" diagnosis a means of acknowledging the social/situational origins of certain psychological problems faced by women. On the other hand, the borderline diagnosis, with its overly ample boundaries and unclear applications, has acquired an increasingly pejorative connotation. The view of one disorder as a consequence of character and the other as a consequence of fate cannot fail to have significant implications for the narratives of both therapist and client. Today, we might characterize BPD and PTSD as the "bad girl" and the "good girl," respectively, of psychiatric labels.

The question raised in this paper is whether, in the context of the long and painful history of the relationship between women and psychodiagnosis, feminist therapists, in "discovering" PTSD, have truly found the diagnostic promised land—or whether widespread acceptance of the diagnosis and the stress paradigm of illness on which it rests represents a further embrace of the medicalization of women's problems. In addressing this question, the present paper explores the implications for women of the effort to redefine BPD as a form of PTSD. It is argued that this effort has resulted in a caste system of diagnosis and treatment that fails either to serve women labeled borderline or to eradicate the pernicious borderline diagnosis altogether. Issues considered include the problematic result for women of the broad application of the stress paradigm of disorder; the paradox inherent in the psychiatric attempt to "normalize" stress responses by calling them disordered; and difficulties created by the attempt to fit BPD into new constructions of trauma-induced disorders.

Borderline Personality Disorder

"Its symptoms are so varied and obscure, so contradictory and changeable." Although these words might well have been found in recent descriptions of the criteria for the diagnosis of BPD, they were, in fact, used in 1833 by an eminent gynecologist, Samuel Ashwell, to describe the symptoms of hysteria, a condition about which he commented: "Few practitioners desire the management of hysterics." Half a century later, another medical man, neurologist Charles K. Mills, called hysteria "preeminently a chronic disease . . . [one] in which it is unsafe to claim a conquest" (quotations cited in Smith-Rosenberg, 1972, p. 665).

Over a century after Mills's pronouncement, we cling to a diagnosis of *our* time—borderline personality disorder—that, despite its status as one of the most widely researched disorders, lacks consistent proof of validity or reliability (Akiskal et al., 1985; Frances & Widiger, 1987; Kroll et al., 1981; Kutchins & Kirk, 1997; Lykowski & Tsuang, 1980). It is a diagnosis that has been applied to women at a rate of about seven to one over men (Swartz, Blazer, George, & Winfield, 1990; Widiger & Weissman, 1991). And, although the diagnosis has been shown to be gender-biased in its application (Adler, Drake, & Teague, 1990; Becker & Lamb, 1994), the psychiatric profession continues, just as did physicians Ashwell and Mills, to wrestle with its protean form, fret over the "management" of patients, and despair about the chronicity of the disease.

The history of the borderline concept and the BPD diagnosis is a history of the shifting sociopolitical contexts in which American psychiatry is embedded. It is not the purpose of this paper to recapitulate that history (Aronson, 1985; Becker, 1997; Fine, 1989), apart from noting that personality disorders, of all psychiatric diagnoses, bear the most remote resemblance to medical disorders. For this reason, they are particularly vulnerable to changes in the social, political, and economic climate (Kroll, 1988). Criteria for the disorder have been shaped over the years in such a way that BPD can now be viewed as an atypical affective disorder, given its core features of mood instability and dysphoria (Kroll, 1993). It seems

hardly coincidental that this transformation began taking shape as interest in and funding for research on affective disorders soared over the past two decades (Kroll, 1988). Since women more frequently report symptoms of dysthymia and major depressive disorder than do men (Kessler et al., 1994; Robins & Regier, 1991), it is not surprising that the centrality of affective criteria in the *DSM-III-R* (American Psychiatric Association, 1987) and *DSM-IV* renderings of BPD has made the diagnosis a better "fit" for women than might previously have been the case (Becker, 1997).

Like that of PTSD, the BPD diagnosis may be arrived at in a multitude of ways, such that one individual diagnosed borderline may not look like another with the identical diagnosis. Stone (1990) found 93 ways in which criteria could be combined and still yield a *DSM-III-R* BPD diagnosis (with the addition of a new criterion in *DSM-IV*, one shudders to think how many combinations are now possible). Given the broad reach of its criteria, it is little wonder that about 15% of inpatients and 8% of outpatients now carry the label "borderline" (Stefan, 1998). In fact, borderline has become the most pejorative of all personality labels, and it is now little more than shorthand for a difficult, angry female client certain to give the therapist countertransferential headaches.

In a study attempting to isolate what they termed markers for BPD, Zanarini, Gunderson, Frankenburg, and Chauncey (1990) identified demandingness/entitlement, treatment regressions, and the ability to evoke inappropriate responses in one's therapist. Use of these behavioral indices as markers for BPD shows us just how far we can go in accepting a label that stands for an aggregate of behavior as a mental disorder (Kutchins & Kirk, 1997). In an extreme variant on this theme, the borderline diagnosis is referred to as if it were equivalent to a symptom (e.g., "the outcome of group treatments was said to be adversely affected when a group member had high levels of dissociation . . . *and a diagnosis of borderline personality disorder*" [Cloitre, 1996, cited in Alexander & Muenzenmaier, 1998, p. 225, emphasis added]). Circular arguments—that a person is demanding because she "has" BPD or that a therapist acted inappropriately because her client "has" BPD—do nothing to advance our understanding of so-called borderline phenomena.

Although the late 1960s ushered in an era in which it became almost de riguer for therapists to treat survivors of incest and sexual abuse, since the 1990s—the era of the recovered memory debate—therapists are increasingly aware of the risks implicit in treating victims of abuse. Among the clients who inspire the greatest anxiety and fear are those "with borderline-type dynamics" (Courtois, 1999, p. 308). BPD has acquired the distinction of being the only diagnosis for which a failure to thrive (so to speak) in treatment and the countertransference reactions of the therapist serve as proofs of validity (Becker, 1997).

In recent years, with the increasing recognition that many women to whom the BPD diagnosis has been applied have suffered physical, sexual, and other forms of childhood maltreatment (G.R. Brown & Anderson, 1991; Coons, Bowman, Pellow, & Schneider, 1989; Goodwin, Cheeves, & Connell, 1990; Herman, 1986; Herman, Perry, & van der Kolk, 1989; Herman, Russell, & Trocki, 1986; Ogata et al., 1990; Stone, Unwin, Beacham, & Swenson, 1988; Surrey, Swett, Michaels, & Levin, 1990; Weaver & Clum, 1993; Westen, Ludolph, Misle, Ruffins, & Block, 1990; Zanarini, Gunderson, Marino, Schwartz, & Frankenburg, 1989), there has been a strong impetus to move away from the characterological blame (Janoff-Bulman, 1985) implicit in intrapsychic explanations for the etiology of BPD toward explanations that take these traumatic antecedents into account. As the antecedents are considered, BPD symptoms are increasingly discussed in terms of their relationship to external forms of stress, and it is this relationship that has been responsible for the frequent pairing of BPD and PTSD in the past decade. This conceptualization of BPD as a special instance of PTSD owes much to the stress paradigm of illness.

The Stress Paradigm

The assumption that there is a correspondence between particular types of disordered behavior and particular types of stress has long been a mainstay of the Western "scientific" or classical paradigm (Cloward & Piven, 1979; Kleinman, 1988). In the contemporary rendering of the classical model, severe stressors—often conceptualized as changes in life events that are menacing or uncontrollable to some degree—produce a strain from which the individual seeks relief by engaging in coping activities intended to restore equilibrium. Those who are exposed to these stressors but who lack adequate social supports or methods of coping will experience mental (or medical) disorder (Kleinman, 1980).

Although, in the aggregate, several sets of recent studies focusing on the effects of environmental ad-

versity have demonstrated that stress and adversity play an important role in the etiology of some psychiatric disorders, much of the evidence associating environmental stressors with *particular* disorders continues to be indirect, and it is unclear what importance to assign to the role of stress vis-à-vis the course of certain disorders (Dohrenwend, 1998). It would appear, too, that in many cases the association between environmental adversity and disorder "is limited to stressful events of considerable magnitude" (Stueve, Dohrenwend, & Skodol, 1998, p. 354).

Any discussion of the relationship between stress and disorder must take into account the social structure within which stressful conditions exist. Such conditions and the options available to us in coping with them are shaped by the sociohistorical context of our lives (Cloward & Piven, 1979). Because the classical view of the causal connection between stress and disorder is both persistent and pervasive, as social changes lead to revisions in the prevalence rates and forms of disordered behavior, we will not only continue to uncover new stresses but may see the forms and distribution of disorder change radically even in the absence of equivalent changes in stress (Cloward & Piven, 1979).

The Big Tent: PTSD and Its Widening Reach

PTSD has recently undergone just such a radical change in form and prevalence. This has been accomplished through an alteration in the description of the precipitants of the onset of PTSD, which has led to a large increase in its prevalence in a brief time span. In less than 20 years, PTSD has been transformed from a newly named syndrome (American Psychiatric Association, 1980) into a widely used and researched diagnosis (Andreason, 1995; Kutchins & Kirk, 1997). In the *DSM-III* description of PTSD, stressful precipitating events had to be "outside the range of usual human experience" (p. 236). Fourteen years later, with the publication of *DSM-IV*, trauma was redefined to include exposure to "an event or events that involved actual or threatened death or serious injury, or a threat to the physical integrity of self or others" (p. 427), events distinctly not outside the range of normal experience. This revision made it possible to conceive of the sexual and physical abuse perpetrated on large numbers of women as stressors that could lead to symptoms development (Kutchins & Kirk, 1997), and it represented, for many, an important acknowledgment of the effects of this abuse.

There is no doubt that consideration of the ways exposure to traumatic stress influences the development of girls and women is vastly preferable to a conceptualization of women's distress as deriving from intrapsychic phenomena. In fact, until their overall effect is appreciated, recent changes in the PTSD diagnosis appear to constitute a much needed validation of and response to the real suffering of victimized women. On balance, however, the benefits to women of these changes are questionable. The redefinition of trauma in *DSM-IV* has increased by millions the number of those eligible for a PTSD diagnosis and has identified those women who qualify for it as having a mental disorder (Kutchins & Kirk, 1997). In addition, as abuse increasingly becomes synonymous with trauma, such a large number of symptoms and syndromes is being subsumed under the category "abuse" that the term may eventually lose all meaning (Cushman, 1995).

There are 175 ways in which PTSD criteria can be combined in order for a PTSD diagnosis to be reached (Kutchins & Kirk, 1997). Because of the amplitude of the category, and the diffuseness of its criteria, some of those individuals brought in under the new, enlarged PTSD tent are barely related; that is, some have no symptoms in common with others so diagnosed. Of course, a smaller tent would necessarily hold less room for insurance-reimbursed service providers in a mental health economy in which supply may well create demand (Frank & Frank, 1991; Haaken & Schlaps, 1991; Kleinman, 1995; Kutchins & Kirk, 1997; Lamb, 1996). Put in historical context, the proliferation of the PTSD diagnosis may rival in scope the epidemic of hysteria and neuroasthenia during the last half of the nineteenth century (Eherenreich & English, 1978; Sicherman, 1977; Wood, 1973).

In her analysis of interviews with more than 40 feminist therapists, Marecek (1999) observed that many of them found PTSD to be the only acceptable (i.e., nonstigmatizing, nonblaming) psychiatric diagnosis for women, as this portion of an interview with one of those therapists illustrates:

Almost all my clients have PTSD and I tell them what it means. I say, "This means you are having a normal reaction to trauma. You're not having a sick reaction to trauma. You're having a normal reaction to trauma." The reason I like PTSD as a diagnosis and I'm glad it's there is that it says right in the definition that this is a normal response to trauma that most people would have. (p. 163)

For all the desire to make it so, the normalization of stress responses cannot be accomplished through our fervent attachment to the PTSD diagnosis. Although the diagnosis seems new in its uses, those uses reflect the application of the classical stress/disease model to age-old stressors. Reliance on the stress model can have disturbing implications for the representation of women's experience. There is no single stressful experience in response to which most individuals develop PTSD (Kessler, Sonnega, Bromet, Hughes, & Nelson, 1995; Yehuda & McFarlane, 1995). Thus, because PTSD is by no means a universal response to abuse, and because its symptoms are considered involuntary, those symptoms can exist only as the constituents of disease (Lamb, 1996). We cannot, as some have suggested, conceptualize PTSD as a "normal" response to trauma (Hamilton & Jensvold, 1992) and call it a disorder at the same time. Of course, as soon as we name a set of responses to stress "disorder," we employ science to justify its medicalization. Not only, then, does acceptance of the widespread use of the PTSD diagnosis for women imply acceptance of a reductionistic theoretical framework that subordinates context to individual reaction, but medicalization further separates that reaction into its psychological and biological components.

Those insistent on viewing psychiatry as a science are bent on validating diagnoses through the identification of so-called biological markers or neurobiological substrates (Andreason, 1995). In the years that have followed the decision to give a name to posttraumatic stress, a disorder that was originally considered to be an acute psychological reaction to a severe stressor in the environment—a mind/body phenomenon—is increasingly being viewed as a biological disorder. Countless studies are now being performed on the biological concomitants of PTSD (Murburg, Ashleigh, Hommer, & Veith, 1994; Shalev, Orr, & Pittman, 1993; van der Kolk & Saporta, 1993; Yehuda & McFarlane, 1995), and it has even been suggested that sex differences in behavioral response to traumatization may be hormonal (Wolfe & Kimerling, 1997). Even where the biology of PTSD is not reified, the dichotomization of the psychological and the environmental persists, as exemplified by Wolfe and Kimerling's statement, "Whether a differential vulnerability for PTSD in women relates to underlying or intrinsic characteristics . . . *as opposed to external factor* remains unclear" (p. 202, emphasis added).

The Overlap between PTSD and BPD

In the age of the "new" PTSD, we are confounded in our ability to view BPD and PTSD as categories separable from each other. Both diagnoses have been termed "catchall" or "wastebasket" categories because of the overinclusiveness of their criteria as well as the amplitude of their boundaries (Kroll, 1993). Not only do they frequently overlap symptomatically, but each is comorbid with so many other disorders that it is difficult to justify the perceived close relationship between the two diagnoses on the basis of comorbidity alone.

Personality disorder categories are by no means mutually exclusive, a fact that has been restated frequently by members of the psychiatric community itself (Lilienfeld, Van Valkenburg, Larntz, & Akiskal, 1986; Oldham et al., 1992; Pope, Jonas, Hudson, Cohen, & Gunderson, 1983; Stangl, Pfohl, Zimmerman, Bowers, & Corenthal, 1985; Widiger & Rogers, 1989). Most individuals who have been diagnosed with a personality disorder such as BPD also meet criteria for at least one additional personality disorder (Fryer, Frances, Sullivan, Hurt, & Clarkin, 1988; Widiger & Rogers, 1989). Almost half of those who qualify for either a BPD or a histrionic personality disorder diagnosis meet criteria for the other disorder.

Zanarini et al. (1988), in studying the pattern of comorbidity of BPD with Axis I disorders, found that the symptoms of female borderline inpatients overlapped frequently with those of mood disorders—and with anxiety disorders and eating disorders as well, but not to such an extent. Rather than viewing this comorbidity as proof of how blurred are the boundaries of BPD, the researchers maintained that these comorbid disorders can "mask" an "underlying borderline psychopathology" (p. 1733), thereby disguising "true" borderline symptoms. Their solution to this dilemma is to maintain that the extensive comorbidity itself serves as a marker, establishing the uniqueness of the diagnosis by discriminating BPD from other Axis II disorders. The fact that 75% of the BPD patients in the study exhibited a certain pattern of comorbidity and 75% of other Axis II patients did not was all the evidence these researchers needed to establish the validity of BPD.

This formulation rests on two erroneous assumptions. One is that the personality disorders are valid categories. Another is that finding what has been put there to find (i.e., finding the affective criteria that have been included in successive revisions of the BPD category by successive *DSM* committees) and applying those same criteria to inpatients constitutes proof of the validity of the disorder. This process is akin to that of parents searching for eggs at an Easter hunt; the outcome is certain even if the legitimacy of the enterprise is suspect.

In this same study of 504 inpatients, Zanarini et al. (1998) found that 56% of those with BPD diagnoses also met the criteria for PTSD. Like BPD, PTSD has criteria that overlap with symptoms of affective disorder. Major depression and dysthymia have been shown to be among the features most frequently found to be comorbid with PTSD (Wolfe & Kimerling, 1997), as well as anxiety symptoms common to social phobia, simple phobia, and panic disorder (Kessler et al., 1995). Research findings indicate that preexisting major depression may increase an individual's vulnerability to PTSD symptoms following exposure to severe traumatic stress (Resnick, Kilpatrick, Best, & Kramer, 1992). Since symptoms of anxiety and depression are frequently experienced by those diagnosed with both BPD and PTSD, and PTSD, like BPD, is significantly more prevalent among women than among men (Breslau, Davis, Andreski, & Peterson, 1991; Kessler et al., 1995), it may be that the study of the relationships among gender, depression, and anxiety will prove more valuable than current attempts to locate the ever-shifting boundaries between the two diagnoses.

The Newest Caste System

There are several current schools of thought about the relationship between BPD and PTSD. One view holds that BPD represents a developmentally based deformation of personality that occurs as a result of early, prolonged experiences of childhood abuse, rendering an individual particularly vulnerable to developing PTSD symptoms in response to later stressors (Gunderson & Sabo, 1993a; Kolb, 1989). Gunderson and Sabo (1993b), proponents of this view, have stated that the person who develops borderline personality features in adulthood "was never previously 'normal'" (p. 1906). Their contention is that, currently, many adults with histories of childhood trauma are being misdiagnosed as having PTSD; that is, that PTSD can "mimic" personality disorders (Kolb, 1989; Ochberg, 1991). This assertion does not admit of the possibility that certain personality configurations may increase individuals' vulnerability to developing chronic symptoms of PTSD, that personality problems may function as a selector of those who are exposed to potentially trauma-inducing situations, or that personality disorder may follow from trauma (Green, Lindy, & Grace, 1985).

Another perspective is that BPD is actually chronic PTSD that has been integrated into the personality structure (Herman, 1992; Herman et al., 1986; Landecker, 1992). According to this conceptualization, chronic (i.e., prolonged and repeated) stress can result in the development of behavior patterns that are adaptive or compensatory but that cannot be distinguished from personality traits (Kroll, 1993), and many women who have been exposed to chronic trauma are incorrectly being diagnosed as having personality disorders, particularly BPD.

BPD as Complex or Chronic PTSD

An ever larger group of advocates suggests that those women with histories of abuse (e.g., physical abuse, sexual abuse, maltreatment) who are currently diagnosed as having BPD suffer from this chronic or "complex" form of PTSD or fit into some category situated between personality disorder and BPD (Alexander & Muenzanmaier, 1998; L.S. Brown, 1994; Courtois, 1999; Herman, 1992; Herman et al., 1989; Lerman, 1996; Zanarini et al., 1998). The case is frequently made that the PTSD diagnosis helps to create a more beneficial treatment context for women currently labeled borderline, since it rids the term of the disagreeable connotations that continue to cling to BPD, while offering the possibility for a situationally focused rather than a more blaming, intrapsychically focused psychotherapy. The notion that construing the client's situation as trauma-based is more likely to elicit from the therapist feelings of warmth and empathy, along with a greater willingness to identify with the client and believe in her ability to change (L.S. Brown, 1994), is indeed a happy thought. The reality, however, may be far different.

There is no doubt that positing situational rather than intrapsychic antecedents for the disorder represents a considerable advance in our thinking about both the etiology and the treatment of BPD. Nonetheless, the move to replace the BPD diagno-

sis with PTSD, "complex" or otherwise, is problematic. It is mistaken to assume that physical and sexual abuse are at the root of all difficulties experienced by women currently diagnosed borderline, or that the existence of abuse alone should determine the focus of psychotherapy. However, this view is apparently held by some therapists, as expressed in the following excerpt from an interview with one of them:

> There's lots of women who get labeled as borderline who have those characteristics but it comes out of twenty years of being beaten by their husbands or a severe incest. If you treat that as borderline personality disorder versus PTSD [laughs] you get really different outcomes. . . . There's a continuum of sexual violence, and most women have experienced some amount by the time they're eighteen, and so I recognize that, and I recognize how it constricts their lives that way. (Marecek, 1999, pp. 162–163)

It has generally been assumed that, because women are more often subject to sexual abuse then men, gender is a risk factor for the development of PTSD (Waites, 1993; Wolfe & Kimerling, 1997), an assumption that is frequently held for BPD as well. Landecker (1992) reiterated this common point of view and its corollary, that posttraumatic stress, as the response to childhood abuse, is "implicit in most borderline diagnoses" (p. 236).

It has been recognized, however, that not all women diagnosed as having BPD have been physically or sexually traumatized, and that multiple factors in interaction with each other can produce the various symptom constellations we currently call BPD. It has also been argued that these symptom constellations under no circumstances should be considered a unitary disorder (Becker, 1997; Kroll, 1988, 1993).

The linear connection among gender, risk for victimization through traumatic sexual/physical abuse, and BPD or PTSD symptoms fails to take into account that the ways in which individuals express distress (i.e., deviate behaviorally from societal norms) are historically and socially determined. As was noted above, individuals' experience of stress is shaped by aspects of the sociohistorical context of stress, by their own interpretations of stressful events, and by their evaluations of the options available to them in coping with those events (Cloward & Piven, 1979). Female development implies exposure to sexualization and devaluation in their many guises, regardless of the occurrence of overt abuse (Becker, 1997; Westkott, 1986). There are differences among individuals, however, in the degree and persistence of exposure to stressful events, as well as in their vulnerability to stressors. There are also differences between the sexes in the perception of what is traumatic—that is, in the interpretation of the conditions they face and how symptoms are expressed (Kessler et al., 1995).

When PTSD was originally considered for inclusion in *DSM-III*, a question arose as to how specific the stressor should be: Should there be a different diagnosis for symptomatic responses to each type of traumatic event? It was quickly determined that PTSD was a unitary disorder that resulted from exposure to many types of traumatic events (Andreasen, 1995). One could argue, however, that within the wide range of individual responses to different dysfunctional environments or traumatic events there are many symptomatic (as well as nonsymptomatic) configurations, only some of which can be thought of as PTSD (Graziano, 1992; Lamb, 1999).

A developmental psychopathology perspective applied to the symptom constellations currently called PTSD and BPD certainly points toward conceptualizing both the severity of the stressor(s) and the experience and expression of distress along continua. We know that the severity of the stressor may or may not predict the kind, severity, or persistence of symptoms (Rutter, 1990). The developmental psychopathology framework accounts for the multiple mediators of stress and response to stress in a way that no diagnostic system—with its insistence on disorders as categorical entities with discrete, delimiting criteria sets—can do. For Herman (1992) to conceive of the sequelae to chronic trauma as a spectrum of conditions as opposed to a single disorder and then insist that the syndrome that results from persistent trauma be given a name of its own (i.e., complex posttraumatic stress disorder) appears contradictory at best.

The trouble with trundling a large group of so-called borderline women off to the shelter of the widening PTSD tent is that it will not serve the purpose of eliminating the borderline diagnosis. It will merely remove those women who have histories of clear-cut traumatic antecedents and PTSD symptomatology from the borderline group, leaving behind a residual group of "true" borderlines. That this is already occurring was made evident by Courtois (1999) in a recent clinical text:

The transference projections of interpersonally victimized patients can be very challenging and difficult to manage and are often similar (if not identical) to those identified with personality disturbances, notably borderline personality. (p. 174)

This statement suggests that the "interpersonally victimized patients" and those with "personality disturbances" are not always one and the same. "Borderlines" become a separable group, identified as "difficult to manage." And the author has unwittingly provided a blueprint for the diagnostic and treatment hierarchy that is now taking shape. The first tier of that hierarchy is occupied by those who have not been severely victimized; the second by those who have been more severely victimized over a prolonged period, or who have borderline personality characteristics—what Courtois, in another section of her book, referred to as "a posttraumatic personality" (p. 87), but which might more aptly be termed a borderline in posttraumatic clothing. When we begin to create hierarchies within the PTSD or complex PTSD categories, are we not still knee-deep in the Big Muddy of psychiatric terrain?

The Good Patient and the Bad

The Burden of the Borderline Diagnosis

No amount of fiddling with the present designations, it would seem, will eliminate use of the BPD diagnosis in actual practice. It has not been demonstrated conclusively that clinicians can make this diagnosis with any reliability (Kutchins & Kirk, 1997), and practitioners continue to find interpersonal difficulties—both within and outside the treatment relationship—sufficient evidence for the existence of BPD (Kutchins & Kirk, 1997; Walker, 1994). Within the confines of offices, agencies, and institutions, the BPD and PTSD diagnoses are often quite loosely and interchangeably applied by clinicians. Witness the following statement by Walker (1994):

Many therapists who treat incest survivors believe that such a diagnostic category [PTSD] would permit greater access to appropriate treatment focusing on the situational trauma and its subsequent sequelae. . . . Other therapists *find the personality disorder diagnosis more to their liking.* (p. 113, emphasis added)

Despite the apparent offhandedness with which both diagnoses are often applied in practice, it is no casual matter for a woman to carry a BPD label. Stefan (1998), in a study of court law, found that women diagnosed with BPD are often considered mentally disabled and, as such, subject to involuntary institutionalization or medication and loss of child custody or parental rights. They likewise are often discredited as witnesses in court cases involving rape or sexual abuse. All of this is in sharp contrast to the way women diagnosed with PTSD are treated. Whereas women who receive diagnoses of PTSD are more likely to benefit under the law on the basis of their disability, women given a BPD diagnosis are not usually thought to be mentally disabled to the extent that would permit them to receive educational or disability benefits, or to recover damages in an abuse case.

Relationship Management:
For Borderlines Only?

The discussion of transference and countertransference in the literature on trauma theory and PTSD differs substantially depending on whether or not the client is a "straight-up" PTSD client or one who is labeled as having BPD or its equivalent (e.g., Courtois's [1999] "posttraumatic personality"). In the trauma/PTSD literature, for example, discussions of countertransference often give a substantial place to descriptions of such phenomena as "vicarious traumatization" (McCann & Pearlman, 1999, p. 520) and "empathic stress" (Wilson & Lindy, 1999, p. 520). Both types of response, it is maintained, can result from continued exposure on the part of therapists to clients' reporting of their trauma stories. These reactions are evoked as a result of the therapist's exposure to the client's *experience*. When the borderline client enters the treatment discussion, however, the client herself and the *relationship* between therapist and client become the focus, as this statement by Ochberg (1991), in a discussion of a treatment model for PTSD sufferers, illustrates:

> Certain coexisting disorders, particularly borderline personality, may be impossible for the posttraumatic therapist to manage according to the principles of PTT. For example, collegiality may be misinterpreted as intimate friendship, and a willingness to intervene with criminal justice may lead to insatiable requests for help with personal affairs. (p. 14)

Again, the term "manage," with its evocation of nineteenth-century "moral management" of the

mad (Showalter, 1985) and ts reminders of more recent calls for "limit setting" and "rigid frames" or boundaries in the treatment of individuals with BPD (Reiser & Levenson, 1984, p. 258) continues to be applied to this subgroup of treatment candidates. Just as much of the literature on treatment of the borderline client often includes lengthy discussions of relational nightmares-to-be, the literature on trauma therapy includes special disquisitions on how to handle the personality-disordered type of client, who is further marginalized even among her alleged sisters in trauma.

In just such an example of treatment segregation, Alexander and Muenzenmaier (1998) have discussed why certain women, those with histories of psychosis, acute suicidality, and substance abuse, and those who "have been diagnosed as having borderline personality disorder are generally excluded from trauma groups" (p. 225). They noted that "Research also suggests that women with complex sequelae to early sexual abuse may not benefit from traditional group work" (p. 225). Given the company it keeps here, the term borderline takes on the meaning "chronic" or "severe."

The "Borderline" and
Trauma Therapy

When stress and the responses to stress constitute the symbolic vehicles through which clinician and client attend to the client's idiosyncratic experience (Cloward & Piven, 1979, Kleinman, 1988), trauma becomes centralized "as an essential category of human existence, rooted in individual rather than social dynamics and reflective more of medical pathology than of religious or moral happenings" (Kleinman, 1995, p. 177). In their discussion of incest resolution therapy, Haaken and Schlaps (1991) argued that this centralization of trauma in psychotherapy may obscure other events and relationships that exist alongside, or predate, the sexual abuse trauma, and that it comes to define the client's sense of self, thereby potentially foreclosing other important domains available for exploration. The therapist's persistent focus on sexual abuse may be perceived by clients as a demand, both tacit and overt, to focus on this issue, and many women, seeking to be "good," responsive clients, will not resist this demand. The centralization of trauma in treatment may also put those clients at a disadvantage who cannot be considered either victims of specific abuse or compliant, well-behaved victims. "Borderline" women, many of whom are diagnosed with BPD precisely because they present relational challenges in treatment as elsewhere, may fall into this group.

Paradoxically, trauma-focused therapy fits well into the medical model, notwithstanding its proponents' views and sentiments to the contrary (Marecek, 1999). When trauma is centralized, not only do medical metaphors such as wound, injury, brokenness, and pain pervade the language of the therapeutic encounter, but healing and recovery become the goals of psychotherapy (Marecek, 1999). The diagnostic criteria for PTSD emphasize the persistence of symptoms, and the experience of post-traumatic stress is deemed pathological because it persists, a view that implies that it is not normal for individuals who have been traumatized to continue to suffer (Kleinman, 1995). In fact, the view of suffering implicit in the *DSM* is that we humans should not have to endure it—that suffering should be terminated. As our Western ideology would have it, we need endure nothing; we can even "work through" our memories (Kleinman, 1995).

Whereas for PTSD sufferers, "recovery," "resolution," or "reparenting" are held out as possible—even probable—outcomes, for those labeled with BPD hope is not often proffered, even though the facts do not support the perception of a wide disparity in the chronicity of the two disorders (Kessler et al., 1995; Kroll, 1993). In one of a number of child custody cases involving women diagnosed with BPD, the court found that the mother, because of her disorder, was

> not likely to benefit from counseling, . . . not likely to respond to treatment [and] that such persons . . . are resistant to social services and are very unlikely to recognize or deal with their problems, and that the [mother] is in that category. (Stefan, 1998, p. 252)

Conclusion

While the notion of recovery fits well with our American ideas about the power of human agency to overcome great odds, of late we find ourselves revering the victim, leaning toward the reactor rather than the actor (Lamb, 1996, 1999). It may be that such a preference implies, as Kaminer (1993) has suggested, a societal sense of resignation—a posture of defeat in a world in which little makes sense, much is accident without explanation, and character is separable from fate. Mention was

made earlier of the false distinction between character and fate that has affected our current conceptualizations of BPD and PTSD. In the absence of that distinction there would be no "bad girls" and "good girls," just women whose suffering—and the context of whose suffering—needs to be understood.

It may also be that our continued attachment to the stress paradigm, and to PTSD as its current diagnostic exponent, causes us to fail our women clients in the very task that we had hoped to accomplish, namely, altering the conceptualization of their suffering as a highly individualized phenomenon. It has been this very view that has persistently justified the separation of women's distress from its sociopolitical contexts on the basis that stress has universal effects on individuals (Kleinman, 1995). Medicalization contributes to the social control of women through expansion of the definition of madness and leads us in pursuit of cures for the "disease" of PTSD.

The promised land of PTSD has turned out to be a wasteland, most particularly so for the "bad girl" borderline client. Our deference to the gods of medicine, who have so kindly allowed us the PTSD diagnosis, has not helped us to resolve the societal dilemmas implicit in male-to-female abuse. It has simply deferred the abolition of the borderline diagnosis and its hideous connotations for another day, and perhaps a much later day at that.

References

Adler, D. A., Drake, R. E., & Teague, G. B. (1990). Clinicians' practices in personality assessment: Does gender influence the use of DSM-III Axis II? *Comprehensive Psychiatry, 31*, 125–133.

Akiskal, H. S., Chen, S. E., Davis, G. C., Puzantian, V. R., Kashgarian, M., & Bolinger, J. M. (1985). Borderline: An adjective in search of a noun. *Journal of Clinical Psychiatry, 46* (2), 41–48.

Alexander, M. J., & Muenzenmaier, K. (1998). Trauma, addiction, and recovery: Addressing public health epidemics among women with severe mental illness. In B. L. Levin, A. K. Blanch, & A. Jennings (Eds.), *Women's mental health services: A public health perspective* (pp. 215–239). Thousand Oaks, CA: Sage Publications.

American Psychiatric Association. (1980). *Diagnostic and statistical manual of mental disorders* (Third ed.). Washington, DC: Author.

American Psychiatric Association. (1987). *Diagnostic and statistical manual of mental disorders.* (Third ed., rev.). Washington, DC: Author.

American Psychiatric Association. (1994). *Diagnostic and statistical manual of mental disorders.* (Fourth ed.). Washington, DC: Author.

Andreason, N. (1995). Posttraumatic stress disorder: Psychology, biology, and the Manichean warfare between false dichotomies. *American Journal of Psychiatry, 152,* 963–965.

Aronson, T. A. (1985). Historical perspectives on the borderline concept: A review and critique. *Psychiatry, 48,* 209–222.

Becker, D. (1997). *Through the looking glass: Women and borderline personality disorder.* Boulder, CO: Westview Press.

Becker, D., & Lamb, S. (1994). Sex bias in the diagnosis of borderline personality disorder and posttraumatic stress disorder. *Professional Psychology: Research and Practice, 25,* 55–61.

Breslau, N., Davis, G. C., Andreski, P., & Peterson, E. (1991). Traumatic events and posttraumatic stress disorder in an urban population of young adults. *Archives of General Psychiatry, 48,* 216–222.

Brown, L. S. (1994). *Subversive dialogues: Theory in feminist therapy.* New York: Basic Books.

Brown, G. R., & Anderson, B. (1991). Psychiatric morbidity in adult inpatients with childhood histories of sexual and physical abuse. *American Journal of Psychiatry, 148,* 55–61.

Cloward, R. A., & Piven, F. F. (1979). Hidden protest: The channeling of female innovation and protest. *Signs: Journal of Women in Culture and Society, 4,* 651–669.

Coons, P. M., Bowman, E., Pellow, T. A., & Schneider, P. (1989). Post-traumatic aspects of the treatment of victims of sexual abuse and incest. *Psychiatric Clinics of North America, 12,* 325–335.

Courtois, C. A. (1999). *Recollections of sexual abuse: Treatment principles and guidelines.* New York: Norton.

Cushman, P. (1995). *Constructing the self, constructing America: A cultural history of psychotherapy.* Reading MA: Addison-Wesley.

Dohrenwend, B. P. (1998). Overview of evidence for the importance of adverse environmental conditions in causing psychiatric disorders. In B. P. Dohrenwend (Ed.), *Adversity, stress, and psychopathology* (pp. 523–538). New York: Oxford University Press.

Eherenreich, B., & English, D. (1978). *For her own good: 150 years of the experts' advice to women.* Garden City, NY: Anchor Press/Doubleday.

Fine, R. (1989). *Current and historical perspectives on the borderline patient.* New York: Brunner/Mazel.

Frances, A., & Widiger, T. A. (1987). A critical review of four DSM-III personality disorders: Borderline, avoidant, dependent and passive-aggressive. In G. L. Tischler (Ed.), *Diagnosis and classification in psychiatry: A critical appraisal of DSM-III* (pp. 269–289). New York: Cambridge University Press.

Frank, J. D., & Frank, J. B. (1991). *Persuasion and healing: A comparative study of psychotherapy.* Baltimore: Johns Hopkins University Press.

Fryer, M. R., Frances, A. J., Sullivan, T., Hurt, S. W., & Clarkin, J. (1988). Comorbidity of borderline personality disorder. *Archives of General Psychiatry, 45,* 348–355.

Goodwin, J. M., Cheeves, K., & Connell, V. (1990). Borderline and other severe symptoms in adult survivors of incestuous abuse. *Psychiatric Annals, 20,* 22–31.

Graziano, R. (1992). Treating women incest survivors: A bridge between "cumulative trauma" and "post-traumatic stress." *Social Work in Health Care, 17,* 69–85.

Green, B. L., Lindy, J. D., & Grace, M. C. (1985). Posttraumatic stress disorder: Toward *DSM-IV. Journal of Nervous and Mental Disease, 173,* 406–411.

Gunderson, J. G., & Sabo, A. N. (1993a). The phenomenological and conceptual interface between borderline personality disorder and PTSD. *American Journal of Psychiatry, 150,* 19–27.

Gunderson, J. G., & Sabo, A.N. (1993b). Borderline personality disorder and PTSD [Reply to H. S. Kudler]. *American Journal of Psychiatry, 150,* 1906–1907.

Haaken, J., & Schlaps, A. (1991). Incest resolution therapy and the objectification of sexual abuse. *Psychotherapy, 39,* 39–46.

Hamilton, J. A., & Jensvold, M. (1992). Personality, psychopathology, and depression in women. In L. S. Brown & M. Ballou (Eds.), *Personality and psychopathology: Feminist reappraisals* (pp. 116–143). New York: Guilford Press.

Herman, J. L. (1986). Histories of violence in an outpatient population: An exploratory study. *American Journal of Orthopsychiatry, 56,* 137–141.

Herman, J. L. (1992). *Trauma and recovery.* New York: Basic Books.

Herman, J. L., Perry, J. C., & van der Kolk, B. A. (1989). Childhood trauma in borderline personality disorder. *American Journal of Psychiatry, 146,* 460–465.

Herman, J., Russell, D., & Trocki, K. (1986). Long-term effects of incestuous abuse in childhood. *American Journal of Psychiatry, 143,* 1293–1296.

Janoff-Bulman, R. (1985). The aftermath of victimization: Rebuilding shattered assumptions. In C. R. Figley (Ed.), *Trauma and its wake: The study and treatment of posttraumatic stress disorder* (pp. 15–35). New York: Brunner/Mazel.

Kaminer, W. (1993). *I'm dysfunctional, you're dysfunctional: The recovery movement and other self-help fashions.* New York: Vintage.

Kessler, R. C., McGonagle, K. A., Zhao, S., Nelson, C. B., Hughes, M., Eshleman, S., Wittchen, H-U., & Kendler, K. S. (1994). Lifetime and 12-month prevalence of DSM-III-R psychiatric disorders in the United States: Results from the National Comorbidity Survey. *Archives of General Psychiatry, 51,* 8–19.

Kessler, R. C., Sonnegra, A., Bromet, E., Hughes, M., & Nelson, C. B. (1995). Posttraumatic stress disorder in the National Comorbidity Survey. *Archives of General Psychiatry, 52,* 1048–1060.

Kleinman, A. (1988). *Rethinking psychiatry: From cultural category to personal experience.* New York: Free Press.

Kleinman, A. (1995). *Writing at the margin: Discourse between anthropology and medicine.* Berkeley: University of California Press.

Kolb, L. C. (1989). Heterogeneity of PTSD [Reply to P.E. Ciccone]. *American Journal of Psychiatry, 146,* 811–812.

Kroll, J. K. (1988). *The challenge of the borderline patient: Competency in diagnosis and treatment.* New York: Norton.

Kroll, J. K. (1993). *PTSD/borderlines in therapy: Finding the balance.* New York: Norton.

Kroll, J., Sines, L., Martin, K., Lari, S., Pyle, R., & Zander, J. (1981). Borderline personality disorder: Construct validity of the concept. *Archives of General Psychiatry, 38,* 1021–1026.

Kutchins, H., & Kirk, S. A. (1997). *Making us crazy: DSM—The psychiatric bible and the creation of mental disorders.* New York: Free Press.

Lamb, S. (1996). *The trouble with blame: Victims, perpetrators, and responsibility.* Cambridge, MA: Harvard University Press.

Lamb, S. (1999). Constructing the victim: Popular images and lasting labels. In S. Lamb (Ed.), *New versions for victims: Feminists struggle with the concept* (pp. 108–138). New York: New York University Press.

Landecker, H. (1992). The role of childhood sexual trauma in the etiology of borderline personality disorder: Considerations for diagnosis and treatment. *Psychotherapy, 29,* 234–242.

Lerman, H. (1996). *Pigeonholing women's misery: A history and critical analysis of the psychodiagnosis of women in the twentieth century.* New York: Basic Books.

Lilienfeld, S., Van Valkenburg, C., Larntz, K., & Akiskal, H. (1986). The relationship of histrionic personality disorder to antisocial personality and somatization disorders. *American Journal of Psychiatry, 143,* 718–722.

Lykowski, J. C., & Tsuang, M. T. (1980). Precautions in treating DSM-III personality disorder. *American Journal of Psychiatry, 137,* 110–111.

Marecek, J. (1999). Trauma talk in feminist clinical practice. In S. Lamb (Ed.), *New versions for victims: Feminists struggle with the concept* (pp. 158–182). New York: New York University Press.

McCann, L., & Pearlman, L. A. (1999). Vicarious traumatization: A framework for understanding the psychological effects of working with victims. In M. J. Horowitz (Ed.), *Essential papers on posttraumatic stress disorder* (pp. 498–517). New York: New York University Press.

Murburg, M. M., Ashleigh, E. A., Hommer, D. W., & Veith, R. C. (1994). Biology of catecholaminergic systems and their relevance to PTSD. In M.M. Murburg (Ed.), *Catecholamine function in posttraumatic stress disorder: Emerging concepts* (pp. 175–188). Washington, DC: American Psychiatric Association Press.

Ochberg, F. M. (1991). Post-traumatic therapy. *Psychotherapy, 28,* 5–15.

Ogata, S. N., Silk, K. R., Goodrich, S., Lohr, N. E., Westen, D., & Hill, E. M. (1990). Childhood sexual and physical abuse in adult patients with borderline personality disorder. *American Journal of Psychiatry, 147,* 1008–1013.

Oldham, J. M., Skodol, A. E., Kellman, H. D., Hyler, S. E., Resnick, L., & Davies, M. (1992). Diagnosis of DSM-III-R personality disorders by two structured interviews: Patterns of comorbidity. *American Journal of Psychiatry, 149,* 213–220.

Pope, H. G., Jonas, J., Hudson, J., Cohen, B., & Gunderson, J. (1983). The validity of DSM-III borderline personality disorder. *Archives of General Psychiatry, 40,* 23–30.

Reiser, D. E., & Levenson, H. (1984). Abuses of the borderline diagnosis: A clinical problem with teaching opportunities. *American Journal of Psychiatry, 141,* 1528–1532.

Resnick, H. S., Kilpatrick, D. G., Best, C. L., & Kramer, T.L. (1992). Vulnerability-stress factors in development of posttraumatic stress disorder. *Journal of Nervous and Mental Disease, 180,* 424–430.

Robins, L. N., & Regier, D. A. (1991). *Psychiatric disorders in America: The Epidemiologic Catchment Area Study.* New York: Free Press.

Rutter, M. (1990). Psychosocial resilience and protective mechanisms. In J. E. Rolf, A. S. Masten, D. Cicchetti, K. H. Neuchterlein, & S. Weintraub (Eds.), *Risk and protective factors in the development of psychopathology* (pp. 181–214). New York: Cambridge University Press.

Shalev, A. Y., Orr, S. P., & Pittman, R. K. (1993). Psychophysiologic assessment of traumatic imagery in Israeli civilian patients with posttraumatic stress disorder. *American Journal of Psychiatry, 150,* 620–624.

Showalter, E. (1985). *The female malady.* New York: Pantheon.

Sicherman, B. (1977). The uses of a diagnosis: Doctors, patients, and neurasthenia. *Journal of the History of Medicine, 32,* 33–54.

Smith-Rosenberg, C. (1972). The hysterical woman: Sex roles in nineteenth century America. *Social Research, 39,* 652–678.

Stangl, D., Pfohl, B., Zimmerman, M., Bowers, W., & Corenthal, C. (1985). A structured interview for the DSM-III personality disorders. *Archives of General Psychiatry, 42,* 591–596.

Stefan, S. (1998). Impact of the law on women with diagnoses of borderline personality disorder related to childhood sexual abuse. In B. L. Levin, A. K. Blanch, & A. Jennings (Eds.), *Women's mental health services: A public health perspective* (pp. 240–278). Thousand Oaks, CA: Sage.

Stone, M. H. (1990). Toward a comprehensive typology of personality. *Journal of Personality Disorders, 4,* 416–421.

Stone, M. H., Unwin, A., Beacham, B., & Swenson, C. (1988). Incest in female borderlines: Its frequency and impact. *International Journal of Family Psychiatry, 9,* 277–293.

Stueve, A., Dohrenwend, B. P., Skodol, A. E. (1998). Relationships between stressful life events and episodes of major depression and nonaffective psychotic disorders: Selected results from a New York risk factor study. In B. P. Dohrenwend (Ed.), *Adversity, stress, and psychopathology* (pp. 341–357). New York: Oxford University Press.

Surrey, J., Swett, C., Michaels, A., & Levin, S. (1990). Reported history of physical and sexual abuse and severity of symptomatology in women psychiatric

outpatients. *American Journal of Orthopsychiatry, 60,* 412–417.

Swartz, M., Blazer, D., George, L., & Winfield, I. (1990). Estimating the prevalence of borderline personality disorder in the community. *Journal of Personality Disorders, 4,* 257–272.

van der Kolk, B. A., & Saporta, J. (1993). Biological responses to psychic trauma. In J. P. Wilson & B. Raphael (Eds.), *International handbook of traumatic stress syndromes* (pp. 25–34). New York: Plenum Press.

Waites, E. (1993). *Trauma and survival: Posttraumatic and dissociative disorders in women.* New York: Norton.

Walker, L. E. A. (1994). *Abused women and survivor therapy: A practical guide for the psychotherapist.* Washington, DC: American Psychological Association.

Weaver, T. L., & Clum, G. A. (1993). Early family environments and traumatic experiences associated with borderline personality disorder. *Journal of Consulting and Clinical Psychology, 61,* 1068–1075.

Westen, D., Ludolph, P., Misle, B., Ruffins, S., & Block, J. (1990). Physical and sexual abuse in adolescent girls with borderline personality disorder. *American Journal of Orthopsychiatry, 60,* 55–66.

Westkott, M. (1986). *The feminist legacy of Karen Horney.* New Haven: Yale University Press.

Widiger, T. A., Frances, A., Spitzer, R. L., & Williams, J. B. W. (1988). The DSM-III-R personality disorders: An overview. *American Journal of Psychiatry, 145,* 786–795.

Widiger, T. A., & Rogers, J. H. (1989). Prevalence and comorbidity of personality disorders. *Psychiatric Annals, 19,* 132–136.

Widiger, T., & Weissman, M. (1991). Epidemiology of borderline personality disorder. *Hospital and Community Psychiatry, 42,* 1015–1021.

Wilson, J. P., & Lindy, J. D. (1999). Empathic strain and countertransference. In M. J. Horowitz (Ed.), *Essential papers on posttraumatic stress disorder* (pp. 518–543). New York: New York University Press.

Wolfe, J., & Kimerling, R. (1997). Gender issues in the assessment of posttraumatic stress disorder. In J. P. Wilson & T. M. Keane (Eds.), *Assessing psychological trauma and PTSD* (pp. 192–237). New York: Guilford Press.

Wood, A. D. (1973). "The fashionable diseases": Women's complaints and their treatment in nineteenth-century America. *Journal of Interdisciplinary History, 4,* 25–52.

Yehuda, R., & McFarlane, A. C. (1995). Conflict between current knowledge about posttraumatic stress disorder and its original conceptual basis. *American Journal of Psychiatry, 152,* 1705–1713.

Zanarini, M. C., Frankenburg, F. R., Dubo, E. D., Sickel, A. E., Trikha, A., Levin, A., & Reynolds, V. (1998). Axis I comorbidity of borderline personality disorder. *American Journal of Psychiatry, 1553,* 1733–1739.

Zanarini, M. C., Gunderson, J. G., Frankenburg, F. R., & Chauncey, D. L. (1990). Discriminating borderline personality disorders from other Axis II disorders. *American Journal of Psychiatry, 147,* 161–167.

Zanarini, M. C., Gunderson, J. G., Marino, M. F., Schwartz, E. O., & Frankenburg, F. R. (1989). Childhood experiences of borderline patients. *Comprehensive Psychiatry, 30,* 18–25.

CARON ZLOTNICK
JILL MATTIA
MARK ZIMMERMAN

25

Clinical Features of Survivors of Sexual Abuse with Major Depression

Introduction

Recently, there as been increased interest in the relationship between childhood sexual abuse and depression (e.g., see the review article by Weiss, Longhurst, & Mazure, 1999). In part, this interest is due to the consistent finding of community-based studies that there is a significantly higher rate of major depression in survivors of childhood sexual abuse compared to individuals without histories of childhood sexual abuse (e.g., Burnam et al., 1988; Russell, 1984; Saunders, Villeponteaux, Lipovsky, Kilpatrick, & Veronen, 1992). Based on this body of research, it has been estimated that nearly 60% and 39% of the overall prevalence of lifetime major depression in women and men, respectively, is associated with a history of childhood sexual abuse (Cutler & Nolen-Hoeksema, 1991). In clinical settings, 50 to 70% of female patients report histories of sexual abuse (Craine, Henson, Colliver, & Maclean, 1988; Palmer Chaloner, & Oppenheimer, 1992). Among female patients with major depression, 38% report histories of sexual abuse (Zlotnick, Ryan, Miller, & Keitner, 1995). Further, sexual abuse survivors who seek treatment show significantly higher rates of major depression than a psychiatric control group and the Epidemiologic Catchment Area population (Margo & McLess, 1991; Pribor & Dinwiddie, 1992). In clinical samples, sexual abuse survivors compared to patients without sexual abuse report higher levels of depressive symptoms (Bryer, Nelson, Miller, & Krol, 1987; Surrey, Swett, Michaels, & Levin, 1990). In

a review of the literature, Finkelhor (1986) concluded that depression is the most commonly reported symptom in adult survivors of sexual abuse.

Research has also shown that childhood trauma is related to a chronic course of depression. A study using a large community sample found that chronicity was strongly associated with childhood adversity (neglect, physical and/or sexual abuse) (Brown, Harris, Hepworth, & Robinson, 1994). Clinical features such as previous depressive episodes, age of onset, and the presence of a personality disorder were relatively unimportant in predicting chronicity compared with childhood adversity. These findings were replicated in a clinical sample of female patients with major depression (Brown et al., 1994). Another study of female inpatients with major depression found that depressed women without a history of abuse were nearly four times more likely to recover from their illness by 12 months than depressed women with histories of childhood abuse (Zlotnick et al., 1995). At a five-year follow-up of these patients, a history of childhood sexual abuse was significantly related to a chronic course of depression (Zlotnick et al., 1995). Further, among patients with an anxiety disorder and comorbid major depression, those who reported histories of lifetime trauma, including childhood sexual abuse, were less likely to remit from their major depressive illness over a five-year period compared to a nontraumatized control group (Zlotnick, Warshaw, Shea, & Keller, 1997). Despite the accumulating literature regarding the salient role of childhood sexual abuse in the onset and course of depression, there is a paucity of data on whether depressed patients with histories of childhood sexual abuse differ in their clinical presentation from other depressed patients. Knowledge concerning the specific needs of a subgroup of patients with major depression would enable treatment providers to formulate effective treatments to address the coexisting pathology.

Currently, only one study has examined the characteristics of depressed patients with histories of sexual abuse. This study found that depressed women who reported childhood sexual abuse were significantly more likely to have borderline personality disorder and a greater degree of self-destructive behaviors compared to depressed women without such histories (Gladstone, Parker, Wilhelm, Mitchell, & Austin, 1999). However, with further analysis, the study showed that the relationship between childhood sexual abuse and adult behaviors of self-harm (history of self-injury, past and current suicidal attempts) was mediated by a higher degree of borderline traits. These findings suggest that factors other than early experiences of childhood sexual abuse may contribute to the dysfunctional behaviors frequently present in this particular group of depressed patients.

Aims of the Study

The present study from the Rhode Island Methods to Improve Diagnosis and Services (MIDAS project) attempted to expand upon the existing literature by examining whether depressed patients with histories of childhood sexual abuse compared to those without childhood sexual abuse histories have a greater degree of trauma-related disorders (borderline personality disorder, posttraumatic stress disorder, eating disorder, and substance abuse). Another aim of this study was to clarify the role of childhood sexual abuse in specific clinical features of depressed patients. These specific clinical features (i.e., current suicidal behavior, poor affect dysregulation, and a prolonged episode of depression) were selected on the basis of being strongly associated with childhood sexual abuse (Briere & Runtz, 1986; Stepakoff, 1998; van der Kolk et al., 1996; Zlotnick et al., 1995) as well as with a diagnosis of borderline personality disorder or posttraumatic stress disorder (Linehan, Armstrong, Suarez, Allmon, & Heard, 1991; Thase, 1996; van der Kolk et al., 1996). Thus, this study examined whether childhood sexual abuse provides an independent risk factor (i.e., above and beyond coexisting pathology) for certain adult disturbances in a sample of depressed patients.

Method

Five hundred patients were evaluated with semi-structured diagnostic interviews in the Rhode Island Hospital Department of Psychiatry outpatient practice (Zimmerman & Mattia, 1998, 1999a, 1999b). Ths private practice group predominantly treats individuals with medical insurance (including Medicare but not Medicaid) on a fee-for-service basis, and it is distinct from the hospital's outpatient residency training clinic that predominantly serves lower-income, uninsured, and medical assistance patients. The Rhode Island Hospital institutional review committee approved the research protocol, and all patients provided informed, written consent. Only patients between the ages of 18 and 65 years and who spoke English sufficiently to understand the consent form as well as the diagnostic interview were included in the study. Of the total number of patients who attended the outpatient practice and received diagnostic interview, 60.3% participated in the study. Compared to the patients who were evaluated with diagnostic interviews, patients who were not evaluated with diagnostic interviews were significantly more often female (69.0% vs. 60.4%, $\chi^2 = 6.03$, p < .05), widowed (13.4% vs. 2.4%, $\chi^2 = 34.6$, p < .001), older (M = 47.4, SD = 19.1 vs. M = 38.8, SD = 13.1, t = 7.01, p < .001) and significantly less likely to have married (29.2% vs. 36.7%, $\chi^2 = 4.34$, p < .05), and to have graduated high school (83.3% vs. 91.5%, $\chi^2 = 9.44$, p < .01).

Of 500 outpatients who attended a hospital-based outpatient practice and who consented to participate in a formal evaluation instead of a routine, unstructured clinical evaluation, 235 (47%) met criteria for current major depression and are the target sample for this study.

Psychiatric Diagnoses

Briefly, prior to an initial psychiatric evaluation, subjects were administered by a trained diagnostic rater the Structured Clinical Interview for DSM-IV (SCID) for Axis I (First, Spitzer, Williams, & Gibbon, 1997). At this time, subjects were also administered the Structured Interview for DSM-IV Personality (SIDP) modules for borderline personality disorder and antisocial personality disorder (Pfohl, Blum, & Zimmerman, 1997). In this study, current Axis I disorders were used, and current was defined as experiencing the diagnostic criteria at the time of the evaluation. During the course of the study, joint interview diagnostic reliability information was collected on 17 patients. Of the disorders of interest in this study, Kappa coefficients were obtained for the following disorders: posttraumatic stress disorder (k = 1), BPD (k = 1), and major depression (k = 1). The diagnostic category of any substance abuse included dependence or abuse of alcohol or drugs and excluded nicotine dependence. Eating disorder included anorexia, bulimia, binge eating disorder, and eating disorder not otherwise specified (NOS).

Childhood Sexual Abuse

Data concerning a history of sexual abuse were obtained during the SCID module for posttraumatic stress disorder. For the assessment of childhood sexual abuse, patients were classified as sexually abused if they reported that they had experienced sexual assault (e.g., rape or attempted rape) by a family member, someone they knew, or by a stranger before 18 years of age, or if they had experienced sexual contact (e.g., contact with genitals, breasts) with someone who was five or more years older than they before 18 years of age.

Clinical Features

Supplementing the SCID interview were items from the Schedule for Affective Disorders and Schizophrenia (SADS) on social functioning within the past five years, past psychiatric hospitalization, and suicide attempts within the past year (Spitzer & Endicott, 1978). The Clinical Global Index of depression severity was rated on all patients (Guy, 1976).

To assess affect regulation, the inability to adaptively manage or tolerate intense emotions, the Regulation of Affect and Impulses subscale of the Structured Interview for Disorders of Extreme Stress (SIDES; Pelcovitz et al., 1997) was administered. Using data from the present study, the individual subscale of affect dysregulation was found to have good internal consistency with a Cronbach coefficient alpha of .86. The Regulation of Affect and Impulses subscale consists of several dimensions that tap affect regulation, modulation of anger, self-destructive behavior, suicidal preoccupation, and excessive risk-taking behavior. Patients were asked about these behaviors when not in an episode of their current psychiatric disorder. Prior research has shown that this subscale of the SIDES has good convergent and divergent validity (Zlotnick & Pearlstein, 1997) and good interrater reliability (Pelcovitz et al., 1997).

Statistical Analyses

Chi-square and t tests were used to compare patients with childhood sexual abuse and those without childhood sexual abuse along the various dimensions of interest (i.e., trauma-related disorders and the selected clinical features). A Mann-Whitney U, a nonparametric test, was used for the variable duration of index depressive episode, because the variable was not normally distributed. To examine whether borderline personality disorder and posttraumatic stress disorder mediated the relationship between childhood sexual abuse and duration of index episode, degree of affect dysregulation, and at least one suicidal attempt within the past year, a series of regressions (multiple and logistic) were conducted. In these regressions, borderline personality disorder and posttraumatic stress disorder were the covariates, childhood sexual abuse was the independent variable, and the variables of interest were the dependent variables. A significance level of p < .01 was used a priori in an attempt to reduce the chances of Type 1 error due to multiple comparisons.

Results

The sample of 235 study subjects with current major depression had an average age of 40.58 (SD = 14.03). These subjects were predominantly Caucasian (85%), female (65%), and high school graduates (16.6%). Most subjects were married or cohabiting (49.1%), and the remaining were single (23.4%) or separated, widowed, or divorced (27.5%).

Fifty-eight (25%) of the 235 subjects with major depression reported a history of sexual abuse. Of those patients with a history of sexual abuse, the average age of onset of the abuse was 7.57 years (SD = 7.57), and 52% of the patients were sexually abused by a family member. The only significant difference in demographic variables between the two groups (i.e., patients with and those without histories of sexual abuse) was that those who reported histories of sexual abuse were significantly more often female (85%) compared to those who did not report such experiences (58%), χ^2 (1, N = 235) = 13.22, p = .0003.

Table 25.1 shows that patients with histories of sexual abuse had significantly elevated rates for posttraumatic stress disorder, borderline personality disorder, and multiple Axis I disorders compared to those without histories of sexual abuse. Significantly more patients with histories of child-

Table 25.1 Differences in Clinical Features between Patients with and without Sexual Abuse Histories in a Sample of Patients with Major Depression (N = 235)

Variable		Sexual Abuse Present n = 58	No Sexual Abuse n = 177	χ^2	t	p
Comorbidity						
Borderline Personality Disorder[a]	n	17	19	9.24		0.002
Posttraumatic Stress Disorder	n	24	19	28.54		0.000
Substance Abuse/Dependency	n	23	37	3.17		0.741
Any Eating Disorder[b]	n	3	12	.18		0.663
Multiple Axis I Disorders	M SD	3.31 (1.37)	2.54 (1.37)	3.57		0.000
Clinical Feature						
Poor Social Functioning in the Past 5 Years	n	20	4		2.24	0.23
Global Assessment of Functioning	M SD	44.98 (12.51)	49.00 (8.88)		2.00	0.007
Clinical Global Index	M SD	3.27 (.74)	3.11 (.62)		1.45	0.114
Duration of Index Episode (weeks)[c]	M SD	544.94 (394.62)	172.39 (394.623)		3483	0.000
Age of Onset (years)	M SD	20.76 (14.09)	29.93 (14.27)		4.26	0.000
Affect Dysregulation[a]	M SD	8.85 (7.73)	5.40 (5.36)		3.39	0.001
At Least One Suicide Attempt in Past Year	n	8	3		14.26	0.000
At Least One Hospitalization	%	22	35		7.27	0.007

[a]For borderline personality disorder, 42 subjects had missing data, and for the measure of affect dysregulation, 72 subjects had missing data.
[b]Fisher's Exact Test.
[c]Mann-Whitney U Test.

hood sexual abuse relative to those without such histories manifested a longer duration of the index depressive episode, an earlier age of onset of major depression, lower Global Assessment of Functioning Scale (GAF) scores, and higher frequencies of at least one previous hospitalization. Sexual abuse survivors also differed from the comparison group in that they were more likely to report at least one suicide attempt within the past year as well as a higher degree of affect dysregulation.

Table 25.2 shows that childhood sexual abuse status was related to a longer index episode, independent of borderline personality disorder and posttraumatic stress disorder. In contrast, childhood sexual abuse status was not independently related to affect dysregulation and suicidal attempts. To explore whether this relationship was specific to childhood sexual abuse, we examined the relationship between childhood physical abuse status (obtained from the SCID module for posttraumatic stress disorder) and a longer index episode, independent of borderline personality disorder and posttraumatic stress disorder. There was no significant association between these two variables.

When all the analyses were repeated with sex as the covariate, all variables maintained their original significance levels.

Discussion

The present study found that having a history of childhood sexual abuse substantially increased the risk of psychiatric morbidity in patients with major depression. More specifically, our study found that, among patients with major depression, those who reported histories of childhood sexual abuse compared to those who did not report such experiences were significantly more likely to present with elevated rates of posttraumatic stress disorder, borderline personality disorder, and multiple Axis I disorders. The overall high degree of comorbidity found in our sample of depressed patients with childhood sexual abuse is consistent with other research that has shown that a history of childhood sexual abuse is a risk factor for a broad range of psychiatric disorders (Pribor & Dinwiddie, 1992; Saunders et al., 1992). In terms of specific morbidity, Gladstone et al. (1999) also found that in a

Table 25.2 Regressions of Relationship between Duration of Index Depressive Illness, Affect Dysregulation, Suicidal Attempts, and Childhood Sexual Abuse Status, Independent of Borderline Personality Disorder and Posttraumatic Stress Disorder in a Sample of Patients with Major Depression

Variable	t	df	β	p
Duration of Index Depressive Illness	2.802	3,188	.214	0.006
Affect Dysregulation[a]	.892	3,139	.073	0.3741
At Least One Suicidal Attempt in the Past Year Wald χ^2	3.36	3,188	.089	0.935

[a]For the measure of affect dysregulation, 72 subjects had missing data.

sample of patients with major depression, childhood sexual abuse status was strongly related to elevated rates of borderline personality disorder and, like the present study, substance abuse was not significantly associated with childhood sexual abuse. In the general literature, many authors view childhood sexual abuse as a factor that is of etiological significance for borderline personality disorder. At the same time, these authors caution that the development of borderline personality disorder is complex and stems from an intermingling of negative childhood experiences that often includes trauma (Zanarini, 1997). Our finding that a large proportion of depressed patients with histories of sexual abuse had posttraumatic stress disorder was not surprising because other studies have reported high rates of childhood sexual abuse among individuals with posttraumatic stress disorder (Breslau, David, Peterson, & Schultz, 1997; Herman, Perry, & van der Kolk, 1989), high rates of posttraumatic stress disorder among survivors of sexual abuse (Rowan & Foy, 1993; Zlotnick, 1997) and high rates of co-occurrence of posttraumatic stress disorder with depression (Kessler, Sonnega, Bromet, Hughes, & Nelson, 1996).

A central question of our study was whether a history of childhood sexual abuse has severe effects in several domains of functioning, independent of the influence of borderline personality disorder and posttraumatic stress disorder. For our study group of depressed patients, childhood sexual abuse appeared to be an independent factor of duration of index episode, controlling for borderline personality disorder and posttraumatic stress disorder. This finding suggests that there may be certain enduring disturbances associated with the experience of childhood sexual abuse that play a pivotal role in maintaining a depressive episode. Identifying the nature of these disturbances (i.e., biological, psy-

chosocial, or psychological) may shed light on our understanding of the mechanisms of a chronic depression. In contrast to the present study, Gladstone et al. (1999) did not find that exposure to childhood sexual abuse was related to a longer duration of the index depressive episode. However, their sample was limited to patients with a major depressive episode that lasted 24 months or shorter. By excluding individuals with chronic depression they reduced the variability in the illness duration variable, and thus, they failed to find a significant association. Indeed, when we limited our sample to patients with a major depressive episode of 24 months or shorter, like Gladstone et al., we found no significant relationship between length of episode and childhood sexual abuse.

The present study found that the relationship between childhood sexual abuse and adult disturbances of affect dysregulation and suicidal attempts was determined more by the influence of borderline personality disorder and posttraumatic stress disorder. Therefore, these adult disturbances may be a function of having the diagnosis of borderline personality disorder and/or posttraumatic stress disorder, instead of having experienced childhood sexual abuse per se. Prior research has reported higher rates of suicidal behavior (Briere & Runtz, 1986; Stepakoff, 1998) as well as higher levels of affect dysregulation (van der Kolk et al., 1996; Zlotnick, 1997) in survivors of sexual abuse compared to their nonabused counterparts. These studies, however, failed to include intervening processes, such as borderline personality disorder and/or posttraumatic stress disorder. The strong relationship found in this study and other studies between sexual abuse and posttraumatic stress disorder (e.g., Rowan & Foy, 1993; Zlotnick, 1997) and BPD (e.g., Links, Steiner, Offord, & Eppel, 1988; Ogata et al., 1990) suggests that the experience of childhood sexual abuse may predispose an individual toward developing certain associated features of posttraumatic stress disorder and borderline personality disorder, such as affect dysregulation and suicidal behavior.

A limitation of this study was the cross-sectional design which, of course, does not allow for conclusions of causal links between sexual abuse and later psychopathology in adulthood. Other mediating conditions that potentially could impact later adjustment include the relational quality of the family (Harter, Alexander, & Neimeyer, 1988), reactions after disclosure (Lange et al., 1999), and an aberrant parental environment (Gladstone et al., 1999). Likewise, other factors may act as a link between childhood sexual abuse and a prolonged episode of depression. Another limitation of this study was that there was an absence of independent corroborating evidence concerning the reports of childhood sexual abuse and, therefore, the veracity of these reports are unknown. Even if these reports are only subjective perceptions, the present study found a distinct pattern of psychiatric morbidity associated with sexual abuse that might still be of clinical interest to those who treat patients with major depression. Finally, it could be argued that the differing clinical manifestations found between patients with histories of sexual abuse and those without such histories in this study were likely the result of mood state effects. Our study, however, found no significant differences between the two groups in severity of depressed mood. Further, our finding of no significant differences between the two groups in social functioning argues against a perceptual bias as depressed survivors of sexual abuse did not uniformly recall more negative material than those depressed patients without sexual abuse histories.

In conclusion, the results of this study suggest that sexual abuse is associated with a distinct set of clinical features among patients with major depression. The high rates of comorbidity found in this study for depressed patients with histories of childhood sexual abuse underscore the need for clinicians to screen for sexual abuse histories in patients with major depression. Moreover, in those patients with major depression and histories of childhood sexual abuse, clinicians need to assess for posttraumatic stress disorder and borderline personality disorder. Since adult survivors of childhood sexual abuse appear to share features similar to patients who are poor responders to existing treatments for depression (such as a greater duration of the index episode and a greater degree of comorbidity), existing treatments for depression may not be effective for this subgroup of depressed patients. Unfortunately, to date, no treatment for major depression has been developed or tested that addresses the specific needs of depressed patients with histories of sexual abuse.

Supported in part by NIMH grant #MH-48732 to Dr. Zimmerman.

The authors thank Sharon Hunter, Ava Nepal, Melissa Torres, and Sharon Younkin for assistance in collecting the data.

References

Breslau, N., David, G. C., Peterson, E. L., & Schultz, L. (1997). Psychiatric sequelae of posttraumatic stress disorder in women. *Archives of General Psychiatry, 54,* 81–87.

Briere, J., & Runtz, M. (1986). Suicidal thoughts and behaviors in former sexual abuse victims. *Canadian Journal of Behavioral Science, 18,* 413–423.

Brown, G. W., Harris, T. O., Hepworth, C., & Robinson, R. (1994). Clinical and psychosocial origins of chronic depressive episodes II. A patient inquiry. *British Journal of Psychiatry, 165,* 457–465.

Bryer, J. B., Nelson, B. A., Miller, J. B., & Krol, P. A. (1987). Childhood sexual and physical abuse as factors in adult psychiatric illness. *American Journal of Psychiatry, 144,* 1426–1430.

Burnam, M. A., Stein, J. A., Golding, J. M., Siegel, J. M., Sorenson, S. B., Forsythe, A. B., & Telles, C. A. (1988). Sexual assault and mental disorders in a community population. *Journal of Consulting and Clinical Psychology, 56,* 843–850.

Craine, L. S., Henson, C. E., Colliver, J. A., & Maclean, D. G. (1988). Prevalence of a history of sexual abuse among female psychiatric patients in a state hospital system. *Hospital and Community Psychiatry, 3,* 300–303.

Cutler, S. E., & Nolen-Hoeksema, S. (1991). Accounting for sex differences in depression through female victimization: Childhood sexual abuse. *Sex Roles, 24,* 425–437.

Finkelhor, D. (1986). *Sexually victimized children.* New York: Free Press.

First, M. B., Spitzer, R. L., Williams, J. B. W., & Gibbon, M. (1997). *Structured clinical interview for DSM-IV (SCID).* Washington, DC: American Psychiatric Association.

Gladstone, G., Parker, G., Wilhelm, K., Mitchell, P., & Austin, M. (1999). Characteristics of depressed patients who report childhood sexual abuse. *American Journal of Psychiatry, 156,* 431–437.

Guy, W. (1976). *ECDEU assessment manual for psychopharmacology.* U.S. Department of Health, Education, and Welfare publication ADM 76–338. National Institute of Mental Health, Rockville, MD.

Harter, S., Alexander, P. C., & Neimeyer, R. A. (1988). Long-term effects of incestuous child abuse in college women: Social adjustment, social cognition, and family characteristics. *Journal of Consulting and Clinical Psychology, 56,* 5–8.

Herman, J. L., Perry, I. C., & van der Kolk, B. A. (1989). Childhood trauma in borderline personality disorder. *American Journal of Psychiatry, 146,* 490–495.

Kessler, R. C., Sonnega, A., Bromet, E., Hughes, M., & Nelson, C. B. (1996). Posttraumatic stress disorder in the National Comorbidity Survey. *Archives of General Psychiatry, 52,* 1048–1060.

Lange, A., De Beurs, E., Dolan, C., Lachnit, T., Sjollema, S., & Hanewald, G. (1999). Long-term effects of childhood sexual abuse: Objective and subjective characteristics of the abuse and psychopathology in later life. *Journal of Nervous and Mental Disease, 187,* 150–158.

Linehan, M. M., Armstrong, H. E., Suarez, A., Allmon, D., & Heard, H. L. (1991). Cognitive-behavioral treatment of chronically parasuicidal borderline patients. *Archives of General Psychiatry, 48,* 1060–1064.

Links, P. S., Steiner, M., Offord, D. R., & Eppel, A. (1988). Characteristics of borderline personality disorder: A Canadian study. *Canadian Journal of Psychiatry, 33,* 336–340.

Margo, G. M., & McLess, E. M. (1991). Further evidence for the significance of a childhood abuse history in psychiatric inpatients. *Comprehensive Psychiatry, 32,* 362–366.

Ogata, S., Silk, K. R., Goodrich, S., Lohr, N. E., Westen, D., & Hill, E. M. (1990). Childhood sexual and physical abuse in adult patients with borderline personality disorder. *American Journal of Psychiatry, 147,* 1008–1013.

Palmer, R. L., Chaloner, D. A., & Oppenheimer, R. (1992). Childhood sexual experiences with adults reported by female psychiatric patients. *British Journal of Psychiatry, 160,* 261–265.

Pelcovitz, D., van der Kolk, B., Roth, S., Mandel, F., Kaplan, S., & Resick, P. (1997). Development of a criteria set and a structured interview for measurement of disorders of extreme stress. *Journal of Traumatic Stress, 10,* 3–16.

Pfohl, B., Blum, N., & Zimmerman, M. (1997). *Structured interview for DSM-IV personality.* Washington, DC: American Psychiatric Association.

Pribor, E. F., & Dinwiddie, S. H. (1992). Psychiatric correlates of incest in childhood. *American Journal of Psychiatry, 149,* 52–56.

Rowan, A. B., & Foy, D. W. (1993). Post-traumatic stress disorder in child sexual abuse survivors: A literature review. *Journal of Traumatic Stress, 6,* 3–20.

Russell, D. E. H. (1984). *Sexual exploitation: Rape, child sexual abuse, and work.* Beverly Hills, CA: Sage.

Saunders, B. E., Villeponteaux, L. A., Lipovsky, J. A., Kilpatrick, D. G., & Veronen, L. J. (1992). Child sexual assault as a risk factor for mental disorders among women. *Journal of Interpersonal Violence, 7,* 189–204.

Spitzer, R. L., & Endicott, J. (1978). *Schedule for affective disorders and schizophrenia.* New York: Biometric Research, New York State Psychiatric Institute.

Stepakoff, S. (1998). Effects of sexual victimization on suicidal ideation and behavior in U.S. college women. *Suicide and Life Threatening Behavior, 28,* 107–126.

Surrey, J., Swett, C., Michaels, B. A., & Levin, S. (1990). Reported history of physical and sexual abuse and severity of symptomatology in women psychiatric outpatients. *American Journal of Orthopsychiatry, 60,* 412–417.

Thase, M. E. (1996). The role of Axis II comorbidity in the management of patients with treatment-resistant depression. *Psychiatric Clinics of North America, 19,* 287–309.

van der Kolk, B. A., Pelcovitz, D., Roth, S., Mandel, F. S., McFarlane, A., & Herman, J. L. (1996). Dissociation, somatization, and affect dysregulation: The complexity of adaptation to trauma. *American Journal of Psychiatry, 153,* 83–93.

Weiss, E. L., Longhurst, J. G., & Mazure, C. M. (1999). Childhood sexual abuse as a risk factor for depression in women: Psychosocial and neurobiological correlates. *American Journal of Psychiatry, 156,* 816–828.

Zanarini, M. (1997). Evolving perspectives on the etiology of borderline personality disorders. In M. C. Zanarini (Ed.), *Role of sexual abuse in the etiology of borderline personality disorder* (pp. 517–552). Washington, DC: American Psychiatric Press.

Zimmerman, M., & Mattia, J. I. (1998). Body dysmorphic disorder in psychiatric outpatients: Recognition, prevalence, comorbidity, demographic, and clinical correlates. *Comprehensive Psychiatry, 39,* 265–270.

Zimmerman, M., & Mattia, J. I. (1999a). Is posttraumatic stress disorder underdiagnosed in routine clinical settings? *Journal of Nervous and Mental Disease, 187,* 420–428.

Zimmerman, M., & Mattia, J. I. (1999b). Psychotic subtyping of major depressive disorder and posttraumatic stress disorder. *Journal of Clinical Psychiatry, 60,* 311–314.

Zlotnick, C. (1997). The relationship between posttraumatic stress disorder and trauma-related disorders and symptomatology among incarcerated women. *Journal of Nervous and Mental Disease, 7,* 761–763.

Zlotnick, C., & Pearlstein, T. (1997). Validation of the structured interview for disorders of extreme stress. *Comprehensive Psychiatry, 38,* 243–247.

Zlotnick, C., Ryan, C. E., Miller, I. W., & Keitner, G. I. (1995). Childhood abuse and recovery from major depression. *Child Abuse & Neglect, 19,* 1513–1516.

Zlotnick, C., Warshaw, M., Shea, M. T., & Keller, M. B. (1997). Trauma and chronic depression among patients with anxiety disorders. *Journal of Consulting and Clinical Psychology, 65,* 333–336.

26

Panic Disorder and Self States: Clinical and Research Illustrations

Introduction

The view of panic disorder presented in this article is based on the assumption that panic functions as a signal of danger to the self and is comprised of various unconscious personal fantasies about the self. Based on self psychological theory, and particularly on Heinz Kohut (1977), it is purported that panic relates to selfobject failures (specifically empathic failures) which result in disorganization and fragmentation experiences. At issue is the explanation of panic offered by cognitive theorists, namely, the catastrophic misinterpretation construal. According to that model, panic results from a misattribution of somatic or psychological experiences misinterpreted as dangerous. Using clinical material from a single case report along with material from this author's research, attempts will be made to demonstrate the applicability of self psychological tenets to the treatment of panic.

Panic Disorder and the Current Concept of Disorder

Our current nosological system, the *Diagnostic and Statistical Manual of Mental Disorders-IV* (APA, 1994) states that panic is a discrete feeling of intense fear or discomfort in which four or more of the following symptoms develop and reach a peak within 10 minutes: (1) palpitations, pounding heart, or accelerated heart rate; (2) sweating, trem-

bling, or shaking; (3) sensations of shortness of breath or smothering; (4) feeling of choking; (5) chest pain or discomfort; (6) nausea or abdominal distress; (7) dizziness, feeling faint; (8) derealization (feeling of unreality) or depersonalization (being detached from oneself); (9) fear of losing control or going crazy; (10) fear of dying; (11) paresthesias (numbness or tingling sensations); (12) chill or hot flashes (p. 395).

Panic disorder is distinguished from generalized anxiety disorder (GAD) in that persons with panic are far more preoccupied with physical symptoms, whereas persons with GAD (chronic worriers) are more concerned with cognitive symptoms. Additionally, persons with panic typically first present to nonpsychiatric physicians (i.e., emergency rooms) convinced that their symptoms reflect a catastrophic medical event such as a heart attack or stroke. GAD patients, on the other hand, are more likely to present to mental health professionals complaining of tension and the inability to relax (Gorman, Papp, and Coplan, 1995).

The evolution of the concept from *DSM-III* to *DSM-IV* reflects the realization that a psychological factor—the fear of panic—is an essential component of the syndrome (McNally, 1994). This view is consistent with the positivist position of reality, which contends that all knowledge is derived from observation—reality is an independent entity that exists independently of individuals. Thus, individuals are diagnosed with panic disorder if they exhibit the aforementioned symptoms. The definition presumes an objective reality through which the person's behaviors may be measured (Palombo,

1992). Pathology is defined as deviations from the norm, usually seen in statistical terms.

In contrast to the *DSM* conceptualization of disorder, Wakefield (1992), in acknowledging the role of cultural norms in diagnosis, proposes that

> a condition is a mental disorder if and only if a) the condition causes some harm or deprivation of benefit to the person as judged by the standards of the person's culture, and b) the condition results from the inability of some mental mechanism to perform its natural function, wherein a natural function is an effect that is part of the evolutionary explanation of the existence and structure of the mental mechanism. (p. 385)

Wakefield's formulation of disorder is more consistent with the constructivist view of reality in that it reflects our cultural context. It is assumed that no inquiry can be value-free; in fact, the values of the culture determine whether the condition will be considered a disorder. Additionally, his definition accounts for dysfunction in the underlying psychobiological mechanisms. The constructivist position can be contrasted with the view held by the rationalists, which holds that the function of the brain is to mirror reality accurately and that "adaptive behavior" is then guided by such a reflection. The underlying assumption of the cognitive models is that psychological problems (in this case, panic) result from distortions in reality and that it is the correction of these distortions that promote change (Safran and Segal, 1990).

The purpose of this paper is to present a model for panic that is informed by self psychological principles. This model is based on the constructivist position in that a strong emphasis will be on examining the subtleties of the individual's subjective experience of panic. First, I present a brief overview of the biological and psychological literature on panic, highlighting the distinctions between the cognitive model of panic and a self psychological view of panic. I then attempt to assist the practicing clinical social worker in implementing a self psychological approach to the treatment of panic by demonstrating the model's applicability to clinical work.

Review of Literature

Biological Models

Controversies surrounding the etiology of panic revolve around the mind-body problem. Is panic a biological or psychological entity? Biomedical professionals and psychopathologists, respectively, have promoted drastically different explanations of panic.

The medical illness (MI) model assumes that panic disorder is associated with a biochemical abnormality in the nervous system to which there is a genetic vulnerability. Stressors are considered to have a nonspecific exacerbating role rather than a causal one (Margraf and Ehlers, 1989). Klein (1993) also holds that panic arises from the misfiring of an evolved suffocation alarm. Curiously, this hypothesized alarm is activated not only by rising levels of brain carbon dioxide, but also by nonbiological stimuli (e.g., entrapment) that signal loss of oxygen. Panic attacks may also be experimentally induced by an infusion of lactate (Gabbard, 1994). Recent biological research conducted by LeDoux has also shown that the neocortex, the site of the brain where it is theorized that conscious thoughts and decisions occur, sometimes is out of touch with the portion of the midbrain, dubbed the "emotional brain" by LeDoux. Primal emotions, like panic and rage, are theorized to reside in the midbrain.

One of the central debates related to panic revolves around the mind-body dialectic. Are mental mechanisms related to this disorder? Cooper (1985) argues that neurobiological theory does not suggest that all anxiety is nonmental in content. A distinction, he proposes, must be made between psychological coping and adaptive efforts to regulate miscarried brain functions that create anxiety with little or no environmental input and psychological coping and adaptive efforts to regulate disturbances of the intrapsychic world that lead to anxiety and are environmentally sensitive (p. 1398).

Psychodynamic Paradigms

The psychodynamic paradigms (Nemiah, 1988), particularly the classical psychoanalytic view, distinguish between realistic and neurotic anxiety. Freud (1926) regarded realistic anxiety as a reaction to the perception of external danger, whereas neurotic anxiety resulted from the perception of internal danger—when unconscious impulses emerge to consciousness and the defense mechanisms fail. Severe anxiety and panic states were a form of current or actual neurosis and were believed to have a somatic etiology; that is, the psychological experience of the somatic sexual drive was not fulfilled. In *Inhibitions, Symptoms, and Anxiety*, Freud pointed out the progression of possible anxieties: fear of loss of the object, the danger of castration, and the fear of the superego to the latency period. He notes "all of these danger-situations and determinants of anxiety can persist side by side and cause the ego to react to them with anxiety at a period later than the appropriate one" (p. 142).

Object relations theorists (e.g., Fairbairn, Winnicott, Guntrip) replaced Freud's formulations in postulating that the infant's relationship with the maternal object is central to understanding anxiety states. Anxiety, in this scheme, points the way to real or imagined failures of the actual maternal object to protect and serve the infantile self. Absence of the nurturant, protective mother is the danger (Roose and Glick, 1995). Cohen (1985), in studying agoraphobia as a disorder in early object relations, found that derealization and depersonalization (symptoms of panic) were seen as associated with a temporary loss of a sense of one's own reality and boundaries. He attributed the etiology of agoraphobia to unresolved dependence needs, concluding that recollections of childhood revealed that the maternal object encouraged dependency rather than movement toward autonomy.

Shear, Cooper, and Klerman (1993) hypothesized that an inborn fear of unfamiliar situations, augmented by frightening, overcontrolling parental behaviors, predisposes to incomplete conflict between dependence and independence and results in panic. The method included pilot interviews with nine patients who met the *DSM III-R* criteria for panic. Their formulations were also based on published reports of psychological characteristics of panic and data from infant animal research on temperament. The results of the interviews revealed themes related to early anxiety and shyness, unsupportive parental relationships (patients remembered parents as angry and critical), and a chronic sense of being trapped. Resentfulness and discomfort with aggressive feelings were also noted.

Other psychodynamic theories (Gabbard, 1994) emphasize the higher incidence of stressful life events, separation issues (panic triggered by a significant loss), and psychological trauma. It was suggested (Gabbard, 1994) that the etiology of panic might involve the unconscious meaning of events, while the pathogenesis may involve neurophysiologic factors triggered by the psychological reactions to the events. In other words, an external stressor may or may not lead to the onset of panic in a neurophysiologically susceptible individual; a psychological factor related to the interpretation of events might mediate between panic onset and external events.

Cognitive Models

Much of the psychological research on anxiety and panic concerns work done in the cognitive tradition. Beck and Emery (1985) propose that an upset in the regulatory system of the cognitive system leads one to indiscriminately interpret environmental events as dangers. The person may overreact to experiences that are perceived as making him or her susceptible to disease, loss of control, or diminished psychological functioning. Within the cognitive tradition, Clark (in McNally, 1994) also postulated a theory about the onset of panic. His theory holds that panic attacks result from the catastrophic misinterpretations of certain bodily sensations. Regardless of the origin of the symptoms (biological or psychological), the bodily sensations will not develop into a panic state unless the individual misinterprets them as signs of imminent danger. For example, heart palpitations might be construed as a sign of a heart attach, dizziness as a sign of a brain tumor.

Even though cognitive psychology brought the issue of mentalism to the fore (at a time when mental processes were being dismissed by the radical behaviorists), many criticisms have been issued against cognitive psychology. One such criticism is the strategy to ignore general theorizing. It has exploded into a constellation of individual theories that appear unrelated to each other except for a common terminology (Kendler, 1987). It has been noted that cognitive psychology needs to establish a connection with neurophysiology (Kendler, 1987) and that developmental psychology must become an integral part of cognitive psychology. The initial research area of experimental cognitive psychology was the higher mental processes of adult humans. Piaget, however, attempted to demonstrate that adult cognition cannot be fully understood independent of its developmental history. A final criticism relates to the question, How can cognitive functions be understood outside the context of action and emotion?

Cognitive Therapy and Its Implications for Panic Disorder   According to Beck (1976), the goals of cognitive therapy are the examination of faulty self-representations and an increase in the patient's ability to process knowledge about the world and oneself realistically. Thus, the treatment centers on identifying the "faulty" thought patterns and self-perceptions and countering them by using more "effective" coping strategies. In terms of the treatment of panic disorder, cognitive therapy incorporates elements of behavioral treatment (e.g., exposure to feared situations), while emphasizing the importance of altering persistent tendencies to misinterpret bodily sensations catastrophically (McNally, 1994). Cognitive restructuring involves refuting these misinterpretations through Socratic questioning and through an assessment of evidence for and against their validity (the empirical approach).

Considerable evidence (Beck and Emery, 1985; Beck and Clark, 1988) confirms the efficacy of cognitive treatment for spontaneous panic attacks. Baker (1989), however, suggests that the successful treatment of panic will require a broad-based approach that addresses the underlying vulnerabilities and sources of stress in addition to the presenting problem. Implicit in the cognitive construal is the notion that the individual's reactions to panic are maladaptive and that the person needs to learn to counter these "faulty" thinking patterns (and conform to some objective sense of what is considered adaptive) in order to be cured (in this formulation, "cure" is usually seen as a reduction of panic symptoms).

A model of panic that can account for the emotional and cognitive meaning of panic to the patient, while appreciating the idiosyncrasies of the patient's phenomenological experience, is needed. Unconscious and preconscious processes need to be considered within such a model. Also, the notion of cure needs to be broadened to include more than the amelioration of symptoms.

Summary of Literature

The literature on panic and its treatment mainly addresses the neurobiological and cognitive processes associated with this disorder. Several researchers (Shear, Cooper, and Klerman, 1993; Gabbard, 1994) have attempted to integrate aspects of both the neurophysiological and psychological models, suggesting that psychological variables mediate between external events and panic onset. Common themes in the psychodynamic literature center on separation issues, overcontrolling parental behaviors leading to a sense of being trapped, and the absence of the nurturant and protective mother.

Studies conducted in the cognitive tradition provide a vivid and thorough description of the cognitive components of panic and threat reactions. Several weaknesses, however, were also cited, centering around the following: (1) the tendency to neglect to consider unconscious processes in relation to human functioning; (2) criticisms related to ignoring the developmental context; and (3) lack of consideration of the affect states that underlie panic. According to the cognitive model, it is pre-

sumed that all persons who experience panic catastrophically misinterpret bodily sensations. Unless the developmental context is incorporated, along with the subtleties of the patient's phenomenology, the idiosyncratic meaning that the individual attaches to panic is lost. A theory of panic must be proposed that would offer a comprehensive framework for the construction of the meaning of panic to the individual who suffers from panic. A self psychological view of panic, particularly the notion of self-fragmentation, provides a broader lens with which to view panic. What were thought to be misattributions by the patient could be reconsidered when there is an empathic immersion into the patient's phenomenological world.

Self Psychology Principles

The concept of self is central to self psychology, a theory of development promulgated by Heinz Kohut and his followers. The self psychologists define the essence of human psychology in terms of the individual's need to organize his or her psychological experience into a cohesive configuration of self. The self is the center of initiative and the repository of the individual's nuclear ambitions, ideals, talents, and skills (Wolf, 1998). Selfobjects, a term used by Kohut, are objects whose functions are experienced as part of the self and its own workings or in the service of maintaining and restoring the self (Tolpin and Kohut, 1980). The selfobject functions are provided by other persons who are part of the selfobject matrix, usually consisting of the paents or parental substitutes. Briefly stated, the selfobject needs are (1) mirroring needs, which include the need to feel admired, affirmed, and recognized; (2) idealized needs, which include the need to experience oneself as beng part of the admired selfobject; and (3) twinship (or alterego) needs, which include the need to experience an essential alikeness with the selfobject (Wolf, 1998). This model is considered to be a deficit model (as opposed to a conflict model) in that it presumes an individual's behavior is motivated by the need to maintain cohesion via the internalization of structure (the selfobject functions).

Another concept central to self psychology is empathy, defined by Kohut (1984) as "the capacity to think and feel oneself into the inner life of another person" (p. 82) Kohut also spoke of approaching the treatment from an "experience-near" vantage point, meaning that the analyst experiences an empathic immersion into the patient's inner life (Kohut, 1977). Fragmentation, or the lessened coherency of the self, results from faulty selfobject responses or from other regression-producing conditions. Fragmentations can be expressed along a continuum, ranging from a mildly anxious selfobject disconnectedness to the panic of total loss of self-structure (Wolf, 1998).

Related to psychopathology, proponents of the Kohutian paradigm view pathology in relation to thwarted mirroring, idealizing, and twinship needs (Rowe and MacIsaac, 1991). The self disorders are characterized by the significant failure of the self to achieve vigor, cohesion, and harmony. Defensive reactions are usually understood as related to narcissistic injury and narcissistic rage, whereby the individual aims to protect (in the case of narcissistic injury) or destroy (narcissistic rage) himself or herself from the threatening/offending object.

Wolf (1998) notes that the primary aim of treatment is the strengthening of the self both in terms of structure (the restoration of the structural—mirroring, idealizing, etc.—deficits) and the selfobject matrix. The restoration of the selfobject transference occurs through proper interpretation of the transference disruption, seen as inevitable empathic failures that represent reenactments of earlier failures in the original selfobject matrix. Self cohesion describes the organization of different sensory, motor, and conceptual experiences into a unitary sense of self and involves having a sense of being a nonfragmented, physical whole with boundaries and a level of integration (Stern, 1985).

Panic from a Self Psychological Perspective

Wolfe (1995), in reconsidering cognitive theory, postulates that it is the patient's inability to stay in touch with the meaning of panic that brings on the fear of panic. The meaning of panic is lost, according to Wolfe, due to the unavailability of crucial affect states. In a similar vein, Diamond (1985) notes that these feeling states, repressed because they were unempathetically responded to in childhood, are excluded from self-representation or are deeply embedded in the patient's defensive structures. The patient's life seems out of control and dangerous due to the intrusion of these primitive feelings.

According to this theoretical scheme, anxiety reflects a state of the self and its vulnerability to disorganization or fragmentation experiences. Emphasis is placed on selfobject failures in protecting nurturing the infantile self. The vicissitudes of ties to the archaic selfobject are registered as fragmentation anxieties of the self, which ultimately color

all later dangers. As Roose and Glick (1995) note, "A patient's anxiety signals structural deficits in the self, resulting from psychic deficiency states in development" (p. 7).

Little attention in the literature has been paid to the relationship of panic to selfobject failures. Only one study (Diamond, 1985) of those reviewed directly addressed self-fragmentation as being at the psychopathological core of panic attacks. The patient's premorbid functioning, viewed in relation to selfobject failures, is often overlooked in other formulations. Kohut (1977) also believed that panic states were related to selfobject failures in childhood, resulting in a vulnerability to disorganization or fragmentation experiences. Panic, according to Kohut, results when the selfobject reacts hypochondriacally to the child's mild anxiety, leading the child to either draw into a noxious merger or actively try to escape it by walling himself or herself off from the noxious response of the selfobject.

The early selfobject failures—to protect the infantile self and to respond to selfobject needs—lead to diminished capacity to regulate anxiety and self-soothe later in life. Severe recurrent anxiety states during development may be later organized as a loss of sense of self (resulting from the noxious merger that Kohut discussed) or may result in withdrawal or avoidance (efforts to escape from the noxious selfobject response).

Summary

Under consideration are clinical and research questions about the neurobiology of panic, the psychological nature of panic, and the proliferation of research on the efficacy of cognitive therapy in relation to panic. Psychodynamic theories of anxiety highlight the shift of emphasis from castration anxieties (Freudian structuralism) to the anxiety generated in the relationship with the internal maternal object (object relations) to the anxiety that signals danger to the self and self organization (self psychology). Cognitive models of threat, particularly the catastrophic misinterpretation construal, purport that panic results from misinterpretations of somatic or psychological experiences as dangerous. This article questions this notion, arguing that thoughts of catastrophe relate to selfobject failures and that early selfobject responses to anxiety set the stage for the meanings of panic in subsequent development. The following case report also focuses on developmental sensitivities and unconscious processes, experiences that receive little attention in the cognitive literature.

Case Material

Presenting Complaint/ Current Functioning

Dawn is a 40-year-old, married, white female who has been seen in twice-weekly treatment for 18 months. She originally complained of a recurrence of panic symptoms with agoraphobia. Her symptom picture includes palpitations, a sense of being off-balance, derealization, and worries about fainting. She is not currently housebound; however, her fear of having another panic attack prevents her from entering into grocery stores and other unfamiliar situations unaccompanied. She is unable to hold down a "normal" job.

Two months before entering into treatment with me, she experienced a resurgence of panic symptoms while on a baseball field, leading her to seek psychopharmacological treatment (Xanax and Prozac). Realizing that the medications could only lessen the symptoms, she discontinued taking them and decided to pursue psychotherapeutic treatment. Initially, Dawn was unable to identify precipitants to the panic and also experienced severe bouts of depression following a panic episode. Her panic attacks began 20 years ago during her sophomore year in high school. Her mother reacted to her panic attacks by telling her that she was "crazy" and that she would be taken away in a straitjacket. She was depressed while in high school and developed a drinking problem around the same time that the symptoms began. She is currently taking Xanax and Effexor, prescribed by a psychiatrist whom she sees on a regular basis.

Dawn has been married for four years and relies on her husband, John, to accompany her to stores and office visits. She maintains several relatively close friendships, limiting socializing to her "safety zone" (within approximately 15 miles from her home). She rarely sees her oldest brother, Bob, and is estranged from her younger brother, Ron. Dawn does not have a clear sense of career ambition. She baby-sits for her friend, Gail, but wishes that she could find a job utilizing her talents. She was told by one of her teachers in high school that she possessed artistic talent, but has no idea how to apply herself.

Developmental History

Dawn was born and raised in a midwestern city. She is the middle child in a sibship of three. Her recollections of childhood involve incidents of abuse and neglect. She characterized her relationship with her mother as "pretty good" up until the age of 5. She recalled telling her mother that she would remain with her forever and her mother's pleased response. Dawn also remembered feeling loved and taken care of by her mother whenever she was sick. At the age of 5, she was separated from her immediate family while her mother was hospitalized for ovarian tumors. Dawn stayed with her maternal aunt while her brothers remained with another aunt. She recalled feeling confused and lonely, wondering when she would return to her family.

Several incidents of profound abuse were noted as she recalled her childhood. At the age of 10, her mother struck her with an object because she refused to go to school. She remembered being overwhelmed with fear until her father arrived home from work. In another incident, she was almost burned by her mother as punishment for playing with matches. She related that her brother, Ron, was her mother's co-conspirator; he held Dawn down while her mother lit the matches. She denied that either parent abused alcohol.

When she was 15, her mother was rehospitalized for benign tumors. Dawn feared that her mother had cancer and that she might develop cancer as well. She suffered from depression and began to have panic attacks, resorting to food and alcohol in an effort to assuage her sense of sadness and helplessness. When she was 18, her father was frequently hospitalized for heart problems. Each time he returned home from the hospital, her mother harassed him. Dawn queried, "Was she trying to kill him?" Dawn took care of him until he died (she was 21 at the time), and became housebound following his death. Her mother blamed her for his death, concluding that Dawn's decision to drop out of high school contributed to his eventual collapse. To Dawn, his death represented the demise of her "knight in shining armor—my only calming influence."

Treatment Issues

When Dawn entered into treatment with me, she was somewhat puzzled about the resurgence of the panic symptoms and worried that she would become housebound again. She voiced worries that she might be dying from "some weird illness," interpreting the feelings of faintness and dizziness as signs of a possible brain tumor. Further questioning revealed that her mother was recently diagnosed with various physical problems, mainly leading to the reactivation of the panic symptoms. A psychiatric evaluation was recommended due to the severity of the panic symptoms. Dawn, in her usual sardonic way, reacted by saying, "I knew, Doc, that you thought I was a nut case. You think I need a shrink too." When her feelings about the recommendation were explored, it became clear that Dawn worried that I viewed her as a "nut case," even though she had been referred to a psychiatrist in the past and was not aware of assigning such an interpretation to the referral. It should also be noted that Dawn's mother accompanied her to my office for the first couple of times that I saw Dawn. Despite my efforts to bring up the issue without embarrassing Dawn, I managed to embarrass her nonetheless. The following interchange ensued:

Therapist: Dawn, I couldn't help but notice that your mother—I assume it's your mother—accompanies you to the sessions. You mentioned before that your husband, John, frequently accompanies you because you are afraid of being along when you panic. Is it similar with your mother?

Dawn: You're right. That's my old lady out there. She's bored. She doesn't have anything better to do.

Therapist: That's the only reason?

Dawn: Well, no. I need my mommy with me, okay? (She laughs, then pauses.) Seriously, it scares me to be without her sometimes, even though she treats me like crap. I'm afraid that something bad will happen to her unless she's with me. (Her eyes well up with tears.)

Early on, the treatment focus shifted from her preoccupations with her bodily sensations to an almost exclusive focus on her relationship with her mother. She revealed that much of her day was devoted to complying with her mother's wishes and needs. For example, when she arrived home from babysitting, she would play back hostile messages left on her answering machine by her mother. Her mother, she said, would be enraged with her because Dawn was not available to her "at all times." Dawn, who was quite artistically talented, began to bring in drawings to the sessions that depicted a beast with blood dripping from its hands. Dawn reluctantly revealed her fear to me that I would hospitalize her for bringing in such a picture. When her fear was explored, it became clear that she worried that I would threaten to put her into a straitjacket (which could be seen as a metaphor for how

confined and victimized she felt by her mother). She also feared that I viewed her as "nuts," meaning that she would be forever plagued by her mental anguish.

Discussion

Considering Dawn's developmental history and current problems with panic and phobias, two dominant themes emerge: (1) the traumatic effects of being physically and verbally abused by her mother, and (2) the meaning of the death of her father. Her disturbance appears to be, in the main, related to disavowed affects associated with failed selfobject needs. The drawings of the beast represented the disavowed rage associated with feeling compelled to comply with her mother's wishes and demands. To Dawn, the expression of these affects represented a risk to maintaining her selfobject tie to her mother.

Goldberg (1995) discusses splitting in the context of disavowal when he notes, "The split in the self leads to the convenient practice of disowning parts of the world that one finds disagreeable. . . . He views himself and the world in essentially all positive or all negative terms. A split is demanded in order to stay connected to a parent who was a sustaining selfobject" (pp. 64–68). Related to Dawn, her panic and agoraphobic symptoms functioned as a way to remain connected to her mother. Her world was essentially divided into a series of binary issues: "sick" and "well," "good" and "evil," "safe" and "dangerous." She feared that she was plagued by a "weird illness," which evoked memories associated with being separated from her mother when her mother was hospitalized for tumors. Maintaining her view of herself as "nuts," which was confirmed by her feelings of fragmentation when she panicked, ensured that her mother would not abandon her. Because she lacked an identification with soothing, idealized selfobjects, she relentlessly hoped that her mother would provide the selfobject functions that she so desperately needed. Her fantasy was that her mother would be transformed into a nurturing mother by Dawn's constant compliance to her mother's needs. This dynamic was reenacted in the transference when she expressed her fear that I would also view her as "nuts." She also worried that the expression of anger in the sessions would threaten her connection to me. Shortly after bringing in the pictures of the beast, she started to bring in gifts to me, such as coffee mugs and the like. When it was interpreted that a reenactment of the original parental situation might be going on, and that she may have feared that her relationship with me would sever lest she take care of me, her compulsive caretaking quieted and eventually ceased.

Much of the treatment centered on helping Dawn to identify and modulate her intense affect states, particularly anger. A pivotal experience in Dawn's narrative was the death of her father. Ostensibly, her agoraphobic symptoms began at this point because she was left alone to deal with the intense feelings that surfaced around that time. Her intense fears of abandonment and loss were revisited during our sessions, an experience that enabled Dawn to have the opportunity to connect with a usable selfobject. The soothing and organizing selfobject functions that were provided by me helped Dawn to better integrate her father's death into her narrative and restored some sense of self-cohesion.

The treatment proved to be quite effective for Dawn in that her panic symptoms began to subside and she began to expand her "safety zone." At the end of treatment she was no longer worried about becoming housebound again because she understood the metaphoric connection between the agoraphobia and being imprisoned by her mother's neediness. She also realized that much of the panic was fueled by her worries about being ceaselessly available to her mother and began to set limits with her mother in that regard.

This approach is quite different from a cognitive approach to the treatment. A cognitive therapist might focus on identifying the distorted thinking patterns (i.e., Dawn's tendency to see herself as crazy) and work toward restructuring or changing her thoughts to more "constructive" thoughts. This view certainly has profound implications in terms of the question, Who is the final arbiter of reality, the patient or the therapist? Who decides what a cognitive distortion is? Self psychologists would tend to agree that the patient is the final arbiter, a view that is consistent with the constructivist's position. It should be noted, however, that there is a lively debate among self psychologists about who is the final arbiter of reality.

The Applicability of Self Psychological Principles: Research Evidence

A research study (Mahoney, 1999) was conducted to determine whether there is something about the experience of inadequate selfobject response that prompts the experience of panic. The study was qualitative and theory-formative. The data were narrative in nature, derived from both semistructured and unstructured interviews with a relatively small sample (N = 10). There were four interviews per subject. The interviews were designed to provide a "thick description" (Lincoln and Guba, 1985) of the experience. A brief presentation of some of the results will be offered here to further demonstrate the clinical applicability of the self psychological tenets in relation to panic. The results were organized according to three overarching themes: (1) the fear of breakdown, (2) the fear of being disconnected and alone, and (3) panic as a "not me" experience. The first two themes related to fears that underlie the panic, while the third category attempted to capture the tendency to describe the panic in terms of a "split-off" aspect of the self.

Some of the quotes related to the fear of breakdown included the following: "It's [the panic] a sign of going crazy. . . . I thought I'd jump out of the car," "I tell myself I'm going crazy [when panic occurs]," and "I'm losing my mind on the spot." The experience of panic was characterized as a breakdown of psyche and soma, usually involving a fear of dying or a sense of "going crazy." The underlying fear that was captured by these quotes appeared to be "the loss of humanness" or "disintegration anxiety." Kohut (1984) spoke of disintegration anxiety in the following way: "What is feared is not physical extinction, but loss of humanness: psychological death" (p. 16).

The question then became, What are the underlying conditions that give rise to these fears about going crazy? It followed that the participants discussed intense abandonment fears and concerns about being left alone with the feelings. The fear of being disconnected and alone was poignantly expressed in the following quotes: "What I was exposed to during childhood predisposed me to the panic—I still feel a great sense of abandonment," "I'm terrified of being alone," and "I know what my fears are now—the fear of being alone." A recurrent theme in the narratives was the lack of association with soothing, idealized selfobjects in dealing with separations and losses.

Quotes related to the "It's Not Me" category included the following: "I couldn't function [when he was suffering from panic and agoraphobia]. It was ridiculous. That isn't the real me . . . I'm always an easy-going type of person" and "It's [the panic] like another personality. You're not doing this to me now [as if talking to the panic]. Like it's another person." There seemed to be discordance in relation to how the participants viewed themselves. The conscious self was seen as separate from the "panicking" self. The experience of panic was organized around a sense of being "sick" like a "sick" parent or caretaker. As was stated earlier, the panic appears to function to reenact early scenes of parental dualism (Goldberg, 1995). Recurrent fragmentation experiences lead to incoherence in terms of how they view themselves. Based on childhood and contemporary experiences, the fantasies of the self were informed by limited ways of viewing themselves and the world. The fantasies, as Goldberg noted, serve to maintain the tie to the selfobject, thereby maintaining the panic attacks.

Conclusion

Current approaches to the conceptualization and treatment of panic focus primarily on the amelioration of symptoms, while de-emphasizing or ignoring the idiosyncratic meaning of the symptoms and their aftermath. The approach presented in this article addresses this dimension, underscoring the importance of developmental and unconscious factors. The catastrophic misinterpretation construal was also reconsidered in terms of the contention that panic represents a fragmentation experience, resulting from selfobject failures. While it was not within the scope of this article to present a lengthy case study or account of the research material, it is hoped that it will stimulate further interest in examining panic from a self psychological perspective.

References

American Psychiatric Association. (1994). *Diagnostic and Statistical Manual of Mental Disorders* (4th Edition). Washington, DC: Author.

Baker, R. (Ed). (1989). *Panic Disorder: Theory, Research and Therapy*. New York: Wiley.

Beck, A. T. (1976). *Cognitive Therapy and Emotional Disorders*. New York: International Universities Press.

Beck, A. T. and Clark, D. M. (1988). Cognitive approaches. In C. G. Last & Hersen (Eds.), *Handbook of Anxiety Disorders* (pp. 362–385). New York: Pergamon Press.

Beck, A. T. and Emery, G. (1985). *Anxiety Disorders and Phobias: A Cognitive Perspective*. New York: Basic Books.

Clark, D. (1988). A cognitive model of panic attacks. In McNally, D. (Ed.), *Panic Disorder: A Critical Analysis*. New York: Guilford Press.

Cohen, M. (1985). A theoretical discussion of and strategy of research to investigate agoraphobia as a disorder in early object relations. Unpublished doctoral dissertation. Forest Institute, Des Plaines, Illinois.

Cooper, A. M. (1985). Will neurobiology influence psychoanalysis? *American Journal of Psychiatry*, 142: 1395–1402.

Diamond, D. (1985). Panic attacks, hypochondriasis, and agoraphobia: A self psychological formulation. *American Journal of Psychotherapy*, 39 (1): 114–125.

Freud, S. (1926). Inhibitions, symptoms, and anxiety. *Standard Edition*, 20. London: Hogarth Press.

Gabbard, G. (1994). *Psychodynamic Psychiatry in Clinical Practice*. Washington, DC: APA.

Gorman, J., Papp, L. and Coplan, J. (1995). Neuroanatomy and neurotransmitter function in panic disorder. In S. Roose & R. Glick. (Eds.), *Anxiety as Symptoms and Signal* (pp. 39–56). Hillsdale, NJ: New Jersey Press.

Goldberg, A. (1995). *The Problem of Perversion*. New Haven: Yale University Press.

Kendler, H. (1987). *Historical Foundations of Modern Psychology*. Chicago: Dorsey Press.

Klein, D. (1993). False suffocation alarms, spontaneous attacks, and related conditions: An integrated hypothesis. *Archives of General Psychiatry*, 50: 302–317.

Kohut, H. (1977). *The Restoration of the Self*. New York: International Universities Press.

Kohut, H. (1984). *How Does Analysis Cure?* Chicago: University of Chicago Press.

LeDoux, J. (1996). The emotional brain: The mysterious underpinnings of emotional life. In Mellinger, D. *Anxiety: Two Minds for One Mood*. The Anxiety Disorders Association of America (ADAA) Reporter (summer/fall), pp. 5–7.

Lincoln, Y. and Guba, E. (1985). *Naturalistic Inquiry*. Newbury Park, CA: Sage Publications.

Mahoney, D. (1999). Panic disorder and self states: An ethnomethodological approach. Unpublished doctoral dissertation. Institute for Clinical Social Work, Chicago, Illinois.

Margraf, J. and Ehlers, A. (1989). Etiologic models of panic—medical and biological aspects. In Baker, R. (Ed.). *Panic Disorder: Theory, Research, and Therapy* (pp. 16–26) New York: Wiley.

McNally, R. (1994). *Panic Disorder: A Critical Analysis*. New York: Guilford Press.

Nemiah, J. (1988). *Handbook of Anxiety Vol. I: Psychodynamic Perspective of Anxiety*. New York: Elsevier.

Palombo, J. (1992). Narratives, self-cohesion, and the patient's search for meaning. *Clinical Social Work Journal*, 20(3): 249–270.

Roose, S. and Glick, R. (Eds.). (1995). *Anxiety as a Symptom and Signal*. Hillsdale, NJ: Analytic Press.

Rowe, C. and MacIsaac, D. (1991). *Empathic Attunement: The Technique of Analytic Self Psychology*. New York: Aronson Press.

Safran, J. and Segel, Z. (1990). *Interpersonal Process in Cognitive Therapy*. Northvale, NJ: Jason Aronson.

Shear, M, Cooper, A. M., and Klerman, G.L. (1993). A psychodynamic model of panic disorder. *American Journal of Psychiatry*, 150(6): 859–866.

Stern, D. (1985). *The Interpersonal World of the Infant*. New York: Basic Books.

Tolpin, M. and Kohut, H. (1980). The disorders of the self: The psycho-development of the first years of life. In J. Greenspan and E. Pollack (Eds.), *The Course of Life, Vol. I.* (pp. 7–30). New York: Free Press.

Wakefield, J. (1992). The concept of mental disorder: On the boundary between biological facts and social values. *American Psychologist*, 47: 373–388.

Wolf, E. (1998). *Treating the Self*. New York: Guilford Press.

Wolfe, B. (1995). The meaning of panic symptoms. *Anxiety Disorders of America (ADAA) Reporter* (summer/fall), pp. 2, 20.

27

Obsessive-Compulsive Symptomatology: A Goal-Directed Response to Anticipated Traumatization?

I will use clinical material to illustrate how one individual's efforts to prevent anticipated traumatization evolved into obsessive-compulsive illness. I am proposing that his obsessive-compulsive symptomatology was trauma-induced and progressed with this predictable pattern: an anticipatory state, activated by traumatic antecedents, compelled a goal-directed response that became maladaptive.

I have divided the discussion into separate sections about traumatic antecedents, anticipatory arousal, and a potentially adaptive motivational state that becomes maladaptive in obsessive-compulsive illness. In the first section about traumatic antecedents, I argue that we must expand our diagnostic use of the term traumatization to include forms of interpersonal threat. I also propose that we must discover how each patient's symbolizing efforts, informed by implicit memory, shape the uniquely personal form of symptomatology. In the second section, I discuss anticipatory anxiety, its mediation by the cortical-subcortical system, and its activation of a motivational state. Finally, I propose that the motivational state observed in obsessive-compulsive symptomatology represents a goal-directed process to prevent anticipated threat and, in consequence, achieve the rewards of relief and mastery.

Ultimately, the goal of this article is to generate a hypothetical construction for trauma-induced obsessive-compulsive illness that will stimulate empirical research about this complex biopsychosocial symptomatology.

Clinical Material

History of Present Illness

Matt, a 22-year-old undergraduate with plans for law school, was referred after two near-lethal suicide attempts, his desperate efforts to escape a consuming compulsion to enact rituals designed to "restore synchrony" within his body. In the preceding two years, Matt had attributed potent threat to certain proprioceptive sensations: he was vigilant to cues for asymmetrical movement, pressure, and balance. Any sensed asynchrony triggered anxiety, to which he responded with a compulsion to *correct* the abnormality through the deliberate manipulation of his joints, in accordance with elaborate rules. Matt explained, "If I can tell something is wrong, such as any particular pressure in my body, I feel anxiety and immediately compelled to equalize it [through the manipulation of joints]. If I achieve balance and synchrony [the goal], as a result of these manipulations, I am exhilarated. It means that everything is OK. If I do not achieve balance, I cannot rest until I do." His relief, of course, was fleeting, lasting only until he noticed a new imbalance.

Notable in my patient's history is the alarm he experienced when, in a high school brawl, he sustained multiple fractures to both hands. He recalled a helplessness associated with temporary deformity and functional limitation. In the ensuing years, as Matt participated not only in college sports and body-building, but also in girl-watching, he became increasingly focused on potential injury, gradually attaching to injury new and threatening attributions of deformity and undesirability. In consequence, he became increasingly vigilant, tuned to his body for signs of danger. Specifically, he attributed to *asymmetrical* bodily feedback the significance of danger. By the time he entered treatment, two years after his initial symptoms, his attribution of threat had generalized to a broad number and variety of asymmetrical proprioceptive changes.

Believing that he could determine a means to prevent bodily danger, Matt had gradually developed an elaborate set of body-focused rituals designed to achieve bodily synchrony. Because he predictably experienced some relief, albeit temporary, when he completed his ritualized joint manipulations, he concluded that he had discovered the means to prevent bodily danger. He used ritualizing as a medium through which he sought complete protection: "The rituals can prevent further asymmetry [the threatening stimuli], if only I can *perfect* them."

Matt concluded that because he predictably experienced some relief (tied to his belief that he had achieved through enactment of his rules some degree of subjectively determined bodily synchrony), he could develop new, more perfect rules to afford total synchrony. "If 1 hour of a total body ritual is failing to achieve sustained synchrony, then 2 hours will," or, "If manipulating just my extremities is insufficient to achieve harmony, then I will proceed to manipulate my eye muscles." He repeatedly voiced the expectation that he could discover a new ritual that would guarantee complete and lasting bodily synchrony.

Developmental History

Matt lost his mother when he was 6. They had been great buddies. After three weeks of hospitalization following an aneurysm, she died without a goodbye. Matt recalled, "She kept telling me that she would come home to make my birthday cake. She never came." Left with a bereft older sibling, he missed his father, who withdrew into work. He remembered growing up quite alone, initially excited at 9 to welcome a stepmother, only to find that she

doted on her own children and insisted on household order. Matt also recalled persistent power struggles to extract her interest from her preoccupation with order and cleanliness. Finally, he turned his competitive attentions to math, sports, and art.

Within weeks of leaving home for college, Matt reportedly began to assign excessive order to the placement of his possessions within his dorm room. He recalls that over the next two years he gradually transferred the focus of his compelling need for order to his body. He remembered that aches and pains after strenuous sports made him anxious and mobilized fears that he might seriously endanger his body. (He recalled the vulnerability he experienced in high school with his fractured hands.) My patient indicated that he linked his fears of bodily injury with losing the opportunity to marry and have a son because of deformity and undesirability. He emphasized that the hope to actualize a family was what sustained him: this destiny was the only reparation for his catastrophic loss at age 6. In the ensuing years, in his determined efforts to protect this hope from danger, he became severely symptomatic with obsessive-compulsive disorder (OCD).

Psychodynamic Impressions

The reader may be asking, How is this patient's obsessive-compulsive symptomatology trauma-based? I hope to show that my patient, during late adolescence, when his strivings toward attachment were reawakened, was reminded of catastrophic loss and, in response, began to anticipate further loss. He eventually formulated a goal-directed strategy to prevent this anticipated traumatization. Although some readers may compare Matt's story to that of Freud's Little Hans and conceptualize his symptoms as manifestations of an Oedipal conflict, I believe instead that Matt suffered the profound traumatization of prematurely losing a mother who had repeatedly told him, "You are the apple of my eye!" With her death, he experienced the catastrophic loss of the caregiving other who, in time, can become internalized as an abiding and encouraging presence (Mahler, Pine, and Bergman 1975; Winnicott 1958). Matt never recovered from the bereftness associated with her loss and desperately sought to rediscover this kind of life-giving relationship, determined to find it again with a family of his own. His obsessive-compulsive symptoms evolved from his goal-directed efforts to protect this hope from danger.

The idea of injury, registered in midadolescent memory as alarm associated with experiences of temporary limitation and deformity, was rendered potentially terrifying in late adolescence because of new attributions of meaning. In my patient's mind's eye, injury became the potential threat to achieving that which was essential, that is, a recovery of what had been lost, through discovery of another life-giving relationship. Protecting this hope from danger warded off eschatological despair.

Bowlby (1980) noted persistent, though disguised, strivings to recover the one who has been lost as a critical element of mourning. His evidence suggested that, even after prolonged periods, individuals would reexperience grief and reactivate their searches for those lost. During late adolescence, when biological strivings are awakened for partnership and family, my patient experienced renewed longings for attachment. However, these strivings mobilized memories of loss and anticipation of further loss. Bowlby also referred to the compelling need to protect attachment: "Any situation that seems to be endangering the bond elicits action designed to preserve it; and the greater the danger of loss appears to be the more intense and varied are the actions elicited to prevent it" (p. 42). Therefore, from Matt's perspective, it is understandable that the idea of injury, evocative of alarm associated with images of deformity and limitation, could endanger his search for new attachment in late adolescence. His response to this perceived threat was a highly focused anticipatory vigilance for body-focused alarms as well as a goal-directed motivational state aimed at preventing danger.

However, a potentially adaptive response to trauma became a pathological process. How? I now address the role of traumatic antecedents, anticipatory arousal, and the subsequent motivational state in an effort to begin to operationalize the process of trauma-induced obsessive-compulsive symptomatology.

The Role of Traumatic Antecedents

Nature of Traumatization

Is there a subset of OCD patients whose illness is triggered by traumatic antecedents? Needing the confirmation of empirical data, I agree with the proposal by Dinn, Harris, and Raynard (1999), who conceptualize one form of OCD symptoms as adaptations to protracted and genuine threat. To support their theory they emphasize the prevalence of psychopathology in the families of OCD patients, noting that children "who find themselves enmeshed in a state of chronic insecurity may respond with heightened vigilance to threat-related stimuli" (p. 314). These authors stress the role of protracted interpersonal threat as a form of childhood traumatization that might activate an anticipatory watchfulness for changes in parental moods and intentions, and ultimately enhance the responsiveness of cortical-subcortical systems. What is the nature of traumatic antecedents in obsessive-compulsive symptomatology? Do we need to broaden our diagnostic conceptualization of trauma to include interpersonal threat?

Anxiety is, of course, the affect that signifies an appraisal of threat. Both psychoanalytic and learning theorists have concluded that "anxiety is the result of traumatic learning experiences" (Le Doux 1996, p. 235). Thus these theorists have concluded that it is only through the medium of experience that a stimulus can be appraised as potentially dangerous. However, Nesse (1996) suggests that the potential for many fears are preplanted, "prepared fears of ancient dangers" (p. 214). His proposal makes excellent sense if we consider the hazards of our ancestral environment, such as separation from caregivers or close encounters with environmental dangers. It seems highly plausible that many of our fears have an innate or prepared potential, waiting for experience to activate them. For example, consider the infant who does not demonstrate a fear of heights until his crawling permits him an opportunity to know through experience the potential dangers of falling. Or the infant who comes to know, through his experiences of separation from his caregivers, the dangers of being without those whose very faces are the maps of his psychological life. The developmentalists have repeatedly emphasized that threats to secure attachment, whether originating from physical separations or from psychological rejections, have traumatic effects on the developing mind and body (Bowlby 1980; Mahler et al. 1975; Stern 1985). My patient suffered a series of catastrophic interpersonal threats to his sense of secure attachment.

As opposed to the clearly identifiable role of threat to physical integrity in posttraumatic stress disorder (PTSD), the role of threat to psychological integrity may emerge as a more typical stressor in OCD. In addition to the compulsive washing and checking behaviors that are attempts to ward off physical threats to home and body, many compulsive symptoms may be manifestations of efforts to prevent intra- or interpersonal psychological traumatization. For decades, psychoanalytic schools have emphasized the role of unconscious intrapersonal conflict in obsessive-compulsive symptoms. Fenichel (1945) suggested that what the patient feared most was a loss of self-respect. Cognitive behavioral theorists have stressed that the typical OCD patient holds himself excessively responsible for outcomes (Menzies et al., 2000). Insel (1990) proposed that an internalized sense of overresponsibility, intolerance or uncertainty, and the resultant struggle for control would predictably induce symptoms. We need careful empirical investigation to determine if and how forms of interpersonal threat, perhaps expressed as critical appraisals or exorbitant expectations by important others, might have shaped these internalized representations in obsessive-compulsive patients.

In addition to Matt's early catastrophic loss, he endured a protracted form of interpersonal traumatization, that is, continual criticisms from his stepmother. Witness to her compulsive behaviors regarding order, he subsequently faced the painful consequences of shame and alienation if he did not comply with her anxiety-driven rules. Her attention to her household at his expense induced potent narcissistic injury and outrage. I suspect that her insistence on household order may have shaped my patient's belief that the maintenance of order was critically important for a sense of well-being and relief from tension. Dinn and colleagues (1999) have observed that, in response to prolonged interpersonal stress, children may evolve not only a hypersensitivity to cues that signify potential alarm, but also a "distinct cognitive style characterized by exaggerated threat appraisal and magical beliefs" that confer a sense of control and predictability in chaotic conditions (p. 313).

These same authors suggest that the orbitofrontal system, part of the mediating circuitry for OCD and vital for the processing of complex social stimuli, may be especially sensitive to interpersonal threat (Dinn et al., 1999). We know that "OFC lesions produce a pseudo psychopathic condition, in which individuals appear deficient in feelings of guilt, shame anxiety, and concern for social norms as opposed to those individuals with OCD (heightened OFC activity) who appear to be excessively concerned with how their actions will affect others" (Zald and Kim, 1996, p. 259).

From a developmental perspective, Schore (1997) has addressed how the maturation of a system in the infant orbito-prefrontal cortex that regulates psychobiological states is dependent on the interpersonal experience between baby and caregiver. He is proposing a predisposition to psychopathology based upon experience-dependent systems in the organizing brain. Given what we have come to understand about the ontological necessity of safe attachment for continued healthy development (Bowlby 1980; Mahler et al. 1975; Stern 1985), I wonder how we can continue to exclude *forms of interpersonal threat* from our diagnostic definition of traumatization.

Symbolization of Traumatization

I agree with the theorists Franzblau, Kanadanian, and Rettig (1995), who have emphasized that a model of OCD must recognize the phenomenological experience of those who engage in compulsive behaviors. We need to know how these individuals have symbolized their experiences with traumatization and their strategies of seeking relief. Therefore, in addition to identifying the essential nature of the stressor, we must consider how the intrinsic has been transformed into the uniquely personal through the symbolizing efforts of the individual. That process has, of course, been the focus of psychoanalytic theory.

Guided by the tenets of psychoanalytic theory, my patient and I simultaneously sought ascending doses of selective serotonin reuptake inhibitors (SSRIs), cognitive-behavioral consultations, and his complex story of traumatization. Mindful of our goal to translate the unconscious into the conscious or thought-about, I wondered if my patient's obsessive-compulsive symptomatology was the enacted outcome of an unremembered story whose early chapters had been encoded primarily through implicit memory. Recall that implicit memory, composed essentially of emotional and sensory experiences, can directly influence behavior, bypassing conscious awareness (Schacter 1987). The basal ganglia may have a central mediating role in shaping motor behavior informed by implicit memory (Squire 1992).

Was it possible that Matt's early traumatizing experiences, encoded primarily in implicit memory, influenced his later compulsive behavior? The following are some of the many questions that my patient and I asked: How might a boy of 6 have experienced the catastrophe of his beloved mother's death? Did he symbolize her damaged body? How did he make sense of what happened? Did mid- and late adolescent experiences with injury trigger implicitly encoded memories of vulnerability and aloneness? Was his choice of preventative strategy shaped by his stepmother's compulsive pursuit of order? Was Matt eventually compelled to prevent anticipated injury because bodily damage had become inextricably linked with catastrophic loss?

My patient and I wondered how two ideas might become inseparably linked in the mind. Kandel (1999) suggests that Freud's concept of psychic determinism provides the answer: "any mental event is causally related to its preceding mental event" (p. 510). He further states that "in learning to associate two stimuli, a subject does not simply learn that one stimulus precedes the other. Instead, in learning to associate two stimuli, a subject learns that one stimulus comes to predict the other" (p. 510). I concluded that Matt linked ideas of bodily damage with catastrophic loss, and over time began to anticipate that injury would inevitably entail loss. It was this idea of injury that became symbolized as the focus of potential threat. This symbol intruded in the obsessional forms of alarming bodily sensations that activated persistent anticipatory arousal.

Anticipatory Arousal

The individual will have made an important advance in his capacity for self-preservation if he can foresee and expect a traumatic situation of this kind which entails helplessness, instead of simply waiting for it to happen. Let us call a situation which contains the determinant for such expectation a danger situation. It is in this situation that the signal of anxiety is given. (Freud, 1926/1957, p. 166)

Thus, Freud spoke about anxiety as a signal that activates the self-preservative function of anticipating, and in consequence, preparing for threat, if time permits. Severe immediate threats activate highly stereotyped responding, as might be expected in a fight-or-flight response (Barlow 1988). However, if one has been ambushed by trauma, caught unexpectedly, he may decide (or does the brain decide for him?) that he will do what he can to foresee potential threat. He understands the value of anticipation (as Freud suggests). He has the opportunity to prepare a self-protective strategy if he anticipates.

Critchley, Mathias, and Dolan (2001) conclude that anticipatory arousal is an index of implicit risk-related learning that may directly influence behavior by affecting the choice between high-risk decisions potentially offering immediate rewards and low-risk decisions resulting in long-term gain but little short-term reward. They have demonstrated that outcome uncertainty and anticipatory arousal increase orbitofrontal cortical activity. Zald and Kim (1996) emphasize the strategic location of the orbitofrontal cortex (OFC), "positioned at the point of interface between sensory association cortices, limbic structures, and subcortical regions involved in the control of autonomic and motor effector pathways" (p. 249). They propose that the OFC is a major contributor to the recognition of reinforcers, stimulus-reinforcer learning, modulation of responses based on changes in reinforcement contingencies, mediation of social-affiliative behavior, mnemonic functions, and rule learning.

Functional neuroimaging studies in obsessive-compulsive disorder have found abnormally elevated activity in the orbitofrontal cortex, anterior cingulate gyrus, caudate nuclei, and thalamus (Breiter et al. 1996). Dinn et al. (1999) propose that it is specifically "the trauma-induced sensitization of the orbitofrontal system that renders the patient particularly susceptible to aversive conditioning and the development of anxiety reducing strategies" (p. 321). Agreeing that the heightened OFC activity in OCD may reflect a greater vulnerability to anticipatory anxiety and a particular efficiency at recognizing conditioned aversive reinforcers, Zald and Kim (1996) suggest that the OFC participates with the fear-conditioning circuits that transform stimuli, through associative processing, into triggers. Paredes and colleagues (1998) comment: "The vigilance reaction would appear to require more decision making and information processing . . . to which stimuli to respond" (p. 171). Unlike the processing of reminders of potent trauma in PTSD patients which trigger immediate, albeit crude subcortical appraisals through a rapid thalamoamygdalar route (Le Doux 1996), OCD patients in their vigilant anticipatory mode have a high level of stimulus specificity, presumably due to more discriminating circuitry.

Thus, it appears that threat stimuli might be evaluated through a prepotent subcortical route first, inducing prompt emotional appraisal and compelling automatic behavioral and mental action programs. If response time is permitted, the coordination of responses from the orbitofrontal cortex with the amygdala will allow the individual to plan and execute a course of more flexible and creative cognitive and/or behavioral action. Rolls (2000) states that the adaptive value of emotional and motivational states, mediated by the orbitofrontal cortex and amygdala, is to allow an interface between sensory inputs and action systems. He believes that appraisals of reward and punishment, manifest through emotional states, will ultimately specify behavioral goals. In other words, appraisals of stimuli can compel or activate motivational or behavioral systems.

A Goal-Directed Motivational State

The Search for the Reward of Anxiety Relief

I am specifically proposing that anticipatory arousal, associated with threat evaluation, may activate a goal-directed motivational state that seeks to prevent anticipated threat and to achieve the reward of relief from anxiety. Mayr (1988) concluded that it is useful for us to represent behavior in goal-directed terms, that is, *something is done in order to.* He stated that behavioral programs do not evolve, according to Darwin's theory, unless they are done in order to enhance either the survival or reproductive success of the organism. Anxiety, the affect associated with threat appraisal, is understandably such noxious feedback, given its evolutionary significance for survival, that it insists on response. Is relief of anxiety (and all that is signifies) a sufficient *reward* to motivate goal-directed behavior aimed at prevention of anticipated threat? Recall that my patient, when he achieved his subjective appraisal of bodily harmony, described a feeling of exhilaration, the feeling that generally accompanies reward.

Panksepp (1998) has conceptualized a motivational state, driven by the mesolimbic cortical dopaminergic circuits, that mediates our ability to anticipate rewards. He states that, most likely, this system interacts with higher brain mechanisms, such as the frontal cortex and hippocampus, to generate plans and expectations of reward. Knowing that the dopaminergic system is intimately involved in reward-seeking (Panskepp 1998) and that animal studies have confirmed the role of dopamine in compulsive behavior (Goodman et al. 1990; Pittman 1991), we need to clarify the complex interaction between the dopaminergic and serotonergic systems in OCD. Although Stein (2000) suggests that dopamine-serotonin interactions are probably critical for a range of stereotypic behaviors, he also argues that so broad a neurochemical characterization has little explanatory power. However, I propose that it might be a useful starting place to conceptualize compulsive behavior in

trauma-induced obsessive-compulsive illness as goal-directed, seeking the *specific reward* of anxiety reduction through prevention of threat. From this perspective we might see more easily the common denominators between compulsive phenomena and addictive processes (which seem more obviously reward-driven).

The Goal-Directed Process toward Mastery

Is relief from anxiety the primary reward in goal-directed compulsive behaviors? My patient's goal-directed behavior possibly originates from a broad-based motivational state seeking the rewards of mastery. Hendrick (1942, 1943) emphasized that compulsive behavior, consistently observed throughout development in the mastery of functions such as walking and talking, was the goal-directed manifestation of an instinctual insistence toward mastery. He believed that individuals were compelled to seek efficient use of their central nervous system in order to perform ego functions that would enable them to control or alter their environment. He proposed that compulsivity would predictably stop whenever the individual had achieved competence with the desired skill. We have all observed aspects of this ontological process, in which the child is compelled instinctually to pursue simple, then more complex aims. He pursues not only mastery of physical and linguistic skills, but also the achievements of psychological autonomy, meaningful attachments, and exploration of inner and outer worlds. When the child has achieved a specific mastery, the compulsive behavior associated with mastery attainment diminishes. Pertinent to our discussion is the repeated observation that many children, receptive to the anxiolytic rhythms and repetitions inherent in simple rituals, discover a means of mastery (through their compulsive habits) over threatening separations such as bedtime. When the perceived threat has past, they predictably discard their ritualistic behaviors.

White (1959) similarly proposed that there is a motivation toward competence, fulfilling what he believed is an evolutionary need to interact competently with the external world. Influenced by White's ideas, Franzblau and colleagues (1995) have suggested that "compulsive behaviors be viewed as behavioral strategies to increase feelings of self-efficacy" (p. 99), "based upon the assumption that people need to have control over their lives, initiated and maintained by their own actions" (p. 108).

A statewide high school math champion, a talented artist and competitive athlete, Matt had repeatedly experienced the satisfactions of mastery. He often referred to his favorite book, Hemingway's *Old Man and the Sea*, fully believing that he, like the old man, would never tire of the fight for what he knew he must do. Determined to conquer potential threat, and believing that he could, Matt was motivated to *perfect* his preventative strategies to achieve the goal of complete and lasting protection from bodily harm. Obviously, his goal-directed attempt to prevent danger became seriously maladaptive.

A Potentially Adaptive Goal-Directed Response Turned Pathological

False Alarms

What may have originated from an innate goal-directed search for mastery evolved into a futile and irrational compulsive process. While it is beyond the scope of my understanding to address further how a potentially adaptive response to traumatization became such a tyrannizing illness, I will briefly comment on what may have become obvious to the reader. Matt sought to prevent *virtual dangers* that had been triggered by *false alarms*: that error in threat appraisal compromised his efforts to extinguish anxiety.

Critchley et al. (2001) state: "Adaptive behavior requires an ability to make advantageous decisions by predicting the likelihood of future success based upon previous experience" (p. 537). Matt's insistent belief that he could prevent danger was very probably based on his acknowledgments of previous successes with mastery over other challenges. However, with this particular challenge, he failed miserably in his predictions: his capacity to make accurate appraisals of danger based on previous experience was impaired.

Like other OCD patients, my patient selectively attended to specific cues (asymmetrical sensations) and exaggerated the probability of harm (Kozak, Foa, and McCarthy 1988). Recall that those who have experienced traumatization may lose the capacity to discriminate actual threatening stimuli from reminders of remembered threat (Pittman and Orr 1990). Because so much of traumatic experience is encoded through implicit memory in somatosensory fragments (van der Kolk 1996), clarifying the overlap between explicit and implicit memory systems may illumine how implicitly remembered threat becomes translated into conscious obsessional cues. Fenichel (1945) referred to obsessions as conscious "derivatives" of what had been originally feared (p. 268). Asymmetrical body sensations, somatosensory reminders of former injury, activated my patient's obsessional thought, "My body is out of order." These triggers, although threat-related, were benign stimuli: they were false alarms. Because Matt's focus had been seized by false alarms, to which he then attributed danger, he was misled into formulating a strategy that sought to prevent a virtual threat, the symbolized form of danger.

Failure to Extinguish Anxiety

Furthermore, we know that once an individual has been sensitized by fear-inducing stimuli, decreasingly intense external stimuli have the power to elicit the same neural activation (Perry et al. 1995). We would then expect Matt, over time, to associate new forms of asymmetrical sensations with anxiety. Attributing to more and more stimuli threatening significance, my patient became increasingly anticipatory, continually attending to possible cues from his body signifying danger. He could not extinguish his anticipatory arousal activated by more and more false alarms. Zald and Kim (1996) suggest that the OFC might contribute to obsessive-compulsive symptoms by maintaining internally generated representations of the reinforcers: "The individual may repeatedly perform behaviors aimed at reducing the anxiety associated with the representation, but because the representation continues to be maintained, the individual feels compelled to repeat the behaviors again" (p. 258). Le Doux (1996) proposes that, over time, the prefrontal cortex is actually altered by stress and may release its brakes on the amygdala, making new learning stronger and more resistant to extinction.

We can safely speculate that with repeated experiences of body-focused cues evoking alarm and subsequent relief-finding through rituals, Matt was inadvertently strengthening specific patterns of neural activation; in turn, he was reinforcing his symbolized representations of danger and relief (in the form of erroneous conclusions based on predictable information from his experiences). He reasoned: "Because these sensations predictably evoke alarm, they must signal danger. I must pay attention and respond. In addition, because I can predictably find only temporary relief through my rituals, I must find a means to perfect them."

Conclusion

I have proposed that one form of obsessive-compulsive symptomatology evolves from a specific goal-directed response to anticipated traumatization. This hypothetical construction depends on an expanded definition of traumatization to include interpersonal threat. Inherent in the proposal is the conclusion that only when we discover how the individual's symbolized forms of threat, shaped by implicit memory, direct his particular strategies for relief can we truly begin to address how a potentially adaptive process becomes pathological. I hope that this conceptualization of trauma-induced obsessive-compulsive symptomatology will stimulate empirical study that might further illumine how these psychological processes are representations of their neurobiological underpinnings.

References

Barlow, D. *Anxiety and Its Disorders: The Nature and Treatment of Anxiety and Panic.* Guilford Press, 1988.

Bowlby, J. *Loss.* Basic Books, 1980.

Breiter, H., Rauch, S., Kwong, K., Baker, J., Weisskoff, R., Kennedy, D., Kendrick, A., Davis, T., Jiang, A., Cohen, M., Stern, C., Belliveau, J., Baer, L., O'Sullivan, R., Savage, C., Brady, T., Jenike, M., and Rosen, B. Functional magnetic resonance imaging of symptom provocation in obsessive compulsive disorder. *General Archives of Psychiatry* (1996) 53:595–606.

Critchley, H., Mathias, C., and Dolan, R. Neural activity in the human brain relating to uncertainty and arousal during anticipation. *Neuron* (2001) 29:537–45.

Dinn, W., Harris, C., and Raynard, R. Post-traumatic obsessive-compulsive disorder: A three-factor model. *Psychiatry* (1999) 62:313–24.

Fenichel, O. Obsession and compulsion. In Fenichel, O., ed., *The Psychoanalytic Theory of Neurosis* (pp. 268–310). Norton, 1945.

Franzblau, S., Kanadanian, M., and Rettig, E. Critique of reductionistic models of obsessive-compulsive disorder: Toward a new explanatory paradigm. *Social Science and Medicine* (1995) 41:99–112.

Freud, S. Inhibitions, symptoms, and anxiety. (Original work published 1926) In J. Strachey, ed. and trans., *The Standard Edition of the Complete Psychological Works of Sigmund Freud* (Vol. 20, pp. 77–175). Hogarth Press, 1957.

Goodman, W., McDougle, C., Price, L., Riddle, M., Pauls, D., and Lackman, J. Beyond the serotonin hypothesis: A role for dopamine in some forms of obsessive compulsive disorder? *Journal of Clinical Psychiatry* (1990) 51:36–43.

Hendrick, I. Instinct and ego during infancy. *Psychoanalytic Quarterly* (1942) 11:33–58.

Hendrick, I. Work and the pleasure principle. *Psychoanalytic Quarterly* (1943) 12:311–29.

Insel, T. Phenomenology of obsessive compulsive disorder. *Journal of Clinical Psychiatry* (1990) 51:4–9.

Kandel, E. Biology and the future of psychoanalysis: A new intellectual framework for psychiatry revisited. *American Journal of Psychiatry* (1999) 156:505–24.

Kozak, M., Foa, E., and McCarthy, P. Obsessive-compulsive disorder. In C. Last and M. Hersen, eds., *The Handbook of Anxiety Disorders* (pp. 87–108). Pergamon Press, 1988.

Le Doux, J. *The Emotional Brain.* Simon and Schuster, 1996.

Mahler, M., Pine, F., and Bergman, A. *The Psychological Birth of the Human Infant.* Basic Books, 1975.

Mayr, E. The multiple meanings of teleological. In *Toward a New Philosophy of Biology.* Beknap Press, 1988.

Menzies, R., Harris, L., Cumming, S., and Einstein, D. The relationship between inflated personal responsibility and exaggerated danger expectancies in obsessive-compulsive concerns. *Behaviour Research and Therapy* (2000) 38:1029–37.

Nesse, R., *Why We Get Sick: The New Science of Darwinian Medicine.* Vintage Books, 1996.

Panksepp, J. *Affective Neurosciences.* Oxford Press, 1998.

Paredes, J., Winters, R., Schneiderman, N., and McCabe, P. Afferents to the central nucleus of the amygdala and functional divisions of the periqueductal gray: Neuroanatomical substrates for affective behavior. *Brain Research* (1998) 887:157–73.

Perry, B., Pollard, R., Blakley, T., Baker, W., and Vigilante, D. Childhood trauma, the neurobiology of adaptation and use-dependent development of the brain: How states become traits. *Infant Mental Health Journal* (1995) 2–35.

Pittman, R. Historical considerations. In J. Zohar, T. Insel, and S. Rasmussen, eds., *Psychobiology of Obsessive Compulsive Disorder.* Springer-Verlag, 1991.

Pittman, R., and Orr, S. The black hole of trauma. *Biological Psychiatry* (1990) 27:469–71.

Rolls, E. Memory systems in the brain. *Annual Review of Psychology* (2000) 51:599–630.

Schacter, D. Implicit memory: History and current states. *Journal of Experimental Psychology* (1987) 13:501–18.

Schore, A. Early organization of the nonlinear right brain and development of a predisposition to psychiatric disorders. *Developmental Psychopathology* (1997) 9:595–631.

Schore, A. The effects of early relational trauma on right brain development, affect regulation and infant mental health. *Infant Mental Health Journal* (2001) 22:201–69.

Squire, L. Declarative and non-declarative memory: Multiple brain systems supporting learning and memory. *Journal of Cognitive Neuroscience* (1992) 4:232–43.

Stein, D. Neurobiology of the obsessive-compulsive spectrum disorders. *Biologic Psychiatry* (2000) 47:296–304.

Stern, D. *Interpersonal World of the Infant.* Basic Books, 1985.

van der Kolk, B. Trauma and memory. In B. Van der Kolk, A. McFarlane, and L. Weisaeth, eds., *Traumatic Stress* (pp. 279–302). Guilford Press, 1996.

White, R. Motivation reconsidered: The concept of competence. *Psychological Review* (1959) 66:297–333.

Winnicott, D. The capacity to be alone. *International Journal of Psycho-Analysis* (1958) 39:416–20.

Zald, D., and Kim, S. Anatomy and function of the orbital frontal cortex, II: Function and relevance to obsessive-compulsive disorder. *Journal of Neuropsychiatry* (1996) 8:249–61.

CATHERINE N. DULMUS
NANCY J. SMYTH

28

Early-Onset Schizophrenia: A Literature Review of Empirically Based Interventions

Twelve percent of American children suffer from mental disorders (National Institute of Mental Health, 1990), with diagnoses ranging from mild anxiety to psychosis. The Office of Technology Assessment (1986) reports that at most, only one-third of those children will receive the services they need. A lack of diagnosis, treatment, and services can have devastating results for the individual child, the family, and society as a whole as the mentally ill child grows up to become a mentally ill adult (Dulmus & Wodarski, 1996).

Schizophrenia is a major psychiatric illness which strikes approximately 1.5% of the general population (Torrey, 1995), often with devastating impact on the lives of both patients and their family members (Mueser & Gungerich, 1994). It is a complex, multifaceted disorder (or group of disorders) which has escaped precise definition after almost a century of study (Russell, 1994). It involves disturbances of the brain's chemistry, anatomy, and physiology, which in turn distort perception and subjective experiences in the affected individual (Maxmen & Ward, 1995). Symptomology includes hallucinations, delusions, and thought disturbances. Though primarily thought of as an illness that strikes young adults, children also can be afflicted with this debilitating illness. Early onset of schizophrenia, which strikes prepubertal children, is atypical and represents a particularly severe and chronic form of the illness (J.R. Asarnow, Thompson, & Goldstein, 1994). A large population of child and adolescent schizophrenic patients present with severe schizophrenia in later life (J.R. Asarnow

et al., 1994). In the general population one child in 10,000 will develop a schizophrenia disorder (Remschmidt, Schulz, Martin, Warnke, & Trott, 1994), with males being inflicted more frequently than females (Kallman & Roth, 1956), though sex differentiation is not noted after the age of 14 (Remschmidt et al., 1994). Torrey (1995) reports childhood-onset schizophrenia appears to have some genetic roots and has been determined to be a brain disease, as demonstrated by the findings of abnormalities on electroencephalographs and enlarged cerebral ventricles on MRI scans in children with this disorder. He further reports that these children also have an excess number of minor physical anomalies and that their mother's history often finds excess pregnancy and birth complications. Gordon and colleagues (1994), when referring to early-onset schizophrenia, state, "Earlier onset might result from a heavier genetic load or a more potent environmental insult. Earlier onset of illness may reflect a more salient environmental insult (e.g., intrauterine viral infection), premature endocrine influence on brain development, fewer protective factors, or greater psychosocial stress."

Early-onset schizophrenia is a rare disorder, estimated to occur 50 times less frequently than adult-onset schizophrenia (Karno & Norquist, 1989). Of all schizophrenia disorders only 0.1–1% manifest before the age of 10, with 4% before the age of 15 (Remschmidt et al., 1994). Unfortunately, those patients whose schizophrenic psychoses manifest before the age of 14 have a poorer prognosis (Remschmidt, 1994). Age and developmental stage are important factors that influence symptoms, course, and outcome (Remschmidt et al., 1994). The majority of cases involving childhood (preadolescent) mode of onset is insidious, with general behavioral disturbance that gradually evolves into psychosis. This is in contrast to most reports of adolescent- and adult-onset cases, which report a higher proportion of acute onset (Russell, 1994). There is a remarkable increase in schizophrenia during adolescence (Remschmidt et al., 1994). About the same rate of adolescents and adults with schizophrenia reach full remission (23%), but only 25% of adolescent-onset schizophrenia subjects achieve partial remission, compared with about 50% of adult schizophrenia patients. A chronic course can be observed in 52% of adolescent schizophrenia subjects, compared with 25% in adults (Remschmidt et al., 1994). Eggers (1989) reported remission in 27% of children with onset of schizophrenia before age 14 at follow-up evaluations conducted 6 to 40 years later (J.R. Asarnow et al., 1994). Studies of early-onset schizophrenia have been motivated partly by the hope that such cases may prove particularly informative for isolating etiological factors and pathways (J.R. Asarnow, 1994).

Schizophrenia has been described in children throughout at least the past century (J.R. Asarnow et al., 1994). Descriptions of various psychotic symptoms in children began to appear in the psychiatric literature at about the same time as descriptions of psychotic symptoms in adults (R.F. Asarnow & Asarnow, 1994). Before 1980, a diagnosis of childhood schizophrenia was often used to denote a group of children with profound impairments of early onset, which by today's standards would result in some receiving an alternative diagnosis, such as infantile autism or a pervasive developmental disorder (Spencer & Campbell, 1994).

It is generally believed that early-onset childhood and later-onset schizophrenia are related disorders (J.R. Asarnow, 1994). The symptoms of schizophrenia in children are very similar to those of adult schizophrenia, with the exception that their content is age-related (Torrey, 1995). It is now clear that schizophrenia in children can be reliably diagnosed using criteria derived from studies of adult patients with schizophrenia, as there is a continuity between childhood- and adult-onset schizophrenia when adult criteria are used to diagnose schizophrenia in children (R.F. Asarnow & Asarnow, 1994). Early findings suggest that early-onset schizophrenia may be a more familial and, unfortunately, a more severe variant of the disorder (J.R. Asarnow, 1994). The *Diagnostic Manual of Mental Disorders (DSM-III)* (American Psychi-

atric Association, 1980), recognizing that symptomatology and other diagnostic features of early-onset schizophrenia are similar to late-onset in adults, stopped using separate diagnostic criteria. This practice continues in *DSM-IV* (American Psychiatric Association, 1994), where identical criteria are used for diagnosis of schizophrenia regardless of age of onset (Gordon et al., 1994).

Remschmidt and colleagues (1994) report that the patient's premorbid personality appears to be of great importance, stating that a poor prognosis can be found in patients who were cognitively impaired, shy, introverted, and withdrawn before the beginning of their psychotic state. They also report that children with high IQ show more positive symptoms (delusions, hallucinations, thought disorder) and fewer negative symptoms (apathy, social withdrawal, poverty of thoughts, blunting of emotions, slowness of movement, lack of drive) than low-IQ children. Formal thought disorder in children has not been reported prior to 6 years of age, with hallucinations identified more frequently in children over 8 years of age (J.R. Asarnow, 1994). This supports the view that developmental changes exert significant influences on the expression of schizophrenic symptoms. Patients with acute manifestation of their disorder, having hallucinations and delusions (positive symptoms), have a better prognosis than those with an insidious onset with continuous impairment of cognitive functions and/or depressive states (Remschmidt et al., 1994).

Children with schizophrenia often meet criteria for additional diagnoses. Russell, Bott, and Sammons (1989) report a study where 68% of their sample met criteria for another diagnosis, the most common of which were conduct/oppositional disorder (31%) and atypical depression or dysthymic disorder (37%). Often these children are affected by other disorders, such as seizures, learning disabilities, mild retardation, neurological symptoms, hyperactivity, or other behavioral problems (Torrey, 1995). Young children have more immature language and cognitive development, which may inhibit their abilities to describe their experiences (Cantor, 1988), which can further complicate the assessment process.

Major advances in child assessment techniques have facilitated reliable and systematic assessment of schizophrenic symptoms and syndromes (J.R. Asarnow, 1994). There are currently a number of well-researched and validated psychiatric interview schedules that assess schizophrenic symptoms (J.R. Asarnow, 1994). Most of these interviews are designed to be administered with parents or other caretakers, as well as individually with the child. Recent advances in assessment methodologies should contribute to more consistent diagnostic procedures across laboratories and facilitate progress in our knowledge regarding childhood-onset schizophrenia (J.R. Asarnow, 1994). Recent years have witnessed major advances in the assessment of psychopathology in children. Techniques for assessment include interview schedules, rating scales, and measures of formal thought disorder (J.R. Asarnow, 1994). These techniques assist the clinician in accurately diagnosing schizophrenia and ruling out any differential diagnosis with overlapping symptomatology.

When providing services to this population it is essential that treatment be integrated with education and job skills training. The child should continue to live at home whenever possible unless there is some contraindication, and services must be flexible and well coordinated (Torrey, 1995). Unfortunately, though, there is a very high risk of out-of-home placement among children diagnosed as schizophrenic (J.R. Asarnow, 1994).

With regard to treatment of schizophrenic psychoses in children and adolescents, Remschmidt and Martin (1992) identify five specific areas that must be integrated into a child's treatment plan: (1) pharmacologic treatment of acute psychotic states, (2) pharmacologic prevention of relapses, (3) a psychotherapeutic component, (4) a family component, and (5) specific measures of rehabilitation. This paper will review controlled intervention studies located in the *Psychological Abstracts* database related to these five areas in the treatment of early-onset schizophrenia and will conclude with recommendations for practice and further research.

Pharmacologic Treatment

Children diagnosed with early-onset schizophrenia present with positive and negative symptoms that require treatment. During acute states of schizophrenia, neuroleptic treatment is absolutely necessary (Remschmidt et al., 1994). Unfortunately, there is a scarcity of data regarding psychopharmacologic treatment of early-onset schizophrenia. In a review of the literature eight studies (Englehardt, Polizos, Waizer, & Hoffman, 1973; Spencer & Campbell, 1994; Wolpert, Hagamen, & Merlis, 1967; Frazier et al., 1994; Spencer, Kafantaris, Padron-Gayol, Rosenberg, & Campbell, 1992; Faretra, Dooher, & Dowling, 1970; Le Vann, 1969; Mores et al., 1994) were located that examined the effectiveness of neuroleptics with children.

Medications tested for effectiveness in treating early-onset schizophrenia were haloperidol (Faretra et al., 1970; Le Vann, 1969; Spencer et al., 1992; Englehardt et al., 1973; Spencer & Campbell, 1994), fluphenazine (Faretra et al., 1970; Englehardt et al., 1973), clozapine (Mores et al., 1994; Frazier et al., 1994), thiothixene (Wolpert et al., 1967), and trifluoperazine (Wolpert et al., 1967).

Inpatient settings were used for all studies except one (Englehardt et al., 1973). Children age 12 and under were the subjects in all eight studies, with three studies also including adolescents in their samples (Wolpert et al., 1967; Frazier et al., 1994; Le Vann, 1969). Only one study (Le Vann, 1969) sample included children with other behavioral disturbances in addition to those with an early-onset schizophrenia diagnosis.

Haloperidol (Haldol) was found to have the same effectiveness in children as in the adult schizophrenia population (Faretra et al., 1970) and was superior to placebo (Spencer et al., 1992). Specific symptoms that decreased in children on haloperidol were hyperactivity, excitability, poor appetite (Le Vann, 1969), anxiety, provocativeness, and autism (Faretra et al., 1970). It was found to be quicker-acting than fluphenazine (Prolixin) (Faretra et al., 1970). One study indicated a reduction in assaultive behavior in children treated with haloperidol (Le Vann, 1969) while another study did not support this finding (Faretra et al., 1970).

A study comparing thiothixene (Navane) to trifluoperazine (Stelazine) found both medications to have the same degree of effectiveness (Wolpert et al., 1967). Fluphenazine had varying results, with one study indicating 50% of children as improved (Faretra et al., 1970) and another study finding 93% much or very much improved (Englehardt et al., 1973).

Clozapine (Clozaril), a dibenzodiazepine antipsychotic known to have minimal extrapyramidal side effects (Meltzer, 1992), has only recently become available for use with children. One double-blind, randomized open trial study (Frazier et al., 1994) of adolescents and one report of four case studies (Mozes et al., 1994) of children were found in the literature. Both reported substantial improvement of both negative and positive symptoms, with one study (Frazier et al., 1994) indicating clozapine was more effective than haloperidol. Of interest was that all participants in these studies had previous unsuccessful trials of neuroleptics with numerous side effects noted. Though clozapine is expensive and requires frequent blood monitoring and children may have slightly greater risks of developing agranulocytosis (Alvir, Lieberman,

Safferman, Schwimmer, & Schaaf, 1993), this particular medication holds much promise for the treatment of early-onset schizophrenia and warrants additional research on children with this disorder.

Of the eight pharmacological studies located, only two were double-blind and placebo-controlled with randomized assignment (Spencer et al., 1992; Spencer & Campbell, 1994), four were double-blind with randomized assignment but without placebo (Frazier et al., 1994; Englehardt et al., 1973; Faretra et al., 1970; Wolpert et al., 1967), one was open-controlled (Le Vann, 1969) with results not reported by diagnosis, and one presented case studies only (Mozes et al., 1994). Sample sizes for the most part were small. Certainly the amount of data is modest and much more research is required, but these studies do indicate that some children with early-onset schizophrenia do benefit from neuroleptics. Once stabilized on psychotropics, relapse prevention is possible with continued neuroleptic medication use (Remschmidt et al., 1994), which is particularly important during childhood when patients have not yet finished school.

Psychosocial Interventions

Surprisingly, no controlled studies of psychosocial treatments of early-onset schizophrenia could be identified in the *Psychological Abstracts* database. J.R. Asarnow's review (1994) of the literature on this topic found a similar lack of controlled research. However, because the criteria for this disorder are the same as that for adult-onset schizophrenia, and given the results from the pharmacological studies that suggest the efficacy of the medications used with adults in the treatment of children, the literature on psychosocial interventions with adult-onset schizophrenia was examined for possible relevant interventions. Two types of psychosocial interventions that are promising for intervention with children are social skills training and family intervention.

Social Skills Training

One psychotherapeutic approach to the treatment of early-onset schizophrenia is to address social skill deficits through cognitive-behavioral social skills training. Social skills training is a general therapy approach aimed at increasing performance competence in critical life situations and emphasizes the positive, educational aspects of treatment

(Goldsmith & McFall, 1975). It may be one of the more effective treatment procedures in working with a variety of child problems (LeCroy, 1994). A review of the literature does not indicate that any social skills training research has been conducted to date on children with early-onset schizophrenia. Social skills training would seem to be a relevant intervention when one considers that children with early-onset schizophrenia may not gain necessary social skills due to their illness. Social skills training may prove to be a universal psychotherapeutic approach for children with this diagnosis that should be incorporated in all treatment plans.

Five research studies were identified on social skills training with adults with schizophrenia (Bellack, Turner, Hersen, & Luber, 1984; Goldsmith & McFall, 1975; Wallace & Lieberman, 1985; Wallace, Leiberman, MacKain, Blackwell, & Eckman, 1992; Finch & Wallace, 1977). Because early-onset schizophrenia is diagnosed using the same criteria as adult-onset schizophrenia, what is learned from these studies is worth reviewing as it may be applicable to children, particularly since social skills interventions are so effective for other child problems.

Adult males with schizophrenia on an inpatient unit were the sample for four studies, with only one study utilizing both adult males and females in a day treatment setting (Bellack et al., 1984). Four study designs utilized a control group, with randomized assignment in the fifth, using an open trial design (Wallace et al., 1992). Sample sizes were adequate for all studies.

Results indicate that social skills training resulted in improvements on measures of loudness, fluency, affect, latency, eye contact, content, self reported assertiveness (Finch & Wallace, 1977), grooming and hygiene, self-management, coping, engaging in friendly conversation, participating in recreational activities (Wallace et al., 1992), better social adjustment (Goldsmith & McFall, 1975), and decreased relapses (Wallace & Lieberman, 1985; Goldsmith & McFall, 1975). One of these studies included a follow-up study which indicate improvement was maintained one year later (Wallace et al., 1992).

Utilizing a cognitive-behavioral approach through social skills training, basic skills can be addressed that improve social functioning and reduce relapse rates in adults. Schizophrenic patients can indeed acquire, generalize, and durably maintain social and conversational skills (Wallace & Lieberman, 1985). It is likely that children with early-onset schizophrenia particularly would benefit from improving these practical skills. Further research should investigate the impact of social skills training on children with early-onset schizophrenia.

Family Intervention

Environmental stress has been identified as an important factor in the relapse of schizophrenic adult patients receiving optimal drug therapy (Falloon et al., 1982). An association has been established between the level of expressed emotion (EE) (an environment stress) shown by relatives and the outcome of schizophrenia in patients living with them (Leff & Vaughn, 1981). The characteristics of expressed emotion are being overly critical, hostile, overinvolved and overidentified with the ill family member, intrusive, and highly expressive of emotions (Torrey, 1995). Behavioral family management is an intervention whereby significant family members (i.e., parent, spouse, sibling) participate in a time-limited psychoeducational and behavioral family intervention in an effort to reduce the expressed emotion of family members, consequently reducing the relapse rates of their family member with schizophrenia. The intervention enables family members to identify and reduce environmental stressors associated with relapse rates in schizophrenics. The intervention, which would appear to be potentially beneficial to families and their children diagnosed with early-onset schizophrenia, has three components: education regarding the etiology, symptoms, course, and management of schizophrenia; training in problem-solving skills; and conversational skills training. These are accomplished through an array of techniques, including lecture, role playing, rehearsal, and homework.

Clearly, the family must be included in the therapy of children with early-onset schizophrenia. Surprisingly, a review of the literature did not locate any intervention studies specific to families of children with early-onset schizophrenia. However, six intervention studies (Hogarty et al., 1986; Tarrier et al., 1988; Randolph et al., 1994; Falloon et al., 1982; Glick et al., 1985; Leff, Kuipers, Berkowitz, & Sturgeon, 1985) were identified that investigated the effectiveness of family interventions for adults diagnosed with schizophrenia. Again, because children and adults are both diagnosed utilizing the same criteria, these studies' findings may be transferable to families of children with early-onset schizophrenia.

All studies tested the effectiveness of family behavioral therapy in reducing relapse rates in schizophrenic adults. Samples in each study included families of both males and females, with the exception of one study including only families of males (Randolph et al., 1994). All schizophrenic patients were living in the community. All six study designs utilized a control group with randomized assignment. Sample sizes ranged from a rather small one of 36 patients (Falloon et al., 1982) to an adequate size of 103 (Hogarty et al., 1986). Age ranges of subjects varied, with the youngest sample including 15–35-year-olds (Glick et al., 1985) to the oldest reporting the sample ages to be 16–65.

Results indicate that family behavioral therapy was successful in reducing relapse rates in schizophrenic adults in all studies. Ranges of relapse rates were from a low of 6% compared to 44% in the control group (at nine-month follow-up) (Falloon et al., 1982) to a relapse rate of 33% compared to 59% in the control group (at two-year follow-up) (Tarrier et al., 1989). Falloon and colleagues suggest that optimal, long-term management of schizophrenia may need to combine low-dosage maintenance neuroleptic drug therapy with psychosocial interventions directed at modifying the impact of environmental sources of stress as addressed in family behavioral therapy (J.R. Asarnow et al., 1994). This treatment approach should be considered for early-onset schizophrenia, which is a particularly severe and chronic form of the disorder.

Though to date their work has not been conducted on early-onset schizophrenia, McFarlane, Link, Dushay, Marchal, and Crilly's (1995) approach to working with families may hold promise for this population also. Utilizing a Psychoeducational approach to working with families in multiple groups, they have reported success in reducing relapse rates for patients with schizophrenia. This approach emphasizes educating families about schizophrenia so they can participate in the recovery and rehabilitation process from an informed position. Delivered in a group modality, it establishes links between families in similar circumstances.

Rehabilitation

Approximately 40% of children and adolescents with schizophrenia need a rehabilitation program after the treatment of their acute episode (Remschmidt et al., 1994). These patients are not able to continue with school or professional training immediately after discharge from the hospital (Remschmidt et al., 1994). Unfortunately, a review of the literature did not reveal any intervention studies regarding rehabilitation for children with early-onset schizophrenia. Confirming this is J.R. Asarnow's (1994) review of the literature that found no controlled trials of psychosocial interventions for this population. It would appear that early-onset schizophrenia is in its early stages of diagnosis by recent *DSM* criteria, and that it is in its infant stages in regard to treatment. Limited thought has been given to rehabilitation of this population, or to management of symptoms. This is not surprising when one considers that rehabilitation in the adult schizophrenic population has only recently begun to be utilized (Anthony, Cohen, & Farkas, 1990). Adult rehabilitative interventions are characterized by a focus on vocational rehabilitation (Anthony et al., 1990) and, therefore, would have a very different focus from rehabilitative interventions for children.

Recommendations for Practice

While there has been little intervention research on early-onset schizophrenia in children, practitioners still must confront the task of choosing interventions until such time that empirical findings are forthcoming. The minimal research that has been conducted on psychotropic medication for this population suggests that some adult medications may be useful with children. In addition, the intervention research conducted with adults with schizophrenia, specifically social skills training and behavioral family therapy, may prove promising with this population, particularly given their effectiveness with other child problems. This strategy of utilizing related research to inform practice is consistent with developmental research, a model for developing new interventions for a given group of clients (Thomas, 1984).

Combining pharmacologic with psychosocial interventions (social skills training and behavioral family therapy) might yield special benefits for children with schizophrenia, especially in the context of intensive service settings, such as day and residential treatment. These specialized services play important roles in the habilitation and rehabilitation of this population in that they can provide intensive treatment within a structured, therapeutic environment. In this way, both settings can provide ongoing, consistent intervention with children and provide a context that is particularly rich for the implementation of skills-oriented interventions as well as the administration and monitoring of medication regimens. While social skills training can be easily delivered in treatment groups, individual modeling and reinforcement of skills can also be provided in a therapeutic milieu through the structuring of reward and privilege systems.

Given the state of knowledge base, intervention with this population will require close monitoring and evaluation of client progress in order to assess treatment responsiveness and make appropriate treatment decisions. Developmental research procedures (Thomas, 1984), including use of single-case evaluation, can again assist in identifying the need for modification of interventions to better suit this group of children. The ongoing contact with children in day and residential treatment settings makes these settings uniquely suited to begin exploring the applicability of these interventions for this population. For example, a day treatment program could easily start a pilot program to offer social skills training to a portion of the children in the program. A comparison in the outcomes for the pilot participants versus participants not receiving the pilot would then provide some indication of the usefulness of this intervention for this challenging population.

Recommendations for Research

A review of the literature indicates that there is a dearth of intervention studies specific to treating early-onset schizophrenia in children or rehabilitative measures for these children once they are stabilized. Schizophrenia, as defined in *DSM-III* (American Psychiatric Association, 1980) has been described in children as young as 5 years (Green, Padron-Gayol, Hardesty, & Bassiri, 1992). However, little systematic research has focused on early-onset schizophrenia. There is an urgent need for controlled studies focusing on the efficacy of pharmacological and psychosocial treatments for children with schizophrenia. Certainly a clear priority in the years ahead is to develop both treatment and rehabilitation interventions for children diagnosed with early-onset schizophrenia.

To date, there has been no systematic study of early-onset schizophrenia. Perhaps it has not been actively pursued because of the rarity of this disorder and its previous lack of diagnostic specificity. However, the recent refinement of diagnostic classification, which began with *DSM-III* (American Psychiatric Association, 1980) and culminated with *DSM-IV* (American Psychiatric Association, 1994), together with recent advances in genetic methodology, brain imaging, and psychopharmacology (Rapoport, 1994) make such study timely. Future work is needed to resolve questions regarding age-specific variation in the expression of the disorder, as well as the etiological and clinical significance of the atypical early onset (J.R. Asarnow, 1994).

Antipsychotic drug treatment in early-onset schizophrenia has been minimally studied and what data there are suggest that responsiveness is much the same as in the adult population. However, many neuroleptics have yet to be tested on children with schizophrenia. Those that have been tested need to be replicated. In addition to a medication's effectiveness, questions regarding risk factors, side effects, and long-term use of psychotropics specific to this population need to be examined.

Psychotherapy interventions need to be tested to determine which ones are of benefit to children with schizophrenia. Do these children benefit from different theoretical applications? Is cognitive-behavioral the best approach? Social skills training has been found to reduce relapse rates in adults with schizophrenia. Is the same true for children? Future research should examine if children with schizophrenia do benefit from social skills training and, if so, which specific skills are most helpful for them to acquire.

There is a need for additional research on early-onset schizophrenia that uses more precise and developmentally appropriate measures and examines the special needs of these children and their families. Future work is needed to clarify the effect of family stress on the course of early-onset schizophrenia. What are the special needs of families with a schizophrenic child? Does treating the family ultimately benefit the child? Family behavioral therapy has been found to reduce relapse rates in adult schizophrenics. Does this hold true for children whose parents participate in this therapy? Do parents themselves benefit from intervention?

It is also imperative to develop rehabilitative interventions for this population whose illness strikes at a time when education and skill building is at its prime. How best would these children be rehabilitated, once stabilized? What needs to be rehabilitated? How would rehabilitation be affected when a child relapses? Measures to assess deficits along with developmentally appropriate interventions need to be designed.

In looking toward future research recommendations it would be amiss not to suggest that preventive interventions also be examined, in hopes of decreasing the number of children annually diagnosed with this debilitating illness. Mental illness takes its emotional and financial toll on each child affected, the family, and society as a whole. Early-onset schizophrenia is a particularly debilitating illness with a severe and chronic course. Researchers must continue to work toward defining an empirically based treatment and rehabilitative protocol for this population.

References

Alvir, J. M., Lieberman, J. A., Safferman, A. Z., Schwimmer, J. L., & Schaaf, J. A. (1993). Clozapine-induced agranulocytosis: Incidence and risk factors in the United States. *New England Journal of Medicine, 329* (3), 162–167.

American Psychiatric Association. (1980). *Diagnostic and statistical manual of mental disorders* (3rd ed.). Washington, DC: Author.

American Psychiatric Association. (1994). *Diagnostic and statistical manual of mental disorders* (4th ed.). Washington, DC: Author.

Anthony, W., Cohen, M., & Farkas, M. (1990). *Psychiatric rehabilitation.* Boston: Boston University.

Asarnow, J. R. (1994). Annotation: Childhood-onset schizophrenia. *Journal of Child Psychology and Psychiatry, 35* (8), 1345–1371.

Asarnow, J. R., Tompson, M. C., & Goldstein, M. J. (1994). Childhood-onset schizophrenia: A follow-up study. *Schizophrenia Bulletin, 20* (4), 599–617.

Asarnow, R. F., & Asarnow, J. R. (1994). Childhood-onset schizophrenia: Editors' introduction. *Schizophrenia Bulletin, 20* (4), 591–597.

Bellack, A. S., Turner, S. M., Hersen, M., & Luber, R. F. (1984). An examination of the efficacy of social skills training for chronic schizophrenic patients. *Hospital and Community Psychiatry, 35* (10), 1023–1028.

Cantor, S. (1988). *Childhood schizophrenia.* New York: Guilford Press.

Dulmus, C. N., & Wodarski, J. S. (1996). Assessment and effective treatment of childhood psychopathology: Responsibilities and implications for practice. *Journal of Child and Adolescent Group Therapy, 6* (2), 75–99.

Eggers, C. (1989) Schizoaffective disorders in childhood: A follow-up study. *Journal of Autism and Developmental Disorders, 19,* 327–342.

Englehardt, D. M., Polizos, P., Waizer, J., & Hoffman, S. P. (1973). A double-blind comparison of fluphenazine and haloperidol in outpatient schizophrenic children. *Journal of Autism and Childhood Schizophrenia, 3* (2), 128–137.

Falloon, I. R., Boyd, J. L., McGill, C. W., Razani, J., Moss, H. B., & Gilderman, A. M. (1982). Family management in the prevention of exacerbations of schizophrenia: A controlled study. *New England Journal of Medicine, 306* (24), 1437–1440.

Faretra, G., Dooher, L., & Dowling, J. (1970). Comparison of haloperidol and fluphenazine in disturbed children. *American Journal of Psychiatry, 126* (11), 146–149.

Finch, B. E., & Wallace, C. J. (1977). Successful interpersonal skills training with schizophrenic inpatients. *Journal of Consulting and Clinical Psychology, 45* (5), 885–890.

Frazier, J. A., Gordon, C. T., McKenna, K., Lenane, M. C., Jih, D., & Rapoport, J. L. (1994). An open trial of clozapine in 11 adolescents with childhood-onset schizophrenia. *Journal of the American Academy of Child and Adolescent Psychiatry, 33* (5), 658–663.

Glick, I. D., Clarkin, J. F., Spencer, J. H., Haas, G. L., Lewis, A. B., Peyser, J., DeMane, N., Good-Ellis, M., Harris, E., & Lestelle, V. (1985). A controlled evaluation of inpatient family intervention. *Archives of General Psychiatry, 42,* 882–886.

Goldsmith, J. B., & McFall, R. M. (1975). Development and evaluation of an interpersonal skill-training program for psychiatric inpatients. *Journal of Abnormal Psychology, 84* (1), 51–58.

Gordon, C. T., Frazier, K. M., Giedd, A. Z., Zahn, D. H., Hong, W., Kaysen, D., Albus, K. E., & Rapoport, J. L. (1994). Childhood-onset · schizophrenia: An NIMH study in progress. *Schizophrenia Bulletin, 20* (4), 697–712.

Green, W., Padron-Gauol, M., Hardesty, A., & Bassiri, M. (1992). Schizophrenia with childhood onset: A phenomenological study of 38 cases. *Journal of the American Academy of Child and Adolescent Psychiatry, 5,* 968–976.

Hogarty, G. E., Anderson, C. M., Reiss, D. J., Kornblith, S. J., Greenwald, D. P., Javna, C. D., & Madonia, M. J. (1986). Family psychoeducation, social skills training, and maintenance chemotherapy in the aftercare of schizophrenia. *Archives of General Psychiatry, 43,* 633–642.

Kallman, F. J., & Roth, B. (1956). Genetic aspects of preadolescent schizophrenia. *American Journal of Psychiatry, 112,* 599–606.

Karno, M., & Norquist, G. S. (1989). Schizophrenia: Epidemiology. In: Kaplan, H. I., & Sadock, B. J., eds. *Comprehensive textbook of psychiatry V.* Vol. 1. Baltimore, MD: Williams & Wilkins.

LeCroy, C. (1994). *Handbook of child and adolescent treatment manuals.* New York: Lexington.

Leff, J., Kuipers, L., Berkowitz, R., & Sturgeon, D. (1985). A controlled trial of social interventions in the families of schizophrenia patients: Two year follow-up. *British Journal of Psychiatry, 146,* 594–600.

LeVann, L. J. (1969). Haloperidol in the treatment of behavioral disorders in children and adolescents. *Canadian Psychiatric Association Journal, 14,* 217–220.

Maxmen, J. S., & Ward, N. G. (1995). *Essential psychopathology and its treatment.* New York: Norton.

McFarlane, W. R., Link, B., Dushay, R., Marchal, J., & Crilly, J. (1995). Psychoeducational multiple family groups: Four-year relapse outcome in schizophrenia. *Family Process, 34,* 127–144.

Meltzer, H. Y. (1992). The importance of outcome with clozapine. *British Journal of Psychiatry, 160* (17), 46–53.

Mozes, T., Toren, P., Chernauzan, N., Mesterm, R., Yoran-Hegesh, R., Blumensohn, R., & Weizman, A. (1994). Clozapine treatment in very early onset schizophrenia. *Journal of the American Academy of Child and Adolescent Psychiatry, 33* (1), 65–70.

Mueser, K. T., & Gungerich, S. (1994). *Coping with schizophrenia.* Oakland, CA: New Harbinger.

National Institute of Mental Health. (1990). *Research on children and adolescents with mental, behavioral and developmental disorder.* Rockville, MD: National Institute of Mental Health.

Office of Technology Assessment, U.S. Congress. (1986). *Children's mental health: Problems and services.* Washington, DC: U.S. Government Printing Office.

Randolph, E. T., Eth, S., Glynn, S. M., Paz, G. G., Leong, G. B., Shaner, A. L., Strachan, A., Van Vort, W., Escobar, J. I., & Lieberman, R. P. (1994). Behavioral family management in schizophrenia: Outcome of a clinic-based intervention. *British Journal of Psychiatry, 164,* 501–506.

Remschmidt, H., Schulz, E., Martin, M., Warnke, A., & Trott, G. (1994). Childhood-onset schizophrenia: History of the concept and recent studies. *Schizophrenia Bulletin, 20* (4), 727–745.

Russell, A. T. (1994). The clinical presentation of childhood-onset schizophrenia. *Schizophrenia Bulletin, 22* (4), 631–646.

Russell, A. T., Bott, L., & Sammons, C. (1989). The phenomenology of schizophrenia occurring in childhood. *Journal of the American Academy of Child and Adolescent Psychiatry, 28,* 399–407.

Spencer, E. K., & Campbell, M. (1994). Children with schizophrenia: Diagnosis, pheno-menology, and pharmacotherapy. *Schizophrenia Bulletin, 20* (4), 713–725.

Spencer, E. K., Kafantaris, V., Padron-Gayol, M. V., Rosenberg, C. R., & Campbell, M. (1992). Haloperidol in schizophrenic children: Early findings from a study in progress. *Psychopharmacology Bulletin, 28* (2), 183–186.

Tarrier, N., Barrowclough, C., Vaughn, C., Bamrah, J. S., Porceddu, K., Watts, S., & Freeman, H. (1989). Community management of schizophrenia: A two-year follow-up of a behavioral intervention with families. *British Journal of Psychiatry, 154,* 635–628.

Thomas, E. J. (1984). *Designing interventions for the helping professions.* Beverly Hills, CA: Sage.

Torrey, E. F. (1995). *Surviving schizophrenia: A manual for families, consumers and providers.* New York: HarperCollins.

Wallace, C. J., & Lieberman, R. P. (1985). Social skills training for patients with schizophrenia: A controlled clinical trial. *Psychiatry Research, 15,* 239–247.

Wallace, C. J., Lieberman, R. P., MacKain, S. J., Blackwell, G., & Eckman, T. A. (1992). Effectiveness and replicability of modules for teaching social and instrumental skills to the severely mentally ill.. *American Journal of Psychiatry, 149* (5), 654–658.

Wolpert, A., Hagamen, M. B., & Merlis, S. (1967). A comparative study of thiothixene and trifluoperazine in childhood schizophrenia. *Current Therapeutic Research Press, 9* (9), 482–485.

B. Problems of a Psychosocial Nature

BONNIE BRANDL
DEBORAH L. HORAN

29

Domestic Violence in Later Life: An Overview for Health Care Providers

Elder abuse is a growing but often hidden problem in the United States. It is estimated that only one in five cases of elder abuse is reported. During the 10-year period between 1986 and 1996, reported cases of domestic elder abuse increased 150% with more than 450,000 older individuals abused or neglected in domestic settings annually. About 90% of elder abuse cases are perpetrated by people known to the victim. Two-thirds of these known perpetrators were adult children or spouses. This form of abuse is often referred to as domestic elder abuse or family violence in later life (National Center on Elder Abuse 1998a).

As of 1998 there were more than 45 million individuals 60 years of age or older (U.S. Bureau of the Census 1998). During the next several decades, the United States will witness a dramatic increase both in the number of elderly persons and in the proportion of elderly persons in the general population (Siegel 1996). Currently, persons age 65 or older constitute 12.6% of the population; in 2040, one in five Americans or 20.5% of the population will be age 65 or older (Administration on Aging 2000b), with more females than males.

Since elderly victims regularly use the health care system and older battered women may seek medical treatment for physical injuries that occurred during an assault, for psychosomatic complaints such as nervousness, gastrointestinal problems, or headaches, or for depression, anxiety, and symptoms of posttraumatic stress disorder (PTSD), health care providers are in a unique position to identify elder domestic abuse, intervene, and pro-

vide appropriate referrals. Early identification and intervention can improve the quality of life for older victims and may reduce their reliance on health care services. Addressing the root of the patient's problem, rather than solely treating the presenting symptoms, can save health care providers time and health care costs. This article will identify common presentations of abuse in later life and provide guidance on appropriate intervention.

Definitions and Dynamics of Elder Abuse and Domestic Violence in Later Life

State law defines the elderly and the recognized forms of elder abuse. Most states define elderly as age 60 or 65 and older, but some states include elder abuse in laws that address abuse against vulnerable adults, who are generally defined as persons with physical and/or cognitive difficulties that limit their ability to protect themselves (Administration on Aging 2000). Legally, elder abuse generally includes physical and sexual abuse, financial exploitation, neglect, and self-neglect. (We do not consider self-neglect here.) These forms of abuse are often accompanied by emotional abuse (e.g., threats, coercion, and isolation). Table 29.1 contains commonly used definitions of the types of elder abuse and the presenting signs and symptoms.

Why do spouses and other family members hurt older women? The stress of caregiving, the depen-

Table 29.1 Types and Presentations of Elder Abuse

Type of Abuse	Presentations (includes, but are not limited to, the following)
Physical abuse—the infliction of physical pain or bodily harm	• Fractures • Welts • Bite marks • Burns (unusual location, type, or shape similar to an object such as an iron or cigarette burn) • Bruises (presence of old and new, shape similar to an object like a belt or fingers, bilateral on upper arms from holding or shaking, clustered on trunk from repeated shaking)
Sexual abuse—any form of sexual contact or exposure without consent or when the victim is incapable of giving consent (e.g., rape, fondling, forcing victim to watch pornography or participate in unwanted sexual acts)	• Difficulty in walking or sitting • Pain, itching, bruising, or bleeding in genital area • Unexplained veneral disease or genital infections
Financial exploitation—illegal or improper exploitation of funds or other assets (e.g., stealing money or property, committing fraud through undue influence)	• Inaccurate, confused, or no knowledge of finances • Unexplained or sudden inability or unwillingness to pay bills, purchase food or personal care items • Unprecedented transfer of assets from an older person to other(s) • Extraordinary interest by family member in older person's assets
Neglect—the refusal or failure to fulfill caregiving obligations, such as abandonment or isolation; denial of food, shelter, clothing, medical assistance, or personal needs; or the withholding of necessary medication or assistive devices (e.g., hearing aids, glasses, false teeth)	• Dehydration • Malnutrition • Hyper/hypothermia • Excessive dirt or odor • Inadequate or inappropriate clothing • Absence of eyeglasses, hearing aids, dentures, or prostheses • Unexpected or unexplained deterioration of health • Decubitus ulcers • Signs of excess drugging, lack of medication, or other misuse (e.g., decreased alertness, responsiveness, and orientation)

dency of the victim, the psychopathology of the abuse, or learned behavior have all been proposed as responses to this query (Wolf 2000). Early interventions, such as adult protective services (APS), were created based on the belief that caregiver stress was the primary cause of elder abuse. The services were designed to relieve stress and to improve relationships between the elder and family members or caregivers. But, according to Wolf, while stress may be a contributing factor, research does not support that stress is the primary cause of elder abuse. Rather, family violence in later life often involves

an abuser using a regular pattern of coercive acts to control, dominate, and/or punish the victim. These dynamics are similar to the experiences of younger battered women (Pillemer & Finkelhor 1988; Podnieks 1992; Wolf 1998).

When abusers believe they are entitled to "run the show," they will use any means necessary to meet their needs. An adult son may order his mother to do the laundry, cook his meals, and turn over her Social Security check. If she doesn't, he may threaten her or hit her. An elderly man may have been battering his wife for 50 or 60 years to "keep her in line." Abusers feel their actions are justified and that they have a right to control their victim, often because of stereotypical views about women or older people. Perpetrators often believe they deserve unquestioned obedience from the victim (Schechter 1987).

Understanding that domestic abuse in later life is most likely an issue of power and control is critical for health care providers. Professionals may offer vastly different remedies depending on how the problem is perceived and defined. Unfortunately, too often well-meaning professionals assume that elder abuse is due to caregiver stress and make several crucial errors that further isolate and endanger the victim. Some health care providers may believe the abuse is caused because the person is difficult to care for. They may suggest that the victim try harder to do more for herself (whether this is possible or not), actions that blame the victim for the abuse and supports the abuser's contention that if the victim tried harder, he would not have to hit her.

Health care providers who see the victim as frail, old, and dependent on the abuser (even if this is not true) may make decisions for the victim rather than use an empowerment strategy to assist the victim in helping herself. Dangerous practices can include believing the abuser's account that the victim is not competent or demented without doing an assessment; telling the victim what to do; or medicating the victim rather than identifying the abuse.

When abuse is viewed as caregiver stress and only social service agencies are contacted, there may be failure to understand that domestic violence at any stage of life can be a criminal act. Some health care providers do not consider discussing legal remedies with older patients, assuming this to be a private family matter. However, many older women do take advantage of restraining/protective orders and other legal remedies when these options are made available to them. To provide safety and support to elderly victims, service models and legal remedies long established for younger victims of domestic abuse should be employed (Pillemer & Finkelhor 1989; Podnieks 1991; Vinton 1991).

Identification through Universal Screening

In addition to clinical presentations previously identified, there are a number of behavioral indicators that should alert the health care provider to the possibility of abuse. Some of the common behaviors exhibited by victims as well as by abusers can be found in Table 29.2. While it is important to recognize physical and behavioral red flags for domestic abuse in later life, abused woman may present with few of these symptoms. To increase the likelihood of identification, health care providers should adopt universal screening for every female patient and every person who is over age 60 and/or has a disability. When possible, questions should be asked in private, and not in the presence of an accompanying family member. Patients should be advised that a positive response might prompt mandatory reporting to law enforcement and/or social services. (At the time of publication, all but six states, Colorado, New Jer-

Table 29.2 Behavioral Indicators

Patient	Abuser
• Repeated "accidents" • Frequent vague or somatic complaints • Delayed presentations • Exhibits anxiety, depression, suicidal ideation • Expresses a sense of isolation—no access to money, friends, family, job, transportation, church, etc. • Refers to a family member's "anger" or "temper" or consistently defers to caregiver • Alcohol or drug abuse • Unable to follow through with medical care • Unable to follow through with medical care due to abuser's control or missed appointments • Presents as a "difficult" patient	• Verbally abusive or overly attentive or charming to the patient or health care staff • Attempts to convince health care workers that the patient is incompetent or insane • Controls most of patient's daily activities • Overly protective or controlling of family member (e.g., refuses to leave the room during exam or treatment)

sey, New York, North Dakota, South Dakota, and Wisconsin, have mandatory elder abuse reporting laws. State adult protective services agencies can provide information about requirements for reporting elder abuse and/or domestic violence.) The patient should have an opportunity to talk freely and confidentially without fear of retaliation. If necessary, a reliable interpreter who is not a family member should be available for non-English-speaking or hearing impaired patients.

Screening should include a review of medical indicators and questions about family abuse. Indirect questions about the patient's life should be asked first and lead up to direct questions about specific acts. Evidence shows that victims of family violence generally respond positively to sensitive questioning from concerned professionals (Warshaw 1998). Providers should identify any injuries and ask about how they occurred. Suggested questions include the following:

- Do you live alone?
- Who does your cooking?
- Who controls your finances?
- How often do you go out with friends?
- Are you afraid of anyone?
- Does anyone slap you? Pull your hair? Touch you in a rough way? Hit you?
- Does anyone threaten to do any of these things?
- Does anyone force you to do sexual acts you do not want to do?

Providers should identify any injuries and ask about how they occurred. Explanations of injuries that are inconsistent with findings or multiple injuries in various stages of healing should be discussed.

An older person may deny that abuse is occurring of refuse to talk about the possibility. There are a variety of reasons for nondisclosure. Language and cultural barriers may prevent the patient from confiding in her health care provider. Immigrant women may fear deportation. Lesbians may fear repercussions from friends, family members, or the community if they have not disclosed their relationship. The victim may believe she cannot escape the abuse and will be in greater danger if she reveals what is happening to her. Her past attempts to get help may have been futile and/or resulted in an escalation of the violence. Victims stay out of fear of being alone, real or perceived financial dependency, health concerns, generational ties, or spiritual and cultural values. Many elderly victims fear retaliation, and, in fact, research reveals that victims are often at greatest risk of being seriously harmed or killed when

they seek help or attempt to leave the abusive relationship (Bachman & Saltzman 1995). Nevertheless, it is important to remember that screening in and of itself is a powerful intervention. It is helpful to leave open the possibility of future discussions. Often victims remember kind, supportive words of encouragement and referrals, even if they do not take action immediately.

Competency

Providers who are concerned that they are working with a patient who is not competent to make decisions about safety should follow their institution's medical protocol to determine competency. If a patient is assessed and determined to be incompetent, contact the county APS agency for consultation on the remedies (including legal options) and services available.

Competency should be tested only if there is evidence that the person has cognitive limitations. Keep in mind that many of the symptoms of dementia, depression, and delirium such as poor judgment, confusion, lethargy, and inability to communicate clearly are also common and normal responses to victimization. The mental condition of many patients improves significantly within a few days when they feel safe and have had food, proper doses of medication, and sleep. Discomfort with a victim's choices is not sufficient reason to declare someone incompetent.

Health Care Provider Response

Busy health care providers often feel they do not have time to adequately respond to the needs of victims of family violence. However, if simple protocols are established, physicians can easily incorporate screening into the health care visit and direct the patient's to other staff members if abuse is disclosed. For example, other professionals, such as a domestic violence advocate or social worker, can be contacted to work directly with victims to ensure safety and offer ongoing support.

However, health care providers have an important role, whether they see a patient only once or have an ongoing relationship with her. Deciding what to do and implementing a plan of action can be a long, complex process for many older women. Health care providers can offer supportive messages, document and photograph, ensure confidentiality, plan for safety, provide referrals, and honor her decisions.

Offer Supportive Messages

Batterers often use a variety of tactics intended to make victims feel unsure of themselves. For example, some batterers may hide things, lie, or use medications inappropriately so that victims will appear confused. Often abusers tell victims of abuse repeatedly that they are to blame for the abuse. Health care providers can provide support and assurance to victims by listening empathetically to their stories and offering supportive statements such as "You are not responsible for the violence and abuse. The abuser's actions are wrong and not your fault," or "I understand how hard this must be for you to talk about. I believe you."

Many victims feel they are the only ones experiencing abuse. Education about the frequency of domestic violence and elder abuse may be especially helpful. Let the victim know that abuse rarely ends on its own; it may continue or escalate without some type of outside intervention. Assure the patient that her reactions are common for victims of abuse and praise her personal courage and strength. Validate and support the choices the victim makes to stay safe and alive.

People who live with domestic abuse often want the abuse to end but do not necessarily want to end the relationship. Expressing concerns about the patient's health and the extent of her injuries and/or emotional trauma may be helpful. Information from professionals that confirms a patient's fear, reassures her that the abuse is not her fault, and reinforces that the abuse may escalate can help the patient more realistically explore options.

Document and Photograph Injuries

Documentation is critical for victims of family abuse who may later go to court. After obtaining consent, document injuries by taking photographs or using a body map. The medical record should include verbatim accounts from the patient about who caused the injury and how the injury occurred and note that the injuries are consistent with the patient's explanation of the cause. Write complete notes about what was said, observed, and done. Include direct quotes of what the patient said happened and/or statements made by the suspected abuser. Avoid language such as "alleges," which suggests the information given is questionable. Avoid judgment statements about the victim such as "She was hysterical and overreacting." Finally, document what interventions were offered (e.g., police, social services, safety planning) and the outcomes (e.g., accepted brochures, consulted with a social worker). If abuse is reported to APS or law enforcement, document the date and time of the call.

Ensure Confidentiality

Health care providers are responsible for ensuring confidentiality so that they do not put patients at risk. Family abuse screening should be done with only the patient and health care provider present, unless an advocate or interpreter is requested. The patient's chart should be placed where the abuser and other unauthorized persons cannot have access to it. Case discussions should be held in private. Other patients and health care providers uninvolved in the case should not be included or able to overhear the discussion. Documentation should go in the patient's chart, not on other family member records. Phone calls or mail should not be directed to the patient's home to discuss abuse without permission from the patient. When filing sensitive information, consider who may have access to files and computer records, particularly if a victim's family member or friend works in a medical setting.

Plan for Safety

Safety planning is an ongoing process. Ideally, the health care provider and victim discuss safety options for the victim's particular set of circumstances. Safety planning tools often are available from local or statewide domestic abuse programs and from a variety of national health care organizations. Questions may include the following:

- What have you done to keep safe in the past?
- If the violence escalates, do you have a place to go?
- Can you call the police or a neighbor, etc.?
- If you need to leave the abuser, where can you go?
- What do you need to bring?
- If you decide to return, how can you plan for your safety and get support?

Sometimes safety planning requires creative thinking. For example, health care providers may write the crisis line telephone number on medical papers such as prescriptions. The telephone number can be disguised as administrative codes so that the victim will be able to keep the number handy without raising abuser suspicion. Another suggestion is to use a personal emergency system for safety. In some communities, a personal emergency system such as a lifeline (necklace with a button to contact emergency medical personnel) has been used for both medical emergencies and domestic abuse cases. The lifeline staff calls the subscriber's home when the button is depressed. If the elderly individual does not return the call or if the emergency personnel are prevented from talking directly with the woman, the police are notified to investigate.

Refer to Available Services

The services offered to a victim of abuse will depend on the wishes and needs of the patient. Many victims of abuse benefit from free domestic abuse services, including emergency shelter (if they choose to leave the abuser), support groups, peer counseling, and crisis lines. A support group may be extremely helpful, especially a group with people who are the same age as the victim. Older abused women's support groups exist in many communities (Seaver 1996).

Some victims will use the legal system to have the abuser arrested, secure a restraining order or divorce, or establish a financial guardian (conservatorship). Other victims may benefit from services offered by an aging network such as transportation, peer support, supportive home care, home-delivered meals, or financial counseling.

Often APS is involved in elder abuse cases. APS or their equivalents are social service agencies mandated to investigate cases of elder abuse or abuse of a vulnerable adult. Calls come to a central agency, which assigns a trained worker to investigate the allegations of abuse and/or neglect. State statutes vary on how immediately a worker must respond. In some states, alleged victims may refuse the investigation. In other states, an investigation is completed, but competent patients have the right to reject services.

Honor Her Decisions

The decision to end a relationship with a new spouse/partner, a long-term spouse/partner, or an adult child or grandchild can be painful. Few victims leave the first time they reach out for help. While it may be frustrating to the health care provider, some victims of family violence stay with abusive family members. Others may leave only to return home after a few days or months. Change of this magnitude often comes slowly and over time,

especially for the elderly, who by virtue of aging may already be experiencing many losses, such as health and social support (Seaver 1996). Communicating support for the patient and the patient's health, no matter what decision is made, plays an important part in the victim's finding strength to make difficult choices.

Dangerous Interventions

The following actions may place an abused older person at increased risk. Health care professionals should exercise caution before doing any of the following:

Prescribing antidepressants or sedatives without a thorough abuse assessment. Older people and victims of family violence frequently are offered medications rather than support and assistance to live free from violence. Prescribed medications may lessen a person's ability to respond effectively in a crisis. Medications can also send a message to the patient that "you are the problem" or mimic messages from the batterer that "you are crazy."

Recommending couples or family counseling without treatment for the batterer. Couples and family counseling is contraindicated unless the abuser has successfully completed a batterer's treatment program, fully accepts responsibility for the abuse, and has stopped the violence (Golden & Frank, 1994; Schechter 1987).

Blaming the victim. Professionals often wonder why victims stay with their abuser. They may offer remedies that suggest that if the patient would try a little harder, the abuse would not occur. Without an understanding of the dynamics of family abuse, health care providers may be frustrated by patients who use the health care system regularly without leaving the abusive relationship (Worcester 1992). Rather than focus on the patient's choices, it is important to remember that abusers are solely responsible for their behavior and must be held accountable for their actions.

Colluding with the batterer. It is important for health providers to differentiate between temporary caregiver stress and domestic violence. If it is assumed the abuse is caused by temporary loss of control rather than imposition of control over another person, messages to the abuser may inadvertently justify his behavior. Expressing concerns about how difficult it is to be providing care to an elder may justify or reinforce the abuser's belief that it is acceptable to use whatever means necessary to get his way. Blaming alcohol/drug use, stress, anger, or mental illness for the abuse is ill-advised. Abusers must be held accountable for their actions before they will change their behavior (WCADV 1999).

Minimizing the potential danger to the victim or health care provider when help is offered. Arrange for appropriate security for the victim, yourself, and staff when working with a potentially lethal batterer (e.g., he has made homicidal/suicidal threats or plans, owns weapons). When the victim is in danger, the provider and staff may be as well.

Health Care System Response

Health care providers have an obvious stake in joining the community's efforts to end family violence. To eliminate domestic violence in later life, systemic change is crucial. Health care providers can join other professionals to create services and challenge societal beliefs and norms that perpetuate a culture where family abuse continues to grow. Several ways health care providers can participate in systemic change are listed below.

- Work with domestic violence specialists to establish an older women's support group at local hospitals or clinics.
- Help educate other health care professionals and the public (including the media) on elder abuse and domestic violence.
- Join a multidisciplinary team or a coordinated community response effort.
- Become a board member or fundraiser for a local domestic abuse program, aging agency, or statewide coalition against domestic violence.
- Participate in local or statewide efforts to improve options for battered women and elder abuse victims such as public awareness campaigns or lobbying.
- Join the efforts of health care organizations working to eliminate family violence.

Conclusion

Older women suffer from abuse and neglect primarily at the hands of family members. Health care providers can affect the quality of life and improve the health of older female patients through recognizing domestic abuse. Providers can accomplish this through universal screening of all patients, documentation, and referrals that include safety planning and reporting abuse to authorities. Joining systemic efforts to prevent family violence also is consistent with the provision of high-quality health care.

References

Administration on Aging. (1996) Aging into the 21st Century. Washington, DC. U.S. Department of Health and Human Services.

Administration on Aging. (2000a) Fact Sheet: Elder Abuse Prevention. Washington, DC. U.S. Department of Health and Human Services.

Administration on Aging. (2000b) Fact Sheet: The Growth of America's Older Population. Washington, DC. U.S. Department of Health and Human Services.

Brandl, B., & Raymond, J. (1997) Unrecognized Elder Abuse Victims: Older Abused Women. *Journal of Case Management* 6(2):62–68.

Bachman, R., & Saltzman, L. (1995) Violence against Women: Estimates from the Redesigned Survey. Washington, DC, Bureau of Justice Statistics.

Golden, G., & Frank, P. (1994) When 50-50 Isn't Fair: The Case against Couple Counseling in Domestic Abuse. *Social Work* 39(6):636–7.

National Center on Elder Abuse. (1998a) National Elder Abuse Incidence Study. Washington, DC. American Public Human Services Association.

National Center on Elder Abuse. (1998b) Fact Sheet: Violence against Women Is an Older Women's Issue. Washington, DC. National Center on Elder Abuse.

Pillemer, K., & Finkelhor, D. (1988) The Prevalence of Elder Abuse: A Random Sample Survey. *Gerontologist* 28, 51–7.

Pillemer, K., & Finkelhor, D. (1989) Causes of Elder Abuse: Caregiver Stress versus Problem Relatives. *American Journal of Orthopsychiatry* 59(2):179–87.

Podnieks, E. (1992) National Survey on Abuse of the Elderly in Canada. *Journal of Elder Abuse & Neglect* 4:5–8.

Seaver, C. (1996) Muted Lives: Older Battered Women. *Journal of Elder Abuse & Neglect* 8:10.

Schechter, S. (1987) Guidelines for Mental Health Workers. Denver, CO. National Coalition against Domestic Violence.

Siegel, J. (1996) Aging into the 21st Century. National Aging Information Center and the US Administration on Aging. Washington, DC. U.S. Department of Health and Human Services.

Tjaden, P., & Thoennes, N. (1998) Prevalence, Incidence, and Consequences of Violence against Women. Findings from the National Violence against Women Survey. Research in Brief. Washington, DC. U.S. Department of Justice, Office of Justice Programs, NCJ 172837.

U.S. Bureau of the Census. (1998) Population Estimates Program. Population Division, U.S. Bureau of the Census. Washington, DC.

Vinton, L. (1991) Abused Older Women: Battered Woman or Abused Elders. *Journal of Women & Aging* 3:5–19.

Warshaw, C. (1998) Identification, Assessment and Intervention with Victims of Domestic Violence. In: Warshaw C., Ganley, A. L. Improving the Health Care Response to Domestic Violence: A Resource Manual for Health Care Providers (pp. 49–86). San Francisco. Family Violence Prevention Fund.

Wisconsin Coalition against Domestic Violence. (1999) *Elder Abuse, Neglect and Family Violence: A Guide for Health Care Professionals.* National Clearinghouse on Domestic Violence in Later Life. Madison, WI.

Wolf, R. (1998) Studies Belie Caregiver Stress as Key to Elder Mistreatment. *Aging Today* November–December.

Wolf, R. (2000) Introduction: The Nature and Scope of Elder Abuse. *Generations* 24(2).

Worcester, N. (1992) The Role of Health Care Workers in Responding to Battered Women. *Wisconsin Medical Journal* 91(6):682–6.

Deborah Fisk
Michael Rowe
Dori Laub
Lisa Calvocoressi
Kathleen DeMino

30

Homeless Persons with Mental Illness and Their Families: Emerging Issues from Clinical Work

Our purpose in this brief clinical study is to explore several family-related issues that emerged in our early work with homeless persons with mental illness in a comparison site for the federally funded Access to Community Care and Effective Services and Support (ACCESS) homeless outreach initiative. The emergence of these issues surprised us, because we expected that homeless persons with mental illness would, for the most part, be isolated from and have no connection to their families. We draw from our experiences to suggest that clinicians and case managers offer a family-focused approach to clinical treatment of this population. A family-focused clinical treatment approach may offer clinicians and case managers relevant information to engage clients in clinical and rehabilitative services and to help clients successfully transition from homelessness to independent living.

There has been relatively little clinical and research attention devoted to the relationship between homeless persons and their families. This is the case despite early research on skid row men that linked disaffiliation from family and social support networks to an increased risk for homelessness (Bahr, 1973). There was a peak of interest in these family relationships after a 1989 study of General Assistance City Welfare recipients found that families can help to prevent homelessness by providing family members with financial and emotional supports (Rossi, 1989); however, Rossi did note that there were limits to the amount of support that families could provide their members when they were poor, or when family members had disabling conditions such as mental illness. Further research revealed that homeless persons have reduced family

and social support when compared with the general population (Cohen & Sokolovsky, 1989; Bassuk & Rosenburg, 1988); that homeless persons with mental illness have reduced family and social support when compared to homeless persons without mental illness (Rosnow, Shaw, & Concord, 1985; Farr, Koegel, & Burnam, 1986; Tessler & Dennis, 1989; Toomey, First, Rife, & Belcher, 1989); and that the more severe the mental illness, the less families are able to provide support to these members (Tessler, Gamache, Rossi, Lehman, & Goldman, 1992). Clinical studies have examined how homeless persons experience their families (Reilly, 1993), the perception that homeless women have of their families of origin (Anderson, 1996), and how homeless mothers with children experience homelessness (Baumann, 1994). Other than one clinical study that emphasizes the importance of understanding the meaning of "home" to homeless persons with mental illness (Koegel, 1992), however, the relationship between homeless persons with mental illness and their families has not been explored in the clinical literature.

The lack of research about the relationship between homeless persons with mental illness and their families may be partially explained by the fact that these individuals have reduced contact with their families. As such, researchers and clinicians may not view these family relationships as a fruitful area for study or clinical work. However, from a family-systems perspective, the behavior of each family member affects all others, regardless of whether there is current actual contact among family members (Rhodes, 1986). It is from this perspective that we suggest that the relationship between homeless persons with mental illness and their families is important and deserves focused clinical attention.

It is not our intention in this article to suggest that there is a simple and direct causal relationship between homelessness among persons with mental illness and family problems or issues. The problem of homelessness among mentally ill persons results from a complex interaction between structural and personal factors. Structural factors include the erosion of affordable housing and the rise in unemployment and poverty (Burt, 1992; Koegel, Burnam, & Baumohl, 1996); reduced finances of mentally ill persons (Burt & Pittman, 1985); de-institutionalization policies (Bassuk & Lamb, 1986); and inadequate and fragmented community mental health service systems (Bassuk & Lamb, 1986). Personal factors include various physical and mental disabilities, substance abuse, and family issues (Koegel et al., 1996). Homeless persons with mental illness have often turned to their families for financial and emotional support prior to becoming homeless, but there are limits to the supports that families can offer to their vulnerable members (Rossi, 1989).

As the numbers of homeless persons and homeless persons with mental illness reached alarming heights in the mid- to late 1980s, the federal government convened the Federal Task Force on Homelessness and Mental Illness to develop a national agenda to end homelessness among persons with mental illness. The task force recommended a national demonstration project that would identify innovative approaches to integrated services and systems of care. The national ACCESS initiative was a five-year, 18-site research demonstration project funded by the Center for Mental Health Services (CMHS). In each of nine states, an experimental site provided both enhanced services and leadership to develop an integrated system of care, while a comparison site offered enhanced services alone (Randolph, 1995). Two key goals of the ACCESS demonstration project were to identify promising approaches to systems integration to evaluate their effectiveness in providing clinical and rehabilitative services to homeless persons with mental illness, and to foster enduring partnerships to improve the integration of services among federal, state, local, and voluntary systems that provide services to homeless persons with mental illness (Randolph, 1995).

The first and third authors of this article began conducting psychiatric interviews with homeless persons with mental illness who were reluctant to receive clinical services from the local community mental health clinic. These interviews took place at a local homeless shelter, several community soup kitchens, and various city street locations. After evaluating 10 clients, we noted that certain family issues were common to most of these clients, even in cases where clients were physically separated from and had no contact with their families. These clinical findings were discussed with the second author of this paper, who helped to locate these issues within a sociological framework. Finally, the last two authors brought a sharp focus to these issues within a family therapy framework. The benefit of this interdisciplinary effort was our ability to bring a unique multidimensional perspective to this clinical study; however, our varying perspectives also presented us with the challenge of producing a final draft of this article. Previous drafts ranged from having a more psychoanalytic focus to having a stronger focus in family therapy.

Because the first and third authors collaborated on the first 10 client cases, we draw primarily from these cases to illustrate the issues outlined in this article; however, we also draw from our experiences of providing clinical supervision to a staff of clinicians and case managers who have provided clinical and rehabilitative services to more than 400 homeless persons with mental illness. Contrary to our initial expectations, homeless persons with mental illness had varying levels of involvement with their families. Others who had no current contact with their families maintained a powerful emotional connection to them. Many clients, regardless of the degree of family contact, insisted that clinicians help them with family issues. As we listened to our clients over time, we noted the emergence of three family-related issues: (1) conflict and structural changes in the family that may increase the risk of homelessness for certain clients; (2) the emotional connection individuals have to their families, and the relationship between this connection and their homelessness; and (3) the ways individuals' relationships with their families influence their transition from homelessness to independent living. In this paper, we examine these three family-related issues.

Family-Related Issues

Conflict or Structural Changes in the Family

For many clients, family conflict seemed to contribute to an increased risk of homelessness. Abrupt or chronic conflict had the potential to scar family relationships, as well as to cause shifts in those relationships. In some cases, the individuals had been expelled from their homes; in others, individuals had reduced or no contact with family members. Three distinct types of family conflict emerged from our clinical work: overt conflict, covert conflict, and veiled conflict expressed through delusional beliefs.

Overt conflict was clear, and clients spoke openly about it. Overt conflict involved disputes about financial issues, role expectations, responsibilities of daily living, and relationships within and outside the family. In some cases, conflict erupted in some dramatic episode, either with or without violence. A case example of overt family conflict is depicted by a female client we will call Ann. Ann is a woman in her early thirties who was homeless for the first time when she met the outreach staff. She told staff that she had a tense relationship with her mother that began in her early adulthood, when Ann's symptoms of depression interfered with her ability to work. Ann said that her mother resented her inability to be self-sufficient. One night, Ann angered her mother when she covered the family dog with a blanket from the family living room. Her mother told her to remove the blanket. Ann refused and they argued. Ann's mother finally called the police and had them forcibly remove Ann from the family home.

The second type of family conflict is covert. Often, we could infer the nature of the conflict from information that emerged over time in clinical sessions or from the clients' behavior. Clients expressed anger and sadness about family events or family members. They described episodes of what appeared to be unprovoked violence toward family members or recounted other conflicts. When the exact nature of the conflict is not immediately evident, clinicians need to attend to all information that clients reveal about their families and attempt to elicit additional family information. A client we will call Joe provides a case example of covert family conflict. Joe is a man in his early thirties with schizophrenia who had slept on the streets for eight years. He had a serious conflict with his sister, but the details were obscure to his clinician. He said that his sister had obtained a restraining order against him just prior to his becoming homeless. Because his sister and her two children lived with his mother, he was not allowed to visit his family for several months; however, he consistently violated the restraining order by going to the home at least monthly to pick up his Social Security check. Joe's clinician periodically asked him whether there were family issues he wanted to discuss. He usually said no. After almost nine months of clinical sessions, Joe described his conflict with his sister,

and told his clinician that she needed to carefully attend to his story to understand his homelessness. Early one evening, Joe was drunk, had a fistfight with a neighbor, and came home with blood on his shirt. When his sister saw his bloody shirt, she called the police. His sister encouraged the police to take him to the local psychiatric unit because he was "crazy." She did this, Joe said, because she hated him. After he returned to the family home, he was verbally abusive toward his sister. She called the police again and obtained a restraining order against him. Joe harbors a simmering resentment against his sister and feels that she has physically separated him from his family and expelled him into homelessness. He denies that he bears any responsibility for the conflict.

The third type of family conflict is veiled. This type of conflict is similar to covert, but clients express the conflict through delusional beliefs about family members, which nonetheless hold a kernel of truth. While the delusional nature of the belief may preclude clarity, the clinician can narrow the focus of the conflict to certain family members or important family events; however, due to the lack of clarity, clinicians must avoid a specific interpretation of conflict in these cases. A client we will call Jim provides an example of this type of family conflict. Jim is a 40-year-old man with schizophrenia who slept under a highway bridge for two years. He described a conflict that he had with his father that dated from his late teens. He told his father that he wanted to join the Marines. His father supported Jim's wish to enlist in the armed services, but objected to his joining the Marines. Jim complied by joining the Army. During Jim's tour of duty, the Marines were involved in heavy combat and many servicemen were killed. Jim returned to live with his family after he left the armed services, but left after several years saying that he was not able to continue living with his father. He had been sleeping outside for four years at the time that the outreach staff met him. Shortly thereafter, he moved into a local homeless shelter. In clinical sessions, Jim punctuated discussions about this event both with anger toward his father and with delusions that he was dying from various illnesses. Jim was in good health. Although we could not find a clear interpretation for his somatic delusions, it seemed that Jim felt guilty for not having been involved in this military combat and that he blamed his father for preventing him from enlisting in the Marines. His somatic complaints and fears of death may be linked to his pervasive guilt, and he may feel that he does not deserve to continue to live while so many others were killed in combat.

A structural change may take place in the family immediately prior to or simultaneously with an episode of homelessness. Family events, such as the birth or death of a family member, marriage, divorce, or the unexpected addition of children into families, often require a shift in family relationships and a reassignment of family responsibilities and roles. When this occurs, caring for a mentally ill member may be more of an emotional or financial strain for the family than in the previous family configuration. A client we will call David is a 40-year-old man with symptoms of depression but no history of psychiatric treatment. At the time the outreach staff met him, he had been staying at a local shelter for three months. He told clinical staff that he had lived with his mother all his life and had worked as a laborer. When his mother died, his siblings decided, against David's wishes, to sell the family home. David quit his job, moved out of state, and became homeless within six months of his mother's death.

Clients' Emotional Connections to Their Families

Homelessness among persons with mental illness, as we noted above, is a complex interaction of structural and personal factors, and families often extend themselves to their limits to help prevent their members with mental illness from becoming homeless (Rossi, 1989). In our clinical work, we noted that in many cases homeless persons maintained powerful emotional connections with their families, regardless of whether they had current contact with their families. Some clients who were estranged from their families yearned to resolve issues and reconnect with them. Other clients who maintained limited involvement with their families talked of returning to live with their families. In some cases, family reunification was possible; in others it was not. Even in the latter cases, the connections that these individuals had with their families was powerful, and many continued to insist that reunification was possible, even imminent.

The powerful emotional connections that clients had with their families seemed to relate to their homelessness in certain cases. Some clients seemed to use their homelessness to tell their families that they need help or want to be invited home. These individuals may even endure longer periods of homelessness in the hope that their families will offer them help or invite them back. Ann, the woman described earlier who became homeless for the first time after being evicted from the family home by her mother, initiated contact with the outreach staff and asked them if her family had made any attempts to find her. She refused emergency shelter, cash assistance, assistance in applying for entitlements and housing programs, and mental health and vocational rehabilitation services that the staff offered her. In all of her contacts with staff, she asked whether her family had called to look for her. She also asked for lists of programs that helped homeless people. Ann then called these programs, not to ask for services, but to ask if her family had called their agency to try to find her. Throughout this time, she slept on the steps of a church just a few blocks from the family home. Although there may have been factors that contributed to this woman's homelessness that were not known to the outreach staff, it seemed, at least in part, that she remained homeless with the hope that her family would look for her and invite her back home.

For other clients, homelessness may reflect, in part, a self-imposed punishment for real, imagined, or delusional wrongs that they perpetrated on family members. Some clients painfully told their clinicians that they deserved to be exiled from their families and did not deserve to have a home. These clients seemed to use their homelessness, in part, to make amends to their families for their real or imagined harm. A client we will call Peter is a man with schizophrenia who was homeless and slept outdoors for 14 years. He believed that he had sexually molested his sister and had killed a man in his hometown. He traveled throughout the country as a drifter and felt that, because of his crimes, he deserved to live life as an outcast. After forming a relationship with clinical staff, he agreed to a trial of antipsychotic medications. The medications cleared some of his delusions, and, although he realized that he did not commit the murder, he was not sure about the sexual abuse. He moved into an apartment at this time and initiated and resumed regular contact with his family, who lived out of state. During one of his visits, Peter asked his sister if he molested her. She said no. Within weeks, he invited many of the clinical and case management staff to visit him at home. He had a section of a bookcase devoted to family pictures and brought staff to see these pictures first. Psychiatric medications eliminated Peter's delusional thoughts about having murdered another person, and this, in turn, seemed to lessen his need to feel punished and exiled. It seemed as though he felt more deserving of a connection to his family once he knew he was not a murderer. His renewed relationship with his family and his sister may have provided the additional reassurance that he was indeed worthy of having a home and of not sleeping on the streets.

Family Relationships and Transition to Independent Living

Transitions into housing, even if they are successful, are rarely smooth and may be filled with difficult moments. Regardless of whether the transition is successful, family issues and dynamics may be positive or negative factors in these transitions.

Changes in the family system or changes in individuals' relationships to their families that minimize or resolve conflicts can help clients to be less ambivalent about moving into an apartment, and the transition from homelessness to housing can proceed with some expectation of success. Resolution of other family issues may also help individuals make a successful transition to housing. A client we will call Shirley is a woman in her mid-thirties who was homeless for the first time. She had no previous history of psychiatric treatment. Six months before our meeting her, she attempted suicide after she moved from another state to live near her brother, who then told her he wanted nothing to do with her. She then exhibited symptoms of depression, anxiety, and paranoia, and she actively abused cocaine. We learned that her two oldest brothers violently committed suicide, one by hanging and the other by shooting his wife and then himself. She said sadly that she was estranged from her remaining two brothers and had no hopes for reconciliation. Over the course of a nine-month trial of psychiatric treatment, Shirley made only limited gains despite receiving various clinical and case management services and trials of medications. She was approved for a subsidized apartment program, but her psychiatric symptoms and substance use interfered with her ability to move into her apartment. Approximately nine months later, the brother who had sent her away from his home contacted her, saying that he wanted to resume their relationship. A clinician met with Shirley and her brother several times. They talked about the painful issue of Shirley's suicide attempt, their feelings about this event, their perspectives on the conflict between them at that time, and the traumatic deaths of their brothers. Shortly after these family meetings, Shirley's psychiatric symptoms reduced dramatically and she was taken off all medications. She stopped using drugs, started attending 12-step meetings, and referred herself to a substance-abuse inpatient and day treatment program. She got a job

after completing this treatment program and moved into an apartment.

Family issues can also hinder individuals' transitions from homelessness. Soon after they move into housing, clients may have a dramatic increase in psychiatric symptoms, stop taking their prescribed medications, start taking drugs or drinking alcohol, stop attending to their hygiene or other daily activities, stop paying their rent, and/or become problem tenants. Some of these individuals may become homeless again. A closer examination of some of these cases may reveal conflicted family situations in which there had been little or no resolution of family issues, or an emergence of additional family issues after the client's move into housing. A client we will call Jerry is in his early forties and has a bipolar disorder. He accepted psychiatric treatment and housing after being homeless and refusing treatment for 10 years, since his brother evicted him from the family home after he had a violent fight with his mother. He talked with his clinician about his mother's terminal illness and explored ways to make peace with her before she died, but she died before this could happen. When he heard the news of her death, he said, "Well then what is this all for? I got this apartment to show her that I'm not a bum living on the streets." He then moved out of his apartment to sleep in a car. It appeared that Jerry had moved into his apartment, at least in part, as a final effort to make peace with his mother before her death. He had hoped she would see that he was no longer a "street person," but that he was safe and secure in an apartment. She died before he could convey this message to her, and he became homeless again.

In cases where family issues are unresolved, the client's transition from homelessness to independent living may evoke painful memories of past or current family issues and generate intense emotions about the current family situation. While these family issues may be present when individuals are homeless, clients are often preoccupied with the challenge of meeting their basic needs and surviving homelessness. Once situated in their apartments, they have more time to dwell on these family issues. Or it may be that when they close the doors of their new apartments, they are met with family memories that they associate with home. Clinical and case management staff can be instrumental in helping clients discuss and manage their emerging feelings about "home," which may help them during the critical early period of their transition into housing. A client we will call Ron, a depressed, alcoholic man in his mid-forties, moved into an apartment after sleeping outdoors for a year. About one month later, he complained that he was worse off in his apartment than he had been when he slept on the streets. He refused to leave his apartment or let anyone in, closed his windows and drew the blinds, stopped bathing and eating, and chain-smoked. Clinical staff visited him regularly. He told them of his immense pain over his early childhood memories. His father left the family when he was a young boy. As the only boy, Ron felt responsible for being the man of the house. He felt robbed of his childhood and could not remember ever having fun. He said that when he was in his midadolescence, he physically and sexually abused his siblings. He hated himself for this, and said that he did not deserve to have a home. Project staff visited him often and shared coffee and meals with him in his apartment. They brought him necessary household items and helped him decide how to decorate his rooms. Over several months, Ron improved, and there may be several reasons why. He may simply have benefited from human companionship when staff visited him, or having his own room where he could sleep indoors and be safe and warm each night may have provided him some stability. It could also be that staff provided an opportunity for him to talk about his painful family issues, and provided him with the support that he needed to achieve some resolution of these issues, which helped him to accept his apartment as his home.

For some clients, their relationship with outreach staff may help them to heal family losses or cope with past and current family issues, and provide them with the sustained support they need to make the transition from homelessness to "home." A client we will call Edward is a man in his late forties who has a diagnosis of schizophrenia and has been homeless for more than 30 years. He became homeless after viciously attacking his parents and siblings when he was psychotic. Immediately following the assault on his family, he was hospitalized in a psychiatric unit and the family severed all contact with him. For four years, he tolerated only brief contacts with the outreach staff. Then, after an extended stay in a psychiatric inpatient unit, Edward agreed to move into an apartment that staff found for him. After moving in, he looked for staff on a daily basis and asked them to stop by and visit him at his home. During these visits, he offered to serve them coffee or cook them meals. He sometimes asked for specific household or food items. Although his thoughts were often quite disorganized and he was delusional, his references to his family increased dramatically after he moved

into his apartment. He told staff that as the oldest male in an Italian family he stood to inherit the family home upon the death of his father. He held to this hope, despite the fact that his father had died 10 years earlier and his family had made no efforts to contact him in more than three decades. At the time of this writing, he has been housed for one year. Staff continue to meet him three times per week to share meals at his apartment and at the community soup kitchen.

It may be interesting to examine the resemblance between outreach staff and families. Outreach workers and families alike interact with clients in their private living spaces. They visit clients to check on their progress and to address their practical needs such as food, housing, and health care. They engage in problem-solving discussions with clients about accessing available resources and supports. The fact that outreach workers are not family members affords them a level of detachment from clients that may be necessary to maintain an ongoing relationship with certain individuals who have a serious mental illness. Their ability to separate themselves physically (at the end of the work shift), and to a certain degree emotionally, may also enable them to demonstrate an almost unconditional acceptance of clients' illnesses and issues.

Practice Principles

The case material in this article was selected to illustrate the importance of family issues in the lives of homeless persons with mental illness. While family-related issues were certainly not central in all cases, they were pivotal for many of the individuals we served. Based on our preliminary clinical findings, we propose that homeless outreach programs consider the following practice principles.

1. *Homeless outreach programs can more effectively serve persons with mental illness when they employ an interdisciplinary staff.* The combination of case management staff and clinical staff equips homeless outreach programs with a broad range of knowledge and skills to effectively engage and provide services to homeless persons with mental illness. Case managers offer knowledge about various community resources, about entitlement programs, vocational rehabilitation programs, and housing. Clinicians and psychiatrists bring a unique perspective to street work that includes an understanding of human behavior and the complexity of interpersonal, especially family, relationships. Clinical staff also understand the characteristics of the therapeutic process and the range of interventions

available to help individuals improve their levels of functioning. By working together, case managers and clinicians can develop a comprehensive understanding of the individuals' problems and support clients in accessing the psychiatric and support services that they need.

2. *A family treatment perspective allows clinicians and case managers to more comprehensively assess homeless persons with mental illness and to develop individualized clinical and case management interventions.* Family theorists have long argued that an individual's problems can be best understood and managed when there is an extensive understanding of the individual's family, even in cases where there is an absence of contact between the person and his or her family (Rhodes, 1986). Our clinical findings support this perspective.

Pertinent data about an individual's family are often offered by, or can be elicited from, clients in early outreach encounters. It is essential that clinicians and case managers value any information that clients share about their families, even if it does not seem important at the time. If clients do not spontaneously offer family data, clinicians and case managers can encourage clients to tell "stories" about their families. They should pay particular attention to family events that occurred in the year prior to the client's homelessness: important events in the life cycle, current family conflicts and problems, and the current status of family relationships. A client's behavior may also provide clinicians and case managers with relevant family information. One client in our project had slept in his car for several years, but several times a week visited his childhood home and asked the new owner if she would sell it to him. Although the client's behavior did not provide specific details about the family issues that affected him, it provided a clue that family issues were important to him.

The clinical data about clients and their families that outreach staff collect become a rich source that clinicians and case managers can draw from to assess clients' problems and their homelessness. Staff can use this family information over the course of clients' treatment to creatively craft and effectively time clinical and case management interventions. Clinical interventions may include supporting clients to grieve family losses, helping clients reconnect with the families, or inviting families to participate in clinical sessions with clients. Case management interventions focus on the more practical needs of clients, such as securing entitlements or finding employment, applying for housing programs and renting apartments, and connecting with agencies that can provide ongoing assistance in various areas, such as obtaining food, clothing, psychiatric treatment, and medical care. It is most effective when clinical and case management interventions are intertwined and build on each other. Providing housing to a client may not be successful until certain family issues are recognized and resolved to some degree. For example, some individuals may need help in understanding that their families do not intend to invite them home, and in starting to grieve this loss. At some point in the grieving process, they may feel prepared to move from the shelter into an apartment. Moving forward with clients at an appropriately sensitive time may be critically important. The proper timing of interventions is crucial to facilitating the clients' ongoing involvement in clinical and case management services.

3. *Transitions from homelessness into housing, or from outreach programs to office-based services, present a crisis for many clients. An understanding of the client's family issues can guide clinicians and case managers to help individuals make these transitions successfully.* As might be expected, homeless outreach programs view the move of their clients into permanent housing as a major success, and as a point where client cases are reviewed for transfer to a less intensive clinical and case management service program. We suggest that the transition into housing, as well as transitions to other clinical or case management service programs, are crises for many clients. Careful consideration should be given to the timing of such transitions.

The first several months that clients are housed on their own is a critical time. Often when clients move into their apartments they reflect on their associations of home, and some of them may associate home with painful and difficult memories. Other clients may long to reconnect with their estranged families. The continued involvement of clinical and case management staff who are familiar with the clients and their family issues is essential during this transition. During the transitional period, staff can monitor the clients' adjustment to independent living and assess their need for additional clinical and case management supports. If necessary, staff may increase visits to clients or actively engage with them in more unconventional activities such as shopping for necessary household items, helping to decorate their apartments, and cooking and sharing meals together.

Once a client is successfully moved into an apartment, most programs immediately plan to transfer the individual to another mental health or community resource agency. Instead, the transition to stable housing should be viewed as a time of potential crisis, possibly necessitating greater involvement from support staff with whom the client has an established rapport. Thus, client transfers should be carefully timed: clients must be receptive and ready to begin to develop a new relationship with a clinician or a case manager in another agency. In contrast, in some cases, transfers can be initiated before clients secure independent housing. When staff inadvertently bypass an opportunity to transfer client cases to locate housing for them, they may miss the clinical marker point for transition. An improperly timed transition may precipitate an additional crisis that could lead to regression into homelessness.

These aforementioned principles of practice can be used by other agencies that provide services to homeless persons with mental illness. Clinicians in mental health agencies and case managers in public shelters or in residential programs can integrate a family treatment perspective into their work with this population, regardless of whether clients are in active contact with their families. An understanding of clients' family issues can serve to guide staff to help clients make the transition successfully from homelessness to independent living. For example, some clients who are estranged from their families may be reluctant to move out of public shelters. A decision to have a home of their own ends the dream of being reclaimed by their families. Their relationships with staff and other shelter residents may provide a substitute for conflicted or absent family relationships. Shelters can develop creative strategies for providing support to these clients. They can visit clients in their new apartments, invite them back to the shelter for meals or community activities, or offer them volunteer jobs within the shelter.

These clinical findings may be applied to other outreach and human service delivery programs that serve homeless persons. Every recipient of clinical or case management services is a member of a family. Clinical and case management staff can provide more effective services by gaining an understanding of clients' relationships with their families and exploring their personal meanings of family and of "home." This comprehensive understanding can guide clinicians and case managers as they assist these individuals to reach an optimal level of functioning, including stable independent housing.

Conclusion

We suggest that further attention be given to the previously unexplored area of the relationship between homeless persons with mental illness and their families. While this area of study may have been neglected to avoid blaming families for the homelessness of their mentally ill family members, neither family members nor clients are to blame for homelessness among these individuals. In studying family relationships among homeless people, we may be able to develop integrated family treatment methods focused on engaging homeless individuals in clinical treatment and moving them toward independent living. We can gain a better understanding of the interaction between the personal and structural factors in contemporary homelessness.

The authors' work on this paper was supported in part by their involvement with the New Haven site of the national ACCESS demonstration project, through a grant from the federal Center for Mental Health Services to the State of Connecticut. The authors would like to thank John Strauss, MD, and Dale Bick Carlson who gave helpful comments on drafts of this paper.

References

Anderson, D. G. (1996). Homeless women's perceptions about their families of origin. *Western Journal of Nursing Research, 18,* 29–42.

Bahr, H. M. (1973). *Skid row: An introduction to disaffiliation.* New York: Oxford University Press.

Bassuk, E., & Lamb, H. R. (1986). Homelessness and the implementation of deinstitutionalization. In E. Bassuk (Ed.), *The mental health needs of homeless persons.* San Francisco: Jossey-Bass.

Bassuk, E. L., & Rosenberg, L. (1988). Why does family homelessness occur? A case-control study. *American Journal of Public Health, 78,* 783–788.

Baumann, S. L. (1994). No place of their own: An exploratory study. *Nursing Science Quarterly, 7,* 162–169.

Burt, P. (1992). *Over the edge: The growth of homelessness in the 1980's.* New York: Russell Safe Foundation.

Burt, P., & Pittman, K. J. (1985). *Testing the social safety net.* Washington, DC: Urban Institute Press.

Cohen, C., & Sokolovsky, J. (1989). *Old men of the Bowery: Strategies for survival among the homeless.* New York: Guilford Press.

Farr, R., Koegel, P., & Burnam, A. (1986). *A study of homelessness and mental illness in the skid row area of Los Angeles.* Los Angeles: Los Angeles County Department of Mental Health.

Koegel, P. (1992). Through a different lens: An anthropological perspective on the homeless mentally ill. *Culture, Medicine and Psychiatry, 16,* 1–22.

Koegel, P., Burnam, M. A., & Baumohl, J. (1996). The causes of homelessness. In J. Baumohl (Ed.), *Homelessness in America* (pp. 24–31). Phoenix, AZ: Oryx Press.

Randolph, F. (1995). Improving service systems through systems integration: The ACCESS program. *American Rehabilitation, 21,* 36–38.

Reilly, F. E. (1993). Experience of family among homeless individuals. *Issues in Mental Health Nursing, 14,* 309–321.

Rhodes, S. L. (1986). Family treatment. In F. J. Turner (Ed.), *Social work treatment: Interlocking theoretical approaches* (pp. 432–453). New York: Free Press.

Rosnow, M., Shaw, T., & Concord, C. (1985). *Listening to the homeless: A study of homeless mentally ill persons in Milwaukee.* Milwaukee, WI: Human Services Triangle.

Rossi, P. (1989). *Without shelter: Homelessness in the 1980's.* New York: Priority Press Publications.

Tessler, R. C., & Dennis, D. L. (1989). *A synthesis of NIMH-funded research concerning persons who are homeless and mentally ill.* Rockville, MD: National Institute of Mental Health.

Tessler, R. C., Gamache, G. M., Rossi, P. H., Lehman, A. F., & Goldman, H. H. (1992). The kindred bonds of mentally ill homeless persons. *New England Journal of Public Policy, 8,* 265–280.

Toomey, B. G., First, R. J., Rife, J. C., & Belcher, J. R. (1989). Evaluating community care for homeless mentally ill people. *Social Work Research and Abstracts, 24*(4), 21–26.

31

Shyness and Social Phobia: A Social Work Perspective on a Problem in Living

Among the anxiety disorders described in *Diagnostic and Statistical Manual of Mental Disorders* (DSM-IV-TR) (American Psychiatric Association, 2001) is *social phobia*. Although not new to the nomenclature, the disorder has received a great deal of attention in the professional and popular press in recent years as a condition that is prevalent and is treatable. Of concern to me is the extent to which social phobia, of which shyness can be considered a mild form, is being conceptualized as a mental disorder with an emphasis on its treatment with medication.

Social phobia provides a striking example of the pathologizing of personality characteristics and the willingness of many consumers and professionals to accept or condone such stigmatization. This article describes the characteristics of social phobia, considers its status as a mental disorder, and discusses the kinds of nonmedical interventions that can be offered to those who seek to overcome it. I will refer to the condition most often as "social anxiety" to reflect my position that it represents a "problem in living" rather than a mental disorder. A *problem in living* is a person-environment transaction that blocks an individual's experience of satisfactory social functioning (Karls & Wandrei, 1994). A *mental disorder* is conceptualized as a dysfunction occurring primarily within the person (American Psychiatric Association, 2001).

The profession of social work is characterized by a consideration of systems and the reciprocal effect of people and their environments. Whereas strong arguments exist for the biological origins of some conditions, such as bipolar disorder and schizophrenia, the evidence is less compelling for many others. From a transactional perspective, most problems in living, including shyness, arise from a variety of factors and can be resolved by altering one's relationship to the environment rather than by using drugs. Furthermore, from an empowerment perspective, people who are shy should not be encouraged to relinquish judgments about the nature of the mental status to professionals who maintain a medical orientation and perceive many problems as being caused by biological abnormalities. Social workers tend not to classify individuals as abnormal or disordered, because this tends to place problems "within" people.

Anxiety and Social Phobia

Anxiety is an unpleasant but normal and functional effect that provides people with warning signs for perceived threats (Rapee, 1996). Its physical and psychological symptoms prepare an individual to confront or avoid the threat. A person's genetic temperament, psychosocial development, past experiences, and cognitive appraisals of events all influence its regulation (Kaplan & Sadock, 1998). Anxiety begins as a physiological reaction to a threatening stimulus, and its symptoms include tension, autonomic nervous system hyperactivity (for example, racing heart, blushing, perspiring, dry mouth, trembling, difficulty swallowing, muscle twitches), and hypervigilance. Anxiety becomes problematic when it creates a sense of powerlessness, suggests a danger that is unrealistic, or produces a level of self-absorption that interferes with social functioning (Campbell, 1996).

Social phobia, also known as social anxiety disorder, is a fear of social situations and interactions. It is a fear of being judged negatively by others and leads to feelings of inadequacy, embarrassment, humiliation, and depression (Den Boer, 1997). People with social phobia may experience distress when being introduced to other people, being teased or criticized, being the center of attention, or being watched while doing something. Such people understand that their anxiety is irrational. The phobia may be considered a mental disorder when it interferes significantly with the person's interpersonal and social lives (American Psychiatric Association, 2001). Social anxiety is distinguished from other anxiety disorders by its early age of onset, occasional symptom remissions followed by relapses, and exclusive association with social and performance situations (Liebowitz, 1999). The condition does not usually become prominent until ages 15 to 20, with a mean age of onset of 16 years (Magee, 1996).

There is an apparent inconsistency in the *DSM-IV* subtypes of the disorder. The specific subtype refers to the fear of speaking in front of groups—one-third of people with the disorder have this fear exclusively (Kessler, Stein, & Berglund, 1998). It is less persistent, less impairing, and less often associated with other *DSM* disorders. In the second subtype, generalized social phobia, the person is anxious in most social situations. He or she perceives negative social events as catastrophes and negatively interprets ambiguous social events (Stopa & Clark, 2000). The psychiatric manual offers no concept of a continuum that might support the significance of person-in-environment processes in the initiation, maintenance, and possible extinction of social anxiety over time

Everyday shyness can be considered a mild form of social phobia. To be *shy*, according to Webster (Random House, 1999), is to be timid or easily frightened; uncomfortable in the presence of, and thus avoiding contact with, others; extremely self-conscious; and cautious, wary, and showing distrust. Zimbardo (1977), whose popular book on shyness was in print for 30 years, was reluctant to pathologize the condition. He placed shyness on a continuum, with people who are not distressed by their introversion on the milder end. He also considered the positive aspects of shyness: people who are shy may appear discreet and introspective, be able to preserve personal privacy, experience the pleasures of solitude, tend not to intimidate or hurt others, add an element of peace to social settings, be selective in relating to others, have opportunities to observe and then act cautiously, avoid interpersonal conflicts, be valued as good listeners, and benefit from the protections of anonymity. What is termed social phobia is shyness at the other end of the continuum, where the fear of social situations is less bounded. It is likely that such a person with a social phobia might want to be more socially adaptive, but it may be unfair to label that person as "ill."

Statistics on Social Phobia

The problem-in-living that is termed social phobia is the third largest psychological disorder in the United States, with a lifetime prevalence of approximately 13% (Magee, 1996). It is more common in females, people with low educational attainment, people with a lack of social supports, and people who use psychiatric medications (Furmark et al., 1999). There may be an increasing prevalence of the condition in recent years among white educated married people (Heimberg, Stein, Hiripi, & Kessler, 2000). People with social anxiety have a high comorbidity for other disorders. They are four times more likely to have other anxiety and mood disorders (Lamberg, 1998). A seven-year cross-sectional study of young adults who attended college found that people with the condition had a 2% to 5% higher likelihood of having an alcohol use disorder than those without the condition (Kushner, Sher, & Erickson, 1999). They tended to drink to increase their sociability and social functioning (Himle et al., 1999). Socially anxious people who abuse alcohol have higher self-reports of alcohol dependence, although the drink no more than people without social anxiety (Thomas, Thevos, & Randall, 1999).

Causes of Social Anxiety

Social anxiety may have a variety of causes. The psychiatric literature often emphasizes genetic and biological causes. Many writers assert, however, that it is only the generalized form of the anxiety that is inherited. Stein, Chartier, et al. (1998) found a high rate of phobias among relatives of people with generalized social phobia. They added that avoidant personality disorder, which is sometimes comorbid with social phobia, also seems to have a familial base. Symptoms of the anxiety may begin in childhood (often before age 5), with another risk period just before puberty. The anxious child may demonstrate a fear of strangers as early as 7 months, and behavioral inhibitions may be observed at 21 to 31 months (Rosenbaum, Biederman, Hirschfeld, Bolduc, & Chaloff, 1991). There is no need to assume a genetic or biological basis for transmitted emotional or behavioral patterns, because social learning theory can also account for them (Bandura, 1977). That is, children born into families with anxious adults may acquire related behaviors through modeling and subsequent reinforcement.

Some researchers state that there is an altered brain structure in people with many anxiety disorders, including social phobia. LeDoux (1996) described the functional evolution of certain brain pathways in which a stimulus can be apprehended as a threat before it registers cognitively. The amygdala, the portion of the brain associated with the alarm response, receives a stimulus before the cortex, which governs cognitive function, receives a stimulus. Although this process is adaptive for species survival, an overactive amygdala, said to be present in some anxiety disorders, can foster an extreme reaction to a perceived threat. Other brain conditions postulated as being significant in anxiety disorders include serotonin and dopamine dysfunction (in the striatal system) and an overactive sympathetic nervous system (Tiihonen, Kuikka, Bergstrom, Koponen, & Leinonen, 1997). Biological theorists maintain that, as a result of these dysfunctions, a person with social phobia develops a low arousal threshold and has difficulty assimilating novel stimuli.

Cognitive and behavioral theorists argue that the condition results from an individual's development over time of cognitive distortions based on social learning patterns. Young schoolchildren with social anxiety demonstrate a low expected performance level, high negative self-talk on social evaluation tasks, and social skills deficits. They are less likely to receive positive evaluations from their peers (Spence, Donovan, & Brechman-Toussaint, 1999). A person's biased assessments of social situations and negative self-evaluations can become so ingrained in patterns of thought (schema) that they may persist even after social success experiences (Poulton & Andrews, 1996). That is, positive social interactions can produce negative responses in people with social anxiety. Still, the implication is not that the anxiety is necessarily biological in origin. Cognitive and behavioral patterns may be quite rigid, and interventions must include considerable rehearsal and repetition by the client to break through these patterns (Wallace & Alden, 1997).

In summary, considering the perspectives discussed, I present a view of the etiology of social anxiety that incorporates biological, psychological, and social influences. The condition may reflect an outcome of situations in which a person's constitutional temperament interacts with family and social factors such as chronic exposure to environmental stressors or experiences of humiliation and criticism in early life. Social anxiety may be more or less severe depending on the person's schema, comfort with various levels of external stimulation, and reinforcement patterns.

Intervention

A variety of interventions are available for people who seek professional help to alleviate their social anxiety. These include medication and psychosocial interventions, which may be provided together or separately.

Medication

Medication has become a primary, and sometimes the only, intervention for people with social anxiety. One set of researchers laments that only one of six people with the disorder receives medication (Stein, McQuaid, Laffaye, & McCahill, 1999). Some physicians believe that the ability of general practitioners to assess social anxiety is crucial, because this ability would allow the practitioners to prescribe medication for social anxiety among people who seek treatment for other problems (Spence et al., 1999). Others advocate for the medical profession's formal adoption of the term "social anxiety disorder" rather than "social phobia" to further its legitimacy as an illness requiring medication (Liebowitz, Heimberg, Travers, & Stein, 2000).

The types of medication used to treat social anxiety include all classes of antidepressants (that is, MAO inhibitors, cyclic drugs, and serotonin reuptake inhibitors, or SSRIs), the benzodiazepines, and the beta-blockers (Bentley & Walsh, 2001). There is also evidence for the effectiveness of the anticonvulsant drug gabapentin (Saklad, 2000). All of the medications work by alleviating the physiological symptoms of anxiety so that the consumer is less inhibited by them.

At present the SSRIs are the first-line drug therapy for social phobia. There is evidence that these drugs have effects on the brain's noradrenergic neurotransmission system, which appears to be important in regulating mood and anxiety (Gorman & Kent, 1999). The SSRIs also lack many of the adverse effects of the older drugs. Paroxetine is probably the most widely used drug intervention, because it has FDA approval as a specific treatment for social phobia (Mechcatie, 1999). In a 12-week multicenter study submitted to the FDA for approval of paroxetine (N = 183), 55% of people on the medication improved compared with only 24% on placebo (Stein, Liebowitz, et al., 1998). Brunello et al. (2000) have reviewed the pharmacological literature documenting the usefulness of paroxetine and other SSRIs, although they note that the medications are often only partially effective. An International Consensus Group on Depression and Anxiety recommends that SSRI therapy be continued for 12 months, or longer if symptoms persist, at a dose level of 20 mg to 40 mg daily (Ballenger et al., 1998).

There is no question that medications can be effective, although they are effective for only about 50% of consumers when compared with placebos under control conditions (Valenstein, 1998). Long-term positive and adverse effects of the newer drugs are unknown because of their limited time on the market. There are other limitations of drug therapy. The older drugs produce adverse physical effects for many consumers (Bentley & Walsh, 2001). The MAO inhibitors present the possibility of a hypotensive reaction if dietary restrictions are not followed. The cyclic antidepressants produce anticholinergic effects of sedation, dry mouth, constipation, weight gain, and blurred vision. The SSRIs produce fewer adverse effects, but the consumer may experience anxiety, weight loss, headache, sexual dysfunction, and gastrointestinal discomfort. The experience of these adverse effects varies among consumers. The consumer also must manage the expense of medication, which is sometimes considerable, particularly with the newer drugs.

Adolescent and young adult consumers of medication may not develop motivation to make cognitive or behavioral changes for combating their anxiety (Gadow, 1991). The process may negatively affect the self-image of consumers as self-directed change agents. They may generalize that many problems of living can be resolved by using drugs. Furthermore, some consumers may feel stigmatized as having a mental illness. Although some professionals might argue that this is not a negative effect, it may conflict with social work values of the dignity of the individual.

Because clinical practice should always be individualized, appropriate intervention may consist of medications alone, medications along with other therapies, or psychotherapy alone. Some clients are not comfortable with the idea of taking medication or participating in other therapies. Although I argue that drug therapies are overused, I believe that clients should be encouraged to make informed choices about the types of intervention they receive and should not be stigmatized if they choose drug therapy.

Psychosocial Intervention

There is empirical evidence that medication is often not sufficient, and may not be necessary, as an intervention for adults and adolescents with social anxiety (Albano, 2000; Barlow, Esler, & Vitali, 1998). Cognitive and behavioral interventions have consistently demonstrated effectiveness with these clients (Plaud & Vavrosky, 1998). Clients who receive these interventions often have lower rates of relapse than those who rely on medication alone (Liebowitz, 1999). Circumscribed phobias are particularly amenable to behavioral interventions. Specific techniques include cognitive restructuring, self-instruction training, problem solving, guided imagery, exposure, social skills training, relaxation training, and stress management (Beck & Emery, 1985; Gruber & Heimberg, 1997; Rapee, 1996). Taylor et al. (1997) found that cognitive interventions have an additive effect on exposure therapies for people with generalized social phobia.

Many of these interventions are similar in structure (Hepworth, Rooney, & Larsen, 2002). The client, with the support and guidance of a social worker and perhaps a group, identifies situations or thoughts that produce social anxiety. The client learns techniques or new thinking patterns that help to overcome the anxiety. He or she practices the new thoughts or behaviors, first in artificial and then actual situations. All such interventions must be targeted to the client's negative cognitive appraisals of social challenges, perceived self-efficacy, and perceived emotional control (Hofmann, 2000b). Repetition is an essential component of intervention, particularly for clients whose thinking and behavior patterns are rigid. This is because initial success experiences can lead to clients' development of self-protective and limited social goals, negative retrospective emotional states, and beliefs that others will now assume unrealistic expectations of them (Wallace & Alden, 1997). Clients' confidence levels regarding the management of social situations seems to increase more quickly than their ability to perceive these situations as non-threatening (Foa, Franklin, Perry, & Herbert, 1996).

Several examples from the literature illustrate the nature of successful cognitive-behavioral interventions for people with social anxiety. Heimberg and Juster (1994) described a program of cognitive-behavioral group therapy that included 12 sessions of $2^1/_2$ hours duration per session. The intervention included six elements: (1) explanations of social anxiety, (2) exercises to recognize maladaptive thinking, (3) exposure to simulated situations that provoke anxiety, (4) cognitive restructuring for control maladaptive thoughts, (5) homework assignments to prepare for real-life situations, and (6) self-administered cognitive restructuring routines. The group format was found to be effective in modifying each member's cognitive distortions because of the immediate and varied feedback they received. Scholing and Emmelkamp (1996) conducted an experimental study of three cognitive and behavioral treatment conditions, with follow-up measures at three and 18 months. Although all interventions were effective, the group intervention featuring cognitive therapy first and in vivo practice later was most effective, followed, respectively, by individual interventions and integrated cognitive-behavioral group therapy. Barrett, Dadds, and Rapee (1996) conducted an experiment including two treatment conditions and one waiting-list control group for children with anxiety ages 7 to 14 years. The greatest gains at 12-month follow-up were seen in the cognitive-behavioral group that included family management consultation (95% no longer met diagnostic criteria). Gains were also significant for the group without family consultation (70%). In the control group, 26% no longer met diagnostic criteria.

Hofmann (2000a) tested the effectiveness of a group program in which 23 clients with social phobia received eight weeks of exposure therapy in groups of four to six members each. The pre- and posttest measures documented that participants experienced significantly fewer negative thoughts after treatment and also had lower scores on a measure of social phobia. Beidel, Turner, and Morris (2000) performed an experimental study of 67 children between ages 8 and 12 years who were randomly assigned to either a behavioral intervention program to enhance social skills and decrease social anxiety or to a control group focused on academic anxiety management. Both groups met for 12 weeks. The experimental program included weekly individual and group therapies focused on education, skills development, peer support, and in

vivo rehearsal. The control group included weekly individual and group treatment for control of classroom test and performance anxiety. The children in the experimental group acquired significantly higher levels of social skills and interaction practices and significantly less social anxiety. Sixty-six percent of the children in the experimental group no longer met the diagnostic criteria for social phobia compared with 5% of the controls. Treatment gains were maintained after six months.

Cottraux et al. (2000) randomly assigned 67 adults with social phobia to cognitive-behavioral (CBT) and supportive (ST) therapies. The CBT clients received eight one-hour sessions of individual therapy for six weeks, followed by six two-hour weekly group sessions for social skills training. The ST clients received nonspecific individual therapy for anxiety reduction for 12 weeks. Findings indicated that CBT clients achieved greater gains than the ST group members on the main social phobia measure and maintained these gains throughout the course of the study. All participants experienced symptom reduction.

People who experience social anxiety also may help themselves overcome their limitations without professional intervention. For example, Zimbardo (1977) devoted half of his book to self-help exercises, and Davis, Eshelman, and McKay (1995) wrote another popular self-help book on managing anxiety.

Discussion

The social work profession has always had an uneasy relationship with the *DSM* and its medical perspective on problems in living. This diagnostic process perpetuates the myth that an independent entity—a disorder—exists within a person. The *DSM* views people in isolation, fails to address interactive problems, and obscures the role played by systems. The social work profession's person-in-environment (PIE) classification system (Karls & Wandrei, 1994) takes a more balanced perspective on problems in living. It offers an alternative to the *DSM* in organizing assessment around the four themes of social functioning problems (social roles, types of problems, their severity and duration, and the client's coping ability), environmental problems (social system contexts, types of problems, and their severity and duration), mental health problems (Axes I and II of the *DSM* system), and physical health problems. The broad classification scheme helps to ensure that a client's range of needs are addressed and avoids the label of mental illness.

Unfortunately, PIE is not sanctioned for use in most clinical settings.

It is sometimes said that conceptualizing problems in living as mental disorders reduces stigma, because the person need not then feel responsible for the condition. This is no doubt true for some people and perhaps for some disorders, but the perspective also supports the interests of medical professionals, who dominate the health care field. Social workers need to preserve their perspective that difficulties in social functioning, whether in terms of behavior or neurotransmitter function, need not be synonymous with illness and that treatment need not always imply drugs or drugs alone. Still, as long as extreme shyness is conceptualized as mental disorder, it is likely that drugs, at times appropriate, will persist as the sole intervention. Research indicates that psychosocial interventions such as those described in this article, all of which can be provided by social workers, are effective and do not include risks for adverse physical and psychological effects. In keeping with professional values, they also may help clients develop a greater sense of self-efficacy.

References

Albano, A. M. (2000). Treatment of social phobia in adolescents: Cognitive behavioral programs focused on intervention and prevention. *Journal of Cognitive Psychotherapy, 14*(1), 67–76.

American Psychiatric Association. (2001). *Diagnostic and statistical manual of mental disorders* (4th ed., text rev.). Washington, DC: Author.

Ballenger, J. C., Davidson, J. R., Lecrubier, Y., Nutt, D. J., Bobes, J., Beidel, D. C., Ono, Y., & Westenberg, H. G. (1998). Consensus statement on social anxiety disorder from the International Consensus Group on Depression and Anxiety. *Journal of Clinical Psychiatry, 59*(Suppl. 17), 54–60.

Bandura, A. (1977). *Social learning theory.* Englewood Cliffs, NJ: PrenticeHall.

Barlow, D. H., Esler, J. L., & Vitali, A. E. (1998). Psychosocial treatments for panic disorders, phobias, and generalized anxiety disorder. In P. E. Nathan & J. M. Gorman (Eds.), *A guide to treatments that work* (pp. 288–318). New York: Oxford University Press.

Barrett, P. M., Dadds, M. R., & Rapee, R. M. (1996). Family treatment of childhood anxiety: A controlled trial. *Journal of Consulting and Clinical Psychology, 4,* 333–343.

Beck, A. T., & Emery, G. (1985). *Anxiety disorders and phobias: A cognitive perspective.* New York: Basic Books.

Beidel, D. C., Turner, S. M., & Morris, T. L. (2000). Behavioral treatment of childhood social phobia. *Journal of Consulting and Clinical Psychology, 68,* 1072–1080.

Bentley, K. J., & Walsh, J. (2001). *The social worker and psychotropic medication: Toward effective collaboration with mental health clients, families, and providers* (2nd ed.). Pacific Grove, CA: Brooks/Cole.

Brunello, N., den Boer, J. A., Judd, L. L., Kasper, S., Kelsey, J. E., Lader, M., Lecrubier, Y., Lepine, J. P., Lydiard, R. B., Mendlewics, J., Montgomery, S. A., Racagni, G., Stein, M. B., & Wittchen, H. U. (2000). Social phobia: Diagnosis and epidemiology, neurobiology and pharmacology, comorbidity and treatment. *Journal of Affective Disorders, 60*(1), 61–74.

Campbell, R. J. (1996). *Psychiatric dictionary* (7th ed.). New York: Oxford University Press.

Cottraux, J., Note, I., Albuisson, E., Yao, S. N., Note, B., Mollard, E., Bonasse, F., Jalenques, I., Guerin, J., & Coudert, A. J. (2000). Cognitive behavior therapy versus supportive therapy in social phobia: A randomized control trial. *Psychotherapy and Psychosomatics, 69*(3), 137–146.

Davis, M., Eshelman, E. R., & McKay, M. (1995). *The relaxation and stress workbook* (4th ed.). New York: MJF.

Den Boer, J. A. (1997). Social phobia: Epidemiology, recognition, and treatment. *British Medical Journal, 315*(7111), 796–781.

Foa, E. B., Franklin, M. E., Perry, K. J., & Herbert, J. D. (1996). Cognitive biases in generalized social phobia. *Journal of Abnormal Psychology, 105,* 433–450.

Furmark, T., Tillfors, M., Everz, P., Marteinsdottir, I., Gefvert, O., & Fredrickson, M. (1999). Social phobias in the general population: Prevalence and sociodemographic profile. *Social Psychiatry and Psychiatric Epidemiology, 34,* 416–414.

Gadow, K. D. (1991). Clinical issues in child and adolescent psychopharmacology. *Journal of Counseling and Clinical Psychology, 59,* 842–852.

Gorman, J. M., & Kent, J. M. (1999). SSRIs and SNRIs: Broad spectrum of efficacy beyond major depression. *Journal of Clinical Psychiatry, 60*(Suppl. 4), 33–39.

Gruber, K., & Heimberg, R. G. (1997). A cognitive-behavioral treatment package for social anxiety. In W. T. Roth (Ed.), *Treating anxiety disorders* (pp. 245–279). San Francisco: Jossey-Bass.

Heimberg, R. G., & Juster, H. R. (1994). Treatment of social phobia in cognitive-behavioral groups. *Journal of Clinical Psychiatry, 55*(Suppl. 2A), A67–A83.

Heimberg, R. G., Stein, M. B., Hiripi, E., & Kessler, R. C. (2000). Trends in the prevalence of social phobia in the United States: A synthetic cohort analysis of changes over four decades. *European Psychiatry, 15*(1), 29–37.

Hepworth, D., Rooney, R., & Larsen, J. (2002). *Direct social work practice: Theory and skills* (5th ed.). Belmont, CA: Brooks/Cole.

Himle, J. A., Abelson, J. L., Haghighgou, H., Hill, E. H., Nesse, R. N., & Curtis, G. C. (1999). Effect of alcohol on social phobic anxiety. *American Journal of Psychiatry, 156*, 1237–1244.

Hofmann, S. G. (2000a). Self-focused attention before and after treatment of social phobia. *Behaviour Research & Therapy, 38,* 717–725.

Hofmann S. G. (2000b). Treatment of social phobia: Potential mediators and moderators. *Clinical Psychology Science & Practice, 7*(1), 3–16.

Kaplan, H. I., & Sadock, B. J. (1998). *Synopsis of psychiatry* (8th ed.). Baltimore: Williams & Wilkins.

Karls, J. M., & Wandrei, K. E. (Eds.). (1994). *Person-in-environment system: The PIE classification system for social functioning problems.* Washington, DC: NASW Press.

Kessler, R. C., Stein, M. B., & Berglund, P. (1998). Social phobia subtypes in the National Comorbidity Survey. *American Journal of Psychiatry, 155,* 13–17.

Kushner, M. G., Sher, K. J., & Erickson, D. J. (1999). Prospective analysis of the relation between DSM-III anxiety disorders and alcohol use disorders. *American Journal of Psychiatry, 156,* 723.

Lamberg, L. (1998). Social phobia—not just another name for shyness. *Journal of the American Medical Association, 20,* 685–689.

LeDoux, J. (1996). *The emotional brain: The mysterious underpinnings of emotional life.* New York: Simon & Schuster.

Liebowitz, M. R. (1999). Update of the diagnosis and treatment of social anxiety disorder. *Journal of Clinical Psychiatry, 60*(Suppl. 18), 22–26.

Liebowitz, M. R., Heimberg, R. G., Travers, J., & Stein, M. B. (2000). Social phobia or social anxiety disorder: What's in a name? *Archives of General Psychiatry, 57,* 191–192.

Magee, W. J. (1996). Agoraphobia, simple phobia, and social phobia in the National Comorbidity Survey. *Journal of the American Medical Association, 75,* 1046.

Mechcatie, E. (1999). Paroxetine first drug approved for social phobia. *Family Practice News, 29*(12), 15–17.

Plaud, J. J., & Vavrosky, K. G. (1998). Specific and social phobias. In B.A. Thyer & J. S. Wodarski (Eds.), *Handbook of empirical social work practice: Volume 1. Mental disorders* (pp. 327–341). New York: Wiley.

Poulton, R. G., & Andrews, G. (1996). Change in danger cognitions in agoraphobia and social phobia. *Behavior Research and Therapy, 34,* 413–422.

Random House. (1999). *Webster's unabridged dictionary.* New York: Author.

Rapee, R. M. (Ed.). (1996). *Current controversies in the anxiety disorders.* New York: Guilford.

Rosenbaum, J. F., Biederman, J., Hirschfeld, D. R., Bolduc, E. A., & Chaloff, J. (1991). Behavioral inhibition in children: A possible precursor to panic disorder or social phobia. *Journal of Clinical Psychiatry, 52*(Suppl. 11), 5–9.

Saklad, S. R. (2000). Gabapentin used to treat patients with social phobia. *Psychopharmacology Update, 11*(1), 3.

Scholing, A., & Emmelkamp, P. M. G. (1996). Treatment of generalized social phobia: Results at long-term follow-up. *Behavior Research and Therapy, 34,* 447–453.

Spence, S. H., Donovan, C., Brechman-Toussaint, M. (1999). Social skills, social outcomes, and cognitive features of childhood social phobia. *Journal of Abnormal Psychology, 108,* 211–221.

Stein, M. B., Chartier, M. J., Hazen, A. L., Kozak, M. V., Tancer, M. E., Lander, S., Furer, P., Chubaty, D., & Walker, J. R. (1998). A direct-interview family study of generalized social phobia. *America Journal of Psychiatry, 155,* 90–98.

Stein, M. B., Liebowitz, M. R., Lydiard, R. B., Pitts, C. D., Bushnell, W., & Gergel, I. (1998). Paroxetine treatment of generalized social phobia (social anxiety disorder): A randomized controlled trial. *Journal of the American Medical Association, 280,* 708–713.

Stein, M. B., McQuaid, J. R., Laffaye, C., & McCahill, M. E. (1999). Social phobia in the primary care medical setting. *Journal of Family Practice, 48,* 514.

Stopa, L., & Clark, D. M. (2000). Social phobia and interpretation of social events. *Behavior Research and Therapy, 38,* 273–283.

Taylor, S., Woody, S., Koch, W. J., McLean, P., Paterson, R. J., & Anderson, K. W. (1997). Cognitive restructuring in the treatment of social phobia. *Behavior Modification, 21,* 487–511.

Thomas, S. E., Thevos, A. K., & Randall, C. A. (1999). Alcoholics with and without social phobia: A comparison of substance use and psychiatric variables. *Journal of Studies on Alcohol, 60*(14), 472.

Tiihonen, J., Kuikka, J., Bergstrom, U. L., Koponen, H., & Lcinonen, E. (1997). Dopamine reuptake site densities in patients with social phobia. *American Journal of Psychiatry, 154,* 239–243.

Valenstein, E. T. (1998). *Blaming the brain: The truth about drugs and mental health.* New York: Free Press.

Wallace, S. T., & Alden, L. E. (1997). Social phobia and positive social events: The price of success. *Journal of Abnormal Psychology, 106,* 416–425.

Zimbardo, P. G. (1977). *Shyness: What it is, what to do about it.* Reading, MA: Addison-Wesley.

SOPHIA F. DZIEGIELEWSKI
JAMIE A. EATER

32

Smoking Cessation: Increasing Practice Understanding and Time-Limited Intervention Strategy

Someone once said that if the effects of cigarette smoking appeared on our skin instead of our lungs—where it can't be seen—no one would smoke.

—American Cancer Society, 1996

Tobacco use has been cited as the number one avoidable cause of illness and death in our society. It is responsible for more than 400,000 deaths in the United States each year. Smoking is a known cause of cancer, heart disease, stroke, and chronic obstructive pulmonary disease (Kaplan & Weiler, 1997; Solberg, Maxwell, Kottke, Gepner, & Brekke, 1990; U.S. Department of Health and Human Services, 1996). Each year there are more deaths due to tobacco use than there are from the combined effects of acquired immunodeficiency syndrome (AIDS), suicide, homicide, alcoholism, cocaine use, heroine use, traffic accidents, and fire (Glynn, Greenwald, Mills, & Manley, 1993; Solberg et al., 1990; Warner, 1987).

Although tobacco smoking has long been known to have negative health consequences, more than one-quarter of the U.S. adult population still smoke (Skarr et al., 1992). Additionally, it is estimated that, in the next 10 years, smoking-related diseases will kill 4.5 million people in the United States, and more than 50,000 nonsmokers will die each year as a result of secondhand exposure to tobacco smoke (Kaplan & Weiler, 1997).

Study after study continues to support that smoking is not only dangerous to your health, but often fatal. Consequently, the surgeon general deems it necessary to put appropriate warnings on all tobacco products. When is it, then, that one in four American adults continues to smoke? Why does it appear that smoking prevalence among adolescents seems to be rising? In a 1988 report about the health consequences of smoking, the surgeon general offered evidence not only that smoking is a social habit but that it is a chemical pharmacological dependency on nicotine as a drug, similar to an addition to heroin and cocaine (Brautbar, 1995; Moncher, Schinke, & Holden, 1992).

According to Phelps and Nourse (1986), nicotine, a plant alkaloid similar in structure to the opium narcotics, is one of the substances capable of temporarily satisfying the physiological hunger an additive person suffers because of a proposed inborn metabolic error. Nicotine, a deadly poison even in very small doses, is probably the most addictive substance known to man. This substance can take a firm grip on the user, and "it stands to reason that any substance taken into the body ten, twenty, thirty, or more times a day is likely to have a potent addicting effect" (p. 138).

According to the American Lung Association (1995), nicotine works on the brain and other parts of the central nervous system simultaneously. Since nicotine is ingested through smoking, it reaches the brain faster than many other drugs and is drawn into the lungs, pumped through the bloodstream, and sent directly to the brain within seven seconds. This sudden burst of nicotine causes an instant "high." In addition, nicotine makes the heart beat faster, which increases the breathing rate and causes the body to use more oxygen. While these reactions are occurring, blood vessels narrow and the blood travels more slowly, causing a possible increase in blood pressure. For years, the tobacco companies claimed that cigarettes were used to provide sensory pleasure and not to satisfy an addiction. Today, however, scientists, physicians and the Food and Drug Administration (FDA) categorize nicotine as a drug and cigarettes as tools to deliver the drug.

> Experts report that smokers show three classic signs of addiction: (1) they become dependent, (2) they want to quit and cannot, (3) they become tolerant, initially having to increase their dosage in order to achieve the same effect, and (4) those who quit often suffer associated symptoms of withdrawal. (Brautbar, 1995, p. 263)

Furthermore, it has been proved that nicotine has direct effects on the brain's biochemistry, and blood levels of epinephrine, dopamine, and norepinephrine are shown to rise in dose-related increases (Pomerleau & Pomerleau, 1984). Subsequent studies have shown a significant correlation between nicotine and the neurotransmitter dopamine (Came, 1993; "Inside the Addict's Brain," 1994; Nash, 1997; Peck, 1996; "Science of Smoking," 1996) and that the release of neurotransmitters triggered by nicotine can jam the system temporarily, preventing the receptor from working. Research continues to suggest that several of the neuroregulators modified by nicotine administration show both positive and negative behavioral reinforcements, such as pleasure enhancement by increased dopamine, norepinephrine, and beta-endorphin levels and reduction of anxiety and tension through the elevation of endorphins (Brautbar, 1995; Came, 1993).

In summary, the scientific community appears to have significant proof that nicotine is a powerfully addictive agent, yet, regardless of this proven scientific information, one-quarter of the American adult population continues to use nicotine. This suggests that

> at some point after continued repetition of voluntary drug-taking, the drug "user" loses the voluntary ability to control its use. At that point, the "drug misuser" becomes "drug addicted" and there is a compulsive, often overwhelming involuntary aspect to continuing drug use and to relapse after a period of abstinence. (O'Brien & McLellan, 1996, p. 237)

According to Orleans (1985), 90% of American smokers would like to quit smoking and 60% have actually tried. National survey statistics repeated indicate high motivation and readiness for change, but limited success because smoking is a complex addictive behavior influenced by powerful physical, emotional, and social factors. Quitting requires extreme control of these factors in addition to general health motivation; throughout the years, smokers have had limited assistance and access to self-help guides and programs that teach successful cessation skills.

The purpose of this article is to explore current nicotine-addiction and smoking-cessation interventions and to make suggestions for an integrated approach for counseling professionals. The fine line between physiological and psychological addiction is explored. A multi- or interdisciplinary team approach is encouraged that incorporates (1) pharmacological treatments such as nicotine-replacement therapy (nicotine patches or gum); (2) brief treatment using cognitive-behavior modification (including skills training and problem solving); and (3) social support (professional encouragement and assistance).

Diagnostic Impressions of the Nicotine-Dependent Client

According to the American Psychiatric Association's *Diagnostic and Statistical Manual of Mental Disorders*, fourth edition (1994), "The essential feature of Substance Dependence is a cluster of cognitive, behavioral, and physiological symptoms indicating that the individual continues use of the substance despite significant substance-related problems" (p. 176). Oftentimes there is a pattern of repeated self-administration that usually results in tolerance (a need to increase the dose to achieve the desired effect). Furthermore, clients frequently suffer from withdrawal (using the drug to relieve withdrawal symptoms) and compulsive drug-taking behavior (unsuccessful efforts to cut down on the drug or stop using it, and continuing to use it despite knowing of the potential harm to self or others). The degree to which tolerance develops varies greatly across substances. For nicotine addiction, the smoker's tolerance increases over time, which creates a need to smoke more to achieve the same effect that was once achieved by smoking one cigarette (American Psychiatric Association, 1994).

Recovery from addition is regarded as a tormenting process that is often lifelong, with no guarantee of success. Research indicates that the nicotine found in cigarettes is the most addictive substance known, and the path back to normalcy can be long and agonizing. Yet, during the past 25 years, approximately 50 million Americans have quit smoking, and 90% of them did it on their own (Riessman & Carroll, 1996).

For us to understand why one person can quit and why another cannot, it is important to address two types of addiction: simple and complex. According to Riessman and Carroll (1996), simple addiction is considered a superficial dependence in that it does not involve physical cravings and withdrawal symptoms when the substance is removed. Complex addition, however, is a physical and psychological dependency associated with good feelings, loss of control over the addiction, and the compulsion to continue use despite the consequences. Addiction to nicotine is unique because, even in its "simple" form, it is one of the most difficult addictions to overcome. As researchers struggle to design smoking-cessation programs it is important to assess the concepts of simple and complex additions when considering the success of intervention approaches.

The single most important reason individuals have for quitting smoking is concern about their health, and those who quit for health reasons or in response to physician advice are more likely to make repeated attempts and permanently stop smoking cigarettes (Orleans, 1985). For many smokers who want to quit, self-initiated willpower is not enough to beat the cravings. As with other addictive drugs, withdrawal from nicotine can include symptoms of irritability, frustration, anger, anxiety, difficulty concentrating, restlessness, and tobacco cravings (Nordenberg, 1998). Fortunately, with the treatment options available today, the client is not forced to rely on willpower alone.

Pharmacological Therapy

"Drugs, the mainstay of many smoking cessation attempts, have been used for two purposes—to help overcome the smoking habit and to help overcome withdrawal symptoms" (Health and Policy Committee, American College of Physicians, 1986,

p. 283). Two common types of pharmacotherapy include nicotine-replacement therapies and mental health medications.

Nicotine-Replacement Therapies

Throughout the years, several drug therapies, such as nicotine replacement, have been used to curb or eliminate nicotine-withdrawal symptoms. Transdermal nicotine-replacement therapies (e.g., the nicotine patch) have been recommended as efficacious smoking-cessation treatments that have proved effective across diverse settings and when used with a variety of psychosocial interventions (U.S. Department of Health and Human Services, 1996).

For most, it appears that a NicoDerm CQ 21-mg transdermal nicotine patch can be used as an intervention tool, especially during the initial phases of therapy for smoking cessation. Nicotine-replacement therapy appears to offer success because it works as a temporary aid to help smokers quit smoking by reducing nicotine-withdrawal symptoms, including nicotine craving. Nicotine patches (and nicotine gums) provide a lower level of nicotine to the body's blood than cigarettes do, and allow the smoker's body to gradually do away with the body's need for nicotine (SmithKline Beecham, 1996). Because nicotine replacements do not contain the tar or carbon monoxide of cigarette smoke, they do not represent the same dangers connected with tobacco. However, the main addictive ingredient, nicotine, is still being ingested into the body's system.

According to an article titled "Methods for Stopping Cigarette Smoking," which appeared in *Annals of Internal Medicine* (Health and Policy Committee, American College of Physicians, 1986), it has been speculated that only nicotine, delivered independently of cigarettes, can replace cigarette smoking. Furthermore, in five meta-analysis studies that were published in 1992, primary results indicated successful interventions with nicotine transdermal systems, especially when combined with psychosocial approaches (as cited in U.S. Department of Health and Human Services, 1996).

Research has been consistent in suggesting that nicotine replacement generally increases rates of smoking cessation. Therefore, except in the presence of serious medical precautions, nicotine-replacement therapy should be given serious consideration by clinicians and physicians. Medical precautions to be considered include physician monitoring, particularly during pregnancy and for the risks and benefits of use among particular cardiovascular patent groups (U.S. Department of Health and Human Services, 1996). Clients should not use nicotine-replacement therapy if they (1) have heart disease, irregular heartbeat, or history of heart attacks (because nicotine can increase blood pressure); (2) have high blood pressure not controlled with medication; (3) take prescription medicine for depression or asthma without consulting a physician; and (4) are allergic to adhesive tape or have skin problems (50% of transdermal patches cause skin rashes). In addition, it is important to know that nicotine patches have enough nicotine to poison children and pets. Also, if the client continues to smoke while wearing the patch or chewing the gum, nicotine overdose can occur (SmithKline Beecham, 1996).

Medication Use

For almost all individuals, significant health benefits have been associated with smoking cessation. Nevertheless, additional concerns have been raised with regard to the mental health status of persons who quit smoking. Recent studies indicate a link between cigarette smoking and certain psychiatric disorders, particularly depression. The possibility that tobacco use may provide psychological relief for some mental health conditions increases concerns in the health industry about the emotional consequences of smoking cessation (Apgar, 1997).

Sequential research initially suggests that the link between smoking cessation and depression or other psychiatric disorders can be treated simultaneously with the administration of medication. Although numerous drugs (e.g., amphetamine, benzedrine sulfate, methylphenidate, fenfluramine, diazepam, phenobarbital, hydroxyzine, and mepromate) other than nicotine have been tried to ease the physiological and psychological withdrawal symptoms of cigarette smoking, their usefulness has been limited (Heath and Policy Committee, American College of Physicians, 1986). In 1989, research found a plausible link when the FDA approved Bupropion, a relevant dopamine-specific antidepressant, for release. Preliminary tests indicate the antidepressants currently being marketed as Wellbutrin and Zyban Bupropion HCl might aid in smoking cessation while combating the effects of withdrawal and other psychiatric symptoms. The chemical lobeline, extracted from the lobelia flower, may also be helpful (Key, 1994).

"Over the past year, several scientific groups have made the case that in dopamine-rich areas of the brain, nicotine behaves remarkably like cocaine" (Nash, 1997, p. 68). This is not surprising, because both of these chemicals are addictive drugs that falsely mimic neurotransmitters to induce the body's release of dopamine. This release, in turn, brings about the desired feelings of pleasure and elation. Pharmacologically speaking, addiction remains similar to the other mental health disorders in terms of its effects on the brain (Nash, 1997). According to Key (1994), Wellbutrin was effective in getting individuals to quit smoking, as it is believed to stimulate the neurotransmitter dopamine, causing the same pleasurable responses associated with nicotine ingestion.

Even with the empirically validated efficacy of pharmacotherapy, most professionals discourage the belief that medication alone will solve the drug problem. In addition to using psychosocial interventions such as psychotherapy and 12-step programs (Nash, 1997), cognitive-behavioral therapies (CBTs) may be necessary because the techniques used are designed to equip individuals with new coping skills within a brief treatment context. These learned skills may create a change in the chemical activities occurring in the brain by increasing the natural release of dopamine through modified thoughts, feelings, and behaviors.

Cognitive-Behavioral Interventions

"Cognitive-behavioral therapy (CBT) uses performance-based and cognitive interventions to produce changes in thinking, feeling, and behavior" (Kendall & Panichelli-Mindel, 1995, p. 107). This type of modification involves both the external environment and the individual's internal processing of the world. In CBT, professional therapists take on several modifying roles to provide help to the client, including providing ideas for experimentation and help with sorting through past experiences. The therapists also introduce problem-solving skills, coping skills, and educational tools that influence clients to think for themselves while maximizing personal strengths and altering their past thoughts and behaviors. The primary objective of CBT, in its most basic form, is to change the stimulus and response patterns that cause smoking (classical conditioning) and/or to reward clients for not smoking while teaching them how to avoid it (operant conditioning and social learning) (*Harvard Mental Health Letter*, 1997, May, June). While CBT is perhaps most successful when professionally designed and administered, in today's time-limited and brief therapeutic environment, self-modification should also be considered as an optional alternative when professional services are not available or affordable. For most, cognitive-behavioral changes can be straightforward and easily implemented by clients who have a commitment to change.

First, it is important to understand the relationship between smoking and the brain. Current studies indicate that the neurotransmitter dopamine is more than a chemical responsible for transmitting pleasure signals and that is relationship to addiction is pronounced (Brautbar, 1995; Came, 1993; Nash, 1997; Peck, 1996). In the field of neuroscience, specific brain receptors have been identified and cloned for every major drug of abuse. Scientists have realized that almost all of the major drugs of abuse affect a single brain circuit, the mesolimbic pathway, which is mediated by dopamine (Peck, 1996). "The dopamine hypothesis provides a basic framework for understanding how a genetically encoded trait—such as a tendency to produce too little dopamine—might intersect with environmental influences to create a serious behavioral disorder" (Nash, 1997, p. 68).

When treatment options are examined, it is important to remember that neurotransmitters such as dopamine underlie every thought and emotion that leads to memory and learning. The pivotal question appears to be, If neurotransmitters are, in fact, the carriers of signals between all nerve cells or neurons in the brains, how can cognitive-behavioral modifications work against such a strong physiological addiction? Given its association with pleasure and elation, dopamine could indeed be elevated by social interactions such as hugs, kisses, or words of praise shared during an evening spent with friends, as well as by the potent pleasures that come from mind/mood altering drugs (Nash, 1997). Thus, simple cognitive and behavioral modifications may naturally increase dopamine release, eliminating the long-term need for pharmaceutical or other drug-related treatments.

One of the first steps in applying CBT involve helping clients to change their views about cigarettes. The habitually pleasurable thoughts of smoking must be replaced with new thoughts grounded in the reality that smoking often kills. In addition, smokers must begin to realize that nicotine addiction has another drawback: it is a habit that controls their lives. To break the cycle, users must become aware and gain some control over their dysfunctional thoughts and behaviors. Smokers who generally succeed in quitting have clearly defined motivations, expectations, self-management skills, and quitting strategies, and, when possible, they have access to social supports and psychosocial resources for both quitting and permanently abstaining from smoking (Orleans, 1985).

Key points for success in time-limited CBTs include the following:

(1) *Help the client to find a smoking-cessation plan that requires a specific day to stop, and be sure that there is support of a group or social network in place to help the client throughout the process.* Although numerous smoking-cessation programs exist, they vary greatly in price and proven success rates. For instance, the Mayo Nicotine Dependence Center in Rochester, Minnesota, runs a series of eight-day residential programs in an ordinary hospital setting offering exercise programs, pharmacotherapies, and individual counseling. This program has a success rate of 50% and costs about $2,850. The Cooper Wellness Program in Dallas, Texas, offers a two-week program at an average cost of $8,000 (Armour, 1997). In self-administered programs, smokers can purchase a week's supply of nicotine patches for approximately $27 that also includes weekly support programs and materials. Thy can also incorporate short-term individual weekly counseling to support and help plan the intervention process.

(2) *It is essential to help clients realize that in order to fight the desire to smoke, resistance must be identified and accompanied with a change in "thinking."* One of the major concepts of cognitive therapy is cognitive restructuring. This skill involves modifying the thoughts, ideas, and beliefs that maintain the client's abnormal behaviors, such as self-statements or self-talk (DeSilvestri, 1989; Dush, Hirt, & Schroeder, 1989). In time-limited CBT, defining the problem, selecting a goal, and generating alternative solutions that alter thoughts and behaviors are encouraged. Thought-stopping involves consciously stopping the negative thought and replacing it with a positive or more adaptive one. When smokers face nicotine cravings, they must consciously choose to change thinking patterns. This can be accomplished alone or in combination with other behavioral modifications. For example, clients should be instructed to say no to the craving and think about why they want to quit. Constant reminders of how well the client is doing on the plan need to be made available for support in times of weakness. Also, mixing the thought-stopping with behavioral intervention is important. For example, help the client to plan to think about something else that is action related, such as getting up, changing positions, or simply walking outside. The client needs to identify and plan to become involved in nonsmoking activities, such as going to church, the gym, or the mall or just talking a walk.

(3) *Always select some type of standardized measurement that can be used to help compare pretest/posttest scores, and use some type of self-report instrument to help the client see the changes that have been made.* In this type of intervention, standardized measures are considered essential to measure outcome results. Fischer and Corcoran (1994) provide a rich selection of scales that can be used in this area. Two measurement scales that might be of particular interest are the Self-Rating Anxiety Scale (SAS) and the Smoking Self-Efficacy Questionnaire (SSEQ). The SAS, a 20-item instrument consisting of the most commonly found characteristics of an anxiety disorder, is used to assess anxiety as a clinical disorder and to quantify anxiety symptoms (Zung, 1971). The SSEQ, a 17-item instrument, is used to measure beliefs about one's ability to resist the urge to smoke (Colletti, Supnick, & Payne, 1985).

(4) *In the intervention strategy, never use food as a reinforcer or substitute.* A primary concern for many individuals who are contemplating smoking cessation is the fear of gaining weight. The majority of smokers who quit smoking do gain weight. Most will gain fewer than 10 pounds, but a general sense of foreboding can interfere with the cessation motivation process (Williamson et al., 1991). Postcessation weight gain appears to be caused by both increased food consumption and by metabolic adjustments; however, regardless of caloric intake, once nicotine leaves the system, the body's metabolism goes through a period of temporary gradual arrest until it can rebalance itself naturally (Hatsukami, LaBounty, Hughes, & Laine, 1993; Hofstetter, Schutz, Jequier, & Wahren, 1986; Klesges & Shumaker, 1992).

Phelps and Nourse (1986) suggest that certain food replacements and exercise can positively combat the addictive process, as long as the smoker is willing to also change his or her patterns of behavior. According to these authors, proper nutrition is essential to beating the body's addictions; nutritional enrichment, based on frequent sugar-free feedings to stabilize the blood sugar and large doses of vitamins and minerals to reverse the body's long-standing depletion, can help in this process. In addition to better nutrition, daily exercise is recommended as an essential element in self-treatment and professional-based programs. Exercise aids in the body's release of natural biochemical neurotransmitters such as dopamine and endorphins. This, in turn, tones and conditions cerebral circulation while acting as a powerful antidote to the depression many recovering addicted persons encounter (Phelps & Nourse, 1986).

Examples of simple behavior-change strategies include having the individuals (a) change where and when they eat (e.g., going to different restaurants, always sitting in the nonsmoking section, consciously changing diet, and avoiding sugar and caffeine); (b) add exercise to their daily routines (e.g., dancing around the house, taking short walks, parking their car in the furthest space, completing isometric exercises while driving and sitting); and (c) learn to use relaxation techniques (talking at least five deep breaths and visualizing a soothing, pleasurable situation).

(5) *Help the client to develop a strategy for change that involves real options such as "time out" while giving up feelings of deprivation and the illusion of having "just one."* When examining CBTs, simple behavioral modifications may be warranted in addition to thought modifications, because overt behavior is often easier to change than thinking habits. One of the principle factors in behavioral therapy is classical conditioning, which involves the pairing of existing patterns of stimulus and response with new stimuli to create new responses. A second factor is operant conditioning, or patterning reward and punishment to alter behavior (*Harvard Mental Health Letter*, 1997, May, June).

During withdrawal, the smoker can use planned avoidance; for example, the smoker can leave a "smoking area" and call a family member or friend. Dangerous situations can be anticipated by preplanning activities that will keep the client busy and focused during times of cravings. Other behavioral changes can include reading a book, starting a diary, gardening, or engaging in music- or art-related activities. In each situation, concentration on either the reward for completion of the successful behavior or the seeking of new stimuli (e.g., calling a friend for socialization) can create new responses.

(6) *Help the client realize that he or she has choices and not smoking must be a self-initiated option.* The smoker must embrace choice and remember that the temporary physical discomforts associated with nicotine withdrawal can and will subside in a few short days. The client needs to be aware that no one will take the smoker's cigarettes away, that quitting is entirely voluntary, and that, if failure occurs, intervention can still be resumed. The longer-term psychological dependency can be addressed by changing thoughts and behaviors to increase control of destiny and success.

Even though addiction to nicotine and other drugs appears to be a highly complex brain disorder, the behavioral and social contexts that have been truly embedded in the psyche require complex treatment strategies. The concept is based on what has been called "whole person treatment." Managed care may undoubtedly find it extremely cost-effective to take a longer-term, comprehensive perspective, using appropriate treatments with the appropriate patient and applying treatments that last long enough to have an effect (Peck, 1996).

(7) *Clients need support (social and professional) during and after the intervention process.* Research repeated confirms that physical addiction is only one factor to be considered when designing cessation-treatment programs. Many individuals continue to smoke because they enjoy the smoking behaviors and they become conditioned to "lighting up" in certain situations. A smoker's entire day is filled with cues that trigger the desire for a cigarette: having the first cup of coffee in the morning, driving in the car to work, sitting down at the computer, reading the paper, or finishing a meal. Although pharmacotherapies and cognitive-behavioral strategy may assist in smoking cessation, support from family, friends, and professionals remains a key ingredient to achieve success in sustaining the will to quit.

When alcoholics and "illicit"-drug addicts decide to "get clean," they are often encouraged by family, friends, and professionals to participate in 12-step programs such as Alcoholics Anonymous or Narcotics Anonymous, or to check themselves into supportive inpatient treatment programs. Because nicotine addiction is just as (if not more) powerful as other drug addictions, these same strategies need to be implemented into the smoker's daily routine. Furthermore, "flooding" the client with this kind of support can increase the will for abstinence, thus increasing the odds for success.

According to Cohen, Stookey, Katz, Drook, and Smith (1989), many smokers who have expressed a desire to quit may resist enrolling in various organized smoking-cessation programs. This type of participation, however, is particularly important for smokers who also have limited social support systems. Furthermore, to facilitate intervention, physician involvement is paramount because health care providers are in a key position for influencing the smoking habits of their patients (Cohen et al., 1989). According to Hughes (1996), however, many primary care physicians shy away from treating smoking because they feel their training is limited in the area and view counseling as too complex and time-consuming. In addition, it is suggested that other health care professionals, such as social workers, therapists, chemical dependency clinicians, and psychiatrists, also ignore smoking because nicotine dependence does not cause immediate adverse psychosocial consequences or severe intoxication as do alcohol and illicit drugs.

To add insult to injury, and in spite of a wealth of empirical data, it is possible that professionals are reluctant to accept the responsibilities of treating smokers who wish to quit because they do not take notice of the severity of this specific addition. Many experienced health care workers fail to see or choose to ignore the need for smoking-cessation programs, because they believe that most smokers voluntarily choose to quit on their own and are successful. Many primary care professionals often overlook that smoking is a form of drug dependence and that it should be treated as such.

(8) *Help clients to understand and address stress.* Many research studies highlight withdrawal symptoms such as irritability, frustration, anger, anxiety, difficulty concentrating, and restlessness, but a search of the literature revealed no mention of the negative consequences that can occur as a result of these symptoms. Research suggests that stress can have significant effects on the human body. Basically, psychological and/or physiological stress can affect the immune system by affecting the number of white blood cells and by decreasing lymphocyte production (Herbert, 1994). It is believed that stress can affect the body in unpredictable ways, similar to when individuals who experience allergy-stress reactions have sensitized or acutely sensitive reactions. Once a reaction is programmed, even the slightest intimation of stress can trigger a case of chemical reactions in the brain and body (Carpi, 1996).

According to Herbert (1994), stress activates primitive regions of the brain, such as the areas that control the immune system. When stress levels begin to rise, the nerve circuits ignite the body's fight-or-flight mechanisms. Stress predominantly attacks the hypothalamus and the pituitary gland. When stress sets off the neurological communications, adrenal glands manufacture and release the "true" stress hormones: dopamine, epinephrine, norepinephrine, and cortisol. This is highly relevant for practice because of the correlation between neurotransmitters and addictions and neurotransmitters and stress. Research also suggests a connection between the duration of the stress and the amount of immune change. Both physiological and behavioral mechanisms provide possible explanations as to why and how emotional states can alter individual immune systems.

Furthermore, persons experiencing tremendous stress tend to sleep less, avoid exercise, have poorer diets, smoke more, and use alcohol and other drugs more often than nonstressed people (Carpi, 1996).

When relating this to smoking cessation, it is important to acknowledge the national statistics that have repeatedly indicated that smokes have high motivation and a readiness for change but limited success, because smoking is a complex addictive behavior influenced by powerful physical, emotional, and social factors. Quitting requires extreme control of these factors (Orleans, 1985).

Conclusions and Future Considerations

This article has addressed the correlation between physiological/psychological addiction and successful smoking cessation within a time-limited intervention framework. Furthermore, it appears that for professional helping to be facilitated, the following suggestions need to be addressed. First, it appears that the psychopharmacological aspects in terms of addiction remain important considerations in helping to promote smoking cessation, especially for eliminating the physical craving. Second, special attention must be given to what to do when environmental stressors become overwhelming. The environment and family supports cannot be minimized, as they can clearly influence the continuance and completion of the intervention process. For social workers, the "person-in-environment" stance that has long been the cornerstone of professional practice may bring some valuable insight. For many clients, life stressors (e.g., divorce) that are not the focus of the actual intervention can clearly hamper intervention attempts. This means that in the first session of the intervention process, environmental concerns as well as social and family support should be assessed. For example, clients should be encouraged to attend a nicotine-support group or use any 12-step program supports such as telephone therapy or go through a formal class/support structure (e.g., American Cancer Society's no-smoking group "Smoke-enders"). Also, plans for including the friends and family members as supporters in the intervention process should be clearly outlined.

For counseling professionals, an empirically driven triadic intervention can present as a sound way to initially quit smoking, but the psychosocial factors should be clearly identified and subsequent plans to address them need to be made early in treatment. Also, the client must clearly show the desire to quit and be willing to plan to act on the intervention plan accordingly. Exogenous factors that create stress must be clearly identified, and plans to address them must be considered. Increased stress leads to a decreased ability to sustain smoking cessation. Therefore, decreased stress levels through more comprehensive planning of potential blocks to intervention success may increase the chances of longer-term success. Psychopharmacological treatment may be critical to addressing physiological dependency, allowing the smoker a window of opportunity for behavioral change. Cognitive-behavioral therapy can counteract thought processes for the short term; however, longer-term changes must be in tandem with increased use of social supports. Last, clearly evaluating social support and supportive counseling cannot be underestimated in the intervention process. Support groups are highly encouraged as a means of gaining low-cost support and assistance. Techniques of recovery borrowed from Alcoholics Anonymous, such as telephone therapy, sponsorship, and most important, the concept of "one drag" versus "one drink," could be used. In addition, social workers need to assist clients in estimating and preparing for "system" difficulties (e.g., clearly identifying marital issues, family members, and events that can impede the counseling process).

Implications for Professional Practice

The social work profession in general has historically committed itself to addressing the needs of women, persons of color, children and adolescents, and other oppressed groups who are increasingly vulnerable to the harmful effects of tobacco use (Kaplan & Weiler, 1997). However, at present, social work practice has invested minimal involvement in the development of programs and policies related to smoking cessation and other health-related behaviors (Dziegielewski, 1998). Even though extensive literature continues to clearly reveal the hazards and harmful effects caused by smoking cigarettes, social workers remain virtually unknown in this field.

Throughout the years, social work has been a profession awaiting empowerment, from governments that hold back funds and from other helping professionals who maintain decision-making responsibility. Nevertheless, as social workers move toward an alignment with health-restoration practice, a rationale will need to be created for the addition of social work involvement (Valentich, 1994). As a profession, social work can offer services in mental health agencies, the criminal justice system, health facilities, social service departments, and places of employment. In addition, we come into contact with the majority of high-risk children and teens in the school system (NASW policy, 1987).

Social workers can and must increase their collective voice to become the leaders in this field by (1) becoming better educated in the multifactorial nature of smoking as a form of drug addiction; (2) looking at supplementing the counseling approach to therapy with pharmacological supports, such as the nicotine patch or medication intervention; (3) remaining aware that the long-term psychological dependencies are powerful and must be counteracted through a more balanced use of the treatment plan and other resources; (4) using a multi- or interdisciplinary framework for collateral support (e.g., physicians and nutritionists) in the intervention process; (5) harnessing social supports such as support groups and indigenous resources, such as persons in the community who have already quit; and (6) taking a preventative stance by being proactive about increasing awareness among clients by advocating that smoking is a form of drug addiction. The profession can act as an industry watch dog for mass media that promote smoking in order to prevent children from beginning to smoke in the first place. Furthermore, from a developmental standpoint, intervention with early smokers (e.g., teens) is a top priority.

References

American Cancer Society. (1996). *The decision is yours.* (Brochure.)

American Lung Association. (1995). *Facts about nicotine addiction and cigarettes.* (Brochure.)

American Psychiatric Association. (1994). *Diagnostic and statistical manual of mental disorders* (4th ed.). Washington, DC: Author.

Apgar, B. (1997). Major depression after smoking cessation. *American Family Physician, 56*(2), 582.

Armour, L. A. (1997). Beyond cold turkey: Where to quit if you need a little help: Six serious smoke-cessation programs (residential programs). *http://www.fcla.ufl.edu/cgi-bin/cgiwrap/~louisr/cgids/NO19964856.*

Brautbar, N. (1995). Direct effects of nicotine on the brain: Evidence for chemical addiction. *Archives for Environmental Health, 50*(4), 263–266.

Came, B. (1993). Clues in the brain. *Maclean's, 107*(29), 40–42.

Carpi, J. (1996). . . . Stress . . . it's worse than you think (psychological effects). *Psychology Today, 29*(1), 34–39.

Cohen, S. J., Stookey, G. K., Katz, B. P., Drook, C. A., & Smith, D. M. (1989). Encouraging primary care physicians to help smokers quit: A randomized, controlled trial. *Annals of Internal Medicine, 110*(8), 648–652.

Colletti, G., Supnick, J. A., & Payne, T. J. (1985). The Smoking Self-Efficacy Questionnaire (SSEQ): Preliminary scale development and validation. *Behavioral Assessment, 7,* 249–260.

DeSilvestri, C. (1989). Clinical models in RET: An advanced model of the organization of emotional and behavioral disorders. *Journal of Rational-Emotive and Cognitive-Behavior Therapy, 7,* 51–58.

Dush, D. M., Hirt, M. L., & Schroeder, H. E. (1989). Self-statement modification in the treatment of child behavior disorders: A meta-analysis. *Psychological Bulletin, 106,* 97–106.

Dziegielewski, S. F. (1998). *The changing face of health care social work: Practice in the era of managed care.* New York: Springer.

Fischer, J., & Corcoran, K. (1994). *Measures for clinical practice: A sourcebook* (2nd ed., Vol. 2, Adults). New York: Springer.

Glynn, T. J., Greenwald, P., Mills, S. M., & Manley, M. (1993). Youth tobacco use in the United States: Problem, progress, goals, and potential solutions. *Preventive Medicine, 22,* 568–575.

Harvard Mental Health Letter. (1997, May). Lester Grinspoon, editor, *13*(11), 1–8.

Harvard Mental Health Letter. (1997, June). Lester Grinspoon, editor, *13*(12), 1–8.

Hatsukami, D., LaBounty, L., Hughes, J., & Laine, D. (1993). Effects of tobacco abstinence on food intake among cigarette smokers. *Health Psychology, 12,* 499–502.

Health and Policy Committee, American College of Physicians. (1986). Methods for stopping cigarette smoking. *Annals of Internal Medicine, 105,* 281–291.

Herbert, T. B. (1994). Stress and the immune system. *World Health, 47*(2), 4–6.

Hofstetter, A., Schutz, Y., Jequier, J., & Wahren, J. (1986). Increased 24-hour energy expenditure in cigarette smokers. *New England Journal of Medicine, 314,* 79–82.

Hughes, J. R. (1996). The future of smoking cessation therapy in the United States. *Addiction, 91*(12), 1797–1803.

Inside the addict's brain. (1994). *Psychology Today, 27*(5), 37–39.

Kaplan, M. S., & Weiler, R. E. (1997). Social patterns of smoking behavior: Trends and practice implications. *Health & Social Work, 22*(1), 47–52.

Kendell, P. C., & Panichelli-Mindel, S. M. (1995). Cognitive-behavioral treatments.

Journal of Abnormal Child Psychology, 23(1), 107–122.

Key, K. K. (1994, December 5). Smoking issues: Alternative drugs may help kick the habit. *Cancer Research Weekly,* 11–12.

Klesges, R. C., & Shumaker, S. A. (1992). Proceedings of the National Working Conference on Smoking and Body Weight. *Health Psychology, 11,* 1–22.

Moncher, M. S., Schinke, S. P., & Holden, G. W. (1992). Tobacco addiction: Correlates, prevention, and treatment. In E. M. Freeman (Ed.), *The addiction process: Effective social work approaches* (pp. 222–236). New York: Longman.

Nash, J. M. (1997). Why do people get hooked? Mounting evidence points to a powerful brain chemical called dopamine. *Time,* 149(18), 68–74.

NASW policy on alcohol and other drugs: Alcoholism and other substance abuse-related problems. (1987, November). *Policy Statement from NASW Delegate Assembly.* Washington, DC.

Nordenberg, T. (1998). It's quittin' time: Smokers need not rely on willpower alone. *http://web.lexisnexis.com/universe/docum.*

O'Brien, C. P., & McLellan, A. T. (1996). Myths about the treatment of addiction. *Lancet,* 347(8996), 237–240.

Orleans, C. T. (1985). Understanding and promoting smoking cessation: Overview and guidelines for physician intervention. *Annual Review of Medicine, 36,* 51–61.

Peck, R. L. (1996). The addicted brain: An era of scientific breakthroughs. *Behavioral Health Management, 16*(5), 33–35.

Phelps, J. K., & Nourse, A. E. (1986). *The hidden addiction and how to get free: Recognizing and breaking the habits that control your life.* Boston: Little, Brown.

Pomerleau, O. F., & Pomerleau, C. S. (1984). Neuroregulators and their reinforcement of smoking: Towards a behavioral explanation. *Neuroscience Behavior Review, 8,* 503–515.

Riessman, F., & Carroll, D. (1996). A new view of addiction: Simple and complex. *Social Policy, 27*(2), 36–41.

Skarr, K. L., Tsoh, J. Y., McClure, J. B. Cinciripini, P. M., Friedman, K., Wetter, D. W., & Gritz, E. R. (1992). Smoking cessation 1: An overview of research. *Behavioral Medicine, 23*(1), 5–9.

SmithKline Beecham. (1996). NicoDerm CQ stop smoking aid nicotine transdermal system. *Consumer Healthcare, L.P.* Pittsburgh, PA.

Solberg, L. I., Maxwell, P. L., Kottke, T. E., Gepner, G. J., & Brekke, M. L. (1990). A systematic primary care office-based smoking cessation program. *Journal of Family Practice, 30*(6), 647–654.

The Science of Smoking. (1996). *The Economist,* 339(7965), 22.

U.S. Department of Health and Human Services. (1996). *Smoking cessation: Information for specialists* (AHCPR Publication No. 96-0694). Rockville, MD: U.S. Government Printing Office.

Valentich, M. (1984). Social work and the development of a smoke-free society. *Social Work, 39*(4), 439–450.

Warner, K. E. (1987). Health and economic implications of a tobacco-free society. *Journal of the American Medical Association, 258,* 2080–2086.

Williamson, D. F., Madans, J., Anda, R. F., Kleinman, J. C., Giovino, G. A., & Beyers, T. (1991). Smoking cessation and severity of weight gain in a national cohort. *New England Journal of Medicine, 324,* 739–745.

Zung, W. K. (1971). A rating instrument for anxiety disorders. *Psychosomatics, 12,* 371–379.

SHARI A. SINWELSKI
LINDA VINTON

33

Stalking: The Constant Threat of Violence

Stalking is unlike other types of crimes because it may include individual actions that are legal, but when put together, these acts cause victims to be fearful of injury or death (Bureau of Justice Assistance, 1996). Stalking did not receive much recognition until the 1989 shooting death of actress Rebecca Shaeffer shed light on the potentially violent consequences of stalking (de Becker, 1997) and celebrities such as David Letterman, Theresa Saldana, Janet Jackson, Madonna, and Steven Spielberg revealed that they have been victims of some form of repeated harassment (McCann, 1995).

Publicity surrounding such cases put pressure on state legislatures in the 1990s to draft legislation to protect those who are repeatedly and persistently followed, harassed, and physically intimidated or threatened in some other way. As with other forms of interpersonal violence, many hidden victims soon came forward to tell their stories and seek protection and remedy for being stalked. Although a precise number of stalking cases has not yet been determined, the National Violence Against Women Survey, a comprehensive survey of violence against women conducted by the Center for Policy Research, found that of the 16,000 respondents, 8% of the women and 2% of the men had been victims of stalking at some time in their lives (Tjaden, 1997). A projection of the findings to the 1995 U.S. population indicated that about 1.4 million persons (1 million women and 400,000 men) per year were affected by stalking; thus, the problem appears to be more prevalent than was previously believed.

This article reports on the history of stalking as a social and legal problem and contemporary efforts to define and regulate stalking behavior. The dynamics of stalking are described along with various profiles or typologies of stalkers. Interventive strategies for working with victims and stalkers are also discussed.

Background

All the states and the District of Columbia have antistalking laws, most of which were passed in the 1990s. Prior to this legislation, the police could not arrest stalkers unless victims were physically attacked or injured. Although the legislation on stalking is new, the phenomenon is not. Historically, some behaviors that would be included in today's definitions of stalking were referred to as *erotomania*, which has been considered a pathological form of love since ancient times, with references to it in the writings of Hippocrates, Plutarch, and Galen (Kurt, 1995). Although the psychiatrists Hart (1912) and Kraepelin (1921/1976) alluded to erotomania in their writings on mental disorders, de Clérambault (1942), A French psychiatrist, is credited with describing the clinical features of erotomania. The phenomenon has even been referred to as *de Clérambault's syndrome* or *psychose passionnelle* (Segal, 1989).

What appears to be missing from these early descriptions of stalking as a psychiatric disorder is the sociopolitical context of the behavior. Although psychoanalytic interpretations may suggest that women gain power through stalking, the contemporary reality is that more than twice as many women as men are stalked (Tjaden, 1997). Furthermore, it has been estimated that as many as

90% of the women who were murdered by their husband or boyfriend were stalked prior to their deaths (Beck et al., 1992).

Although stalking gained attention during the late 1980s with the death of actress Rebecca Shaeffer, the stage was set during the 1960s and 1970s to accept stalking as a social problem with recognition of child and wife abuse as societal problems. The first law against stalking was passed in California in 1990, and by 1994, 48 states and the District of Columbia had passed such legislation (Dziegielewski & Roberts, 1995). Although Maine does not have an antistalking law, the state has a statute on terrorizing to address stalking behavior (Bureau of Justice Assistance, 1996).

Although the legal definitions of stalking vary from state to state, most definitions suggest that the stalker must have exhibited criminal intent of inducing fear in the victim and engaged in threatening behavioral patterns toward the victim. Most laws also have a course-of-conduct criteria clause that refers to the stalker's behavior as a series of acts that have taken place over time, and the laws of some states require that the victim must be fearful for his or her personal safety or bodily injury or death as a result of the stalker's actions (Dziegielewski & Roberts, 1995).

One of the toughest antistalking laws in the country was unanimously approved by the Florida legislature in 1992 (Dziegielewski & Roberts, 1995). According to Florida Statute 784.048, a victim must prove that she or he has been repeatedly followed or harassed by another person to file a charge of stalking against an alleged stalker but does not have to provide evidence of overt threats of death or severe injury. If found guilty, the stalker is convicted of a first-degree misdemeanor and faces a fine of up to $1,000 and up to one year in a county jail. As stated in Florida Statute 784.048 (§ 775.083), a misdemeanor escalates to the level of a felony (also called aggravated stalking) when a person "willfully, maliciously, and repeatedly follows or harasses another person, and makes a credible threat with the intent to place that person in reasonable fear of death or bodily injury" or violates an injunction for protection against repeated violence or for domestic violence. A person who is convicted of aggravated stalking faces a fine of up to $5,000 and up to five years in prison. Like Florida, most states have laws that distinguish between a misdemeanor and a felony charge of stalking.

In 1996, the National Institute of Justice released the Model Antistalking Code as a guide for states on writing antistalking laws that are neither too vague nor too specific. The Model Antistalking Code is distinguished from many state statutes in that it does not list specific types of behavior that constitute stalking (and thus avoids the implication that certain behaviors are the only ones) and does not use the term *credible threat* (which means that actual verbal or written threats would not be required as evidence of a threat that caused fear in a victim). In addition, the Violence Against Women Act of 1998 provides for stalkers who have restraining orders against them to be prosecuted when they travel across state lines.

Stalking Behaviors

As indicated by the various legal definitions, stalking behaviors range on a continuum of severity and intensity. They may begin with acts that individually may seem insignificant, such as repeated, unwanted contact in the form of telephone calls, beeper codes, e-mail messages, or letters. If left unchecked, these contacts may escalate to unwanted physical contacts or the stalker's "coincidental" appearance wherever the victim goes. Sometimes the contacts are in the form of unwanted gifts, such as flowers or jewelry. At other times, stalkers spread false rumors about their victims to the victims' family members, friends, or employers or lie to frighten or coerce their victims. One stalker, for instance, falsely informed the victim, his ex girlfriend, that he had AIDS. In addition, many stalkers go to the extreme of vandalizing, stealing, or destroying the victims' personal property. For example, one woman reported that her stalker mutilated her cat and left it in her yard, and another reported that her stalker left a pig's head on her doorstep (Pathé & Mullen, 1997).

Two studies used the Stalking Incident Checklist to assess stalking behaviors (Coleman, 1997; Wright et al., 1996). Wright et al. constructed a list of defining characteristics of stalking behavior that were organized around victimology, frequent crime scene indicators, common forensic findings, investigative considerations, and search warrant suggestions that were reviewed by FBI agents who were working on stalking cases. They then reviewed anecdotal cases, the literature, and newspaper accounts of stalking, along with 10 self-reports and 20 additional cases reported to the Trauma and Violence Office at the University of Pennsylvania, to refine the instrument to a 46-item checklist, which was pilot-tested at a victim assistance agency. The Stalking Incident Checklist included background information, number or frequency of incidents, length of time the behavior has been directed at the victim, location of the behavior, level of aggression, style and content of communication during the stalking incident, typology, victim's level of risk, stalker's motive, and outcome.

Coleman (1997) used a version of the Stalking Behavior Checklist (SBC) along with the Conflict Tactics Scale (CTS) to measure abusive behavior in her study of 141 female undergraduate psychology students. We assume that availability dictated the choice of sample. Coleman stated that stalking often takes place in cases in which there is a romantic or even imagined relationship. The participants were divided into three groups: (1) controls (who answered no when asked if they ever ended a relationship that resulted in repeated, unwanted attention by a former partner), (2) harassed (who answered yes to the same question and to questions based on Florida's antistalking law), and (3) stalked (who answered yes to all these questions and affirmed the malicious intent of and fear caused by their former partner's acts). The vast majority of the participants (90) were controls; 38 and 13 were in the harassed group and the stalked group, respectively.

Coleman examined the three groups' demographic characteristics, reports of former partner's behavior, and use of violent tactics to resolve conflict during former relationships and found no statistically significant demographic differences between the groups. The participants' mean age (23.6 years) and race (78% were White) matched the mean age (24.6 years) and race (81% were White) of their former partner. Gender of the former partners was not among the demographic information collected.

The results of a factor analysis indicated that two factors accounted for 45.5% of the variance in scores on the SBC. Factor 1 (34.7%) consisted of items on the violent behavior subscale of the SBC (physically harming the victim, breaking into the victim's house or car, and violating a restraining order), and Factor 2 (10.8%) consisted of items on the harassing behavior subscale (made repeated telephone calls to the victim, followed or watched the victim, and went to the victim's home or workplace). Post hoc analyses distinguished the women in the stalked group as reporting more violent and harassing behaviors than those in the control and harassed groups. With respect to the CTS, Coleman found that the stalked participants reported using more reasoning conflict-resolution strategies during their relationships with the stalkers than did those in the other two groups; this finding led her to suggest that men who are abusive during rela-

tionships are more likely to demonstrate harassing or violent behavior after the relationships have ended.

Characteristics of Stalkers

A few studies have examined the characteristics of stalkers. In one such study, Zona, Sharma, and Lane (1993) examined case files categorized as erotomanic, love obsessional, or simple obsessional that were collected by the Los Angeles Police Department's Threat Management Unit. Stalkers in the first two groups had delusions that they were passionately loved by their victims, with whom they had little or no contact. In contrast, those in the simple obsessional category had prior relationships with their victims, whom they felt had wronged or mistreated them; had more frequent contact with their victims (by telephone, letter, or in person); and were the only ones to cause bodily or property harm. However, as Coleman (1997) pointed out, from a methodological standpoint, Zona et al.'s study did not include a control population and did not examine specific demographics of stalkers and victims.

Wright et al. (1996) did not report the victims' or stalkers' gender, age, race, educational level, or marital status for the 30 stalking cases they examined. In terms of typology, they found that 16 of the 30 cases were domestic (the stalkers and victims had relationships); 15 of these 16 stalkers were nondelusional, and 4 of the remaining 14 stalkers were delusional.

Similar to other types of partner violence, the motives of the 30 stalkers were classified primarily as anger-retaliation (12 cases) and possession (10 cases), followed by infatuation (6 cases) and other motives (2 cases). With regard to the victims' level of risk, 13 victims (43%) were considered to be at high risk, 12 (40%) were considered to be at medium risk, and 5 (17%) were considered to be at low risk. Of the 30 cases, 16 were dispatched to the legal system, and 4 received psychiatric treatment; 7 stalkers committed suicide, and for the remaining 3 cases, the outcomes were not known. Of the 30 victims, 6 were murdered by their stalkers. Wright et al. (1996)described three such cases in which the stalker-murderers were either ex-husbands or ex-boyfriends; again, the similarity to scenarios of homicides in domestic violence cases is evident.

In their article, Wright et al. (1996 referred to "targets" as well as victims and stated that the terms are not necessarily interchangeable. A target is the primary recipient of the stalker's attention, but there may be victims other than the targeted person, including relatives and friends. Wright et al. may have drawn this distinction because of their law enforcement, rather than victim assistance, perspective, as is evident when they described persons other than the target that the stalker may harm as "innocent parties." The implication is that the targets of stalkers are not innocent or are somehow implicated in the stalking behavior.

The National Violence Against Women Survey of 8,000 women and 8,000 men, conducted from November 1995 to May 1996, collected data on the prevalence of stalking, characteristics of stalkers and victims, characteristics of stalking behaviors, victims' perceptions of the reasons they were stalked, incidence of stalking with domestic violence, victims' responses, and the psychological and social consequences of stalking (Tjaden, 1997). Of those who were surveyed, 10% (8% of the women and 2% of the men) had experienced stalking at some time. Of these cases, the women were significantly more likely than the men to have been stalked by a current or former partner (79%), and 87% of the stalkers were men. Half of the male victims' stalkers were reported to have had accomplices (typically a friend or girlfriend), whereas the women's stalkers tended to act alone.

The survey found no difference in the rate of stalking between White and minority women, but among minority women, Native American women were at a greater risk of being stalked. Behaviors that the stalkers demonstrated included spying on or following the victim (reported by 75% of the victims), making overt threats (45%), vandalizing the victim's property (30%), and threatening to kill or killing the victim's pets (10%). Most of the female victims (and many of the male victims) believed they were being stalked because their partner or ex-partner wanted to scare or control them and keep them in the relationship. In 60% of the cases, the stalking behaviors started before the relationship had ended; 80% of the women reported being physically assaulted and 31% sexually assaulted by their partner during the relationship.

Victim's Perceptions

With respect to victims' responses to stalking, Tjaden (1997) reported that half the victims reported stalking behaviors to law enforcement personnel. A disproportionately greater number of female victims than male victims obtained restraining orders, 80% of which were violated. Slightly fewer than 25% of the women's cases against the stalkers were prosecuted, compared to 19% of the men's cases. About one third of the victims sought psychological help in the aftermath of the stalking, which usually stopped one to two years after the first episode. Twenty percent lost work hours, and 7% said they did not return to work because of the stalking. When asked what made the stalking cease, 20% of the victims said they had moved away, and 15% attributed the cessation to involvement by the police. Others noted that the stalking stopped when the assailants remarried or had new girlfriends.

Romans, Hays, and White (1996) conducted a study of 10 staff members of a counseling center who had been stalked by their clients. Of the 10 stalkers, five were female and three were male; the gender of the remaining two was not specified. The reported ages of the male stalkers ranged from 17 to 25, and the female stalkers' ages ranged from 20 to 40. According to the counselors, 6 of the 10 stalkers had presenting problems elated to Axis II personality disorders in the *Diagnostic and Statistical Manual of Mental Disorders* (4th ed.) (American Psychiatric Association, 1994). Although this study shed light on the stalking of professional helpers, it was limited by its small sample size and the selective sample (stalkers who had sought counseling).

Lowney and Best (1995) examined the construction of stalking as a crime problem and classified claims from 1980 to 1994. From 1980 to 1988, the term *psychological rape* was used to describe stalking claims. The dynamics of psychological rape were considered to be men harassing women, usually in nonviolent ways; obsessed offenders; and victims who may have shared responsibility for the harassment—these claims resulted in occasional media coverage. From 1989 to 1991, the claims were termed *star stalking* because the victims tended to be celebrities and the offenders were of either gender. In these cases, the victims tended not to be viewed as sharing responsibility for the stalking; the offenders were thought of as suffering from erotomania, and violence and homicide were seen as possible outcomes. The response was increased media coverage and the passage of California's antistalking law.

From 1992 to 1994, the term *stalking* was used to describe claims, and in these claims, the dynamics of psychological rape and star stalking were combined. In the stalking claims, men tended to harass women, victims and offenders were often former intimates or current partners, the victims were not responsible for the harassment, and homicide was often the outcome. According to Lowney and

Best (1995), some of the sociocultural aspects of stalking are vulnerability to harassment, violence by men, and the victimization of women. Contemporary resources in combating stalking include the crime victims' movement, battered women's advocates, and law enforcement.

Effects of Stalking

Pathé and Mullen (1997) explored the effects of stalking on 100 victims (whose gender and race were not reported). They found that 94 of the victims experienced changes in their work or social lives. The types of changes they experienced varied, but 53% either changed jobs or stopped working, and 39% moved as a result of being stalked (among those who moved, seven moved to another state and three moved overseas). Most of the victims (82%) modified their usual activities because of their experiences, including avoiding places that the stalker might be or forbidding their children to answer the door, and many (73%) took measures to increase their security, such as changing telephone numbers or obtaining unlisted numbers, getting post office boxes, or even changing their names. Others purchased security systems for their homes, and three used security guards at their place of employment. Some victims took more aggressive approaches; for example, five took self-defense courses, and four kept makeshift weapons under their bed.

With respect to psychological responses, 83% of the victims in Pathé and Mullen's (1997) study reported increased anxiety and "jumpiness, shakes, panic attacks, hypervigilance and exaggerated startle response" (p. 14), 74% cited chronic sleep disturbance and 55% reported nightmares or intrusive flashbacks. Many victims exhibited some symptoms of posttraumatic stress disorder (PTSD), and 37% were diagnosed as having PTSD; 24% reported suicidal ruminations.

Physical reactions to the stalking, including appetite disturbances (48%), persistent nausea (30%), and indigestion (27%), were also common. More than 20% of the victims reported increased alcohol or cigarette consumption, and more than 50% said they were excessively tired. Other physical problems noted were headaches and a worsening of existing physical problems, such as psoriasis or asthma.

Gross (1994) suggested that victims of stalking go through the five grief stages described by Kübler-Ross (1969). In the first stage, the victims may deny the seriousness of the stalker's behavior or fail to label it as stalking. In the second stage, they may bargain with the stalker if the stalker is known to them. In the third stage, the victims, particularly women, may feel guilty or assume some of the fault for the stalker's behavior because of women's gender socialization, which places more responsibility for relationships on women. In the fourth stage, the victims may feel angry at the stalker for disrupting their lives and making them feel afraid. In the fifth and final stage, the victims may come to accept that the burden for protecting themselves from the stalker rests with the victims themselves.

Interventions

Because stalking is such a new crime, the victims may not know where to go for help, and the people they approach for help may be as confused as the victims about the crime of stalking and the rights of victims. Because they often feel ashamed and embarrassed by the stalking, victims tend to isolate themselves and not tell others what is happening to them. They may blame themselves for their problem and ask themselves what they did to deserve being stalked. This way of thinking creates the illusion that if they would change their behavior in some way, the stalking would stop, whereas in reality, it is the stalkers who are responsible for the behavior, and only they can make it stop. Victims cannot control their stalker's behavior; they can only take precautions and do the best they can to cope.

According to Dziegielewski and Roberts (1995), three events typically cause victims to seek treatment: escalation of the incidence or severity of the stalking episodes, inflicted injury, and problems with a relationship or job. In other words, the precipitating event is viewed as the last straw—that is, the victims can no longer use their normal coping mechanisms to get through the situation, and a crisis state follows.

When victims seek treatment, it is important that they are taken seriously and not blamed for the stalking behavior. If they approach someone for help who does not understand the dynamics of their problem and how to treat it, they are likely to try to continue to cope on their own. Unfortunately, stalking is such a new crime that little has been written about strategies for treating its victims or which interventions are more effective for various groups: women or men, same-sex versus opposite-sex victims and stalkers, or victims and stalkers with mental or physical disabilities. In general, helpers must consider both the legal and psychosocial aspects of the crime as well as the safety of the victims.

Legal Interventions

The police response to the crime of stalking has been varied, perhaps because only 50% of the police departments in states with antistalking laws provide formal training to their officers, and hence police officers may not completely understand the dynamics of the crime (Dziegielewski & Roberts, 1995). However, some police departments have developed model programs to protect victims.

In response to a number of stalking incidents against celebrities, the Los Angeles Police Department established a four-member Threat Management Unit, also known as the Stalking Squad, in its Mental Evaluation Unit (Lane, 1992). Another innovative aid to stalking victims, a pendant with a small beeper, was developed by ADT security systems working directly with police departments and is used by two agencies in Florida and New Jersey that have coordinated victim assistance programs (Dziegielewski & Roberts, 1995). If a victim sees the stalker, she or he presses the pendant, which triggers an alarm at the ADT monitoring station that immediately informs the police. This aid may serve many stalking victims who are in protected places, but it will not help those who are directly exposed to their stalker because no matter how quickly the police are notified, it will still take some time for them to arrive on the scene.

Stalking victims have the legal option of obtaining restraining orders against their assailant. Restraining orders do not guarantee protection, however; they simply give victims legal recourse if the orders are violated. Requirements for restraining orders vary, but most states require that the offensive behavior already has occurred. An advantage of restraining orders is that they help to document the fear perceived by the victims, which it is necessary to show under most state statues. After completing a three-year follow-up study of 200 randomly selected persons against whom orders were issued, Meloy (1997) found that more than 80% of the persons who violated the orders were not subsequently arrested for crimes against the victims whom the orders wee supposed to protect.

Interventions to Empower Victims

Meloy (1997) advocated using a team consisting of "the victim, an emotionally supportive companion, a mental health professional, a local police officer familiar with the case, a local prosecutor, and in some cases, a private attorney and private security guard/investigator" (p. 175). Victim advocates may also be helpful to victims dealing with their responses to stalking and navigating the legal and other support systems. In addition, there should be a coordinator among the team members who maintains networking efforts on behalf of the victim. Depending on the needs of the victim, the focus of the group and involvement of its members may change.

According to Meloy (1997), clinicians should emphasize to stalking victims that they are primarily responsible for their own safety—that no one, including the police, has the power or ability to protect them from harm at all times. Although it is important for victims to take responsibility for their safety, they should not be made to feel responsible for the fact that they are being stalked. In taking personal responsibility, victims can develop a proactive approach by attempting to minimize risk when possible, such as by not walking to their car alone, adding security systems at home, and developing safety plans, that is, what they can do if they spot their stalker nearby.

Because most stalking victims find their usual coping mechanisms inadequate for dealing with their predicament, it is often helpful for them to seek the assistance of victim advocates or mental health professionals who are familiar with the dynamics of stalking. An advocate can help a victim manage the situation by giving support and guidance. Initially, the advocate can validate the victim's feelings and help empower the victim to take action. An advocate can also inform a victim of the laws in his or her state with regard to stalking.

After forming a trusting relationship with the victim, the advocate can help the victim deal with the stalker. The first thing the victim should do is tell the stalker explicitly that he or she does not want a relationship with the stalker and do so briefly because the stalker may misinterpret the victim's intentions. To build confidence and empower the victim, the advocate can help the victim rehearse what she or he will say and, if safety considerations permit, be present when the victim confronts the stalker. Victims should never be alone with stalkers because their personal safety may be at risk. Once a victim confronts the stalker, she or he should have no further contact with the stalker. Any communication, whether positive or negative can stimulate the stalker to continue to contact the victim.

Obviously, not all stalkers stop harassing their victims after they are confronted. In these cases, the victims may choose to file police reports or injunctions for protection. Documentation is of utmost importance in these cases. It is helpful for a victim who is working with the legal system to keep a log or journal of all attempts the stalker makes to contact her or him; each entry should include the date, time, and place of the contact; a description of the incident and how it affected him or her; and the names of any witnesses who were present.

Two sites on the World Wide Web may be helpful to stalking victims. The Stalking Victim's Sanctuary (http://www.stalkingvictims.com) offers information about stalking, tips on how to cope, and an online support group, and Survivors of Stalking (http://www.soshelp.org/) provides information about a national support group for stalking victims.

Prevention

Although the prevention of stalking is not within the victim's control, there are "red flags," according to de Becker (1997), who has written extensively about safety issues and stalking. As the result of working with victims of stalking on enhancing their security, de Becker believes that there are warning signs or behaviors that stalkers demonstrate before they actually stalk their victims. Knowing these signs can enhance awareness and therefore security; thus, de Becker refers to such "survival signals"—that is, behaviors that may indicate that a person will become a stalker—as forced teaming, charm or niceness, the use of too many details, "typecasting," "loan-sharking," unsolicited promises, and discounting the word *no*. As was pointed out earlier, these individual behaviors do not necessarily indicate that stalking will follow, but joined in a pattern over time, they can be intimidating or threatening.

According to de Becker (1997), in forced teaming, a stalker tries to establish a bond with the victim by creating the illusion that they share a common predicament, with the goal of establishing premature trust between them. A stalker who uses forced teaming may use phrases such as, "How are *we* going to get through this?" Charm can seem alluring and attractive but is used by stalkers to compel or control the victim for personal gain.

A stalker uses "too many details," according to de Becker (1997, p. 58), when he or she is lying and feels compelled to back up the lie with details because the lie "doesn't sound credible" even to him or her. A stalker who uses typecasting may say, "You are probably too busy to hear this, but . . . ," which may impel the listener to try to prove the stalker wrong by having a conversation with him or her.

Loan-sharking is used when a stalker does unsolicited favors for or gives gifts to the victim, which often makes the victim feel indebted to the stalker. According to de Becker (1997), there is often a motive behind unsolicited favors, and a person should be cautious if someone overextends himself or herself. "The unsolicited promise is one of the most reliable signals because it is nearly always of questionable motive" (p. 61). Unsolicited promises are little more than attempts by the speaker to convince the victim of something and thus should be viewed with caution. The final red flag is discounting the word *no*. A person should be able to say no to a question or request without feeling the need to defend it. A speaker who attempts to persuade another person to back down when the person has a strong belief about an issue sends the message that the speaker is in charge; this feeling of control can be dangerous.

Working with Stalkers

According to Meloy (1997), therapeutic interventions with stalkers must take into account that stalkers exhibit antisocial behaviors and are angry or out of touch with reality (or both). Thus, the stalker needs to experience both social repercussions and psychological treatment. The criminal justice system can attempt to protect the victim and send the stalker a message that society will not tolerate this type of behavior, but such treatment is not always effective. Sometimes the attention that stalkers receive through the legal system reinforces their stalking behavior; for example, Arthur Jackson, the man who stalked and attempted to murder the actress Theresa Saldana, continued to stalk her after he was released from incarceration (Markman & La Brecque, 1994). Other stalkers may like the notoriety that being in prison brings them. According to Rhonda Saunders (*Crazy for You*, 2000), a Los Angeles prosecutor who interviewed Robert Hoskins, who was incarcerated for stalking crimes against the singer Madonna, Hoskins painted "The Madonna Stalker" in his jail cell and appeared to enjoy being referred to as "the material guy" by his cell mates.

By its nature, stalking raises questions about the mental stability, maturity, and level of aggression of people who engage in it. Small-scale, descriptive studies of stalkers are now being conducted, but little is known about how stalkers are distinguished from the general population and whether legal or psychological treatment was effective in cases in which it was employed. Some states, such as Minnesota and Wisconsin, have recognized the dual nature of stalking and require the courts to order mental health evaluations and counseling for all stalking defendants (Bureau of Justice Assistance, 1996). In these cases, psychological treatment is usually left to the discretion of mental health professionals.

A few states have tried an unusual approach to curbing stalkers' obsessive behavior. They require convicted stalkers to wear electronic devices that signal to the police when they are in locations that are in violation of the stalker's probation (McCann, 1995). These devices take some of the responsibility for staying away from the victims off the victims and place it back on the offenders.

Conclusion

Historically, stalking received attention only when an obsessional stalker, either a man or a woman, pursued or harmed a public figure. It is now known that stalking is not a rare occurrence, and though it can happen to anyone (particularly in nondomestic cases), proportionately more women than men are victims. Some victims do not realize that stalking may have serious consequences and therefore do not take personal or legal measures against it when it starts.

Antistalking legislation was passed in swift response to the death of an actress in California in 1989. Since 1990, each state has taken steps to criminalize stalking behavior. Because legislation was passed rapidly, the need for modifications to these laws is already evident. The Model Antistalking Code (National Institute of Justice, 1996) offers useful guidelines to the states in this regard, and dialogues have begun among the many persons who work with and on behalf of the stalking victims, including law enforcement personnel and the treatment community.

Although the psychopathological characteristics of nondomestic stalkers need further examination, the dynamics of stalking in situations involving persons who are known to each other appear similar to those of abusive relationships. In stalking situations involving people who know one another, the number of male perpetrators is disproportionate, the motives seem to be power and control, and the former relationship between stalker and victim may have been emotionally and/or physically abusive. Individuals who have worked in the domestic violence community for

the past 30 years can undoubtedly relate stories of women who were stalked by their ex-husband or ex-partner. Hence, the sociopolitical context of stalking, like domestic violence, should not be ignored in the focus on stalkers' psychopathology or victims' characteristics.

Just as there is a growing awareness that dating relationships can be violent, greater attention is being paid to people of high school and college age who are being stalked by ex-boyfriends or ex-girlfriends. Through our work with college students and contacts with victim advocacy centers on college campuses, we have found that cases of stalking routinely come to the attention of advocates and counselors. Although little has been written about persons seeking counseling in the community at large, Meloy (1997) offered some beginning guidelines for clinical practice with stalking victims. It is hoped that the growing literature on the characteristics of stalkers and the effects of stalking on victims will lead to research on the effectiveness of interventions with both victims and stalkers. Such research should include diverse and large enough samples to allow the examination of the effect of factors like gender, sexual orientation, disability, and race-ethnicity on the effectiveness of treatment.

References

American Psychiatric Association. (1994). *Diagnostic and statistical manual of mental disorders* (4th ed.). Washington, DC: Author.

Beck, M., Rosenberg, D., Chideya, F., Miller, S., Foote, D., Manly, H., & Katel, P. (1992, July 13). Murderous obsession. *Newsweek*, 60–62.

Bureau of Justice Assistance. (1996). *Regional seminar series on developing and implementing antistalking codes.* Washington, DC: National Criminal Justice Association.

Coleman, F. L. (1997). Stalking behavior and the cycle of domestic violence. *Journal of Interpersonal Violence, 12*, 420–432.

Crazy for you [Online]. (2000, February 15). Available: http://www.cpnet.com/cpress/arts/popculture/docs

de Becker, G. (1997). *The gift of fear.* Boston: Little, Brown.

de Clérambault, C. G. (1942). Les psychoses passionelles [Passion psychoses]. In *Oeuvres psychiatriques* (pp. 315–322). Paris: Presses Universitaires de France.

Dziegielewski, S., & Roberts, A. R. (1995). Stalking victims and their survivors. In A. R.

Roberts (Ed.), *Crisis intervention and time-limited cognitive treatment* (pp. 73–90). Thousand Oak, CA: Sage.

Gross, L. (1994). *To have or to harm: True stories of stalkers and their victims.* New York: Warner Books.

Hart, B. (1912). *The psychology of insanity.* New York: G. P. Putnam.

Kraepelin, E. (1921/1976). *Manic-depressive insanity and paranoia.* New York: Arno.

Kübler-Ross, E. (1969). *On death and dying.* New York: Macmillan.

Kurt, J. L. (1995). Stalking as a variant of domestic violence. *Bulletin of the American Academy of Psychiatry and Law, 23,* 219–231.

Lane, J. (1992). Threat management fills void in police services. *Police Chief, 59*(8), 27.

Lowney, K. S., & Best J. (1995). Stalking strangers and lovers: Changing media typifications of a new crime problem. In J. Best (Ed.), *Images of issues: Typifying contemporary social problems* (2nd ed., pp. 33–57). New York: Aldine de Gruyter.

Markman, R., & La Brecque, R. (1994). *Obsessed: The stalking of Theresa Saldana.* New York: William Morrow.

McCann, J. T. (1995). Obsessive attachment and the victimization of children: Can antistalking legislation provide protection? *Law & Psychology Review, 19,* 95–112.

Meloy, J. R. (1997). The clinical risk management of stalking: "Someone is watching over me. . . . " *American Journal of Psychotherapy, 51,* 174–184.

National Institute of Justice. (1996). *Domestic violence, stalking, and antistalking legislation: An annual report to Congress under the Violence Against Women Act.* Washington, DC: U.S. Department of Justice.

Pathé, M., & Mullen, P.E. (1997). The impact of stalkers on their victims. *British Journal of Psychiatry, 170,* 12–17.

Romans, J.S.C., Hays, J. R., & White, T. K. (1996). Stalking and related behaviors experienced by counseling center staff members from current or former clients. *Professional Psychology: Research and Practice, 27,* 595–599.

Segal, J. (1989). Erotomania revisited: From Kraepelin to DSM III-R. *American Journal of Psychiatry, 146,* 1261–1266.

Tjaden, P. (1997). The crime of stalking: How big is the problem? *National Institute of Justice Research Preview, November 1997* [Online]. Available: http://www.fiu.edu/~victimad/natstudy.html

Wright, J. A., Burgess, A. G., Burgess, A. W. Laszlo, A. T., McCrary, G. O., & Douglas, J. E. (1996). A typology of interpersonal stalking. *Journal of Interpersonal Violence, 11,* 487–502.

Zona, M. A., Sharma, K. K., & Lane, J. L. (1993). A comparative study of erotomania and obsessional subjects in a forensic sample. *Journal of Forensic Sciences, 38,* 894–903.

FAYE MISHNA
BEVERLEY J. ANTLE
CHERYL REGEHR

34

Social Work with Clients Contemplating Suicide: Complexity and Ambiguity in the Clinical, Ethical, and Legal Considerations

Introduction

Most social workers, whatever their area of clinical practice, have worked with individuals who view suicide as their only option to relieve suffering. This situation probably more than any other clinical condition forces the practitioner to confront complex and difficult ethical, legal, and psychological questions while simultaneously managing an emotionally charged and urgent circumstance (Amchin, Wettstein, & Roth, 1990). On first inspection, the social worker's responsibilities seem clear. Congress (1998), for instance, asserts that the NASW Code of Ethics principle permitting a social worker to break confidentiality in working with a suicidal client is "widely accepted, except by the most radical of thinkers" (p. 43). However, applying this principle to highly complex individual situations is not always s straightforward. This became abundantly clear when the authors, all professors of social work with over 20 years of clinical experience, had different views on the clinical management and ethical obligations in working with a person who is suicidal.

Our review of the literature and Social Work Codes of Ethics (CASW, 1994; NASW, 1999) revealed diverse obligations and guiding principles for practice in the United States and Canada. Indeed, significant room exists for clinical judgment, as is embodied in the 1994 NASW resolution granting social workers freedom to choose the role they may or may not play in assisted suicides (Callahan, 1996; Miller, Hedlund, & Murphy, 1998). Further exploration showed that there are few clear ethical guidelines or legal precedents in the United States or Canada to assist the social worker in navigating this thorny terrain (Burgess & Hawton, 1998). Social workers often work with clients contemplating suicide either in an acute or chronic situation (Callahan, 1994, 1996). Social workers must be familiar with the law and the profession's regulatory and ethical standards and practice accordingly while also taking into account clinical issues (Bongar, 1992; Miller et al., 1996). The crisis, depression, and suicide literature focuses on risk assessment, management including referral for medication, and the identification of risk factors (Bongar, 1992; Simon & Sadoff, 1990). Clearly, these are priorities. However, given the pervasiveness of suicidal behavior—thoughts, gestures, attempted and completed suicides—and the large number of people affected, it is equally important for social workers to be aware of and engage in discourse on the dilemmas. Such dialogue is lacking in the literature but is especially critical because in certain situations the social worker may face an ethical choice between respecting a client's right to choose suicide and intervening to protect the client's life.

This article reviews the ethical and legal issues related to suicide. In spite of the tremendous stigma and the willingness to override individual freedoms to prevent it, suicide remains a significant health problem. The clinical and moral dilemma that occurs when a client communicates the intent or plan to commit suicide is explored. This paper suggests that social workers should grapple with these issues, beginning with social work training and continuing in the workplace, whether in an agency or private practice. We did not advance one answer, but rather stress that social workers must fully consider the complexities and ambiguities of a client's lived experiences as well as their own clinical, ethical, and legal obligations. Since the laws related to children are unique (Szasz, 1989), this paper refers specifically to adults.

Suicide

Historically, different societies and cultures have held varying attitudes toward suicide. Suicide has been accepted and viewed as noble, an important freedom, and even as a form of martyrdom (Heyd & Bloch, 1999; Schmidt & Zechnich, 1999). More commonly, suicide has been seen as unacceptable, morally wrong, a crime, irrational, a sign of mental illness, or as unjust to the state and/or God (Atkinson, 1991; Burgess & Hawton, 1998; Heyd & Bloch, 1999; Schmidt & Zechnich, 1999). Undeniably, considerable stigma continues to surround suicide (United States Surgeon General, 2001).

Today, attempted and completed suicide has serious social and public health consequences throughout the world (Heyd & Bloch, 1999; Jamison & Baldessarini, 1999; Sim, 1997; United States Surgeon General, 2001). There is insufficient evidence that recent advances in pharmaceutical and clinical interventions, including the newer and safer antidepressant medication, have decreased suicide rates (De Man & Labreche-Gauthier, 1991; Jamison & Baldessarini, 1999). Experts acknowledge that if sufficiently determined, a person will eventually succeed in committing suicide whether or not this individual is in a hospital or in seemingly appropriate treatment (Chiles & Strosahl, 1995; King, Baldwin, Sinclair, & Campbell, 2001; Simon & Sadoff, 1990). Indeed, King and colleagues report that 25 to 40% of persons who commit suicide have had contact with psychiatric services in the year preceding their death. Yet an assumption remains in Western society that suicide should and can be prevented (Nelson, 1984; Simon & Sadoff, 1990; United States Surgeon General, 2001).

Suicide's endurance challenges the assumption that suicide can be prevented and the precept held dear by our society of the sacred value of life (Atkinson, 1991; Heyd & Bloch, 1999). Suicide poses immense hardships for family and friends and is one of the most difficult and demanding aspects of clinical work (Burstow, 1992; Corey, Corey, & Callanan, 1998; Heyd & Bloch, 1999; Pulakos, 1993). Convictions about the value of life may lead a practitioner to experience a client's suicidal behavior as a personal threat and/or as a challenge to religious or moral beliefs (Heyd & Bloch, 1999; Sim, 1997). Indeed, Portenoy and colleagues (1997) found that professionals, including social workers, who espoused religious beliefs were less likely to be willing to endorse assisted suicide. A practitioner may concurrently feel both powerless and responsible for stopping an individual from committing suicide (Chiles & Strosahl, 1995).

Alternate Views of Suicide

Much of the controversy stems from opposing conceptualizations, viewing suicide either as a symptom of mental illness or as a rational choice (Heyd & Bloch, 1999). The prevailing approach in our society considers suicide to be based on factors beyond a person's control and thus neither rational nor autonomous (Amchin et al., 1990; Narveson, 1986; Nelson, 1984). There is general agreement that the individual who is suicidal is either mentally ill or depressed and reacting to feelings of hopelessness and despair (Finkenbine, Redwine, Hardesty, & Carson, 1998; Heyd & Bloch, 1999; Jamison & Baldessarini, 1999). These states are seen as impeding the person's ability to reason and make rational decisions and as treatable and thus amenable to change with the appropriate interventions (Callahan, 1994; McGee, 1997). Accordingly, society is believed to have a moral obligation to intervene to prevent the suicide (Amchin et al., 1990; Heyd & Bloch, 1999; Nelson, 1984). Thus, suicide prevention is the priority, notwithstanding a person's expressed wish to die (Nelson, 1984; Pulakos, 1993). Heyd and Bloch observe that the value of life is so fundamental and unquestioned in our society that the very fact of an individual questioning this value is considered irrational and a sign of illness.

There are criticisms of this prevailing view (Bentley, 1993; Burgess & Hawton, 1998; Burstow, 1992; Kapp, 1988; Szasz, 1989). Berghmans (1998) points out that "mental illness as such does not preclude competence" (p. 134). Bentley (1993) contends that this form of labeling "leads to an intolerable 'global indictment' of the population by characterizing them as inept and unfit and may lead to unnecessary or inappropriate decision making by third parties" (p. 102). This may indeed be reflective of the persistent stigma about mental illness (Burt, 2001; Finlay, Dinos, & Lyons, 2001). It has been more than 30 years since Goffman's (1959, 1961, 1963) classic essays on the experiences of the institutionalized mentally ill and the impact of social conventions and mores on defining and shaping normative behavior. Yet there has been little appreciable change in the devastating impact of stigma on the lived experience of individuals who have mental health conditions (Burt, 2001).

Those who challenge the prevailing perspectives on suicide maintain that the freedom to commit suicide is a fundamental right (Amchin et al., 1990; Burstow, 1992; Report of the Task Force on Physician-assisted Suicide, 1995; Szasz, 1989). In contrast to the traditional approach in which prevention is the goal, suicide intervention recognizes that suicidal feelings may be chronic and that suicide may not be preventable (Nelson, 1984; Pulakos, 1993). According to this nontraditional view, there is no assumption that intervention is justified, regardless of the strength of the association between suicide and mental illness (Burstow, 1992; Heyd & Bloch, 1999; Warnock, 1998). Further, suicide is not automatically presumed to be irrational or a reflection of psychopathology (Amchin et al., 1990; Burgess & Hawton, 1998; Narveson, 1986; Nelson, 1984). According to this view, some individuals who are rational and able to make decisions may have sufficient reasons to choose suicide (Report of the Task Force on Physician-assisted Suicide, 1995). Amchin and colleagues argued that in labeling a suicidal person as having a mental illness and therefore as irrational, society has bypassed the ethical issue embedded in suicide, which is the individual's right to self-determination. Chiles and Strosahl (1995) argue, for instance, that any individual can become suicidal if a situation causes emotional pain that is experienced as intolerable and thought to be never-ending.

More recently, the right to self-determination in ending one's life has emerged in the context of chronic and debilitating health conditions, particularly among those living with HIV/AIDS (R.L. Barret, 2000; B. Barret, Kitchener, & Burris, 2001; Goggin, Sewell, Ferrando, Evans, Fishman, & Rabkin, 2000), but also within the disability community (Meslin & Senn, 1993). Proponents of the right to choose the way their life will end highlight that uncertain nature of the progression of these conditions, the painful and debilitating side effects, and the awareness of inevitable death. Here suicide is contemplated as a rational and understandable response to devastating and life-limiting conditions. One might argue that the physical representation of suffering and loss inherent in progressive physical illnesses forms an acceptable moral foundation for suicide, whereas the enduring and less visible emotional suffering of a chronically depressed person whose symptoms cannot be alleviated by treatment is not accorded the same support.

In both instances, stigma shapes the outsider's view. In the first instance, public fears of disfigurement and disablement (Hebl & Kleck, 2000; Houser, 1997) converge to permit empathy for those living with a progressively disabling condition, even to the extent of support should they wish to take their own life. The level of suffering and lack of hope for alleviation of symptoms may be similar in the case of the person with a chronic and untreatable depression. However, the public perception that mental health problems reflect internal weakness or dangerous flaws (Burt, 2001; Crisp, 2001; Finlay et al., 2001) inhibits empathy for those living with debilitating mental illness. It is significant that disability rights advocates have raised concerns that stigma about disability actually contributes to inappropriate complacency in the face of expressions of suicide ideation (Fine & Asch, 1995; Zandrow, 2001). Advocates argue that practitioners in this context are not vigilant enough in diagnosing depression in persons with debilitating physical conditions, given the predominant bias that a desire to die in the face of severe disablement would be "normal."

Intervention

Even those writers who argue for the right of an individual to commit suicide underscore the ethical and legal obligations of mental health professionals to help the suicidal person who desires it (Burstow, 1992; Szasz, 1989). There is consensus that the practitioner is obliged to do absolutely whatever he or she can to help the suicidal client find a way to live and that most individuals who express the wish to die can be helped to want to live (Burstow, 1992; Narveson, 1986). The onus is placed on the practitioner to take all reasonable steps to provide help (McGee, 1997; Sim, 1997). The practitioner must determine whether the person is rational (Sim, 1997) and able to make an autonomous decision (Fairbairn, 1998), and whether he or she truly intends to die rather than seek help (Heyd & Bloch, 1999; Sim, 1997). Schmidt and Zechnich (1999) comment on how very difficult and complicated it is to ascertain when a suicidal person is rational. The prevailing opinion is that if it is unclear whether the person can make a rational and autonomous decision, the practitioner should err on the side of caution and intervene when possible. The choice to intervene may provide an opportunity for a second chance and can always be reconsidered (Heyd & Bloch, 1999; Mayo, 1984).

Although suicidal clients are often grouped together, it is important to differentiate between individuals who are acutely suicidal and those who are chronically suicidal (Burgess & Hawton, 1998; Finkenbine et al., 1998; Heyd & Bloch, 1999; Motto, 1983; Rosenbluth, Kleinman, & Lowy, 1995). Determining how to respond to a person who is acutely suicidal generally poses less of an ethical dilemma, as the need to intervene seems more obvious. In contrast, work with the person who is chronically suicidal is much more complex and confusing.

The situation that is particularly ethically challenging is one in which an individual's mental illness or suicidal condition is considered intractable or incurable (Burgess & Hawton, 1998; Heyd & Bloch, 1999; Motto, 1983; Warnock, 1998). The chronic and unbearable pain experienced by this population may go on for years and years without relief for the individual, because he or she is not terminally ill (Berghmans, 1998; Burgess & Hawton, 1998; Warnock, 1998). Available treatments may have been tried time and again with no significant or lasting improvement to the quality of their lives. In these circumstances, some authors have suggested that there is ample justification for these individuals' decision to die (Burgess & Hawton, 1998; Nelson, 1984), reflecting a desire for relief rather than a wish to die. If a person is living with intractable depression, and his or her suffering is evident and prolonged, then the professional obligation to protect and support life competes with the obligation to alleviate suffering.

In the case of chronic and unremitting mental illness, a practitioner's conviction that suicide can and must be prevented may reflect an avoidance of the ethical dilemma and responsibility (Hey & Bloch, 1999). The continuation of enforced treatment may only intensify the unbearable pain and distress for the suicidal individual (Heyd & Bloch, 1999; Narveson, 1986). Narveson writes that the intervention may be "what the professional insists is 'treatment,' and what the subject regards as, simply, a refined variety of torture" (p. 107). Some writers suggest that if a practitioner is able to hear the client's unbearable suffering and death wishes empathically, this may build trust in the relationship with the therapist. They speculate that, paradoxically, this may foster some hope in the client (Berghmans, 1998; Nelson, 1984).

Last, those individuals whose suicidal thoughts emerge in the context of an illness or disability require additional consideration. Research reflects that individuals with life-threatening conditions (such as HIV/AIDS or cancer) or life-limiting conditions (such as multiple sclerosis) are at greatest risk of suicide (Hughes & Kleepsies, 1998; Mancoske, Wadsworth, Dugas, & Hasney, 1995; United States Surgeon General, 2001). Miller and colleagues (1998) provide a clinical framework for assessments when working with those who are terminally ill. They highlight the need to understand the meanings of the illness and suicidal thoughts, the cultural context of the person and his or her family, and the potentially erroneous fears about the end stages of their disease.

We would encourage practitioners who are working with those who are chronically depressed or living with a chronic health condition or disability to develop a more complex understanding of the rationale for the client's suicidal ideation, including active exploration of the role that social stigma may play in individual circumstances. Additionally, such assessments must take place with an integrated knowledge of legal obligations and ethical principles.

Legal Obligations

In considering the legal obligations regarding a social worker's conduct with suicidal individuals, the two main factors consist of the standard of care that the practitioner is required to provide and the duty to disclose confidential information that a client may be suicidal Physicians have a well-defined duty under the law to try to prevent suicide. Both Canadian and U.S. legislation clearly identifies the roles and responsibilities of physicians to assess individuals for risk of self-harm and to admit them to a psychiatric facility either voluntarily or involuntarily as required. If physicians, particularly psychiatrists, do not take adequate measures to protect life or are found to be negligent in meeting the standard of care, they may be held liable (for review of liability and malpractice, see Simon & Sadoff, 1990). The failure to prevent suicide is one of the leading reasons for malpractice suits against mental health professionals and institutions in the United States (Corey et al., 1998). Malpractice claims against social workers have escalated in the United States (Besharov & Besharov,

1987; Coale, 1998), paralleling the experience of other professions.

Claims for malpractice occur when a professional does not perform duties in a manner consistent with an established standard of care. That is, the professional did not act in the manner in which an ordinary, reasonable, and prudent professional would act under the same circumstances (Reamer, 1995). To ensure protection from this conclusion, therefore, social workers must be aware of and follow standards of care in working with suicidal clients. This includes conducting thorough assessments, providing recommended treatments, and being informed of and following findings related to breaching confidentiality when a client threatens self-harm. Assessment and intervention with suicidal clients is a vital aspect of clinical practice and consequently practice guidelines can be easily located in social work, psychiatry, and psychology textbooks.

Despite the varied sources, guidelines are remarkably similar. Because an expectation of social workers in any context is to provide competent practice (CASW, 1994; NASW, 1999), the first important guideline is that clinicians must determine their own level of competence to work with high-risk clients and must ensure that they have adequate training to manage difficult situations (Simon, 1998). If any questions or uncertainties arise, practitioners are strongly advised to seek consultation (CASW, 1994; Simon & Sadoff, 1990). The social worker must conduct a though assessment of risk, including contributing biological, cognitive, affective, and social factors, and of the client's competence to make a free and informed decision regarding suicide (Jobes, Berman, & Martin, 2000; Reinecke, 2000; Simon & Sadoff, 1990). This assessment must be carefully documented (Corey et al., 1998). Next, the social worker must, within the context of the therapeutic alliance, discuss alternative courses of action and attempt to develop a mutually agreed upon solution (Bongar, 1992; Jobes et al., 2000).

Questions regarding the duty to report confidential information occur when the client has determined that suicide continues to be the only viable alternative. Confidentiality is central to the provision of both social work and medical services (CASW, 1994; CMA, 1978; NASW, 1999), yet increasingly legislators and the courts have moved to override principles of confidentiality (Glancy, Regehr, & Bryant, 1998a, 1998b). For example, physicians in Canada are required to report any person suffering from a communicable disease to the Medical Officer of Health (Health Protection and Promotion Act, 1990). Further, in all jurisdictions in Canada and the United States, it is mandatory to report child abuse disclosures. In addition, subsequent to the famous *Tarasoff* decision in California (1976), all mental health practitioners have a positive duty to protect third parties who may be at risk of harm at the hands of a client (Glancy et al., 1998a; Glancy, Regehr, Bryant, & Schneider, 1999). In these situations, the mandatory duty to report overrides the client's request for and right to confidentiality.

The duty to protect becomes less clear with regard to suicide. To date the *Tarasoff* ruling has not been extended to situations where a person poses a threat to himself or herself, and consequently there is no affirmative duty under the law for social workers to report information regarding suicidal intent (Amchin et al., 1990). Nevertheless, there is no evidence on which to judge how the law might handle a situation where a social worker faced a civil action for breaking the confidentiality of a client that he or she believed to be suicidal. If the social worker reasonably believed that a client would harm himself or herself and thus acted in good faith, the practitioner would likely be protected in law for breach of confidentiality if he or she reported the suicidal intentions to a family member or a physician. Similarly, it is not evident whether social workers may be held liable if they do not disclose risk of suicide in an individual who is vulnerable, dependent, in crisis, or in a transitory situation. Thus, in summary, the law provides little guidance on how a social worker should proceed; yet the threat of potential malpractice litigation must still be borne in mind as mental health practitioners face an increasingly litigious environment (Bongar, Greaney, & Peruzzi, 1998).

Professional Codes of Ethics and Regulatory Obligations

While social workers may turn to codes of ethics for guidance in difficult clinical situations, this source provides limited concrete advice with regard to work with suicidal clients. In general, codes of ethics do not address the assessment and care of people with suicidal ideation, but rather address the issue of whether the social worker should disclose this information to others. Further, within social work codes of ethics, there is not one clear guideline regarding permission to disclose.

The duty to breach confidence to protect a suicidal client must be examined in relation to the statutorily entrenched duty to protect confidential information. Social workers in Canada and the United States operate under regulatory and licensing bodies at the provincial and state level, respectively (Association of Social Work Boards, 2001; CASW, 2000). In general, in a therapeutic relationship the social worker must protect the confidentiality of the information provided by the client (CASW, 1994; NASW, 1999). The social worker may, however, disclose the information when required or allowed by law or when a client has consented to the disclosure. In fact, NASW's most recent revisions to the Code of Ethics (1999) section 1.02 states, "Social workers respect and promote the right of clients to self-determination and assist clients in their efforts to identify and clarify their goals" (p. 7). However, the expectation that social workers will keep information confidential does not apply when disclosure is necessary to prevent serious, foreseeable, and imminent harm to a client. In this instance, the social worker is obliged to do what is best for the client (Callahan, 1994). With regard to disclosure in the case of a suicidal client in Canada, there is inconsistency across provinces. The Canadian Association of Social Workers' Code of Ethics (1994) requires social workers to report information of suicidal intent to a family member. Some provinces are consistent with this in expecting social workers to disclose when there is a clear risk that the client intends harm to self or others (Saskatchewan Association of Social Workers, 1995). Contrary to this position however, the Ontario College of Social Workers and Social Service Workers (2000) states that disclosure of confidential information of a client's potential suicide is discretionary (section 4.3.5, p. 13).

Ethical Principles

In considering a course of action in difficult clinical situations, social workers must weigh not only their legal obligations, the professional standards as defined by the Code of Ethics and existing professional regulatory standards and practice guidelines, but also their own ethical views (Miller et al., 1998; Woody, 1990). A primary ethical conflict facing the social worker with a suicidal client is the choice between self-determination and beneficence, which is the duty to bring about good and minimize possible harm (Weijer, Dickens, & Meslin, 1997).

Self-determination is central to the ethics and values of social work (Callahan, 1994; Rothman, 1989; Spicker, 1990) and a fundamental human right in Western society (Freedberg, 1989; Rothman, 1989). Nevertheless, there have always been limits to self-determination (Schmidt & Zechnich, 1999). In part, this is due to the fact that self-determination "involves individuals being able to formulate and carry out their own plans, desires, wishes, and policies, thereby determining the course of their own life" (Atkinson, 1991, p. 104). This then requires that the decision maker be competent to weigh the alternatives, evaluate the risks and benefits, and choose the option that is most advantageous. In consenting to health care, for instance, provisions are made for alternative decision makers should an individual be deemed incapable of understanding the relevant treatment information and of appreciating the reasonably foreseeable consequences of a decision or lack of decision (Health Care Consent Act, 1996, 1998; Substitute Decisions Act, SO 1992, 2001, ss.6 & 45). Although lack of capacity does not necessarily result from mental illness (Mental Health Act, 1990), there is evidence that those suffering from mental illness have impairments in decisional capacity and may not make the same decisions when the illness has abated subsequent to treatment (Grisso & Appelbaum, 1995). However, as identified earlier, in the face of chronic and debilitating mental illness, the potential rationality of suicide must be appreciated and considered as well as the sense of autonomy that persons may derive from contemplating suicide in that there is an option for control of the suffering.

The ethical guideline of beneficence is often contentious due to the question of who determines what constitutes the greater good, a particular concern in this circumstance wherein, as highlighted earlier, those contemplating suicide often live with considerable stigma (Bergeron & Handley, 1992; Crisp, 2001; Finlay et al., 2001; Houser, 1997). Arguments are advanced both for intervening to prevent suicide and for allowing an individual the freedom to choose death. Some suggest that since not all clients have the capacity for self-direction, other moral values such as beneficence at times outweigh self-determination (Schmidt & Zechnich, 1999). Kapp (1988) contended that when all other options have been tried and when a person's personal safety is at stake, beneficence is called for. Other authors assert that taking away an individual's choice to live or die is unjustified (Burstow, 1992; Szasz, 1989) and smacks of paternalism (Murdach, 1996).

This conflict between autonomy and paternalism reveals social work's long-standing dichotomy whereby the practitioner must balance responsibility to the community with responsibility to the individual's self-determination (Corey et al., 1998; Freedberg, 1989; Regehr & Antle, 1997). The practitioner must wrestle with the benefits of suicide prevention versus the costs of the deprivation of individual rights and of potential suffering (Amchin et al., 1990; Rosenbluth et al., 1995).

Social work ethics also calls for attention to social justice and the fair distribution of burdens and benefits, which may sometimes limit individual freedoms (Regehr & Antle, 1997). With regard to suicide, questions are also raised about the greater good in society. For example, the freedom to choose one's actions in life is limited by the potential of those actions to harm others. Might it then be argued that the actions of an individual to end his or her own life may harm others? Goldney (2000) estimates that for every person who engages in suicidal behavior, five or six others are affected. Thus, another potential ethical dilemma for practitioners consists of determining whether they are primarily responsible to the client or the client's relatives who will be profoundly affected by a successful suicide (Sim, 1997). If the practitioner concludes that the person has the right to commit suicide and that telling his or her family may interfere, the practitioner may be required morally to say nothing. However, if the practitioner concludes that the client is not rational and thus is not making an autonomous decision, the practitioner may be compelled ethically to warn the family in order to protect the client and family's interests.

Finally, the tremendous stigma associated with having a physical disability might potentially contribute to endorsing a disabled person's suicidal intentions (Fine & Asch, 1995; Zandrow, 2001). Some have argued that the needs of a larger and vulnerable disabled population to be protected from the devastating impacts of sigma outweigh individual burdens. In a similar fashion, the United States Supreme Court and the Supreme Court of Canada have both ruled on the matter of assisted suicide and have unambiguously stated that individual do not have the right to an assisted suicide (Callahan, 1996; Meslin & Senn, 1993). In Canada, this ruling surrounded the petition of a woman, Susan Ridriquez, with a profound disability, who expressed that her right to self-determination was limited by her disability in that she would not have the strength to kill herself. The Court's ruling affirmed the interests of the many who may suffer in the future over the interests of an individual who was indeed suffering in the present.

Implications for Social Work Practice

In summary, our work with clients who may be suicidal is complex and fraught with many competing demands. Clear, practical, and ethical guidelines and laws that determined the most appropriate course of action in each case would reduce the pressure that individual social workers face. Presently, professional codes of ethics and legal precedents do not clarify our responsibilities and duties in all situations. It is essential, therefore, that social workers grapple with the dilemmas and issues that may arise when clients contemplate suicide. Factors to consider include clients' ability to make rational choices based on their current mental and physical state and social situation, the sources of their suffering, and the often invisible influences of stigma. If there are means to alleviate their distress, we must do everything in our power to ensure that these options are made available to our clients.

For those whose contemplation of suicide is chronic and/or associated with debilitating illness or disability, engaging with clients in a deeper exploration of the sources of their suffering may open up an opportunity for understanding and perhaps even hope. Social workers must rely on practice guidelines, which call for careful evaluation, a good therapeutic alliance, and consultation. However, in the end, the social worker may be faced with an ethical choice between the right to choose suicide and the duty to protect life.

Beyond our clinical work with the individual client, social workers have other vital roles to play. Specifically, this includes working with families and communities affected by suicide and addressing the contributing factors. Individuals and communities need to become aware of the multiple sources of suicide, including oppressive social systems, the stigma, and the desperation that may underlie the suicidal intent of those with mental illness, chronic medical conditions, and physical disability. Social workers can take the lead in educating the community about suicide in a way that gives voice to the complexity of personal, professional, social, legal, and ethical issues. Further education into suicide prevention and/or intervention is needed, as is work to reduce the blame and shame associated with suicide.

References

Amchin, J., Wettstein, R. M., & Roth, L. H. (1990). Suicide, ethics, and the law. In S. J. Blumenthal, & D.J. Kupfer (Eds.), *Suicide over the life cycle* (pp. 637–781). Washington, DC: American Psychiatric Press.

Association of Social Work Boards. (2001). *Licensing information.* Association of Social Work Boards [October 30].

Atkinson, J. (1991). Autonomy and mental health. In P. J. Barker, & S. Baldwin (Eds.), *Ethical issues in mental health* (pp. 103–126). London: Chapman & Hall.

Barret, B., Kitchener, K. S., & Burris, S. (2001). Suicide and confidentiality with the client with advanced AIDS: The case of Phil. In J. R. Anderson (Ed.), *Ethics in HIV-related psychotherapy: Clinical decision making in complex cases* (pp. 299–314). Washington, DC: American Psychological Association.

Barret, R. L. (2000). Confidentiality and HIV/AIDS: Professional challenges. In J. J. Gates (Ed.), *Privacy and confidentiality in mental health care* (pp. 157–171). Baltimore, MD: Paul H. Brookes.

Bentley, K. J. (1993). The right of psychiatric patients to refuse medication: Where should social workers stand? *Social Work, 38*(1), 101–106.

Bergeron, J. P., & Handley, P. R. (1992). Bibliography on AIDS-related bereavement and grief. *Death Studies, 16*(3), 247–267.

Berghmans, R. (1998). Commentary on "suicide, euthanasia, and the psychiatrist." *Philosophy, Psychiatry, & Psychology, 5*(2), 131–135.

Besharov, D. & Besharov, S. (1987). Teaching about liability. *Social Work, 32*(6), 517–522.

Bongar, B. (1992). *Suicide: Guidelines for assessment, management, and treatment.* Oxford: Oxford University Press.

Bongar, B., Greaney, S., & Peruzzi, N. (1998). *Risk management with suicidal patients.* New York: Guilford Press.

Burgess, S., & Hawton, K. (1998). Suicide, euthanasia, and the psychiatrist. *Philosophy, Psychiatry, & Psychology, 5*(2), 113–126.

Burstow, B. (1992). *Radical feminist therapy: Working in the context of violence.* Newbury Park, CA: Sage Publications.

Burt, R. A. (2001). Promises to keep, miles to go: Mental health law since 1972. In L. E. Frost (Ed.), *The evolution of mental health law* (pp. 11–30). Washington, DC: American Psychological Association.

Callahan, J. (1994). The ethics of assisted suicide. *Health and Social Work, 19*(4), 237–244.

Callahan, J. (1996). Social work with suicidal clients: Challenges of implementing practice guidelines and standards of care. *Health and Social Work, 21*(4), 277–282.

Canadian Medical Association [CMA]. (1978). *Code of Ethics.* Ottawa: Canadian Medical Association.

CASW. (1994). *Code of Ethics.* Ottawa: Canadian Association of Social Workers.

CASW. (2000). *Status of social work legislation in Canada: A summary.* Canadian Association of Social Workers. Available: http://www.casw-acts.ca/Legislation.htm.

Chiles, J. A., & Strosahl, K. D. (1995). *The suicidal patient: Principles of assessment, treatment, and case management.* Washington, DC: American Psychiatric Press.

Coale, H. (1998). *The vulnerable therapist: Practicing psychotherapy in an age of uncertainty.* Binghamton, NY: Haworth Press.

Congress, E. P. (1998). *Social work values and ethics.* Chicago: Nelson-Hall.

Corey, G., Corey, M. K. S., & Callanan, P. (1998). *Issues and ethics in the helping professions* (fifth edition). Pacific Grove, CA: Brooks/Cole.

Crisp, A. (2001). The tendency to stigmatise. *British Journal of Psychiatry. Special Issue, 178*(Mar.), 197–199.

De Man, A., & Labreche-Gauthier, L. (1991). Suicide ideation and community support: An evaluation of two programs. *Journal of Clinical Psychology, 47*(1), 57–60.

Fairbairn, G. J. (1998). Suicide, language, and clinical practice. *Philosophy, Psychiatry, & Psychology, 5*(2), 157–169.

Fine, M., & Asch, A. (1995). Disability beyond stigma: Social interaction, discrimination, and activism. In N. R. Goldberger (Ed.), *The culture and psychology reader* (pp. 536–558). New York: New York University Press.

Finkenbine, R., Redwine, M. B., Hardesty, S., & Carson, W. H. (1998). Ethical approach in contemporary psychiatry: A pragmatic approach in a psychiatry access center. *General Hospital Psychiatry, 20,* 231–234.

Finlay, W. M. L., Dinos, S., & Lyons, E. (2001). Stigma and multiple social comparisons in people with schizophrenia. *European Journal of Social Psychology. Special Issue: New Directions in Social Comparison Research, 31*(5), 579–592.

Freedberg, S. (1989). Self-determination: Historical perspectives and effects on current practice. *Social Work, 34*(1), 33–38.

Glancy, G., Regehr, C., & Bryant, A. (1998a). Confidentiality in crisis: Part I, The duty to inform. *Canadian Journal of Psychiatry, 43*(12), 1001–1005.

Glancy, G., Regehr, C. & Bryant, A. (1998b). Confidentiality in crisis: Part II, Confidentiality of treatment records. *Canadian Journal of Psychiatry, 43*(12), 1006–1011.

Glancy, G., Regehr, C. & Bryant, A., & Schneider, R. (1999). Editorial: Another nail in the coffin of confidentiality. *Canadian Journal of Psychiatry, 44*(6), 83.

Goffman, E. (1959). *The presentation of self in everyday life.* Harmondsworth, England: Penguin.

Goffman, E. (1961). *Asylums: Essays on the social situation of mental patients and other inmates.* Garden City, NY: Doubleday Anchor.

Goffman, E. (1963). *Stigma. Notes on the management of spoiled identity.* Englewood Cliffs, NJ: Prentice-Hall.

Goggin, K., Sewell, M., Ferrando, S., Evans, S., Fishman, B., & Rabkin, J. (2000). Plans to hasten death among gay men with HIV/ADS: Relationship to psychological adjustment. *AIDS Care, 12*(2), 125–136.

Goldney, R. D. (2000). The privilege and responsibility of suicide prevention. *Crisis, 21*(1), 8–15.

Grisso, T., & Applebaum, P. (1995). The MacArthur treatment competence study, III: The ability of patients to consent to psychiatric and medical treatments. *Law and Human Behaviour, 19*, 149–174.

Health Care Consent Act (1996, 1998).

Health Protection and Promotion Act, R.S.O. (1990). c.H.7, ss.25–26.

Helb, M. R., & Kleck, R. E. (2000). The social consequences of physical disability. In T. F. Heatherton, R. E. Kleck, M. R. Hebl, & J. G. Hull (Eds.), *The social psychology of stigma* (pp. 419–439). New York: Guilford Press.

Heyd, D., & Bloch, S. (1999). The ethics of suicide. In S. Bloch, P. Chodoff, & S. Green (Eds.), *Psychiatric ethics* (third edition; pp. 441–460). Oxford: Oxford University Press.

Houser, J. A. U. I. (1997). Stigma, spread and status: The impact of physical disability on social interaction. *Dissertation Abstracts International Section A: Humanities & Social Sciences, 58*(5-A).

Hughes, D., & Kleepsies, P. (1998). Suicide in the medically ill. *Suicide & Life Threatening Behavior. Special Issues: Background Papers to the National Suicide Prevention Conference. October, 31*(1, Suppl), 48–59.

Jamison, K. R., & Baldessarini, R. J. (1999). Effects of medical interventions on suicidal behavior. *Journal of Clinical Psychiatry, 60*(suppl 2), 4–6.

Jobes, D., Berman, A. & Martin, C. (2000). Adolescent suicidality and crisis intervention. In A. Roberts (Ed.), *Crisis intervention handbook: Assessment, treatment and research* (pp. 131–151). New York: Oxford University Press.

Kapp, M. B. (1988). Forcing services on at-risk older adults: When doing good is not so good. *Social Work in Health Care, 13*(4), 1–13.

King, E. A., Baldwin, D. S., Sinclair, J. M., & Campbell, M. J. (2001). The Wessex recent in-patient suicide study; 2: Case-control study of 59 in-patient suicides. *British Journal of Psychiatry, 178*, 537–542.

Mancoske, R. J., Wadsworth, C. M., Dugas, D. S., & Hasney, J. A. (1995). Suicide risk among people living with AIDS. *Social Work, 40*(6), 783–787.

Mayo, D. J. (1984). Confidentiality in crisis counseling: A philosophical perspective. *Suicide and Life-Threatening Behavior, 14*(2), 96–112.

McGee, E. M. (1997). Can suicide intervention in hospice be ethical? *Journal of Palliative Care, 13*(1), 27–33.

Mental Health Act, R.S.O. [1990] c.M7, ss29(2) and (3).

Meslin, E. M. & Senn, J. (1993). A discussion of the Rodriguez decision. *Ethical Effects, 1*(4), 1–4.

Miller, P. J., Hedlund, S. C., & Murphy, K. A. (1998). Social work assessment at end of life: Practice guidelines for suicide and the terminally ill. *Social Work in Health Care, 26*(4), 23–36.

Motto, J. A. (1983). Clinical implications of moral theory regarding suicide. *Suicide and Life-Threatening Behavior, 13*(4), 304–312.

Murdach, A. (1996). Beneficence re-examined: Protective intervention in mental health. *Social Work, 41*(1), 26–32.

Narveson, J. (1986). Moral philosophy and suicide. *Canadian Journal of Psychiatry, 31*, 104–107.

NASW. (1999). *Code of Ethics.* Washington, DC: National Association of Social Workers.

Nelson, F. L. (1984). Suicide: Issues of prevention, intervention, and facilitation. *Journal of Clinical Psychology, 40*(6), 1328–1333.

Ontario College of Social Workers and Social Service Workers. (2000). *Code of ethics and standards of practice.* Toronto: Ontario College of Social Workers and Social Service Workers.

Portenoy, R. K., Coyle, N., Kash, K. M., Brescia, F., Scanlon, C., O'Hare, D., et al. (1997). Determinants of the willingness to endorse assisted suicide: A survey of physicians, nurses, and social workers. *Psychosomatics, 38*(3), 277–287.

Pulakos, J. (1993). Two models of suicide treatment: Evaluation and recommendations. *American Journal of Psychotherapy, 47*(4), 603–612.

Reamer, F. (1995). Malpractice claims against social workers: First facts. *Social Work, 40*(5) 595–600.

Regehr, C., & Antle, B. J. (1997). Coercive influences: Informed consent in court-mandated social work practice. *Social Work, 42*(3), 300–306.

Reinecke, M. (2000). Suicide and depression. In F. Dattilio & A. Freeman (Eds.), *Cognitive behavioural strategies in crisis intervention.* New York: Guilford Press, 84–121.

Report of the Task Force on Physician-assisted Suicide. (1995). *Physician-assisted suicide: Toward a comprehensive understanding.*

Rosenbluth, M., Kleinman, I., & Lowy, F. (1995). Suicide: The interaction of clinical and ethical issues. *Psychiatric Services, 46*(9), 919–921.

Rothman, J. (1989). Client self-determination: Untangling the knot. *Social Service Review, 63*(4), 598–612.

Saskatchewan Association of Social Workers. (1995). *Standards of ethical practice for professional social workers in Saskatchewan.* Regina: Saskatchewan Association of Social Workers.

Schmidt, T. A., & Zechnich, A. D. (1999). Suicidal patients in the E: Ethical issues. *Emergency Medicine Clinics of North America, 17*(2), 371–383.

Sim, J. (1997). *Ethical decision-making in therapy practice.* Oxford: Butterworth-Heinemann.

Simon, R. I. (1998). Psychiatrists awake! Suicide risk assessments are all about a good night's sleep. *Psychiatric Annals, 28*(9), 479–485.

Simon, R. I., & Sadoff, R. L. (1990). *Psychiatric malpractice: Cases and comments for clinicians.* Washington, DC: American Psychiatric Press.

Spicker, P. (1990). Social work and self-determination. *British Journal of Social Work, 20,* 221–236.

Substitute Decisions Act, SO 1992, 2001, ss.6 & 45.

Susman, J. (1994). Disability, stigma and deviance. *Social Science & Medicine, 38*(1), 15–22.

Szasz, T. S. (1989). A moral view on suicide. In D. Jacobs, & H. N. Brown (Eds.), *Suicide: Understanding and responding* (pp. 437–447). Madison CT: Universities Press.

Tarasoff v. Regents of the University of California. (1976). 17 Cal. Rptr. 3rd (U.S.).

United States Surgeon General. (2001). *National strategy for suicide prevention.* United States Department of Health and Human Services. Available: http://www.mentalhealt.org/suicideprevention/default.asp.

Warnock, The Baroness Mary (1998). Commentary on "suicide, euthanasia, and the psychiatrist." *Philosophy, Psychiatry, & Psychology, 5*(2), 127–130.

Weijer, C., Dickens, B., & Meslin, E. (1997). Bioethics for clinicians: 10. Research ethics. *Canadian Medical Association Journal, 156,* 1153–1157.

Woody, J. (1990) Resolving ethical concerns in clinical practice: Towards a pragmatic model. *Journal of Marital and Family Therapy, 16*(2) 133–150.

Zandrow, L. F., Jr. (2001). Misguided mercy: Hastening death in the disability community. *Topics in Spinal Cord Injury Rehabilitation, 6*(4), 76–82.

35

Posttraumatic Stress Symptoms Following Near-Death Experiences

More than half of all Americans are exposed to a life-threatening traumatic event at least once, and one-quarter of Americans more than once (Kessler, Sonnega, Bromet, Hughes, & Nelson, 1995). Although there are many possible psychological and biological responses to traumatic events, almost half of those exposed to such events may develop the particular avoidance and hyperarousal symptoms of posttraumatic stress disorder (PTSD) (Kessler et al., 1995). Many of the symptoms of PTSD overlap with those of depressive and anxiety disorders. What distinguishes PTSD is a biphasic pattern of reliving the trauma through intrusive memories, alternating with avoidance of reminders and numbing (Davidson, 1997).

The *DSM-IV* diagnostic criteria for PTSD focus on intrusive memories and disordered arousal as its distinguishing characteristics, with other symptoms understood as strategies to ward off emotions, somatic sensations, and personal meaning schemes associated with the trauma (van der Kolk et al., 1996). There are four diagnostic criteria for PTSD that address symptoms (and two others that address duration and degree of impairment): (a) exposure to a traumatic event that induces fear, helplessness, or horror; (b) persistent reexperiencing of the traumatic event; (c) avoidance of trauma-related stimuli or numbing; and (d) hyperarousal (American Psychiatric Association, 1994).

Several studies in recent years have suggested that dissociative experiences at the time of trauma are a significant long-term predictor of the later development of PTSD (Koopman, Classen, & Spiegel, 1994; Marmar et al., 1994; Shalev, Peri, Canetti, & Schreiber, 1996; van der Kolk et al., 1996). One distinctive type of dissociative experience in the face of life-threatening danger is the so-called transcendental near-death experience (NDE), in which persons close to death may believe they have left their physical bodies and transcended the boundaries of the ego and the confines of time and space. These NDEs include cognitive elements, such as accelerated thought processes and a "life review"; affective elements, such as intense feelings of peace and joy; purportedly paranormal elements, such as sensation of being out of the body or visions of future events; and transcendental elements, such as an experienced encounter with deceased relatives or an unearthly realm (Bates & Stanley, 1985; Greyson, 1983a; Noyes & Kletti, 1976; Owens, Cook & Stevenson, 1990). Because NDEs involve perceptions, cognitions, and emotions that are disconnected from mainstream consciousness, they can be considered a type of dissociation (Greyson, 1997b) or depersonalization (Noyes & Kletti, 1976). People who report NDEs also report more everyday dissociation than do other trauma survivors, although they report far less dissociation than do patients with pathological dissociative disorders (Greyson, 2000).

Although the term "near-death experience" was not coined until 1975, transcendental experiences near death were reported in the medical literature of the 19th century (Anonymous, 1894; Wiltse, 1889), and the phenomenon had been described as a discrete syndrome toward the end of that century, when Heim (1892) published a collection of such cases. NDEs probably occur to between 9% and 18% of individuals who experience documented cardiac arrest (Greyson, 1998b), and often produce a consistent pattern of change in beliefs, attitudes, and values (Greyson, 1998a; Noyes, 1980).

In general, retrospective studies of survivors of NDEs have shown them to be psychologically healthy individuals who do not differ from comparison groups on measures of mental health (Gabbard & Twemlow, 1984; Greyson, 1991; Locke & Schontz, 1983). However, some experiencers report considerable distress or psychosocial impairment that appears to be related to recurrent intrusive memories of their close brush with death or to difficulty integrating the NDE and its sequelae into their lives (Greyson, 1997a). Some report typical PTSD symptoms of diminished interest in activities, estrangement from others, restricted range of effect, and a sense of foreshortened future (Greyson, 1997a).

Because, by definition, NDEs involve a threat of death or serious injury, it would be surprising if they were not associated with some symptoms of PTSD. However, near-death experiencers rarely respond with the intense negative affects required to meet the *DSM-IV* criteria for PTSD. They may report recurrent, intrusive recollections of the event, but these recollections are rarely distressing. Those who have had the experience rarely report efforts to avoid reminders of the NDE, difficulty recalling parts of the experience, or hyperarousal.

Thus, although dissociation at the time of trauma may predict subsequent PTSD, the particular type of dissociation seen in NDEs does not. In fact, uncontrolled clinical anecdotes suggest that NDEs may serve a defensive function, protecting against the later development of PTSD. However, to date such clinical speculation remains untested.

The present study compared the incidence of PTSD symptoms in a nonclinical sample of NDE survivors and in persons who came close to death but did not have NDEs. Only a small percentage of people with PTSD ever seek professional help, and those who do may be atypical of the total population with these problems (Solomon & Davidson, 1997). For that reason, a nonclinical sample was used to provide an assessment of normative responses to life-threatening stress, which could not be obtained from studies of clinical populations.

Method

Sample

The sample was recruited from among individuals who contacted the author to share accounts of their close brushes with death, following reports in the public media about the author's prior reports in the public media about the author's prior research on NDEs. No effort was made to solicit such contacts, but once contact was made, correspondents were invited to participate in this research. Participants were not paid, and were told that the purpose of the research was to further understanding of the emotional effects of a close brush with death.

The study sample included 194 individuals who claimed to have come close to death, all of whom completed the NDE Scale (see below). Of those, 148 participants (76%) claimed to have had NDEs at the time of their close brush with death and described experiences that scored at or above the cut-off criterion of seven points on the NDE Scale (M = 17.5, SD = 6.3). The remaining 46 participants (24%) denied having had NDEs and described experiences that scored below the cut-off criterion (M = 1.6, SD = 2.1). The 15.9-point difference (95% CI = 14.0 to 17.7) in the scores of these two groups was significant (t = 16.70, df = 192, p < .001). Among the 194 participants, the traumatic event that precipitated the close brush with death was an accident in 56 cases (29%), illness in 52 cases (27%), surgery in 40 cases (21%), childbirth in 21 cases (11%), suicide attempt in 6 cases (3%), and "other" in 19 cases (10%). Mean elapsed time since the close brush with death was 18.4 (SD = 14.2) years with a range of less than 1 year to 67 years.

Of the 194 participants, 122 (63%) were female and 72 (37%) male. Their mean age was 49.8 (SD = 12.4) years, with a range of 22–82 years. Of the 193 participants who indicated a religious preference, 86 (44%) described themselves as Protestant, 41 (21%) as Roman Catholic, 9 (5%) as Jewish, 19 (10%) as "other," and 38 (20%) as "none."

Procedure and Instruments

After a complete description of the study was sent to the participants, written informed consent was obtained. Participants were mailed questionnaires that included the two study instruments. When returned, completed questionnaires were identified only by coded participant number.

NDE Scale   The NDE Scale is a reliable and valid 16-item, self-report, multiple-choice questionnaire for identifying and quantifying NDEs and differentiating such experiences from other responses to a close brush with death (Greyson, 1983a, 1990). Cronbach's alpha was .91 for the 16-item scale in the current study, and a score of seven or higher (out of a possible 32) was used as the standard criterion for identifying an experience as an NDE (Greyson, 1983a). The scale includes questions about cognitive processes (e.g., "Did time seem to speed up or slow down?), affective processes (e.g., "Did you have a feeling of peace or pleasantness?"), purportedly paranormal processes (e.g., "Did you feel separated from your physical body?"), and experienced transcendence (e.g., "Did you seem to enter some other, unearthly world?").

Impact of Event Scale   The IES is a reliable and valid 15-item, self-report, multiple-choice questionnaire for measuring the stressful effects of specific traumatic life events (Horowitz, Wilner, & Alvarez, 1979). The instrument categorizes these stressful effects into two clusters: intrusion and avoidance. The seven items measuring intrusive symptoms include the penetration of thoughts, images, feelings, and dreams, and distressing repetitive behavior (e.g., "I had dreams about it"). The eight items measuring avoidant symptoms include psychic numbing, denial, behavioral inhibition, and counterphobic activities (e.g., "I tried not to think about it").

Analyses

A score of seven or greater on the NDE Scale was used to determine the presence of an NDE. Scores on the intrusion and avoidance subscales of the IES were used as continuous measures of intrusive and avoidant posttraumatic stress symptoms.

The hypothesis that individuals with NDEs would report higher numbers of intrusive and avoidant posttraumatic stress symptoms than would those who came close to death without NDEs was tested by comparing the mean scores of those two groups on the IES and its subscales, using two-tailed t-tests for independent samples. Secondary analyses comparing the two study groups on age and time elapsed since the close brush with death were conducted using two-tailed t-tests for independent samples; and those comparing the two study groups on gender, religion, and traumatic event were conducted using Pearson chi-square tests.

Finally, multiple regression analyses were conducted using forward stepwise variable selection, with a criterion of the probability of $F \leq 0.05$ to enter a variable, and a criterion of the probability of $F \geq 0.10$ to remove a variable. One regression analysis was conducted for the overall IES score and one each for the intrusion and avoidance subscales in order to assess the effect of NDEs while controlling statistically for the potentially confounding covariates of years elapsed since the close brush with death, gender, age, religion (dichotomized into Christian vs. other), and traumatic event (dichotomized into accident vs. other). All analyses were performed using SPSS for Windows, version 9.0.

Results

Sample Demographics

Comparisons on demographic variables between the 148 participants who had NDEs and the 46 who did not are presented in Table 35.1. Two-thirds of the participants with NDEs, but only half of those without NDEs, were female. The mean difference in age between the two groups was a nonsignificant -3.1 years (95% CI = -7.2 to 1.1). Time elapsed since the trauma was significantly longer for those without NDEs; the difference in elapsed time between the two groups was -7.8 years (95% CI = -12.5 to -3.3). A higher percentage of participants with than without NDEs described themselves as Christian. The two groups did not differ significantly in type of traumatic event that precipitated the close brush with death.

Posttraumatic Stress Symptoms

The mean score of the 194 participants was 17.5 (SD = 14.6) on the overall IES, 11.6 (SD = 9.4) on the intrusion subscale, and 5.9 (SD = 7.4) on the avoidance subscale. Comparisons on posttraumatic stress symptoms between the 148 participants who had NDEs and the 46 who did not are presented in Table 35.2. On the overall IES, those with NDEs scored 9.0 points (95% CI = 4.3 to 13.7) higher than those without NDEs. Nevertheless, the mean IES score of participants with NDEs was 1.2 standard deviations below the mean score of 39.5 among a criterion sample of patients with PTSD (Horowitz et al., 1979). Likewise, on the intrusion subscale, those with NDEs scored 8.4 points (95% CI = 5.6 to 11.3) higher than those without NDEs.

Table 35.1 Sample Characteristics: Participants with (N = 148) and without (N = 46) NEDs

Item	NDEs	No NDEs	Statistic	df	p
Female	67%	50%	$\chi^2 = 4.20$	1	0.038
Age: yrs (SD)	49.0 (11.9)	52.1 (14.0)	$t = 1.47$	192	0.144
Yrs since Trauma	16.6 (12.9)	24.5 (16.6)	$t = 3.37$	192	0.001
Religion			$\chi^2 = 12.17$	4	0.016
Protestant	46%	39%			
Roman Catholic	25%	9%			
Jewish	3%	9%			
Other	10%	11%			
None	16%	33%			
Traumatic Event			$\chi^2 = 6.16$	5	0.290
Accident	26%	37%			
Illness	27%	26%			
Surgery	20%	24%			
Childbirth	13%	4%			
Suicide	3%	4%			
Other	12%	4%			

Again, the mean intrusion score of participants with NDEs was 0.8 standard deviation below the mean score of 21.4 among a criterion sample of patients with PTSD (Horowitz et al., 1979). On the avoidance subscale, the mean scores of those with and without NDEs were comparable (mean difference = 0.6, 95% CI = −1.9 to 3.0), and were 1.1 standard deviations below the mean score of 18.2 among a criterion sample of patients with PTSD (Horowitz et al., 1979).

Table 35.3 presents the multiple regression analyses carried out with forward stepwise selection of variables. For the overall IES, NDEs and years elapsed since the traumatic event met criteria to be entered as variables, whereas gender, religion, age, and type of traumatic event did not. In that analysis, NDEs were a significant predictor of IES scores (B = 7.59; 95% CI = 2.78 to 12.39). For the intrusion subscale, NDEs, years elapsed, and female gender met criteria to be entered as variables, whereas religion, age, and type of traumatic event did not. In that analysis also, NDEs were a significant predictor of intrusion scores (B = 7.02, 95% CI = 4.08 to 9.97). For the avoidance subscale, none of the variables met criteria to be entered into the analysis.

Discussion

This study suggests a distinctive pattern of post-traumatic symptoms among people who report NDEs. Compared to research participants who had come close to death without having had NDEs, those with NDEs scored significantly higher on the total IES and on its intrusion, but not its avoidance, subscale. Thus, although experiencers do report more intrusive thoughts and memories of their close brush with death than comparison group participants, they do not report greater efforts to avoid thoughts or reminders of that event.

Table 35.2 Impact of Event Scale Scores: Participants with (N = 148) and without (N = 46) NDEs

Scale	NDEs M (SD)	No NDEs M (SD)	(df = 192)	p
Impact of Event	19.6 (14.5)	10.6 (12.9)	3.76	<0.001
Intrusion subscale	13.6 (9.2)	5.2 (6.5)	5.77	<0.001
Avoidance of subscale	6.0 (7.5)	5.4 (7.3)	0.45	0.65

Table 35.3 Multiple Regression Analyses of Impact of Event Scale (IES) Scores

Dependent Variable	Variable Included	b	Partial r	t	P	Incremental R^2
IES[a]						
Step 1	NDE	0.22	0.22	3.12	0.002	0.069
Step 2	Yrs elapsed	−0.18	0.18	2.50	0.013	0.030
Intrusion[b]						
Step 1	NDE	0.32	0.32	4.71	<0.001	0.148
Step 2	Yrs elasped	−0.19	0.20	−2.86	0.005	0.030
Step 3	Fem. gender	0.13	0.15	2.03	0.044	0.017
Avoidance[c]	None					

[a]Excluded variables: gender, religion, age, type of trauma
[b]Excluded variables: religion, age, type of trauma
[c]Excluded variables: NDE, years elapsed, gender, religion, age, type of trauma.

On the total IES and on both subscales, the experiencers scored substantially lower than did the criterion sample of patients with PTSD (Horowitz et al., 1979), and lower than the recommended cutoff point for PTSD "caseness" in a community sample (McFarlane, 1988). These data suggest that survivors of NDEs do not, as a group, suffer the degree of distress or impairment that patients with PTSD do. The clinical relevance of IES scores that are elevated yet still below the PTSD diagnostic threshold is unclear. Given the importance of subsyndromal levels of depressive symptoms (Frasure-Smith, Lespérance, & Talajic, 1995; Judd, 2000), it may be premature to assume that subsyndromal levels of intrusive thoughts are not clinically relevant in the prognosis of trauma survivors. However, it is noteworthy that in these participants with NDEs, the elevation of IES scores was entirely due to the scores on the intrusion subscale, and not on the avoidance subscale.

There is some evidence that catastrophic events, such as military combat, produce greater intrusion, whereas more commonplace stressful events, such as bereavement or personal injuries, may produce greater avoidance (Schwartzwald, Solomon, Weisenberg, & Mikulincer, 1987). Longitudinal studies suggest that intrusive phenomena may be a nonspecific marker of inadequate cognitive processing of a traumatic event rather than symptomatic of psychiatric disorder; many survivors of life-threatening crises report intrusive symptoms without ever developing PTSD or other stress-related disorders (McFarlane, 1992).

The profile of near-death experiencers on the IES, with moderate elevation on the intrusion subscale and none on the avoidance subscale, is therefore consistent with a nonspecific response to catastrophic stress with a low specificity for PTSD (McFarlane, 1992). This profile is also in keeping with clinical observations that NDE survivors tend to be preoccupied with their experience and its sequelae but do not generally view it as a negative influence on their lives. Of course, some individuals who report having had NDEs my also suffer PTSD as a result of their close brush with death or the associated subjective experience (Greyson, 1997a), but the intrusive symptoms commonly reported by near-death experiencers do not in themselves appear sufficient to suggest the presence of PTSD.

Although peritraumatic dissociation has been shown to predict subsequent PTSD (Koopman et al., 1994; Marmar et al., 1994; Shalev et al., 1996), this study suggests that dissociative NDEs do not. One feature that distinguishes most NDEs from other forms of peritraumatic dissociation is the strong positive affect (Bates & Stanley, 1985; Greyson, 1983a; Noyes & Kletti, 1976; Owens et al., 1990), in contrast to the fear and terror that accompany most dissociative responses to catastrophic events. It is plausible that the positive affect in NDEs might help defend against the subsequent development of full-blown PTSD.

The cross-cultural commonalities among NDEs suggest that humans may be programmed to have such experiences in the face of life-threatening danger. If so, we might speculate about the possible survival value of having NDEs when close to death. For example, the peacefulness and behavioral relaxation of the NDE might conserve energy, prolonging life where agitation or panic might hasten death; the splitting off of the threatened individual's consciousness as a detached observer, separated from the imperiled body, might protect against paralyzing pain and cognitive disorganization; and the accelerated mental processes might facilitate extraordinary rescue efforts in the face of life-threatening danger (Greyson, 1983b; Noyes & Kletti, 1976). The present study suggests that there may, in addition, be a long-term adaptive function of NDEs: namely, strong positive affect at the time of the trauma may forestall or mitigate the subsequent development of the more maladaptive PTSD symptoms.

Limitations of the Study

Findings of the current study must be interpreted with caution because of its reliance on self-selected participants, who may conceivably differ from persons who do not come forward voluntarily. For example, it is possible that individuals who experience fewer intrusive symptoms may be less motivated to participate in research, or that those who experience more avoidant symptoms may be reluctant to participate in research that may arouse traumatic memories. It is also conceivable that those who volunteer for research may feel they are "doing something about" their experience, and that activity may thereby shield them form the more distressing PTSD symptoms experienced by nonvolunteers. No attempt was made to corroborate these participants' proximity to death, a factor that may influence some features of NDEs (Owens et al., 1990). Furthermore, no attempt was made to conduct diagnostic interviews with these participants to confirm the presence or absence of PTSD. For these reasons, it may be valuable to repeat this study with an unselected cohort for whom proximity to death has been well documented.

Conclusions and Implications

This study corroborates clinical observations that near-death experiencers report more intrusive memories of their close brush with death than do other survivors of a near-fatal crisis, whereas they do not report greater efforts to avoid reminders of that event. Survivors of NDEs do not generally suffer the degree of distress or impairment that patients with PTSD do, although their lower level of symptoms may still have clinical relevance and may warrant counseling. The profile of posttraumatic symptoms reported by near-death experiencers suggests a nonspecific response characterized by in-

adequate cognitive processing of a catastrophic event rather than symptoms of a discrete psychiatric disorder.

Although dissociation at the time of a crisis generally increases the risk of developing subsequent PTSD, NDEs apparently do not. NDEs differ from other forms of peritraumatic dissociation by their strong positive affect. It is plausible that this positive affect might insulate the survivor against the subsequent development of full-blown PTSD.

References

American Psychiatric Association. (1994). *Diagnostic and statistical manual of mental disorders* (4th ed.). Washington, DC: Author.

Anonymous. (1894). What drowning feels like. *British Medical Journal, 2*, 823–824.

Bates, B. C., & Stanley, A. (1985). The epidemiology and differential diagnosis of near-death experience. *American Journal of Orthopsychiatry, 55*, 542–549.

Davidson, J. R. T. (1997). Repairing the shattered self: Recovering from trauma. *Journal of Clinical Psychiatry, 58*(suppl. 9), 3–4.

Frasure-Smith, N., Lespérance, F., & Talajic, M. (1995). Depression and 18-month prognosis after myocardial infarction. *Circulation, 91*, 999–1005.

Gabbard, G. O., & Twemlow, S. W. (1984). *With the eyes of the mind: An empirical analysis of out-of-body states*. New York: Praeger.

Greyson, B. (1983a). The Near-Death Experience Scale: Construction, reliability, and validity. *Journal of Nervous and Mental Disease, 171*, 369–375.

Greyson, B. (1983b). The psychodynamics of near-death experiences. *Journal of Nervous and Mental Disease, 171*, 376–381.

Greyson, B. (1990). Near-death encounters with and without near-death experiences: Comparative NDE Scale profiles. *Journal of Near-Death Studies, 8*, 151–161.

Greyson, B. (1991). Near-death experiences precipitated by suicide attempt: Lack of influence of psychopathology, religion, and expectations. *Journal of Near-Death Studies, 9*, 183–188.

Greyson, B. (1997a). The near-death experience as a focus of clinical attention. *Journal of Nervous and Mental Disease, 185*, 327–334.

Greyson, B. (1997b). Near-death narratives. In S. Krippner & S.M. Powers (Eds.), *Broken images, broken selves: Dissociative narratives in clinical practice* (pp. 163–180), Washington, DC: Brunner/Mazel.

Greyson, B. (1998a). Biological aspects of near-death experiences. *Perspectives in Biology and Medicine, 42,* 14–32.

Greyson, B. (1998b). The incidence of near-death experiences. *Medicine and Psychiatry, 1,* 92–99.

Greyson, B. (2000). Dissociation in people who have near-death experiences: Out of their bodies or out of their minds? *Lancet, 355,* 460–463.

Heim, A. (1892). Notizen über den Tod durch abstruz [Remarks on fatal falls]. *Jahrbuch des Schweitzerischen Aplenclub [Yearbook of the Swiss Alpine Club], 27,* 327–337.

Horowitz, M., Wilner, N., & Alvarez, W. (1979). Impact of Event Scale: A measure of subjective stress. *Psychosomatic Medicine, 41,* 209–218.

Judd, L. L. (2000). Adverse outcome of subsyndromal and syndromal levels of depressive symptom severity. *Psychosomatic Medicine, 62,* 472–473.

Kessler, R. C., Sonnega, A., Bromet, E., Hughes, M., & Nelson, C. B. (1995). Posttraumatic stress disorder in the National Comorbidity Survey. *Archives of General Psychiatry, 52,* 1048–1060.

Koopman, C., Classen, C., & Spiegel, D. (1994). Predictors of posttraumatic stress symptoms among survivors of the Oakland/Berkeley, Calif., firestorm. *American Journal of Psychiatry, 151,* 888–894.

Locke, T. P., & Schontz, F. C. (1983). Personality correlates of the near-death experience: A preliminary study. *Journal of the American Society for Psychical Research, 77,* 311–318.

Marmar, C. R., Weiss, D. S., Schlenger, W. E., Fairbank, J. A., Jordan, B. K., Kulka, R. A., & Hough, R. L. (1994). Peritraumatic dissociation and posttraumatic stress in male Vietnam theater veterans. *American Journal of Psychiatry, 151,* 902–907.

McFarlane, A. C. (1988). The aetiology of posttraumatic stress disorders following a natural disaster. *British Journal of Psychiatry, 152,* 116–121.

McFarlane, A. C. (1992). Avoidance and intrusion in posttraumatic stress disorder. *Journal of Nervous and Mental Disease, 180,* 439–445.

Noyes, R. (1980). Attitude change following near-death experiences. *Psychiatry, 43,* 234–242.

Noyes, R., & Kletti, R. (1976). Depersonalization in the face of life-threatening danger: An interpretation. *Omega, 7,* 103–114.

Owens, J. E., Cook, E. W., & Stevenson, I. (1990). Features of "near-death experience" in relation to whether or not patients were near death. *Lancet, 336,* 1175–1177.

Schwartzwald, J., Solomon, Z., Weisenberg, M., & Mikulincer, M. (1987). Validation of the Impact of Event Scale for psychological sequelae of combat. *Journal of Consulting and Clinical Psychology, 55,* 251–256.

Shalev, A. Y., Peri, T., Canetti, L., & Schreiber, S. (1996). Predictors of PTSD in injured trauma survivors: A prospective study. *American Journal of Clinical Psychiatry, 153,* 219–225.

Solomon, S. D., & Davidson, J. R. T. (1997). Trauma: Prevalence, impairment, service use, and cost. *Journal of Clinical Psychiatry, 58* (suppl. 9), 5–11.

van der Kolk, B. A., Pelcovitz, D., Roth, S., Mandel, F. S., McFarlane, A., & Herman, J. L. (1996). Dissociation, somatization, and affect dysregulation: The complexity of adaptation to trauma. *American Journal of Psychiatry, 153* (suppl. 7), 83–93.

Wiltse, A. S. (1889). A case of typhoid fever with subnormal temperature and pulse. *Saint Louis Medical and Surgical Journal, 57,* 355–364.

36

Lost Boys: Why Our Sons Turn Violent and How We Can Save Them

At a time when people around the country are mindlessly talking about zero tolerance, video cameras, and cracking down, it is refreshing to come to Smith College to speak at a conference titled *Safe Schools: Building Fortresses* or *Opening the Doors to Community.* I am also pleased that a student led this conference off, a student who spoke unashamedly about optimism, about values, and about doing good with her life. Many people are mired in hopelessness, in shortsighted thinking, and in the emotional immobilization that has taken place in our country in recent years. I think that optimism and hope are worth beginning with today as we talk about the issue of violence.

There was a time not that long ago when the issue of lethal youth violence was marginalized. The worst example of this I encountered about ten years ago, when I worked in Chicago. I received a call from the office of a senator in Washington who was considering hearings on youth violence. An aide was sent out to spend the day in Chicago and other major cities to collect background information. A month later, the aide called to say that he had completed his report for the senator. In his report, he concluded that the problem of lethal youth violence was primarily confined to poor minority kids. The senator's response had been, "Well, that's good news. Then we don't have to have hearings." His exact words were, "Let them kill each other off."

Well, we're a long way from that response to having a White House summit on youth violence a year ago in May in the wake of the Littleton shootings in Colorado. What's changed is that now all of America—including middle-class White America—can look in the newspaper and see their kids involved with or victim to violence. That makes it a national issue worthy of presidential attention, worthy of hearings, worthy of programs. We need to understand the legacy of racism and classism that informs this issue and defines it in many ways, but at the same time we need to make use of this mobilization of energy. Simply because entry is mobilized does not mean that people will do the right thing. Constructive change does not simply involve mobilizing energy and getting people's attention. It requires us to do something that we, as Americans, don't do very well: think deeply about the issue.

If it's action you want, Americans are number one. It's known around the world that if you want something done, get an American. Probably the slogan "Just do it!" should be our national motto. This is really our strong suit. If a kid's stuck in a well someplace, we're the ones to handle it. We'll mobilize, we'll set up scholarships, we'll dig, and everyone will think it's terrific. But if what is needed is to think more deeply about the issue, it's necessary to lean on a much more European tradition, where theory and deep analysis have a longer history and greater kind of social credence.

There was a German psychologist named Kurt Lewin who worked in the United States and tried to bring this European approach to America. Lewin (1935) once wrote "There is nothing so practical as a good theory," which to an American often sounds like a contradiction in terms. We tend to think theoretical is over *here* and practical over *there*. Lewin understood that to do good practice you have to understand things deeply. This is evident in many sound programs.

For example, in almost every state around the country, home visiting is being offered as a strategy for preventing child abuse, and with good reason. Research and program development done 20 years ago by psychologist David Olds (Olds et al., 1997) resulted in a home visiting program that was very effective in reducing child abuse. He spent a lot of time thinking through the interrelationship behind child development, family development, and intervention. When he got it all right theoretically, he came up with the nurse home visitor program, where nurses begin visiting during the prenatal period and continue for two years after birth. Now, 17 years later, Olds's research shows that the nurse home visitor is very powerful in protecting children from being abused. But the minute the program was turned over to the local health department, people who hadn't made the same investment in understanding the theory behind it started making changes. Somebody said, "Well, you know, you've got caseloads of 10 families per nurse; we'll get a lot more bang for the buck if we have 30 families per nurse. Let's make it 30." Somebody else said, "Well, you have nurses doing this visiting. It would be a lot cheaper if we had volunteer laypeople do it—let's have volunteer laypeople." Somebody else said, "Well, you know, it's not convenient to begin visiting before the babies are born. Why don't we just wait until after they are born because then we'll have birth certificates?" When you start cavalierly changing the key elements that are grounded in the theory of a program, the program does not work the same way any more. This is dangerous, but it's also very characteristic of America. "Just do it!"

To approach the issue of violence and safe schools, we need to think *more deeply*. Another way to make that point is with a parable. A parable, of course, is a teaching story and this parable has something to teach us as Americans. It's called the parable of the lamppost. In the parable of the lamppost, Joe is on his way home from a meeting one night. He comes upon his friend George, who is on his hands and knees on the street, groping around under a lamppost. Joe stops and says, "George, what's the matter?" George says, "Well, Joe, I have lost my car keys. I live 35 miles away and I can't go home until I find them." "Well," says Joe, "Let me help you." So like a good American, he rolls up his sleeves and he gets down on the street and starts groping around under the lamppost looking for the keys. Some time passes

with no result, so Joe says, "Wait a moment, George. Maybe we need a more systematic approach. Maybe we need a *public health approach*." From his pocket he pulls a piece of chalk and draws a grid on the street under the lamppost, and labels the boxes A through Z and 1 through 26. "Now," He says, "we can search systematically." So they search: Box A1, Box A2, Box A3, Box A4, on an on until they get to Box Z26. But they haven't found the car keys. After thinking a moment, Joe says, "Maybe we need a more *behaviorist approach*." So from his other pocket, he pulls a bag of M & Ms. He says, "George, I am going to fee you these M & Ms to get your behavior under control." He gets George moving left and right, and back and forth. It was very impressive, but they still hadn't found the car keys. So Joe says, "Maybe we need a more *psychoanalytic, psychodynamic approach*." He asks George about early experiences of loss in his life. Soon George remembers when he was 4 years old an he lost his teddy bear, and his feelings of loss come flooding back to him now with the loss of the car keys. Soon George is getting great insight, but he still can't go home. "Well," says Joe, "maybe we need a *support group*." So he gets out his cell phone and calls other people who have lost their car keys. They talk to George and soon George is feeling okay about losing his car keys. "Well," says Joe, "that didn't work. Maybe we need a more *educational approach*." So he pulls out from his bag a book titled *History of the Key in Western Civilization*. They read about how Ingmar Bergman used the key as a metaphor in his films, and how Woody Allen picked up on that metaphor in his films: it was quite enlightening. But they still can't find the keys. Finally Joe is really depressed and says, "All right, George, let's take a really radical approach. Where exactly were you when you dropped the keys?" George says, "I was about 150 yards up the road when I dropped the keys." So, of course Joe says, "Why are we looking here?" George replies, "The light is much better here!"

The reason this parable is applicable to us today is that there are so many forces at work around us and inside us to get us to look where the light is good: where you can get funding, where there are grants, where you can get corporate sponsors, where it doesn't rock the boat, and where it is personally comfortable. The point of the parable is that if the real issues often lie up the road somewhere, in the dark places where people don't want to go, working where the light is good will yield few results beyond the appearance of action. If we don't look in those dark places, we won't solve the problem.

To dig deeper into this issue, and not just have some meager, popular response, we need to improve what I like to call our *conceptual toolbox.* Every professional carries around a toolbox, and there's a series of five or six tools I would put in our box to address the issue of violence. The first is an *ecological perspective on human development.* When you look at research on human development with your eyes wide open, you find rarely, if ever, a simple cause-effect relationship. Cause-effect relationships are always shaped and conditioned by culture, society, community, gender, race, ethnicity, and historical period. If the question is "Does X cause Y?" the best answer is "It depends; it depends on the context in which X and Y are occurring."

The issue of violence raises a lot of striking examples of the importance of context. Twenty-five years ago a study by Mednick (1988) asked the question "Are kids who are born with minor neurological damage more likely to end up as violent teenagers than biologically normal children?" (Well, now you know the answer: it depends.) It turned out if they were growing up in well-functioning families, they were no more likely than biologically normal children to end up as violent teenagers. But if neurotically damaged children were growing up in abusive families and dysfunctional communities, they were four times as likely to end up as violent teenagers than biologically normal children. The impact of biological leaning, or disability, or vulnerability depends on the context in which a child grows up.

This is a finding that has tremendous implications for the practice of child welfare. If you're dealing with high-risk kids who have a tradition, a heritage of risk, you better be very careful about where you place them. That's one reason why kinship foster care is a risky proposition in many cases. Take, for example, the case of the 6-year-old boy in Michigan who shot and killed his first-grade classmate. He had been living with his mother, who was part of an illicit drug ring. He and his brother were sent to live with their uncle, her brother, who was also part of the illicit drug ring. The kingpin of the drug ring was the boy's maternal grandmother. Would you want to place that child in foster care with his maternal grandmother? Eventually they placed him with his aunt, his mother's sister. You'd sure want to know if she's a part of the same drug-abusing family system because if she is, you are almost dooming that boy to replicate his father's criminal record and imprisonment.

Other studies on violence speak in the same way about the role of family context and community context. The point is that when there is massive social risk, it tends to be overwhelming. The relevance of the subtle difficulties in thinking and feeling may be diminished because the overwhelming character of the context blows kids away. If you're in a situation of zero risk in terms of social environmental factors, then naturally it stands to reason that the only kids who are going to be in big trouble are the kids who have some neurological predisposition.

A study conducted by German psychologists Friedrich Losel, Doris Bender, and Thomas Bliensener tells a very similar story. For a long time people have suspected or said they'd known that kids who are prone to bullying are temperamentally not like other kids. By the same token, kids who are prone to victimization are not like other kids. Kids prone to victimization are kids who are hypersensitive because bullies try their bullying out on everybody and eventually realize that some kids really get upset by it. The kids are prone to bullying because they have a belligerent temperament. The German study looked at the base heart rate of bullies, victims, and kids who were neither bullies nor victims; but they also looked at context. They looked at the heart rates in high-risk and low-risk families. In low-risk families, they found a difference in the base heart rate. Bullies had an average heart rate of 65 beats per minute, victims had an average heart rate of 75 beats per minute, and kids who were neither bullies nor victims had an average heart rate of 70 beats per minute. But in the high-risk families, all three groups had heart rates of 70 beats per minute. In a high-risk environment, it didn't take a temperamental predisposition to produce a bully or a victim; the environment is so overwhelming it crashes down on you.

The second key concept for our toolbox is the *accumulation of risk and opportunity* in children's lives. Once again it starts from research that shows that rarely, if ever, does a single risk factor or a single opportunity factor account for much in the outcome of children. So if we're trying to account for violence, we can't look at one single factor. My book *Lost Boys* happened to come out the morning of the Littleton shootings, so it got lots of extra attention. Journalists kept asking, "What is the cause for this tragedy?" And I kept trying to say there's no *cause*, there's only the accumulation of risk. It's as if a boy is building a tower of blocks, block after block after block, and finally he puts one more block on the tower and it falls over. You can't really say that the last block is the cause of the fall because if that block were there by itself, it wouldn't fall over. If some other block came last, it would look like the cause. Indeed, the research shows that it is the accumulation of risk factors that does the damage.

A classic study demonstrating this notion of accumulation of risk was done by University of Michigan psychologist Arnold Sameroff and his colleagues (1987). The Sameroff study looked at the accumulation of risk and its impact on intellectual development. Intellectual development is relevant to the issue of violence because it is known that average intellectual functioning is one of the pillars of resilience; it affects the ability to deal with adversity. It stands to reason that having both hands free is more adaptive than having both hands tied behind your back. The Sameroff study is about how risk accumulation affects intellectual development, which ultimately plays a role in violence and aggression. Here are the risk factors he looked at: poverty, absence of a parent, drug abuse in a parent, mental illness in a parent, low educational attainment in a parent, child abuse in the family, exposure to racism, and large family size. When none of these risk factors are present, the average IQ scores were 119. We say 100 is the average, but that's average for everybody.

As risk accumulates, the story becomes very interesting. With one risk factor, the IQ scores were still 116; with two risk factors, 113. Now that's really good news for the human enterprise: life does not have to be totally risk-free in order for kids to thrive. Most kids can thrive with two risk factors, but when you go from two to four risk factors, any four, the IQ scores go down to 93. That's where you get into jeopardy. Most kids can cope with two risk factors, but few can cope with four. By the time you get to eight risk factors, scores drop to 85. That is the effect of the accumulation of risk. It has tremendous implications for our thinking about programs. Life does not have to be risk-free, and none of those issues is a problem in and of itself. The problem isn't poverty, the problem isn't child abuse, and the problem isn't absent parents. Most kids can deal with any of those. The problem is too many of them. When we put too many burdens on a kid's shoulders, he can't stand up under the weight.

On the other side, you have the accumulation of opportunity. More and more people are using the term "asset" to refer to these developmental opportunities. You may be familiar with the Search Institute in Minneapolis, Minnesota, where they researched 40 developmental assets. These assets range from things inside the kid and inside the family, to things inside the school and inside the community. The list is incredibly diverse, including assets such as family life provides high level of support; child goes to church or religious institutions at least an hour a week; and young person is optimistic about his future. It's an incredible range of items. What they found is that the more assets a kid has in his life, the less likely he is to have problems.

Let's look at violence from this perspective. For the Search Institute study, the violent category was defined as having engaged in three or more acts of hitting, fighting, injuring a person, carrying a weapon, or threatening physical harm in the past 12 months. Of the kids who had 31 to 40 assets, only 6% were found to be in the violent category. Of the kids who had 21 to 30 assets, 16% were in the violent category. Of the kids who had 11 to 20 assets, 35% were in the violent category. And of the kids with 0 to 10 of these assets, 61% were in the violent category. The issue is not which asset you have, but rather, how many assets you have. It is a mirror image of risk accumulation.

An issue worth considering, however, is the 6% of children with between 31 and 40 assets who *were* in the violent category. How could they be violent? With kids who have between 0 and 10 assets we can say, "Well, sure, what do you expect?" But notice that even with 0 to 10 assets, 39% *aren't* in the violent category. A third of them were still hanging in there being pro-social. Kids are resilient even when they've got nothing going for them. The 6% of the kids who are violent even though they have all these assets might be called asset-resistant. Think about a boy like Dylan Klebold, one of the shooters at the school in Littleton, Colorado. Dylan had assets coming out of his ears: loving, competent, caring parents; good school; no poverty; affluence—you name it, he had it. What right does he have to be so screwed up? Well, maybe he was an asset-resistant kid with a troubled inner life we need to find out about. When you look at kinds who kill, 90% are not surprising at all. Their lives are full of abuse, trauma, deprivation, impoverishment, and oppression. But 10% of the kids who kill are of this more mysterious kind that comes out of nowhere socially.

This assets approach also opens our eyes to opportunities for intervention. For example, of those assets, about 10 are very much a function of the school a child attends. Some school climates provide a caring, encouraging environment; parents are actively involved in helping young people succeed in school; youngsters feel safe at home, at school, and in the neighborhood; school provides clear rules and consequences, and so on. What kinds of schools are most likely to provide these assets to kinds, thus making them safer for themselves, from themselves, and for the community? An issue to consider is size.

Research from the 1950s (Barker and Gump, 1964) showed us that small high schools create a different social climate from big high schools. The assets associated with schools include such things as participation in music or theater and art at least three hours a week; participation in sports or youth organizations; and parents actively involved with school programs. In a small high school, everyone is needed, not because the teachers and the principal go to inclusiveness workshops or have had their consciousnesses raised, but because the context demands participation. The research found that in small high schools, kids were much more likely to have all these assets than in a big high school. This was particularly true for marginal students, those at risk of dropping out, those who are disaffected, those whose parents don't support their education, those with lower IQ scores; for those kids, the research found that small schools were better.

In a big school, you try out and because most kids don't make the cut, most kids don't participate. They don't feel they're in a caring environment. They don't participate in activities; they don't feel safe. The research found that when high schools got bigger than about 500 for grades 9–12, they very quickly crossed over into the dynamic of bigness. In 1955, the average size of America's high schools was 500; by 1975 it was about 1,500.

The third concept we need to bring to our toolbox is *humility about resilience*. I've used that term before: resilience, the ability to deal with adversity, the idea that we can cope but we also have limits. In American society, however, the term resilience has a kind of dark side to it. In this judgmental society, it's a short step between celebrating coping and judging those who are not coping. The worst example I encountered was when I was testifying in the murder trial of a 16-year-old boy. My job was to explain to the jury how the accumulation of risk in the absence of assets should be understood in making sense of what the boy did—not just to excuse what he did, but to make sense of it. In the cross-examination the prosecutor asked. "What's wrong with this boy that he isn't resilient?" And I realized that instead of being in celebration of coping, we are now making a deficiency judgment.

Two studies really give you an intellectual foundation for the humility we need in thinking about resilience. Brigadier-general S. L. A. Marshall, the official U.S. military historian of World War II in Europe, commissioned the first study. He asked the question: If regular soldiers go into combat and stay

in combat for 60 days, what percentage end up as psychiatric casualties? When the data came in, it turned out that after 60 days of combat, 98% of the soldiers became psychiatric casualties. Now what is the intellectual justification for judging those soldiers as being deficient, when 98% become psychiatric casualties? Particularly because, when the researchers looked at the 2% who didn't break down, they found they were not robust, healthy, well-adjusted men—they were all psychopaths. That gives us a perspective on resilience: the only people who didn't go crazy already were.

Psychologist Pat Tolan (1996) from the University of Illinois has done the domestic equivalent to that study when he asked what percentage of kids would break down under the burden of various levels of additional risk factors. He measured "breaking down" either in academic terms (needing remedial special education) or in mental health terms (needing professional mental health intervention). The risk factors he considered included living in violent, impoverished neighborhoods; abuse and neglect; being between the ages of 13 and 15; being male; and being a person of color. Tolan wondered what percentage of children with all five of these risk factors would show one or both forms of breakdown. Not surprisingly, the answer was 100%. That doesn't mean the kids' lives are over. Many of them find a way back, but anyone with that burden takes a major hit.

Let me make it even more concrete to you personally. How many people in this room would say you are in good shape because you work out or do aerobics? Okay, let's group the work-out folks in one section and the couch potatoes in another. If I were then to ask which group has better lung capacity, better resilient breathing, surely it would be the aerobic group. But then, if you asked which group would last longer on the surface of the moon, the answer would be neither group. All the aerobic breathing in the world isn't going to protect you on the surface on the moon; that's the starting point for humility about resilience, resilience in context. And there but for the grace of God go any of us.

The fourth concept for our toolbox is the issue of *temperament*—the recognition that children come to us with different packages of attributes: active, passive, soothable, unsoothable, and so on. Now if you don't have any children, you may not believe in temperament; you may think all children are alike. If you have one child, you may still not believe in temperament. But if you have two or more children, you tend to believe in temperament; you tend to believe children come in many flavors and varieties.

Temperament, however, is not destiny. It is probability. Temperament is what the child offers up to the world as a possibility and a challenge, or a direction. Without knowledge, without resources, without intelligence, without insight, temperament shapes patterns of behavior that lead kids down different pathways. If you're the parent of an easy baby, life is pretty darn good. You wake up every day thinking about what further evidence you will be shown to confirm what a wonderful parent you are. If you're the parent of a difficult baby, you wake up thinking, "Oh god, what further evidence of my incompetence and ineptitude will I be presented with today?" More recent research, however, has highlighted that temperament is not destiny. If temperament is a challenge, how do parents succeed in meeting that challenge? It is important to understand how the child sees and experiences the world. As I said before, temperament takes place in context, too: temperament predicts violence in some situations but not in others, and we can override temperament to a large degree.

The next key concept to put into this equation is *rejection*. Anthropologist Ronald Rohner (1975) studied rejection in 118 cultures around the world and found that in every one, kids who are rejected turn out badly, and they turn out badly in ways that are culturally appropriate. They develop whatever is bad in that culture, so much so that Rohner called rejection a psychological malignancy or psychological cancer. This is very important because one of the themes for kids who are violent is the problem of rejection. It may be interpersonal rejection in the family or in school, or it may be linked to homophobia, to racism. In any case, it is internalized as rejection of who you are as a person, of your identity. Rejection produces shame, shame produces anxiety about psychiatric annihilation (you feel you will cease to exist), and violence is one sure way to demonstrate to yourself and to others that you do indeed exist. A man in prison once said to a colleague of mine, "I'd rather be wanted for murder than not be wanted at all." If positive acceptance isn't provided, there is always the negative route. The experience of being wanted and needed is one of the psychological anchors that keeps kids steady.

The last addition to this toolbox is the concept of *spirituality*: the recognition that human beings are not simply animals with complicated brains, but spiritual beings as well. Not meeting your spiritual needs can produce damage in much the same what that not meeting your physical, nutritional, emotional, and intellectual needs does.

Among the kids I've interviewed who have killed, spiritual emptiness is perhaps the most com-mon thread. I think there are at least three reasons why a spiritually empty kid is in jeopardy. First, a spiritually empty kid has a kind of hole in his heart, and that hole must be filled with some sense of meaningfulness. If it is not filled by the positive meaningfulness of a universe of love and a reverence for life, then it will be filled with a Marilyn Manson who offers a kind of demonically meaningful interpretation of life.

Second, a kid who is spiritually empty has no sense of limits. A spiritually grounded kid has a sense that he exists in a meaningful spiritual universe, that he's not acting alone, and that there are limits on him and on what he can do. Reverence for life comes naturally. A spiritually empty kid says, "I'm on my own in here, it's me and you. You make me angry, you deserve to die. You make me afraid, you deserve to die. You make me feel bad, you deserve to die."

Third, a spiritually empty kid has no emotional floor to fall back on when he gets sad. A grounded kid could say, "I may feel lousy, but at least I know I live in a meaningful universe and there's a comfort to that." The spiritually empty kid is on his own. He can go into emotional free fall and can fall as low as a human being can possibly go.

If you start to put all these concepts together—spirituality, rejection, temperament, accumulation of risk, ecological perspective, humility about resilience—you begin to have the tools to look at the different pathways that kids take. With these tools, it becomes clear that 90% of the kids who are put on the pathway that includes abuse, deprivation, and oppression develop a chronic pattern of aggression, bad behavior, acting out, and violating of others' rights by the time they are 10. These are behaviors that might meet the diagnostic standard for conduct disorder. We know (Dodge et al., 1997) that 30% of kids diagnosed with conduct disorder by age 10 end up as delinquents in adolescence. But even then, context has its effects: in some neighborhoods that figure is 65%; in other neighborhoods it's 15%—same pattern of behavior, different ramifications. It depends on the context in which they grow up, the context of peer support, the context of gun availability, and the context of media imagery.

I was in Canada a few weeks ago on the day of a school massacre. In Ottawa, a 15-year-old boy attacked his school. Their TV images looked just like our TV images: ambulances, police cars, girls crying into each other's shoulders, boys trying to hold back their tears, distraught parents. They sent five kids to the hospital, all of whom were released with minor injuries because the only thing the attacker could come up with was a knife. Put that same boy on our side of the border and there would have been a gun, and it would not have caused minor injuries. That's part of the toxicity in which these troubled kids are drowning.

A couple of years ago a survey of the youth prison system (Edens & Otto, 1997) found that 85% of the boys in prison have conduct disorders. How surprising! How else do you get in prison except by showing a chronic pattern of aggression, bad behavior, acting out, and violating the rights of others?

Now remember that 90% of the kids who develop a chronic pattern of aggression, bad behavior, acting out, and violating of others' rights come from backgrounds including abuse, deprivation, and oppression. They go down the route of conduct disorder. Whether they end up as killers or not depends a lot on how toxic or benign the culture is around them. But as I said before, there's that other 10% who aren't abused, who don't develop early conduct disorder, but who become so troubled in their thinking and feeling that they really lose their way in the world. Ironically, they often try to keep that a secret. They develop a secret life because they don't want to disappoint their parents; their parents love them. They don't want to disappoint their teachers; their teachers care for them. Boys in particular keep this secret world.

We're doing a study at Cornell called "The Secret Life of Teenagers," asking college students to talk about the most dangerous/illegal things they did when they were teenagers, things their parents still don't know about. Some of the stories we're hearing are hair-raising. And this is among Ivy League students who are in human development.

Kip Kinkel, the school shooter in Springfield, Oregon, was hearing voices and never told anybody because he didn't want to disappoint his parents. Michael Carneal, the boy from West Patuka, Kentucky, who shot up a prayer meeting, had a photographic memory: total recall for every insult he had ever experienced in his life going back to age 3. Nobody knew this; it hadn't leaked out until his secret life burst forth in a barrage of bullets.

The real challenge for us in thinking about school safety and safe schools is to find a way to use these concepts to understand the development of every kid who walks in the door, whether they're prone to be in the 90% or the 10%. We need to develop the infrastructure of mental health services, of caring, of participation, of character education to support, accept, and nurture kids in a way that will meet their spiritual as well as their emotional needs. And if we do this and we keep our eyes open, then we can probably have safer schools.

References

Barker, R., & Gump, P. (1964). *Big school, small school.* Stanford, CA: Stanford University Press.

Dodge, K. A., Pettit, G. S., & Bates, J. E. (1997). How the experience of early physical abuse leads children to become chronically aggressive. In C. Cicchetti & S. L. Toth (Eds.), *Developmental psychopathology: Vol. 9. Theory, research, and intervention* (pp. 263–288). Rochester, NY: University of Rochester Press.

Edens, J. F. F., & Otto, R. K. (1997, Spring). Prevalence of mental disorders among youth in the juvenile system. *Focal Point: A National Bulletin on Family Support and Children's Mental Health, 1,* 6–7. Portland, OR: Portland State University.

Lewin, K. (1935). *A dynamic theory of personality.* New York: McGraw-Hill.

Mednick, S. (1988). *Biological bases of antisocial behavior.* Norwell, MA: Kluwer.

Olds, D., Eckenrode, J., Henderson, Jr., C. R., Kotzman, H. K., Powers, J., Cole, R., Sidosa, K., Morris, P., Pettit, L., & Luckey, D. (1997). Long-term effects of home visitation on maternal life course and child abuse and neglect: 15-year follow-up of a randomized trial. *Journal of the American Medical Association, 278,* 637–643.

Rohner, R. (1975). *They love me, they love me not.* New Haven, CT: Human Relations Area Files Press.

Sameroff, A., Seifer, R., Barocas, R., Zax, M., & Greenspan, S. (1987). Intelligence quotient scores of four-year-old children: Social environmental risk factors. *Pediatrics, 79,* 343–350.

Search Institute, 700 S. Third Street, Suite 210, Minneapolis, MN 55415. *www.search-institute.org*

Tolan, P. (1996, October). How resilient is the concept of resilience? *Community Psychologist, 4,* 12–15.

C. Problems with a Physical Basis

CHARLES A. EMLET
KATHLEEN J. FARKAS

37

A Descriptive Analysis of Older Adults with HIV/AIDS in California

HIV/AIDS has been a growing area of concern for social workers and other health care professionals since the early 1980s; HIV/AIDS has become a disease common in later life. More cases of AIDS have been diagnosed in the geriatric population than in younger children (Ory & Mack, 1998). As of June 2000, 22,014 cases of AIDS had been reported in people age 60 and over compared with 12,669 cases in children and adolescents age 0 to 19 years (Centers for Disease Control and Prevention [CDC], 2000). New cases of AIDS have risen twice as fast in people age 50 and over compared with the younger population (CDC, 1998). One physician recently described the increasing HIV-positive rate among elderly men as spreading like a "forest fire" (Palmer, 2000).

The primary transmission route for HIV in older adults is sexual exposure, and the highest-risk behavior associated with HIV transmission is older men having sex with an infected male partner (Puleo, 1996). Exposure to HIV among older people, however, is changing substantially (Emlet, 1997). In the past 10 years, there has been a significant increase in the numbers of older people infected through heterosexual contact (Gordon & Thompson, 1995; Ory & Mack, 1998; Puelo, 1996), injection drug use (Gordon & Thompson; Ory & Mack), and undetermined or unidentified exposure (CDC, 1998; Ory & Mack, 1998), whereas the proportion of older people infected through blood transfusions has declined significantly (Gordon & Thompson; Ory & Mack, 1998). Improved health and increased levels of interest in sexual activity as well as pharmaceu-

tical assistance from Viagra have given rise to concerns about the transmission of HIV in older people (Palmer, 2000). The increase in sexual transmission rates, both same sex and heterosexual, have implications for prevention and treatment initiatives with the elderly population.

Older women are especially disadvantaged because of the simultaneous exclusion of both women and older people from HIV/AIDS research and intervention (Zablotsky, 1998). Clinicians do not expect older women to be infected with HIV, so symptoms often go undiagnosed, misdiagnosed, or diagnosed late in the disease process (AIDS Alert, 1995; American Association of Retired Persons [AARP], 1994; El-Sadr & Gettler, 1995; Schable, Chu, & Diaz, 1996). Because most prevention activities for women focus on women of childbearing age, older women are neither targeted nor reached by current prevention strategies (AARP; Zablotsky). Older women themselves may not see the need to practice safe sex because they may not see themselves as at risk of pregnancy, HIV/AIDS, or other sexually transmitted diseases. Older women may not have the knowledge or skills that allow them to insist on or initiate safe sex behaviors.

Little has been written on the similarities and differences between elderly HIV/AIDS populations and their younger counterparts. This article describes the characteristics of people participating in California's system of HIV/AIDS case management programs and compares selected characteristics across age groups. The analysis provides information on the similarities and differences of the

HIV/AIDS groups ages 50 and older and gives direction to prevention and interventions strategies with elderly people.

Service Delivery Systems in California

California has maintained a significant portion of the AIDS cases diagnosed nationally. By the end of 1998, 17% of all AIDS cases diagnosed in the United States were in California (California Department of Health Services [CDHS], 1998).

In 1986 California initiated case management services for people with symptomatic HIV (then referred to as AIDS-related complex or ARC) and AIDS. These services were made available to local jurisdictions (primarily counties) through a competitive grant process. Although grant funds initially came exclusively from state government, funding from the Health Resources and Services Administration later augmented these grants.

The case management programs' services included an interdisciplinary team consisting of a social worker and a nurse case manager, the client or his or her representative, and the attending physician; initial and ongoing client assessments, development of a service plan, and coordination of services; attendant care, homemaker services, skilled nursing, nutritional counseling, benefit and psychosocial counseling, transportation, and food and housing subsidies (CDHS, 1998). To be eligible for these services, an individual must have a diagnosis of symptomatic HIV or AIDS certified by a physician, reside in a participating county, and be under the care of a primary care physician.

As funds became available, additional case management programs were funded, with the goal of expanding services statewide. By 1996 the Office of AIDS had contracts with 43 local health department and community-based agencies administering services in 53 of California's 58 counties (CDHS, 1996). The few counties without these services were very rural counties with few or no diagnosed cases of AIDS. Because these programs were initially pilot programs, contractors were required to collect service utilization data on each client as part of the contractual agreement with the Office of AIDS. Data collected by case managers were uniform across all programs including the data fields, operationalization of variables, and data reporting software used. The availability of data on older people with HIV/AIDS made this a valuable resource for exploring older people with

HIV/AIDS throughout California. As of June 30, 1996, California had a cumulative total of 96,120 cases of AIDS of which 62,153 individuals had died, leaving 33,967 people living with AIDS in California at that time. With 2,266 individuals in the data set who received an AIDS diagnosis, we suggest that the full data set represented approximately 6.6% of the total number of people living with AIDS in California at that time.

Method

This research project involved a cross-sectional secondary analysis of data from the CDHS, Office of AIDS. All data presented in this article were provided to the first author. No data were obtained directly from clients.

Sample Description

The data used in this study were obtained from CDHS, Office of AIDS, Community-Based Care Section. The study included individuals who were enrolled in case management programs between July 1, 1995 and June 30, 1996. These individuals represented a wide geographic spectrum of people living with AIDS throughout California, including urban, suburban, and rural areas.

The sample was derived from a data set of 2,659 cases. All cases of individuals age 50 and over were included in the analysis (281 cases). To construct a comparison group of almost equal size, a randomly selected sample of 350 cases (age 30 to 49) was chosen using SPSS commands for random selection. This resulted in a total sample of 631 cases. Examination of the data revealed one site in which large amounts of data were missing. The decision was made to eliminate that site from the analysis, which reduced the sample by 60 cases, resulting in a final sample of 571. The final sample included 63 cases age 60 and over, 190 cases age 50 to 59, and 318 cases 30 to 49 years of age.

Measures

Earlier research in the area of HIV/AIDS and aging has provided no consistent direction for the measurement of age. Multiple studies, however, dichotomized age groups into those under age 50 and those 50 and over (CDC, 1998; Ferro & Salit, 1992; Justice & Weissman, 1998; Ory & Mack, 1998; Schable et al., 1996; Ship, Wolff, & Selik, 1991). We felt that by combining all individuals age 50 and over, differences across age groups might not become apparent. Therefore it was decided to divide the sample into three age categories:

1. People age 30 to 49, not considered "older" by any definition; however, the majority of AIDS cases in the United States (71%) have been identified in people in this age group (CDC, 2000), and theorists in life span development consistently place a developmental transition at approximately age 30 (Gould, 1978; Levinson, 1978; Riegel, 1975).
2. People Age 50 to 59.
3. Individuals age 60 and over. Individuals in the final age group met criteria established under the Older Americans Act as being "aged," and therefore can be considered aged by criteria of the federal government.

Multiple studies related to this topic have chosen to categorize age into three distinct categories using slightly different cut-off points (Carre et al., 1994; Lemp, Payne, Neal, Temelso, & Rutherford, 1990; Sutin, Rose, Mulvihill, & Taylor, 1993).

Other variables in this research included gender, ethnicity, HIV exposure, living arrangements, poverty level, insurance coverage, residence in a metropolitan statistical area (MSA), having received an AIDS diagnosis, functional disability, and mortality. Gender, ethnicity, living alone, and HIV exposure were all coded categorically. Low income, defined as a reported income falling below 300% of federal poverty guidelines, was coded dichotomously. Having private insurance and receiving Medicaid were both coded as dichotomous indicator variables. MSAs were coded dichotomously. If the zip code was not in a federally defined MSA or less than 50% of the zip code was in an MSA, the variable was coded as 0.

Functional dependence was measured using the Karnofsky Performance Scale (KPS). The KPS is the most widely used health status measure in HIV medicine and research (O'Dell, Lubeck, O'Driscoll & Matsuno, 1995) and consists of an 11-point rating scale ranging from normal functioning = 100 to dead = 0 (Mor, Laliberte, Morris, & Wiemann, 1984). The Karnofsky has been significantly correlated with other instruments that measure functional status, including the Katz Activity of Daily Living Scale ($r = .73$) and the Instrumental Activities of Daily Living Index ($r = .66$). The KPS has been found to yield interrater reliability coefficients of .97 across multiple disciplines (Mor et al.). AIDS diagnosis was determined by whether the individual had received an AIDS diagnosis as opposed to

having symptomatic HIV disease. Regarding mortality, individuals were coded dichotomously according to whether they had died during the study.

Results

The final sample ranged in age from 30 to 81 years (M = 46.1, SD = 10.6). Individuals age 60 and over made up 11% of the sample, with individuals age 50 to 59 accounting for 33.3%. The majority of the sample was male (86%) with a slight majority being white (58%). African Americans made up 21.5% of the sample, with Hispanics accounting for 16.9%. Approximately 28% of the sample lived alone. With regard to the exposure category, 68.4% of subjects identified their exposure to HIV as men having sex with men. Injection drug use was identified as the risk factor in 16.8% of the cases, heterosexual contact in 19.2%, and exposure through contaminated blood products in 5.5% of all cases. It is important to remember that individuals may have identified more than one category of exposure to HIV, thus percentages in risk categories do not equal 100%. In regard to medical coverage, 38.8% identified themselves as having private insurance, and 51.4% were documented as having or being eligible for Medicaid. More than 95% of the sample was designated by zip code as living inside of an MSA. Regarding diagnosis and functional status, 86% of the sample had received a formal diagnosis of AIDS, with the remaining 14% having symptomatic HIV disease. KPS scores for the sample ranged from a low of 20 to a high of 70 (M = 53.8, SD = 15.7), with 59% being assessed as having a KPS score of 60 or below. The significance of a score of 60 on the KPS is based on the findings of Crooks, Waller, Smith, and Hahn (1991), who found that KPS scores that approximate 60 or below were highly predictive of outcomes such as hospitalizations and mortality. At the end of the study period, 88.6% of the sample were still living.

The analysis of the sample was conducted to examine differences in the variables under study across age groups. Age effects for the relationship examined in this study were generally nonlinear, most often changing abruptly for the oldest group only. Thus, analysis of age by categories rather than modeling as a continuous measure provided the best fit to the data.

When the sample was examined by age, particular patterns became apparent. Whereas females accounted for 14% of the full sample, that proportion nearly doubled in individuals age 60 years and over (Table 37.1). Whereas 12.6% of individ-

Table 37.1 Sample Description, by Age, in Percentages

Variable	All Ages (N = 571)	Age 30–49 (n = 318)	Age 50–59 (n = 190)	Age 60+ (n = 63)
Female*‡	14.0	12.6	13.7	22.2
Race/ethnicity				
White	58.0	53.2	65.1	61.3
African American	21.5	23.7	18.0	21.0
Hispanic	16.9	19.6	14.3	11.3
Asian/Pacific Islander	2.3	1.6	2.1	6.5
Native American	.5	.6	.5	0
Exposure[a]				
Men having sex with men*	68.4	74.1	64.7	52.6
Injection drug use	16.8	17.8	18.4	7.9
Heterosexual	19.2	17.4	21.6	21.1
Blood products**	5.5	3.0	5.9	15.8
Lives alone**	28.8	23.3	30.3	53.0
≤300% of poverty level	58.5	63.0	51.4	60.0
Medicaid	51.4	54.1	51.0	40.0
Private insurance*‡	38.8	35.6	37.9	56.3
Metropolitan statistical area	95.3	95.3	95.1	96.1
AIDS diagnosis	86.0	85.8	86.8	84.1
Karnofsky ≤ 60	59.0	59.0	58.0	62.0
Fatal illness during study*	11.4	9.7	12.1	17.5

NOTE: For race/ethnicity, percentages do not total 100 because of missing data.
[a]Exposure categories are not mutually exclusive and do not add to 100%.
*$p < .05$. **$p < .01$. ***$p < .001$. ‡Significance is between youngest and oldest groups only.

uals 30 to 49 were female, the percentage increased to 13.7% in those age 50 to 59 and to 22% in the oldest group. Differences in the proportion of females between the youngest and oldest age groups were statistically significant [$\chi^2(1, N = 381) = 4.02, p < .05$].

Differences in ethnicity across age groups did not indicate any particular pattern. The two older age groups 50 to 59 and 60 years and over, had a larger proportion of white people, similar to recently documented national trends (CDC, 1998). This difference, however, was not significant.

When exposure to HIV was examined, patterns appeared to reflect national trends. The proportion of individuals exposed to HIV from men having sex with men decreased with each successive age group. A chi-square statistic found the differences in this category of exposure to be significant [$\chi^2(2, N = 296) = 7.07, p < .05$]. Exposure through injection drug use also declined in the older age groups. In those age 60 and over, 7.9% had been exposed to HIV through this means compared with 18.4% in those 50 to 59 years and 17.8% in those age 30 to 49. Not surprisingly, HIV exposure through blood products increased significantly as the sample aged [$\chi^2(2, N = 292) = 9.77, p < .01$]. Expo-

sure through heterosexual contact also increased in the older groups; however, this increase was not statistically significant (Table 37.1). The increase in heterosexual exposure to HIV disease is consistent with the findings of other researchers (Gordon & Thompson, 1995; Ory & Mack, 1998).

Age was significantly associated with living arrangements in this sample. The proportion of individuals living alone was greater in the older groups. More than twice as many people age 60 and over were found to live alone compared with those below age 60 [$\chi^2(2, N = 250) = 11.01, p < .01$]. The significance increased further when comparing those 60 years and over with those 30 to 49 ($p < .001$).

Age appeared to have little influence on poverty rates, with no clear pattern of income relative to age groups. In regard to Medicaid status, people 60 and over were less likely to be Medicaid recipients than people in the other two age groups. The likelihood of having private insurance increased significantly in the same from 35.6% for people age 30 to 49 to 56.3% in those 60 years and over [$\chi^2 (1, N = 174) = 5.52, p < .05$]. This may reflect an increase in a more stable household economy and earning power in older individuals. Age had little influence on the percentage of people who had an AIDS diagnosis rather than symptomatic HIV disease. The largest proportion of individuals who had received an AIDS diagnosis was found in the 50 to 59 age group. The percentages of individuals with AIDS, however, varied by less than 3% across all age categories. When functional status was examined, individuals age 60 and over had a slightly higher proportion of cases in which the KPS scores were at 60 or below; the differences, however, were not statistically significant. The area in which age did appear to affect the sample was mortality. The mortality rate increased steadily in older age groups, from 9.7% in those age 30 to 49 to 12.1% in those age 50 to 59 to 17.5% for people age 60 and over. Nearly twice the percentage of people age 60 and over had died by the end of the study compared with those age 30 to 49.

These results identified four variables in which significant differences across age groups may be explained by age effect: (1) gender, more specifically the proportion of females, (2) living arrangements, (3) having private insurance, and (4) mortality. To understand the extent to which these differences may be associated with natural trends in the general aging population, the data from this study were compared with the general aging population in the United States (Table 37.2).

Compared with data from the general population (U.S. Census Bureau, 1999), the sample had a smaller percentage of females in all age categories (Table 37.2). The increase in the proportion of females across age categories, however, is higher in the study sample than the overall population (an increase of 60% versus 8%). The importance here is to reinforce the fact that older women do become infected with HIV in later life and need to be considered in viewing at-risk populations.

The proportion of individuals living alone in the study group was higher than the general population for all age categories (Table 37.2). The increase in the proportion of individuals living alone may be reflective of population trends, but it should be noted that the study population had a higher base to begin with in all age groups. These findings also serve to draw attention to the fact that social support networks for older people with HIV disease may be more limited than for their non-HIV-infected counterparts. For both the sample and the general population, the percentage of individuals with private health insurance increased, although the general population had higher rates of private insurance overall. The sample data, however, do not reflect population trends.

The death rate for the sample was higher overall than for the general population (Table 37.2). Al-

Table 37.2 Comparison of the Proportion of Age Categories in the Study Sample and the U.S. Population, by Females, Living Alone, Private Insurance, and Mortality

Variable	Study Sample (n = 571) % (CI)	Population Data (%)
Proportion of females		
Age: 39–49	12.6 (10, 17)	50.5
50–59	13.7 (10, 20)	51.6
60+	22.2 (14, 34)	56.0
Proportion living alone		
Age: 30–49	23.0 (19, 28)	9.7
50–59	30.3 (24, 37)	13.1
60+	53.0 (41, 65)	26.7
Proportion with private health insurance		
Age: 30–49	35.6 (31, 41)	60.1
50–59	37.9 (31, 45)	74.7
60+	56.3 (44, 68)	67.0
Proportion who died during study		
Age: 30–49	9.7 (.07, .14)	0.2
50–59	12.1 (.08, .17)	.6
60+	17.5 (.10, 29)	3.1

NOTE: CI = confidence interval.

SOURCE OF GENERAL POPULATION DATA: U.S. Census Bureau. (1999). *Statistical abstracts of the United States, 1999* (Table 49, p. 50; Table 61, p. 57; Table 185, p. 127). Washington, DC: U.S. Government Printing Office.

though the sample had a higher proportion of mortality, the increase in deaths did not increase as substantially as in the overall population. Perhaps the increase in death rates seen in this sample can be explained, at least in part, as age effect.

Discussion

The descriptive analysis of this sample reveals important trends with regard to sociodemographic characteristics. These trends include issues related to gender, HIV exposure, living arrangements, and mortality. The percentages of women nearly doubled between the 30 to 49 age group and the 60 years and over group. These findings are consistent with other research on AIDS in older populations (Ship et al., 1991). Older women with HIV/AIDS have been described as the "invisible victims" of the HIV epidemic, virtually ignored by health care providers, researchers, and policymakers (AIDS Alert, 1995). The problems of invisibility may be systemic, proliferated not only by practitioners and researchers, but also by older women themselves. Many physicians do not view older women as being at risk off HIV and may not evaluate them with the same clinical rigor as younger women; this problem is compounded by the fact that older women do not see themselves as being at risk of HIV (AARP, 1994; CDC, 1998). Many postmenopausal women equate the inability to become pregnant with freedom from HIV and thus engage in unprotected sex (AARP). At the same time, HIV/AIDS prevention and education efforts are targeted at women of childbearing age, often ignoring postmenopausal women (Zablotsky, Fullmer, & Roberson, 1997).

Despite the documentation of HIV risks for older women, the development of gender- and age-appropriate education and intervention methods have been minimal at best (Linsk et al., 1997). HIV/AIDS prevention efforts need to be broadened to include a focus on older women. This focus is often difficult given that HIV/AIDS care and treatment issues are vetted in policy arenas such as the Ryan White CARE Act Consortia, where the needs of older people are not usually salient. The current study's data reinforce the fact that older women are at risk of HIV/AIDS and that the proportion of women increases in the older cohorts. Public information strategies targeted to elderly, sexually active populations are warranted; research strategies to evaluate the effectiveness of different prevention methods need to be developed. One noteworthy example of a public information effort is the video

"HIV/AIDS It Can Happen to Me" (1995) produced by AARP.

The descriptive analysis also identified trends in the exposure categories as the sample aged. Specifically, exposure through men having sex with men decline in the older age groups, whereas those exposed through blood products and heterosexual risk increased. These trends are consistent with recent national figures (CDC, 1998). Such findings reinforce the need for services and prevention strategies for the heterosexual population, particularly among older people.

The proportion of people living alone increased significantly in the older age groups, whereas the proportion living with blood relatives was larger in the younger group. Such trends suggest that older people with HIV/AIDS may be at higher risk of social isolation, requiring additional assistance to be linked to appropriate services. Depression, social isolation, and social stigma are common psychosocial issues confronting older people living with AIDS (Linsk, 1994; Solomon, 1996). Many older gay men, for example, are unwilling or unable to explore new relationships (including nonsexual friendships) after the loss of a lifetime partner (Anderson, 1996). Service systems designed specifically to reach older people with HIV/AIDS are developing in larger metropolitan areas such as New York City and Miami, Florida (Anderson, 1996; Emlet et al., 1997). Such outreach efforts must be expanded through national service delivery systems such as the Ryan White Consortia and Area Agencies on Aging.

When insurance coverage was examined, the data revealed an overall increase in the proportion of individuals in the older age groups who had private insurance. These findings are consistent with other data on private insurance (Lillard, Rogowski, & Kington, 1997). The incidence of having Medicaid decreased in older age groups. Although having private insurance is often associated with better medical care, it may also mean lack of accessibility to home and community-based services such as homemaker services, Medicaid waiver programs for people with HIV/AIDS, and adult day care.

The final noteworthy trend found in this analysis was the increase in mortality in the older age groups. Nearly twice the proportion of individuals 60 and over died during the study compared with individuals 30 to 49 years of age. These findings are consistent with other studies that found increased age associated with higher rates of mortality in people with transfusion-related AIDS (Sutin et al., 1993) and people with various risk factors

(CDC, 1998; Lemp et al., 1990). Various reasons have been presented as the cause of higher mortality rates among older people with HIV/AIDS, including the possibility that AIDS-associated illnesses are more severe in older people, that opportunistic infections develop differently, that other aging-related diseases affect survival (Aupperle, 1996), or that older people are not diagnosed until later in the disease continuum (CDC, 1998). The data were unable to determine why the higher mortality rate existed in the study population. It appears, however, that the increase may be, in part, associated with age effect. Providers of HIV and aging services need to be aware of the continued potential for high mortality in older HIV/AIDS clients and assist clients in planning accordingly.

Implications for Practice

Prevention

Although knowledge concerning HIV/AIDS has increased during the past decade, older adults continue to have a lower level of knowledge than the general population (Strombeck & Levy, 1998). Without proper knowledge of HIV and how the virus is transmitted, older adults continue to engage in behaviors that place them at risk. With 17 million prescriptions for Viagra being written for older Americans in the past two years (Palmer, 2000), education to prevent HIV is more important than ever. Social workers are employed in settings in which they can contribute to the knowledge and education of older adults about HIV/AIDS. Social workers who come in contact with older people through senior services organizations, Area Agencies on Aging, AIDS services organizations, and hospitals can help improve older people's knowledge by first being aware of these issues themselves. Model educational programs have been developed that focus specifically on older adults (Anderson, 1998). Social workers need to recognize the importance of such prevention efforts.

Care and Services

Although care and services to this population could come from the aging professionals and AIDS organizations, these systems have been slow to respond to older people, leaving them caught between systems. The aging network continues to be in denial about the extent to which HIV is infecting and affecting the elderly community (Anderson, 1998).

AIDS service providers are not used to working with older clients and may not see the need for age-specific services. Specially trained workers with a background in gerontological social work would be excellent additions to agencies currently working with HIV/AIDS outreach and treatment agencies. Assisting clients with the stigma and loneliness they may experience, helping facilitate communication with family members, and advocating for older HIV-infected people across systems of care are all skills that social workers possess. Awareness by social workers of the issues related to this emerging vulnerable population can move social work practice and advocacy beyond helping individual clients to macro levels of practice that will be needed in the coming years.

Conclusion

The demographic characteristics of the sample were similar to other samples of HIV/AIDS populations, but the results cannot be generalized beyond the limits of the sample, nor can conclusions about causation be made.

Research on the emerging topic of HIV/AIDS in older people will take on continued importance in the coming years. Once considered a terminal disease with little chance of survival beyond a few years, people infected in their forties, and perhaps even in their thirties, can see the potential of growing into old age with HIV disease. HIV transmission among older people has changed substantially over the past 15 years. Older adults exposed through heterosexual sex, for example, rose from 0 to 12% between 1982 and 1997 (Linsk, 2000). Even greater increases are found in older people infected through injection drug use. Social workers and other health care providers need to acknowledge the risk of HIV infection with older clients and be aware of their own ageist beliefs concerning sexuality, drug use, and old age. As shown in this study, the consideration of HIV infection in older women must not be overlooked.

These data suggest that the social support network for older people with HIV may be more limited than for their younger counterparts, with older people more likely to live alone. Adequate assessment of social support networks, including recent changes in those networks, is necessary to provide adequate care to older individuals with HIV/AIDS. Older people may have been alienated from adult children because of their diagnosis while at the same time less likely to have had living parents to provide necessary support. Special care should be taken when assessing the social support networks of these individuals.

Despite advances in HIV care and treatment, people continue to die from HIV/AIDS. As shown in this study, a significant increase in deaths occurred in older age groups. According to CDC data, 14,033 people age 45 and over died from AIDS between June 1998 and 2000 Nearly 4,600 of them were age 55 and over. Terminal care for people with HIV/AIDS continues to be an important aspect of the continuum of care. Particular attention may need to be paid to older individuals who have comorbid conditions that may complicate or even hasten death.

Finally, service delivery models for older people with HIV need to be considered and evaluated in contrast to integrating older people into HIV-related services for individuals of all ages. Social workers have and must continue to play a pivotal role in moving this agenda forward.

The authors thank Raphael Hess, California Department of Health Services, Office of AIDS, for his assistance with the data and Sondra Purdue, DrPH, and Beth Kalikoff, PhD, from the University of Washington, Tacoma, for their assistance with the preparation of the manuscript.

References

AIDS Alert. (1995, June). *Providers not diagnosing HIV in older women*. Atlanta: American Health Consultants.

American Association of Retired Persons. (1994). *Midlife and older women and HIV/AIDS*. Washington, DC: Author.

Anderson, G. (1996). The older gay man. In K. M. Nodes (Ed.), *HIV/AIDS and the older adult* (pp. 63–79). Bristol, PA: Taylor and Francis.

Anderson, G. (1998). Providing services to elderly people with HIV. In D. M. Aronstein & B. J. Thompson (Eds.), *HIV and social work: A practitioner's guide* (pp. 443–450). New York: Harrington Park Press.

Aupperle, P. (1996). Medical issues. In K. M. Nokes (Ed.), *HIV/AIDS and the older adult* (pp. 25–31). Bristol, PA: Taylor and Francis.

California Department of Health Services. (1996). *California and the HIV/AIDS epidemic: The state of the state report*. Sacramento: Author.

California Department of Health Services. (1998). *California and the HIV/AIDS epidemic 1998: The state of the state report*. Sacramento: Author.

Carre, N., Deveau, C., Belanger, F., Boufassa, F., Persoz, A., Jadand, C., Rouzioux, C.,

Delfraissy, J. F., & Bucquet, D. (1994). Effect of age and exposure group on the onset of AIDS in heterosexual and homosexual HIV-infected patients. *AIDS, 8,* 797–802.

Centers for Disease Control and Prevention. (1998). AIDS among persons 50 years—United States, 1991–1996. *Morbidity and Mortality Weekly Report, 47(2),* 21–27.

Centers for Disease Control and Prevention. (2000). *HIV/AIDS Surveillance Report, 12(2),* 1–45.

Crooks, V., Waller, S., Smith, T., & Hahn, T. J. (1991). The use of the Karnofsky Performance Scale in determining outcomes and risk in geriatric outpatients. *Journal of Gerontology: Medical Sciences, 46,* M139–M144.

El-Sadr, W., & Gettler, J. (1995). Unrecognized human immunodeficiency virus infection in the elderly. *Archives of Internal Medicine, 155,* 184–186.

Emlet, C. (1997). HIV/AIDS in the elderly: A hidden population. *Home Care Provider, 2,* 69–75.

Emlet, C., Linsk, N., Goodkin, K., Nazon, M., Williams, C., Delgado, V., Witten, T., & Eisodrfer, C. (1997, November). *Older persons with HIV/AIDS: Challenges for assessment and service delivery*. Symposium presented at the 50th Annual Scientific Meeting on Aging of the Gerontological Society, Cincinnati.

Ferro, S., & Salit, I. E. (1992). HIV infection in patients over 55 years of age. *Journal of Acquired Immune Deficiency Syndrome, 5,* 348–355.

Gordon, S. M., & Thompson, S. (1995). The changing epidemiology of human immunodeficiency virus in older persons. *Journal of the American Geriatrics Society, 43,* 7–9.

Gould, R. (1978). *Transformations and change in adult life*. New York: Simon & Schuster.

Justice, A. C., & Weissman, S. (1998). The survival experience of older and younger adults with AIDS: Is there a growing gap in survival? *Research on Aging, 20,* 665–685.

Lemp, G. F., Payne, S. F., Neal, D., Temelso, T., & Rutherford, G. W. (1990). Survival trends for patients with AIDS. *Journal of the American Medical Association, 263,* 402–406.

Levinson, D. J. (1978). *The season of a man's life*. New York: Knopf.

Lillard, L., Rogowski, J., & Kington, R. (1997). Long-term determinants of patterns of health insurance coverage in a Medicare population. *Gerontologist, 37,* 314–323.

Linsk, N. (1994). HIV and the elderly. *Families in Society, 75,* 362–372.

Linsk, N. (2000). HIV among older adults: Age-specific issues in prevention and treatment. *AIDS Reader, 10,* 430–440.

Linsk, N., Perkell, J., Poindexter, C., Fowler, J., Zablotsky, D., & Fullmer, E. (1997, November). *Impacts of HIV/AIDS on older women: Consumer and caregiver impacts.* Symposium presented at the 50th Annual Scientific Meeting on Aging of the Gerontological Society, Cincinnati.

Mor, V., Laliberte, L., Morris, J. N., & Wiemann, M. (1984). The Karnofsky Performance Status Scale: An examination of its reliability and validity in a research setting. *Cancer, 53,* 2002–2007.

O'Dell, M. W., Lubeck, D. P., O'Driscoll, P., & Matsuno, S. (1995). Validity of the Karnofsky Performance Status in an HIV-infected sample. *Journal of Acquired Immunodeficiency Syndromes, 10,* 350–357.

Ory, M. G., & Mack, K. A. (1998). Middle-aged and older people with AIDS. *Research on Aging, 20,* 653–664.

Palmer, L. D. (2000, March 12). Unsafe sex in age of Viagra: Rising HIV rates show seniors often ignore risks. *Austin American-Statesman,* pp. A19, A22–A233.

Puleo, J. H. (1975). The scope of the challenge. In K. M. Nokes (Ed.), *HIV/AIDS and the older adult* (pp. 1–8). Bristol, PA: Taylor and Francis.

Riegel, K. F. (1975). Adult life crises: A dialectic interpretation of development. In N. Datan & L. H. Ginsberg (Eds.), *Life-span development psychology* (pp. 99–128). New York: Academic Press.

Schable, B., Chu, S. Y., & Diaz, T. (1996). Characteristics of women 50 years of age and older with heterosexually acquired AIDS. *American Journal of Public Health, 86,* 1616–1618.

Ship, J. A., Wolff, A., & Selik, R. M. (1991). Epidemiology of acquired immune deficiency syndrome in persons aged 50 and over. *Journal of Acquired Immune Deficiency Syndrome, 4,* 84–88.

Solomon, K. (1996). Psychosocial issues. In K. M. Nokes (Ed.), *HIV/AIDS and the older adult* (pp. 33–46). Bristol, PA: Taylor and Francis.

Strombeck, R., & Levy, J. A. (1998). Educational strategies and interventions targeting adults age 50 and over for HIV/AIDS prevention. *Research on Aging, 20,* 912–936.

Sutin, D. G., Rose, D. N., Mulvihill, M., & Taylor, B. (1993). Survival of elderly patients with transfusion related acquired immunodeficiency syndrome. *Journal of the American Geriatrics Society, 41,* 214–216.

U.S. Census Bureau. (1999). *Statistical abstracts of the United States: 1999* [Online]. Available: http://www.census.gov/rpod/99pubs/99statab/sec01.pdf.

Zablotsky, D. L. (1998). Overlooked, ignored and forgotten: Older women at risk for HIV infection and AIDS. *Research on Aging, 20,* 760–775.

Zablotsky, D. L., Fullmer, E., & Roberson, T. (1997, November). *Developing appropriate HIV/AIDS education and intervention messages for midlife and older women.* Paper presented at the 50th Annual Scientific Meeting on Aging of the Gerontological Society, Cincinnati.

Hasida Ben-Zur
Batya Rappaport
Ronny Ammar
Gideon Uretzky

38

Coping Strategies, Lifestyle Changes, and Pessimism after Open-Heart Surgery

Coronary heart disease is a major physical illness and one of the main causes of death in Western society (Fitzgerald, Tennen, Affleck, & Pransky, 1993; Trzcieniecka-Green & Steptoe, 1994). People who do not die an early and sudden death may have to consider a major surgical treatment, the most prevalent being coronary artery bypass graft surgery (CABG). More than 350,000 such operations are performed annually in the United States alone (Kulik & Mahler, 1993). This operation prolongs the life of patients in cases of triple-vessel disease (Passamani, Davis, Gillespie, & Killip, 1985). It also improves patients' quality of life (Jenkins, Stanton & Jono, 1994), thus providing them with the opportunity for successful rehabilitation.

The present research investigated physical and behavioral rehabilitation of patients after CABG, assessed by improvements in their functional capacity, daily activities, and lifestyle. The study used patients' anxiety and mood states as distress indicators. The research examined the extent to which these outcomes were associated with dispositional coping and pessimism. Such research findings may contribute to the planning of short-term interventions by social workers and other health professionals for use with patients following CABG.

CABG Surgery Outcomes

During the first several weeks after CABG surgery, states of high anxiety or depression are usu-ally observed (see, for example, Pick, Molloy, Hinds, Pearce, & Salmon, 1994; Trzcieniecka-Green & Steptoe, 1994). In long-term research (that is, approximately one year after the operation), the results present a more positive trend in terms of elevation in positive moods (King, Porter, Norsen, & Reis, 1992; King, Reis, Porter, & Norsen, 1993), as well as an increase in quality of life (Kulik & Mahler, 1993). Such outcomes can be accounted for by illness severity factors. In addition, in recent years, the individual's personality and coping characteristics have been investigated as important determinants of post-CABG patients' emotional reactions and rehabilitation.

Coping Strategies

Lazarus and Folkman (1984) defined *coping* as the behavioral and cognitive efforts invested by an individual to deal with stressful encounters. Coping is described as having two main components: (1) problem-focused coping, aimed at changing, managing, or tolerating the stressful encounter, and (2) emotion-focused coping, aimed at changing or managing the affective and physiological outcomes of the stressful situation, without actually changing the encounter itself. Following Lazarus and Folkman, Carver, Scheier, and Weintraub (1989) developed a classification of coping according to 15 strategies characterized as problem- or emotion-focused strategies and discussed their adaptive and maladaptive values. Problem-focused strategies usually are found to be adaptive or effective when the stressful situation is manageable. The use of emotion-focused strategies seems to be appropriate in the context of uncontrollable situations. However, emotion-focused strategies differ in their presumed effectiveness, and some, such as ventilation or avoidance, are found to be ineffective even when the stressful occurrence is not under the individual's control (see Ben-Zur, 1999; Carver et al., 1989).

The two components of coping have been extensively investigated, but few studies have dealt with coping strategies and patients' adjustment after CABG surgery. Carver and Scheier (1993) correlated avoidance and vigilant coping in relation to the medical situation, and well-being after CABG. Their results suggest that the use of either type of coping strategy is related to a high distress level and sometimes to a low quality of life and slow rehabilitation.

Dispositional optimism is defined as the generalized expectancies that good outcomes will occur when confronting major problems (Scheier et al., 1989). It is considered to be a determinant of continued efforts to deal with problems, as opposed to turning away and giving up. Scheier et al. found dispositional optimism to be related positively to situation-specific problem-focused coping, as well as to a high quality of life, six months after surgery. Recently, King, Rowe, Kimble, and Zerwic (1998) found associations of optimism with mood, but not with functional ability, among women who recovered from CABG, with the effects of optimism mediated by the use of cognitive coping strategies.

Research Aims and Hypotheses

The aim of the present research was threefold: (1) to assess post-CABG patients' rehabilitation and distress; (2) to assess post-CABG patients' recovery from the operation by comparing their anxiety, coping, and pessimism levels with the levels observed in a community sample; and (3) to examine associations between coping and pessimism with post-CABG distress and rehabilitation.

The research hypotheses were that

- Emotion-focused coping with pessimism would be associated with higher distress and a lower level of rehabilitation.
- Problem-focused coping would be associated with lower distress and a higher level of rehabilitation.

Method

Participants and Sampling Procedures

CABG Sample   A convenience sampling was used by selecting 400 Hebrew-speaking patients from the lists of a large medical center that serves the population in the north of Israel. The patients were chosen if they were between the ages of 40 and 70 and had undergone CABG surgery for the first time two to 20 months prior to study initiation.

A questionnaire was mailed to the patients from May through September 1995. The return rate was approximately 50%, with 50 of the questionnaires returned uncompleted because of a wrong address. The final sample included 171 people (81 men), with a mean age of 61.45 (SD = 6.24). The majority (87%) were married, 5% were divorced, and 8% were widowed; the average number of children was 3.02 (SD = 1.79). Most of the respondents had a high school (42%) or higher level of education (26%). Fifty-eight percent of the respondents worked during the six-month period prior to surgery, and 42% reported working following surgery.

A comparison of the sample with the CABG population from the same time period revealed no differences on gender, education (p > .05), or age distribution (p > .01).

Community Sample   One hundred and fifty community residents (45% men) were selected from a large database collected as part of a community research project on stress and coping in everyday life (Zeidner & Ben-Zur, 1994). These participants were selected according to the same age range (40 to 70) as the post-CABG patients (M = 49.33, SD = 7.90). The majority were married (85%), with an average number of 3.12 children (SD = 1.63). Most had a high school (51%) or higher level of education (32%).

Ethical Procedures

The questionnaires were mailed to the post-CABG patients with the assurance that the study was voluntary and personal details were kept confidential. Accordingly, data were coded and analyzed using code numbers only, and the same procedures applied to the community sample data.

Measures

Physiological and Behavioral Rehabilitation   The following data were collected from the post-CABG patients only:

- Functional capacity—A scale including the four descriptions of the New York Heart Association's functional capacity classification was used (O'Rourke, 1994). Participants were asked to indicate the description that best fitted their current state. The highest functional capacity was indicated by 1 ("I do not experience pain or have any restrictions in everyday activity"), and the lowest by 4 ("I feel disabled and experience pain during periods of rest and when making the smallest effort").
- Daily activity, life habits, and compliance— Respondents were asked to report the number of hours spent on each of the following daily activities, both preceding and following surgery: paid job, volunteer job, hobbies, physical exercise, social/family gatherings, courses/studies, house maintenance, movies/concerts, television viewing/reading, and sleep. They marked the instructions given by physicians concerning medication and life habits, including physical activity, sexual activity, smoking, appropriate nutrition (low-fat, low-salt, or low-sugar diet). They were also asked whether they took the prescribed medication and engaged in these life habits both before and after the operation.

Psychological Measures   The following data, except for the current mood scale, are available for both samples:

- Distress—Current anxiety was measured by a five-item State-Anxiety scale, taken from the State-Trait Personality Inventory (Spielberger et al., 1979) and translated into Hebrew (Ben-Zur & Zeidner, 1991). The items were rated on a four-point scale (ranging from 1 = not at all to 4 = very much; $\alpha = .86$). A high score, based on the sum of the five items, indicates high anxiety. Current mood and feelings were measured by six new items created for the present study and rated on the same four-point scale: bad mood, feeling helpless, angry mood, changing mood, depressed mood and sensitization. A composite mood score was created based on a one-factor solution ($\alpha = .88$). Since anxiety and mood were highly correlated (r = .84), they were com-

bined to create a general distress score to be used in the correlational analyses.
- Pessimism—The Life Orientation Test (LOT) (Scheier & Carver, 1985) was used its Hebrew version (Zeidner & Ben-Zur, 1994). It includes eight items, rated on a five-point scale (ranging from 1 = strongly agree to 5 = strongly disagree). A high score indicates a pessimistic tendency, and a low score an optimistic tendency ($\alpha = .59$).
- Coping strategies—The COPE scale (Carver et al., 1989) was used in its shortened Hebrew form (Zeidner & Ben-Zur, 1994). Respondents mark their use of each of the coping options in dealing with stressful encounters in everyday life on a scale ranging from 0 = not at all to 3 = great extent. The Hebrew scale includes 15 subscales, each composed of the sum of two items per subscale. Following factor analysis, two main scales were computed: (1) a problem-focused scale composed of active coping; planning, positive reinterpretation, instrumental social support, suppression of competing activities, and restraint, and (2) an emotion-focused scale composed of emotional/social support, religion, ventilation of emotion, mental disengagement, behavioral disengagement, and alcohol or substance use (the COPE includes an additional three subscales that did not form a scale: humor, acceptance, and denial). Alpha levels were .80 and .72 for the problem-focused and emotion-focused scales, respectively.

Data Analysis

In light of the number of statistical operations performed on the data, we used a conservative p = <.01 level of significance.

Results

Physical and Behavioral Rehabilitation in the CABG Sample

Functional Capacity   Following CABG, 30 people reported the highest level of functional capacity, 55 a medium level, 46 a low level, and 24 reported the lowest level. Frequencies of functional capacity for the general population of patients during the period preceding surgery in 1995 and 1996, as assessed by physicians on the same scale used for participants, were, from highest to lowest, 6, 189, 243, and 267.

Thus, more than 50% of the post-CABG patients showed high to medium capacity compared with fewer than 30% in the pre-CABG population [$\chi^2(3,150) = 138.2$, p < .0001]. These data imply an improvement following the CABG surgery.

Daily Activities, Life Habits, and Compliance   As can be seen in Table 38.1, after the operation, the average number of working hours was greatly reduced (t = −7.12, p < .0001; these data do not include retired or disabled respondents), whereas number of hours spent on physical exercise increased (t = 3.31, p < .005).

Overall scores for life habits before and after surgery were created by summing up all answers given in a positive direction. A positive overall change in life habits following the operation was observed (t = 6.56, p < .0001) (Table 38.2). Positive changes in nutrition were reported most frequently, whereas sexual activity showed a small change in the opposite direction.

When asked about instructions pertaining to medication, 98% reported receiving instructions to take medication after surgery, and 93% reported compliance with these instructions (Table 38.2). Respondents reported receiving instructions on the following daily life habits: smoking (78%), dietary habits (93%), physical exercise (82%), and sexual activity (63%).

To measure compliance, the data for engagement in each life habit after surgery were crossed with the data pertaining to instructions concerning the habit. The percentages of people reporting that they received instructions and followed them are given in Table 38.2. The highest levels of compliance were found for the nutrition and smoking habits.

Comparisons between CABG and Community Samples

Anxiety   The anxiety mean of the CABG participants was compared with the mean of the community sample in a two-way, sex sample analysis of covariance (ANCOVA), controlling for age. Significant effects for both sample and sex, with no interaction, were found: women reported higher anxiety than men, with corrected means of 10.48 and 9.29, respectively, [F(1, 282) = 6.22, p = .01]. More important, the post-CABG patients were more anxious than the community sample, [corrected means of 10.62 and 9.15, respectively, F(1, 282) = 6.09, p = .01].

Coping Strategies and Pessimism   No differences were observed between the two samples on either the emotion- or problem-focused coping subscales or on pessimism. A clear trend was observed in our sample, as was noted in earlier research (Zeidner & Ben-Zur, 1994), to report a more frequent use of problem-focused strategies compared to emotion-focused strategies [M = 3.54 (SD = 1.20) and 2.11 (SD = 1.10), respectively; t = 14.68, p < .0001].

Association among Distress, Rehabilitation, Coping, and Pessimism

Pearson correlation analyses showed positive correlations between distress and emotion-focused

Table 38.1 Means of Reported Daily Activities before and after Cardiac Bypass Graft Surgery

Activity	Before Surgery		After Surgery	
	M	SD	M	SD
Paid job	6.77	3.69	4.07	3.99
Volunteer job	0.28	0.88	0.21	0.73
Hobbies	1.14	1.95	1.06	1.89
Physical exercise	0.50	0.80	0.85	1.16
Social/family gatherings	1.89	1.84	1.77	1.65
Courses/studies	0.28	0.80	0.15	0.57
House maintenance	1.69	1.88	1.55	1.60
Movies, concerts	0.66	1.92	0.63	1.64
Television/reading	3.20	2.00	3.50	2.23
Sleep	6.69	1.54	6.88	1.85

NOTE: ns = 123 to 155, except for paid job, for which ns = 110 to 114.

Table 38.2 Positive Answers Concerning Life Habits before and after and Compliance after Cardiac Bypass Graft Surgery

Activity	Presurgery (%)	Postsurgery (%)	Compliance (%)
Physical exercise	46.6	57.7	52.4
Sexual activity	69.5	63.2	47.2
Not smoking	77.4	96.0	75.6
Appropriate nutrition	48.1	81.7	75.8

NOTE: ns = 149 to 159 for presurgery data, 144 to 156 for postsurgery data, and 123 to 145 for compliance data.

coping or pessimism (r = .52, p < .0001). Emotion-focused and problem-focused coping were correlated differentially with pessimism (r = .40, p < .001 and r = −.22, p < .01, respectively). Of the demographic variables, people with less education reported a high level of emotion-focused coping, a high level of pessimism, and a low level of problem-focused coping (r = −.24, −.28, and .20, respectively, p < .01).

Difference scores were used for overall changes in life habits and in hours spent on daily activities (not including sleep). The compliance measure was based on the sum of combinations of receiving instructions in relation to life habits and engagement in these habits.

Distress was highly correlated with functional capacity, and both measures were negatively related to changes in life habits, with distress related to changes in activity levels (Table 38.3). Thus, people who experienced high distress also reported low functional capacity, less activity, and less positive changes in life habits. Distress and functional ca-

pacity after surgery were correlated highly with emotion-focused coping and pessimism. It should be noted that surgery-related variables, or time elapsed between operation and questionnaire completion, did not correlate with any of these variables.

The preceding analyses show emotion-focused coping to be positively related to distress and functional capacity. Therefore, we investigated correlations between these outcomes and the specific emotion-focused strategies. High distress was found to be mainly associated with ventilation, alcohol or substance use, and behavioral disengagement (r = .62, .35, and .33, p < .001), as well as emotional support, religion, and mental disengagement (r = .28, .26 and .21, p < .01). Low functional capacity was related to religion (r = .30, p < .001), ventilation, and emotional support (r = .28 and .27, p < .01).

Multiple Regressions and Hypotheses Testing   Table 38.4 presents five regression analyses. Each of the

Table 38.3 Correlations between Measures of Distress, Functional Capacity, Rehabilitation, Coping, and Pessimism

Variable	Distress	Functional Capacity	Compliance	Life Habit Difference	Activity Difference
Functional capacity	−.46**				
Compliance	−.19	−.11			
Life habit difference	−.26**	−.23**	.26***		
Activity difference	−.35***	−.13	.07	.31**	
Problem-focused coping	−.02	−.10	.26**	.06	.02
Emotion-focused coping	.55****	.36****	−.11	−.21**	.02
Pessimism	.50****	.28***	−.14	−.26**	−.28**

NOTE: ns = 121 to 155.

**p < .01. ***p < .001. ****p < .0001.

Table 38.4 Multiple Regressions (Standardized β Weights) of Distress, Functional Capacity, and Rehabilitation Measures on Coping, Pessimism, and Demographic Variables

Variable	Distress	Functional Capacity	Compliance	Life Habit Difference	Activity Difference
Problem-focused coping	.02	−.09	.32**	−.11	−.19
Emotion-focused coping	.43****	.32***	−.10	.18	.19
Pessimism	.37****	.13	.00	.14	−.42****
Family status	.13	.26**	.18	−.04	−.07
Education	−.04	−.11	.11	−.07	.07
Gender	.10	.22	−.03	−.07	.07
Age	−.11	−.02	.07	.25**	.13
Multiple R^2	.50****	.30****	.15*	.18**	.18**

NOTE: ns = 109 to 114 for all except compliance, for which n = 100; β weights significance was tested by t values.

*p < .05. **p < .01. ***p < .001. ****p < .0001.

five main outcome measures (that is, distress, functional capacity, compliance, life habits difference, and activities difference scores) was regressed on the coping and pessimism scales, as well as education, sex, marital status, and age. Emotion-focused coping is related significantly to high distress and low functional capacity, and pessimism is related to high distress and small activities changes. These results support the first hypothesis in regard to distress and some of the rehabilitation measures. Problem-focused coping is related only to high levels of compliance, and therefore the second hypothesis is not supported for distress and most of the rehabilitation measures.

Discussion

Rehabilitation and Distress of Post-CABG Patients

The present research focused on distress and rehabilitation of individuals following CABG surgery. On the one hand, participants' reports indicated a very high level of compliance concerning medication and physician follow-up, with a large positive change in nutrition habits and with positive changes in smoking and physical exercise. On the other hand, very small changes were noted in daily activity, with a major reduction in hours spent on paid work. Moreover, the anxiety of respondents was higher than that of a comparison sample and did not change over time in a cross-sectional testing.

The fact that the distress of postsurgery patients is not reduced over time is alarming insofar as it

may interfere with rehabilitation, impair quality of life, and affect health. Several possible explanations can be offered in regard to this finding. First, although the operation was successful for these patients and their functional capacity was improved, it still consisted of a major life-threatening event, with long-term trauma leading to anxiety and other mood changes that are difficult to overcome. Moreover, these patients may have realized their vulnerability for the first time, and the possibility of death may have become more concrete than ever before. Second, patients might have hoped that their level of functioning would be highly improved and their hopes were not entirely fulfilled. Such disappointment may underlie their continued anxiety and mood changes, and may lead to uncertainty concerning future health.

Distress and Rehabilitation as Correlates of Coping and Pessimism

Our results concerning associations between low pessimistic tendency and lifestyle changes are in accordance with earlier findings (Scheier et al., 1989). In addition, those who reported low postsurgery functional capacity also reported a high level of emotion-focused coping. In contrast, problem-focused coping was not correlated highly with rehabilitation and life-change measures. In addition, distress was associated mainly with certain emotion-focused coping strategies considered to be ineffective—that is, the ventilation or avoidance strategies (Carver et al., 1989), which were found to correlate with post-CABG distress in other studies (Carver & Scheier, 1993).

Although postsurgery distress, functional capacity, pessimism, and emotion-focused coping were found to be strongly associated in this study, it should be remembered that the investigated variables are reciprocally determined. Thus, distress may affect and be affected by functional capacity and may augment the use of emotion-focused coping and pessimism; emotion-focused coping and pessimism, in turn, may elevate distress and prevent improvements in functional capacity.

Methodological Limitations

First, all postsurgery data were based on patients' self-reports, including postsurgery functional capacity. Second, the changes in anxiety over time were assessed by a cross-sectional and not by a within-individual test. Third, all data were collected at one time point. Nevertheless, the comparisons made between the CABG and community samples showed no differences on the coping and pessimism measures, suggesting that these tendencies might indeed be stable enough not to be affected by CABG and its related physical and psychological effects. However, future studies should include pre- and postsurgery psychological and medical assessments made during several time points.

Implications for Intervention

The present results indicate strong associations between postsurgery distress, functional capacity, and dispositional emotion-focused coping strategies, whereas distress and changes in life habits and daily activity reveal an association with pessimism. In addition, positive changes in life habits and changes toward more activity following the operation were shown to be related negatively to high distress and a low level of functional capacity.

These results suggest that after CABG surgery, patients who possess a tendency toward either high pessimism or high emotion-focused coping are at a high health risk emanating from both high distress and a slow rehabilitation process. This calls for the creation of intervention procedures that will aid patients and their families in the post-CABG adaptation period by changing their outlook on life and teaching effective coping strategies. Such a perspective presents a challenge for social workers to develop patient intervention programs for the specific population of highly anxious and pessimistic CABG patients. The aim of these programs would be to implement cognitive and behavioral techniques (see Cameron & Meichenbaum, 1982; Horne, Vatmanidis, & Careri, 1994), for changing individual coping strategies in dealing with anxiety, as well as for focusing on personal motivation to change unhealthy life habits.

Several facets of these interventions can be delineated. First, credible and positive information should be provided, both before and after CABG. Earlier studies have shown positive effects of preoperative health care–relevant information on indices of postoperative pain, distress, and recoverly (Devine, 1992; Johnson, 1999). The postoperative information should emphasize the patient's active role in the recovery and rehabilitation process and aim at creating feelings of control and mastery. It can be based on written material covering topics such as risk-reduction activities and ways to safe recovery (Thomas, 1995) as well as a graphic or video presentation of a model patient (Burish, Snyder, & Jenkins, 1991) that went through the various stages of surgery successfully. The provision of such information is intended to lower patients' anxiety, feelings of helplessness, and overindulgence in either emotional expression and ventilation or in mental and behavioral disengagement.

Second, short-term intervention programs can be devised using cognitive-behavioral preparation methods such as relaxation and cognitive coping strategies. CABG patients participating in a program including relaxation, information, and counseling reported on general improvements in emotional state, functional level, and social activity (Trzcieniecka-Green & Steptoe, 1994). Thomas (1995) found that a collaborative patient-staff educational intervention lowered CABG patients' anxiety at hospital discharge. This program offered opportunities to identify individual needs regarding recovery and presumably strengthen the patients' sense of power, choice, and control through active involvement.

Third, patients' participation in social support group sessions should be recommended. Such groups have been used with people with chronic illnesses, the evidence suggesting that this type of intervention helps patients cope (Taylor & Aspinwall, 1993). Furthermore, several studies have shown that for cardiovascular patients social support is important in smoking cessation, weight loss, and exercise maintenance (Crossman & Eyjolfsson, 1991). Thus, support through patient group sessions can be used to strengthen effective coping strategies and compliance with treatment recommendations.

These proposed interventions can be implemented by medical social workers in the various stages of diagnosis, treatment, and recovery of CABG patients. However, the best results in terms of rehabilitation probably can be achieved if an interdisciplinary team that includes social workers, physicians, occupational therapists, and nurses cooperate in the effort to strengthen the appropriate messages. Such a team can best direct patients toward the types of actions that are most effective in lowering distress, bolstering optimism, and developing coping strategies, and consequently, improving their quality of life.

References

Ben-Zur, H. (1999). The effectiveness of coping metastrategies: Perceived efficiency, emotional correlates and cognitive performance. *Personality and Individual Differences, 26,* 923–939.

Ben-Zur, H., & Zeidner, M. (1991). Anxiety and bodily symptoms under the threat of missile attacks: The Israel scene. *Anxiety Research, 4,* 79–95.

Burish, T. G., Snyder, S. L., & Jenkins, R. A. (1991). Preparing patients for cancer chemotherapy: Effect of coping preparation and relaxation interventions. *Journal of Consulting and Clinical Psychology, 59,* 518–525.

Cameron, R., & Meichenbaum, D. (1982). The nature of effective coping and the treatment of stress related problems: A cognitive-behavioral perspective. In L. Goldberger & S. Breznitz (Eds.), *Handbook of stress: Theoretical and clinical aspects* (pp. 695–710). New York: Free Press.

Carver, S. C., & Scheier, M. F. (1993). Vigilant and avoidant coping in two patient samples. In H. W. Krohne (Ed.), *Attention and avoidance: Strategies in coping with aversiveness* (pp. 295–319). Seattle: Hogrefe & Huber.

Carver, C. S., Scheier, M., & Weintraub, J. K. (1989). Assessing coping strategies: A theoretically based approach. *Journal of Personality and Social Psychology, 56,* 267–283.

Crossman, J., & Eyjolfsson, K. (1991). Perceptions of participants regarding the long-term impact of an education and support program for heart attack and heart surgery patients and their partners. *Journal of Community Psychology, 19,* 333–336.

Devine, E. C. (1992). Effects of psychoeducational care for adult surgical patients: A meta-analysis of 191 studies. *Patient Education and Counseling, 19,* 129–142.

Fitzgerald, T. E., Tennen, H., Affleck, G., & Pransky, G. S. (1993). The relative importance of dispositional optimism and control appraisals in quality of life after coronary artery bypass surgery. *Journal of Behavioral Medicine, 16,* 25–43.

Horne, D. J. de L., Vatmanidis, P., & Careri, A. (1994). Preparing patients for invasive medical and surgical procedures 1: Adding behavioral and cognitive interventions. *Behavioral Medicine, 20,* 5–13.

Jenkins, C. D., Stanton, B. A., & Jono, R. (1994). Quantifying and predicting recovery after heart surgery. *Psychosomatic Medicine, 56,* 203–212.

Johnson, J. E. (1999). Self-regulation theory and coping with physical illness. *Research in Nursing and Health, 22,* 435–448.

King, K. B., Porter, L. A., Norsen, L. H., & Reis, H. T. (1992). Patient perceptions of quality of life after coronary artery surgery: Was it worth it? *Research in Nursing and Health, 15,* 327–334.

King, K. B., Reis, H. T., Porter, L. A., & Norsen, L. H. (1993). Social support and long-term recovery from coronary artery surgery: Effects on patients and spouses. *Health Psychology, 12,* 56–63.

King, K. B., Rowe, M. A., Kimble, L. P., & Zerwic, J. J. (1998). Optimism, coping and longterm recovery from coronary artery surgery in women. *Research in Nursing and Health, 21,* 15–26.

Kulik, J. A., & Mahler, H. I. M. (1993). Emotional support as a moderator of adjustment and compliance after coronary artery bypass surgery: A longitudinal study. *Journal of Behavioral Medicine, 16,* 45–63.

Lazarus, R. S., & Folkman, S. (1984). *Stress, appraisal and coping.* New York: Springer.

O'Rourke, R. A. (1994). Introduction to the general evaluation of the patient. In R. C. Schlant & R. W. Alexander (Eds.), *The heart* (pp. 201–203). New York: McGraw-Hill.

Passamani, E., Davis, K. B., Gillespie, M. J., & Killip, T. (1985). A randomized trial of coronary artery bypass surgery: Survival of patients with a low ejection fraction. *New England Journal of Medicine, 312,* 1665–1671.

Pick, B., Molloy, A., Hinds, C., Pearce, S., & Salmon, P. (1994). Post-operative fatigue following coronary artery bypass surgery: Relationship to emotional state and to the catecholamine response to surgery. *Journal of Psychosomatic Research, 38,* 599–607.

Scheier, M. F., & Carver, C. S. (1985). Optimism, coping and health: Assessment and implications of generalized outcome expectancies. *Health Psychology, 4,* 219–247.

Scheier, M. F., Matthews, K. A., Owens, J. F., Magovern, G. J., Lefebvre, R. C., Abbott, R. A., & Carver, C. S. (1989). Dispositional optimism and recovery from coronary artery bypass surgery: The beneficial effects on physical and psychological well-being. *Journal of Personality and Social Psychology, 57,* 1024–1040.

Spielberger, C. D., Barker, L., Russell, S., Silva De Crane, R., Westberry, I., Knight, J., & Marks, E. (1979). *Preliminary manual for the State-Trait Personality Inventory (STPI).* Tampa: University of South Florida.

Taylor, S. E., & Aspinwall, L. G. (1993). Coping with chronic illness. In L. Goldberger & S. Breznitz (Eds.), *Handbook of stress: Theoretical and clinical aspects* (pp. 511–531) (2nd ed.). New York: Free Press.

Thomas, J. J. (1995). Reducing anxiety during phase I cardiac rehabilitation. *Journal of Psychosomatic Research, 39,* 295–304.

Trzcieniecka-Green, A., & Steptoe, A. (1994). Stress management in cardiac patients: A preliminary study of the predictors of improvement in quality of life. *Journal of Psychosomatic Research, 38,* 267–280.

Zeidner, M., & Ben-Zur, H. (1994). Individual differences in anxiety, coping and post-traumatic stress in the aftermath of the Persian Gulf war. *Personality & Individual Differences, 16,* 459–476.

MIGUEL O. AGUAYO
NICK F. COADY

39

The Experience of Deafened Adults: Implications for Rehabilitative Services

For the purposes of this article "adventitious deafness" (Benderly, 1980) is the term used for profound hearing loss acquired after having learned speech and language, rather than deafness from birth. Other common terms in the literature for this phenomenon include late deafness (Rothschild & Kampfe, 1997), postvocational deafness (Schein & Delk, 1974), and sudden severe deafness (Levine, 1981). The impetus for this study is the conviction that adventitious deafness is a social problem that is underrecognized, underresearched, and undertreated.

The criteria for being defined as a deafened person vary, but are always conservative. Usually, this requires a loss of 70 decibels or greater in the better ear, which makes audition useless for understanding oral communication (Rothschild & Kampfe, 1997). Using the definition "at best, can hear and understand words shouted in the better ear," the 1990 and 1991 Health Interview Surveys of the National Center for Health Statistics yielded the estimate that about .5% of the population age 3 years and older are deaf (Ries, 1994). This amounts to about 1.15 million deaf people over the age of 2 in the United States (Ries, 1994). What is not commonly recognized, however, is that approximately three of four deaf people lose their hearing after the age of 19 (Ries, 1994; Schein & Delk, 1974). Thus, there are close to 1 million adventitiously deafened adults in the United States, and they represent the vast majority (75%) of deaf people.

A recent survey (Boone & Scherich, 1995) of 348 members of the Association of Late-Deafened Adults (ALDA) in the United States documented some of the causes of adventitious deafness. Forty percent of respondents reported medical causes (for example, illnesses such as meningitis or Menière's syndrome, viruses, or reactions to medication), 13% reported surgical causes (for example, complete or partial removal of the auditory nerves to alleviate another condition, such as neurofibromatosis Type-2 or acoustic neuroma), 5% reported traumatic injury (such as automobile or workplace accidents or near-fatal drowning) as the cause, and 42% reported progressive hearing loss that was mostly unexplained (idiopathic). This latter category of progressive hearing loss can sometimes be attributed to heredity, aging, or overexposure to excessive noise; however, the causes usually remain unknown. Most people who experience such progressive hearing loss detect a mild decline in hearing ability in adolescence, which deteriorates to profound deafness by middle adulthood. Although the results of this study should be viewed cautiously because of the small and nonrandom sample, the study provides important information about the various causes of adventitious deafness.

The psychological and social effect of adventitious hearing loss can be devastating. In addition to the general difficulty of living without hearing, compared with the experience of those who are congenitally or prelingually deafened, deafness is not ingrained into the core identity of people who become deafened as adults; they are confronted with the loss of their self-image (David & Trehub, 1989). Furthermore, people who experience profound hearing loss after being socialized as a hearing person must face the task of learning a new way to cope with the world without dependence on the auditory sense (David & Trehub, 1989).

Luey (1980) reported that deafened adults often feel as if they are stuck between the deaf and hearing worlds. They no longer can function effectively among hearing people as they were accustomed to doing. Because speech reading is not an easily acquired skill, a deafened person must resort to guessing to fill the gaps of dialogue. Many deafened people have reported that social gaffes in the form of inappropriate responses to the comments and questions of others are common. The resulting embarrassment and humiliation leads the deafened person to withdraw from social settings and limits the opportunity to discover positive coping strategies.

Impediments to convenient conversation with people from their premorbid life often result in damaged relationships—especially family members (Kyle & Wood, 1987). Glass and Elliott (1992) reported that people who experience severe to profound hearing losses have reported higher divorce rates than the nondisabled population. Even when marriages remained intact, the structure and quality of relationships in the family often deteriorated (Kyle & Wood, 1987; Meadow-Orlans, 1985). This is attributed to the added stress placed on the nondisabled spouses, who often take on additional responsibilities to compensate for their partner's disability (Goffman, 1963).

Because acquired deafness is a well-studied subject in the medical and audiological professions, it might be natural to assume that the deafness rehabilitation system would be well-equipped to provide a range of services. Unfortunately, such research has focused narrowly on restoring deafened individuals to preloss functioning through medical and audiological intervention. However, documented reports from people who have experienced profound hearing loss indicate that this approach does not address the significant psychosocial stressors experienced by deafened people. The repetitive theme found in surveys (David & Trehub, 1989), personal interviews (Glass & Elliott, 1992), and focus groups (Aguayo & Avena, 1994) with deafened adults is that the rehabilitation they typically receive does not help them cope. A common refrain from the respondents in these studies is that the professionals who were responsible for their care did not understand the complex repercussions of the condition and offered services more appropriate for either congenitally deaf people or people with mild hearing loss.

Although some hearing health professionals have argued that denial of the hearing loss and social withdrawal delay the entry of deafened adults into rehabilitation and prevent them from obtaining available services (Glass & Elliott, 1992; Meadow-Orlan, 1985), it seems clear that a gap exists in rehabilitation services. Santos (1995) noted that the deafness rehabilitative system is geared more toward early intervention for congenitally deaf children than toward services for individuals who become deaf as adults. Luey (1980, 1994) noted that even social workers often simply refer deafened clients to physicians and audiologists, apparently unaware that these professions are not equipped to recognize or deal with the psychosocial effects of profound hearing loss.

The limited literature on adventitious deafness has identified in a general sense the inadequacy of the rehabilitative system for this condition. It has not, however, documented in detail the rehabilitative care that deafened people receive after experiencing a profound hearing loss. Similarly, the literature lacks in-depth accounts from deafened adults about the psychological and social effect of adventitious deafness. This study addresses both of these issues.

Method

Sample

A request for volunteers for this study was mailed to the 25 Ontario residents who subscribed to a newsletter written for deafened people in Canada. A demographic survey was enclosed (along with a self-addressed stamped envelope) to aid in the selection of a purposive sample. Purposive samples are often used to ensure the inclusion of a range of affected individuals (Erlandson, Harris, Skipper, & Allen, 1993). For this study, we felt it was important to obtain diversity within the sample with regard to cause of deafness, age at onset, present age, gender, and geographical location (that is, rural or urban).

Eight of the 10 individuals who responded affirmatively to the request for participation in the study were selected for the sample. The sample contained an even gender distribution, and all respondents were white. Four respondents resided in a major city, two in medium-sized cities, and two in rural areas. The mean age of participants was 49 years (range = 31–68 years). The mean age of the participants at the onset of hearing loss was 32 years (range = 13–40 years). The mean number of years with a hearing loss was 17 (range = 2–39 years). Three causes of deafness—medical (two respondents), surgical (three respondents), and progressive-idiopathic (three respondents)—were represented in this sample. In terms of the rapidity of hearing loss, four respondents experienced gradual decline; one participant's hearing deteriorated at a rapid pace; and the remaining three experienced sudden deafness as a result of removal of the auditory nerve.

Data Collection

In-depth individual interviews were the source of data. The interviews were semistructured and an interview schedule of open-ended questions was used flexibly to explore respondents' experiences in becoming deaf and in dealing with the deafness rehabilitation system. The literature review and the first author's experience in becoming a deafened adult were used to develop the interview schedule, which was then pretested with a late-deafened adult. The first author conducted all interviews. Five respondents were interviewed in person with the help of computer-assisted real-time translation (CART) stenography. The CART stenography converted verbal dialogue into typed text that was shown on a computer monitor. This allowed respondents to read the interviewer's questions and produced a word processing record of their responses. Although the interviewer was fluent in American Sign Language (ASL), the CART stenography was necessary to compensate for the low level of sign language skill of the respondents. The interviews lasted approximately two hours. Because of the remote geographical location, two interviews were conducted by e-mail exchanges over a period of weeks. One interview was conducted by telephone using a telecommunication device for the deaf (TDD/TTY), which generated a visual display of questions and answers on a computer monitor.

Data Analysis

The general process of qualitative analysis used in this study was adapted from Lincoln and Guba (1985). All interviews were converted to transcript form, which the first author analyzed. Transcripts were reviewed a number of times to achieve intimate familiarity with the respondents' experiences. The data were then broken down

into units, coded as themes, and sorted into categories of themes.

Results

A major art of the original study's results included a detailed account of each respondent's experience (Aguayo, 1998). It is beyond the scope of this article to report the individual stories. This article presents an overview of the across-respondent themes related to the psychological and social effects of becoming deaf and experiences with rehabilitative services.

Psychological and Social Effects of Becoming Deaf

Three themes emerged in this first category: emotional trauma; oppression, exclusion, and isolation within the family; and general oppression, exclusion, and social isolation (Table 39.1).

Emotional Trauma The respondents' accounts were extremely moving with regard to the emotional trauma that they suffered in becoming deaf and coping with ongoing deafness. Anxiety, grief, and mourning were the emotions that all respondents experienced deeply. Each respondent reported anxiety related to feelings of inadequacy, self-doubt, and uncertainty about the future. Many respondents felt bewildered when they became deaf and had fears for their personal safety. Six of the eight respondents also spoke of the anger and frustration they experienced at their inability to function "normally." Embarrassment and shame were other common feelings described in this regard.

Oppression, Exclusion, and Isolation within the Family As would be expected, after the onset of deafness all eight participants experienced significant communication difficulties with their families. For the majority of the respondents, severe communication problems persisted and led to a sense of isolation within the family. Although six of the eight respondents learned ASL, the families of only two learned and continued to use ASL (two other families learned ASL but abandoned its use). Although the two families continued to use ASL, often they overlooked the deafened person's communication needs. All respondents reported that they felt excluded from family interaction to some degree, and five of them believed that the root cause of such neglect was familial denial of the deafness. These

Table 39.1 Psychosocial Effects of Deafness

Subtheme	Quote
Emotional trauma	I felt so helpless . . . I got caught in a cycle of "can'ts."
	I had to pull off the road to cry for half an hour [after diagnosis of permanent biaural deafness].
	I think that I nearly died then [on sudden realization of deafness postsurgery].
	After I went through all this, meningitis, the heart attack, the cancer . . . nothing was as bad as the deafness . . . it's the worst thing I have ever faced. The silence made me a different person. Let me put it this way, take the criminals' hearing away rather than put them to death, and you will see the prison they get.
Oppression, exclusion, and isolation within the family	I felt so unimportant to them [family members].
	My family did not discuss my hearing loss . . . my father told others it was a "small problem."
	I just sat there [at a family gathering] watching all these little conversations that I didn't hear. The family became so overwhelmed at times (about my deafness), that they forgot about my feelings.
	My husband was not patient with my hearing loss. He said many very mean things to me. I remember him yelling and yelling because I didn't understand something he said. Sometimes he got physical . . . it was horrible.
General oppression, exclusion, and social isolation	I was left out of most cliques. Always picked last to join a [sports] team and always given the old "rolling eyes" whenever paired with someone on a class assignment.
	There is no social life.
	They [friends] were shocked that I would let deafness bother me.

respondents felt that the magnitude of their hearing loss was minimized or ignored outright.

Many of the respondents reported more severe family problems. Half of the respondents reported feeling discriminated against, oppressed by, or abused by some family members. One respondent described how her family of origin taught her to conceal and feel ashamed of her deafness. Another respondent, who subsequently divorced, described how her husband was embarrassed by her deafness and would ridicule and blame her. Only one respondent described his family as consistently understanding and supportive.

General Oppression, Exclusion, and Social Isolation   All of the respondents reported social difficulties that led to increased social isolation. Respondents described how deafness caused them to feel embarrassed, fearful, inadequate, and incompetent in social situations. They also described how they frequently were neglected, shunned, or discriminated against by others. One respondent, who became deaf gradually, reported how high school peers would sometimes taunt and ridicule him. Another respondent described how she was the victim

of obvious discrimination in a job competition. A third respondent noted how the awkwardness of well-intentioned friends in communicating with him made him feel uncomfortable.

Respondents reported similar reactions to, or way of coping with, social oppression and exclusion. Many respondents learned to conceal their deafness from others or to bluff their ability to understand verbal dialogue. Also, to varying degrees, all respondents used strategies of general social withdrawal or selective avoidance of anxiety-provoking situations. These understandable coping strategies led to further social isolation.

Experiences with Rehabilitative Services

Two themes emerged with regard to experiences with rehabilitative services: the exclusive medical orientation and revolving door nature of rehabilitation services and respondents' dissatisfaction with rehabilitative services.

Exclusive Medical Orientation and Revolving Door in Rehabilitative Services   As would be expected with any physical disorder or illness, all of the respondents sought medical attention when they became aware of hearing loss. The eight respondents consulted a total of 36 health care providers. Of all the health care practitioners consulted, 33 were trained medical professionals and three had paraprofessional medical training. Among the health care professionals were 13 family physicians; 10 ear, nose, and throat (ENT) specialists; eight audiologists; and two neurologists. The three other professionals were a hearing aid dispenser without training in audiology, an occupational therapist, and a military hearing examiner whose hearing health training was in the operation of an audiometer to screen-test the hearing of new recruits.

Respondents went through a minimum of three stages in rehabilitative services, and most went through such stages more than once (Table 39.2). For some respondents, rehabilitation services may have been separated by a number of years. For example, the cochlear implantation for two respondents occurred several years after the earlier rehabilitative processes. Respondents reported several common experiences in the stages of rehabilitative services received.

Stage one of rehabilitative services primarily consisted of initial intake, assessment of the condition, and referral to a second practitioner. A general practitioner was the initial contact for all but one of the respondents. The only stage-one health

Table 39.2 Aural Rehabilitation: Stages and Treatments Received

Informant	Stage One	Stage Two	Stage Three	Stage Four
A	Physician	Hearing aid vendor	Hearing aids	
	Physician	ENT	Audiologist	Termination[a]
				Audiograms
	Physician	ENT	Cochlear implant	
B	Physician	ENT	Audiologist	Termination[b]
	Physician	ENT	Audiologist	Hearing aids
	Physician	ENT	Audiologist	Cochlear implant
C	Physician	ENT	Audiologist[c]	
	Physician	ENT	Audiologist	Hearing aids
D	Physician	ENT	Neurologist	Surgery
	Physician	ENT	Neurologist	Surgery
E	Examiner	Termination[d]		
	Physician	ENT	Termination[e]	
	Physician	ENT	Audiologist	Hearing aids
F	Physician	ENT	Surgery	
G	Physician	Neurologist	Surgery	
H	Physician	ENT	Steroid treatment	
			Audiologist	Hearing aids
			Hearing health counselor	Resource info.
			ENT	Audiologist

NOTES: Treatments are represented by shaded boxes.
[a]Cochelar implant candidacy rejected.
[b]Misdiagnosis.
[c]Referral not used by respondent.
[d]Faulty audiogram assessment.
[e]ENT assumed respondent would reject hearing aid use.

care provider who was not a physician was a military paramedic who was trained to operate an audiometer.

In the second stage, services to respondents were further assessments and referrals to another health care specialist. The breakdown of service providers in this stage included 13 ENT specialists, one neurologist, and one hearing aid dispenser (who was not an audiologist).

In stage three, respondents received a total of 12 referrals to medical practitioners, five treatments, and one termination. Of the referrals, one went unconsummated at the respondent's discretion. The referrals were distributed among eight audiologists, two neurologists, one ENT specialist, and one hearing health counselor. The five treatments that were provided included one hearing aids prescription, one cochlear implantation, two surgeries, and one pharmaceutical regimen.

Stage four was the most treatment-laden. The respondents received a total of nine treatments that included two surgeries (on one individual), four hearing aids prescription, one cochlear implantation, one recommendation for annual audiograms, and one provision of hearing loss resource information. Two rehabilitation processes were terminated at stage four because no treatment could remedy these respondents' hearing loss. No respondents received further treatment after stage four.

In examining the rehabilitative services experienced by the study's participants, two issues stand out. First, it is striking that no mental health professionals were involved to help address the participants' psychosocial needs. Second, for most participants the multiplicity of stages of treatment and of professionals involved conjures up the image of an ineffective, revolving door of services.

Dissatisfaction with Rehabilitation Services   Given the revolving door nature of rehabilitative services received, it is no surprise that many participants expressed dissatisfaction with the competence of the medical professionals they encountered. Participants complained about shortcomings in professional knowledge and skill, including the inability to provide correct diagnoses and the lack of knowledge about appropriate services and resources. The following quotes illustrate some of these complaints:

The medical people didn't do me much good.

They should have been the authorities but they didn't have the information.

There would be nothing [in the way of referrals for social rehabilitation] . . . just a gaping hole where my inner ear is located.

Other dissatisfactions about the medical professionals related to poor professional manner and interpersonal sensitivity and lack of attention to the emotional, psychological, and social effect of deafness. Participants said:

They had kind of an attitude . . . there was no empathy.

They forgot about my feelings.

I was told: "Don't worry about it. Look at how well you've coped so far." Then he [ENT] told me to find a deaf club.

Although some respondents had more positive experiences with rehabilitative services than others, overall the rehabilitation that was provided was woefully inadequate.

Discussion

The participants' stories attest to the commonsense acknowledgment in the literature (David & Trehub, 1989; Glass & Elliott, 1992; Luey, 1980) that the transition to deafness after living as a hearing person is marked by emotional trauma and extensive problems in social functioning. As others (for example, Meadow-Orlans, 1985) have noted, of particular concern is that the psychosocial needs of deafened adults often are neglected or responded to inadequately by family members.

The participants' stories also confirm accounts in the literature that rehabilitation for deafened adults often consists exclusively of medically oriented services and that counseling services to address the psychosocial needs of the individual are overlooked (Aguayo & Avena, 1994; David & Trehub, 1989; Glass & Elliott, 1992; Rothschild & Kampfe, 1997). Although medical intervention is a natural first step in rehabilitative care, clearly forgotten in the pursuit to provide a "cure" is that adventitious deafness is not only a medical condition, but also a psychosocial phenomenon. Psychosocial interventions are required when deafness and hearing loss are diagnosed—especially if the individual's hearing loss is irreversible, as was the case for all eight respondents in this study. Psychosocial interventions are particularly necessary when the irreversibility and suddenness of hearing loss can be predicted, as was the case for the three respondents for whom surgeons controlled the exact month, date, and hour that the patient would become deaf.

The rehabilitation system's neglect of the psychosocial needs of deafened adults represents a major shortcoming, as reflected in the satisfaction levels of the sample. In addition to complaints about inadequate training and knowledge, respondents were critical of insensitivity of professionals to the psychosocial effects of deafness. Respondents were clear in advocating for the various types of formal (that is, individual, family, and group) and informal (for example, individual, and group peer support) interventions.

Although varying in individual competences, the medical professionals in each aspect of the respondents' rehabilitation performed as they were trained to do. The general practitioners made preliminary evaluations and referred the respondents to the appropriate specialist. This professional, either an ENT or a neurologist, used a treatment that seemed most appropriate for the services that they offered and referred the respondents to an audiologist or a rehabilitation professional. Each of these service providers offered the type of therapy consistent with their expertise. Unfortunately, the ability to assess and treat psychosocial needs fell outside the limits of their practice.

This adherence to a narrow medical rehabilitative approach to deafened adults is widespread. The respondents' stories about the shortcomings of their rehabilitative experiences were consistent across rural, small town, and large city environments. Furthermore, although this study took place in Canada, there are reasons to suspect that the results can be generalized to the United States. First, despite the differences in health care policy and funding between these countries, the training and practice of medical professionals is based on the same body of knowledge. Second, most of the studies that document deafened people's dissatisfaction with their rehabilitation were conducted in the United States (Glass & Elliott, 1992; Luey, 1980, 1994; Luey, Glass, & Elliott, 1995; Meadow-Orlans, 1985; Rothschild & Kampfe, 1997).

The findings of this study support the call that others have made for social workers to become involved in rehabilitation for adventitious deafness (Luey, 1980, 1994; Luey et al., 1995). Any type of acquired disability involves a multitude of difficult changes for the affected person and his or her family. The onset of deafness marks the beginning of a transition from being a hearing person to being a deaf person, a change involving a fundamental shift in personal identity affecting all members of the immediate family. Family stress and social isolation increase, and adaptation to such changes is not smooth or painless. Social workers, as change agents, are trained to work with the relationship systems of families and the social support resources in the broader environment to support social functioning. In the case of adventitious deafness, social workers could fulfill many functions.

First, a social worker could offer grief counseling to the affected individual. Such counseling could help the deafened adult work through emotional reactions to the loss and develop coping strategies to gain a sense of control (Luey, 1980; Rothschild & Kampfe, 1997). Second, a social worker could link the deafened person to peer support to normalize the condition and reduce the social isolation that can occur. Third, a social worker could engage the family of the deafened person in counseling to help them deal with the emotional and practical effects and to prevent familial neglect or oppression of the deafened person. Acting as a mediator during family counseling sessions, the social worker could bring important issues, such as adapting to new communication and familial roles, into the open and help the family problem-solve around such issues. Fourth, a social worker could act as a broker for resources and information for the deafened individual and the family. This should include mediating and advocating with the medical and audiological professionals and with the place of employment of the deafened individual.

Although social workers could fill existing gaps in the treatment of adventitious deafness, medical professionals need to be better informed about the traumatic effects of adventitious deafness so that they can show better understanding of, and support for, deafened people (David & Trehub, 1989). Studies have demonstrated that support, concern, and understanding from medical professionals can help alleviate symptoms for individuals with hearing disorders (Rothschild & Kampfe, 1997). Furthermore, hearing health professionals also should help lead the deafened individual to appropriate psychosocial rehabilitation by including referrals to social workers in their treatment plans. Toward this end, social workers should be included in interdisciplinary teams that diagnose and treat deafness.

References

Aguayo, M. O. (1998). *Rehabilitation for deafened adults: A puzzle with missing pieces*. Unpublished master's thesis, Wilfrid Laurier University, Waterloo, Ontario.

Aguayo, M. O., & Avena, K. (1994). *Fact sheet on deafened adults*. Unpublished manuscript.

Benderly, B. L. (1980). *Dancing without music: Deafness in America*. Garden City, NJ: Anchor Press/Doubleday.

Boone, S., & Scherich, D. (1995). Characteristics of ALDAns: The ALDA member survey. *ALDA News*. (Available from Association of Late-Deafened Adults, 1131 Lake Street, #204, Oak Park, IL 60301.)

David, M., & Trehub, S. (1989). Perspectives on deafened adults. *American Annals of the Deaf, 134*, 200–204.

Erlandson, D. A., Harris, E. L., Skipper, B. L., & Allen, S. D. (1993). *Doing naturalistic inquiry*. Newbury Park, CA: Sage Publications.

Glass, L., & Elliott, H. (1992, January/February). The professionals told me what it was, but that's not enough. *SHHH Journal*, pp. 26–28.

Goffman, E. (1963). *Stigma: Notes on the management of spoiled identity*. Englewood Cliffs, NJ: Prentice Hall.

Kyle, J., & Wood, J. (1987). *Adjustment to acquired deafness*. London: British Association of Deafened People.

Levine, E. S. (1981). *The ecology of early deafness*. New York: Columbia University Press.

Lincoln, Y. S., & Guba, E. G. (1985). *Naturalistic inquiry*. Beverly Hills, CA: Sage Publications.

Luey, H. S. (1980). Between worlds: The problems of deafened adults. *Social Work in Health Care, 5*, 253–265.

Luey, H. S. (1994). Sensory loss: A neglected issue in social work. *Journal of Gerontological Social Work, 21*, 213–265.

Luey, H. S., Glass, L., & Elliott, H. (1995). Hard-of-hearing or deaf: Issues of ears, language, culture, and identity. *Social Work, 40*, 177–182.

Meadow-Orlans, K. P. (1985). Social and psychological effects of hearing loss in adulthood: A literature review. In H. Orlans (Ed.), *Adjustment to adult hearing loss* (pp. 35–57). San Diego: College Hill Press.

Ries, P. W. (1994). Prevalence and characteristics of persons with hearing trouble: United States, 1990–91. National Center for Health Statistics, data from National Health Interview Survey, Series 10, Number 188.

Rothschild, M. A., & Kampfe, C. M. (1997). Issues associated with late onset deafness. *JADARA, 31*, 1–16.

Santos, K. D. (1995). Deafness. In R. L. Edwards (Ed in Chief), *Encyclopedia of social work* (19th ed.) [CD-ROM]. Washington, DC: NASW Press.

Schein, J. D., & Delk, M. (1974). *The deaf population in the United States*. Silver Spring, MD: National Association of the Deaf.

40

Challenges of Type 2 Diabetes and the Role of Health Care Social Work: A Neglected Area of Practice

Diabetes mellitus is one of the most prevalent and serious chronic diseases facing the U.S. health care system. According to the Centers for Disease Control and Prevention (CDC) (1998), diabetes affects 15.7 million people in the United States, 10.3 million of whom have been diagnosed and 5.4 million of whom are unaware that they have this disease. The American Diabetes Association (ADA) (1998) estimates that in 1997 alone medical care for diabetes cost $44.1 billion. Diabetes exacts an equally devastating physical toll; it is the leading cause of blindness, end-stage renal disease, non-injury-related lower limb amputations, and cardiac disease, and it is the seventh leading cause of death in this country (CDC, 1998). Currently, social work involvement with this chronic disease is limited. For instance, as of 1998, social work clinicians made up less than 1% (n = 57) of the professionals listed with the American Association of Diabetes Educators, the principal organization of diabetes professionals. As a topic of research, a review of the social work literature identified 13 articles on diabetes-related topics (see Table 40.1). Although there are probably many social workers treating and researching diabetes, their involvement seems inconspicuous. Considering the ability of diabetes and its treatment to challenge an individual's biopsychosocial functioning, social workers have the potential to make remarkable differences in the lives of people coping with this disease. Nevertheless, according to Sidell (1997),

mental health professionals "typically receive little training specifically designed to help them assist people with chronic illnesses" (p. 10).

To assist people with diabetes, social workers first need to understand the disease, how it challenges patients, and then ways to become involved. This article outlines the basic aspects of Type 2 diabetes, its incessant challenges, and several interventions health care social workers may use to assist adults with this chronic disease.

Diabetes Mellitus

Diabetes mellitus is a cluster of endocrine diseases characterized by the body's complete or partial inability to absorb glucose, the principal source of energy, from digested foods into cells (Harris, 1995b). Unabsorbed glucose accumulates in the bloodstream, eventually exceeding physiologically tolerable levels, damaging blood vessels and capillaries. According to the National Institutes of Health (NIH) (1995), diabetic complications include blindness, renal failure, peripheral neuropathy, and peripheral vascular disease. People with diabetes are also at greater risk of cardiac disease, strokes, amputations, retinopathy, cataracts, glaucoma, and gestational complications compared with people of similar age without diabetes (CDC, 1998; NIH, 1995).

Table 40.1 Social Work Articles Investigating Diabetes Mellitus

Authors	Year	Subject Population
Amir, Rabin, & Galatzer	1990	Diabetic adults (N = 70)
Auslander, Anderson, Bubb, Jung, & Santiago	1990	Diabetic children and their families (N = 42)
Auslander, Bubb, Rogge, & Santiago	1993	Newly diagnosed diabetic children and their families (N = 53)
Auslander, Thompson, Dreitzer, & Santiago	1997	Mothers/female caregivers of children with diabetes (N = 158)
Blackburn, Piper, Woolridge, Hoag, & Hanan	1978	Dialysis patients with and without diabetes (N = 22)
Daley	1992	Adolescents with diabetes (N = 54)
Fair	1993	Diabetic children with ocular disease—conceptual paper (N = 0)
Hill & Hynes	1980	School-age diabetic children and families—program review (N = 0)
Kanter	1996	Depressed adult male with diabetes (N = 1)
Piening	1984	Families of diabetes patients—conceptual paper (N = 0)
Rabin, Amir, Nardi, & Ovadia	1986	Adult women with diabetes (N = 9)
Safyer et al.	1993	Prepubescent diabetic children and their parents (N = 49)
Vest, Ronnau, Lopez, & Gonzales	1997	Mexican American adults with diabetes (N = 36)

NOTE: The literature review was conducted using *Social Work Abstracts PLUS* (SWAB + CD-ROM) from 1977 to 1999, all years currently available in this database, to identify articles by social workers or from journals that were clearly targeting social workers on any topic related to diabetes mellitus.

Distinguishing Type 2 from Type 1 Diabetes

There are primarily two forms of diabetes. In Type 1 diabetes, formerly called "insulin-dependent diabetes mellitus," the pancreas produces very little or no insulin, necessitating an injected supply of insulin. Type 1 accounts for between 5% and 10% (from 515,000 to 1.3 million) of diagnosed cases (CDC, 1998). Although Type 1 diabetes is the most frequent chronic childhood disease, formerly referred to as "juvenile diabetes," 60% (from 309,000 to 780,000) of cases are among people over 19 years of age (LaPorte, Matsushima, & Chang, 1995). The focus of this article is Type 2 diabetes, a disease in which either the insulin secreted or the body's use of insulin is less effective compared with nondiabetics; it is treated through initially diet, exercise, and oral medications, although insulin injections may be required as the disease progresses (Hillson, 1996).

Although previously termed "noninsulin-dependent diabetes mellitus," 40% of adults with Type 2 diabetes need supplemental insulin (CDC, 1998). Labeled "adult onset diabetes" because of its common onset after age 40, Type 2 diabetes makes up approximately 90% to 95% (from 9.2 to 9.7 million) of diagnosed cases (CDC, 1998). During the 1990s, however, the incidence of Type 2 diabetes among adolescents, referred to as maturity-onset diabetes of the young, rose to epidemic proportions among some groups, particularly African American and Native American children (Dabelea, Pettitt, Jones, & Arslanian, 1999). The signs and symptoms for both types of diabetes include sudden weight loss, blurred eyesight, fatigue, frequent infections, increased thirst, hunger, and urination (Davidson, Davidson, & Richard, 1998).

Risk Factors

Although the precise etiology of Type 2 diabetes is unclear, researchers have identified four major risk factors: (1) age, (2) obesity, (3) family history, and (4) ethnicity. The incidence of diabetes increases rapidly with age, so that people over the age of 64 are 3.5 times more likely to be diagnosed (Kenny, Aubert, & Geiss, 1995). Overweight adults are also at greater risk; mean and women 20% above their desirable weight, a common indicator of obesity, are twice as likely to be diagnosed with Type 2 diabetes (Harris, 1995a). A family history of diabetes (parent, grandparent) also increases the risk.

Rewers and Hamman (1995) found that adults with a diabetic parent were four times as likely to contract diabetes. Several ethnic minority groups are also at greater risk of diabetes. The CDC (1999) reported that non-Hispanic black people, Latino Americans, and Asian Americans and Pacific Islanders are twice as likely, and American Indians and Alaskan Natives almost three times as likely, as non-Hispanic white people of similar ages to acquire diabetes. Although family history and ethnicity indicate a genetic cause, behavioral and lifestyle variables (diet, alcohol consumption, physical inactivity, socioeconomic status, and urbanization) also heighten a person's risk of diabetes (Rewers & Hamman, 1995).

Treatment

To date, research with Type 2 diabetes (Kumamoto Study, University Group Diabetes Program, and Veterans Affairs Cooperative Study on Glycemic Control and Complications in Type 3 Diabetes) and similar studies with Type 1 diabetes (Diabetes Control and Complications Trial) decisively support the aggressive control of blood glucose levels as the paramount treatment approach to reduce many diabetic complications (ADA, 1999b; Cerveny, Leder, & Weart, 1998; Herman & Eastman, 1998).

A typical treatment plan striving to achieve tight glycemic control in Type 2 diabetes may include oral medication or insulin supplements, home monitoring of glucose levels, diet, exercise, and strategies to minimize psychological stress (ADA, 1999b). To meet the requirements of such a regimen demands that patients learn a remarkable amount of information (for example, basic diabetes pathology and physiology, symptoms of hypo/hyperglycemic reactions, and dietary guidelines), master several skills (for example, glucose monitoring and insulin injections), and make multiple life adjustments (such as eating habits, regular exercise, and healthy stress management) (Davidson et al., 1998). Common tasks may include finger sticks to test blood glucose levels before meals, oral medication compliance, calculated meal planning, and 20 minutes of daily cardiovascular activity—all on a time schedule (Hillson, 1996).

Plans also may involve weight loss (Nuttall & Chasuk, 1998) and abstaining from alcohol or cigarettes (Rimm et al., 1993). Treatment, therefore, demands significant involvement, responsibility, and change from patients and their families across an array of challenges. It is important to note that even with perfect compliance, blood sugars still may fluctuate, and complications occur (Feinglos & Bethel, 1998).

Diabetic Challenges

Diabetes Self-Care Knowledge and Skills

For patients, diabetes treatment involves much information and skill, requiring them to become "self-regulating" (Toobert & Glasgow, 1991). To manage effectively Type 2 diabetes, a person must understand the basic pathological and physiological nature of diabetes, for example, what causes blood sugars to rise and fall as well as the effects of these high and low blood sugars (Hillson, 1996). Although patients need not become "diabetes experts," adequate self-care requires a working knowledge of the interaction between personal behavior and immediate glucose control and complications (Assal, Jacquemet, & Morel, 1997). According to Clement (1995), patients also must master self-monitoring of glucose (for example, meter use, recording and interpreting results, and disposing of biohazardous materials), become adept at recognizing and treating hypo- or hyperglycemic episodes, planning and executing an exercise program, skin and foot care, ketone testing, care during a cold of flu (sick care), as well as a multitude of diet-related issues (that is, healthy meal planning, grocery shopping, food preparation, and restaurant choices).

Knowledge and skills also may be needed to manage oral medications or insulin, the latter involving proper storage, dosage calculation and timing, and administration of injections or continuous infusions with computerized pumps. Patients also must master navigation of health care systems (that is, clinics, hospitals, and insurance companies), self-advocacy, and successful interaction with a host of professionals (dieticians, physicians, nurses, and social workers) (Rubin, Biermann, & Toohey, 1997).

Depth of understanding and mastery of skills vary according to the patient's intellectual capacity and education and often are impeded by the sheer volume of material (Glasgow, 1995). The onset of diabetes may be the first time many adults have had extended involvement with health care professionals and systems, and thus they lack familiarity with the medical culture (that is, language, role expectations, and norms) (Graziani, Rosenthal, & Diamond, 1999). The learning process also may be hindered by a sense of urgency to get the disease "under control," the presence of other health problems or disabilities, preexisting learning challenges (for example, attention deficit disorder or dyslexia), mental retardation, psychosocial problems (such as thought or mood disorders or family problems), language incompatibility with the professionals, illiteracy, level of emotional acceptance, access to diabetic education (for example, programs, professionals, and materials), absence from diabetic classes or appointments, or insufficient time to study (Overland, Hoskins, McGill, & Yue, 1993).

Diabetes-informed social workers are an asset to diabetes educators and programs, serving as the resident behavioral science experts (Daley, 1992). Social workers can interject, affirm, and interpret relevant psychosocial factors during initial assessments and progress evaluations, highlighting strengths, needs, family involvement and functioning and the effects of patient, family, and group cultures on outcomes (Auslander, Bubb, Rogge, & Santiago, 1993). They are invaluable as consultants or instructors to diabetic clients also dealing with cognitive deficits, learning disabilities, or chronic mental illnesses. Likewise, social workers are indispensable in designing and implementing education programs and materials tailored to meet the information and skills needs of people with learning challenges or educational deficits and especially young or elderly patients. In particular, social work practitioners are ideally suited to develop and teach the psychosocial component of a diabetes program that may include presentations on behavior modification, emotions, depression, stress and time management, and community resources. Social workers also can serve as resources to those lacking access to traditional diabetes programs, such as rural, homebound, uninsured, or underinsured populations or in medical settings with limited diabetes education resources.

When client or family psychosocial issues inhibit the educational process, social work intervention can help resolve or contain the problem, allowing continued instruction. Facilitating a family-centered approach—family as the focus of intervention—among the multidisciplinary diabetes team may be a more preventive approach for addressing resistance (Ell & Northern, 1990). Family-centered interventions may include soliciting and addressing family concerns, encouraging family attendance and participation at appointments, fostering shared responsibility and credit for treatment outcomes, incorporating family members' talents and health needs in the care plan, enlisting participation in classes, and selling everyone on the benefits of healthy habits for wellness and delaying or preventing the onset of diabetes.

To improve participation in outpatient programs, social workers can identify and address client barriers to keeping appointments, such as inadequate transportation, noncooperative employers or family members, limited financial or child care resources, or even poor client motivation. Pairing newly diagnosed patients with "diabetic sponsors"—individuals who are experienced and successful at managing their diabetes—also may enhance attendance. Rather than relying on clients to come to clinics, social workers may need to bring the clinics to clients by organizing diabetic health fairs, outreach, or training programs in work settings, church facilities, or community centers.

Diet and Exercise

For people with Type 2 diabetes, medical nutritional therapy (MNT) is often the "first-line therapy of choice" (Lipkin, 1999). The goal of MNT is to maintain near-normal glucose levels by matching dietary consumption with actual caloric (energy) needs, necessitating that the right foods in correct proportions be eaten at prescribed times (Nuttall & Chasuk, 1998). For many, MNT may include a secondary goal: weight loss. In meeting either goal, the person must become aware of his or her individual food consumption patterns and basic caloric needs for height, weight, age, and level of activity; be able to prepare and plan well-balanced meals using fresh foods as often as possible; be able to read and interpret nutritional information on food labels; and be able to incorporate regular meal times into work and home schedules (ADA, 1999c; Franz et al., 1994).

Nutritional self-management or compliance with a prescribed diet can be handicapped by many of the same factors that impede self-care knowledge and skill mastery. The hectic schedules of patients and caregivers may not allow adequate time or energy to prepare healthy meals, learning different cooking methods, or shop more frequently for fresh foods. Time and energy limitations plague women with diabetes responsible for food preparation in a family of nondiabetics who protest eating "diabetic food," although educators emphasize that what is good for a person with diabetes is good for someone without diabetes (Rubin et al., 1997).

For some, the availability or ability to acquire nutritionally adequate and safe foods may be limited or uncertain, a circumstance referred to as "food insecurity" (Campbell, 1991). Although predominately attributed to low income, several other factors have been found to contribute to food insecurity: the absence of supermarkets in either remote rural or urban inner-city settings, poor health, limited physical mobility, inadequate transportation, sudden unemployment, homelessness, and budget cuts or poor access to government or private food assistance programs (American Dietetic Association, 1998; Andrews, Nord, Bickel, & Carlson, 1999; Campbell, 1991). In MNT, food assumes an almost medicinal quality, and many may resist altering long-held consumption patterns, inasmuch as food plays a part in their cultural heritage or serves as a source of pleasure; therefore, dietary changes are interpreted as loss of either function. For others, as Quatromoni et al. (1994) discovered with Caribbean Latinos, a belief in destiny or a sense of fatalism may inhibit changes in dietary or health behaviors; clients surrender their diabetes care and lives to fate, luck, or God. Alcohol or substance abuse also hinders dietary compliance (W.M. Cox, Blount, Crowe, & Singh, 1996).

Exercise is one of the most important and effective methods for managing diabetes. Exercise improves glycemic control, cholesterol levels, cardiovascular fitness, physical strength, and flexibility; decreases blood pressure; and aids weight loss. Also, exercise may prevent or delay the onset of Type 2 diabetes (ADA, 1999b). The ADA recommends an accumulation of 30 minutes of daily moderate physical activity. Most people are encouraged to meet this goal as long as existing diabetic complications are monitored and they are in good glucose control (ADA, 1999a). For some, exercise necessitates well-established self-management skills, pre- and postexercise glucose monitoring, and medication or insulin adjustments according to the proposed activity.

Poor exercise may result from a lack of time or energy, competing domestic tasks, family needs, or work demands (Glasgow, 1995). Diabetic complications or medical problems (heart disease, pulmonary disease, arthritis) also may hinder activity. In contrast, many may lack motivation because of the absence of complications, depression, or embarrassment over personal appearance (Swift, Armstrong, Beerman, Campbell, & Pond-Smith, 1995). Living in high-crime areas also may limit

establishing adequate exercise routines (Maillet, D'Eramo-Melkus, & Spollett, 1996).

Again, social workers' behavioral science background; ability to work with individuals, groups, or families; cultural competence; and ecological approach can be useful to patients and diabetes programs. In group, classroom, and individual sessions, the practitioner can provide instruction and assistance with behavior modifications, targeting diet and exercise habits in a manner respectful of cultural differences. Families can be engaged as change agents, enlisted to assist and support the patient in altering diet and activity habits, and used as a target for intervention itself through the alteration of family dietary and activity patterns (Rolland, 1994). Specialized behavior plans and monitoring can be developed for challenging patients (that is, noncompliant or behaviorally or cognitively challenged) or those in institutional settings (for example, nursing homes, group homes, assisted living centers, or state hospitals). Given the difficulty of these lifestyle changes, social workers also can provide supportive counseling to patients and their significant others. Developing a buddy system, as used with adolescents (Daley, 1992), to partner newly diagnosed people with experienced diabetic mentors (sponsors) is another possible social work intervention.

For some patients, making these lifestyle changes may require assistance with concrete resources. As resource brokers, social workers can assess needs and link clients with community agencies for nutritional assistance, fitness training, additional diabetic education (professionals or material), medical care, health insurance, insulin and glucose monitoring supplies, prescription assistance, transportation, and counseling or support groups.

Resource brokering also is realized when the social worker serves as a community resource expert for other professionals. As recognized by Vest, Ronnau, Lopez, and Gonzales (1997), many social workers may not appreciate and accommodate viable alternative treatment resources (such as herbal medicine, osteopathy, and therapeutic touch), foster understanding of these practices among professionals, and assist clients with incorporating these with conventional treatment. Community-level interventions may focus on neighborhood safety, walk-and-talk exercise groups based in area churches or community centers, food insecurity, or dietary compliance when meals are prepared outside the home (for example, in senior citizen centers, meals-on-wheels programs, or nursing homes). Again, traditional mental health interventions may be necessary to address challenges frustrating compliance with the diabetes diet and exercise plans.

Time Management

As the treatment regime suggests, diabetes care requires significant investments of time and energy and a degree of punctuality. Wdowik, Kendall, and Harris (1997) found that poor time management was the leading barrier to diabetes management among college students. For example, skipping lunch, eating a late dinner, taking medication or injecting insulin too early or too late, or exercising before breakfast all had immediate and long-term effects. Accommodating the temporal demands of diabetes self-care assumes that life is predictable and orderly and that work or home environments conform to a rigid time schedule, which may in effect curtail spontaneity and add an additional layer of stress for some patients and families.

Social workers can instruct diabetes patients in the area of time management principles and skills, aiding them in prioritizing life activities and accommodating diabetic self-care demands within their personal, family, and work schedules. Social workers may encourage self-advocacy or advocate on behalf of clients for adequate time in the workplace for glucose monitoring, for equitable divisions of household labor, or for greater awareness of the challenges and needs of people with diabetes among family, friends, and the community. Although advances with insulin pumps have increased flexibility and spontaneity for many, the technology is not without problems (for example, pump failure or catheter occlusions) and requires a highly motivated patient with good glycemic control and mastery of additional technical information and skills (American Association of Diabetic Educators, 1997; Dunn, Nathan, Scavini, Selam, & Wingrove, 1997; Lorenz, 1999). In short, diabetes self-care requires a lifestyle change, and social workers can be indispensable in guiding clients through this process.

Stress

Understandably, patients experience a great deal of psychological stress at the onset of diabetic symptoms, when diagnosed, while adjusting to treatment, and during complications, in addition to stress from ongoing life events and challenges (Rubin et al., 1997). Stress during acute events (for example, the death of a partner or an automobile accident) can double or triple glucose levels (Greenberg, 1993). Accumulations of chronic stress from work or home may elevate glucose as much

as 25% above normal (Aikens, Wallander, Bell, & McNorton, 1994). There is also evidence that stress indirectly affects glycemic control through forgetfulness, accidents, or poor coping habits such as denial, isolation, avoidance, increased eating, alcohol consumption, and cigarette smoking (Delamater, Kurtz, Bubb, White, & Santiago, 1987; Peyrot & McMurry, 1992). Essentially, patients need to recognize the signs and symptoms of the sources of stress (positive and negative stressors) and then implement remedies (for example, alter perceptions, eliminate or reduce stressors, expose themselves to humor or fun, or engage in relaxation techniques).

Stress management often is constrained by time and resource limitations, pessimism, unassertiveness, inadequate emotional support, limited access to educational or treatment programs, insufficient control over living or work environments, Type A personality traits, or, unbeknown to many Americans, an addiction to stress itself (Greenberg, 1993). For some, poor diabetes self-care, erratic glucose levels, complications, and stress can become entwined, necessitating professional intervention (Rubin et al., 1997).

As stated earlier, the principal social work intervention may be to provide didactic and experiential lessons on stress management, and relaxation techniques to enhance the patients' ability to detect signs and symptoms of stress, foster effective and healthy ways of coping, and encourage relaxation techniques such as progressive muscle relaxation, diaphragmatic deep breathing, or guided imagery. It is important for clients to understand the effects of stress on blood glucose control and the tendency, when stressed, to revert back to earlier, less healthy, coping mechanisms like smoking, overeating, or drinking alcohol (Peyrot & McMurry, 1992). In individual sessions, social workers can identify and assist patients and families with stressors (for example, inadequate resources or problematic life events), offer supportive counseling, or provide guided relaxation instruction. Mediation also may be necessary to ameliorate conflictive relationships between patients and family or patients and frustrated health professionals. Ideally, a staff or on-call social worker can provide immediate assistance to clients during periods of crisis.

Emotions

In addition to the educational, behavioral, and temporal challenges, chronic diseases like diabetes also bring about significant emotional challenges (Ivinson, 1995; Sidell, 1997). Patients and families face a "literal torrent of affect" throughout their lifetimes with such a disease (Rolland, 1984). Jacobson (1996) asserted that the state of "emotional adjustment" might have a significant influence on the success of glycemic control. Focusing on anticipatory loss in physical illness, Rolland (1994) suggested that patients and families experience an "emotional roller coaster" shaped by their ethnic, gender, and cultural frameworks and the "illness life cycle" (Rolland, 1984)—that is, the temporal phases in a disease: crisis (initial onset and diagnosis), chronic (ongoing adaptation), and terminal (impending death). Although it is beyond the scope of this article to detail a diabetes–specific-stage theory of emotional adjustment, the literature and my clinical experience suggest that people typically encounter six emotion-oriented challenges in various degrees and orders: denial, anger, fear or anxiety, guilt, grief or sadness, and depression.

Denial   Denial can be a feeling of utter disbelief at the diagnosis, a belittling of the seriousness or chronic nature of the disease, or an avoidance of the consequences (Ivinson, 1995). Denial also occurs as a refusal to acknowledge the disease strategically when overindulging at mealtimes or as a defense mechanism against being overwhelmed by multiple losses (that is, loss of control, independence, and health), the treatment regimen, or complications (S. Cox, 1994). As Ivinson suggested, denial serves a viable function: it allows the person or family to gradually process the event, information, and life changes. Despite its psychological value, denial can be physically devastating to a body battling diabetes. Chronic denial is common and easy for adults who are asymptomatic or erroneously diagnosed as having "borderline diabetes" (NIH, 1995).

Anger   Anger is common for people with diabetes (S. Cox, 1994; Rubin et al., 1997). When well-being is threatened, anger serves as an initial defense, a "primal reaction" associated with the fight-or-flight response (Greenberg, 1993). Anger is also a classic response to the unanswerable paradox of why "bad things happen to good people" (Kushner & Fetterman, 1997). It may be a product of the bombardment of "have to, must, and should," sometimes referred to as "infantilization" (Rabin, Amir, Nardi, & Ovadia, 1986). Anger can be directed at the diabetes nurse educator, dietitian, or occasionally the physician. Often, though, it is patients themselves or loved ones that bare the brunt of this emotion. Although appropriate, excessive or chronic anger can be destructive to glycemic control, mental health, and personal relationships (Rubin et al., 1997).

Fear and Anxiety   After leaving the protective state of denial and the feeling of control sometimes associated with anger, the fearful reality of diabetes becomes clear (S. Cox, 1994). Pollin (1995) noted that individuals with chronic diseases like diabetes often fear the loss of control, self-image, and independence, as well as being stigmatized, abandoned, isolated, disabled, or overwhelmed by anger. Diabetes can be a constant reminder of the fragility of life and inevitable mortality, with the unrelenting treatment protocols robbing a person of traditional defense mechanisms like repression and suppression. As with denial and anger, diabetes warrants a reasonable dose of fear and respect (Hendricks & Hendricks, 1998). Nevertheless, fear as well as anxiety has a limited capacity to motivate treatment compliance or behavioral changes and may be debilitating, leading to avoidance, inaction, and depression (Rubin et al., 1997).

Guilt   Guilt and self-blame are also common emotions among people with diabetes (S. Cox, 1994; Rubin et al., 1997). Because "bad things" are supposed to happen to "bad people," adults with diabetes may blame themselves (because of obesity, improper diets, and stress) for being diagnosed and for poor glycemic control or when diabetic complications surface. Parents may feel a sense of guilt for genetically "passing on" diabetes to their children. Dependency can be a source of guilt among those who feel they are a burden to family, friends, or health care providers (Rubin et al., 1997). Guilt also can stem from self-care mistakes, inactivity, procrastination, or overindulgence or as a chronic means of penance (Amir, Rabin, & Galatzer, 1990). As with other emotions, guilt is appropriate and purposive, serving as an indicator for deviations from treatment protocols. Chronic guilt, however, is destructive; perfect glycemic control is a laudable goal, but unreachable given the unpredictable nature of diabetes.

Grief and Sadness   Grief and sadness are expected reactions to the losses encountered from diabetes (S. Cox, 1994; Rubin et al., 1997). As Zemars (1984) suggested, someone with a chronic illness "can never fully return to his or her preillness state of health. Thus the experience of loss ensues" (p. 44). Rolland (1994) suggested that patients and families facing threatened loss of control, disruption of individual role functions, and the ambiguity of disease and its treatment might lead to "frenetic behavior or immobilization." Sadness also may accompany the loss of bodily control, behavioral freedom, culinary culture, family traditions, uncertainty for the future, or loss of vision or renal function, or an amputated limb (Rubin et al., 1997). A period of "bereavement" for losses is appropriate, although if unchecked and without resolution may lead to depression (Peyrot & Rubin, 1999).

Depression   Under the circumstances it is understandable why adults with diabetes might feel overwhelmed, vulnerable, and out of control, which can lead to clinical depression (Peyrot & Rubin, 1999; Rubin et al., 1997). Adults with diabetes are five times as likely as the general public to suffer from major depression at least once during their lifetime (Carney, 1998). Among adults with poorly controlled diabetes, the presence of depression can go undetected by health care providers who mistake its symptoms for those of hyperglycemia (characterized by fatigue and sleepiness) and hypoglycemia (characterized by shaky or anxious feelings, despondence, lethargy, and agitation) (Jacobson, 1996). In contrast, patients may attribute physiological symptoms of poor glycemic control to their psychological disposition. Depression is a debilitating illness, but when it is combined with diabetes, its effects (for example, depressed mood, decreases in activity, fatigue, anhedonia, weight loss or gain, sleep disturbance, and poor concentration) can have disastrous consequences for a person's glucose control, and for some may lead to an untimely death. As Black and Markidel (1999) found among older Mexican Americans, when depression was comorbid with diabetes, mortality rates were substantially higher than those in comparable groups. Psychopharmacological interventions may have negative side effects as well, with antidepressants increasing or decrease glucose levels either physiologically or through changes in eating and exercise habits (Jacobson, 1996).

Emotional challenges may be complicated by several factors. First, unresolved personal issues, marital or family difficulties, and preexisting psychological or alcohol and substance abuse problems can prolong and complicate emotional balance (Rolland, 1994). Normal adult development (for example, identity, career, and retirement) or common life events (for example, marriage, divorce, birth, and death) of patients, family, or friends also can affect emotional reactions. Finally, the severity of the diabetes, presence of complications, or level or ease of glycemic control can complicate these challenging emotions (Lustman, Freedland, Griffith, & Clouse, 1998).

Assuming a counseling role, a social worker is invaluable in aiding patients through these typical emotional challenges. Initially, this may be accomplished by assessing the patient and family's illness belief systems and previous coping patterns related to emotions (Ivinson, 1995; Rolland, 1994). A social worker may also educate patients and families about these emotional challenges within a psychosocial module during a diabetes self-care class or through individual or family counseling sessions—normalizing responses, identifying resources, and enabling coping mechanisms (Piening, 1984). In addition, patients can be helped or educated to differentiate between physical sensations associated with high and low blood glucose levels (such as anxiousness, irritability, and lethargy) versus psychosocially based emotion, with the former easily confused with the latter (Rubin et al., 1997).

Psychoeducational groups for newly diagnosed patients or those with ongoing challenges with self-care skills, self-esteem, or assertiveness or those making the transition from professional to self-based care also are advisable (Rabin et al., 1986). More intensive social work interventions may be necessary when these emotional challenges are complicated by preexisting mental health concerns.

As a therapist, the social worker may practice independently or in conjunction with other professionals (such as psychiatrists and psychologists) to treat more serious mental health issues inhibiting the management of diabetes. In this role a social work practitioner may screen and treat illnesses with high rates of comorbidity among diabetes patients, such as major depression or eating and anxiety disorders (Jacobson, 1996). The social worker also may ensure the management of preexisting chronic mental illnesses like schizophrenia, bipolar disorder, and alcohol or substance abuse. Often the stress of diabetes or complications may exacerbate existing social or work dysfunctions or revive unresolved personal issues (for example, adjustment disorders and identity and self-esteem problems) or family issues (for example, domestic violence and role conflict or strain), also necessitating social work interventions. For some, the potential or actual occurrence of diabetic complications such as amputations, blindness, and kidney failure can prove overwhelming, leading to suicide ideation or attempts. Serious treatment noncompliance may require skilled therapeutic interventions to identify and deal with psychological obstacles within the individual or family systems. Strained supportive resources and relationships also may require assistance to restore personal and family functioning.

Diabetic Complications

Diabetes itself presents several short-term and long-term challenges. Hypoglycemia, an abrupt drop in blood sugars, typically less than 50 mg/dL, although the precise level when symptoms occur varies from person to person, is the most prevalent and feared short-term diabetic complication (Hillson, 1996). As defined by Davidson et al. (1998), symptoms may include feeling shaky; being tired, hungry, and sweaty; having blurred vision, headaches, and numbness or tingling in mouth or lips; and experiencing irritability, confusion, or combativeness. In some instances an individual may be unable to swallow or may become unconscious, requiring an injection of glucagon. By taking too much medication or insulin, skipping or eating meals at the wrong time, or engaging in excessive physical activity, patients frequently "overtreat" hypoglycemia, raising glucose levels too high. Even with correct treatment, clients typically feel ill for hours or a full day after a low blood sugar episode.

In contrast, hyperglycemia is persistently elevated glucose levels, markedly above normal, more than 180 mg/dL, often the result of treatment noncompliance such as eating too much or engaging in insufficient exercise, taking inadequate medication or insulin, being physically ill, or being psychologically stressed (Davidson et al., 1998). Patients often experience thirst, hunger, increased urination, dry itchy skin, feeling tired or sleepy, vision problems, infections, or slow-healing cuts and sores. A serious consequence of prolonged hyperglycemia is a condition called ketoacidosis, the dangerous accumulation of an acidic byproduct called ketones from the body's use of fat as a source of energy (Hillson, 1996). Indicated by blood sugars above 240 mg/dL and ketones in the urine, patients experience symptoms similar to hyperglycemia as well as weight loss, upset stomach, vomiting, fruity-smelling breath, or rapid or shallow respirations. Untreated, ketoacidosis inflicts serious damage to the body and may lead to a coma or death (CDC, 1999). In the long run, poorly controlled glucose levels cause irreversible damage, often unknowingly until long-term complications arise.

Regardless of how infrequently these complications occur, they demonstrate the ability of diabetes to seize control of the body and interrupt life, for both newly diagnosed and experienced patients regardless of glycemic control. Frequent reoccurrences may signal deteriorating glucose control and necessitate reevaluation of diet and activities, closer monitoring, or intensive care management. Although diabetes can be managed effectively and these short-term complications delayed for years, it is a progressive chronic disease and, unfortunately, long-term complications (for example, cardiovascular diseases, neuropathy, and retinopathy) inevitably occur, disturbing experiences that can be aided by either individual or group-based counseling.

As diabetes case (care) managers, social workers may provide an impressive array of services. They can coordinate a comprehensive assessment, treatment plan, and intervention, striving for an optimal level of collaboration among professionals, patients, and families. Financially, social work case management can effectively and efficiently use community resources, creating an optimal environment that promotes glycemic control to delay complications and reduce hospitalizations (Kanter, 1996). They also can establish continuity of care through a comprehensive approach by coordinating interagency efforts, providing ongoing evaluations, and monitoring planned follow-ups. In short, this amalgamation of roles maximizes patient and family functioning through an informed appreciation and skilled assistance with diabetic challenges.

Conclusion

Adults with diabetes confront a remarkable array of challenges, from both the disease and its treatment. Given the nature of diabetes, its escalating presence, and patient-dependent treatment regimen, social workers have immense potential to improve the lives of people facing this chronic illness through well-established roles of educator, advocate, counselor, therapist, community developer, and resource broker. Although social workers in traditional health care settings such as acute and rehabilitation hospitals, clinics, dialysis units, home health, or hospice agencies must increase their awareness of and involvement with diabetes, the same holds true for social work practitioners in other areas of practice (for example, adult protection, mental health, substance abuse, and public health). Social work researchers also should become more involved by developing and testing interventions, exploring compliance and outcome predictors, and improving empirical understanding of the psychosocial experiences of adults dealing with the challenges of diabetes mellitus.

An earlier version of this article was presented at the Tennessee Conference on Social Welfare, March 1999, Nashville. The author thanks the anonymous reviewers of *Health & Social Work*, social work scholar Dr. John Orme, endocrinologist Dr. Douglas Gordon, diabetes educator Claire Groff, dietician Charlotte Kilburn, and director Peggy Bourgeois and staff of the Diabetes Center, Memphis, for their numerous contributions in the conceptual development and writing of this article.

References

Aikens, J. E., Wallander, J. L., Bell, D. S., & McNorton, A. (1994). A nomothetic-idiographic study of daily psychological stress and blood glucose in women with Type 1 diabetes mellitus. *Journal of Behavioral Medicine, 17*, 535–548.

American Association of Diabetes Educators. (1997). AADE position statement: Education for continuous subcutaneous insulin infusion pump users. *Diabetes Education, 23* 397–398.

American Diabetes Association. (1998). Economic consequences of diabetes mellitus in the U.S. in 1997. *Diabetes Care, 21*, 296–309.

American Diabetes Association. (1999a). Diabetes & exercise. *Diabetes Care, 22*(Suppl. 1), S1–S11.

American Diabetes Association. (1999b). Implications of the United Kingdom prospective diabetes study. *Diabetes Care, 22*(Suppl. 1), S27–S31.

American Diabetes Association. (1999c). Nutrition recommendations and principles for people with diabetes mellitus (Position Statement). *Diabetes Care, 22*(Suppl. 1), S42–S45.

American Dietetic Association. (1998). Position of the American Dietetic Association: Domestic food and nutrition security. *Journal of the American Dietetic Association, 98*, 337–342.

Amir, S., Rabin, C., & Galatzer, A. (1990). Cognitive and behavioral determinants of compliance in diabetics. *Health & Social Work, 15*, 144–151.

Andrews, M., Nord, M., Bickel, G., & Carlson, S. (1999). *Household food security in the United States, 1999* (U.S. Department of Agriculture, Economic Research Service). Washington, DC: U.S. Government Printing Office.

Assal, J. P., Jacquemet, S., & Morel, Y. (1997). The added value of therapy in diabetes: The education of patients for self-management. *Metabolism, 46*(Suppl. 1), 61–64.

Auslander, W. F., Anderson, B. J., Bubb, J., Jung, K. C., & Santiago, J. V. (1990). Risk factors in diabetic children: A prospective study from diagnosis. *Health & Social Work, 15*, 133–142.

Auslander, W. F., Bubb, J., Rogge, M., & Santiago, J. V. (1993). Family stress and resources: Potential areas of intervention in children recently diagnosed with diabetes. *Health & Social Work, 18* 101–113.

Auslander, W. F., Thompson, S. J., Dreitzer, D., & Santiago, J. V. (1997). Mothers' satisfaction with medical care: Perceptions of racism, family stress, and medical outcomes in children with diabetes. *Health & Social Work, 22*, 190–199.

Black, S. A., & Markidel, K. S. (1999). Depressive symptoms and mortality in older Mexican Americans. *Annals of Epidemiology, 9*, 45–52.

Blackburn, S. L., Piper, K., Wooldridge, T., Hoag, J. D., & Hanan, S. L. (1978). Diabetic patients on hemodialysis. *Health & Social Work, 3*, 91–104.

Campbell, C. C. (1991). Food insecurity: A nutritional outcome or a predictor variable? *Journal of Nutrition, 121*, 408–415.

Carney, C. (1998). Diabetes mellitus and major depressive disorder: An overview of prevalence, complications, and treatment. *Depression and Anxiety, 7*, 149–157.

Centers for Disease Control and Prevention. (1998). *National diabetes fact sheet: National estimates and general information on diabetes in the United States* (rev. ed.). Washington, DC: U.S. Government Printing Office.

Centers for Disease Control and Prevention. (1999). *Diabetes: A serious public health problem* (CDC Publication No. PDF-268K). Washington, DC: U.S. Government Printing Office.

Cerveny, J. D., Leder, R. D., & Weart, C. W. (1998). Issues surrounding tight glycemic control with Type II diabetes mellitus. *Annals of Pharmacotherapy, 32*, 896–905.

Clement, S. (1995). Diabetes self-management education. *Diabetes Care, 18*, 1204–1214.

Cox, S. (1994). How I coped emotionally with diabetes in my family. *Professional Care of Mother and Child, 4*, 139–141.

Cox, W. M., Blount, J. P., Crowe, P. A., & Singh, S. P. (1996). Diabetic patients' alcohol use and quality of life: Relationships with prescribed treatment compliance among older males. *Alcoholism, Clinical and Experimental Research, 20*, 327–331.

Dabelea, D., Pettitt, D. J., Jones, K. L., & Arslanian, S. A. (1999). Type 2 diabetes mellitus in minority children and adolescents:

An emerging problem. *Endocrinology and Metabolism Clinics of North America, 28,* 709–729.

Daley, B. J. (1992). Sponsorship for adolescents with diabetes. *Health & Social Work, 17,* 173–182.

Davidson, M. B., Davidson, A. I., & Richard, Z. (Eds.). (1998). *Diabetes mellitus: Diagnosis and treatment* (4th ed.). Philadelphia: W. B. Saunders.

Delamater, A. M., Kurtz, S. M., Bubb, J., White, N. H., & Santiago, J. V. (1987). Stress and coping in relation to metabolic control of adolescents with Type I diabetes. *Journal of Developmental and Behavioral Pediatrics, 8,* 136–140.

Dunn, F. L., Nathan, D. M., Scavini, M., Selam, J. L., & Wingrove, T. G. (1997). Long-term therapy of IDDM with an implantable insulin pump: The implantable insulin pump trial study group. *Diabetes Care, 20,* 59–63.

Ell, K., & Northen, H. (1990). *Families and health care: Psychosocial practice.* New York: Aldine de Gruyter.

Fair, R. G. (1993). The interdisciplinary care of children with insulin dependent diabetes mellitus. *Child and Adolescent Social Work Journal, 10,* 441–453.

Feinglos, M. N., & Bethel, M. A. (1998). Treatment of Type 2 diabetes mellitus. *Medical Clinics of North America, 82,* 757–790.

Franz, M. J., Horton, E. D., Bantle, J. P., Beebe, C A., Brunzell, J. D., Coulston, A. M., Henry, R. R., Hoogwerf, B. J., & Stacpoole, P. W. (1994). Nutrition principles for the management of diabetes and related complications (tech. rev.). *Diabetes Care, 17,* 490–518.

Glasgow, R. E. (1995). A practical model of diabetes management and education. *Diabetes Care, 18,* 117–126.

Graziani, C., Rosenthal, M. P., & Diamond, J. J. (1999). Diabetes education program use and patient-perceived barriers to attendance. *Family Medicine, 31,* 358–363.

Greenberg, J. S. (1993). *Comprehensive stress management* (4th ed.). Dubuque, IA: WCB Brown & Benchmark.

Harris, M. I. (1995a). Classification, diagnostic criteria and screening for diabetes. In *Diabetes in America* (NIH Publication No. 95-1468, 2nd ed., pp. 15–36). Washington, DC: U.S. Government Printing Office.

Harris, M. I. (1995b). Summary. In *Diabetes in America* (NIH Publication No. 95-1468, 2nd ed., pp. 1–13). Washington, DC: U.S. Government Printing Office.

Hendricks, L. E., & Hendricks, R. T. (1998). Greatest fears of Type I and Type II patients

about having diabetes: Implications for diabetes educators. *Diabetes Education, 24,* 168–173.

Herman, W. H., & Eastman, R. C. (1998). The effects of treatment on the direct costs of diabetes. *Diabetes Care, 21*(Suppl. 3), C19–C24.

Hill, F. M., & Hynes, J. E. (1980). Fostering self-esteem in families with diabetic children. *Child Welfare, 59,* 576–582.

Hillson, R. (1996). *Practical diabetes care.* New York: Oxford University Press.

Ivinson, M. H. (1995). The emotional world of the diabetic patient. *Diabetic Medicine, 12,* 113–116.

Jacobson, A. M. (1996). The psychological care for patients with insulin dependent diabetes mellitus. *New England Journal of Medicine, 334,* 1249–1253.

Kanter, J. (1996). Depression, diabetes and despair: Clinical case management in a managed care context. *Smith College Studies in Social Work, 66,* 358–369.

Kenny, S. J., Aubert, R. E., & Geiss, L. S. (1995). Prevalence and incidence of non-insulin dependent diabetes. In *Diabetes in America* (NIH Publication No. 95–1468, 2nd ed., pp. 47–65). Washington, DC: U.S. Government Printing Office.

Kushner, H. S., & Fetterman, B. V. (1997). *When bad things happen to good people.* New York: Schocken Books.

LaPorte, R. E., Matsushima, M., & Chang, Y. (1995). Prevalence and incidence of insulin-dependent diabetes. In *Diabetes in America* (NIH Publication No. 95-1468, 2nd ed., pp. 37–45). Washington, DC: U.S. Government Printing Office.

Lipkin, E. (1999). New strategies for the treatment of Type II diabetes. *Journal of the American Dietician Association, 99,* 39–44.

Lorenz, R. A. (1999). Modern insulin therapy for Type I diabetes mellitus. *Primary Care, 26,* 917–929.

Lustman, P., Freedland, K., Griffith, L., & Clouse, R. (1998). Predicting response to cognitive behavior therapy of depression in Type II diabetes. *General Hospital Psychiatry, 20,* 302–306.

Maillet, N. A., D'Eramo-Melkus, G., & Spollett, G. (1996). Using focus groups to characterize the health beliefs and practices of black women with non-insulin-dependent diabetes. *Diabetes Education, 22,* 39–46.

National Institutes of Health. (1995). *Diabetes in America* (NIH Publication No. 95-1468, 2nd ed.). Washington, DC: U.S. Government Printing Office.

Nuttall, F. Q., & Chasuk, R. M. (1998). Nutrition and the management of Type II diabetes. *Journal of Family Practice,* 47(Suppl.), S45–S53.

Overland, J. E., Hoskins, P. L., McGill, M. J., & Yue, D. K. (1993). Low literacy: A problem in diabetes education. *Diabetic Medicine, 10,* 847–850.

Peyrot, M. F., & McMurry, J. F. (1992). Stress buffering and glycemic control: The role of coping styles. *Diabetes Care, 15,* 842–846.

Peyrot, M. F., & Rubin, R. R. (1999). Persistence of depressive symptoms in diabetic adults. *Diabetes Care, 2,* 448–452.

Piening, S. (1984). Family stress in diabetic renal failure. *Health & Social Work, 9,* 134–150.

Pollin, I. (1995). *Medical crisis counseling: Short-term therapy for long-term illness.* New York: Norton.

Quatromoni, P. A., Millbauer, M., Posner, B. M., Carballeira, N. P., Brunt, M., & Chipkin, S. R. (1994). Use of focus groups to explore nutrition practices and health beliefs of urban Caribbean Latinos with diabetes. *Diabetes Care, 17,* 869–873.

Rabin, C., Amir S., Nardi, R., & Ovadia, B. (1986). Compliance and control: Issues in group training for diabetics. *Health & Social Work, 11,* 141–150.

Rewers, M., & Hamman, R. F. (1995). Risk factors for non-insulin-dependent diabetes. In *Diabetes in America* (NIH Publication No. 95-1468, 2nd ed., pp. 179–200). Washington, DC: U.S. Government Printing Office.

Rimm, E. B., Manson, J. E., Stampfer, M. J., Colditz, G. A., Willett, W. C., Rosner, B., Hennekens, C. H., & Speizer, F. E. (1993). Cigarette smoking and the risk of diabetes in women. *American Journal of Public Health, 83,* 211–214.

Rolland, J. S. (1984). Toward a psychosocial typology of chronic and life-threatening illness. *Family Systems Medicine, 2,* 245–262.

Rolland, J. S. (1994). *Families, illness, and disability: An integrative treatment model.* New York: Basic Books.

Rubin, R. R., Biermann, J., & Toohey, B. (1997). *Psyching out diabetes: A positive approach to your negative emotions.* Los Angeles: Lowell House.

Safyer, A. W., Hauser, S. T., Jacobson, A. M., Bliss, R., Herskowitz, R. D., Wolfsdorf, J. I., & Wertlieb, D. (1993). The impact of the family on diabetes adjustment: A developmental perspective. *Child & Adolescent Social Work Journal, 10,* 123–140.

Sidell, N. L. (1997). Adult adjustment of chronic disease: A review of the literature. *Health & Social Work, 22,* 5–11.

Swift, C. S., Armstrong, J. E., Beerman, K. A., Campbell, R. K., & Pond-Smith, D. (1995). Attitudes and beliefs about exercise among persons with non-insulin-dependent diabetes. *Diabetes Education, 21,* 533–540.

Toobert, D. J., Glasgow, R. E. (1991). Problem solving and diabetes self-care. *Journal of Behavioral Medicine, 14,* 71–86.

Vest, G. W., Ronnau, J., Lopez, B. R., & Gonzalez, G. (1997). Alternative health practices in ethnically diverse rural areas: A collaborative research project. *Health & Social Work, 22,* 95–100.

Wdowik, M. J., Kendall, P. A., & Harris, M. A. (1997). College students with diabetes: Using focus groups and interviews to determine psychosocial issues and barriers to control. *Diabetes Education, 23,* 558–562.

Zemars, I. S. (1984). Adjustment to health loss: Implications for psychosocial treatment. In S. E. Milligan (Ed.), *Community health care for chronic physical illness: Issues and models* (pp. 44–48). Cleveland: Case Western Reserve University Press.

Judith Dobrof
Arlene Dolinko
Elena Lichtiger
Jaime Uribarri
Irwin Epstein

41

Dialysis Patient Characteristics and Outcomes: The Complexity of Social Work Practice with the End-Stage Renal Disease Population

Measuring patient outcomes has become especially crucial in the competitive world of healthcare, where patient outcomes are studied in relation to medical and cost effectiveness (Epstein, Zilberfein, & Snyder, 1997; Nurius & Vourlekis, 1997). For patients with end-stage renal disease (ESRD), understanding and reporting on the interconnection between dialysis patient characteristics and outcomes can inform social workers' interventions and advocacy efforts in support of continued federally mandated involvement of professional social workers with this population. Because psychosocial factors have a strong influence on how patients progress on dialysis (Vourlekis & Rivera-Mizzoni, 1997), and social work interventions can affect patients' psychosocial situation (Furr, 1998), social work services are critical to positive outcomes among the ESRD population.

This article describes a demonstration project funded by the National Kidney Foundation's Council of Nephrology Social Workers (CNSW) and is designed to employ "clinical data-mining" (Epstein, 1998) to explore the association of psychosocial risk and resiliency factors, social work interventions, and adherence and other health-related outcomes among hemodialysis and peritoneal dialysis patients. In doing so, it demonstrates the complexity of social work interventions with dialysis patients and the crucial role for social workers in enhancing patient outcomes.

Demographic and Psychosocial Factors and Health-Related Outcomes Among Dialysis Patients

A substantial literature centers on the interplay between demographic and psychosocial characteristics and ESRD outcomes. Much of this literature focuses specifically on adherence because of its obvious relationship to ESRD patients' morbidity, mortality, and overall quality of life. Measurements of compliance generally focus on adherence to (1) restrictions in diet and fluid intake; (2) the medication regimen; and (3) treatment appointment schedules (Bame, Petersen, & Wray, 1993; Brownbridge & Fielding, 1994; Christensen, Benotsch, & Smith, 1997; Davis, Tucker, & Fennel, 1996; Furr, 1998; Kaplan De-Nour & Czaczkes, 1972; Kimmel et al., 1998; Leggat et al., 1998; McKevitt, Jones, Lane, & Marion, 1990). Family and social support (Boyer, Friend, Chlouverakis & Kaloyanides, 1990; Burton, Kline, Lindsay, & Heidenheim, 1988; Davis et al., 1996; Kimmel et al., 1998; Levenson & Glocheski, 1991; O'Brien, 1990), demographic characteristics (Bame et al., 1993; Christensen et al., 1997; Davis et al., 1996; Leggat et al., 1998), and psychological variables (Brownbridge & Fielding, 1994; Kaplan De-Nour & Czaczkes, 1972; Kimmel, Weihs, & Peterson, 1993; Levenson & Glocheski, 1991) are among many factors associated with patient compliance. Other studies focus on outcomes such as quality of life (Kutner & Brogan, 1990, 1994; Wolcott, Nissenson, & Landsverk, 1988; Killingworth & Akker, 1996) and general health status (Ozminkowski, White, Hassol, & Murphy, 1997). Finally, there are articles that attend to the kinds of interventions that health care providers, including social workers, can use to enhance outcomes among renal patients (Furr, 1998; Gorman & Anderson, 1982; Hener, Weisenberg, & Har-Even, 1996; Homedes, 1991; Kirschenbaum, 1991; Streltzer & Hassell, 1988; Vourlekis & Rivera-Mizzoni, 1997).

This study is unique in focusing on an urban, low-income, minority population; in employing an interdisciplinary research team to guide the research process; in retrospectively reviewing available data contained within medical records; and in focusing on interventions and outcomes over time rather than at one point in patients' dialysis history.

The Setting

The study project took place at Mount Sinai Hospital, a large, urban academic medical center with approximately 950 inpatient beds and a comprehensive ambulatory care division. The hospital is surrounded by very diverse neighborhoods, from middle class and wealthy to its catchment area that includes a very poor, largely Latino community. The study focused on patients at two dialysis sites: one that is hospital-based and includes approximately 35 hemodialysis and 65 peritoneal dialysis patients, and a nearby satellite unit that has capacity for 190 hemodialysis patients.

The Study Population

The study population consisted of 100 adult hemodialysis and peritoneal dialysis patients who began dialysis between December 1, 1996, and April 1, 1998, *and* received at least two months of outpatient dialysis at either of the sites. Only those who had been dialyzed on an outpatient basis for at least two months were included because, in general, after two months of outpatient dialysis, patients would be assumed to be medically and psychosocially stable and to have received some education and training regarding the treatment regimen. Therefore, it was presumed that medical and psychosocial outcome measures would have increased stability. Eight patients'

medical records were unable to be located and they were therefore not included in the study. All other patients who met these criteria were included until the sample numbered 100 patients. (Approximately five other patients met the criteria.) The sample was limited to *100* patients to facilitate data collection and analysis of findings in this demonstration project.

Methodology

Using Available Clinical Information

The methodology for the project parallels an approach successfully employed at Mount Sinai Hospital, utilizing routinely available patient chart information to study retrospectively psychosocial risk factors and treatment outcomes among liver transplant patients (Epstein et al., 1997). A retrospective methodology using available data has several advantages:

1. It is less intrusive to patients and staff than questionnaires administered directly to patients. Daily patient care routines are less likely to be disrupted when data collection focuses on available medical record documentation rather than direct contact with patients (Epstein et al., 1997).
2. The problems presented by a potentially low response rate and the time involved in administering a questionnaire to patients can be avoided and data can be gathered more quickly.
3. Data are potentially more agency and practice relevant because they are generated from actual documentation by the medical and social work team (Epstein et al., 1997).

The Interdisciplinary Research Team

The interdisciplinary research team guiding the process included the medical director of Mount Sinai Hospital's on-site dialysis unit, the unit's nurse manager, three master's-level renal social workers with a combined experience of nine years with dialysis patients, a renal nutritionist, and the lead author, who is an assistant director in the Department of Social Work Services with clinical and supervisory experience in nephrology social work. A research consultant from Hunter College School of Social Work who facilitated the liver transplant study was consultant to the team throughout the project. The team met periodically throughout the study and focused on establishing the study population, developing the data collection instrument, planning for data analysis, and analyzing and interpreting the findings. The purpose of involving an interdisciplinary team, including social workers, throughout the research process was that it would enhance cohesiveness among them; provide clarity as to professional decision making, roles, and practice; and enhance the validity of the study instrument and outcomes (Ben Shahar, Auslander, & Cohen, 1995; Epstein et al., 1997). Moreover, the credibility of the findings would be especially enhanced since this process captures the medical and psychosocial perspectives of staff actually caring for dialysis patients.

The Data Collection Instrument

A quantitative data collection instrument from the liver transplant study was revised by the research team to reflect psychosocial determinants, social work interventions, and outcomes related to ESRD patients. Altering an existing instrument that had been successfully implemented in a previous study was more time- and cost-efficient than developing an entirely new one for this study. In addition, use of the instrument will facilitate comparison and replication in the future at other sites.

The instrument measures three sets of variables:

Independent variables: from medical record demographic information and initial medical and psychosocial assessments. They include demographic data, psychosocial factors (e.g., employment history, living situation), and medical information (e.g., comorbid conditions, time on dialysis).

Intervening variables: include interventions performed by social work staff in order to address patients' presenting problems and documented in initial psychosocial assessments, ongoing progress notes, and patients' care goals. Examples are individual, family, and group counseling and referral for benefits and community-based services.

Outcome variables: adherence and other medical and psychosocial outcome measures obtained from available data such as ongoing medical or social work progress notes and patient care goals. Examples include missed treatments, emergency department visits, hospitalizations, and ability to perform activities of daily living (ADLs).

The data collection instrument identified patients through a code number so that patient confidentiality would be assured.

In addition to making the instrument ESRD relevant, other important revisions to the liver transplant instrument were made to enrich the research findings. First, the liver study had focused on data on patient obstacles to coping with transplant. In the dialysis study, resiliency factors to assist coping capacity were also captured. Social workers and other team members then benefit from knowing about both the problems that affect managing the illness and the strengths patients bring that can be reinforced (Barnard, 1994; McCubbin, McCubbin, Thompson, Han, & Allen, 1997).

Second, rather than collecting data at two points in time as had been done in the liver transplant study, social work interventions and outcome measures on the dialysis data collection instrument were divided into quarters to reflect more accurately patients' medical and psychosocial history. Data were collected beginning with the first outpatient dialysis treatment and collected for every quarter in which the patient received treatment. Since length of time on dialysis has been shown to be a significant predictor of compliance (Boyer et al., 1990; O'Brien, 1990), other outcomes can also be expected to differ according to how long patients have received treatment. It was hoped that designing the instrument to compare data at quarterly intervals would provide a more comprehensive picture of the complexity of the experience of being on dialysis over time and thus strengthen the findings and their practice implications.

Data Collection

Data were collected from March through July 1998 by four social workers who were presently working or had previously worked at the dialysis sites. Benefits of including social workers practicing with renal patients as data collectors include (1) enhanced validity and reliability since the data collectors knew the patients and families well and were intimately involved in the myriad medical and psychosocial issues they presented (Epstein, 1998); (2) time efficiency since the social work staff knew where variables in the medical record were recorded and therefore spent minimal time searching for data; (3) heightened commitment to the project since three of the social workers were also part of the research team and therefore were involved from conceptualization through data analysis.

The instrument was initially piloted to promote its reliability. To do so, all the social workers collected data on the same patient and then met to compare results. In general, there was agreement on most responses. When there were differences, they were resolved through discussions among staff. These meetings were also used to clarify any additional confusion about the instrument. Decision-making rules for data extraction were then formulated.

Table 41.1 Patient Characteristics

		%
Gender	Female	57
	Male	43
Age (mean 54)		
	Less than 40	23
	40 through 65	48
	More than 65	29
Ethnicity	African American	44
	Latino	34
	Caucasian	15
	Other	6
Marital Status	Never married	26
	Married/common law	25
	Separated/divorced	22
	Widowed	20
	Other	2
Lives alone		37
Lives with	Child	51
	Spouse	32
	Other	19
	Parent	12
	Sibling	12
	Other relative	8
	Significant other	6
	Home attendant	5
	Friend	2
Insurance	Medicaid	64
	Medicare	49
	Private insurance	23
	Other	3
	Uninsured	2
Primary Language	English	75
	Spanish	16
	Other	5
History of Employment	72	
Employed at Assessment	10	
Resumed Working	13	

Table 41.2 Resiliency Factors and Impediments Affecting Coping

Resiliency factors	%	
	69	Support by family/friends/caregiver
	48	Good family relationships
	27	Adequate physical functioning
	21	Ability to understand ESRD/treatment
	18	Cultural religious/spiritual beliefs
	17	General ability to cope with adversity
	16	Other
	9	Employment/student status
	8	Ability to maintain compliance
	7	Ability to cope with multiple medical illnesses
	3	Financial status
	1	Insurance status
	1	Adequate housing
	11	No strengths noted
Impediments		
	28	Coping with ESRD
	24	Other
	23	Poor physical functioning
	16	Coping with multiple medical illnesses
	13	Financial
	12	Insurance
	8	Lack of understanding of ESRD/treatment
	8	Mental health problems
	7	Coping with compliance requirements
	7	Lack of support by family/friends
	6	Bereavement
	5	Housing
	3	Poor family relationships
	2	Divorce/separation
	2	Substance abuse
	2	Language barrier
	1	Impact of cultural/religious beliefs on treatment
	1	Coping with other family member's illness
	0	Sexual problems
	0	Employment/student status
	21	No problems noted

Data Analysis

Using SPSS, univariate and bivariate analysis was done of patient characteristics, social work interventions, and patient outcomes. Analysis focused on associations among demographic, psychosocial, and medical factors and compliance and other health-related outcomes as well as detailed descriptions of the complex interventions used by social workers in working with dialysis patients and their families over time.

Findings

Patient Characteristics

Demographics: Table 41.1 describes the demographics of the study population at the time of the social workers' initial psychosocial assessment. The population is racially and ethnically diverse and primarily low-income. Although a little over a third (37%) live alone, of note is the fact that about half (51%) of patients live with a child (either adult child or younger) and almost a third (32%) with a spouse. Also noteworthy is the fact that although 72% have a history of employment, only 10% are employed in the initial days of treatment. Only 13% of patients who had previously worked resumed employment once they began dialysis treatments.

Resiliency factors and impediments affecting coping: Table 41.2 enumerates resiliency factors and impediments to coping cited in patients' initial psychosocial assessments. Resiliency factors are indicators of patients' strengths that helped them manage ESRD while impediments are factors that hindered coping. These factors were developed from the renal social workers' practice and from their knowledge of regularly documented patient strengths and problems. Thus, the predominant resiliency factor was support by family and friends (69%) and good family relationships (48%). Although many patients in this population had a general ability to cope with illness and adversity, in the social worker's initial assessment over a quarter (28%) were having general difficulty coping. Among approximately a quarter (24%) of the pa-

tients, a range of impediments listed in the "other" category included a variety of psychological, cognitive, and resource issues such as memory problems, anxiety, and lack of adequate transportation and home care services. No apparent strengths were noted in 11% of initial assessments, while in 21% of assessments, no impediments were noted.

Patient anxiety, depression, and need for assistance with ADLs: Table 41.3 demonstrates that in the first three months of patients' dialysis experience, many were assessed by social workers as being anxious and depressed. Thus, in the first quarter, 52% of patients were noted as anxious and 43% depressed. Although the percentage decreases over time, anxiety continued to present a problem for 30% of patients even after 10 months of treatment. In all quarters, about half of this population had need for some assistance with ADLs either from family members and friends or from formal home care services.

Social Work Interventions

Nephrology social workers provide psychosocial assessment, counseling, and referral to community services to assist patients on dialysis and their families (American Kidney Foundation, Council of Nephrology Social Workers, 1993). In the study population, 57% received social work counseling in the first three months of outpatient treatment. Although the degree to which social workers counseled patients declined over time, approximately a third (32–37%) of patients were receiving counseling in any one quarter in the first year of treatment. According to patient records, only 9% of family members received counseling in the first quarter with only a slight rise to 11% in months 4–6. (The questionable validity of this finding will be discussed later in the paper.)

In relation to the content of social work counseling, not surprisingly, patients often talked about issues directly related to being on dialysis, especially

Table 41.3 Percentage of Patients Experiencing Anxiety/Depression/Assistance with ADLs by Quarters*

	Months			
	1–3	4–6	7–9	10–Present
Anxiety	52 *(N = 90)*	30 *(N = 89)*	25 *(N = 58)*	30 *(N = 39)*
Depression	43 *(N = 88)*	18 *(N = 90)*	17 *(N = 58)*	10 *(N = 38)*
Some assistance	51 *(N = 95)*	51 *(N = 78)*	51 *(N = 51)*	47 *(N = 34)*

*Excluding nonapplicable/missing data/no notation

in the first few months of treatment. Thus, in the initial three months of treatment, almost three quarters (72%) of patients focused on coping with their diagnosis and treatment and slightly over a quarter (26%) discussed this topic in months 4–6. Other topics discussed in the first months of dialysis included how to cope with multiple medical illnesses (43%), decreased physical functioning (39%), mental health issues such as feelings of anxiety or depression (39%), difficulty understanding the ESRD diagnosis (32%), and how to maintain compliance with the treatment regimen (22%). Patients also focused on concrete issues: 38% in the first quarter focused on coping with insurance problems while 29% were concerned about financial issues. Over half (51–57%) of family members whose social work counseling was documented in the medical record in the first two quarters talked about their lack of understanding of ESRD treatments while 36% initially discussed how to cope with the patient's diagnosis and treatment. Similarly to patients, families also discussed more concrete issues: almost a third (31–32%) were having difficulty coping with financial problems in the first six months of treatment.

In addition to counseling, nephrology social workers provide assistance to patients and families through referral for community resources and benefits. Assistance was most frequently provided in the first quarter of treatment and often centered on referral to obtain government or work-related benefits, insurance, transportation, and home care services.

Nonadherence Indicators

Table 41.4 highlights the extent of nonadherence among this population. For hemodialysis patients, at least 25% missed their hemodialysis treatments a minimum of once per month in the first three quarters of outpatient treatment, increasing to 44% of patients in the fourth quarter. Patients also frequently asked to be taken off the hemodialysis machine early, with more than a third exhibiting this behavior in any of the four quarters. Although these behaviors may be associated with noncompliance, there are also other reasons that patients request an early end to treatment; for example, some experience painful leg cramps. Nonetheless, in relation to noncompliance with diet among hemodialysis and peritoneal dialysis study patients, a large majority (76–85%) were assessed by staff as failing to follow the prescribed diet regimen.

Patient Characteristics, Presenting Problems, and Nonadherence Outcomes

Bivariate analysis was done to explore the association of patient characteristics and the following outcomes (occurring at least once over four quarters): (1) emergency department (ED) visit(s); (2) hospitalization(s); (3) missed hemodialysis treatment(s); (4) asking to be taken off hemodialysis machine; (5) weight gain between treatments (hemodialysis) or between physician visits (peritoneal patients). Although ED visits and hospitalizations can result from a variety of factors, they were viewed as negative patient outcomes. Only those practice-relevant patient characteristics that are either closely or significantly associated ($p < .05$) with these outcomes will be discussed.

ED visits: Educational level and poor physical functioning were associated with patients coming to the ED at least once within the four quarters in which data were collected. Hence, patients with lower educational levels were more likely to go to the ED. More specifically, 61% of patients with a high school degree or less visited the ED as compared with 31% of those with at least some college experience (Chi-square = 7.159, df = 1, $p < .01$). Not surprisingly, 61% of patients with poor physical functioning as identified in their initial psychosocial assessment had at least one ED visit compared with 34% where this was not identified as a problem (Chi-square = 5.211, df = 1, $p < .05$).

Hospitalizations: Living with their child (most likely an adult child, given the age range of the pop-

Table 41.4 Percentage of Patients Exhibiting Nonadherence Behaviors by Quarters*

	Months			
	1–3	4–6	7–9	10–Present
Missed hemodialysis treatment				
	31 *(N = 79)*	28 *(N = 73)*	27 *(N = 44)*	44 *(N = 25)*
Asked to be taken off machine early	35 *(N = 79)*	37 *(N = 72)*	40 *(N = 42)*	41 *(N = 24)*
Diet nonadherence	83 *(N = 74)*	85 (N = 69)	76 (N = 46)	80 (N = 30)

*Excluding nonapplicable/missing data/no notation

ulation) significantly decreased chances of being hospitalized in the first four quarters of treatment. Thus, only 42% of patients who lived with a child were admitted to the hospital compared with 75% of patients who did not (Chi-square = 7.099, df = 1, p < .01).

Missed hemodialysis treatments: Age, Medicare status, insurance and financial problems, work status, and having difficulty coping with ESRD were significantly related to whether patients missed hemodialysis treatments. In relation to age, elderly patients were less likely to miss treatments than those less than 65 years of age. Only 35% of elderly patients missed treatments at least once in any quarter in contrast to 75% of patients aged 40–65, and 61% of patients less than 40 years of age (Chi-square = 11.928, df = 2, p < .01). Patients without Medicare at the start of dialysis and those that initially were experiencing insurance or financial problems were more likely to miss treatments. In other words, 78% without Medicare, as compared to 41% with, missed treatments (Chi-square = 14.733, df = 1, p < .01). All patients who reported having an insurance problem did not attend at least one treatment in comparison to 55% who were not concerned about insurance (Chi-square = 8.876, df = 1, p < .01), while 85% with financial problems missed treatments in contrast to 57% who did not have financial problems (Chi-square = 3.613, df = 1, p = .06). Regarding work status, patients with a history of paid employment and those who were working when dialysis was initiated had a higher incidence of missing hemodialysis appointments. Hence, 68% of patients with a work history missed treatments while only 33% who had not worked in the past missed treatments (Chi-square = 7.263, df = 2, p < .05). All patients working at the start of outpatient dialysis did not attend at least one treatment as compared with 57% who were not working (Chi-square = 7.000, df = 1, p < .01). Finally, 75% of those initially assessed by social workers as having difficulty coping with their disease were likely to miss treatments, while 55% not assessed has having this problem were noncompliant with their dialysis schedule (Chi-square = 3.388, df = 1, p = .07).

Taken off machine early: Insurance and financial issues were significantly related to patients asking to be taken off the hemodialysis machine at least five minutes early. Thus, 44% of patients without Medicaid (although possibly with other insurance) asked to be taken off early at least once in contrast to 12% with Medicaid (Chi-square = 12.890, df = 1, p < .01). Ninety-two percent of patients with insurance problems requested an early departure compared with 15% without insurance concerns (Chi-square = 33.801, df = 1, p < .01),

while 69% of patients with financial problems at the time of initial psychosocial assessment exhibited this behavior in comparison to 17% who were not experiencing financial problems (Chi-square = 16.492, df = 1, p < .01).

Weight gain: For hemodialysis and peritoneal dialysis patients, weight gain recorded at least once between appointments, a sign of noncompliance with fluid restrictions, is associated with race/ethnic background, Medicare status, and difficulty coping with multiple medical illnesses. Latino patients had the highest incidence of weight gain (44%) compared with African Americans (23%) and Caucasian or other racial/ethnic backgrounds (19%, Chi-square = 5.588, df = 2, p = .06). Patients with Medicare at the start of dialysis were less likely to experience weight gain over time than those without it. In other words, 20% of patients who had Medicare gained weight between appointments compared with 37% of those who did not have Medicare (Chi-square = 3.445, df = 1, p = .06). Finally, 50% of patients who were assessed by social workers as having difficulty managing multiple medical illnesses gained weight between appointments in contrast to 25% who were not assessed to have this problem (Chi-square = 3.951, df = 1, p < .05).

Discussion

The study sample is predominantly low income and African American or Latino, reflecting Mount Sinai Hospital's catchment area population. In relation to resiliency factors and impediments to coping, the majority of patients *do* have the familial and social supports that in other studies have been shown to buffer against depression, increase compliance, and contribute to positive health outcomes (Burton et al., 1988; Christensen et al., 1997; Furr, 1998; Kimmel et al., 1998). Some patients bring to the treatment a general ability to understand their diagnosis and treatment and an ability to cope with adversity, while, in contrast, others are having difficulty coping with the crisis of being diagnosed with ESRD. For some patients, resource issues surface, such as financial and insurance problems, that negatively affect illness management. Certainly, there is an intertwining of psychological strengths and impediments along with patients' "concrete" needs that point to the multifaceted complexity of social work practice with this population.

Most patients had documented strengths, demonstrating that social work staff are recognizing and reinforcing patient characteristics and beliefs that can contribute to success on dialysis.

However, one fifth of patients' initial psychosocial assessments had no recorded apparent obstacles to coping. This finding may stem from a variety of factors: (1) patients' reticence to discuss programs when they first are interviewed; (2) patients' ability to cope with ESRD because they have experience managing other chronic illnesses; (3) the benefits of increased access to care and socialization that dialysis affords some patients (Kutner & Brogan, 1990, 1994); and, (4) in some instances, social workers' failure to identify problems among some patients.

Concerning patients' mental health, it is important that social workers continually monitor levels of anxiety and depression since this study and others demonstrate their prevalence among nephrology patients (Davis, Krug, Dean, & Hong, 1990; Illic, Djordjevic, & Stefanovic, 1996; Kitner, Fair, & Kutner, 1985). Because depression especially has been shown to negatively influence patient outcomes (Furr, 1998), attention to patients' psychological status is crucial. Especially in the initial months, many of these patients were experiencing anxiety and depression and, social work researchers in our study acknowledged, counseling interventions at this time are especially intense. Although feelings of anxiety and depression lessened over time, a finding similar to Kutner et al.'s (1985), even after at least 10 months of treatment, almost a third continued to feel anxious. At the same time, social workers should also continually assess patients' capacity to perform ADLs since approximately half of the population needed some to total assistance over the months of the study period.

In relation to work status, although almost three quarters of patients have previously worked, very few are working at the time of diagnosis or are able to resume working. Considering that so many patients are of working age, for some, their nonworking status could possibly be attributed to a lack of education and skills for jobs that allow for the physical and time demands of the dialysis regimen. On the other hand, since vocational activity has been correlated with generally superior adaptation to dialysis (Wolcott et al., 1988), interventions to increase employment among this population would be an important area to work on in order to enhance patient outcomes.

Findings on social work interventions reflect the interconnection between working with patients and families to help them cope psychologically with illness and ensuring that resources are in place to help them manage the disease. Especially given that the study cohort comprises low-income, minority patients, many of whom experienced anxiety and depression along with more concrete financial and in-surance problems, social worker interventions frequently focused on providing psychosocial counseling at the same time that referrals were made for benefits and community services. Subsequent analysis of the data in this study will focus on the impact of social work counseling on health-related outcomes such as ED visits and hospitalizations.

One of the most striking findings is the extent to which patients received counseling, particularly early in their treatment. Over the four quarters, however, the help provided by the social workers gradually decreased, possibly because as patients became accustomed to dialysis, their need for intensive counseling and resource help might have decreased. However, certainly high levels of anxiety continued, as did patients' need for assistance with ADLs. Therefore, another, less positive explanation for decreasing social work intervention over time may concern the need for social work staff to prioritize among their caseload. More specifically, as the volume of patients for which renal social workers are responsible increases and presenting problems become more complex (LePard, 1991), social workers might be faced with "rationing" their services. It is possible that those newest to dialysis are seen frequently to assist them in coping with treatment and ensure that adequate resources are in place. Then, as they stabilize, social workers must turn to the next round of new patients who are viewed as most in need. Social workers may do much more outreach to newer patients, while relying on those who have been on dialysis longer to ask for help as needed. Within such a context, social workers should be particularly alert to patients who may not be able to request assistance and establish mechanisms that facilitate patient self-referral. High-risk criteria can be established using the findings of this study and others so that renal team members who see patients at every treatment can refer patients who warrant ongoing psychosocial intervention.

In contrast to the high rate of patient counseling, social workers seemed to rarely counsel family members even though the impact of ESRD is so profound (Burton et al., 1988). Social workers involved in the study thought that it was likely that the number of family members who receive counseling, especially in the first months of treatment, is actually much higher than the findings indicate, but that time constraints result in incomplete recording of family contacts.

In regard to adherence, patients' difficulties following the treatment and diet regimen is considered a major problem among the ESRD population (Bame et al., 1993; Kimmel et al., 1998; Leggat et al., 1998) and is particularly disturbing since it is associated with serious medical complications and decreased survival (Christensen et al., 1997). For the study population, it is also a striking phenomenon. Among the hemodialysis population, noncompliance actually increased over time, a finding consistent with Boyer et al.'s (1990) research. In her study of long-term hemodialysis patients, O'Brien (1990) argues that some experienced dialysis patients develop "reasoned" rather than "ritual" adherence (p. 209) that can actually be adaptive. In other words, patients become adept at knowing where they can "cheat" on their diet, for example, without encountering serious consequences. Leggat et al. (1998) hypothesize that patients who occasionally shorten hemodialysis treatments are a "little bit" (p. 144) noncompliant may benefit from gaining a greater sense of control without adverse consequences. Further analysis would be needed to ascertain whether nonadherence among this study's patients was "reasoned" or something more serious. However, renal team members might help patients to better adhere by identifying with the them areas of the treatment regimen with which they *must* comply to prevent negative outcomes and where they can be a "little bit" noncompliant.

Regarding the impact of educational level on patient outcomes, Ozminkowski et al. (1997) found that educational level did not significantly influence general health status dimensions for ESRD patients. However, our finding that lower educational level is significantly associated with ED visits has practice implications for our social workers and other renal team members. For example, proactive steps can be taken to teach patients with lower levels of education about compliance or ways to avoid emergency medical visits. In addition, patients with less education who may not have had access to comprehensive, continuous medical care prior to starting dialysis may require direction about how to contact their physician when they have a medical need that does not require an emergency room visit. Clearly, for some dialysis patients, emergent care is necessary. Further research would be needed to ascertain the reasons behind dialysis patients' ED visits and the extent to which they are medically necessary or related to issues such as nonadherence, alcoholism, or the inability to access a primary care physician (Parboosingh & Larsen, 1987; Pierce, Kellerman, & Oster, 1990).

Obviously, subsequent research would be needed to understand how living with a child is associated with decreased hospitalizations. However, an adult child who provides some amount of care to the dialysis patient and reinforces the need for adherence could possibly be a significant buffer against inpatient stays. Dialysis staff should there-fore support children and other family members who assist in caring for patients and target those patients who do not have these supports to ensure that efforts are made to prevent unnecessary hospitalizations.

Although missing at least one hemodialysis treatment per quarter was prevalent across the population, elderly patients (and patients with Medicare at the time of diagnosis, a potential proxy for elderly status) were more likely to adhere to their schedule than those under 65. Other research has also found that older patients are generally more compliant (Bame et al., 1993; Boyer et al., 1990; Christensen et al., 1997; Furr, 1998; Leggat et al., 1998). Our study found that patients 40–65 years of age were most likely to miss treatments, although younger patients also frequently did not adhere to the schedule. This finding is contrary to Leggat et al.'s that young adults tend to be the most noncompliant group on a variety of measures. Furr uses continuity theory to explain some outcome variations among dialysis patients. Thus, patients who can maintain some continuity in their previous psychosocial functioning will make a smoother adjustment to dialysis. In this context, patients under 65 may have multiple family and work-related responsibilities and may be more active (Kutner & Brogan, 1990), and, therefore, find the treatment schedule especially disruptive to their lifestyle. In addition, older patients may be more accustomed to managing chronic illnesses than younger and therefore adhere more easily. Similarly, patients who had a work history and/or were working at the time of diagnosis also were significantly more likely to miss treatment. The rigid treatment regimen for this group might have been especially jarring and a likely deterrent to complete adherence.

Significantly, insurance and financial issues were found to be associated with missing treatments, being taken off the machine early, and weight gain. Patients without Medicare and those experiencing insurance and financial problems at the time that treatment was initiated were generally less adherent on these measures. It is possible that patients with Medicare represent an older or disabled population that is more experienced coping with illness and therefore more readily adjust and adhere. Alternatively, patients without sufficient insurance and those with financial problems may represent the lower-income population that other studies have demonstrated has more difficulty managing (Bame et al., 1993; Furr, 1998). O'Brien (cited in Hoover, 1989) suggests that for low-income patients, having *enough* food may be more of a priority than following a prescribed diet. Certainly, insurance and financial problems may be a predic-

tor of noncompliance, and patients with these presenting issues should be viewed as high-risk for negative outcomes.

As expected, patients having difficulty coping
with ESRD were more likely to miss treatments,
and patients having difficulty coping with multiple
medical illnesses were more likely to experience
weight gain between appointments. These findings
point to social workers' accurate assessments of impediments to coping that can potentially have negative consequences. Patients having difficulty coping initially can also be identified as high-risk,
requiring intensive interventions to improve their
medical and psychosocial outcomes.

In relation to racial/ethnic background and adherence, Latino patients were more likely to experience weight gain between treatments than African
American, Caucasian, and other patients. In a recent study of Medicare ESRD Program beneficiaries, Ozminkowski et al. (1997) found that health
status among Hispanic persons was often lower
than other ethnic groups. It is possible that fluid
and diet restrictions may be particularly difficult for
certain patient groups to follow because of cultural
norms, therefore leading to poorer medical outcomes. Providing nutritional counseling that is culturally sensitive and working with patients to tailor diets to their specific needs, where possible, may
increase their ability to comply. However, in general, demographic variables such as race and ethnic background have not proven to be consistently
related to adherence among the dialysis population
(Bame et al., 1993; Christensen et al., 1997). For
example, in two studies of hemodialysis patients,
O'Brien (1990) did not find statistically significant
associations between race and adherence outcomes,
whereas Bame et al. report that African Americans
and Latinos were more compliant with fluid restrictions than White patients. Bame et al. point out
that demographic factors such as race are an efficient way to categorize patients at high risk but do
not explain reasons for nonadherence. They call for
further research that explores the associated factors
that motivate patients to comply with their treatment regimen.

Secondary Practice, Organizational, and Research Benefits

Using existing clinical information within an interdisciplinary team approach to explore patient characteristics, social work interventions, and outcomes
has considerable practice, organizational, and research benefits.

- Practice is enhanced as social workers reflec-
tively review their work and gain valuable insights into patients' behavior in relation to
dialysis (Ben Shahar et al., 1995). In addition,
social workers and other health care providers
can become more knowledgeable about patients potentially high risk for negative medical and psychosocial outcomes and tailor
their interventions accordingly.
- Chart reviews highlighted areas where documentation was vague or lacking, for example,
regarding adherence to the peritoneal dialysis
treatment regimen or in relation to some patients' impediments to coping. Certainly, social
workers involved in the project had a heightened awareness of the practice benefits, for example, of documenting in the initial assessment
problems in coping in order to work with patients toward enhanced outcomes. Furthermore, other renal staff and patients benefit if
practice documentation is strengthened.
- For the interdisciplinary team, working together on a creative project away from daily
patient care can enhance cohesion among
members (Epstein et al., 1997).
- For the social work supervisor, coordinating
the project resulted in closer working relationships with renal staff and an invitation to
attend biweekly renal management meetings.
- For the social work department, the leadership role of the department in outcomes research relating to patient care constitutes a
contribution to a critically important area of
research within the hospital.
- Finally, since ESRD is one of the few mandated areas of social work practice in health
care, it is fertile ground for research on social
work interventions and outcomes.

Although these findings are consistent with a
variety of other studies of the dialysis population,
they may not be applicable to other renal settings
with differing patient populations. However,
replication of this study at other sites would result in valuable information about outcomes
among other renal populations. Presently, the
study is being implemented in Israel and will possibly be replicated with a rural population in the
southern United States.

In addition, although there was sufficient information in medical records to make record review
a highly feasible methodological strategy, some aspects of patients' experiences were not documented,
and the lack of documentation could affect the validity of our findings. Finally, although there is po-

tential bias among practitioner-researchers studying their own patients, the secondary benefits to their practice and the efficiency brought to the project far outweighed the possible negative consequences.

Conclusion

Providing psychosocial services to dialysis patients involves complex tasks associated with helping patients and families manage an intricate and tedious treatment regimen and dramatic lifestyle changes. It entails an understanding of the impact of renal disease on patients and families and the strengths and programs they bring that affect their ability to manage the illness. It also requires that social workers be able to respond to the need for psychological support and at the same time attend to resource needs. Achievement of balance between the psychosocial and the concrete necessitates a high level of social work knowledge and skill. Equally demanding is the need in many cases to provide help to the patient and family members at the same time, a task that requires understanding of and ability to work with the family as a psychosocial system.

What can be so rewarding for renal social workers—and so challenging—is intervening with patients where the physical, psychological, and socioeconomic impacts are so intertwined. This study of available clinical information clearly demonstrates the complexity of social work practice with the ESRD population and the critical role of professionally trained social workers in contributing to positive patient outcomes.

This research was supported by a grant from the National Kidney Foundation's Council of Nephrology Social Workers.

References

Bame, S. I., Peterson, N., & Wray, N. P. (1993). Variation in hemodialysis patient compliance according to demographic characteristics. *Social Sciences Medicine, 37*(8), 1035–1043.

Barnard, C. P. (1994). Resiliency: A shift in our perception? *American Journal of Family Therapy, 22*(2), 135–144.

Ben Shahar, I., Auslander, G., & Cohen, M. (1995). Utilizing data to improve practice in hospital social work: A case study. *Social Work in Health Care, 20*(3), 99–111.

Boyer, C. B., Friend, R., Chlouverakis, G., & Kaloyanides, G. (1990). Social support and demographic factors influencing compliance of hemodialysis patients. *Journal of Applied Social Psychology, 20*, 1902–1918.

Brownbridge, G. & Fielding, D. M. (1994). Psychosocial adjustment and adherence to dialysis treatment regimes. *Pediatric Nephrology, 8*, 744–749.

Burton, H. J., Kline, S. A., Lindsay, R. M., & Heidenheim, P. (1988). The role of support in influencing outcome of end-stage renal disease. *General Hospital Psychiatry, 10*, 260–266.

Christensen, A. J., Benotsch, E. G., & Smith, T. W. (1997). Determinants of regimen adherence in renal dialysis. In D. S. Gochman (Ed.), *Handbook of health behavior research II: Provider determinants* (231–243). New York: Plenum Press.

Davis, B., Krug, D., Dean, R. S., & Hong, B. A. (1990). MMPI differences for renal, psychiatric, and general medical patients. *Journal of Clinical Psychology, 46*, 178–184.

Davis, M. C., Tucker, C. M., & Fennel, R. S. (1996). Family behavior, adaptation, and treatment adherence of pediatric nephrology patients. *Pediatric Nephrology, 10*, 160–166.

Epstein, I. (1998, January). *Using clinical information in practice-based social work research: Mining for silver while dreaming of gold.* Paper presented at the 2nd International Conference on Social Work in Health and Mental Health. Melbourne, Australia.

Epstein, I., Zilberfein, F., & Snyder, S. (1997). Using available information in practice-based outcomes research: A case study of psychosocial risk factors and liver transplant outcomes. In E. J. Mullen & J. L. Magnabosco (Eds., *Outcomes measurement in the human services: Cross-cutting issues and methods* (224–233). Washington D.C.: NASW Press.

Furr, L. A. (1998). Psycho-social aspects of serious renal disease and dialysis: A review of the literature. *Social Work in Health Care, 27*(3), 97–118.

Gorman, D., & Anderson, J. (1982). Initial shock: Impact of a life-threatening disease and ways to deal with it. *Social Work in Health Care, 7*(3), 37–46.

Hener, T., Weisenberg, & Har-Even, D. (1996). Supportive versus cognitive-behavioral intervention programs in achieving adjustment to home peritoneal kidney dialysis. *Journal of Consulting and Clinical Psychology, 64*(4), 731–741.

Homedes, N. (1991). Do we know how to influence patients' behavior? Tips to improve patients' adherence. *Family Practice, 8*(4), 412–423.

Hoover, H. (1989). Compliance in hemodialysis patients: A review of the literature. *Journal of the American Dietetic Association, 89*(7), 957–959.

Illic, S., Djordjevic, V., & Stefanovic, V. (1996). Psychological status of ESRD patients on hemodialysis. *Dialysis & Transplantation, 25*(12), 871–880.

Kaplan De-Nour, A. K. & Czaczkes, J. W. (1972). Personality factors in chronic hemodialysis patients causing noncompliance with medical regimen. *Psychosomatic Medicine, 34*(4), 333–344.

Killingworth, A., & Den Akker, O. (1996). The quality of life of renal dialysis patients: Trying to find the missing measurement. *International Journal of Nursing Studies, 33*(1), 107–120.

Kimmel, P. L., Peterson, R. A., Weihs, K. L., Simmens, S. J., Alleyne, S., Cruz, I., & Veis, J. H. (1998). Psychosocial factors, behavioral compliance and survival in urban hemodialysis patients. *Kidney International, 54*, 245–254.

Kimmel, P. L., Weihs, K., & Peterson, R. A. (1993). Survival in hemodialysis patients: The role of depression. *Journal of the American Society of Nephrology, 4*(1), 12–27.

Kirschenbaum, D. S. (1991). Integration of clinical psychology into hemodialysis programs. In J. J. Sweet, R. H. Rozensky, & S. M. Tovian (Eds.), *Handbook of clinical psychology in medical settings* (567–586). New York: Plenum Press.

Kutner, N. G., & Brogan, D. (1990). Expectations and psychological needs of elderly dialysis patients. *International Journal of Aging and Human Development, 31*, 239–249.

Kutner, N. G., & Brogan, D. (1994). Life quality as a function of aging with a chronic illness: Differential assessment by older Blacks and older Whites. *Research in Sociology of Health Care, 11*, 127–150.

Kutner, N. G., Fair, P. L., & Kutner, M. H. (1985). Assessing depression and anxiety in chronic dialysis patients. *Journal of Psychosomatic Research, 29*(1), 23–31.

LePard, L. F. (1991). Psychosocial aspects of dialysis in the '90's. *Dialysis & Transplantation, 20*(10), 600–601.

Leggat, J. E., Orzol, S. M., Hulbert-Shearon, T. E., Golper, T. A., Jones, C. A., Held, P. J., & Port, F. K. (1998). Noncompliance in hemodialysis: Predictors and survival analysis. *American Journal of Kidney Diseases, 32*(1), 139–145.

Levenson, J. L., & Glocheski, S. (1991). Psychological factors affecting end-stage renal disease: A review. *Psychosomatics, 32*(4), 382–389.

McCubbin, H. I., McCubbin, M. A., Thompson, A. I., Han, S. Y., & Allen, C. T. (1997). Families under stress: What makes them resilient. *Journal of Family and Consumer Sciences, 89*, 2–11.

McKevitt, P. M., Jones, J. F., Lane, D. A., & Marion, R. R. (1990). The elderly on dialysis: Some considerations in compliance. *American Journal of Kidney Diseases, 16*(4), 346–350.

National Kidney Foundation Council of Nephrology Social Workers. (1993). *Renal administrator's handbook on nephrology social work.* New York: National Kidney Foundation.

Nurius, P. S., & Vourlekis, B. S. (1997). Comments and questions for outcomes in measurement in mental health and social work. In E. J. Mullen & J. L. Magnabosco (Eds.), *Outcomes measurement in the human services: Cross-cutting issues and methods* (144–148). Washington, D.C.: NASW Press.

O'Brien, M. E. (1990). Compliance behavior and long-term maintenance dialysis. *American Journal of Kidney Diseases, 15*(3), 209–214.

Ozminkowski, R. J., White, A. J., Hassol, A., & Murphy, M. (1997). General health of end stage renal disease program beneficiaries. *Health Care Financing Review, 19*(1), 121–144.

Parboosingh, E. J. & Larsen, D. E. (1987). Factors influencing frequency and appropriateness of utilization of the emergency room by the elderly. *Medical Care, 25*(12), 1139–1146.

Pierce, J. M., Kellerman, A. L., & Oster, C. (1990). "Bounces": An analysis of short-term return visits to a public hospital emergency department. *Annals of Emergency Medicine, 19*(7), 752–757.

Streltzer, J. & Hassell, L. H. (1988). Noncompliant hemodialysis patients: A biopsychosocial approach. *General Hospital Psychiatry, 10*, 255–259.

Vourlekis, B. S., & Rivera-Mizzoni, R. A. (1997). Psychosocial problem assessment and end-stage renal disease patient outcomes. *Advances in Renal Replacement Therapy, 4*(2), 136–144.

Wolcott, D. L., Nissenson, A. R., & Landsverk, J. (1988). Quality of life in chronic dialysis patients: Factors unrelated to dialysis modality. *General Hospital Psychiatry, 10*, 267–277.

42

Senile Dementia of the Alzheimer Type

Introduction

Five million Americans are diagnosed with Alzheimer's. This number is projected to triple by the year 2050. Ten percent of people 65 years old, and nearly 50% of those age 85 or older are affected by Alzheimer's disease (Alzheimer's Disease and Related Disorders Association, 1997). The average life span 100 years ago was 49 years. Now it is 76. People are living longer, healthier lives. Alzheimer's may become one of the pressing health problems for this longer-lived, baby boomer generation (Kuhn, 1999).

"Alzheimer's disease is a progressive, degenerative disease of the brain in which brain cells die and are not replaced. It results in impaired memory, thinking, and behavior, and is the most common form of dementing illness" (Alzheimer's Disease and Related Disorders Association, 1996). Kuhn (1999) refers to Alzheimer's disease as an "unwelcome stranger" that makes its "presence known slowly and gradually." Nuland (1993, 91) states, "The severity and nature of the patient's dementia at any given time are proportional to the number and location of cells that have been affected." Alzheimer's Disease intrudes on the lives of the patient and the family, robbing the mind, changing the person, assaulting the relationships, forcing dependency, changing the course of life, and challenging one's faith or life view.

History and Treatment of Alzheimer's Disease

Alzheimer's disease received its name from a German physician, Alois Alzheimer, in 1907, when he examined under a microscope the brain of a woman who died at age 51 after progressive memory and brain impairment. He found tiny abnormalities or lesions called amyloid plaques and neurofibrillary tangles in her gray matter (Kuhn, 1999; Mace and Rabins 1981; Zarit, Orr, and Zarit 1985). In the 1960s, scientists linked this unusual disease of middle-aged people to the common condition of senility observed in the elderly. Both had similar symptoms and exhibited the same lesions in the brain.

Nearly 100 years after Dr. Alzheimer's discovery, "the basic questions about whether amyloid plaques and neurofibrillary tangles are causes or effects of the disease are not fully answered" (Kuhn, 1999, 14). Little is known about the underlying causes of Alzheimer's disease.

Age and family history with Alzheimer's disease are identifiable risk factors for the disease. Scientists are exploring the role of genetics in the development of Alzheimer's, focusing on chromosome 19. Rarer forms of the disease which strike people in their 30's and 40's often run within families and appear to be related to chromosome 1, chromosome 14, and chromosome 21. (Alzheimer's Disease and Related Disorders Association, 1997)

Definite risk factors for developing the disease include advanced age, a family history of Alzheimer's disease in a first-degree blood relative, genetics, Down syndrome, history of head trauma, and low educational and occupational status (Kuhn, 1999). Possible risk factors include being female, having had small strokes or cerebrovascular disease, Parkinson's disease, race and ethnicity (African Americans have five times the rate as European Americans), environmental toxins, diet, lack of exercise, stress, and depression before the onset of Alzheimer's disease (Kuhn, 1999). Lack of knowledge of the causes impacts the development of prevention, effective treatments, and cure.

There is no known medical treatment to stop or cure the progression of Alzheimer's disease. The FDA approved two drugs in 1994 and 1996, tacrine (Cognex) and donepezil hydrochloride (Aricept), which may temporarily improve symptoms (Alzheimer's Disease and Related Disorders Association, 1997). Kuhn (1999) reports that the FDA has two other drugs under review: rivastigmine (Exelon) and metrifonate (ProMem). These drugs are known as cholinesterase inhibitors, which work by inhibiting the breakdown of a key brain chemical, acetylcholine, and have the effect of slowing the disease process by 6 to 12 months (Kuhn, 1999). The practical benefits of these drugs are stated by Kuhn:

> About half the people in the early and middle stages of Alzheimer's disease who take them respond favorably, at least for a while, either in terms of improvement or stability. Improvements in memory, thinking, and concentration are the most frequently reported positive changes. . . . Problems such as repeating questions, misplacing objects, or becoming confused in new surroundings may be eased, and mood and behavior may also be improved. (64)

Kuhn predicts that in the coming years the two dozen drugs in various phases of testing at research centers may offer more meaningful and longer-lasting benefits for people with Alzheimer's disease. Approaches under study to treat, slow, or prevent Alzheimer's disease include cholinesterase inhibitors, anti-inflammatory drugs, estrogen-replacement therapy, antioxidants, complementary and alternative medicine, the "use-it-or -lose-it" approach, and a vaccine (Kuhn, 1999). The most exciting and perhaps most promising of the approaches under study is the experimental vaccine known as AN-1792 being tested at the research centers of the Elan Corporation in south San Francisco. The vaccine was injected into mice that had the type of brain changes connected with Alzheimer's disease and withheld from another group of mice that also had the same brain changes. After seven months, the disease was stopped or reversed in the mice that were vaccinated (Kuhn, 1999).

Diagnosis

David Bennett, M.D., director of Rush Presbyterian-St. Luke's Alzheimer's Disease Center in Chicago, states in the foreword to Daniel Kuhn's latest book on Alzheimer's,

> A sort of conspiracy exists between the person with the disease, their family and friends, and their physician. There is a silent agreement not to talk about the memory problems until the disease has progressed to a more advanced stage, when the signs and symptoms cannot be concealed and the condition cannot be denied. (Kuhn, 1999, vi)

This conspiracy results in loss of precious time to plan for the future, make decisions, and treat the signs and symptoms. The fear of all that Alzheimer's is a death sentence stealing the mind, destroying relations, and changing personality may be the reason for high denial of early symptoms. Kuhn refers to the disease as lasting from three to 20 years and that "becoming familiar with the challenges of its initial stages can help you to prevent or minimize crises later on" (1). He goes on to quote the old adage: "You cannot control the wind but you can adjust your sails."

Alzheimer's disease can be confirmed as the cause of dementia only by autopsy (Kuhn 1999; Mace and Rabins 1981; Zarit, Orr, and Zarit 1985). Kuhn states that a "probable diagnosis" can be made based on close scrutiny of the person's symptoms and differentiation from less common forms of dementia. Alzheimer's disease is the leading cause of dementia. Other diseases that cause dementia and act like Alzheimer's include Creutzfeldt-Jakob disease, multi-infarct dementia, normal pressure hydrocephalus, Pick's disease, Parkinson's disease, Lew body disease, Huntington's disease, and depression (Alzheimer's Disease and Related Disorders Association, 1997). There are also reversible forms of dementia such as pernicious anemia, brain tumors, hypothyroidism, infections, and nutritional deficiencies that can mimic the symptoms associated with Alzheimer's disease. (Kuhn, 1999). A differential diagnosis is necessary to distinguish between reversible and irreversible forms of brain failure. Components of diagnostic testing include history and physical exam, neurological exam, cognitive screening exam, blood tests, and brain scan (CT or MRI). Components sometimes included are psychological tests, spinal tap, brain scan (PET or SPECT), HIV blood test, and brain biopsy (Kuhn, 1999). The accuracy rate of diagnosis of Alzheimer's disease by experienced physicians is 85%, as confirmed by autopsy (Kuhn, 1999). The criteria established for "probable" diagnosis follows:

1. There must be a gradual and progressive worsening in short-term memory and in at least one other brain function such as orientation, language, judgment, and concentration.
2. These deficits must cause significant impairment in social and occupation functioning and represent a decline in the person's previous level of functioning.
3. Other medical conditions that otherwise could account for the progressive deficits must be ruled out. (Kuhn, 1999)

Kuhn (1999) recommends that the physician sensitively explain the test results, diagnosis, treatment options, causes of Alzheimer's disease, progression, and educational and supportive services to the patient, family, and significant others. "The benefits of telling the truth about the diagnosis invariably outweigh the perceived benefits of secrecy" (22). Disclosing the diagnosis allows the patient and family to participate fully in decisions about the present and future choices about research studies and legal and financial plans in an atmosphere of openness.

Symptoms

Early Symptoms

Many months or years may pass before the gradual memory loss of a person with Alzheimer's disease develops a pattern that is identified. Memory impairment is the early symptom and key feature. Subtle changes in language, orientation, perception, and judgment may also appear in the early stages (Kuhn, 1999). Forgetting an encounter, losing or misplacing items, and needing to have regular reminders about tasks occur early on, while the person appears to think and behave normally most of time. The person with early Alzheimer's often makes attempts to hide or compensate for the memory impairments. Recent memory of events, which took place within the past hour, day, or week, is most impaired. Remote memory of events, places, or people from the past often remains intact in the early stages. Persons may not remember what they ate for breakfast two hours earlier but can tell in great detail the events of their high school graduation party

50 years ago. The early symptoms do not mark the beginning of the disease. "Changes in the brain have probably been occurring for years before manifesting as symptoms" (24). The common belief that there is a decline in memory with aging can result in allowances for an elderly person's memory loss and deter diagnosis. "Many people with Alzheimer's disease are able to continue compensating for their symptoms, keeping them hidden from others, even their spouses, for months or years. They may deliberately avoid embarrassing situations that challenge their faulty memory" (27).

People with early symptoms of Alzheimer's may retire, turn over responsibilities to others, avoid new or unfamiliar places, or rely on old memories in conversations to compensate. Stressful situations such as the death of a spouse, lifestyle changes, change in routine or vacation (Kuhn, 1999) may bring the symptoms to awareness. "Abilities to store, prioritize, and recall new information are brain functions that slowly break down with the onset of Alzheimer's disease" (28). A pattern begins to emerge. Other early stage troubling symptoms may include difficulty with reasoning, disorientation, difficulty with language, poor concentration, difficulty with spatial relations, poor judgment, personality changes, delusional thinking, changes in sexuality, diminished coordination, and diminished sense of smell (Kuhn, 1999). There are many practical ways these symptoms may be manifested. A person may have difficulty with the logical steps of handling money or doing calculations. Cooking a meal, driving a car, or using household appliances may present a challenge. A person may lose his or her sense of direction and become lost. A person may have trouble retrieving words, concentrating, or reading.

Middle and Late Stages

Kuhn (1999, 24) limits his description of the disease to the early symptoms: Physicians have made numerous attempts to categorize the different stages of Alzheimer's disease, but these classifications have fallen short for one simple reason: there is great variability among affected people in how the disease is first manifested and progresses over time, although impairment of recent memory is the common feature.

Zarit, Orr, and Zarit (1985, 16) review Reisberg's five progressive stages of the disease as follows:

In the first stage, memory deficits are observed, along with mood disturbances (anxiety, depression). As memory worsens, there is a loss of ability to perform complex activities (stage 2). Stage 3 and 4 involve increased impairment of memory and the loss of ability to function independently. Eventually, all verbal and self-care abilities are lost (stage 5).

The Patient's Experience

Kaufman (1986, 6) states, "The old Americans I studied do not perceive meaning in aging itself; rather, they perceive meaning in being themselves in old age. . . . Mental health depends upon ensuring a continuous sense of self across the adult life span." Alzheimer's disease robs persons of being able to find meaning in being themselves and creates discontinuity due to lack of memory. A sense of loss of self can be experienced by the Alzheimer's patient. Rowe and Kahn (1997, 433) define successful aging "as including three main components: low probability of disease and disease-related disability, high cognitive and physical functional capacity and active engagement with life." Alzheimer's disease strips a person of control, cognition, and active engagement with life while often leaving a functional physical body that can survive for many years. Normal and successful aging is subverted by the disease of Alzheimer's.

By the very nature of the disease "self reflection is limited by forgetfulness" (Kuhn, 1999, 81). Common feelings reported include alienation, loneliness, fear, and worry of being abandoned. Kuhn (82) quotes Cary Henderson's description in *Partial View: An Alzheimer's Journey* of his experience:

Being dense is a very big part of Alzheimer's. Although I'm not as bad as I sometimes am, it comes and goes. It's a very come and go disease. When I make a real blunder, I tend to get defensive about it; I have a sense of shame for not knowing what I should have known. And for not being able to think things and see things that I saw several years ago when I was a normal person—but everybody by this time knows I'm not a normal person, and I'm quite aware of that. . . . I think one of the worst things about Alzheimer's disease is that you are so alone with it. Nobody around you really knows what's going on. And half the time, or most of the time, we don't know what's going on ourselves.

To further explain the patient's experience, Kuhn (83) also quotes Christine Boden in *Who Will I Be*

When I Die?: "But we can't help the way we are—we know that there is something terribly wrong with us, and we seem to be losing touch with even who we are."

Not all experiences consist of being alone, afraid, or alienated. The disease allows for decreased intellectualization which fosters awareness of feelings. Ronald Reagan is quoted as saying "I now begin the journey into the sunset of my life" (Kuhn, 1999, 84). Jan Soukop is quoted as telling this story:

One day, as I fumbled around the kitchen to make a pot of coffee, something caught my eye through the window. It had snowed and I had forgotten what a beautiful sight a soft, gentle snowfall could be. I eagerly dressed and went outside to join my son who was shoveling our driveway. As I bent down to gather a mass of those radiantly white flakes on my shovel, it seemed as though I could do nothing but marvel at their beauty. Needless to say, my son did not share in my enthusiasm. To him it was nothing more than a job; but to me it was an experience. Later, I realized that for a short period of time, God granted me the ability to see snowfall through the same innocent eyes of the child I once was, so many years ago. Jan is still there I thought, and there will be wonders to behold in each new day. They will just be different now. (Kuhn, 1999, 91)

In this quote it is obvious that Soukop was able to experience the present, with all its pleasure, as a child. Paradoxically, the ability to be present in the here and now is countered by the growing sense of losing oneself and one's place in the world. Atchley (1989, 184) states:

Internal continuity is defined by the individual in relation to a remembered inner structure, such as the persistence of a psychic structure of ideas, temperament, affect, experiences, preferences, dispositions, and skills. Internal continuity requires memory. What is disconcerting to us about people with Amnesia or Alzheimer's disease is precisely their inability to use memory to present continuity of identity and self. They do not know who their character was or is, how it fits with other characters in the everyday drama, or even what the drama is about. Obviously, then, lack of internal continuity can be not only a source of distress to the individual who has no orientation that can be used to get a sense of direction, make decisions, or take action, but also to those who are accustomed to interacting with him or her and expect a degree of predictability.

People with Alzheimer's have varying degrees of how they perceive their symptoms. Tobin (1991, 63) states that for the Alzheimer's patient "the dissolution of the self is catastrophic for the person who is aware of the dissolution in him or herself." An awareness of symptoms and limitations may allow the person to accept help readily but may also increase his or her frustration because of an awareness of failings. Frustration about the disease may be misplaced onto loved ones. People who are unaware of limitations may experience help as demeaning and it will be difficult to elicit their cooperation. "For most people in the early stages, personal awareness fluctuates but generally remains at a lower level than expected, as insight into the nature and degree of their impairments is blunted by the disease" (Kuhn, 1999, 89). Over time, as the disease progresses, the patient becomes less aware and more dependent on significant others. Lustbader (1991, ix) states, "The chief consequence of dependency is that we are forced to count on the kindness of others."

The Family's Experience

The relationship between the person with Alzheimer's disease and the family members, especially the caregiver, must change and will never be the same again. The nature of the disease prevents persons with Alzheimer's from fulfilling roles in relationships as they have in the past. The caregiver is called on to accept the disease, give up denial for reality, and assume the overall well-being of the person with Alzheimer's. She or he must become a leader as the power shifts in the relationship, intuitively know the different levels of dependence and independence as these change, and care for and about the loved one while preserving the patient's dignity and balance his or her own limits on time, energy, and patience. This is a tall call. The demands on the caregiver's time and energy are an enormous undertaking. Levin (1993, 225–226) states, "The stresses of family members who are caretakers include: Fear of loss and becoming orphaned. Fear of repeating ancient childhood narcissistic insults. Guilt over not being adequate caretakers. Ambivalence. Competitiveness with siblings. Fears about rage. Fears about their own vulnerability and mortality and about being next."

Providing care can be frustrating, draining, and painful. Kuhn (1999, 104) states, "If you are assertive without being domineering, helpful without being overbearing, and kind without being patronizing, then the person with the disease is likely to respond positively to your good intentions." Lustbader (1991, 17) states, "Helping to the right extent, at the right time, for the right reason, and in the right way has never been something easy. What is truly merciful changes from day to day, even from hour to hour. Often, we have to go to the extremes of doing too much or too little for someone before we can find the right extent of helping."

The caregiver's life will change drastically. Ten signs of caregiver stress are: denial, anger, social withdrawal, anxiety, depression, exhaustion, sleeplessness, irritability, lack of concentration, and health problems (Alzheimer's Disease and Related Disorders Association, 1995). Support is available through support groups, the Department of Aging, and the Alzheimer's Association. Calling on family members to share the responsibility is essential.

The grief of the loss of the loved one in the way he or she has been known in the past must be experienced. "Grief associated with a chronic illness seems to go on and on. Your feelings may shift back and forth between hope that the person will get better and anger and sadness over an irreversible condition. Just when you think you have adjusted the person may change and you will go through the grieving experience over again" (Mace & Rabins 1981, 64). Watching a loved one suffer can increase the sadness related to grief. Feelings of depression, sadness, discouragement, guilt, despair, and being alone are common. The ambiguity surrounding Alzheimer's disease can increase depression in families. The loved one with Alzheimer's is physically present but psychologically dying. Walsh and McGoldrick (1991, 13) state, "When the dying process has been prolonged, family care-giving and financial resources are likely to be depleted, with needs of other members put on hold. Relief at ending patient suffering and family strain is likely to be guilt-laden."

How We Die

We are born alone and we die alone. Our uniqueness is expressed, not only in how we live our life, but in how our spirit enters and leaves this earth. Nuland (1993, 8) states,

Many of us hope for a swift death or a death during sleep, "so I won't suffer" we at the same time cling to an image of our final moments that combines grace with a sense of closure; we need to believe in a clear-minded process in which the summation of a life takes place—either that or a perfect lapse into agony-free unconsciousness.

Dying with dignity and meaning, so often expressed in our society, is not part of Alzheimer's disease. Alzheimer's is slowly but relentlessly progressive in robbing the person of all awareness of life and the ability to live life. "To live until we say good-by" (Kubler-Ross 1978) is not possible.

The universal factor in all death is loss of oxygen (Nuland, 1993). Dementia is often proceeded by a series of small strokes affecting cerebral circulation. There is no immediate significant symptoms to indicate what has taken place. The accumulation of little strokes and the evidence of gradual deterioration becomes evident with time. Nuland quotes Dr. Walter Alvarez's description of a wise old lady:

> She saw that with each attack of dizziness or fainting or confusion she became a little older, a little weaker, and a little more tired; her step became more hesitant, her memory less trustworthy, her handwriting less legible, and her interest in life less keen. She knew that for 10 years or more, she had been moving step by step towards the grave.

A patient may die of a stroke or myocardial infarction. The course of Alzheimer's disease eventually results in the person becoming unaware of the deterioration, including complete dependency, a vegetative state, and the loss of all higher brain functions. The slow progression includes inability to walk, forgetting to chew or swallow food, starvation, malnutrition, incontinence, immobility, and bedsores. Incontinence may require catheterization and result in urinary tract infections. The inability to swallow may cause aspiration and pneumonia. "The great majority of people in an Alzheimer's vegetative state will die of some sort of infection, whether it arises in the urinary tract, in the lungs, or in the fetid, bacteria-choked swamp of a bedsore" (Nuland, 1993, 104).

Families are faced with difficult decisions regarding nursing home care, feeding tubes, hydration, and the enormous expense to sustain a family member indefinitely in a vegetative state with virtually no hope of recovery. "Controversy over medical ethics, religious beliefs, patient/family rights, and criminal prosecution extend to the most fundamental questions of when life ends and who should determine that end" (Walsh & McGoldrick, 1991, 13). This can be further complicated if the person with Alzheimer's disease has not communicated his or her wishes in writing before becoming unable to do so. The difficulty for families in making decisions is compounded by the difficulty of living with what has been decided.

The cost of Alzheimer's disease is considerable to both the patient and the family. The only relief is death. Yet death is only a partial relief for family members, for memories live on.

> There is no dignity in this kind of death. It is an arbitrary act of nature and an affront to the humanity of its victims. If there is wisdom to be found, it must be in the knowledge that human beings are capable of the kind of love and loyalty that transcends not only the physical debasement but even the spiritual weariness of the years of sorrow. (Nuland, 1993, 117)

Case Examples

Theoretical Orientation

The elderly who presents in psychotherapy often have issues surrounding loss, retirement, illness, death of family and friends, and concerns of mortality. Issues of the meaning of one's life and acceptance of the diverse experiences of a lifetime are paramount. Developmental theory and exploration of the life span cycle form a basis for understanding the challenges, crises, and transitions in the later stages of life. Tensions between integrity and an opposing sense of despair or hopelessness may persist. When an individual with undiagnosed, early-stage Alzheimer's disease seeks outpatient psychotherapy, the issues may resemble this late-life stage transition. The first case that follows illustrates a client whose symptoms related to anxiety and panic may be interpreted as triggering unresolved early losses brought on by the current death of family members and friends. The temptation to proceed in psychotherapy with this articulate, engaging individual is balanced by family clarification of current events and my own internal alertness and countertransference awareness of a need for a differential diagnosis and a more comprehensive medical assessment. Referral to a gerontology center provided not only a differential diagnosis, but also available family support groups, educational groups, and anticipatory needs for caregivers over time. The possibility of the family members remaining in psychotherapy is beyond the scope of this paper, as are ethically informed judgments about medical care at the end of life.

The second case example of a late-stage Alzheimer's patient in a nursing home challenges social workers and health care professionals to a broader therapeutic orientation. Psychotherapy ceases to be relevant to the late-stage Alzheimer's patient because physical needs have taken over. What is needed when care is at its most basic level is a holding environment and the common human response of touch, voice, music, and human presence.

Early Stage Intervention

Sophia had been seen in the emergency room two times in one month for symptoms related to anxiety, heart palpitations, disorientation, and confusion. Both occasions occurred when she and her husband had traveled to their summer home. Medical problems were ruled out as the cause of the heart palpitations or confusion. The emergency room physician referred Sophia to psychotherapy. Her husband and her 48-year-old daughter accompanied Sophia to her first therapy appointment. Her husband reported that prior to seeing the ER doctor Sophia was confused and had difficulty telling him what she was experiencing. He said, "It was almost as though she had no words to tell me what was wrong." When the ER doctor arrived, Sophia's confusion lifted and Sophia described in great detail the couple's second home at a nearby resort area where they had been vacationing. The doctor and the couple apparently had a pleasant conversation. Sophia could not remember her earlier heart palpitations and disorientation.

Sophia was an attractive, 82-year-old woman with white hair. Her attire was colorful and accented with silver jewelry. She had three children and 10 grandchildren. She was delightfully pleasant and gracious. Despite her pleasing attitude, she appeared quite perplexed about her appointments for psychotherapy. She seemed to view therapy as a social event and was delightfully congenial. Sophia was unable to describe with consistency the details of her physical problems or the recent emergency room visits. She was confused regarding the sequence of events and the details of recommendations. She would forget the content of the sessions from week to week. Sophia would describe in great detail experiences of her childhood, her adoption by an aunt, and some family misunderstandings that occurred prior to her marriage. Family members stated these misunderstandings had been re-

solved years prior. Sophia had begun to build a delusional system around actual events that had occurred. She felt betrayed by an adopted sister. Family members continually reminded Sophia that the adopted sister had died prior to the events described.

Sophia's daughter, Kathleen, had several concerns regarding her mother's functioning. Although close family members and friends had died, Sophia talked as though they were still alive. On two occasions, Sophia had become confused when driving and arrived at Kathleen's home when her destination had been her daughter-in-law's home. On one occasion Sophia had arrived at Kathleen's home wearing her house slippers. This was unusual for Sophia in that she paid special attention to her appearance. In my interactions with Sophia I sensed a charm and an ability to cover over memory lapses with stock phrases. I became curious about the troublesome symptoms described by the family. Symptoms such as confusion, frustration when not able to find the right words, loss of orientation regarding familiar places, clear memory for past events but not for recent ones, and the noted delusional experience of a family dispute represented possible early Alzheimer's disease.

As I listened to the family's current concerns, my own reverie emerged. I remembered the early stages of my own mother's Alzheimer's disease. She was a teacher and could very easily cover her memory lapses with engaging stories, making you forget what the original discussion surrounded. She loved to walk and soon lost her ability to find her way home. The most upsetting symptom was when she developed a delusion that people were living in our basement. Parts of her story were based on seemingly truthful occurrences. I remembered how hard it was for me to believe that dementia really existed even in face of all the evidence.

As my thoughts returned to Sophia, I questioned if Alzheimer's disease was making its presence known as an insidious, gradual, unwelcomed stranger, as Kuhn (1999) describes. I gathered the family members together, made note of the symptoms that they described, and made a referral to a local hospital program specializing in geriatric assessments and differential diagnosis. Kathleen immediately asked if I thought dementia was present. I told her that "a clear memory of the past but confusion about current events is a concern, as well as difficulty in finding direction in familiar places." I spoke honestly, providing education as well as recognizing that further medical assessment was necessary. Although there is no conclusive testing for the diagnosis of Alzheimer's disease, by ruling out other possible causes of the symptoms I helped the family begin a process of obtaining education, support, and the ability to plan for the future. Kuhn (1999) speaks of replacing fear with knowledge in the hope that knowledge will bring empowerment.

Late-Stage Intervention

Genevieve was a 79-year-old widow with two children and three grandchildren. Her son lived out of state. He had made arrangements for her nursing home care six years ago when Genevieve was diagnosed with dementia and no longer able to live alone in her home. Genevieve's daughter, age 55, recently had her foot amputated due to diabetes. The daughter's visits to her mother had ceased during her own operation and recovery. Genevieve had stopped eating and lost weight, going down to 95 pounds. Genevieve ate slowly and often forgot to swallow. She had become increasingly withdrawn. Genevieve had ceased walking two years ago. She depended on staff to mobilize her around the nursing home in her wheelchair. She no longer spoke in sentences. Many of her vocalizations were not actual words. She could not verbally communicate her needs. Nursing homes were required by law in the early 1990s to provide intravenous feeding if a patient's weight dropped to a dangerous level. The son objected to intravenous feeding and requested hospice services. Genevieve fit the hospice criteria of six months or less to live, given her current weight loss and dementia. Hospice workers worked as a team to provide services. The hospice program provided a nurse two times per week, a nursing assistant three times per week for bathing and eating assistance, a chaplain, social worker, and volunteer. Hospice care has a fluidity of professional roles. As the hospice staff became intensively involved with Genevieve, she began to smile, laugh, and recognize faces. The nurse's aid would patiently take time to feed her and remind her to swallow continually. Hospice staff would take Genevieve outside to the garden area for a walk. Time was spent holding her hand, noticing little things, and saying very simple sentences. Genevieve would occasionally say one word, such as "pretty" or "thank you." She did not seem to mind silence and appeared to find comfort in being with someone. The chaplain would often arrive in time to take her to the Christian service in the nursing home. Genevieve would tap her feet to the traditional hymns, make the sign of the cross, and say "Amen."

As a social worker, my role is challenged by a client who does not speak or reflect within. I found a new way of relating in the silence of a relationship that can be communicated only with touch, eye contact, facial gestures, human presence, and pleasure in the simplest aspects of life. The fragility, vulnerability, and primitive needs of the Alzheimer's patient, which parallel the needs of the child in a cradle, evoke in the professional a sense of helplessness. I found I was confronted with my own discomfort with silence, illness, suffering, the meaning of pain, powerlessness, and finiteness and in making my social work meaningful to the patient. Nuances of pleasure, time, and meaning have changed for the Alzheimer's patient. Providing a holding environment, attention to primitive physical needs and human presence, is what brings comfort and a mutual experience for the patient. I experienced silence as a fluent expression of care that provided a merger that lessened loneliness and brought solace. The nuances of pleasure are seen when engaging silently in the appreciation of the warm sun streaming through the window, the breeze on the patio, the wonder of a colorful plant, a tender hand holding a frail one, the sound of music playing in the background while feet are tapping, a cool sip of water, the soothing of hand lotion, and the feel of human touch or combing of the hair. Wendy Lustbader (1999–2000) describes these sacred moments with the frail individual:

> To behold another is a spiritual act. In the context of illness, knowing and seeing are reflexive. Once my helper takes the trouble to know me, I will begin to feel seen. In the course of feeling seen, I will reveal more of myself into the safety of being known. Our giving and receiving will move into a sacred dimension. This knowing and seeing will be expressed in small moments of intimacy which will loom large to both of us.

The awareness that the fate of the patient could be our own fate is pervasive, and the rift between health and illness is pronounced. One gains a new understanding of the absent family members and their need to flee the silent humiliation of the aging empty faces in the filled wheelchairs. Silence and emptiness is something our society tends to flee. Efforts to contact Genevieve's son, Jim, who had power of attorney for medical care, resulted in being informed that he only wanted to communicate with the nurse or doctor when needed. He had competently addressed practical plans regarding his mother's will, finances, and preplanned funeral arrangements. Across the years, Jim had watched the succession of little deaths narrow the horizons for recovery. The extended suffering of his mother had resulted in knowledge of the reality of her deterioration, experiencing anticipatory grief, withdrawing emotionally, and reinvesting in the present and future. His mother's diminished capacity for normal living made death acceptable. Reinvestment in the process of his mother's dying was too painful to embrace.

Outreach to Genevieve's daughter, Eleanor, revealed multiple grief experiences occurring simultaneously with her recent amputation of her foot and the inability to be present in the nursing home for her mother. Guilt pervaded. Support was provided in helping Eleanor differentiate her own legitimate needs from those of her mother. Information was provided to Eleanor regarding her mother's adjustment and response to hospice care, thus reducing her anxiety. Eleanor spoke of aging as sometimes a graceful event, bringing wisdom and insight, but the demeaning disease of Alzheimer's had robbed her mother's mind and their relationship. She expressed anger related to the experience of her mother's and her own illnesses, the unfairness, impotency, and frustration with dependency. Permission to express and ventilate these feelings was provided as well as recognition of the normalcy of these feelings. Eleanor's grief contained contemplation of her own illness, annihilation, and existential anxiety.

Genevieve began to gain weight and no longer fit the guidelines for the hospice program. Hospice was required to withdraw. There was concern that Genevieve would again decline without the environmental stimulation that she had been receiving. Four months later, I returned to the nursing home to see another patient. As I walked into the day room, Genevieve caught my eye. She had a big smile and said, "Where have you been?" This was the only complete sentence Genevieve had said in years. This case brings up many questions both for Genevieve and others. Given an attentive environment, nurturance, and stimulation, can the process of deterioration be slowed down? When family members are unavailable or estranged, how can these needs be provided for the patients?

Discussion

Sophia and Genevieve were at two different stages of the progression of senile dementia of the Alzheimer type. The challenge for Sophia's care was to recognize symptoms, obtain a differential diagnosis, educate family and patient, and facilitate an active, supportive environment. Sophia was still capable of making choices and of planning her care. Medical technology has extended options for the patient and slowed the progression of the disease with tacrine and donepezil hydrochloride, which are now approved by the FDA. Education and support groups will not stop the progression of the disease but can help explain what to expect as well as lessen the fear of the unknown.

Genevieve's disease had progressed beyond the stage of awareness, beyond the ability to make decisions and the ability to worry about the unknown. Many dying patients fear the process of dying rather than the actual event of dying. Kohut (1984, 18) states, "What leads to the human self's destruction is its exposure to the coldness, the indifference of the nonhuman, the nonempathically responding world. . . . It is not physical extinction that is feared, but the ascendancy of a nonhuman environment in which our humanness would permanently come to an end." Genevieve's thoughts did not allow her to ponder the process of her deterioration, but her positive response to the hospice team did challenge professionals to recognize that the need for human attention and connection remains until the last breath. Kohut (198) states, "When a friend puts his hand on our shoulder when we are troubled, this symbolic gesture indicates without a doubt that a self-selfobject relationship is being established, that our fragmenting, weakening, or disharmonious self is made more coherent, is being invigorated, or is having harmony restored via the friend qua selfobject." Kohut goes on to state that we need to maintain this "continuous stream of supportive experiences . . . during all periods of life . . . in old age, and ultimately in death." Kohut proposes that we need further investigation of the special selfobject needs of the elderly as they shift to a new cultural milieu, deal with a debilitating illness, or confront death.

References

Alzheimer's Disease and Related Disorders Association. (1995). *Caregiver stress.* (Brochure).

Alzheimer's Disease and Related Disorders Association. (1996). *Is it Alzheimer's? Warning signs you should know.* (Brochure).

Alzheimer's Disease and Related Disorders Association. (1997). *An overview of Alzheimer's disease and related dementias.* (Brochure).

Atchley, R. C. (1989). A continuity theory of normal aging. *The Gerontologist*, 29, 2 (183–190).

Kaufman, S. R. (1986). *The ageless self: Sources of meaning in late life*. Madison, University of Wisconsin Press.

Kohut, H. (1984). *How does analysis cure?* Chicago, University of Chicago Press.

Kubler-Ross, E. (1978). *To live until we say good-by*. New York, Fireside Books.

Kuhn, D. (1999). *Alzheimer's early stages: First steps in caring and treatment*. Alameda, CA, Hunter House.

Levin, Arnold M. (1993). Psychotherapy with the elderly. In *Aging in good health: A quality lifestyle for the later years*. Ed. Lieberman,
F. & Collen, M., New York, Plenum Press.

Lustbader, W. (1991). *Counting on kindness: The dilemmas of dependency*. New York, Free Press.

Lustbader, W. (winter 1999–2000). Thoughts on the meaning of frailty. *Generations*, American Society on Aging.

Lustbader, W. & Hooyman, N. R. (1994). *Taking care of aging family members*. New York, Free Press.

Mace, N., & Rabins, P. (1981). *The 36-hour day*. Baltimore, Johns Hopkins University Press.

Nuland, S.B. (1993). *How we die: Reflections on life's final chapter*. New York, Vintage Books.

Rowe, J. W. & Kahn, R. L. (1997). Successful aging. *The Forum*, 37, 4 (433–440).

Tobin, S.S. (1991). *Personhood in advanced old age: Implications for practice*. New York, Springer.

Vaillant, G. E. (1977). *Adaptation to life*. Boston, Little Brown.

Walsh, F. & McGoldrick, M. (1991). *Living beyond loss*. New York. Norton.

Zarit, S., & Orr, N., & Zarit, J. (1985). *The hidden victims of Alzheimer's disease: Families under stress*. New York, New York University Press.

PART III

ELEMENTS OF DIVERSITY TO BE ADDRESSED IN OUR DIAGNOSES

The third group of articles for this volume focuses on that component of the social structure in which various groups of persons in the human family are identified as having special characteristics viewed as making them different from other persons. In recent decades we have come to refer to this spectrum of designated differences by the generic term "diversity." Such perceived differences can be based on such things as place of origin, color of skin, religion, gender, ethnic identity, worldviews, values, cultural identity, color of hair, language, political ideology, socioeconomic class, accent, occupation, and more. Depending on whose viewpoint is being considered, such differences are assessed as being ranged along a status continuum extending from favored status for some to equal status for all to cruel and punitive rejection and persecution of others.

Social work has always been aware of the importance and complexities of the many components of diversity and of their differential impact for various groups in society, albeit in an earlier day in a somewhat naïve way. Over the decades we have tended to overfocus on some aspects of diversity, such as race, class, culture, and religion, usually seeing these qualities of humans as distinct factors with little if anything in common. As well, we have tended to coidentify terms such as race, culture, and ethnicity as some type of minority status, failing to recognize that all of us have some identification with some aspect of virtually all the categories mentioned above. This results in very complex patterns of social identity and social adjustment. Too often in our writing and in our practice we have focused

on only one component of a client's diversity identity, and in so doing we have failed to appreciate both the strengths and challenges that other aspects of identity bring. In recent years there has been growing awareness in our profession of the complex ways in which the many facets of diversity interact and interface both in the self-perception of individuals and in the way various other systems and persons respond.

As a profession we reached a major point in our own maturational process by moving from the perception that we were value-free and could assess and help our clients from a value-neutral perspective. Now we have become aware that much about us, including the curricula of our schools, comes to us from a particular view of the world and a particular segment of its diverse population. Thus, our contemporary professional task is to focus considerable effort on striving to understand our own diverse makeup to better understand how it responds to and is responded to by others, both those close to us and those with whom we have little contact. This has been a difficult journey for us as a profession but one that has resulted in a much more responsive and sensitive ability to recognize, assess, and effectively interact with persons different from ourselves, sometimes in only minor ways but at other times in very critical and essential ways.

The great progress that has been made in our own self-understanding has taught us to see that the operational variable is diversity and its multiple components, not any one component of it. This has helped us to see much commonality in the ways that different aspects of diversity function in similar ways in the identity of individuals and groups but also interface with other diversity facets. We have also learned that it is very difficult to view all forms of diversity as of equal importance and how easy it is to work from a position that sets our own cluster, whatever it may be, as the keystone against which all other systems are measured. In North America we were frequently accused, and perhaps rightly so, of viewing the profession in a unitary way, acting as if there were only one social work profile, that which is practiced in North America. Viewed as "the truth," this profile exported throughout the world as the canon. Surely, all forms of diversity are not of equal weight and impact on our clients and our profession. But thankfully, we have become much more global in our view of the profession and ourselves and now see the great advantages of interacting with colleagues in other parts of the world.

In our search for articles for this volume we were impressed with the richness of diversity material available in contemporary social work literature. To ensure that we have breadth and depth in our learning and our practice in the area of diversity, it is evident that our writing is steering in three directions. I am not suggesting that this is the result of some type of master strategy on the part of the publishers of our various journals. Rather, I suggest that this tripartite diversity comes from an inherent recognition that this is the way we need to look at this critical area of practice.

First, there are articles that look at the major issues concerning diversity, such as emigration, ethnicity, culture, and racial and biracial sensitivity. The strength of these articles is the help they provide us in looking at common features of particular forms of identity. Second, there are articles that deal with specific cultural groups. Certainly this type of article does not imply that every person from a particular group will fit the profile of that group. Rather, such articles present us with overviews of central tendencies in a group that give us a general understanding of the group and provide the basis for sensitive response to individuals and for understanding their customs, resources, structures, and policies. Such examinations of particular groups are also useful in helping us become more sensitive to the complexity of factors that are shaped and influenced by specific cultures. The third type of article included in this section looks at specific aspects of a culture which are viewed as differences within that culture. These assure that we do not adopt stereotypical views not only of other cultures but of groups within our own society. This theme is reflected in topics such as rural families, spirituality, children of the military, and migrants.

Over and over again the data stress the need to avoid seeing differences as a problem area for the person. Being a member of a diversity category is not a diagnostic problem category, although it may lead us to understand problems, just as it may lead us to understand areas of strength on which we can build in our practice.

It is clear that one could compile a very rich collection from contemporary literature on many aspects of diversity. It is also clear that as a profession we have much to contribute to learning for our ourselves and colleagues in other disciplines as to how to best incorporate the diversity profile of our clients in interaction with our own into rich and responsive diagnoses and plans of intervention.

A. SPECIFIC COMPONENTS OF DIVERSITY

43

Africans and Racism in the New Millennium

All men are born free and equal both in dignity and in rights.
—4th United Nations Educational, Scientific, and Cultural Organization's Statement
on Race, Paris, 1967, quoted in Benedict (1983, p. 1979).

[An African American's dream is] to be in Africa, to walk outside to see lions and leopards running
around; that would have been good!
—Statement in documentary film *An American Love Story* (Fox, Fleming, & Fox, 1999)

There's a struggle between the dreamers of inclusion and the dream busters of exclusion.
—Jesse Jackson, at a church in Tallahassee, Florida, in *Miami Herald* (Sept. 27, 1999, p. 1B)

When they [European immigrants] got off the boat, the second word they learned was "nigger." Every
immigrant knew he would not come as the very bottom. He had to come above at least one group—
and that was us.
—Toni Morrison (1989, p. 120)

A branca é mais bonita que a negra, e quem prospera troca automaticamente de carro. The White
woman is more beautiful than the Black, and whoever is prosperous automatically changes cars.)
—The Brazilian historian Joel Rufino dos Santos, quoted in Pinto (1998, p. 43)

The Past: Dead or Alive?

Many observers of African or world history have a fixed idea of the African past and its evolution to the present: slavery, colonialism, independence, postindependence. However, those of us who know better, due to our experience in the eye of the hurricane or in the belly of the civilized monster, would make some adjustment to show that slavery and colonialism are not really dead, that independence has been nominal and superficial, and that postindependence is a euphemism for neocolonialism. The latter, concretized by the inhuman acts of military and civilian dictators, has witnessed the depletion, if not destruction, of Africa's human and natural resources to such an extent that the best minds as well as the worst are scurrying off in search of life more abundant abroad, specifically in Euramerica.

The author of this article is among the ever-growing number of these dreamers who find soon enough, to their dismay and disappointment, that the dream is very close to a nightmare and that no matter where Africans find themselves, they are faced with the problem of race and color. Yet, we Africans, wanderers of the world, resilient in our search for a better place away from home, convinced that we can shed our sufferings and shame like some past events that our masters call historical constructs, insist on reenacting the slavery of centuries past, with the distinct difference that, unlike our forebears who were forcibly carried across the Atlantic into an existence worse than that of horses and dogs, the eve-of-the-new-millennium slaves are offering ourselves willingly, prepared to do anything, just to feel free. We do not care to think that this so-called freedom may be another bondage or, indeed, a continuation of that first bondage that has left an indelible and painful mark on the psyche of our people. So, here we are in civilization,[1] slaving away, contributing to the construction of citadels on top of which others perch like peacocks, while we remain at the bottom to prop up the edifice and make sure that it does not collapse.[2]

The reason for our status vis-à-vis others, including the implacable masters, is the madness called *racism*. One would not dare proffer a definitive definition here, for that is not the point. Intellectual discourse is not our objective. The incontrovertible fact is that for the African, the color of his skin and his race immediately make him less than the others. It is what Toni Morrison (1989), the African American Nobel laureate, calls "the pain of being black." We agree with Ruth Benedict (1983) that "racism stultifies the development of those who suffer from it, perverts those who apply it, divides nations within themselves, aggravates international conflict and threatens world peace" (p. 179). But in our estimation, what it does most and worst is to make everyone else feel superior to Blacks. It is the opprobrium visited upon Black people because of our race, color, and Africanity. Manifested by prejudice or discrimination, it is a question of belief or behavior, of attitude or action. No matter how many theories may be propounded by "experts" who try to highlight the impact of class and economics, of culture and civilization, and of individual ignorance, racism has continued to rear its ugly head, and Blacks, including and particularly those hoodwinked into believing in their emancipation (salvation)? by material or professional success, are often urged to return to the ancestral jungle to live among the apes and chimps. This in spite of Rosa Parks and her refusal to sit at the back of the bus; Martin Luther King, the March on Washington, and the myriad achievements of the civil rights movement; W. E. B. DuBois, Kwame Nkrumah, and the glory of pan-Africanism; Frederick Douglass and abolition and emancipation and nationhood in African countries. This in spite of General Colin Powell, son of Jamaican immigrants who rose to the very top of American military hierarchy; and Michael Jordon, the basketball megastar, symbol of deracialization, whose larger-than-life image on the side of Chicago skyscrapers made Louis Farrakhan, Black Muslim leader, appreciate "that process of transformation [of Black]" and his interlocutor, Henry Louis Gates Jr. (1996), exclaim in awe, "He's a walking phallic symbol. Here's this black man, very dark complexion, obviously being used as a sex symbol. That wouldn't have happened when I was growing up" (p. 159).

Optimists of Black movement up the ladder could also point to Brazil, often cited as symbol of deracialized society, of the much vaunted policy of racial democracy, in essence, the epitome of "rainbow coalition." Brazil is the nation where the vast majority of Blacks have refused to see themselves as Black. Yet, one must again urge caution, because the myth of deracialization and democracy is now being debunked by those who know better (Nascimento, 1978). "The wonderful Brazilian landscape, a melange of blacks and browns and tans and taupes, of coppers and cinnamons and at least a dozen shades of beige" (Robinson, 1999, p. 10), is basically a convoluted construct of escapism, driven by the fear to face facts and the hypocrisy of a racist society: Black is at the bottom, imprisoned in the *favela* (slum or ghetto). It is only logical that given the slightest opportunity, everyone would deny his pedigree, even if it means living a lie.

It is significant that the conference at which these comments are being made is organized in Salvador-Bahia,[3] the center of African presence in Brazil and the capital of a state epitomizing the political absence of Blacks and their socioeconomic enslavement. "The question of political representation in Bahia is symbolic of the situation in the nation as a whole. In this 'antiracist' state, an African majority of close to ninety percent is governed by an all-white democratic minority" (Nasciemento, 1992, p. 112).[4] As opposed to past recidivist efforts to cover up the criminality of an establishment bent on eradicating all African elements in Brazil by preaching deracialization, some Brazilians are now speaking out, affirming and confirming what certain observers as well as victims of the oppressive system have been condemning: racism is a problem in Brazil.

Unfortunately, however, such intellectual gatherings as those of Salvador, organized by descendants and adherents of a Eurocentric society and visibly and almost exclusively populated by them, hardly constitute the way out for victims of racism. This critic has already commented on the peculiarities of the 1997 *congreso* (see Gates, 1996). The 1999 experience is supposed to be less scientifically oriented, that is, more popular, more open, and more committed to the cause of antiracism. Yet, as one witnesses the comings and goings of conferees, as one listens to comments from inside and outside the cavernous, definitely highbrow Centro de Convenções da Bahia, one wonders whether much has changed. In a country where the minimum wage is about R$140 (reais), each participant at the conference has been asked to pay R$100. It is therefore not surprising that the very people whose lives are being discussed are largely on the outside looking in, objects of elitist notions and still instruments for promoting careers and causes far removed from the hell to which they have been banished. In essence, the Salvador congress, in a very subtle manner, reaffirms the reality of racism, derived as it does from a position of power. One would like to ask: Who is present? Whose voice is heard? Who is in control? Who oils and directs the sociopolitical machine? Who decides the nation's destiny?

Defining the African

The answer to each of the above questions would no doubt indicate that powerlessness is inextricably linked to the fact of Blackness or, more precisely, of Africanness. In other words, the closer one is to Africa, the more likely one would be a victim of racism. One cannot forget that in Africa, Africans do not define themselves according to their color. The debate on color and culture has been going on for years, and no one has proffered a universally accepted solution or definition. At the 1956 First International Congress of Black Writers and Artists, Louis-Thomas Achille, from Martinique, asked whether Africans called themselves Black, "an expression that, indeed, has been imposed from outside, by the colonizing nations" (*Présence Africaine*, 1956, p. 219). In response, Alioune Diop, from Senegal, made the clarification that it is necessary to distinguish between Blacks, Arabs, and Whites. This does not lessen the import or impact of Achille's food for thought, for notwithstanding the relevance of specificity of one's Africanity, one is often mystified by certain diasporic postures on the question of Africa.

Perhaps one should not be astonished: during slavery, one major factor for determining the slaves' place in the human (civilized) hierarchy was linkage to Africa. The most recent arrivals, the *Congo*, the *African*, were at the bottom of the ladder. One recalls the story of Mag, a mulatto woman, in Harriet E. Wilson's (1859/1983) novel, *Our Nig*. Mag fell in love with a White man:

> She knew the voice of her charmer, so ravishing, sounded far above her. It seemed like an angel's, alluring her upward and onward. She thought she could ascend to him and become an equal. She surrendered to him a priceless gem, which he proudly garnered as a trophy, with those of other victims, and left her to her fate. (p. 6)

Thus abandoned and ostracized by society, the pregnant Mag goes into exile in another community. The baby soon dies. Mag is a nonentity in everyone's eyes, save in those of "a kind-hearted African," Jim, her fuel supplier who sums up courage to ask her to marry him. For the inferior man, it is a unique opportunity at superioration. She is close to White: "He thought of the pleasing contrast between her fair face and his own dark skin. . . . 'She'd be as much of a prize to me as she'd fall short of coming up to the mark with white folks.'" So, he declares to her, "'I's black outside, I know, but I's got a white heart inside. Which you rather have, a black heart in a white skin, or a white heart in a black one?'" (pp. 11–12). When she agrees to marry the African, Mag is clear in her mind that it is not a question of love but of necessity and that she has taken one more step toward absolute ignominy: "Poor Mag. She has sundered another bond which held her to her fellows. She has descended another step down the ladder of infamy" (p. 13).

We must note here the nascent amalgamation or confusion between color and culture and, more important, the evolution of the African exiled in America into Negro-nigger-Black-colored-Afro-/African American[5] as he strives to realize the legendary American dream. With the abolition of slavery and emancipation, the process of de-Africanization continued apace. Ex-slaves and their descendants were encouraged to go back to civilize continental Africans. Even those who returned to settle back on the continent considered themselves superior for having been to the "new world"; such was the attitude of the coastal Liberians and Sierra Leoneans. Later, with the advent of pan-Africanism, the element of superiority was notably reduced; nonetheless, there remained a condescending attitude toward the colonized Africans who were to be helped to shed their shackles.

Again a survey of the 1956 Paris congress shows the tension between the African American and the African. James Baldwin (1985), then living in Paris, was an interested observer. He saw himself as "a black westerner." He was struck by "that gulf which yawns between the American Negro and all other men of color." He lamented,

> This is a very sad and dangerous state of affairs, for the American Negro is possibly the only man of color who can speak of the West with real authority, whose experience, painful as it is, also proves the vitality of the so transgressed western ideals. (p. 44)

In Baldwin's opinion, the Negro is fortunate to be "born in a society, which, in a way quite inconceivable for Africans, and no longer real for Europeans, was open, and, in a sense which has nothing to do with justice and injustice, was free" (p. 45). It is a society offering many more possibilities than one could ever imagine elsewhere—indeed, a superior society. For Baldwin, Africa, which he calls "a country," is "a mystery" (p. 46), with strange people and an "extremely strange language," not to forget a "hypothetical African heritage," a culture that "may simply be, after all, a history of oppression" (p. 49). Baldwin is categorical in his position that American Negroes are Americans before being anything else. In their privileged position, they can help other Negroes only because they, Americans, and the connecting link between Africa and the West know the protocol and process of climbing the mythical ladder of civilization.

Baldwin's position is supported by the objection raised by the American delegation to the following statement by one of the acclaimed fathers of Negritude, Aimé Césaire:

> This common denominator [among the conferees] is the colonial situation. And our American brothers themselves are, by the game of racial discrimination, placed in an artificial manner and within a great modern nation, in a situation that can be understood only in reference to a colonialism, certainly abolished, but whose consequences have continued to echo in the present. (*Présence Africaine*, 1956, p. 190)

J. A. Davis makes it clear that as Americans, they are builders, "pragmatic people," working hard to achieve "equal status as citizens" and "making tremendous progress in this regard" (p. 215). Césaire is forced to apologize for daring to posit a racial and cultural unity based on African ancestry.

In Brazil, there is a unique example of racist de-Africanization, with categorization being decidedly anchored on a policy of Afrophobia. Brazil was the last country in the Americas to abolish slavery (in 1888), and when it did, something peculiar happened: the minister of finance, Ruy Barbosa, decreed in 1891 that all documents and archives related to slavery be burnt. Thus began the process of trying to destroy any African presence in the country. No doubt that much success has been achieved. Even today, with the conscientization among Afro-Brazilian groups, such as the Movimento Negro Unificado, it is not unusual to find

people staring at anyone wearing an African dress on the streets of Salvador, center of Candomblé, the Afrocentric religion, and symbol of African culture and continuity. It is not unusual to hear Blacks refusing to be called *Black*. A Black American foreign correspondent, Eugene Robinson (1999), recently recounted his experience of this racial dilemma. Individuals whom he considered Black denied being so, preferring to call themselves White. At first, he was elated by this newfound freedom to name oneself:

> I was in a world where race seemed to be indefinite, unfixed, imprecise—a world where, at least to some extent, race was what you made it. Instead of what it made you. . . . Many individuals fit into that nether region where there was no absolute racial identity, just broad categories.

Gradually, however, he began to realize the danger in a situation where solid walls are absent. This dawns on him when he visits the *favelas*, slums, most visibly and vividly populated by Blacks, and when, at *carnaval*, he witnesses subtle but well-defined segregation, including the dehumanization of Black entertainers:

> Black was more than just a color. It was a condition. It was an identity about which some of them might have been ambivalent, that some of them might even have rejected, but that suddenly, for me, had a clarity and a pertinence that changed everything. (p. 24)

Thus, the American visitor comes to understand that Brazil, far from representing the glorious America future of a mixed society, actually symbolizes the deliberate attempt to eradicate Blackness through a process of dehumanization so that Blacks may categorically deny their color and culture and, to which one must add, their Africanness. Interestingly enough, although he indirectly made this last point, Robinson did not dwell at length on it, for a reason that we shall soon suggest. He rightly affirmed, "In Brazil, most people with some measure of African blood demand *not* to be thought of as black. . . . In Brazil, most black people do not seem to feel themselves at all in conflict with white society" (p. 24). He noticed that the factors for naming anyone Black are usually pronounced as African features: kinky hair, flat nose, among others. Anyone fortunate to have escaped from the slums, to become empowered through education, certainly ceases to be called

Black. Why, then does the Black American (Robinson does not use the term *African American*) not recognize the fact of de-Africanization in the Brazilian example? From Robinson's account of life in South Carolina, what is of utmost importance is the question of Blackness, that is, the racism encountered by his people in the hands of Whites and the struggle to affirm their Americanity. In Brazil, he is an American, albeit Black, but not an American conscious of his Africanity. Therefore, it is with relief that he concluded that Brazil does not have anything to teach America and that in America, Blacks constitute a presence: "Despite all *our* [italics added] problems, I could put together a dozen magazine covers of black role models that included more than basketball players and soap opera stars" (p. 24).[6]

What is common between the American and the Brazilian realities is the refusal to recognize African heritage as a viable, positive factor in the lives of diasporic Africans; indeed, the very word *African* is foreign, strange, if not absolute anathema. Nonetheless, to this critic's mind, being African—not as a matter of citizenship or nationality, not as a question of racial or cultural imprisonment or restriction, but as a fact of an affiliation offering possibilities for affirming one's humanity—cannot but be a force and a factor in the presence and survival of those now belonging to the new world. For, after all, the European who becomes American has never forgotten his heritage. He takes it for granted, because his presence and empowerment are a matter of course, and his way of life is the standard, the mainstream. As for the Chinese, the Japanese, the Indian, and other transplanted nationalities, it is noteworthy that they also take for granted the viability of their cultures, which they live without shame or any second thought.

It is left to us Africans to find out why the hesitation, the self-hate, the self-denial. Whether we like it or not, the words of Abdias do Nascimento (1992) ring true:

Blackness is not a question of skin color. The color of our skin, in all its varied and sundry shades, functions only as a badge of our African origin, the root of our identity. *Mulato, cafuso, negro, escurinho, moreno*: all the famous euphemisms converge toward this identity, which the ruling elites in Brazil have always tried to disclaim. Therefore, when we are denied a job or shown the service entrance, it is not only our skin color that provokes the discrimination, but above all the African identity announced by the color of our skin. (pp. 71–72)

The Malady and the Madness: Racism Is Alive and Well

What makes the Brazilian example particularly troubling is that descendants of Africans are so many in number but so marginalized and dehumanized that the prognosis for the future is very discouraging. The following information is supplied online by Láldert Produções Multimídia: 75% of Blacks run the risk of being arrested, 70% work in the nontechnical sector, 80% live in *favelas*, and 87% of Brazilian children who are out of school are Black. Only 15% of Blacks complete college. Among dropouts, there are 65% more among Blacks; 37.7% of Black women are illiterate, as opposed to 17.7% of White women. Of Black men, 40.25% are illiterate, as compared to 18.5% of White men. An average Black family earns R$689, whereas a White family earns R$1,440.

In such a situation, one can easily imagine how the idea of miscegenation would be widespread. The myth is that Brazilian society is a model of conviviality, cordiality, and total harmony. The reality is that Blacks, having internalized a complex of inferiority, would use the White woman as a stepping stone, a means of upward mobility, and for their offspring, life in racial paradise. Recently, an Afro-Brazilian magazine, *RAÇA* (it reminds one of *Ebony*), published an article, "Por que eles preferem as loiras?" ("Why do they [economically successful Black men] prefer blond women?") (Pinto, 1998). The thesis is quite simple and straightforward: Black men prefer White women—any White woman—to Black because White is superior and makes the man better. The magazine quotes several anthropologists and psychologists to buttress the point. Sergio Ferreira da Silva, Black psychologist, affirmed,

Os homens negros preferem as loiras por medo de perpetuar a raça. Quando você olha o negro, vê o sujo, o piche, o macaco. É o que ele vive quando criança na escola e traz para a vida adulta. Aí, quando ele pensa em casar, sai em busca da mulher branca como objeto de negação da própria cor. (Black men prefer blondes out of fear of perpetuating the race. When you see Black, you see filth, tar, monkey. That is what he lives through at childhood and brings to adulthood. So, when he thinks of getting married, he goes out in search of the White woman as symbol of denial of his own color.) (Pinto, 1998, p. 42)

Ana Lúcia Valente, anthropologist, saw reciprocity in the relationship between a Black man and a

White woman and a reaffirmation of the ambiguity of racial relations in Brazil: "A loira ao lado do negro, de alguma maneira, mostra que não é racista" (The blonde by the side of the Black man, somehow, shows that she is not a racist) (p. 42). If the affair goes bad, the woman can claim to know Black men and their behavior. Valente also quoted comments by those observing such biracial couples: "Ele deve ser rico! Senão, não conseguiria sair com uma loira dessas" (He must be rich! If not, he would not succeed in going out with such a blonde). "Ela deve estar numa pior" (She must be in dire straits). "Esse cara deve ser muito bom de cama" (That guy must be very good in bed) (p. 42).

Joel Rufino dos Santos, a blunt, chauvinistic, and racist historian, explained why Black men lust after White women:

> A parte mais obvia da explicação é que a branca e mais bonita que a negra, e quem prospera troca automaticamente de carro. Quem me conheceu dirigindo um Fusca e hoje me vê de Monza tem certeza de que já não sou um pé-rapado: a carro, como mulher, é um signo. (The most obvious explanation is that the White woman is more beautiful than the Black, and any successful person automatically changes cars. Whoever knew that I used to drive a Fusca sees me today driving a Monza is convinced that I am no longer an underdog: the car, like woman, is a symbol.) (Pinto, 1998, p. 43)

In the meantime, some of the magazine's respondents stood firm on the side of the mixed couples. According to a businessman, "Não é uma questão de preferência, é uma questão de coincidência" (It is not a question of preference, it is one of coincidence) (Pinto, 1998, p. 42). Sueli Carneiro, of the Institute of the Black Woman, saw mixed couples as representative of the ongoing universal changes in racial and social relations.

> Não são objetos de consumo, símbolo de status nem garantia de mobilidade social: são companheiros e companheiras, seres humanos, que não simbolizam êxito, mas a possibilidade do encontro, da solidariedade, do amor entre grupos étnicos e raciais diferentes. (They are neither consumer objects, symbols of status, nor guarantee of social mobility: They are companions, human beings, that do not symbolize success but the possibility of coming together, of solidarity, of love between two different ethnic and racial groups). (Pinto, 1998, p. 43)

Such a notion, one need comment, would be the ultimate ideal in a society without any racial problems, in a community where everyone's humanity was taken for granted, and in a world where skin color, social status, indeed any factor for divisions or separation, did not exist. That would be paradise, not the human society at the end of the 20th century.

The most striking aspect of the *RAÇA* article is the lack of perception in using a classic of Black revolutionary writing to support the sensationalist standpoint. The text in question is Eldridge Cleaver's (1968) *Soul on Ice* in its Portuguese edition of *Alma no Exílio*. Quoting out of context, the author, journalist Tania Regina Pinto (1998), included statements about the Black man's obsession with the White woman. For example, it is stated that he cannot help himself in craving madly for this superior flesh. He has, indeed, concluded that there can never be love between Black men and women, thus supposedly giving support and explanation for the Black Brazilian's lactifying lust. "There is no love left between a black man and a black woman" (Cleaver, 1968, p. 159): "Every time I embrace a black woman I'm embracing slavery, and when I put my arms around a white woman, well, I'm hugging freedom" (p. 160). Pinto (1998) went on to inform the reader,

> Homens negros, no tudo, ou em parte, concordam com sua analise . . . porque o branco representa realmente essa grandeza. Acho que sempre relacionei a mulher negra ao retrocesso." (Black men, wholly, or in part, agree with his [Cleaver's] analysis . . . because White really represents that greatness. I always linked the Black woman to retrogression.) (p. 41)

Unfortunately for the reader and for the editors of the magazine, the whole article lacks focus and depth. Cleaver's (1968) text is, indeed, the confession of a sickness resulting from the experience of racism, a disease that must be cured; more important, it is an honest, blunt analysis of the malady, with the resolve to find a solution within the context of Black. It is a soul-searching journey through psychological hell toward the light provided by consciousness of one's culture, race, and humanity. Cleaver never made an absolute statement regarding the Black woman or the White. Besides, the experience of the young Cleaver is not presented as a monologue; he shared his trauma with other prisoners, and *RAÇA* fails to distinguish between the various personages in the affirmations quoted in the article.

Most significant, Cleaver found his way back home, to the Black woman, his Black Queen. The last chapter of *Soul on Ice* is a message, "To All Black Women, From All Black Men:"

Queen-Mother-Daughter of Africa
Sister of My Soul
Black Pride of My Passion
my Eternal Love. (p. 205)

Cleaver outlined the Black man's hurt and humiliation, his fear and shame, and "the naked abyss of negated masculinity," in short, the 400 years of dehumanization that left him not only impotent but also incapable of accepting responsibility toward himself and his woman. He declared, "Flower of Africa, it is only through the liberating power of your *re*-love that my manhood can be redeemed. . . . Only, only, only you and only you can condemn or set me free" (p. 207). Africa, it cannot be overemphasized, plays a major role in this process of liberation and rehabilitation. It is the past, but also the present and the path to the future.

The past is an omniscient mirror: we gaze and see reflected there ourselves and each other—what we used to be, what we are today, how we got this way, and what we are becoming. To decline to look into the Mirror of Then, my heart, is to refuse to view the face of Now. (p. 207)

Cleaver (1968) made another very thought-provoking point: that contrary to what everyone might like to believe, the abolition of slavery and the enacting of laws proclaiming equality and other human rights have not led Blacks to earthly paradise. "It's all jungle here, a wild and savage wilderness that's overrun with ruins" (p. 210). Together, Black man and Black woman are therefore called on to build a new nation over the ruins. The Black Brazilian bourgeoisie would know nothing of such resolve; they are engaged in self-denial and self-destruction. On the streets of Salvador, the commonest sight is that of a Black man oozing some ill-defined pride in his Rastafarian dreadlocks, walking hand in hand with his elated blonde and preaching Black power while swaying to the music of Bob Marley blaring out of the giant amplifiers in a nearby bar. If and when the couple makes babies, the offspring would blend into the supposedly deracialized society. But would they? *RAÇA*, in another recent issue (Bertlolino, 1998), raises the question of the experience and behavior of siblings of different color shades, "Irmão de sangue, porém com tom de pele diferente" ("Blood siblings, but with different skin color"). Implication: There does exist difficulty in paradise.[7]

In the United States, in spite of declarations of tremendous progress made in regard to racial relations, everyone remains obsessed with race and with good reason: racism is endemic to the system; it is embedded in the culture; it is entrenched in the air we breathe. In fact, race remains the issue, and precisely, it is the dichotomy between Black and White. As Morrison (1989) asserted, "Black people have always been used as a buffer in this country between powers to prevent class war, to prevent other kinds of real conflagrations" (p. 120) Everyday, in every major-city newspaper—the *New York Times*, the *Washington Post, Los Angeles Times*—some outrageous, racist act is reported, with Black as victim of White. At the end of the century that has witnessed a move beyond modern to postmodern civilized savages are on the prowl, more daring than ever before, more barbaric in their actions.

In Bryant, Texas, a Black man is tied to the back of a truck by two White supremacists, who then go on a joy ride on the town's dirt road, dragging along their innocent victim. His body is shredded to pieces. In New York, an African immigrant is arrested and sodomized almost to death by a White police officer in the presence of other unprotesting officers. Two pipe bombs are detonated at Black Florida A & M University (FAMU) in Tallahassee, after many Black churches have been victims of similar hate crimes. Racial profiling is a daily fixture on public roads, and DWB (Driving While Black) has become a theme of discussion in bars and bistros, with Black men finding themselves, as usual, categorized as irresponsible criminals culpable for being Black. A police offers said with conviction. "To be honest, my sense of suspicion is greater towards black males than any other race of people" (*Washington Post*, Sept. 26, 1999, p. A1). The Ku Klux Klan, hiding behind constitutional provisions, marches with impunity on main streets. And one remembers O. J. Simpson and Rodney King and the racial divide defining their cases. And one recalls that this is not the early 20th century, not the times when Blacks were lynched for having the audacity to look at a White woman; not the 1950s or 1960s, when Blacks were fighting to ride in front of a bus or obtain service in a bar. This is the postmodern era, when Blacks are supposed to be free: free to walk tall, to sit where they want, to use any toilet, to attend any school of their choice, and to date any person they want. And, indeed,

they are doing all that; however, somewhere, someone, by an act of hate, supported by a system that
allows such madness to thrive, reminds us that we
are living in a fool's paradise.

Africans and Racism: A Question of Inclusion or Exclusion

One is fascinated by how easily we Africans—and
here we are, including all those on the continent
and in the diaspora—overlook the reality of our
lives to gravitate toward *Eldorado*, a dreamland
that allows us peace of mind but not much else.
The individualism encouraged by capitalism contributes to this spurious search for peace and pros-
perity. The West has taught us that attachment to
community is the bane of primitive society and that
the hallmark of modern society is the ability and
desire to compete, to assert oneself, to be oneself,
to set one's goals, and to be the best that one can
be in a setting that rewards the outstanding individual willing and able to beat the competition. So
the goal of the progressive Black is to get out of
the ghetto by all means necessary. As for the leaders, their objective is to lead the followers into the
melting pot of American mainstream to attain the
almighty American dream.

Talking of leadership, one finds a certain confusion among those of the diaspora. On the continent, leaders are afflicted by decadence. First, the
diasporic leadership. One observation made by
Baldwin (1985) resonates with relevance and co-
gency: Black leaders, the new bourgeoisie, have a
special relationship to the West, a relationship that
they must deal with, with honesty and sincerity of
purpose; otherwise, they will have difficulty leading their people in the right direction. Frantz Fanon
(1952, 1961) called these leaders "men of culture,"
that is, those who have "penetrated into the heart
of the great wilderness which was Europe and
stolen the sacred fire" (Baldwin, 1985, p. 54).

In the case of the African American, there is a
tendency to eschew Black nationalism and opt for
American nationalism. Note that it is an element
peculiar to the Black struggle to consider everything
in phases of progression, delineating and distinguishing movements, generations, and personalities
as historical constructs so that the past is forgotten
as the present welcomes something better that is
closer to and more acceptable by the mainstream.
Several questions arise: Is it true that racism has
been eradicated? What should Blacks do in a society that considers them inferior and liable to return
to the level of their cousins living on trees in Africa?

Is it wrong to proclaim one's Blackness, to promote
it, to protect it, and to live one's culture based on
values extant in the motherland? For Blacks to survive in the West, correct answers must be found to
these questions. In the United States, not only is
there lack of leadership interested in such questions,
but those standing out among the crowd are too
often engaged in bickering among themselves,
struggling to be the most visible and vocal, the most
viable candidate for whatever is available because,
rather than think of the people's destiny, they are
busy thinking of their image (individualism) and
the so-called larger society (American nationalism).

One of the most prominent leaders of the Black
community is the Reverend Jesse Jackson. At a
gathering used to express support and encouragement for the students and faculty of the Florida university where those bombs exploded, the good reverend stated,

> There is a struggle between the dreamers of in-
> clusion and the dream busters of exclusion. . . .
> This is not racists, this is fascists. This is shoot-
> ing children in Los Angeles. . . . This is not black
> and white, it's wrong and right. Whether it's
> Jews in Los Angeles or FAMU in Florida, peo-
> ple of conscience know none of us are safe un-
> til all of us are safe. . . . Black and white to-
> gether, that's power. When we register to vote,
> that's power, and when we pray, that's power.
> (*Miami Herald*, Sept. 27, 1999, pp. 1B–2B)

Of course, one easily notices the preacher's rhetoric
and the rousing style of the civil rights era: relevant, one might say, but also confusing and confused. Perhaps one mistake committed then and
continued now is to link the Black struggle to others, thus diluting it, making it commonplace, hood-
winking the people, and giving them a false notion
of their condition. Fascists, anti-Semitic bigots,
child killers, and ethnic cleansers are all criminal
monsters, yes; but although their crimes may be
categorized in the general construct that would include racism against Blacks, it must not be forgotten that being Black is indeed considered to be a
crime, at birth. Jackson and others are often more
engaged in assimilationist politics than in combating racism. Precisely, Jackson's Rainbow Coalition,
in its attempt to be all-embracing to cut across the
color and other lines, so as to be all-American, compels one to note that, after all, Black is not a color
of the rainbow.

Another Black leader whose actions leave one
in doubt of a clear understanding of the Black condition and his commitment to the community is the

Black Muslim Louis Farrakhan. His whole organization is, to a certain extent, representative of a misunderstanding of culture and heritage; for, if Christianity has been the bane of Africans, Islam has been no less an instrument of imperialism. To reject one and embrace the other, therefore, might be regarded as a matter of jumping from the frying pan into the fire. But, then, how can one sincerely blame the Black Muslim or the Baptist in the United States when continental Africans are engaged in religious zealotry and bigotry as servants of messiahs and masters from abroad while they continue to condemn their own original beliefs as paganism? Farrakhan would appear to think first and foremost in terms of maligning and embarrassing the oppressive system in his country and cooperating with whoever stands against the system, without paying much attention to issues of major concern to his culture and community. This would explain, for instance, his visit to the late Nigerian dictator, Abacha.

A quick look at the situation in Brazil confirms the kind of confusion and lack of focus noticeable in the American setting. Only there the situation is worsened by the deliberate lack of opportunity made available to the Afro-Brazilian. At least the United States does throw up umpteen possibilities if there is a concerted effort to avail oneself of them. By successfully promoting a faceless brand of nationalism, Brazilian establishment has reduced the level of militancy among Blacks. And within the rank of the militant minority, engagement is dissipated in sectional struggles when not mired in the mysterious myopia of religious mysticism. Ironically, unlike in the United States, the vast majority of Afro-Brazilians (one could actually say most Brazilians) admit adherence to African religion, which holds the potential for self-determination, affirmation, and progress within the society. The problem is that the faith favors resignation, an acceptance of the status quo, and an inertia that imprisons the acolytes in the shrine, even as the leaders corner socioeconomic power.

Black ambiguity is exacerbated by the machinations of an establishment that discourages communal action. Elements of solidarity are definitely more noticeable among African Americans than their counterparts in Brazil. Nonetheless, both countries have their share of mongrelization. If Brazil's racial democracy has effectively reduced to a minimum adherence to one's Blackness, American individualism is continually arousing thoughts of biracial and bicultural egalitarianism. Thus, miscegenation, more and more visible, appears to be a fad, a way of showing the great possibilities of a

society accepting Black and White on the same level. Stories of biracial couples abound in books and articles and, most recently, a documentary, *An American Love Story* (Fox et al., 1999), which was broadcast on public television. The film raises questions about the whole process of Americanization. Rather than level the playing field, as it were, the outcome seems to be de-conscientization. At best, the offspring of interracial marriage would be human beings, neither Black nor White; at worst, they could be simply mad. Of the many themes addressed in the documentary—which, by the way, reminds this viewer of an earlier docudrama, *Roots*—the one on the Africanness of a biracial child is of most interest to us here.

Cicily Wilson, daughter of a Black blues musician and a White corporate manager, is a student at Colgate University in upstate New York. She travels for a summer semester in Nigeria in company of other students: seven White, seven Black, and two mixed blood (she and her only friend in the group, Nicole). The sojourn reveals the tension and latent hate between mulatto and Black Americans. It also reveals the tension between African Americans and Africans, not to forget the mutual ignorance of both American and African Blacks.

Cicily's trip is a fulfillment of sorts of her father Bill's dream of going to Africa and waking up "to walk outside to see lions and leopards running around." His daughter does not see lions and leopards but visits a zoo and see chimpanzees as well as human beings. Her opinion evolves from ignorance through confusion to some acceptance of her Africanness. She falls in love with a young Nigerian, Tony, who, significantly, cannot hide his yearning for the American dream. Indeed, his fawning and cringing toward the American woman is reminiscent of many an African prepared to do anything to become part of the human cargo of the postmodern slave ship.

The relationship between Cicily and her African American colleagues is sad, because it takes the trip to Africa to bring both sides to live together. On the other hand, it is symbolic that by going back to the ancestral continent, both sides come face to face with their color and, particularly, their culture. Perhaps, back home in the United States, Cicily, now a working woman, would convince her parents that it is important to live and understand her "Black side," a side that, subconsciously, she and her family have downplayed or denied.

According to Census Bureau statistics, since 1990, the annual number of marriages between

Blacks and Whites has nearly doubled: in 1997, it was 13% of all weddings (311,000). "They offer an intriguing lens through which to look at the ever-perplexing role of race in America" (*Washington Post*, Sept. 9, 1999, p. C9). The thrust of the American love story would seem to be the potential to create a cocoon of humanity or humanism, precisely American, with no thoughts of another place or presence, so that lovers may live their life in this earthly paradise. Unfortunately, the truth is otherwise. The very fact that the two children of this all-American family bear different surnames—the first takes the mother's name, Wilson, whereas the younger takes the father's, Sims—constitutes a loud comment on the spuriousness of such a sense of family. And when Bill Sims visits his extended family, one cannot help thinking of the African concept of community, with family as nucleus of a well-grounded unity, complementarity, and continuity. Such elemental configurations are hardly accorded importance in American society.

Cicily's visit to Nigeria also underscores the way Africans contribute to the racist perception and misrepresentation perpetrated by the West. The Americana mannerisms of the young men and women around her make the perplexed student remark, "I didn't think I was going to see people striving to be like Americans!" If one condemns American media for heir Afrophobic propaganda, as they emphasize only and always the negative (violence, misery, death, official corruption, lack of material development, with the jungle as symbol), one must also condemn Africans for aiding and abetting the propaganda: there are innumerable Tonys approving of any negative statement on Africa and serving as mouthpiece for American state departments by warning the foreigner to steer clear of "the dark continent." Moreover, if one feels nauseated by Western officialdom for failing to recognize Africa as part of the world—the world that for them seems to begin and end between the United States and Europe, with outposts in Asia and Latin America—one must simultaneously feel outraged by the actions of African dictators, money-mongering monsters with designs at self-perpetuation in power and the patriotic objective of reducing their countries to rubble. Meanwhile, it is conveniently forgotten that past colonizers and present imperialists are also culpable in this art of debauchery and destruction; they prop up the abominable dictators who readily serve as pimps in the prostitution of Africans. The West cannot claim innocence from the tragedies exemplified by Angola, Burundi, the Congo, Liberia, Rwanda, Sierra Leone, Somalia, and Nigeria.

For the African American or Afro-Brazilian or Afro-Cuban or any descendant of Africans returning to the continent, there is the need to know Africa's history, not from the perspective of the invaders who exploited the land and peoples and are now collaborating with internal colonizers but from the point of view of Africans, aware of their past and how it has led to the present and committed to using those experiences to genuinely liberate the beleaguered culture and civilization. Such visitors from abroad would come to understand that Africa is not just the land of safari, not the jungles depicted on television and postcards, not the land of filth and corruption and coups d'état. They would find out that Africa has a culture and a civilization from which others borrowed and stole without making any acknowledgment. They would learn that that culture represents a continuity in their new homeland and that they would do best to recognize and draw from that living culture for their own benefits.

Conclusion: A Millennial Pan-Africanism

If this sounds like another call for a return to roots, that would be an unfortunate misunderstanding, because no one in his right mind would tell citizens of other countries, with the commitment of nationalism and patriotism, to reject their nation for other habitats that in reality are geographical conglomerations concocted by vainglorious exploiters. The coming together being proposed here is based on not only the shared experiences of colonialism but many manifestations of a common ethos. In addition, this article has proved that African ancestry has been used by racist detractors to keep down Africans. It is therefore only logical to rehabilitate the downtrodden by returning value to their culture and rehumanizing them.

As Morrison (1989) has asserted in disgust, "One black person is all black people" (p. 120)—that is, when the particular individual has perpetrated something considered negative, evil. On the contrary, when a Black person does good, shows signs of brilliance, or affirms his or her genius, then he or she is an exception to the rule. Our proposal here is that we reject the ruse of individualism while reviewing and revamping our cherished ethos of community: to begin with, we must perceive the bad eggs as an exception to be rehabilitated and the exceptional talent as representing the potential for widespread excellence. In other words, we must reject the habit of having others write our history.

To date, we have allowed them to make our history not even on our behalf but over our dead bodies, using us as objects to promote their various agendas. In the new millennium, the image of Africa has to change: Africa, the most exploited, the most expendable, the least aided, and the most afflicted by the AIDS virus has to give way to another Africa, conscious of its values and its humanism; prepared to make sacrifices to make its people survive; clean again, as it used to be in generations past, when dignity, probity, and honor were essential aspects of commitment; and committed, not to oneself, but to all. An Africa of achievers, with research institutions where foreigners went to study; an Africa that contributed immensely to human development. That is the Africa of which every son and daughter can be proud. It is the Africa to which the mentally enslaved and the socially deprived will not hesitate to return to drink from its well of wisdom and its source of strength and to continue the struggle against racism.

In the face of this persistent racism, the worst that could happen is polarization of Africans along continental and national lines. And the temptation is very strong, what with the United States' emergence as the "only world superpower" and the African Americans' tendency to prioritize their adhesion to this superior society to the detriment of their Africanity. That worst scenario can only hurt, not help, the cause of all descendants of Africa, including the African American. It would constitute the apotheosis of determined efforts at de-Africanization (call it "civilizing the savage") begun centuries ago. In this process of dispersal, dilution, and dissipation, diasporic Africans have come to believe that "the best and brightest" were saved from the motherland.[8]

There appears to be a growing support for the theory that Africans themselves must bear the blame for slavery and that Euramericans were only exercising their God-given right to free trade. As outrageous as it may sound, such an idea was expressed back in 1966 by a Brazilian, Clarival do Prado Valladares, who after the First World Festival of Negro Art in Dakar, Senegal, declared, "Whites did not hunt blacks in Africa, but bought them peacefully from black tyrants" (Nascimento, 1992, p. 114). Thus, whereas reparations are being paid in multimillion dollars to Jews for the Holocaust, Africans are being compelled to engage in another set of arguments about their culpability in the heinous crimes committed against them.[9]

Indeed, it is only with us Africans that people dare suggest that the past be doctored or buried and forgotten, either because of shame or because,

we are told, the very thought of it is too painful to bear. Yet, other programs, at best comparable in bestiality to our enslavement, are constantly kept on the front burner, so that the perpetrators of the evils may continually ponder the past and pay for it—so that any potential monsters may think a million times before rearing their ugly heads.

How can we as Africans become self-sufficient and self-fulfilled to survive in the new millennium, given all the odds against us? How can we thrive in a so-called global village where Black has not ceased to be globally marginalized and dehumanized? Where others are aware and proud of their past, which they have used to carve out their niche in the present, without denying or being ashamed of their heritage? Why are we always apologetic and afraid? Why do we need anyone's permission to propagate programs that will promote our culture and affirm our humanity? To this writer's mind, the most appropriate action must be based on the complementarity among the various African communities spread across the world. Each nationality would evolve new configurations of self, taking cognizance of Africa as an essential presence. After all, the qualifier—*Afro* or *African*—already admits such a presence. The increasing number of continental immigrants also attests to the rising possibilities for new formations. Contrary to the widespread stereotype of the African as vagrant, drug courier, credit card defrauder, and con artist, most Africans in the diaspora are hard-working professionals and artisans engaged in constructive rather than destructive enterprises. It would be worthwhile, for instance, to provide data on these responsible citizens. Apart from debunking certain myths, the exercise would, it is hoped, make for well-deserved respect and open the door toward solidarity among all of Africa's children.

The Yoruba, one of the major nations to which diasporic Africans can trace their roots, affirmed, *Àpàpò̩ ówó l' afí só àyà* (We use the whole hand, with all the fingers together, to beat our chest). And *È̩nìkán k'~i jé àwà de* (An individual cannot be called the community). The notion of community, serving as underpinning for communality, has been successfully used in great kingdoms on the continent and in the diaspora. It was, indeed, an essential aspect of maroon societies (Colombia, Cuba, Haiti, Jamaica, Venezuela) and the Republic of Palmares in Brazil[10] remains a symbol of pride for all African descendants who know their history. Such solidarity has remained our source of strength, even in this age of selfishness and individualism. If we return to our ethos based on the cycle of life, we would be able to forge a new ideology. We would thus synthesize the best elements of the cultural nationalism of Quilombismo, Negritude, and indigenism; the pride and zeal of Harlem's New Negro; the commitment to freedom of the original pan-Africanism; the militancy of Black Power; the artistic and sociocultural return to the roots of Black Aesthetics—all anchored on Mother Africa's unwavering humanism.

To anyone who might wish to condemn this as proof of retrogression, let us respond, with conviction, that a call to go back to understand, appreciate, and live one's culture—a constant in human existence—cannot but be the height of progressiveness, particularly because our experience of dehumanization was actually precipitated on a systematic alienation from that culture. In essence, to become human again, to combat and conquer the ills of oppression, exploitation, and racism, we have to find our way back home. Let us note that when, years ago, such a call was made, the proponents were imbued with a mixture of superiority complex vis-à-vis Africa and a sense of inferiority in their relationship with America. And those who heeded the call, the reputed leaders of Africa's struggle for independence, stood a chance to lead their countries out of bondage; but confused in their colonized minds, they soon became collaborators with our oppressors and murderers of their own people. Today's call comes from those who realize the deep confusion and lack of commitment raging in the community. With this perspicacity, all Africans can come together and walk through the tunnel into the light of a new day.

Notes

1. The word *civilization* is used ironically throughout this article to connote a society that purports to epitomize the zenith of humanism while, in reality, actualizing savagery and dehumanizing fellow human beings.

2. Years ago, in 1939, the Haitian writer Jacques Roumain (1972) captured this image of African slaves in his poetry, "Bois d'ébène."

3. Congresso Mundial Sobre Racismo, September 28 to October 1, 1999. An earlier gather (August 17–20, 1997) took place in the same city: V Congresso Afro-Brasileiro, which addressed several sociocultural issues, including racism. From that congress emanated a book, edited by Jeferson Bacelar and Carlos Caroso (1999), *Brasil: Um Paí de negros?* See Femi Ojo-Ade's (1999) chapter in the book.

4. See also Ojo-Ade (1996a, pp. 228–260).

5. For comments on this evolution in nomenclature and psyche, see Ojo-Ade (1996b, pp. 181–186), "Afterword: What's in a Name?"

6. Robinson's (1999) *we* is defined as all Americans, Black and White. Of course, one can easily context his statement with other facts. The truth about Black Brazilian role models is hardly different for their American counterparts. Michael Jordan, Oprah Winfrey, Bill Cosby, and Quincy Jones, all entertainers, are at the top of any list of role models.

7. It is noteworthy that several of the issues being lately addressed in Brazil have caught the attention of people in the United States. Indeed, the tendency is to think that America has already dealt with and resolved such problems. On the contrary, one finds that what America does is deal cursorily with many problems without finding solutions or with superficial ones. Legislation, a historical marker, records official action but not the beliefs and actions of human beings. Furthermore, it is amazing how easily the establishment as well as the marginalized also forget. Group amnesia attends many seminal works by Blacks, including Cleaver's (1968). Often enough, personalities themselves suffer from the disease: Cleaver metamorphosed from revolutionary to reactionary, a Republican propagandist and a conservative Christian whose words and works came to belie the position held in *Soul on Ice*. Chester Himes's (1972) novel *The Third Generation* analyzes the problem of color shades among siblings. Spike Lee's movie *School Daze* does a similar analysis of students at an all-Black college. The film certainly ruffled many a complacent, contented feather.

8. One vividly remembers the nighttime television talk show hosted by Arsenio Hall. His guest was another popular African American personality, Bryant Gumbel, host of the morning-time *Today* show. It was 1990, the year Nelson Mandela was freed from his 27-year incarceration by South Africa's apartheid government, and Gumbel was planning to take his show on the road to South Africa. He and Hall were having fun talking of the past and present and were visibly enthralled by the notion that the best and brightest had crossed the Atlantic during slavery.

9. A present source of controversy is the public television documentary by Henry Louis Gates Jr. of Harvard University and one of the officially recognized voices of the African American community. *Wonders of the African World* is the subject of ongoing e-mail exchanges and a collection of essays to be published by Africa World Press. This author intends to be a contributor.

10. Zumbi was the king of this Afro-Brazilian nation, *quilombo*. The republic of Palmares resisted armed colonizers for more than a century (1594–1696).

References

Bacelar, J., & Caroso, C. (1999). *Brasil: Um país de negros?* [Brazil: A Black country?]. Rio de Janeiro, Brazil: Pallas.

Baldwin, J. (1985). *The price of the ticket.* New York: St. Martin's.

Benedict, R. (1983). *Race and racism* (2nd ed.). London: Routledge & Kegan Paul.

Bertlolino, É. (1998). Irmãos de sangue, porém com tom de pele diferente. *RAÇA, 3*(28), 52–56.

Cleaver, E. (1968). *Soul on ice.* New York: Dell.

Fanon, F. (1952). *Peau noire, masques blancs.* Paris: Eds. Du Seuil.

Fanon, F. (1961). *Les damnes de la terre.* Paris: Maspero.

Fox, J., & Fleming, J. (Producers), & Fox, J. (Producer). (1999). *An American love story* [Documentary film]. London: BBC2.

Gates, H. L., Jr. (1996). Farrakhan speaks. *Transition, 70,* 159.

Himes, C. (1972). *The third generation.* New York: World Publishing.

Morrison, T. (1989, May 22). The pain of being Black. *Time,* pp. 120–122.

Nascimento, A. (1978). *O genocídio do negro brasileiro* [The genocide of the Brazilian Negro]. Rio de Janeiro, Brazil: Editora Paz e Terra.

Nascimento, A. (1992). *Africans in Brazil.* Trenton, NJ: Africa World Press.

Ojo-Ade, F. (1996a). *Being Black, being human.* Ile-Ife, Nigeria: Obafemi Awolowo University Press.

Ojo-Ade, F. (Ed.). (1996b). *Of dreams deferred, dead, or alive: African perspectives on African American writers.* Westport, CT: Greenwood Press.

Ojo-Ade, F. (1999). *O Brasil, Paraíso ou Inferno para o Negro? Subsídios para uma Nova Negritude* [Brazil, paradise, or hell for Blacks? Toward a new negritude]. In J. Bacelar & C. Caroso (Eds.), *Brasil: Um País de negros?* (pp. 35–50). Rio de Janeiro, Brazil: Pallas.

Pinto, T. R. (1998). Por que eles preferem as loiras? *RAÇA, 3*(26), 40–43.

Présence Africaine. (1956). Le ler Congrès International des Ecrivains et Artistes Noirs [First International Congress of Black Writers and Artists]. Issue 8-9-10.

Robinson, E. (1999, August 1). On the beach at Ipanema. *Washington Post Magazine,* pp. 8–13/21–24.

Roumain, J. (1972). Bois d'ébène. In *La Montagne ensorcelée* (pp. 229–235). Paris: Les Editeurs Français Réunis.

Wilson, H. E. (Ed.). (1983). *Our nig.* London: Allison & Busby. (Original work published 1859)

Anna Y. Nobles
Daniel T. Sciarra

44

Cultural Determinants in the Treatment of Arab Americans: A Primer for Mainstream Therapists

In the United States, 50% of the minority group members, compared to 30% of whites, terminate counseling after the first session (Sue & Sue, 1990). The difference is significant and due in part to minority clients' negative experiences stemming from counselors' lack of sensitivity to the client's culture (Fukuyama, 1990; Gladding, 1992). However, with a burgeoning of multiculturalism—referred to as the "fourth force in counseling" (Pedersen, 1991)—awareness, knowledge, and skills are now acknowledged as the three broad areas in which competence is needed for working effectively across cultures (Sue et al., 1982; Sue, Arredondo, & McDavis, 1995).

The number of Arab Americans, currently estimated at 3 million (Abudabbeh, 1996), is steadily increasing. Their cultural background, however, is little understood and, because of hostile relations between the United States and some Arab countries, there is considerable prejudice against Arab Americans. Thus, they often find it difficult to secure mental health services that are sensitive to their cultural background.

Arab Culture

The Arab world consists of 21 countries divided geographically into two major parts, one in Southwest Asia, the other in North Africa. These nations cover considerable territory and vary in size and population. Furthermore, they are politically diverse, including monarchies, military governments, and socialist republics (Nydell, 1987). Such heterogeneity might seem to preclude such a thing as an Arab culture. However, Arab regimes that arose after the partition of Palestine and the creation of the state of Israel (e.g., Syria, Egypt, and Jordan, which were defeated in the 1967 Arab-Israeli war) are committed to nationalism and the union of Arab nations (Abudabbeh, 1996). These regimes do not seem themselves as separate nations inhabiting separate political entities. In their view, all Arabs constitute one nation, the boundaries dividing them are temporary, and sooner or later they will be united (Patai, 1973; Mansfield, 1992).

A general description of any cultural group runs the risk of engendering stereotypes and overlooking intragroup differences. The following delineation is meant to be representative of the broad lines of Arab culture, which will not be reflected in every Arab, nor in all to the same degree. A good rule of thumb for mainstream therapists is to question the extent to which a particular client conforms to and differs from what the therapist knows about his or her cultural background (Gushue & Sciarra, 1995).

Cultural Roots

In prebiblical and biblical times, Arabs were a nomadic people inhabiting the Arabian Peninsula.

With the rise of Islam in the 7th century A.D. and its expansion over parts of Asia, Africa, and Europe, Arabic culture and language spread. As millions in the Middle East and North Africa adopted the Arabic language and integrated Arabic culture with that of their own, Arab identity lost its purely ethnic roots. Thus, the word Arab today is a cultural, linguistic, and to some extent political term, since it refers to all the countries that were Arabized through conquest by the Muslim Arabs. Arabization was accomplished by intermarriage, conversion to Islam, or adoption of the Arabic language (Abraham, 1995). As a result, some populations (e.g., the Christian communities of Copts in Egypt and Maronites in Lebanon) are Arabs by speech, not by race or religion (Atiyah, 1958).

Political History

The 7th and 8th centuries marked the peak of the Arab empire. Arabs tend to look back on it as a glorious and ideal period, when political harmony was the norm in the expansion effort (Hottinger, 1963; Mansfield, 1992). The 13th century saw Europe prosper and the Arab empire begin to decline as they were invaded by Mongols, then Crusaders, and finally Turks, who established more than 100 years of hegemony in the Arab world (Isenberg, 1976). Division of the Arab world continued during World War I, as the Allied forces occupied the entire North African coast. The 1917 agreement (the Balfour Declaration) between the British and the Jews to make Palestine the latter's homeland came as a blow to Arabs in general and to Palestinian Arabs in particular, perceiving their homeland occupied by outsiders.

The impact of this history of decline on Arab ideas and feelings cannot be overemphasized. Many Arabs deeply resented the domination of Europeans, which saw the imposition of foreign languages and culture, and the insinuation of the United States into the Arab-Israeli conflict; they felt that history had betrayed them (Mansfield, 1992), and the psychological wounds are still open. Some Arab thinkers tend to hold European colonialism responsible for Arab poverty, psychological conflicts, and, most of all, the "bloody tragedy" of Palestine (Patai, 1973).

As Isenberg (1976) noted, these experiences have left a negative impression of the West on Arabs, many of whom believe that the West is capable of taking away their moral values and family ties in the same manner that it once took their freedom. Since the mid-1970s, the return to Islamic fundamentalism has spread throughout the Islamic East, popularized as an antidote to Western domination and influence (El Guindi, 1995).

Religion

Though not all Arabs are Muslim,* or Muslims Arab, it is hard to overestimate the influence of Islam on the Arab world, in which religion regulates everyday behavior through positive and negative commandments that are carefully observed (Patai, 1973). Religion is not just one aspect of life but its center, effecting all activity, thought, and feeling. The practice of Islam (which means "submission to God") ideally results in a psychological certainty of inward protection from serious harm, allowing the believer a high level of tolerance and dignity (Patai, 1973). Equally important is the belief in fatalism:

> Neither the individual himself nor external factors can change a man's God-given character, which remains with him throughout his life and which destines him to a certain way of life. (p. 148)

Since deeds and behavior are predetermined, individuals have no choice and consequently cannot be held morally responsible for what they do. Furthermore, long-term planning is considered sinful, since it indicates a lack of trust in divine providence (Patai, 1973).

Nydell (1987) summarize the basic Arab religious attitudes as follows: (1) Everyone believes in God, acknowledges God's powers, and has a religious affiliation. (2) Humans cannot control all events; some things depend on God (i.e., "fate"). (3) Piety is one of the most admirable characteristics in a person. (4) There should be no separation between church and state; religion should be taught in schools and promoted by governments. (5) Religious tenets should not be subjected to "liberal" interpretations or modifications, which can threaten established beliefs and practices.

Language

Arabic is the native and official language of all the Arab countries. In 1973, it became the sixth official language of the United Nations and the fourth

---

*For example, Iran was part of the Arab empire during the spread of Islam and remains Muslim to this day; however, it never became Arabized. On the other hand, Christians in Lebanon, Syria, Iraq, and Palestine are direct descendants of early Arabs.

most widely spoken in the world (Nydell, 1987). Approximately 130 million people speak Arabic (Abudabbeh, 1996), which is also the language of the Koran. According to Savory (1976):

> The most important formative factor creating the Arab consciousness is the Arabic language, which is the bearer of their culture, the vehicle of their history and the sacred tongue of the religion of the majority. (p. 147)

The Arabic language is complex. Spoken dialects (colloquial Arabic) can be as different as Spanish and Italian. They are all different from classical Arabic, which is spoken by educated Arabs and, as the written version of the language, is substantially the same throughout the Arab world. Patai (1973) has suggested that the existence of colloquial varieties causes psychological problems. A good command of classical Arabic is highly admired (Abudabbeh, 1996) and considered a function of the higher, idealized self (Mansfield, 1992); since less educated Arabs are unable to speak it, they may feel inferior to those who do.

In Arabic, the way something is said is just as important as its content. Nydell (1987) pointed out that Arabs use many repetitions of phrases and themes, along with exaggerated reports and descriptions, to stress the importance of what is being said. In times of anger, they may threaten, make promises, or use nationalistic slogans, but these are not intended to be taken literally. This is a creative and metaphorical use of language, a form of fantasy for the sake of emotional satisfaction and expression of feeling.

Arab thinking tends to extremes, with little capacity for accepting the gray areas of reality. Arabs tend to use descriptors such as "excellent," "magnificent," "great," "terrible," "disgusting," and "stupid," and very seldom use qualifiers. Patai (1973) referred to the many Arab scientists who hold that such extremes are partly the result of the desert climate, noted for its own extremes of daytime heat, nighttime cold, dry summers, and bitter winters. Arabs also use many euphemisms for uncomfortable situations such as death, illness, or disaster (Nydell, 1987). For example, instead of saying someone is sick, an Arab may say she or he is a little tired.

Arab Americans

Abraham (1995) felt that the 1990 census estimate of 870,000 Arab Americans living in the United States (U.S. Bureau of the Census, 1990) is inaccurate, since some Arabs, suspicious of government authorities, conceal their ethnic affiliation. In any case, the number of Arab immigrants to North America is growing with continuing political instability in the Arab world (El-Badry, 1994), and unofficial estimates place the number of Arab Americans at closer to 3 million.

Immigration Patterns

Historically, Arab Americans arrived in the United States in three major waves, each under special circumstances that affected the acculturative process (Barazangi, 1989).

First wave   Occurring in the late 19th century, the first wave of Arab immigration comprised primarily Arab Christians from Syria and Lebanon (Abraham, 1995). They were predominantly males who had left their families behind, intending to stay in the United States only until they had earned sufficient money to improve their lives back home (Abu-Laban & Suleiman, 1989). From this early wave emerged a group of poets, artists, and writers (e.g., Kahlil Gibran) who became permanent residents of the United States, settling in such major urban centers as New York and Boston (Abraham, 1995).

Second wave   The second wave of immigration took place about the middle of the 20th century and included many more Muslims than did the first (El-Badry, 1994). Many of them were Palestinians displaced after the establishment of Israel in 1948. Also included in this wave were Iraqis and Syrians who were escaping political conflict in their countries of origin.

Third wave   Starting in the mid-1960s and continuing to the present, the third wave includes many professionals and entrepreneurs fleeing political unrest and wars (Abraham, 1989) who would otherwise have remained in their country of origin (El-Badry, 1994). This group is more educated, young, and affluent than the average Arab, and most have become U.S. citizens. They held executive positions in their homelands and, in bringing their entrepreneurial skills to the United States have proved attractive to the corporate world (El-Badry, 1994).

Stereotypes

During eight years of television viewing (starting in 1975), Shaheen (1984) documented over 100 popular entertainment programs, cartoons, and major documentaries telecast on network, independent, and public channels and totaling nearly 200 episodes that related to Arabs. He found that all channels portrayed Arabs as billionaires, bombers, belly dancers, or unfriendly desert dwellers with veiled harems. Discussing the reinforcement of Arab stereotypes by American television, films, and other media, Shaheen (1997) pointed out that in reality only 2% of the present-day Arab population live a nomadic or harem life, and that these were never among the prevailing customs of most Arab countries. While some of the stereotypes depicted by Shaheen (1984) have since lost their appeal, one that has endured is that of rebel and terrorist bomber (Said, 1979). This is partly due to media coverage of sensational bombings, especially of Israelis by Palestinians, which has left the impression that all Arabs are political radicals. The recent U.S. military strikes against Osama bin Laden have contributed to this stereotype. Shaheen (1984) wrote:

> Stereotyping of Arabs is just as wrong as assuming that Blacks are lazy, Hispanics are dirty, Jews are greedy and Italians are criminals. . . . Like every national or ethnic group, Arabs are made up of good decent people with the usual mix of one percenters, the bad apples found in any barrel. (p. 25)

Second-Culture Acquisition

Arab Americans take pride in their cultural heritage and its many contributions to philosophy, literature, medicine, architecture, art, mathematics, and the natural sciences. At the same time, they feel misunderstood and wrongly characterized by most Westerners (Nydell, 1987) defamed in the news media, Hollywood productions, and political speeches. Barazangi (1989) pointed out that the stereotyping of the Arab American community in the United States has made its member feel like sojourners, very different from the mainstream culture. As a result, many have experienced, and are still experiencing, marginalization, which has led to ways of coping that can be divided into three major types.

Denial of ethnic identity Arab Americans from all groups—recent immigrants, assimilated immigrants, or native born—may choose to deny their ethnic background (Abraham, 1995). B. Abu-Laban and Suleiman (1989) pointed out that some Arabs never reveal their ethnic background because

of stereotyping. They give as an example the consumer advocate Ralph Nader, who has seldom (if ever) referred to his Arab lineage. Such denial was particularly true of first-wave immigrants who, since they were mostly Christian and isolated from their homeland, tended to marry and assimilate more readily into the dominant culture.

Withdrawal Most of the Arab Americans who have chosen to withdraw from American society are third-wave immigrants, including recent arrivals (S. Abu-Laban, 1989). Unlike earlier immigrants, these Arab Americans coexist in two social, psychological, and physical worlds. They are able to stay in touch with their country of origin through advances in telecommunications; this reinforces their sense of Arab community and tradition, intensifying a preference for living in ethnic Arab neighborhoods or near other Arab Americans in the suburbs. Finding their ethnic identity and religious traditions alien to the dominant American culture, they prefer to stay withdrawn in order to prevent assimilation (Abraham, 1995).

Engaging mainstream society Arab Americans who engage with the dominant culture tend to have distant ancestral ties, be successful, have high leadership positions, advocate secularism, or identify with Christianity. Concerned with acceptance into the dominant society, they emphasize the commonalities between Arab and American cultures, or between Islam and Christianity (Abraham, 1995). They identify themselves as Americans who happen to be of Arab ancestry.

Cultural Differences

While intragroup differences exist among Arab Americans in terms of second-culture acquisition and cultural identity, some of the differences between the values and traditions of Arab culture and those of the dominant culture of the United Sates are noteworthy.

Family As Nydell (1987) explained, Arab society is built around the extended family system, creating a strong bond among blood relatives. Family is the first priority, exceeding obligations to work—an attitude understood by Arab employers, who will excuse an employee's absence or tardiness if family obligations or duties are involved. Budman, Lipson, and Meleis (1992) wrote: "Arabs do not see themselves primarily as individuals but rather as members of group, especially family groups" (p. 360).

Family members support each other both emotionally and financially (Nydell, 1987). Arabs consider family the place of refuge that provides them with security and reassurance in an unpredictable world. The reputation of a family member reflects upon the entire family: "One's family name is a ready-made identification which reveals to all both one's reputation and one's access to assistance" (El Saadawi, 1993, p. 14). Irresponsible behavior that is apt to destroy the perpetrator is also apt to destroy the entire family.

The importance of family can give power and control over its individual members, who may be pressured to abide by acceptable behavior patterns at the cost of development of their own personality. Parents seldom encourage independence and like to remain involved in their children's lives for as long as possible. "It is not uncommon for Arab parents to make such major decisions for their children as to choice of a career or marital partner" (Budman et al., 1992, p. 361).

Well-defined cultural norms dictate that the oldest son be trained at an early age to become head of the extended family.

He [the eldest son] is given every privilege, according to the means of the family, with the exception that, as an adult, he will care for his aging parents and younger siblings, especially any unmarried sisters. (Najjar, 1994, p. 41)

The significant role of the eldest son begins at birth, when his father and mother become known by his name (El Saadawi, 1993); for example, if the oldest son's name is Sammi, his parents will be called "Um Sammi" and "Abu Sammi" ("mother/father of Sammi").

Socioeconomic Status   An Arab family's social, economic, or political status determines its role as an instrument of control (Tucker, 1993). For instance, a wealthy family functions as an extended unit whose main concern is to maintain its economic status. Although arranged marriages (in which parents choose suitable mates for their children) are no longer practiced in the same manner as in ancient days, preferred marriages among the wealthy, even today, are to first or second cousins (Nydell, 1987), a pattern ensuring that its wealth and inheritance remain within the family. On the other hand, lower-class families are much less concerned about careful marriage choices (Tucker, 1993). Barakat (1985) reported that field studies conducted in diverse Arab communities indicated an overall rate of only 3%–8% for endogamous marriages but a significantly higher rate for such marriages in traditional and isolated communities.

Arab culture places certain limitations on the activities of the wealthy in order to maintain their status and a good public image. For example, the upper-class person will refuse to engage in any kind of manual labor, even washing the car or sweeping the sidewalk. Physical appearance is important; proper clothing (even traditional Islamic dress) reflects social standing as well as wealth (which is why Arabs are often surprised to see rich and educated foreigners wearing old clothes and faded jeans, which they associate with being poor and lower class).

It is worth noting that Arab Muslim families are more intensely affected by cultural traditions, which are linked to Islamic teachings, than are Arab Christian families.

Child-Rearing Practices   Most Arab children grow up among numerous loving and nurturing caregivers, not only their parents but extended family members, who share caretaking responsibilities (Nydell, 1987). The presence of numerous authority figures appears to be universal in Arab culture. The traditional preference for male over female offspring stems from the general belief that men contribute more to their family's influence and effectiveness. This is beginning to change in the Arab community at large, but is still evident in some traditional families.

Among Arab children, the attachment to the mother is usually affectionate, while that to the father is based more on respect and fear, largely because of the different treatment received from each parent (Patai, 1973; Abudabbeh, 1996). Stereotypically, the father is the stern, authoritarian figure, while the mother is loving and compassionate.

According to Nydell (1987), Arabs tend to administer more corporal punishment than do Westerners. Children are expected and taught to behave in a certain way in order to maintain an acceptable social image. They are not conditioned to judge or criticize their own behavior in terms of right or wrong, which would give rise to guilt for bad behavior, but in terms of acceptability, which gives rise to shame for behavior that does not meet social expectations. Consequently, children are more concerned with how other people seem them than with how they see themselves, and there is great social pressure to conform. The strong religious context of Arab culture intensifies such conformity and establishes in the child's mind a close association between sin and nonconformity.

Sexuality   The realm of sex and sexual relationships is a much more personal and sensitive area of life for Arabs than for Westerners (Patai, 1973), resulting in a paucity of writing about Arab sexual mores (Mansfield, 1992). Timini (1995) indicated that Muslim Arabs generally have a positive view of sexuality, believing that sexual union within marriage is the highest good in the eyes of God. For Arabs in general, social and religious values determine when sex is good and when it is bad.

As Davis and Davis (1993) have emphasized, Arab cultural ideals and reality are often contradictory. For example, the restrictions placed on women are not shared by men, so that a single man can experiment sexually with women but will marry only a virgin. Moreover, a woman who commits any sexual offense loses her honor forever and destroys not only her own but her family's reputation, since it is held accountable for her actions by the local community. As a rule, Arab women are expected to prove their virginity on their wedding night. Najjar (1994) wrote of the cultural differences regarding women:

> I know that the women's movement in this country [United States] has yet a long way to go, but compared to the restrictions on women may society has, this culture is liberating. (p. 41)

Najjar was a university student in the United States when she started to struggle with issues of dating and sexual intimacy. Although she was 24 years old and free to do as she pleased, her ingrained perceptions of what was proper behavior continued to restrict her.

The emancipation of women in Arab culture continues to be a vibrant and complex process. For instance, even though they had been influenced by Western ideas under the leadership of the Shah, millions of Iranian women supported (apparently with no coercion from their husbands) a return to Islamic fundamentalism and the more traditional role of women under Ayatollah Khomeini. Social change in many Arab countries can be reduced to the role of women in society (Mansfield, 1992). Throughout the 20th century, the status of women in the Arab world has fluctuated as a result of conflicts between reformists, who reinterpret the Koran on the basis of reason, and militant scripturalists, who adhere fundamentally and even violently to those texts that favor men over women (Altorki, 1995). Thus, the current status of women in a particular Arab country can be a good indicator of which group, reformist or spiritualist, is dominant.

Hospitality   Arabs are famous for their hospitality. Kanafani (1993) traced the origin of this tradition

to the Bedouins, who saw a need to protect travelers who were passing through their hostile desert. In Nydell's (1987) words,

> Social formalities and rules of etiquette are extremely important in Arab society. Good manners constitute one of the more salient factors in evaluating a person's character. (p. 57)

Because people are judged by how they receive and threat their guests, hospitality is the most frequently used measure for increasing one's self-respect (Patai, 1973). For Arabs, hospitality and generosity are so closely related as to have the same meaning (Nydell, 1987). For instance, guests never leave a home, shop, or business without being offered something to drink; whereas Westerners might ask guests if they would like something to drink, Arabs would ask whether they preferred coffee or tea. Or, if two friends meet on a bus, each will insist on paying the other's fare until one gives way and accepts the offer.

Arab culture insists that a guest is always welcome, whatever the inconvenience—the only exception being when a woman is at home alone and a man calls unexpectedly. Arabs enjoy inviting guests to their home for meals, at which their ultimate form of generosity is exhibited in the serving of great quantities of food and varieties of dishes.

Expression of Feelings   Certain cultural beliefs have endured over sufficient time to have become central to the development of what might be called the Arab personality. First, while they subscribe to the law and historical events, Arabs are more concerned about people and their feelings. They may be more subjective in their approach to certain situations than are Westerners, who are taught to attempt objectivity and try to prevent emotion from interfering with their behavior. On the other hand, Arabs (even men) express their emotions freely, talking openly about pain and sorrow and weeping, even lamenting, when death occurs. Such behavior can shock Westerners, who may see it as a loss of control. Nydell (1987) concluded that Arabs beliefs are centered around the assumptions that "everyone loves children, wisdom increases with age, and the inherent personalities of men and women are vastly different" (p. 15).

Implications for Treatment

Like many nondominant groups that struggle with issues of second-culture acquisition, Arab Americans are at risk of developing problems associated with emotional well-being and psychological health. Their acculturative stress is exacerbated by the discrimination and prejudice they commonly face upon arrival in the United States (Pollara & Meleis, 1995).

Second-Culture Acquisition

Acquiring a second culture can create great ambivalence in Arab Americans as they strive to maintain their cultural roots, of which they are proud, while trying to become familiar with and integrated into American culture (Meleis, 1991). The result can be a feeling that they belong to neither culture. In their homes, Arab Americans may speak the colloquial Arabic of their origin and exhibit the authoritarian attitudes normal in traditional Arab society, while at work they speak English and behave like Americans. The result may be a psychological struggle among different attitudes, thought processes, and behavioral patterns (Patai, 1973). Unable to identify emotionally with either culture, Arab Americans can find themselves clinging to the traditional Arab culture even though they feel that modernization is desirable. This conflict can pull them apart, and the task of therapy is to help integrate the conflicting forces into a new and more fruitful cultural configuration and bicultural identity.

Family Issues

Arab American parents struggle continuously for balance in helping their children maintain their ethnic identity while acquiring entrance into the larger culture. Pollara and Meleis (1995), in a study of 30 Christian Jordanian mothers of adolescents in the Los Angeles area, found that their greatest source of stress was in the attempt to raise their children in a different cultural context. The mothers reported intense and persistent worry, despair, guilt, confusion, and fear of losing respect and control over parenting. Their feelings were intensified by the perception that people in their new environment did not understand the depth of their concerns and the extent of their fears.

Adolescent Identity   Adolescence in Arab countries tend to be early, brief, and less stormy than in the West. While Western adolescents develop their individual identities by separating from their families and forming strong peer relationships, Arab culture demands that adolescents shape themselves to fit their family environment (Pollara & Meleis, 1995).

Arab American parents do not expect their adolescent children to act out, become self-centered, or engage in nonconformist behavior. They consider adolescence a period of hormonal imbalance with mood changes evidenced by impatience, nervousness, frustration, low tolerance in the male, and a certain degree of withdrawal in the female (Budman et al., 1992).

As a result, issues of identity and belonging can be somewhat traumatic for Arab American adolescents. They experience negative discrimination from a dominant culture that has a different set of expectations for puberty, dating, marriage, and attitudes toward parents and elders than their own culture (Bowen & Early, 1993). They are caught between the two cultures—on the one hand seeking acceptance from their families, on the other hand tugged by peer pressure to seek acceptance in American society (Timini, 1995). This dilemma can result in either enmeshment or disengagement between adolescents and their parents. Fear of losing their adolescent to the new culture can make parents overprotective, preventing the child from developing his or her own identity (Jackson, 1991). Disengagement occurs when adolescents feel pressured to accept the family's values and lifestyle but choose to reject their minority cultural background and adopt the dominant culture of their peers. Timini concluded that Arab American adolescents were likely to develop guilt feelings if they abandoned their family's traditions and refused to abide by its rules.

Clinical Intervention

Clinicians providing mental health services to Arab Americans are likely to encounter certain expectations and types of behavior in their clients. Some awareness of the cultural factors already discussed, combined with the following observations, should help ensure a degree of cultural sensitivity in rendering the services.

1. Because of their fatalistic attitudes, a high degree of resistance to cooperation should be expected from Arab American clients, especially Muslims.
2. Arab families seek mental health services only as a last resort, and are more likely to telephone for help than come in person for treatment (Abudabbeh, 1996).
3. Be aware of the impact of negative stereotyp-ing and discrimination on Arab Americans.

4. While Arabs tend to be highly emotional and full of zest for life, they are also bounded by stringent rules and expectations.

5. In the Arab culture, the behavior of an individual reflects on the entire family. Clients' immediate issues, therefore, are likely to be accompanied by such factors as guilt, shame, dependence, and low self-esteem.

6. The themes of honor and shame are the main components of everyday life in Arab society.

7. Arab families encourage their members to remain dependent, discouraging self-reliance and differentiation.

8. Social hierarchies in the Arab culture influence individual behavior (e.g., men from different social classes would be embarrassed if they found themselves invited to the same event).

9. Discussion of matters related to illness, death, or other painful event is uncomfortable for Arab clients. It is advisable to avoid direct reference to them, since it can worsen a bad situation or cause such intense hurt and resentment that the client may terminate therapy.

10. Arabs are brought up to view disadvantages (physical, economic, etc.) and relational problems as shameful and might resist admitting to them.

11. Therapists should be careful about disclosure of personal information, since negative data about family life or relationships may adversely affect their image and status in an Arab client's eyes. On the other hand, positive information (e.g., successful events or connection to famous persons) can induce admiration.

12. Be hospitable; an Arab client who is not invited to participate when the therapist is eating or drinking is likely to be offended.

13. In general, Arabs stand and sit closer to each other than is the norm for Westerners. The space that Westerners assume for intimate conversations would be considered comfortable for ordinary conversations by Arabs. Individuals of the same gender touch each other repeatedly during a conversation (e.g., it is common to see two women or two men holding hands—this is a sign of friendship—and kissing on both cheeks is customary in greeting someone of the same sex).

14. In conversation, Arabs are accustomed to repetitions of the same idea or issue for the purpose of emphasis. Repeated responses are therefore needed for reassurance: if a statement is made softly and not repeated, an Arab may wonder if the speaker really means what he or she is saying. This originates in the Arabic language, which uses many different phrases with the same meaning. Therapists should not be surprised if a client keeps asking for reassurance by asking "Really?"

15. Family intimacy is achieved indirectly in Arab society; family members rely more on unspoken expectations than on overt verbalization and are not accustomed to confronting each other. Although family therapy is recommended as a modality for treating Arab Americans, because of Arab family structure, asking family members to address each other in therapy is likely to cause frustration and resistance.

16. The transition of an Arab immigrant family from an extended family support system to a sudden nuclear family situation can give rise to feelings of isolation, disengagement, and enmeshment. The trained clinician should be able to explore these issues and respond to the often desperate need for support.

17. Believing that dressing well is essential to self-respect, Arab clients are reassured by a presentable appearance (including no long hair for men or revealing clothes for women).

18. Be considerate of Arab etiquette. In terms of nonverbal behavior, this includes not sitting so that the soles of one's shoes face the other person (an insult); not standing carelessly, for example, leaning against the wall or keeping hands in pockets (lack of respect); and not failing to shake hands when clients arrive and depart (very rude and cold).

19. An Arab American client family is likely to become attached and consider the therapist a member of the family, which might give rise to an invitation to their home. However, a polite refusal is usually accepted.

20. Be sensitive to any characteristics of the dominant culture that an Arab client may be acquiring, which will be affected by such variables as client's socioeconomic status, age, gender, religious affiliation, and language. Nominal membership in a cultural

group does not necessarily indicate possession of all that group's characteristics.

21. Termination can be stressful and traumatic for Arab clients if not handled with great care. The family will not expect the relationship to end; therefore, therapists should refer to termination as temporary, indicating that the family should feel free to contact them any time a difficult situation arises. Otherwise, client and family may consider therapist untrustworthy, cold, and inconsiderate.

Conclusion

While it has only scratched the surface, this article has attempted to open up some of the issues that the mental health community must face in providing culturally sensitive services to Arab Americans. Their political history, strong religious background, and significant differences from the dominant culture of the United States complicate issues of second-culture acquisition for Arab Americans. Furthermore, little is known about this population's use of mental health services. More research is needed to determine the extent and effectiveness of that use, as well as Arab Americans' perceptions of mental health treatment.

At present, the mental health literature in English that might further the understanding of practitioners about Arab American clients is sparse. Nevertheless, it is essential that those who work with this clientele become as knowledgeable as possible about its culture. Equally necessary is a sensitivity to that culture and to the issues with which its members must cope in living in a dominant culture in which some mores are radically different from their own. In therapeutic work with Arab American clients, therapists must bring to bear all the information and awareness at their disposal, while keeping in mind that the encounter is also a potential source of enrichment for both client and therapist. Such considerations might go far to ameliorate any tendency to regard the dominant culture as the norm to which clients of any nondominant culture should aspire. Therapists must take care to give this kind of cultural imperialism a wide berth because it silences the discourse of the nondominant culture and imposes that of the dominant culture.

The rise in the population of Arab Americans in the United States offers the mental health community yet another opportunity to transcend its frequent role as the handmaiden of the status quo and reach out to those maligned by discrimination, bigotry, and racism.

References

Abraham, N. (1989). Arab-American marginality: Mythos and praxis. In B. Abu-Laban & M. W. Suleiman (Eds.), *Arab American: Continuity and change* (pp. 17–43). Belmont, MA: Association of Arab-American University Graduates.

Abraham, N. (1995). Arab Americans. In J. Gale, A. Sheets, & R. Young (Eds.), *Gale encyclopedia of multicultural America* (Vol. 1). Detroit: Gale Research.

Abudabbeh, N. (1996). Arab families. In M. McGoldrick, J. Giordano, & J. K. Pearce (Eds.), *Ethnicity and family therapy* (pp. 333–346). New York: Guilford Press.

Abu-Laban B., & Suleiman M. (1989). *Arab Americans: Continuity and change.* Belmont, MA: Association of Arab-American University Graduates.

Abu-Laban, S. (1989). Identity and adaption among Arab-American Muslims. In B. Abu-Laban & M. W. Suleiman (Eds.), *Arab Americans: Continuity and change* (pp. 45–63). Belmont, MA: Association of Arab-American University Graduates.

Altorki, S. (1995). Role and status of women. In J. L. Esposito (Ed.), *The Oxford encyclopedia of the modern Islamic world* (pp. 323–327). New York: Oxford University Press.

Atiyah, E. (1958). *The Arab's world.* Baltimore, MD: Penguin Books.

Barakat, H. (1985). The Arab family and the challenge of social transformation. In E. Fernea (Ed.), *Women and the family in the Middle East: New voices of change* (pp. 27–48). Austin: University of Texas Press.

Barazangi, N. (1989). Arab Muslim identity transmission: Parents and youth. In B. Abu-Laban & M. W. Suleiman (Eds.), *Arab-Americans: Continuity and change* pp. 65–82). Belmont, MA: Association of Arab-American University Graduates.

Bowen, D., & Early, E. (1993). Introduction. In D. L. Bowen & E. A. Early (Eds.), *Everyday life in the Muslim Middle East* (pp. 77–80). Bloomington: Indiana University Press.

Budman, C., Lipson, J., & Meleis, A. (1992). The cultural consultant in mental health care: The case of an Arab adolescent. *American Journal of Orthopsychiatry, 62,* 359–370.

Davis, D., & Davis, S. (1993). Dilemmas of adolescence: Courtship, sex, and marriage in a Moroccan town. In D. L. Bowen & E. A. Early (Eds.), *Everyday life in the Muslim*

Middle East (pp. 84–90). Bloomington: Indiana University Press.

El-Badry, S. (1994). The Arab-Americans. *American Demographics, 16*(1), 22–30.

El Guindi, F. (1995). Hijab. In J. L. Esposito (Ed.), *The Oxford encyclopedia of the modern Islamic world* (pp. 108–111). New York: Oxford University Press.

El Saadawi, N. (1993). Women and sex. In D. L. Bowen & E. A. Early (Eds.). *Everyday life in the Muslim Middle East* (pp. 81–83). Bloomington: Indiana University Press.

Fukuyama, M. (1990). Taking a universal approach to multicultural counseling. *Counselor Education and Supervision, 30,* 6–17.

Gladding, S. (1992). *Counseling: A comprehensive profession.* New York: Macmillan.

Gushue, G. V., & Sciarra, D. T. (1995). Culture and families. In J. G. Ponterotto, J. M. Casas, L. A. Suzuki, & C. M. Alexander (Eds.), *Handbook of multicultural counseling* (pp. 586–606). Thousand Oaks, CA: Sage Publications.

Hottinger, A. (1963). *The Arabs: Their history, culture, and place in the modern world.* Los Angeles: University of California Press.

Isenberg, I. (1976). *The Arab world.* New York: H. W. Wilson.

Jackson, M. L. (1991). Counseling Arab Americans. In C. C. Lee & B. L. Richardson (Eds.), *Multicultural issues in counseling* (pp. 197–206). Alexandria, VA: American Association for Counseling and Development.

Kanafani, A. (1993). Rites of hospitality and aesthetics. In D. L. Bowen, & E. A. Early (Eds.), *Everyday life in the Muslim Middle East* (pp. 128–135). Bloomington: Indiana University Press.

Mansfield, P. (1992). *The Arabs* (3rd ed.). London: Penguin Books.

Meleis, A. (1991). Between two cultures: Identity, roles, and health. *Health Care for Women International, 12,* 365–377.

Najjar, R. (1994). A Palestinian's struggle with cultural conflicts. In J. M. Bystydzienski & E. P. Resnik (Eds.), *Women in cross-cultural transitions* (pp. 39–44). Bloomington, IN: Phi Delta Kappa Educational Foundation.

Nydell, M. K. (1987). *Understanding Arabs: A guide for Westerners.* Bangor, ME: Intercultural Press.

Patai, R. (1973). *The Arab mind.* New York: Scribners.

Pedersen, P. (1991). Multiculturalism as a fourth force in counseling. *Journal of Counseling and Development, 70,* 6–12.

Pollara, M., & Meleis, A. (1995). Parenting their adolescents: The experience of Jordanian immigrant women in California. *Health Care for Women International, 16,* 195–211.

Said, E. (1979). *Orientalism.* New York: Random House.

Savory, R. (1976). Christendom vs. Islam: 14 centuries of interaction and co-existence. In R. M. Savory (Ed.), *Introduction to Islamic civilization* (pp. 127–135). London: Cambridge University Press.

Shaheen, J. G. (1984). *The TV Arabs.* Bowling Green, OH: State University Popular Press.

Shaheen, J. G. (1997). *Arab and Muslim stereotyping in American popular culture.* Washington, D.C.: Center for Muslim-Christian Understanding.

Sue, D. W., Arredondo, P., & McDavis, R. J. (1995). Multicultural competencies and standards: A call to the profession. In J. G. Ponterotto, J. M. Casas, L. A. Suzuki, & C. M. Alexander (Eds.), *Handbook of multicultural counseling* (pp. 624–643). Thousand Oaks, CA: Sage Publications.

Sue, D., Bernier, J., Duran, A., Feinberg, L., Pedersen, P., Smith, E., & Vasquez-Nuttall, E. (1982). Position paper: Cross-cultural counseling competencies. *Counseling Psychologist, 43,* 301–308.

Sue, D. W., & Sue, D. (1990). *Counseling the culturally different: Theory and practice* (2nd ed.). New York: Wiley.

Timini, S. (1995). Adolescence in immigrant Arab families. *Journal of Psychotherapy, 32*(1), 141–149.

Tucker, J. (1993). The Arab family in history: "Otherness" and the study of the family. In J. Tucker (Ed.), *Arab women* (pp. 195–207). Bloomington: Indiana University Press.

U.S. Bureau of the Census. (1990). *Statistical abstracts of the United States: 1990* (110th edition). Washington, D.C.: U.S. Government Printing Office.

CECILIA CHAN
PETULA SIK YIN HO
ESTHER CHOW

45

A Body-Mind-Spirit Model in Health: An Eastern Approach

Looking to the East for Solutions

In response to the overspecialization of the health care profession and the failure of Western medicine to provide satisfactory cures (Taylor, 1979), there is a growing interest in how the Eastern philosophies of Buddhism, Taoism, Confucianism, energy work, body-mind connection, and traditional medicine can shed new light on patients' physical and mental health (English-Lueck, 1990; Hansen, 1992; Legge, 1964; Y.S. Leung, 1988; Needham, 1970; Pachuta, 1989; Tsuei, 1992; Yang, 1995a, 1995b). Western medicine fixes its gaze on isolated symptoms rather than on the patient himself. Its practitioners, therefore, tend to pay more attention to external sources of the disease at the expense of the internal dynamics of the patient's body. Under such circumstances, it may be illuminating to explore the Eastern philosophy of health and healing, which treats patients in the totality of their body-mind-emotion-spirit-environment (Chan, 1997a; Chan et al., 1998; Lei, 1988; Pachuta, 1989; People's Medical Publishing House, 1984).

The purpose of this paper is to bring to the attention of the clinical social workers the Eastern body-mind-spirit approach in health and healing (Lei, 1988; Yang, 1995a, 1995b). Health and well-being, in the traditional Chinese medicine paradigm, result from the achievement and maintenance of a state of harmonious balance of Life Energy[1] (Qi) between the internal integrated whole of the person and the external environment, the nature and the universe Pachuta, 1989; Reid, 1989; Vercammen, 1996; Yang, 1995b). Traditional Chinese medical practi-

tioners are trained to appreciate the dynamic interaction between the internal and external systems of a patient, his or her individual uniqueness, interrelations, and reactions, and the circular effect within the overall unified wholeness (Tsuei, 1992; Yin et al., 1994). By observing, listening, smelling, pulse reading, and inquiring about the patient's family relation, work, and emotions, traditional Chinese medical practitioners are able to make a comprehensive, in-depth diagnosis (Yin et al., 1994). Treatment typically consists in a prescription for herbal soups, recommendation for physical and therapeutic exercises, and some suggestions on how to improve the patient's family relations—the so-called mind-body-family wholeness treatment (Koo, 1982, 1989a, 1989b; Sheikh & Sheikh, 1989; Topley, 1978). This may sound esoteric to the practitioners of Western medicine. But the fact is alternative approaches to healing, such as qi-$gong$,[2] tai-$jiquan$,[3] $yoga$,[4] nutrition, aromatherapy,[5] herbal medicine,[6] acupuncture,[7] acupressure,[8] moxibustion,[9] massage, and temple healing are now being practiced widely by patients and their family members around the world (Chan, 1997c; Harold, 1994; R. Lee, 1978, 1984; Ng, 1995; Sheikh & Sheikh, 1989; Yang, 1995b).

Dualistic Western philosophy splits the spiritual and physical realms into two hostile and mutually exclusive spheres and attaches greater value to the former (Reid, 1989). Under the influence of the Western medical model, health care professionals in Hong Kong, including social workers in most health care settings, tend to see themselves as the caretakers of their patients' physical health. The psychosocial and spiritual needs of patients are often neglected (Chan, Chow et al., 1996; Chan, Ho et al., 1996; Chan, 1997c; Chang & Chan, 1994). Growing up in a predominantly Chinese society, social workers in Hong Kong are aware of the wide adoption of traditional Chinese medical practices as complementary methods to healing. However, as professionals, they have little to contribute in this area, because they are not familiar with the analytical framework concerning an individual's total well-being within the context of the balance of the five elements,[10] the attainment of *yin-yang* equilibrium, and its associated interventions (Lei, 1988).

In this article, we introduce several useful concepts in traditional Chinese medicine and discuss how they can be applied in clinical social work interventions with patients and their family members in Hong Kong (Chan, 1997a, 1997b, 1997c). By working with patients suffering from cancer, stroke, systemic lupus erythematosis (SLE), rheumatoid arthritis (RA), and diabetes and bereaved wives and postdivorced single mothers in groups (Chan, Ho et al., 1996; Chan et al., 1998; P. Lee, 1995; Man, 1996; Wan, 1996), we have developed a model of an individual's body-mind-spirit total well-being. This intervention, which focuses on the total well-being of the client's body, emotions, and spirituality (Chan et al., 1998), aims at empowering the client at a personal level. (For details of the body-mind-spirit intervention, please read Appendix 1 and 2.) Pre- and postintervention research results show significant improvement among patients who participated in treatment and self-help groups. They score higher on both physical health and communication with professionals and develop a sense of control of their illness and emotional well-being (Chan, Ho et al., 1996; Chan et al., 1988; Chow, 1995; Man, 1996; Wan, 1996).

Traditional Chinese Medicine

Traditional Chinese medicine originates from the Taoist philosophy of one's harmony with the universe (Reid, 1989). Under this philosophy, an individual's health and personal needs vary according to the weather and environmental conditions. One can attain physical, mental, and spiritual health only when one is able to strike an inner balance and harmony between the *yin*, the passive or feminine force, and the *yang*, the active or male force (Koo, 1982; Reid, 1989).

Health is thus seen as a harmonious equilibrium between the *yin* and *yang*, the five elements (*earth, wood, water, metal,* and *fire*), the internal environment (*dry, wet, hot, cold, wind,* and *flame*), the other external conditions (*physical harm, insect bites, poison, overeating,* and *overworking*), and the seven emotions (*joy, sorrow, anger, worry, panic, anxiety,* and *fear*) (Yin et al., 1994). This represents a holistic approach similar to the ecological and systems approaches practiced in the field of social work. It highlights an important difference between Western and Eastern typology: while Western typology divides the body, the mind, cognition, emotions, and behavior into discrete entities, Eastern typology regards the physical and spiritual as indivisible yet distinctly different aspects of the same reality, with the body serving as the root for the blossom of the mind (Reid, 1989). One's physical, emotional, and spiritual well-being are taken as an integrated whole, underlying a systemic and cybernetic conception of the equilibrium of human existence.

The Body-Mind Connection

Given this holistic body-mind-spirit conception of health and well-being, one can easily understand how one's emotional states affect one's physical well-being and vice-versa (Borysenko & Rothstein, 1987; Chan, 1995). For example, the degree of physical and psychiatric morbidity of bereaved persons is found to be higher than that of the normal population (Kararn, 1994; Parkes, 1986; Stroebe & Stroebe, 1993). Our research provides further evidence of this body-mind connection. One-third of the members in our groups of divorced women are seeing psychiatrists for their emotional and physiological problems, such as anxiety attacks, anger, suicidal tendencies, depression, and insomnia (Chan et al., 1998). Two-thirds of cancer patients of our groups are suffering from depression and/or anxiety attacks (Chan, Chow et al., 1996). Indeed, the New Age body-mind conception links somatic complaints to emotional deficits (Tsang, 1992), providing a basis for the development of interventions with an integrated perspective.

In Western philosophy, patients are taught to fight their illness (Simonton et al., 1978; Siegel, 1986). They refuse to accept chronic illness, misfortune, loss, and death. The treatment philosophy and strategy is to confront and attack (Kaplan et al., 1993). Western medicine combats the disease, tries to kill the bacteria, and radically cuts out defective body parts. Like a ruin in a battlefield, the patients are left to heal on their own. In contrast, Eastern philosophy regards disease as symptomatic of the patient's bodily dysfunction and inner disharmony. The treatment therefore focuses on strengthening the patients' entire bodily system and restoring his or her inner balance, instead of tackling only the physical manifestations of the illness (Yin et al., 1994). Since one's organs and emotions, the environment (diet, weather, color, taste, and sound) and spirits (values, life philosophy, and beliefs) are all connected to one another, an equilibrium between these elements is the key to one's health and well-being. Prescriptions thus vary according to the climate and the patient's mood, emotions, physical strength, and social relationships (Yin et al., 1994). Training and prescription for the patient's total well-being under such a cybernetic framework should be useful to social workers, especially to those working with clients in the process of healing. Table 45.1 shows the symbiotic interaction among body parts, emotions, and the mind within the classification system of the five elements, which will be useful in the diagnosis and treatment of the patient's psychosocial problems related to physical illness (Reid, 1989; Tsuei, 1992; Vercammen, 1996; Yin et al., 1994).

Emotions and Physical Well-Being

It is obvious that one's physical functioning is linked to one's emotional expression and sense of well-being (see Table 45.1). An individual's inter-nal systems of liver, heart, spleen, lungs, and kidney (the Chinese internal systems are different from the organs referred to in Western anatomy) will have a bearing on his or her mood and emotion (sorrow, fear, anger, joy, and worry). For example, if a person has a hot liver, it is likely that he or she would be hot-tempered and "liverish." If a person has weak lungs, he or she is likely to be depressive and sorrowful.

Nancy (34/F, social worker) developed tuberculosis (TB) in January 1998. Two years earlier, her mother had developed pancreas cancer, and Nancy took care of her mother at home during the terminal stages of her cancer. When her mother died in November 1997, Nancy was exhausted and depressed. Two months later, she developed TB. Her sorrow weakened her lungs and immune system. Not until she turned to therapy did Nancy realize that her illness was a manifestation of the grief she felt for the loss of her mother.

"I Am Sick and Tired of Being Sick and Tired"

Physical illness and discomfort can be annoying, irritating, depressing, and anxiety provoking. They can seriously affect patients' emotion, weaken their

Table 45.1 Categorization of the Body and the Mind under the Symbiotic Interaction of the System of Five Elements

	Five Elements				
Category	Wood	Fire	Earth	Metal	Water
Emotions	Anger	Joy	Worry	Sorrow	Fear
Expression	Yell, Grasp	Laugh, Grieve	Sing, Nag	Cry, Cough	Moan, Tense
Body (Yin, Yang) Organs	Liver, Gall Bladder	Heart, Small Intestine	Spleen, Stomach	Lung, Large Intestine	Kidney, Urinary Bladder
Tissue	Tendons	Vessels	Muscle	Skin	Bone
Sense Organs	Eye	Tongue	Mouth	Nose	Ear
Organs Being Supported	Heart (fire)	Spleen (earth)	Lung (metal)	Kidney (water)	Liver (wood)
Affecting Organs	Spleen (earth)	Lung (metal)	Kidney (water)	Liver (wood)	Heart (fire)
Mind/ Spirituality	Benevolence Soul Humanity	Faith Mind Authenticity	Politeness Idea Reason	Justice Spiritedness Wisdom	Intelligence Will Faith

Source: Tsuei, 1992, p. 90; Yin et al., 1994, p. 20,

immune system, and create a whole range of imbalances inside the body (Zhang & Guo, 1991). The sicker they feel, the more depressed they become. It is easy for individuals to get into a vicious cycle of worsening physical and mental health. According to traditional Chinese medicine, these are all the consequences of an imbalance or a disharmony that exists between the interrelationships and dynamic interactions among the various subsystems and five main elements (Tsuei, 1992; Yin et al., 1994). The key to successful healing therefore lies in identifying the efficient elements and strengthening them through health education and mood control.

For the Chinese, a healthy person is someone who can always keep his or her emotions under control, take time to cultivate the mind artistically, and behave moderately. The book *Shen Chien* states "In order to nourish the spirit, anger, pity, happiness, care and anxieties must at all costs be moderated" (quoted in Needham, 1970). In another classic, *All Men Are Brothers*, it is pointed out that "The ancients have said that a soft temper is the root of long life and a high (hot) temper is the beginning of Trouble" (Buck, 1967). Excessive emotions can affect bodily functions. How often have we seen unhappy people or bereaved or divorced women approach the health care system for somatic complaints? The Asian population is known to somatize rather than to seek help for emotional stress (Lau et al., 1981).

According to the systems of five elements, excess joy can affect the heart, small intestine, tongue, and blood vessels. The emotions of excess anger can affect the organ system of liver, gall bladder, eyes, and tendons. Excess worry can affect the digestive system of the spleen, stomach, mouth, and muscles. Excess sorrow can affect the lungs, large intestine, nose, and skin. Excess fear and anxiety can affect the kidney, urinary bladder, ears, and bones (Yin et al., 1994). The dysfunctional systems will subsequently affect other bodily organs and their functioning (Lei, 1988).

When Flora (42/F, housewife) discovered her husband was having extramarital affairs, she began to develop symptoms of insomnia, mood swings, dryness of the eyes, knee pain, rough lines on her nails, and poor liver functions. These symptoms were all related to her excess emotions of anger. She participated in a Reiki class (hands-on healing) and started working on her anger by putting her hands on the right side of her lower rib cage, where the liver is situated. She learned that she would have to let go of her

anger to regain her health. She immersed herself in volunteer services and finally came to forgive her husband for his infidelities. Her condition improved two years after the therapy.

The first author has observed a *qi-gong* master at work. A woman complained about sores on her elbows and the *qi-gong* master asked her, "Why are you so angry?" The woman said, "Yes, there are things that I am very angry about." The *qi-gong* master said, "Let go of your anger or the pain on your elbows will stay." This is characteristic of *qi-gong* masters and doctors of traditional herbal medicine who often provide their patients with advice on how to control their emotions, behave properly, and live well. In this sense, these healers are doctor, counselor, spiritual leader, and exercise instructor, all in one.

There is much that social workers can learn from traditional Chinese medicine. By making the connection between emotional states and health, they can improve their clients' physical health and well-being by helping them let go of their excess emotions. A patient's discomfort in the liver system, for example, may be relieved by urging him or her to reflect on the virtue of benevolence, humanity, and service to other people (see Table 45.1). In short, we have to facilitate our clients' understanding of the emotional and spiritual origin of their physical discomfort/losses and their ability to heal through the process of giving and volunteerism (Lei, 1988).

Restoring Emotional Balance Through Working with the Mind

In Table 45.1, we can see that the relief of emotional strain can be achieved through physical training of the body as well as spiritual reflection on the meaning of life (Barnard, 1990; Frankl, 1984). Indeed, practitioners of traditional medicine under the influence of Buddhist[11] and Taoist schools of thought are always ready to preach by telling their patients what to do and how to live (Chan, 1995, 1997c; Lei, 1988). For them, benevolence, helping other people, lovingkindness, respect for humanity, forgiveness, and finding new meanings in life are the cures for excess anger, while trust in other people, sincerity, and respect for nothingness can reduce excessive joy. Resorting to reason, discounting gains and losses, and humility are antidotes to excessive worry (Y. S. Leung, 1988; Yin et al., 1994). This reflects the heavy influence of the Buddhist teaching that "the more one wants, the more one suffers"

(Chan, 1997b; Yang, 1995a) and the Taoist philosophy that one should accept life as ever changing and unpredictable (Chan, 1997b; Yang, 1995b).

This growing interest in the link between one's emotional and physical well-being is not confined to Chinese societies. In the West, there is an increasing number of publications on spirituality and the meaning of life, such as *Chicken Soup for the Soul* and *Inner Simplicity*, which addresses the issues of morality and value. Given such zeitgeist, clients may be more receptive to a holistic, body-mind-spirit-environment intervention. But before we set out to help our clients to get in touch with and control their innermost feelings, we may have to do some soul-searching on our own first.

Lucy (35/F, housewife) developed breast cancer when she was about to divorce her husband, who had been abusing her for 15 years. Depressed and suicidal, she approached the Hong Kong Cancer Fund for counseling. Other cancer survivors helped her understand that having cancer was not the end of the world. She began to take part in the Fund's weekly meetings and learned about diet, acupressure, qi-gong, and alternative healing. She then became a voluntary worker herself and spent much time helping other cancer patients. She believed that having cancer changed her life. No longer self-pitying and bitter about life, she grew into a person who appreciated life and was devoted to helping others. She has found new meaning in her life through serving on the hotline. She accepted her misfortunes in life and took them as challenges to accomplish personal growth.

Body Work

Working with the formula of body-mind-spirit interaction, social workers can lead their clients on the pathways to cure through their body, their mind, and their spirit. The flow of energy (*qi*) through the meridians is one of the most important and unique concepts in traditional Chinese medicine and acupuncture (Tsuei, 1992). The flow of *qi* along the fourteen meridians governs the well-being of our internal systems. Popular approaches to healing such as *qi-gong, tai-jiquan, yoga*, acupressure, moxibustion, massage, *qi* meditation, Reiki, hands-on healing, and reflexology[12] are modifications of using concepts of meridians and acupuncture points in the human body. Chinese physicians regarded message and gymnastics as some of the

best ways to harmonize the *qi*, to nourish the body, and to expel noxious tumors from the body (Koo, 1982). Acupressure and moxibustion at acupuncture points in the body can be employed to maintain health and relieve symptoms.

Many of these techniques can be taught to clients during the process of their healing and recovery. For instance, we can teach them acupressure and *qi-gong* exercises in therapeutic and support groups to help them regain a sense of control. There is also a whole range of treatment exercises and massage programs that they can practice to help themselves. A 38-year-old SLE patient said, "I felt empowered by the group because there are things that I can do to help myself recover." In China, the Cancer Clubs popularize a type of *qi-gong*, called walking guo-lin *qi-gong*, which the patients practice four to five hours every day in the parks (Shanghai Cancer Club, 1993; Zhang, 1994). Apart from physical exercises, patients are able to gain from the practice group support, mutual reinforcement, and social interaction (Chan, 1997b; Shanghai Cancer Club, 1993). Such a practice can also be used as a psychological distraction from the patient's illness and a kind of stress inoculation training (Michenbaum, 1985).

Massage is another means widely used in our groups to promote the health and well-being of our clients. Women in our postdivorce single parent group love facial massage (Chan et al., 1998). Cancer patients in our groups are taught what acupuncture points to press to enhance their immune system and help restore their bodily functioning (P. Leung, 1997). Bereaved wives love hugging and group massage activities as they are deprived of physical intimacy and touch after the death of their husbands, especially in a Chinese society that discourages physical contact (Chow, 1995). Fourteen out of 16 members of the SLE group reported improvement after practicing acupressure and massage exercises for six weeks.

Physical Exercises to Handle Emotions

Physical well-being can restore emotional balance, too. Physical exercise can lift clients out of depression. A simple physical exercise is designed to facilitate emotional expression and augment a sense of satisfaction (Chan et al., 1998). Some seemingly trivial bodily movements, such as a blink of the eye, star jumps, hip swings, hand massage, and ear massage, are fond to be very useful in helping clients ventilate their emotional tensions and frustrations, as well as increasing their sense of satisfaction (Chan et al., 1998).

Alexander Lowen (1975) has designed a school of body-work called bioenergetics[13] by blending psychoanalysis with physical exercise and body-work. The adoption of the harmonious flow of *qi* in the body is actually an easier framework to follow. *Qi-gong* exercises can relax the person and transport him or her into a state of tranquility and peace of mind (Shanghai Cancer Club, 1993). Research on this topic has shown that physical exercise can reduce depression. Our research also found that participation in our body-mind-spirit-environment groups improved the patients' physical, emotional well-being and enhanced their sense of pride in life (Chang, Chow et al., 1996; Zhang, 1994).

In fact, physical exercise is sometimes an effective alternative to counseling (Chan et al., 1998). Not all individuals can articulate or want to share their feelings and emotions with other people. By practicing the breathing exercises, acupressure, and *qi-gong* exercises, they can develop a sense of emotional and spiritual well-being (Shanghai Cancer Club, 1993; Zhang, 1994). Action speaks louder than words.

Spiritual Transformation: Growth through Pain

Some of our clients have a hard time getting over their traumatic experiences, loss, and pain. Overwhelmed by a strong sense of loss of control, they are resentful of their God, the supernatural creator, who made life so difficult for them. By turning depressed and angry, sad and fearful, dispirited or aggressive, bitter and cynical about life, jealous and suspicious, revengeful and unforgiving, self-pitying and socially destructive, they are a miserable lot stuck with the negativities in life (Barnard, 1990; Chan et al., 1998; Kleinman, 1988; Miller, 1983; Ngan et al., 1994).

But there are clients who behave otherwise. Despite their misfortunes and bad experience, they come out positive, charming, energetic, loving, forgiving, generous, kind, and full of life. They are the winners who grow and learn through pain and suffering by transforming their traumatic experiences into a platform for personal growth (Chan, 1997a; Frankl, 1984; Leick & Davidsen-Nielsen, 1991; LeShan, 1989; Yang, 1995a). This willingness to "hang in there" and meet the difficulties head-on is the necessary first step we must take in waking the Hero/Buddha within us (Shanghai Cancer Club, 1993; Yang, 1995a).

Philosophical and Spiritual Intervention

Qi-gong practices also emphasize the morality of life, promote meditation and letting go (Yang, 1995b). Under Taoist teaching, meditation promotes respect for nature (Hansen, 1992) and a detached, easygoing, and noncompetitive mentality (J. Lee, 1995; Cloke, 1993). It contrasts sharply with the Western values of striving for excellence, competition, achievement, and success in life.

The Eastern concepts of accepting life as being unpredictable, tolerating hardship, finding meaning in suffering, letting go of the self and expectations of others, self-affirmation and empowerment are some of the key components of treatment in our groups (Chan, 1997a, 1997c; Chow, 1995; P. Leung, 1997). Being able to help others is an effective way of giving meaning to suffering. It is also consistent with the helper-therapy principle of personal growth through helping others (Jeffers, 1993; J. Lee, 1995; Shanghai Cancer Club, 1993). Under the concept of Karma, it pays to help others as by doing so one will be rewarded in heaven (Chan, 1995, 1997b; Lei, 1988; Yang, 1995a).

Forgiveness and letting go are common themes in our work (Benson, 1992; Chan, Chow et al., 1996; Chan et al., 1988; DiBlasio & Proctor, 1993; McCullough & Worthington, 1994; Wanderer & Cabot, 1978). The negative emotions of anger, hatred, worry, and self-pity can suffocate and exhaust cancer patients and bereaved or divorced persons, draining their energy to grow and change. Through reexamining the meaning of life, exploring the concept of letting go, and learning how to acknowledge and work with emotions, our group members have strengthened their mental resources. Even if their illness or situation worsens, their ability to handle loss and distress is enhanced.

Changing the Environment: A Social Worker's Work Is Never Done

Since Chinese find it hard to talk about their emotions, they have a natural tendency to somatize their emotional frustrations (Cheung, 1986; Cheung et al., 1984; Cheung & Lau, 1982; Lau et al., 1981). As pragmatic people, Chinese are always willing to comply with medical instructions, usually preferring psychoeducational classes to psychoanalytic psychotherapy (P. Leung, 1997).

Owing to the strength of family as an institution and the support network it provides in Hong Kong, patients are actually better off than they are usually given credit for (Chan, Ho et al., 1996; Oen, 1991; Tang, 1994). Survivors of physical and mental illness are willing to help new patients by sharing their experiences. For them, it is a way to reestablish self-worth and repay society (Chan, 1997b; Chan et al., 1992, 1993; J. Lee, 1995; Williams, 1989; S. Wong, 1993; D. Wong & Chan, 1994).

To effect real changes, we must also work with the patient's family (Biegel et al., 1991; Dillon, 1985; Ma et al., 1993), the social system (Conrad & Kern, 1986), the legislature, and the environment (Jeffrey & Madden, 1991). While health is still closely linked to poverty, social environment, and access to service, social workers have to take on an advocate's role in bringing about changes (Blackburn, 1991; Chan et al., 1992; D. Wong & Chan, 1994; Davis, 1986; Ikeda, 1974; World Health Organization, 1981).

Conclusion

Transcending the Western typology of body-mind duality, seeing health as a harmonious interplay between an individual's body-mind-spirit components and the environment can energize social work intervention. We can, for example, help clients improve the inner workings of their bodies by showing them how to handle their emotions. The teaching of such skills as *qi-gong*, acupressure, and massage is not only good for clients' physical health; it introduces an element of fun and variety in our intervention. Fostering a sense of spiritual gain through loss and pain is also effective in enhancing clients' strength and resilience to misfortunes. We are still a long way from developing elaborate interventions with the body-mind-spirit approach. Yet with the encouraging results of the research we have done in Hong Kong, we have every reason to believe this approach will soon render itself very useful to social work intervention in health settings.

Notes

1. The *qi* energy is a cosmic life force that flows through the human body in a very orderly and logical way. Balance and harmony of the flow of *qi* results in health. The imbalance or disharmony of the flow leads to illness (Lei, 1988).

2. With a history of 2,000 to 3,000 years, *qi-gong* exercise combines motion with stillness and involves different forms and demands. *Qi-gong* can be done in the form of a walking exercise for relaxation, respiration training, breath control, and mental regulation (sometimes referred to as meditation). It consists of five kinds of regulation exercises: regulation of mind, posture, respiration, voice production, and combined exercises. New *qi-gong* is proven to have a definite effect on chronic diseases, including cancer and cardiovascular disease. The principles of roundness, softness, and extensiveness in movement should be observed in practice. Essential attributes for doing New *qi-gong* exercises well are confidence, determination, and perseverance (Tsuei, 1992).

3. *Tai-jiquan*, which has its origins in the Taoist philosophies, accords with the principles of traditional Chinese medicine. It stresses the need to harmonize with nature, and is a Chinese health-enhancement practice for the prevention and treatment of disease. *Tai-jiquan* should be practiced on a regular basis, which takes about 30 minutes to complete one circle of exercise consisting of movements linked together in a series of continuous steps. It requires a focused mind with a strong sense of purpose and coordinates with deep, calm breathing patterns (Nash, 1996).

4. Originated in India over 4,000 years ago, yoga means "union," being at one, at harmony with oneself and everything in creation. It is a holistic training for the body-mind-emotions-spirit that emphasizes self-control through a series of exercises, levels of breathing, postures, relaxation, and meditation (Sheikh & Sheikh, 1989).

5. *Aromatherapy* is an ancient mediated practice recorded in the writing of early civilizations including Egypt, India, and China. It is a treatment of common ailments and health problems with highly concentrated oils that have been extracted from plants and trees. These oil essences are believed to contain properties of natural healing power. They are often used in massage or hand and foot baths. There are more than 130 different oils whose uses can be classified into the following three major categories: refreshing and uplifting, regulating and toning up of body, and relaxing and soothing. Essences of aromatic plants have been used for beauty and healing purposes (Nash, 1996).

6. *Herbal medicine* had been used by different cultures of ancient civilizations such as Egyptians, Greeks, Romans, Chinese, and Indians. Herbal

medicine is basically the Chinese ancient pharmacology, and is heavily influenced by Taoism in its accordance with the *yin* and *yang* practices. It has been used as a natural way of improving health with great emphasis on the holistic approach in treating the physical, emotional, and spiritual needs of patients. Basically a plant-based medicine, its ingredients consist of minerals, animal components, and extracts of flowers, fruit, leaves, roots, stems, and seeds. It is especially used for strengthening and regulating the deficient properties of patients' body systems (Lei, 1988).

7. *Acupuncture*, the best-known Chinese therapeutic technique, is a way of influencing bodily functions by inserting needles in the *xue meridians*). According to traditional Chinese medicine, there are 14 main meridians running from the hands and feet to the body and head. Acupuncture helps to maintain health and restore the balance between the physical, emotional, mental, and spiritual aspects of patients, the *yin-yang* balance, and the Law of Five Elements, helping the individual to arrive at a natural state of harmony. There are many factors that can upset the balance, disturb the flow of *qi*, and cause disharmony and ill-health, including excess emotions, poor eating habits, drugs, environmental and occupational conditions, change of weather, and the like.

8. *Acupressure* is a massage technique widely used in China and Japan for over 3,000 years. Instead of using needles as in acupuncture, the therapist uses his or her palms, thumbs, and fingertips to apply firm pressure massage on the pressure points along the body's energy paths, or meridians. Acupressure balances the flow of energy, enhances natural vitality, and promotes maintenance of health and self-healing. It is believed to be highly effective in relieving stress and preventing illness and is used for beauty purposes and treating ailments (Tsuei, 1992).

9. *Moxibustion* is the burning of moxa, a kind of herb collected, dried, and prepared by the herbalists themselves. Moxa is thought to be *yang* in nature and is suitable for warming. One of the common treatments is to use a cylindrical moxa stick and move it along the track of the meridians. The burning stick can also be held over the meridians to cause heat to enter the body. Moxa used directly on kin will leave a dark mark after treatment. Regular moxa treatment is believed to be helpful in preventing disease (Sheikh & Sheikh, 1989).

10. The Law of Five Elements constitutes the fundamental analytical framework of traditional Chinese medicine, its concepts of bodily functions and the systems of healing. It is derived from Taoist philosophy. The five elements (wood, fire, earth, metal, and water), called *wuxing*, are the five basic components that govern the universe. They are intertwined within two basic relationships: a productive relationship, whereby one agent helps to create another; and a controlling relationship, whereby one agent limits the impact of another. For example, wood produces fire; fire produces earth; earth produces metal; metal produces water; and water produces wood. Earth is controlled by wood; wood is controlled by metal; metal is controlled by fire; fire is controlled by water; and water is controlled by earth. This complex system of relationships can be explained through the *yin-yang* theory. It is also believed that any relationship between the various elements of the universe can be seen as a kind of *wuxing* relationship, allowing for a systematic categorization of things and their interactions. According to this framework, our body, mind, and emotions can be compatible with the law of five elements. This is the fundamental schema with which Chinese physicians categorize the human body's organs, emotions, expression, mind, and spirituality into the system. Table 45.1 provides further information on how different sets of relations can be integrated into one single system and their causative and consecutive relations with the body-mind-spirit functions (Yin et al., 1994).

11. Buddhism originated in India. It spread into China and came under the influence of Taoism. Buddhism believes one should never cause harm to any living thing. It emphasizes compassion and peaceful coexistence. Through mediation, Buddhists hope to reach a state of "nothingness," or "emptiness," the liberation or freedom from desires. Buddhism believes in reincarnation, that each person will be born again and again until he or she reaches the state of emptiness. It is important to practice the Four Noble Truths and the Noble Eightfold Path of Buddha. The Four Noble truths are: Life is full of suffering and is created by humans; the suffering continues if man keeps on his pleasurable things; it is only when a person surrenders his luxurious life and seeks the reason of why humans suffer that he begins the footsteps of the Buddha. The Noble Eightfold Path is as follows: Right views (positive thinking, good in oneself, in others, and in creation), Right thoughts (caring for other and everything in nature), Right speech (tell the truth and be kind in words), Right action (do not kill, steal, or hurt), Right livelihood (do not cheat or harm others), Right effort (practice and

work hard to follow the path), Right mindfulness (be aware of the consequences of thoughts and actions), and Right concentration (calm, peaceful state of mind) (Lei, 1988).

12. *Reflexology,* a kind of natural therapy, applies massage to major reflex areas on the soles of the feet. It is believed that there are spots on the feet associated with different parts of the body. Treatment consists of applying special massage techniques to the appropriate spots (Nash, 1996).

13. *Bioenergetics* was developed by Lowen (1975) and is a way of understanding the personality in terms of the body and its energetic processes. These include breathing, movement, feeling, sexuality, and self-expression. Lowen's well-known exercise is the bow, which aims to build up the energetic charge of the body.

References

Barnard, D. Healing the damaged self: Identity, intimacy and meaning in the lives of the chronically ill. *Perspectives in Biology and Medicine* 33(4) 535–546, summer 1990.

Benson, C. K. Forgiveness and the psychotherapeutic process. *Journal of Psychology and Christianity* 11(1) 76–81, 1992.

Biegel, D. E., Sales, E., Schulz, R. *Family Caregiving in Chronic Illness.* Newbury Park, California: Sage, 1991.

Blackburn, C. *Poverty and Health: Working with Families.* Milton Keynes: Open University, 1991.

Borysenko, J, Rothstein, L. *Minding the Body, Mending the Mind.* Reading, MA: Addison Wesley, 1987.

Buck, Pearl S. *All Men Are Brothers.* Taipei, Taiwan: First Northern, 1967.

Chan, C. The application of Eastern philosophy and Western techniques of imagery in psychosocial support for Chinese cancer patients. Paper presented at the Second International Congress on Psycho-Oncology. October 19–22. Kobe, Japan, 1995.

Chan, C. Social work in health settings. In Chi, I, Cheung, S. K. (Eds.) *Social Work in Hong Kong.* Hong Kong: Hong Kong Social Workers Association, 1996, 69–79.

Chan, C. The application of Eastern philosophy in cancer counseling. Paper presented at the 14th Asian Cancer Conference and 4th Hong Kong International Cancer Congress, November 18, 1997a.

Chan, C. Chinese values and group counseling. Paper presented at the Third International Conference of Social Work Education in Chinese Societies, April 22–25, Taipei, 1997b.

Chan, C. Introduction. In Chan, C. and Rhind, N. (Eds.) *Social Work in Health Care.* Hong Kong: Hong Kong University, 1997c, 3–22.

Chan, C., Chan, Y., Law, W. F., Wong, F. L., Yu SC. *Manual for Emotional Healing for Divorced Women.* Hong Kong: University of Hong Kong. Department of Social Work and Social Administration (in Chinese), 1998.

Chan, C., Chow, A., Au, T., Leung, P., Chau, P., Chang, F., Ma, J., Cheng, B. Y., Tam, V. *Therapeutic Groups in Medical Settings (Resource Paper No. 25).* Hong Kong: University of Hong Kong, Department of Social Work and Social Administration, 1996.

Chan, C., Ho, J., Ng, H. S., Chau, M. *Quality of Life for Chronic Patients: Report of the Community Rehabilitation Network. (Resource Paper No. 27).* Hong Kong: University of Hong Kong, Department of Social Work and Social Administration, 1996.

Chan, C., Sham, J., Wei, W. Contribution of self-help to mental health of larygectomees in Hong Kong. *Asia Pacific Journal of Social Work* 3(1) 24–35, 1993.

Chan, C., Wong, D., Ho, P., Ip, F., Tong, H. *Report of a Survey of the Members of Self-help Groups for Persons with Chronic Illness in Hong Kong. (Resource Paper Series No. 19).* Hong Kong: University of Hong Kong, Department of Social Work and Social Administration, 1992.

Chang, F., Chan, C. Alternative social work intervention approaches in hospital setting—patient resource centre. *Community Development Resource Book 1993–1994.* Hong Kong: Hong Kong Council of Social Services, 1994, 141–151.

Cheung, F. M. Psychopathology among Chinese people. In Bond MH (Ed.) *The Psychology of Chinese People.* Hong Kong: Oxford University, 1986.

Cheung, F. M., Lau, B. W. K. Situational variation of help-seeking behavior among Chinese patients. *Comprehensive Psychiatry* 23(3) 252–62, 1982.

Cheung, F. M., Lau, B. W. K., Wong, S. W. Paths to psychiatric care in Hong Kong. *Culture, Medicine and Psychiatry* 8 207–28, 1984.

Chow, A. Y. M. The development of a practice model for working with the bereaved relatives of cancer patients. Unpublished master's dissertation, Department of Social Work and Social Administration, University of Hong Kong, 1995.

Cloke, K. Revenge, forgiveness, and the magic of meditation. In special issue: Beyond technique: The soul of family mediation. *Mediation Quarterly* 11(1) 6–78, 1993.

Conrad, P., Kern, R. (Ed.). *The Sociology of Health and Illness: Critical Perspectives.* New York: St. Martins, 1986.

Davis, S. (Ed.). *Tree of Life: Buddhism and Protection of Nature (with a Declaration on Environmental Ethics from the Holiness the Dalai Lama).* Geneva: Buddhist Perception of Nature, 1986.

DiBlasio, F. A., Proctor, J. H. Therapists and the clinical use of forgiveness. *American Journal of Family Therapy* 21(2) 175–84, 1993.

Dillon, C. Families, transitions, and health: Another look. *Social Work in Health Care* 10(4) 35–44, 1985.

English-Lueck, J. A. *Health in the New Age: A Study of California Holistic Practices.* Albuquerque: University of New Mexico, 1990.

Frankl, V. *Man's Search for Meaning.* New York: Simon & Schuster, 1984.

Hansen, C. *A Taoist Theory of Chinese Thought: A Philosophical Interpretation.* New York: Oxford University Press, 1992.

Harold, E. *Know Yourself, Heal Yourself: A Complete Guide to Natural Healing.* Victoria, Australia: Penguin, 1994.

Ikeda, D. *Protecting Human Life.* Tokyo: Soka Gkkai, 1974.

Jeffers, S. *The Journey from Lost to Found.* Toronto: Random House, 1993.

Jeffrey, D. W., Madden, B. (Eds.). *Bioindicators and Environmental Management.* London: Academic, 1991.

Kaplan, R. M., Sallis, J. F., Patterson, T. L. *Health and Human Behavior.* New York: McGraw-Hill, 1993.

Kararn, E. G. The nosological status of bereavement-related depressions. *British Journal of Psychiatry* 165 48–52, 1994.

Kleinman, A. *The Illness Narratives: Suffering, Healing, and the Human Condition.* New York: Basic, 1988.

Koo, L. *Nourishment of Life: Health in Chinese Society.* Hong Kong: Commercial Press, 1982.

Koo, L. Ethnonutrition in Hong Kong: Traditional dietary methods of treatment and preventing disease. *Hong Kong Practitioners* 11(5) 221–231, 1989a.

Koo, L. A journey into the cultural aspects of health and ill health in Chinese society in Hong Kong. *Hong Kong Practitioners* 11(2) 51–58, 1989b.

Lau, B. W. K., Cheung, F. M. C., Waldmann, E. Somatization among Chinese depressives in general practice. *International Journal of Psychiatric Medicine* 10(4) 361–374, 1981.

Lee, J. An exploratory study of leadership in self-help organizations in Hong Kong.

Unpublished master's dissertation, Department of Social Work and Social Administration, University of Hong Kong, 1995.

Lee, P. An exploratory study of the effectiveness of relaxation techniques on rheumatoid arthritis patients. Unpublished master's dissertation, Department of Social Work and Social Administration, University of Hong Kong, 1995.

Lee, R. Interaction between Chinese and Western medicine in Hong Kong. In Anthropological Psychiatrics and Public Health Studies (Eds.) *Culture and Healing in Asian Society.* Cambridge, MA: Schenkman Publishing, 1978, 289–319.

Lee, R. Chinese and Western health care systems: Professional stratification in a modernizing society. In King, A., Lee, R. (Eds.) *Social Life and Development in Hong Kong.* Hong Kong: Chinese University of Hong Kong, 1984.

Legge, J. trans. *1 Ching (Book of Change).* New York: University Books, 1964.

Lei, J. N. *Body-Mind-Spirit Total Health.* Taipei: Liuleikwong Publishing House (in Chinese, 1988.

Leick, N., Davidsen-Nielsen, M. *Healing Pain: Attachment, Loss and Grief Therapy.* Translated by Danish and David Stoner. London: Tavistock, 191.

LeShan, L: *Cancer as a Turning Point.* New York: E.P. Dutton, 1989.

Leung, P. Stress management for cancer patients: A psycho-educational-support group. In Chan C, Rhind N (Eds.) *Social Work in Health Care.* Hong Kong: University of Hong Kong, 1997, 85–103.

Leung, Y. P. Coping strategies of cardiovascular disease patients. Unpublished master's dissertation, Department of Social Work and Social Administration, University of Hong Kong, 1996.

Leung, Y. S. *Taoism, Buddhism and Confucianism in China.* Hong Kong: Suen Doe Publishing (in Chinese), 1988.

Lowen, A. *Bioenergetics.* New York: Penguin, 1975.

Ma, J., Chan, C., Chi, I., Sham, J. Social support for cancer patients in Hong Kong. *Asia Pacific Journal of Social Work* 3(1) 36–51, 1993.

Man, W. K. The empowering of Hong Kong Chinese families with a brain damaged member: Its investigation, measurement and intervention. Unpublished doctoral dissertation, Department of Social Work and Social Administration, University of Hong Kong, 1996.

McCullough, M. E., Worthington, E. L. Encouraging clients to forgive people who have hurt them: Review, critique, and research prospectus. *Journal of Psychology and Theology* 22(1) 3–20, 1994.

Michenbaum, D. *Stress Inoculation Training.* New York: Pergaman, 1985.

Miller, J. F. *Coping with Chronic Illness: Overcoming Powerlessness.* Philadelphia: F. A. Davis, 1983.

Nash, B. *From Acupressure to Zen.* London: Hunter House, 1996.

Needham, J. *Clerks and Craftsmen in China and the West.* London: Cambridge University Press, 1970.

Ng, H. Y. Healing in the Chinese temples: A challenge to clinical social work practice. *Hong Kong Journal of Social Work* 24(2), 10–17, 1995.

Ngan, Y. S., Tang, G. W. K., Lau, O. W. K. Psychosocial study on Hong Kong Chinese with gynecological cancer. *Journal of Psychometric Obstetrics and Gynecology* 15 111–17, 1994.

Oen, S. L. An exploratory study on the family support for patients of the day hospital at Yaumatei Psychiatric Center. Unpublished master's dissertation, Department of Social Work and Social Administration, University of Hong Kong, 1991.

Pachuta, D.M. Chinese medicine: The law of five elements. In Sheikh, A. A., Sheikh, K. S. (Eds.) *Healing East and West: Ancient Wisdom and Modern Psychology.* New York: Wiley, 1989, 64–90.

Parkes, C. M. *Bereavement: Studies of Grief in Adult Life.* London: Tavistock, 1986.

People's Medical Publishing House. *The Chinese Way to a Long and Healthy Life.* Hong Kong: Joint Publishing, 1984.

Rehr, H. Introduction. *Social Work in Health Care* 18(3/4) 101–102, 1993.

Rehr, H., Epstein, I. Evaluating the Mount Sinai Leadership Enhancement Program: A developmental perspective. *Social Work in Health Care* 18(3/4) 79–93, 1993.

Rehr, H., Rosenberg, G., Blumenfield, S. Enhancing leadership skills through an international exchange: The Mount Sinai experience. *Social Work in Health Care* 18(3/4) 13–33, 1993.

Reid, D. *The Tao of Health, Sex and Longevity: A Modern Practical Approach to the Ancient Way.* London: Simon & Schuster, 1989.

Shanghai Cancer Club (Ed.). *Challenging Life: The Experience of the Members of the Shanghai Cancer Club.* Shanghai: Shanghai Cancer Club (in Chinese), 1993.

Sheikh, A. A., Sheikh, K.S. (Eds.). *Eastern and Western Approaches to Healing: Ancient Wisdom and Modern Knowledge.* New York: Wiley, 1989.

Siegel, B. *Love, Medicine and Miracles.* New York: Harper and Row, 1986.

Simonton, O. C., Matthews-Simonton S, Creighton J. L. *Getting Well Again.* New York: Bantam Books, 1978.

Stroebe, M. S., Stroebe, W. The mortality of bereavement. In Stroebe, M. S., Stroebe, W., Hansson, R. O. (Eds.) *Handbook of Bereavement.* Cambridge, England: Cambridge University, 1993.

Tang, W. H. Quality of life of gynecological cancer patients. Unpublished master's dissertation, Department of Social Work and Social Administration, University of Hong Kong, 1994.

Taylor, R. *Medicine Out of Control.* Melbourne: Sun Books, 1979.

Topley, M. Chinese and Western medicine in Hong Kong. In Kleinman A. (Ed.) *Cultural and Healing in Asian Society.* Cambridge, MA: Schenkman, 1978.

Tsang, L. W. *Understanding the New Age Movement.* Hong Kong: Suen Doe Publishing, 1992.

Tsuei, W. *Roots of Chinese Culture and Medicine.* Jaya, Malaysia: Pelanduk Publications, 1992.

Vercammen, D. Theory and practice of Chinese medicine. In Alpen, J. V., Aris, A, *Oriental Medicine: An Illustrated Guide to the Asian Arts of Healing.* Boston: Shambhala, 1996.

Wan, W. K. An exploratory design of an empowerment group for the stroke survivors. Unpublished master's dissertation, Department of Social Work and Social Administration, University of Hong Kong, 1996.

Wanderer, Z., Cabot, T. *Letting-Go.* New York: Bantam, 1978.

Williams, G. H. Hope for the humblest? The role of self-help in chronic illness: The case of ankylosing spondylitis. *Sociology of Health and Illness* 11(2) 135–59, 1989.

Wong, D., Chan, C. Advocacy and self-help for patients with chronic illness: The case of Hong Kong. *Prevention in Human Services* 11(1) 117–139, 1994.

Wong, S. Y. E. A study of self-help movement in Hong Kong: Implications for the role and involvement of social workers. Unpublished master's dissertation, Department of Social Work and Social Administration, University of Hong Kong, 1993.

World Health Organization. *Managerial Process for National Health Development: Guiding Principles for Use in Support of Strategies for Health for All by the Year 2000.* Geneva: World Health Organization, 1981.

Yang, K. A. *Buddhism and Health*. Heilungjiang: Heilungjiang Xinhua Books (in Chinese), 1995a.

Yang, K. A. *Taoism and Health*. Heilungjiang: Heilungjiang Xinhua Books (in Chinese),1995b.

Yin, H. H., Zhang, B. L., Zhang, C. Y., Zhang, S. C., Meng SM (Eds.) *Foundations of Chinese Medicine*. Shanghai: Shanghai Scientific (in Chinese), 1994.

Zhang, Z. W. Overview of comprehensive cancer rehabilitation care in China. Paper presented at the Hong Kong International Cancer Congress, Hong Kong, November 28–30, 1994.

Zhang, Z. W., Guo, Y. R. Studies of psychological factors and cancer in China. In Cooper, C. L., Watson, M. (Eds.) *Cancer and Stress: Psychological, Biological and Coping Studies*. Chichester: Wiley, 1991, 125–143.

Appendix 1 A Body-Mind-Spirit Intervention for Cancer Patients in Hong Kong

Cognitive Dimension	Behavioral Dimension	Emotional Dimension	Physical Dimension	Spiritual Dimension
Cognitive restructuring	Meditation & guided imagery	Emotional healing	Breathing exercises	Faith
Positive thinking	Relaxation training	Skills for dealing with emotions	Physical exercises	Goal & meaning of life
Secondary gains	Affirmations	Traditional Chinese perspectives		Sense of self-worth & dignity
	Love & forgiveness	Mutual support & understanding		
	Laughter & play			
	Life enrichment plan			

The social workers attempt to bring about change in the patterns through intervening at five levels of cognitive, behavioral, physical, emotional, and spiritual dimensions. Each session of the group meeting deals with a few dimensions and the group is run as a Cancer Fighter Training Course. Patients are more willing to come to a training course than a counseling group. Pre- and postgroup research results show significant improvements among group members on their physical, emotional, and social well-being.

Source: P. Leung, 1997, p. 93.

Appendix 2 Themes and Contents of the Cancer Fighter's Training Course

Session	Theme of Session	Specific Objectives	Contents
1	**You Can Fight Cancer**	• Introduce purpose of the group • Explain concept of body-mind connection, cancer, stress, & relaxation • Inspire lighting spirit & confidence in self-healing • Obtain commitment from members • Get acquainted	• Informal lecture • Sharing about background & expectation among patients • Goal setting and contracting • Meditation* • Breathing exercise • Encouraging song I • Home assignments

(continued)

Appendix 2 Themes and Contents of the Cancer Fighter's Training Course (*Continued*)

Session	Theme of Session	Specific Objectives	Contents
2	**Enjoy Peace of Mind**	• Cognitive restructuring • Introduce positive thinking, power of thought, & will power • Encourage appreciation of life & nature	• Report back on home assignment • Sharing about secondary gains • Informal lecturing • Meditation II* • Physical exercise I • Encouraging song II • Home assignments
3	**Love, Foregiveness, & Letting Go**	• Relaxation training • Explain therapeutic effect of love, forgiveness, & letting go • Introduce Chinese philosophy of acceptance, holding on, & letting go • Introduce ways to love & to forgive • Promotion of acceptance	• Report back • Progressive muscle relaxation • Informal lecture • Mirror work • Cushion exercise • Meditation III* • Physical exercise II • Encouraging song III • Home assignments
4	**Taking Control of Your Life**	• Explain relationship between emotion & well-being • Dealing with emotions • Talk on cancer personality	• Report back • Video appreciation • Informal lecture • Sharing ways to deal with emotions • Test on cancer personality • Meditation IV* • Physical exercise III • Encouraging song IV • Home assignments
5	**Inspiring Hope & Search for the Purpose of Life**	• Introduce affirmations • Develop life enrichment plan • Evaluation and summary	• Report back • Sharing of feelings and achievement • Evaluation questionnaire & recommendations • Meditation V* • Encouraging song V

*Meditation in each session was based on the same theme as that of the session.

Source: P. Leung, 1997, p. 100

46

Does Social Work Oppress Evangelical Christians? A "New Class" Analysis of Society and Social Work

"Injustice anywhere is a threat to justice everywhere," wrote Martin Luther King (1992, p. 85). When injustice is tolerated against a specific group, ultimately everyone's access to justice is at risk. Indeed, since its foundation, social work has recognized the deleterious effects of social injustice and incorporates as one of its six guiding ethical principles the need to understand and ameliorate oppression (NASW, 2000).

Recognition of injustice, however, is a perplexing issue. How does discrimination against a particular group enter one's consciousness? It is clear that the actual existence of oppression is a minimal criterion at best. For a century and a half, segregated restaurants, hotels, schools, and buses existed without being acknowledged as a problem. Similarly, the internment of coastal-dwelling Asian Americans during World War II was not widely perceived as discriminatory when it occurred, but only long after the internment was an accepted fact.

As Edelman (1990) noted, ideologically oriented class issues keep oppressions concealed. Indeed, the most deeply obscured instances of discrimination stem from ideological premises that are so widespread in people's everyday language that they are not recognized as ideological at all but are accepted as the way the world is constituted. For example, to generations of educated white people socialized to see black people as a less-evolved form of life, segregation reflected the reality of the cosmos, not a matrix of oppression.

Accordingly, social work has attempted to uncover oppression by deconstructing the prevailing dominant ideology using a modified Marxist analysis. As Hamilton and Sharma (1997) observed, a clash between ideologies or worldviews, along with a power differential, sets the stage for oppressive conditions. Because the class or group holding power inclines toward oppressing those without access to power, serving its own ideological interests, deconstructing the dominant class tends to reveal the populations who face oppression.

The profession has done a commendable job applying this framework in the areas of race, ethnicity, gender, age, sexual orientation, and so forth, but one area has been overlooked: religion. Although the *Code of Ethics of the National Association of Social Workers* (NASW, 2000) stipulates that "social workers should obtained education about and seek to understand the nature of social diversity and oppression with respect to . . . religion" (p. 9, 1.05c) few, if any, articles have explored the oppression of religious populations.

Definitions

This article's discussion of religious oppression uses a number of terms. The most specific, *Evangelicals*, refers to a transdenominational, ecumenical Protestant movement that emphasizes the following three points: (1) salvation only through existential, personal trust in Christ's finished atoning work, (2) a spiritually transformed life marked by moral conduct and personal devotion such as scripture reading and missions, and (3) the Bible as authoritative and reliable (Marsden, 1987). Because of their status as the nation's largest spiritual tradition—approximately 25% of the population—Evangelicals often are used as a proxy for a family of discrete religious groups that are frequently referred to as religious conservatives (Green, Guth, Smidt, & Kellstedt, 1996).

Religious conservatives, or orthodox believers, are defined as individuals who derive their value system from an external transcendent source, often manifested in a particular sacred text (Hunter, 1991). In North America these individuals are primarily *theists*, defined as people who believe in a personal God of transcendent existence and power, who seek to ground their lives in the Bible (Gallup & Castelli, 1989). In keeping with the accepted practice of using self-designations for the population being described, this article uses the term "people of faith" interchangeably with religious conservatives/historically orthodox believers. This term is used by Evangelicals (Reed, 1996; Wolfe, 1998) to refer to themselves and other orthodox believers. It is this community of historically orthodox believers, and Evangelicals in particular because of their status as the nation's largest religious minority group, that a new dominant class seeks to oppress.

Emergence of the "New Class"

Traditional Marxism posits the existence of two classes: the middle class and the working class. The emergence of a third class—the "new class," or knowledge class—has been adopted by a number of sociologists to explain changes that have occurred in Western societies since World War II (Berger, 1986; Bruce-Briggs, 1979; Ehrenreich, 1990; Frow, 1993; Gouldner, 1979; McAdams, 1987; Schmalzbauer, 1993; Szelenyi & Martin, 1991). As observers have noted, what was once a large middle class has split into two ideologically demarcated entities. It is between these two relatively privileged groups that Western culture's predominant societal conflict occurs. As Berger put it, "Contemporary western societies are characterized by a protracted conflict between two classes, the old middle class (occupied in the production and distribution of material goods and services) and a "new class" (occupied in the production and distribution of symbolic knowledge)" (p. 67).

The rise of the "new class" is traced to the sustained economic growth Western societies have experienced since World War II in conjunction with rapid technological advancement. The information, government, and financial sectors that increasingly underlie Western economies have led to a substantial increase in the knowledge occupations. Whereas employment in manufacturing has been trending down, both relatively and absolutely since the turn of the 20th century, the number of knowledge-producing occupations tripled from 1900 to 1959 and then doubled from 1960 to 1980, at which juncture it accounted for approximately 34% of the U.S. gross national product (GNP) (Frow, 1993; Hunter, 1991). Because many social workers depend on social welfare spending for their economic livelihood, it is interesting to note that government spending for social welfare is 22% of the GNP in 1995.

The "new class" has been demarcated in various fashions (Schmalzbauer, 1993). The broadest definition of the class includes all professionals. Conversely, more narrow interpretations define the group as those who work in the "cultural production" occupations (for example, academia, media) and professions whose self-interest is served by the expansion of government (for example, social work).

Regardless of how the new class is defined, empirical tests with national survey data have found a distinct ideology associated with political liberalism, the rejection of traditional moral values, and functional secularism (Ladd, 1979; McAdams, 1987; Schmalzbauer, 1993). The surveys demonstrate that the new class differs substantially from the middle class and "working class" as well as other groups and differs radically from numerous cultural groups and workers (who were the traditional means of production) on religious affiliation, moral and sexual issues, national priorities, foreign and defense policy, personal values, and party affiliation (Ladd, 1979; McAdams, 1987). For example, Schmalzbauer, using 17 years of General Social Survey data, surmised that the ideological framework held by the new class is distinct from and frequently at odds with groups such as the working class and Evangelicals.

The new class wields political and cultural power disproportionate to its relatively small size. This power flows from its ability to control the labels and manipulate the symbols by which the broader population understand themselves and their purposes in life (Lipset, 1979). Indeed, as feminists have noted (Luepnitz, 1988), the ability to apply labels is one of the most fundamental expressions of power.

As Bruce Briggs (1979a) noted, because of professional and educational status, the new class is "favored in income, status, freedom, power, and other presumed benefits of life" (p. 9). Although distinct from the "old money" socioeconomic group, the new class generally occupies the upper-middle socioeconomic strata (Gouldner, 1979; Szelenyi & Martin, 1991). However, given their ability to define and direct the parameters of public discourse, the members of the new class enjoy a measure of prestige and power that surpasses even that of the upper level of the traditional bourgeois class.

Yet, despite the new class's power and prestige, its members actively engage in reshaping society. Because they hold the keys to cultural discourse, it is inevitable that the members of the new class could influence public perceptions, even if they attempted to maintain objectivity (Sermabeikian, 1994). However, as is the case in any class struggle, the new class seeks to influence and persuade, to advance its own ideological interests at the expense of other constructions of reality in an effort to achieve cultural hegemony.

Gouldner (1979) an advocate of the new class, who is widely praised for his conceptualization of the this new cultural group (Szelenyi & Martin, 1991), delineated the ground rules for engaging the old middle class and opposing interests as follows: "Short of going to the barricades, the "new class" may harass the old, sabotage it, critique it, expose and muckrake it, express moral, technical, and cultural superiority to it, and hold it up to contempt and ridicule" (p. 17). As Gouldner noted, in the struggle between the new class, the middle class, and the working class, any tactic will be used to ensure that the new class interests prevail.

Secular Ideology of the "New Class"

Among the many characteristics that distinguish the new class, one of the most pertinent is its functional secularism. Indeed, the differences in metaphysical beliefs and practices between new class professionals and members of the middle and working classes has been documented with nationally representative data sets (McAdams, 1987; Schmalzbauer, 1993). The culture of critical discourse on which the new class is based is thought to engender a secular orientation (Gouldner, 1979). More broadly, transcendent truth claims, such as those posited by theistic traditions, are eroded by the new class means of production in favor of a relativistic, lib-

eral, or progressive set of morals and values and heterodox religious beliefs.

Social work serves as a pertinent example. Illustrating the corrosive effects of new class status on theism, 44% of Sheridan and associates' (1992) sample of Virginia-based clinical social workers (N = 108) no longer participated in the religious tradition of their childhood, with the change in religious affiliation from childhood to present occurring predominantly in a shift away from Christianity to "none" or "other." Significantly, over one-third (36%) of workers reported a range of sentiments from ambivalence to strong agreement when presented with the statement "I feel negative about the religious experiences in my past." Similarly, nationally representative data indicated that 20% of NASW members (N = 2,069) reported negative childhood religious experiences (Furman, Canda, & Benson, 2001).

Because in Marxist theory cultural and socioeconomic status engenders a distinct set of metaphysical beliefs, a dramatic difference in cosmologies has developed between social workers and the middle class and working classes, the more traditional members of society. National survey data indicate that anywhere from 95% (Canda & Furman, 1999) to 66% (Gallup & Castelli, 1989) of the general population believe in a personal God, the sine qua non of theism (Lauer, 1967; Ludwig, 1987). Conversely, studies, using a scale adapted from Lehman (1974) that presents individuals with six discrete options ranging from belief in a personal God to views that notions of God or the transcendent are illusions and irrelevant, have found that roughly similar percentages of social workers affirm nontheistic beliefs. Sheridan and associates' studies of clinical social workers (N = 108) and social work educators drawn from 12 southeastern states (N = 280) found that, respectively, 70% (Sheridan et al., 1992) and 62% (Sheridan, Wilmer, & Atcheson, 1994) rejected belief in a personal God. The elevated rates of nontheistic belief among practitioners and educators are congruent with data on the beliefs of NASW members (Furman, Canada, & Benson, 2002).

Functional secularism is demonstrated by the lack of importance attributed to religion. Whereas 57% of Sheridan and associate's (1992) sample of clinical social workers (N = 108) reported either limited or no involvement in any organized religion or spiritual group, 86% of the general population reported that religion was either very or fairly important to them (Gallup & Castelli, 1989). A study of Midwestern Evangelicals (N = 76) found that 75% (n = 57) of respondents perceived social workers to be less religious than the general population; 90% indicated social workers were less religious than themselves (Furman, Perry, & Goldale, 1996).

Correspondingly, because the new class largely determines the topics of public discourse, an Evangelical perspective receives minimal exposure (Carter, 1993; Neuhaus, 1984). Because their theistic cosmology holds little meaning for the new class, the tendency of this group is to ignore it. For example, empirical investigation in such new class fields as prime time fictional television (Skill, Robinson, Lyons, & Larson, 1994), popular periodicals (Perkins, 1984), social science research (Larson, Sherrill, & Lyons, 1994), and psychology (Bergin, 1980) and social work textbooks (Cnaan, 1999; Hodge, Baughman & Cummings, 2002), documents that almost complete exclusion of Evangelical religious expression. As Kuhn (1970) noted, salient information falling outside the reigning ideology is disregarded.

In sum, because an Evangelical perspective holds little relevance to the new class, the tendency is to reflect that stance in its spheres of influence by excluding it from meaningful discussion. Both past and present constructions of reality are largely devoid of an Evangelical narrative. American history textbooks essentially omit its historical presence (Boyer, 1996), and the New York Times bestseller list has historically excluded Evangelical works from its lists, including the top-selling book of the 1970s (Hunter, 1991). Although this approach effectively disenfranchises the Evangelical community, recently a more aggressive tactic has been adopted.

Active Oppression of Evangelicals

As implied earlier, most Evangelicals, along with other people of faith, are members of the traditional middle and working classes associated with the production and delivery of goods and services. Furthermore, Evangelicals, Catholics, Orthodox Jews, Muslims, Mormons, and other people of faith hold value positions (for example, on abortion) that are at odds with those held by the new class (Schmalzbauer, 1993). In fact, Hunter (1991), formerly a new class theorist (Hunter, 1980), has since posited the cultural conflict in terms of epistemologically derived values, with orthodox believers committed to transcendent truth on one side and progressives or heterodox believers who understand truth in a relativistic manner on the other.

Put different, the new class, or knowledge class has so effectively assimilated large segments of the middle class that a key, and perhaps now the primary, obstacle to advancing its interests are people of faith and their competing worldview. In other words, the new class tactics have so eroded the middle class that Evangelicals and other people of faith are one of the few remaining independent of new class means of knowledge production. Thus, attacking the largest religious minority, Evangelicals, weakens what remains of the middle class and a competing construction of reality.

Accordingly, as the new class has grown more secure in its cultural dominance, overt hostility against Evangelicals and other people of faith has become increasingly evident in new class forums. The necessary conditions for oppression, a clash between ideologies, along with a power differential, have been set in place (Hamilton & Sharma, 1997). Evangelicals sense an increased level of hostility, as evidenced by Smith's (1998) research with a nationally representative sample of self-identified Evangelicals (N = 430), which found that 92% of respondents felt that "Christian values are under serious attack in the United States."

Content analysis has revealed pejorative depictions of conservative Christians and their beliefs in television (Skill & Robinson, 1994), comic strips (Lindsey & Heeren, 1992), and textbooks for grade school (Vitz, 1985), high school (Bellitto, 1996; Hillocks, 1978; Sewall, 1995), and college-level marriage (Glenn, 1997), psychology (Lehr & Spilka, 1989), and social work courses (Hodge, Baughman, & Cummings, 2002). Analysis of the DSM III-R disclosed that Christianity was unduly associated with psychopathology (Larson, Milano, & Lu, 1998). In a manner analogous to Gilligan's (1993) critique of Kohlberg's (1981) work, researchers have illustrated that moral development research is biased against people of faith, assigning them a lower level of moral development because of their belief in basic theistic tenets (Richards & Davison, 1992).

Using a sampling frame of all faculty (N = 356) at every American Psychological Association (APA)-approved psychology doctoral program in the nation, Gartner (1986) studied the likelihood of being admitted to graduate psychology programs. Applicants who mentioned they were Evangelicals or stated that they desired to integrate their beliefs into their studies were more likely to be denied admission than comparable secular applicants who had not stated such a belief or desire.

Furman and colleagues' (1996) study of a midwestern sample of Evangelicals (N = 76) found "a profound difference" in the beliefs and values between social workers and Evangelicals. Eighty-three percent of Evangelicals felt that social workers did not understand their religious beliefs and values, and among those with counseling experience, the response rate rose to 94%. As a result, Evangelicals were hesitant to receive services from social workers and particularly felt they could not trust social workers with their female adolescent children.

In a series of studies using national samples, Neumann and colleagues demonstrated that professionals in the physical and social sciences discriminated against Evangelicals because of the difference in value systems (Neumann, Harvill, & Callahan, 1995; Neumann & Leppien, 1997a, 1997b; Neumann, Thompson, Woolley, 1991). Typical is their national study of graduate-level social workers (N = 131) affiliated with Veterans Affairs, which used vignettes to ascertain how liberal and Evangelical value systems would affect nonclinical, professional decisions (Neumann, Thompson, & Woolley, 1992). In every instance, vignettes that contained Evangelical values (for example, Christ as the one and only son of God) received lower approval ratings than vignettes that contained liberal values (for example, Christ as an excellent teacher and example), suggesting that social workers may exclude Evangelicals and other theists from teaching or publishing in professional social work forums.

Ressler and Hodge (1999) explored perceptions of religious discrimination in social work in their national survey of workers (N = 222) affiliated with the National Association of Christians in Social Work supplemented by students from three state university MSW elective classes on spirituality. These authors found that religious conservatives, almost exclusively Evangelicals, were 142% more likely to experience discrimination than religious liberals or progressives. Although the quantitative results indicated systemic, professionwide discrimination, incidents of discrimination occurred disproportionately in university settings, an expected finding given the instrumental function academia plays in propagating new class ideology (Gouldner, 1979). In spite of constitutional guarantees prohibiting religious discrimination (Clinton, 1995; Riley, 1998), students cited being denied funds to go to religiously affiliated conferences, being denied the right to write papers dealing with religion or spirituality or being given lower grades for writing on the topic, being denied practicum experiences in religiously affiliated agencies, being denied admittance to graduate school

because of religious undergraduate affiliation, and being denied the opportunity to finish their degree because of their Christian beliefs. Similarly, faculty reported being fired or threatened with firing, being denied funds for travel, and being denied tenure. A follow-up, quantitative study of respondents (N = 12) confirmed that conservative narratives are systematically silenced in social work settings (Ressler & Hodge, in press).

Failure of Social Work to Deconstruct Its Ideology

How did the profession arrive at the point where it is producing social workers who are either consciously or unconsciously antagonistic toward Evangelicals and many other people of faith? The question is especially troubling given that Evangelicals were instrumental in founding social work. As Karger and Stoesz (1998) noted, the two were "inextricably linked" during the profession's formative years in the 19th century (Marsden, 1991). Indeed, the profession's values as articulated in the *Code of Ethics*, including its unique commitments to social justice, respect for all individuals, and service to poor and oppressed people, are derived from biblical mandates. For example, while many 19th-century academics were advocating social Darwinism—the application of the "survival of the fittest" doctrine—to society by withdrawing assistance to widows, orphans, poor people, and the like so the "less fit" would die at an enhanced rate, Evangelicals led the fight against social Darwinism, helping give birth to a profession rooted in biblical values as part of the struggle to provide services to disenfranchised populations (Magnuson, 1977; Olasky, 1992).

How did the profession shift from a position of acceptance toward diverse populations to a stance of antagonism toward one of its founders? The answer lies in the profession's failure to deconstruct the new class ideology that increasingly pervades the profession. To its credit, social work has been quick to grasp an essential philosophical implication of postmodernism: that value bias pervades all human endeavors (Sermabeikian, 1994). The profession's tendency, however, is to see only the new class cultural opponents as being informed by ideology, as when authors single out "right wing Christian ideologues" (Karger & Stoesz, 1998, p. 16). There is less willingness to engage in self-examination to discover specific areas in which social work's ideology fosters bias, despite the *Code of Ethic's* (NASW, 2000) injunction to engage in "responsible criticism of the profession" (p. 24, 5.01b).

Others, however, have observed that new class ideology is pervasive in social work (Berger, 1986; Hunter, 1980) and that it inhibits diversity and the free exchange of ideas (Bruce-Briggs, 1979b). Apparently only by excluding contradictory narratives can it be ensured that its version of truth will prevail. As Gouldner (1979) put it, "The 'new class' seeks to *control* everything, its topic and itself, believing that such domination is the only road to truth. The 'new class' begins by monopolizing truth and by making itself its guardian" (p. 85) [emphasis in original].

Accordingly, when an area of disagreement occurs between religious values and new class values (for example, sexual orientation), the profession's guiding ethical principles are superseded by its ideologically inspired drive to control the parameters of the debate by excluding divergent voices. Thus, articles appear in the literature implicitly recommending the expulsion of the few faith-based institutions from the profession (Jones, 1996) and the exclusion of conservative faith-based constructions of reality from curriculum content (Van Soest, 1996). Authentic diversity, in other words, allowing differing constructions of reality or truth, cannot be tolerated, as this would prevent the profession from monopolizing truth and being its sole arbitrator.

Inverting these examples helps clarify the degree to which the ideological drive to restrict the parameters of discussion occurs in the profession. The *Code of Ethics* (NASW, 2000) "does not specify which values, principles, and standards are most important and ought to outweigh others in instances when they conflict" (p. 3). In other words, there is no hierarchy regarding religion and sexual orientation. The *Code of Ethics* stipulates that workers are to respect both, recognizing that tensions exist between differing values. Thus, whereas Jones (1996) and Van Soest (1996) essentially argued that orthodox religious constructions of reality should be excluded from the profession because these perspectives allegedly inhibit engendering respect for gay men and lesbians, it is just as valid to advocate the opposite on the basis of the *Code of Ethics*. Yet it is difficult to conceive of an article appearing in the literature arguing that gay and lesbian narratives should be excluded from the profession's curriculum because such perspectives inhibit fostering respect for Muslims, for instance (Halstead & Lewicka, 1998).

Indeed, the completeness with which new class ideology controls the terms of the social work discussion is crystallized in the academic literature. As McMahon and Allen-Meares (1992) noted, published articles establish the issues of discussion in the profession, effectively defining the terms of debate. Publication legitimizes a perception and informs researchers and academics concerning significant issues. Asking how a professor's religion affects her or his interaction with gay men and lesbians fosters certain perceptions (Van Soest, 1996), whereas asking how a professor's homosexuality affects his or her interaction with people of faith fosters others. Recognizing the power inherent in publication, prominent social work journals attempt to foster the inclusion of diverse constructions of reality by stating they welcome even controversial articles that challenge the conventional wisdom (Witkin, 1998).

However, as the following analysis reveals, articles that present constructions of reality that deviate from new class norms are rarely published. McMahon and Allen-Meares (1992) noted that *Social Work, Families in Society, Social Service Review,* and *Child Welfare* are the leading, opinion-forming journals that cover a broad range of issues and have been used for a number of content analyses. Titles, abstracts, and descriptors were examined in *Social Work Abstracts Plus* 1977–1999/2003 for the most recent 10-year period for these four periodicals. These three areas are particularly significant because titles usually represent the author's attempt to convey the general ethos of the article, descriptors convey the main themes, and abstracts summarize the article's content. Together, they provide a thorough guide for understanding what themes and subjects are being addressed in the social work literature.

Whereas searches using "gay," "lesbian," and "homosexual" revealed more than 35 articles, and searches using "black" and "African American" resulted in more than 60 articles, searches using "Evangelical," "conservative Protestant," and the more pejorative "fundamentalist" revealed no articles. Even using "Christian" and associated terms resulted in only three articles. In all three cases, the term appeared in the abstract and was peripheral to the main themes of the article. Two articles chronicled the contributions of African Americans during the early 1900s through their involvement in the YWCA and YMCA; the third discussed the religious dimensions of the foster care system in India. Significantly, none of the articles dealt with the intersection of Evangelicalism and contemporary North American society. Similarly, examining Canda, Nakashima, Burgess, and Russel's (1999) exhaustive compilation of articles on spirituality revealed no listings in their section on Christianity during the past 10 years in the four specified journals.

Even using the broadest descriptors in *Social Work Abstracts Plus*, "religion" and "spirituality," elicited only 16 articles. When these 16 articles touched on the subject of Evangelicalism, they often associated it with negative characteristics, revealing new class ideological bias. For instance, Cornett (1992) discussed the "dangerousness" of conservative Protestants imposing their values in clinical settings on gay people and others who hold progressive or liberal values. There was no similar discussion concerning the dangers of nontheists imposing their liberal values on Evangelicals and other people of faith. New class ideology dictates that one side of the value conflict is highlighted while the other is ignored. Furthermore, given the divide in values between social workers and Evangelicals chronicled earlier, and the extant evidence indicating that Evangelicals are hesitant to receive services from social workers and do not trust social workers with their children (Furman et al., 1996), presumably because of fear of social workers imposing their values, it would seem that a discussion of the latter value conflict would be more appropriate.

The central point, however, is that in the forum of the leading social work journals, the voice of Evangelicals—a quarter of the population—is not heard (Green et al., 1996). Whereas the 1969 Stonewall riots that sparked the politicization of gay men and lesbians is delineated (Poindexter, 1997), the 1973 nationally profiled Kanawha County strikes against new class oppression that sparked Evangelical politicization is ignored (Martin, 1996). Once control of the debate has been established by essentially eliminating alternative constructions of truth from the literature, classrooms, and the like, voiceless populations can be redefined in keeping with the requirements of the dominant ideology. Thus, social work's agenda as applied to Evangelicalism is, a Gouldner (1979) put it, to "sabotage it, critique it, expose and muckrake it, express moral, technical, and cultural superiority to it, and hold it up to contempt and ridicule" (p. 17) to further the new class goal of cultural dominance.

Consequently, in social work textbooks and journal articles, Evangelicals are framed as being against "women's rights" (Hutchison, 1999, p. 241), and their beliefs are associated with promotion of "violence against women and children" (Longres, 1995, p. 83). Devout believers are depicted as snakehandlers (Pittman, 1990), and the "religious right" is said to support the "enforcement of morality" (Whitaker & Federico, 1990, p. 176). "Fundamentalists," "rocked" by "scandals," are partisan zealots who are against freedom of speech and freedom of religion (DiNitto, 1995, p. 27). Biblical beliefs are depicted as "wildly anachronistic," worthy of "ridicule" (Fabricant & Burghardt, 1998, p. 55), and inspiring "racism" (Spencer, 1998, p. 25). Evangelicals and other people of faith are called "minions" (Fabricant & Burghardt, 1998, p. 54) and are associated with the Ku Klux Klan, Nazis, and armed militias preparing for violent insurrection (van Wormer, 1997).

It is difficult to imagine any other population being characterized in such a disparaging light in prominent social work literature. It is also hard to conceive of a more egregious violation of the *Code of Ethics's* injunction to recognize "the strengths that exist in all cultures," (NASW, 2000, p. 9, 1.05a) or the four standards (1.05c, 2.01b, 4.02, 6.04d) that specifically mention religion as a category toward which the profession should strive to exhibit cultural sensitivity.

Yet, to recall Edelman's (1990) observation, it is important to note that new class ideologies may be so ingrained that some are tempted to understand the above characterizations as accurate, as reflecting reality. For example, a critic may respond that some Evangelicals attempt to use legislative action to advocate for values they believe in, such as further restrictions on partial birth abortion. Thus, describing them as supporting the "enforcement of morality" is essentially accurate, and therefore arguably congruent with the profession's ethical standards.

However, as social work is cognizant of, values infuse all legislation (Sermabeikian, 1994). All laws represent an attempt to legislate or enforce a perceived public good (Sayyid, 1997). Some members of the new class, including social workers, also attempt to use legislative action to advocate for values they believe in, such as further restrictions on firearms. It is difficult to see how singling out Evangelicals as supporters of the enforcement of morality, when social workers' own legislative efforts represent a similar attempt to impose their values (NASW, 2000), is a practice that promotes and demonstrates respect for the social and cultural differences of Evangelicals. Similarly, on an international level, stating that the Vatican is an outpost of "modern religious fanaticism," that Irish Catholics "have just enough religion to make [them] hate," and that Muslims commit "crimes against humanity" (van Wormer, 1997, pp. 507, 509, 511) would seem to do little to "promote con-

ditions that encourage respect for cultural and social diversity within the United States and globally"
(NASW, 2000, p. 27, 6.04c). Such characterizations, however, do serve to further new class ideological aims of discrediting people of faith and their
worldviews.

Numerous other tactics also are used to deni-
grate people of faith. In a profession that places a
special emphasis on helping poor people (NASW,
2000), perhaps the most potent means of disparaging Evangelicals in social work literature is to
characterize them as being antagonistic toward this
vulnerable population. Thus, social work history
reports that the Protestant ethic was "inimical" to
efforts to assist poor people (Macarov, 1995, p. 86)
and that in the 1980s "a firestorm of fundamentalism swept across the nation" restricting services
to marginalized groups (Karger & Stoesz, 1998,
p. 33). In the 1990s "religious conservatives" were
depicted as one of the three groups "spearheading"
the "war against the poor" (Gans, 1995, p. 90).
The "radical right" sought to "abolish the welfare
state" (Midgley & Jones, 1994, p. 116). "Religious
fundamentalists" were associated with "harsh
treatment of society's underdogs" (van Wormer,
1997, p. 507), and the Christian Coalition reportedly believed the poor "must be attacked" (Fabricant & Burghardt, 1998, p. 54).

Despite the inflammatory nature of such comments, little in the way of empirical evidence is provided. Research with nationally representative data
sets has repeatedly revealed that religious conservatives hold more favorable attitudes toward poor
people than religious liberals (Clydesdale, 1990,
1999; Davis & Robinson, 1997; Hart, 1992; Iannaccone, 1993; Pyle, 1993; Regnerus, Smith, &
Sikkink, 1998; Wuthnow, 1994).

For example, Wuthnow (1994) found that "religious conservatives are substantially more likely
to have thought about [their responsibility to the
poor] than either moderates or liberals" (p. 196).
Regnerus and colleagues (1998) examined patterns
of personal giving to antipoverty organizations.
These authors found that Evangelicals were more
pro-poor than liberal Protestants. Furthermore, individuals who used conservative Christian leaders
and organizations such as the Christian Coalition
to help them in voting were more likely to give to
antipoverty organizations. Compared with their
counterparts, these individuals were 60% more
likely to give to poverty relief organizations.
Clydesdale (1999) examined attitudes toward
economic restructuring using the General Social
Surveys from 1984 to 1996. Using beliefs about the
Bible as a proxy for religious conservatism, he ex-

amined four areas. Religious conservatives were as
likely as liberals, and more likely than moderates, to
agree that "the government in Washington should
see to it that every person has a job and a good standard of living." However, religious conservatives
were more likely than both liberals and moderates
to agree that "the government in Washington should
do everything possible to improve the living standards of all poor Americans," "too little money is
being spent in this country on assistance ot the
poor," and "the government in Washington ought
to reduce the income differences between rich and
poor, perhaps by raising taxes on wealthy families
or by giving income assistance to the poor."

Views concerning poor people are not the only
area in which Evangelicals are misrepresented. Indeed, the extensive array of strengths research has
associated with Evangelicalism, including, for example, autonomy (Hodge, 2000; Pargament et al.,
1987), diversity (Smith, 2000), empowerment (Maton & Salem, 1995), forgiveness (Gorsuch & Hao,
1993), interpersonal friendliness (Ellison, 1992),
and self-esteem (Ellison, 1993) are largely ignored
in social work depictions of Evangelicals. That
these traits, which echo those that social workers
profess to uphold, should be evidenced among
Evangelicals should surprise no one. As noted earlier, Evangelicals were largely responsible for
founding the profession and articulating its guiding values.

Also troubling is the repeated use of negative labels ascribed to Evangelicals and other people of
faith. A case in point is the widely used label "fundamentalists." To disarticulate believers, the new
class has verbally isolated Christians by redescrib-
ing them first as traditionalist, then as orthodox,
next as ultra-orthodox, and finally as fundamentalists, while concurrently the belief system has
remained static (Johnson, 1995). As Hunsberger
(1995) observed, the label has been constructed by
the new class as a pejorative term, implying "bigotry, ruthlessness, hatred and a commitment to terrorism and militancy" (p. 119). Accordingly, the
label "fundamentalist" has roughly the same emotional force when applied to people of faith as the
label "queer" does to gay men and lesbians. The
term is used by the dominant class to exclude alternative narratives by signifying that people of
faith should be understood as "other," as nonnormal, as outside the bounds of legitimate discourse
(Sayyid, 1997).

If it is assumed that the textbooks and journal
articles containing such derisive depictions of Evangelicals do in fact "teach" future practitioners
something about the population, that the educa-

tional process creates a lens through which Evangelicals are viewed, it is little wonder that social workers have either consciously or unconsciously adopted an antagonistic stance toward Evangelicals. And given the disparity between the values that lens attributes to Evangelicals and empirical reality concerning the values Evangelicals actually hold, it is also not surprising that 94% of Evangelical consumers felt social workers did not understand their values (Furman et al., 1996). Nor is it surprising that Evangelicals in social work were 142% more likely than progressives to report being discriminated against in the profession (Ressler & Hodge, 1999).

Addressing the Problem

Deconstructing the profession's new class ideology, creating awareness, in other words, is the initial step in addressing the oppression of Evangelicals. Open acknowledgment, discussion, and research on the bias of some social workers in various social work forums would be productive. To facilitate critical assessment skills, classroom exercises could deconstruct social work texts, exploring how Evangelicals and other people of faith are labeled compared with other populations, in light of the *Code of Ethic's* injunctions to treat all populations with respect and dignity. Professors might highlight how some authors (Karger & Stoesz, 1998) refer to believers as "right wing Christian ideologues" (p. 16) without comparable references to, for example, left-wing feminist ideologues, implicitly marginalizing Christians in the eyes of readers.

Similarly, in terms of the profession's written materials, the *Code of Ethics* should be applied impartially, "recognizing the strengths that exist in all cultures" (NASW, 2000, p. 9, 105a). This goes beyond merely substituting another label for "fundamentalists" while leaving the central message intact. Rather, just as, for example, gay men, lesbians, and feminists are treated with sensitivity and respect, so too should Evangelicals, Catholics, and Muslims.

Social work texts, for example, could include people of faith in sections dealing with discrimination, noting how they are oppressed in new class venues. Historical accounts could highlight the Bible's influence on the *Code of Ethics*, or Evangelicals' struggle against social Darwinism on behalf of poor people, instead of pejoratively suggesting their belief system was opposed to assisting disenfranchised groups (Karger & Stoesz, 1998; Macarov, 1995). Likewise, journals could feature

Evangelical constructions of reality equally with the perspectives of other groups. The central point is to ensure that each population is given a voice and is treated in a manner that they feel respects their worldview, instead of interpreting populations through the ideological lens of the dominant class.

A deeper problem is the metaphysical imbalance between the profession and the populations it is called to serve. Given the hostility frequently expressed against them in social work, Evangelicals and other people of faith have been discouraged from choosing social work as a career (Ressler & Hodge 1999). Consequently, the profession is no longer representative of the general population or of many ethnic or cultural minority groups. Although many social workers continue to self-identify as Christian, their heterodox beliefs, such as rejecting belief in a personal God of transcendent existence and power (Sheridan et al., 1992; Sheridan et al., 1994), indicate that they identify with value systems radically different from those affirmed by mainstream Christianity and other theistic traditions (Lauer, 1967; Ludwig, 1987).

For example, 70% of Virginia-based clinical social workers (N = 108) affirm belief systems that place them outside the mainstream articulations of the world's major theistic religions: Christianity, Islam, Judaism, Sikhism, and Zoroastrianism (Richards & Bergin, 1997; Sheridan et al., 1992). Conversely, African Americans, Hispanics, poor people, elderly people, recent immigrants, and many other populations outside of the purview of the new class report high levels of theism (Davis & Robinson, 1996; Gallup & Castelli, 1989). More than 50% of African Americans, for instance, are Evangelicals (Richards & Bergin, 1997).

For many individuals, their faith is central to their personal ontology (Gallup & Castelli, 1989). Consequently, the profession is in danger of losing touch with large segments of the general population and the disenfranchised groups that have been central to its historic mission. For example, Muslims, perhaps now the largest theistic population after Christians (Melton, 1999), are often hesitant to receive services from professional counselors because of concerns related to therapists new class values (Altareb, 1996; Daneshpour, 1998). But the problem is not limited to adherents of theistic traditions. Many immigrants from nontheistic traditions, such as Hindus, find they have more in common with the values of conservative Christians than those affirmed by the new class (Fenton, 1988). In short, the profession risks losing its ability to provide services to any population whose worldview conflicts with the new class construction of reality.

Accordingly, attempts should be made to increase the numbers of Evangelicals in the profession so that social work is more representative of society. Although 25% of the general population are Evangelicals (Green et al., 1996), Sheridan and associates' (1994) study of full-time faculty (N = 280) at 25 schools in 12 southeastern states found that only 3% of social worker educators were Evangelicals. In other words, increasing the number of Evangelical faculty members by 700% would result in social work educational institutions that reflect the general population.

In addition to hiring more Evangelical faculty, a more immediate method for facilitating an Evangelical perspective is to provide a climate of support for Evangelical faculty members to disclose and discuss spiritual frameworks in classroom setting in the same manner as gay men, lesbians, and feminists are encouraged to discuss their personal perspectives (Cain, 1996). Not only do such disclosures challenge ingrained new class stereotypes concerning Evangelicals, but they support Evangelicals and other students of faith by making spiritual concerns visible and by facilitating discussion of related issues. Such activities help create "save zones" for students, encouraging them to continue in their programs while the profession addresses some of the more time-intensive issues such as recruitment and developing culturally sensitive texts.

Conclusion

Beyond the issues raised by the *Code of Ethics*, the oppression of Evangelicals and other people of faith should concern every social worker, for authentic diversity is an intrinsic good that enriches society. The sharing of alternative constructions of reality promotes understanding and fosters points of congruence among diverse populations. Indeed, it is through the uncensored sharing of narratives that society becomes aware of discrimination and can work toward ameliorating it. As North American society experiences increasing numbers of ideologically based conflicts as a result of the increasing multiculturalism of the population, the free exchange of discrete cultural narratives must be facilitated to foster a society in which all cultures can coexist in an atmosphere of mutual respect.

Furthermore, the profession has the ethical tools to become a broker of peace in the new multicultural reality. However, the effective use of these instruments is predicated on deconstructing its own ideological biases. If the profession hopes to serve all segments of the population, it must apply its ethics in its own house. As Gandhi observed, one must be the change one wishes to see in the world.

The author thanks Georgeanne Greene, Karen Cochran, Philip Shpakowsky, and the three anonymous reviewers for *Social Work* for their encouragement and comments, which substantially improved the manuscript.

References

Altareb, B. Y. (1996). Islamic spirituality in America: A middle path to unity. *Counseling and Values, 41*(1), 29–38.

Bellitto, C. M. (1996). Incomplete pictures: Religion in high-school textbooks on European history. *Social Studies, 87,* 274–280.

Berger, P. L. (1986). *The capitalist revolution.* New York: Basic Books.

Bergin, A. E. (1980). Psychotherapy and religious values. *Journal of Consulting and Clinical Psychology, 48,* 95–105.

Boyer, P. (1996). In search of the fourth "R": The treatment of religion in American history textbooks and survey courses. *History Teacher, 29*(2), 195–216.

Bruce-Briggs, B. (1979a). An introduction to the idea of the "new class." In B. Bruce-Briggs (Ed.), *The "new class"* (pp. 1–19). New Brunswick, NJ: Transaction Books.

Bruce-Briggs, B. (1979b). *The "new class"?* New Brunswick, NJ: Transaction Books.

Cain, R. (1996). Heterosexism and self-disclosure in the social work classroom. *Journal of Social Work Education, 32,* 65–76.

Canda, E. R., & Furman, L. D. (1999). *Spiritual diversity in social work practice.* New York: Free Press.

Canda, E. R., Nakashima, M., Burgess, V. L., & Russel, R. (compilers). (1999). *Spiritual diversity and social work: A comprehensive bibliography with annotations.* Alexandria, VA: Council on Social Work Education.

Carter, S. L. (1993). *The culture of disbelief: How American law and politics trivialize religious devotion.* New York: Basic Books.

Clinton, W. J. (1995). Memorandum for the U.S. secretary of education and the U.S. attorney general. Retrieved November 11, 1999, from w3.trib.com/FACT/1st.pres.rel.html.

Clydesdale, T. T. (1990). Soul-winning and social work: Giving and caring in the Evangelical tradition. In R. Wuthnow & V. A. Hodgkinson and associates (Eds.), *Faith and philanthropy in America* (pp. 187–210). San Francisco: Jossey-Bass.

Clydesdale, T. T. (1999). Toward understanding the role of Bible beliefs and higher education in American attitudes toward eradicating poverty, 1964–1996. *Journal for the Scientific Study of Religion, 38*(1), 103–118.

Cnaan, R. A. (1999). *The newer deal.* New York: Columbia University Press.

Cornett, C. (1992). Toward a more comprehensive personology: Integrating a spiritual perspective into social work practice [Op-Ed]. *Social Work, 37,* 101–102.

Daneshpour, M. (1998). Muslim families and family therapy. *Journal of Marital and Family Therapy, 24,* 355–390.

Davis, N. J., & Robinson, R. V. (1996). Religious orthodoxy in American society: The myth of a monolithic camp. *Journal for the Scientific Study of Religion, 35*(3), 229–245.

Davis, N. J., & Robinson, R. V. (1996). A war for America's soul? The American religious landscape. In R. H. Williams (Ed.), *Cultural wars in American politics* (p. 39–61). New York: Aldine de Gruyter.

DiNitto, D. M. (1995). *Social welfare: Politics and public policy* (4th ed.). Boston: Allyn & Bacon.

Edelman, M. (1990). *Constructing the political spectacle.* Chicago: University of Chicago Press.

Ehrenreich, B. (1990). The professional-managerial class revisited. In B. Robbins (Ed.), *Intellectuals: Aesthetics, politics, and academics* (pp. 173–185). Minneapolis: University of Minnesota Press.

Ellison, C. G. (1992). Are religious people nice? Evidence from the national survey of black Americans. *Social Forces, 71,* 411–430.

Ellison, C. G. (1993). Religious involvement and self-perception among black Americans. *Social Forces, 71,* 1027–1055.

Fabricant, M., & Burghardt, S. (1998). Rising from the ashes of cutback, political warfare and degraded services: Strategic considerations for community building: An editorial essay. *Journal of Community Practice, 5*(4), 53–65.

Fenton, J. Y. (1988). *Transplanting religious traditions.* New York: Praeger.

Frow, J. (1993). Knowledge and class. *Cultural Studies, 7,* 240–281.

Furman, L. D., Canda, E. R., & Benson, P. W. (2001). *Implications of religion and spirituality in social work practice: Descriptive findings from U.S. survey.* Unpublished manuscript.

Furman, L. D., Perry, D., & Goldale, T. (1996). Interaction of Evangelical Christians and social workers in the rural environment. *Human Services in the Rural Environment, 19*(3), 5–8.

Gallup, G. J., & Castelli, J. (1989). *The people's religion: American faith in the 90s.* New York: Macmillan.

Gans, H. J. (1995). *The war against the poor.* New York: Basic Books.

Gartner, J. D. (1986). Antireligious prejudice in admissions to doctoral programs in clinical psychology. *Professional Psychology: Research and Practice, 17,* 473–475.

Gilligan, C. (1993). *In a different voice: Psychological theory and women's development.* Cambridge, MA: Harvard University Press.

Glenn, N. (1997). *Closed hearts, closed minds: The textbook story of marriage.* New York: Institute for American Values.

Gorsuch, R. L., & Hao, J. Y. (1993). Forgiveness: An exploratory factor analysis and its relationship to religious variables. *Review of the Religious Research, 34,* 333–347.

Gouldner, A. W. (1979). *The future of intellectuals and the rise of the "new class."* New York: Seabury Press.

Green, J. C., Guth, J. L., Smidt, C. E., & Kellstedt, L. A. (1996). *Religion and the culture wars.* New York: Rowman & Littlefield.

Hallstead, J. M., & Lewicka, K. (1998). Should homosexuality be taught as an acceptable alternative lifestyle? A Muslim perspective. *Cambridge Journal of Education, 28*(1), 49–64.

Hamilton, T., & Sharma, S. (1997). The violence and oppression of power relations. *Peace Review, 9,* 555–561.

Hart, S. (1992). *What does the Lord require? How American Christians think about economic justice.* New York: Oxford University Press.

Hillocks, J. G. (1978). Books and bombs: Ideological conflict and the schools—A case study of the Kanawha County book protest. *School Review, 86,* 632–654.

Hodge, D. R. (2000).Do faith-based providers respect client autonomy? A comparison of client and staff perceptions in faith-based and secular residential treatment programs. *Social Thought, 19*(3), 39–57.

Hodge, D. R., Baughman, L. M., & Cummings, J. A. (2002, February 24–27). *Moving toward spiritual competency: Deconstructing religious stereotypes and spiritual prejudices in social work literature.* Paper presented at the 48th annual program meeting, Council on Social Work Education, Nashville.

Hunsberger, B. (1995). Religion and prejudice: The role of religious fundamentalism, quest, and right-wing authoritarianism. *Journal of Social Issues, 51*(2), 113–129.

Hunter, J. D. (1980). The "new class" and the young evangelicals. *Review of the Religious Research, 22,* 155–169.

Hunter, J. D. (1991). *Culture wars.* New York: Basic Books.

Hutchison, E. D. (1999). *Dimensions of human behavior.* Thousand Oaks, CA: Pine Forge Press.

Iannaccone, L. R. (1993). Heirs to the Protestant ethic? The economics of American fundamentalists. In M. E. Marty & R. S. Appleby (Eds.), *Fundamentalisms and the state* (pp. 342–366). Chicago: University of Chicago Press.

Johnson, P. (1995). God and the Americans. *Commentary, 99*(1), 25–45.

Jones, L. E. (1996). Should CSWE allow social work programs in religious institutions and exemption from the accreditation nondiscrimination standard related to sexual orientation? No! *Journal of Social Work Education, 32,* 302–310.

Karger, H. J., & Stoesz, D. (1998). *American social welfare policy* (3rd ed.). New York: Longman.

King, M. L. (1992). Letter from Birmingham jail, April 16, 1963. In J. M. Washington (Ed.), *I have a dream: Writings and speeches that changed the world* (pp. 84–100). San Francisco: Harper San Francisco.

Kohlberg, L. (1981). *The philosophy of moral development: Moral stages and the idea of justice.* San Francisco: Harper & Row.

Kuhn, T. S. (1970). *The structure of scientific revolutions* (2nd ed.). Chicago, University of Chicago Press.

Ladd, E. C. J. (1979). Pursuing the "new class": Social theory and survey data. In B. Bruce-Briggs (Ed.), *The "new class"* (pp. 101–123). New Brunswick, NJ: Transaction Books.

Larson, D., Milano, G. M., & Lu, F. (1998). Religion and mental health: The need for cultural sensitivity and synthesis. In S. O. Okpaku (Ed.), *Clinical methods in transcultural psychiatry* (pp. 191–210). Washington, DC: American Psychiatric Association.

Larson, D. B., Sherrill, K. A., & Lyons, J. S. (1994). Neglect and misuse of the r word. In J. S. Levin (Ed.), *Religion in aging and health* (pp. 178–195). London: Sage Publications.

Lauer, R. Z. (1967). Theism. In W. J. McDonald (Ed.), *New Catholic encyclopedia* (Vol. 14, pp. 9–11). New York: McGraw-Hill.

Lehman, E. C. (1974). Academic discipline and faculty religiosity in secular and church-related colleges. *Journal for the Scientific Study of Religion, 13,* 205–220.

Lehr, E., & Spilka, B. (1989). Religion in the introductory psychology textbook: A comparison of three decades. *Journal for the Scientific Study of Religion, 28,* 366–371.

Lindsey, D. B., & Heeren, J. (1992). Where the sacred meets the profane: Religion in the comic pages. *Review of Religious Research, 34*(1), 63–77.

Lipset, S. M. (1979). The "new class" and the professoriate. In B. Bruce-Briggs (Ed.), *The "new class"* (pp. 67–89). New Brunswick, NJ: Transaction Books.

Longres, J. F. (1995). *Human behavior in the social environment* (2nd ed.). Itasca, IL: F. E. Peacock.

Ludwig, T. M. (1987). Monotheism. In M. Eliade (Ed.), *The encyclopedia of religion* (Vol. 10, pp. 68–76). New York: Macmillan.

Luepnitz, D. A. (1988). *The family interpreted.* New York: Basic Books.

Macarov, D. (1995). *Social welfare: Structure and practice.* Thousand Oaks, CA: Sage Publications.

Magnuson, N. (1977). *Salvation in the slums: Evangelical social work 1865–1920.* Grand Rapids, MI: Baker Book House.

Marsden, G. M. (1987). Evangelical and fundamental Christianity. In M. Eliade (Ed.), *The encyclopedia of religion* (Vol. 5, pp. 190–197). New York: Macmillan.

Marsden, G. M. (1991). *Understanding fundamentalism and evangelicalism.* Grand Rapids, MI: Eerdmans.

Martin, W. (1996). *With God on our side.* New York: Broadway Books.

Maton, K. I., & Salem, D. A. (1995). Organizational characteristics of empowering community settings: A multiple case study approach. *American Journal of Community Practice, 23,* 631–656.

McAdams, J. (1987). Testing the theory of the "new class." *Sociological Quarterly, 28*(1), 23–49.

McMahon, A., & Allen-Meares, P. (1992). Is social work racist? A content analysis of recent literature. *Social Work, 37,* 533–539.

Melton, J. G. (1999). *The encyclopedia of American religions* (6th ed.). London: Gale Research.

Midgley, J., & Jones, C. (1994). Social work and the radical right: Impact of developments in Britain and the United States. *International Social Work, 37,* 115–126.

National Association of Social Workers. (2000). *Code of ethics of the National Associations of Social Workers* [Online] Available: www.naswdc.org/Code/ethics.htm. Retrieved January 20, 2000.

Neuhaus, J. R. (1984). *The naked public square: Religion and democracy in America.* Grand Rapids, MI: Eerdmans.

Neumann, J. K., Harvill, L. M., & Callahan, M. (1995). Impact of humanistic, liberal Christian, and Evangelical Christian values on the self-reported opinions of radiologists and psychiatrists. *Journal of Psychology and Theology, 23,* 198–207.

Neumann, J. K., & Leppien, F. V. (1997a). Impact of religious values and medical specialty on professional inservice decisions. *Journal of Psychology and Theology, 25,* 437–448.

Neumann, J. K., & Leppien, F. V. (1997b). Influence of physicians' religious values on inservice training decisions. *Journal of Psychology and Theology, 25,* 427–436.

Neumann, J. K., Thompson, W., & Woolley, T. W. (1991). Christianity versus humanism: The influence of values on the nonclinical professional decisions of Veterans Administration psychologists. *Journal of Psychology and Theology, 19,* 166–177.

Neumann, J. K., Thompson, W., & Woolley, T. W. (1992). Evangelical vs. liberal Christianity: The influence of values on the nonclinical professional decisions of social workers. *Journal of Psychology and Christianity, 11*(1), 57–67.

Olasky, M. (1992). *The tragedy of American compassion.* Wheaton, IL: Crossway.

Pargament, K. I., Echemendia, R. J., Johnson, S., Cook, P., McGath, C., Myers, J. G., & Brannick, M. (1987). The conservative church: Psychosocial advantages and disadvantages. *American Journal of Community Psychology, 15,* 269–286.

Perkins, H. W. (1984). Religious content in American, British, and Canadian popular publications from 1937 to 1979. *Sociological Analysis, 45,* 159–165.

Pittman, F. (1990). The rattle of God. *Family Therapy Networker, 14*(5), 43–46.

Poindexter, C. C. (1997). Sociopolitical antecedents to Stonewall: Analysis of the origins of the gay rights movement in the United States. *Social Work, 42,* 607–615.

Pyle, R. E. (1993). Faith and commitment to the poor: Theological orientation and support for government assistance measures. *Sociology of Religion, 54,* 385–401.

Reed, R. (1996). *Active faith.* New York: Free Press.

Regnerus, M. D., Smith, C., & Sikkink, D. (1998). Who gives to the poor? The influence of religious tradition and political location on the personal generosity of Americans toward the poor. *Journal for the Scientific Study of Religion, 37,* 481–493.

Ressler, L. E., & Hodge, D. R. (1999, March 10–13). *Religious discrimination in social work: an exploratory study.* Paper presented at the 45th annual program meeting, Council on Social Work Education, San Francisco.

Ressler, L. E., & Hodge, D. R. (in press). Silenced voices: Social work and the oppression of conservative narratives. *Social Thought.*

Richards, P. S., & Bergin, A. E. (1997). *A spiritual strategy.* Washington, DC: American Psychological Association.

Richards, P. S., & Davison, M. L. (1992). Religious bias in moral development research: A psychometric investigation. *Journal for the Scientific Study of Religion, 31,* 467–485.

Riley, R. W. (1998). Religious expression in public schools [Online]. Available: www.ed.gov/Speeches/08-1995/religion.html. Retrieved November 7, 2000.

Sayyid, B. S. (1997). *A fundamental fear.* New York: St. Martin's Press.

Schmalzbauer, J. (1993). Evangelicals in the "new class": Class versus subcultural predictors of ideology. *Journal for the Scientific Study of Religion, 32,* 330–342.

Sermabeikian, P. (1994). Our clients, ourselves: The spiritual perspective and social work practice. *Social Work, 39,* 178–183.

Sewall, G. T. (1995). *Religion in the classroom: What the textbooks tell us.* New York: American Textbook Council.

Sheridan, M. J., Bullis, R. K., Adcock, C. R., Berlin, S. D., & Miller, P. C. (1992). Practitioners' personal and professional attitudes and behaviors toward religion and spirituality: Issues for education and practice. *Journal of Social Work Education, 28,* 190–203.

Sheridan, M. J., Wilmer, C. M., & Atcheson, L. (1994). Inclusion of content on religion and spirituality in the social work curriculum: A study of faculty views. *Journal of Social Work Education, 30,* 363–376.

Skill, T., & Robinson, J. D. (1994). The image of Christian leaders in fictional television programs. *Sociology of Religion, 55*(1), 75–84.

Skill, T., Robinson, J. D., Lyons, J. S., & Larson, D. (1994). The portrayal of religion and spirituality on fictional network television. *Review of the Religious Research, 35,* 251–267.

Smith, C. (1998). *American Evangelicalism.* Chicago: University of Chicago Press.

Smith, C. (2000). *Christian America?* Los Angeles: University of California Press.

Spencer, M. S. (1998). Reducing racism in schools: Moving beyond rhetoric. *Social Work in Education, 20,* 25–36.

Szelenyi, I., & Martin, B. (1991). The three waves of "new class" theories and a postscript. In C. C. Lemert (Ed.), *Intellectuals and politics* (pp. 19–30). London: Sage Publications.

U.S. Bureau of Census. (1999). *Statistical abstract of the United States* (119th ed.). Suitland, MD: Author.

Van Soest, D. (1996). The influence of competing ideologies about homosexuality on nondiscrimination policy: Implications for social work education. *Journal of Social Work Education, 32,* p53–64.

van Wormer, K. (1997). *Social welfare.* Chicago: Nelson-Hall.

Vitz, P. C. (1985). Religion and traditional values in public school textbooks: An empirical study. In *Equality in values education: Do the values education aspects of public school curricula deal fairly with diverse belief systems?* [Microfilm]. Washington, DC: National Institute of Education.

Whitaker, W. H., & Federico, R. C. (1990). *Welfare in today's world* (2nd ed.). New York: McGraw-Hill.

Witkin, S. L. (1998). "Greetings." *Social Work, 43,* 101–103.

Wolfe, A. (1998). *One nation, after all.* New York: Viking.

Wuthnow, R. (199). *God and mammon in America.* New York: Free Press.

ANN K. CARRUTH
CYNTHIA A. LOGAN

47

Depressive Symptoms in Farm Women: Effects of Health Status and Farming Lifestyle Characteristics, Behaviors, and Beliefs

Introduction

Rural life has frequently been depicted as slower, healthier, and less stressful than its urban counterpart. In reality, farming is one of the most dangerous occupations[1] and stress associated with farm life affects men, women, and children. Because the majority of farms in the United States are family owned,[2] the stress associated with farm life is predicated by the constant threat of occupational risks and hazards even as families share life experiences. In fact, the National Institute of Occupational Safety and Health[3] has identified stress in occupational workers as a serious problem. Women, often active as agricultural partners in farm operation, may be at higher risk for depressive symptoms as they attempt to juggle a multitude of farm and family responsibilities. Feelings of isolation and loneliness are compounded by the rural location of farms and the nature of farm work. Taken together, these environmental and social influences may contribute to depressive symptoms. Therefore, the objective of this study was to examine the impact of personal and farming lifestyle characteristics, behaviors, and beliefs on depressive symptoms in farm women.

Health and Depressive Symptoms

Many researchers have examined the relationships between stress and disease; others have focused on stress and psychological outcomes. In this study, the relationship of farm lifestyle characteristics, conceptualized as potential stressors, as well as perceived health status are examined as predictors of depressive symptoms. Limited research exists that examines women's perceptions of their health. Instead, much of the research that addresses the psychological sequelae of chronic illness focuses on the impact of exhibiting various disease patterns and symptoms. This narrow focus limits the opportunity to take into account individual self-evaluation of health status. Chronic illness has been conceptualized as a stressor that impacts personal relationships,[4] work function,[5] and ability to carry out roles.[6] And as women age, declining health may contribute to depressive symptoms, as was the case in a study of older residents in which 15% reported depressive symptoms.[7]

Farm Characteristics

Farm families are exposed to a multitude of hazards, many with serious consequences. These include exposure and long-term ill effects from fertilizers and pesticides, the psychosocial hazards related to stress, and hazards identified with farm equipment.[8] Women, unlike men, experience stress not only related to day-to-day farm operation but also to the impact of the farming operation on the physical, social, and financial well-being of all family members. In many instances, women take on increasing responsibilities both on and off the farm, which allows husbands or sons to hold more lucrative off-the-farm jobs, ensuring the economic viability of the farm operation.

Fatigue, related to increasing role strain, increases the risk of injury. The threat of injury is of concern not only for themselves but other family members as well. Distress related to increased burden on spouses and potential injury of children performing farm chores contributes to the burden shouldered by farm women. The reality of the strain has been supported by Walker and Walker,[9] who surveyed farmers' self-reported stress levels and found women and farmers who were younger, worked off the farm, or worked in mixed farming enterprises were more likely to experience trouble relaxing, loss of temper, and fatigue.

Farm pressures, which affect both husband and wife, have a tendency to strain the marital relationship and influence the well-being of children.[10] Paykel[11] argues that married women with children at home are more vulnerable to stress. While single women have lower rates of depressive symptoms, women who are divorced or widowed often have high depressive symptoms.

A qualitative study by Kidd, Scharf, and Veazie[12] explored stress and injury by analyzing focus group transcripts of interviews of 70 farmers and/or spouses. Respondents' comments suggested that farmers and their spouses were well aware of the dangerous nature of equipment, animals, and chemicals and their accompanying stressors. The number and complexity of tasks, lack of access to workload-relieving resources, and time-consuming safety features were perceived to increase farmers' workload. Furthermore, physical injury, illness, and disability were identified with the common theme of chronic strain, which was a recognized consequence of farm work stress.

Specific work of farming and its impact on health and well-being has been extensively examined. What is lacking is an examination of the impact of these perceived hazards on depressive symptoms. The use of pesticides has long been of concern to farmers. Sheep farmers reported symptoms which they attributed to the use of organophosphates in sheep dips.[13] The farmers reported a variety of symptoms affecting their health status, including depression, memory loss, respiratory problems, joint pain, and lethargy.

Farm size has been investigated for its potential as a stressor with conflicting results. In a survey of 500 English and Welsh farmers[13] researchers found that 79% of respondents were worried about finances, but those most vulnerable to financial problems were the operators of small or mixed farms. In contrast, Zhou and Roseman,[14] found that large-scale operations may experience more economic pressure and/or greater exposure to hazards than smaller operations. Moreover, the authors found that injury patterns occurred at certain peak times, including afternoons and Saturdays, when fatigue could be a factor. Another possible factor was the link between weekend drinking and the Saturday peak of injuries. Drinkers were three times more likely to have been injured on Saturdays rather than other days of the week. An associated factor influencing Saturday injuries was the prevalence of part-time workers' injuries on Saturdays, which may suggest that part-timers had to work faster and harder on Saturdays to make up for lack of time during the week or that part-timers lacked experience and thus were more likely to be hurt. The long hours worked by farmers have also been cited by others as stressful.[13]

Farm families not only consistently report stress as the fundamental cause of farm injury[15] but also readily perceive the potential harmfulness and daily risks of the occupation. Other factors have been linked to adverse psychological outcomes, such as lack of safety measures,[16] economic hardships and suicide,[17,18] and role overload and ambiguity.[19] Furthermore, farmers also felt that occupational health and safety needs went unmet.

Injury as a Stressor

While it has been established that stress contributes to injury, very little is known about the effects of injuries on depressive symptoms. Farm injuries may have long-lasting physical and psychological effects. Swanson, Sachs, Dahlgren, and Tinguely[20] reported that a significant number of farm injuries in children were associated with long-term disability and other problems. Expensive, long-term treatment adds to the economic stressors already felt by farm families. In farming situations the family receives no paid leave and may have to travel considerable distance and accumulate additional debt to care for injured children.[18] Since women commonly assume primary responsibility for the care of children, dealing with the daily stress of long-term care is shouldered by women.

Potential risk factors for injuries to women were studied by Stueland et al.,[21] who found that increased risk of injury faced by women expanded their already burdensome balancing act. Furthermore, a significant predictor of injury was the total number of hours worked by women, with most injuries occurring in the barn. As men increasingly sought high-paying off-farm work to relieve economic pressure, women assumed more responsibility for farm work. May[22] also note that the complexities of farm life that lead to increased stress exist simultaneously with underutilization of mental health resources for generally ignored psychiatric problems. Several authors report alcohol-related problems as a factor.[17,23]

Depressive Symptoms

Although stress has been identified as an important concern, little is known about farm women and the risk factors contributing to depressive symptoms. Compared to men, women report more depression,[24] a rate of approximately three times that of men worldwide.[25] Attempts to explain this difference have resulted in the identification of women's multiple roles with limited support as a risk factor for depression. Other factors, which are more common among women, such as poverty, single parenting, and economic dependence, have been linked to depression. Farm women frequently typify this description. The "third shift phenomenon" label has been created to characterize farm women's multiple responsibilities when working outside the home, caring for families, and also working on the farm.[26]

A positive correlation has also been noted between age and depressive symptoms for women.[27] Not surprisingly, females who have a greater average life expectancy constitute a majority of the older population in urban and rural areas, spending more time alone. Since older women have multiple health care concerns and needs and may have mobility and/or transportation problems, health care access becomes an even greater obstacle. Isolation and loneliness may be a natural consequence of the rural setting, health concerns, and the changing family structure.[28] The availability of wellness programs, such as stress reduction and depression screening, may also be limited by the type of health care coverage individuals have.[29]

The crippling conditions of depression and depressive symptoms are commonly seen in primary care. While 2 to 10% may suffer from major depression, even more astonishing is that 20% of persons may struggle with depressive disorders less severe than major depression. While the effect on well-being and function is well-known, an association between depression and other medical problems, such as heart disease, also exists.[30] Stallones, Leff, Garrett, and Gillan[31] administered the Center for Epidemiologic Studies Depression Scale (CESD) to 872 individuals on 485 Colorado farms, selected

by stratified probability sampling. Four hundred and two individuals were female. Although the percentage of participants who admitted experiencing depressive symptoms did not exceed the rate for nonfarm individuals, the authors found that a total of 9.3% of participants admitted having depressive symptoms, 7.9% of males and 11.1% of females. Interestingly, high depressive symptoms were found more often in individuals who lived on a farm but were not actively involved in farm work, a position regularly occupied by women.

Methods

This cross-sectional survey design study included women 18 years old and older whose family participated in a farming operation. The sample of farm women was selected from a sampling pool of 4,804 farm owners obtained from mailing lists maintained by LSU Agricultural Centers and Farm Service Agency in 10 parishes across southeast Louisiana. The parishes were selected based on agricultural diversity and location. Postcards identifying the university and the research center were sent to farms prior to beginning survey work to promote the creditability of the project and encourage participation. Data were collected in summer 1998 under the Louisiana Farm Health and Injury Survey to conduct 30-minute computer-assisted telephone interviews. Callers participated in an extensive training program to minimize threats to validity.

The survey instrument was adapted from the Women Farm Health Interview Survey and the Children Farm Health Interview Survey developed by the Southeast Center for Agricultural Health, Injury Prevention, and Education at the University of Kentucky for the Kentucky Farm Family Health and Hazardous Surveillance Project. The Louisiana Farm Health and Injury Survey consisted of two sections: farm women's health and farming lifestyle characteristics, behaviors, and beliefs, and children's health and safety behaviors. Questions elicited information about women's farm work associated with the operation of the farm; general health status and access to health care; associated factors related to farm and nonfarm injuries, attitudes related to hazards, and demographic information.

To determine the prevalence of depressive symptoms respondents were asked if they had experienced feelings of sadness or depression within the past year. Sadness was conceptualized as a pervasive feeling of disillusionment and unhappiness that influences the meaning of life events and decision making.[32] The authors theorize that inability to resolve sadness leads to feelings of depression. The intent of the study was not to classify patterns of depressive symptoms but rather to determine the presence of the feelings in the past year. Therefore, it was deemed appropriate to use a categorical response to capture the phenomenon of depressive symptoms.

Self-reported health status was grouped as poor, fair, good, very good, or excellent. Time to the nearest facility was determined as a means of evaluating the degree of geographic isolation as it relates to accessing health care. Categories consisted of <15 minutes, 15–29 minutes, 30–59 minutes, and greater than one hour.

Questions regarding farm lifestyle characteristics, behaviors, and beliefs were used to evaluate risk factors for depressive symptoms. Farm type was determined by asking respondents to describe their principal farming activity. Fifteen farm-related tasks, coded as yes/no, were collapsed into four role categories: Management/Oversight of Farm, Care/Use of equipment, Care of Animals, and Crop Management. Answering yes to any task within these categories indicated participation in that role. Labor affiliation was created by combining responses to two variables: time commitment to farm operation each week and off-the-farm employment status. To calculate time commitment to the farm operation each week, the average number of hours worked each day was multiplied by the average number of days worked each week. Six groups were created for labor affiliations: <20 hours/week and no off-farm work; <20 hours/week and part-time off-farm work; <20 hours/week and full-time off-farm work; >20 hours/week and no off-farm work; >20 hours/week and part-time off-farm work; >20 hours/week and full-time off-farm work. Number of acres was grouped as <20; 20–99 acres; 100–499 acres; >500 acres. Years farming since eighteenth birthday were grouped less than and greater than 20 years. Hazards of farming were determined by asking respondents to identify hazards they felt existed while farming. These hazards were coded yes/no for each type identified. Injuries that women sustained within the past year were coded as none, farm-related, or non-farm-related.

Marital status was grouped as married, divorced or single/widowed. Educational background was grouped less than high school, high school/GED, or beyond high school. Age was determined by asking birth date, and regrouped in 15-year intervals. Race was grouped as white and nonwhite. Farm income was grouped 0–$9,999; $10,000–19,999; $20,000–29,999; $30,000–39,999; $40,000–49,999; $50,000–74,999; $75,000–99,999; $100,000–124,999; >125,000. Children <18 years of age at home were coded yes/no.

Women over the age of 18 years were eligible for participation if their family participated in a farm operation. In the event two women were eligible, the woman who perceived having the most involvement was selected and asked to participate. A stratified sampling design with parishes composing the strata and simple random sample without replacement selected within each stratum was employed. Because each of the 10 parishes was unequal in the number of farm operations, proportional allocation of the participating counties/parishes was employed to provide representative participation in keeping with population density.[33] Once eligibility was determined and the woman agreed to participate, the interview proceeded. Of those who completed the eligibility screen, 657 (participation rate 57.6% among known eligible farms) southeast Louisiana farm residents completed full interviews.

Data analyses were undertaken using the SPSS computer statistical software package and EpiInfo 6.0. Cross-tabulation and frequencies were used to describe demographic data. Univariate odds ratios were used to determine which explanatory variables to include in final adjusted logistic regression model.

Results

The demographic composition of farm characteristics revealed that the majority of women were married, white, had a twelfth-grade education or higher, and lived within 30 minutes to one hour from the health care facility that they use most often (Table 47.1). In the majority of cases, the family home was located on the farm (n = 577, 88.0%). In addition, over 300 husbands (n = 302) worked off the farm, with 80.6% working a full-time job.

Overall, 24% of the 657 farm women reported depressive symptoms (95% C.I. 20.9–27.5). The age-specific prevalence estimates of depressive symptoms for southeast Louisiana farm women are given in Table 47.2. Those over 65 years of age had the highest prevalence of depressive symptoms compared to the other age groups.

Univariate odds ratios for significant (p < 0.05) risk factors are summarized in Table 47.1. Variables correlated in expected directions with prevalence of depressive symptoms.

Table 47.1 Percentages of Demographics and Univariate Odds Ratio for Risk Factors of Depressive Symptoms for Southeast Louisiana Farm Women

Variable	Farm Women in Sample	Percent	Odds Ratio[a]	95% C.I.
Age (years)				
18–34	72	11.0	1.0	NA
35–49	204	31.1	1.87	.90–3.87
50–64	243	37.0	1.43	.69–2.96
>65	138	21.0	1.97	.93–4.20
Education				
<HS	62	9.4	1.54	.84–2.81
HS/GED/Trade	278	42.3	1.19	.80–1.76
>HS	317	48.2	1.0	NA
Net Farm Income				
0–$9,999	416	63.3	.33	.08–1.39
$10,000–19,999	100	15.2	.36	.08–1.59
$20,000–29,999	40	6.1	.28	.06–1.41
$30,000–39,999	29	4.4	.26	.05–1.49
$40,000–49,999	16	2.4	.37	.06–2.29
$50,000–74,999	13	2.0	.17	.02–1.45
$75,000–99,999	15	2.3	.10	.01–1.07
$100,000–124,999	4	.6	.35	.01–8.73
>$125,000	8	1.2	1.0	NA
dk/refused	16	2.4		
Race				
White	615	93.6	.83	.44–1.56
Other	42	6.4	1.0	NA
Marital Status				
Married	589	89.6	1.0	NA
Divorced	53	8.1	5.33	1.74–16.37
Single/widowed	13	2.0	.91	.46–1.81
Child < 18 Years at Home				
Yes	177	26.9	1.01	.67–1.53
No	480	73.1	1.0	NA
Health Status				
Poor	17	2.6	7.85	2.86–21.57
Fair	73	11.1	3.52	1.76–7.02
Good	196	29.8	2.83	1.59–5.03
Very Good	228	34.7	1.51	.83–2.74
Excellent	143	21.8	1.0	NA
Time to Nearest Health Care Facility				
Does not go anywhere	10	1.5		
<15 minutes	174	26.5	1.0	NA
15–29 minutes	249	37.9	1.56	.96–2.53
30–59 minutes	177	26.9	1.48	.87–2.49
>1 hour	47	7.2	1.36	.62–2.99
Farm Type				
Beef Cattle or Dairy	457	69.6	.76	.52–1.11
Other	200	30.4	1.0	NA
Acres				
<20	238	36.2	1.0	NA
20–99	233	35.5	.76	.49–1.16
100–499	161	24.5	.88	.54–1.42
>500	25	3.8	.95	.36–2.45

(continued)

Table 47.1 Percentages of Demographics and Univariate Odds Ratio for Risk Factors of Depressive Symptoms for Southeast Louisiana Farm Women (*Continued*)

Variable	Farm Women in Sample	Percent	Odds Ratio[a]	95% C.I.
Years Farming since 18th Birthday				
20 years and less	307	46.7	1.0	NA
>20 years	350	53.3	1.88	1.28–2.75
Hazards				
None	491	74.7	1.0	NA
Animals	52	7.9	.79	.97–3.29
Equipment use	43	6.5	.86	.39–1.86
Tractor use	29	4.4	2.37	1.08–5.20
Pesticides	19	2.9	4.29	1.74–10.61
Long-term exposure	13	2.0	3.84	1.26–11.62
Milking	6	.9	.46	.03–6.75
Crops	4	.7	—[b]	
Injury Event				
None	544	82.8	1.0	NA
Injury Non-farm work	79	12.0	1.94	1.18–3.22
Injury Farm work	34	5.2	2.27	1.10–4.70
Labor Affiliation				
<20 hours and no off-farm work	247	37.6	1.0	NA
<20 hours and part-time off-farm work	51	7.8	.98	.60–1.59
<20 hours and full-time off-farm work	163	24.8	.70	.34–1.46
>20 hours and no off-farm work	139	21.2	1.22	.48–3.08
>20 hours and part-time off-farm work	25	3.8	.68	.42–1.11
>20 hours and full-time off-farm work	32	4.9	.57	.21–1.53
Type of Task Involvement				
Management/Oversight of Farm Operation				
Yes	584	88.9	1.35	.75–2.44
No	73	11.1	1.0	NA
Care of Farm Animals				
Yes	396	60.3	.72	.49–1.04
No	261	39.7	1.0	NA
Care/Use of Farm Equipment				
Yes	465	70.8	1.01	.68–1.50
No	192	29.2	1.0	NA
Crop Management				
Yes	279	42.5	1.34	.93–1.93
No	378	57.5	1.0	NA

Reproduced with permission of the copyright owner.
[a]Odds ratios weighted to adjust for unequal sampling probabilities.
[b]Too few observations.

Table 47.2 Estimates of Prevalence Rates for Depressive Symptoms (CI 95%) among Southeast Louisiana Farm Women

Age	Prevalence Rate	95% Confidence Interval
18–34 years	18.0	10.3–29.3
35–49 years	26.9	21.1–33.7
50–64 years	21.4	16.5–27.2
>65 years	27.5	20.4–35.9
Total	24.0	20.9–27.5

Table 47.3 presents the adjusted odds ratios and confidence limits from the logistic regression analyses of potential risk factors for depressive symptoms. The likelihood of depressive symptoms was 3.68 times greater for farm women who were divorced. Adjusting for the other variables, poorer health status yielded an increased risk for depressive symptoms. When other potential risk factors were controlled, depressive symptoms became statistically significant with good, fair, or poor health status. Having had an injury in the past year while engaging in farm work increased the risk of distress by 2.15 times. And the use of pesticides and tractors, perceived hazards, contributed significantly to depressive symptoms by 2.83 and 2.88 times, respectively.

Discussion

This study is one of the few investigations to examine depressive symptoms among southern farm women. The overall prevalence of depressive symptoms of 24% for southeast Louisiana farm women warrants the attention of the public health and medical communities. Given that self-reported depressive symptoms may be underreported, the true prevalence may be greater than the data from this survey would indicate. While no other study exists to compare the prevalence of depressive symptoms among Louisiana farm women, the rate exceeds the prevalence of depressive symptoms reported in previous studies among farm women[31] and a national health survey.[34]

One limitation to the study is the use of self-reported survey data to analyze relationships between risk factors and depressive symptoms. Un-

Table 47.3 Adjusted Odds Ratios[a] for Personal and Lifestyle Risk Factors for Depressive Symptoms for Farm Women

Risk Factors	Odds Ratio[b]	95% C.I.
Marital Status[d]		
Married	1.0	NA
Single/Widowed	.92	.44–1.91
Divorced	5.00	1.51–16.57
General Health Status[e]		
Excellent	1.0	NA
Very Good	1.56	.83–2.93
Good	2.88	1.57–5.33
Fair	3.12	1.49–6.51
Poor	7.85	2.65–22.72
Injury Event[f]		
None	1.0	NA
Injury—Non-Farm Work	1.92	1.12–3.27
Farming Hazards		
Pesticide Use	3.28	1.08–7.42
Tractor Use	3.11	1.30–6.34
Long-term Exposure	5.97	1.81–19.67
Farming >20 years	1.61	1.08–2.42

[a]Odds ratio weighted to adjust for unequal sampling probabilities.
[b]Adjusted for other risk factors included in the model.
[c]95% confidence intervals from logistic regression analyses.
[d]Odds ratio for comparisons with marital status: married.
[e]Odds ratio for comparison with general health status: excellent.
[f]Odds ratio for comparison with injury event: none.

willingness to admit symptoms to an interviewer may contribute to the underestimation of the prevalence of depressive symptoms. The results of this study apply only to southeast Louisiana farm women and should not be extended to other rural women, men, or migrant farmers in the area. Causality of the observed association cannot be established due to the cross-sectional survey design.

It might have been expected that the relatively high prevalence of depressive symptoms would have been reflected in women experiencing economic hardships. Unlike other studies that found financial status to be related to depressive symptoms, the results of this study did not support this finding.[7] This may be explained by the fact that many of the women and their spouses work additional off-the-farm jobs, significantly improving the economic status of the farm operation. Evaluating the extent of financial security beyond farm net income was not possible in this study.

Even though this study affirms a consistent pattern that older women experience a higher prevalence of depressive symptoms,[27,35] age was not a predictor of depressive symptoms in this study. Caring for children at home, typically done by younger women, was not found to contribute to depressive symptoms. Because the prevalence of depressive symptoms is higher in this sample than what has been reported in other studies, the need for women of all age groups to be screened for depressive symptoms is evident.

Marital status was predictive of depressive symptoms. Consistent with a study conducted as part of the Iowa Youth and Families Project, divorced women suffer greater stress and negative events than other unmarried women.[36] One possible explanation is that divorced women experience more depressive symptoms due to changes in emotional and financial support in maintaining the farm operation and the fulfillment of multiple roles and responsibilities without the benefit of a supportive partner. An alternative explanation is that being divorced in a farm community contributes to depressive symptoms because women lose the association of married couples working interdependently together in their work.[37] Another contributing factor is that women experience the loss of relationships more intensely.[9,38,39] Being divorced, as opposed to being widowed, may be more traumatic to women living in rural communities.

Consistent with other research, diminished health status was associated with greater depressive symptoms.[40] This finding highlights the importance of women's perceptions of the impact of the quality of their health on mental health and supports the need to screen farm women for depressive symptoms who are experiencing medical conditions or physical ailments.[11] Future research is needed to further explore the impact of perceptions of health status on mental well-being among this group of women. Further exploration is also needed to determine women's norms and expectations about health and their willingness to participate in various preventive health practices.

Aspects of farm life, potentially stressful, were analyzed for their ability to predict depressive symptoms. While other studies report stress associated with type of farming,[42] no association was found in this study. Stallones, Leff, Garrett, and Gillan[31] reported high depressive symptoms present in those who lived on a farm but were not actively involved in farm work. Unlike in their study, labor affiliation and task involvement were not predictive of depressive symptoms in southeast Louisiana women.

Several farm-related variables predictive of depressive symptoms reflect the threat of hazards women face on a daily basis. Women were more likely to report depressive symptoms if driving a tractor applying pesticides and long-term exposure was considered hazardous. They were also more likely to report depressive symptoms if they had sustained a farm-related injury within the previous year. These findings are similar to those found in recent research on hazards of farming and depressive symptoms.[42]

Women involved in the farm operation longer than 20 years were 1.88 times more likely to experience depressive symptoms. The findings of this study underscore the reality that women's concerns and awareness of potential threat of injury may affect mental well-being. The ever-present threat of harm to self and family members is one of the burdens farm women face while balancing multiple family roles and responsibilities. Future research should be encouraged to explore coping mechanisms and other mediating variables among women who do and do not experience depressive symptoms.

This project is supported through a cooperative agreement with the Centers for Disease Control and Prevention and the National Institute of Occupational Safety and Health (U07/CCU612017-03). The authors gratefully acknowledge the Southwest Center for Agricultural Health, Injury Prevention, and Education for sponsoring the project. Appreciation is also extended to the research team at the

Notes

Southeast Center for Agricultural Health and Injury Prevention for consultative support.

1. National Safety Council. *Accident Facts.* 1998 Edition. Itasca, IL: National Safety Council.

2. United States Department of Agriculture. (1999). *1997 Census of Agriculture.* (NASS AC 97-A-51). Washington, D.C.: US Government Printing Office.

3. NIOSH. 1996. *National occupational research agenda, 67.* DHHS (NIOSH) Pub No. 115. Cincinnati, Ohio: U.S. Department of Health and Human Services, Public Health Service, Centers for Disease Control and Prevention. National Institute for Occupational Safety and Health.

4. Lichtman, R., Taylor, S., & Wood, J. Research on the chronically ill: Conceptual and methodological perspectives. In A Baum and J Singer (Eds). *Advances in Environmental Psychology: Methods and Environmental Psychology,* Hillsdale, NJ: Erlbaum. 1985, pp 43–74.

5. Yelin, E. Social problems in persons with chronic disease. *Soc Sci Med* 1980;13: 13–20.

6. Reisine, S., Goodenow, C., & Grady, K. The impact of RA on the homemaker. *Soc Sci Med* 1987; 25: 189–195.

7. Craft, B. J., Johnston, D. R., & Ortega, S. T.: Rural urban women's experience of symptoms of depression related to economic hardship. *J Women Aging* 1998;10:3–18.

8. Lusk, S. L. Agricultural workers. *AAOHN Journal* 1998; 46:465.

9. Walker, J. L., Walker, L. S. & MacLennan, P. M. An informal look at farm stress. *Psychol Rep* 1986; 59: 427–430.

10. Field, B. Managing farm-related stress for safety's sake [Online] Available: http: persephone.agcom.purdue.edu/agcom/Pubs/S/S-86.htm, 1998.

11. Paykel, E. S. Depression in women. *Br J Psychiatry* 1991;22–29.

12. Kidd, P., Scharf, T., Veazie, M. Linking stress and injury in the farming environment: A secondary analysis of qualitative data. *Health Educ Q* 1996; 23: 224–237.

13. Simkin, S., Hawton, K., Fagg, J., Malmberg, A. Stress in farmers: A survey of farmers in England and Wales. *Occup Environ Med* 1998;55:729–734.

14. Zhou, C., Roseman, J. Agricultural injuries among a population-based sample of farm operators in Alabama. *Am J Ind Med* 1994;25:385–402.

15. Reis, T. J., Elkind, P. D. Influences on farm safety practice in eastern Washington. In KJ Donham, R Rautiainen, SH Schuman, and JA Lay (Eds). *Agricultural Health and Safety: Recent Advances.* New York: Haworth Medical Press, 1997, pp 193–205.

16. Gerrard, C. E. Farmers' occupational health: Cause for concern, cause for action. *J Adv Nurs* 1998; 28:155–163.

17. Osborne, S. J. Farmers' suicides: What can be done? *Social Sciences in Health* 1998;4: 163–175.

18. Wright, K. Management of agricultural injuries and illness. *Rural Nursing* 1993;28:253–266.

19. Keating, N. C. Reducing stress of farm men and women. *Family Relations: Journal of Applied Family and Child Studies* 1987;36:358–363.

20. Swanson, J. A., Sachs, M. I., Dahlgren, K. A., Tinguely, S. J. Accidental farm injuries in children. *American Journal of Disabled Children* 1987;141:1276–1279.

21. Strueland, D. T., Lee, B., Nordstrom, D., Layde, P. M., Wittman, L. M., Gunderson, P. D. Case-control study of agricultural injuries to women in central Wisconsin. *Women's Health* 1997;25:91–103.

22. May, J. Agriculture: Work practices and health consequences. *Seminars in Respiratory Medicine* 1993;14:1–7.

23. Farr, K. A., Wilson-Figueroa, M. Talking about health and health care: Experiences and perspectives of Latina women in a farmworking community. *Women's Health* 1997;25: 23–40.

24. Tevis, C. Stress. *Successful Farming* 1982; 80:27–42.

25. Notman, M. T. Depression in working women. *Surgical Services Management* 1997;3:47–48.

26. Gallagher, E, Dellworth, U. The third shift: Juggling employment, family, and the farm. *Journal of Rural Community Psychology* 1993;12: 21–36.

27. Stromquist, A. M. Rapporteur report: Mental health. *Journal of Agromedicine* 1997;4:179–180.

28. Thelin, A. Epilogue: Agricultural occupational and environmental health policy strategies for the future. *Am J Ind Med* 1990;18:523–526.

29. Weisman, C. S. Proceedings of Women's Health an Managed Care: Balancing cost, access, and quality. *Women's Health and Managed Care* 1996;6:1–4.

30. D'Epiro, P. Depression and medical illness: Understanding the links. *Patient Care* 1999;33:34.

31. Stallones, L., Leff, M., Garrett, C., Criswell, L., Gillan, T. Depressive symptoms among Colorado farmers. *Agric Saf Health* 1995;1:37–43.

32. Gramling, L. F., McCain, N. L. Grey glasses: Sadness in young women. *J of Adv Nurs* 1997;26: 312–319.

33. Lunsford, T. R., & Lunsford, B. R. The research sample, Part I: Sampling. *Journal of Prosthetics and Orthotics* 1995;7:105–112.

34. Sayetta, R. B., Johnson, D.P. Basic data on depressive symptomatology. United States, 1974–75. *Vital Health Stat* 1980;11:1–37.

35. Musil, C. M., Haug, M. R., Warner, C. D. Stress, health, and depressive symptoms in older adults at three points over 18 months. *Issues Ment Health Nurs* 1998;19:207–224.

36. Simons, R. L. *Understanding Differences between Divorced and Intact Families: Stress, Interaction, and Child Outcome.* London: Sage Publications.

37. Rosenblatt, P., Anderson, R. Interaction in farm families: Tension and stress. In R. Cow-ard & W. Smith (Eds.), *The Family in Rural Society*. Boulder, CO: Westview Press; 1981, pp 147–166.

38. Berkowitz, A. D., Perkins H. W. Correlates of psychosomatic stress symptoms among farm women: A research note on farm and family functions. *J Human Stress* 1985;11:76–81.

39. Wollersheim, J. P. Depression, women, and the workplace. *Occup Med* 1993;8: 787–795.

40. Scarth, R. D., Stallones, L., Zwerling, C., Burmeister, L. F. The prevalence of depressive symptoms among Iowa and Colorado farmers. *Am J Ind Med* 2000;37:382–389.

41. Clancy, C., Massion, C. T. (1992). American women's health care: A patchwork quilt with gaps. *JAMA* 1992;268:1918–1920.

42. Deary, I. J., Willock, J., McGregor, M. Stress in farming. *Stress Medicine* 1997;13: 131–136.

48

Social Work with Immigrants and Refugees: Developing a Participation-based Framework for Anti-Oppressive Practice

Introduction

Modern migration flows bring about increasing ethnocultural diversity in most states. Groups of differing ethnocultural backgrounds fashion patterns of coexistence and niches in their new home societies. While numerically large groups, which have settled over long periods of time, have gradually become well-established communities, those groups that have arrived more recently still face the multiple tasks of resettlement. A growing arena of contemporary social work and the organized social service system is that of immigrant and refugee resettlement and integration.[1]

Over time, different groups have presented the social work profession with fresh and novel service challenges. Social work's strong ties to context in time and space guide the field into distinct specializations which nonetheless are linked by its fundamental values of humanism and social justice. Resettling immigrants and refugees forms an activity for which social work and social services must be aptly shaped.

In this essay, the Finnish experience of immigration and refugee incorporation is explored using an analytic frame based on societal participation (see Isoplan, 1995). Some of the main findings of two recent studies are presented and discussed in order to highlight specific areas of current concern. The societal participation construct is used for organizing and understanding resettlement phenomena and as a matrix for locating barriers, or points of "oppression" in the integration process.

The Context of Resettlement in Finland

When compared with other European countries, the proportion of foreigners in the Finnish population is still low. After half a century of minimal in-migration and two decades of heavy out-migration to Sweden, Finland had become in the late 1980s a country of net in-migration. At present, the foreign-born form only 2.3% of the population, but in-migration has been steadily on the rise. Categories include special returning ethnic migration,[2] regular return migration, spouses, and humanitarian immigration (refugees). Labor immigration has so far been highly selective and does not form a major category. By and large, labor market demand has been met domestically.

Recent refugee quotas are introducing new ethnocultural diversity into the relatively homogeneous society of Finland. The field of reception and resettlement has become part of the social work agenda since the inception of a national refugee resettlement program one decade ago. Under the auspices of the United Nations High Commissioner for Refugees (UNHCR), between 1,000 and 2,000 refugees are resettled annually.[3]

The state assumes the main responsibility for resettling refugees in a comprehensive program that is implemented by the municipalities. At the national level, the program is administered from the Ministry of Labor, but a wide range of official and public bodies are involved at various levels in service provision. Generally, immigrants can avail themselves of language courses and social services. Refugees, however, have been targeted for a more compact and centrally organized orientation program comprising health, housing, language education, income support, and other components. In Finland, most resettlement programs have been outgrowths of the extensive welfare state, as a consequence of which the interface with officials is very high during this initial period.

The Resettlement Field in Finland

This section looks at resettlement in Finland, using qualitative data from fieldwork conducted in stages between 1994 and 1998 among refugees and immigrants, including groups from Vietnam, Somalia, and the Middle East (Valtonen, 1997, 1999). The target groups comprised 240 individuals, who were interviewed either individually or through the medium of focus groups. The majority of the people in the target groups arrived in the early 1990s. Resettlement took place in the context of an advanced welfare state. Universality is a central characteristic of the Finnish system, meaning that all citizens and permanently residing persons are covered. The state maintains a relatively high level of benefits and social protection, implemented through a comprehensive system of redistributive economic and social service mechanisms.

The empirical data that follow are organized in different participatory spheres. Observed areas of oppression, or blocked participation, are presented and discussed in relation to tasks and approaches for resettlement social work. The scope of the study reported here does not extend to proposing specific types of intervention. The organizational context will influence and determine, to a large extent, what level and type of involvement is possible for social workers functioning in different professional scenarios of immigrant resettlement and integration.

Economic Sphere

Labor market programs cater to resettling immigrants. Language courses are available to resettling groups as part of the central policy thrust toward employment. Individuals generally participate in training programs and temporary on-the-job placements arranged through the labor office. Immigrants are well catered to in this "preemployment" arena of the labor market. Yet, high unemployment[4] indicates that they are still in a very marginal position in the labor market, in spite of the accessibility of official employment services and the fact that they participate actively in the available range of training programs and courses.

The qualitative data point to a high level of independent job-seeking activity. Individuals reported that they use a broad range of job-seeking channels. They have, by this time, acquired greater familiarity with the geography of the employment market. Their job searches include inquiries and information seeking through the official labor exchange, following up newspaper announcements or other leads via telephone, written applications and/or personal visits, as well as spontaneous inquiries at likely places of employment, and follow-up inquiries.

Young adult job seekers, in particular, seem to have inculcated the message of persistence in job seeking, which seems also to be reinforced by lively job search activity in immediate social circles. Underlying the formal contacts with the labor market, there is dense networking and information exchange in informal groups.

A common experience among the numerous youths who were interviewed has been rejection at the first "gate" (e.g., telephone inquiry stage) of the employment market. There have been barriers for the most basic levels of employment. As one subject explained: "I tried to get to cleaning work in the evening, but I cannot get even there." Such comment were routine. A research informant explained that some cleaning firms have had very positive experience with young workers from immigrant/refugee backgrounds. They would prefer to hire them as there have been fewer problems with absenteeism. However, a cleaning firm's client companies can dictate their own terms and throw up barriers.

The repeated experiences of young job seekers at the first stage of the employment market point to the existence of attitudinal and institutional factors of resistance along the boundaries of the employment market. It is significant that, in their case, in spite of job search activity, many individuals are not able to penetrate the outer boundaries of the employment market. Similar experiences were also recounted by young adults who have a considerable level of educational and vocational training in

Finland. Their systematically increasing stock of human and social capital has not improved their employment situation during this decade.

The resettling groups comprise a cross-section of education levels. The population includes persons who, in their own countries, have already acquired an academic or professional background in the humanities or sciences, for example in teaching professions at basic and higher education levels, medicine and nursing, and engineering. The interview data indicate that the more highly educated have, as a rule with few exceptions, not been able to obtain work commensurate with their qualifications. They have not been able to use their education or experience in the Finnish labor market.

Applicants with subjects taken to professional level seem to be at a greater disadvantage, in the long term, than those with less education and training. Taking into account the many barriers faced in the employment market, efforts to achieve accreditation do not seem worthwhile. On the other hand, alternative employment opportunities for their skills are difficult to find.

How does social work related to the problem of labor market exclusion? The profession is strategically situated at the junction of the social services and the labor market, at the stage where welfare services intervene to allay the economic hardship caused by unemployment and to guarantee a minimum standard of material welfare. In the Finnish welfare system, which is built partially on corporatist principles, employment relations also determine in a decisive way the ultimate level of long-term benefits and social insurance, for example, against the risks of sickness, disability, unemployment, and old age.

Considering the central significance of employment in settlement and integration, social work faces pressure to relate to unemployment not only in the areas of benefit and social service delivery. Labor market exclusion, for resettling persons, implies social as well as economic vulnerability. The social utility of employment in generating nonmaterial as well as material aspects of well-being is well recognized (see, e.g., Sen, 1985). Social status is derived invariably from one's occupational status. Welfare dependence is a disempowering state which is hard to justify and a category that is not accepted in the eyes of the receiving society. The capacity for self-determination is lessened. Unemployment is also dysfunctional from the perspective of community and ethnic relations. It is difficult to develop the roles and relationships that would effectively compensate for active employment and links with the formal labor market.

Social workers in the resettlement field cannot ignore the fundamental problem of lack of employment. Generally, immigrants initiate close contact with social workers and the social services during the initial orientation period. Practical social service transactions and contacts can lay the initial basis for effective integration work in many key areas. Social work is one of the few service sectors with a firm foundation of client contact which would serve as a basis for building links with the outside institutions and networks. While social work's major concentration is on the delivery of specific services, it is vital that professional networking does not exclude central institutions such as the labor market and its agencies. Social work links with the institutions with which resettling persons are seeking to establish relations should be part of the holistic bridging effort that is at the heart of integration work. The nature of resettlement services is not problem-centered in the orthodox sense. The essential approach can be defined as one of initiating newcomers into the societal processes and networks within which they take up new roles and exercise the citizen's repertoire of rights and duties in the new social context. Resettlement social work requires, in addition to linkage to clients, a considerable breadth of knowledge of the society, as well as a base of functioning multisectoral networks which together constitute this field's distinct instruments for facilitating the newcomer's transition into the new home society.

"Indirect social work practice embodies interventions that have relevance to this area of concern. Indirect work refers to the social worker's intervention in clients' environments and collaboration with others in bureaucracies or clients' social networks in an attempt to alleviate clients' difficulties" (Johnson, 1999). In indirect social work practice the worker is seen as a "pivotal link," playing an important role as liaison in the widest sense (Flexner, 1915). Johnson also stresses that indirect work is not only time-consuming but requires, above all, skill and expertise.

Notes

1. The term "immigrant" is used in the text when referring to issues common to most types of immigrants, including refugees. "Refugees" is used when the issue refers specifically to this group.

2. The return migration of persons of Finnish descent who may belong to the third or fourth generation living abroad, and have been permitted un-

der certain conditions (e.g., possession of a level of Finnish language skill) to "return" and reside in Finland. The flow of this type of returning ethnic migration is mainly from areas of the Former Soviet Union since 1990.

3. This figure includes family reunification and special humanitarian categories.

4. Unemployment across immigrant groups was 43% at the end of 1997.

References

Flexner, A. (1915) Is social work a profession? Paper presented at the national Conference of Charities and Correction, Baltimore.

Isoplan, Institute for Development Research, Economic and Social Planning GmbH (1995) Measurement and Indicators of Integration. Documentation of a meeting organized by the Council of Europe's Specialist Group on Equality of Opportunities for Immigrants, Strasbourg, 4–6 October.

Johnson, Y. M. (1999) Indirect work: Social work's uncelebrated strength. *Social Work,* 44 (4), pp. 323–34.

Sen, A. (1985) A sociological approach to the measurement of poverty: A reply to Professor Peter Townsend. *Oxford Economic Papers,* 37 (4).

Valtonen, K. (1997). *The Societal Participation of Refugees and Immigrants: Case Studies in Finland, Canada and Trinidad,* Turku, Institute of Migration.

Valtonen, K. (1999). *The Integration of Refugees in Finland in the 1990s,* Helsinki, Ministry of Labour.

DONNA E. HURDLE

49

Native Hawaiian Traditional Healing: Culturally Based Interventions for Social Work Practice

Cultural competence is an emerging focus of social work practice that is encouraged by both major social work professional organizations, NASW and the Council on Social Work Education, and reflects the reality of America's multicultural society. As described by Lum (1999), social work practice with people of color and various ethnic groups has evolved over the past two decades from ethnic-sensitive approaches, to cultural awareness, to cultural diversity, and finally to cultural competence. Each of these approaches has a different focus, ranging from the development of enhanced awareness in practitioners to greater knowledge of specific cultural groups and finally to the more integrated concept of cultural competence. Cultural competence is a practice method also used by other helping professionals to refer to the development of adequate professional skills to provide services to ethnic, racial, and cultural groups. With the development of common terminology and scholarship, training and content in cultural competence can now be compared across the helping disciplines. At the present time, counseling psychology seems to have the most clearly articulated set of competences, ethics, and training requirements (Lum, 1999; D. Sue et al., 1998).

Although cultural competence is a relatively new concept for the social work profession, it developed from a long tradition of providing services to people from a variety of ethnic and racial backgrounds. This article describes the elements of cultural competence as conceptualized by the current leading theorists in different disciplines. The use of culturally grounded social work interventions is identified as a core skill in culturally competent practice. As this concept is best understood through the use of examples, the article describes two interventions with Native Hawaiians. Culturally grounded interventions based on traditional healing practices may have the most chance for success in working with ethnic groups because they reflect the culture and tradition of a particular group. A culturally based approach to social work practice could be developed from the healing traditions of many ethnic groups and is a new area for development of cross-cultural practice skills.

Cultural Competence in the Helping Professions

Perhaps the first identification of cultural competence was provided by the Child and Adolescent Services Technical Assistance Program (CASSP) at Georgetown University, Washington, D.C. (Cross, Bazron, Dennis, & Isaacs, 1989). This conceptualization identified the elements of cultural competence for individual practitioners, agencies, and systems of care. *Cultural competence* was defined as a set of behaviors, attitudes, and policies that enable systems, agencies, or professionals to work effectively in cross-cultural situations (Cross et al., 1989). The focus of the CASSP model was on defining effective services for children from ethnic minority groups who have severe emotional disturbances. The strength of this model was its inclusion of both self-awareness and behaviors of practitioners, as well as its recognition of the need for incorporating particular elements in agency systems. This framework continues to be a foundation of the theory and descriptions of cultural competence in social work and other helping professions (Lum, 1999; Pierce & Pierce, 1996).

In the 1990s the Association for Multicultural Counseling and Development developed a framework of cultural competences for professional counselors in the field of counseling psychology. This model served as an inspiration for the social work cultural competence framework developed by Lum (1999). It includes three dimensions: (1) counselor awareness of personal values and biases, (2) understanding the worldview of culturally different clients, and (3) developing appropriate intervention strategies and techniques. Each of these areas further include competence in attitudes and beliefs, knowledge, and skills (D. Sue et al., 1998). Characteristics of culturally competent organizations also are identified in this framework. It is believed that the combination of personal awareness, knowledge of different cultures of clients, and the development of appropriate skills allows mental health professionals to ably provide services to clients who are culturally different from themselves. This is seen as a necessity in the multicultural world of the United States in the 21st century. Multicultural counseling and therapy, originally called "cross-cultural counseling/therapy," recognizes that both Western and non-Western approaches to helping may be necessary, as well as culturally appropriate awareness, knowledge, and skills (D. Sue et al., 1989).

Significant work in cultural competence also has occurred in the field of family therapy. McGoldrick (1998) noted that all families are embedded in and bounded by socioeconomic status, culture, gender, and race; how a society defines and values these relationships is critical to understanding how family processes are structured. The "culture" of families is seen as a multidimensional construct consisting of levels of identification with various identities: ethnicity, race, gender, socioeconomic status, and sexual orientation(Laird, 1998).

Other factors in understanding the cultural nature of a family include migration and acculturation, ecological context (including interaction with the community, work, and social institutions), stage of family life cycle, and family organization (Falicov, 1995). Each of these dimensions varies by country, culture, religion, socioeconomic status, and acculturation, among other variables. Assessment tools have been developed to articulate the role of culture in particular families, such as the cultural genogram (Hardy & Laszloffy, 1995), culturagram (Congress, 1994), and the multidimensional comparative framework (Falicov, 1995).

Another crucial factor is the stance of the therapist working with culturally different families. Whereas awareness of one's cultural background, biases, prejudices, and stereotyping is important, the attitude with which a practitioner approaches a family is equally influential to the outcome of therapy. Adopting an ethnographic perspective with a sense of curiosity and naïveté enables practitioners to collaborate with clients to learn about their culture and how it influences their behavior (Dyche & Zayas, 1995). This has also been termed "cultural humility" (Tervalon & Murray-Garcia, 1998). Therapists can best understand the multidimensional nature of family culture by using a narrative approach that enables a family to tell its story, including aspects that are "problem-saturated" as well as those reflecting family strengths and values (Laird, 1994, 1998). This approach moves practitioners away from a predetermined assessment framework to examining the unique aspects of the culture of each family.

Cultural competence also has been a focus in the field of nursing, evolving from transcultural nursing practice. This tradition focused on understanding the health care practices of people from different cultures, their varying ways of defining health and illness, and how caring is conceptualized in their cultures (Leininger, 1985). In an analysis of the concept of cultural competence from a nursing perspective, L.S. Smith (1998) identified the components of the model, as well as their antecedents and consequences. The antecedents or prerequisites for cultural competence are practitioner self-assessment of assumptions, biases, and values; an open attitude; and development of new knowledge. The components of cultural competence in this framework parallel those discussed earlier (that is, cultural awareness, cultural knowledge, and cultural skill). To these are added cultural sensitivity, participation in cultural encounters, and liaison and linkage for health care resources and services.

After increasing their knowledge and awareness in these areas, culturally competent nurses are able to empower clients, decrease their anxiety or fear of the health care system, engage clients more effectively in treatment, and improve their health status and satisfaction with services. This conceptualization further enriches the literature on cultural competence and adds important additional elements.

Cultural Competence in Social Work

Several models of cultural competence have been developed in the profession of social work (Green, 1999; Lum, 1999; McPhatter, 1997). *Cultural competence in social work* can be defined as the ability to understand the dimensions of culture and cultural practice and to apply them to clients and their cultural-social environment (Lum, 1999). This model has evolved from earlier social work literature on the dual-perspective (Norton, 1993) ethnic-sensitive practice (Devore & Schlesinger, 1987; Granger & Portner, 1985), and social work with ethnic minority groups (Chau, 1989; Lum, 1982, 1996). It also has been influenced by the literature on cultural competence in other helping disciplines.

Lum (1999) identified four areas of cultural competence in social work: (1) personal and professional awareness of ethnicity by the practitioner, (2) knowledge of culturally diverse practice, (3) skill development in work with culturally diverse clients, and (4) inductive learning; he further identified the levels of these competences for both general and advanced practice. Some of these aspects paralleled other models of cultural competence, such as personal awareness, knowledge of cultural groups, and development of skills.

Regarding personal awareness, Lum developed a useful self-assessment that helped social workers identify their experiences with people of color and different cultures. In the knowledge component of his model, Lum went beyond a focus on racism, prejudice, and discrimination to discuss cultural values and practice theories, such as social construction, that led to new models of practice, such as narrative approaches to treatment. The last component of the model, inductive learning, referred to the development of critical thinking and lifelong learning about culturally diverse practice. This component is essential to the development of culturally competent social workers, as the process of continuing to develop new knowledge and enhanced perspective, questioning the accuracy and relevance of one's existing knowledge base, and using clients as "cultural informants" to further develop specialized information must be ongoing. Cultural competence is not a static process of acquiring ability but an ongoing process of attuning oneself to the ever-changing cultures of various client groups.

McPhatter's (1997) concern was cultural competence in child welfare, where there is an overrepresentation of children from ethnic minority groups in state care. Her cultural competence attainment model consisted of three overlapping spheres of information: (1) grounded knowledge base, (2) enlightened consciousness and (3) cumulative skill proficiency. There are similarities between this model and others described earlier; enlightened consciousness refers to the restructuring of the worldview of the social worker as one moves from a monocultural to a multicultural position embracing both the positive and negative aspects of one's own culture and that of clients. A grounded knowledge base includes knowledge of the history, culture, traditions and customs, language, values, spirituality, art forms, and healing beliefs of clients; it also includes critiquing psychological theories that have traditionally guided social work practice but reflect the dominant culture. Feminist psychologists have criticized the psychodynamic theories of Freud and the developmental theories of Erikson and Kohlberg for their lack of applicability to the experiences of girls and women (Gilligan, 1982). The knowledge base further includes social problems, dynamics of oppression and racism, diverse family structures, and neighborhood and community profiles. McPhatter's final component of cultural competence was cumulative skill proficiency, which referred to appropriate assessment and intervention skills for clients of color, with an emphasis on cross-cultural communication skills.

Green (1999) defined a cultural competent services provider as one who delivers services in "a way that is congruent with behavior and expectations normative for a given community and that are adapted to suit the specific needs of individuals and families" (p. 87). He approached cultural competence from an anthropological perspective and emphasized ethnographic interviewing, familiarity with cultural descriptions, participant observation, and use of cultural guides. Green also was concerned with the help-seeking behaviors and traditions of healing for different cultures; these influence when and how a client system interacts with a helping system, of which social workers are a part. Culture influences how problems are defined, as well as the nature of problem resolution. Without recognition of these variables, social workers cannot know what type of assistance clients may be seeking that would be compatible with their cultural views of problem resolution.

Many of these models of cultural competence imply that after social workers acquire specific skills, enhance their knowledge and awareness, and learn new intervention techniques, they will become "culturally competent." However, this formula-driven approach does not take into account the fact that cultures continually change over time, as do individual, family, and community expressions of culture. Cultural competence is an evolutionary process that needs continual attention from the helping professionals. Social workers must continually focus on issues of culture in their clients and in themselves, knowing that their knowledge and skills must grow and develop over time.

To apply this discussion of cultural competence to social work practice, it is useful to examine examples of culturally competent interventions with particular cultural groups. By looking at specific culturally based interventions, it is possible to identify the knowledge and skill components that are necessary, as well as the values and cultural worldview of a unique client group. Because cultural worldviews are so diverse, social workers must have knowledge of particular groups and their cultures to provide therapeutic interventions that are relevant and appropriate. This article discusses culturally specific interventions that have been found to be useful with one indigenous Native American group, Native Hawaiians: a direct practice intervention used with Native Hawaiian families, and a community-based intervention used with a Native Hawaiian community.

Culturally Based Interventions

The models of cultural competence reviewed all encourage social workers to use cultural diverse intervention skills that are appropriate for different practice levels: micro, meso, and macro (Lum, 1999). According to Lum, the results of these strategies are empowerment, parity, and maintenance of culture and should be based in the unique experience of cultures. Indigenous interventions, such as those described in this article, are ways of helping based on the history and culture of a particular ethnic group. As stated by Shook (1985), practitioners should "cloak therapy in the garments of the client's cultural milieu" (p. 30). S. Sue and Zane (1987) suggested that using culturally compatible helping strategies builds credibility with culturally different clients, which is a key variable in successful interventions.

Some literature has developed in social work and other disciplines concerning the use of traditional healing practices and folk healing with specific ethnic groups. *Folk healing* can be defined as "health beliefs and practices derived from ethnic and historical traditions that have as their goal the amelioration or cure of psychological, spiritual, and physical problems" (Applewhite, 1995, p. 247). The advantage of indigenous therapies is that the values and philosophical basis of the interventions are compatible with client's own cultural tradition. As the majority of these interventions occur in a family or group setting, these natural support systems also are activated to assist the client. Cultural approaches to healing are consistent with a strengths perspective on social work practice Saleebey, 1996). A traditional healing approach requires an ethnographic orientation to specific cultures, as these interventions may need to be learned from indigenous practitioners or elders within a particular culture, and then adapted for use by helping professionals. Some scholars suggest that particular helping skills are needed for work with members of a particular culture. Weaver (1999) found that Native American social workers and students suggest that practitioners use containment skills with Native American clients, which involve patience, the ability to tolerate silence, listening, and limited verbalizations.

A variety of indigenous healing approaches have been used therapeutically with different cultural groups. Folktales communicate culture-specific values, customs, and wisdom as well as problem-solving methods and coping skills; they can be used in counseling with both children and adults (Alexander & Sussman, 1995). One example of this is the use of *dichos*, or Latino folk sayings, as metaphors in therapeutic work with Latino clients (Zuniga, 1992). Other approaches have been developed by mental health providers in other countries and brought to the United States for use with clients from those countries, such as Morita therapy, a Japanese treatment for anxiety disorders (K. Smith, 1981). In many non-Western and indigenous cultures, healing is performed by a medicine man or woman or shaman through the use of ceremonies, herbs and medicinal cures, trances, and other mechanisms. Many of these traditions are active today in indigenous cultures in the United States and other countries (Lee & Armstrong, 1995; Voss, Douville, Little Soldier, & Twiss, 1999). Often family-centered methods of intervention are suggested with clients from ethnic minority cultures, as most of these cultures have a strong emphasis on extended family (Pedersen, 1997).

Culturally Based Intervention with Native Hawaiians

Native Hawaiians are the indigenous peoples of the former monarchy of Hawaii, which was colonized by the United States in the mid-1800s; they originally migrated to the Hawaiian Islands from Tahiti about 750 A.D. After generations of intermarriage with other Asian and Pacific Islander groups (Chinese, Japanese, Filipino, Samoans, Tongans), as well as Europeans and Americans, the population of Hawaii is now primarily of mixed ethnic heritage. Current estimates of the Native Hawaiian population range from 12.5% of the population of the state of Hawaii (138,742) by the 1990 U.S. Census to 21.5% (240,000) by the 1993 State of Hawaii Health Department, with several hundred others living on the mainland (University of Hawaii, 1994). In recent years, there has been a resurgence of cultural identity among Native Hawaiians, which has included using the Hawaiian language, reclaiming traditional land, and developing Hawaiian music and dance (hula) forms, traditional healing practices, and culturally based programming in health care and social services.

Native Hawaiians have significant social, health, and mental health problems that indicate an urgent need for social work intervention (Mokuau, 1990; Mokuau & Matsuoka, 1995). Native Hawaiians have a 34% higher death rate than other ethnic groups in the United States, which reflects higher incidence rates of heart disease, cancer, and cerebrovascular disease (Mokuau, 1990). They also have a shorter life expectancy and higher rates of suicide, child abuse and neglect, substance abuse, and criminal conviction than other ethnic groups in the state of Hawaii (Mokuau, 1990). Additional indicators of dysfunction include low incomes, infrequent use of prenatal care resulting in high incidences of low birth rate and premature infants, and limited use of health care (University of Hawaii, 1994).

There are a number of efforts underway by health and human services organizations to address these problem areas. Congress passed the Native Hawaiian Health Care Improvement Act in 1988 (P.L. 100-579) that funded programs on most of the islands to provide culturally based health care and health education and promotion. These services incorporate traditional Hawaiian values and healing practices into their program design and delivery; congruence is therefore achieved between the Hawaiian worldview and the assessment, intervention, and evaluation stages of services delivery (Mokuau, 1990). Social services agencies have incorporated traditional healing practices into their human services interventions with families, in prisons, in schools, and in residential treatment centers (Nishihara, 1978; Shook, 1985). The adaptation of cultural traditions into health and human services is a unique emphasis that has resulted in increased participation by Native Hawaiians in health and human services programs.

Culturally based interventions in Hawaii provide an example of how human services interventions can be grounded in the culture of an ethnic group so that they reflect the worldview, values, and traditions of the culture. This approach can be adapted to other cultural groups to develop intervention approaches suited to their unique characteristics.

Ho'oponopono: A Family Conflict Resolution Process

Ho'oponopono, or setting to rights, is a family-based conflict resolution process that was originally performed in ancient Hawaii by *kahuna* (traditional healers) to maintain harmony in the community. It fell out of use with the colonization of Hawaii and the introduction of the Christian religion (Pukui, Haertig, & Lee, 1972). However, in the early 1970s a therapeutic children's center in Honolulu, Hawaii, became aware that Native Hawaiian children were not progressing in treatment or changing their dysfunctional behaviors with the Western psychotherapeutic approaches that were used at that time. To address this issue, the mental health staff began meeting with Hawaiian elders and kahuna to develop more culturally syntonic ways of treating the children. Over time, the group began to revitalize the use of ho'oponopono, an ancient Hawaiian conflict-resolution process, in the center and with the families of the residents (Shook, 1985). Social workers from the School of Social Work at the University of Hawaii later became involved in this effort, and a training film was eventually made. This method also has been adapted for use in residential treatment centers for youths (Shook, 1985), in schools (Nishihara, 1978), and in Hawaiian churches (Ito, 1985).

The ho'oponopono process was originally used by extended Native Hawaiian families to discuss and settle arguments, assuage hurt feelings, mediate angry words, and deal with other types of interpersonal problems (Pukui et al., 1972). This conflict resolution model is embedded in the traditional

Hawaiian values of extended family, need for harmonious relationships, and restoration of good will, or *aloha*. It has several specific stages that must be followed in a particular order, with a protocol as to how family members must conduct themselves during the ritual. Traditionally it was led by a kahuna within the extended family; however, this role is now taken by an elder family member or a therapist when used in a professional setting. An explanation of the stages of the process is necessary to fully understand this family conflict-resolution process.

To begin the ho'oponopono, the leader calls the family members together, with the understanding that they will participate in the process until it is complete, which may take a number of hours or even several sessions on multiple days (Shook, 1985). All family members involved in the conflict must attend; these typically include the nuclear family and some members of the extended family system. The rules of the process include the control of all communication by the leader and a prohibition on expression of emotional excess; this prevents individuals from directly confronting each other and eliminates the risk of further escalation of the problem or the creation of additional misunderstandings. The goal of the ho'oponopono is the restoration of harmony within the family and the development of a solution to the problem.

The ho'oponopono is opened with a prayer, which is followed by the identification of the problem, in both a general and a specific manner (Shook, 1985). This includes a description of the *hala*, or transgression, and the negative entanglement, or *hihia*, thus created. Each participant who has been affected by the problem, either directly or indirectly, is asked to share his or her feelings (*mana'o*). An emphasis is placed on self-scrutiny, honest and open communication, and avoidance of blame. If participants become emotional during the process, the leader may declare a cooling-off period of silence (*ho'omalu*). After the discussion phase, the resolution phase begins with the *mihi*; this is a confession of wrongdoing and the seeking of forgiveness, which is expected to be forthcoming. To establish mutuality, the wronged party also asks forgiveness for his or her reactions to the offense. This is a unique part of the process because all parties to the conflict ask forgiveness of each other, which establishes equal status among them. Restitution for the offense may be appropriate, and if so a plan for this may be determined. The *kala* concludes this phase, whereby the conflict and hurt are released, and the negative entanglement is broken. The closing phase, *pani*, includes a summary of the process, a reaffirmation of the family's strengths and enduring bonds, and a final prayer. The problem that has been worked out is then declared closed and should not be brought up again. If subsequent sessions are needed to work out other layers of the problem, the final pani is delayed until that time. After the completion of the ho'oponopono, a meal is often shared by all participants.

An example of this process as described by Shook (1985) concerns problems within a family following a child's refusal to complete her chores. In this example, the father conducted the ho'oponopono with members of a nuclear family group. The process opened with a prayer and a request for honest discussion about the problematic family interrelationships. The father asked each family member to recount his or her view of the presenting problem; as the process unfolded, it became apparent that the teenager's failure to complete the chore resulted from anger over past interactions with her mother and brother. After all family members individually discussed their participation in the present and past events, the father directed the teenager to ask forgiveness of other family members and then asked the other family members to ask forgiveness for their roles in past events and the tension and anger they had experienced. After this, the father summarized the discussion, praised family members for their honesty and openness, and closed the process with a prayer.

This Hawaiian conflict-resolution process includes many aspects of therapeutic interventions used by social workers: identification of the problem with all involved parties, discussion of the effect on the family system, identification of possible solution to the problem, and then implementation of the selected solution. It is implemented in an extended family system, which is similar to some methods of family therapy that use a network approach (Attneave, 1985). However, it is also very different from these interventions in that the process is based on a shared cultural tradition with understood roles for participants; there is a spiritual focus and an impetus for resolution to restore harmony. The formal nature of the ritual lends an aura of solemnity and importance to the process, which is crucial to many forms of traditional healing.

The model of ho'oponopono described above was developed by Shook (1985) after surveying native Hawaiian social workers who had extensive experience providing this intervention. In this research, she identified the common elements of the process as described by a number of practitioners and formulated a composite model that could be taught to students in schools of social work. The ho'oponopono technique can be used by social workers from different cultural heritages and is applicable to work with all types of families and their problems as well as to interventions with groups of nonrelated people, such as in residential care settings (Shook, 1985). This is an excellent example of traditional healing that has been adapted for modern use by helping professionals.

The ho'oponopono method of conflict resolution can be used by mental health professionals of various cultural backgrounds after they learn the process; it has been used in residential treatments and in schools with children of various cultural backgrounds with much success (Ito, 1985; Mokuau, 1990; Shook, 1985). Although no studies have yet identified the precise nature of the effectiveness of the ho'oponopono technique, one can speculate that its basis in the culture and values of Native Hawaiians may enable families to engage in the process in a comfortable manner. In addition, the spiritual component of this process is reflective of the integration of spirituality with healing in many indigenous cultures.

Culture-centered Community-based Practice

Community development activities that recognize and build community strengths, understand the culture and values of ethnic communities, and work as partners with them have the best chance of success (Gutierrez, Alvarez, Nemon, & Lewis, 1996). To be an effective and culturally competent community organizer requires many of the cultural competence skills discussed earlier, such as understanding one's own cultural heritage and gaining knowledge of the ethnic group with which one is working, including its history, traditions, and values. Recognition of the strengths of communities of color is a key factor, particularly the family and community support networks and collectivist worldview (Gutierrez et al., 1996). Often there is a need for interpreters or cultural mediators to ensure that communication is fully understandable to the community; these roles should not be held by community organizers because they are an excel-

lent vehicle for developing indigenous community leadership (Heskin & Heffner, 1987).

Ho'opono Ahupua'a: A Native Hawaiian Community Development Project

In the mid-1990s, a Hawaiian foundation, the Queen Emma Foundation, targeted several rural communities on the island of Oahu for assistance because they had high concentrations of Native Hawaiians and had significant health and education problems. To facilitate the involvement of the indigenous community, the foundation developed a culturally competent community development strategy with the goal of enabling the communities to identify their own problems and help create needed programs and services. In 1995 the foundation adopted the Ahupua'a Access and Support Model, a plan for development of healthy Native Hawaiian communities based on ancient Hawaiian values (Janoff & Weisbord, 1997). This model outlines a framework for support of communities based on levels of access; all levels are interdependent and holistic and rest on the foundation of *lokahi* (unity). The primary support system is the family, both nuclear and extended, with the community (*malama'ohana*) being of secondary support. The community level is envisioned to support a *pu'uhonua* (place of refuge); historically, this was a particular location that provided refuge and protection to people in need. The pu'uhonua is now being reframed as a community center that provides services such as outpatient medical care, counseling services, or respite care (Janoff & Weisbord, 1997).

To initiate the community development project, the rural communities participated in a future-visioning process in which they developed their "ideal" community (Janoff & Weisbord, 1997). The several-day conference, with participation from representatives of all areas of the community, resulted in a master community plan for the development of a variety of programs and services. Task groups were formed to plan and initiate programming in various topical areas. The project was so successful that at follow-up a year later, the community had created a child care center, a farmer's market, and a health promotion program; also they had developed a healthy lifestyle program that included nutritional instruction based on a Native Hawaiian diet. In addition, they had integrated Native Hawaiian healers into local medical clinics (Janoff & Weisbord, 1997). Foundation funding was used for several of these projects. It was apparent that the community development process was responsible for the tremendous progress that these previously marginally functioning communities had made in self-determination and mobilization of resources.

This example of culturally based community development used many of the principles of multicultural community organizing. The project was based on the values and worldview of the Native Hawaiian communities it served, and it built on community strengths by integrating cultural practices into program delivery, such as the use of Native Hawaiian healers and dietary instruction based on the Native Hawaiian diet. Community members became leaders of task groups to plan and initiate the development of needed community services. The funding foundation worked as a partner with the community rather than sending in staff to develop programs for the community. The articulation of Native Hawaiian values into the guiding principals of the foundation was a key aspect of the success of this project (Janoff & Weisbord, 1997).

Conclusion

Cultural competence requires the use of intervention skills that are a good fit with the cultural worldview and values of specific ethnic groups. Developing cultural competence requires social workers to engage in an ongoing cultural knowledge development process, as well as learning about traditional healing practices that can be applied to work with ethnic clients. A primary focus needs to be on empowering the client systems to determine the problems to be addressed and the solutions they envision. The intervention process then uses culturally based interventions to achieve these goals. This process requires a trusting relationship to be developed with clients, which is facilitated by the use of culturally based social work practice.

The two different types of interventions, based on traditional Hawaiian values and practices, discussed in this article provide assistance to families and to the community and reflect the importance of cultural values and spirituality in the intervention process. They are also examples of how traditional indigenous healing practices can be applied to contemporary social work practice. For client systems in the Hawaiian Islands, both Native

Hawaiians and members of other cultures, use of these intervention methods is very appropriate. These methods also may be useful with other cultural groups on the mainland, as the ho'oponopono process has been found to be effective with members of various cultural groups (Shook, 1985). These two Hawaiian methods also may serve as examples of different ways in which indigenous cultural healing concepts and practices can be integrated into direct social work practice with families and communities. Because the literature on these types of culturally based interventions is very limited, this is an area in which further research and development is needed.

References

Alexander, C. M., & Sussman, L. (1995). Creative approaches to multicultural counseling. In J. G. Ponterotto, J. M. Casas, L. A. Susuki, & C. M. Alexander (Eds.), *Handbook of multicultural counseling* (pp. 375–384). Thousand Oaks, CA: Sage Publications.

Applewhite, S. L. (1995). *Curanderismo*: Demystifying the health beliefs and practices of elderly Mexican Americans. *Health & Social Work, 20,* 247–253.

Attneave, C. L. (1985). Practical counseling with American Indian and Alaska Native clients. In P. Pedersen (Ed.), *Handbook of cross-cultural counseling and therapy* (pp. 135–140). Westport, CT: Greenwood Press.

Chau, K. L. (1989). Sociocultural dissonance among ethnic minority populations. *Social Casework, 70,* 224–230.

Congress, E. P. (1994). The use of culturagrams to assess and empower culturally diverse families. *Families in Society, 75,* 531–539.

Cross, T., Bazron, B. J., Dennis, K. W., & Isaacs, M. R. (1989). *Towards a culturally competent system of care: Volume I. A monograph on effective services for minority children who are severely emotionally disturbed.* Washington, DC: CASSP Technical Assistance Center, Georgetown University Child Development Center.

Devore, W., & Schlesinger, E. G. (1987). *Ethnic sensitive social work practice* (2nd ed.). Columbus, OH: Merrill.

Dyche, L., & Zayas, L. H. (1995). The value of curiosity and naivete for the cross-cultural psychotherapist. *Family Process, 34,* 389–399.

Falicov, C. (1995). Training to think culturally: A multidimensional comparative framework. *Family Process, 34,* 373–388.

Gilligan, C. (1982). *In a different voice: Psychological theory and women's development*. Cambridge, MA: Harvard University Press.

Granger, J. M., & Portner, D. L. (1985). Ethnic- and gender-sensitive social work practice. *Journal of Social Work Education, 21*, 38–47.

Green, J. W. (1999). *Cultural awareness in the human services: A multi-ethnic approach* (3rd ed.). Needham Heights, MA: Allyn & Bacon.

Gutierrez, L., Alvarez, A. R., Nemon, H., & Lewis, E. A. (1996). Multicultural community organizing: A strategy for change. *Social Work, 41*, 501–508.

Hardy, K. V., & Laszloffy, T. A. (1995). The cultural genogram: Key to training culturally competent family therapists. *Journal of Marital and Family Therapy, 21*, 227–237.

Heskin, A. D., & Heffner, R. A. (1987). Learning about bilingual, multicultural organizing. *Journal of Applied Behavioral Science, 23*, 525–541.

Ito, K. L. (1985). Ho'oponopono, "to make right": Hawaiian conflict resolution and metaphor in the construction of a family therapy. *Culture, Medicine and Psychiatry, 9*, 201–217.

Janoff, S., & Weisbord, M. R. (1997). Speaking with the ancients. *Healthcare Forum Journal, 40*, 26–34.

Laird, J. (1994). "Thick description" revisited: Family therapist as anthropologist-constructivist. In E. Sherman & W. J. Reid (Eds.), *Qualitative research in social work* (pp. 175–188). New York: Columbia University Press.

Laird, J. (1998). Theorizing culture: Narrative ideas and practice principles. In M. McGoldrick (Ed.), *Re-visioning family therapy: Race, culture, and gender in clinical practice* (pp. 20–36). New York: Guilford Press.

Lee, C. C., & Armstrong, K. L. (1995). Indigenous models of mental health intervention: Lessons from traditional healers. In J. G. Ponterotto, J. M. Casas, L. A. Susuki, & C. M. Alexander (Eds.), *Handbook of multicultural counseling* (pp. 441–456). Thousand Oaks, CA: Sage Publication.

Leininger, M. M. (1985). Transcultural caring: A different way to help people. In P. Pedersen (Ed.), *Handbook of cross-cultural counseling and therapy* (pp. 107–115). Westport, CT: Greenwood Press.

Lum, D. (1982). Toward a framework for social work practice with minorities. *Social Work, 27*, 244–249.

Lum, D. (1996). *Social work practice with people of color: A process-stage approach* (3rd ed.). Pacific Grove, CA: Brooks/Cole.

Lum, D. (1999). *Culturally competent practice: A framework for growth and action*. Pacific Grove, CA: Brooks/Cole.

McGoldrick, M. (1998). Introduction: Re-visioning family therapy through a cultural lens. In M. McGoldrick (Ed.), *Re-visioning family therapy: Race, culture, and gender in clinical practice* (pp. 3–19). New York: Guilford Press.

McPhatter, A. R. (1997). Cultural competence in child welfare: What is it? How do we achieve it? What happens without it? *Child Welfare, 76*, 255–278.

Mokuau, N. (1990). The impoverishment of Native Hawaiians and the social work challenge. *Health & Social Work, 15*, 235–242.

Mokuau, N., & Matsuoka, J. (1995). Turbulence among a native people: Social work practice with Hawaiians. *Social Work, 40*, 465–472.

Native Hawaiian Health Care Improvement Act of 1988, P.L. 100-579, 102 Stat. 2916.

Nishihara, D. P. (1978). Culture, counseling, and ho'oponopono: An ancient model in a modern context. *Personnel and Guidance Journal, 56*, 562–566.

Norton, D. G. (1993). Diversity, early socialization, and temporal development: The dual perspective revisited. *Social Work, 38*, 82–90.

Pedersen, P. B. (1997). *Culture-centered counseling interventions: Striving for accuracy*. Thousand Oaks, CA: Sage Publications.

Pierce, R. L., & Pierce, L. H. (1996). Moving toward cultural competence in the child welfare system. *Children and Youth Review, 18*, 713–731.

Pukui, M. K., Haertig, E. W., & Lee, C. A. (1972). *Nana I Ke Kumu (Look to the source)* (Vol. 1). Honolulu: Hui Hanai.

Saleebey, D. (1996). The strengths perspective in social work practice: Extensions and cautions. *Social Work, 41*, 296–305.

Shook, E. V. (1985). *Ho'oponopono: Contemporary uses of a Hawaiian problem-solving process*. Honolulu: University of Hawaii Press.

Smith, K. (1981). Observations on Morita therapy and culture-specific interpretations. *Journal of Transpersonal Psychology, 13*, 59–69.

Smith, L. S. (1998). Concept analysis: Cultural competence. *Journal of Cultural Diversity, 5*(1), 4–10.

Sue, D. W., Carter, R. T., Casas, J. M., Fouad, N. A., Ivey, A. E., Jensen, M., LaFromboise, T., Manese, J. E., Ponterotto, J. G., &

Vazquez-Nutall, E. (Eds.). (1998). *Multicultural counseling competencies: Individual and organizational development.* Thousand Oaks, CA: Sage Publications.

Sue, S., & Zane, N. (1987). The role of culture and cultural techniques in psychotherapy: A critique and reformulation. *American Psychologist, 42,* 37–45.

Tervalon, M., & Murray-Garcia, J. (1998). Cultural humility versus cultural competence: A critical distinction in defining physician training outcomes in multicultural education. *Journal of Health Care for the Poor and Underserved, 9,* 117–125.

University of Hawaii, John A. Burns School of Medicine. (1994, June 18). *Native Hawaiian health briefing paper.* Honolulu: Author.

Voss, R. W., Douville, V., Little Soldier, A., & Twiss, G. (1999). Tribal and shamanic-based social work practice: A Lakota perspective. *Social Work, 44,* 228–241.

Weaver, H. N. (1999). Indigenous people and the social work profession: Defining culturally competent services. *Social Work, 44,* 217–225.

Zuniga, M. E. (1992). Using metaphors in therapy: Dichos and Latino clients. *Social Work, 37,* 55–60.

ROBERT G. MALGADY
LUIS H. ZAYAS

50

Cultural and Linguistic Considerations in Psychodiagnosis with Hispanics: The Need for an Empirically Informed Process Model

Migration from Latin America has moved large numbers of Hispanic immigrants, mostly Spanish monolingual or limited English-proficient, into major urban areas in the United States (Rogler, 1994). Coupled with the already substantial numbers of resident Hispanics, most of whom are Spanish-dominant (U.S. Bureau of the Census, 1991), members of this growing population must cope not only with stressors associated with lower socioeconomic status (SES), but also with stress associated with the language and cultural demands of the host American society. When unacculturated Hispanics with limited English proficiency turn to organizations delivering mental health services, on intake they often face a common problem of language and cultural distance from service providers because there is a severe shortage of bilingual and bicultural clinicians in the mental health services system (Bernal & Castro, 1994; Cross, Bazron, Dennis, & Isaacs, 1989). Inasmuch as clinical social workers are involved in the diagnosis of immigrant clients from ethnic minority groups, using *DSM-IV* in such wide-ranging practice settings as primary care clinics, outpatient psychiatric clinics, medical and psychiatric inpatient services, hospital consultation-liaison services, residential treatment centers, substance abuse treatment facilities, and private practice, it seems imperative to consider at some length the issue of how ethnicity and language influence diagnostic decision making. Furthermore, as social work researchers continue to expand their roles in mental health research, similar considerations are

useful in advancing our research knowledge on the influence of language and ethnicity on the diagnostic process. Therefore, this article gives attention to both practice and research concerns.

There is likely to continue to be a large gap between the mental health needs of ethnic minority populations and the availability of bilingual and bicultural services providers. The reality of this situation is that, even when a fuller understanding of cultural competence is achieved, the availability of bilingual and bicultural social workers remains limited, and is even more so in psychology and psychiatry. The practical consequences of this gap are such that social workers who do belong to ethnic minority groups and other mental health professionals need to be trained to provide culturally sensitive diagnostic and treatment services to clients from ethnic minority groups. Fundamental to the development of such training programs is the study of the process of how accurate diagnoses are made when the client and clinician are matched ethnically and linguistically, but more important are the processes that distinguish accurate and inaccurate diagnoses when they are not matched. In the Hispanic mental health literature, there has been considerable speculation and concern that biases in diagnosis occur when bilingual Hispanic clients are interviewed in English by non-Hispanic clinicians, even when a translator is pressed into service (for example, Lewis-Fernandez & Kleinman, 1994, 1995; Malgady, Rogler, & Costantino, 1987; Marcos, 1994).

In the history of the American Psychiatric Association's *Diagnostic and Statistical Manual of Mental Disorders*, the publication of the fourth edition (*DSM-IV*) (APA, 1994) reflects an unprecedented recognition of the importance of the cultural diversity of clients in psychiatric evaluations. Despite the importance of accurate psychodiagnosis in the delivery of mental health services, empirical research on this topic has been equivocal, and theoretical formulations have been limited (Malgady, Rogler, & Marcos, 1997). Given the attention to the consideration of cultural and linguistic diversity in the formulation of diagnostic criteria in the *DSM-IV* (for example, "ethnic and cultural considerations," p. xxxiv) and its glossary of "culture-bound syndromes," there is a critical need now to understand the diagnostic process in the light of such considerations. However, there has been no attempt to model systematically the dynamic interpersonal process by which language and ethnic diversity affect the behavior and communications of clients during the psychiatric interview and how these in turn affect the diagnostic impression of mental health clinicians. Lessons drawn from Spanish-dominant and bilingual Hispanics may help social workers in the diagnostic process with other ethnocultural and linguistic minority groups and immigrants.

The sheer dearth of research on this topic is surprising because accurate psychiatric diagnosis is fundamental to epidemiological assessment of mental health needs in ethnic minority populations, determination of patterns of utilization of mental health services, appropriate choice of psychotherapeutic and psychopharmacological intervention, and monitoring of posttreatment adjustment. This article critically reviews research on the diagnostic process with Hispanics, one of many ethnic and linguistic minority groups in this country. Because the diagnosis research literature on Hispanics has focused primarily on adults, we have not included children and adolescents because they present unique diagnostic challenges based on developmental factors and different pace of acculturation and English-language acquisition.

pared with other ethnic groups (Moscicki, Rae, Regier, & Locke, 1987; Rogler, Malgady, & Rodriguez, 1989). In contrast, other epidemiological studies have found higher levels of symptom severity among Hispanics, but not higher prevalence rates of *DSM-IV* disorders (Shrout et al., 1992).

The recent report of lifetime and 12-month prevalence of *DSM-III-R* disorders from the National Comorbidity Survey (NCS) (Kessler et al., 1994) has revealed unexpectedly high prevalence rates of disorder prevalence rates of disorder and comorbidity among Hispanics, particularly major depression and alcohol dependence. Kessler et al. reported that Hispanics have significantly higher prevalence of current affective disorders (that is, major depression, manic episode, dysthymia, and other affective disorders) and higher prevalence of active comorbidity compared with non-Hispanic white people and African Americans. Indeed, there were no disorders in which Hispanic prevalence rates were lower than those among non-Hispanic white people.

Other risk factors include acculturation problems and low SES, which have been linked in many studies to increased stress and consequently higher risk of mental disorder among Hispanics (Rogler et al., 1989). Consistent with this research, the prevalence rates of almost all disorders were inversely related to income and education in the 1994 NCS study. This places Hispanics at increased risk given their generally low income and educational profile relative to white people (U.S. Bureau of the Census, 1991). This problem is compounded by Hispanics' underutilization of mental health services and high dropout rate after initial contact with service providers (Rodriguez, 1989; Sue & Zane, 1987). Part of the underutilization and premature termination among Hispanics and other ethnolinguistic minority groups may be attributable to the cultural distance that affects the diagnosis and treatment process. The same is true of the manner in which services are designed and delivered, approaches that do not facilitate engagement in mental health services. These findings have implications for social workers involved in psychiatric diagnoses with language-minority and ethnic-minority clients.

Mental Health Services Needs among Hispanics

There is some evidence from epidemiological studies to suggest that members of Hispanic populations are at higher risk of certain mental disorders, such as schizophrenia and major depression, com-

Language Effects and Expressions of Distress

Researchers have suggested that misdiagnosis of bilingual Hispanic clients may stem from the language used to express distress during a psychiatric interview (Gomez, Ruiz, & Rumbaut, 1985; Marcos, Alpert, Urcuyo, & Kesselman, 1973; Price & Cuellar, 1981). Language affects the bilingual client's ability to express thoughts, feelings, and emotions and the clinician's understanding and interpretation of the client's verbal and nonverbal responses. Manson (1996) noted that clients bring a richly varied lexicon of emotions from their cultures. Unbiased assessment of a client's orientation, presenting symptoms, judgment, and other mental functions requires accurate communication; hence biases may intrude into the diagnostic process to the extent that the interview language promotes misinterpretations of the client's verbal and nonverbal responses to diagnostic inquiry. Guarnaccia (1996) also emphasized the importance of assessing language abilities and multilingualism in the diagnostic process.

Research has examined the effect of the language spoken during psychiatric interviews on clinical judgments of symptom severity. However, the findings are equivocal regarding which language—English or Spanish—spoken by bilingual clients leads to clinical judgments of greater or lesser pathology. In a case study, Del Castillo (1970) described several clinical episodes in which Spanish-speaking clients appeared overtly psychotic during a Spanish interview, but much less so when interviewed in English. Del Castillo speculated that when the clients were interviewed in their nonnative language they exerted more effort to communicate, which produced greater vigilance and control over their emotions.

On the other hand, Marcos and his associates (1973) reported opposite findings. The symptomatology of Spanish-dominant schizophrenics was rated as more severe when they were interviewed in English. Although Marcos conducted a more controlled study than Del Castillo's (1970) case study, interview language and ethnicity of the clinician evaluated the English interviews and a Hispanic clinician evaluated the Spanish interviews. In an attempt to eliminate such confounding, Price and Cuellar (1981) investigated the effect of interview language on symptom severity ratings but held clinician ethnicity constant, using bilingual Hispanic clinicians to evaluate both the English and Spanish interviews. Their results contradicted Marcos's findings and supported Del Castillo's findings, because symptoms were rated as more severe in Spanish interviews.

A general problem with all these studies is that they were based on extremely small samples. Del Castillo's (1970) observations were based on only a handful of interviews, and Marcos and colleagues

(1973) interviewed only 10 patients, and Price and Cuellar only 32 patients. Thus, the discrepant outcomes may reflect the unreliability produced by the small sample size in each study. In a sense, the empirical literature in this arena represents intriguing and suggestive pilot studies rather than a systematic body of knowledge.

With respect to language mismatches, Marcos and his associates (1973, 1976, 1979) have studied extensively the effects of Spanish-language translators in diagnostic interview situations. Marcos and associates (1973) found that in actual clinical settings, almost any available Spanish-speaking person tends to be pressed into service as an interpreter; family members, friends, or hospital staff. Moreover, there is rarely any assessment of the interpreter's bilingual or mental health treatment competence. Errors identified by Marcos under such circumstances include grossly inaccurate translation from English to Spanish, intrusion of the interpreter's feelings and interpretations of the client's Spanish-language disclosures, and interference with the development of rapport between client and clinician, an element considered essential in the social work interview.

Others have argued, however, that with proper translation and mental health training, it is possible to use interpreters to enhance the quality of services to ethnic minority clients (Acosta & Cristo, 1981; Liebowitz, 1995). This issue is likely to become more critical in the years to come, not only because of the shortage of bilingual/bicultural social workers and, especially, other mental health professional staff, but also because the training of lay interpreters is an economical solution to the problem in light of an already overburdened health care system.

Individual Differences

Another consequence of this sample size limitation is that there has been no investigation of individual differences among clients, such as how chronicity, acculturation, and demographic factors may influence the effect of interview language on mental health evaluations. Some suggestive evidence of the influence of such variables comes from studies in the general Hispanic population. For example, in a national survey of Mexican Americans, Ortiz and Arce (1983) found that the relationship between interview language and expressed symptoms was dependent on SES. Mexican Americans with lower SES disclosed more depressive and psychosomatic symptoms when interviewed in Spanish; however, middle-class Mexican Americans reported more depressive and psychosomatic symptoms when interviewed in English. These results suggest how individual differences, such as SES, can mitigate the influence of language variations on mental health evaluations. Because SES is associated with language dominance and level of acculturation, the findings suggest that greater pathology would be revealed in the dominant Spanish language.

The type and chronicity of a client's disorder are other factors that may influence the outcome of a social work psychiatric interview. The studies by Marcos (1973, 1976) and Price and Cuellar (1981) were limited to schizophrenics, so we have no knowledge of whether their results generalize to clients expressing other symptom configurations, such as affective disorders. Chronicity of disorder was suggested by Vasquez (1982) as a reason for the equivocal findings. Whereas Marcos studied recent admissions, Price and Cuellar studied chronic hospitalized patients who were more experienced with their psychiatric setting. As Vasquez remarked, patients inexperienced in a psychiatric setting may exhibit increased anxiety and tension when speaking a nondominant language during an intake interview and thus may be evaluated as more pathological. However, earlier interview experience together with speaking Spanish, the dominant language, may promote greater self-disclosure and hence may reveal actual pathology.

Ethnic Matching of Client and Clinician

In addition to language considerations, the ethnic similarity of the client and clinician may be a factor influencing the evaluation of Hispanic clients. In a review of psychiatric diagnoses of patients from ethnic minority groups in clinical settings, Adebimpe (1981) concluded that members of ethnic minority populations are at increased risk of misdiagnosis because of the sociocultural distance between clinician and client. Research has indicated that ethnic similarity between client and clinician enhances the clinician's ability to identify cultural modes of expressing symptoms, to comprehend the meanings associated with particular experiences, and to understand linguistic variation in thought and expression that often does not occur when clinician and client differ in ethnicity (Malgady et al., 1987).

Several studies have demonstrated that clinicians of diverse ethnicities render significantly different diagnoses of similar patients (Baskin, Bluestone, & Nelson, 1981; Malgady et al., 1997). Based on 148 diagnostic interviews of Hispanics, Malgady and his associates examined interview situations by either a Hispanic or non-Hispanic white clinician, either in Spanish, English, or bilingually. Results indicated that Hispanic clinicians consistently rated symptoms as more severe than non-Hispanic white clinicians. Rating of symptom severity and diagnostic sensitivity were the highest in bilingual interviews, followed by Spanish interviews, and lowest in English interviews.

Lopez and Nunez (1987) remarked that the *DSM-III-R* provided no guidelines for taking cultural factors into consideration in formulating a diagnosis. Other research suggests that practicing clinicians do not concur on what cultural factors are crucial in the diagnostic process (Lopez & Hernandez, 1987). The *DSM-IV* provides greater attention to culture than its predecessors; however, there is limited empirical and virtually no theoretical basis for understanding how to make a culturally sensitive diagnosis. The absence of practical strategies to incorporate culture into diagnosis in *DSM-IV* has been discussed (Mezzich, Kleinman, Fabrega, & Parron, 1996), and some basic guidelines have been proposed (Mezzich, 1969). Kleinman (1996) noted that linguistic categories are derived from cultural models of the world, the person, and the illness—aspects that may not be shared by clinician and client when they are culturally distant. Indeed, clinical practice is a culturally patterned event, and diagnosis is an interpretation by the clinician of an interpretation rendered by the client based on his or her own cultural categories, words, images, and feelings for expressing symptoms and distress (Kleinman, 1996; Wintrob, 1996).

Mezzich (1996) described a cultural formulation guideline for *DSM-IV*, which includes assessing the client's cultural identity, cultural explanations of the person's illness, cultural factors related to psychosocial environment and levels of functioning, cultural elements of the relationship between the individual and the clinician, and overall cultural assessment for diagnosis and care. However, these guidelines remain at a general level of conceptualization and operationalization, and, furthermore, have not made their way into mainstream diagnostic practices, or into *DSM-IV*, but social workers may be in positions to extend the mental health field's knowledge in this area. Thus, there is a need to asses the independent and possible interactive effects of language of interview and ethnicity of the social worker and other clinicians in the mental health evaluation process.

Client–Social Worker Interactive Processes

If the outcome of a psychiatric interview is influenced by the language spoken during the interview and the ethnic match of client and clinician, questions arise about the processes by which language and cultural factors affect the behavior and communication of clients during psychiatric interviews and how these in turn affect the diagnostic impression of social workers and other mental health professionals. There is a limited body of research that has examined the effect of process variables on the course of a psychiatric interview. For instance, in a structured interview a client tends to mimic the interviewer's speech, length of utterance, and response latency (Matarazzo, 1978). Accordingly, the language and ethnicity of the social work clinician may influence a Hispanic client's attitudes and emotions in the interview, which in turn affect the client's verbal behavior (for example, self-disclosure or emotional expressiveness) and nonverbal behavior (for example, facial affect or gestures). The question then arises of whether such verbal and nonverbal behavior in the interview process have the effect of biasing the diagnosis or the perception of symptom severity. To the extent that client behavior is responsive to language and cultural conditions, the information elicited in the interview is vulnerable to distortion, misunderstanding, and diagnostic bias.

A number of interview behaviors have been reported to change a result of language and ethnicity. In the Marcos (1976) study, Spanish-dominant clients were less verbally fluent and more likely to switch languages, emit incoherent sounds, have long silent pauses, and speak slowly during English interviews. These speech patterns in English made the flow of thought appear more illogical and confused compared with verbal behavior in Spanish interviews. In the Price and Cuellar (1981) study, clients disclosed more symptomatic information during Spanish-language interviews than during English interviews, although self-disclosure did not correlate with symptom severity ratings. Thus, there is a suggestion from the little research on this topic that Hispanic clients may be more self-revealing in a Spanish interview administered by a Hispanic social worker, and that such interviewing conditions will reveal more pathology.

Emotional expressiveness of the client in a psychiatric interview has been identified as a critical factor by Gonzalez (1978), who reported that His-panic clients expressed more discomfort and hostility in Spanish interviews than in English interviews. This finding coincides with Del Castillo's (1970) argument that speaking a nondominant language produces a vigilance over emotions. Therefore, verbal behavior indicating hospitality or other emotions—which are suggestive of a mood disorder—might be inhibited during English interviews of Spanish-dominant clients. Cultural factors, such as the premium placed on deferential behavior toward professionals and people of authority, also may be misinterpreted as passivity, impoverished language or cognition, withdrawal, or obsequiousness. Similarly, Guttfreund (1990) found that bilingual people expressed more anxiety and depression symptoms when speaking Spanish, regardless of whether Spanish or English was their first language.

In regard to nonverbal expressions indicative of cognitive difficulty, Marcos (1976) found that when bilingual people verbalized similar topics in their two languages, more speech-related hand movements (reflecting active cognitive encoding) were used during verbalization in the nondominant language. However, more body-focused movements such as touching, soothing, and stroking (reflecting emotional states) were used in the dominant language. Marcos and his associates (Grand, Marcos, Freedman, & Barroso, 1977) later found that expression of symptoms during English-language interviews was correlated with nonverbal cognitive signs, such as hand movements, whereas in Spanish interviews symptoms were associated with nonverbal emotional signs, such as body movements. In effect, symptoms increased with cognitive effort or emotional expression, depending on the language of the interview. This suggests that Spanish-dominant Hispanic clients would be diagnosed as having more affective disorders in Spanish interviews because of the increased intensity of emotional movements, but in English interviews as having more thought disorders (for example, schizophrenia) because of the greater cognitive load of speaking in the nondominant language. Therefore, there is a need to consider the effects of the interview situation on clients' nonverbal expressive behavior and especially how such behavior mediates the influence of interview language and ethnicity on severity ratings and diagnosis.

Implications for Social Work Practice and Social Work Research

To overcome the problems of culture and language in the diagnostic process and move beyond "objective" criteria set forth as if culture were not a social construction that influences mental health, social work clinicians and researchers must consider the process variables in the diagnostic interview. In the assessment of the mental health of immigrant, ethnolinguistically different clients, the interaction of client and social worker in the diagnostic interview and the language used by both participants requires attention to arrive at a diagnosis.

We agree with Marcos (1979) that people who are not mental health professionals should not be pressed into service as translators. Inaccurate translations, the injection of value judgments and biases, and the intensity or magnitude of the distress being described through particular idiomatic expressions may mislead the diagnostician. Indeed, in our experience, similar mistranslations have occurred with other non-Hispanic immigrant clients, such as Southeast Asians and Serbo-Croatians. In cases where professional mental health personnel are not available for translation, social workers can take leadership in training mental health paraprofessionals from linguistic and ethnic minority groups. This process of development would start with paraprofessionals possessing the requisite language skill—Spanish in our discussion, but applicable to other groups—and training them with the unique translation skills needed in the diagnostic processes.

In his most recent discussion of the diagnostic process involving bilingual people, Marcos (1994) identified four major categories of client behavior that are susceptible to distortion and misinterpretation. These categories can prove useful process guidelines for social work clinicians conducting diagnostic interviews. Moreover, they may represent an important initial step in developing research approaches for examining process variables. One category is the client's "general attitude toward the examiner and the interview situation." Clients struggling with a language barrier often behave self-effacingly, leading clinical social workers to infer guarded behavior, uncooperativeness, or reluctance to communicate. Limited English-proficient Hispanic clients can have a negative attitude toward English, which may permeate that general predisposition toward the non-Hispanic English-speaking clinician and the interview situation itself.

A second category is the client's "motor activity, speech, and stream of talk." The quality and quantity of a client's motor activity poses a challenge for social work clinicians to distinguish between language-induced problems and true underlying symptoms. Speech disturbances and language mixing or primary language intrusion, which tend to occur in clients' responses to emotionally charged questions and in high-stress situations (Javier & Alpert, 1986; Javier & Marcos, 1989; Manson, 1996), also may lead social workers and other mental health clinicians to infer that the flow of thought is less logical and more confused. Within language behavior, the social work diagnostician needs to be concerned with fluency measures (that is, word, type, sentence counts, and ratios), client-versus therapist-initiated statements, number of self-disclosures, affective expression (affective tone and lability, hostility, discomfort, monotone vocal emphasis, and voice level), speech rate, latency to respond to query, speech disturbances (hesitations and silent pauses), language switching (English to Spanish, Spanish to English), and expressive gestures (body and postural movements suggestive of tension or apprehension or relaxation). But, to be sure, not all of the tension seen in clients comes from a mental disorder; much may be attributed to the natural anxiety of participating in the diagnostic interview, as pointed out by Vasquez (1982).

A third category relates to the "affective and emotional tone" that clients present in the clinical encounter. According to Marcos (1994), flattened affect is common among bilingual individuals, leading clinicians to infer emotional withdrawal or inappropriate emotional reaction. We add to this category the variation in how different cultural groups express different emotional experiences (Manson, 1996). Some groups may proscribe the exuberant display of joy over an achievement, for example, based on a cultural belief about humility and pride. Within this category, facial affect also must be clearly attended to and understood by clinicians. Guttfreund's (1990) findings that bilingual people express more anxiety and depression when speaking Spanish is highly relevant to the social worker's considerations during diagnostic interviews.

A fourth category suggested by Marcos (1994) is the manner in which culturally and linguistically different clients present their "sense of self." Marcos argued that clients may express a different sense of identity depending on which language they speak. Speaking a second language may lead to a clinical impression of less intelligence and poorer self-esteem. In cultures that respect the spirits of deceased loved ones and of communication with the departed, descriptions of connections with these individuals may lead to diagnostic misunderstandings of depersonalization, derealization, or delusions, yet have valid, culturally based explanations (Mezzich et al., 1996). Marcos pointed to an array of barriers that place demands on the social worker to discriminate between artificial language-induced symptoms and actual pathological symptoms.

Based on the early work of Marcos and his associates (1973, 1976, 1979), the main categories of verbal behavior consist of client fluency, self-disclosure, emotional expression, speech disturbance, and language switching. These verbal behaviors include client and clinician self-reports and the assessment by each of honesty, trust, credibility, quality of rapport, warmth, giving and exchange, insight gained into problem, progress made toward resolution, and overall satisfaction and helpfulness. Mezzich (1996) pointed out that the client's cultural identity is an important factor in the assessment and that cultural elements associated with interpersonal relations influence the manner in which the client interacts with the social work clinician. Consider also that using one's native tongue permits greater self-disclosure (Vasquez, 1982).

A Process Research Agenda

There is a clear need for social work clinicians in mental health settings to include important process variables in their work on diagnosis of ethnic and linguistic minority groups in the United States, such as Hispanics. Yet, we cannot stop at suggesting guidelines for direct practice only; social workers practicing as researchers not only constitute part of the readership of this journal [*Social Work*], but also are expanding their roles in the mental health research area in larger numbers than ever before. For social work research into the diagnostic interview, aspects of the Roter Interactional Analysis System (RIAS) (Roter, 1990) may be adapted from the medical interview situation to the psychiatric interview situation. The RIAS codes each phrase or complete thought expressed by both client and clinician into mutually exclusive and exhaustive content categories.

Basic to the interaction analysis system are such issues as information giving (procedures and tests and treatments) and how questions are posed by the examiner (that is, general, closed, or open questions). Four aspects of the RIAS can be incorporated in social work research on the mental health diagnostic process that focuses on members of ethnocultural and linguistic minority groups: (1) concerns for social workers' competence (technical and interpersonal), (2) social workers' capacity for partnership building with clients, (3) client socioemotional behavior (body movements, social conversation, positive talk, and negative talk), and (4) amount of communication between clinician and client. The RIAS, and other proposed guidelines

(for example, Mezzich, 1996), may offer some grounds on which researchers can build in the quest for a more empirically based process model of diagnosis than that currently available, most prominently represented by *DSM-IV*'s emphasis on meeting specific criteria for diagnosis without adequate room for the impact of language and culture.

Although there is some literature on client interview behaviors, there has been no research undertaken to systematically specify and test the causal sequence from language and ethnicity to particular verbal and nonverbal process behaviors and from such mediating process behaviors to social workers' diagnoses and judgments of symptom severity. The *DSM-IV* provides numerous considerations of culture in diagnosis and in its glossary of culture-bound syndromes, but provides little direction regarding how culture influences the psychiatric diagnostic process. Clearly, there is a need for training both social workers and other mental health services providers of ethnic minority populations and those who are not in the processes by which the language and cultural dynamics of the diagnostic interview lead to correct diagnoses or misdiagnosis of ethnic minority clients. However, to make this training valid, research must document how these dynamics operate and influence diagnosis. Then, teachable approaches can be developed.

Because both psychotherapeutic and psychopharmacological treatment planning are predicated on accurate psychiatric diagnosis, understanding the roots of potential cultural or language diagnostic bias has critical implications for the delivery of effective mental health services to ethnic and linguistic minority populations. Given the increasing ethnic minority population in the mental health services system, coupled with a persistent shortage of ethnic minority service providers, there is a growing need to understand the circumstances under which accurate and inaccurate diagnostic decisions take place when practitioners who do not belong to ethnic minority groups provide mental health services to a growing ethnic minority clientele.

References

Acosta, F., & Cristo, M. (1981). Development of a bilingual interpreter program: An alternative model for Spanish-speaking services. *Professional Psychology, 12,* 474–482.

Adebimpe, V. (1981). White norms and psychiatric diagnosis of black patients.

American Journal of Psychiatry, 138, 279–285.

American Psychiatric Association. (1994). *Diagnostic and statistical manual of mental disorders* (4th ed.). Washington, DC: Author.

Baskin, D., Bluestone, H., & Nelson, M. (1981). Ethnicity and psychiatric diagnosis. *Journal of Clinical Psychology, 37,* 529–537.

Bernal, M. E., & Castro, F. G. (1994). Are clinical psychologists prepared for service and research with ethnic minorities? Report of a decade of progress. *American Psychologist, 49,* 797–805.

Cross, T. L., Bazron, B. J., Dennis, K. W., & Isaacs, M. R. (1989). *Toward a culturally competent system of care.* Washington, DC: Georgetown University, CAASP Technical Assistance Center.

Del Castillo, J. (1970).The influence of language upon symptomatology in foreign-born patients. *American Journal of Psychiatry, 127,* 242–244.

Gomez, R., Ruiz, P., & Rumbaut, R. (1985). Hispanic patients: A linguo-cultural minority. *Hispanic Journal of Behavioral Sciences, 7,* 177–186.

Gonzalez, J. R. (1978). Language factors affecting treatment of bilingual schizophrenics. *Psychiatric Annals, 8,* 68–70.

Grand, S., Marcos, L. R., Freedman, N., & Barroso, F. (1977). Relation of psychopathology and bilingualism to kinesic aspects of interview behavior in schizophrenia. *Journal of Abnormal Psychology, 86,* 492–500.

Guarnaccia, P. J. (1996). Cultural comments on multiaxial issues. In J. E. Mezzich, A. Kleinman, H. Fabrega, Jr., & D. L. Parron (Eds.), *Culture and psychiatric diagnosis: A DSM-IV perspective* (pp. 335–338). Washington, DC: American Psychiatric Press.

Guttfreund, D. G. (1990). Effects of language usage on the emotional experience of Spanish-English and English-Spanish bilinguals. *Journal of Consulting and Clinical Psychology, 58,* 604–607.

Javier, R. A., & Alpert, M. (1986). The effect of stress in the linguistic generalization of coordinate bilinguals. *Journal of Psycholinguistic Research, 15,* 419–435.

Javier, R. A., & Marcos, L. R. (1989). The role of stress on the language-independence and code-switching phenomenon. *Journal of Psycholinguistic Research, 18,* 449–472.

Kessler, R. C., McGonagle, K. A., Zhao, S., Nelson, C. G., Hughes, M., Eshleman, S., Wittchen, H. U., & Kendler, K. S. (1994). Lifetime and 12-month prevalence of DSM-III-R psychiatric disorders in the United States. *Archives of General Psychiatry, 51,* 8–19.

Kleinman, A. (1996). How is culture important for DSM-IV? In J. E. Mezzich, A. Kleinman, H. Fabrega, Jr., & D. L. Parron (Eds.), *Culture and psychiatric diagnosis: A DSM-IV perspective* (pp. 15–25). Washington, DC: American Psychiatric Press.

Lewis-Fernandez, R., & Kleinman, A. (1994). Culture, personality and psychopathology. *Journal of Abnormal Psychology, 103,* 67–71.

Lewis-Fernandez, R., & Kleinman, A. (1995). Cultural psychiatry: Theoretical, clinical and research issues. *Psychiatric Clinics of North America, 18,* 433–447.

Liebowitz, M. R. (1995). *Ethnically sensitive interventions in Hispanics with major depression disorder.* Research grant application submitted to the National Institute of Mental Health.

Lopez, S., & Hernandez, P. (1987). When culture is considered in the evaluation and treatment of Hispanic patients. *Psychotherapy, 24,* 120–126.

Lopez, S., & Nunez, J. A. (1987). Cultural factors considered in selected diagnostic criteria and interview schedules. *Journal of Abnormal Psychology, 96,* 270–272.

Malgady, R. G., Rogler, L. H., & Costantino, G. (1987). Ethnocultural and linguistic bias in mental health evaluation of Hispanics. *American Psychologist, 42,* 228–234.

Malgady, R. G., Rogler, L. H., & Marcos, L. R. (1997). *Culture and behavior in the psychodiagnosis of Puerto Ricans* (Report prepared under Grant No. R01MH45939). Rockville, MD: National Institute of Mental Health.

Manson, S. M. (1996). Culture and DSM-IV: Implications for diagnosis of mood and anxiety disorders. In J. E. Mezzich, A. Kleinman, H. Fabrega, Jr., & D. L. Parron (Eds.), *Culture and psychiatric diagnosis: A DSM-IV perspective* (pp. 99–113). Washington, DC: American Psychiatric Press.

Marcos, L. R. (1976). Bilinguals in psychotherapy: Language as an emotional barrier. *American Journal of Psychotherapy, 30,* 552–560.

Marcos, L. R. (1979). Effects of interpreters on the evaluation of psychopathology in non-English speaking patients. *Archives of General Psychiatry, 136,* 171–174.

Marcos, L. R. (1994). The psychiatric examination of Hispanics across the language barrier. In R. G. Malgady & O. Rodriguez (Eds.), *Theoretical and conceptual issues in Hispanic mental health* (pp. 143–154). Melbourne, FL: Krieger.

Marcos, L. R., Alpert, M., Urcuyo, L., & Kesselman, M. (1973). The effect of interview language on the evaluation of psychopathology in Spanish-American schizophrenic patients. *American Journal of Psychiatry, 130,* 549–553.

Matarazzo, J. D. (1978). The interview: Its reliability and validity in psychiatric diagnosis. In B. B. Wolman (Ed.), *Clinical diagnosis of mental disorders: A handbook* (pp. 899–932). New York: Plenum Press.

Mezzich, J. E. (1996). Culture and multiaxial diagnosis. In J. E. Mezzich, A. Kleinman, H. Fabrega, Jr., & D. L. Parron (Eds.), *Culture and psychiatric diagnosis: A DSM-IV perspective* (pp. 327–334). Washington, DC: American Psychiatric Press.

Mezzich, J. E., Kleinman, A., Fabrega, Jr., H., & Parron, D. L. (Eds.). (1996). *Culture and psychiatric diagnosis: A DSM-IV perspective.* Washington, DC: American Psychiatric Press.

Moscicki, E. K., Rae, D., Regier, D. A., & Locke, B. Z. (1987). The Hispanic health and nutrition examination survey: Depression among Mexican-Americans, Cuban Americans, Puerto Ricans. In M. Gaviria & J. D. Arana (Eds.), *Health behavior: Research agenda for Hispanics* (pp. 145–149). Chicago: University of Illinois at Chicago Circle.

Ortiz, V., & Arce, C. H. (1983). Language orientation and mental health status among persons of Mexican descent. *Hispanic Journal of Behavioral Sciences, 6,* 127–143.

Price, C. S., & Cuellar, I. (1981). Effects of language and related variables on the expression of psychopathology in Mexican-American psychiatric patients. *Hispanic Journal of Behavioral Sciences, 3,* 145–160.

Rodriguez, O. (1989). *Hispanics and human services: Help-seeking in the inner city* (Monograph No. 14). Bronx, NY: Fordham University, Hispanic Research Center.

Rogler, L. H. (1994). International migrations: A framework for directing research. *American Psychologist, 48,* 701–708.

Rogler, L. H., Malgady, R. G., & Rodriguez, O. (1989). *Hispanics and mental health: A framework for research.* Melbourne, FL: Krieger.

Roter, D. L. (1990). *The Roter Interactional Analysis System coding manual.* Baltimore, Johns Hopkins University Press.

Shrout, P., Canino, G., Bird, H., Rubio-Stipec, M., Bravo, M., & Burnam, M. (1992). Mental health status among Puerto Ricans, Mexican Americans, and non-Hispanic whites. *American Journal of Community Psychology, 20,* 729–752.

Sue, S., & Zane, N. (1987). The role of culture and cultural techniques in psychotherapy: A critique and reformulation. *American Psychologist, 42,* 37–45.

U.S. Bureau of the Census. (1991, September). *1990 census of population and housing* (Summary tape file 1A). Washington, DC: Data User Services Division.

Vasquez, C. (1982). Research on the psychiatric evaluation of the bilingual patient: A methodological critique. *Hispanic Journal of Behavioral Sciences, 4,* 75–80.

Wintrob, R. M. (1996). Cultural comments on culture-bound syndromes II. In J. E. Mezzich, A. Kleinman, H. Fabrega, Jr., & D. L. Parron (Eds.), *Culture and psychiatric diagnosis: A DMS-IV perspective* (pp. 313–320). Washington, DC: American Psychiatric Press.

51

Working with Victims of Persecution: Lessons from Holocaust Survivors

Fueled partly by geopolitical manipulation, the numbers of people experiencing severe political, religious, ethnic, and social persecution are rising. These displaced populations are created by civil wars, ethnic conflict, economic depressions, and wars between countries (Amnesty International, 1997; Drachman, 1995; U.S. Committee for Refugees, 1998).

Social workers have a long history of advocating for and promoting the psychosocial adjustment of displaced and traumatized populations, as was the case in the aftermath of the Holocaust. Similarities exist between problems observed in Holocaust survivors and those seen in current victims of persecution in regard to behaviors exhibited under extreme stress and transmission of the trauma to subsequent generations (Danieli, 1988, 1994; Rosenbloom, 1995; Solkoff, 1992). Other lessons that may be extrapolated from the Holocaust include the consequences of unquestioning conformity, abdication of individual responsibility, and the ruthless application of the prodigious creations of the 20th century: science and technology (Milchman & Rosenberg, 1996; Rosenbloom, 1995).

Scope and Importance of Immigration

Data Considerations: Practice Problems in Counting Refugees

Statistics on refugees and other displaced populations are often inexact and controversial because of the following. First, because definitions vary from country to country—one country's refugee is another country's illegal alien. Today's internally displaced person may be tomorrow's refugee. Therefore, government tallies cannot always be trusted to give full and unbiased accounts of refugee movements (U.S. Committee for Refugees, 1998). Second, in emergency situations it is not always possible to provide a reliable estimate because of the ongoing nature of the influx. Third, significant forced displacements may be over- or underreported. Fourth, in large-scale refugee situations, camp populations are often fluid, moving in and out often without notifying relevant organizations or authorities. Finally, statistics can become quickly outdated as a result of sudden new arrivals or departures (U.N. High Commissioner for Refugees, 1998).

Overview of Displaced People at the International Level

Currently available statistics underscore the overwhelming magnitude of these dislocations. It is estimated that 25 to 30 million people are forced to leave their homes because of human rights violations or threats to their lives. Many of these people are displaced within their own borders. It is estimated further than in their search for safety, an additional 13 million people have been displaced. Almost 90% of these people come from the poorest countries in the world, including Afghanistan, Azerbaijan, Bangladesh, Ethiopia, Liberia, and Somalia (Table 51.1). Such massive dislocations at the international level result in significant numbers of diverse, persecuted populations seeking asylum in the United States, including Cambodians, Caribbean Islanders, Central Americans, Eastern and Central Europeans, Iranians, sub-Saharan Africans, and Vietnamese (Amnesty International, 1997; Castex, 1994; Fong & Mokuau, 1994; Padilla, 1997; Partida, 1996; U.S. Committee for Refugees, 1998; U.S. Immigration and Naturalization Service, 1998).

It is critical to note that women and children constitute the fast majority of those who are displaced; women are particularly at risk before, during, and after they flee. Rape increasingly has been used to torture and terrorize women into flight, especially in Afghanistan, Rwanda, and the former Yugoslavia. Women also are forced to leave their homelands because of gender-related oppression in addition to reasons of war or civil strife. In some countries, women suffer severe persecution solely because of their gender and government authorities that tolerate or condone the local populations' harsh or inhuman treatment of women (Amnesty International, 1990, 1997; U.S. Committee for Refugees, 1998).

Traumas Suffered by Displaced Populations

Although the exact numbers of refugees and asylum seekers who have been exposed to situations producing massive psychic trauma are unknown, organizations such as Amnesty International, the U.N. High Commissioner for Refugees, and the

Table 51.1 Refugee and Asylum Seekers Worldwide, by Region, 1997

Region	Number
Middle East	5,708,000
Africa	2,944,000
Europe	2,020,000
South and Central Asia	1,743,000
Americas and the Caribbean	616,000
East Asia and the Pacific	535,000
World total	13,566,000

NOTE: This table includes statistics from the *World Refugee Survey* (U.S. Committee for Refugees, 1998) for two categories of uprooted people: (1) refugees who are unwilling or unable to return to their home countries because they fear persecution or armed conflict and lack a durable solution and (2) asylum seekers who are awaiting a refugee status determination.

U.S. Committee for Refugees have made great strides in obtaining international demographic data and information on the type and magnitude of human rights abuses.

Many current refugees and asylum seekers have endured the traumatic exposure to genocide. In the 1994 Rwandan genocide, up to a million people were murdered. In the period that immediately followed, 1994–96, the combination of genocide and civil war left more than 40% of the country's estimated 7 million people dead or uprooted.

In the Sudan, where there is a long-standing conflict between north and south Sudan because of racial, cultural, religious, and political differences, civilian populations have been targeted and exploited by all sides in the civil war. A study conducted by the U.S. Committee for Refugees concluded that since 1993, 1.3 million southern Sudanese had died otherwise avoidable deaths because of war, war-related famine, disease, and Sudanese government policies. Countless others survived these horrors, only to live with constant bombings of civilian targets by the Sudanese government, targets that include displaced-persons camps and hospitals (U.S. Committee for Refugees, 1998).

Torture—including beatings, psychological abuse, sexual abuse, witnessing the torture of loved ones, deprivation, and burns—is another traumatic experience endured by many of today's refugees and asylum seekers. It is estimated that as many as 400,000 victims of torture now reside in the United States, with many survivors suffering in silence. They endure the ongoing physical and emotional anguish that their torturers intended, ranging from chronic pain in muscles and joints to severe depression, constant anxiety, and frequent thoughts of suicide. Many are talented, educated, productive people—including doctors, business people, lawyers, and legislators—who were purposefully disabled by their governments (Center for Victims of Torture, 1998). Thus, the challenge for social workers is twofold: to discover this often hidden, vulnerable population and to serve them.

Patterns of Immigration

The number of immigrants continues to increase annually and consists of two parts: legal and illegal. In 1996 there were 915,000 legal immigrants admitted to the United States and an estimated 300,000 to 400,000 entering illegally (Federation for American Immigration Reform [FAIR], 1997; U.S. Immigration and Naturalization Service, 1998). This is four times the number of immigrants that the United States was receiving only 40 years ago. In the next 50 years, the U.S. population is projected to rise from 260 to 400 million people; 70% of that growth will result from post-1995 immigration (FAIR, 1997).

The overall view of immigration to the United States reflects many changes from the 1950s to the 1990s. Among the most notable has been the shift of immigration from Europe and Canada (almost 52% of all immigrants to the United States in 1964) to Asia (36.4% of all immigrants in 1994). By 1995 Asian immigration was at its highest (37%), followed by North American (32%) and European immigration (17.8%). This reversed a trend of nearly two centuries (U.S. Immigration and Naturalization Service, 1998).

Finally, in 1994 total immigration from Europe more than doubled, from 63,042 in 1985 to 160,916 in 1994. This change has been largely attributed to the effect of the Immigration Act of 1990 (P.L. 101-649) that revised the numerical limits and preferential categories used to regulate immigration. Specifically, the act increased the level of employment-based immigration and allotted a higher proportion of visas to highly skilled immigrants. This preference resulted in a rise in immigration from most European countries (Karger & Levine, 2000; U.S. Immigration and Naturalization Service, 1998).

Refugee and Asylum Seeker Resettlement

During 1997 the United States hosted about 451,000 refugees and asylum seekers in need of protection. This included nearly 398,000 pending asylum applications, about 22,300 people granted asylum during the year, and more than 70,000 newly settled refugees. The largest number of asylum seekers were from Mexico (18,684); however, they had among the lowest approval rating for asylum status (0.3%) of any nationality. The next largest nationality group applying for asylum was Guatemalans, with 9,886 applicants, and an approval rate of 6.9%. Salvadorans represented the third largest group, with 7,894 applying during the year, and an approval rate of 3.3%. The next largest groups were Chinese (5,771; approval rate of 5.5%), Haitians (5,230; approval rate of 15%), and Asian Indians (4,926; approval rate of 26%). Among the nationalities with the highest approval rates for asylum status were Iraqis (94.7%), Afghans (72.8%), and Burmese (61.2%) (U.S. Committee for Refugees, 1998).

Current political trends in the United States reveal ambivalence about accepting all categories of immigrant groups, even refugees and asylum seekers, because of concerns about the burdens they may place on health, education, and social welfare systems. Although an underlying xenophobia has been suggested to play a strong role in covertly driving recent immigration legislation, cost containment efforts are overtly presented as the driving force for limiting the number of immigrants this country can accept and limiting services available to them. Yet, when immigrants make a successful transition into the mainstream of U.S. society, research strongly suggests that everyone can benefit because the arrival of immigrants frequently increases economic activity and creates jobs for local residents (Taylor, 1997).

Clearly, world conditions and events continue to create large populations of displaced people. Consequently, the United States continues to receive significant numbers of refugees and asylum seekers. This influx clearly necessitates the attention of human services professionals to the complex systems of services needed to assist them all (FAIR, 1997; Karger & Levine, 2000; Le-Doux & Stephens, 1992; Padilla, 1997; Taylor, 1997).

Lessons from Holocaust Survivors

Among all the populations experiencing the trauma and stress associated with persecution, the most is known about Holocaust survivors. This is attributable to several factors. First, Holocaust survivors began immigrating to the United States in the middle 1940s. Therefore, social workers and other mental health providers have over 50 years of experience with survivors and their families. Second, survivors and their families have been willing to talk about their experiences and to participate in designated research to facilitate further understanding of the psychosocial effects of their traumas. Third, self-help groups of survivors' children have publicized the problems experienced by their parents and themselves. Fourth, a large number of research studies have shed light on the coping mechanisms used by survivors. Fifth, willingness of the media to publicize the Holocaust has encouraged survivors and their families to feel freer in speaking out. Finally, Jewish organizations have helped focus public attention on the Holocaust, thereby encouraging dialogue by survivors.

Methodological Concerns

Over the past 50 years, mental health professionals have conducted numerous studies on Holocaust survivors and their families. Generally these studies have attempted to understand the effects of massive psychic trauma on survivors and to examine the transmission of trauma from the survivors to their children. Whereas these studies have yielded much useful information, there also are criticisms about their methodologies. Such criticisms have acknowledged that studying Holocaust survivors and their families is difficult because of the number and complexity of variables involved.

Regarding studies that have focused on Holocaust survivors, questions have been raised about the usefulness of the concept of survivor guilt and the dearth of information about the pretrauma personalities of survivors; the loss of family members; their age at exposure to the trauma; their adaptive strategies; and the countries in which they grew up. Re garding studies that examine the intergenerational transmission of trauma, major concerns about methodology also have emerged and include absence of data about the personality of the parent who is not a Holocaust survivor; lack of information about competent parenting by Holocaust survivors; overgeneralizations from the sample to the entire second generation; absence of relevant and properly constituted control groups; and definitions of pathology applied to children of survivors (Rosenbloom, 1995; Solkoff, 1992; Zilberfein, 1996).

Recent research, which has tended to focus on the second generation, has become more methodologically sound. However, deficiencies still noted include failure to analyze potential gender differences in children's responses to parent's Holocaust experiences; problems with sampling procedures; and use of psychometric instruments specifically developed for studying this population that have not been demonstrated to be valid and reliable (Solkoff, 1992). Despite these methodological criticisms, there are several recurring themes that emerge in studies of Holocaust survivors and their children.

Major Effects of the Holocaust on Survivors

First, clusters of similar reactions to massive psychic trauma have been observed for Holocaust survivors regardless of other factors such as pretrauma ethnicity, socioeconomic status, or global level of functioning (Stenitz, 1983). These clusters were initially dubbed the "Survivor Syndrome" and were the forerunner to what became known as post-traumatic stress syndrome (PTSD). Major universal reactions to the long-term effects of massive psychic trauma observed in Holocaust survivors include chronic and severe depression; disturbances in memory and cognition; feelings of guilt (about their survival while others died) marked by anxiety, fear, hallucinations, and sleep disturbances; syndromes of pain, muscle tension, psychosomatic diseases, and occasional personality changes (Niederland, 1961).

Second, the life cycle of aging may be experienced as highly traumatic by survivors. Old age may elicit a recapitulation of Holocaust experiences, most prominently separation from children and the deaths of family and friends (Davidson, 1980). These recollections of loss may supersede any positive cultural or personal associations with old age, such as a time for sharing knowledge and wisdom or assuming the mantle of family matriarch or patriarch.

Third, normative events that typically occur during old age—such as illness and loss of functioning—may elicit exaggerated feelings of anxiety, panic, and depression. Memories of the Holocaust, a prior period of catastrophic loss, are once again triggered. Survivors remember that not being able-bodied in concentration camps signified certain death (Danieli, 1994). Should the survivor need hospitalization or institutional placement (for example, nursing home), extreme reactions may occur because these transitions are an admission of sickness and deterioration. The associated feelings of helplessness may cause psychotic-like delusions of being in a concentration camp. The caregiver's uniforms, overhead sound systems, and the background noise of ambulance sirens of life flight helicopters all serve to trigger further flashbacks of the concentration camp experiences. Invasive medical procedures can further invoke a loss of control and trigger feelings of revictimization (Danieli, 1994; Karger & Levine, 2000; Zilberfein & Eskin, 1992).

Fourth, the strength and vitality of Holocaust survivors emerges throughout the literature. There are many who went on to create successful careers, start families, and make contributions to society. Those survivors who coped most successfully appear to make conscious efforts to interpret their survival as a special obligation to give meaning to their lives—neither denying the trauma or their ordeal nor succumbing to it (Danieli, 1994; Davidson, 1980; Katz & Keleman, 1981; Rosenbloom, 1995; Solkoff, 1992).

Finally, research clearly underscores that survivors and their families are not a homogeneous group of vulnerable, dysfunctional individuals (Solkoff, 1992). Instead, they have displayed a wide range of adaptive coping strategies. In fact, there are many who exceed the level of functioning displayed by peers who have not endured exposure to such massive trauma.

Long-Term Effects of the Holocaust on the Second Generation

As a sequel to their massive personal losses, many Holocaust survivors started families, albeit often small. Adult children therefore are called on to enact multiple roles that would normally be assumed by extended family members. This may place additional burdens on adult children who also struggle to maintain their own families as well as careers. In addition, adult children may be unrealistic about or underestimate the care needs of elderly, medically ill Holocaust survivors. This may arise from beliefs about their parents as heroic, almost superhuman figures for having survived the vicissitudes of the Holocaust. Adult children of survivors also may perceive that having survived the Holocaust their parents can survive anything—especially without the help of formal or informal caregivers (Danieli, 1994; Karger & Levine, 2000).

Children of survivors also may feel a great burden to spare their parents any more pain and suffering. Their rationale is that survivors have already endured enough misfortune. Although a caring and noble sentiment that is highly understandable given the circumstances, this perspective may sometimes result in conflicts with formal caregivers. These caregivers may be misperceived as not attending to survivors' best interests or causing them needless pain. Because of a desire to protect the Holocaust survivor, children may not always be receptive to explanations about the current realities of limited institutional and community resources or the unavoidable discomfort caused by numerous medical procedures (Danieli, 1994; Davidson, 1980; Karger & Levine, 2000; Zilberfein & Eskin, 1992).

Finally, researchers consistently have reported a high degree of separation anxiety by both Holocaust survivors and their children. For some survivors, this may be manifested by discouraging their children's attempts to develop autonomous activities, peer friendships, or romantic relationships. Bereavement-related issues have been suggested to play a role, with some survivors not being able to fully grieve the loss of dead relatives. Many survivors may even have attempted to replace lost loved ones with their current offspring. As a result, even in their adult years, some children of Holocaust survivors may experience a significantly greater threat of separation from their parents than peers who are not children of survivors (Katz & Keleman, 1981; Stenitz, 1983; Yeheskel, 1995; Zilberfein, 1996).

Thus, difficulties in helping Holocaust survivors also may extent to their families. As discussed earlier, some children of Holocaust survivors may be overprotective of their parents, and both may feel revictimized when institutional needs supersede client needs. This is especially true in medical settings where hospitals stays are shortened and the need for strict compliance with health care providers' treatment plans and recommendations are required (Danieli, 1994; Zilberfein & Eskin, 1992). Taken together, these factors can result in exaggerated difficulties in developing a therapeutic alliance with survivors and their families.

Lack of Public Resources Allocated for Mental Health Services to Holocaust Survivors

The age-old use of torture has continued to be a part of modern life since World War II. The use of torture by the Gestapo was revealed to the world in the Nuremberg trials of war criminals and led to the clear statement in the Universal Declaration of Human Rights that no one shall be subjected to torture or to cruel, inhuman, or degrading treatment or punishment (International Rehabilitation Council for Victims of Torture, 1998).

Yet, even though Holocaust survivors have endured massive traumas, initial plans for their readjustment entirely overlooked their need for psychological assistance. Despite the cry from some mental health professionals (as early as 1948) and the vast literature documenting the destructive emotional effect of the Holocaust, there were never any government programs developed in the United States to address their psychological needs (Danieli, 1988). Mental health services were provided through the auspices of self-help groups, private religious organizations, or individual mental health providers (Danieli, 1988; Neipris, 1992).

Resulting from this lack of public attention to the psychological aftermath of the Holocaust was a conspiracy of silence, a glossing over or ignoring of the survivor's traumatic experiences. Denial of the Holocaust survivor's psychic pain occurred not just for society at large but also from many mental health providers. Consequently, many survivors were left alone to struggle with their profound sense of isolation, loneliness, and alienation (Danieli, 1988; Neipris, 1992).

Thus, another lesson emerges from the experience of Holocaust survivors: that silence about atrocities perpetuates victims' mistrust and alienation, thereby impeding their tasks of mourning, emotional healing, and social reintegration.

Implications for Social Work Practice: Framework for Assisting Current Victims of Persecution

As discussed earlier, of all the populations who have experienced the traumas associated with persecution, the most is known about Holocaust survivors. Therefore, examining the effects of trauma on survivors and their families has become a case study for other victims of persecution (Stenitz, 1983). Based on extrapolations from research on Holocaust survivors and their families, the following framework suggests guidelines for social work intervention with current victims of persecution.

Assess and Intervene from a Systems Perspective

Research on Holocaust survivors and their children has shown that the effects of massive traumas are systemic and multigenerational (Danieli, 1994; Davidson, 1980; Karger & Levine, 2000; Katz & Keleman, 1981; Rosenbloom, 1995; Solkoff, 1992; Stenitz, 1983; Yeheskel, 1995; Zilberfein, 1996; Zilberfein & Eskin, 1992). Therefore, it is imperative that social workers assess and intervene with current victims of persecution from a systems perspective. This framework is critical even when the refugee or asylum seeker needs assistance as an individual because family members are deceased, missing, in their country of origin, or in displaced persons camps. Although data obviously cannot always be obtained from other family members, a systems perspective is essential for developing a holistic understanding of individuals in their social, psychological, cultural, and economic contexts.

Because each family is unique, social workers must use a systems framework that enables them to analyze and understand the behavior of the individuals in relation to the ongoing operations of the family group. It is also critical when assisting this population to devote special attention to the family context component of the assessment. This includes the family's access to basic resources such as food, health care, housing, or job training. Clearly, providing assistance to meet basic survival needs must take precedence over interventions to change family dynamics (Hepworth, Rooney, & Larson, 1997).

Undertake Culturally Competent Assessments and Interventions

Despite universal responses to massive psychic trauma (for example, PTSD, Survivors Syndrome), it is crucial not to view current refugee and asylum groups as homogeneous. Holocaust survivors came from every continent, and their diverse cultural and ethnic perspectives influenced both their reactions and adaptations to extreme stress (Danieli, 1994; Davidson, 1980; Milchman & Rosenberg, 1996; Rosenbloom, 1995). The current populations of refugees are also highly diverse in both their demographic and socioeconomic profiles. Consider, for example, that Hispanic refugees come from 26 nations in North and Central America, the Caribbean, and South America. Asians and Pacific Islanders include Chinese, Filipinos, Koreans, Vietnamese, Laotians, Cambodians, and many others.

There are significant differences among these nationalities, including languages, customs, educational systems, and status structures. The historic experiences of each country with the United States also vary considerably. This too may affect refugee attitudes toward this country and receiving assistance through its auspices (Castex, 1994; Fong & Mokuau, 1994).

Assess and Intervene from a Strengths Perspective

Despite their traumatic experiences, the strength and vitality of Holocaust survivors and their families underscore the fact that assessment and intervention with current persecuted groups should emphasize strengths (Katz & Keleman, 1981; Rosenbloom, 1995). Strengths shown to sustain the viability of immigrant families include reliance on cultural attachments, values, and social support from family, kin, and community (Padilla, 1997).

Social workers are encouraged to facilitate partnerships with these clients through sharing power and de-emphasizing the stigmatizing diagnostic categories that often reinforce passivity. Working from a strengths perspective has been shown to diminish the feelings of victimization, low self-esteem, and loss of control that arise in those who strug-

gle to cope with the emotional sequelae of persecution, victimization, and catastrophic losses
(Hepworth et al., 1997). Finally, using a strengths
perspective with this population helps to ameliorate the effects of resettlement—a life crisis caused
by the loss of all that is familiar (Hulewat, 1996).

Use Empowerment and Political Advocacy Skills

Empowerment is defined as a process through
which people become strong enough to participate
in, share in control of, and influence events and institutions affecting their lives and those they care
about (Gutierrez, 1994; Parsons, 1991). Self-help
groups such as the American Jewish Joint Distribution Committee (JDC), a humanitarian organization represented and supported by the various
segments of the U.S. Jewish community, demonstrate how one persecuted group empowered itself
in the face of catastrophic losses. After World War
II, as the representative of organized U.S. Jewry,
the JDC carried responsibility for the Jewish residents of displaced persons camps, provided assistance for physical reconstruction of communal
buildings and synagogues, provided personal physical rehabilitation through medical and health
services, and provided economic rehabilitation of
communities and individuals. The latter was carried out through the support of educational and vocational programs and the development of indigenous services for aid to individuals in need of social
and psychological services (Neipris, 1992).

Current self-help efforts for Holocaust survivors
and their second generation include nonprofit Israeli organizations such as AMCHA. Named after
the code word (*amcha*) that helped identify fellow
Jews in war-ravaged Europe AMCHA provides a
range of psychosocial support services, including
psychotherapy, support groups, clubs for aging survivors, and volunteer services to homebound survivors. Their clientele includes the three population
groups most affected by the Holocaust: older survivors who experienced the Holocaust as adults,
"child survivors" who were in concentration camps
during their youth (often not remembering their
families or where they came from), and children of
survivors (AMCHA, 1998).

These examples of one persecuted group's self-
help efforts can be useful in developing empowerment-based interventions with current groups.
Plans for psychosocial intervention must include
access to mental health services to help traumatized
individuals cope with psychological sequelae such
as depression and anxiety (Center for Victims of

Torture, 1998). Microlevel interventions focus on
promoting participatory behavior, skill acquisition,
and differing forms of self-efficacy attributions (for
example, self-esteem), leading to an increased sense
of personal control. At the mezzo level, the use of
group modalities can result in the development of
collective problem-solving skills, affiliate behavior,
normalization of emotional responses, and joint
feelings of efficacy and control. At the macro level,
research should be conducted to document the adverse effects of unmet needs (for example, mental
health services) on the social, educational, and economic outcomes of refugees and asylum seekers,
the possible gender-related responses to massive
psychic trauma, and the identification of torture
survivors within the general clinical and social services populations (Center for Victims of Torture,
1998; Gutierrez, 1994; Padilla, 1997; Parsons,
1991). Finally, social workers also can facilitate
community organizing efforts so that victims and
potential victims of human rights abuses can empower themselves toward achieving the goals of social justice and participatory decision making.

Victims who become empowered may be able
to focus public attention on the crimes of their oppressors and accomplish remarkable acts of restitution. For example, Jewish groups, on behalf of
remaining Holocaust survivors and their heirs, are
currently engaged in efforts to expose past government collaborations with the Nazis—especially by
the Swiss. Through the World Jewish Restitution
Organization, a class action suit was filed against
Swiss banks that failed to return the claimants'
undisclosed assets. Brokered by the U.S. State Department, this has resulted in a $1.25 billion set-
tlement against the banks, which must now compensate Holocaust survivors and heirs of victims
who deposited money prior to or during World
War II. This agreement came as the U.S. Senate
Banking Commission on Switzerland prepared to
apply pressure against the Swiss banks if they did
not comply. This success empowered Holocaust
victims to seek further compensation. In another
class action suit, these victims are suing seven European insurance companies for a $1 billion settle-
ment. These companies convinced victims who
feared Nazi persecution to buy policies to protect
their families and then used some of the funds
to enrich Nazi leaders. Finally, another class action lawsuit brought by Holocaust survivors is
against German companies—including Volkswa-
gen, BMW, Audi, and Daimler-Benz—that forced
inmates in Nazi concentration camps to work as
slave laborers ("Holocaust survivors file suits,"
1998; Simon Wiesenthal Center, 1998).

These examples illustrate the power of using empowerment and political advocacy skills, thereby facilitating progress by persecuted groups toward achieving social and economic justice. Therefore, I encourage social workers not only to enact their historical role as advocates for vulnerable and oppressed groups but also to facilitate ownership of the skills needed to advocate by the persecuted themselves.

Advocate and Intervene to Prevent a Conspiracy of Silence

For refugees and asylum seekers who have in varying degrees experienced violence and deprivation, mental health problems are critical issues that often go unaddressed, despite extensive research that shows this group to have significantly higher rates of mental health problems than the general population (Danieli, 1988; Karger & Levine, 2000). This has been partially attributed to the crisis of resettlement and exposure to war, violence, and deprivation. If left unaddressed, torture and other war-related traumas can lead to depression and anxiety, inability to concentrate, memory problems, disruptive behavior, learning difficulties, and acts of fighting and other violence (Center for Victims of Torture, 1998).

Thus, a critical aspect of being able to successfully resettle and join the mainstream of society is the availability of mental health services (Danieli, 1988; Karger & Levine, 2000; Padilla, 1997). Yet, after the initial resettlement period when most emotional problems begin to manifest themselves, there are only limited public funds for mental health services. Even if mental health problems were to be present during the reception period, only 15% of funds for refugee and asylum services are available for nonemployment-related services, mental health counseling being only one of several funding categories (Le-Doux & Stephens, 1992; Padilla, 1997).

The lack of public resources designated to help people cope with the psychological aspects of forced immigration, especially crucial for victims of persecution, can contribute to a conspiracy of silence, as was the case for Holocaust survivors after World War II. Social workers must advocate for mental health services to meet the needs of this traumatized and underserved group. Refugees and asylum seekers also should be encouraged to talk openly about their traumatic experiences with the goal of becoming their own advocates. They can be the most persuasive voice for bringing attention to human rights abuses and for getting help in resettlement. They can also take the leadership role in helping to prevent a conspiracy of silence.

Develop Strategies to Cope with Effects of Vicarious Trauma

Vicarious trauma occurs when helping professionals cannot help but absorb some of the emotional pain from bearing witness to their clients' traumas and victimization (Nelson, 1998). Research on the emotional responses of mental health professionals who counseled Holocaust survivors supports this idea and reveals important themes, including bystander's guilt (for example, "I feel an immense sense of guilt because I led a happy and protected childhood while these people have suffered so much"); overwhelming feelings of rage; shame about the potential boundlessness of human evil; dread and horror; grief and mourning; and the tendency to dwell excessively on the Holocaust, thereby neglecting the survivor as a whole person (Danieli, 1988).

These themes are relevant to helping professionals who are exposed to disturbing content through listening to contemporary victims of persecution recount their experiences in civil wars, genocides, and "ethnic cleansings." Social workers must recognize their vulnerability and know the warning signs, such as when a specific case is consuming their thoughts and entering into their personal life. The symptoms of PTSD can affect the helpers as well as the primary victims of the trauma. Those who help victims of persecution are not immune to nightmares, hypervigilance, avoidance, or a preoccupation with the trauma (Nelson, 1998).

To hep stave off the deleterious effects of vicarious trauma, it is essential for helping professionals to develop anticipatory coping strategies. First, the helper should be made aware that having intensive emotional reactions to the disturbing material is normative. Second, effort should be placed on developing social supports to ameliorate the toll of these reactions. Earlier research on job stress and coping has examined factors in the work setting and in individuals' lives outside of work that may influence their reactions to work-related stress. Evidence about the relationships among work stressors, social support, and stress strongly support the buffering role of social support (Levine, 1997). Peer supervision, friends, and personal therapy all can be helpful toward increasing social supports for the helpers of those who have been traumatized.

Conclusion

The Holocaust serves as a reminder of how hate-based policies and political movements can affect the destiny of millions of people. In Nazi Germany respected judges participated in writing racial laws, physicians conducted gruesome medical experiments, and engineers built the chambers for extermination (Milchman & Rosenberg, 1996; Rosenbloom, 1995). Around the world there continue to be destructive policies and political movements resulting in human rights abuses and genocides. As was the case after the Holocaust, present-day consequences include vast numbers of traumatized, displaced people—including children—who desperately seek asylum (Amnesty International, 1997; U.S. Committee for Refugees, 1998). Given social work's historical tradition of advocating for social justice, it is essential for members of the profession to engage in international efforts toward changing these present-day human rights abuses.

Lessons from the Holocaust also serve to act as a catalyst for future research and reflection in this country about the history and continuing effects of genocide. Questions for exploration include: How can social workers deal with the experiences of people who have been tortured and oppressed by our own government through international military operations or by its support of unjust governments that commit genocide? How do social workers cope with assisting victims of persecution, genocide, and torture who have suffered at the hands of the same group to whom the social worker belongs?

Social workers can learn from and help Holocaust survivors and contemporary victims of persecution. Survivors can teach social workers how to rebuild a life torn by unimaginable horrors and how to adjust to a foreign society that has little understanding of genocide, torture, and disappearances. Although unique, many coping mechanisms used by Holocaust survivors translate into other vulnerable populations.

Human services professionals also need to take responsibility for obtaining the skills and knowledge that can best facilitate their efforts—on individual, group, organizational, and community levels—to best assist current victims of persecution. Human history is replete with many shameful chapters; however, these periods can provide useful information on how to best ameliorate the deleterious effects of such horrors. This article has reflected on some lessons from the Holocaust available for those who want to make a difference—for those who strive to fulfill their moral, ethical, and professional mandates to pursue social justice in a world that continues to undermine this pursuit.

References

AMCHA. (1998). *What is AMCHA?* [Online]. Available: www.virtual.co.il/orgs/orgs/amcha/whatsit.htm.

Amnesty International. (1990). *Reasonable fear: Human rights and United States refugee policy.* New York: Author.

Amnesty International. (1997). *Refugees: Human rights have no borders.* New York: Author.

Castex, G. (1994). Providing services to Hispanic/Latino populations: Profiles in diversity. *Social Work, 39,* 288–296.

Center for Victims of Torture. (1998). *Who we are* [Online]. Available: www.cvt.org.

Danieli, Y. (1988). Confronting the unimaginable. In J. Wilson, Z. Harel, & B. Kahana (Eds.), *From human adaptation to extreme stress* (pp. 219–238. New York: Plenum Press.

Danieli, Y. (1994). As survivors age: Part 1. The National Center for Post-Traumatic Stress Disorder. *Clinical Quarterly, 4,* 1–8.

Davidson, S. (1980). The clinical effects of massive psychic trauma in families of Holocaust survivors. *Journal of Marital and Family Therapy, 6,* 11–21.

Drachman, D. (1995). Immigration statuses and their influence on service provision, access and use. *Social Work, 40,* 188–197.

Federation for American Immigration Reform. (1997). *Immigrant related provisions of the Welfare Reform Bill* [Online]. Available: www.fairus.org/04124609.htm.

Fong, R., & Mokuau, N. (1994). Not simply Asian Americans: Periodical literature review on Asian and Pacific Islanders. *Social Work, 39,* 298–305.

Gutierrez, L. (1994). Beyond coping: An empowerment perspective on stressful life events. *Journal of Sociology and Social Welfare, 21,* 201–219.

Hepworth, D., Rooney, R., & Larsen, J. (1997). *Direct social work practice.* Pacific Grove, CA: Brooks/Cole.

Holocaust survivors file suits, having slaved for German companies. (1998). *Nando Times* [Online]. Available: www.nando.com.

Hulewat, P. (1996). Resettlement: A cultural and psychological crisis. *Social Work, 41,* 129–135.

Immigration Act of 1990, P.L. 101-649, 104 Stat. 214.

International Rehabilitation Council for Victims of Torture. (1998). *The history of the IRCT* [Online]. Available: www.irct.org/about irct.htm.

Karger, H., & Levine, J. (2000). Social work policy and practice with European immigrants. In P. Balgopal (Ed.), *Social work with immigrants and refugees* (pp. 167–197). New York: Columbia University Press.

Katz, C., & Keleman, F. (1981). The children of Holocaust survivors: Issues of separation. *Journal of Jewish Communal Service, 57,* 257–263.

Le-Doux, C., & Stephens, K. (1992). Refugee and immigrant social service delivery: Critical management issues. *Journal of Multicultural Social Work, 2,* 31–45.

Levine, J. (1997). *Conflicted helping: The mediator role of social work discharge planners in a rapidly changing health care environment.* Ann Arbor: University of Michigan Dissertation Services.

Milchman, A., & Rosenberg, A. (1996). Two kinds of uniqueness: The universal aspects of the Holocaust. In R. Millen (Ed.), *New perspectives on the Holocaust* (pp. 3–5). New York: New York University Press.

Neipris, J. (1992). *The American Jewish Joint Distribution Committee and its contribution to social work education.* Jerusalem: Jewish Joint Distribution Committee.

Nelson, T. S. (1998). *Vicarious trauma: Bearing witness to another's trauma* [Online]. Available: www.uic.eduorgsconvening/vicariou.htm.

Niederland, W. G. (1961). The problem of the survivor: Some remarks on the psychiatric evaluation of emotional disorders in survivors of Nazi persecution. *Journal of the Hillside Hospital, 10,* 233–247.

Padilla, Y. (1997). Immigrant policy: Issues for social work practice. *Social Work, 42,* 595–606.

Parsons, R. (1991). Empowerment: Purpose and practice principles in social work. *Social Work with Groups, 14,* 7–21.

Partida, J. (1996). The effects of immigration on children in the Mexican-American community. *Child and Adolescent Social Work Journal, 13,* 241–254.

Rosenbloom, M. (1995). Implications of the Holocaust for social work. *Families in Society, 76,* 567–576.

Simon Wiesenthal Center. (1998). *Lawsuit information and mandates* [Online]. Available: www.wisenthal.com.

Solkoff, N. (1992). Children of survivors of the Nazi Holocaust: A critical review of the literature. *American Journal of Orthopsychiatry, 62,* 342–358.

Stenitz, L. (1983). Psychosocial effects of the Holocaust on aging survivors and their families. *Journal of Jewish Communal Service, 60,* 331–336.

Taylor, J. (1997). *An interactive model of immigration, employment, poverty and welfare* [Online]. Available: www.migration.sucdavis.edu/mm21/Taylor10-6.htmil.

U.N. High Commissioner for Refugees. (1998). *REFWORLD* [Online]. Available: www.unhcr.ch/refworld/refbib/refstat/1998/98intro.htm.

U.S. Committee for Refugees. (1998). *World refugee survey.* Washington, DC: Immigration and Refugee Services of America.

U.S. Immigration and Naturalization Service. (1998). *INS statistics* [Online]. Available: www.ins.usdoj.gov/stats/200html.

Yeheskel, A. (1995). The intimate environment and the sense of coherence among Holocaust survivors. *Social Work in Health Care, 20,* 25–35.

Zilberfein, F. (1996). Children of Holocausts survivors: Separation obstacles, attachments, and anxiety. *Social Work in Health Care, 23,* 35–55.

Zilberfein, F., & Eskin, V. (1992). Helping Holocaust survivors with the impact of illness and hospitalization: Social work role. *Social Work in Health Care, 18,* 59–70.

52

Migrants and Their Parents: Caregiving from a Distance

My aim in this article is to report on a study of transnational migrants and their relationships with their elderly parents "back home." The article is based on the assumption that these migrants make a contribution to the caregiving of their parents through letters, telephone calls, and return visits, which has not been acknowledged in the literature on aged care. My definition of *caregiving* incorporates both the practices and emotions of caring about—illustrated by frequency of contact, the sense of loss when apart, and the importance of visits—and the practices and emotions of caring for—through participation in decision making about issues of health and well-being and the actual hands-on caregiving during return visits.

Theoretical Rationale

Studies of intergenerational family relationships have been an important component of family research for some time now. Some of the early research on the topic was inspired by attempts to extend and partially refute Parsonian theory regarding the so-called modern nuclear family. Concepts such as the "modified extended family" (Litwak, 1960) were used to disprove the notion of an isolated nuclear family; research focused on the emotional and financial support provided by parents to their adult children as they moved away from home and set up families of their own. The relevance of geographical proximity to the maintenance of such family support systems was one of the important is-

sues under consideration. Following Litwak, authors agreed that geographical proximity was not a prerequisite for maintaining close family bonds (Bengston, Rosenthal, & Burton, 1996; Cicirelli, 1995). In fact, modern means of communication and high technology were seen to enhance close contact between kin living at a distance from one another (De Vaus, 1994; Litwak & Kulis, 1987). At the same time, researchers argued that the quantity and quality of interactions may vary depending on distance: certain activities and support tasks were simply not feasible when family members lived far away (Silverstein & Litwak, 1993).

Possibly due to the intersection of family studies and gerontology, the focus of research has shifted in recent years, more attention now being given to support by adult children to their parents than by parents to their children. In fact, the question now asked repeatedly is how much caregiving adult children provide for their parents as they age. Research has shown that adult children are initially little prepared to take on a caregiving role, still assuming that parents are there to help them (Remnet, 1987, p. 342). However, with the development of "filial maturity" (Blenkner, 1965), closeness between adult children and parents grows, and children gain a sense of moral responsibility to give care to their parents as both children and parents age (Brubaker, 1985; Nydegger, 1991). Researchers have noted that adult children become particularly responsive to parental needs when parents become widowed (Remnet, 1987, p. 348). Daughters are generally expected to help our more than sons (Lin & Rogerson, 1995, p. 311).

Interestingly, most of the researchers who have considered caregiving practices by adult children for their parents have assumed a very close relationship between caregiving and geographical proximity. For example, it has been argued that geographic distance reduces not only frequency of visiting and telephone contact or help with chores, but it also limits the support that could be provided from a distance, such as giving advice or comfort (Rossi & Rossi, 1990, p. 455). When people are young, they tend to move away from their parental home to establish independent lives, but in later years children may move toward greater proximity, or parents will move to be near an adult child for support and social contact (Teaford, 1993). The adult child who is geographically closest then tends to take on the role of caregiver (Aldous & Klein, 1991). Lin and Rogerson (1995) concluded on the basis of such findings that "because caregiving often requires close proximity, it is important to understand the demographic and geographic availability of adult children" (p. 304).

There is then an interesting paradox in research on intergenerational family relationships. On the one hand, it is well established that geographic proximity is not necessary to the maintenance of close family bonds (and specifically to the provision of financial and emotional support by parents to their adult children). On the other hand, there is a persistent tendency to assume that caregiving is dependent on close proximity, with the implication that parents who do not have children living close by are bereft of their children's support. As noted by Climo (1992, p. 11), the preoccupation with geographic proximity in the caregiving literature means that very little research has been done on the relationships between aging parents and adult children who live at a distance; consequently, these relations remain invisible. The few researchers who have explored issues of distant care, in fact, have made observations that refute some of the well-established "truths" regarding caregiving and geographic proximity. Climo, for example, in a study of university professors and their distant parents, specifically refuted the notion that only adult children who live near their parents provide face-to-face services and health care. He found that although some services required proximity, distant children still gave a great deal of help and support. Cicirelli (1995), in another important study, showed that differences between siblings in caregiving of aging parents disappeared as geographic distance increased.

My personal experiences as a transnational migrant who moved from Europe to New Zealand and subsequently to Australia inspired my own research on this subject. I had maintained close family bonds and caregiving relationships with my parents back home over a very long distance for many years. These were relationships characterized by lengthy periods of absence followed by brief, intense reunions. I had not encountered any description of such experiences in the academic literature. This article is a preliminary attempt to provide such an account and to throw light on the caregiving practices and emotions of adult children in a situation in which, due to distance, maintaining family bonds would appear particularly difficult.

Methodology

I interviewed 12 people, seven women and five men, in a total of 11 interviews (one interview was with a couple). All but two of the people I interviewed came to Australia from an English-speaking country, mainly from the United Kingdom or North America. Four worked in university administration; the others were on the teaching staff of a university. Eight of them had both their parents at the time they left their home country; at the time of interview, this applied only to one person. In the seven instances in which only one parent was still alive, it was the mother. Four of the mothers were still very active and mobile; the others required various degrees of caregiving. Some of the parents had died in recent years; they had required caregiving before their death.

Interviews generally took between 45 minutes and one hour and they were recorded and subsequently transcribed. The questions I asked reflected the issues to which I sought answers for myself. I asked about frequency of contact (by phone, letter, or visits) and the actual hands-on caregiving from a distance or during return visits back home. I dealt also with questions of identity—the sense of Australianness and the notion of "home" as tied to family connections—and the likelihood that people would ever return to their country of birth to care or to be cared for. I was interviewed myself by one of my colleagues, and I include my own data as the backdrop against which my interviews took place. All interviews occurred in 1996.

Leaving Home

To place stories in context, I began each interview by asking when people had left their home country, the family networks they left behind, and the extent to which they saw themselves as migrants. I had departed more than 30 years ago, leaving my parents, my sister, aunts, uncles, and many friends behind, all healthy, active people busy with their own affairs. I did not see myself as a migrant and claimed I would stay away for, at most, three years. There was some sadness at my departure, one elderly aunt among the many who bade me farewell at the airport crying that she would never see me again. But generally people went on with their own lives, and although later my mother often said she had not believed I ever would return, no one expressed the feeling that I should not go. Indeed, I was given "license to leave."

What was the situation for those I interviewed? Eight of my interviewees came to Australia in the late 1960s or early 1970s and thus had lived abroad for 20 to 30 years. Even the four more recent arrivals, having departed their home country in the 1980s, had been in Australia from 10 to 15 years. Six of them (five women and one man) were single when they left their country of birth; all but one of these found a partner in Australia, and three of them became parents. Two of those who came to Australia with partners subsequently divorced and remarried Australians.

Like me, most of them did not seem themselves as migrants and did not consider their initial move away from their own country a permanent one. In several instances, this may have been due to the fact that they were single at the time they moved to Australia. Some already had lived away from home for many years and coming to Australia was, one interviewee said, "an adventure, it was something else, another country to come to." The geographic mobility often required of university lecturers also would have played a part: several had left home to study at university, and this had led to jobs; the move to Australia appeared little different from any other move. It is also relevant that most moved within the British Commonwealth. One interviewee remarked, "No, there was no intention to migrate permanently and in the early 1970s . . . you just walked into the country. So it did not require a deliberate desire and process to come and work in Australia in those days."

Not all of the people I interviewed were, like me, given license to leave. Five of them, all women—four of them single when they left—indicated that their parents had been upset about their decision to depart. When one of them told her parents that she was migrating to Australia, her father would not talk to her until she left (a period of about nine months), and her mother told everyone

that her daughter was going on a two-year working holiday. Another said that it took her mother 15 years before she finally could say that she was happy for her daughter to be in Australia. A third, who had been away from her country of birth for 25 years, spoke of her parents:

> They did not really want me to go. I think every time that I went back they always asked, well when are you coming back? So they never saw this as permanent, and probably even some of the other members of my family wouldn't still see it as permanent. . . . They still say, well are you ever going to move back?

On the other hand, none of the men I interviewed gave the impression that their parents resisted their departure. In fact, several suggested that they had been encouraged in their plans; they used statements such as "She was very encouraging of me traveling" and "They saw it as an exciting situation."

These differences in parental attitudes were not connected to the size of the family networks my interviewees left behind. Two of the men who were encouraged to migrate were only sons who left behind widowed mothers with limited family support networks, and four of the women who said that they had been put under pressure to remain came from large families. In listening to the respondents talk, it seemed to me that gender was the decisive factor: sons were allowed to venture out in the world, whereas daughters were expected to stay close to home. The women who migrated against their parents' wishes described themselves as "rebellious," often in "conflict" and with radically different political values.

Only one of my respondents appeared to have given conscious thought at the time of leaving to the possibility that parent or parents might one day require caregiving or die. Because his father died suddenly when he was only 19, this interviewee had been prepared for the possibility of the sudden death of his mother all his adult life:

> I can remember a stage, probably when we first came out here, where I used to be quite scared of the telephone—late night telephone. . . . I have always been apprehensive that somebody was going to be . . . I mean, that it's going to be too late.

The likelihood that parents would age and need care did not enter the other interviewees' thoughts.

In the words of one interviewee, "You don't think when you are 30 that your parents are going to [die]. . . . You just don't think about it."

Staying in Touch

It is one of the broad expectations of family relations that when children move away from home, parents and children must remain in contact with each other (Moss & Moss, 1988, p. 656). Indeed, having settled in the new environment, the people I interviewed all established regular patterns of staying in touch with their distant families. The patterns changed considerably over time, and the character of communication changed as parents aged, but what impressed was the regularity and frequency of contact over so many years.

When I moved to New Zealand in the 1960s, and when my interviewees came to Australia in the 1970s, the common mode of contact was by mail. Telephones were used sparingly in those days: connections were not always good, and it was the convention to reserve the phone for Christmas, New Year's, or birthdays, and, of course, emergencies. Every letter I wrote was immediately responded to by my mother, which meant we each received mail once a fortnight. Most of my interviewees developed similar regular patterns, some writing even more frequently. One said, "I used to write every week and the response would be weekly as well."

The telephone became gradually more important, and those of my interviewees who came to Australia in the 1980s started a pattern of letter writing combined with phone calls from the beginning. At the time of interview, for most, the contact was by phone. The overall frequency of telephone calls was high: several interviewees called their mother once a week or once a fortnight, and one respondent said he had an arrangement in which he phoned every Wednesday and his mother phoned every Sunday and "so we have big telephone bills." Another still wrote letters and estimated that "on average we speak to each other about a dozen times a year and write each other a dozen letters a year." Staying in touch was especially important on birthdays and at Christmas time and involved letters and sometimes presents also to other relatives. One interviewee said she "got into trouble one year" when she forgot a birthday.

The other major pattern of staying in touch involved visits by parents (and other relatives) and return visits back home. All but one of my interviewees had at least one visit from their parents, and some had as many as four or five. The return trip home, however, had been a much more frequent occurrence in most cases. Two of the interviewees waited quite a while before returning home, but all others had made the first return visit within three years of leaving their home country. Subsequent trips occurred at regular intervals, sometimes yearly, and only three interviewees had ever been away from their home country for longer than three years. One traveled back home three times one year when a parent was ill. At the time of this study, four interviewees (this included one couple) traveled back home every year. It is noteworthy that these frequent visits were undertaken by people who had lived in Australia for many years, some for half of their lifetime or more.

Frequent return visits to the home country are not unique to the people in this study. Baldassar (1997), for example, found in her research among Italian immigrants to Australia a high frequency of return visits. There, however, such visits were postponed until people were older and financially better off. That so many trips were possible for my interviewees was probably due to the fact that they all worked in a university context. The long Christmas university break in the southern hemisphere allowed return visits at that time, and sabbaticals, conference and research travel, as well as long-service leave offered opportunities for travel back home. These are times when other colleagues might take trips to more varied destinations.

The opportunity that teaching staff in my sample had for study leave and conference travel provided not only an opportunity to combine visits home with paid work but also to defray some of the costs, with the university granting the travel money. The fact that there was free accommodation at the other end also helped; it was apparent that interviewees usually stayed with their relatives when attending conferences or when on research leave. The interviewees who worked in administration used annual and long-service leave for trips home—notably without the defrayment of travel costs that lecturing positions provide.

Notwithstanding the benefits of university "subsidy" and free accommodation, the trips made to visit parents were very costly, and most of the people I interviewed also indicated they spent a great deal of time and energy on those return visits. Some were given financial assistance by their relatives to make the trip. Others who did not receive such assistance found it a considerable burden, especially because they could not afford a trip somewhere else. One commented, "The problem is a lot of your paid leave seems to go in these what are often obligatory visits. . . . I'd love to just go to a little holiday home or just something, you can't afford it, because it [the money] all goes over there." The extent to which sacrifices are made in this regard was clear from the comment of a university administrator who said, "It takes quite a bit of my income, but it is something we'll have to try and build in our budget because otherwise I know I will be feeling ever so guilty."

Distant Care, Practices, and Process

Death of a Parent from a Distance

The realization of the fragility of life and the probability that parents age and need caregiving came to most of my interviewees after they had left their home country when one of their parents died. In my own case, I had been aware of my parents' health problems for some years prior to my father's death in 1990. My mother had written to me about any personal health issues and deaths in the family in her regular letters, and my sister also kept me informed of illnesses and hospitalizations of my parents. In fact, the timing of my very first return trip in the late 1960s had been motivated by my mother's serious illness and subsequent surgery. During a visit in 1987 (combined with outside studies leave), I assisted my sister in her attempt to persuade my parents that they should move to a hostel. These were clearly instances of involvement in caregiving. However, I was not consciously aware of this and had no sense of a major responsibility. There was also a certain element of protectiveness toward the absent family member. Unexpected telephone calls to me were introduced with the words "Nothing serious. . . . " When there was a death in the family or some other crisis, I was not always told immediately; usually my mother would use her fortnightly letters for a carefully worded account of such events.

It was my father's death that brought a drastic change 25 years after I had left home. He died suddenly, but I was able to attend the funeral, help comfort my mother, and assist my sister with some of the financial and other arrangements. This close contact and involvement in family continued after my return to Australia. I began a pattern of weekly phone calls with my mother, and my sister began to provide me with detailed information about my mother's well-being, financial matters, and any other issues requiring action. In this, my advice was sought, and it appeared that my involvement was

appreciated. Return visits also began to accelerate, sometimes combined with conferences and research travel, but also specially arranged for family occasions. For example, although I had not attended my parents' fortieth and fiftieth wedding anniversaries, I now made a special effort in 1993 to attend my mother's ninetieth birthday. As my mother's physical and mental health deteriorated, contact with my sister became more intense, regular letters back and forth replacing the correspondence my mother was now no longer able to draft.

Caring from a distance, I became aware that my sister's caregiving as the only close relative was becoming stressful. Travel back home then became increasingly an effort to relieve the caregiver, to provide support to my sister and not just to my mother. Together, we visited nursing homes, sorted my mother's belongings, and created a "living memory" photo album in anticipation of our mother's move from hostel to nursing home. Again, the final visit to attend my mother's funeral was an occasion to assist with practical matters as well as for mutual support.

Notwithstanding my close involvement in the caregiving process, my role as a caregiver was at all times only partial. I did not have to deal with the day-to-day issues that my sister did. For example, my ability to provide assistance with personal hygiene when we visited mother was very limited; in any case, my mother—only confident with my sister's caregiving—would not accept much help from me. I participated primarily in decision making related to funeral arrangements, accommodation needs, and some purchases. My participation may have been of some comfort to my sister, but she also involved me in a deliberate effort to ensure I would not feel left out: major decisions sometimes already had been made, and my advice was sought for confirmation only.

How did my interviewees deal with such experiences? For seven interviewees, the first death of a parent became a reality fairly soon after they moved to Australia. In six instances, these were events in which they could not participate to any great extent. They were unable to visit their parent in his or her final illness or, if they did, they could not attend the funeral. Several respondents expressed considerable regret that they had not been able to do more for the parent who died and for their family. For example, one, who had briefly visited her mother before her death but missed her funeral, remarked, "I was feeling guilty, I guess, that my sisters were having to do this all the time . . . and also I guess afterwards that they had to take care of all the decisions of cleaning up, even clothes and all these sort of things." Another recalled being discouraged by his sister back home from visiting his dying mother and from attending the funerals of both his parents "because there was nothing gained from it." He was still very unhappy about this many years later, saying, "I cannot really even recall without much effort how long ago it was my parents died, but I can easily recall I don't feel good about [not attending the funerals]."

Only one interviewee had an opportunity to be closely involved in the caregiving of the first parent to die after she moved to Australia. When her father became terminally ill, she "put everything here on hold and went back home to be with him for the year of his illness." She had been in Australia about seven years by then. She said, "[The family] asked me. And it was clear to me and to them that it was part of my responsibility to go back." Her father was cared for at home, and during that period—six to seven months—she shared the caregiving with her grandmother "whilst [her] mother and brother went to work." This was an important experience to her, "too significant to miss."

Caring for the Surviving Parent

When there was only one surviving parent, the interviewees' preoccupation with caregiving appeared to gain a special intensity. For eight of the interviewees, this was no doubt due to the immediacy of the situation. Although some of the parents were in good health, they were getting older and attention needed to be given to their care. Because most of my interviewees were established in their careers and were no longer responsible for very young children, they had more opportunities for conference and research travel. This allowed them to visit home more frequently, enhancing their awareness of the caregiving their parents now needed. In three instances, no other relatives were available to care, and this intensified for these interviewees the importance of providing care and support.

The intensity of responses, however, indicated that there was more at play: greater awareness of one's own mortality, perhaps, and of the importance of contact between the generations, which does not occur until people get older. I had not developed a conscious awareness of what it may mean to parents that their children live at such a distance until my own children moved abroad. As my interviewees became older and had children of their own, they similarly appeared to develop a greater sense of their parents' needs. In this vein, one said of his mother, "I've felt a guilt mainly in terms of the fact of her not having extended family and not

having her grandchildren around and those sorts of things which are sources of satisfaction to elderly people." Another respondent said that if I had interviewed him 12 years ago (before the birth of his own child), he would have responded differently. As he became older, the connection with his family had become more important, and it had been particularly important to him that his daughter had the opportunity to know her grandmother. This, in turn, had made him more aware of his own need to be in close touch with his mother.

Caregiving Practices

What were the caregiving practices in which my interviewees were involved? All interviewees who were still caregiving for their elderly parents at the time of my research were in frequent touch with their parent or parents, mostly by phone. In addition, they all in recent years had established arrangements with neighbors or close relatives so that they could be warned if and when there were emergencies. One described this as something she had to do in a roundabout way because otherwise she would not find out what was going on: "You have to be a bit inventive at times."

While at a distance, they took a close interest in health-related matters. Their narratives imply that they made certain they were kept informed and that if there appeared to be a problem, they would travel back home to take stock. One interviewee, for example, after discovering that her father had serious health problems, "played detective" by phoning relatives and in that way discovered that his medicine might have been to blame. When she subsequently visited, she accompanied him to the doctor, with the result that the medication was discontinued and her father much improved. Other decision-making issues were also dealt with from a distance: one interviewee helped her mother over the phone with funeral arrangements for another relative, and another routinely attended to his mother's business concerns.

Return visits had in some instances become a lot more frequent. One interviewee said "and so little by little, I'd been going very three years, then every two years . . . every year for the last four years." When there, interviewees dealt with a range of caregiving issues. Several would hire a car and take their mother on holidays or to visit relatives; they would also organize birthday parties. The male interviewees returning home inevitably were drawn into financial matters and issues of house maintenance and repair. When I interviewed the couple, the husband commented, "I run a lot of business for the family; they really do rely on me." He also ensured during his regular visits that his mother's car was properly serviced. As his wife remarked jokingly, "It's good she does not drive it too often." Another interviewee had safety devices, double glazing, and better insulation installed in his mother's house when he visited last. On the other hand, female interviewees who had siblings back home said their brothers took care of all financial matters and repairs.

All of these interviewees had tried to persuade their mother (and, in one case, parents) to come to live with them in Australia or visit for extended periods. One interviewee had his mother live with his family for a while, but she subsequently decided to return home. All other parents had visited, but none had agreed to stay permanently. The dynamics that lead some parents of migrants to join their children in Australia while others do not would be an important subject for research. It is interesting that one issue always came up when I asked this question. Interviewees inevitably told me that the parent had close, well-established networks of friends and neighbors at home whom they would not want to leave.

In fact, most respondents assured me—and possibly themselves—that their parent or parents lived in a country town and close-knit community where people would look after them. One spoke with a sense of relief that when he went back to investigate his mother's housing and health care needs, "I began to realize there was much more of a network there than I'd ever had any idea of." Another found out "quite by accident," she said, that her parents' nice neighbors, who "have always been in touch with my parents and just generally helped them," were actually in touch with her brother back home, and "when they notice that something is wrong or needs to be checked out, they get in touch with my brother, who then works it out from there." Their narratives, then, emphasized the existence of a "strong, caring community" and "very good support networks."

I felt that it was important to my interviewees to have this assurance partly because of the fact that, notwithstanding the close contact and involvement they had with their parents, all felt they were not doing quite enough. They fretted about not going over frequently enough ("It is like a guilt thing, that if you don't go you'll be regretting it the next year," said one); they were worried because "anything can happen at any time"; and they expressed sadness and loss about "not being there." Several remarked that their parents did not make demands or make them feel guilty, but that it was

their own need to care and their own need to give that was responsible for their sense of guilt. As one said, "I owe a lot to her. . . . I think the need [to care] is more from my side than from her side."

All respondents wrestled during the interview with the vexed question of what would need to happen if and when their parents were no longer able to live alone or if their current caring arrangements became inadequate. Their comments on how to deal with this situation reflected, I think, both cultural differences and personal experiences. Some suggested that they could never put their mother in a nursing home and acknowledged the possible consequences of this for their lives. For example, one said he would not know what to do if the current arrangements for his mother would cease. She was 92 and lived with several siblings in one house, cared for by a younger sister. In case that would fall through, he thought "we'd have to bring her here. . . . If we put her in an old-age home, that would definitely kill her off." Others had not discarded the possibility that they might need to return home for long periods to care for their mother, although one expressed the concern that "if she got so used to me being there, I would not be able to leave." On the other hand, some, brought up in a different cultural tradition, expected that nursing home care would be found.

Identity and Distant Care

Becoming Australian

I now turn to the final issues I dwelled on with my interviewees, their sense of national identity and the extent to which this had any connection with their care for distant parents. As I mentioned earlier, most people I talked to saw their move away from their home country initially as temporary and were inclined to think that they would return home. However, all have lived in Australia for many years now and could be defined as permanent settlers. How did they account for this process?

My curiosity on this issue was aroused by the fact that I had undergone a sharp shift in my sense of identity at the time my father died. Having lived in many countries, I always had defined myself as a "citizen of the world" with limited allegiance to one country. I had given up my original nationality when I married and later became an Australian, partly for convenience. When I reaffirmed my connection with my mother and sister after the death of my father, I also rediscovered my home country, taking increased pleasure in "going home" and experiencing, as I wrote once in my diary, "a sense of well-being, of being in the right place." When my daughter later settled in my country of birth, this added to my pleasure in going back. Nonetheless, during a recent return visit, I wrote in my diary, "The more I am here, the more Australian I feel."

What was the process for my interviewees? Read (1996, p. 33) suggested that the two common turning points in the life of a migrant are the death of parents in the home country and the birth of one's own children; this seemed to have some application here. All 12 interviewees were adamant that they no longer saw themselves as temporary visitors to Australia. For six of them, the fact that they had married Australians, that their children were born in Australia and/or identified with this country had been the most important considerations. One considered Australia a good place for her children to grow up and said, "I really want my kids to feel Australian." In all six cases, the pull of their family bonds in Australia had increased their sense of belonging in the country and had made them embrace a sense of Australian identity.

In some instances, changes in family relations back home had an impact on their national identity. When I asked interviewees when they began to see themselves as permanent settlers, one woman, who had been under considerable pressure from her mother to return home, said, "My mother's dying was probably one thing that made a difference. . . . Somebody who's all the time telling you you have to come back home is no longer doing that." In another case, the interviewee's mother put less pressure on her to return home after her father's death, and this also consolidated her own sense of Australianness.

The strength of feeling expressed about Australia did not signify that these people had not retained strong bonds with their home country—even in those cases in which their parents were no longer alive. Several, in fact, had become closer to their siblings in recent years, and most had remained in touch with friends. For example, one of the male interviewees who had traveled back home every 18 months to visit his mother, spending all his time with her during the trips, thought this had led to an estrangement from his own country. After her death, now that his mother was no longer the focus of his travel, he had been able to rediscover his country and even revisit friends and relatives he had not seen for many years. Only one interviewee had given up traveling back home after his parents died, and the university lecturers whose parents were still alive did not expect that they would give up their research- and con-

ference-related visits to their home country after their parent's death. In some instances, as in mine, the next generation had settled in the home country, thereby reinforcing their parents' bonds with their country of birth.

Push-pull factors such as these contributed to a sense of ambiguity about their national identity among several interviewees. Only two had embraced their Australianness to such an extent that they felt no more allegiance to their home country. Three others accepted their dual nationality as a fact of life; they were American Australians or Canadian Australians, they said, and they saw no difficulty with this situation. But several voiced the kind of uncertainty so well expressed by Modjeska (1990) in *Poppy*, when she said, "I still don't understand what it means to consider myself Australian when I know I am not" (p. 261). One interviewee commented, I still feel I'm not totally an Australian. I don't belong anywhere or I belong in both places." Another said poignantly, "You don't really belong there, you don't really belong here. Or you belong in both. . . . On your good days you think you belong in both. But I certainly sometimes think that I won't grow old here."

Returning Home?

I asked all interviewees whether they would ever consider returning permanently to their country of birth. Interestingly, all the women I interviewed could contemplate this possibility, some after their retirement from paid work, notwithstanding the fact that they had lived in Australia for many years and considered themselves now to be permanent settlers. I appeared to me that, for them, this was associated with an awareness that they might end up alone in later life. They had seen parents die, and the surviving parent (usually the mother) lived alone; they knew this could happen to them. They made comments such as "If my children migrate there, and there is no one else here, then I'll probably end up going there myself" and "If my sister and I would end up being alone, we might live in the same community." It was clear, then, that where their children, other close relatives, and friends lived as they grew older—and possibly needed to be cared for themselves—was an important consideration, given the possibility that their partner might die before they did.

On the other hand, none of the male interviewees expressed such concerns. Those whose mother was still alive could contemplate returning home for extended periods to provide care and support, and 1 considered returning for employment reasons. However, the possibility that they would be on their own in old age was not raised by any of them.

Discussion and Conclusions

This project began out of an interest to share my own experiences with people who had faced the same concerns of distant care. I was richly rewarded in this respect. Interviewees were very generous in sharing their life stories with me, and I believe the interviews were mutually enriching experiences, illuminating to both respondents and researcher. Beyond this, however, the interviews unearthed a wealth of data highly relevant to the fields of family studies and gerontology.

The Care of the Aged and Geographic Proximity

As my study showed, these transnational migrants were all very much involved in the caregiving process. Their caregiving practices gained momentum over time and became especially intensive when their parent became widowed. I found it revealing to what extent the contributions to caregiving by these distant carers were part of a negotiated set of decisions between kin, the transnational migrant being incorporated in family help patterns—called on if and when other kin were unavailable or to provide support for other kin. While at a distance, the caregiving practices of these migrant children differed from those of siblings living in close proximity to their parents: clearly, emotional support was more in evidence than day-to-day hands-on caregiving. However, during return visits, the contribution made to caregiving by distant children was, on occasions, as important as or more than that of adult children living close by. In some instances, the distant child—as an only or favored child—was the only source of support for the aging parents at all times, whether the migrant was aboard or visiting back home.

It is recognized in the literature that people who are caregivers for elderly parents within their own residence or in close vicinity face extreme burdens on a day-to-day basis (e.g., Ungerson, 1990). Their caring responsibility may affect their ability to remain in paid work, but it also may be relieved (albeit only to a limited extent) by respite services. The responsibilities of distant carers such as the people I interviewed are compartmentalized. While they care from afar, in letters and telephone calls,

their stress and anguish remain invisible. At a practical level, it is not likely to affect their paid work. However, I found that such distant carers may use all their long-service and annual leave not to relax and restore their energies but to "go home" and become caregivers for their elderly parents. Other people may see this travel back to the home country as holiday, and the fact that the travel is actually an instance of compassionate leave is not acknowledged.

Literature on carers (e.g., Ungerson, 1983, 1990) tends to see caring as a gender-specific issue. I began this research with a similar assumption. However, on the basis of the data I have collected so far, a simple gendered construct of caring from a distance cannot be maintained. I found that male and female interviewees retained close communication and support networks with their parents; sons as well as daughters made the frequent trips home to care for and comfort these parents. Male as well as female migrants relied on (or could not rely on) siblings back home to provide care. This, then, supports Cicirelli's (1995) finding that sibling differences in caregiving disappear as geographic distance increases.

Inasmuch as gendered care did occur, it related to the type of tasks performed; it appeared that male migrants (as well as male siblings back home) were more involved in looking after business affairs, repairs, or maintenance issues, and women were especially (but by no means exclusively) concerned with health issues and with emotional support. A further gendered issue that arose related to the reluctance parents had shown to give their daughter license to leave. It may be this that led some of the women I interviewed to express a sense of guilt at not doing more and a sense of obligation to caregiving not expressed quite so strongly by male interviewees.

Overall, my research has provided important insights in the richness of extended family relations and obligations across space and time. In this respect, it adds to the spate of recent family studies (e.g., Blieszner & Bedford, 1995; Gubrium & Holstein, 1990; McDonald, 1995) that attempt to break away from conventional, narrow-based concepts of "the family." Blieszner and Bedford have drawn attention to the need for a more inclusive concept of the family through greater emphasis on family relations in later life. My study suggests that to focus on family relations in later life implies not only the study of connections and obligations between family members who live in close vicinity but also of the range of family interactions and caregiving that occurs across vast geographic distances.

There are two aspects to the caregiving practices and emotions of these transnational migrants that appear to differ from those of other distant children. First, due to the excessive costs and long complex journeys involved, travel back home tends to be planned a long time ahead and with great care. I found that university lecturers may sustain professional contacts over long periods of time with colleagues in their country of origin not only because this allows them to pursue academic interests, or not even primarily for that reason. They sustain these contacts because it gives them a chance to combine such research with return visits to their families. They schedule sabbaticals and conference travel to coincide with visits to their elderly parents and siblings. In other words, their private family needs determine to a considerable extent the public, international contacts they maintain and on which for some their professional standing is based. In this instance, it is not the private sphere of the family that is used to aid and assist the public sphere (the common understanding, especially in much feminist writing; e.g., Sassoon, 1987) but rather the public domain that is invoked to aid and support the private.

Second, continued close communication with family in the country of birth led some of these transnational migrants to a sense of ambiguity about national identity many years after their settlement in their new country. Their commitment to fulfilling their family obligations contributed to sometimes emotionally painful reflections about the question of who they were and where they belonged. In this sense, transnational migrants who seek to be involved in caregiving for their elderly parents face an extra burden, not carried by distant children who remain within their country of birth, even if far from home.

The Need for Further Research

This was an exploratory study, and much more extensive investigation is required. My decision to interview migrants working in the context of a university who care about and have cared for parents in their country of birth is a limited approach to the issue of distant care. A comparison between my kind of sample (professional people who are able to travel a great deal) and other migrant groups is in order. My findings, then, have opened up avenues for a range of further studies using transnational distant caregiving as their main theme, but taking into account the varying contexts in which distant care for elderly parents takes place.

In such studies, a number of important further questions need to be answered. For example, why in some instances do elderly parents follow their children to distant lands, whereas in other cases they cannot be persuaded to leave their home country? What are the processes of negotiation between siblings as to who plays the central role in caring for parents if one of the siblings lives at great distance? My research has suggested (see also, e.g., Bedford, 1995) that siblings who live far away from the primary caregiver experience considerable conflict. There was an example in one of my interviews that caregivers may prevent their distant sibling from participating in the caring process, whereas other interviews suggested that primary caregivers encouraged—or even demanded—assistance from distant siblings. My research also raised some interesting questions regarding migration, national identity, and caregiving that I believe warrant further study. Why, for example, did the death of a parent in some cases release migrants, whereas in other cases it reinforced their past national identity?

This is an extended version of a paper I gave at the annual conference of the Australian Sociological Association, Tasmania, December 1996. I thank Loretta Baldassar, Patricia Harris, Victoria Rogers, and three of my interviewees for helpful comments on this article. I am grateful to the 12 respondents for their participation in the project.

References

Aldous, J., & Klein, D. M. (1991). Sentiments and services: Models of intergenerational relationships in mid-life. *Journal of Marriage and the Family, 53,* 595–608.

Baldassar, L. (1997). Home and away: Migration, the return visit and "transnational" identity. *Communal/Plural: Journal of Transnational and Cross Cultural Studies, 5,* 69–94.

Bedford, V. H. (1995). Sibling relationships in middle and old age. In R. Blieszner & V. H. Bedford (Eds.), *Handbook of aging and the family* (pp. 201–222). Westport, CT: Greenwood.

Bengtson, V., Rosenthal, C., & Burton, L. (1996). Paradoxes of families and aging. In R. H. Binstock & L. K. George (Eds.), *Handbook of aging and the social sciences* (4th ed., pp. 253–282). San Diego, CA: Academic Press.

Blenkner, M. (1965). Social work and family relationships in later life with some thoughts on filial maturity. In E. Shanas & G. Streib (Eds.), *Social structure and the family: Generational relations* (pp. 46–59). Englewood Cliffs, NJ: Prentice Hall.

Blieszner, R., & Bedford, V. H. (Eds.). (1995). *Handbook of aging and the family.* Westport, CT: Greenwood.

Brubaker, T. H. (1985). *Later life families.* Beverly Hills, CA: Sage.

Cicirelli, V. G. (1995). *Sibling relationships across the life span.* New York: Plenum.

Climo, J. (1992). *Distant parents.* New Brunswick, NJ: Rutgers University Press.

De Vaus, D. (1994). *Letting go: Relationships between adults and their parents.* New York: Oxford University Press.

Gubrium, J. F., & Holstein, J. A. (1990). *What is family?* Mountain View, CA: Mayfield.

Lin, G., & Rogerson, P. A. (1995). Elderly parents and the geographic availability of their adult children. *Research on Aging, 17,* 303–331.

Litwak, E. (1960). Geographic mobility and extended family cohesion. *American Sociological Review, 25,* 385–394.

Litwak, E., & Kulis, S. (1987). Technology, proximity and measures of kin support. *Journal of Marriage and the Family, 49,* 649–661.

McDonald, P. (1995). *Families in Australia: A socio-demographic perspective.* Melbourne: Australian Institute of Family Studies.

Modjeska, D. (1990). *Poppy.* Ringwood, Australia: Penguin.

Moss, M. S., & Moss, S. Z. (1988). Reunion between elderly parents and their distant children. *American Behavioral Scientist, 31,* 654–668.

Nydegger, C. (1991). The development of paternal and filial maturity. In K. Pillemer & K. MacCarthney (Eds.), *Parent-child relations throughout life* (pp. 93–112). Hillsdale, NJ: Lawrence Erlbaum.

Read, P. (1996). *Returning to nothing: The meaning of lost places.* Cambridge, UK: Cambridge University Press.

Remnet, V. L. (1987). How adult children respond to role transitions in the lives of their aging parents. *Educational Gerontologist, 133,* 341–355.

Rossi, A. S., & Rossie, P. H. (1990). *Of human bonding: Parent-child relations across the life course.* New York: Aldine.

Sassoon, A. S. (Ed.). (1987). *Women and the state.* London: Hutchinson.

Silverstein, M., & Litwak, E. (1993). A task-specific typology of intergenerational family structure in later life. *The Gerontologist, 33,* 258–264.

Teaford, M. H. (1993, November). *Availability of adult children and residential mobility of older widows.* Paper presented at the annual meeting of the Gerontological Society of America, New Orleans, LA.

Ungerson, C. (1983). Women and caring: Skills, tasks and taboos. In E. Garmarinikov, D. Morgan, J. Purvis, & D. Taylorsson (Eds.), *The public and the private* (pp. 62–77). Portsmouth, NH: Heinemann.

Ungerson, C. (Ed.). (1990). *Gender and caring.* Hemel Hempstead, UK: Harvester Wheatsheaf.

B. Generic Diversity Factors

53

Biracial Sensitive Practice: Expanding Social Services to an Invisible Population

Introduction

Social work practitioners are faced with the task of providing services to clients characterized as biracial. Biracial clients comprise a group they may have had little or no practice experience with as a separate entity. Although the literature acknowledges the existence of a biracial population, there has been minimal discussion of the significant differences and similarities indicative of biracial clients and how these difference and similarities might impact the provision of services. Instead, discussions regarding services tend to incorporate biracial clients into groups on the basis of skin color and/or racial criteria rendering them invisible. In the aftermath, practitioners ask: What are the comprehensive criteria for service delivery to biracial clients? In what ways are biracial clients diverse, and in what ways are they similar? Finally, what are the implications for biracial clients perceived as members of something other than their native group based on racial attributes?

In the backdrop of these queries, biracial clients pose increasing challenges to social work practitioners. The size of this historically invisible group is increasing rapidly, and indicators such as dating and marital patterns suggest the need for more comprehensive delivery of services. In answer to the aforementioned queries, this article profiles the biracial population in the United States. It very briefly discusses the dynamics faced by said group in the context of race and identity theory. As an alternative to racial paradigms, identity across the life span is put forth as a more comprehensive model for biracial clients who must negotiate for social services with social work practitioners.

Biracial Census: A California Profile

The United States 2000 census has made available an identity category separate from traditional race to accommodate biracial Americans (Census, 2000). Hitherto, the federal Census Bureau **had not** collected data profiling the U.S. biracial clientele. Consequent to criticisms from an increasingly vocal and active biracial population, federal agencies have begun to modify standards for collecting race and ethnic data. However, such information remains unavailable for public consumption. Fortunately, states such as California have acted with deliberate speed to accommodate racial changes in the state population.

In California a biracial person is defined as one descended from more than one racial category (Tafoya, 2000, p. 4). Because maternal/paternal race data are organized by monoracial criteria, it is impossible to report the biracial status of parents. Thus, the number of biracial births reported in the same data may be biased downward. Conversely, since racial status of children in the California data are derived rather than self-identified, it may actually overestimate the number of biracial births.

California today has one of the nation's most diverse populations vis-à-vis immigration. While legal barriers to intermarriage were abandoned relatively early compared to other states, this has otherwise enabled little more than a moderate increase in biracial births within a 15-year period. However, taken as a percentage of state data in toto, biracial births rose from just under 12% in 1982 to just over 14% in 1997. In real numbers this increase accounts for about 50,000 births in 1982 and about 70,000 in 1997 (Tafoya, 2000, p. 4).

Despite modest rates of increase, the number of biracial births in California is significant and substantial. In fact, said births exceeded that of Asian and African Americans for the state of California in 1997 (Tafoya, 2000, p. 6). The increasing size of this biracial population provides a context for understanding the concerns raised by biracial Americans as pertain to identity. Furthermore, the task of accurately assessing this population complicates traditional tabulation procedures for monitoring civil rights. For example, it has yet been determined nationally how and if statistically smaller biracial populations will be aggregated into traditional race categories. Considering aggregate group data, it will then be incumbent upon census agencies to construct more comprehensive procedures for categorization.

Due to level of immigration California boasts the distinction of having one of the nation's most racially diverse populations. That diversity, however, has not necessarily accounted for its biracial birthrate. The California data compared the births of native-born citizens with that of immigrants. Biracial births to native-born Californians increased from 14% to 21% between 1982 and 1997. This increase represents a 50% population differential. In contrast, fewer than 8% of California's biracial births were attributed to immigrant mothers during the same time period (Tafoya, 2000, p. 5). Hence, the biracial birthrate is not necessarily attributable to immigration.

In 1997 births to couples in which one partner was white non-Hispanic and the other was Hispanic, Asian, or black accounted for an estimated 75% of all biracial births. The major portion of such births—53%—were to Hispanic/white couples. Births to Hispanic/black, Hispanic/Asian, and Asian/black couples accounted for 15% of biracial births. The remaining births were to couples composed of Native, Alaskan, Hawaiian, Pacific Islander Americans, etc. (Tafoya, 2000, pp. 6–7). As a bellwether state, it is plausible to suggest that what exists in California provides a glimpse of the biracial population that will eventually characterize the nation as a whole.

Racial Identity vis-à-vis Racism

Racism, according to Banton (cf Kitano, 1985), refers to the efforts of a dominant race group to exclude a dominated race group from sharing in the material and symbolic rewards of status and power. It differs from the various other forms of exclusion in that qualification is contingent on observable and assumed physiological traits (Wilson, 1992). Said traits imply the inherent superiority of dominant race groups that are then rationalized as a natural order of the biological universe (Minor & McGauley, 1988).

The most zealous proponents of racism proclaim their superiority on the basis of race as a matter of scientific fact (Welsing, 1970). They postulate that they alone have been endowed with capacities necessary to bring about civilization. So-called advancing civilization was a thinly veiled form of racism devoted to rationalizing the right of one race to embark on a worldwide mission aimed at conquering others (Pinderhughes, 1982; Daly, Jennings, Beckett & Leashore, 1995). By way of conquest and colonization, dominant race groups left no terrain of the world untouched by their professed superiority. After centuries of domination, the mission to "civilize" has necessitated a universal, almost mystic belief in the power of race to define identity (Hyde, 1995).

Consequent to identity vis-à-vis race, racism has prevailed as one of the most subtle, but no less devastating, and tenacious social problems in the modern era (Hernton, 1965; Kovel, 1984). Volumes of literature have contributed little to its demise. Germane to the American version is a biracial population rendered invisible by virtue of race categorization. The biracial identity by definition is predicated on the notion that there are no pure races and/or biologically sound racial concepts apart from racism (Stember, 1976). About the importance of this assumption there should be no doubt. Notwithstanding current levels of diversity, to characterize identity in a narrow racial context does disservice to the scientific method. It enables the absurd rhetoric of hierarchy within a single species and in fact provides a conduit for the continued social, economic, and political oppression of biracial persons nationwide.

Among biracial Americans manifestations of a racial identity are a direct result of domination.

Domination by racist concepts allowed for the exportation of racial values, which biracial Americans internalized. As pertains to skin color, the uppermost in status became those who most approximate dominant race groups and the darkest a lesser extreme. In an attempt to conform, biracial Americans adhered to the racial prescripts of identity. Their efforts facilitated a value system that is in many ways not only physiologically alien to them but psychologically brutal to same (Keefe, 1984; Soule, 1992). The result is a configuration of identity whereby cultural and familial experience are all but totally irrelevant to the assessment of biracial clients. That being so, it is imperative to acknowledge the intimate associations between identity and power.

In the absence of power, the perpetuation of self-definition becomes ineffectual. Associated with power, racism perpetuates the racial model of identity. As a logical consequence, dominant race groups maintain superior numbers, cohesion, and resources to sustain the current identity system (Schermerhorn, 1978). Biracial Americans are frequently their descendants, that is, mulatto, Eurasian, and so on (Russell, Wilson & Hall, 1992). They may lack numerical superiority but in fact are cohesive and share a common experience of identity ambiguity extended from the race paradigm—an ambiguity that has galvanized their numbers.

Subsequent to biracial ambiguity, identity vis-à-vis race in the United States is generally regarded as rooted in culture (Hall, 1997). By lack of any biologically significant criteria, social scientists have determined race to be a matter of subjective interpretation. Thus, any biological traits that extend from identity based on race may vary from one culture to another. Skin color, hair texture, and the like ultimately interact differentially to determine biracial identity; therefore, identity is in fact a pliable cultural phenomenon. A biracial Puerto Rican, for example, may be identified as moreno in Puerto Rico and African American on the U.S. mainland (*Felix v Marquez*, 1981). In the aftermath, biracial Americans are racially diverse by any given system of identity. Individuals may be simultaneously perceived in the United States as Euro-, Native, African, or Asian American dependent on circumstances. However, a biracial identity that suggests African descent may be the most socially damning of all statuses. But even then, to look white forces the biracial individual to identify as white to engage a better quality of life.

As pertains to biracial Americans, traces including African blood necessitates their status as "minorities" (Kitano, 1997). It is their most potent

and salient feature because an African phenotype contrasts with the dominant group ideal (Hall, 1990). African identity may have an effect on every phase of life, including self-concept (Owusu, 1994). It is a "master status" which differentiates the race category of biracial clients from the dominant group as an inferior element of society (Gacia & Swenson, 1992; Herrnstein & Murray, 1994). So potent is this "master status" that it has recently served as grounds for litigation between persons of light and dark skin color but belonging to the same African-descended race group (*Morrow v IRS*, 1990; Hiskey, 1990). A resort to legal tactics is an indication that for some, identity has been particularly painful given the psychologically conflicting implications of race. That is, biracial Americans have idealized much of the dominant culture but unlike members of the dominant race group are prohibited from structural assimilation into it (Kitano, 1997). Their willingness to assimilate regardless reflects a desire not to devalue themselves but to improve their quality of life and live the "American Dream." In so doing, they may develop a racist disdain for dark skin because the disdain is an aspect of Western culture (Anderson, 1991; Martinez, 1993). They are cognizant of the fact that African blood is regarded by various institutions as an obstacle that might otherwise afford them the opportunities necessary to succeed. For those who labor, unaware of the inherent limitations, failure is the end result. Furthermore, since quality of life closely correlates with having a color identification with the racial mainstream, light skin has emerged as critical to the biracial's ability to prosper (Hughes & Hertel, 1990).

Self/Other Identification

When asked to identify themselves by traditional race categories, biracial Americans are often resentful or confused. All too frequently the racial criterion has been used to categorize some as African American who may subsequently experience serious identity conflict (Tizard & Phoenix, 1995). As a result, it is incumbent upon the social work practitioner to consult with biracial clients regarding their identity. They must be sensitive to the possibility that biracial clients—upon reaching adolescence—may have experienced a dramatic change in social status attributable to the U.S. system of racial identification. Such a change can directly impact social and psychological well-being, self-esteem, and interactions with others.

When asked to describe their identity, most biracial child clients will first respond with a reference to their home and family life. If one were to ask them about any broader self-identification, the term biracial would until recently rarely be their response. The significance of these queries has implications for both identity and quality of life. Work is perhaps the most important decision confronting Americans regardless of race (Hall, 1990). It is in fact the major variable in determining quality of life. As practitioners assist biracial clients in their decisions, contradictions become even more apparent. Equality of opportunity for all Americans has only recently become a societal goal (Foster, 1993). Biracial clients in their youth observe prevailing racism in the high rates of unemployment and poverty in African American communities. They know that hard work for them may not result in the realization of career objectives. Aspiring youth must then decide whether or not they will invest their time and energies developing competencies around an identity, because of which, society may not allow them to fully evolve. The decision to pursue a particular line of work is thus contingent upon risk. For biracial youth the risk incurred by embracing a stigmatized identity involves their emotional well-being. If they invest themselves totally in the effort and the effort doesn't pay off, if they see that equality in the job market has eluded them in the process, they will face a profound devastation, and lose all respect for societal institutions (Shams & Jackson, 1994). American communities are rife with casualties of previous generations. They consist of talented folk like themselves who struggled only to become alcoholics, prostitutes, and other societal derelicts. The alternative to taking the risk, particularly if one is a light-skinned biracial, is to distance oneself from the stigmatized community. Embracing mainstream society via passing for 'white' or the creation of a new identity under the circumstances are seemingly viable alternatives.

Being biracial in America requires/enables living a life of multiple identities (Mills, Daly & Longmore, 1995). At the very least, biracial Americans are the result of a predominantly black/white society that demands adherence to certain race-based social norms (Phinney & Alipuria, 1996). Alternatively, today's less overt and more covert racism facilitates a separate biracial identity evolving its own set of applicable criteria. Being biracial then requires two processes. One the one hand, it may precipitate a conscious distancing from the stigmatized group—usually African-descended. On the other hand, it may involve the creation of a new identity based in part on an inability to be accepted without reservation by either composite race group.

Living as a biracial person in a racist society demands identity diffusion in the traditional Eriksonian (1968) sense; at the same time, a biracial life may exemplify the functional identity of a "black" or "white" citizen (Sowards, 1993). Given their experiences, by the time they become of age biracial Americans may be conflicted by identity (Tizard & Phoenix, 1995). As per the stigma associated with dark skin, the ambitious confront major decisions pertaining to where they are going and how to get there. In a racist milieu that affects them personally they must prioritize American values, standards, and ideals. The bright and talented cannot possibly ignore the inherent contradictions between those values, standards, and ideals and their personal lives. The middle class who may have been sheltered from such a reality encounter stinging consequences by the time they reach adolescence.

Identity across the Life Span

In contrast to the traditional race models is the idea that identity as a fluid social construction that extends across the life span of human development (Brown & Montague, 1992). In this view, identity is no more static than any other social entity (i.e., custom, class, or experience). Advocated as a model, the idea that identity is shaped by social circumstances is radical and politically charged. In fact, especially for the biracial, identity is multifaceted, subject to change, and a malleable component of the social universe. Such experience-based models expose the perception of race models as thinly veiled manifestations of racism. Furthermore, the self as multiple identities is well demonstrated in an analysis of biracial clients whose skin color is associated with more than one racial category (Brown & Montague, 1992). Enlightened conclusions offer skin color and the development of a biracial identity model to point out how racial models have become obsolete and/or function to reinforce various social and political objectives.

The need of biracial Americans for a separate identity contrasts with the degree to which race remains imperative (Hall, 1997). While numbers may be few, those who prefer to distance themselves from their African heritage must—for mental health reasons—have the option to do so. This contrast highlights the power of achieved identity as a cultural concept that is to be developed preceding adulthood. But for biracial Americans, racist imperatives are unyielding, rendering other than race-based identities questionable. The race dynamic is possible because the biracial identity is removed from its historical and political context. As a result, biracial lives are assumed unrelated and unresponsive to social circumstances, history, or culture. This allows for the idealization of race in mythic proportion conveyed by Western culture and its belief systems (Hall, 1993). The construction of an essentially racial identity then inhibits fluidity and models that incorporate development across the life span. Models of identity that emerge are inculcated by pseudo-scholars who perpetuate hegemony, resulting in the many layers of victimization that biracial Americans frequently endure.

The development of identity across the life span serves as a powerful alternative to the pathologizing influence of racial canons and to approaches emphasizing racial characteristics to the exclusion of others. It suggests a very different model from the traditional view. This set of concerns involves personal and social recognition that one's race/skin color is not wholly definitive. Generally, this includes understanding the nature of personal preferences and valuing them in spite of their existence within a stigmatizing social universe. Initially, the breadth of meaning for the new identity may be uncertain: it may also mean a new perception of the biracial self.

In the interest of mental and emotional health, Americans who perceive themselves as biracial must counterdefine the social and political universe. In the face of two powerful barriers—racism and culture—this characterizes the viability of their existence. Scholars of cultural diversity stress the process of self-acknowledgment and the proclamation of existence as the first critical step in personal and, later, social acceptance of what is different (Long, 1991). For biracial Americans, this simple proclamation is a revolutionary act in its repudiation of a culturally imposed stigma. They are unique in that their defining difference on the basis of skin color may be racially nondefinitive. Since they can literally choose their identity—via straddling racial categories—the affirmation of identity may be complicated for otherwise absurd racist reasons. Thus, to the degree that identity is actually a culturally constructed phenomenon, biracial Americans develop their identities under a unique set of circumstances (Biracial kids endure . . . , 1995). Consolidation of it is more impacted by ambiguity with few positive and many negative consequences. The characteristic ambiguity of "passing-for-white" is nearly always one of difficult consideration. But it is a necessity of slowly and painfully appreciating

an identity wholeness that cannot be understood via race canon ideology.

Antithetical to the racial traditions is coming to an appreciation of the cultural myths pertaining to race. Some of these myths are the obvious negative stereotypes about the associations of dark skin with inferiority and the superiority of European ancestry (Hall, 1992). Others are less well articulated, maintaining that some among biracial Americans, particularly the light-skinned, having European ancestry are arrogant and/or self-centered (Jones, 1994; Gatson, 1994). To the degree that these views have been consciously incorporated, they are easy to challenge, but they must be challenged by demythologizing personal contact. Such occurrences as recognizing other aspects of identity will slowly modify the more deeply entrenched assumptions.

The disadvantages of racial criteria as an identity paradigm in social work stem from a methodology rooted in cultural tradition—not science. Fortunately, such disadvantages have begun to manifest in the practitioner's push for a scientific explanation of social phenomena. Conversely, by adhering to cultural tradition, the practitioner is forced to view identity from a culturally constructed perspective. This necessitates identity by racial criteria rather than reflecting reality. Under such circumstances a traditional preexisting view of the identity universe is reinforced. The more scientific, logically constructed nature of identity across the life span is then overlooked accordingly. To reverse this trend and enable more biracial-sensitive practice, the social worker attempting to service biracial clients will find it helpful to:

- Determine what the class, social, and familial circumstances of the client are
- Be sensitive to the possibility that people who are in crisis or who are experiencing powerful emotions may resent erroneous assumptions about their identity
- Seek biracial support systems if such action seems appropriate
- Review the literature pertaining to biracial clients

Conclusion

When determining a biracial client's identity, it is imperative to consider the social context in which that identity evolved. A biracial individual may in fact assume a multiplicity of identities, including African, Asian, Latino, and Native American, when negotiating with macro institutions such as social services. Biracial clients comprise a composite group with enough feelings of solidarity to aid coalition forming when confronting institutional structures, which in turn may find it convenient to regard them by race—making them all but invisible. In other situations this sense of solidarity need not be called into play, as in a racially diverse neighborhood where class or ancestral heritage serve as the predominant identity criterion.

Macro institutions and the society at large have heretofore invalidated the biracial identity. In many respects, biracial clients being racially labeled is the result of and a response to oppression and exploitation: one might speak of the labels "half-caste" and "half-breed" as indicative of such oppression. By a purification of terms, such labels are assumed derogatory in designation. But life span experience may transcend terminology in the search for a comprehensive biracial identity. Pertinent to situations where racial identification may be important, the social worker will find it helpful to let clients identify themselves, to remember that interpretations of identity may vary by social context, and to remember that individuals may not see themselves as members of the group they have been institutionally identified with.

For the entirety of U.S. history, biracial Americans have been oppressed by virtue of their inability to be rendered visible (Kitano, 1997, p. 317). Particularly those perceived as black have suffered from discrimination, violence, and disrespect. The cultural suppression of their biracial heritage, sanctioned by the state at various institutional levels, led to the acknowledgment of the population now referred to as biracial. That biracial population began to form a separate identity, as part of a diversity cultural theme in the social services profession. This process has led to an increasing group consciousness among biracial populations both organizationally and symbolically, as indicated by the addition of identity categories to the 2000 census.

Whatever cohesion existent among biracial populations extended from racial criteria is the product of traditional racism. When confronted with the special needs and challenges of such a large and growing populace, U.S. institutions began labeling without meaningful input from affected groups. Individuals then tended to identify themselves as biracial or not depending on their level of interactions with other systems, facilitating conflict.

Evolution of a model of human development across the life span minimizes identity conflict and complies with the genesis of a new awareness in theory and practice. It is increasingly evidently pertinent to the study of identity, self-image, family dynamics, and so on. It is a necessity in a nation fast becoming not only racially but also ethnically and culturally diverse. The subsequent diversity in higher education has facilitated assertions on the part of "minorities" to define identity for themselves. Their findings have validated the importance of self-experience as having a direct correlation to psychological well-being. Furthermore, there are implications for the mental health of biracial clients in that they require the option, at least, to identify themselves rather than be identified by superficial racial characteristics. In the aftermath biracial clients will be rendered visible, resulting in validation of identity models that prevail less on the basis of what race they are, vis-à-vis skin color, and more on the basis of who they are, vis-à-vis experience, extended across the life span.

References

Anderson, L. (1991). Acculturative stress: A theory of relevance to Black Americans. *Clinical Psychology Review*, 11(6), 685–702.

Biracial kids endure society's obsession with appearance. *Los Angeles Sentinel* (1995), July, 13, Sec A, p. 14, col 1.

Brown, A. & Montague, A. (1992). Choosing sides (mixed race children). *New Stateman & Society*, 5, 14–15.

Census 2000. *Complete Count Committee Handbook for Local Governments*. (April, 1998). U.S. Bureau of the Census, Washington, D.C.

Daly, A., Jennings, J., Beckett, J., & Leashore, B. (1995). Effective coping strategies of African Americans. *Social Work*, 40(2), 40–48.

Erickson, E. (1968). *Identity, youth and crisis*. New York: Norton.

Felix v. Marquez, 78-2314, (U.S. Dist. Ct. Dist. Of Columbia, 1981).

Foster, P. (1993). Some problems in establishing equality of treatment in multi-ethnic schools. *British Journal of Sociology*, 44(3), 519–535.

Garcia, B., & Swenson, C. (1992). Writing the stories of white racism. *Journal of Teaching in Social Work*, 6(2), 3–17.

Gatson, S. (July, 1994). Aristocrats of color: The black elite, 1880–1920. *Contemporary Sociology*, 23(4), 524–525.

Hall, R. E. (1990). The projected manifestations of aspiration, personal values, and environmental assessment cognates of cutaneo-chroma (skin color) for a selected population of African Americans (Doctoral dissertation, Atlanta University, 1989). Dissertation Abstracts International, 50, 3363A.

Hall, R. E. (1992). Bias among African-Americans regarding skin color: Implications for social work practice. *Research on Social Work Practice*, 2(4), 479–486.

Hall, R. E. (1993). Clowns, buffoons, and gladiators: Media portrayals of African-American men. *Journal of Men's Studies*, 1, 239–251.

Hall, R. E. (1997). Human development across the lifespan as identity model for biracial males. *Journal of African American Men*, 3(2), 65–80.

Herrnstein, R. & Murray, C. (1994). *The bell curve*. New York: Free Press.

Hernton, C. (1965). *Sex and racism in America*. New York: Grove.

Hiskey, M. (1990, February 1). Boss: Skin hue, firing unrelated. *Atlanta Journal-Constitution*, pp. 1, 4.

Hughes, M. & Hertel, B. (1990). The significance of color remains: A study of life chances, mate selection and ethnic consciousness among Black Americans. *Social Forces*, 68 (4), 1105–1120.

Hyde, C. (1995). The meanings of whiteness. *Qualitative Sociology*, 18(1), 87–95.

Jones, R. (1994). The end of Africanity? The bi-racial assault on blackness. *Western Journal of Black Studies*, 18(4), 201–210.

Keefe, T. (1984). Alienation and social work practice. *Social Casework*, 65(3), 145–153.

Kitano, H. (1985). *Race relations*. Englewood Cliffs, NJ: Prentice-Hall.

Kitano, H. (1997). *Race relations*. Englewood Cliffs, NJ: Prentice-Hall.

Kovel, J. (1984). *White racism: A psychohistory*. New York: Columbia University Press.

Long, V. (1991). Masculinity, femininity and women scientists self-esteem and self acceptance. *Journal of Psychology*, 125(3), 263–270.

Martinez, E. (1993). Beyond black/white: The racisms of our time. *Social Justice*, 12(51-52), 22–34.

Mills, J., Daly, J. & Longmore, A. (1995). A note on family acceptance involving interracial friendships and romantic relationships. *Journal of Social Psychology*, 129, 349–351.

Minor, N. & McGauley, L. (1988). A different approach: Dialogue in education. *Journal of Teaching in Social Work*, 2(1), 127–140.

Morrow v the Internal Revenue Service, 742 F. Supp. 670 (N.D. Ga. 1990).

Owusu, B. (1994). Race, self-identity and social work. *British Journal of Social Work*, 24(2), 123–136.

Phinney, J. & Alipuria, L. (1996). At the interface of cultures: Multiethnic/multiracial high school and college students. *Journal of Social Psychology*, 136, 139–158.

Pinderhughes, E. (1982). Black geneology: Self liberator and therapeutic tool. *Smith College Studies in Social Work*, 52(2), 93–106.

Russell, K., Wilson, M., & Hall, R. E. (1992). *The color complex*. New York: Harcourt Brace Jovanovich.

Schermerhorn, R. (1978). *Comparative ethnic relations*. Chicago: University of Chicago Press.

Shams, M. & Jackson, P. (1994). The impact of unemployment on the psychological well-being of British Asians. *Psychological Medicine*, 24(2), 347–355.

Soule, S. (1992). Populism and black lynching in Georgia. *Social Forces*, 71(2), 431–449.

Sowards, K. (1993). Assigning racial labels to the children of interracial marriages in Brazil: Patterns in child mortality. *Social Science Quarterly*, 74, 631–644.

Stember, C. (1976). *Sexual racism*. New York: Elsevier Scientific.

Tafoya, S. (2000). Mixed race and ethnicity in California. *California Counts: Population Trends and Profiles*, 1(2) 1–12. Public Policy Institute of California.

Tizard, B. & Phoenix, A. (1995). The identity of mixed parentage adolescents. *Journal of Child Psychology and Psychiatry and Allied Disciplines*, 36, 1399–1410.

Welsing, F. (1970). *The Cress theory of color confrontation and racism*. Washington, D.C.: C-R Publishers.

Wilson, M. (1992). What difference could a revolution make? Group work in the new Nicaragua. *Social Work with Groups*, 15(2/3), 301–314.

54

Constructing Ethnicity: Culture and Ethnic Conflict in the New World Disorder

For scholars of the postmodernist persuasion, the great insight into ethnicity—ethnic identity, nationalism, culture, history, or most everything else that is social, for that matter—is that ethnicity is socially constructed: not a given but rather a made thing, and thus potentially unstable, inconstant, and negotiable. Taken to an epistemological extreme, most elegantly perhaps by Richard Rorty, this position exercises different sorts of foundationalists, truth-correspondence theorists, and conservatives, and has generated tremendous turmoil in the teapot of the academy. But what makes this insight worth pursuing (and it is, at least in the long run, essentially correct) is that it so sharply flies in the face of what most ethnic "actors," the players themselves, believe. For they are convinced beyond doubt that their group—its "culture" (more on this troublesome term later), its customs, traditions, language, religious beliefs, and practices—stretches back in an unbroken chain to some primordial antiquity.

Many have remarked on this tension between the observers of ethnicity and the players: "Traditions," wrote Hobsbawn (1983), "which appear or claim to be old are often quite recent in origin and sometime invented" (p. 1). Referring to nationalism (a special genre or manifestation of ethnicity broadly conceived), Anderson (1983) noted the "objective modernity of nations to the historian's eye versus their subjective antiquity in the eyes of the nationalists" (p. 5). But the notion of "invention" takes us only part way in understanding how ethnicity is constructed. Eller (1999) has pointed out that the prime

raw material for constructing ethnicity is usually the past—"history," as transparently conceived by the ethnics themselves (even if such "history" is legend, myth, or worse to outsiders, i.e., "objective" analysts or opposing ethnics). And consideration of collective construals of the past means that supplementing mechanical invention demands the many arts of memory: of remembering *and* forgetting; above all of interpretation.

Let me give an example close to home. Many Americans (and, perhaps especially, African Americans) even now view the December festival called Kwanza as an ancient (if generic) African celebration, as old as Christianity and Christmas. In a generation of two, after exposure to multicultural K–12 education, almost all Americans will believe this. In fact, Kwanza is quite new. It was invented (out of African cultural materials, certainly) in 1966 by Maulana Ron Karenga, an African American academic and black nationalist who was quite explicitly politically motivated to create in America an *African* cultural counterweight to Christian Christmas and Jewish Hanukkah. But Hanukkah in fact is an earlier variation on the same theme. It is a traditionally minor Jewish festival that over time was blown up in importance in the United States to serve American Jews as a cultural counterweight—to shield their culturally vulnerable children from an unstoppable combination of mythos, spirituality, and consumerism: from the powerful allure of Christmas.

Taking the long, or longitudinal, view to the insight of the constructed nature of ethnicity is properly the province of the historian. But the historical, or diachronic, view is not the only way to get a look at ethnicity's constructedness. My own insight came—appropriately for a cultural anthropologist—synchronically, in the course of ethnographic fieldwork, interacting with that epitome of postmodern encounters, The Other.

At the Hotel Splendid

I was 25 years old, sitting anxiously in a room at the Hotel Splendid in Rabat, waiting for permission to come through from the Ministry of Interior that allow me to reside for a year or so in a Moroccan village and "do" my doctoral fieldwork. It was a bad time to seek this permission, worse than usual, according to old Moroccanist hands. In Spain, Generalissimo Franco was sick and dying, and Moroccan newspapers were already reflecting the government's line that a new era was dawning in the struggle against colonialism, that the future of Spanish Sahara lay in its "reintegration" to Morocco. The noises from Spain were that, after Franco, this old remaining bit of the Empire would, indeed, be jettisoned. But the noises from the colony itself, from its indigenous *saharouis*, were quite different. Talk there was of independence from both Spain and Morocco. The *saharouis* claimed that they were never part of Morocco's Maghrebian empire.

This was the beginning of a movement, soon to be called the Polisario, which would engage Morocco in a draining insurgency war for decades. But in fact in those days—commencing in September of 1975—Morocco's main worry was not the Polisario guerrillas, but rather Algeria's (and to a lesser extent, Mauritania's) potential interest in the Spanish Sahara. It was war with Algeria that frightened Morocco the most, and put the country, its ministries and armed forces, in a state of high alert. In November, King Hassan II sent hundreds of thousands of Moroccans down south in what was called *la marche verte*, "a green march of peace," to claim the territory for the kingdom by virtue of their physical presence in it, well before Spanish troops even left. All transportation in the country was mobilized to move the marchers southward; all other work in the ministries stopped.

So I sat in Rabat, waiting out my three-month's tourist visa and hoping daily for word from the Ministry. From down the hall, every afternoon, came the pungent smell of a *tajine* being cooked (illicitly) in a room, and one day Mohammed, the cook, invited me in to share some.

Mohammed was, to my American eyes, a young black man about my age. He was excited to hear I was an American, and told me he was in Rabat trying to get a passport so that he could leave Morocco and go to France or, better yet, America. (Couldn't I help him? Didn't I have a job for him? Perhaps my father did?) Increasingly worried about my own prospects for job and career should doctoral fieldwork collapse completely, I reflected on this: he, a Moroccan national, in the capital trying to wring the bureaucracy in order to get out; me, a foreigner, trying to wring it in order to be allowed in.

One day I asked him why he wanted to leave. "Ah," he said, "I come from the south, and things there are bad and they are going to get worse. The worse thing is the Africans," he added. "The who?" I said, taken aback. "The Africans," he said, "*les noirs*. They are lazy and deceitful and not to be trusted. God help us if they ever get any power." I looked at him, confused. *Les noirs?* What did he think he was? I said: "I'm sorry, I'm confused, aren't you, too, African?" His eyes flashed angrily. "*Non! Je suis Arabe!* My father is a sheikh, I am a prince and a sherif, a descendant of the Prophet. I am no more African than you are."

At 25, this was my first direct contact with ethnicity's essentially postmodern sensibility. True, I had come from multiethnic and polyglot Brooklyn and bethought myself a big-city sophisticate in racial matters and what we today call "diversity." But despite this and my advanced training in the social sciences and all-but-doctoral status as an anthropologist, in fact I was culture-bound and cognitively trapped in my own ethnic and racial categories and calculus, and had never been confronted by another's. I was also a little angry, given something Mohammed had said with great self-righteousness the day before. So I said to him, not aiming to enhance the ethnographer's rapport, "But you know, Mohammed, in America, you would be thought of as a black man."

It was as if I slapped him. He reared and said: "No! You are lying. I am as white as you are." And then, forsaking the *tajine* and further contact (I knew), I rudely put my arm next to his and said with mock mildness: "We are the same color?" Mohammed looked down at our arms and spit: "Yes, we are. But do you know why mine looks darker?" And before I could way a word, he said: "Because unlike you, you rich and spoiled American bastard, I have had to work outdoors in the sun all of my life, and not in an office. If I had your life and your money in America, and you mine in the south, you would be black and I would be white."

"Well," I said as I gathered my wits, a thoroughly ungrateful guest as well as a hopeless fieldworker, "that may be. But if ever you make it to America, Mohammed, to Los Angeles or Chicago or Houston, and you are stopped by the police one night in your car, you would do best to remember, for your own safety that, like it or not, you are a black man." (Twenty years later, watching the awful video of Rodney King's beating for the *n*th time, Mohammed's face and that entire afternoon at the Hotel Splendid came back to me with a frightening clarify. Today, I realize also that I was then instinctively a good enough native informant of American culture to have recognized the mordant contingencies of what some call "driving while black.")

That day in Rabat, looking at me aghast, gathering his wits now, I thought, Mohammed repeated to me what he had said the day before, that which had gotten me angry in the first place. "Yes," he'd said, after denigrating once again the Africans who stole from his father, *les noirs* whose laziness was surpassed only by their deceitfulness, "Yes," he'd said, "America is a great country except for one great problem." "What is that?" I'd asked. "But of course," he said, "but of course you know, everybody does: it is *le racisme*."

Ethnicity and Culture

This encounter was revelatory for me in 1975 (which, indeed, is why one does fieldwork in foreign places—or teaches undergraduates about them); but by 2001, it must seem passé. Now there are many accounts that ring familiarly of this: of the chagrin—to reverse figure and ground—that some African Americans feel on being classified, by their African brothers and sisters, as "Europeans" in many parts of Mother Africa (Lee, 1984); or the unhappiness of American Jewish immigrants to Israel (who often traded an American materially good life for a less good one, but one that "maximized" their Jewishness) on being called "Anglo-Saxons" by other Israelis (Avruch, 1981); or how the "subjective" perception of skin color seems to vary by "objective" social class in parts of Brazil (the higher you go, the lighter you are) (Skidmore, 1974).

The next time I ran into the Moroccan paradigm was on the other side of the African/ Arab/Muslim world, in the Sudan. There "black" (to the eye of our paradigmatic Los Angeles patrolman—or university/corporate equity officer, for that matter) northern (Muslim, Arabophone) Sudanese know themselves to be Arabs, and thus utterly different from the African (i.e., "black") southern (Christian, non-Arabophone) Sudanese, with whom they have struggled in a bloody civil war for more than two decades now.

One of the effects of looking at ethnicity as socially constructed was to change our orientation from regarding it as a thing completed (Narroll, 1964)—a unit-vessel filled with cultural content (which is how the ethnic actors themselves continue to view it)—to regarding it as a work-in-progress. (The completist impulse never disappears completely; nevertheless, I give short shrift here to the position, expressed by Van den Berghe [1987], that roots ethnicity in ethology or evolutionary theory; here, ethnicity is a vessel stuffed with DNA.) We focus less on the assumed "primordiality" of the cultural content of ethnicity, and more on the processes of the production of this cultural content (Fox, 1990).

This revision has largely replaced an older concern in the ethnicity literature, a concern expressed by the Parsonian distinction between expressive and instrumental modalities. Both modalities sought after the uses of ethnicity, but use-values were differently construed. The expressivists saw the actors' concerns with ethnicity as self-evident ends in themselves or, if not quite self-evident, perhaps as means toward identity integration or "authenticity." This naturally led them to focus on the cultural content of ethnicity, especially as it dovetailed with religion. The instrumentalists, in contrast, saw actors' use of ethnicity as a strategy for the mobilization of resources and personnel. Like Barth (1969), these scholars were mostly not interested in ethnicity at all, but in ethnic groups. Ethnic groups organized actors to compete for scarce resources against other groups. What mattered most were the boundary-maintaining mechanisms that separated one group from another, not the rubbery cultural content—tradition, custom, cult, kinship: ethnicity—inside the boundaries.

In a consummate elucidation of this view, Cohen (1969) demonstrated how changeable this cultural content really was. He traced how, in postcolonial Nigeria, the Hausa of Sabo, in order to protect their monopoly of the north-south cattle and cola nut trade from other groups, transformed the basis of their group solidarity from "tribal" Hausa (the colonial locution) to "religious" Tijaniyya-Muslim (acceptable in a postcolonial political environment that proscribed open appeals to tribalism). Today, of course, in the midst of worsening Muslim-Christian violence exacerbating regional conflicts, many Nigerians rue this turn in the postindependence era to confessional identity.

Now, fast-forward to a modern classic of the constructivist view of ethnicity, Handler's (1988) treatise on nationalism and the politics of culture. Handler demonstrated how, over the course of several decades, Quebecois nationalists sought self-consciously to construct a satisfying version of Quebecois culture. Some of the cultural "raw material" available to them, that which "naturally" set them off from the Anglophone majority—the French language, the Roman Catholic Church, and indigenous rural village Quebec mores and folkways—were all, in one way or another, ultimately unsatisfactory to the intellectuals and elites who were the self-appointed culture producers.

As to language (with French language here standing metonymically for French culture as well), a perception of France as the "neglectful mother," combined with a sense of inferiority to metropolitan (i.e., Parisian) French—abetted by the typical ungraciousness of the metropolis's speech community to all other variants (Marseilles or Nancy, much less Montreal or Quebec City)—rendered this suboptimal. As for the Church, the bulwark of Francophone Canadian identity and solidarity through the 19th century, it struck many liberal or leftist intellectuals by the late-middle twentieth century as theocratic, rigid, and reactionary. As to authentic, indigenous village culture, demographically Quebec was an increasingly urban society by the 1970s; the village as prototypically Quebecois was already a thing of the past. And besides, rural Quebecois—the genuine Quebecois "folk"—romanticism aside, were in the end villagers with wooden shoes and fiddle dances—folkish—*rustre* after all.

So the intellectuals were caught in a bind: How to construct a satisfying culture when one rejects the "real" culture that is lying around? In the radical 1960s, one solution was to follow Fanon (1986) and declare Quebecois culture a "culture born of oppression," a culture thus shared with other victims of colonial oppression, like the Algerians. (The colonial oppressors were anglophone Canadians. However, comparing themselves to Algerians, just out of a very bloody war, had limited political appeal.) But if the intellectuals bickered and faltered, the politicians knew exactly what to do. First gaining provincial power under the Parti Quebecois in the 1976 elections, one of the things they did was to empower a Ministry of Culture, charged with bureaucratically *creating* a culture for the ministry's *fonctionnaires* to administer. Gaining further power, as the 1980s and 1990s went on, the party spearheaded a move to separate from Canada.

Ultimately, they (re)turned to the French language to make their points. Within Quebec, they and the revivified culture makers enacted a series of anti–English language and educational laws that have seemed unacceptably repressive to liberal champions of individual rights, as well as very frightening to the so-called *allophones*—the non-native French or English speakers: new immigrants in increasing numbers, and aboriginal, First Nation peoples. Separatists later charged that it was these people (especially new immigrants in Montreal) that provided the very thin margin of votes that defeated the last sovereignty referendum in 1995.

Works such as that of Handler (1988) show some of the complications in connecting "culture" to "ethnicity." These are not isomorphic concepts, either conceptually (deployed by the analyst) or practically, as used by ethnic actors, politicians, and entrepreneurs. Objectively speaking, it can take a very little bit of cultural content—cultural *difference*—to mark off one ethnic group from another; and, as Cohen's (1969) Nigerian work demonstrated decades ago, the "choice" of that content (from fictive kinship to religion; from language to dress) can be labile in the extreme. Ethnicity utilizes bits of culture that have been "objectified" by political actors, projected publicly, and then resourcefully deployed by actors for political purposes (Avruch, 1998). "People who live their culture unproblematically tend not to be ethnic in the proper sense of the word," Eller noted (1999, p. 11), and went on to argue that ethnic groups in conflict are not fighting *about* culture but *with* culture. Indeed, this is one reason (among several) why one must treat the "clash of civilizations" approach to New World Order ethnic or national conflict with some skepticism (Huntington, 1996).

Works such as Handler's can also be refracted through the lens that the older perspective for understanding ethnicity provides. One thing that comes into focus is power. Holding Barth and Cohen, on the one hand, and Handler, on the other, in the same frame, it would appear that the instrumentalists' view of ethnicity in effect presaged that of the postmodern constructivists, at least with respect to the transformable nature of ethnicity's cultural content. This is so because both regard ethnicity, whether viewed as resource or discourse, as a way that parties organize in order to contest with one another for power. Both see ethnicity as necessarily implying social conflict.

The Barthian instrumentalist is likely to see all this as groups occupying some socioecological "niche" and in conflict for the resources of the niche. The postmodernist is likely to see groups as social congeries in more or less frangible states, competing for the fruits of hegemony, control over the dominant discourse of the society. The constructivist dismisses Barth's instrumentality for its ethnocentric "market model" of ethnic conflict. Seeking rather to reintegrate expressivist concerns with identity with instrumentalist ones of profit, the constructivist argues for the "constituting effect on individuals" of ethnic conflict (Fox, 1990, p. 6). From the contest flows identity. But does not the concern with power remain central to both views? Does it matter if the vocabulary is hegemony or market share? Curriculum or cola nuts? Why fight to control the discourse if not to control the resources? (Gramsci *was* a Marxist.)

Looked at from the perspective of power, there is perhaps little, or less than one thought, to differentiate the postmodern from the instrumentalist view of ethnicity—or, indeed, the parameters of ethnic conflict in the "postindustrial" and "pre/postindustrial" (!) eras. Power seems to remain the obdurate social primitive in all manner of ethnic calculi. But there is another variable—hinted at in Handler's analysis—that perhaps serves better to distinguish ethnicity and ethnic conflict in the new world disorder, and that is the intervention of state (or, as we shall see, suprastate) bureaucracy in the matter of ethnic identity construction. There is, I shall argue in the last part of this paper, a new superethnic category in the making, one that transcends the traditional particularist confines of blood, cult, and shared history, but is yet crucial for their articulation. I refer to the category of international refugee, created, on the one hand, as a fall-out of the contests of states—this being an old process—and, on the other, and rather more recently, by the new world order of United Nations and nongovernmental organizations (NGOs), in developing concert with the militaries of yet other states, and all in the context of new, 21st-century political-cum-bureaucratic briefs like "conflict resolution," "peacekeeping," and "humanitarian assistance."

Ethnic Conflict after World War II

In his prescient analysis of ethnicity, first published in 1975—just about the time the term itself was making its way into the social scientist's lexicon—Harold Isaacs (who himself preferred the term "basic group identity," which never quite caught on) pointed to the forces that, since 1945, made ethnic conflict an inevitably increasing part of the world's political order. The main impetus came from the

collapse of power systems that had hitherto held together disparate clusters of people, the collapse acting as a sort of political centrifuge that broke the clusters apart and sent them flying off in different directions. One result is what is today called "transnational" or "globalized" institutions or personnel. Isaacs mentioned four sorts of power systems that seemed to be disintegrating in the post-1945 world: postcolonial, postimperial, postrevolutionary, and postillusionary.

Postcolonial

In Africa, for example, most of the national boundaries were drawn by Europeans in Berlin in 1882. The retreating Europeans—some of the final backwash was what I ran into in Morocco in 1975—left behind them African nationalist movements that cross-cut older tribal/ethnic identities, just as the boundaries of the new African states sundered some ethnic groups and bound together others. Biafra, the Ogaden War, the Polisario, and so on, all came out as unfinished business in the wake of European colonialism.

Postimperial

Some time after the last European troops left and the Colonial Office disbanded, the "periphery" returned the favor of colonialism, in some measure, and came as immigrants to he old colonial centers: North Africans in France, Moluccans in Holland, Indians and Pakistanis in the United Kingdom. This movement was connected to broader labor flows, for example the phenomenon of the guest-laborer that also brought Turks to Germany and Sicilians to Scandinavia, a not quite postimperial manifestation. As their numbers grew and certain of their institutions and practices, especially those connected to Islam, became more visible, these migrants engendered ethnic and racial conflict in Northern and Western European democratic states—the very sort of conflict that in the past, *pace* Myrdal, could be ascribed to the United States, alone.

Postrevolutionary

Here—in 1975—Isaacs seemed most dismissible, as he predicted the collapse of the Soviet Union and even China, the "revolutionary" states of modern times, the spinning off of their holdings (Eastern Europe and the Soviet republics) and conflict among their minority "nationalities." From our perspective in 2001 (post-Ukraine and post-

Chechnya, with Tiananman Square as unfinished business), Isaacs seems most prescient.

Postillusionary

Here, finally, Isaacs turned his eye on the United States—the "illusion" he referred to was that of white supremacy—and the progressive weakening of American apartheid since Truman integrated the Army, Eisenhower sent troops to Little Rock, and Johnson pushed forward the Civil Rights legislation of 1964. Following this came black power, black nationalism, and the ethnic revivals of the late 1960s and 1970s, which changed American society and would make of ethnicity and ethnic conflict, for the two decades since Isaacs wrote, the hottest areas of social scientific inquiry.

For all his prescience, however, Isaacs could not see a fifth post-1945 (and specifically, a post-1989, end-of-the-cold-war) dynamic: that ethnic conflict in the postcolonial world, especially, could never stay isolated in the periphery. Partly as a precipitate of postimperial forces, which physically brought the lately decolonized to the centers, ethnic clashes in the unstable periphery threatened increasingly to involve the old colonial/imperial centers in their violent conflict. For example: disturbances in Algeria send yet more Algerians fleeing to France, which exacerbates interethnic tensions there. Chechnya, once regarded as the "tombstone of Russian power" (Lieven, 1998) retains a destabilizing potential for subsequent governments. Indonesian repressions send Ambionese to Holland. The reabsorption of Hong Kong into the Peoples Republic of China precipitates a potential immigration crisis for the United Kingdom and reconfigures the true worth of a Commonwealth passport overnight.

Often enough the disturbances in the periphery are played out with acts of terrorism in the cities of the old center. Yet, even if they wanted to, the old imperial centers find it difficult to disengage entirely from their peripheries, for the formerly colonized now reappear not just as labor migrants but also as political refugees, as ethnic problems waiting to happen. One response to this has been to declare immigration crises and tighten increasingly restrictive immigration laws: keep the refugees out. Linked to this is the rising electoral success of ultranationalist (and, some argue, racist or protofascist) parties throughout western and central Europe.

When things get really bad—when the warlords and the civil war disrupt the harvest and famine comes; when the ethnic cleansing produces mass graves and the new world order of concentration camps—they also appear, thanks to CNN and satellite communications, on the television screens of citizens throughout Europe and North America. Especially the children appear. Now, the visibility of refugees presents a different sort of problem for the governments of the center. Keeping them out is only a partial solution. (And neither the Europeans nor the North Americans have been overly successful even in keeping them out.) For now, one's own citizens clamor that they be helped. And one's own security analysts argue that the best way to keep them out is to address the problems "out there," in the first place.

Thus is born, along with new bureaucracies, the new international organizations (IO and NGO) and large-scale humanitarian assistance, as well as a new role for the formerly disengaged center: "peacekeeping operations," under the UN or some regional (NATO, OAU, ECOWAS, etc.) consortium. Here, military operations get blended with an emerging rhetoric of conflict resolution (Charters, 1994; Durch, 1993). When that circle cannot be squared—and it is not easily squarable on the face of it, as Somalia demonstrated (Clarke & Herbst, 1997)—its critics call the reengagement neocolonialism. But that is hardly the whole story, if only because many of the so-called neocolonialists seem on the whole more Conrad than Kipling; they seem deeply conflicted and unenthusiastic about the task.

Refugees and the New Ethnicity

In some sense, of course, the refugee is as old as a neolithic clash between any two groups, in which one group vanquishes the other, destroys or occupies its habitation, and thus compels the other to flee to some new place. These refugees melded themselves into existing settlements, or started new ones, or perished somewhere between the two. This sort of refugee is as old as history. But the modern sense of refugee entails the state system, and refers to the human precipitate of the conflict dynamics of states: interstate warfare, intrastate terrorism and repression, state collapse. There are no longer any land bridges to cross over to empty continents. The territories to which these refugees flee are no longer the virgin forests of the neolithic; they are usually territories that are in the domain of some other state, and more often than not already occupied by citizens of that state.

Refugees may come as individuals or as family units to their place of refuge, and some are even admitted under special provisions of the refuge state's immigration law (the so-called political refugee). But the dynamics of state conflict or state collapse mean that refugees often flee en masse and must be dealt with en masse. The emergent socioecological setting—the niche, in Barthian terms—for this is the refugee camp, administered by a congeries of new bureaucracies—governmental and nongovernmental, public and private—but most often and paradigmatically by the United National High Commissioner for Refugees. Increasingly, too, the refugee camps are part of larger third-party operations organized under the rubrics of peacekeeping, humanitarian assistance, and conflict resolution.

What are some of the implications for ethnic conflict of these new sociopolitical forms?

First, these forms are the hitherto neglected manifestations of ethnic conflict in the postindustrial world, the newest, post–cold war extensions of what Isaacs (1975) called postcolonial and postimperial disturbances. Although played out most often in the former periphery, these forms represent ways in which the centers get—willy-nilly and not always with great enthusiasm—reengaged in their collapsing affairs. The newest form of engagement with ethnic conflicts outside the centers is in the form of "peacekeeping" operations, in which militaries are invited to reinvent themselves. The newest areas of the military crafts are denoted by the acronym OOTW: Operations Other Than War.

Second, the refugee camps themselves are veritable hothouses for the forced growth and nurturance of ethnic (or national) identifies. Probably the paradigmatic case is that of the Palestinians—also one of the first refugee groups to have been administered by the UN, under the United Nations Relief Works Agency for Palestinians Refugees, established in 1948 a part of the first Arab-Israeli armistice. Palestinian camps scattered in Gaza, the West Bank, and Lebanon provided the fighters for the most militant PLO factions such as Fatah, as well as its ideological elite. (Financial resources came from elsewhere.) Schools—crucial elements in ethnogenesis—turned out the fiercest anti-Zionists and the most committed Palestinian nationalists. Increasingly, schools are combining with other social service–providing institutions under Islamist influences, like Hamas, thus marrying Palestinian nationalism to Islamism. The Palestinian state may well be the first state in history whose underlying governance structures were partially built on the formative framework of the refugee camp.

Although paradigmatic, Palestinians are hardly the only example of this. Work by Malkki (1990,

1995) on Hutu refugees from Burundi in Tanzania in the 1980s contrasts those living in organized camps with those who chose to live among Tanzanians in the nearby city. She pointed out that the "camp Hutus," by creating and fostering a compelling "mythico-history" (as Malkki called it) of their relations with the Tutsi and their victimization, maintained a strong sense of "pure" Hutu identity, while the city-dwellers sought to assimilate, even to intermarry with Tanzanians. The camp Hutus strongly stressed their eventual return to Burundi (and, alas, their planned revenge on the Tutsis), while the city Hutus did not. Moreover, the camp Hutus directed some of their greatest hostility against their city-dwelling coethnics, whom they regarded as traitors and cowards.

If, as I said at the beginning of this essay, ethnicity is a constructed affair, then one of the prime sites of its construction is the refugee camp. Moreover, considering the range of political goals that ethnic groups can aspire to, the camp is especially important for constructing the sort of ethnicity that feeds overtly nationalistic movements, those claiming the existence of a unique *nation* entitled to sovereign control over a territory: a *state* (Connor, 1994; Smith, 1991).

But more than this—and third—"refugee" itself is a newly constructed category and, as my comparison of Palestinian and Hutu indicates, it can be construed as a sort of superethnicity. For it may be used to constitute a social group that is closely bounded, ecologically situated, with a shared history (oppression, persecution, ethnic/religious identity), a shared present (famine, isolation, uncertainty, the "wards" of UN and NGOs and reluctant host refuge states), and shared visions of the future (a state of their own, a return to a homeland, revenge taken on their oppressors). What is also shared, increasingly, is their formative exposure to the "culture" of the "international community"— the militaries, IOs, and NGOs— which certifies refugee status and creates, supports, and administers the camps.

Finally, to return at last to the issue of culture, one might ask what is the "cultural content" of the category *refugee*? Surely, the Palestinian and the Hutu and the Bosnian Muslim do not share the same "culture"? Well, of course not. Or at least not the way "culture" was traditionally bestowed. But they do. To a great extent, it is the culture shared by all those unfortunate enough to be the human precipitate of the struggle or collapse of states. And it is a cultural "content" shared by dint of the shared cultures of the postindustrial institutions and bureaucracies (UN, NGO, PVO, ICRC, USAID, OXFAM, etc., etc.)—as well as the various "aid industries" (Hancock, 1989; Maren, 1997)—that conjoin to create and sustain them, and each other.

References

Anderson, B. (1983). *Imagined communities.* London: Verso.

Avruch, K. (1981). *American immigrants in Israel: Social identities and change.* Chicago: University of Chicago Press.

Avruch, K. (1998). *Culture and conflict resolution.* Washington, DC: United States Institute of Peace Press.

Barth, F. (Ed.). (1969). *Ethnic groups and boundaries.* Boston: Little, Brown.

Charters, D. (Ed.). (1994). *Peacekeeping and the challenge of civil conflict resolution.* Halifax: Centre for Conflict Studies, University of New Brunswick.

Clarke, W., & Herbst, J. (1997). *Learning from Somalia: The lessons of armed humanitarian intervention.* Boulder, CO: Westview Press.

Cohen, A. (1969). *Custom and politics in urban Africa.* Berkeley: University of California Press.

Connor, W. (1994). *Ethnonationalism: The quest for understanding.* Princeton: Princeton University Press.

Durch, W. (Ed.). (1993). *The evolution of UN peacekeeping.* New York: St. Martin's.

Eller, J. D. (1999). *From culture to ethnicity to conflict.* Ann Arbor: University of Michigan Press.

Fanon, F. (1986). *The wretched of the earth.* New York: Grove Press.

Fox, R. (Ed.). (1990). *Nationalist ideologies and the production of national culture.* Washington, DC: American Anthropological Association.

Hancock, G. (1989). *Lords of poverty: The power, prestige and corruption of the international aid business.* New York: Atlantic Monthly Press.

Handler, R. (1988). *Nationalism and the politics of culture in Quebec.* Madison: University of Wisconsin Press.

Hobsbawm, E. (1983). Introduction: Inventing traditions. In E. Hobsbawm & T. Ranger (Eds.), *The invention of tradition* (pp. 1–14). New York: Cambridge University Press.

Huntington, S. (1996). *The clash of civilizations and the remaking of world order.* New York: Simon & Schuster.

Isaacs, H. (1975). *Idols of the tribe: Group identity and political change.* Cambridge, MA: Harvard University Press.

Lee, R. B. (1984). *The Dobe! !Kung.* New York: Holt, Rinehart & Winston.

Lieven, A. (1988). *Chechnya tombstone of Russian power.* New Haven, CT: Yale University Press.

Malkki, L. (1990). Context and consciousness: Local conditions for the production of historical and national thought among Hutu refugees in Tanzania. In R. Fox (Ed.), *Nationalist ideologies and the production of national culture* (pp. 32–62). Washington, DC: American Anthropological Association.

Malkki, L. (1995). *Purity and exile: Violence, memory, and national cosmology among Hutu refugees in Tanzania.* Chicago: University of Chicago Press.

Maren, M. (1997). *The road to hell: The ravaging effects of foreign aid and international charity.* New York: Free Press.

Narroll, R. (1964). Ethnic unit classification. *Current Anthropology, 5,* 283–312.

Skidmore, T. E. (1974). *Black into white: Race and nationality in Brazilian thought.* New York: Oxford University Press.

Smith, A. (1991). *National identity.* Reno: University of Nevada Press.

Van den Berghe, P. (1987). *The ethnic phenomenon.* New York: Praeger.

S. Sudha
Elizabeth J. Mutran

55

Race and Ethnicity, Nativity, and Issues of Healthcare

"Age and Health in a Multiethnic Society: Health Care Issues," the special issue of *Research on Aging* (January 2001), highlights two very important social facts of the early 21st century. U.S. immigration is at new highs, paralleling the influx of persons at the beginning of the century and contributing to greater heterogeneity. The second social fact is the ever-increasing emphasis on health, health care, and health policy as expressed in political campaigns and in President Bill Clinton's call for Healthy People 2010.

While it is well-known that America's elderly population is growing ethnically diverse, in-migration as an appreciable contribution to growing ethnic diversity is less often pointed out. The end of the 20th century saw the numbers migrating to this country approximate the level of the first decade of the century: 7,338,000 in the 1980s compared with 8,795,000 in 1900–10 (Table 55.1). However, the larger population base at the end of the century makes the proportion of immigrants smaller now than at the beginning of the century. After the changes in the immigration laws of the 1960s, much in-migration to the United States has been from non-European countries composed of both work and family reunification streams. Thirty years later, the impact of this increasingly diverse in-migration can be seen in the changing composition of American elders, especially in terms of both ethnicity and nativity (Table 55.2). The proportion of White non-Hispanic persons among those age 65 and older declined between 1990 and 1999, while that of every other ethnic group increased (column 3 vs. column

6). Strikingly, we see that the proportion of foreign-born among elderly persons has increased for every ethnic group except non-Hispanic Whites (percentages shown in columns 1 and 2 vs. 4 and 5). For Asian and Pacific Islanders, the foreign-born substantially outnumber the native-born increasingly over the decade. For those of Hispanic ethnicity too, the proportion of foreign-born almost equals that of those who were born in the United States. Although these Census figures do not tell us the ages at which the foreign-born immigrated and thus the length of time they participated in the U.S. work and benefits system, it appears increasingly evident that issues of ethnicity and nativity will be relevant for researchers and planners concerned with reducing health disparities among elderly persons in the United States.

At the same time, President Clinton in his radio address of February 21, 1998, committed the nation to two ambitious goals: to increase the quality and years of healthy life, and to eliminate health disparities among different segments of the population. The evidence that links race and ethnicity to health disparities is very compelling and emphasizes the burden of illness and death experienced by African Americans, Hispanics, American Indians and Alaska Natives, and Pacific Islanders compared with the U.S. population as a whole. The American Medical Association (AMA) (1999) calls attention to these disparities in access to and satisfaction with health care. The AMA reports that 29% of minorities in comparison to 16% of Whites say they have little or no choice

Table 55.1 Immigration and Emigration by Decade: 1901–90 (numbers in thousands)

Period	Immigrants to the United States	Emigrants from the United States	Net Immigration	Ratio: Emigration/ Immigration
Total, 1901–90	37,869	11,882	25,987	0.31
1981–90	7,338	1,600	5,738	0.22
1971–80	4,493	1,176	3,317	0.26
1961–70	3,322	900	2,422	0.27
1951–60	2,515	425	2,090	0.17
1941–50	1,035	281	754	0.27
1931–40	528	649	−121	1.23
1921–30	4,107	1,685	2,422	0.41
1911–20	5,736	2,157	3,579	0.38
1901–10	8,795	3,008	5,787	0.34

SOURCE: U.S. Department of Justice, Immigration and Naturalization Service (1999).

about where to get health care; 21% of minority adults have problems with language differences in receiving care, with about one-fourth of those who do not speak English as a first language needing an interpreter when seeking health care services; 60% of Whites in contrast to 46% for minorities say they are satisfied with their health care; and 15% of adults in all minority groups believe their medical care would be better if they were a different race.

At the same time, the AMA reports from the Physician Payment Review Commission (PPRC) on Monitoring Access of Medicare Beneficiaries that African American beneficiaries continue to have access problems, which is reflected in their use of emergency rooms more than other beneficiaries, further suggesting the lack of a customary physician. The PPRC analysis was especially concerned about the older population, as Medicare reduces the primary barrier of financial limitations. On the more positive side, however, the AMA sees encouragement in studies that report (1) neighborhood clinics and hospital outpatient departments are offering care to minority groups "comparable"

Table 55.2 Population Age 65+ by Ethnicity and Nativity, 1990–99 (numbers in thousands, percentage of total in parentheses)

	1990			1999		
	Foreign-Born	Native-Born	Total	Foreign-Born	Native-Born	Total
Total	2,733.00 (8.79)	28,351.00 (91.21)	31,084.00	3,206.00 (9.28)	31,334.00 (90.72)	34,540.00
White non-Hispanic	1,784.40 (6.60)	25,259.90 (93.40)	27,044.95 (87.01)	1,575.60 (5.45)	27,349.50 (94.55)	28,925.59 (83.75)
African American non-Hispanic	73.70 (3.01)	2,376.30 (96.99)	2,450.03 (7.88)	123.30 (4.47)	2,635.40 (95.53)	2,758.75 (7.99)
American Indian, Eskimo, Aleut, non-Hispanic	2.20 (2.03)	106.4 (97.97)	108.60 (0.35)	4.7 (3.28)	138.5 (96.72)	143.20 (0.41)
Asian and Pacific Islander non-Hispanic	306.30 (69.60)	133.7 (30.04)	440.11 (1.42)	600.1 (78.10)	168.1 (21.90)	768.39 (2.22)
Hispanic	565.6 (48.69)	595.9 (51.31)	1,161.71 (3.74)	891.2 (49.30)	916.3 (50.70)	1,807.78 (5.23)

SOURCE: U.S. Census Bureau, Population Division (2000).

NOTE: These figures are estimations and projections based on the 1990 Census. The 2000 Census figures were not yet available at the time of writing.

to services provided by private physicians, (2) minority groups receiving regular care from such facilities report access comparable to patients with private physicians, and (3) providers who are similar to their patients in race or ethnicity are filling a critical void for minority patients.

These reports suggest that attention needs to be paid to differences in ethnicity and immigrant status in considering access to health care and quality of and satisfaction with the care received. The articles included in this issue illustrate aspects of these interrelationships.

The article by Kuo and Torres-Gil on factors affecting utilization of health services and home- and community-based care programs by older Taiwanese in the United States illustrates the need for studies examining the interaction of specific ethnic/cultural subgroups, particularly those who are recent immigrants, with the U.S. health care system. Such studies raise the question of whether the health care system serving seniors can meet the challenges of growing ethnic diversity by providing specific services for diverse linguistic or national subgroups, or by considering the special needs of immigrants in contrast with older-established minorities, or by some combination of the two. Such studies demonstrate that the broad-based publicly funded or organized health system for seniors needs to interact closely with community-based organizations that are most familiar with the intricate cultural details of each group.

Specifically, Kuo and Torres-Gil examine which factors influence use of health care services and home- and community-based services by elderly Taiwanese residents of California. Most of these residents immigrated after retirement. They find that the Andersen behavioral model of health service used (Andersen 1995; Andersen et al. 1995) in its most recent form is applicable in studying immigrant ethnic minority groups. Kuo and Torres-Gil find that use of nondiscretionary services (hospital stay) is mainly related to structural enabling and need factors such as acute health conditions, living alone, ability to speak English, and increasing years since immigration. The use of discretionary services such as doctor visits are related to predisposing cultural factors, including children living in the region, using alternative medicine, and preferring providers of a similar cultural background. Similarly, use of home- or community-based services is also influenced by these cultural factors, as well as having functional limitations.

In a similar vein, Baxter, Bryant, Scarbro, and Shetterly examine patterns of rural Hispanic and non-Hispanic Whites' use of health care in the San Luis Valley Health and Aging Study. These authors also use Andersen's behavioral model (Andersen 1995; Andersen et al. 1995) as a mechanism to inform us of potential differences in access to care and to cultural norms related to need and appropriateness of care. The factors that have generally been found to predispose persons to use health care include measures of demographic attributes, social structure, and cultural beliefs, while the enabling characteristics include family and community resources related to health care use. The need factors are the perceived and objective health status. On many of these variables, Hispanics differ from the non-Hispanic White population. In general, Hispanics have less education, are more likely to live in poverty, have lower-paying jobs, and are less likely to have health insurance. Without insurance, they are less likely to have a regular provider or to have annual visits to the physician. Yet, given all of this, their review of health care use shows a great deal of inconsistency. Perhaps part of the reason is that the Hispanic population itself is ethnically diverse, with Mexican Americans, Puerto Rican Americans, Cuban Americans, and "other Hispanics."

The study by Baxter et al. focuses on Mexican Americans and "other Spanish/Hispanic" persons who live in the rural area of the San Luis Valley of southern Colorado. Their study replicates findings reported by the AMA that minority groups who receive regular care from neighborhood clinics and hospital outpatient departments report access comparable to patients with private physicians. The residents of the San Luis Valley have access to a community health center, and Baxter et al. find that the rates of outpatient visits, hospitalization, and having a regular source of care do not vary significantly by ethnicity. In this particular location, language is also not a barrier, and the authors note that the San Luis Valley has a relatively stable population with little recent immigration from Mexico. The authors comment on the quality of the community health clinic that provides services to the entire valley at no or reduced cost. In addition, the provider and staff have experience and competence with the diverse population they serve. Interviewers for the study were all bilingual.

The primary differences in utilization revolve around the use of nursing homes and professional home-nursing services. A significantly smaller proportion of the Hispanic population was living in nursing homes at the time of the study, but Hispanics use more professional home-nursing services. More professional nursing services vary by acculturation levels, with larger percentages of people with low or medium acculturation levels using these services, but this relationship disappears after controlling for education. Differences in nursing home use persist after all controls for enabling and need factors are included in the model.

Caring for elderly persons, whether in their own homes or the homes of family members, is more customary in many ethnic and minority groups in comparison to the majority White population. This may rest on a value system, or it may be a response to perceived barriers to access or to the financial costs of nursing homes and other types of facilities that provide personal care to elders who are unable to live independently, such as rest homes, board and care homes, or adult care homes.

This is the topic of the article by Mutran, Sudha, Desai, and Long. They examine the issue of satisfaction with care in facilities and are called "adult care homes" in the state of North Carolina. These are the facilities that are more colloquially called "rest homes" by the general population. Many of these homes serve persons who are predominantly members of one racial/ethnic group or the other. While the authors do not look at the effect on satisfaction with care due to similarity between the care providers and the care recipients—the subject of the article by Berdes and Eckert—they do examine the differences in satisfaction based on the percentage of African Americans in the home, which captures whether the person is living with others of the same race. The authors find that African Americans are less satisfied with their care and that the variables that explain their satisfaction, or lack thereof, are different from the variables that contribute to White satisfaction. The finding that Whites in contrast to minorities are satisfied with their health care, as reported in the AMA (1999) document, can be extended to facilities that provide personal care and service.

The authors identify three dimensions of satisfaction. First, there is the satisfaction that results from a sense of familiarity, a sense of being "at home." Second, there is an expression of satisfaction with staff and the care they deliver. And third, there is an overall assessment of satisfaction with the facility. This study of adult care homes finds that African Americans have a greater feeling of being at home in residences that house six or fewer people and when the older individual takes part in the decision to enter a home. They are also more satisfied with being in a facility when they have more need of physical assistance, leading to the suggestion that perhaps African Americans more than Whites use "need" to rationalize the decision to enter such a home. The research also shows that

African Americans have difficulty adjusting to the facility the more recent the move. Whites, on the other hand, feel more at home when frequency of family contact increases. And White women are more satisfied than White men are.

Similar variables explain African Americans' satisfaction with the staff, with one exception. This group is more satisfied when there are fewer private rooms. The authors interpreted this as an indication of the social climate of the home. More private rooms may reflect a greater number of higher-paying clientele who are likely to be accommodated first. For Whites, satisfaction with the staff is greater among women than among men. One variable does affect the satisfaction levels of both African Americans and Whites: their satisfaction with their own health. This variable is added to control for a tendency of persons to say "All is well," when in truth it is not. Second, it may be that those who are satisfied with their health find it easier to be satisfied in other areas.

In looking at the pattern of results, it appears that African Americans are dealing with a new phenomenon. They prefer facilities that are smaller, take more time to adjust, want to be in on the decision making, and enter a home with fewer private rooms and with lower changeover in the staff. Their overall satisfaction is linked to satisfaction with the "like home" and staff qualities. On the other hand, the satisfaction of Whites is predicted by fewer variables. Gender (women), age (being older), frequency of family contact, and being dependent affects one or the other measure of satisfaction. Only satisfaction with staff is related to the overall satisfaction of Whites.

The next article in this issue is written by Howard, Konrad, Stevens, and Porter, and examines the racial matching of physician and patient in effectiveness of care, use of services, and patient satisfaction. They address one of the findings mentioned earlier in the report of the AMA (1995) that providers who are similar to their patients in race or ethnicity fill a critical void for minority patients. The authors of this article present two alternative views of why physicians' ethnicity and patients' health might be linked. One is the belief, based on historical patterns of geographic distribution and service provision, that increased numbers of African American physicians will increase the availability of physicians to African American communities, increasing access and improving outcomes. The alternative belief asserts more subtly that African American patients require ethnically similar physicians to receive optimal medical care; that is, African American physicians will understand the cultural and social context of illness in this community and thus more effectively communicate with the patient.

Howard et al. fill a gap in the existing literature by examining a sample of elderly African Americans and Whites who have identified an African American or a White physician as their usual health care provider. They are also able to examine the relationship between the social and clinical characteristics of the survey respondents along with the characteristics of their usual care physicians. The authors look at several dependent variables: the elders' pattern of care for hypertension, whether the respondent delayed seeking care quite often, emergency department visits as a proportion of total visits, and elders' satisfaction with care. Their study population is drawn from the Piedmont Health Survey of the Elderly (PHSE) conducted by the Duke University Center for Aging and Human Development as part of the Established Populations for Epidemiologic Studies of the Elderly.

Their work shows the importance of considering the setting in which the physician works and the predominance in the number of White physicians versus African American physicians. The PHSE has only 34 physicians who are African American, 31 of whom serve 720 African American elders, while 3 serve 36 White elders. Of 243 White physicians, 87 serve 696 African American elders, while 156 serve 1,415 White elders. The African American and White physicians are statistically similar in gender, age, and years since graduating from medical school. But African American physicians are less likely to be board certified than White physicians are and more likely to work in primary care and in community health centers.

Howard and his colleagues find that race of the elder is related to being told about high blood pressure, being give blood pressure medication, and taking the medication but also putting off care quite often. African Americans are known to have higher rates of hypertension, more severe conditions, and a worse prognosis for cardiovascular morbidity and mortality. The authors speculate that physicians may be more sensitive to these patterns and their deadliness to African American elders. African American physicians appear to be more effective in securing elders' compliance with taking their medications than White physicians.

Perhaps the most perplexing finding of this study, though, is the relationship of satisfaction with care and the dyad of racially similar physician and patient. African American elders with African American physicians are less satisfied than other types of dyads. The authors offer several explanations for this finding, which include history and experience in a "separate but unequal" medical care system in which African American physicians might be inadvertently associated with inferior quality. On the other hand, African American physicians might also be delivering care in settings where constraints from scarce resources affect the quality of care. Thus, paradoxically, clinics that may be in the local community and serving primarily people associated with these communities, and have culturally competent staff, are likely to have fewer resources. So, on one hand, there are positives about help from a community source, as in the article by Baxter et al., but negative effects if the resources are stretched too thin.

The contribution by Berdes and Eckert provides an important reminder of how the social facts of ethnicity and nativity influence quality of care, not only from the perspective of consumers' interaction with the upper-level providers such as doctors, nurses, home administrators, and so forth but also from the rank-and-file staff such as nurse's aides, who carry out the instructions of the health care professionals and provide the daily interaction and personal care for the residents. Studies have long documented the twin facts that many nurse's aides are both foreign-born and from less privileged socioeconomic backgrounds (e.g., Tellis-Nayak and Tellis-Nayak 1989). Nurse's aides tend to be female African Americans or foreign-born and have the least education and lowest skills and pay, and thus the lowest occupational status in health care. The institutional culture of the nursing home reinforces their negative situation, ignoring the aides' affective needs and doing nothing to bolster their self-esteem. The nursing home becomes a menial job in an impersonal setting serving difficult-to-please managers and clientele.

Berdes and Eckert provide new evidence for the ongoing presence and corrosive effects of racism and xenophobia faced by nurse's aides. This study uses qualitative methods to explore the world of interpersonal relations between nursing home residents and the caregiving staff and among the staff themselves. The article focuses on race relations. They find that one-third of the residents exhibit race-related attitudes, which take two forms: anachronistic racism (language not acceptable today but commonly used in the past) and malignant racism (comments intended to be offensive). Nurse's aides discount the former, attributing it to residents' age, social background, lack of education, or mental competence, and use various coping strategies to maintain a caring attitude, or they sometimes successfully reeducate residents to use more acceptable language. Malignant racism, however, could not be coped with by these means. Ethnic minority nurse's aides experience racism from residents and from their coworkers. In particular, immigrant workers face a conflation of racism and xenophobia, where they encounter additional prejudice from native-born ethnic minority coworkers. The authors conclude that racial differences between residents and nurse's aides will continue to be a problem as long as nursing homes are effectively segregated in terms of ethnicity of residential clientele. Their study indicated that more than three-quarters of nurse's aides experience racism on the job, which they describe as a "monumental problem and deserving of urgent attention."

The articles included in this second and final issue of the special edition on age and health in a multiethnic society focus on the ways ethnicity and nativity of clients and service providers interact to influence access to care and quality of care. They provide a representation of the many complex issues that face those who are engaged in crafting policies and plans related to reducing disparities in the health of seniors. On one hand, some of the studies suggest that similar conceptual models underpin the experience of diverse groups' interaction with the health care system (such as the Andersen model of health service use or quality-of-care frameworks). These models serve to highlight the similarities in the way different ethnic groups engage with the health care system, as well as the different specific variables that influence use for each group. They highlight commonalities as well as differences. Community-based organizations, on the other hand, often do well when they customize their services to clients of a specific ethnic or cultural subgroup. For them too, however, periodic communication and cooperation across groups at different levels serves to improve services and build bridges for their clientele with the overall health care system. These articles represent only the tip of the iceberg; much further research is needed to explore the complex and changing health issues facing ethnic minority seniors in America today.

This research was partly supported by the Resource Center on Minority Aging Research under the auspices of the NINR, NIA, and ORMH Grant RO1 NR 03406. We thank Kevin Harrell for assistance with manuscript preparation.

References

American Medical Association. 1999. *Report on Racial and Ethnic Disparities in Health Care: Board of Trustees Report 50-1-95 Recommendations* [Online]. Available: http://www.ama-assn.org/ama/downloads/minority/html/263.html.

Andersen, Ronald M. 1995. "Revisiting the Behavioral Model and Access to Medical Care: Does It Matter?" *Journal of Health and Social Behavior* 36:1–10.

Andersen, Ronald, N. Harada, V. Chiu, and T. Makinodan. 1995. "Application of the Behavioral Model to Health Studies of Asian and Pacific Islander Americans." *Asian American and Pacific Islander Journal of Health* 3 (1): 128–41.

Tellis-Nayak, Vivian, and Mary Tellis-Nayak. 1989. "Quality of Care and the Burden of Two Cultures: When the World of the Nurse's Aide Enters the World of the Nursing Home." *The Gerontologist* 29 (3): 307–13.

U.S. Census Bureau, Population Division. 2000. Last revised May 10. Online. Available: http://www.census.gov/population/estimates/nation/nativity/for9099q.txt; http://www.census.gov/population/estimates/nation/nativity/nat9099q.txt; http://www.census.gov/population/estimates/nation/nativity/fbtab002.txt; http://www.census.gov/population/estimates/nation/nativity/nbtab002.txt.

U.S. Department of Justice, Immigration and Naturalization Service (1999). Last revised July 27. Online. Available: http://www.ins.usdoj.gov/graphic/aboutins/statistics/300.htm.

JAMES E. DOBBINS
JUDITH H. SKILLINGS

56

Racism as a Clinical Syndrome

Nearly a century ago, in a seminal treatise on racism in America, Sociologist W. E. B. Du Bois (1903/1961) put forth a concept of "dual consciousness" that is especially relevant now to discussions of the clinical impact of racism. Although DuBois used dual consciousness to describe the social effects of racism on people of African descent, the concept of race reactance can be applied not only to people of color but to members of mainstream American culture as well. For both ethnic minorities and members of the dominant culture, dual consciousness implies a self/not-self splitting of the persona; whereas the former represents healthy drives, needs, and cognition, the largely unacknowledged "not-self" is composed of intrapsychic mechanisms that organize thoughts, behavior, and attitudes around racial themes in order to compensate for manifestations that are inconsistent with our inherent attributes. Rather, the organization of the not-self, a concept akin to Jung's notion of the shadow self, is consistent with the realities of societal stereotypes and prejudices. For members of nondominant or target groups, this dual consciousness involves an authentic self, which recognizes that the environment may be oppressive, and an "oppressed self," which must somehow suppress self-efficacy in order to adapt to the demands of oppression. For members of mainstream culture, the split is between an authentic (i.e., egalitarian) self and a socially generated, falsely entitled self.

The pervasiveness of the dysfunction created by racism is confounded by historically interactive influences of culture and science that have distorted our definitions of mental health, especially for the dominant cultures. Thus, we need not only to re-consider our notions of mental health but to develop accurate clinical definitions of prejudice and racism. The ensuing discussion will frame the intrapsychic mechanisms of racism as a functional problem, similar to an addiction.

Functional paradigms emphasize the utility of focusing on behavioral content and its consequences, rather than on personality variables. When the focus is on treating behavior that is racist, the related faulty cognition and emotional responses will present themselves for treatment or undergo a process of self-correction. Treating faulty cognitive/emotional components without focusing on immediate behavior change is like treating an alcoholic or addict without requiring a cessation or, minimally, a consistent reduction of the habit. Further, like addiction, the healing process is rarely an overnight, "I've seen the light" conversion experience. With treatment, however, the progress of the dysfunction can be arrested, while other supports are put in place to encourage growth and supersede racist coping styles. Personal accountability for behavior change is given greater weight in this model than is the expectation that mass demonstrations and political processes alone will change racists or the impact of their behavior.

Social Definitions of Racism: A Functional Paradigm

Investigators have used a wide variety of terms to describe ethnic and cultural groups affected by racism. The terms "whites," "mainstream," "Anglos," and "European Americans" are among those often used to identify individual members of American culture who are the primary agents or hosts of racism in the United States (Skillings & Dobbins, 1991). Targets of racism have been described as belonging to various ethnic or racial groups referred to by such terms as "blacks," "African Americans," "Asian/Pacific Islanders," "Native Americans," "Indians," "Chicanos," "Hispanics," "people of color," and "ethnic minorities." Marden and Meyer (1973) coined the generic terms "dominant culture" and "nondominant culture," respectively, for agents and targets of racial transactions. These terms are preferred in this discussion because abuse of power is the quintessential functional element that differentiates racism. Those who hold institutional power constitute the dominant culture; they are the people whom the larger social system inherently serves. Members of nondominant groups are the likely targets of overt and covert institutional power manipulations, or the targets of institutional and personal neglect.

For purposes of this discussion, it is important to note the power differential among prejudice, ethnocentrism, and racism. Prejudice is a human phenomenon, apparent in all individuals and all cultures. At its lowest level, a prejudice may be a simple preference such as a favorite food or a highly prized piece of music. As it intensifies, it may involve preferences among human attributes, such as variations in body shape or facial features. Such preferences frequently are coupled with judgments and sentiments about the superiority or worth of these particular choices and features over others. It is to be expected that various ethnic groups judge their own culture to be preferable to outgroup variations; we call this "essential ethnocentrism." However, when ethnocentrism is combined with the power to enforce one's own preferences and prejudices, and to punish or ignore a different arrangement of preferences held by a presumed outgroup, then the ground is fertile for the seeds of racism.

Although there are parallels between ethnocentrism and racism, the latter is far more damaging—to the individuals who hold racist views, as well as to those in the target groups. Both racism and prejudice are often associated with an affect of antipathy toward members of a less preferred outgroup or nondominant group. When there is also an extraordinary power imbalance, such as exists in the United States, discriminatory behavior creates privilege for dominant-group members to the detriment of nondominant-group members. The problem that tends to be overlooked, however, is the extent to which this arrests and erodes the development of a healthy intercultural, interpersonal style in members of the dominant culture.

The use of race labels represents a taxonomy directed at various groups seen as originating in parts of the world different from the European. Although the term is popular in secular circles as well as in science, several investigators (Allport, 1980; Dobbins & Skillings, 1991; DuBois, 1961; Dunn, 1951; Leiris, 1951; Thomas & Dobbins, 1985) have noted that race, as a descriptor of ethnic groups, is a loose generalization with no biological precision. Little wonder, then, that the construct of race has remained such an inconclusive set of observations in most social science research, with virtually no predictive utility for social science practice.

Van den Bergh (1967) proposed a logical reformulation of race, noting that it is not of itself a biological reality but the use of biological realities for social purposes. Following on this construct, racism may be thought of as the purposeful use of biological features to create and support an artificial need for social distance. For example, an Anglo father forbidding his Anglo daughter to marry "out of her race" really means that he intends that she not marry out of her color caste. Thus, social distance is asserted to be the motive at the core of racist behavior, as maintained by individual, institutional, and cultural structures of privilege for members of the dominant group.

According to Taylor (1980) and Jones (1972), racism can take many forms—individual, institutional, and cultural—and can be intentional or inadvertent. Some people are overt racists; others hold the same faulty, negatively charged generalizations about nondominant cultures, but are guarded in their public behavior (i.e., covert racists); still others, who do not see themselves as racist, are nonetheless deeply ingrained with stereotypical patterns of race awareness and reactance (i.e., unconscious racists).

Institutional and cultural aspects of racism are as important as individual manifestations; indeed, people act out individually because there are cultural and institutional supports to do so. Pinderhughes (1989) eloquently underscored this point by noting that the "features of the dominant culture symbolize a marker of privilege within the larger social system." These markers are so pervasive that children, as well as adults, are socialized into the syndrome. The negative impact of cultural racism on children from nondominant groups can be observed in the extent to which they are assaulted by images of dominant-culture heroes. Children of both nondominant and dominant groups encode and decode subtle messages about how they are like or unlike the power figure in various television shows, advertisements, books, and cartoons. Whether it is Power Rangers, VR Troopers, or the Masked Rider, the leader of the "action team" is invariably a white male; the images are ceaseless, and their effects may be clinically significant for many children.

This barrage of cultural bias is also damaging to children of the dominant culture. They are led to believe, and to behave as though, it is a given that, in a group context, people who look like them will be the leaders. Thus is conveyed to the child a message about how relevant he or she is within the larger scheme of things. Increasingly, the message leads to an accommodation, a belief on the part of the children that they are successfully adapting to a predictable future. Adults and children of both groups are shaped to see the preferences of the dominant culture as morally superior. Since the dominant culture controls the institutions of media and advertising, such generalizations serve to reinforce views that are inconsistent with democratic values and with the realities of the rapid multicultural shifts taking place in the wider society.

The reportedly widespread Anglo reaction to O. J. Simpson's acquittal is an example of the unpreparedness of adult members of the dominant culture to remain open-minded when the system doesn't mitigate as institutional racism says it should. The position of dominance, whether sought after or not, isolates members of the dominant group in a way that activates self-centeredness, a sense of entitlement, and a certain compulsivity about eliminating or explaining away threats to an illusory sense of a morally superior order. Often, without even consciously intending to do so, the dominant power structure is invoked as a defense, a means of making things right by invoking dominant cultural standards.

Since there are obvious functional advantages for those who hold power, the system tends to be self-perpetuating; it offers little motivation for change to those in a position to alter it. However, as noted above, there are profound repercussions at the individual level that stem not only from being a target of racism but also from being a recipient of privilege in such a brutal system. Racism depersonalizes and dehumanizes, it is, at its core, a violent form of social distancing with overt and covert manifestations. In the context of these social definitions of race and racism, this paper will consider the clinical issues associated with racism.

Clinical Issues

Impact on Nondominant-Group Members

It is safe to say that if members of nondominant groups could do so, they would choose not to experience the social and psychological manifestations of racism. Thus, racism may be characterized as unsolicited and unwarranted violence—whether physical or mental; covert or overt; transpiring within individuals, institutions, or cultural transactions.

The social science literature is replete with works that discuss the negative psychological impact of racism on members of nondominant groups (Adams, 1990; Akbar, 1991; DuBois, 1961; Fanon, 1967; Grier & Cobbs, 1968; Ho, 1987; Pinder-hughes, 1989; Milliones, 1980; Welsing, 1970). However, DuBois's assertion of a dual consciousness among blacks went largely unrecognized before Fanon's allegorical writings suggested a clinical application. The work of Fanon, like that of DuBois, was generally treated as irrelevant by the dominant academic culture until Grier and Cobbs, focusing on internalized rage as a causal factor for race-related pathology, recapitulated the theme of dual consciousness and greatly elaborated Fanon's insights on racism as it manifests itself in the psychiatric disorders of men and women of color. Subsequent investigations of personality development in nondominant populations supported the validity of dual consciousness and the pathological effects of racism (Adams, 1990; Akbar, 1991; Asante & Anderson, 1973; Harrell, 1979; Jones 1991; Semaj, 1981; Welsing, 1970).

Adams (1990), noting that prejudice and exclusion are social traumata for nondominant persons, maintained that such exclusion maintained that such exclusion is a stressor that interferes with the mental and social adjustment of many Americans in both dominant and nondominant cultures:

> Among the social traumata in the current societal scene, exclusion and prejudice, having structural as well as mentalistic aspects, are high in both prevalence and pathogenicity. (p. 362)

Akbar (1991) asserted that, as a consequence of adjusting to racism, the African American suffers routinely from a number of clinical syndromes (e.g., alien self disorder, anti-self disorder, self-destructive disorders, and organic disorders) related to dual consciousness. Jones (1991) stated that, for

African Americans, there is a politics to personality, that is, the need for a dual consciousness to satisfy social ends, which results in their having to

> struggle with their duality, an African heritage which bestows degradation and insult, and an American heritage which seems to offer promise and opportunity. As a result, being Black in America often leads to a bifurcation of self. (p. 307)

According to Jones, the politics of personality implies that the nondominant group is projected as "the problem." Thus, the bearers of the symptom are the ones who must work out the solution, both for the perpetrator and for themselves. This dynamic mimics the battering syndrome that has been so well studied in clinical psychology. The perpetrator is able to maintain ego-syntonic balance by rationalizing that "the victim deserved it" or "I didn't really mean to do it." Racially battered people often acquiesce to the anxieties of the dominant culture "to keep the peace." As Jones put it,

> personal strategies for survival often create a conflict between . . . behavior regarded as appropriate in mainstream America and that . . . judged to be an expression of self and circumstance. (p. 309)

Modes of Coping   Harrell (1979) posited six coping styles as a supplemental diagnostic system for assessing the impact of racism on blacks. Like Jones (1991) and Adams (1990), Harrell found these modes of coping to have both positive and pathological dimensions. The first of Harrell's six styles is Continued Apathy, a situation in which one's response to racism is to have no mitigating plan of action. As with victims of chronic battering, continued apathy in the face of racism describes an individual who sees no way to escape and seeks no relief. Although, on the face of it, this response, or lack thereof, seems pathological, it may embody a paradoxically positive coping strategy, that is, the apparent apathy may serve as a means of conserving energy, mitigating the stress of futile defensiveness, and avoiding unproductive confrontation or violence. However, in pathological applications of this style, people fail to make appropriate use of available resources against racism; rather (as in Akbar's anti-self syndrome), they become bound to their nemesis by means of anticipatory invalidation of their own humanity, that is, obsequiousness and self-deprecatory attitudes and behavior.

The second coping style Harrell termed Seeking a Piece of the Action, making oneself a "marketable commodity" for the system. Asante and Anderson (1973) described those who do so as "assimilationists." On the positive side, this style is oriented toward achievement and the acquisition of material goods, not for the purpose of conspicuous consumption but to enhance one's material standing and security according to the values of mainstream culture. When this coping style becomes pathological, individuals lose connection with their ethnic and cultural identity by placing personal agendas ahead of critical group agendas. Thus, the style represents a dialectical struggle between two worldviews: the individualistic priorities of Eurocentric culture versus the more group-oriented Afrocentric priorities.

Harrell's third style, Obsession with Counter-Culture Alternatives, is an attempt to escape having to deal with racism. In this mode, members of the nondominant group attempt to find a "personal solution" by altering their consciousness via drugs, religiosity, and so on. At pathological levels, one quickly loses ground in being able to express—or even know—one's authentic self, and there is marked erosion in the ability to distinguish between abuse and addiction or, more generally, fantasy and reality.

The fourth style, dubbed the Black Nationalist Alternative, emerges from a debate about the depth of self-examination necessary for an individual to project a valid nationalistic identity. Although the ideology of black nationalism is such that those committed to it would be reluctant to label their approach to racism as a coping style, Harrell viewed the positive aspects of this style as countering the system of victimization, as an alternative to the stereotypical ways in which black people have been socialized to think about themselves. However, there are pathological aspects to this style for those who have a limited base of requisite life experience to support the ideology. If the black nationalist lifestyle becomes a way to flee from the dominant culture, rather than a mode of self-assertion or the expression of preferred values, the individual's adjustment is likely to be less healthy; nationalism, at its pathological extreme, is marked by a kind of "cyclopean, paranoid approach to reality" (Harrell, 1979, p. 104), in which individuals are likely to ascribe to racism all manner of personal, social, and familial problems.

In the fifth of Harrell's styles, Identification with an Authoritarian Solution, positive effects include the development of disciplined belief and struggle toward a common goal. Since the perception of discipline is a valued attribute, an internal sense of resolution may take the form of an ideological or quasi-religious set of beliefs. The danger here is that use of this style often depends on overidentification with ideology or group identity. Jones (1991) assessed these types of coping responses as useful because they give "a better account of positive developments in black personality, but seem to limit it to group personality" (p. 313).

The final coping style, Historically Aware Cognitive Flexibility, involves a grasp of the history of the struggle of black people, and especially of the complexity of their present position. Harrell's description is in accord with the latter stages of other models of black consciousness (Cross, Parham, & Helms, 1991; Milliones, 1980). This style reflects readiness to take action toward ending racism, which, according to Harrell, involves "creating new theory, practicing anti-racist ideology and consequently maintaining new hope." On the positive side, racism is responded to in a "nonparanoid, nondefensive manner [based on a] creative offensive" (p. 105). This style moves toward pathology when flexibility descends into confusion (although, in the view of the present authors, those who reach this level of coping may need to guard against burnout more than confusion).

In sum, the modes of coping with racism outlined by Harrell and others suggest that such responses are far more complex and varied than that of merely internalizing rage or self-hate. Although most nondominant people internalize racism at some point, using this as the focus of treatment is apt to be overly simplistic. As Jones (1991) put it:

> The old view sees self-hate as the only response to racism. This may have been more *apropos* in its time, but it greatly overstates the case then and is of relatively little use to us now. (p. 313)

While, as the above discussion suggests, the effects of racism constitute a serious mental health concern for nondominant groups, it is the purpose of this paper to explicate racism as a critical mental health issue for members of the dominant culture as well.

Impact on Dominant-Group Members

Over the past half-century, a great deal of research has been conducted to help explain the personality and attitudinal structures of people who practice racist behavior. Post–World War II researchers (Adorno, 1950; Pettigrew, 1981; Rokeach, 1951) hypothesized that an identifiable pattern of attitudes predict behavior related to race prejudice. However, the work devoted to this hypothesis yielded inconclusive results about racism's impact on the personality or mental health of members of the dominant culture (Pettigrew, 1981). As a result, social scientists have tended to view racism as an artifact of social forces and structures, and clinicians have generally circumvented diagnostic consideration of overt racist expressions, in much the same way that they might work around a client's political views or religious affiliations (i.e., as relevant only if it is the explicit focus of investigation). In sum, we tend to look at the forces that shape these attitudes but not at how the attitudes shape the person that holds them. The main thrust of social/psychological research and practice, then, has shifted toward examinations of structural causes, rather than the clinical significance, of racism.

In challenging this trend, we can point to other areas of clinical concern in which allowing abusive attitudes to go unchallenged has proven dysfunctional. For example, in treating individuals with histories of spouse abuse, child molestation, or drug addiction, even where these may not be part of the client's presenting problem, the latent discovery of such attitudes and behavior has profound implications for the client's adaptation in all life spheres and brings the issues properly into the treatment arena. The very presence of the attitude makes it legitimate clinical material and, in the case of racism at least, may have a bearing on the appropriateness of the therapist-patient match.

There are several reasons racism should be regarded as a relevant clinical issue, whether or not the client perceives it as a problem. The most obvious is that racism, as do the other forms of abusive behavior noted above, harms people. On this ethical basis alone, it may be argued that those who hold racist views (whether consciously or unconsciously) have emotional and physical correlates that merit systematic attention. Although the literature has shifted away from the mental health "deficits" of racists, clinicians continue to struggle with the relationship of racism to mental health. Whether or not a client articulates white supremacist views, for example, is likely to have a bearing on whether or not that person is able to make a healthy adaptation to an increasingly multicultural society. The following vignette may serve to illustrate the point:

Al is a 53-year-old Caucasian veteran of the Vietnam War, who has been diagnosed with posttraumatic stress disorder (PTSD), with depression as the major clinical factor. His primary character defense is a postwar sense of self-worth built on a belief in his own toughness—both mental and physical. He prides himself on his leadership abilities, which in recent times have been expressed by freely sharing advice with associates about how they might improve their approach to life. He believes, with a passion just loud enough to drown out the horrors of war, that, "It's a man's duty to fight for his country, freedom, and democracy."

Al would not consider himself a racist, He has numerous African American friends. However, he has bought—hook, line, and sinker—into a white, male supremacist model that allows him, by virtue of meeting the criteria of being white and male, to see himself as being appropriate to the role of designated leader. He believes that, by right or destiny, it is his place to serve as the arbiter of right and wrong for those around him.

Increasingly, Al finds himself isolated and lonely, although he cannot show weakness by acknowledging this. More and more, as his health fails, he is unable to exert enough control to ensure that he can be the primary decision maker in the world in which he travels. Further, his faith in the purity of the Vietnam mission is steadily eroding under the assault of what is continuously revealed about U.S. foreign policy—both then and now. But Al has been raised to be an autocrat, and there is nothing in his personal history that has prepared him for being other than "right." The idea of cultural preferences is totally foreign to him. He has grown severely depressed, and contemplates suicide. Al's method of choice is carbon monoxide poisoning. On his bad days he sits in his car in a closed garage, trying to decide whether to end his life.

Surely, this veteran's socialization to a white, male role of dominance is as important to his psychopathology as is the PTSD diagnosis that he carries. However, the symptom that the clinician sees is suicidal ideation. The fact that Al does not articulate racist verbiage does not mean he is free from racism, or that it is not a contributing factor in his psychological deterioration.

Considering racism as a clinical syndrome in light of one's behavior toward others, as well as one's internalized beliefs, suggests some challenging reformulations of the clinical importance of racism—its etiology, process, and potential for redemption in the dominant culture. In terms of the definition of racism offered earlier, a racist could be characterized as one who mistakes personal preferences for morally superior behavior and who is accustomed to invoking the power of the dominant culture to indulge these preferences. For example, if, in October 1995, when thousands of African Americans stayed home from work in support of the Million Man March, a supervisor who disapproved of the event decided to have all those who stayed away from work "written up," that supervisor could be said to have exhibited a racist coping style, that is, invoking the power of the dominant culture to enforce personal preferences. When this style is resorted to chronically, it is at the expense of developing more sophisticated and flexible coping devices.

As we have argued previously (Skillings & Dobbins, 1991), given the dominant cultural bombardment that exists, most Americans struggle, to one degree or another, with having internalized European American standards. We suggest, therefore, that clinically significant racism is a syndrome whereby some of the signs of the disorder may be subclinical at various times and may not manifest as a complete systemic breakdown. However, when these symptoms and signs are taken in aggregate form and observed over time, the progression and effect of the syndrome may be seen. Further, when more sophisticated defenses break down, the primitive defenses often present as intrinsic to the basic pathology.

For example, the leading causes of death of African Americans are stress-related diseases and homicides. By analysis of the preceding section, one might hypothesize that these statistics are a reflection of failed coping mechanisms against racism or the enactment of self-hate as manifested in internalized individual and cultural racism. The one statistic that holds constant for race-related syndromes is the correlation between race and stress, such that for some nondominant groups it is safe to say that skin color alone is a risk factor (Thomas & Dobbins, 1985).

Conversely, given that the leading cause of death among those in the dominant culture is cardiovascular disease, it can be hypothesized that the maintenance of an active drive to hold on to privilege (status, money, or market dominance) exacerbates cardiovascular morbidity. Further speculation suggests that this drive may be directly fueled by the advantage of the dominant cultural position vis-à-vis rewards in American society. Additionally, there are considerable cognitive/emotional gymnastics required to turn a blind eye to the covert and overt violence on which the system is predicated, and to maintain this homeostasis. Such a competitive, "Type A"-like position can be said to constitute a chronic stressor consistent with the profile that correlates highly with heart disease.

Models of Mainstream Behavior   Functional models of mainstream racist behavior offer an alternative to the personality research perspective and can help clinicians better understand the impact of racism on members of the dominant culture. Noting that not all negative cross-cultural interactions are motivated by conscious racist hostility, Taylor (1980) used the term "racialism" to describe race-related varieties of individual, cultural, and institutional behavior. Taylor's model differentiates intentional racist behavior motivated by conscious white supremacist beliefs from other, more contextual forms of racial behavior, which he referred to as "non-racism." However, in defining racism as the ability to enforce one's preferences as a means of achieving social distance based on ingroup/outgroup physical traits, we would argue that Taylor's dimensions can more accurately be said to distinguish overt racism from inadvertent, or unconscious, racism. Nevertheless, Taylor's approach allows one to determine whether behavior is an artifact of situational or intentional factors and helps establish the construct validity of diagnostic nosology of racist behavior.

Taylor's model specified six sociogenic variables that define the etiology of racialistic (racist and nonracist) behavior. In his Frustration Aggression variable, for example, routine conflicts at home may lead one to attempt intrapsychic resolution by taking frustration out on a nondominant target (e.g., someone at work). Although his behavioral outcome is situational, in the sense that it was not initially prompted by issues of racism but by dysfunction in the home, it also reflects cultural values and beliefs about the utility of nondominant persons as accessible scapegoats for the casual frustrations of dominant-culture persons. Under more prolonged displacements, this not only reflects situational and cultural influences, but more deeply seated personality issues that mediate and sustain this form of displacement in lieu of healthier coping styles. It also serves the societal function of maintaining social distance "on the front lines."

For Taylor, another powerful sociogenic variable is Identification, in that it mediates beliefs about the worth and status of nondominant and dominant members of the culture. If someone identifies with a parent or other such figure who models racism, it is easy to see how stereotypic behavior will be incorporated into that person's response repertoire via a process of identification. For example:

In a mainstream, white American family, a son had been taught by his bigoted father not to touch African Americans because they are "dirty." When placed as an apprentice to an African American electrician, the young man assiduously avoided bodily contact, as he had seen his father do with any number of African Americans, even when passing tools to his new mentor.

In Taylor's model, insofar as it was his father's belief system and not his own that he was acting on, the son's behavior would be defined as racialistic and not overt bigotry. However, the privilege of power to interact in such an interpersonally insulting manner fell to this man as a member of the dominant culture. In this sense, it is nonetheless a form of racism.

The third of Taylor's variables, Internalization, hypothesizes that there are powerful rewards or incentives for adopting or changing one's beliefs to conform to those of significant others who are racist. The practice of social distance is based on the belief that such adaptation can bring one the same privileges (i.e., status, power, control) perceived in the role models. Thus, internalization may be linked to identification:

A pattern such as this was exemplified by David, a young man with an IQ of roughly 70, who struggled through high school. David proudly graduated and, with great diligence, landed a job at a local fast-food store. Unfortunately, the store was staffed by Klan sympathizers. Although David had, in fact, come from a family that did not perceive itself as racist, but rather expressed support for civil rights, he quickly adopted the neo-Nazi attitudes of his coworkers because, in his very limited world, these were associated with the power-bearers. Even after David lost his job at the store, he continued to espouse his doctrines of hate.

Taylor's fourth internal state, Ego Defense, involves vicarious use of racist beliefs in the service of an otherwise failing or weakened ego. Those who do so project nondominant status onto others as a means of feeling better about themselves, even in cases where their own social status may be marginal or questionable by comparison. This form of race-related behavior is reminiscent of the authoritarian personality described by Adorno (1950). It might be exemplified by a person whose business is failing for all the reasons that businesses fail (e.g., changing market, new competition, undercapitalization, or even poor management). Such organized self-references are projected so that the store owner blames his demise on "black shoplifters." If there were no blacks, or other ethnic groups, such ego-defensive racists. (Dobbins, 1974) would find another scapegoat to blame in order to protect their own fragile self-system.

The concept of functional attitudes (Katz, 1960) helps to explain how this type of process operates in the service of the ego. Functional attitudes organize opinions about targets, even to the point of distortion, in helping individuals avoid examination of ego-threatening aspects of their personalities (e.g., "I am not an efficient manager"). In the interest of strongly internalized needs reinforced by social payoffs, social distance seems a small price to pay. Thus, if the business fails, the cause has nothing to do with personal attributes nor (most unfortunately) with any condition that requires work on the self.

Taylor's last two sociogenic variables are contextual. His concept of Social Effect holds that race-related behavior may serve a need to create a favorable impression in a valued social context. For example, when one hears racist jokes or name-calling by dominant-culture members, failure to challenge such behavior may stem from not wanting to be ostracized by people who are socially significant to the listener's psychosocial comfort and well-being. Unlike the person who has internalized the racist behavior and values of others, individuals in this category understand that this is not appropriate behavior. Social effect is instrumental in helping individuals gain or maintain social desirability so that, whether momentarily or as a matter of trait, they collude with behavior they know to be insensitive or violent. Ultimately, by their silence, they declare racial slurs and jokes to be socially acceptable.

The final variable in Taylor's model, also contextual, has no intended social effect. This race-related behavior, referred to by Taylor as Instrumental Racialism, occurs when a preference is acted on independent of ethnic or cultural influences, but the direction of the choice happens to parallel dominant values. For example:

A member of the dominant culture is hiring someone for a job. A dominant-culture candidate and one from a nondominant group apply. The applicant from the dominant culture is given the job because that candidate applied first. Since the interviewer and the successful applicant are of the same race, it might appear on the surface that race was a significant factor when, in actuality, it had virtually no influence on the choice that was made.

Although such situations occur frequently and are not intrinsically racist, they may set the stage for other types of racist interactions (e.g., the employer angrily dismissing an inquiry from the rejected candidate about whether or not affirmative action standards were followed in the hiring process). Such a dismissal would be called frustration aggression (displacement) in Taylor's typology.

Indeed, review of Taylor's model underscores the point that a conceptualization of racism as merely a set of hostile attitudes only scratches the surface of what we need to know about the correlates of racist motives and behavior in the dominant culture. Racism takes many forms, some of which are readily identified as being grounded in white supremacist values; most, however, are far more subtle and easier to overlook within ourselves. Habitual access to power, for example, can create an insidious reliance on the source of that power: in seeking to sustain their sense of well-being, individuals in the dominant culture become addicted to the perquisites of power. Thus, while it would be simpler to think of racism as an ingroup/outgroup phenomenon that will fade with cross-group contact, the proper framing of this problem requires that we probe more deeply into the addictive properties of racism.

Racism as an Addiction

It is the thesis of the present authors that racism is maintained in members of the dominant culture as a result of their becoming addicted to the exercise of power, that is, having relatively unrestricted access to "doing it our way." At the same time, projection of blame helps to maintain a system of denial, so that people learn, early on, to feel covertly or overtly justified in continuing the use of maladaptive, unresponsive behavior to negotiate the oppressive system in which we all function. This system inculcates in dominant-culture children the "schema of irrelevance" (Skillings & Dobbins,

1991) with respect to the needs of nondominant groups. It is this learned concept of irrelevance that resolves cognitive dissonance created by the conflict between egalitarian values and the maintenance of social distance—that allows Thomas Jefferson, in the 18th century, to declare that "All men are created equal" while continuing to own slaves; the white Women's Suffrage Movement, in the late 19th century, to write off their African American sisters; and large portions of the nation, in the late 20th century, to dismiss the integrity of the yearlong evaluation of evidence by 12 jurors in the Simpson case. Thus, historically and currently, the dominant culture socializes addiction to privilege.

In considering racism as an addiction, a couple of analogies may be illuminating. One is to drunk driving, in which the pathological behavior is often ego-dystonic to the alcoholic, who never intended to place other lives at risk when setting out for an evening of fun and partying. Innocent people are as likely to be the targets of the drinker's behavior as is the drinker. Further, despite legislation directing that people not drink and drive, the penalties are poor deterrents due to the underlying addiction to the abused substance. Another common way of conceptualizing addiction is as a love affair, the addict being "in love" with the addictive substance. The organizing dynamic of the pathology of addiction may thus be thought of as ways the addict tries to protect access to a love object; any threat to this association will trigger defenses that have been developed to protect the pathological relationship. These defenses, which will be examined in detail below, are generally seen as serving the maintenance of the addict's denial. They have been described in various ways but at their core, as any addiction counselor can attest, is profoundly impaired self-esteem, stemming from the circumstance of feeling trapped in inauthentic choices.

In Defense of Denial

One type of defense used to maintain denial in racism is rationalization. According to the 1981 edition of the *Random House Dictionary*, to rationalize is to ascribe (one's acts, opinions, etc.) to "causes that superficially seem reasonable and valid but that actually are unrelated to the true, possibly unconscious causes." An example might be parents who offer no objection when their child is bussed five miles across town to a school in a more affluent neighborhood, but who protest loudly that they want their child to enjoy the benefits of a local school when, the following year, bussing would take the child five miles away to a school in a poorer neighborhood with a high number of children of nondominant groups.

Grandiosity, another defense that serves denial, tends to go hand in hand with a sense of entitlement. One example would be the person who takes the stance, "I know the nuclear waste dump shouldn't go on the Reservation, but where else is there to put it?" Another may be found in the white reaction to the Simpson verdict, and to the African American celebration of it as reported in the media. What was left out of that discussion may be as pertinent as what was said: Even if Simpson *is* guilty, the U.S. justice system has seen countless acquittals of guilty white men whose victims were from nondominant groups, and countless convictions of innocent members of nondominant groups whose alleged victims were from the dominant culture. The Simpson verdict was intolerable to many dominant-group members not because it was a miscarriage of justice (they have tolerated these well in the past), but because it offended a sense of entitlement so grandiose as to preclude miscarriages of justice that go against the wishes or interests of the dominant group. It is not disagreement with the verdict in the Simpson case that is pathological, it is the outrage in the dominant culture at a violated sense of entitlement. If there seemed to be an inability on the part of the white community to take a different perspective on the jury's decision, it may be because the coping style of dominant privilege has precluded the development of other, healthier coping styles.

A third way that denial is maintained in most classical addiction patterns is through selective comparison. The person who gets drunk only after work or on weekends points to others who are in even less control of their illness and declares that the way he accommodates his disease is therefore acceptable. This is akin to the dominant-group member who asserts, "It's all right that I shop at the grocery store of a racist, because I told him I disagreed with him when he was spewing racial epithets," yet who continues to support the business, and thus the power base, of someone whose views are offensive.

Another earmark of addiction is protection of one's source. That one's drug connection, for example, is also dealing to children is not sufficient motive to turn him in. Protecting the source takes precedence over the damage being done to the neighborhood or, potentially, even to one's own offspring. In a parallel process, again with reference to the Simpson case, more distressing than the words or actions of Mark Furhman (the Fuhrmans of the world being fairly easy to identify) were the thousands of people who must have suspected that he planted the glove, yet failed to give voice to their concern during or after the trial. Using the construct of an addiction to privilege, this is a form of "protecting the source." ("We don't agree with this particular abuse of power but we'll not turn in the player because, in the long run, his game works well for us.")

For some, the addiction to racism leads to pathological denial; for others, the denial may be overcome by internal consequences such as extreme guilt and confusion over discriminatory behavior that is in conflict with personal values. This might occur when a person has a first-hand experience that challenges cognitive dissonance beyond the capacity to rationalize privilege or apply childhood lessons of irrelevance about nondominant persons and their traits. Helms (1984) termed this the "contact" level of awareness for members of the dominant culture. The delusion may also be broken as a result of external consequences, such as cultural insensitivity leading to loss of a job. However, for most people, neither of these circumstances will be sufficient to induce change. Rather, social conflict or social protext at individual or larger social levels is the stimulus that more often breaks through false entitlement.

Unfortunately, even for those who have broken through their denial and acknowledged the obvious ways in which racism directly benefits them at the expense of others, there is a strong tendency to minimize the degree to which the disease has made inroads into the addict's life. This is a central issue in successful recovery. Members of dominant groups tend to stumble because the sweet aroma from the pipes of power is so very intoxicating. Often, they will have an awakening event, perhaps attend a week-long confrontation; afterward, the wish is to be "over it" *now*, to be magically blessed with a cultural sensitivity and interpersonal flexibility, despite the fact that major portions of their cognitive set were developed to exclude, avoid, and deny this very sensitivity (Skillings & Dobbins, 1991).

The Road to Recovery

There is a saying in recovery that there's nothing worse than a head full of AA and a belly full of beer. It is easy to "talk the talk"; walking the walk is tougher. In the case at hand, agreeing that skin color is a marker of privilege by which to access power is only a beginning step in a recovery process.

Grieving the loss of privilege that is often deeply entangled with dominant members' sense of security in the world and in themselves is a long process. For members of the dominant culture striving to release a privileged lifestyle, access to power may be all too pervasive and much too tempting. The response of whites to the Simpson verdict is but one in a host of examples where people who declare themselves nonracist become reactive when the nondominant culture fails to be "appropriately grateful."

Consider, for example, the mind-set of many members of the dominant culture who do not perceive themselves to be racist, but who have been indoctrinated with the cultural value that work and worth are rewarded by money. They tend to be torn between beliefs in equity and equality. A sense of equity leads them to feel that less affluent, nondominant people have not contributed to the society as equals and therefore do not deserve the same benefits (Jones, 1981). This runs counter to civil rights philosophy, which posits that everyone should have equal opportunity to the same resources. In terms of equality, true recovery requires, for example, that a successful job applicant turn down the position in an all-white workplace if it is revealed that a better-qualified applicant from a target group had been denied the job.

Equity, however, is the cognitive framework that is most often influenced by false entitlement. The dominant group feels that it has put in more of the essential effort to sustain the culture, and therefore deserves greater access to upward mobility and societal resources. Of course, denial precludes their accurately perceiving the importance of contributions from nondominant persons; thus, the delusion envelops more of their perceptual vigilance, and their addiction progresses. In confirmation hearings during the early days of the Clinton administration, there was widespread, albeit brief, attention paid to the employment by several high-ranking appointees of "illegal aliens" as child care and household workers. Apparently, these poor people from "other" (i.e., subservient) cultures were the only ones who could be made to work for the low wages these affluent lawyers wished to pay. Using the addiction model, recovery requires relinquishing such abuses of power wherever they occur—not just where letting them go will have minimal impact on one's privileged lifestyle.

It is our contention (Skillings & Dobbins, 1991) that people learn racism as part of a biologically innocent process by which they seek to organize data into efficient categories with high predictability. As a result, members of the dominant culture learn to ignore, or view as irrelevant, data regarding nondominant groups before they even know what the term white supremacy means. This cognitive style is reinforced by unquestioned access to the privileges of power (e.g., dining at a restaurant and not having to worry whether you'll be served as well as other patrons, or trusting that a teacher is going to assume your child is college material). Members of dominant groups, who drink at this well of entitlement from the moment of birth, soon become addicted to its pleasures. The addiction is maintained by the schema of irrelevance—a form of societal delusion—and further cemented in place on an individual basis by the defenses described above. It should be stressed that, as with other addictions, it is not an individual's fault that he or she has contracted the addiction. No one person is responsible for being taught the irrelevance of nondominant peoples and rewarded for abusing the power of privilege. However, we are responsible for doing something about it once we have been made aware that we are addicts, carriers of this disease called racism.

This model has a logical etiology, in that it puts the treatment focus on changing learned behavior as opposed to restructuring personalities. Arrest the behavior and the personality will restructure itself. Obviously, as with any addiction, there are individuals who are simply unwilling to tolerate the pain of withdrawal and the implications of their own racism. In such cases, one can only hope that the consequences of their disease will stop them sooner or later, before they do further damage to self and others.

Treatment and Remediation

Racism is a phenomenon that manifests itself on multiple levels; the individual is the basic unit, but institutional sanction is the key to how racism operates as a sociopolitical force. Investigators have been divided, however, on how to conceptualize the psychosocial aspects of racism, and especially on how to develop effective interventions. The literature reflects consensus that social protests and civil rights litigation have been effective in changing the face of overt, individual racism (Pettigrew, 1981; Wellman, 1977). Unfortunately, covert racism—both intentional and unintentional—remains pervasive.

If simple affiliation and negative consequences were enough to change the course of racism, we would no longer be seeing the symptoms that have been analyzed in this paper. Michelle Norris, an African American journalist, participating in a tele-

vision talk-show with two Caucasian panelists in the aftermath of the Simpson verdict, summed up the deep division between the white and African American perspectives. We eat together, work together, play together, go to school together, and talk together, she observed, but we go home to very different worlds. As for the celebrated trial, it was as startling to her that the dominant-group journalists could assume a guilty verdict to be the only logical outcome as it was to the nondominant journalists that acquittal might be possible. Socialization of the two groups, rubbing shoulders even among the journalistic fraternity, does not seem sufficient to bring us together ideologically.

This phenomenon is consistent with the addiction model advocated here. As in the case of substance abuse, racism is dynamic in its properties, with intrapsychic resistance and defensiveness at the core of its maintenance. In short, racism is a mental health disorder (Adams, 1990; Delany, 1991; Skillings & Dobbins, 1991; Welsing, 1970).

This notion is contrary to the stratification hypothesis advanced by structuralist investigators who maintain that racism does not involve internal states or, necessarily, a motive to disenfranchise nondominant groups. Racism, in the structuralist framework, is simply a symptom of social stratification. Presumably, of social stratification is a natural consequence of social organization, then racism can be ameliorated as we remove barriers to social mobility (Wellman, 1977). This view seems to assume that individuals' psychological adjustment to their world can be divorced from their perception of their status in society. It implies that those of high status will not use this perception to inflate their self-esteem, rather than developing more substantial reasons for celebrating self-worth. It also implies that those of low status will not need to shape their psyches to accommodate, circumvent, or directly oppose the persistent message that they are of less value. Unfortunately, a lessening of physical distance does not necessarily equate with a lessening in social distance; the defenses that may originally have been created by social distance now serve to maintain that distance, even in circumstances of greater physical proximity.

The civil rights protests, and the legislative mandates and affirmative action policies to which they gave rise, have been with us for nearly half a century. While racism has changed in form over that time, social stratification remains in place. It would appear, then, that racism in its present manifestation is rooted primarily within people, rather than institutions—and that it is present more in the form of an addiction than an adjustment or mood disorder. Adjustment disorders tend to abate when relief from the precipitant psychosocial stressor is provided; addictions are not cured simply by changing the context of the abuse.

Institutional sanctions are needed, of course, but institutional change will occur when people change. Interventions at both levels are essential. Awareness, sensitivity, and multiculturalism are essential in American contexts, and so is treatment of the clinical syndrome of racism as it manifests in the individual. Another truism from the substance abuse field is that addicts must come to hate what the drug is doing to their lives more than they love the drug and what it does, or they hope it does, for them. Sanctions are vital in helping dominant-group members experience negative consequences from their failure to let go of their abuses of power. However, intervention at an individual level is necessary to help people identify their assumptions of privilege and learn how it is in their best interest to relinquish them.

Interventions need to be broad-based. Large-scale social actions serve to heighten awareness about problems in equity and equality and set the stage for laws and policies that provide an institutional context for change. However, once individuals become aware of their problematic behavior and its potential for undesirable consequences, other types of intervention are called for. Self-help groups have been proposed to help individuals acknowledge and change racist thinking or behavior, for example:

In a case known to the authors, the dean of a large department in a state university was charged with being defamatory and discriminatory in his approach to hiring, promotion, and tenure by one of his African American faculty. When these allegations were substantiated by school authorities, the dean was removed from his post. He was also instructed to obtain sensitivity training as a form of correction. Although it is likely that this dean had already experienced sensitivity training, it is equally likely that this was not followed by ongoing treatment or support to maintain whatever benefits were acquired. A European American trying to work on his racism alone, because he had his hand slapped once, is like an alcoholic trying to develop a sober lifestyle while still surrounded by his drinking buddies. Who is there to confront him on his negative behavior and attitudes? By virtue of belonging to a dominant group, he is insulated from feedback in the natural course of events. Treatment that fails to take this into ac-

count is little more than a Band-Aid that lets one pretend to be healed.

There are a variety of group formats, each of which may be appropriate to the needs of different people. Although the 12-step model has been criticized for having been applied to circumstances and behavior beyond that which it was designed to address, we nonetheless find it to be particularly useful within our addiction model of racism. While certainly not the only treatment paradigm for racists seeking recovery, it contains several components that we have found to be effective.

The approach is helpful in breaking through the dominant denial and enabling individuals to admit—at least to themselves, and perhaps to others as well—that, whether willingly or not, they harbor ethnocentric thoughts and feelings (i.e., that they are affected by racist ideology). In this process, it is important to acknowledge that we are powerless to change the fact that racism has affected us—that, whatever our wishes to the contrary, it has made us hosts to the disease in ways that we never consciously welcomed. From this single admission, a watershed of healing becomes possible. It opens the path for the next step, which is to acknowledge that the toxic lifestyle of benefiting from another's loss is not working, nor is amassing personal power at the expense of people with less access to the source of such power.

In this context, people understand the signpost of addiction, the notion that "our lives had become unmanageable." It involves essentially the same intervention process used with those who are chemically dependent. The framework includes group discussions and pairing individuals with others (i.e., sponsors) who have longevity and experience in changing their own beliefs and behavior. Sponsors are necessary because deficits in self-honesty and open-mindedness are so difficult to detect in oneself; it is the sponsor who can serve as a guide in breaking through the grandiosity, violence, denial, and dishonesty that define the progression of the functional disorder we call racism.

In cases where the development of healthier coping styles has been sorely neglected, or where the individual's self-esteem rests so heavily on the status of dominant-group membership that a great deal of ego defensiveness has been triggered, individual therapy is indicated. Ego strength is assumed to be an important mediator of how people in dominant positions use people in nondominant positions as scapegoats or targets. Those who are very resistant to change, especially in the face of consequences, might be assessed via the use of traditional personality measures in order to calibrate their potential for insight and change. This also suggests a possible variation in intervention style. For example, with people reliably diagnosed as having antisocial personality disorders, the addiction paradigm is modified, since these individuals do not generally find it motivating to acknowledge that their behavior has caused harm to others (e.g., killed someone while driving drunk; spent parents' rent money on crack); the emphasis in such cases is focused instead on consequences to self (e.g., revocation of driving privileges; having to stay at a homeless shelter instead of the parental home). Likewise, with people who score high on measures of personal rigidity, the intervention could be tightly focused on making multicultural flexibility more consistent with their personal values. The F-Scale (Adorno, 1950), scales of racialism (Taylor, Dobbins, & Wilson, 1972), and scales of multicultural awareness (Ponterotto, Casas, Suzuki, & Alexander, 1995) might also be used to identify those in need of individualized behavioral plans.

However unlikely it may be to elicit positive response from those in denial, treatment should not be limited to people professing a desire for change. As noted above, an addiction to power, an assumption of privilege, and expectations of entitlement are fostered in members of the dominant culture by forces that have little to do with individual choice or consciously chosen values. These char-acteristics, while forming the underpinnings of racism, are also underlying issues in a vast array of already diagnosed psychopathology. They sprout symptoms such as suicidal depression when one is not being treated well, and anxiety when one is not in control. To treat the symptom and not the cause is like ignoring problem drinking or drug use in someone who comes to therapy to work on marital dysfunction.

Identifying the need to treat the individual for racism does not constitute what Wellman (1993) has termed the "medicalization" of racism. Rather, we seek to provide additional tools with which to confront the contagion of false beliefs and false entitlements that distort reality for many Americans. No one can convince others that racism plays an integral part in their psychic adjustment, one that they would be well advised to start weeding out. What we can do is offer objective feedback, establish consequences, and refused to cooperate with manifestations of the disease. Ultimately, self-diagnosis is required in order for someone to accept the need for change. Once that self-diagnosis is made, however, self-help groups—as well as competent therapists—can be indispensable in charting a course that will enable individuals to stay on track, acknowledge and begin to relinquish their sense of entitlement, accept their imperfections, and ultimately abstain from the abuse of power whenever the opportunities for such abuse may arise.

References

Adams, P. L. (1990). Prejudice and exclusion as social traumata. In J. D. Noshpitz & R. D. Coddington (Eds.), *Stressors and the adjustment disorders* (pp. 362–391). New York: Wiley.

Adorno, T. W. (1950). *The authoritarian personality*. New York: Harper.

Akbar, N. (1991). Mental disorder among African Americans. In R. L. Jones (Ed.), *Black psychology* (pp. 339–352). New York: Harper & Row.

Allport, G. (1980) *The nature of prejudice*. Reading, MA: Addison-Wesley.

Asante, M., & Anderson, P. (1973). Transracial communication and the changing image of black Americans. *Journal of Black Studies, 4,* 69–79.

Cross, W. E., Jr., Parham, T. A., & Helms, J. E. (1991). The stages of black identity development: Nigrescence models. In R.L. Jones (Ed.), *Black psychology* (pp. 319–338). New York: Harper & Row.

Delaney, L. T. (1991). The other bodies in the river. In R. L. Jones (Ed.), *Black psychology* (pp. 597–607). New York: Harper & Row.

Dobbins, J. E. (1974). *A construct validational study of ego-defensiveness*. Unpublished manuscript, University of Pittsburgh.

Dobbins, J., & Skillings, J. (1991). The utility of race labeling in understanding cultural identity: A conceptual tool for the social science practitioner. *Journal of Counseling and Development, 70,* 37–43.

Du Bois, W. E. B. (1961). *The souls of black folks*. Greenwich, CT: Fawcett Publications. (Original work published 1903)

Dunn, L. G. (1951). *Race and biology*. Paris: UNESCO.

Fanon, F. (1967). *Black skin, white masks*. New York: Grove Press.

Grier, W., & Cobbs, D. (1968). *Black rage*. New York: Basic Books.

Harrell, J. P. (1979). Analyzing black coping styles: A supportive diagnostic system. *Journal of Black Psychology, 5,* 99–108.

Helms, J. E. (1984). Toward a theoretical explanation of the effects of race on counseling: A black and white model. *Counseling Psychologist, 12,* 153–165.

Ho, M. K. (1987). *Family therapy with ethnic minorities*. Newbury Park: Sage Publications.

Jones, J. (1972). *Prejudice and racism*. Reading, MA: Addison-Wesley.

Jones, J. (1981). The concept of racism and its changing reality. In B.P. Bowser & R.G. Hunt (Eds.), *Impacts of racism on white Americans* (pp. 27–50). Newbury Park: Sage Publications.

Jones, J. M. (1991). The politics of personality: Being black in America. In R. L. Jones (Ed.), *Black psychology* (pp. 305–318). New York: Harper & Row.

Katz, D. (1960). The functional approach to the study of attitudes. *Public Opinion Quarterly, 24*, 163–176.

Leiris, M. (1951). *Race and culture*. Paris: UNESCO.

Marden, C. F., & Meyer, G. (1973). *Minorities in American society*. New York: Van Nostrand.

Milliones, J. (1980). Construction of a black consciousness measure: Psychotherapeutic consequences. *Psychotherapy: Theory, Research and Practice, 17*, 175–182.

Pettigrew, T. (1981). The mental health impact. In B. P. Bowser & R. G. Hunt (Eds.), *Impacts of racism on white Americans* (pp. 88–96). Newbury Park: Sage Publications.

Pinderhughes, E. (1989). *Understanding race, ethnicity, and power*. New York: Free Press.

Ponterotto, J. G., Casas, J. M., Suzuki, L. A., & Alexander, C. M. (Eds.). (1995). *Handbook of multicultural counseling*. Thousand Oaks, CA: Sage Publications.

Rokeach, M. (1951). "Narrow-mindedness" and personality. *Journal of Personality, 20*, 234–251.

Semaj, L. (1981). The black self, identity, and models for a psychology of black liberation. *Western Journal of Black Studies, 6*, 116–122.

Skillings, J., & Dobbins, J. (1991). Racism as a disease: Etiology and treatment implications. *Journal of Counseling and Development, 70*, 206–212.

Taylor, J. (1980). Dimensionalizations of racism and the black experience: The Pittsburgh Project. In J. M. Jones (Ed.), *Black psychology* (pp. 384–400). New York: Harper & Row.

Taylor, J., Dobbins, J., & Wilson, M. (1972). Racialistic inventory. Unpublished paper, University of Pittsburgh.

Thomas, J., & Dobbins, J. (1985). The color line and social distance in the genesis of essential hypertension. *Journal of the National Medical Association, 78*, 532–536.

van Den Berghe, P. (1967). *Race and racism: A comparative perspective*. New York: Wiley.

Welsing, F. C. (1970). *The Cress theory of color confrontation and racism (white supremacy)*. Washington, DC: C-R Publishers.

Wellman, D. T. (1977). *Portraits of white racism*. Cambridge, MA: Cambridge University Press.

Wellman, D. T. (1993, May). *Racism as a disease*. Paper presented at the annual meeting of the American Orthopsychiatric Association, San Francisco.

C. INTRA CULTURAL FACTORS OF DIVERSITY

57

Constructing a Place for Religion and Spirituality in Psychodynamic Practice

Introduction

A story about the Protestant theologian Paul Tillich tells of his beginning one of his lectures by sweeping into the classroom, pausing for dramatic effect and then uttering one word, "GOD." The students have their pencils poised for THE answer of what God is as defined by this famous and brilliant man. Tillich then says, "Whatever you have been thinking is not God. . . . God is mystery" (Gray, 1998). The idea that perceptions of God, a supreme being, and/or spirituality is filled with unknown and unexplainable ideas and experiences has been a source of difficulty in articulating a coherent framework for the inclusion of religion and spirituality in clinical work. A constructivist framework is premised on the relativity of truth; all knowledge is shaped by our interpretations of it. Such a framework lends itself well to grappling with the ambiguities and often polarized positions inherent in discussions with colleagues and clients about religion and spirituality. Consequently, Tillich's provocative challenge provides a fitting starting place for this article's consideration of how to make room for religion and spirituality in psychodynamic psychotherapy and the ways constructivism can be helpful in this process.

As a practitioner and an educator, this author has found psychodynamic theories helpful for understanding the internal world of clients. However, these theories, at best, have been ambivalent about the inclusion of religion and spirituality in treatment. Often clients' belief systems are understood to represent only their internal object world (e.g., Rizutto, 1979). Perhaps out of the desire to not be viewed as less than scientific and influenced by Freud's (1927; Rothenberg, 1997) dismissiveness of religion as an illusion, psychodynamic practitioners have not articulated guidelines as to how to include spiritual dimensions in their work. In addition to the lack of guidelines, there is an estrangement between the two fields that emanates from "the very conceptual structure of psychoanalysis . . . founded upon a metapsychology that enshrined drives, causality, and determinism as the exclusive motivational underpinnings of an emerging science of the mind" (Rothenberg, 1997, p. 57). With such a deterministic philosophy it is very difficult to reconcile a treatment approach that looks for definitive connections and insights with a spiritual arena that is dominated by vagueness, paradox, and biases.

In contrast to psychodynamic theories, constructivism is not a practice theory per se, but a conceptual framework that can inform practice approaches. "Constructivist theories posit that humans cannot know (perceive) objective reality absolutely" (Franklin & Nurius, 1998, viii). Tillich's beginning exercise parallels the philosophical stance inherent in constructivism—that no one has the corner on "truth" (although his belief that God is mystery represents *his* version of truth). One of the primary influences of postmodernism on psychotherapy is that the central issue has shifted from finding insights or answers to helping our clients find meaning (Saari, 1991, 1999). The process of finding meaning is reminiscent of existential therapies; however, constructivism is coming from a much broader philosophical base. There are numerous texts that explain this philosophical base as well as the various schools of thought within constructivism that vary in their orthodoxy (Franklin & Nurius, 1998; Granvold, 1998; Mahoney, 1998; Carpenter, 1996). These philosophical schools will not be discussed in this paper, however. Instead, the focus will be on the practice guidelines for this meaning-making process as it relates to the inclusion of religious and spiritual issues.

While constructivism is helpful for orienting the clinician in practice, it does not require that the clinician throw the baby out with the bathwater. In practice and in teaching, psychodynamic theories have been informative and relevant. At the conclusion of Bernhard Schlink's *The Reader* (1995) the central character states, "The tectonic layers of our lives rest so tightly one on top of the other that we always come up against earlier events in later ones, not as matter that has been fully formed and pushed aside, but absolutely present and alive" (p. 217). However, Schlink's character also states that "there are many different stories in addition to the one I have written. The guarantee that the written one is the right one lies in the fact that I wrote it and not the other versions" (p. 217). The influence of past development is critical in the present, but it is not the only influence. The present "negotiation" of past, present, and future is continually evolving and equally influential.

The dilemma, then, is how to conceptualize treatment in a way that allows for the insights of psychodynamic theories while opening the door on diverse value systems and much ambiguity. The purpose in this paper is to use the general philosophy of constructivism to elicit and/or allow spiritual and religious issues to emerge in the treatment relationship while drawing on psychodynamic training to provide some practice guidelines. Kelley's (1996) discussion of narrative theory, which "borrows from the constructivists in the field of literary criticism, where narratives are taken apart and analyzed for meaning, and from the social constructionists in the field of social psychology, where reality is viewed as co-constructed in the minds of individuals in interaction with other people and societal beliefs" (p. 462), is an important influence as well. Kelley uses White and Epston's (1990) stages in the narrative approach, which include deconstruction and reconstruction. These influences shape this discussion in the following areas: definition of terms, self-awareness, deconstruction of clients' narrative, assessment of strengths and vulnerabilities, and reconstruction of a useful narrative.

Definitions

One of the principles of postmodernism is that we cannot separate ourselves from what we are studying; our own constructions must be taken into account (Franklin & Nurius, 1998). If one agrees that truth is at least in part a construction that one helps create, then it is critical in therapeutic work to be clear about how the construction of the ideas of religion and spirituality takes place. Joseph (1988) defines religion as "the external expression of faith . . . comprised of beliefs, ethical codes, and worship practices" (p. 44). Spirituality, on the other hand, can be defined as "the human quest for personal meaning and mutually fulfilling relationships among people, the nonhuman environment, and for some, God" (Canda, 1988, p. 243). However, it is not always useful to divide and consequently reduce religion and spirituality to descriptions of external practices versus internal experience. For example, Bishop Ramirez (1985) describes the faith experience for Hispanics as a legacy: "The heart of spirituality touches not only the spiritual, as a mere interior and private event, but [it] is also one that affects their total lives . . . including moral and external behavior, including religious and social relationships. The social aspect brings people in touch with past spirituality of their ancestors. Thus, spirituality is about more than an isolated or private experience—it is also a legacy" (p. 6).

For some clients it may be helpful to make the distinction between religion and spirituality. A homosexual client of mine grew up with missionary parents in a conservative religion. He struggled to continue to view himself as a spiritual being while in a homosexual relationship because homosexuality had been condemned by his denomination. For him it was important to divorce religion from his spirituality. In a similar manner, some clients may not conceptualize a supreme being as part of their spirituality. Still other clients may find no need to draw a distinction between religion and spirituality, finding them compatible and intricately interwoven. In true postmodern fashion, these definitions may change for clients over the course of their treatment and even after treatment officially ends. Utilizing constructivism compels the clinician to articulate his or her understanding of the concepts, to ask for the client's definitions, and also suggests that the act of discussing these concepts with clients produces a third definition—one that is constructed between the client and clinician. The definitions by Joseph, Canda, and Ramirez represent starting places only.

Self-Awareness

As one might expect, both constructivism and psychodynamic theories consider it important for the clinician to understand his or her own religious/spirituality beliefs and practices. Bullis (1996) describes two exercises that can be helpful in understanding the influences in our own lives. The first is a spiritual genogram. As most social work clinicians are aware, a genogram is a graphic representation of genealogy. Similarly, spiritual genograms depict one's spiritual heritage. A spiritual genogram can demonstrate "those persons, places, ideas, and experiences that have formed one's current spiritual identity" (p. 34) or a perceived lack of one. After constructing a spiritual genogram, one should be able to answer the following questions:

> Who were the most significant persons and what were the most significant events in my spiritual development?
> How have they affected my spiritual growth and development?
> How have I changed my spiritual stance in the past five years?
> Was there one particular experience (or experiences) that had a lasting spiritual impact on me?
> What are the current spiritual ideas, books, authors, persons, or events most important to me? (pp. 34–35)

A second exercise is establishing a time line. Drawing a time line of one's religious experiences, either in an elaborate or simple graph or chart, chronologically depicts beginning spiritual experiences, principal spiritual events, and current experiences. "The value of the time line is that the chronology of spiritual experiences makes it possible to place spiritual journeys in perspective over a long period of time" (Bullis, 1996, p. 35). Once the time line is constructed, the following questions can be answered:

> How long have I been on a conscious spiritual journey?
> Did my spiritual journey begin from my deliberate effort or did it begin from a spontaneous, unplanned event?

> Have there been large gaps in my spiritual growth and development or has my spiritual growth been regular and consistent?
> Have I changed my spiritual outlook or position since my childhood upbringing? If so, how? (p. 35)

Once we understand our own history and our current comfort level with spirituality and religion it is helpful to consider the possible countertransference and ethical dilemmas can undermine the therapist's attempts to understand the client's experience. For example, the clinician may envy the client's religious experience (Hall & Hall, 1997). If the clinician is going through a particularly trying time of uncertainty and the client is "sure" of the answers for himself or herself, the treatment can raise a number of conflicting emotions in the therapist; envy and devaluation may be two such emotions. Certainly there are times when religious beliefs and practices can serve defensive purposes. However, clinicians who interpret clients' religious beliefs as always defensive may be acting out countertransference feelings through devaluing these clients' experiences. Consequently, clinicians may attempt to correct "resistant" clients' positions through extended philosophical discussions with no specific therapeutic value (Kochems, 1993) other than to "convert" clients to their way of thinking. This type of countertransference may be particularly relevant when client and therapist have different beliefs or if they are at opposite ends of the conservative-liberal debate.

However, shared religious beliefs do not create immunity to countertransference. For example, similar external religious practices may lead the clinician and the client to assume "we know what we mean by concepts such as sin, grace, God's will, truth, etc." (Giglio, 1993). Such collusion around avoiding therapeutic investigation can extend to painful areas such as abortion, the role of women, and homosexuality and (Narramore, 1994). Shared religious communities also can lead to blurring of therapeutic boundaries and dual relationships (Carbo & Gartner, 1994). Pastoral counselors will inevitably produce grist for the mill when they are in the position of giving communion and providing transference-based psychotherapy. When clinicians and clients share a common belief system, clients can respond to therapeutic inquiries by giving a "catechistic" response (the "correct" one rather than a "personal" one), or by "confessing" out of guilt (Kehoe & Guthiel, 1984; Raines, 1999). Clinicians also can over identify with clients' struggles; "window shop" by vicariously gratifying personal fantasies through exploiting clients' "sinful" experiences; or believe "my way is Yahweh" by assuming that clients who are theologically similar are the most psychologically mature and therefore healthier (Case, 1997; Raines, 1999).

In accordance with our professional code of ethics, clinicians should recognize the limit of their expertise and provide only the services or techniques for which they are qualified by education, training, or experience. It would be unethical for a clinician not trained as a minister or spiritual guide to advertise or purport to be an expert in that area. Likewise, as members of the social work profession, we are to respect our clients' beliefs and values by not imposing our value system through the use of techniques without the client's understanding and consent. Saari (1999) has articulated in her discussion of guidelines for evaluating new meaning that "the absence of known universal truth requires the clinician to pay careful attention to the ethics and values of the profession, particularly that of self-determination" (p. 9). The ambiguity of postmodernism does not make treatment a free-for-all value system.

Deconstruction Stage

The components present in the deconstruction stage of narrative-based treatment include listening to the client's story, externalizing the problem, and deconstructing the dominant story (Kelley, 1996). Often, conflicts around religion and spirituality are not the presenting problems, as most clients interested in focusing on these issues select a clinician in the religious community or someone designated as a spiritual guide. However, utilizing a narrative format is helpful, whether it is used to focus on the presenting problem or is used with issues such as religion and spirituality that may emerge later in treatment.

Listening to the Client's Story

As stated at the beginning of this article, often clinicians are hesitant to broach the subject of religion and/or spirituality for fear clients will think they are going to be coerced into believing or acting in a way that is contrary to their beliefs. However, the act of taking a religious/spiritual history can validate religion as an important part of the client's life and may identify it as a potential coping resource. Also, including this subject area in an initial history highlights any negative experiences that

might impact current functioning. "Working through" (Freud, 1914) this negative experience may allow for the current utilization of religion or spirituality in a more supportive way. In addition, once the clinician knows the status of religious or spiritual practices of the client, he or she can work with the client to determine whether any interventions should include representatives of the client's religious community.

When information about religion and spirituality is included in the initial inquiry, the heat or tension around the subject is diffused for the practitioner and the client. Samples of the type of history-taking questions are as follows:

> What positive or negative experiences with religion or spirituality have you had in the past?
> What importance does religion/spirituality have for you today?
> What type of religious behaviors or spiritual practices do you engage in today? What attitudes do you have about these behaviors? Why are they performed?
> Has religion/spirituality been helpful in the past when dealing with stressful life situations or events? To what extent do you use religion/spirituality for such purposes today?
> Is a supreme being part of your spirituality? If so, how do you view that supreme being? Angry? Concerned? Loving? Punishing? Distant? Uninterested? Uninvolved?

Externalizing the Problem

The kind of initial questions listed above allow clients to step back and look at their beliefs in a manner that can facilitate needed distance from an area of their life that may be laden with affect, painful or otherwise (Scharfenberg, 1988). Both psychodynamic and constructivist frameworks support articulating these narratives. An ego psychological perspective proposes that the act of putting experiences into words can also strengthen the observing aspect of the ego (Katan, 1961; Northcut, 1991). A postmodern perspective proposes that language shapes meaning and reflects personal and cultural values (Kelley, 1996). One step in the process of helping clients form helpful life narratives is to examine the ways they have constructed their stories; particularly relevant here are the narratives around religious and spiritual experiences.

Including both of the terms *religion* and *spirituality* in initial discussions allows room for those clients who oppose organized religion yet embrace spirituality. It also will raise the possibility of a separation of the two concepts, which may be helpful later on in treatment if there is internal conflict over values and behaviors. For example, clients may feel ashamed about behavior or beliefs that are contrary to their religious upbringing. The mere act of suggesting that religion and spirituality are two different yet related concepts paves the way for later discussions with clients that could result in validation of a spiritual life that may not adhere to religious doctrine that has ceased to have positive meaning.

Deconstructing the Dominant Story

The process of deconstructing the client's stories include the sound clinical practice of summarizing, assessing for impacts on the client of his or her story, and looking for contradictions or other interpretations/meanings. The use of some variation on the self-awareness exercises discussed earlier can help clients tell their religious/spiritual story while recognizing that this story is being reshaped in the telling. Most psychodynamic clinicians no longer believe the Freudian view that we can uncover intact memories. The memories of events or experiences are shaded by the affect associated with the experience, by the circumstances since the events, and by the context in which the story is being told (i.e., the relationship with the clinician). Understandably then, the therapeutic relationship is essential to facilitate the unfolding and reshaping of these personal stories.

What is it the clinician listens for as he or she hears clients' stories? Clinical training and skill help us identify themes that characterize aspects of a client's narrative. These themes can develop at any stage of treatment and certainly have to be explored for their meaning within the context of "Why might this be surfacing now?" In addition, it is important to listen for an overarching theme that may be emerging in relation to religious or spiritual issues. Cornett (1998, p. 21) describes one model of spirituality that includes six elements that may emerge as spiritual themes in treatment:

1. Meaning in life—Does the client worry he or she has missed out on *the* meaning of life? Is he or she having difficulty creating *a* personal meaning in life?
2. Values—Are there conflicts between the client's temperament and/or experiences and his or her values?
3. Mortality—Does the client fear death or struggle with the physical finiteness of life?
4. Organization of the universe—Does the client operate under the belief that some type of God or supreme being controls the universe?
5. Suffering—Does the client believe suffering is supposed to bring you closer to God or to a mystical experience? Is he or she questioning "Why do bad things happen to good people?"
6. Transcendence—Is the client questioning what happens after death? Is there something "larger than life"?

There are many different themes that can shape these clinical discussions. Fleischman (1989) has delineated similar categories, that is, witness to significance, lawful order, affirming acceptance, calling, membership, release, worldview, human love, sacrifice, meaningful death. Families also have important narratives just as they have myths and rituals. Exploring the meaning of their religious/spiritual stories will be helpful for the whole system to hear and consequently reshape.

The choice of a relevant focus relies on the clinician's ability to read the client's confirmation or disconfirmation when she or he attempts to identify a theme. Rather than the clinician providing an interpretation, establishing a focus is a dynamic process that is composed of raising hypotheses and having clients determine whether the language accurately reflects their struggles and experiences. Together, client and clinician identify a narrative them that "fits." Saari (1999) further suggests that the clinician should pay attention "to the coherence of that narrative and its ability to explain the client's experiences in ways that are compatible with the perspectives of both client and therapist" (p. 10).

Assessment of Strengths and Vulnerabilities

One of the difficulties of constructivism is the lack of clear guidelines for assessment. In fact, it could be argued that the concept of assessment is antithetical to a postmodern type of treatment because of its implications for diagnosis (Dean, 1993). However, the fact remains that clinicians are still ultimately responsible for the course of treatment and must make some determinations regarding client functioning. To date, a few authors have offered specific assessment guidelines (Franklin & Jordan, 1998; Neimeyer, Hagans, & Anderson, 1998) but generally speaking, most have adhered to a particular treatment technique (Berg & De Jong, 1998; Biever & Franklin, 1998). As mentioned earlier, Saari (1993, 1999) has articulated general guidelines for evaluating new meaning. These guidelines assume that through the client and therapist dialogue a healthy and "complex, multifaceted identity" will develop. The framework of constructivism allows for use of multiple models of assessment as long as it is clear they are heuristic devices and not "the one way to truth." Of course, the language in the models of assessment chosen must also be understood in terms of its ability to shape treatment.

In utilizing psychodynamic theories to assess client functioning and spirituality it is important to remember also that the purpose is not to reduce spirituality to psychological functioning. But it is important to have some framework for figuring out whether the religion/spirituality can be drawn on as a source of support or whether it is a source of conflict or in what ways it might be both. It is also important to remember that for some clients the very act of discussing spirituality entails introducing ambiguity and consequently complexity, which can be threatening. In addition, raising questions about clients' belief systems can make them feel you are judging their beliefs. It is helpful in the beginning of treatment to assess the degree to which clients will be open to allowing for ambiguity or chaos in their belief systems. The psychodynamic theories help clinicians know how and when to explore client meaning systems.

As part of a usual psychodynamic assessment many experienced clinicians routinely will check, almost without thinking, client's current ego functioning. Included in the group of ego functions considered relevant for assessing mental health are reality testing, judgment, defenses, and impulse control. Object relations also are considered in terms of assessing social relationships and the capacity for intimacy. Rizutto (1979) has made a strong case for the correlation with inpatients between level of object relatedness and conceptions of God. While considering ego functioning is certainly not the definitive tool for determining health, it does provide one means of assessing cognitive and behavioral functioning. If these areas appear intact, then the clinician can move to examine spirituality and religious belief in depth through exploring narratives.

One problem in examining spirituality and religion occurs when these experiences described by clients don't seem healthy from the clinician's subjective position. To help contain the clinician's bias, and to determine whether spiritual experiences

were ego enhancing, the following questions may be helpful: Are the beliefs representative of his or her religious group, community, and family? How does the client articulate the strengths and weaknesses of his or her belief system? How is his or her functioning affected following religious/spiritual experiences? What is the client's concept of God/truth? The goal is to determine if clients' narrative is "sufficiently anchored in the broader meaning system of the client's cultural surround," if there are strengths that will help them grow in desired ways, if the meaning of these experiences is "consonant with the best available understanding of human development and functioning," and if clients' narrated identity enhances their capacity for intimacy with others (Saari, 1999, pp. 9–10). These kinds of constructivist guidelines build on the knowledge base of assessing ego functioning.

The issue of social relatedness is particularly relevant with clients diagnosed as schizophrenic who may describe "mystical experiences." The critical factor in determining whether these experiences are helpful is the degree to which they ultimately enhance social functioning or increase social isolation (Bullis, 1996). Certainly if the clinician makes the determination that a client's experiences may not have been ego enhancing, it does not mean that the clinician tries to talk the client out of those experiences. As with good clinical practice the focus remains on the client's understanding of the experience. But in addition to determining the client's capacity for social relations one also has to determine in ego psychological terms when a client needs shoring up of his or her ego functions and when there are sufficient strengths to uncover more information.

For example, one of my clients described feeling "one with God" in a manner that some clinicians on the clinical team thought was evidence of some form of psychosis. When I explored further with the client, I was able to determine that these unitive experiences helped her cope with loss and separation both from me and from other significant figures in her life. Unfortunately, when she described these experiences they alienated her from others because they came across as grandiose and narcissistic. Over the course of treatment, as she was able to articulate the impact of my unavailability during vacations and the loss of other relationships, the tenor of her experiences changed. She still had periods when she felt she was close to God, but these experiences enhanced her ability to connect with others rather than distancing her from those she cared the most about. When I was not open to the possibility that her experiences were spiritual and saw them only as evidence of faulty object relations, she clammed up and would not elaborate. If I saw them only as mystical experiences that did not need further exploration, I lost the understanding of their function in her psychological world. Both elements were important to ascertain a fuller understanding of her spiritual world, which had enormous potential as a source of support and strength.

Historically, mystics have described a "dark night of the soul" similar to that of St. John of the Cross (Bullis, 1996). This phenomenon also can be differentiated from clinical depression or other mental health problems through the understanding of psychodynamic theories and constructivist ideology. With depression there is little felt sense of spiritual connection or blessing, a sense of worthlessness and inappropriate guilt, and few spiritual insights. This type of depression occurs in response to emptiness and hopelessness. With the "dark night of the soul," depression can result from the outgrowth of a spiritual journey that includes experiences of spiritual fullness and the consequential letdown. There is a sense of unworthiness in the presence of the divine and a sense of appropriate guilt. While the spiritual insights may feel overwhelming, they also can cultivate a sense of blessing and grace.

It is important for the clinician to be familiar with the descriptions of these contrasting experiences to ascertain the sometimes subtle differences. As with any clinical material, the clinician needs to understand the spiritual material and the role it may be serving. For example, new spiritual material could be a prodromal symptom signaling the onset of a manic episode, particularly if there is a dramatic change in belief or behavior. While there would need to be certain safeguards put into place (e.g., medication, interpretations, extra sessions) if the spiritual content emerged in connection to manic depression, clinician and client would still need at some point to construct together the meaning this material has for the client. Finding and articulating the meaning of the spiritual experiences also may serve to help contain the experience, preserve the helpful components, and strengthen the therapeutic relationship.

Reconstruction Phase

Once the clinician has assessed a client's spiritual functioning the challenge is to determine how a client's strengths can be mobilized in order to augment his or her vulnerabilities. This process constitutes the reconstruction phase of treatment. Saari (1999) suggests that "the identity created should bring out existing but dormant abilities in the client such that the client can grow in desired ways" (p. 10). While there are steps in this process, they are not meant to be utilized in a linear manner. As is true in good practice, including religious and spiritual issues in treatment does not mean the clinician adheres to a rigid prescriptive format.

It is helpful for the clinician to reexamine any personal biases regarding the goals of treatment. The clinician also should review with the client the client's goals for treatment. The client and clinician should consider if there are ways religion or spirituality can help or hinder these goals. If religion or spirituality has been a source of support in the past, it can be helpful for the clinician to encourage clients to consider how it might be helpful now or what might be standing in the way of its being helpful. If at all possible, any ideas or initiative should come from the client to guard against feelings of coercion in response to the clinician acting out his or her countertransference. If past experience with religion or spirituality has been difficult or painful, together client and clinician can determine if focusing on these difficulties is beyond the scope of the treatment contract or relevant for the current issues.

Once there has been concrete work done to determine whether religion or spirituality will have an overt role in treatment, the clinician still needs to listen for themes that may reflect spiritual struggles (similar to Cornett or Fleischman). The clinician's job is to verbalize those themes and monitor clients' reactions to the labeling of problems in these spiritual terms. If the language chosen is on target, the clients should respond with relief at having someone understand. They also may show emotion and sadness as a result of having an area of tremendous pain articulated (Cornet, 1998).

In addition to religious themes, client and therapist continue to work together to determine what events, outcomes, or beliefs cannot be explained by the dominant religious or spiritual narrative. Based on the assessment of ego functioning, the clinician determines how to best point out any variations or contradictions in the client story. Clients will need assistance in assessing the effects of any discrepancies and in making a decision of what if anything should be done about that discrepancy. The goal is to "broaden" clients' life stories," rather than "polishing" them (Kelley, 1996, p. 470).

The therapeutic relationship continues to be essential in determining whether other supportive resources are needed to assist the client. It is important that clinicians not be too quick to refer to an outside resource. Zealous referrals communicate discomfort with the subject and impede ongoing therapeutic work. In a similar manner, refusal to consider an appropriate referral due to biases or values will derail the therapeutic process. When possible, clinicians should try to develop collateral relationships with relevant clergy or religious representatives. At the very least, the clinician should become knowledgeable about the authority of church elders, for example, and the attitudes the religious group has toward psychotherapy and medication.

Conclusion

Empowering clients to utilize their religious or spiritual resources to assist them with their problems requires general, sound practice skills. There is nothing magic or gimmicky about good clinical practice. Like all interventions, the efforts to include religion and spirituality should be thoughtfully conducted with the client's well-being and the therapeutic goals that have been mutually decided upon always in mind. Awareness of psychodynamic theories and treatment techniques assists the clinician in understanding and responding to the various meanings religion and spirituality can have for clients. Drawing on the postmodern ideology represented by constructivist practice allows clinicians to not burden themselves or their clients with predetermined answers to therapeutic challenges. The influence of narrative theory provides a framework that guides client and clinician to deconstruct and reconstruct more helpful stories and identities that allow for the complexity and experiences in life. Clinicians can more effectively augment client strengths and reduce client vulnerabilities through understanding psychodynamic theories and constructivist informed practice. Including religion and spirituality in clinical work only enhances this goal.

A version of this paper was presented at the fourth National Clinical Social Work Conference, Washington, D.C., May 2, 1999.

References

Berg, I. K. & De Jong, P. (1998). Solution-building conversations: Co-constructing a sense of competence with clients. In C. Franklin & P. S. Nurius (eds.) *Constructivism in practice: Methods and challenges.* Milwaukee, WI: Families International (235–258).

Biever, J. L. & Franklin, C. (1998). Social constructionism in action: Using reflecting teams in family practice. In C. Franklin & P. S. Nurius (eds.) *Constructivism in practice: Methods and challenges.* Milwaukee, WI: Families International (259–278).

Bullis, R. K. (1996). *Spirituality in social work practice.* Bristol, PA: Taylor & Francis.

Canda, E. (1988). Spirituality, religious diversity, and social work practice. *Social Casework,* 69(4), 238–247.

Carbo, R. A. & Gartner, J. (1994). Can religious communities become dysfunctional families? Sources of countertransference for the religiously committed psychotherapist. *Journal of Psychology and Theology,* 22, 264–271.

Carpenter, D. (1996). Constructivism and social work treatment. In F. J. Turner (ed.) *Social work treatment: Interlocking theoretical approaches,* 4th edition. New York: Free Press (146–167).

Case, P. W. (1997). Potential sources of countertransference among religious therapists. *Counseling and Values,* 41, 97–106.

Cornett, C. (1998). *The soul of psychotherapy.* New York: Free Press.

Dean, R. G. (1993). Constructivism: An approach to clinical practice. *Smith College Studies in Social Work,* 63(2), 127–146.

Fleischman, P. R. (1989). *The healing zone: Religious issues in psychotherapy.* New York: Parragon House.

Franklin, C. & Jordan, C. (1998). Qualitative assessment: A methodological review. In C. Franklin & P. S. Nurius (eds.) *Constructivism in practice: Methods and challenges.* Milwaukee, WI: Families International (97–114).

Franklin, C. & Nurius, P. S. (1998). *Constructivism in practice: Methods and challenges.* Milwaukee, WI: Families International.

Freud, S. (1914). Remembering, repeating, and working through. *Standard Edition,* 12, 145–156. [1927] London: Hogarth Press.

Freud, S. (1927). The future of an illusion: *Standard Edition,* 21, 5–56. London: Hogarth Press, 1959.

Giglio, J. (1993). The impact of patients' and therapists' religious values on psychotherapy. *Hospital and Community Psychiatry,* 44, 768–771.

Granvold, D. (1998). Constructivist psychotherapy. In C. Franklin & P. S. Nurius (eds.) *Constructivism in practice: Methods and challenges.* Milwaukee, WI: Families International (141–164).

Gray, H. (1998). Consilium keynote speaker. Unpublished manuscript. Loyola University of Chicago. July 7.

Hall, M. E. L. & Hall, T. W. (1997). Integration in the therapy room: An overview of the literature. *Journal of Psychology and Theology*, 25(1), 86–101.

Joseph, M. (1988). Religion and social work practice. *Social Casework*, 69, 443–452.

Katan, A. (1961). Some thoughts about the role of verbalization in early childhood. *Psychoanalytic Study of the Child*, 16, 184–188. New York: International Universities Press.

Kehoe, N. C. & Gutheil, T. G. (1984). Shared religious belief as resistance in psychotherapy. *American Journal of Psychotherapy*, 38, 579–585.

Kelley, P. (1996). Narrative theory and social work treatment. In F. J. Turner (ed.) *Social work treatment: Interlocking theoretical approaches*, 4th edition. New York: Free Press (461–479).

Kochems, T. (1993). Countertransference and transference aspects of religious material in psychotherapy: The isolation or integration of religious material. In M. L. Randour (ed.) *Exploring sacred landscapes: Religious and spiritual experiences in psychotherapy* (34–54). New York: Columbia University Press.

Mahoney, M. J. (1998). Continuing evolution of the cognitive sciences and psychotherapies. In C. Franklin & P. S. Nurius (eds.) *Constructivism in practice: Methods and challenges*. Milwaukee, WI: Families International (3–24).

Narramore, S. B. (1994). Dealing with religious resistances in psychotherapy. *Journal of Psychology and Theology*, 12, 15–23.

Neimeyer, G. J., Hagans, C. L., & Anderson, R. (1998). Intervening in meaning: Applications of constructivist assessment. In C. Franklin & P. S. Nurius (eds.) *Constructivism in practice: Methods and challenges*. Milwaukee, WI: Families International (115–140).

Northcut, T. B. (1991). *The level of referential activity in time-limited dynamic psychotherapy*. Unpublished doctoral dissertation, Smith College, Northampton, MA.

Raines, J. C. (1999). Dissertation proposal: Countertransference issues with spiritually similar clients. Unpublished manuscript. Loyola University, Chicago, IL.

Ramirez, B. R. (1985). Hispanic spirituality. *Social Thought*, 11(3), 6–13.

Rizutto, A. M. (1979). *The birth of the living god: A psychoanalytic study*. Chicago: University of Chicago Press.

Rothenberg, D. J. (1997). Formulation, psychic space, and time: New dimensions in psychoanalysis and Jewish spirituality. In C. Spezzano and G. J. Gargiulo (eds.) *Soul on the couch: Spirituality, religion and morality in contemporary psychoanalysis*. Hillsdale, NJ: Analytic Press.

Saari, C. (1991). *The creation of meaning in clinical social work*. New York: Guilford Press.

Saari, C. (1993). Identity complexity as an indicator of health. *Clinical Social Work Journal*, 21(1), 11–23.

Saari, C. (1999). Therapeutic dialogue as means of creating identity complexity. Submitted to *Smith College Studies in Social Work*.

Scharfenberg, J. (1988). The therapy: Healing through language. In *Sigmund Freud and His Critique of Religion*, trans. O. C. Dean, Jr. (76–100). Philadelphia: Fortress.

Schlink, B. (1995). *The Reader*. Trans. C. B. Janeway. New York: Vintage Books.

White, M. & Epston, D. (1990). *Narrative means to therapeutic ends*. New York: Norton.

58

Mental Health and Social Justice: Gender, Race, and Psychological Consequences of Unfairness

On the face of it, social justice and mental health are strange bedfellows. Social justice is concerned, as its name would suggest with the "social." Its focus is on the distribution of, in particular, material goods as between different groups. Mental health, or at least mental ill health, some conventional wisdom might suggest, is an individual issue. The state of mental ill health resides within the individual, and the proper focus of treatment is on the person with the mental illness. Some views from the antipsychiatric movement, which, however, tend to have rather less currency among the most influential circles than in the past, would indicate that mental ill health is less a property of the individual than of groups, which create rules whose transgression is labeled as mental illness.

However, few would contest the idea that mental ill health has a social context, as opposed to a social content. This can operate in two ways. Part of the identification of mental illness requires unraveling, for the individual sufferer, the meaning of the content of ideas to the individual. This can help understanding, for example, of the nature of depressed mood, or the extent to which there is a delusional content in ideas of an individual. The social context, furthermore, can be relevant in a way more obviously related to social justice. The link between the distribution of material goods and the mental health state of social groups has been a proper focus for the study of social psychiatry for many decades.

Even where limited to the issue of material goods, therefore, there seems some connection between social justice and mental health. We can ask, for example, What is the connection between the distribution of material wealth of different groups in society and the epidemiology of mental illness? This is no academic question. The position of some on the new right would suggest that there is no such thing as social justice or, more precisely, that the only coherent notion of social justice is the distribution of material goods according to the working of the market (Hayek, 1974). This view, which would generally be considered extreme in Western industrial society, would reasonably lead to the question: Are there mental health consequences to a distribution based on market principles? Indeed, in view of the experience of Britain under Thatcher, or of the United States in relation to the Republican right, we could legitimately ask a more subtle question: To what extent does a greater adherence to market principles have an impact on the mental health state of differently rewarded social groups? Such a question would immediately link the political commitment of governments with the personal experience of mental health and illness in individuals and groups.

Behind this lies a notion of *fairness*: that we should seek to be fair in the distribution of material good between individuals and groups. This, in turn, relates to the issue of equality, not a simple one whereby all individuals or groups should be equal in all aspects of life. Rather, social justice has, at its heart, the notion of equal *treatment* for all. In general this is viewed in three dimensions: in terms of rights, in terms of desert, and in terms of need (Franklin, 1998). A socially just notion of rights would be that we would all have equal rights under the law (for example, to inheritance of wealth from relatives). One based on desert would entail that people would receive reward for individual effort or punishment for morally opprobrious behavior. Need is at the heart of social justice where social response is based on disadvantage: for example, those who are poorest would, as a result of their poverty, be given access to material goods which would limit the effects of their disadvantage. Plainly these principles do not always lead in the same direction: allowing inheritance would advantage rich families the most (despite the appearance of equality in the right itself), while a needs-based response to poverty would tend to limit material inequality.

It is the notion of need that would appear to be the clearest base for a link between social justice and mental health. To what extent, this line would run, do inequalities in society lead to a state of need (mental ill health) which is differential as between different social groups? Where different population groups suffer differing rates of mental ill health, this raises the question about the extent to which equality of treatment, in the broadest sense, is being experienced by these population groups, when compared with other population groups, or the population as a whole. The idea of need here is linked to the notion of harm, particularly significant harm. An individual or group is in a state of need where the state of affairs that they are experiencing is likely to lead to their suffering significant harm (Miller, 1976). Doyal and Gough (1991) identify the most basic of needs to relate to autonomy and health (and, of course, life, since neither of these would be possible otherwise). British welfare professionals are well aware of the use of the term *significant harm* as an important legal dimension to the protection of children.

However, a notion of need, or inequalities, based simply on the distribution of material wealth would provide us with a very limited way of examining the link between social justice and mental health, even though this relationship is itself a proper focus for study. We need rather to understand not just the *material* dimension of social justice but also the *symbolic* dimension. By the latter, I mean the influence of values, attitudes, expectations, and norms on the ways social groups operate, how these groups relate to each other, and the ways individuals within groups and the wider so-

ciety interact. This would lead to the question: To what extent do the material and symbolic arrangements of a society have a systematic and differential effect on the mental health and ill health of its constituent groups?

This, in turn, leads to a focus on the cultural and normative arrangements of the society and groups within it. Are the normative expectations of different groups within society such that they differentially affect their opportunity for mental health and illness? Are the norms adopted by sections within society such that they are likely to manifest behaviours which will systematically harm, in terms of mental health, particular groups? Such questions allow us to move towards the issue of discrimination. However discrimination is a social act (or set of acts). We are concerned with their psychological consequences. We need, therefore, to consider the intervening mechanisms by which particular social acts or arrangements, which involve the production of disadvantage or discrimination, can be linked with, and lead to, differential mental health states in different social groups.

It would not do, however, to focus on a simplistic, overarching notion of mental health or ill health. The general idea of mental illness covers a wide and diverse range of psychological states. Each of these manifests different characteristics and has different causal elements. Just as it makes sense to concentrate on social justice in terms of need—because mental ill health would be seen to be the consequence of particular systems of social relations, and because they would lead to the significant harm of mental ill health—so it is necessary to look at particular systems of social relations in relation to particular mental ill health. Within this general framework of ideas we shall look at the link between race and schizophrenia, specifically the vulnerability in particular of young Afro-Caribbean males to the diagnosis of schizophrenia. We will also look at the link between gender and depression. We shall be concerned with both of these in two dimensions: the ways in which social relations help produce mental ill health and the response of mental health services to these social groups.

It should be emphasized that I do not here wish to get into the issue of biological versus psychological and social factors in the genesis of mental ill health as a whole. To state that there are social causes or influences on mental ill health is not to exclude the possibility of biological dimensions. Likewise, if there are biological dimensions, this does not exclude social factors. Furthermore, where they do influence facets of mental ill health, they may influence different forms, and different aspects of them, variably. Rather, what I seek to do is highlight some aspects of social life that may be considered systematically to disadvantage some social groups to a greater degree than others.

Inequality of Distribution of Mental Ill Health

Disadvantage and discrimination tend to go hand in hand. That this is the case with mental ill health has been established for a number of decades. In the middle of the past century, a number of studies, using methods admittedly less sophisticated than those of today, established a relationship between class, poverty, and mental disorder. Work by Hollingshead and Redlich (1958) showed a strong relationship between social class and patient status (whether or not subjects were patients). The trend of low social class associated with patient status was strongest in those suffering schizophrenia. Similar results were found by Myers and Bean (1968) and Birtchall (1971). Likewise, early community studies showed a similar trend, where those with the lowest socioeconomic status were likely to suffer higher rates of mental disorder (Srole et al., 1961). More recent studies have found similar trends (Cochrane and Stopes Roe, 1980; Muntauer et al., 1999; Bebbington et al., 2000).

Gender has also been the base for greater frequency of mental disorder. As with other areas, this rather depends on *which* mental disorder you are looking at. While there is a tendency for more men to suffer from schizophrenia (on data from patient status), women have been shown consistently to suffer from depression with a far greater frequency than men. This is the case with inpatient statistics (Pilgrim and Rogers, 1999) and has been shown with community samples. In study after study in Western industrial countries, women have been shown to suffer from depression at a rate around twice that of men (Weissman and Klerman, 1977; Schwartz and Schwartz, 1993). Where poverty and gender disadvantage go hand in hand, the rates get even higher, and Moss and Plewis (1977) and Richman et al., (1982) found rates of symptoms to rise above 50% in deprived urban populations. In Brown and Harris's (1978) classic study, they found just under a quarter of working-class women suffered the onset of psychiatric disorder over one year, four times the rate of middle-class women.

Race presents a picture with still further differences. It is more difficult to obtain data on ethnic groups, because until recently such monitoring did not take place (with a few exceptions). There appears to be a tendency for lower rates of mental disorder among, for example, Asians than Afro-Caribbeans. This is clearly the case with compulsory admissions (Barnes et al., 1990). In the latter case (Afro-Caribbeans), and particularly in relation to young males, there seem to be considerably higher rates of schizophrenia than in the general population as a whole (Regier et al., 1994). Again, therefore, the issue of the specific mental illness comes to the fore. However, there is some question about the extent to which the diagnosis of schizophrenia is, in fact, an artifact of the diagnostic criteria themselves, or the ways that they are applied, rather than this representing a real picture of differences according to ethnicity. One study that did, however, take considerable care to apply diagnostic criteria in a way consistent with local community perspectives nevertheless found far higher rates among Afro-Caribbean males (Harrison et al., 1988).

How do adverse social circumstances contribute to mental health problems?

Environment, Racism, and Mental Disorder

Adverse environmental circumstances, both material and in terms of social interaction, are systematically associated with mental disorder. What, then, is the link between these circumstances and high rates of schizophrenia identified in young black Afro-Caribbean males? There is little doubt that, as a whole, Afro-Caribbeans live in considerably greater disadvantage in economic, material, and opportunity terms when compared with the white population. Afro-Caribbeans are systematically disadvantaged in terms of life opportunities in areas such as education, housing, and employment and are, of course subject to racial harassment and discrimination (Drew, 1995; Troyna et al., 1997; Connolly and Troyna, 1998). The discrimination, while experienced in a day-to-day fashion, in general harassment, the language used and racially motivated violence experienced, also operates systematically in the ways, for example, employment opportunities are denied, the consequences of which are reflected, among other things, in the higher rates of unemployment experienced by young Afro-Caribbean males. Where they are employed, this tends to be more frequently, compared with the general population, in lower-status, more menial work. This itself is not helped by poorer educational performance, which is associated with an education system that is perceived as not to meet their needs properly and from which many young black people feel alienated.

There is evidence of a subjective perception by Afro-Caribbeans that disadvantage does play a major part in contributing to rates of mental disorder. One study focused on the views of Afro-Caribbean mental health service users about the impact of environmental pressures on mental health state. They identified a number of such contributory problems. These included growing up in a hostile environment, with few positive and many negative images of black people, the alienating nature of the education system, and problems of adolescence (a problem shared with their white counterparts, but that had particular resonance because of the wider racism). They also felt that some confusion over identity, arising from the predominant white British culture, played a significant part in generating mental health problems (Frederick, 1991). These have a general theme emphasizing stress as a cause of mental health problems.

However, this does not help us to understand why one particular mental disorder and not another is the result of this stress. In the case of young black Afro-Caribbean males, schizophrenia rather than any other mental disorder is highlighted. There is no direct evidence as to how stress experienced should manifest itself in this particular way. However, the link between expressed emotion and schizophrenia in general may provide some idea of the connection. Expressed emotion (EE) has been studied primarily in terms of the family context for schizophrenia (Leff and Vaughn, 1984; Kuipers, 1994; Hashemi and Cochrane, 1999). The basic finding is that where the family manifests high levels of expressed emotion, and when this is associated with sufficient face-to-face contact between the person with schizophrenia and high EE relatives, the likelihood of relapse is significantly higher. These findings, it should be emphasized, relate to relapse rather than onset of schizophrenia, although in the detailed study by Leff and Vaughn there was some indication, from the interviews with family members, that high EE was a sustained feature of these families and that this may have preceded onset.

Expressed emotion was measured mainly in terms of hostility, emotional overinvolvement, and critical comments, but the primary factor seems to be critical comments. While these studies have been confined largely to families, they do seem to point to the significance of demeaning and threatening critical comments. The effect of high EE is considerable, and people with schizophrenia often seek avoidance strategies, particularly exiting themselves from social interaction, when confronted with it. The aggressive, esteem-reducing nature of routine racism experienced by Afro-Caribbeans, and which, of course, would not be experienced by their white counterparts, may well play a contributory part in higher rates of schizophrenia.

A simple two-stage model of genesis is not unusual, which involves (1) vulnerability and (2) provoking factors, the combination of which is required to produce mental disorder in any individual. The vulnerability is some factor that predisposes the individual toward the particular illness, without, on its own, leading to that illness. The provoking agents are factors that, *in addition to* the vulnerability, are necessary to produce the illness. The vulnerability might, in principle, be biological, psychological, or social. We could assume a similar vulnerability to schizophrenia in different population groups, but that one population group (Afro-Caribbeans) would be far more likely to experience provoking agents than others. The provoking agent, in this case, would be high expressed emotion in the form of routine experience of racism. The result would be higher rates of schizophrenia among Afro-Caribbeans. This might help explain the specificity of this mental disorder, while linking it with the experience of racism. Higher rates of schizophrenia, on this model, would, in Afro-Caribbean males, be an indicator of their experience of oppression.

Environment, Gender, and Depression

The link between social environment and higher rates of depression found in women may be understood, to a considerable degree, in terms of sex role and sex role stereotyping. Where traditional sex roles predominate, there is evidence that women are likely to suffer higher rates of depression. The general thesis of a number of feminist writers (e.g., Corob, 1988; Smith and Nairne, 1995) is that traditional sex roles are likely to engender, to a greater degree in women than in men, low self-esteem, feelings of helplessness, and an external locus of control. It would follow, of course, from this, that where women were able to move away from traditional sex roles and to have wider opportunities for personal development, we would expect the rates of depression to fall. Hence, the thesis being offered here is that the greater the extent to which social relations encourage traditional sex roles, the greater the likelihood of women suffering systematically higher rates of depression. The key to this is in understanding the relationship between facets of traditional female sex roles and psychological features specifically associated with depression. Of particular importance here is the significance, on the one hand, of the ways traditional sex roles act to encourage low self-esteem and a sense, respectively, of helplessness and external locus of control and, on the other, the link between self-esteem, helplessness, and depression.

Sex role stereotyping emerges in the socializing processes occurring from childhood. This socializing process is of particular significance, because it provides from the earliest stages in a person's life the opportunity for "imprinting" particular attitudes, expectations, and cognitions that can contribute to a sense of helplessness or low self-esteem. Many feminists argue that women in families with traditional sex role values have shown a tendency to prefer boys to girls. This means that they start life with parental attitudes that are liable to leave them with feelings of being second best. The fact of their femaleness encourages a sense of inferiority, of being less highly regarded, when compared with males. Welburn (1980) quotes a woman who damns with faint praise on the birth of her daughter, saying that she "did not mind because you can dress them pretty."

This tendency to male preference evident in traditional sex role–oriented families does seem to be showing some decline in recent years. There is evidence, for example, through surveys of pregnant women, that the majority of women did not mind what sex their child was going to be. Of the rest, there was a rough equivalence between women whose preference was for a boy and those whose preferred choice was a girl (Cambridge Centre for Family Research, 1993). While this does not amount to a ringing endorsement of girls, it does point toward a greater equality of preference between the sexes. Of course, many adult women grew up at a time when this greater attitude for equality was not prevalent, so they will not have benefited from these changes, which may be expected to take effect on girls who are currently growing up. Certainly, there is evidence that it is still true that many women feel that their brothers were and are more important to their parents than they are (Billington, 1994). It is in this subjective feeling of inferiority that a reduced sense of self-esteem is encouraged in women.

One key way this can be manifested is in fewer educational opportunities being made available to girls. Girls may be subject to a relative lack of encouragement for their education, and educational achievement, when compared with boys. In traditional sex role families, the role of the male as sole breadwinner (a feature that has been in decline in recent years, as women increasingly take part in part-time work) makes this preference for male education understandable, if not defensible. The relatively low encouragement for a girl's education implies that the girl is less likely to be "important as an individual" when she enters the wider world (Spender, 1982). Education affects life chances: those with a better education are likely to have better job prospects, a greater opportunity to pursue a career, greater job security, and higher pay. There would be less of a sense of control over the direction of one's life, and hence a greater sense of helplessness. It is also associated with depression. One large study of young mothers found a highly significant relationship between education and depression, one that exercised an *independent* effect in a multivariable analysis (M. Sheppard, 1997). The poorer the education received, the more likely were women, as adults, to be suffering a major depression.

The quality of nurturance received may also have considerable impact. There are, of course, significant class and racial differences in, for example, the amount of physical contact expressed in families (Howe, 1995). However, findings from classic psychological research have shown definite differences in the ways parents behave toward their children, according to the sex of the child (Shaffer, 1999; Richardson, 2000). In one study, for example, adults given a baby to handle responded quite differently according to whether they believed the child was a girl or a boy (Maccoby and Jacklin, 1974). The lack of nurturing results in what Chesler (1972) has called "submission conditioning," whereby women feel they have to grow up behaving in ways that essentially respond to what others want, rather than what they would like to be, in order to obtain the desired affection and value. They, in turn, learn that, to be loved and approved by others they must be nurturing and emotionally giving (Eichenbaum and Orbach, 1985). This "other-regarding" orientation leaves their self-worth dependent on other's approval, leaving a locus of control in important areas of their life in an external rather than internal location: they have less control over the circumstances that are likely to make them feel good about themselves. There is evidence that the potential positive effects of personal characteristics on mental well-being of adolescent girls is affected by traditional sex role expectations within their familial context (Obeidallah et al., 1996) and that failing to perform adequately according to internalized sex role expectations can lead to self-criticism and depressed mood (Grimmel, 1998). Extreme lack of nurturance, furthermore, in the form of the experience of child abuse has been shown to be a major factor related to depression in adult women (Bifulco and Moran, 1999).

As adults, women's traditional roles have also been associated with depression; child care is an obvious dimension of women's traditional responsibilities as female parent. Women are overwhelmingly the primary caregivers for children. Where separation occurs, it is generally the mother left "holding the baby." According to the British Census of 1991, around 90% of single parents are women. Traditionally women have been regarded widely as the "natural" childcarers (M. Sheppard, 1993). The basis for this, it has been generally assumed, is some kind of biological "programming" which underlies motherhood and through which the strong bond between mother and child is created. This has been reflected, and further reinforced, by Bowlby's early ideas about attachment and the woman's central role in creating and maintaining a strong bond with the child for its stable development (ideas that have, admittedly, been subsequently developed and changed) (Howe, 1995; J. Sheppard, 2000).

The idealized image of motherhood as one that is fulfilling and safe that has been projected in the media is, however, frequently not reflected in the reality of women's lives. The transition to parenthood for many women involves stressful responsibility for the child's life and well-being. The problem of postnatal depression is well-known, and although this has frequently been considered a predominantly biological issue, there is clear evidence of highly significant social factors. Many of the elements of disadvantage identified with "wider [nonpostnatal]" depression have been identified for postnatal depression itself (Cox et al., 1994; Murray et al., 1995). There is also clear evidence from an authoritative review of studies of social support and postnatal depression that a combination of poverty and traditional sex role segregation is likely to increase vulnerability to depression (M. Sheppard, 1994).

The early years, in particular, can emphasize the woman's "entrapment" in the role of mother. The relentless demands placed by children on the mother, particularly one who predominantly is the primary caregiver, can leave the mother with a limited sense of self, her identity subsumed as she responds to the child's needs. The responsibilities of child care can both help create new social contacts, by, for example, contact with other mothers, or restrict their former capacity for such contacts, as the responsibilities of child care reduce opportunities for socializing. Furthermore, their feelings of entrapment and subsumed identity contrast strongly with media images of motherhood as a fulfilling and rewarding activity, leaving women with a sense of having failed to live up to standards that "most other" women are able to achieve. The larger the family, furthermore, the greater the problem. There is clear evidence that large families present a vulnerability factor for depression, with three or more children age under 14 being of particular significance (Brown and Harris, 1978). It would seem that the demands placed by children on the mother, particularly working-class mothers, mean they fail to live up to their own expectations and standards, with the consequence of a negative effect on their self-esteem. Likewise, single mothers are more vulnerable to depression (Brown, 1986). This can again be related to demands being placed on them (without the support of a partner) and the greater likelihood of living in strained financial circumstances, leaving them pressured and feeling less in control of their lives. The extreme consequences of this is evident in the links between maternal depression and child protection and consequent social work involvement (M. Sheppard, 2001).

Housework carries in general a low status and is unlikely to enhance a sense of self-esteem. Those who seek esteem from its performance are not focusing on an activity highly valued. Often it is taken for granted and contrasted with the "real work" of paid employment. Furthermore, the activity itself is not experienced by many women to be very rewarding. It does, unlike much paid work, carry a lack of supervision and high level of autonomy. However, particularly where it is carried out routinely, there are no dramatic results. The house simply remains neat, with little positive change. It is difficult to know when you have done enough, and monitoring can only be done by your own standards. Indeed, of course, the best efforts can be quickly undone by active children or partners. The work is never ending, invisible, routine, and often boring. These facets seem to be strongly related to a raised likelihood of depression (Siedal, 1978; Miles, 1988: Bracegirdle, 1991). Most men and women, when asked, would usually say that household tasks should be shared. However, in practice, most families do not have an equal division of household labor between the woman and her (male) partner, even where the woman is working in paid employment full time or part time (Harman, 1993; Bird, 1999).

The employment status of women can exert a positive effect. Brown and Harris (1978) found that employment could have a protective effect in relation to depression. Paid employment is not just a source of income, but also a means for wider social contacts (Bromberg and Mathews, 1994). In principle it can raise self-esteem by giving a sense of making a valued or useful contribution (Glass and Fujimoto, 1994). Women with young children who prefer employment but have to remain at home have reported higher levels of depressive symptomatology (Hock and DeMeiss, 1990). However, the picture is not straightforward. Women remain more frequently involved in part-time and more insecure employment, with lower wages, by comparison with men. Such work can itself be monotonous and morale sapping. Where the pressure of paid work and child care and home responsibilities become too great, however, depressive symptoms can be the result (Glass and Fujimoto, 1994). While paid work can provide opportunities for women to broaden horizons, have greater financial independence, or at least contribution, and hence a greater sense of control over their lives, women are frequently required to continue to take primary responsibility in the home while nevertheless holding down a job. Where paid employment occurs within an otherwise traditional sex role–oriented family, the pressures can contribute to psychological ill health (Parry 1986, 1987).

Culture, Stereotypes, and the Response of Mental Health Services

Black Afro-Caribbeans and Schizophrenia

Psychiatry, it has been suggested, has been affected by long-held prejudices of black inferiority, which stems from the time of slavery (Rack, 1982; Fernando, 1988). Deeply held racist views of white superiority are insidiously incorporated into the discipline of psychiatry, where mental illness, and in particular some of its more virulent types, such as schizophrenia, are highly stigmatized. Where particular ethnic groups are found to suffer such illness to a systematically greater extent than other population groups, this provides a clear and stigmatizing impression of racial inferiority. Whether or not one agrees with Szasz (1976) as a whole, it is difficult to argue with his view that psychiatry, particularly in relation to psychotic disorders, has the capacity for degradation of individuals and groups. Psychiatry becomes, perhaps inadvertently, a significant means for the perpetration of racism and racist views.

On this view (unlike that propounded above, that mental ill health is an index of the real experience of oppression by some minority ethnic groups), high rates of mental illness, particularly those most stigmatizing, are a mere artifact, manufactured by the individual practices of psychiatrists or, more widely, systematically through institutional racism that exists in psychiatry. One line of criticism is that there is a high degree of ethnocentricity in the practical conduct of psychiatry, dominated as it is by Western, white (and male) ethnic groups (Littlewood and Lipsedge, 1997; Fernando, 1988, 1995). White psychiatrists, it is suggested, have little appreciation of major cultural differences between their own and minority ethnic groups. Such psychiatrists are oblivious to nuances of perceptions and behavior, the result of which is a misunderstanding of the meaning of acts by minority ethnic groups. What appears as evidence of a delusion to a white psychiatrist may be quite meaningful behavior within the cultural context of the individual's own ethnic group. This may extend to psychiatric studies, as well as the day-to-day practice of psychiatrists. Where cultural stereotypes feature in studies, Fernando (1988) suggests, it is difficult to make accurate estimates of prevalence, while misclassification can have a considerable effect on perceived rates of mental illness (Francis et al., 1989).

Part of this problem lies in the positivist commitment of psychiatry. Psychiatry is seen as a branch of medicine, a knowledge-based activity based on objectivity (Busfield, 1986; Tyrer and Steinberg, 1998). There can be a tendency to read this objectivity to mean similar behaviors should be regarded similarly, without reference to ethnic group and cultural differences. Although it would be quite wrong to suggest that psychiatry is generally perceived by psychiatrists to be entirely biophysically based, the sensitivity to the significance of culture is likely to be diminished by the emphasis placed on the biophysical in psychiatry. The absence of attention to ethnic differences and cultural nuance can lead, as Littlewood and Lipsedge (1997) have commented, to the use of terms such as *cannabis psychosis* and *schizophrenia* when black people appear to display disturbed behavior, while conditions like depression may be underdiagnosed. They draw attention to the difficulties experienced by psychiatrists in diagnosis, by noting the greater frequency with which black patients, compared with their white counterparts, have changes of diagnosis over time.

Scheff's (1984) concept of residual rule breaking may help account for this. Scheff's work has been largely ignored by mainstream psychiatry because of its association with, for them, the discredited antipsychiatry movement of the 1960s. However, it is not necessary to accept a hard-line notion of labeling causing mental illness (to the exclusion of other factors) to recognize that some aspects of his theory have considerable interest in examining the possibility of racism in psychiatry. Scheff distinguished between explicit rules and residual rules. The former are stated or written down and appear in the form of, for example, legal rules, rules of etiquette, and club rules. They are overt. Residual rules, on the other hand are not rules that are explicitly identified, but taken for granted. These are rules of social behavior, which separate, broadly speaking, what is considered "normal" from what is considered "odd" or "strange." Such behaviors are considered to be odd or strange because they are incomprehensible: they do not make any sense.

Scheff suggests that those actions or perceptions that are considered to be symptoms of mental illness are contraventions of these residual rules. Hence hallucinations, delusions, withdrawal, or continual muttering by individuals are examples of residual rule breaking. Residual rules, defining the borderline between normal and strange, are culture-related. What may appear normal in one culture appears strange in another. A belief in being possessed by devils, a belief acceptable in some cultures, would not, in general, be perceived as normal in white groups in 21st-century Britain. On the other hand, praying (apparently to nothing at all), provided it is carried out in the appropriate context, would not generally be considered evidence of mental illness.

These ideas do not preclude the possibility that, to a greater or lesser extent, behavioral disturbance is the result of biophysical facets. Indeed, we can be quite agnostic about this. Residual rules relate to the interpretation of behavior and perceptions. The notion of residual rules indicates strongly that, in the understanding of normal or strange behavior, a proper understanding of culture and cultural context is required. Where psychiatry, suffused by positivist scientism and dominated by white ethnic groups, comes into contact with disadvantaged groups with different expectations, the opportunity for misinterpretation is considerable.

Of course, this notion—that higher rates of mental disorder are an artifact of psychiatric practice—would seem to contrast with the idea that mental disorder might be caused by social factors, and rates could reflect the degree of oppression experienced by these groups. Are social causation and social reaction theories contradictory? There has been a tendency to view these as such (Fernando et al., 1998). The overrepresentation of Afro-Caribbean males can only be *either* the result of racist attitudes inappropriately labeling these people with mental illnesses, *or* the result of real social causes with real psychological consequences. However, these explanations are not necessarily contradictory at all. It is perfectly plausible that disadvantage, social attitudes, behaviors, and experiences of oppressed groups have deleterious psychological consequences, *at the same time* as suggesting, for example, that cultural difference between diagnoser and diagnosed can have a tendency to raise rates of mental disorder higher than that merited by its real experience.

The influence of race and culture is reflected in the processes of mental health provision. Where racism and the stigmatizing effect of labeling people mentally ill plays a significant part in the psychiatric process, we would expect the overrepresentation of stigmatized groups in the most draconian service responses. One of these involves compulsory admission. Barnes et al. (1990) undertook a large study of compulsory admission assessments involving Approved Social Workers (ASWs). They show how there is systematic overrepresentation of Afro-Caribbeans in the compulsory admission process. In a study of 10 local authorities with significant ethnic minority populations, they found overrepresentation of Afro-Caribbeans in referral for compulsory admission (by a ratio of about 2:1 compared with the overall sample), and a greater likelihood, when referred, that they would be compulsorily admitted. One contributory factor in this excess of Afro-Caribbeans in referrals (a considerable proportion of which did not emanate from the psychiatric services) could be described as cultural distance. This is the idea that the greater the cultural distance between, in this case, referrer and referred, the more likely the referred are to be labeled mentally ill (Horowitz, 1977).

Where emergency applications for compulsory admission were concerned (section 4 of the Mental Health Act), Afro-Caribbeans were more likely to be admitted than those from other ethnic groups.

While 80% of Afro-Caribbeans referred for emergency admission were admitted, this was the case with only 59% of other groups. There was a strong emphasis on schizophrenia, furthermore, this being the diagnosis of choice with 74% of males and 60% of females. The tendency for more young Afro-Caribbean males to be referred, they felt, was likely to be associated with the idea of "dangerousness"—that they were "bad or mad." Barnes et al. (1990, p. 171) commented that "the cumulative decisions made by these workers is indicative of a racist response to the mental health problems of those referred to them."

The criminal justice system, when related to mental disorder, provides another venue for over-representation of Afro-Caribbean males. The police (who are, of course, part of the agencies concerned with criminality) are also significant in relation to Afro-Caribbeans (Rogers and Faulkener, 1987). Under section 136 of the Mental Health Act, they have the power to take to a place of safety an individual who, in a public place, appears to be suffering from a mental disorder and is in immediate need of care and control. They can be taken to a place of safety for up to 72 hours. Bean et al. (1991) have shown that, when compared with white people living in the community, Afro-Caribbeans proportionately have a rate of detention that goes up to over twice that of white people. As with compulsory admissions involving approved social workers, furthermore, those Afro-Caribbean people who are detained have a greater tendency to be young and male.

Another aspect of criminal proceedings—the courts and prisons—play a part. This is covered in part 111 of the Mental Health Act and relates to mentally disordered offenders. As with compulsory admissions, young black males are likely to be involved with mental health services more than their white counterparts, only to a vastly greater extent. McGovern and Cope (1987; Cope, 1989) found that second-generation and migrant Afro-Caribbeans were referred 29 *times* more frequently than white males. Likewise, Norris's (1984) study of those discharged from special hospitals found the proportion of black males was higher than would be expected from the general population.

Gender and Professional Responses

As with race, so in relation to gender, social explanations of mental ill health do not preclude our

examining social reaction. These may be considered in terms of the views of the general population. Horowitz (1977) found that women were more likely to be labeled by kin group and friends as having psychiatric problems. Jones and Cochrane (1981) found that, in the general population, the characteristics used to describe the mentally healthy man were very different from those used to describe the mentally ill man. However, those used to describe the mentally ill woman were not very different from those of the mentally healthy women. It may well be, therefore, that mental illness is widely seen to have an essentially feminine quality (especially when applying traits recognizable in traditional sex roles).

There is evidence, furthermore, that the practices of mental health professionals contribute to the labeling and stigmatizing of women. A classic study of the attitude of mental health professionals (Broverman et al., 1970) examined the extent to which the decisions of mental health clinicians are based on sex-stereotypical assumptions. They were asked to choose, from a number of characteristics, those that are typical of the healthy, mature, and socially competent person, with the sex unspecified. That which was considered to be healthy for adults was also considered to be healthy for men. However, this was not the case for women. Women who were healthy were considered, for example, to be more submissive, passive, dependent, emotional, excitable, and concerned with their appearance. In effect, if they were to be considered healthy people, the women could not have the characteristics that were considered to be womanly, or they could keep their womanhood and be considered not to be healthy adults. They could not win either way. These results have been replicated in other studies in the 1970s (Fabrikant, 1974; Aslin, 1977).

Of course, both the general population's and mental health professionals' view may have changed in the period from the 1970s. However, there is some evidence of continued problems relating to gender and mental health beliefs from Kaplan et al. (1990; Heesacker et al., 1999). They found, interestingly that although male psychiatrists tended to identify undifferentiated gender characteristics as optimal for the mental health of both sexes, women psychiatrists rated masculine traits as optimal for female patients. There may be some circularity here. Busfield (1982) suggested there may be some differentiation in type of disorder in terms of sex characteristics. Abnormality and femininity may converge, for example, with phobic disorders, to the extent that women are expected and permitted to be more fearful than men.

Medical attitudes and use of tranquilizers can reflect conventional attitudes to women, alongside a predisposition to a biophysical response to problems. Barrett and Roberts (1978) found GPs sought to smooth away "surface anxieties" and adjust women to a life largely located in the home. Doctors frequently used medical-moral language to offer a set of social prescriptions reflecting conventional wisdom in their own social milieu. The use of tranquilizers provides a further means for dealing, in a medical way, with emotional problems that can be rooted in more social, gender-based factors. Women consume psychotropic drugs to a far greater extent than do men (Olfson and Pincus, 1994). Nevertheless, women show a very strong dislike about using drugs to solve their problems (Gabe and Lipshitz-Phillips, 1982). Pilgrim and Rogers (1999) note that there has been a general decline in the use of minor tranquilizers since the 1970s. Nevertheless, they state that, by 1980, the excess of female consumption over that of males was estimated to be a ratio of 2:1, with four-fifths of that consumption involving the use of minor tranquilizers. This drug use comes at a price. Valium is a case in point (Koumjian, 1981). This is an extensively prescribed drug to deal with anxiety and stress (a frequent accompaniment to depression). It can have severe withdrawal symptoms, including dizziness, nausea, vomiting, panic, anxiety, and depression. Valium prescription is frequently related to an individual's social functioning: the person's ability to live up to the social ideals, social expectations, and the physician's judgment, according to Koumjian, are factors present in some diagnoses. Individual distress, at times related to gender issues, is dealt with in a framework of a medical model of relief, alleviating symptoms, rather than responding to gender-based social issues with psychological consequences for the individual.

As with race, compulsory admission under the Mental Health Act, according to research by M. Sheppard (1991), has implications for gender. Barnes et al.'s (1990) exhaustive study of compulsory admission assessments involving Approved Social Workers showed a considerable excess of female over male referrals, although roughly equal proportions of both were compulsorily admitted. This meant that both in referral and admission, there was an excess of females over males. Sheppard explored this further in relation to medical, particularly GP, involvement. He found that the excess of female over male referrals were accounted for practically entirely by those emanating from GPs. Furthermore, despite their being expected to

have greater psychiatric experience and expertise than the lay public and nonmedical occupations, GP referrals, particularly women, were significantly more likely to be diverted from compulsory admission as a result of subsequent specialist assessment, including ASWs. Examining this further, he found that female referrals were more frequently for those married with children, and that major features in the assessment related to the performance of traditional roles of homemaker, family manager, and housewife. These formed three types: those involved in active familial disruption, passive withdrawal from their usual role, and escape from familial circumstances. Much of their disorder was recognizable in social terms, for which GPs were seeking solutions through compulsory action. Interestingly, diversion from compulsion was significantly more likely to occur where a male relative was consulted. The clear gender dimensions of these processes of course raise concerns on what Sheppard called "the social control of women" through attempted compulsory action.

Conclusion

We need not labor the points here. There does seem to be a relationship between social justice and mental health problems, particularly where we are prepared to consider symbolic as well as material dimensions. Where disadvantage occurs, mental health problems will be experienced to a greater degree than where this is not the case. In this sense, social injustice has psychological consequences. The form of these consequences will, however, vary, and it is important to be aware of the ways social injustice may be translated into particular psychological conditions. It is also important to be aware how these are not fixed and unchanging. For example, to the extent that differences in female rates of depression is a reflection of widespread adoption of traditional sex roles, a move away from these may be expected to reduce the difference in rates between men and women.

However, it can also have consequences for provision of services. Cultural differences, when related to mental health, have subtle consequences, in which the taken-for-granted residual rules of behavior can have a major part to play. We may accept the legitimacy of the use of what sociologists term residual rules as a means of identifying mental health or illness, but this then requires the recognition that these residual rules may be different between different cultures. It becomes necessary, when diagnosing mental ill health, to have a high level of appreciation of those residual rules. This, it appears is not present as widely as might be considered desirable. Residual rules appreciation would not of itself undermine all the potential varieties of racism, and it is incumbent on all mental health professionals to be aware of these and take account for them in their practice.

Social injustice, therefore, is not just about material wealth, and its absence, and differential distribution of resources within society. It is not simply a matter of fairness or unfairness. It should be no surprise that disadvantage and despair can go hand in hand. It is perhaps this relationship to which differential rates of mental health problems point when we compare different groups in society.

References

Aslin, A. L. (1977) Feminist and community mental health centre psychotherapists' expectations of mental health for women, Sex Roles, 3 (6), pp. 537–44.

Barnes, M., Bowl, R. and Fisher, M. (1990) Sectioned: Social Services and the 1983 Mental Health Act, London, Routledge.

Barrett, M. and Roberts, H. (1978) Doctors and their patients: The social control of women in general practice, in Smart, C. and Smart, M. (eds) Women, Sexuality and Social Control, London, Routledge and Kegan Paul.

Bean, P., Bingley, W. and Bynoe, I. (1991) Out of Harm's Way: MIND's Research into Police and Psychiatric Action under Section 136 of the Mental Health Act, London, MIND.

Bebbington, P., Brugha, T., Meltzer, H., Farrell, M., Ceresa, C., Jenkins, R. and Lewis, G. (2000) Psychiatric disorder and dysfunction in the UK national survey of psychiatric morbidity, Social Psychiatry and Psychiatric Epidemiology, 35, pp. 191–7.

Bifulco, A. and Moran, P (1999) Wednesday's Child: Research into Women's Experience of Neglect and Abuse in Childhood, and Adult Depression, London, Routledge.

Billington, R. (1994) The Great Umbilical, London, Hutchinson.

Bird, C. E. (1999) Gender, household labour, and psychological distress: The impact of the amount of division of housework, Journal of Health and Social Behaviour, 40 (1), pp. 32–45.

Birtchall, J. (1971) Social class, parent social class, and social mobility in psychiatric patients and general population controls, Psychological Medicine, 1 pp. 209–2.

Bracegirdle, H. (1991) The female stereotype and occupational therapy for women with depression, British Journal of Occupational Therapy, 54, pp. 193–4.

Bromberg, J. and Mathews, K. (1994) Employment status and depressive symptoms in middle aged women: A longitudinal investigation, American Journal of Public Health, 84 (2), pp. 202–6.

Broverman, I., Broverman, D., Clarkson, F., Rosenkrantz, P. and Vogal, S. (1970) Sex role stereotypes and clinical judgments of mental health, Journal of Consulting and Clinical Psychology, 34, pp. 1–7.

Brown, G. W., Andrews, B., Harris, T. O., Adler, Z. and Bridge, L. (1986) Social support, self esteem and depression, Psychological Medicine, 16, pp. 813–31.

Brown G. W. and Harris, T. O. (1978) Social Origins of Depression, London, Tavistock.

Busfield, J. (1982) Gender and mental illness, International Journal of Mental Health, 11, pp. 46–66.

Busfield, J. (1986) Managing Madness, London, Hutchison.

Cambridge Centre for Family Research (1993) Survey, quoted in Guardian, 21 March.

Chesler, P. (1972) Women and Madness, New York, Doubleday.

Cochrane, R. and Stopes Roe, M. (1980) Factors affecting the distribution of psychological symptoms in urban areas of England, Acta Psychiatrica Scandinavica, 61, pp. 445–60.

Connolly, P. and Troyna, B. (ed.) (1998) Researching Racism in Education: Politics, Theory and Practice, Buckingham, Open University Press.

Cope, R. (1989) The compulsory detention of Afro Caribbeans under the Mental Health Act, New Community, 15 (3), pp. 343–56.

Corob, A. (1988) Working with Depressed Women, Aldershot, Gower.

Cox, J., Murray, D. and Chapman, G. (1994) A controlled study of the onset, duration and prevalence of post natal depression, British Journal of Psychiatry, 16, pp. 27–31.

Doyal, I. and Gough, L. (1991) A Theory of Human Need, London, Macmillan.

Drew, D. (1995) Race, Education and Work: The Statistics of Inequality, Aldershot, Avebury.

Eichenbaum, L. and Orbach, S. (1985) Understanding Women, Harmondsworth, Penguin.

Fabrikant, B. (1974) The pychotherapist and the female patient: Perceptions, misconceptions and change, in Franks, V. and Burtle, V. (eds), Women, the Family and Social Work, London, Tavistock.

Fernando, S. (1988) Race and Culture in Psychiatry, London, Tavistock/Routledge.

Fernando, S. (1995) *Mental Health in a Multi Ethnic Society*, London, Routledge.

Fernando, S., Ndegwa, D. and Wilson, M. (1998) *Forensic Psychiatry, Race and Culture*, London, Routledge.

Francis, E., Pilgrim, D., Rogers, A. and Sashidran, S. (1989) Race and schizophrenia: A reply to Ineichen, *New Community*, 17, pp. 161–3.

Franklin, J. (ed.) (1998) *Social Policy and Social Justice*, Cambridge, Polity Press.

Frederick, J. (1991) *Positive Thinking for Mental Health*, London, The Black Mental Health Group.

Gabe, J. and Lipshitz-Phillips, S. (1982) Evil necessity? The meaning of benzodiazapine use for women patients from one general practice, *Sociology of Health and Illness*, 4, pp. 210–11.

Glass, J. and Fujimoto, T. (1994) Housework, paid work and depression among husbands and wives, *Journal of Health and Social Behaviour*, 35 (2), pp. 179–91.

Grimmel, D. (1998) Effects of gender role self-discrepancy on depressed mood, *Sex Roles: A Journal of Research*, 39 (3/4), pp. 204–14.

Harman, H. (1993) *The Century Gap*, London, Vermillion.

Harrison, G., Owen, D. and Holton, A. (1988) A prospective study of severe mental disorder in Afro-Caribbean patients, *Psychological Medicine*, 11, pp. 289–302.

Hashemi, A. and Cochrane, R. (1999) Expressed emotion and schizophrenia: A review of studies across culture, *International Review of Psychiatry*, 11, pp. 219–24.

Hayek, F. (1974) *Law, Legislation and Liberty*, Vol 2, London, Routledge and Kegan Paul.

Heesacker, M., Wester, S., Vogel, D., Wentzel, J., Mejia-Millan, C. and Goodholm, C. (1999) Gender based emotional stereotyping, *Journal of Counseling Psychology*, 46, pp. 483–95.

Hock, E. and DeMeiss, D. (1990) Depression in mothers of infants: The role of maternal employment, *Developmental Psychology*, 26, pp. 285–91.

Hollingshead, A. and Redlich, F. (1958) *Social Class and Mental Illness*, John Wiley, New York.

Horowitz, A. (1977) The pathways into psychiatric treatment: Some differences between men and women, *Journal of Health and Social Behaviour*, 18, pp. 169–78.

Howe, D. (1995) *Attachment Theory for Social Work Practice*, Aldershot, Avebury.

Jones, L. and Cochrane, R. (1981) Stereotypes of mental illness: A test of the labelling hypothesis, *International Journal of Social Psychiatry*, 27, pp. 99–107.

Kaplan, M., Winget, C. and Free, N. (1990) Psychiatrists' beliefs about gender appropriate behaviour, *American Journal of Psychiatry*, 147, pp. 910–2.

Koumjian, K. (1981) The use of valium as a form of social control, *Social Science and Medicine*, 15e, pp. 245–9.

Kuipers, L. (1994) The measurement of expressed emotion: Its influence on research and clinical practice, *International Review of Psychiatry*, 6, pp. 187–99.

Leff, J. and Vaughn, C. (1984) *Expressed Emotion in Families*, London, Guilford Press.

Littlewood, R. and Lipsedge, M. (1997) *Aliens and Alienists*, 3rd ed., Harmondsworth, Penguin.

Maccoby, E. and Jacklin, C. (1974) *The Psychology of Sex Differences*, Stanford, Stanford University Press.

McGovern, D. and Cope, R. (1987) The compulsory detention of males of different ethnic groups with special reference to offender patients, *British Journal of Psychiatry*, 150, pp. 505–12.

Miles, A. (1988) *Women and Mental Illness*, Brighton, Wheatsheaf.

Miller, D. (1976) *Social Justice*, Oxford, Oxford University Press.

Moss, P. and Plewis, I. (1977) Mental distress in mothers of pre school children in Inner London, *Psychological Medicine*, 7, pp. 641–52.

Muntauer, C., Eaton, W., Diala, C., Kessler, R. and Sorlie, P. (1999) Social class, assets, organisational control and the prevalence of common groups of psychiatric disorders, *Social Science and Medicine*, 47, pp. 2043–5.

Murray, D., Cox, J., Chapman, G. and Jones, P. (1995) Childbirth: Life event or start of a long term disability? Further data from the Stoke on Trent controlled study of post natal depression, *British Journal of Psychiatry*, 166, pp. 595–60.

Myers, J. and Bean, L. (1968) *A Decade Later: A Follow Up of Social Class and Mental Illness*, New York, John Wiley.

Norris, M. (1984) *Integration of Special Hospital Patients into the Community*, Aldershot, Gower.

Obeidallah, D., McHale, S. and Silbereisen, R. (1996) Gender role socialisation and adolescents' reports of depression: Why some girls and not others? *Journal of Youth and Adolescence*, 25, pp. 775–85.

Olfson, M. and Pincus, H. (1994) Use of benzodiazapines in the community, *Archives of Internal Medicine*, 154, pp. 1235–40.

Parry, G. (1986) Paid employment, life events, social support and mental health in working class mothers, *Journal of Health and Social Behaviour, 27*, pp. 47–58.

Parry, G. (1987) Sex role beliefs, work attitudes and mental health in employed and non employed mothers, *British Journal of Social Psychology, 26*, pp. 193–208.

Pilgrim, D. and Rogers, A. (1999) *A Sociology of Mental Health and Illness,* 2nd ed., Buckingham, Open University Press.

Rack, P. (1982) *Race, Culture and Mental Disorder*, London, Tavistock.

Regier, D., Farmer, M., Rae, D. and Myers, J. (1994) One month prevalence of mental disorders in the United States and sociodemographic characteristics, *Acta Psychiatrica Scandinavica, 88*, pp. 35–47.

Richardson, K. (2000) *Developmental Psychology*, London, Macmillan.

Richman, N., Stevenson, J. and Graham, H. (1982) *Preschool to School: A Behavioural Study*, London, Academic Press.

Rogers, A. and Faulkener, A. (1987) *A Place of Safety*, London, MIND.

Scheff, T. (1984) *Being Mentally Ill: A Sociological Theory*, 2nd ed., Chicago, Aldine.

Schwartz, A. and Schwartz, R. (1993) *Depression: Theories and Treatment*, New York, Columbia University Press.

Shaffer, D. (1999) *Developmental Psychology: Childhood and Adolescence*, London, Brooks/Cole.

Sheppard, J. (2000) Learning from practice experience: Reflexions on social work practice with mothers in child and family care, *Journal of Social Work Practice, 14* (1), pp. 37–51.

Sheppard, M. (1991) General practice, social work and mental health section: The social control of women, *British Journal of Social Work, 21*, pp. 663–83.

Sheppard, M. (1993) The external context for social support: Towards a theoretical formulation of social support, child care and maternal depression, *Social Work and Social Sciences Review, 4* (1), pp. 27–59.

Sheppard, M. (1994) Post natal depression, child care and social support: A review of findings and their implications for practice, *Social Work and Social Sciences Review, 5*, pp. 24–47.

Sheppard, M. (1997) Depression in female health visitor consulters: Social and demographic facets, *Journal of Advanced Nursing, 26*, pp. 921–9.

Sheppard, M. (2001) *Social Work Practice with Depressed Mothers in Child and Family Care*, London, Stationery Office.

Siedal, H. (1978) Women, Housework and Depression, unpublished M.Phil thesis, University of London.

Smith, G. and Nairne, K. (1995) *Dealing with Depression*, London, Women's Press.

Spender, D. (1982) *Invisible Women: The Schooling Scandal*, London, Writers and Readers.

Srole, L., Langer, T., Michael, S. and Opler, M. (1961) *Mental Health in the Metropolis*, New York, McGraw Hill.

Szasz, T. (1976) *The Myth of Mental Illness*, New York, Harper and Row.

Troyna, B., Sikes, B. and Rizvi, F. (1997) *Researching Race and Social Justice in Education*, Stoke on Trent, Trentham.

Tyrer, P. and Steinberg, D. (1998) *Models for Mental Disorder*, London, John Wiley.

Weissman, M. and Klerman, G. (1977) Sex differences and the epidemiology of depression, *Archives of General Psychiatry, 34*, pp. 98–117.

Welburn, V. (1980) *Post Natal Depression*, Glasgow, Fontana.

59

Impact of the Threat of War on Children in Military Families

Since 1990, the number of United States military personnel deployed for war and operations other than war has been at an all-time high. Active-duty and reserve military personnel constantly train and prepare for war and deployment. But how prepared for war are the 3.36 million *children* of military parents? What is it like for children who have parents who could be deployed at any moment? To what extent does living with the threat of war cause fear, anxiety, or other emotional responses in children? How do children cope with this pervasive threat to their security and family structure? Are military health care providers overlooking a need for anticipatory guidance or intervention for military families?

Military children are not insensitive to the cues about war that surround them. Jensen (1992) observed that children in military families experience many repeated stressors, including "the threat of wartime conditions affecting the security and stability of the care taking figures and the structure of the family" (p. 986). Even if war never materializes, the threat of war may have a benign, positive, or negative effect on "children's developing security and emerging personality" (p. 986). Research suggests that ongoing adversity has a greater influence on child psychopathology than do discrete life events (Jensen, 1992). The potential impact of the threat of war on children's worldview, social map, and moral development remains uncharted territory (Garbarino, Kostelny & Dubrow, 1991). The aim of the present study was to describe military and civilian children's perceptions of war and to

examine variables that may reflect the impact of those perceptions.

Theoretical Framework

The theoretical framework used for this study was an integration of Lazarus's theory of stress, coping, and emotions and Rachman's theory of fear acquisition. A stressor (e.g., threat of war) is a demand that results in "a particular relationship between the person and the environment that is appraised by the person as taxing or exceeding his or her resources and endangering his or her well-being" (Lazarus & Folkman, 1984, p. 19). Fear is a reaction to certain externally threatening stimuli, or stressors, and is acquired through direct and indirect conditioning (Rachman, 1976, 1977). Direct experience with the stressor. Indirectly, fear is acquired vicariously through modeling or learned through information and instruction. Fear is manifested as subjective experience, avoidance behavior, and psychophysiological disturbance (Lazarus, 1991; Rachman, 1976). Coping strategies are learned, deliberate, and purposeful emotional and behavioral responses to stressors that serve to mediate the impact of a stressor (Lazarus & Folkman, 1984).

Children and War

In the 1990s, most research focused on the direct conditioning effects of war on children, with particular emphasis on posttraumatic stress disorder, for exxample, children of the Gaza strip in Palestine (Thabet & Vostanis, 2000), Croatia (Woodside, Santa Barbara, & Benner, 1999), Bosnia (Stein, Comer, Gardner, & Kelleher, 1999) and Afghanistan (Mghir & Raskin, 1999). The more subtle effects of indirect conditioning, that is, the *threat of war*, were popular topics during the cold war, when nuclear annihilation was a pervasive threat. The International Children's Project examined the psychological impact of the threat of war on children of the United States, New Zealand, Soviet Union, Sweden, and Hungary (Waterston, 1987). Of several thousand 12–18-year-old children, 79% knew about the effects of nuclear war. Mass media were the primary source of information, while parents and schools were only a minor source. There was no clear evidence that the threat of war affected the children's mental health, however. Waterston cautioned that "more work is needed to distinguish between healthy concerns, which may spur young children to action, and pathological despair, which may lead to mental or physical illness" (p. 1385).

The proximity of war to children is a variable that needs further study. Research findings are mixed up, in a thorough review and synthesis of the literature, Jensen and Shaw (1993) suggested that massive exposure to war overwhelms the child's defenses. Moderate exposure probably leads to development of adaptive, self-protective strategies, but minimal exposure may not invoke self-protective mechanisms. Thus, an important area for research is the effect of minimal exposure to the threat of war, such as that experienced by children in U.S. military families.

Military Families as a Special Population

The existence of a "military family syndrome" (i.e., children of military families having a higher than normal incidence of psychopathology) is controversial. Over 20 years ago, LaGrone (1978) introduced the concept after noting an unusually high number of behavior disorders in children referred to a military children's mental health clinic. LaGrone associated children's behavioral disorders with several problem areas common to nearly all the military families (in all of which fathers were the military personnel), including authoritarian parenting styles, family conflicts, and the transient nature of the family. LaGrone did not compare his findings to a civilian population;

therefore, many of these characteristics may not be unique to military families.

Morrison (1981) challenged LaGrone's view of a military family syndrome by comparing data on 140 children of military families and 234 civilian children from his private psychiatric practice. There were no differences reported in the percentage of *DSM-III* diagnostic categories between the two groups except for a finding of fewer diagnoses of schizophrenia among military dependents. Approximately half the children in each group had behavior disorders. The military dependents were more likely to have a six-month or more separation from their father, and to have an alcoholic father, than were civilian children. Subsequently, Shaw (1987) identified four "critical pressures" experienced by children in military families: high mobility, episodic father absence, exposure to foreign cultures, and early military retirement that results in dramatic lifestyle changes. It is likely that "pile-up" of stressors such as these puts military families at higher risk for family dysfunction (Black, 1993).

A study of psychiatric clinical and community samples of 6–12-year-old children from military families indicated that the children's symptom levels were related to parental psychopathology and life stress (Jensen, Bloedau, DeGroot, Usserey, & Davis, 1990). Jensen (1992) cautioned against making inferences about the larger community based on children seen in clinical practice. Another study of 213 (nonclinical) 6–12-year-old-children at one military post showed that self-report and teacher-report scores on the Child Behavior Checklist (CBCL) did not support the idea that children in military families have higher than normal levels of psychopathology (Jensen, Xenakis, Wolf, & Bain, 1991). Curiously, parents' CBCL ratings of their children were higher than national norms, but there was little evidence that children's actual symptoms matched those ratings. Werkman (1992) insisted that life in a military family can lead to subtle personality disturbances that may not be measurable on available instruments, but that often manifest as clinical problems. None of these researchers considered the "threat of war" as a potential source of stress for children in military families.

Children's Fears

Numerous descriptive studies of 8–16-year-old Australian, British, and American children have shown consistent findings related to children's fears. In general, girls report more fears than boys, the number of fears decreases with age, and the most common fears of 8–11-year-old children are related to physical danger and injury (Carroll & Ryan-Wenger, 1999; Gullone & King, 1993; Ollendick, Matson, & Helsel, 1985; Silverman & Nelles, 1988; Spence & McCathie, 1993). Scores on the frequently used Fear Survey Schedule for Children-Revised (FSSC-R) show moderate positive correlations with self-report measures of anxiety and depression (Mc-Cathie & Spence, 1991; Ollendick & Yule, 1990; Ollendick, Yule, & Ollier, 1991). Rachman's theory of fear acquisition was tested by asking 1,092 Australian and American children about the origin of common fears (Ollendick & King, 1991). Children attributed 36% of their fears to direct subjective experience, 56% to vicarious experience, and 89% to information or instructional factors. Findings suggested that these pathways to fear are interactive and synergistic, so that fear of harm or injury was greatest when there was more than one pathway to fear acquisition.

Although it was not an item on the original FSSC-R, "nuclear war" was added to the instrument in several studies. That item was selected as the first or second most common fear by 55%–72% of children in three studies (King et al., 1989, Mc-Cathie & Spence, 1991; Slee & Cross, 1989). A study comparing children from the United States and the Soviet Union showed that, of many stressors, concerns about nuclear war were highest in USSR children and second highest, after death of a parent, for U.S. children (Chivian et al., 1985). On open-ended questionnaires about children's fears, "war" was an impromptu answer by 56% of children in one study, and "nuclear" war was specified by 33% of those children (Boughton, Kenyon, Laycock, Lewin, & Thomas, 1987). Most children reported that the source of their fear was information from family, friends, and mass media. In a more recent study, 48 school-age children of U.S. civilian families completed a "worry" questionnaire (Neff & Dale, 1996). Even after the end of the cold war, and about five years after Operation Desert Storm, these children ranked "being in a war" as the most worrisome event.

Clearly, the idea of war is on the minds of children in the United States and other countries, but that topic has not been a primary focus of research with children of military or civilian families. The increasing involvement of the U.S. military in war, peacekeeping actions, and humanitarian missions across the globe, and the increasing deployment rate of military mothers and fathers, warrant a sys-

tematic examination of their children's perspectives on this pervasive stressor in their lives.

Methods

This was a descriptive, comparative study of the impact of living with the threat of war on children in active-duty and reserve military families. To avoid the unfair assumption that findings from a military sample are unique, civilian children served as a comparison group.

Sample and Procedure

Based on analysis of variance (ANOVA), alpha=0.05, and a medium effect size, a power analysis indicated that at least 23 subjects per group were required, for a total of 69 subjects (Cohen, 1988). Inclusion criteria for all three groups included: one child per family (to ensure independent observations); ages 8–11; age-appropriate grade in school; parental consent; and child assent to participate. Human subject approvals were obtained from all required agencies. Military nurses and research assistants helped to recruit children from schools, military installations, and reserve units across the United States.

Military human subjects committees require that participation or nonparticipation in research be completely voluntary. There must be no suggestion of coercion or potential for positive or negative personnel actions for the military personnel based on their decision. Thus, measures were taken to assure that families who chose not to have their children participate could remain anonymous; those who wanted to participate were required to make the initial contact with the principal investigator. Information about the study, and a telephone number, was presented at unit meetings, posted on bulletin boards, or placed on tables in military community facilities, and included in unit newsletters. For consistency, similar methods were used in the schools to obtain the civilian sample, except that children were instructed to place a sealed envelope containing a form with the parent's name and telephone number in a designated box in their classroom. While these strategies protected potential subjects, the drawback is that the actual number of families who "declined" participation is not known.

Research assistants conducted 20–30-minute individual, audiotaped interviews with the children in their homes. The children completed two questionnaires and a drawing during that time. The interviews were transcribed verbatim for inductive content analysis.

Instruments

Because there is no standardized, reliable, and valid instrument available to examine children's perceptions of war and the threat of war, a structured interview was devised. For purposes of the interview, "threat of war" was not conceived as a specific event, but as a pervasive stimulus that becomes a part of everyday life. The terms "war" and "threat of war" were left to the children to define for themselves.

The interview consisted of 17 open-ended questions, beginning with items about things that make children happy, sad, or afraid; followed by their ideas and fears about war; and moving on to the origin of those ideas/fears. To increase the content and construct validity of the interview, nine items were borrowed or adapted from the standardized Child Assessment Interview (Hodges, Kline, Stern, Cytryn, & McKnew, 1982; Hodges; McKnew & Cytryn, 1982) and four items from a study of children's fears (Ollendick & King, 1991). Four additional items were developed in consultation with a military child psychiatrist (S. Xenakis). Pilot-testing with six children resulted in only minor adjustments.

Manifest anxiety was measured by the Revised Children's Manifest Anxiety Scale (RCMAS), a 37-item self-report measure of the level and nature of trait, or manifest, anxiety in children and adolescents, 8–19 years old (Reynolds & Richmond, 1985). Manifest anxiety is appropriate to measure when a stressor, or fear, is pervasive and ill-defined, such as living with the threat of war. Items on the RCMAS are scored 1 (yes) or 0 (no). Three subscales measure physiological anxiety, worry, and social concerns. High scores reflect high anxiety. When used with school-age children, reliability correlations were: test-retest, 0.98; internal consistency, 0.83–0.85. Factor analysis showed three factors consistent with the three subscales. Scores on the RCMAS correlated 0.78–0.85 with the Spielberger Trait Anxiety Scale for Children, and 0.08–0.24 with the State Scale, as expected.

Emotional indicators on Human Figure Drawings (HFD) were used as another measure of emotional status. The HFD is a widely used projective technique for children. Psychoanalytic theory suggests that in the process of drawing a human figure, individuals unconsciously externalize their feelings, thoughts, needs, conflicts, and attitudes (Poster,

1989). Drawing is a nonthreatening, developmentally appropriate activity for children. HFDs are analyzed according to 28 mutually exclusive characteristics, called Emotional Indicators (EI). Examples of EIs include poor integration of parts of the figure, gross asymmetry of limbs or teeth, crossed eyes, and omission of commonly drawn parts, such as eyes or legs. EIs are not primarily related to age or maturation or to artistic ability; they are unusual features that occur in fewer than 16% of all HFDs. EIs have clinical validity, having been found to differentiate between children with and without emotional or behavioral problems (Hammer, 1981; Koppitz, 1968). Two or more EIs on a drawing are highly suggestive of emotional problems and unsatisfactory interpersonal relationships.

Coping strategies were measured by the 26-item self-report Schoolage Children's Coping Strategies Inventory (SCSI) (Ryan-Wenger, 1990). Children indicate how frequently they use each coping strategy (frequency scale) and how much the same coping strategies help them to feel better (effectiveness scale) on a scale of 0–3. Range of reliability correlations in several studies have been: test-retest, 0.73–0.82; internal consistency, 0.70–0.89 (Ryan-Wenger, 1997). Children with two or more stress-related symptoms had significantly lower coping scores compared to children with no symptoms (Ryan-Wenger, 1990). The SCSI was later validated for use with black children from low-income families (Ryan-Wenger & Copeland, 1994).

Results and Discussion

Sample Characteristics

The anticipated minimum number of 23 children per group was not attained for the active-duty group. Therefore, study results that specifically describe this group or compare it with others should be interpreted with caution. Complete data were collected from children from active-duty (N = 18), reserve (N = 25), and civilian (N = 48) families, for a total sample size of 91. There were 50 boys and 41 girls; 81 were white, 5 black, 2 mixed, 2 Hispanic, and 1 unknown (i.e., not reported).

Seven states and a wide range of socioeconomic levels were represented. Most of the children came from two-parent families. Of the 43 military families represented, the mother was the military parent of 10 children, the father was the military parent of the other 25; for eight of these 43 children, both mother and father were in the military. Thirteen of the parents had been involved in Operation

Desert Storm, when the children in this sample were 2–6 years old.

Anxiety and Coping

Using ANOVA, there were no significant differences among children of civilian, active-duty, and reserve families on manifest anxiety total or subscale scores (see Table 59.1). The number of EIs on the HFDs ranged from 0 to 7. Because the presence of two or more EIs on a HFD has potential clinical significance, the number of children with two or more were compared across the three groups using a chi-square goodness-of-fit test (Pett, 1997). Again, there were no significant differences among the three study groups ($\chi^2 = 0.96$, p < 0.50).

Findings from these two measures of anxiety and emotional problems provide no evidence of a "military family syndrome" (i.e., more psychopathology in the children of reserve or active-duty families, compared to the children of civilians). ANOVA showed no differences among the three groups for number of coping strategies used or for frequency or effectiveness of coping (Table 59.1), which suggests that if military children experience the pervasive stressor "threat of war," they are quite adaptive and cope as well as civilian children. Post hoc analyses showed no differences in anxiety, coping, or EIs when the military parent was the mother only, father only, or both parents.

The richness of research data is in the individual items that make up an instrument, and item analysis often provides information that may be applicable to practice. One the anxiety scale, active-duty children were significantly more likely to say that they "worry about what my parents will say to me" ($\chi^2 = 6.8$, p = 0.03). This concern may be related to the "authoritarian" parenting style that is attributed to military families (LaGrone, 1978). All but one of these boys and girls had fathers in the military who had been deployed one or two times.

Active-duty children also were more likely to have two specific EIs in their drawings: "poor integration of parts," which is indicative of impulsivity ($\chi^2 = 18.52$, p = 0.001), and "arms pressed close to the body," which is indicative of timidity ($\chi^2 = 7.94$, p = 0.02). Significantly more reserve children drew "arms shorter than waistline," an indicator of timidity ($\chi^2 = 7.02$, p = 0.05).

A few coping strategies stood out among the military children. Significantly more active-duty children used "fight with someone," "bite my nails," and "daydream" to cope with stressors ($\chi^2 = 5.8$–7.0, p = 0.05), while reserve children were more likely to "do something about it" ($\chi^2 = 9.7$, p = 0.01). "Do something about it" is a problem-focused strategy that is more likely to mediate the impact of, or change, a stressor than are aggressive emotional strategies (Lazarus & Folkman, 1984).

When asked about the most helpful strategies, active-duty children were most likely to say "fight with someone" and "yell or scream" ($\chi^2 = 5.8$, p = 0.05), which fits with the impulsivity described above, but not the timidity. There are few instances in which these two aggressive strategies would be considered adaptive or even socially acceptable. If this pattern holds in future studies, researchers should explore how and why some active-duty children find physically and verbally aggressive methods of coping to be effective for them. Reserve and civilian children were more likely than active-duty children to find the strategy "try to relax" to be helpful ($\chi^2 = 8.4$, p = 0.02). Relaxation is an ap-

Table 59.1 Manifest Anxiety and Coping Scale Scores by Total Sample and by Group

Scale	$\alpha^{coeff.}$	Possible Range	Total Sample	Civilian	Reserve	Active	F^a	Sig.
Anxiety								
Total	0.85	0–28	10.6 (5.79)	10.7 (6.05)	9.5 (5.49)	11.8 (5.50)	0.838	0.436
Physiological	0.64	0–10	4.1 (2.28)	4.2 (2.32)	9.5 (5.49)	4.4 (2.28)	0.695	0.502
Social	0.53	0–7	2.0 (1.59)	2.0 (1.69)	1.8 (1.46)	2.2 (1.54)	0.220	0.803
Worry	0.78	0–11	4.5 (2.91)	4.4 (3.07)	4.0 (2.82)	5.2 (2.57)	0.901	0.410
Coping								
Number	—	0–26	15.3 (4.31)	15.0 (4.41)	15.5 (4.69)	16.2 (3.50)	0.579	0.563
Frequency	0.74	0–78	24.5 (8.62)	23.5 (8.40)	24.9 (9.25)	26.6 (8.39)	0.834	0.438
Effective	0.78	0–78	32.4 (10.03)	30.8 (9.34)	33.9 (11.43)	34.8 (9.55)	1.421	0.247

NOTE. Scores for total sample and the three groups are means, with standard deviations in parentheses.
[a] F based on ANOVA, $df = 2$, alpha = 0.05; harmonic means used to account for unequal sample size.

propriate emotion-focused strategy to use when the stressor is not under the child's own control (Lazarus & Folkman, 1984).

Perceptions and Threat of War

Children's responses to the interview questions related to war were inductively sorted into categories; frequencies and percentages across groups were then examined using the chi-square goodness-of-fit test (see Table 59.2). As might be expected, children of active-duty and reserve families were more likely to know that Desert Storm was the last war in which the United States was involved. Uniformly across groups, responses to the question "What have you heard about war?" produced statements that had to do with people getting killed, fighting and violence, guns, bombs, and missiles.

The sources of children's beliefs about war were categorized according to direct or indirect conditioning methods, as proposed by Rachman (1977). As expected, none of the children experienced direct conditioning, which requires personal exposure to war. Information and instruction, particularly, are inherent in child rearing, wherein parents teach children which events should be feared, which should not, and how to cope with fears and their evoked responses. In this sample, active-duty children were more likely to obtain information from their teachers and from the movies, rather than from their parents. It may be that the active-duty parents chose not to discuss the idea of war with their children. This hypothesis is consistent with the author's experience in conducting this study: active-duty subjects were the most difficult to recruit. Parents who refused permission often stated that they did not want their children to be questioned about war.

The children's feelings about war did not always match their friends' attitudes:

> Ten-year-old Billy said of his friends, "They think it's cool but that's because they're 12 years old and don't have a bit of war in their area." Another child, Ricky, said, "My friends play weird with pretend grenades and guns and stuff. They think they're cool but I don't."

When asked, "What if the U.S. got into a war? What do you think about [that]?", more active-duty children thought the United States would win (whereas more civilian children thought the U.S. would lose). More active-duty children expressed a fear that they or their parent would die. Many civil-

ian and reserve children expressed moral outrage at the idea of the United States getting into war, indicating, "It's not right." Fewer active-duty children thought that war was not right, or felt "bad" about war. Rather, they were significantly more "afraid" and "sad" about war:

> A 9-year-old boy from a reserve family said, "I don't like it. A lot of bad things happen and people die for no reason, it seems like."

When asked "What would happen in your family if there was war?", more reserve and active-duty children, compared to civilian children, believed that their parent(s) would go to war and that a parent would die:

> An 8-year-old active-duty girl said, "My family would be killed, shot, stabbed, and they might be hurt." A 10-year-old boy from an active-duty family said, "My Dad might have to go to war. He might die and never come back." Another 10-year-old boy whose mother was a reservist said, "It would just be my Dad, my sister, and me. And if they were going to take my Dad, they could take me instead. I'd risk my life for my Dad's."

If the war was thought to be on U.S. soil, significantly more active-duty children believed that their house would be invaded, perhaps because they tended to live near military installations, which are probably prime targets.

To allow for a more positive perspective on the phenomenon of war, children were asked, "What is good about war?" The most frequent responses were "nothing" and the fact that it is "good when it's over." The interview ended with, "What do *you* like about war?" The overwhelming response from all groups was: "Nothing!" Still, some children expressed a liking for the guns and other implements of war, others like the celebrations afterward and stories about war heroes:

> Jeremy, age 11, said, "There's nothing to like about war. People die."

Implications for Research and Practice

While the literature to date has focused primarily on negative effects of war or threat of war on child development, it is important to acknowledge that many military children are quite adaptive and re-

Table 59.2 Categories, Frequencies, and Percentages of Children's Responses to War-related Questions by Total Sample and by Group

Question/Response Category[a]	Total (N = 91) %	(N)	Civilian (N = 48) %	(N)	Reserve (N = 25) %	(N)	Active (N = 18) %	(N)	χ^{2b}	p
What was the last war that the U.S. was involved in?										
Don't know	31	(28)	38	(18)	20	(5)	28	(5)	8.72	<0.02
Desert Storm	28	(26)	15	(7)	40	(10)	50	(9)	18.57	<0.001
Bosnia	11	(10)	10	(5)	12	(3)	14	(2)	0.66	<0.70
WW II	11	(10)	10	(5)	12	(3)	14	(2)	0.66	<0.70
Vietnam	4	(4)	2	(1)	12	(3)	0	(0)	17.97	<0.001
WW III	4	(4)	6	(3)	4	(1)	0	(0)	5.66	<0.01
What have you heard about war?										
People get killed	43	(39)	38	(18)	44	(11)	56	(10)	3.65	<0.10
Fighting and violence	15	(14)	15	(7)	12	(3)	22	(4)	3.23	<0.10
About different wars	13	(12)	10	(5)	16	(4)	17	(3)	2.00	<0.30
Guns, bombs, missiles	10	(9)	10	(5)	12	(3)	6	(1)	2.00	<0.30
Bad things happen	7	(6)	8	(4)	4	(1)	6	(1)	1.34	<0.50
Where did you hear about war?										
Information:										
Teacher	34	(31)	27	(13)	36	(9)	50	(9)	7.08	<0.05
Parents	26	(24)	23	(11)	44	(11)	11	(2)	21.47	<0.001
Books	17	(15)	17	(8)	24	(6)	17	(3)	1.68	<0.30
Vicarious:										
Television	59	(54)	54	(26)	68	(17)	61	(11)	1.60	<0.30
Movies	21	(19)	10	(5)	20	(5)	50	(5)	32.46	<0.001
Friends/Play	20	(18)	15	(7)	28	(7)	22	(4)	3.90	<0.10
What do you think about if the U.S. got into a war?										
People killed or dying	40	(36)	38	(18)	36	(9)	50	(9)	3.58	<0.10
It's not right	23	(21)	25	(12)	32	(8)	6	(1)	17.23	<0.001
Cities bombed/destroyed	13	(12)	17	(8)	8	(2)	11	(2)	3.49	<0.10
The U.S. would win	10	(9)	6	(3)	4	(1)	28	(5)	27.92	<0.001
Me or parent would die	9	(8)	2	(1)	4	(1)	33	(6)	46.31	<0.001
The U.S. would lose	8	(7)	16	(7)	0	(0)	0	(0)	30.00	<0.001
How do you feel about war?										
Bad	51	(46)	56	(27)	56	(14)	28	(5)	11.19	<0.01
Afraid	23	(21)	23	(11)	8	(2)	45	(8)	27.37	<0.001
Worried	12	(11)	14	(7)	8	(2)	11	(2)	1.64	<0.30
Sad	10	(9)	2	(1)	12	(3)	28	(5)	24.58	<0.001
What would happen in your family if there was war?										
Parent would go to war	34	(31)	13	(6)	64	(16)	50	(9)	32.83	<0.001
We'd go somewhere else	21	(19)	21	(10)	12	(3)	33	(6)	10.10	<0.01
Nothing/no change	13	(12)	19	(9)	4	(1)	11	(2)	9.98	<0.01
Parent would die	12	(11)	4	(2)	20	(5)	22	(4)	12.72	<0.01
House would be invaded	9	(8)	8	(4)	0	(0)	22	(4)	24.80	<0.001
We would die	7	(6)	2	(1)	12	(3)	11	(2)	7.31	<0.05
What is good about war?										
Nothing	19	(17)	19	(9)	20	(5)	17	(3)	.26	<0.80
Fighting stops/It's over	14	(13)	10	(5)	20	(5)	17	(3)	3.36	<0.20
It settles things	12	(11)	13	(6)	12	(3)	11	(2)	.16	<0.90
What do you like about war?										
Nothing	63	(57)	52	(25)	80	(20)	67	(12)	5.92	<0.10

[a]Categories with very low frequencies are not reported.

[b]Based on χ^2 goodness-of-fit test; critical value = 5.99, $\alpha = 0.05$.

silient in spite of this potentially chronic stressor. Military children in this sample are not inordinately preoccupied with the threat of war, are not unusually anxious, and cope quite effectively. This is the first study to examine these variables with military children and, although the findings are encouraging, there are limitations to the research. The sample size of active-duty children fell short of the desired 23 per group; therefore, there may be insufficient power to detect real differences across groups using inferential statistics. Further research is needed, with perhaps a smaller effect size hypothesized.

While interviews about children's perceptions of war are revealing, it is difficult to link data from interviews to scores on related variables. Therefore, development of a self-report instrument to measure children's perceptions of war is needed. Future research should link anxiety and coping measures and children's perceptions of war with relevant outcomes, such as psychosomatic symptoms and emotional and behavioral problems. Researchers have not addressed the effects of other relatively rare stressors that children in military families experience, such as the increased likelihood of lengthy maternal absence, now that more women with children are in the military.

Recruitment of subjects for a study such as this has inherent difficulties. Many military parents do not want their children to think about war and what it means to their family. Years ago, Rutter (1974) warned that separation from parents may have more untoward effects on a child if, from child's perspective the reason for separation involves a sense of danger, or if the child is inadequately prepared. Military parents may not be aware that their children *do* think about war, and that children often have misconceptions that may be more dangerous to their psyche than a frank discussion about the facts of war.

At a primary prevention level, military providers should include as anticipatory guidance, at each well-child visit, the suggestion that parents ask about and discuss their children's perceptions of war and the impact of war on their family. Providers in the community can develop and test primary prevention interventions for children that incorporate open discussions at home and school about the unique situation in which military children grow up.

Secondary preventive interventions might involve development of programs for children at highest risk for problems upon parental deployment (another important topic for research), and support programs when troops are deployed and family members are left behind. Providers can develop and implement tertiary prevention interventions for situations when children appear at the school, clinic, or hospital with stress-related symptoms or behavioral or emotional disorders. A high index of suspicion is needed to link children's perceptions about war to their symptoms. Anxiety and coping scales and HFDs can be useful screening tools at all levels of prevention. Unusually high or low scores on individual items are cues for further data collection.

Much more research on the children's perspective is needed, including phenomenological studies. Jensen and Shaw (1993) suggested that research focus less on the negative aspects of war and shift to variables that buffer the impact of war on children, such as social awareness, values, and attitudes. The present study constituted the first opportunity for most of these children to discuss their ideas and fears about war with someone who really wanted to know. The children's perceptions of this study can be summarized by 10-year-old Justin, who said: *"Wow, this is great! No one's ever asked me before!"*

Research was funded by grant N94-006A1 from the TriService Nursing Research Program, Uniformed Services University of the Health Sciences, Department of Defense. Views expressed are those of the author and do not reflect official policy or position of the Departments of the Navy, Army, Air Force, or Defense, nor the U.S. Government.

References

Black, W. G. (1993). Military-induced family separation: A stress reduction intervention. *Social Work, 38,* 273–280.

Boughton, R. C., Kenyon, Y., Laycock, L., Lewin, T. J., & Thomas, S. P. (1987). Australian children and the threat of nuclear war. *Medical Journal of Australia, 147,* 121–124.

Carroll, M. K., & Ryan-Wenger, N. A. (1999). School-age children's fears, anxiety, and human figure drawings. *Journal of Pediatric Health Care, 13,* 24–31.

Chivian, E., Mack, J. E., Waletzky, J. P., Lazaroff, C., Doctor, R., & Goldenring, J. M. (1985). Soviet children and the threat of nuclear war: A preliminary study. *American Journal of Orthopsychiatry, 55,* 484–502.

Cohen, J. (1988). Statistical power analysis (2nd ed.). Hillsdale, NJ: Erlbaum.

Garbarino, J., Kostelny, K., & Dubrow, N. (1991). What children can tell us about living in danger. *American Psychologist, 46*, 376–383.

Gullone, E., & King, N. J. (1993). The fears of youth in the 1990's: Contemporary normative data. *Journal of Genetic Psychology, 154*, 137–153.

Hammer, E. F. (1981). Projective drawings. In A. I. Rabin (Ed.), *Assessment with projective techniques: A concise introduction* (pp. 151–180). New York: Springer.

Hodges, K., Kline, J., Stern, L., Cytryn, L., & McKnew, D. (1982). The development of a child assessment interview for research and clinical use. *Journal of Abnormal Child Psychology, 10*, 173–189.

Hodges, K., McKnew, D., & Cytryn, L. (1982). The Child Assessment Schedule (CAS) diagnostic interview: A report on reliability and validity. *Journal of the American Academy of Child Psychiatry, 21*, 468–473.

Jensen, P. S. (1992). Resolved: Military family life is hazardous to the mental health of children. *Journal of the American Academy of Child and Adolescent Psychiatry, 31*, 984–987.

Jensen, P. S., Bloedau, L., DeGroot, J., Ussery, T., & Davis, H. (1990). Children at risk: I. Risk factors and child symptomatology. *Journal of the American Academy of Child and Adolescent Psychiatry, 29*, 51–59.

Jensen, P. S., Lewis, R. L., & Xenakis, S. N. (1986). The military family in review: Context, risk and prevention. *Journal of the American Academy of Child Psychiatry, 25*, 225–234.

Jensen, P. S., Richters, J., Ussery, T., Bloedau, L., & Davis, H. (1991). Child psychopathology and environmental influences: Discrete life events versus ongoing adversity. *Journal of the American Academy of Child and Adolescent Psychiatry, 30*, 303–309.

Jensen, P. S., & Shaw, J. (1993). Children as victims of war: Current knowledge and future research needs. *Journal of the American Academy of Child and Adolescent Psychiatry, 32*, 697–708.

Jensen, P. S., Xenakis, S. N., Wolf, P., & Bain, M. W. (1991). The "military family syndrome" revisited: By the numbers. *Journal of Nervous and Mental Disorders, 179*, 102–107.

King, N. J., Ollier, K., Iacuone, R., Schuster, S., Bays, K., Gullone, E., & Ollendick, T. H. (1989). Fears of children and adolescents: A cross-sectional Australian study using the Revised-Fear Survey Schedule for Children. *Journal of Child Psychology and Psychiatry & Allied Disciplines, 30*, 775–784.

Koppitz, E. M. (1968). *Psychological evaluation of children's human figure drawings.* New York: Grune & Stratton.

LaGrone, D. M. (1978). The military family syndrome. *American Journal of Psychiatry, 135*, 1040–1043.

Lazarus, R. S. (1991). *Emotion and adaptation.* New York: Oxford University Press.

Lazarus, R.S., & Folkman, S. (1984). *Stress, appraisal and coping.* New York: Springer.

McCathie, H., & Spence, S. H. (1991). What is the revised Fear Survey Schedule for Children measuring? *Behaviour Research and Therapy, 29*, 495–502.

Mghir, R., & Raskin, A. (1999). The psychological effects of the war in Afghanistan on young Afghan refugees from different ethnic backgrounds. *International Journal of Social Psychiatry, 45*, 29–36; discussion 36–40.

Morrison, J. (1981). Rethinking the military family syndrome. *American Journal of Psychiatry, 138*, 354–357.

Neff, E. J., & Dale, J. C. (1996). Worries of school-age children. *Journal of the Society of Pediatric Nursing, 1*, 27–32.

Ollendick, T. H., & King, N. J. (1991). Origins of childhood fears: An evaluation of Rachman's theory of fear acquisition. *Behaviour Research and Therapy, 29*, 117–123.

Ollendick, T. H., Matson, J. L., & Helsel, W. J. (1985). Fears in children and adolescents: Normative data. *Behaviour Research and Therapy, 23*, 465–467.

Ollendick, T. H., & Yule, W. (1990). Depression in British and American children and its relation to anxiety and fear. *Journal of Consulting and Clinical Psychology, 58*, 126–129.

Ollendick, T. H., Yule, W., & Ollier, K. (1991). Fears in British children and their relationship to manifest anxiety and depression. *Journal of Child Psychology and Psychiatry and Allied Disciplines, 32*, 321–331.

Pett, M. A. (1997). *Nonparametric statistics for health care research.* Thousand Oaks, CA: Sage.

Poster, E. C. (1989). The use of projective assessment techniques in pediatric research. *Journal of Pediatric Nursing, 4*, 26–35.

Rachman, S. (1976). The passing of the two-stage theory of fear and avoidance: Fresh possibilities. *Behavioural Research and Therapy, 14*, 125–131.

Rachman, S. (1977). The conditioning theory of fear-acquisition: A critical examination. *Behavioural Research and Therapy, 15*, 375–387.

Reynolds, C. R., & Richmond, B. O. (1985). *Revised Children's Manifest Anxiety Scale [RCMAS] manual.* Los Angeles: Western Psychological Services.

Rutter, M. (1974). Parent-child separation: Psychological effects on the children. *Journal of Child Psychology and Psychiatry, 12,* 233–260.

Ryan-Wenger, N. A. (1990). Development and psychometric properties of the Schoolagers' Coping Strategies Inventory. *Nursing Research, 39,* 344–349.

Ryan-Wenger, N. A. (1997). Schoolagers' Coping Strategies Inventory: Directions for administration and scoring.

Ryan-Wenger, N. A., & Copeland, S. G. (1994). Coping strategies used by black school-age children from low-income families. *Journal of Pediatric Nursing, 9,* 33–40.

Shaw, J. A. (1987). Children in the military. *Psychiatric Annals, 17,* 539–544.

Silverman, W. K., & Nelles, W. B. (1988). The influence of gender on children's ratings of fear in self and same-aged peers. *Journal of Genetic Psychology, 149,* 17–21.

Slee, P. T., & Cross, D. G. (1989). Living in the nuclear age: An Australian study of children's and adolescent's fears. *Child Psychiatry and Human Development, 1,* 270–278.

Spence, S. H., & McCathie, H. (1993). The stability of fears in children: A two-year prospective study: A research note. *Journal of Child Psychology and Psychiatry and Allied Disciplines, 40,* 579–585.

Stein, B., Comer, D., Gardner, W., & Kelleher, K. (1999). Prospective study of displaced children's symptoms in wartime Bosnia. *Social Psychiatry and Psychiatric Epidemiology, 34,* 464–469.

Thabet, A. A., & Vostanis, P. (2000). Post traumatic stress disorder reactions in children of war: A longitudinal study. *Child Abuse and Neglect, 24,* 291–298.

Waterston, T. (1987). Children and the threat of nuclear war. *Lancet,* June 13, 1384–1385.

Werkman, S. (1992). Resolved: Military family life is hazardous to the mental health of children. *Journal of the American Academy of Child and Adolescent Psychiatry, 31,* 984–987.

Woodside, D., Santa Barbara, J., & Benner, D. G. (1999). Psychological trauma and social healing in Croatia. *Medicine, Conflict and Survival, 15,* 355–367; discussion 391–393.

ANDREW I. BATAVIA
RICHARD L. BEAULAURIER

60

The Financial Vulnerability of People with Disabilities: Assessing Poverty Risks

Introduction

The Americans with Disabilities Act of 1990 states, "The Nation's proper goals regarding individuals with disabilities are to assure equality of opportunity, full participation, independent living, and economic self-sufficiency for such individuals."[1] Thus, assisting the 54 million[2] Americans with disabilities (i.e., functional or activity limitations)[3] to be self-sufficient and to live independently in their communities is among the most important objectives of U.S. disability policy.[4] To achieve these goals, people with disabilities need to be able to maintain financial stability, balancing their budgets and absorbing threatening shocks to their financial security such as the costs of illnesses and other short-term emergencies.

As a group, people with disabilities appear to be particularly vulnerable financially due to (1) reduced earning capacity often associated with functional limitations, (2) the often substantial costs of accommodating these limitations, and (3) their high susceptibility to certain financial shocks (LaPlante, 1993; LaPlante, Kennedy & Trupin, 1996; LaPlante, Carlson et al., 1996). Many people with disabilities live at or near the poverty line (Kaye, 1998). These individuals, who have virtually no financial reserves and extremely limited earning potential, have no financial "cushion" to help absorb short-term shocks and are at high risk of poverty. Some are at substantial risk of homelessness, particularly individuals with mental illness. The capacity of people with disabilities living at a subsistence level to maintain

independence can be compromised as a result of a single major adverse event.

However, such vulnerability also has profound implications for people with disabilities who are more financially secure, but whose resources are limited and whose expenses are extraordinary. Challenges to financial stability may threaten their abilities to maintain necessary housing, nutrition, medical care, and other key factors affecting health and survival. The absence of such resources may, in turn, result in further financial vulnerability. Failure to maintain financial stability may, therefore, trigger a downward spiral resulting in bankruptcy, diminished health (both physical and mental), financial dependence on family members and friends, and even homelessness or institutionalization if no family support is available.

Unfortunately, while financial stability is so important to people with disabilities, these individuals also appear to be disproportionately subject to extraordinary costs of living that compromise the ability to maintain stability. These include the high cost of personal assistance services (e.g., attendant care for people with quadriplegia, reader services for blind people, interpreter services for people who are deaf), assistive technology (e.g., wheelchairs, augmentive communication devices, reading machines, and voice recognition computers), and transportation services for some people with disabilities (Nosek, 1991, 1993).

Exacerbating this situation, the inability of many people with disabilities to pay for extraordinary expenses such as personal assistance and transportation costs may increase their vulnerability to health-related financial shocks (Nosek, 1993). Due to their disabilities, many of these individuals have a thinner margin of health than people without disabilities (DeJong, Batavia, and Griss, 1989). Any deprivation of needed resources can compromise their health, causing a major drain of limited financial resources.

Although people who address disability issues understand these factors and relationships in a general manner, such variables have never been studied systematically with the objective of developing insights for reducing financial vulnerability and increasing financial stability. Specifically, no comprehensive model for predicting disability poverty risks has been developed to date. This article constitutes a first effort to develop such a theoretical framework and research agenda for understanding the financial vulnerability of people with disabilities.

The Financial Status of People with Disabilities

As a group, people with disabilities are among the poorest of all Americans (Louis Harris and Associates, 1998, p. 5). Of course, the disabled population is extremely diverse, and there are broad ranges of educational status, employment status, income level, asset level, and other economic indicators among people with disabilities (Louis Harris and Associates, 1986, 1998; Baldwin, 1999). Some, by virtue of their family circumstances, individual efforts, legal settlements, or other good fortune, are wealthy or at least secure in the middle class and not financially vulnerable (except perhaps in a relative sense compared with other people in their social class). However, the vast majority of people with disabilities are not so fortunate. The following parameters fairly characterize the financial circumstances of the average individual with a major disability in the United States.

Poverty Rates

Based on data from the 1995 Current Population Survey (CPS), 38.3% of working-age adults with severe work disabilities (i.e., unable to work due to a disability)[5] live in poverty, compared with 30% of those limited in their ability to work and 10.2% of those not limited in work (Kaye, 1998). The 1998 National Organization on Disability (NOD)/Harris survey found that 33% of people

with disabilities live in households with incomes of less than $15,000; only 12% of adults without disabilities live in such households (Louis Harris and Associates, 1998). According to these data, depending on the extent of disability, people with disabilities are three to four times as likely to live in poverty as nondisabled people.

The 1992 National Health Interview Survey (NHIS) similarly suggests a significant discrepancy between the poverty rates of people with and without disabilities, though a somewhat smaller one. According to NHIS data, 17.1% of people limited in any activity live in poverty compared with 11.2% of people not limited in activity. Some 28.4% of children with a limitation in a life activity live in poverty compared with 17.8% of children who are not limited. Among the elderly population, 11.4% of those with disabilities live in poverty compared with 6.5% of those without disabilities (Kay, 1998).

According to 1992 CPS data, women with severe work disabilities (i.e., conditions that prevent them from working) have the highest rates of poverty of all groups. Some 40.5% of such women live in poverty compared with 31% of men with severe work disabilities, 12.1% of women with no work disability, and 8.1% of men with no work disability (InfoUse, 1999).

Although these estimates of the extent of poverty among the disabled population differ, there is general consensus that a far larger percentage of people with disabilities live in poverty than people without disabilities. This conclusion is particularly disconcerting considering that about half of people who are unable to work due to a chronic disease or illness receive federal cash benefits under the Social Security Disability Insurance (SSDI) program (32.7%), Supplemental Security Income (SSI) program (19.8%), or both (6%). These individuals also quality for Medicare and Medicaid, respectively. Thus, even though many people with disabilities have a stable source of program income and health insurance, they still remain in poverty at rates significantly higher than people without disabilities.

Education

People with disabilities have relatively low levels of education compared with the population generally. According to the NOD/Harris survey, 20% of people with disabilities do not complete high school, compared with 10% of those without disabilities (Louis Harris and Associates, 1998). Based on NHIS data, people with lower education levels consistently report higher levels of activity limitations, with 16.5% of those with eight years of education or less unable to do their major life activity compared with 2.3% of those with 16 years or more (InfoUse, 1996). The relationship between disability and education is complex, and causation is likely to run in both directions.

Employment

According to the NOD/Harris survey, only about 30% of working-age adults with disabilities are employed full or part time, compared with 80% of adults without disabilities (Louis Harris and Associates, 1998). Although 75% of unemployed individuals with disabilities consistently indicate that they would like to have a job, their employment situation has not improved, and may have worsened, in the past decade even with the implementation of legislation designed specifically to improve their economic viability, such as the ADA (Louis Harris and Associates, 1986, 1998; Budetti et al., 2001).

Other national surveys have yielded similar results. CPS data indicate that, of the 16.9 million working-age people with health conditions or impairments that limit their ability to work, 12.1 million people (72.1%) are unemployed (Kaye, 1998). Survey of Income and Program Participation (SIPP) data collected in 1994–95 indicate that 26.1% of people with severe disabilities[6] are employed, compared with 76.9% of people with nonsevere disabilities and 82.1% of people with no disabilities (McNeil, 1997). The following percentages represent the proportion of people with certain disability characteristics who are employed: 22% of working-age wheelchair users; 27.5% of cane, crutch, or walker users; 25% of people unable to climb stairs; 30.8% of people who are unable to see words or letters; and 35.1% of people with mental retardation (Kaye, 1998).

The poor levels of education and training of people with disabilities, combined with prejudicial attitudes and a history of dependence, often conspire to give many people with disabilities short or spotty job histories. This may make them less desirable to employers than other employees. Traditionally, disabled people have tended to make the most significant gains in the workforce when there is a shortage of available labor or when disabled veterans return from a popular war (Berkowitz, 1980; Oberman, 1965; Renz-Beaulaurier, 1996, chap 2). There is little evidence that the employment provisions of the ADA and other disability laws have changed the employment prospects of people with disabilities very much.

Earnings and Other Income

The major sources of income for people with disabilities are well-known. They include a combination of conventional sources of income available to all people (e.g., employment, interest payments, dividends, TANF), as well as income transfer programs specifically targeted at disabled people such as SSI, SSDI, and private disability insurance. Moreover, employer- or government-subsidized benefits such as employment-based health insurance, Medicaid, Medicare, disability trust programs, and sliding scale service programs may serve as in-kind forms of income, or at least provide a way of limiting expenses (Batavia, 1998).

According to SIPP data, the median earnings of people with severe disabilities is about 60% of that for people without disabilities, and "the presence of a disability is associated with an increased chance of having a low level of income" (McNeil, 1997, pp. 3–4). For men 21–64, median earnings for individuals with severe disabilities was $1,262 per month, compared with $2,190 for individuals with no disabilities. For women in this age range, the median earnings for disabled individuals was $1,000 per month, compared with $1,470 per month for women with no disabilities. Some 42.2% of people with severe disabilities have incomes below the median income, compared with 13.3% of people with no disabilities (McNeil, 1997).

Individuals with very low incomes are, of course, particularly vulnerable to high costs of living and exposure to financial shocks. Those who are eligible for federal cash assistance under the federal disability programs SSI and SSDI are less vulnerable in part due to the cash payments, but mostly due to their resulting eligibility for Medicaid and Medicare. Contrary to popular misconception, only 37.1% of people with severe disabilities receive means-tested government assistance (McNeil, 1997). Among those on the disability programs, work incentive provisions in these laws have further increased the earning potential of these individuals. However, the vast majority of people with disabilities still do not attempt to work and remain trapped in a permanent state of subsistence (Batavia & Parker, 1995).

Expenses

The term "expenses" is used in this article to connote financial costs that must be paid out of pocket by the individual (as opposed to costs that may be paid by third parties). People with disabilities generally have the same categories of expenses as other people, as well as a few additional categories. These additional expenses may include housing and workplace modifications, special transportation needs, attendant care, interpreter services, reader services, periodic medical procedures or visits with specialists, and in some cases assistance in organizing care and services for their special needs. The need for personal assistance services increases with age (McNeil, 1997). Depending on their specific needs associated with their impairments and functional limitations, people with disabilities often bear financial burdens far beyond those of people without disabilities.

Obviously, if the individual's expenses exceed income for several years consecutively, this could deplete whatever net assets the individual may have accumulated. Even those people with disabilities who are highly educated and have substantial income levels may also be adversely affected by high costs and financial shocks. For example, an individual with an annual income of $100,000 who requires extensive personal assistance services and who is subject to occasional severe health problems (e.g., decubitus ulcers, severe infections) may be severely impacted in a particularly bad year.

Although it is clear that people with disabilities are subject to high costs of living, little is known about their specific expenses. By virtue of their functional limitations, they tend to be more dependent than other people on costly human assistance and assistive technology. The most expensive component of human assistance for these individuals is services specifically designed to address their disabilities, such as specialized medical services and personal assistance services. However, people with disabilities also tend to have an increased dependence on services also used by nondisabled people such as housekeepers, electricians, plumbers, auto mechanics, and handymen, because many are less able to engage in self-help activities that are physical in nature (e.g., make minor home or car repairs and modifications).

Assistive technology can range from relatively simple devices (e.g., canes, walkers) to highly sophisticated motorized wheelchairs, communication devices, and environmental control units. The more expensive devices can cost tens of thousands of dollars and are virtually unaffordable to those who are not wealthy or who do not have another significant source of payment (e.g., health insurance, workers' compensation, vocational rehabil-

itation). Many insurance plans do not cover assistive devices or cover them only in very limited circumstances.

Stability of Income and Expenses

Almost as important as levels of income and expenses is their stability over time. An occasional dip in income or spike in expenses can have a dramatic effect on an individual's financial situation and risk of poverty. Expense stability may be conceptualized as a continuum, with a range based on stability of impairments, accommodations, housing, and social supports. Almost all expenses are subject to fluctuation, and this can have a particularly adverse impact on people with disabilities.

Automobile expenses are a good example. While insurance, licensing, and even maintenance costs may remain relatively stable, in some years it will be necessary to replace the car or make major repairs, creating extra financial instability. For a disabled person driving a wheelchair-accessible conversion van, such spikes can be particularly dramatic due to the relatively high cost of the accessible vehicle itself (typically over $35,000), as well as to the high cost of nonstandard parts and high labor costs for specialized personnel. Moreover, a person with special transportation needs may not easily be able to find another means of transportation while the van is being repaired. Unlike nondisabled individuals, people with disabilities may not be able to simply rent a car, even if their insurance will pay for them to do so. This can lead to additional expenses or even a loss in employment or employment-related income.

The nature of disability can also influence stability of expenses. Some disabilities change over time and require different adaptations and therefore different expenses over time. Some disabilities are degenerative in nature (e.g., multiple sclerosis, muscular dystrophy) and inherently result in major changes in needs and expenses as the impairment and disability progress. Yet, even people with relatively stable impairments (e.g., spinal cord injury) can have increased expenses over time as they age with their disabilities and develop secondary conditions (e.g., joint deterioration, muscle deterioration, skin breakdown, arthritis, scoliosis).

Like expense stability, income stability may be conceptualized as a continuum, ranging from very stable sources of income to very unstable sources. Some forms of income, such as entitlement program income (e.g., SSI, SSDI) and trust payments, are very stable. Most work-related benefits, however, are limited roughly to the time one is working and are therefore unavailable when a person is unable to work. Because people with disabilities have greater susceptibility to health problems, their risk of losing employment due to health problems is probably also above average. If this is true, income fluctuations are likely to be relatively high for people with disabilities.

Assets and Net Worth

The financial net worth (i.e., assets minus liabilities) of an individual offers an assessment of the individual's financial cushion at any point in time. This cushion can protect the individual during a period of financial shock, such as a severe medical problem. Personal savings and liquifiable assets remain the chief way people of all abilities prepare for the possibility of financial burdens and shocks. Many people with disabilities have almost no financial assets, and even a single year of financial shocks or one substantial shock can put the individual in poverty.

There are few direct data on the net worth of people with disabilities. However, we know that many have almost no net assets by the significant and growing number of SSI and TANF recipients with disabilities. For the most part, assistance under these programs is not designed to allow these individuals to increase what little reserve they may have. In order to qualify, it is generally necessary to show both low income and minimum assets. Once in poverty, financial recovery is extremely difficult.

Health-Related Financial Consequences

All aspects of a person's finances are affected by a substantial disability. However, financial consequences related to health problems deserve specific attention. Numerous studies demonstrate the high susceptibility of many people with disabilities to major health problems (DeJong, Batavia, Griss, 1989; LaPlante, 1993; Max, Rice, Trupin, 1995). Estimates of their health care expenses vary in part based on the definition of disability used. One study found that people with an activity limitation due to a chronic condition spend over four times more than nondisabled people on health care (InfoUse, 1996). The high-risk status of this population has a double impact on the potential for financial stability: an effect on income and on expenses.

First, health problems can substantially affect income in any given year, particularly for the many people with disabilities who have little or no job security (such as individuals who work for wages or on a part-time basis). A major health problem can result in unemployment and/or loss of income even for people with full-time employment.

Second, high susceptibility to health problems has obvious implications for the expenses of people with disabilities. To the extent an individual does not have access to group insurance coverage and is not eligible for government coverage, an individual policy will be extremely expensive and often unaffordable. Moreover, individual policies typically have inadequate coverage, particularly for the needs of people with disabilities. Even if the individual has a good group policy, out-of-pocket expenses can be extremely burdensome in a year in which the individual has a major health problem. The federal tax system attempts to reduce the burden of some health care costs. However, only those qualified health-related expenses that exceed 7.5% of income may be deducted. Therefore, individuals with disabilities often have to bear the burden of thousands of dollars directly out of pocket without any tax relief.

The consequences of increased susceptibility to health problems are major sources of financial shock for people with disabilities. One study found that persons with both musculoskeletal conditions and comorbidity report 18% lower family earnings, 15% lower family income, and 35% fewer assets than the average among all persons their age, while those with such conditions and no comorbidity have earnings, incomes, and assets closer to the average among their peers (Yelin, 1997).

Another study indicates that 89% of an inception cohort of 186 people with rheumatoid arthritis (mean disease duration three years) were affected in at least one socioeconomic area (work capability, income, rest during the daytime, leisure time activity, transport mobility, housing, and social support), and 58% were impacted in at least three of these areas simultaneously. Overall, work disability was 4–15 times higher among these individuals than the general population, with 42% registered as work disabled after three years (Albers et al., 1999). However, we must also recognize that there are enormous differences among people with different impairments, and even among people with the same impairment, with respect to health problems that increase poverty risks (Baldwin, 1999).

It is apparent that health, income, and expenses are very closely related for people with disabilities—even more so than for people without disabilities—and any comprehensive policy to reduce poverty among the disabled population must address their health as well. Conversely, health care policy generally must be concerned about providing adequate access to quality care at a reasonable cost for people with disabilities and ensuring that the burden of health care expenses does not render such individuals disproportionately financially vulnerable (Batavia, 1993b).

Theoretical Framework

A rough assessment of the financial situation of people with disabilities may be depicted through income statements and statements of net worth. However, such a purely financial analysis by itself will not be sufficient to predict an individual's long-term financial security. In order to make such predictions, we must understand those factors that af-

fect income, expenses, assets, and liabilities over time. The risk of poverty, and consequent loss of financial security, is best depicted as the complex interaction of several personal, social, and environmental factors. As illustrated in figure 60.1, each of these factors may be expected to have a weak, moderate, or strong effect (characterized by the narrow, medium, and broad lines, respectively) on income and expenses, and consequently assets and liabilities.

Personal Factors

Among the personal factors that could potentially affect the individual's financial condition are impairment, disability, personality, values, intellectual ability, education, skills, adaptability, and motivation. Some of these are innate in the individual, such as impairment and intelligence. Others are more subject to modification, such as education and

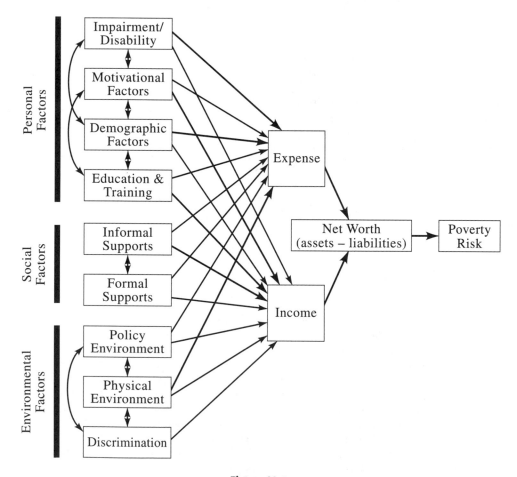

Figure 60.1

motivation. All of these personal factors interact in affecting individuals' abilities to manage their disabilities in a manner that allows them to function in the economy—whether that means attempting to balance their budgets based on program income or attaining optimal productivity to succeed in a competitive environment.

Managing a disability is not an easy task. Effective management typically involves the highly complex financing and coordination of many resources which must work in concert to compensate for the individual's functional limitations and/or to adapt the individual's environment to his or her needs. In most cases, people with disabilities, or their agents, will need to spend considerable time at these management necessities. Moreover, since the best laid plans often go awry due to extrinsic factors, the individual or agent will also spend considerable time troubleshooting when one or more parts of the accommodation strategy develops problems.

People who experience financial crises typically adapt by making contingency plans. If you cannot drive to work, you take the bus. If you cannot afford to each out, you eat in. However, for many people with disabilities, there is a limited array of viable substitute options. If your personal assistant doesn't show up, or your customized wheelchair breaks, or your guide dog dies, what do you do? Even the best managed contingency systems break down on occasion, resulting in particular frustration when contingency options are limited. This suggests that many people with disabilities may be close to the margin not only financially, but also emotionally, in their capacity to maintain independence. Several factors appear important, including the ability to plan in a flexible manner, the ability to deal with stress and frustration, the ability to invest by delaying gratification, and the ability to follow through in ensuring a successful long-term outcome.

The following are our hypotheses concerning how various factors inherent in the individual will affect the individual's income and expenses:

1. *Disability* (i.e., functional deficit) *is a moderate negative predictor of income.* Advocates of disability rights and independent living like to claim that the functional limitations of people with disabilities do not cause reduced employment and income, but rather the interaction between the disability and the environment causes such problems. Although environmental factors appear to impose the most significant barriers to inclusion in all aspects of life for people with disabilities, including employment, the impairments and related disabili-

ties of individuals can inherently preclude employment, either entirely or with respect to certain occupations, or can simply reduce productivity.

A perceptive commentator once observed, "Disability steals time." This insight has substantial implications for both the income-earning potential and spending requirements of people with disabilities. To the extent that the limitations associated with disability require an individual to spend more time on a given task than the task would require in the absence of the limitations, disability reduces the individual's productivity and earning potential. Of course, depending on relative aptitude, skills, attitude, motivation, and a variety of other factors, the individual could still be significantly more productive than his or her peers. The point is that, relative to the individual's potential without the disability, productivity may be reduced to some extent.

Thus, disability deprives the individual of needed income associated with the lost time, or alternatively, deprives the individual of spare time and energy necessary to compensate for the lost time. The type and extent of disability, and the availability of assistive technology to compensate for functional losses, will determine the extent of the lost income.

2. *Age is a moderate positive predictor of income.* Age is among the most important demographic factors affecting poverty risk. All other factors held constant, increased age and related life experience are probably associated with increased income.

3. *Motivation is a strong positive predictor of income.* Perhaps the personal factor that is most difficult to understand or measure is motivation. Some people with disabilities who have every financial advantage completely lack the motivation to become self-sufficient. Others who have no advantages have succeeded admirably. In other words, people with disabilities are not basically different from nondisabled people in this important regard, except that the consequences of their motivation or lack thereof may be greater for people with disabilities. Motivation is certainly affected by values and upbringing, but it also has a strong unpredictable element. It is not unusual to hear successful people with disabilities say that they succeeded to prove their ability to all those who doubted it.

Motivation in people with disabilities is likely to be affected by several factors, including perceptions about stability of their income and expenses and about the prospects that the future will be as good as or better than the present. For example, if individuals believe their hard work will be "re-warded" by a reduction in government benefits, motivation is likely to be diminished. This is prob-ably the strongest reason that very few people ever leave the Social Security disability rolls (Batavia & Parker, 1995). The individual's degree of commit-ment to the independent living philosophy is also likely to affect his or her motivation to become fi-nancially self-sufficient.

4. *Education is a strong positive predictor of in-come.* It is practically a truism that a good educa-tion is the road to opportunity and economic suc-cess. This appears to be particularly true for people with significant disabilities, because the skills and knowledge gained through education can compen-sate for lost functional capacity or can otherwise offer employment opportunities that would not have been available to the individual. For example, obviously a person who is legally blind cannot be employed as a taxi driver (except possibly in Mi-ami). However, such an individual, with the ap-propriate education, can be employed as an attor-ney or a banker. Therefore, education is not only the most promising strategy for employment for many people with disabilities; it is also the strategy with the highest return in terms of income. Unfor-tunately, as indicated above, people with disabili-ties do not achieve levels of education comparable to people without disabilities. Clearly, education is a key variable in any model for predicting financial vulnerability of people with disabilities.

5. *Functional deficit is a strong positive predic-tor of expenses.* In addition to adversely affecting income, disability is likely to increase expenses. This may result from increased costs of rehabilita-tive care, personal assistance services, and assistive devices. Also, to the extent individuals have limited time available to meet those needs they are capa-ble of addressing independently, they must live with needs unattended or must pay for them. For ex-ample, a person with a disability who is capable of doing housework may still need to hire a house-keeper if all his time and energy are consumed man-aging his disability.

6. *Age is a strong positive predictor of expenses.* All other factors held constant, increasing age is likely to exacerbate the costs associated with a dis-ability. A growing literature on ageing with a dis-ability indicates that, as people with disabilities age, their functional and health problems tend to in-crease (DeJong, Batavia, & Griss, 1989). These problems often require expensive medical attention or personal assistance.

7. *Motivation is a weak negative predictor of expenses.* Motivated individuals may find ways to fulfill their responsibilities without incurring addi-tional expenses.

8. *Education is a weak negative predictor of ex-penses.* Educated individuals may have skills or ac-cess to informational resources that can assist them in containing their expenses.

Social Factors

When most people with disabilities experience fis-cal shocks and other sorts of crises, there are a va-riety of social resources that they are able to ac-cess. These constitute our society's formal and informal safety net. They include informal support from family and friends, and formal support through federal, state, local, and not-for-profit pro-grams (Batavia, DeJong, & McKnew, 1991). In-formal support, which is uncompensated, is often inadequate to assist people with disabilities to achieve economic security and the capacity for in-dependent living. The high costs of many special accommodations are beyond the financial capacity of most families. The direct provision of personal assistance services by family members may reduce their capacity to earn income that would benefit the household, including the disabled individual.

There are considerable differences among fami-lies with regard to how they cope with crises (Mc-Cubbin & Patterson, 1983). By the same token, naturally occurring community supports (as defined by Pinderhughes, 1994), such as churches and so-cial organizations, frequently are not able to ac-commodate the often extensive needs of people with disabilities. Therefore, although informal supports are an essential component of the mix of resources needed by people with disabilities to survive eco-nomically, they will never be adequate for the vast majority of people with significant disabilities.

Like all Americans, those with disabilities are potentially eligible for all the government poverty-reduction programs, assuming that they satisfy the programs' non-disability-related eligibility criteria. In addition, there are some programs such as SSI for which disability itself is a primary eligibility cri-terion. Often, however, use of these programs comes at the cost of increased dependence or lim-itations on independence. For example, in order to receive SSI, it is necessary to prove that the indi-vidual is basically unemployable. Other programs may have other restrictions as well. For example, subsidized attendant care may be available in some areas only if the individual is willing to accept highly restrictive conditions (Batavia, DeJong, & McKnew, 1991; Doty, Kasper, & Litvak, 1996; Eg-ley, 1994).

The following are our hypotheses concerning how various factors associated with the individual's social relationships and support networks will affect the individual's income and expenses:

1. *Informal social support is a strong positive predictor of income.* Support provided by family members and friends is probably one of the most important factors in assisting a person with a disability to be able to seek gainful employment and to work at a higher level of productivity than without such support. For example, an individual without informal support may not have adequate personal assistance services or transportation to allow the individual to get to work.

2. *Formal social support is a weak positive predictor of income.* Obviously, formal support from social programs provides direct income or the equivalent in in-kind benefits (e.g., Medicare, Medicaid) for those who are eligible. However, this factor is somewhat ambiguous in its effect because such formal support can create a disincentive to seek gainful employment. On balance, formal support is probably a weak predictor of income.

3. *Informal social support is a moderate negative predictor of expenses.* Informal support from friends and family can directly decrease the expenses of an individual with a disability by providing services that the individual would otherwise have to pay out of pocket (e.g., personal assistance and transportation).

4. *Formal social support is a weak negative predictor of expenses.* Formal support from government programs may increase the individual's ability to care for himself or herself, and thereby contain health care costs.

Environmental Factors

Disability rights advocates often argue that the problems of disabled people have more to do with environmental factors, including discrimination and negative attitudes, than with their physical impairments (Fine & Asch, 1990; Meyerson, 1990). According to this perspective, their problems may be ameliorated or eliminated entirely through environmental modifications, including the use of assistive technology. Unfortunately, many people with disabilities who are working or wish to work do not have access to optimal assistive devices and work in environments that have not been adapted to their needs. Consequently, many such individuals are performing at a level that is below their optimal potential. In a competitive economy, in which incomes reflect productivity, it is likely that these workers are being paid less than what they would earn if accommodated more appropriately.[7]

To some extent, environmental factors and social factors overlap, particularly when we consider how formal and informal supports often affect the environment of people with disabilities. For example, some government programs provide some funding specifically for assistive devices and environmental accommodations. Other programs provide general funds that may be used by individuals or businesses for such purposes. Still, for purposes of conceptualizing financial vulnerability factors, it is valuable to consider the environment as a separate but overlapping category.

The following are our hypotheses concerning how various factors inherent in the individual's environment will affect the individual's income and expenses:

1. *Policy accessibility is a moderate positive predictor of income.* An environment of laws and policies supporting the aspirations of people with disabilities is likely to enhance the individual's ability to attain and maintain gainful employment. To the extent that some states, such as California and Wisconsin, have supportive policy environments, we predict that people with disabilities in such states will have advantages in seeking employment relative to people with disabilities in less supportive states.

2. *Physical accessibility is a moderate positive predictor of income.* An optimally accessible environment is likely to enhance the individual's ability to attain and maintain gainful employment. Conversely, an inaccessible environment can impose an insurmountable barrier to employment. As the ADA has enhanced accessibility in our country, physical accessibility is less of a barrier now than it has ever been.

3. *Discrimination is a moderate negative predictor of income.* Employment discrimination may prevent the individual from being hired or advancing to a higher level of employment. However, it is not deemed a strong factor, in that many individuals have been able to overcome discrimination to become successful in employment.

4. *Policy accessibility is a weak negative predictor of expenses.* A policy environment amenable to the needs of people with disabilities may reduce their burden of managing their disabilities, and could therefore reduce avoidable expenses.

5. *Physical accessibility is a moderate negative predictor of expenses.* An accessible environment is likely to reduce the individual's need for costly assistance. For example, an environment with a highly accessible public transportation system, such

as Washington, D.C., will significantly reduce the individual's transportation expenses.

Conclusions

People with disabilities appear to be among the most financially vulnerable Americans due to their low levels of education, employment, income, and assets. They are also among the people most in need of financial security due to often extraordinary and unstable expenses. There has been no systematic effort to research the relationships among personal, social, and environmental factors and financial vulnerability of people with disabilities. A variety of factors, including social support, environmental modifications, and attitudes about community living, may serve to moderate the effects of impairments and disabilities even in the face of financial crisis.

Significant empirical research is needed to determine factors that affect the financial vulnerability of people with disabilities and implications for economic self-sufficiency and independent living. Specifically what is called for initially is exploratory and descriptive research that can chart in detail how people with disabilities view their financial circumstances. These studies should identify the relevant vulnerability factors, including those that impose extraordinary costs on people with disabilities. Discerning this information is probably best achieved through qualitative research methods using focus groups of people with different disabilities (e.g., quadriplegia, paraplegia, deafness, blindness, mental illness), including an adequate representation of individuals who are living in or near poverty. Subsequently, once specific factors are identified, they must be operationalized as key variables and tested on the broader disability population to determine whether they are generalizable.

The findings of such studies will have important implications at several different levels. At the individual level, they can provide valuable insight for people with disabilities and their families to recognize sources of financial vulnerability and how to avoid them, including coping strategies of successful people with disabilities. At the clinical level, this research can provide similar information to professionals such as social workers and rehabilitation professionals to assist them in empowering their clients with disabilities to gain financial security and avoid poverty. At the broader policy level, such studies will have implications for income maintenance policy, employment policy, health care policy, tax policy, and civil litigation. By reducing the financial vulnerability of people with disabilities, we can help them to improve their lives and enhance their independence and self-sufficiency.

Notes

1. Section 2(a) (8) of the ADA (42 U.S.C. 12101(a) (8)).
2. The estimate of 54 million Americans with disabilities, representing 20.6% of the population, is based on a broad definition of disability including an array of functional and activity limitations. It is estimated that approximately 26 million, or 9.9% of the population, have a severe disability. Approximately 6 million use wheelchairs, 5.2 million use other mobility aides (e.g., cane, crutches, walker), 1.6 million are unable to see, and 1 million are unable to hear (McNeil, 1997).
3. The term disability is used differently by different people and in different contexts. Some people use the term to denote the relationship between the individual's environment and any impairment (e.g., severed spinal cord) or functional limitation (e.g., paraplegia) the individual has—the extent to which the individual is disadvantaged socially (i.e., "handicapped"). For purposes of this paper, we use the Nagi terminology in which disability is synonymous with functional limitation and does not necessarily imply a social disadvantage (Batavia, 1993a).
4. The philosophy of independent living, which has served as the ideological foundation of the independent living movement of the 1970s, includes strong emphasis on consumer control, peer support, self-help, self-determination, equal access, and individual and system advocacy (DeJong, 1979). See section 701 of the Rehabilitation Act of 1973 (29 U.S.C. 796).
5. Specifically, the CPS classifies people as having a "severe work disability" if (1) they did not work in the survey week because of a long-term physical or mental illness that prevents the performance of any kind of work, (2) they did not work at all in the previous year because of illness or disability, (3) they are under 65 years of age and covered by Medicare, or (4) they are either 65 years of age or a recipient of SSI.
6. The SIPP regards a person who is unable to perform, or needs the help of another person to perform, one or more of the following physical functional activities as having a severe functional limitation: (1) seeing ordinary newspaper print (with glasses or contacts if normally used); (2) hearing normal conversation (using hearing aid if nor-

mally used); (3) having speech understood; (4) lifting or carrying 10 pounds; (5) walking a quarter of a mile without resting; (6) climbing a flight of stairs without resting; (7) getting around outside; (8) getting around inside; and (9) getting in and out of bed.

7. This is also true of other workers without disabilities who are not accommodated adequately to meet their individual needs. However, due to the functional limitations of people with disabilities, the potential productivity gain of ad equate accommodations is likely to be greater for them.

References

Albers J. M., Kuper H. H., van Riel P. L., Prevoo M. L., van't Hof M. A., van Gestel A. M., & Severens J. L. (1999), "Socio-economic consequences of rheumatoid arthritis in the first years of the disease." *Rheumatology* May; 38(5):423–30.

Baldwin M. L., (1999). "The effects of impairments on employment and wages: Estimates from the 1984 and 1990 SIPP." *Behavioral Science Law.* 17(1):7–27.

Batavia, A. I. (1993a). "Relating disability policy to broader public policy: Understanding the concept of handicap." *Policy Studies Journal* 21(4):735–39.

Batavia, A. I. (1993b). "Health care reform and people with disabilities." *Health Affairs* 12(1):40–57.

Batavia, A. I., & S. Parker. (1995). "From disability rolls to payrolls: A proposal for social security program reform." *Journal of Disability Policy Studies* 6(1):73–86.

Batavia, A. I., G. DeJong, & L. McKnew. (1991). "Toward a national personal assistance program: The independent living model of long-term care for persons with disabilities." *Journal of Health Politics, Policy and Law* 16(3):525–47.

Berkowitz, E. D. (1980). *Rehabilitation: The Federal Government's Response to Disability 1935–1954.* New York: Arno Press.

Budetti, P., Burkhauser, R., Gregory, J. & Hunt, H. A. (2001). *Ensuring Health and Security for an Aging Workforce.* Kalama Zoo, MI: W. E. Upjohn Institute for Employment Research.

DeJong, G. (1979). "Independent living: From social movement to analytic paradigm." *Archives of Physical Medicine and Rehabilitation* 60:435–46.

DeJong, G., A. I. Batavia, & R. Griss. (1989). "America's neglected health minority: Working-age persons with disabilities."

Milbank Quarterly, 67 (Supplement 2, Part 2): 311–51.

Doty, P., J. Kasper & S. Litvak. (1996). "Consumer-directed models of personal care: Lessons from Medicaid." *Milbank Memorial Fund* 74(3):377–409.

Egley, L. (1994). *Program Models Providing Personal Assistance Services (PAS) for Independent Living.* Oakland, CA: World Institute on Disability.

Fine, M., & Asch, A. (1990). "Disability beyond stigma: Social interaction, discrimination and activism." In M. Nagler (Ed.), *Perspectives on Disability* (pp. 61–74). Palo Alto, CA: Health Markets Research.

InfoUse (1996). *Chartbook on Disability in the United States.* Washington, DC: National Institute on Disability and Rehabilitation Research.

InfoUse (1999). *Chartbook on Women and Disability in the United States.* Washington, DC: National Institute on Disability and Rehabilitation Research.

Louis Harris and Associates. (1986). *NOD/Harris Survey of Americans with Disabilities.* Washington, DC: Author.

Louis Harris and Associates. (1998). *NOD/Harris Survey of Americans with Disabilities.* Washington, DC: Author.

Kaye, H. S. (1998). The Status of People with Disabilities in the United States: A Report of Disability Rights Advocates, Inc. Volcano, CA: Volcano Press.

LaPlante, M. P. (1993). *Disability, Health Insurance Coverage, and Utilization of Acute Health Services in the United States.* Disability Statistics Report (9). Washington, DC: U.S. Department of Health and Human Services.

LaPlante, M., Kennedy, J., & Trupin, L. (1996). *Income and Program Participation of People with Work Disabilities.* Disability Statistics Report, (9). Washington, DC: U.S. Department of Education, National Institute on Disability and Rehabilitation Research.

LaPlante, M. P., Carlson, D., Kaye, S., & Bradsher J. E. (1996). *Families with Disabilities in the United States.* Disability Statistics Report (8). Washington, DC: National Institute on Disability and Rehabilitation Research.

Max, W., Rice, D. P., Trupin, L. (1995). *Medical Expenditures for People with Disabilities.* Disability Statistics Report (12). Disability Statistics Rehabilitation Research and Training Center. Washington, DC: National Institute on Disability and Rehabilitation Research.

McCubbin, H. I., & Patterson, J. M. (1983). "Family transitions: Adaptations to stress.

In H. I. McCubbin & C. R. Figley (Eds.), *Coping with Normative Transitions* (Vol. 1, pp. 5–25). New York: Brunner/Mazel.

McNeil, J. M. (1997). *Americans with Disabilities: 1994–95.* U.S. Bureau of the Census, Current Population Reports, P7 70–61. Washington, DC: U.S. Department of Commerce.

Meyerson, L. (1990). "The social psychology of physical disability: 1948 and 1988." In M. Nagler (Ed.), *Perspectives on Disability* (pp. 13–23). Palo Alto, CA: Health Markets Research.

Nosek, M. (1991). "Personal assistance services: A review of literature and analysis of policy implications." *Journal of Disability Policy Studies* 2(2):1–17.

Nosek, M. (1993). "Personal assistance: Its effect on the long-term health of a rehabilitation hospital population." *Archives of Physical Medicine and Rehabilitation* 74(2):127–32.

Oberman, C. E. (1965). *A History of Vocational Rehabilitation in American.* Minneapolis, MN: T. S. Denison.

Pinderhughes, E. (1994). "Empowerment as an intervention goal: Early ideas." In L. Gutiérrez & P. Nurius (Eds.), *Education and Research for Empowerment Practice* (pp. 17–30). Seattle, WA: Center for Policy and Practice Research.

Renz-Beaulaurier, R. L. (1996). *Health Social Workers' Perspectives on Practice with People with Disabilities in the Era of the Americans with Disabilities Act: An Exploratory-descriptive Study.* Unpublished doctoral dissertation, University of Southern California, Los Angeles.

Trupin, L.., Sebesta, D. S., Yelin, E., & LaPlante, M. P. (1997). *Trends in Labor Force Participation among Persons with Disabilities, 1983–1994.* Disability Statistics Report (10). Washington, DC: U.S. Department of Education, National Institute on Disability and Rehabilitation Research.

Trupin, L, & Yelin, E. H. (1999). *The Employment Experience of Persons with Limitations in Physical Functioning: An Analysis of the 1996 California Work and Health Survey.* Disability Statistics Report (12). Washington, DC: U.S. Department of Education, National Institute on Disability and Rehabilitation Research.

Yelin E. (1997). "The earnings, income, and assets of persons aged 51–61 with and without musculoskeletal conditions." *Journal Rheumatology* Oct; 24(10):2024–30.

PART IV

INTERVENTION: WHAT DOES OUR DIAGNOSIS LEAD US TO DO?

One of the most satisfying components of preparing this volume relates to the topic of this section on intervention. It was not a topic originally envisaged for this discussion of diagnosis through an analysis of recently published materials. Intervention has been viewed as something distinct from diagnosis. It tends to be viewed as a process that one puts into effect as an ongoing outcome of our diagnosis. Also, as social workers, technique is not a topic to which we have given a lot of attention. Most of our writing about intervention is found in the rich literature about the skillful use of the therapeutic relationship through the application of our long-standing methods of individual, group, and family intervention, with some discussion of dyadic work, principally in work with couples. (For the most part, it is implied that such couples are married and heterosexual).

However, as I focused on the practice-based articles written in this new millennium, I was pleased to find a large number that touched directly on differential aspects of intervention. That is, these articles showed very clearly that we have begun to move in two directions from the perspective of our developing practice literature. First, there continues a desirable discussion of specific aspects of our well-established individual, couple, group, family, and community quintet of methodologies. However, in addition to the continuance of this tradition, we are beginning to look at more specific therapeutic activities, most of which could be used as a part of any of the above five methods of intervention. It appears that we have now legitimized, at least in the practice literature, a new and different layer of therapeutic activities.

We have long stressed that to fully understand a person we must understand all significant factors that are influencing his or her life progress. Since many of these influences are positive factors for growth and since the essence of our therapeutic activities is to foster growth in whatever way is ethical and effective, should we not draw on the power of these influences to bring about sought-for change?

One of the most primitive of these factors, yet one most avoided as a therapeutic tool, is the concept of food. Much of our writing and our practice, especially that related to the fostering of a growth-enhancing relationship, uses language and images that imply acts of feeding and nourishing of a client. We know the role that food plays in our lives as both a daily need for survival and a real and symbolic way to relate to people at various significant events and from various significant systems in our lives. Yet consider how little use we have made of this knowledge in our therapy. Indeed, we have frequently cautioned and even admonished our colleagues about the risks, inappropriateness, and unprofessionalism of eating with a client. However, we are now moving beyond this very narrow perception and beginning to see that perhaps one of the most powerful things we can do with and for a client is to make use of food in a therapeutic manner, as exemplified in the Mishna, Muskat, and Schamess article.

This concept of making use of anything that is helpful and ethical is leading us to look at other components of our clients' lives. We are much more comfortable with viewing money, games, the telephone, dreams, technology, art, pets, meditation, and hypnosis as therapeutic tools. The range of articles selected for this section reflects particular uses that have been made of these specific actions or objects as a part of intervention.

Clearly, this is not the first time that such suggestions and reports of their use have been raised. Over the years there have been various efforts to broaden our repertoire of skills, techniques, and resources of treatment, as reflected in such practices as art therapy, bibliotherapy, psychodrama, play therapy, and music therapy. However, much of this type of practice activity gets sidelined, or is of interest to only a few. Often, colleagues interested in a particular intervention have been viewed as cult-like or, nonmainstream or as a special and exclusionary group. Yet some of these practices have established and richly developed knowledge bases. Gradually, we are implementing these more concrete and specific interventions.

Of course, there are risks of developing a mind-set that promotes irresponsible one-up-man-ship if we strive to be the therapist with the newest toy. However, there are checks and balances that can be introduced to operate against this. Certainly one very important way to enhance quality and accountability is for practitioners to contribute to literature that describes, critiques, and permits criticism of the use of various resources found to be helpful in practice. I am comfortable that we will find ways of ensuring quality. More important is to foster a mind-set in the profession that seeks to expand greatly our repertoire of techniques by making use of these very high-life human activities in a therapeutic way. Truly there is nothing more high-life than human relationships. These we have captured and directed into the almost frightening power of the therapeutic relationship that has been the essence of our clinical practice. Let us begin to invest similar interests in other human processes as ways of helping and influencing our clients.

Two other areas exemplify this expanding repertoire of interventive techniques. The first relates to the physical aspect of our clients, that is, the use of the body as a therapeutic resource. I include here such activities as yoga, hypnotism, and eye movement, as exemplified in articles selected for this section. Clearly we need to heed the abundant evidence that demonstrates that such activities are powerful instruments for change, activities that

have already shown that they can bring about desired alterations in the life areas we deal with in our practice. Such interventions are already used by many of our colleagues. This factor of course raises the question of professional boundaries and borders. I am not speaking here of interprofessional turf wars but of the ethical issue of competence. Our body is a part of our biopsychosocial essence, and how we care for and what we do to our body affects how we grow and develop. There is much knowledge available on which we can draw to appropriately utilize these physically related therapeutic activities. This assumes, of course, that as with any kind of intervention, we have the requisite knowledge and training. We cannot claim to be biopsychosocial in context but make use of only the bio or psycho or social interventions.

A second area of development in appropriate intervention in social work practice speaks to our growing comfort in considering theory as a treatment resource. This we do in two ways. The first relates closely to our diagnostic process. One of the advantages of approaching our practice from a multitheory perspective in which each theory is viewed as a separate but interlocking entity is to permit us to shine, different colored searchlights on presenting situations. The advantage of this is that we thereby get a variety of perceptions of clients, of their strengths, aspirations, and limitations, and of how best to influence them. As we know, neither a single theory nor our amalgam of theories gives us a total view of another human being. This is an important concept, one that helps to keep us from viewing any one theory or group of theories as the canon. Rather, it reminds us, as well as strengthens our humility about our knowledge, that theories only reflect our feeble efforts to understand that miraculous reality "person in situation." Theory has an essential role in diagnosis, but it also has a critical role in treatment, for just as each theory brings its own worldview and its own value set, it follows that some theories will fit some of our clients more closely or more sensitively than others and will lead us to shape with the client our therapeutic strategies. The exemplar of this idea, of which there were many in the literature, is found in the Lantz article where he discusses the use of Frankl's logotherapy. This is a helpful example of how theory sharpens our intertwined processes of diagnosis and intervention.

The richness of our diagnosic-based literature is rapidly expanding, in quantity certainly, but more important, in quality and diversity. This reflects our comfort and ability to imaginatively expand our perception of intervention into a rich range of specific activities that underscore our understanding of our clients as biopsychosocial entities. Now that we have legitimized this concept, it is anticipated that in the next few years we will see an even broader discussion of specific strategies, techniques, activities, and instrumentation as part of the armamentarium of our frontline colleagues. Mistakes will be made, out of enthusiasm or undue caution, but overall our value commitment and evaluative skills will help us find an appropriate balance. The conceptual challenge will be to distinguish between method (e.g., individual, family, group) and technique. Is this a clear distinction, or is it rather a spectrum along which, at some point, technique and method blend?

GUYLAINE RACINE
ODILE SÉVIGNY

61

Changing the Rules
A Board Game Lets Homeless Women Tell Their Stories

Introduction

As Milburn and D'Ercole (1991) have noted, many studies of homeless people have tended to assume that their subjects are incompetent, incapable of functioning, or both. Research on homeless women in particular is certainly no exception, with participants often presented as passive, disaffiliated, and unable to help themselves or others (Martin and Nayowith, 1989; Pollio et al., 1996). During the past 10 years, however, there have been more studies that distance themselves from this discourse, choosing to focus on the strengths and skills of the individual, even the most disadvantaged (Banyard, 1995; Banyard and Graham-Bermann, 1995; Berman-Rossi and Cohen, 1988; Breton, 1988, 1979; Glasser and Suroviak, 1988; Hardman, 1997; Johnson and Lee, 1994). There have been several experiments involving group work with homeless people, explicitly or implicitly aimed at constructing interventions that would not disqualify the participants' experience. These interventions focused on the strengths and skills of those involved "rather than on their 'pathologies' " (Pollio et al., 1996: 7). It is in this spirit that this article presents the innovative group activity developed by the workers at Auberge Madeleine, a shelter for homeless women in Montreal, Canada. During a research project on the coping strategies of homeless women,[1] a board game was created to encourage the women to talk about how they viewed their problems and how they dealt with the many difficulties that color their daily lives.

To put the activity into a context, we will begin by describing Auberge Madeleine, followed by a brief history of the creation of a board game called *Strata-Débrouille*, which roughly translates as "strategy + resourcefulness." A description of the game itself will follow, along with information on how the activity was organized and the role of the workers who facilitated it. We will then describe how participating in the game affected the women involved. In the discussion, an attempt will be made to relate the board game to the broader literature on the usefulness of program activities in group work. A few points are discussed that are pertinent to setting up the activity and to the relationship between playing the game and the stages of group development. Finally, although *Strata-Débrouille* was created in a unique context, we conclude by discussing the potential repercussions of this experience on group work with homeless people.

Project Background

Auberge Madeleine, which opened its doors 16 years ago, currently uses its 20 available beds to provide shelter for approximately 250 women a year. The problems most often encountered are related to violence, mental illness and substance abuse, extreme poverty, and social isolation. In addition to offering short- and medium-term shelter, the resource also provides psychosocial intervention services and helps its clientele obtain the social and medical services they need. Since its creation, Auberge Madeleine has been recognized for its innovative intervention practices. One of the main features of the culture of the shelter is its constant desire to reorganize its intervention practices in the interest of the autonomy and equity of its clientele.

The research experience surrounding the creation of the *Strata-Débrouille* game was a perfect fit with the ongoing development of Auberge Madeleine. In fact, the director and workers at the shelter were the actual originators of the project, looking for ways to move away from intervention models that ignored clients' abilities to solve their own problems without "expert" assistance. Although most of the women coming to the shelter were in a very distressed state, workers saw daily examples of their clients' resourcefulness in dealing with extremely difficult living conditions. By participating in a research project based on reflections they themselves had initiated, the workers hoped to develop new intervention tools that would allow them to focus on their shelter residents' strengths and skills. The result was the experience described in this article.

Creation of the Strata-Débrouille *Game*

Many discussions with the workers during project development culminated in an activity centered around the residents' participation in a board game that would allow them to talk together about the strategies they had devised to deal with the various problems they had encountered in their lives. In light of the study requirements and the practice milieu, it was agreed that a group activity would be developed to meet several criteria. The activity would (a) provide an opportunity for the women participating in the study to share their experiences with one another, (b) be adapted to the actual experiences of women living in a shelter,[2] (c) allow the workers to be involved in data collection, and (d) enable the workers to interact with the residents in a context other than that of "expert versus client." The board game not only met these criteria, but was also a good fit with the workers' practice style, taking into account the realities of the intervention and research context[3] and the workers' knowledge of the needs and characteristics of their clientele. What follows is a brief description of the game and how it was played.

Using the popular American board game *Careers* as a model, the director of Auberge Madeleine

and two of the workers created *Strata-Débrouille* (a description and rules of the game are presented in the appendix). The purpose of the game was to help staff to better understand the strategies used by homeless women in dealing with problems encountered in four different domains of their daily life: relationships with family and friends, housing, health, and legal issues.[4] It consisted of 120 questions, about thirty in each of the four domains.[5] The questions were based on fictitious situations that could easily occur in the life of any homeless woman.[6]

Along with the Question cards, there were also Situation squares at various places around the board. If a player's piece landed on a Situation square, she was required to recount a difficult situation that she herself or someone she knew[7] had experienced and how she or her friend had dealt with the situation. While the Question cards were intended to encourage residents to talk about their actions and the resources they used, the Situation squares were designed to find out how participants perceived their problems, that is, what constituted a problem in their eyes. Although the game offered players the opportunity to express their opinions on various subjects that affected them, it also had a definite social and recreational aspect. There were prizes for the winners and Chance cards that required players to answer questions of a less serious nature (for example, a player could be asked to tell a joke or sing a song).

Description of the Activity and Workers' Role

The game activity was first announced to all Auberge Madeleine residents at mealtimes. Once a sufficient number of women were interested in playing (more than two and ideally four), the activity was arranged.[8] Between October 1996 and June 1997 the game was played 10 times by a total of 35 residents. They varied in age from 18 to 60, but most were between 31 and 40. Like most of the shelter clientele, the majority of the participants lived in extreme poverty, in situations marked by violence, mental illness, and substance abuse.

The game was usually played once a month, with three or four women playing at a time. Since no participants played more than once, the group was different for every activity. It is interesting to note that this arrangement never hindered the creation of a bond of trust among the players. Perhaps this easy connection was due to the fact that many of the participants had already gotten to know one another a little bit during their stay at the shelter. For participants who knew each other less well, the game proved to be an opportunity to create bonds with the others. Some of the participants said that if they had not played the game together, they probably never would have spoken to one another.

The activity was always facilitated by a regular Auberge Madeleine worker who presented the game, explained the rules, and made sure all players had a chance to express themselves. The facilitator was also responsible for ensuring that the atmosphere remained one of mutual acceptance and trust. During the exchanges, the worker paid close attention to the needs of the participants, encouraging them to express their emotions, feelings, and thoughts on the situations they shared with the other women present. For most of the activities, the workers played a more active role at the beginning of the game, but gradually reduced their participation to leave as much space as possible for the participants to talk about their experiences together. Participants were quick to "take their place" and moved from addressing the workers directly to sharing their experiences among themselves with no need of the worker's support and encouragement.

The game was played in a closed room to ensure that participants' conversations remained confidential. The entire activity lasted about 90 minutes: the game was played for an hour, with a half-hour discussion period afterward. During the discussion, participants were encouraged to express what they had liked or disliked about the activity, as well as what they had learned about themselves and the others. They were also free to talk about any topic they considered to be pertinent to the experience they had just had. A short pause between the game and the discussion period served for the distribution of prizes and refreshments.

Strata-Débrouille: A Promising Group Activity

The action of forming a group of people around a specific activity does not necessarily guarantee that they will create a cohesive, supportive group likely to bring about change. From observation of the women's interactions during the game activity and conversations afterward, however, it was apparent that the board game encouraged dialogue among the participants, validated their experiences, feelings, and strengths, and fostered a feeling of solidarity.

An Opportunity to Speak Out

Many of the women who played the game spoke of solitude, both their own and that of others. They blamed today's society for the isolation of so many of its members. As one participant put it, "Everyone lives in their own little bubble, their own private space. They eat dinner with their families in front of the TV, their kids come home to an empty house, they walk down the street plugged into their walkmans." Almost all the women talked about their feelings of isolation, of a lack of meaningful individual or social recognition. The game emphasized the suffering of the participants, who were unused to the luxury of having someone listen with interest to what they had to say.

Many explained that playing the game had given them the chance to talk about themselves, to be heard and understood by others. In spite of their initial reserve, most of the participants said that the game had helped them to "open up, express ourselves, to communicate and interact with others." Liza[9] had this to say about her experience: "The questions [asked by the game and other participants] brought me out of my shell, which really helped me a lot. After spending eight years in jail, I needed some contact with other people." Their need to express themselves to a sympathetic audience was so great that most of the women found the game too short.

Their participation in the activity allowed the women to share and validate the knowledge they say they acquired through life experience. Since they felt that their words were heard and not disqualified, they stated their opinions freely and took a strong position on matters that directly affected their lives. In fact, some participants claimed that what they most appreciated about the game was seeing that their words could have an impact on others (both the other players and the worker facilitating the activity). As one woman explained, "If you don't touch someone with your words when you talk, you might as well not bother." Many others requested that Auberge Madeleine provide more opportunities for them to discuss various topics of interest with other shelter residents.

Learning from Others

The game provided an opportunity to hear other women talk about how they cope with the difficulties in their lives. As one woman said, "It gives us the possibility to learn together, find solutions and new ideas. We see other women as sources of information." Many said that what they learned by watching and listening to the others helped them to reconsider their own way of acting or thinking: "Since I'm someone who has trouble making decisions, I find that other women's situations give me ideas." Along with this recognition of the other comes the realization that she is "a little bit the same as me." Before the game, participants saw themselves as "strangers stuck together in a shelter"; after the game, they realized they had something in common. Women who come to the shelter are at a similar point in their lives, a moment of crisis or serious rupture in the fabric of their existence. This is the feeling of being "all in the same boat" so often described in the literature on group work (Shulman, 1988).

During all the game activities, many examples were evident of interactions where concern for the other was palpable. Participants showed each other attention, respect, interest, and empathy. They were touched by the others' experiences, revealing their capacity for support. For example, when one participant wept while describing a violent incident of which she was the victim, the other women comforted her, held her hand, and assured her that she was not responsible for what had happened to her.

This concern for the other was also revealed in small gestures during the game: helping other participants understand how the game was played (explaining one of the rules to a woman who did not understand, for example) or helping them improve their chances of winning (giving a chip to a player who had forgotten to ask for one, explaining a better strategy for accumulating chips, helping another player formulate her answer to a question, etc.). The alliances developed during the game activity were often maintained well after the game had been put away. During the days following, workers observed that women who kept to themselves before playing began to join the others at mealtimes, take part in activities, and give each other advice.[10]

Discussion

The value of activity-oriented experience has long been recognized in group intervention (Heap, 1979; Middleman, 1983; Northen, 1988). In social work with groups, activities can be used for a variety of purposes. An activity like *Strata-Débrouille* facilitated the verbal communication of feelings, ideas, and experiences and "stimulated reflective and problem-solving discussions, leading to understanding selves, others, and situations" (Northen, 1988:78–79). Moreover, since it was a tangible activity that allowed participants to decide on their degree of involvement in the conversations (from telling jokes to discussing very personal subjects), *Strata-Débrouille* made it easier for participants to express themselves. In that sense, the experience reflects one of Northen's (80) observations that "engaging in some activity permits a person to enter into conversation as he is ready to do so, without the sense of pressure that is often present when discussion is the only activity."

The board game also had an impact on the group development process. Although it was never the intention to do an in-depth analysis of how the group developed, every time the game was played the "search for commonality," the initial phase in most groups (Heap, 1979; 78), was made easier by the fact that the game was based on pooling the players' experiences. It also seems that this type of activity can be used as a vehicle to "enhance the development of relationships among the members and the cohesiveness of the group" (Northen, 1988: 78–79). All game activities moved very quickly to a stage of intimacy without going through the stage of power and control described by Garland, Jones, and Kolodny (1965). There are various explanations for this rapid development of intimacy. Perhaps the participants felt more comfortable discussing personal subjects with women they had been seeing on a daily basis at the shelter.

It is also well-known that the events that occur in the life of a group can be catalysts for mutual support if they are wisely managed by the group. Incidents during the activities (a woman being consoled by the others when she wept remembering an episode of violence she had experienced, another woman receiving support for her anger with the legal system) helped to solder the bonds among the players by creating greater cohesion. It is also possible, as suggested by Schiller (1997), that the Garland, Jones, and Kolodny model is not universally applicable for all groups and that "normative group development for women's groups follows a different pathway" (p. 4).

In spite of its singularity, the *Strata-Débrouille* board game represents a creative approach to engaging and working with homeless women. Two elements in particular seemed to attract and hold the interest of this population and facilitate the implementation of the game. First, the fact that the game was presented to participants as an activity designed to recognize and endorse their experience seemed to have had a special appeal for these women. In fact, most of the women who accepted the invitation to participate in the game activity said that they did so because they found in interesting that, for once, someone was showing interest in their knowledge, not just their problems. As one of them said, "All of a sudden, the fact that we live in difficult situations but develop strategies to cope with our problems becomes an asset, something to be proud of . . . and not something to be ashamed of." Playing the game conferred on the participants the status of experts in their own field, whose knowledge was recognized as expertise to be shared. Second, the attitude of the workers involved in facilitating such an activity is crucial to its success. The workers at Auberge Madeleine shared the conviction that the participants had rich, valuable experiences and possessed knowledge and skills that deserved to be recognized. This attitude colored all the games and was undoubtedly one of the factors that contributed to the emergence of a feeling of social usefulness and competence among the participants.

Conclusion

The board game has proved its worth as a group intervention tool. At this stage, it appears to have all the elements of an empowering activity, encouraging participants to acknowledge and identify the strengths they use to deal with their problems. As the participants put it, the experience of telling their stories to others who listened and believed was an extremely powerful one. This kind of experience helps to reduce the emotional isolation of these women (Breton, 1988: 58), thereby "breaking into the spiral of isolation, rejection and social failure" (Heap, 1979: 75). The experience also showed that homeless women have a great capacity for mutual aid. The dialogue among the participants gives each of them the opportunity to learn from the skills and strategies they recognize in the others. The interaction with other women living in similar situations transforms their words, which are no longer centered uniquely on their personal experience of daily survival but expanded to include the words of other women like them. The action of participating in the game thus can produce a collective discourse on the experience of being a homeless woman. This is a first step in allowing people with little access to the traditional seats of power to produce a version of their experience that "*sustains their own personal life story in positive ways*" (Rappaport, 1995: 796).

Taking part in a group activity such as this can also serve as a springboard to the mobilization necessary to bring about change at the macrosocial level with respect to improved living conditions for homeless women. For example, several *Strata-Débrouille* players took advantage of the activity

to present their view of the social context in which they live and the impact of social inequality on their living conditions. For many, these discussions provided a needed opportunity to initiate a reflection on the social and economic factors that contribute to maintaining their status as homeless women.

The involvement of the workers at Auberge Madeleine in developing the *Strata-Débrouille* board game has had significant repercussions on their work. It has encouraged them to redefine their practice to reflect a recognition of complementary skills: the professional expertise of the workers combined with the experiential knowledge of their clients. It has also changed their perceptions of group intervention and their own ability to develop this kind of activity. Since the vast majority of workers in Montreal shelters had had little training in facilitating or developing group interventions, this type of work has often been seen as difficult to implement in their practice milieus. On the one hand, the characteristics of their clientele lead them to assume that homeless women are not ready to play an active role in a group process. On the other hand, many shelter workers see group work as an extremely long process that demands a certain stability in terms of membership, and women living in shelters are only there for a short time. For the workers at Auberge Madeleine, their involvement in creating and facilitating the *Strata-Débrouille* game activity provided concrete evidence of the value of group work. This has already resulted in a move away from their usual practice based on individual intervention models to develop group and collective processes.[11]

Notes

1. Support for this research was provided by the Quebec Council of Social Research.

2. Although the game was originally created to be played by homeless women, it can easily be modified for use with other groups. The game board is set up in such a way that the four domains used by workers at Auberge Madeleine (interpersonal relationships, health, legal issues, and housing) can be adapted by other practice milieus interested in using the activity.

3. Since the women who come to Auberge Madeleine stay for relatively short periods of time (from a few days to a few weeks) and do not necessarily keep in touch with the resource after they leave, it was difficult to plan a long-term activity. Furthermore, the research project specifications demanded that the greatest number of women be

reached over a given period. In this research context, it was thus impossible to attempt to create a group whose membership would remain stable for all of the game activities.

4. The game was structured around three main research objectives: (1) to better understand how homeless women perceive their problems, (2) to find out what resources they use to solve those problems, and (3) to learn what action they took to deal with a given problem.

5. Some examples of Question cards in the four different domains: *Personal relationships*: "Your neighbor is having a hard time living with her alcoholic husband and can't decide whether she should leave him or not. What would you say if she asked you for advice?" "Your sister is going for an abortion and asks you to go with her, but you have a new job and can't risk taking a day off. Who could you ask for help?" "Your 70-year-old mother is suffering from Alzheimer's, but it is impossible for you to help her. Who could you turn to for help?" *Legal issues*: "A friend of yours, who has been accused of assaulting her neighbor, has to appear in court next week. She tells you that she was only defending herself, but is afraid no one will believe her. What do you think she could do?" "Your cousin has just been arrested for shoplifting for the fourth time. Who could help her?" *Health*: "Your denture is too small and causing ulcers on your gums, but welfare won't pay for another one for another year. What can you do?" "You are absolutely exhausted and really need a break. Where would be the best place for you to go and rest?" *Housing*: "Your friend wants to move because she is afraid of her neighbors, who are very violent. She decides to talk to her landlord before taking action. If you were with her, what would you tell her?" "Your landlord tells you that you won't have any water for four days because he has to do some repairs in your bathroom. You get along well with your neighbors and you also know that your sister has a really big apartment. Who would you ask for help?"

6. The Question cards were written by shelter workers based on records of requests for assistance from former residents.

7. This "rule" is intended to minimize discomfort at having to talk about personal situations in front of others. Participants were free to describe situations that were not their own experience. In addition, if the facilitator felt that one of the participants was extremely distressed at any point during the game, she could terminate the activity or take a break for the time it took to comfort the participant in question. Although it often happened that one of the participants expressed distress or cried, it was never necessary to end the game. The support offered by the other participants and the facilitator was sufficient.

8. Four categories of potential participants had to be excluded from playing the game: (1) women whose knowledge of French was insufficient to express themselves easily (women who could understand the gist of the conversations with the facilitator's help were allowed to play, however); (2) women whose mental or psychological health was too fragile; (3) women who were intoxicated (on alcohol or drugs) at the time of the activity; and (4) women whose behavior could disrupt the activity.

9. Names are fictitious.

10. These effects of the game may have been limited in time as there was no way of determining whether the contacts were maintained once the women left the shelter.

11. One of those projects is the Friday breakfast discussion group, where all participants—both residents and workers—talk about the week's current events. These informal sessions have now been taking place for several months. Each person is asked to select an article from the week's newspapers and present it to the group on Friday morning. Sometimes the activity focuses on current events that have a direct effect on those present, such as new laws and cuts in social services, and their impact on the daily lives of homeless women. At other times, discussions can range from international policy, organ donation, the legal system, and how women are presented in the media to lighter fare, such as new movies or a favorite celebrity. The discussion group is extremely stimulating and enriching for everyone involved. It enables participants to situate themselves with respect to what is happening in society and form an opinion on various subjects. Like the board game activity, the discussion group gives shelter residents a space where they can not only talk about themselves, but express opinions on subjects on which they are rarely consulted.

The authors thank the workers at Auberge Madeleine and all the residents who participated in the game. They also thank Cynthia Gates for her assistance with the translation of this article.

The research project described in this article was made possible by a grant from the Quebec Council of Social Research (#RS-2660 095).

References

Banyard, V.L. (1995). "Taking another route": Daily survival narratives from mothers who are homeless. *American Journal of Community Psychology, 23*(6), 871–891.

Banyard, V.L. and Graham-Bermann, S.A. (1995). Building an empowerment policy paradigm: Self-reported strengths of homeless mothers. *American Journal of Orthopsychiatry, 65*(4), 479–491.

Berman-Rossi, T. and Cohen, M.B. (1988). Group development and shared decision making: Working with homeless mentally ill women, *Social Work with Groups, 11*(4), 63–78.

Breton, M, (1988). The need for mutual-aid groups in a drop-in for homeless women: The Sistering case. *Social Work with Groups, 11*(4), 47–61.

Breton, M. (1979). Nurturing abused and abusive mothers: The hairdressing group. *Social Work with Groups, 2*(2), 161–173.

Garland, J., Jones, H. and Kolodny, R. (1965). A model for stages of development in social work groups, in *Explorations in groups work,* ed. Bernstein, S. Boston: Milford House.

Glasser, I. and Suroviak, J. (1988). Social group work in a soup kitchen: Mobilizing the strengths of the guests. *Social Work with Groups, 11*(4), 95–109.

Hardman, K.L.J. (1997). A social work group for prostituted women and their children. *Social Work with Groups, 20*(1), 19–31.

Heap, K, (1979). *Process and action in work with groups: The preconditions for treatment and growth,* New York: Pergamon Press.

Johnson, A.K. and Lee, J.A.B. (1994). Empowerment work with homeless women, in Markin, M.P. *Women in context: Toward a feminist reconstruction of psychotherapy.* New York: Guilford Press.

Martin, M.A. and Nayowith, S.A. (1989). Creating community: Group work to develop social support networks with homeless mentally ill. *Social Work with Groups, 11*(4), 79–93.

Middleman, R, (1983). *Activities and action in groupwork.* New York: Haworth Press.

Milburn, N. and D'Ercole, A. (1991). Homeless women: Moving toward a comprehensive model. *American Psychologist, 46*(11), 1161–1169.

Northen, H. (1988). *Social work with groups.* New York: Columbia University Press.

Pollio, D.E. (1995). Hoops group: Group work with young "street" men. *Social Work with Groups, 18*(2/3), 107–122.

Pollio, D.E., McDonald, M. and North, C.S. (1996). Combining a strengths-based approach and feminist theory in group work with persons "on the streets." *Social Work with Groups, 19*(3/4), 5–20.

Rappaport, J. (1995). Empowerment meets narrative: Listening to stories and creating settings. *American Journal of Community Psychology, 23*(5), 795–807.

Schiller, L. Y. (1997). Rethinking stages of development in women's groups: Implications for practice. *Social Work with Groups, 20*(3), 3–19.

Shulman, L. (1988). Groupwork practice with hard to reach clients: A modality of choice. *Groupwork, 1*(5–16).

Appendix

Rules for Playing *Strata-Débrouille*

Game contents:	1 game board
	4 colored pieces
	1 die
	4 individual scoreboards
	Different colored plastic chips to fill up the scoreboards
	4 sets of yellow and purple cards (family, health, housing, legal) to be placed at specific places on the board
	A set of blue "chance" cards to be placed in the middle of the board
Number of players:	From 2 to 4, as well as a worker to facilitate the activity
Purpose of the game:	Each player tries to fill up the 12 spaces on her scoreboard by answering the questions on the cards.

Rules

1. Before you start playing, appoint one person to be responsible for distributing the plastic colored chips that are earned every time a player answers a question on one of the Question cards.

2. Each player selects a piece, which can then be placed on any of the "Start" squares (there is one for each domain).

3. Place the sets of blue and green cards on a table beside the facilitator and the Chance cards in the middle of the board.

4. Players must decide whether they can be reminded to ask for a chip every time they answer a question or if they want to be responsible for remembering on their own.
5. Players take turns throwing the die. The highest number starts.
6. Pieces must be moved clockwise around the board.
7. Each player throws the die and moves her piece the same number of squares around the board. Each toss of the die is one turn.
8. When a player's piece lands on a square that tells her to go to the entrance of one of the four domains, she must go there immediately, but does not actually enter until her next turn.
9. The four domains: this is where players can collect the most chips they need to fill up their board. When a piece lands on a blue or red square in one of the domains, the player must take a card of the corresponding color and answer the question after having read it aloud. When a piece lands on a green square, the player must talk about a problem that she or someone she knows experienced and explain how the problem was dealt with. She must also explain in a few words why the situation she described was a problem.

Once the player has answered the question or presented a problematic situation, she is entitled to one chip for her scoreboard.

10. Any chance cards collected can be used at any time during the game. If a player uses one to move around the board, she cannot throw the die during the same turn.
11. During the game, if another player lands on a square that lets her ask another player for one of her chips and that player doesn't have any, she doesn't have to give her one!
12. The first player to fill up the 12 spaces on her scoreboard wins the game.
13. If the game has to be interrupted for some reason before one of the players has filled up her scoreboard, the prize goes to the player with the most chips.

62

The Use of Crisis Teams in Response to Violent or Critical Incidents in Schools

Introduction

Increased public awareness of violent incidents in America's schools has prompted a call for school districts to prepare themselves for unthinkable events. School systems have developed an array of plans that include procedures to enhance the flow of communication, the installation of metal detectors or other security devices, and the formation of collaborative relationships between educational institutions and law enforcement agencies.

This paper will first define the types of violent or critical incidents that may affect schools, and then discuss why schools must develop plans for responding to such events. Proactive responses include forming school crisis teams to plan interventions, developing action plans that make it possible to respond quickly and effectively to a variety of crisis situations, and establishing criteria for selecting team members. The paper will then outline the three essential components of a crisis plan and discuss the vital role social workers can play in developing and implementing such plans in school settings.

Types of Violent or Critical Incidents

Thankfully, most schools will not be confronted with massive violence of the type that has recently occurred in Arkansas, Colorado, and California. Research data published in an annual report on school safety (Office of Juvenile Justice and Delinquency Prevention, 1998) state that since 1993, school crime has been declining. Moreover, the statistical findings show that violent crimes and homicides in schools are extremely rare; theft is the crime most frequently committed in schools. Nonetheless, schools must be prepared for violence or other critical incidents that seem likely to traumatize students, families, and staff members. Critical events can include (1) natural disasters (e.g., earthquakes, tornadoes, or hurricanes); (2) deaths resulting from violent or natural causes that involve a student, parent, faculty, or staff member; and (3) threats of in-school violence (e.g., verbal threats, bomb scares, an individual with a weapon).

It is impossible to predict the traumatic effect of any potential incident since so many variables influence how students, teachers, staff, and community will respond. The most significant variables are the severity of the event, the harm inflicted, the relevant relationship of victims to the rest of the school community, and the coping skills and developmental level of the most affected children.

Preparing for Violence

If schools are to develop violence response plans, they must first recognize that violence and other traumatic events can occur within their boundaries. This fact is difficult to assimilate since it challenges most people's view of the world as a safe and secure place. People tend to feel "it could never happen to us," and that violence happens only to "other people." Nonetheless, violent incidents in schools have been happening with depressing regularity over the past decade. In a survey of 1,044 students conducted by the Metropolitan Life Insurance Company (1999), it was found that 25% had been victims of a violent act occurring in or around a school building. The tragedy at Columbine High School in Littleton, Colorado, rocked belief systems across the country, as people were confronted with the fact that violence can and does occur in communities of privilege. Unfortunately, for many years violence has occurred regularly in schools in poorer communities but has, far too often, been tolerated or ignored.

Preparing for violence takes several forms in schools. One perspective, typically offered by law enforcement personnel, is that preparation means installing metal detectors and instituting unannounced locker searchers to keep the tools of violence out of educational institutions. Another perspective involves working with children around issues of civility, bullying, and appropriate ways to express anger. Preparation, however, is only one component of a comprehensive plan. Ideally, such a plan would involve recruiting a crisis team; conceptualizing, agreeing on, and implementing prevention activities; and, if a violent or critical event actually occurs, implementing a mutually agreed upon action plan designed to ameliorate the effects of the event. In a guide issued to schools by the Department of Education (1999), the attorney general and the secretary of education jointly recommend that schools create environments where students feel connected to each other and to the faculty/administration, and where early warning signs are heeded and responded to proactively.

The Crisis Team

Responding effectively to violent incidents in schools requires the development of teams that will assess the need for intervention, develop response plans, and effectively implement agreed upon plans. Although the composition of crisis response teams varies depending on the particular school, teams that are well comprised should include key representatives from every component of the school program. Accordingly, the response team may include school administrators, teachers, paraprofessionals, nurses, office staff employees, counselors/social workers, food service personnel, custodians, and other support staff members such as speech pathologists or physical therapists. Since roles and func-

tions within the school vary, the different team members contribute their own unique perspectives during the assessment and planning phases as interventions are being developed. In general, team members should be full-time staff so they can be contacted immediately in the event the team needs to respond quickly; interested part-time personnel can be included if they are easily accessible.

Generally, because of the organizational structures of schools, it is desirable to choose as team leader a representative of the administrative staff who is committed to the team concept. A contingency plan should be developed in case this administrator is unavailable. The backup person could be the principal, assistant principal, a lead teacher, or a counselor/social worker.

Team members should be evaluated carefully since willingness to participate is not the only membership criterion necessary to ensure optimal development and functioning. The school social worker can play a vital role in the planning phase by helping to identify staff members who possess the characteristics that will contribute to the team's effective functioning. Team members should possess the ability to formulate multisystemic interventions. They should also be flexible, skillful collaborators with good communication skills who are comfortable in dealing with crises and other potentially traumatic events.

Developing the Crisis Plan

Once the crisis team members have been identified, the next step is to develop an intervention plan. The team should not focus on particular critical incidents, but rather should plan for how it will function in response to a range of different emergency situations. Individual roles should be clearly delineated so the agreed upon intervention plan can be implemented quickly. Responsibilities that must be assigned include assembling the team; communicating with the school system's central administration; communicating with the media; providing mental health services for students, families, and/or staff members; and developing informational materials for parents.

If a critical incident occurs, the team must establish safety and security for students and faculty as quickly as possible. It is essential that team members use this principle to guide their thinking as they assess, plan, and intervene. The crisis plan must also consider a range of contingencies and designate backup individuals if team members are unable to participate. In addition, the plan should be made available to all staff in a written form that clearly describes team members' roles and responsibilities. A checklist may be helpful in guiding the assessment and planning phases of the team's response. This tool ensures that crucial aspects of the plan are not forgotten in the confusion generated by a crisis.

Communication is an essential aspect of a coordinated plan. A recognized code word should be used to inform all school personnel that notice of a crisis is being conveyed and that the crisis plan is being implemented. Communicating information to school personnel, parents, community members, and the media will help reestablish safety and security in the school building. Many schools use intercom systems to communicate within the building; however, a contingency plan must be developed for those times when the intercom system is disabled. This plan might, for example, involve choosing individuals to function as messengers with the tasks of imparting instructions and key information to school personnel. A violent act occurring in a school building will also require a response from community agencies such as the police and/or fire departments. Collaboration with these agencies in developing the crisis team and the action plan will help ensure a coordinated response, and is strongly recommended.

Once a plan has been developed, all staff members in the school should attend an orientation session in which the plan's details are presented. At that time, questions can be answered and staff can become familiar with the emergency code word as well as with the initial steps that must be taken (e.g. locking classroom doors or securing the building's outside doors while awaiting further instructions). This training should be repeated annually, and new staff should be provided with the information during their first days on the job.

Responding to a Critical Incident

When the crisis team is called on to respond to a critical incident, it will move through the following three phases: assessment, planning the intervention, and carrying out the plan. A thorough assessment of the situation is necessary since it will determine what interventions are needed. Each situation is different, and the team will have to assess a variety of factors including the severity of the incident, the number of students and/or staff affected, and the developmental level of the victims. For in-

stance, the death of a student will have different meanings for the other students depending on their relationship with the deceased, the cause of death, and their age and cultural understanding of what death means.

During the assessment phase, it is necessary for the team to formulate plans on a multisystemic level, taking the previously mentioned factors into account. For example, a traumatic event in the community that affects a student and his or her family may ripple throughout the entire school community. Students in the child's classroom will, perhaps, experience the most intense reaction, while staff members will have a different response, and students in other classrooms may experience the incident with less emotion. Varying reactions necessitate the development of different action plans to meet the needs of different populations.

The school social worker can play an integral role by formulating a comprehensive assessment of the situation. Social work training emphasizes collaborative skills and an ability to formulate interventions that consider how multiple systems affect individuals. These factors must be carefully considered in order to both to reestablish a sense of safety and security within the school and to meet the needs of those affected by the crisis.

When the assessment is complete, various interventions will be implemented. These should be targeted to specific groups such as an individual classroom or a particular grade level. The team will need to designate individuals to facilitate the plan. Facilitators might include members of the crisis team, other school personnel, or, at times, individuals from the community. It is important that the team reconvene when the crisis is over for at least one debriefing session. During that session the interventions can be evaluated and needs assessed to determine whether further action is necessary. In addition, crisis team members should evaluate the team's functioning and process the members' feelings and reactions to the event. This is a vital but frequently overlooked team function.

A Case Example: An Elementary School's Response to the Columbine High School Tragedy

In 1997, two years before the Columbine tragedy, the social worker at an elementary school in a mid-size New England city decided it would be prudent to develop a crisis plan. The school, which served

750 students from preschool through grade 5, operated in a large building that had some open public access because it housed a systemwide registration center for parents. The city had high rates of poverty and crime. The social worker was experienced in working with children and families affected by trauma. Consequently, she was familiar with the effects of violence and the importance of early intervention in the aftermath of a critical event. She shared her concern with another school counselor, and together they approached the school principal, asking her to authorize the creation of a crisis plan. She agreed and strongly supported them in developing the document. When the draft was complete, school personnel were asked to volunteer to become team members. In addition, other individuals were recruited to ensure that membership consisted of a representative sample of the school staff. The team reviewed the document and offered suggestions that were incorporated into the final draft. The final draft was then presented to the site-based management team, which approved it and forwarded it to the central office administration. The crisis plan was presented at a schoolwide staff meeting and since then has been reviewed annually, at the beginning of each school year.

When school resumed after the spring vacation in 1999, the Columbine High School shootings had occurred. The school counselors and social workers, administrators, and a unit of social work interns convened to determine whether an intervention was necessary in the aftermath of this violent event. There was general agreement that because of the intense media coverage, most students would have heard of the incident during the vacation. The crisis team recommended a school-as-a-whole response. Working in teams, counselors, social workers, and social work interns proposed to visit each classroom to initiate conversations about the shootings. In support of the plan, the school administrator agreed to write a letter informing parents about the intervention. Classroom teachers were approached about their willingness to have students in their classes participate in the conversation. All agreed, and some expressed relief that the dialogue was going to occur since they had not been certain about what to say or whether it would be helpful to say anything.

The classroom conversations varied depending on the developmental level of the students. In the lower grade levels (kindergarten through grade 2), students were asked what they knew about the event. Most were aware that something bad had happened at Columbine. The discussion then moved to issues of safety, and a number of children said they had not felt safe returning to school. They were assured that the adults in the building were doing everything they could to ensure a safe environment. The children were also encouraged to talk to an adult if at any time they felt unsafe or uncomfortable.

Students in grades 3 through 5 had much more knowledge about the events at Columbine High School, and many described graphic images they had seen on television. In discussing their feelings about the events, they too expressed concerns about issues of safety. The team members outlined the procedures in place to ensure student safety. These included the security guard on full-time duty at the school, security cameras, and the policy that all visitors were required to sign in at the office. Students were also encouraged to report any situations they felt might be unsafe to teachers or school administrators.

Implementing this crisis response illustrates that action plans must respond to events that occur both inside and outside of the school. Specific plans must also be flexible enough to accommodate children's different developmental needs. Last, it is important to note that at times, community events require a response that addresses the entire student body.

Conclusion

Violent and other critical incidents that affect schoolchildren are no longer impossible or even difficult to imagine. In spite of one set of reassuring statistics (Office of Juvenile Justice and Delinquency Prevention, 1998), they seem to occur with some regularity. Despite the relative sense of safety enjoyed by most schools, it is important to develop proactive plans that acknowledge the possibility that a crisis might occur. Planning should include activities directed at prevention, the development of a representative crisis team, the development of a crisis action plan, and opening lines of communication to community police and fire units. School staff should be oriented to this plan annually, and new staff should be oriented shortly after starting work at the school so everyone is aware of his or her delineated responsibilities. At times of crisis, when chaos is likely it is essential to have a clearly outlined action plan in place to ensure a prompt and effective response. A well-conceived plan guides the crisis team as it assesses the nature of the incident, conceptualizes an appropriate intervention, and implements an agreed upon intervention. The plan should be flexible enough to address a wide array of crises (from natural disasters to in-house violence) and responsive enough to address the different developmental needs of children who have been affected.

References

Metropolitan Life Insurance Company. (1999). *The Metropolitan Life survey of the American teacher: Violence in America's public schools—five years later.* New York: Metropolitan Life Insurance Company.

Office of Juvenile Justice and Delinquency Prevention. (1998). *Annual report on school safety.* Washington, DC: U.S. Department of Justice.

U.S. Department of Education. (1999). *Early warning, timely response. A guide to safe schools.* Washington, DC: U.S. Department of Education.

63

Nurturing Life with Dreams: Therapeutic Dream Work with Cancer Patients

Dreams can offer an effective vehicle for therapeutic work with patients managing life-threatening illness, a vulnerable group in need of a safe, supportive environment. Because of the stigma and complex emotions attached to advanced medical illness, patients tend to be isolated and inadequately supported by friends and family. Breaking the isolation and providing the requisite nurturing environment, dreams can act as a nonthreatening means to form a connection between therapist and patient. For a population that is often more able to discuss the physical aspects of disease, dreams can provide an effective vehicle for accessing the emotional aspects of that experience. This can help lessen isolation and loneliness and provide a means for discussing multiple issues of loss.

Although some dream work has been done with other patient populations (Bosnak, 1997; Moss, 1998; Muff, 1996; Welman and Faber, 1992), the literature reflects that little has been done with cancer patients. Since this group can be particularly prone to focusing on physical symptoms, treatment options, and the eventual outcome of the disease, including possible recurrences, it seems apparent that dreams could offer a way for them to talk about the associated psychological process. Oncology experts have found these types of discussions to be beneficial (Gore-Felton and Spiegel, 1999). Consistent with this hypothesis, short-term dream work integrated with counseling was offered to cancer patients at a social service agency. This paper will review the literature, discuss similar dream work conducted by other professionals, and present the outcome of the short-term work.

Background Information

Holland, founder of the field of psycho-oncology, has studied the emotional needs of patients diagnosed with cancer. According to her research, 25% of cancer patients present with psychiatric diagnoses, primarily related to anxiety and depression (Rosenthal, 1993). Gore-Felton and Spiegel (1999) report in their paper on breast cancer patients that "two decades of research provide ample evidence that many of the psychosocial problems that chronically ill patients experience respond to psychotherapeutic intervention" (p. 274).

Cancer patients are a vulnerable group in need of a safe, supportive environment to which they feel securely connected. Gore-Felton and Spiegel (1999) describe the sense of isolation experienced by patients: "The stress that is associated with coping . . . combined with the conflicted responses of friends and family can strain interpersonal relationships and exacerbate feelings of loneliness and isolation in the patient" (pp. 277–278). Cancer patients consistently report that friends disappear and family members do not know what to say. This dynamic is often compounded by an escalated sense of isolation when faced with increased symptoms and the process of dying (Gore-Felton and Spiegel, 1999).

Forming a secure therapeutic alliance can help diminish the isolation many cancer patients face and encourage the sharing of painful feelings and fears. Provost (1999) has found that "Dream work approaches seem to 'jump-start' members to move quickly into self-exploration" (p. 79). This is true because, she says, "the sharing of dreams provides a natural way to initiate self-disclosure through the medium of the dream, a way that usually seems less risky than more direct self-disclosure" (p. 79).

In their therapeutic work with cancer patients, Holland's team has found the need to "adapt their tactics for their unusual patient population" (Rosenthal, 1993). Treatment approaches tend to be less analytical and more geared toward helping the patient develop effective coping strategies. Non-traditional methods such as meditation and visualization are often introduced. Holland has also found that when "you are treating someone who may be facing death, you tend toward more existential questions: what is life and what is death" (Rosenthal, 1993). These are questions that make many people uncomfortable and can be difficult even for professionals to discuss.

Gore-Felton and Spiegel (1999, pp. 278–283) have found that "exploring fears associated with the process of dying is a powerful therapeutic tool that reduces anxiety experienced by the threat of death" and that it can help diminish the sense of isolation patients often experience. They also point out how difficult it is to introduce the topic of death and dying, to the point that therapists as well as patients tend to avoid it. Just as dreams can introduce different perspectives and provide a means to experiment with new ways to live, they can also introduce ideas about death (Moss, 1998).

Other professionals have studied the role dreams can play in therapy with terminally ill patients. Muff (1996) describes dream work in which dream images were used to help AIDS patients with the transitions involved in life-threatening illness, including the preparation for death. Welman and Faber (1992) discuss the dreams of a patient with a life-threatening disease. They report that the results of dream work with this patient supported Jung's view of death and dying as critical stages of individuation. Not only did the dream work help the patient come to terms with the dying process, but it also seemed to reduce his sense of isolation.

Practitioners of dream work report results that range from increased self-awareness and personal growth to more controversial ideas such as precognition, detection, and healing of physical ailments (Burch, 1999; Hersh, 1995). Bosnak says that "dreams offer us a clear track to healing and transformation" (Dykema, 1998, p. 1). He "believes that dreams can lead us from depression, dis-

orientation, and ennui to a feeling of aliveness and vitality. . . . Dream work can give us deeper connections in our lives, more direction in our lives and more control over our lives" (p. 1). Berube (1999) supports a similar view: "When the dream content is addressed in an appropriate setting, the dreamer may experience healing a part of the self not previously and explicitly acknowledged. The healing is a step toward wholeness" (p. 99).

Communication with professionals in the field of dream work and with experts Robert Bosnak and Robert Moss, who have worked with AIDS and cardiac patients, supported the validity of using dreams to work with individuals with life-threatening illnesses. These professionals stated that, in their experience, dreams helped establish effective therapeutic relationships. Bosnak felt this was true because "patients are less personally involved in their dream life than in their day life. This opens possibilities for intimacy with slight distance, which then evolves into full-grown intimacy" (personal communication, 2000). These professionals also agreed that dreams provide an effective vehicle for discussing the multiple issues of loss encountered by this population. As Bosnak said, "Because dreams present the issues, and not the therapist, they are experienced as more self-related, less imposed by the therapist." According to another therapist, dreaming of life as it was prior to being sick, as patients often do, can remind them of what they have lost and allow them to grieve.

Dreams were also found to be helpful with improving focus and increasing self-awareness: "Patients get to experience unknown elements of self and of others, increasing [their] ability to suffer through symptoms, finding meaning, and decrease isolation." Bosnak also described the "surprise" aspect of working with dreams: "People expect intellectual understanding and are taken aback by overwhelming emotional experiences." Other therapists have noted that dreams always bring surprising perspectives. The element of surprise in working with dreams may be part of what makes the work of these professionals successful. Patients are often surprised by what their dreams reveal and can be less defended and more open to dream messages. Thoughts they have repressed or have resisted acknowledging can be allowed expression and become a part of consciousness, expanding their awareness and potentially having a profound impact on their life (Bosnak, 1996).

The Dream Work Methodology

Historically, dream work has been used as a component of psychoanalysis for treating neuroses and character disorders. Bosnak, who developed the methodology utilized by the author, employs an innovative approach based on Jung's view of the dream world. A focus on bodily sensations seems to be particularly effective for patients with life-threatening illnesses, although it can sometimes be difficult for patients who have "walled off" feelings. Instead of trying to analyze a dream from a conscious perspective, Bosnak helps the dreamer to reexperience and learn directly from its reenactment. Reexperiencing the totality presupposes feeling all dream emotions, including those of the dreamer and the other characters. Time limitations and the length of the dream often make this impractical, but the intent is to help the dreamer see different perspectives of the dream by experiencing it rather then analyzing it. The insights that come from this kind of work are "cooked" and integrated in the dreamer's psyche rather than figured out and assembled by the mind.

When working on a dream, the dreamer is first asked to say the dream, without reading it. This dialogue is done slowly and in the first person, giving the dreamer a chance to reenter the dream. The therapist then asks about the context of the dream—what was going on in the dreamer's life that may contribute to its meaning. This includes major issues the dreamer might be facing, the mood he or she was in before and after the dream, and any immediate personal meanings he or she might see. The dream itself is then explored in more detail using Jung's technique of amplification (Van de Castle, 1994).

Amplification is an investigation into the personal meanings of the dream images. Using Bosnak's method, this investigation is done with all the senses—sight, sound, taste, smell, and touch. This allows for a visceral response to the dream that can bypass or reduce the intellectual response and allow direct assimilation of the dream material. According to Jung (1974), dream work brings about change when assimilation is done. For cancer patients, who are often cut off from their bodily sensations, the attention to sensate details can also offer a way back into the physical dimension, a way that can help them get in touch with associated feelings that may have remained unexpressed.

The Dreamers

The participants in this dream work were cancer patients and clients of Cancer Care, Inc., a community social service organization. They were women with limited social supports who reported having difficulty coping with their disease. One was not able to continue therapy because she became too sick from chemotherapy. All were quite debilitated by cancer, so the work was done on the phone. This did not seem to be a barrier for the dream work, but illness symptoms and treatment needs did sometimes cause other difficulties. Appointments were often missed, sometimes creating large gaps between sessions. Because the dream work methodology consisted of working on a dream in one session and discussing the ramifications of the dream work in the next session, continuity could be challenging when a few weeks had passed. Fortunately, dream work tended to introduce such compelling feelings and themes that there was generally little difficulty picking up the work, even after lengthy breaks between sessions.

Their Dreams

Pat is a 43-year-old single woman with breast cancer. It had been more than a year since her diagnosis. She was undergoing breast reconstruction surgery after a second mastectomy. Although she was under the care of a psychiatrist for depression, she saw him infrequently, mostly for review of her medication, and had limited familial and social supports. She contacted Cancer Care for financial support and had no interest in individual or group counseling until dream work was proposed.

Pat brought this dream to the first session:

I am entertaining guests in my house. Suddenly my brother is there. I don't know how he got there or how to get him to leave. He is aggressive and hurtful with me. I am shocked, angry, and scared. When I wake up from the dream, I am upset and think, "How did he sneak into my dream?"

Because of time limitations we were able to work only with the dreamer's perspective in this dream. I asked Pat to focus on the feelings she had before her brother arrived:

I am in my apartment with friends and relatives I trust. I am working and doing OK financially. I feel confident. I feel neutral, normal, good.

She was not able to reenter the domain of the dream and reenact its physical sensations, but she was able to experience the confidence and safety engendered by the dream scene—qualities she was sorely missing from her life at that time and pleased to get in touch with.

I then moved with her to when her brother was there, in her house, and asked her to focus on her feelings. These feelings made her very anxious and she did not want to stay with them long:

> I feel anxious because I don't know how to get him out or how he got there. It's my house and he's not supposed to be there. I am shocked at how he acts even though its how he's always acted. This is my house, with my friends, and he shouldn't act like that. I should be able to stop him. Someone should be able to stop him. The others are as shocked as I am and don't say anything. I don't know what to do.

I reminded her of how she felt before he came, trusting and confident, and asked her to try to feel that again. She was able to feel this and became much more relaxed. I asked her if she could then feel the anxiety of her brother's anger again. She did not want to try. We ended the session with her feeling the trust and confidence from the beginning of the dream.

In the next session we discussed the dream further. She indicated that it was very disturbing, but at the same time left her with a feeling of accomplishment and confidence. She also reported feeling more relaxed than usual. This new feeling of strength surprised her. We talked about the other feeling in the dream, the anxiety about her brother being in her house and not knowing how he got there or how to get him out. I asked her if this was a familiar feeling that she had experienced at other times. She brought up past incidents with her brother, other family members, and an old boss. These incidents all involved conflict but were not directly related to her current struggle with cancer.

The idea of using dreams with cancer patients was based on the premise that their dreams would be about cancer or cancer-related issues. This dream did not seem to be. Since the purpose of our work was to address issues related to her cancer, I was unsure of what direction to take with the dream. I remembered that Pat had mentioned feeling apprehensive about her imminent breast reconstruction surgery when she talked about the context of the dream, and I asked if the apprehension might be related to the dream feelings. Had she ever felt toward cancer as she had felt toward her brother in the dream? She said that when she was first diagnosed she had some of the same feelings. She did not know how the cancer got there

and just wanted to get it out as fast as possible, as she felt toward her brother in the dream, but the anxious feelings about her brother seemed much more "deadly" to her than those related to the cancer. Then she remembered other feelings she had about her illness: shock, fear, including morbidity, and anxiety that she would not be able to get the cancer out. "I could die," she said, "and there's so much life left to live."

As we processed this and other dreams, Pat and I discussed the possibility of her death and what it was like to be out of control, overwhelmed, hopeless, helpless, and held back from fully living her life. She was eventually able to experience the bodily sensations contained in her dreams. She described a weight on her shoulders that felt like it would topple her over. It seemed to her that she was carrying bricks on her shoulders while bricks were being thrown at her. She was also able to experience feelings, like the trust and confidence of the first dreams, which invited different perspectives, such as a feeling of empowerment from experiencing the aggressive strength of her mother in the same dream as she experienced the weight of her difficulties in life as bricks on her shoulders.

Joan is a 53-year-old single woman with stage IV colon cancer, metastasized to the liver, pancreas, small bowel, and spleen. She was in the process of undergoing chemotherapy and was quite ill following recent emergency small bowel resection. She was also experiencing difficulty getting around and had hired a part-time home attendant. Despite these challenges, Joan remained optimistic. She contacted Cancer Care for financial assistance and had no interest in counseling until she heard about dream work counseling.

Joan's first dream introduced the concept of death:

> Four bald naked men appeared. Their appearance seemed strange but despite this Joan told her partner, "Ignore them and they'll go away. Live and let live." At the end of the dream, there was a metamorphosis and they became four handsome men, one of whom told her, "Don't worry, everything's going to be OK."

Joan associated the bald men with cancer, chemotherapy, and the possibility of death and the handsome men with health, recovery, and life. This dream, which gave her hope because she believed it meant she would recover, also reflected her ambivalence by portraying her almost simultaneous acknowledgment and denial of the possibility of death.

Joan's second dream introduced the concept of change:

She was in an apartment where the furniture was not her taste and was all in the wrong place. She was very uncomfortable with this until her friend helped her move it. Then she felt better, although it still did not feel like her apartment.

As she worked on this dream, Joan discussed her fear of change. She described it as being like "something was gnawing at her."

By the third dream, Joan had become quite proficient with the process of the dream work. She was able to experience a range of emotions from the dream, including those of her real-life boyfriend, who was a character in the dream:

She was on a cruise ship with her boyfriend. He was there with his wife and Joan was observing him from a distance. She felt his relaxation as he soaked up the nurturing sun, without any fear of cancer. Later, when all the ship passengers ended up in the water, at first the water felt wonderful to Joan. Warm and soothing, it reminded her of happy days in her grandmother's pool. Then she sensed an undertow pulling at her. She said it felt like it had her by the leg. As she was feeling this, she saw her boyfriend and his wife. Swimming between them in the water, her boyfriend looked from one to the other, trying to decide which to save from drowning.

Fortified by reexperiencing the feelings of comfort from the sun and the soothing water, she was able to feel what it was like to have the undertow pull at her and to watch her boyfriend deciding whether he would save her life or his wife's. She was also able to feel all three of these perspectives at once.

In our discussions of this dream, Joan was drawn to the feeling of the undertow. Reminding her of an asthma attack, it was not a sensation she would easily forget. She thought it must be similar to what it would be like to drown. When I asked her if there was anything else about the water that struck her, she said, "It's funny that I'm leaving the choice up to him because I know how to get out of an undertow." She talked about this for a while, concluding on a positive note, "If I put myself in a position in life, I can get out of it." Then she began to sound less positive as we discussed specific ways this applied. She reported that in her current situation with cancer, "it feels like I have no choice. I did have a choice when I was healthy but I don't

anymore." She related her feeling of frustration with not having a choice to the drowning feeling from the dream and said that it would help if she felt more control over situations in her life. A later dream presented images of strength, protectiveness, competence, safety, comfort, and belonging that she could evoke when she felt afraid and/or out of control to gain a sense of mastery over the situation, thus reducing her anxiety and contributing to her state of well-being.

Sophia is an 80-year-old single woman with ovarian cancer and severe arthritis. She was undergoing chemotherapy treatments and was homebound with a part-time home attendant. She had been a client for about two months when she started doing dream work.

The first dream was about a toothbrush that was all broken up:

The brush was jagged like someone had cut pieces out of it. Sophia was holding it and saying, "What the hell is this?" with surprise. She knew she did not cut the toothbrush and wondered who did.

Sophia described her feelings holding the brush as curious, odd, out of control, and not the way things were supposed to be. She also related it to the fact that she could not take care of herself any more. We discussed her feeling of being unable to control her life and her resentment about having to be dependent on others.

The second dream had two characters: Sophia as a young schoolgirl and Rosie O'Donnell, someone she admires very much. Consistent with the dream work methodology, I asked her to experience being Rosie. As this character, she was able to feel successful, peaceful, and satisfied with her life—like she had accomplished what she wanted. She also experienced herself as a schoolgirl and felt uncomfortable, exposed, disapproved of, and anxious. Although it was very uncomfortable and made her tired, Sophia was able to experience both feelings together for a period of time, enabling their assimilation. Through the medium of this dream, Sophia expressed her ambivalence with her life and the possibility of dying without having accomplished all of her goals. At the same time, she said that the dream gave her access to a sense of satisfaction with her life of which she had not been previously aware.

The last dreams she worked on seemed almost like visitations. In both, a young woman appeared by her bed as she woke up in the morning and then quickly disappeared. The discussion that resulted from these visits was an in-depth exploration of death and dying. Sophia talked about reincarnation and what happens when we die. She discussed her fears related to death and shared how she would like to die. She concluded by saying that she was not really afraid of dying and that she saw it not as an ending but as a new beginning, one to which she looked forward.

Conclusion

These case vignettes illustrate how using dreams as a vehicle enhanced the depth of the work accomplished. The work focused on important illness-related issues: the patients' loss of control, their inability to take care of themselves, a feeling of their lives being on hold, ambivalence, and the fear of death. This happened very quickly, generally in the first session, and allowed crucial discussions that may have taken longer to occur in a traditional therapeutic relationship. Despite the fact that these discussions were difficult and brought up intense feelings of fear, loss of control, and being overwhelmed, patients reported feeling more relaxed and optimistic after the sessions. It is also clear that as a result of the dream work, core issues were discussed, bringing about the potential for fundamental change in these clients. All this was done with clients who were initially unwilling to accept counseling and who frequently missed scheduled appointments, possibly indicating ambivalence about the work. Not only did these women conclude that the dream work was helpful, but they did not want to stop when the contracted period of 10 sessions was completed (not all participants completed 10 sessions; some had fewer and some had a few more). When they learned that they could only continue counseling with other therapists who did not do dream work, they still requested referrals.

It also seems that dreams help patients to come to terms with dying. This is particularly apparent in the work with Sophia, who started out telling jokes and making light conversation and through the introduction of dream work moved quickly toward serious topics, including the longing for the new life she thought death might offer.

Implications for Practice

Despite these positive reports on dream work, there has been relatively little work done in the social

work field on dreams (Lucente, 1987). It is my hope that the use of dreams in working with patients with life-threatening illnesses will expand and continue to be explored. Given the frequency of social work practice with the dying and the favorable outcome of this work with cancer patients, dreams could be an effective tool in working with this population. There are many client populations who may also benefit. Studies have been done that show dreams can be beneficial in working with clients who have undergone trauma and other stressful events (Hartmann, 1991, 1995, and 1996; Cartwright, 1991).

These studies indicate that dreams may be an effective modality for therapeutic work with many individuals. There are many approaches to dream work that have merit. As Marie-Louise von Franz, "Jung's foremost living successor" who researched over 65,000 dreams, concludes:

> The healthiest thing human beings can do is pay attention to their dreams. "Dreams show us how to find meaning in our lives, how to fulfill our own destiny, how to realize the greater potential of life within us." (Boa, 1994, p. x)

The author would like to thank Stephanie Stern of Cancer Care, Inc., and Hunter College School of Social Work Professors Michael J. Smith and Judith Rosenberger for their help and support with this project.

References

Berube, Lionel. (1999). Dream work: Demystifying dreams using a small group for personal growth. *Journal for Specialists in Group Work*, 24(1), 88–101.

Boa, Fraser. (1994). *The Way of the Dream*. Boston: Shambhala Publications.

Bosnak, Robert. (1997). *Christopher's Dreams: Dreaming and Living with AIDS*. New York: Dell Publishing.

Bosnak, Robert. (1996). *Tracks in the Wilderness of Dreaming*. New York: Dell Publishing.

Burch, Wanda. (1999). Dream diagnosis, dream healing. *Dream Network*, 18(3), 32–35.

Cartwright, Rosalind D. (1991). Dreams that work: The relation of dream incorporation to adaptation to stressful events. *Dreaming: Journal of the Association for the Study of Dreams*, 1(1), 3–9.

Dykema, Ravi. (1998). Dreaming our way back to life, an interview with Robert Bosnak. *Nexus, Colorado's Holistic Journal*, electronic edition.

Gore-Felton, Cheryl and Spiegel, David. (1999). Enhancing women's lives: The role of support groups among breast cancer patients. *Journal for Specialists in Group Work*, 24(3), 274–287.

Hartmann, Ernest. (1991). Dreams that work or dreams that poison? What does dreaming do? An editorial essay. *Dreaming: Journal of the Association for the Study of Dreams*, 1(1), 23–25.

Hartmann, Ernest. (1995). Making connections in a safe place: Is dreaming psychotherapy? *Dreaming: Journal of the Association for the Study of Dreams*, 5(4), 213–228.

Hartmann, Ernest. (1996). Outline for a theory on the nature and functions of dreaming. *Dreaming: Journal of the Association for the Study of Dreams*, 6(2), 147–170.

Hersh, Thomas R. (1995). How might we explain the parallels between Freud's 1895 Irma dream and his 1923 cancer? *Dreaming: Journal of the Association for the Study of Dreams*, 5(4), 267–287.

Jung, C.G. (1974). *Dreams*. Princeton, NJ: Princeton University Press.

Lucente, Randolph L. (1987). The dream: Mechanisms and clinical applications. *Clinical Social Work Journal*, 15(1), 43–55.

Moss, Robert. (1998). *Dreamgates*. New York: Three Rivers Press.

Muff, Janet. (1996). Images of life on the verge of death: Dreams and drawings of people with AIDS. *Perspectives in Psychiatric Care*, 32(3), 10–23.

Provost, Judith A. (1999). A dream focus for short-term growth groups. *Journal for Specialists in Group Work*, 24(1), 74–87.

Rosenthal, Elisabeth. (July 20, 1993). Listening to the emotional needs of cancer patients. *New York Times*, 142 (49398), C1.

Van de Castle, Robert L. (1994). *Our Dreaming Mind*. New York: Ballantine Books.

Welman, Mark and Faber, Phillip A. (1992). The dream in terminal illness: A Jungian formulation. *Journal of Analytical Psychology*, 37(1) 61–81.

HOWARD PROTINSKY
JENNIFER SPARKS
KIMBERLY FLEMKE

64

Using Eye Movement Desensitization and Reprocessing to Enhance Treatment of Couples

An examination of the controlled-outcomes studies in marital therapy indicates that approximately 50% of couples significantly improve. Only a small number of studies has investigated the longevity of the positive results of couple therapy, and these investigations unfortunately demonstrate that there is a diminishing effect. Couple therapists obviously need to understand more about how to produce change that is lasting. Because the focus in most couple therapy is at the level of changing thinking or behavior, it may be that interventions that are aimed at our rational processes are not sufficiently effective (Atkinson, 1999). Recognizing that affective change should be an important focus in couple therapy has led to an increase in developing and researching emotionally oriented approaches (Johnson & Greenberg, 1994; Johnson & Lebow, 2000).

The creation of effective emotionally oriented interventions (Greenberg, 1993; Greenberg & Pavio, 1997; Johnson, 1996) has emerged through clinical practice and task analysis. The first step in task analysis is the clinical implementation of a nonempirically tested intervention that is based on the clinician's experience, theory, or model of therapy (Greenberg, Heatherington, & Friedlander, 1996). Our purpose is to take this first step in task analysis and introduce eye movement desensitization and reprocessing (EMDR; Shapiro, 1995) as an important and useful clinical technique when it is implemented in the context of an emotionally based experiential approach with couples.

For the past seven years, we have used EMDR in clinical practice and have supervised the implementation of EMDR with individuals and couples who have been treated in an experiential and emotionally based approach. We initially began using EMDR with highly distressed couples who did not have a therapeutic response to standard interventions (e.g., validation, evocative responding, heightening, empathetic conjecture) used in emotionally focused therapy (EFT; Johnson, 1996) or to techniques from various experiential models (e.g., empty chair, two chair, focusing). Our experience with this subset of couples was that EMDR seemed to provide the heightened emotional experience and increased willingness to engage emotionally that research has identified as important to the successful outcome of emotionally based therapy (Johnson & Talitman, 1997). Although EMDR has been classified as one of the behavioral exposure therapies, and Shapiro (1995) has embedded it within information processing, the theoretical basis of EMDR is still the subject of much debate (Van Etten & Taylor, 1998). In this article, we situate its use as a therapy technique in the context of emotion and an emotionally and experientially based relational therapy. This beginning effort to create another context for the use of EMDR hopefully will expand its clinical implementation with couples and lead to future empirical evaluations.

Importance of Emotion

Therapeutically, choosing to focus on emotion is supported from a variety of sources. Research by Gottman (1994) indicates that physiological expression of powerful negative emotion during couple conflict is an important predictor of marital distress. Specifically, emotional flooding can lead to conflictual marital behaviors, such as criticism, contempt, defensiveness, and stonewalling. In extreme cases, partners may eventually develop a bioemotional allergy to each other that interferes with the successful implementation of traditional cognitive and behavioral therapeutic interventions. Gottman's conclusions are supported by recent research in neuroscience (LeDoux, 1996) that demonstrates that emotional processing of simple sensory input is precognitive as affect alarms are initially set off that subsequently direct cognition and behavior toward flight or fight. When such emotional responses are triggered in the amygdala, the neocortex is not activated, and emotion is unregulated by reason. Because the brain may respond emotionally based on the similarity of the present situation to those of the past, a mild current stimulus may activate strong emotional reactivity caused by its relationship to a prior traumatic wounding. For example, an intense emotional response to a powerful event, such as a rape, may be triggered by sexual overtures from a loving partner; or a well-intentioned behavior may inadvertently trigger a childhood abandonment fear.

Jerome Frank (1963), in his classic work on psychotherapy as persuasion and healing, put forth the view that emotional arousal is an essential common factor in successful psychotherapy. In the past two decades, especially, some theorists have recognized that the process of emotional awareness, arousal, and reorganization is crucial to change in psychotherapy and that disorders occur when emotions are avoided, disowned, or underregulated (Greenberg, Watson, & Lietaer, 1998). Recent experiential therapy models also underscore the importance of emotion. For example, Gendlin (1981) has developed an approach that emphasizes a focus on a bodily felt sense to bring neglected inner affective experiences to awareness, and the dialectical-constructivist model (Greenberg & Pascual-Leone, 1997) encourages the therapeutic synthesis of two streams of consciousness: consciously mediated conceptualization and automatic emotional experience. Therapy from these models activates emotional experience to create new meaning.

In some experiential relationship therapies, emotions are at the forefront because they provide information about our intentions, and because they are seen as a powerful organizing force in human interactions. In relationships, we constantly send and read signals about emotional states (especially through our facial expressions) that inform and regulate our interactions (Johnson & Greenberg, 1988). From another relationship perspective (Pierce, 1994), distress is understood to result from attempts by each partner to control or avoid emotion. The fear of experiencing and expressing emotion produces a constriction of experience and interactions, whereas acceptance and expression of emotion lead to more expansive and healthier interactions.

EMDR and Emotionally Based Experiential Therapy

Borrowing liberally from these emotionally and experientially oriented models, we have developed an emotionally based experiential approach for highly distressed couples that uses EMDR as a primary intervention technique. In the early stages of this work, we employed EMDR with a couple only after a lack of success with other emotionally oriented interventions. However, after experiencing repeated positive results, we now time its implementation as we would any other emotionally based intervention. Before using EMDR, we thoroughly inform the couple about this approach; we demonstrate the eye movement technique; we give the couple printed materials to read; and we refer them to Shapiro's (1995) book for a thorough discussion of the EMDR process. With their agreement, EMDR is then implemented in a therapy context that operates within five primary guidelines: creating safety, targeting surface affect, deepening to core problematic experiences, reprocessing, and enhancing intimacy.

Creating Safety

Research over the past several decades has indicated that the therapeutic alliance is the best single predictor of treatment success, and many of the variables that contribute to a successful alliance have been delineated (Safran & Muran, 2000). Therapy approaches that are based on emotion (Greenberg & Pavio, 1997; Johnson, 1996), especially, place an emphasis on the importance of a safe and trusting therapeutic relationship so that clients may explore intense negative affect. Because EMDR may move people quickly and deeply into painful feelings (Manfield, 1998), we often ask our clients what they need to experience a sense of safety. Wanting to be assured that the therapist can handle intense emotion and prevent intense painful feelings from becoming overwhelming is the most common response. Thus, therapists in this approach must not only be able to tolerate and work with extreme client emotions, but they also must have the ability to contain their own emotional reactions, which can be easily triggered in this work. When clients do not perceive the presence of these factors, we have found successful application of EMDR to be unlikely. In addition to these more general ways of creating safety, clients often suggest methods that are unique to them, such as holding a stuffed animal, wrapping themselves in a blanket, keeping a door partially open, playing soft music, and having a brightly lit room.

In our work with couples, all sessions are dyadic because it is therapeutically important to have each partner witness the other's EMDR process. Therefore, clients must feel safe not only with the therapist but also with their partner. If there is a history of abuse or some dynamic that might put one or both partners at risk, EMDR is contraindicated because experiencing emotional vulnerability can create additional risk. Also, Shapiro (1995) does not recommend the use of EMDR with medical conditions, such as cardiac and ocular problems, pregnancy, or severe dissociative disorders because of the potential for intense emotional arousal.

Targeting Surface Affect

Highly distressed couples often present with intense negative emotions that are rarely difficult to identify or activate in the session and are often experienced as overwhelming and unchangeable. Deeper, disowned emotions may lie beneath those that are being expressed initially. Some emotionally oriented treatment models make a distinction between these types of emotion by categorizing them as secondary or primary (Greenberg & Pavio, 1997; Johnson, 1996). Primary emotions are described as fundamental, initial, core responses, whereas secondary emotions are understood to be reactions to primary emotions; for example, intense anger may be a reaction to hurt. Creating a change in secondary and primary emotions can lead to a change in a couple's dysfunctional interactions. Thus, emotionally oriented couple therapists focus on changing interactional patterns from the inside out; that is to say, changing internal emotional experiences precedes behavioral and cognitive changes.

Some approaches that focus on the importance of emotion (Atkinson, 1999; Gottman, 1994) em-

phasize intervening with self-soothing when intense emotion is expressed, to prevent flooding. In our approach, the therapist does not stop the emotional process to promote client self-soothing but, rather, uses the intense primary or secondary emotion as a target for bilateral eye movements. Clients are asked to describe and focus on the elements that are associated with their intense emotions (e.g., body sensations, feelings, images, and behaviors) while the therapist implements sets of eye movements. Our clinical experience supports various EMDR clinical reports (Lipke, 2000; Manfield, 1998; Shapiro, 1995) that prior traumatic events and primary emotions often emerge when secondary emotions are targeted with bilateral eye movements. For example, when targeting the rage that one partner expresses to the other, previously disowned vulnerable, painful feelings may emerge in a rather rapid but manageable manner. In this way, EMDR may quickly process couples through experiencing secondary emotions to the activation of those primary emotions that are fueling dysfunctional interactions.

Deepening to Core Traumatic Experiences

From an information-processing perspective, intensely negative emotional reactions toward a partner may be a result of incompletely processed experiences that are stored in the brain (Shapiro, 1995). These experiences may have been life-threatening traumas, such as rape, or "small t" traumas (Shapiro & Forrest, 1997), such as childhood attachment limitations that have occurred over time. For information processing to be successful, these single-incident traumas or multiple painful incidents from an invalidating past environment must first be accessed to be modified. The importance of accessing these networks receives some support from research that indicates change with adaptive functioning follows specific brain activation (Perry, 1998; Rossi, 1996). Clinical reports indicate that the use of bilateral eye movements is one effective strategy for activating and bringing to consciousness these previously inaccessible painful experiences (Lipke, 2000; Shapiro, 1995).

The effectiveness of EFT with couples has received strong empirical support (Johnson & Lebow, 2000), and the EFT model (Johnson, 1996) has greatly influenced the practice of couple therapy. However, in using emotionally focused interventions, we have sometimes experienced a lack of success at the point of attempting to access and activate primary emotions—a process that clinical research has indicated is important for change (Johnson & Greenberg, 1994). Implementing sets of bilateral eye movements can be a useful addition to the existing list of emotionally oriented interventions because it offers another possible way to lead clients into primary emotional experience. The success of EMDR may be caused by its activation of an intense, orienting response. There is some evidence that bilateral eye movements trigger an ability to engage in continuing attention to painful affect without emotional flooding (Armstrong & Vaughan, 1996). Creating such an orienting response is therapeutically valuable because the ability to access, regulate, and contain intense affective states is important for clients to have a corrective emotional experience (van der Kolk & McFarlane, 1996).

In using this approach with couples, the identification of an "attachment crime" (Johnson, 1996) can be therapeutically useful. The attachment crime is an important concept in EFT; it refers to a critical incident that symbolizes the most significant betrayal in a couple's relationship. The wounded partner experiences this incident as the basic pain underlying many subsequent hurtful relationship experiences. Some clients enter treatment with little memory of the incident, others report the experience as a traumatic flashback, and still others are able to describe many details of the experience. Within the EFT model, the therapist mainly deals with past examples of this attachment crime as they are enacted in present interactions with one's partner. Clients are not typically taken back into the past in an attempt to resolve these hurts; rather, these past experiences are acknowledged primarily to legitimize the couple's present interactional behaviors (Johnson, 1996).

The intensity of the devastation experienced from an attachment crime may sometimes block a couple from achieving a successful therapeutic resolution. In our experience, one explanation for treatment failure is that the attachment crime from the present relationship continues to be associated with past emotionally traumatic events. This association can be of sufficient strength that successful processing may require uncovering its prerelationship origins. For example, in one couple the husband was able to clearly identify the major attachment crime that he felt his wife had committed—one that he could not get over, one that seemed to be the basis of many other disappointments he experienced in their relationship. Anger was his typical response to these hurts, and he was not successful in moving beyond his hostility. The therapist implemented eye movements while the client experienced the emotions, bodily felt sense, and visual images that were associated with that attachment crime. He quickly accessed a core attachment trauma from his childhood that was related to his inability to process the attachment crime in his current relationship. This core trauma subsequently became the focus for therapeutic reprocessing and led to his working through the attachment crime in his current relationship.

Reprocessing

As emotionally and experientially oriented treatment approaches assert, when previously disowned feelings are activated, they can then be reprocessed by uniting them with cognition (Greenberg & Pavio, 1997). There is some research support for the theory that traumatic memories are locked in the right hemisphere in the form of disturbing sensory images and physical sensations without access to left-hemisphere language and reasoning abilities and that visual bilateral brain stimulation may promote the transfer of information between hemispheres (Teicher et al., 1997; van der Kolk, 1998). In this way, painful past hurts that fuel habitual dysfunctional interactions can be activated and linked to cognitive reasoning abilities. Clinical reports indicate that one possible advantage of using EMDR is that this reprocessing experience often occurs in an accelerated fashion without emotional flooding (Lipke, 2000; Manfield, 1998; Shapiro, 1995). The EMDR process is different from the client's usual past experiences in which emotion either has been overregulated by reason or has dominated reasoning abilities.

With successful reprocessing, the current relationship behaviors that activate a couple's emotional reactivity to each other would no longer have a strong association to past painful experiences. Decreasing this association can significantly reduce an overreactivity to a partner's current behavior and provide a basis for interactional change. For example, a critical remark by a partner would no longer have a strong emotional link to significant criticisms of the past. The negative primary emotions from those past experiences would have been accessed, activated, desensitized, and connected to adult reasoning. In addition, the experience of the primary emotions from those incidences would be able to flow naturally from emergence to healthy completion (Greenberg & Pavio, 1997). Because it is important to link the benefits of reprocessing to problematic couple interactions, EMDR should be implemented with both members of the couple to reprocess the emotional experiences that drive each partner's contributions to their dysfunctional patterns.

Enhancing Intimacy

As partners reveal their vulnerabilities, empathy is often evoked from the significant other (Fishbane, 1998). Taking the risk of showing vulnerability creates a "softening event," which research (Johnson & Greenberg, 1988) has identified as an important treatment success marker. Research also suggests that trauma recovery is better predicted by receiving comfort from another than by the trauma history itself (Johnson & Williams-Keeler, 1998). Thus, enhancing intimacy with couples may be conceptualized as the creation of a context where the mutual healing of emotional pain takes place (Baucom, Shoham, Mueser, Daiuto, & Stickle, 1998; Lewis, 1997).

Partner empathy and compassion often increase is proportion to the level of vulnerable self-disclosure (Guerney, 1994; L'Abate & Sloan, 1984). For example, experiencing a partner's deep pain from a childhood trauma may evoke more empathy in the witnessing partner than experiencing a partner's anger over being controlled. In the witnessing process, however, partners may remain self-absorbed and not respond to the newly emerging vulnerabilities with empathy. In this approach, witnessing partners are encouraged and coached to attend with a double focus: to their partners' experiences and to their own internal experiences. Witnessing partners make notes about their emotional responses to their partners' EMDR process to discover any constraints to their ability to be empathic. If present, these constraining emotional states become the focus for EMDR intervention. When such constraints are successfully reprocessed, often a compassionate response is released. For example, as one husband witnessed his wife work with hurtful primary emotions, his initial empathic response returned quickly to an intense secondary anger. After she completed EMDR for that session, his continued anger became the focus of intervention. During several sets of eye movements, he experienced and reprocessed earlier traumatic life events and the associated painful emotions that were fueling his anger. As reprocessing continued, his anger gave way to a more compassionate response.

Case Illustration

A couple presented for marital therapy because of the wife's recent threat to seek divorce after 15 years of marriage. The presenting problem was the husband's intense anger, which he expressed verbally and by breaking furniture. He also had experienced intermittent problems with impotency for the past 10 years of their marriage. One of their primary relationship patterns fit this description: She pursued him for emotional and sexual contact; he reacted in anger; she followed with reactive anger; they then engaged in an escalation of angry confrontation that terminated with both of them withdrawing into emotional distance. Although she was able to acknowledge the sense of hurt and rejection she felt below her anger, he was only able to acknowledge his hostility, which both labeled as "rage."

During the first several sessions, the therapist talked with the husband about his unhappiness with the frequency and intensity of his rage responses to his wife. He related that he had wondered for years why he seemed so "overreactive" and wanted one of the goals of therapy to be his gaining a better insight into and control over his rage. His wife agreed with that goal and added that she would like to get past her anger and hurt so they could rekindle the more intimate relationship that they used to have. The therapist explained the EMDR model and how he used it in an emotionally and experientially based context. All agreed that the husband's rage response from a recent argument between them would be the initial EMDR target. Both were reassured that her troublesome emotional responses would be targeted later. A two hour session was scheduled because this type of EMDR process often demands more than the 50 minute hour.

Before beginning the EMDR procedure, the husband requested that the room be brightened with additional lighting to increase his sense of safety. During the first set of eye movements, he focused on the visual images, thoughts, emotions, and bodily felt experiences that were associated with their most recent marital argument. After several more sets, his anger and muscle tension decreased. With additional sets of eye movements, he experienced prior incidences of marital stress followed by several painful childhood experiences. Experiencing these related life events during EMDR is understood from Shapiro's (1995) information-processing viewpoint as progressing through associated memory networks. The idea is that clients react to a present stimulus with undue anger or anxiety because of other associations linked to it. Therapy progresses as these additional associative experiences are processed.

During what was to be the last eye movement set for that session, further incidences emerged, culminating in his spontaneous experience of having been raped by two men approximately 20 years ago. He had never told anyone of this incident, except for his father, and had always used his "willpower to keep such thoughts away." As he focused on that memory during eye movement sets, his emotional reactions became amplified. The intensity increased to the point where he vomited into a trash can and experienced his body shaking uncontrollably. It is common with EMDR for emotional intensity to increase significantly before abating. Despite that level of intensity, he was able to focus on the therapist's fingers as he continued to guide him through bilateral eye movements. Possibly because of the strong orienting response produced by this EMDR process (Armstrong & Vaughan, 1996), he reported that he was not feeling overwhelmed by the experience and that he wanted to continue. With additional eye movement sets, many details of the traumatic memory emerged and became desensitized and reprocessed. EMDR continued for an additional 45 minutes as he recalled even more details about the rape with significantly less emotional intensity.

Because there is some research evidence that receiving comfort after a trauma may partially alleviate the emotional pain (Johnson & Williams-Keeler, 1998), the therapist asked him to recall his experience during the 24 hours after the rape. He described going home, telling his father about the incident, and experiencing his father's responses as rejecting and shaming. This memory created additional intense emotional and physical responses, and the therapist continued eye movements until he was able to achieve a satisfactory degree of desensitization. Several more sets were implemented as he reprocessed the entire 24-hour period beginning with the rape and ending with his father's rejection.

At the end of this session, he was able to integrate his cognitive functioning with his emotional memory, create a coherent narrative, and relate this past traumatic experience to his current anger and sexual/intimacy issues with his wife. From the viewpoints of EMDR and emotionally oriented therapies, he went on a deep inner search (from secondary to primary emotion) and was able to access, tolerate, self-disclose, and reprocess intensely painful affect. Hypothetically, through the use of bilateral eye movements, emotional memory that was held in the right hemisphere crossed the corpus collosum to the left hemisphere, where the emotional and cognitive neuronal networks became associated (van der Kolk, 1998). The accelerated pace at which reprocessing occurred in this case has been frequently reported in the clinical literature (Lipke,

2000), and we believe that this is one of the main advantages of EMDR.

A successful compassionate witnessing process is crucial for therapeutic success within this approach. Throughout the two hours of EMDR, the therapist frequently coached the client's wife to maintain a dual focus: her husband's pain and her reactions to it. The therapist encouraged her to feel free either to move closer to her husband physically and emotionally during this process or to move away. The therapist assured her that they would spend time discussing her reactions to this experience, but that EMDR itself would be primarily attuned to her husband. However, the therapist gave her permission to interrupt him at any time that she felt she could not safely handle her reactions.

During the most intensely painful parts of EMDR, his wife moved closer, put her arm around him, and gave him physical and emotional comfort. She was clearly moved by his depth of pain and vulnerability. At the end of his EMDR process and vulnerable level of self-disclosure, she reported "a drifting away" of her anger and an increased feeling of connection and compassion. He reported a deep sense of relief, some vulnerability about his self-disclosure, a decrease in his feeling of shame, and a renewed closeness to his wife. Our clinical experience continues to be that EMDR in the context of an experiential and emotionally based approach often produces a rather rapid and deep emotional experience for both partners with an amplification of their sense of connection, that is, a genuine compassionate witnessing. This observation is consistent with reports by other clinicians that intimacy is enhanced by self-disclosure of deep emotional experience (Guerney, 1994; L'Abate & Sloan, 1984).

The therapist employed EMDR in subsequent sessions that targeted some of the husband's unsuccessful sexual attempts with his wife and his feelings of inadequacy and shame. With her, EMDR was used to process through residual anger at her husband, her feelings of being rejected by him, and her subsequent feelings of inadequacy. During her EMDR work, no single traumatic event emerged as it had with her husband. However, many emotionally painful events (attachment crimes) from her childhood spontaneously emerged on which she was able to focus and reprocess during eye movement sets. Her husband's response to her EMDR process was one of increased understanding, compassion, and intimacy.

Further sessions focused on understanding how these traumatic primary emotional experiences had been fueling their current relationship patterns and how their recently experienced sense of renewed intimacy and connection could be used for change. As their core traumatic emotional experiences below their angry pursuer-distancer behaviors were reprocessed, the pattern itself faded for lack of support. Subsequent sessions focused on communication skills and problem-solving approaches, which had not worked in the past. The activation and reprocessing of the deep pain associated with their traumas, combined with mutual compassionate witnessing, seemed to increase their ability to use more cognitive, relational, and behavioral strategies in the service of creating an improved relationship.

Conclusion

Our purpose in presenting this material has not been to provide details of the EMDR model or of the various emotionally oriented therapy models. For the reader who is interested in the specifics of these approaches, excellent presentations of emotionally focused therapy can be found in books by Sue Johnson (1996) and Greenberg and Pavio (1997), and the details of the EMDR procedure are in Francine Shapiro's work (1995). For those MFTs who do not have expertise in the many experiential/emotion-based therapies, *The Handbook of Experiential Psychotherapy* (Greenberg et al., 1998) is a good resource.

It is also not our intention to promote EMDR as the next great "cure-all" or as a replacement for currently used emotionally focused interventions. However, EMDR as an intervention seems to fit well in an emotionally and experientially based treatment approach and can increase its therapeutic effectiveness.

References

Armstrong, M. S., & Vaughan, K. (1996). An orienting response model of eye movement desensitization. *Journal of Behavior Therapy and Experimental Psychiatry, 27*(1), 21–32.

Atkinson, B. (1999). The emotional imperative: Psychotherapists cannot afford to ignore the primacy of the limbic brain. *Family Therapy Networker*, July/August, 22–33.

Baucom, D. H., Shoham, V., Mueser, K. T., Daiuto, A. D., & Stickle, T. R. (1998). Empirically supported couple and family interventions for marital distress and adult mental health problems. *Journal of Consulting and Clinical Psychology, 66*, 53–88.

Fishbane, M. D. (1998). I, thou, and we: A dialogical approach to couple therapy. *Journal of Marital and Family Therapy, 24*, 41–58.

Frank, J. D. (1963). *Persuasion and healing: A comparative study of psychotherapy.* Baltimore, MD: Johns Hopkins University Press.

Gendlin, E. T. (1981). *Focusing.* New York: Bantam.

Gottman, J. M. (1994). An agenda for marital therapy. In S. M. Johnson & L. S. Greenberg (Eds.), *The heart of the matter: Perspectives on emotion in marital therapy* (pp. 256–293). New York: Brunner/Mazel.

Greenberg, L. S. (1993). Emotion and change processes in psychotherapy. In M. Lewis & J. M. Haviland (Eds.), *Handbook of emotions* (pp. 123–135). New York: Guilford.

Greenberg, L. S., Heatherington, L., & Friedlander, M. (1996). The event-based approach to couple and family therapy research. In D. Sprenkle & S. Moon (Eds.), *Research methods in family therapy* (pp. 411–428). New York: Guilford.

Greenberg, L. S., & Pascual-Leone, J. (1997). Emotion in the creation of personal meaning. In M. Power & C. Bervin (Eds.), *The transformation of meaning in psychological therapies: Integrating theory and practice* (pp. 77–102). New York: Wiley.

Greenberg, L. S., & Pavio, S. C. (1997). *Working with emotions in psychotherapy.* New York: Guilford.

Greenberg, L. S., Watson, J. C., & Lietaer, G. (1998). *Handbook of experiential psychotherapy.* New York: Guilford.

Guerney, B. G. (1994). The role of emotion in relationship enhancement marital/family therapy. In S. M. Johnson & L. S. Greenberg (Eds.), *The heart of the matter: Perspectives on emotion in marital therapy* (pp. 124–147). New York: Brunner/Mazel.

Johnson, S. M. (1996). *Creating connection: The practice of emotionally focused marital therapy.* New York: Brunner/Mazel.

Johnson, S. M., & Greenberg, L. S. (1988). Relating process to outcome in marital therapy. *Journal of Marital and Family Therapy, 14*, 175–183.

Johnson, S. M., & Greenberg, L. S. (1994). *The heart of the matter: Perspectives on emotion in marital therapy.* New York: Brunner/Mazel.

Johnson, S., & Lebow, J. (2000). The "coming of age" of couple therapy: A decade review.

Journal of Marital and Family Therapy, 26, 23–38.

Johnson, S. M., & Talitman, E. (1997). Predictors of success in emotionally focused marital therapy. *Journal of Marital and Family Therapy, 23,* 135–151.

Johnson, S. M., & Williams-Keeler, L. (1998). Creating healing relationships for couples dealing with trauma: The use of emotionally focused marital therapy. *Journal of Marital and Family Therapy, 24,* 25–40.

L'Abate, L. N., & Sloan, S. (1984). A workshop format to facilitate intimacy in married couples. *Family Relations, 33,* 245–250.

LeDoux, J. E. (1996). *The emotional brain.* New York: Simon & Schuster.

Lewis, J. M. (1997). *Marriage as a search for healing: Theory, assessment, and therapy.* New York: Brunner/Mazel.

Lipke, H. (2000). *EMDR and psychotherapy integration.* New York: CRC.

Manfield, P. (1998). *Extending EMDR: A casebook of innovative applications.* New York: Norton.

Perry, B. D. (1998). *Diagnosis and treatment of childhood trauma: New developments.* Conference conducted by the Menninger Clinic, Topeka, KS.

Pierce, R. A. (1994). Helping couples make authentic emotional contact. In S. M. Johnson & L. S. Greenberg (Eds.), *The heart of the matter: Perspectives on emotion in marital therapy* (pp. 75–107). New York: Brunner/Mazel.

Rossi, E. L. (1996). *The symptom path to enlightenment: The new dynamics of self-organization in hypnotherapy: An advanced manual for beginners.* Pacific Palisades, CA: Palisades Gateway.

Safran, D., & Muran, C. (2000). *Negotiating the therapeutic alliance: Handbook of experiential psychotherapy.* New York: Guilford.

Shapiro, F. (1995). *Eye movement desensitization and reprocessing: Basic principles. protocols, and procedures.* New York: Guilford.

Shapiro, F., & Forrest, M. (1997). *EMDR: The breakthrough therapy for overcoming anxiety, stress, and trauma.* New York: Basic.

Teicher, M., Ito, Y., Glod, C., Anderson, S., Dumont, N., & Ackerman, E. (1997). Preliminary evidence for abnormal cortical development in physically and sexually abused children, using EEG coherence and MRI. *New York Academy of Sciences, 821,* 160–175.

van der Kolk, B. A. (1998). *Understanding the psychobiology of trauma.* Conference conducted by the EMDR International Association, Baltimore, MD.

van der Kolk, B. A., & McFarlane, A. C. (1996). The black hole of trauma. In B. van der Kolk, A. McFarlane, & L. Weisaeth (Eds.), *Traumatic stress: Handbook of experiential psychotherapy* (pp. 3–19). New York: Guilford.

Van Etten, M. L., & Taylor, S. (1998). Comparative efficacy of treatments for post-traumatic stress disorder: A meta-analysis. *Clinical Psychology and Psychotherapy, 5,* 126–144.

65

Depression, Existential Family Therapy, and Viktor Frankl's Dimensional Ontology

One of the most common problems presented to general medical practitioners, psychiatrists, crisis intervention centers, hospital emergency rooms, social service agencies, individual psychotherapists, and marital and family therapists is depression (Lantz, 1978; Lantz & Thorword, 1985; Maxman & Ward, 1995). Although depression is often described as the kind of problem that responds most effectively to medications and individual psychotherapy (Maxman & Ward, 1995), family therapists have rather consistently pointed out that depression cannot be holistically understood or treated without an adequate understanding of the family context of the symptoms of depression (Andrews, 1974; Lantz, 1978; Lantz & Thorword, 1985). In this article the author seeks to provide an existential family therapy understanding of depression by outlining Viktor Frankl's (1955, 1959, 1967, 1969, 1975, 1978, 1997) existential dimensional ontology from a family-centered point of view. Case illustrations will be presented to show how Frankl's dimensional ontology can be used during existential family therapy to more effectively structure the assessment and treatment of depression within its family context. The author believes that the use of Frankl's dimensional ontology often results in a more effective, precise, and cost-effective treatment experience for couples and families facing depression.

About Depression

Depression strikes between 15 and 25% of the general population of the United States at least once during their lives (Maxman & Ward, 1995). Symptoms of depression can be severe, leading to suicidal attempts to "stop the pain," or less severe yet still unpleasant and disruptive to family life. The etiology of depression is mixed but is generally understood to include biological, neurochemical, genetic, psychosocial, family, developmental, ecological, and existential factors (Maxman & Ward, 1995).

Depression is generally considered to be a treatable problem, and most authorities (Frankl, 1955, 1967; Maxman & Ward, 1995) believe that a flexible treatment approach using medications, environmental modification, and psychotherapy will most frequently be effective. In existential family therapy (Lantz, 1974, 1978, 1993, 2000), Viktor Frankl's dimensional ontology can be utilized as a holistic framework around which to organize a flexible yet systematic approach to the family-centered treatment of depression.

Frankl's Dimensional Ontology

In Viktor Frankl's (1969) *Existenzanalyse* approach to existential family therapy, the "we are" of family existence includes three dimensions and/or levels of understanding. For Frankl (1955, 1969) family existence ("we are—we stand out") includes what we "must" do, what we "can" do, and what we "ought to" do. Using Frankl's dimensional ontology, it is possible to identify three dimensions of family depression: the "must" dimension, the "can" dimension, and the "ought" dimension. An outline of Frankl's dimensional ontology for use during the existential family treatment of depression is presented in Table 65.1.

The "Must" Dimension of Family Depression

In Frankl's (1959, 1969) dimensional ontology, the "must" level of family existence refers to those aspects of family life that cannot be changed by will or choice. For example, all family members must die if deprived of food, water, or shelter for an extended period of time. There is no will or choice in such a situation. In Frankl's (1955, 1969, 1978) dimensional ontology, it is understood that certain physical, genetic, neurological, and/or biochemical "must" factors contribute to family life, and that this "must" level of family existence is an extremely significant factor in the development of many mental health problems, such as depression, mania, and schizophrenia. In an existential family therapy understanding of depression, it is accepted that chemical imbalances in the central nervous system may contribute significantly to the development of depression and that medical intervention is usually necessary on the "must" level of treatment for depression among family members (Frankl, 1955, 1959, 1969; Lantz, 1978, 1993, 2000; Lantz & Thorword, 1985). In existential family therapy, it is believed that family members suffering from biologically based depression "must" continue suffering such depression until biochemical imbalances resulting in such depression are treated through medical interventions such as the use of antidepressant medications (see Table 67.1) (Lantz, 1978, 1993, 2000). In existential family therapy, it is important to help "must" dimension depressed families (as well as other family members) to realize that their "must" level symptoms of depression are not a result of their weakness or any lack of character or will (Frankl, 1969; Lantz, 1978; Lantz & Thorword, 1985). For the existential family therapist (Lantz, 2000), it is extremely important to teach "must" level depression families to avoid anger toward the self about those aspects of depression that family members cannot change through will or choice.

During the past 20 years there has been an explosion in understanding of biochemical ("must" level) depression and in development of medications to help family members cope with or overcome the biological ("must") component of depression (Frankl, 1997; Maxman & Ward, 1995). Such drugs fall into three general categories: the tricyclic drugs, the MAO inhibitors, and a group of second-generation antidepressants that include the newest drugs for the treatment of depression. All of these drugs probably correct biochemical imbalances that result in family member "must" dimension depression and in this way normalize the depressed family member's mood.

In existential family therapy, it is also understood that an important element of "must" dimension depression treatment is to help all family members learn more about the chemical aspects of depression, the symptoms of depression, and family coping mechanisms that can help all family members resist, contain, and manage the impact of depression on family life (Lantz, 1978, 1993; Lantz & Thorword, 1985). In existential family therapy, it is believed that psychoeducational methods can provide considerable relief with families and couples who are trying to deal with "must" level depression (Lantz & Thorword, 1985). The following two case illustrations demonstrate existential

Table 65.1 Family Existence: "We Are—We Stand Out"

"Must" level of family existence	"Can" level of family existence	"Ought" level of family existence
Physical and biological aspects of family existence	Structural, transactional, and pattern aspects of family existence	Meaning and purpose aspects of family existence
Physical capacities and limitations in family existence	The choices in family existence	The call to family existence
Somatic treatments, medications, and psychoeducational methods of family intervention	Structural, behavioral, narrative, transactional, psychodynamic, and solution-focused intervention methods	Existenzanalyse methods of family intervention

family therapy in a clinical situation where the primary element of depression was "must" level depression.

The James Family Mr. and Mrs. James were referred to marital therapy by their priest after Mrs. James complained to her priest about sleeplessness, crying spells, and guilt about "not wanting sex with my husband." Although the couple were willing to follow their priest's advice and engage in marital therapy, both the couple and the existential family therapist quickly realized that Mrs. James was suffering with "must" level (biological) depression that required psychiatric intervention and medications as the primary mode of intervention. Mrs. James was referred to the author's consulting psychiatrist, who started her on antidepressant medications and provided (initially) weekly supportive and educational counseling sessions to help the couple understand and cope with Mrs. James's biologically based "must" depression. Mrs. James responded well to medications, and within three months was free of her depressed mood, crying spells, suicidal ideation, reduced level of libidinal energy, general energy loss, and difficulty eating. Mr. and Mrs. James also experienced a considerably improved marital relationship with the decreased symptoms.

In this clinical illustration, Mrs. James responded well to medications designed to meet her treatment needs at the "must" level of existence. Although significant marital treatment on the "can" and/or "ought" levels of family existence was not needed, it is important to remember that successful "must" level treatment of depression often results in a couple's or family's realizing that additional treatment on the "can" and/or "ought" levels of family existence is also necessary (Frankl, 1955, 1969, 1997; Lantz, 1978; Lantz & Thorword, 1985).

The Jackson Family The Jackson family requested family treatment services after their son overdosed on street drugs. The son stated that he had tried to kill himself "to end the pain." The family was referred to treatment by the physician at the emergency room where the son had been treated for the overdose. At the time of the first family session, the son scored 87 (marked depression), the father scored 53 (minimal depression), and the mother scored 51 (minimal depression) on the Zung (1964) Self-Rating of Depression Scale.

It was difficult to determine any unusual or pathological family interactional patterns in the Jackson family. The parents had an open and nurturing relationship with each other and appeared to be supportive parents who were able to provide appropriate structure, guidance, and warmth to their son. The parents reported that their son's grandfather on the father's side of the family had committed suicide and that his uncle on the mother's side of the family had suffered recurrent major depressions for many years. In view of this history, the son's symptoms, and the apparently stable family atmosphere, the son was referred to a psychiatrist for a medication evaluation at the end of the fourth family treatment session. The son was placed on an antidepressant medication by the psychiatrist. The family continued in family treatment that focused on helping the parents to protect and support the son until it could be determined whether medication was or was not helping.

The son responded very favorably to the medication and reported being free of symptoms five weeks after he started on medication. At this time the family was given a second Zung (1964) Self-Rating of Depression Scale test. The son scored 52 (minimal depression), the mother scored 38 (normal), and the father scored 46 (normal) on the depression inventory. To be noted is that at the second test, there was a decrease of 35 in adolescent depression and also a decrease of 20 in parental depression.

For the Jackson family, parental depression scores decreased in conjunction with a decrease in adolescent depression. A different pattern was observed for the three families suffering "can" level depression who are discussed in the next section of this article. In existential family therapy, it is believed that adolescent depression in "can" level depression families is reactive to and signals a major structural and communication problem within such families. "Can" level depression is often labeled as reactive or exogenous depression in the mental health literature (Frankl, 1955, 1978; Lantz & Thorword, 1985). The adolescent in the Jackson family was apparently suffering from a type of depression that was not reactive or exogenous in nature. His form of "must" level depression is generally labeled as a major or endogenous depression. In the three families suffering exogenous or "can" level depression whose stories follow, a decrease in adolescent depression was accompanied by an increase in parental depression. Such data suggest that exogenous or "can" level adolescent depression may often be reactive to a structural or communication problem within the total family, whereas endogenous or "must" level adolescent depression may often be a function of the adolescent's biochemical tendency toward the development of a major or biochemical form of depression. Lowered levels of depression were maintained by all Jackson family members, and termination of family therapy occurred after 17 family sessions. The son is still being treated by the psychiatrist and is taking antidepressant medications.

The "Can" Dimension of Family Depression

In Frankl's (1955, 1969) dimensional ontology, the "can" dimension of existence refers to those patterns of family life that "can" be affected through will, freedom, responsibility, and choice. The "can" dimension of family depression includes symptoms of depression that are reactive to learned patterns of family interaction that "can" be changed through reflection, practice, and will. Knowledge about the "can" dimension of family depression includes the contributions of existential, structural, behavioral, narrative, transactional, solution-focused, and psychoanalytic family therapy and can help family therapists and their clients understand how patterns of family living often result in depression. Family psychotherapy approaches focusing on helping the family or couple to challenge and change dysfunctional problem-solving and interpersonal patterns can often be extremely effective with a couple or family suffering "can" dimension depression. The following clinical material illustrates how existential family treatment may be useful to a couple or family suffering this type of depression.

The Smith Family   The Smith family requested treatment after their 15-year-old son told the school guidance counselor that he was having problems studying due to concentration difficulties, sleep problems, and a loss of energy. The counselor referred the total family for treatment. At the first session the son scored 73 (severe depression), the father scored 53 (minimal depression), and the mother scored 38 (normal) on the Zung (1964) Self-Rating of Depression Scale. After a few exploratory family sessions, the therapist concluded that the son's depression seemed reactive to a family transactional process in which the parents channeled marital conflict through their relationship with the son. The son felt "trapped" in the middle and ended up feeling "disloyal" to both parents. Intervention was directed toward helping the son to "stay out of the middle" and toward helping the parents to manifest their marital problems to each other in a clear, direct, and congruent way. The son's depression quickly lifted, and during the sixth family

session, the family members were again given the depression rating scale.

On test number two, the father scored 67 (marked depression), the mother scored 79 (severe depression), and the son scored 51 (minimal depression). These test scores reflected a decrease of 22 in adolescent depression and an increase of 55 in parental depression. At this point the focus of treatment changed, and both the therapist and the parents concentrated on improving the parents' marital relationship. Good progress was made and termination occurred after 13 sessions. At termination the father scored 49 (normal), the mother scored 42 (normal), and the son scored 48 (normal) on the Self-Rating of Depression Scale. The Smith family's scores on the depression scale documented an increase in parental depression following a decrease in adolescent depression during conjoint family therapy. This was followed by a decrease in parental depression after the parents worked through some of their marital difficulties.

The Jones Family   The Jones family requested family treatment after their 17-year-old daughter overdosed on her mother's blood pressure medication. The family was referred for treatment after the daughter was released from a medical facility. At the initial treatment session, the daughter scored 73 (severe depression), the mother scored 53 (mild depression), and the father scored 36 (normal) on the depression inventory.

In the Jones family the mother and father had a distant marital relationship and the mother used the daughter as a nurturing object. She was unable to obtain this nurturing from her husband. The daughter's role of "mother's emotional caretaker" inhibited the daughter's ability to spend time with peers and also blocked her natural developmental push toward autonomy and independence. Intervention focused on freeing the daughter from her pathogenic role and helping the parents begin to reestablish mutual nurturing within their marital relationship.

At the eighth family session, the family members were given test number two. At this time Tina (the daughter) was beginning to distance herself from her dysfunctional family role. Tina scored 51 (mild depression), the mother scored 82 (severe depression), and the father scored 68 (marked depression) on the depression inventory scale. Test number two revealed a decrease of 22 in adolescent depression and an increase of 61 in parental depression.

The family remained in treatment for a total of 16 sessions, and at the time of termination, the father scored 39 (normal), the daughter scored 32 (normal), and the mother scored 47 (normal) on the depression inventory. Again in the Jones family, a decrease in adolescent depression coincided with an increase in parental depression at the time of test number two. And once again, at termination, test number three revealed decreased parental depression that coincided with an improved marital relationship and stabilization of a lower level of adolescent depression.

The Hubbard Family   The Hubbard family requested treatment after their daughter complained of energy loss, crying spells, and a sleep disturbance. The family initially contacted their family physician, who referred them for family treatment. In the Hubbard family, the daughter also performed the family system role of being "mother's emotional helper" in reaction to the distant relationship between the parents.

On test number one, the daughter scored 71 (extreme depression), the mother scored 56 (mild depression), and the father scored 47 (normal). Test number two was given during family session 12 after the daughter had begun to have some success moving away from her pathogenic role. On test two, the daughter scored 34 (normal), the mother scored 66 (moderate depression), and the father scored 83 (marked depression) on the depression inventory. There was a decrease of 38 in adolescent depression and an increase of 46 in parental depression on test number two. Termination occurred after 22 sessions. On test number three the father scored 43 (normal), the mother scored 48 (normal), and the daughter scored 38 (normal). Again, the Hubbard family demonstrated an initial increase in parental depression following a decrease in adolescent depression. The level of parental depression then decreased following an improvement in their marital relationship.

In the three previous "can" depression families, an adolescent family member developed severe depression reactive to problems in the parental relationship. In all three families, there was decreased adolescent depression and increased parental depression when the adolescent was helped to "stay out" of the parents' marital problems (Lantz, 1978, 1993, 2000) and the parents began to challenge and change their marital difficulties. The three previously described "can" level depression families are typical examples of families that develop a symptomatic adolescent reactive to structural, interactional, and/or communication problems.

The "Ought" Dimension of Family Depression

In Frankl's (1955, 1997) "ought" dimension of existence, there is a focus on what the couple or family "ought" to do or is "called" by life to accomplish and/or achieve. On the "ought" level of existence, the couple or family is understood to be a recipient of "meaning opportunities" presented to the family by life (Lantz, 1993, 2000). An "ought" dimension understanding of depression includes the awareness that depression is sometimes a direct result of a couple's or family's avoidance or repression of the "call of life" (Frankl, 1955, 1997; Lantz, 1974, 1993, 2000). In such a situation, the couple or family develops an existential-meaning vacuum that becomes filled with symptoms of depression reactive to the family's failure (i.e., bad faith) to respond to the call of life and to the meaning potentials and opportunities presented by life (Frankl, 1975, 1997; Lantz, 1974, 1993, 2000). In Frankl's (1975, 1997) dimensional ontology, finding the "oughts" in a family's life can prevent the occurrence of some depression and can often help the couple or family to overcome the symptoms of depression that grow and flourish in an existential-meaning vacuum. This author believes that only existential family therapy and its practitioners have shown an adequate interest in helping depressed couples and/or families to notice and respond to the meaning potentials and opportunities in life and exploring how this approach can be helpful in the treatment of depression. This existential family therapy approach to the treatment of "ought" dimension depression may be described as existential reflection directed toward discovering Frankl's "unconscious ought" (Lantz, 1993). The following clinical material is presented to illustrate "ought" dimension family depression and its treatment.

Mr. and Mrs. Sampson   Mr. and Mrs. Sampson requested clinical services after the death of their son from an AIDS-related illness. Mr. Sampson indicated that he was having problems sleeping "because my conscience is bothering me." Mrs. Sampson stated she was worried about her husband. Mr. Sampson explained, "I kicked my son out of the house three years ago when he told me he was gay. Knowing my son was gay was a big shock. I didn't handle it well." Mrs. Sampson reported that she, her husband, and the son had eventually reconciled and that the son had lived at home for "the last three months of his life."

Mr. and Mrs. Sampson both said they felt proud they had "been there" for their son when he was dying. The couple also reported that they were "fools" to have "kicked him out of the house," and that they would always feel guilty about their "ignorance." They stated they had "lost a year and a half" with their son because of their "ignorance," and now that the son was dead they would "give anything to get that time back." Mr. Sampson reported that he could not sleep at night because he kept thinking about his "mistake."

In this situation the existential family therapist initially encouraged the couple to talk about their tragedy and their feelings about it. The therapist was very careful not to give advice and simply listened to the couple until they felt comfortable that the therapist had some understanding of their feelings. It was only after the therapist was assured that the couple had perceived him to be an empathic person who had worked hard to understand them that the therapist was willing to give the couple a suggestion.

When empathic trust had been developed, the therapist asked the couple how they might feel about giving talks about "the mistake" to other parents—those who had recently discovered their son or daughter to be lesbian or gay. They initially felt uncomfortable with this idea, but as time went on, decided it was a "really good idea." The couple felt this suggestion gave them a way to "help others" and "help turn a mistake into something useful." Mr. and Mrs. Sampson were linked with a gay rights organization for volunteer work and were also provided with support and training in their public speaking activities. By the time this article was written, they had shared their experience and "mistake" in over 50 speeches. Also, Mr. Sampson no longer experiences difficulty sleeping.

The Roberts Family   Mr. and Mrs. Roberts were referred for treatment by Mr. Roberts's oncologist. Mr. Roberts had throat cancer and could no longer eat solid foods. His feeding process was considerably less than dignified. Mr. Roberts reported that he obsessed about solid food, and Mrs. Roberts reported that "it gets to me that he cannot even enjoy his food." For over 40 years the members of the Roberts family had been sitting down at the dinner table and "sharing bread." The family had abandoned this activity reactive to Mr. Roberts's inability to eat solid food.

In this family the members had always used the family dinner as a ritual to signify, share, and experience meaning. With the loss of this ritual, the family experienced an emptiness in their daily life. They experienced an existential vacuum. The existential family therapist's task with the Roberts family was

complex. One part of the task was to help the family create a new ritual that family members could use to share and experience meaning. After the Roberts family replaced the dinner ritual with poker parties and the game of Fish, Mr. Roberts reported that he no longer was "obsessing about solid foods," Replacing the lost ritual helped the family discover the family "ought" of celebrating the closeness and love that they had shared over the past 40 years as Mr. Roberts approached his death.

The Jabco Family   Mr. Jabco was brought for admission to a psychiatric hospital by his adult son and daughter. His presenting problem was labeled a biological depression by his psychiatrist and the hospital treatment team. Mr. Jabco was 68 years old. The onset of his depression occurred soon after he lost his wife to her year-long fight with cancer.

Mr. Jabco had retired one year prior to his wife's death only to discover that his first year of retirement would be spent helping his wife deal with her deadly disease. Mr. Jabco had never suffered with depression before, and there was no history of depression in his family of origin. Both the son and daughter reported that they were "frantic" because Mr. Jabco had said he was thinking about killing himself. The son and daughter did not want to face the death of both parents. Both the client and his children reported that Mr. Jabco had not been depressed while his wife had been alive.

In spite of the fact that Mr. Jabco exhibited some of the classical symptoms of a biological depression (energy loss, suicidal thinking, crying spells, and sleep disturbance), he was not suffering from merely biological ("must" level) depression. In this clinical situation, Mr. Jabco was also suffering from an existential vacuum. Mr. Jabco and his children had suffered a tragedy. When Mr. Jabco was provided an opportunity to discuss, explore, and challenge the meaning vacuum he was experiencing reactive to the family tragedy, he was able to overcome his depression. His children were also able to overcome their feelings of anxiety.

Mr. Jabco and his adult children were seen together by a family therapist in a conjoint family interview at the request of Mr. Jabco's psychiatrist. During the initial family interview, Mr. Jabco reported that he and his wife had been looking forward to his retirement with great expectations of having fun through both travel and cultural activities. Mr. Jabco reported that for him retirement was now "empty" and, as far as he could see, so was the rest of his life. He indicated that he wanted to die so that he could again see his wife "in heaven." Mr. Jabco believed in an afterlife and felt that life on earth could not be meaningful without his wife. He was not aware of what life might be calling him to do on the "ought" level of existence.

The family therapist asked Mr. Jabco exactly what he and his wife had planned to do and see after his retirement. Mr. Jabco explained in great detail the plans he and his wife had made and the cultural activities they had hoped to experience. Mr. Jabco reported that his wife had always wanted to visit her relatives in Italy. He sobbed as he explained how unfair it was that his wife would not get to have this visit.

At this point, the family therapist asked Mr. Jabco, "Do you think your wife will be disappointed in not getting to hear about your trip to visit her relatives in Italy or your experience of the other activities you and she had planned?" Mr. Jabco immediately stopped sobbing. He remained silent for a few minutes and stared directly at the family therapist. He then laughed and stated, "I always did want to be a reporter." He also told the family therapist, "That is the kind of question that shocks you into seeing a good reason to keep on living."

At the next family interview, Mr. Jabco reported that he had stopped having crying "attacks," that his food tasted better, that he was sleeping well and was getting his energy back. He added, "Killing myself seems like a very bad idea now; I want to get out of this hospital as soon as possible so I can get on with my retirement."

Both adult children reported that they felt much better and believed that the family therapist had performed "magic." The family therapist thanked the son and daughter for the compliment, but said there is no magic in helping individuals remember that their relationship with someone they love can still be meaningful after death.

The existential questions used in this clinical illustration were based on the beliefs and values of the family. Mr. Jabco and his children believed that Mr. Jabco would see his wife again after his death. They also believed that action and behavior are meaningful only if done in a transcendent way for the benefit of those one loves.

The Existenzanalyse question used by the family therapist helped Mr. Jabco to see that he could go on living and enjoy his retirement in a way that was giving to his wife and compatible with the beliefs and values of the family. It allowed him and his children to see a meaning potential in retirement that they had not been able to perceive previously on a conscious level of awareness. Mr. Jabco is presently enjoying his retirement, visiting his children on a frequent basis, and has had no recurrences of depression.

Conclusions

In existential family therapy, it is believed that Viktor Frankl's dimensional ontology can be used as a framework to ensure that families suffering depression will be treated in a holistic manner. Within this framework, family depression is understood to include three levels: the "must" (biological), "can" (interactional), and "ought" (existential) dimensions of family existence. Numerous case examples have been presented to illustrate the treatment of family depression on all three levels of existence.

References

Andrews, E. (1974). *The emotionally disturbed family*. Northvale, NJ: Jason Aronson.

Frankl, V. (1955). *The doctor and the soul*. New York: Vintage Press.

Frankl, V. (1959). *Man's search for meaning*. New York: Simon and Schuster.

Frankl, V. (1967). *Psychotherapy and existentialism*. New York: Simon and Schuster.

Frankl, V. (1969). *The will to meaning*. New York: New American Library.

Frankl, V. (1975). *The unconscious god*. New York: Simon and Schuster.

Frankl, V. (1978). *The unheard cry for meaning*. New York: Simon and Schuster.

Frankl, V. (1997). *Recollections*. New York: Dimension Books.

Lantz, J. (1974). Existential treatment and the Vietnam veteran family. In *Ohio Department of Mental Health Yearly Report* (pp. 33–36). Columbus: Ohio Department of Mental Health.

Lantz, J. (1978). *Family and marital therapy*. New York: Appleton-Century-Crofts.

Lantz, J. (1993). *Existential family therapy: Using the concepts of Viktor Frankl*. Northvale, NJ: Jason Aronson.

Lantz, J. (2000). *Meaning-centered marital and family therapy: Learning to bear the beams of love*. Springfield, IL: Charles C. Thomas.

Lantz, J., & Thorword, S. (1985). Inpatient family therapy approaches. Psychiatric Hospital, *16*, 85–89.

Maxman, J., & Ward, N. (1995). *Essential psychopathology and its treatment*. New York: Norton.

Zung, G. (1964). A self rating of depression scale. *Archives of General Psychiatry, 12*, 63–67.

FAYE MISHNA
BARBARA MUSKAT
GERALD SCHAMESS

66

Food for Thought: The Use of Food in Group Therapy with Children and Adolescents

"Food is more than fodder. It is an act of giving and receiving because the experience at table is a communal sharing; talk begins to flow, feelings are expressed, and a sense of well-being takes over" (Cunningham, 1990, p. ix). In our practice of group therapy with children and adolescents, food or a snack is routinely offered during the sessions. Over time, we have observed the powerful impact that food has on the groups and the wide range of reactions to the food by various groups and group members. These observations led us to wonder whether the impact and meanings of food in group therapy are undervalued and underestimated.

A review of the group therapy literature did not produce many articles related to the use of food or snack in group therapy, nor any empirical studies on food in group (Troester & Darby, 1976). Despite this paucity of literature, the use of food in group therapy seems fairly ubiquitous in the extant literature, and the meanings and importance of food are implicitly recognized and identified. Authors with disparate theoretical, clinical, and technical approaches, who offer diverse ways to understand the purpose and meanings food has for group members, recommend providing food (Cerda, Nemiroff, & Richmond, 1991; Kahn, 1993; Rachman, 1975; Schamess, 1990; Scheidlinger, 1982; Schiffer, 1971; Troester & Darby, 1976). The provision of food is recommended for a large variety of group types and lengths, and with members ranging in age from the very young to the elderly (de Luca, Boyes, Furer, Grayson, & Hiebert-Murphy, 1992; Franko, 1993; Zimpfer, 1987).

According to traditional psychoanalytic theory, providing food is seen as hindering the therapeutic process due to several concerns and has been customarily strongly discouraged (Rachman, 1975). Providing food is thought to foster the individual's dependence on the therapist, rather than encouraging more mature and realistic behavior. In addition, the therapist who provides food is seen as "acting out in the transference relationship with patients" (p. 128) and, therefore, gratifying the members wishes rather than helping them analyze their need to be fed. "Gratification" by the therapist is thought to communicate a message that acting out is acceptable and is thought to interfere with the classical analytic imperative that patients must be helped to engage in self-examination. Another concern is that providing food discourages a group member from expressing negative affect toward the therapist, who is gratifying the member. Finally, a concern is that the therapist may provide food due to his or her own needs, indicative of a counterrtransference problem.

Rachman (1975) maintains that these concerns are not applicable to adolescent group psychotherapy and argues that the actual provision of food by the therapist may in fact contribute to the adolescent group's therapeutic value. He emphasizes the need for an adolescent group to have a group leader who actively demonstrates his or her caring. Accordingly, the provision of food by the group therapist is a way to demonstrate this active caring, which fosters a "positive parental transference and relationship" (p. 128). Other reasons Rachman lists that make food crucial in an adolescent group include (2) self-titration of anxiety; (3) provides direct interaction for familial conflicts; (4) creates a positive psychosocial climate; (5) provides physical modes of behaving; (6) biological and psychological hunger is abated" (p. 128). These same arguments apply to children's group therapy.

The view of food as a significant element in group therapy may represent a way of conceptualizing food in relation to the group therapeutic process that diverges from traditional psychoanalytic theory. The scarcity of discussion of food in the literature may belie group therapists' current views on its use and leaves unanswered questions about the gap in the literature with respect to the use of food in group therapy.

The aims of this article are to highlight the significance of food and to engage in a discussion of how food can be constructively used in group therapy with children and adolescents, as well as how food can trigger salient conflicts. The perspective in this article is that food can be a powerful medium through which central issues and processes emerge and are worked through. We identify common themes and meanings related to the use of food and focus on the interactions between group members and leaders in response to food. We provide several examples of child and adolescent groups that illustrate these themes and issues, along with a discussion of each example.

Literature Review

Articles in which food is mentioned typically describe the structure of each group session. These descriptions often include the provision of food, which varies according to the particular group, for example, as a snack to be eaten together or as a life-skill activity in which members prepare food (Cerda et al., 1991; Mayfield & Neil, 1983; Schamess, 1990). These articles typically do not include the reasons, process, or meanings food may have for the members. Kahn (1993) observed that child and adolescent groups regularly include a snack, which is supported by Zimpfer's (1987) comment that "cake, cookies, coffee, and tea are commonly mentioned in the literature on treatment" in referring to psychiatric groups (p. 53).

Several authors recommend the use of food in group therapy with groups that vary in terms of purpose, format, length, and age of members. These include groups for individuals with bulimia nervosa (Franko, 1993), schizophrenia (Zimpfer, 1987), sexual abuse survivors (de Luca et al., 1992), and

populations considered seriously disturbed, vulnerable, or unique because of their developmental stage (Black & Rosenthal, 1970; Cerda et al., 1991; Rachman, 1975; Raubolt, 1989; Richmond, 1991; Schamess, 1991; Scheidlinger, 1982; Schiffer, 1971; Troester & Darby, 1976).

Paradoxically, food appears to be used both as a fundamental component of group and as a modification with particular or vulnerable populations, which requires a specific rationale. On the one hand, it may be that the provision of food is considered quite standard in group treatment, thus requiring little explanation. On the other hand, it may be that the provision of food is discouraged based on traditional psychoanalytic theory and thus requires a rationale when it is offered.

A common rationale for the use of food is fostering a nurturing atmosphere and communicating the therapists' care for the group members (Black & Rosenthal, 1970; Davis, Geikie, & Schamess, 1988; de Luca et al., 1992; Kahn, 1993; Rachman, 1975; Richmond, 1991; Rose, 1987; Schamess, 1990, 1991; Scheidlinger, 1982; Schiffer, 1971). Researchers with different theoretical and clinical approaches recommend food for emotional nourishment and to enhance rapport, communication, group cohesion, and emotional well-being (Cerda et al., 1991; Davis et al., 1988; de Luca et al., 1992; Kahn, 1993; Rachman, 1975; Schamess, 1990; Scheidlinger, 1982; Schiffer, 1971; Troester & Darby, 1976). Troester and Darby explain that food provides a structure that enables the group members to "simply sit and talk." They maintain that "the meal, then, provides the boys with an enjoyable reason to sit together, and conversation spontaneously and naturally ensues" (p. 99). The food shifts from the foreground, gradually becoming secondary to the discussion (Troester & Darby, 1976).

A related meaning is that of providing tangible nurturing and reducing physical and emotional hunger (Black & Rosenthal, 1970; Cerda et al., 1991; Davis et al., 1988; Kahn, 1993; Mellor & Storer, 1995; Mooney & Schamess, 1991; Rachman, 1975; Richmond, 1991; Rose, 1987; Schamess, 1990; Scheidlinger, 1982; Troester & Darby, 1976; Zimpfer, 1987). The care with which leaders plan the food and other particulars may influence members' comfort and their "perceptions of warmth and safety, and of the respect they hope to receive" (Butler & Wintram, 1991, p. 37; Lee, 1994; Rose, 1987).

Food is understood to be a powerful way to further therapeutic work (Black & Rosenthal, 1970; Cerda et al., 1991; Davis et al., 1988; Kahn, 1993;

Rachman, 1975; Richmond, 1991; Rose, 1987; Schamess, 1990; Schiffer, 1971; Slavson, 1943; Troester & Darby, 1976). As such, food is seen as promoting socialization and prosocial behaviors within a positive milieu (Cerda et al., 1991; Kahn, 1993; Mooney & Schamess, 1991; Rachman, 1975; Slavson, 1943; Troester & Darby, 1976; Zimpfer, 1987). The behaviors and skills identified include socialization, learning manners, and promoting cleanup skills, all of which can be generalized to situations outside of the group (Cerda et al., 1991; Troester & Darby, 1976).

Slavson (1943) linked children's responses to food in group therapy with their family environments. A variety of children's issues, problems, family patterns, concerns, and expectations related to adults have been found to be evoked by food (Black & Rosenthal, 1970; Cerda et al., 1991; Davis et al., 1988; Kahn, 1993; Mooney & Schamess, 1991; Rachman, 1975; Rose, 1987; Schamess, 1990; Schiffer, 1971; Slavson, 1943; Troester & Darby, 1976).

Food may provide an opportunity for group members to express and work through conflicts that could be less amenable to direct verbalization. Scheidlinger (1982) observes, "It is around the theme of food—the buying of it, the bringing of it to the meeting room, the cooking, and serving— that the most dramatic and meaningful interactions occur" (pp. 139–140). A characteristic theme that emerges is the difficulty members may have in sharing (Black & Rosenthal, 1970; Cerda et al., 1991; Kahn, 1993; Rachman, 1975; Schiffer, 1971; Slavson, 1943; Troester & Darby, 1976). Other issues and conflicts include feelings of deprivation (Black & Rosenthal, 1970; Cerda et al., 1991; Kahn, 1993; Schiffer, 1971), fears, anxieties, suspicions, and expectations such as not feeling able to rely on adults (Black & Rosenthal, 1970; Cerda et al., 1991; Davis et al., 1988; Kahn, 1993; Rachman, 1975; Schamess, 1990; Troester & Darby, 1976). Some members are described as reluctant to accept the snacks, whereas others are depicted as grabbing or hoarding food (Schiffer, 1971; Troester & Darby, 1976). In addition, the provision of food may crystallize ways in which group therapists may be misattuned to members needs (Rose, 1987). At these times, it is necessary for group therapists to understand their rationale and reactions (Rose, 1987).

A perusal of the literature indicates that a large variety of food is provided in groups, from dessert and beverages (Schiffer, 1971), to more nutritious offerings (Davis et al., 1988; Troester & Darby, 1976). Some authors advocate involving the members in choosing the particular food items, listening to complaints group members may voice about the food, and, within reason, complying with members requests (Black & Rosenthal. 1970; Rachman, 1975; Troester & Darby, 1976). Others maintain that it is important that the leaders provide the food (Cerda et al., 1991; Davis et al., 1988; Rachman, 1975; Richmond, 1991; Rose, 1987; Schamess, 1990; Schiffer, 1971). Still others note shifts that occur over time, in which the group members may gradually assume responsibility for the food (Richmond, 1991; Slavson, 1943). The general consensus appears to be that the group leaders or sponsoring agencies purchase the food. Group members who contribute food may be understood as participating in mutual aid and/or as conveying their desire and ability to care for themselves and for others (Richmond, 1991); however, expecting group members to purchase the food may be problematic. As some members may not have the funds or ability to purchase or prepare food, this inequity within the group could evoke intense feelings.

Food may be offered either at the beginning or the end or made available throughout the session (Davis et al., 1988; Kahn, 1993; Rachman, 1975; Troester & Darby, 1976). Kahn described providing food at the beginning to welcome the group members and to decrease their actual hunger. Food may be needed to allow members to replenish themselves in order to attend to the work in the group (Mellor & Storer, 1995). Others find that at the end of the group session food restores the members energy, calmness, and a sense of togetherness (Davis et al., 1988; Troester & Darby, 1976).

The intense conflict that the provision of food may evoke suggests that it is necessary for group leaders to be cognizant of the potential effects of these conflicts for the group and its members. The approach advanced by Slavson (1943) to managing conflict evoked by food is one in which the therapist initially purchases, prepares, and provides the food for the group and allows whatever conflicts are stirred up to emerge and be worked out within the group. Conflict may be manifest through members grabbing, spilling, and throwing food and drinks, as well as through other forms of disruptive behavior. An important component of Slavson's approach is the therapist's permissiveness and lack of intervention, although Slavson stressed the need for therapists to adjust their level of intervention according to the children's ages and needs (Slavson, 1986). According to Slavson, by remaining passive, the therapist "gives the group an opportunity to discover for themselves the advantages of orderly behavior, and to evolve techniques of group control" (p. 45). Slavson used "diminishing food anxiety and improved table manners" (p. 45) as an indicator of improvement.

Scheidlinger (1982) advises that the children for whom Slavson's activity group therapy was developed were not severely disturbed. Accordingly, Scheidlinger underscores the importance of the therapist assuming an active role in activity group therapy with children who have more severe ego pathology. Specifically, the therapist is considered responsible for ensuring that each child receives his or her portion of the food, which may include preventing other children from grabbing a group member's food or drink. Scheidlinger cautions that children with severe emotional problems will not experience a leader who does not interfere with developments that the group members perceive to be threatening as warm and helpful. Without the leader's active help, there is a danger that such conflicts may lead to harmful outcomes in which the children reexperience the negative patterns of their lives. In a similar vein, Rachman (1975) recommended that group therapists provide food differentially at various stages of adolescent groups in order not to exacerbate conflicts. For example, initially, cans of soda may be offered, whereas in later stages of the group's development, large bottles of soda may be provided when the members are able to work out the difficulties evoked by the food. In contrast, Black and Rosenthal (1970) allowed group members, described as exhibiting "a high degree of emotional disturbance with severe antisocial symptomatology" (p. 107), to express the intense conflicts raised by food.

Despite recognition in the literature that the provision of food may evoke a range of conflicts for group members, there is little mention of specific problems that could be created. With respect to child and adolescent groups, Kahn (1993) concluded that providing food is universally beneficial, and noted the lack of comments in the literature on negative effects of providing a snack. However positive or benign the provision of food may appear to be, it is important to be cognizant of the intense conflict that food may evoke for group members. As Scheidlinger (1982) discusses, if the group leaders are not aware of potential problems related to food and do not manage conflicts that emerge, there could be harmful consequences for the members; for example, children may be left reexperiencing feelings of deprivation. Other conditions in which the use of food may be problematic are those in which groups include individuals who have eating problems or disorders, or in which the members have been persistently overindulged.

Food in Group Therapy

The following examples illustrate the ways in which providing food in group therapy serves as actual and symbolic nurturing and as a means to evoke and work through conflicts.

Case 1: Symbolic Meaning of Food as Nurturance

The first example is a psychotherapy group for single teenage mothers, conducted by female cotherapists in a community-based family agency. In this group, food was served at every meeting during the last half-hour. As the group progressed, the members actively took part in choosing, preparing, and serving the refreshments. Snack time provided the members with an opportunity to talk casually among themselves and to the therapists, and over time, began to bear a distinct resemblance to family meal times. The snack itself varied from meeting to meeting and at different times included cookies, cake, candy, potato chips, pretzels, soda, and tea. The members were asked to express their snack preferences within a clearly established price range, which the therapists agreed to purchase. Discussions about what snack they wanted were sometimes lengthy and provided ways both of promoting group cohesion and precipitating differences and conflicts among members. Over the first year and a half of the group, the young women were eager for sweets and ate as many as the leaders provided. The themes they discussed included wanting to feed their children healthy food, wanting to be healthier themselves, wanting to slim down to feel better, and wanting to look better so they would be more attractive to men. In the third year, the group members decided to replace the sweets with healthy food, such as vegetables or fruit and crackers. They held to their decision with the exception of special occasions such as Easter, Halloween, and Christmas, when they again wanted sweets. Intermittently, during the later stages of the group, they expressed nostalgia for the sweets in which they had indulged and for their earlier prepregnancy metabolism that allowed them to eat as many sweets as they wanted without gaining weight.

Every Christmas, the mothers expressed their desire to bake Christmas cookies "for their children." Since the agency had a kitchen, it was possible to do this and it became a yearly ritual. For the first three years, the group members finished baking the cookies, sat down for snack, and, as they were chatting together, consumed everything they had baked, sometimes as many as 60 cookies divided among seven or eight members. At the first Christmas baking session, they ate all the cookies, expressing delight in the taste and remembering their own childhood Christmases. They seemed quite unaware of the amount they were eating, and the therapists did not comment. At the end of the session, the members expressed surprise and regret that there were no cookies to take home to their children. Before the second and third back sessions they discussed the first session, which they agreed that they would not permit again. Once again, however, they ate all the cookies even though the therapists commented halfway through their snacking that they had expressed a wish to bring some cookies to their children. They agreed, expressed embarrassment about how much they were eating, and then seemed compelled to finish every last cookie. It was only at the fourth Christmas bake session that they were able to divide the cookies and put aside half to take home for their children and to consume the other half themselves.

Baking (and eating) Christmas cookies allowed the group members to revisit a time in their lives when they felt cared for, with no responsibilities other than to help their mother prepare for the holiday festivities. As the women baked they talked together and remembered (or perhaps imagined) what it had been like to be young and carefree, filled with anticipation of Christmas presents and reassuring family rituals. Baking made the group more cohesive. The mothers felt closer both to each other and to the therapists enacting a restorative fantasy of a functional, symbolic family unit. And as they baked they could momentarily forget the responsibilities and toils of motherhood, becoming, as it were, young children in their own right.

Comments   For this group of teenage, single mothers (and for many others in their situation) the central, recurring, painful conflict was between assuming the responsibilities involved in caring for their children and participating in the excitement, adventure, and turmoil of adolescence. Choosing motherhood had made it impossible for them to do both in full measure. During the first years of treatment, while their conflicts and unmet developmental needs took precedence over everything else, when it was time to eat they could not contain their hunger and sense of deprivation. They seemed to inhale equally the cookies and the aroma of baking that filled the room. Afterward they were contrite and guilty, remembering "too late" their promise to bring cookies to their children. But obliquely, subtly, they hinted about feeling gleeful.

No one had asked them to share. They had eaten their fill, and more. The therapists had not stopped them, warned them about overeating, or reminded them they were depriving their children. The ritual continued yearly until the time came when the young women were developmentally ready, on their own initiative, to really consider their children's wishes: to divide the cookies, pack up, and bring the remaining cookies home. They returned with stories about their children's delight when they presented the cookies.

When the mothers could spontaneously consider their children's wants and needs without feeling deprived themselves, the therapists knew the group would soon be ready to end. Over the course of treatment, baking and eating Christmas cookies served multiple functions: fortifying the group's experience as a symbolic family, enhancing the group "holding environment," gratifying the members' unmet oral needs, promoting cooperation, and marking the mothers' progress toward accepting the responsibilities (and pleasures) of parenthood. It is difficult to imagine any other activity that would have addressed those issues as well.

Case 2: Conflict Evoked by the Provision of Food

This involved a 10-week agency-based group of six boys between 10 and 12 years who had learning disabilities and psychosocial difficulties. One aim of the group was to create a milieu in which group members could experience being accepted by a group of their peers who shared similar experiences and problems. A second objective was to provide an opportunity for the members to enact their conflicts in the here and now. The leaders were active in providing structure and in helping the members work through the conflicts, while ensuring physical and emotional safety.

The boys' difficulties included being isolated, rejected, and bullied by peers; having problems regulating their emotions, particularly anger and anxiety; and suffering from low self-esteem. These boys demonstrated little awareness of their impact on others and of the connections between their behaviors and others' responses. The group structure consisted of a brief check-in, activity and/or discussion, snack, and wrap-up. The group leaders purchased and prepared the snack, which was included in the agency's group program budget. Highly structured activities were required to help the boys maintain their focus. The boys all talked at the same time and engaged in behaviors such as hiding under the furniture and sticking their feet in each other's faces, which they were often unable to stop without help. Although at times it seemed that the members purposely provoked each other, their behaviors were understood as reflecting their anxiety and difficulties with interaction. Despite the boys' eagerness to participate, their impulsivity and reactivity to each other often led to conflicts. The members responded well to leaders interventions, including monitoring redirecting and separating members. A supervisor was in the observation room as a component of providing training for new staff who were coleading the group. The supervisor was introduced and her role was made clear to the children, who incorporated her presence into the group process.

For the seventh group session, the leaders prepared several short activities to match the group members' activity level and in an attempt to minimize conflict. After the activities, the leaders brought out a bag of candies. One boy grabbed the bag and tore it open, when sent the candies flying. Group members scrambled to scoop them up, which resulted in an unequal distribution; a few members ended up with most of the candies. One member who had grabbed the bulk of candies scurried to hide behind a chair in order to protect his stash. Another member, who had stuffed his pocket with candies, ate them voraciously, seemingly oblivious to the anger evoked in the other members. Within seconds the group became very loud and chaotic.

One boy, described as bright, depressed, and critical of himself and others, yelled that the boy behind the chair "is taking too many, as usual!" Another boy tried to break into the cacophony to suggest that they all share, and offered to divide the candies. This boy was described as bright with good ideas, but as typically ignored by peers. Similar to his real-life experiences, this boy was ignored by the group. Only the leaders seemed to hear him, and in vain they asked the others to listen to him. The boy who had collected candies in his pocket continued to eat them and joined the boy behind the chair. Another group member began yelling, "You're hogging them!"

With a mouthful of candy, the first boy behind the chair shouted, "I only ate one, so shut up!" The boy who had complained first hollered back, "You took too many, about 1,000," and said to the group, "He feels he's the best person in the world." The boy behind the chair began crying, which led one boy to suggest that they give him all the candy. The leaders noted that the conflict wasn't just about the candy and wondered what the boys were trying to communicate. One boy answered, "It's about

calling names." The first boy who had become angry said he was bugged "that he gets ten times more than anyone else," to which the boy behind the chair responded by running out of the room, crying, with a leader in pursuit.

After being momentarily silent, the boys began expressing their reactions. They articulated their anger at the boy who left as well as their guilt for having driven him from the room. The leader asked how the boys could solve the problem, to which one replied that they could apologize. A second boy responded that saying sorry would not change the past. The most vocal boy suggested a time machine to allow them to redo the episode. Still another boy replied, "Just because he cried, it's still not fair."

The boy who had run out phoned from the observation room to say that he intended to share but was upset at being called names. This led to a discussion about being called names at school. The group members shared their hope that the group would be a place in which they wouldn't be teased. One boy told of being continually rejected by a peer at school despite repeated attempts to "be nice." The leader commented that many of the boys shared the experience of being bullied. As the group session was coming to an end, some boys indicated their anger that the "candy problem" had not been resolved. The leader acknowledged their frustrations and noted that the difficulties they experienced as a group were similar to conflicts in their lives. The leader added that sometimes hurts could not be sorted out right away, which means that people may leave group feeling "yucky." The leader said it would be important to continue to talk about what had taken place, in the next session. The boys left the group session seeming more settled.

The members resumed discussing what had occurred during the next group session. Based on their understanding of the members, the leaders linked each member's role in the conflict with difficulties for which that individual was referred to group. The boys listened attentively, and either verbally or nonverbally appeared to agree with the leaders' insights. Afterward, the leaders brought out another bag of candies. The members suggested that the leaders give the bag to the boy who had tried to distribute the candy fairly the week before. The members seemed relieved with this solution.

Comments   Since these boys were not physically deprived or hungry, the importance that food assumed can be understood as having symbolic meaning for the members. Prior to this session, the boys had become more cooperative. The structured activities had provided containment, which had promoted the members' ability to participate and have fun, important and rare experiences for these boys. In this session, food was a catalyst that triggered an enactment by the group whereby the problems that emerged were those for which members had initially been referred. The leaders expressed their confusion about the candy's singular importance and ability to disrupt the group, and wondered why the conflict occurred. The boys responded by talking about what had been triggered for them. This was the first group session in which the members divulged their sense that life wasn't fair to them, their belief that others received more than they did, and their pain and anger at being bullied by peers.

The boys who grabbed the candies can be understood as acting to ensure that they would receive their fair share, spurred on by the expectation that they would not receive an equitable share. The strategies these boys employed were not adaptive. Their desperation to obtain the candy triggered intense responses in the others. The boys who grabbed the candies were not motivated to deprive the others, and neither were aware of the consequence of their behaviors. Their motivation seemed to be in protecting their "stashes." Consequently, they were taken aback and hurt by the intensity of the others' anger. Common problems for the members of this group included lack of adaptive strategies to cope with interpersonal situations, lack of awareness of the impact of their behavior on others, and difficulty expressing anger and other feelings appropriately.

The conflict triggered by food was facilitative, as it allowed this group of boys who historically had difficulty expressing themselves verbally to discuss important issues in the group. They did so at first by enacting their outside problems in the here and now of the group (Yalom, 1995). The group leaders then took the opportunity to link the problems that emerged in the group with those identified outside group, and to help the members process the conflict. For example, the boy who grabbed the bulk of candies and ran out crying after creating much conflict had been referred to group due to his tendency to flee from conflicts he had unintentionally created with peers. With the leaders' support, this boy was able to return to the group and face the others. Further, he articulated his upset at being called names, his intention to return the candies, and his need for the other members' reassurance in order to return. The boy who became particularly outraged by the others hoarding candies was able to articulate his sense that others "always" got more than he, which left him feeling less worthy. In the ensuing discussion, this boy was able to make the connection between his intense anger within the group session and the difficulties with which he struggled outside of group. He received validation in two ways. First, the leaders validated his feelings, and second, he recognized that other group members felt similarly. This validation promoted this boy's ability to reflect on and talk about his experiences, which represented a shift from his standard reactions, described as verbal aggression and/or withdrawal. The leaders' provision of a new bag of candies in the following session represented a reparative experience for this boy, in that he received what he perceived to be an equitable share. The leaders' intervention also provided structure to help the whole group find a way to resolve the previous week's conflict. It was essential in this group that the leaders intervened actively to manage the degree of conflict that emerged and thus ensure that the children did not reexperience their problematic patterns of relating, for example, finding life to be unfair to them and feeling powerless to effect any change.

Case 3: Adapting the Food and Timing to Group Members' Needs

The type of food and the timing at which it is offered can be significant for group members. In organizing the food they provide, group leaders should be guided by the members' message, comprised of both direct and indirect communications. The following example is an instance in which the leaders made what they believed to be suitable provisions for food; however, the members' needs differed from what was offered, and the leaders were eventually able to hear and to accommodate what members required.

This was a 25-week, racially diverse group composed of young male offenders with learning disabilities between the ages of 14 and 16. These teenagers belonged to peer groups with whom they engaged in criminal activities. They experienced severe economic disadvantage, and most of them lived in foster homes or with extended families due to significant family problems. The group was co-led by two leaders from a community agency. The purpose of the group included assisting the members to begin to understand the impact of their learning disabilities on their functioning, in particular on their faulty decision-making processes.

The group took place in the late morning, ending at lunchtime. The members had a long history of arriving for school very late and generally turned up just in time for the sessions. The leaders purchased the food, paid for by the agency. The leaders brought bagels to the first session, which they served at the midpoint. The group members complained that the leaders had not brought "real food" and expressed their hunger and need for "real food." The boys also protested about having to wait for the food and complained that they could not concentrate because of hunger. Believing they were responsive, the leaders solicited the boys' requests for food for future groups. The boys gave many suggestions (pizza, meat patties, etc.) with which the leaders complied in subsequent weeks; however, the leaders continued to offer the food halfway through the session in the next two meetings because in their agency food was routinely provided after activities or discussion. Another reason for the leaders' insistence on providing food later in the session related to unarticulated concerns that providing food before "work" had occurred would distract the members and might reduce their incentive to remain for the rest of the session. Although satisfied with the food, the members persisted in their complaints about the timing. After listening to the boys' arguments, the leaders finally understood the importance of altering the time and began offering food at the beginning of group. Once the right food was offered at the right time, the group members settled. They became less agitated, shared more about their lives, and seemed more comfortable. The boys spontaneously began to tidy up by putting plates in the garbage and recycling juice bottles. This was significant because of their reputation of being uncooperative with adults.

Comments   The group members' persistence helped the leaders realize that the boys' actual hunger needed to be addressed before they could "work." This realization helped the leaders understand the meaning food had for this group. Importantly, the leaders came to see that they had provided food in part based on their own comfort and biases (for example, bagels at midmorning). The leaders' increased understanding of the meaning food had for the members and for themselves enabled them to adjust their own behavior. More than a snack, food was actual nutrition. It also symbolized the leaders' willingness and ability to be attuned to, respond to and nurture the boys emotionally. The leaders came to understand their reluctance to altering the time at which they offered the food, a realization that had important clinical implications. The leaders realized that they had not been hearing what the boys were trying to tell them because of their own, largely unaware, preconceived notions both of when food should be provided and of the group members' motivations. The

discussions about food allowed the members to appropriately and assertively communicate their dissatisfaction and resolve the conflict.

Conclusion

Group therapy for children and adolescents provides an opportunity for members to socialize with peers and to work through problems. We argue that the provision of food in group therapy can be a powerful tool and that it is important to examine the meaning food has for a particular group and its members. In some cases, the provision of food provides actual and symbolic nurturance to the group members and is a way group leaders can demonstrate active caring, considered especially important for children and adolescent groups.

Our approach to how food should be offered includes (1) leaders providing specific foods requested by the members (within reason); (2) leaders listening to the members' complaints about the food; and (3) leaders recognizing how their provisions might not satisfy the members' needs. This responsiveness can supply validation for the members, which may foster the therapeutic relationship and the work.

Food may have significant meanings in group therapy. It is therefore essential that group leaders recognize and understand the potential importance and impact of food, which varies from group to group. Food may evoke intense conflict within the group, which puts the members' struggles "on the table." This may be particularly salient for members who are no able to articulate their concerns. On the other hand, the risk of allowing the conflict to emerge is the possibility that it will not be managed properly and will have negative consequences, such as a child or adolescent once again feeling and being deprived. We have demonstrated that the interactions among the members and leaders are critical in contributing to, understanding, and resolving the conflicts and issues that are evoked by food in group therapy for children and adolescents.

References

Black, M., & Rosenthal, L. (1970). Modifications in therapeutic technique in the group treatment of delinquent boys. In H. S. Strean (Ed.), *New approaches in child guidance* (pp. 106–122). Metuchen, NJ: Scarecrow Press.

Butler, S., & Wintram, C. (1991). *Feminist groupwork*. London: Sage Publications.

Cerda, R. A., Nemiroff, H. J. (Wolarsky), & Richmond, A. H. (1991). Therapeutic group approaches in an inpatient facility for children and adolescents: A 15-year perspective. *Group, 15*, 71–80.

Cunningham, M. K. (1990). *The Fannie Farmer cookbook*. Toronto: Bantam Books.

Davis, L., Geikie, G., & Schamess, G. (1988). The use of genograms in a group for latency age children. *International Journal of Group Psychotherapy, 38*, 189–210.

de Luca, R. V., Boyes, D. A., Furer, P., Grayson, A. D., & Hiebert-Murphy, D. (1992). Group treatment for child sexual abuse. *Canadian Psychology, 33*, 168–179.

Franko, D. L. (1993). The use of a group meal in the brief group therapy of bulimia nervosa. *International Journal of Group Psychotherapy, 43*, 237–242.

Kahn, S. R. (1993). Reflections upon the functions of food in a children's psychotherapy group. *Journal of Child and Adolescent Group Therapy, 3*, 143–153.

Lee, J. A. B. (1994). The empowerment group approach. In *The empowerment approach to social work practice* (pp. 208–261). New York: Columbia University Press.

Mayfield, J., & Neil, J. B. (1983). Group treatment for children in substitute care. *Social Casework, 64*, 579–584.

Mellor, D., & Storer, S. (1995). Support groups for children in alternate care: A largely untapped therapeutic resource. *Child Welfare, 74*, 905–918.

Mooney, S., & Schamess, G. (1991). Focused time limited, interactive group psychotherapy with latency age children: Theory and practice. *Journal of Child and Adolescent Group Therapy, 1*, 107–146.

Rachman, A. W. (1975). Structures and functions which enhance ego identity in adolescent groups. In *Identity group psychotherapy with adolescents* (pp. 111–169). Springfield, IL: Charles C. Thomas.

Raubolt, R. R. (1989). The clinical practice of group psychotherapy with delinquents. In F. J. Cramer Azima & L. H. Richmond (Eds.), *Adolescent group psychotherapy* (pp. 143–162). Madison: International Universities Press.

Richmond, L. H. (1991). The influence of the non-member on an adolescent psychotherapy group. *Journal of Child and Adolescent Group Therapy, 1*, 159–163.

Rose, M. (1987). The function of food in residential treatment. *Journal of Adolescence, 10*, 149–162.

Schamess, G. (1990). New directions in children's group therapy: Integrating family and group perspectives in the treatment of at risk children and families. *Social Work with Groups, 13*, 67–92.

Schamess, G. (1991). The group as transitional object: Reflections on the treatment process in a long-term psychotherapy group for unmarried teenage mothers and their infants or toddlers. In S. Tuttman (Ed.), *Psychoanalytic group theory and therapy: Essays in honor of Saul Scheidlinger* (pp. 237–269). Madison: International Universities Press.

Scheidlinger, S. (1982). Experiential group treatment of severely deprived latency-age children. In *Focus on group psychotherapy: Clinical essays* (pp. 113–150). New York: International Universities Press. (Original work published 1960).

Schiffer, M. (1971). Therapeutic play group practice. In *The therapeutic play group* (pp. 25–68). London: Allen & Unwin.

Slavson, S. R. (1943). *An introduction to group therapy*. New York: International Universities Press.

Slavson, S. R. (1986). Differential methods of group therapy in relation to age levels. In A. E. Riester & I. A. Kraft (Eds.), *Child group psychotherapy: Future tense* (pp. 9–27). Madison: International Universities Press. (Original work published 1945).

Troester, J. D. & Darby, J. A. (1976). The role of the mini-meal in therapeutic play groups. *Social Casework, 57*, 97–103.

Yalon, I. D. (1995). *The theory and practice of group psychotherapy* (4th ed.). New York: Basic Books.

Zimpfer, D. G. (1987). Group work with psychiatric patients. *Journal for Specialists in Group Work, 12*, 49–56.

67

"Less Is Best": A Group-based Treatment Program for Persons with Personality Disorders

Group work has become a popular method of providing mental health services in today's managed mental health care environment (MacKenzie, 1996; Rosenberg and Zimet, 1995). This method is being used for a great variety of mental health problems, from depression and anxiety disorders to treatment of persons with more severe mental illness, such as schizophrenia or bipolar disorders. Severe personality disorders can be just as debilitating as any of these Axis I disorders, and many clients are diagnosed with both (American Psychiatric Association, 1994; Benjamin, 1993). Personality disorders can be a challenge to provide services for in even the most resource-rich environment and can seem virtually impossible to serve in a managed care environment. Among the personality disorders, the borderline syndrome is often considered the most intractable and difficult to treat (Gabbard, 1998). Using a group work model can enable clients with personality disorders to function more adaptively in the community and can use staffing resources efficiently.

After a brief introductory discussion on personality disorders, this paper will describe a group-based treatment approach that was developed at a large urban community mental health center in the northwest part of the United States. This method was adapted from Linehan's (1993a, 1993b) dialectical behavior therapy, which will be briefly summarized and contrasted. Lastly, this group-based approach to working with personality disorders will be compared to other group work models frequently used in social work settings.

Personality Disorders and Client Functional Impairment

Nearly half of all clients treated in mental health settings have a personality disorder, either as a sole or concomitant diagnosis (Benjamin, 1997). While the widely used *Diagnostic and Statistical Manual* (American Psychiatric Association, 1994) identifies 11 distinctive personality disorders, other authors have grouped them into clusters (Millon, 1996), traits (Watson, Clark, and Harkness, 1994), or dimensions (Becker, 1998). Controversy exists on which method of describing personality disorders is most accurate and which most clearly reflects a continuum of normal to abnormal personality functioning (Strack and Lorr, 1997). However they are identified, these disorders are associated with long-term impairment, recurrent treatment of both inpatient and outpatient types, and poor treatment compliance (Benjamin, 1997). Certain personality disorders, such as borderline and avoidant, have been studied more extensively, and treatment methods have been developed that are predominantly cognitive or cognitive-behavioral.

Many adults suffering from personality disorders have much difficulty functioning in the community. While there is a range of functioning levels in these clients, those who end up in treatment in the public mental health system tend to be the most impaired. These individuals typically receive entitlements, such as Social Security disability, and are not able to maintain steady employment in the community. Most individuals with borderline personality disorder exhibit a pattern of suicidal gestures or self-mutilating behaviors, typically 70% to 75% (Linehan, 1993a). These actions often result in hospitalizations (psychiatric and physical health), repetitive calls to crisis facilities, and impairment in relationships with partners or friends. Other self-damaging behaviors occur in the areas of sexual functioning, use of alcohol, reckless driving, binge eating, shoplifting, and other violations of the law. Many of these behaviors are shared with persons with other personality disorders, such as those with antisocial and narcissistic patterns. Persons with personality disorders frequently have other mood, cognitive, or substance abuse disorders that further impair their functioning. Often, these individuals are classified as severely mentally ill (SMI), a determination that allows them to receive more extensive public mental health services in many states.

Treatment Methodologies

Treatment of personality disorders is rather underdeveloped when compared to treatment of other mental disorders. In a recent effectiveness study on the treatment of personality disorders, which reviewed articles published between 1974 and 1998, only 15 articles were found to qualify as scientifically rigorous (Perry, Banon, and Ianni, 1999). One notable finding of this study was that the mean length of treatment was 1.3 years in order to establish significant change. The reviewed articles reflected treatment from various theoretical perspectives and included both individual and group therapies. While empirically validated therapies have been developed for other mental disorders, so far none exists for personality disorders according to the American Psychological Association criteria (Benjamin, 1997). However, Linehan's dialectical behavior therapy for treatment of borderline personality disorder is classified as "probably efficacious" an is the only treatment for personality disorders to be so categorized.

The group-based treatment program described in this article was adapted from Linehan's (1993a, 1993b) approach but significantly modified to meet the needs of and impaired client population in a community, rather than research, settling. For clients with borderline personality disorder, while the traditional form of treatment has been individual psychotherapy, the literature reflects the development of several group-based approaches (Nehls, 1992). However, as community mental health centers come under increasing pressure to provide cost-effective treatment, individual therapy approaches severely limit the number of clients who can be served with dwindling grant dollars. Group-based approaches offer the best hope for providing services to all clients in need.

Group-Based Treatment of Personality Disorders

Several treatment programs for individuals with personality disorders have used group-based models. Some programs preface the group therapy experience with individual therapy as a way to engage clients and prepare them for the group experience (Blum and Marziali, 1988). Other programs offered weekly group sessions for a five-month period, led by two therapists, which were structured and focused on giving information (Nehls, 1992). The most empirically validated model of treatment for personality disorders, Linehan's Dialectical behavior therapy for persons with borderline personality disorder, uses a combination of individual and group therapy coupled with telephone consultation with the therapist. All of these programs have been associated with positive outcomes. The treatment model here described has adapted some aspects of these different approaches to provide an integrated group work approach whose aim is to enable clients to cope successfully with their disorder and function well in the community.

"Less Is Best" Treatment Model

This group-based treatment model was designed for an impaired population of clients with personality disorders being served at a community health center in the northwestern United States. While primarily diagnosed with borderline personality disorder, the clients experienced a range of Axis I and II disorders in various combinations and of different levels of impairment. The group-based approach was developed at a time of reductions in grant funding, which limited the amount of client services. Faced with a choice of eliminating treatment for some clients or using groups to serve more, this group-based approach was developed. The program was an adaptation of Linehan's dialectical behavioral therapy model but was tailored to the needs of a functionally impaired client population.

This program came to be known by providers as "Less is Best" when over time this highly structured group-based program yielded improved client functioning in the community and reduced the need for mental health services. Previously, clients had received intensive individual therapy, often for many years, with frequent crises that demanded intensive interaction with therapeutic staff. The group-based program was designed as one year of treatment with breaks for holidays; clients were required to contract for this length of treatment. Services included up to three groups per week: a process therapy group, a skills training group, and an activity/community integration group. Clients also received periodic psychiatric evaluations and medication management. An agency crisis hotline was available to clients in their community setting. Inpatient hospitalization was discouraged; however, a resident temporary respite center was available if a supervised 24-hour setting was necessary. Individual sessions were used as a reward for engagement in therapy and discussion of special topics; however, they were provided infrequently.

Master's-level therapists (social workers and psychologists) provided staffing for the therapy and skill building groups, while bachelor's-level staff led the activity groups. A primary component of this program is the use of a treatment team to deliver services; a team approach was found to be superior as clients remained bonded to some member of the team even when acting out or angry with other team members. This idealization-devaluation dynamic is characteristic of borderline and other personality disorders and often results in premature termination of treatment. By bonding to a team, clients are able to process their intense feelings with other team members and then typically reconcile their feelings with the therapist with whom they were angry. This ensures the continuity of treatment as well as the development of improved coping skills.

The purpose of each type of group was distinct. The process therapy group provided a setting for handling the many crises these clients experience in their daily lives, developing problem-solving methods, and integrating new skills into the client's coping repertoire. The mixture of client diagnoses and personality types provided the opportunity for less functional clients to learn from peers with more adaptive functioning. Most process groups were led by two therapists; this staffing pattern enables clients to observe two role models and experience two therapeutic styles. Clients were expected to attend group weekly and were discharged from treatment for more than three absences. Process groups were run in a manner similar to that used in other types of group therapy, such as the interpersonal group therapy model of Yalom (1995).

The group skills training component of the program consisted of six modules on the following topics: mindfulness, anger management, coping with depression, interpersonal relationships, stress and anxiety management, and abuse recovery. Each module lasted between six and eight weeks and was held weekly for two-hour sessions. While many of these topics are similar to those of Linehan (1993a, 1993b), these groups were presented in a more focused and simplified manner; they were also provided only to clients rather than a mixture of clients and family members. Therapists led at most two different modules, so that clients were exposed to a variety of therapeutic styles and techniques. Skill-building groups were generally run by one therapist for up to 12 clients. The format used was that of psychoeducation; this approach is increasingly common in mental health care and has been adapted also to work with families of borderline clients (Gunderson, Berkowitz, and Ruiz-Sancho, 1997). The sessions were topically focused and included a didactic and a skill-building component with numerous client exercises and homework activities.

The activity therapy/community integration group provided an opportunity for clients to become more involved in community activities, to learn about necessary resources, and to engage in new recreational experiences. This group also provided a more natural setting for developing peer relationships. A variety of recreational activities were provided, including attendance at cultural activities (plays, art museum), sports, outings, and engagement with the natural environment (gardening, hikes). Community resources, such as thrift shops, food banks, low-cost apartments, and the YMCA, were explored through field trips to these facilities. This component of the program enabled clients to live in the community on the minimal income obtained through entitlement programs or part-time work. Additionally, it encouraged clients to form relationships with others who became a source of support and natural problem solving. These groups were led by bachelor's-level staff and typically had up to 12 clients involved. They rapidly became one of the most popular parts of the program, as they were informal, enjoyable, and offered exposure to activities different from those that most clients had experienced.

This group-based program for clients with predominantly borderline personality disorders was developed as a working component of a high-volume community mental health center. As this was not developed as part of a research study, no instruments were used to measure improvements in client functioning. However, evaluation data were derived from regular evaluation of group sessions by clients and from staff feedback. At the end of the first year of treatment, both clients and staff felt that the program was very successful. Most clients had previously experienced an individual therapy approach to treatment, and they overwhelmingly preferred this group-based approach. After participating in the first year of the program, all clients established a more stable community living situation and a minority (fewer than 10%) experienced in-patient hospitalizations. Evaluation of all skills modules were extremely positive, with superlative responses the norm. Leaders of the process groups observed that the clients were generally able to incorporate the skills and knowledge taught in the skill-building groups.

For most team members, one of the greatest changes they observed was the developing capacity of clients to observe their own functioning and methods of responding to life situations. Based on the mindfulness skills of Linehan (1993b), this module in the group-based program also included training in meditation as a method of relaxation. This development of a type of "observing ego" in these chronically mentally ill clients was a new experience for them and for the staff and was critical to their learning new skills and changing their existing patterns of behavior.

Group-Based Treatment of Personality Disorders as Social Group Work

Within the classification of types of social group work, the "Less is Best" model is a treatment approach that includes several types of groups: therapy, education, and socialization (Toseland and Rivas, 1998). The purposes of therapy groups are to change behavior, cope with problems and rehabilitate psychological issues; the process group of the Less is Best model fits into this category. The skill-building group could be considered an educational group, as the group contained a didactic component, homework assignments, and repetitive practice of skills as they were taught. The activity/community integration group would be classified as a socialization group, according to the Toseland and Rivas framework. The purpose of this type of group is to learn social skills and behaviors to enable clients to function more effectively in the community. The activity group accomplished this by using a "learning through doing approach" (p. 26).

Outings to different venues broadened the experience base of clients, provided an opportunity for interaction, and informed them about community resources that could assist them with concrete services, such as food.

As the client population served by this model was functionally impaired, this combination of approaches taught new coping skills, assisted in integration of the skills and problem solving, and provided an opportunity to develop relationships with others. Because several types of groups were integrated into one program, clients had an opportunity to maximize their personal gains in a way that would have been difficult had only one group modality been offered.

Other authors classify group work according to different typologies. According to Anderson's (1997) framework, the Less is Best model has components of group psychotherapy, mutual aid, and structured group approaches. The process therapy group of the model was clearly a psychotherapy group in which members were coping with psychiatric disorders and the group provided a setting to work with issues in the present and gain insight into behaviors and motivation. The program's skill-building and activity groups could be considered mutual aid groups, as they provided a community environment for clients to share concerns and crises, look out for each other, and provide support. This became apparent as members became a network of assistance and support for each other that extended beyond the group meeting period to provide support and friendship in the community. The skill-building component of the model illustrates the structured group approach of Anderson, in which a learning curriculum is used and members practice skills with group norms, allowing the safety to experiment with learning new skills.

The various groups in the Less is Best program model progressed through the typical stages of group development; this was most evident in the process therapy group, which was the least structured program component. In all groups, there was some anxiety and discomfort at the beginning of the program, as is typical of the preaffiliation stage (Berman-Rossi, 1993). While power and control issues were less apparent in the structured skill-building and informal activity groups, all the process therapy groups experienced this inevitable aspect of group development. However, many members were familiar with each other and the leaders as a result of having participated in other, less intensive groups, and that eased the intensity of this stage. The work phase of the process groups was generally characterized by intimacy, sharing of personal experiences and reflections, and offering support to others, as is typical of this group stage (Berman-Rossi, 1993; Toseland and Rivas, 1998).

As several groups were ongoing in nature, incorporating new members as other members finished their work and left, the termination phase was not evident in the process and activity groups. However, as the skill-building group operated on the basis of four- to six-week educational modules, there was a type of termination at the end of each module. Members often voiced their regret that the module was ending and asked for extended time in their evaluations. While sequential modules started immediately, there was often a change of leaders or the addition or loss of client members. Loss or regret at the end of a successful group is often part of the termination experience (Berman-Rossi, 1993).

As clients interfaced with a team of therapists and case managers who led the various groups, they became comfortable and bond to the team and used them as role models and sources of support. Leadership of the groups varied according to their function and ranged from more formal and didactic approaches in the skill-building groups to facilitative and empowerment models in the activity/community integration groups. The process therapy group used the most typical group leadership skills in which individual therapeutic goals were developed and facilitated for each member, and various techniques such as cognitive restructuring, reframing, and role-playing were used at various times. Communication patterns within the group reflected typical patterns, such as maypole, round-robin, free-floating, with the increasing development of group interactive styles over time (Toseland and Rivas, 1998).

The Less is Best program model of providing group-based therapeutic services to adults with personality disorders reflects commonly accepted practices in the social group work literature. There is a variety of types and purposes of groups and an integration of group development into the formats of the various types of groups. Leadership patterns are flexible and tailored to the particular goal and focus of each group. Groups were evaluated through client feedback forms and informal discussions; members were very satisfied with the format and content of the group experiences. In all, this group model is seen as a successful means of enabling impaired clients in community mental health settings to live more successful lives in the community and reduce their use of mental health services. In the current environment of funding reductions, programs such as this can maximize funding and staff resources while at the same time enabling clients to manage their mental health problems in a more adaptive fashion.

References

American Psychiatric Association. (1994). *Diagnostic and statistical manual of mental disorders* (4th ed.). Washington, DC: Author.

Anderson, J. (1997). *Social work with groups: A process model*. New York: Longman.

Becker, P. (1998). A multifacet circumplex model of personality as a basis for the description and therapy of personality disorders. *Journal of Personality Disorders, 12*, 213–225.

Benjamin, L. (1993). *Interpersonal diagnosis and treatment of personal disorders*. New York: Guilford Press.

Benjamin, L. S. (1997). Personality disorders: Models for treatment and strategies for treatment development. *Journal of Personality Disorders, 11*, 307–324.

Berman-Rossi, T. (1993). The tasks and skills of the social worker across stages of group development. *Social Work with Groups, 16*, 69–81.

Blum, J. M., and Marziali, E. (1988). Time-limited, group psychotherapy for borderline patients. *Canadian Journal of Psychiatry, 33*, 364–369.

Gabbard, G. O. (1998). Treatment-resistant borderline personality disorder. *Psychiatric Annals, 28*, 651–656.

Gunderson, J. G., Berkowitz, C., and Ruiz-Sancho, A. (1997). Families of borderline patients: A psychoeducational approach. *Bulletin of the Menninger Clinic, 61*, 446–456.

Linehan, M. M. (1993a). *Cognitive-behavioral treatment of borderline personality disorder*. New York: Guilford Press.

Linehan, M. M. (1993b). *Skills training manual for treating borderline personality disorder*. New York: Guilford Press.

MacKenzie, K. R. (1996, May/June). Group psychotherapy: Managed care's reluctant bride. *Behavioral Health Management*, 18–21.

Millon, T. (1996). *Disorders of personality: DSM-IV an beyond* (2nd ed.). New York: Wiley.

Nehls, N. (1992). Group therapy for people with borderline personality disorder: Interventions associated with positive outcomes. *Issues in Mental Health Nursing, 13*, 255–269.

Perry, J. C., Banon, E., and Ianni, F. (1999). Effectiveness of psychotherapy for personality disorders. *American Journal of Psychiatry, 156*, 1312–1321.

Rosenberg, S. A., and Zimet, C. N. (1995). Brief group treatment and managed mental health care. *International Journal of Group Psychotherapy, 45*, 367–379.

Strack, S., and Lorr, M. (1997). The challenge of differentiating normal and disordered personality. *Journal of Personality Disorders, 11*, 105–12.

Toseland, R. W., and Rivas, R. F. (1998). *An introduction to group work practice* (3rd ed.). Boston: Allyn and Bacon.

Watson, D., Clark, L. A., and Harkness, A. R. (1994). Structures of personality and their relevance to psychopathology. *Journal of Abnormal Psychology, 103*, 18–31.

Yalom, I. D. (1995). *The theory and practice of group psychotherapy* (4th ed.). New York: Basic Books.

68

The Harm-Reduction Approach Revisited: An International Perspective

Illicit drugs have become a global problem following greater movement brought about by political changes such as the collapse of communism in Russia and the formation of international groups of countries to increase trade (Hellawell, 1995). Although there is close cooperation between the law enforcement authorities of different countries, illicit drug use appears to be increasing. Although people in many societies reject legalization or decriminalization of illicit drug use, the search for an alternative approach to zero tolerance to reduce the demand for illicit drugs will become a big issue for most countries in the world.

The harm-reduction approach has been selected for its potential to be the most influential substance abuse prevention, treatment, and rehabilitation approach in Western countries. In the late 1960s and early 1970s, several drug clinics and day centers in London taught injecting techniques and provided rooms in which the addicts could inject. Harm-reduction programs were also adopted by Italy in the 1970s and the Netherlands in the 1980s (Strang, 1992). In addition, there are some experimental projects in some cities of North America. Although there are many researchers and helping professionals who advocate the harm-reduction approach, the mainstream approach in many countries is still the war on drugs, especially in developing countries, which adopt a zero-tolerance policy toward drug taking and require a commitment of total abstinence as an admission criterion for treatment (Samarasinghe, 1995). It may be time for us to reexamine the assumptions and definition of the harm-reduction approach before implementing it in different parts of the world where there may be different cultural contexts.

Assumptions

The harm-reduction approach is based on the assumption that habits can be placed on a continuum. On one end is excessive use. On the other is abstinence. In the middle is moderate use (Marlatt and Tapert, 1993). The harm-reduction approach aims to change the drug taker from excessive to moderate use and then to total abstinence as an ultimate goal. The approach assists drug users to improve along this right direction. Based on this assumption, the harm-reduction approach has unique features, being pragmatic, incremental, comprehensive, scientific, proactive and accessible.

  Pragmatic: As drug use problems cannot be totally eliminated in the short run, the most practical way is to reduce the related harmful effects of drug abuse as much as possible (DesJarlais, 1995). Short-term operational objectives highlight the direction and are indicators for the drug users to achieve progress in reducing drug-related harm.
  Incremental: The harm-reduction approach is a step-by-step process (Carey, 1996; Minkoff, 1996). It strives for even a small slow advancement instead of total abstinence. The following is a good illustration provided by Parry (1989):

If a person is injecting street heroin of un-known potency, harm reduction would con-sider it an advance if the addict were pre-scribed safe, legal heroin. A further advance if he stopped sharing needles. A further ad-vance if he enrolled in a needle-exchange scheme. A much further advance if he moved on to oral drugs or to smoked drugs. A fur-ther advance in harm reduction if he started using condoms and practicing safe sex prac-tices. A further advance if he took advantage of the general health services available to ad-dicts. A wonderful victory if he kicked drugs, although total victory is not a requirement as it is in the United States. (13)

Comprehensive: The harm-reduction approach can be used for all kinds of addictive behav-ior. The effort can be short term or long term. The target levels include individual, commu-nity, and societal. The focus is on health, so-cial, and economic perspectives.

Scientific: The effectiveness of the harm-reduc-tion approach is confirmed by empirical stud-ies of its intervention strategies. In addition, since there is a scale of measurable short-term operational goals, it is easier for the re-searchers and helping professionals to evalu-ate its effectiveness.

Proactive and accessible: The harm-reduction approach adopts a reaching-out approach in making contact with drug users, who are per-ceived as clients in need, not criminals. This approach increases the accessibility of the ser-vice to the needy drug users. For example, in Amsterdam, about 60–80% of addicts are be-ing reached by various kinds of assistance from harm-reduction programs (Engelsman, 1989. However, in New York City, the esti-mate of injected drug users (IDUs) is 200,000 but only 38,000 are participating in publicly funded assistance programs (National Com-mission on AIDS, 1991).

Redefining Harm Reduction

As Single (1995) argued, the concept of harm re-duction is still poorly defined. In fact, harm re-duction has been expanded from illicit drugs to legal drugs and is grounded in the evolving pub-lic health and advocacy movements. Its basic phi-losophy is that some drug users cannot be ex-pected to cease their drug use immediately. The

alternative, then, is to try to provide some short-term measures to ameliorate the undesirable con-sequences.

The harm-reduction approach is designed to re-duce the harm (and risk of harm) associated with addictive behavior (Marlatt and Tapert, 1993). The use of this approach is not confined to the preven-tion and treatment of drug-related harm. It can also be applied to other addictive behavior, for exam-ple, gambling or excessive sex.

The terms "harm reduction," "harm minimiza-tion," and "risk reduction" are always used inter-changeably. Europeans (particularly the Dutch) like to use the term harm reduction. The British prefer harm minimization. However, Americans call this approach risk reduction. Strictly speaking, "harm" is the damage, while "risk" refers to the chance that damage might occur (Marlatt and Tapert, 1993; Strang, 1992).

The harm-reduction approach adopts a prag-matic attitude in dealing with substance-use prob-lems. Drug use is perceived as a reality in Western societies, not as a crime in an absolutely moralis-tic sense (DesJarlais, 1995). The harm-reduction approach places the drug use problem in a contin-uum with different degrees of addiction (see figure 68.1).

Different from the policy of a war on drugs, the goal of the harm-reduction approach is to re-duce drug-related harm by different kinds of out-reach effort combined with respect and accep-tance. The assistance is accessible to needy individuals and communities. The harm-reduc-tion approach does not equate all substance use as equally dangerous and illegal. There is some differentiation between levels of harms caused by different kinds of drugs, for example, soft drugs (alcohol, cannabis, etc.) and hard drugs (cocaine, heroin, etc.). It adopts a tolerance policy toward the soft drugs, but not the hard drugs (Broer and Garretsen, 1995).

Features of Harm-Reduction Approaches

The features of a harm-reduction approach can be characterized by low-threshold access, a public health approach, a tolerance policy, and a normal-ization policy.

Low-threshold compared with high-threshold access to prevention and treatment programs: Low-threshold harm-reduction programs do

Excess   Moderation   Abstinence

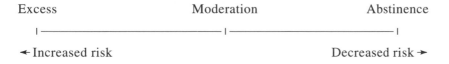

◄ Increased risk   Decreased risk ►

Figure 68.1 Continuum of excess, moderation, and abstinence (Marlatt and Tapert, 1993: 246)

not require for admission a personal commitment by the drug users to abstinence or drug testing (Marlatt, 1996). All the drug abusers have to do is show up and take steps toward reducing harm (Marlatt and Tapert, 1993). The effort aims at improving the physical and social functioning of drug users. The addicts' temporary inability to give up drug taking is well accepted (Engelsman, 1989). As Parry (1989) explained, harm reduction takes steps to reduce, even by a small degree, the harm resulting from the use of drugs.

Public health approach compared with criminal justice approaches to drug addiction: In the United States addicts are both victimized and stigmatized by current drug policies and theories of addiction causation (Mieczkowski, 1992). The criminal justice approach uses law enforcement mechanisms to control the supply of drugs. Illegal drug use is strictly punished by law (Erickson, 1995; Marlatt and Tapert, 1993). Public health policy does not see drug use as a crime. It is a matter of health and social functioning (Engelsman, 1989; DesJarlais, 1995). This problem can be tacked by providing adequate financial resources, professional intervention, and community support.

Tolerance compared with zero tolerance: The principle of zero tolerance insists on an absolute dichotomy between no use and any use whatsoever. This all-or-none theory equates all drug use as being equally harmful and fails to distinguish between different degrees of harmful use (Marlatt and Tapert, 1993). The tolerance approach adopts a realistic attitude, which differentiates between the levels of harm associated with drug use and takes other measures to reduce the harm.

Normalization policy compared with denormalization policy: Denormalization policy considers the drug user to be a loser. No drug use is viewed as safe or normal. Harm reduction adopts a normalization policy which acknowledges the existence of a drug use prob-

lem, but tries to reduce the harm through a variety of specific means.

Mechanism for Behavioral Change

The harm-reduction approach uses three mechanisms for changing the behavior of drug users. First, it tries to change the route of drug administration. For example, in AIDS prevention, needle exchange programs provide clean needles and syringes to drug users (Marlatt and Tapert, 1993). Second, it provides a safer alternative substance to replace the more harmful substance. For example, the Dutch government decriminalized the use of cannabis in 1976 so that drug users would not turn to substances with higher risks. Another famous example is the methadone maintenance programs in many large cities in Western countries in Asia. Third, it tries to reduce the frequency and intensity of ongoing addictive behavior. For example, there are responsible use programs to help drinkers reduce the risk of chronological disease and traffic accidents.

In the treatment process, drug users have only to commit themselves to the degree that they are willing to show up and are ready to improve. The progress will be step by step and the improvement in each step will be reinforcement for the drug users to experience behavioral change in the next step.

Programs of Harm Reduction

Harm reduction covers a variety of previously unrelated programs in the addictive behavior field (Marlatt and Tapert, 1993). The first type is an AIDS prevention program which includes safe sex and condom-use programs as well as needle exchange for injecting drug abusers. Second is treatment programs for ongoing, active addictive behavior, which include methadone maintenance for opiate addiction and nicotine replacement therapy for tobacco smokers. Third is a prevention program for harmful addictive behavior, which includes controlled drinking.

Effectiveness of Harm-Reduction Approach: An International Perspective

There is much evidence to support the effectiveness of harm-reduction programs all over the world. The following are examples from Europe, the United Kingdom, the United States, and Asia.

The Dutch Experience

In the Netherlands, after the implementation of decriminalization in 1976, the prevalence of cannabis use among youth age 10 to 18 was only 4.2%. In 1987, in a household survey in Amsterdam (where drug use is considered to be higher than the national average), the "last-month prevalence" of cannabis use was reported to be 5.5%. In Amsterdam, the proportion of drug users age 21 and younger decreased from 14.4% in 1981 to 4.8% in 1987 (Marlatt and Tapert, 1993: 252).

Another indication of success is the finding that the number of injecting drug users seeking treatment in Amsterdam alone has tripled from 600 in 1981 to 1,800 in 1988. In 1988, only 8% of AIDS patients in the Netherlands were drug addicts, and the prevalence of HIV-positive cases among high-risk injection addicts in Amsterdam was reported to be 30% (Houwelig cited in Engelsman, 1989).

The Scottish Experience

In Scotland, two cities with similar injection drug use problems handled syringe availability differently and had quite different outcomes (Brettle, 1991). In 1981, Edinburgh made it illegal to purchase syringes without a prescription, in an attempt to reduce drug use. This led to considerable needle sharing. More than 50% of all IDUs in Edinburgh were HIV-positive by 1984, and an epidemic of hepatitis B occurred simultaneously. Glasgow had a larger number of IDUs, but did not limit syringe availability and did not suffer an HIV or hepatitis B epidemic, with only 5% of the city's IDUs testing HIV-positive (Brettle, 1991). The success of the harm reduction approach in Glasgow was further supported by an empirical study on the behavior and attitudes of injecting drug abusers in Scotland in 1993 (Frischer et al., 1993).

The U.S. Experience

The New Haven needle exchange program was evaluated for effectiveness by members of the Yale School of Medicine (Kaplan et al., 1991). New infections of HIV among clients were reduced by 33%. Other cities with needle exchange programs have shown decreasing numbers of new cases each year (Buning, 1991). The most common argument against needle exchanges is that they will encourage or increase illicit drug use. This fear has not been supported by the data in many empirical studies in different communities (Watters et al., 1991; Wolk et al., 1990).

The Hong Kong Experience

In Hong Kong, although the use of the harm-reduction approach is still a topic for heated debate in the addictive field, the methadone treatment program has been going on since 1972. In fact, this government-run program is the largest treatment program for substance abusers in Hong Kong. In 1995, there were 10,000 admissions (Hong Kong Action Committee Against Narcotics, 1995). Under the supervision of medical professionals and the guidance of social workers, the dose of methadone is reduced gradually and adjusted according to the needs of each participant. The program enables the participants to retain their jobs and maintain normal life. In addition, the risks of illegal possession and consumption of illicit drugs, and that of transmitting AIDS and hepatitis B by sharing needles, were greatly reduced. As reported by the Hong Kong government, the program maintained a 70% average attendance rate in 1995 (Hong Kong Action Committee Against Narcotics, 1995). This means that the program successfully helped 7,000 substance abusers to maintain a normal lifestyle without taking illicit drugs every day.

Conclusion

Harm reduction is an incremental but practical approach with a realistic attitude to drug-abuse prevention, treatment, and rehabilitation. It takes action through proactive outreach efforts. There are pragmatic values behind the approach. The coverage is wide, ranging from remedial to preventative. It is accessible to drug users. It is supported by empirical research, and the outcome is comparatively easy to evaluate. In terms of resource allocation, to adopt the harm-reduction approach may help to shift resources from law enforcement to treatment and preventative education.

As an approach for substance-abuse prevention, treatment, and rehabilitation, harm reduction has great potential to be the most influential in the addictive field. Although there is a fear that harm-reduction programs will facilitate greater drug abuse among users, its effectiveness has been proven in various evaluation studies in different countries. Although harm reduction is still an alternative approach in many parts of the world, it will become an internationally adopted mainstream approach in the near future.

The author would like to thank Dr. Eric Single and Dr. Charles Chan for their valuable comments on the paper.

References

Broer, J. and H. F. L. Garretsen (1995) Simultaneous Strategies to Reduce Demand for and Problematic Use of Hard Drugs, *Medicine and Law* 14(3–4): 171–9.

Brettle, R. P. (1991) HIV and Harm Reduction for Injecting Drug Users, *AIDS* 5: 125–36.

Buning, E. C. (1991) Effects of Amsterdam Needle and Syringe Exchange, *International Journal of the Addictions* 26: 1303–11.

Carey, K. B. (1996). Substance Use Reduction in the Context of Outpatient Psychiatric Treatment: A Collaborative, Motivational, Harm Reduction Approach, *Community Mental Health Journal* 32(3):291–306.

DesJarlais, D. C. (1995). Harm Reduction: A Framework for Incorporating Science into Drug Policy, *American Journal of Public Health* 85(1): 10–12.

Engelsman, E. L. (1989) Dutch Policy on the Management of Drug-Related Problems, *British Journal of Addiction* 84: 211–18.

Erickson, P. G. (1995) Harm Reduction: What It Is and Is Not, *Drug and Alcohol Review* 14(3): 283–5.

Frischer, M. et al. (1993) Modeling the Behavior and Attributes of Injecting Drug Users: A New Approach to Identifying HIV Risk Practices, *International Journal of the Addictions* 28(2): 129–52.

Hellawell, K. (1995) The Role of Law Enforcement in Minimizing the Harm Resulting from Illicit Drugs, *Drug and Alcohol Review* 14(3): 317–22.

Hong Kong Action Committee Against Narcotics (1995) *Hong Kong Narcotics Report 1995*. Hong Kong: Hong Kong Government Printer.

Kaplan, E. H., E. O'Keefe and R. Heimer (1991) Evaluating the New Haven Needle Exchange Program, paper presented at the meeting of the International Conference on AIDS, Florence, Italy.

Marlatt, G. A. (1996) Harm Reduction: Come as You Are, *Addictive Behaviors* 21(6): 779–88.

Marlatt, G. A. and S. F. Tapert (1993) Harm Reduction: Reducing the Risks of Addictive Behaviours, in J. S. Baer, G. A. Marlatt and R. J. McMahon (eds) *Addictive Behaviour across the Life Span*, pp. 243–73. London: Sage.

Mieczkowski, T. (ed.) (1992) *Drugs, Crime, and Social Policy*. Needham Heights, MA: Allyn and Bacon.

Minkoff, K. (1996) Discussion of Substance Use Reduction in the Context of Outpatient Psychiatric Treatment, *Community Mental Health Journal* 32(3): 307–10.

National Commission on AIDS (1991) *Report: The Twin Epidemics of Substance Use and HIV*. Washington, DC: National Commission on AIDS.

Parry, A. (1989) Harm Reduction (Interview), *Drug Policy Letter* 1(4): 13.

Samarasinghe, D. (1995) Harm Reduction in the Developing World, *Drug and Alcohol Review* 14(3): 305–9.

Single, E. (1995) Defining Harm Reduction, *Drug and Alcohol Review* 14(3): 287–90.

Strang, J. (1992) Drug Use and Harm Reduction: Responding to the Challenge, in N. Healther et al. (eds) *Psychoactive Drugs and Harm Reduction: From Faith to Science*, pp. 3–33. London: Whurr Publishers.

Watters, J. K., Y. T. Cheng, G. L. Clark and J. Lorvick (1991) Syringe Exchange in San Francisco: Preliminary Findings, paper presented at the meeting of the International Conference on AIDS, Florence, Italy.

Wolk, J. et al. (1990) The Effect of a Needle and Syringe Exchange on a Methadone Maintenance Unit, *British Journal of Addiction* 85: 1445–50.

CHRISTINA E. NEWHILL
EDWARD W. SITES

69

Identifying Human Remains Following an Air Disaster: The Role of Social Work

Introduction and Background

Crisis intervention theory and practice have traditionally been within the purview of social work (Fein & Knaut, 1986; Groner, 1978; Hepworth & Larsen, 1993; Lukton, 1982; Newhill, 1989; Slaikeu, 1984). The origin of modern crisis intervention methodology may be traced to the work of Erich Lindemann (1944) and his colleagues following the Coconut Grove nightclub fire in Boston on November 28, 1942 in which 493 people perished. His clinical report on the psychological aftermath of this disaster and the interventions thought to be effective in mitigating the distress of family members of the victims laid the foundation for the development of approaches to disaster response (Newhill, 1989).

The development of disaster relief services and policies has been primarily supported by efforts of the American Red Cross and the federal government, with education and training materials developed by the Red Cross and the Emergency Services and Disaster Relief Branch of the National Institute of Mental Health (Baker & Zakour, 1996). The area of disaster response continues to be an important sphere of crisis intervention work. Such disasters may be divided into three main categories: (1) natural disasters (e.g., earthquakes or floods) (Durkin, 1993; Durkin & Thiel, 1993; Erikson, 1976; Freedy, Kilpatrick & Resnick, 1993); (2) accidental disasters (e.g., major transportation crashes or fires) (Armstrong, Lund, McWright &

Tichenor, 1995; Black, 1987; Butcher & Dunn, 1989; Butcher & Hatcher, 1988; Green, Grace & Gleser, 1985; Harr, 1994; Jacobs, Quevillon & Stricherz, 1990; Popplow, 1984; Williams, Soloman & Bartone, 1988); and (3) human-induced disasters (e.g., war, terrorism, kidnapping) (Artiss, 1963; Terr, 1983; Drory, Posen, Vilner & Ginzburg, 1998). Considerable attention has been given in the literature to strategies for response to natural disasters and certain human-induced disasters, particularly in the area of stress debriefing (Armstrong et al., 1995; Bell, 1995; Mitchell, 1988, 1983; Talbot, Manton & Dunn, 1992; Spitzer & Burke, 1993).

Much of the disaster response literature, however, has focused on the role of professional groups other than social work, for example, psychologists (Jacobs et al., 1990; Talbot et al., 1992), military personnel (Jones, 1985), and nurses (Laube, 1973; Rayner, 1958). More recently, literature has emerged specifically addressing social workers' involvement in traumatic event debriefing work and related responsibilities of disaster response (Baker & Zakour, 1996; Bell, 1995; Shah, 1985; Spitzer & Neely, 1992; Zakour, 1996).

Recovery and Identification of Human Remains

One area of disaster response that has a high risk of inducing trauma in the response workers is recovering and identifying human remains (Dala-hanty, Dougall, Craig, Jenkins & Baum, 1997). Human remains from a disaster event may range from burned, dismembered, or mutilated bodies to relatively intact bodies (Ursano & McCarroll, 1990). Exposure to violent death is a significant psychological stressor that has the potential of creating "secondary disaster victims" (Jones, 1985) or "hidden victims" (Kliman, 1976) of those who assist in recovery work. A small literature exists addressing the specific psychological risks of handling the dead and how people cope with such experiences (Dalahanty et al., 1997).

For example, approximately one-third of the volunteers who recovered bodies from the Mount Erebus air crash in Antarctica initially experienced transient problems of moderate to severe intensity; at three months, about one-fifth reported high levels of stress-related symptoms (Taylor & Frazer, 1982). For those workers who handled bodies following the Jonestown Guyana, mass suicide, youth, inexperience, lower military rank, and degree of exposure to the bodies were associated with high levels of emotional stress eight months after the experience (Jones, 1985). Although it is recognized that exposure to mass death is a significant stressor, the nature of this stressor is not well understood (Ursano, 1987). Few data exist on the psychological effects of exposure to dead bodies and body parts (Hershiser & Quarantelli, 1976; Jones, 1985; Ursano & McCarroll, 1990).

In a recent study, McCarroll, Ursano, Wright, and Fullerton (1993) conducted on-site observations and interviews with individuals who worked with dead bodies to determine significant stressors and how the workers coped with them. Data were collected following three major disasters: the Gander, Newfoundland, air crash of 1985, in which 256 people were killed; the turret explosion aboard the USS Iowa in 1989, in which 47 sailors were killed; and the crash of United States Flight 232 in Sioux City, Iowa, in 1989, in which 112 people died. Participants were asked to describe the nature of their jobs, their experiences, and their observations on the stresses of handling dead bodies.

The first stressful period for many workers is before exposure to the dead (Harr, 1996; McCarroll et al., 1993; Corenblum & Taylor, 1981; Fenz & Jones, 1972). Anticipating how one may react to seeing the dead, lack of information regarding what one will be facing, fearing one's own reaction to the bodies, and concerns about the ability to cope are common stressors during this period. During this stage, social and professional support is essential (McCarroll et al., 1993). Practice drills can be

helpful, along with being "told the worst" to minimize surprise and shock.

The next stressful period is direct exposure to the bodies. Ursano and McCarroll (1990) describe the profound sensory overload produced by handling dead bodies and body parts for those who volunteer or are assigned such duties, including extreme sensory stimulation associated with exposure to and handling of dead bodies, shock of unexpected events associated with the dead, identification or emotional involvement with the dead, and handling children's bodies, as constituting significant stressors for the workers involved. During the period of direct exposure, workers must constantly defend against the "multiple sensory stimuli" associated with handling the dead:

Among [the multiple sensory stimuli] are the sight of bodies, including those that are grotesque, burned, or mutilated; the sounds that occur during autopsy, such as heads hitting tables and saws cutting bone; the smells of decomposing flesh and burned bodies; and the tactile stimuli experienced as bodies are handled throughout the process. All this can be described as sensory overload. (McCarroll et al., 1993, p. 211)

Studies of sensory overload experienced by recovery workers report that the smell is usually described as the most troublesome. "Investigators say that aircraft accidents all have the same distinctive smell, and that once experienced it is never forgotten . . . the reek of . . . jet fuel, the smoldering remains of the plane, the scent of roasted flesh" (Harr, 1996, pp. 39–40). Recovery workers utilize a variety of strategies to cope with the unbearable smells, including smoking cigars, burning coffee, working in the cold if possible, and using strong fragrances such as peppermint or orange oil inside surgical masks (Cervantes, 1988).

Handling dead bodies and body parts creates tactile stress as well as representing a biohazard. Wearing gloves, masks, and bodysuits can both protect the recovery worker from infectious disease (Harr, 1996) and serve to decrease tactile stimulation, reported to be particularly difficult with decomposed and burned bodies (McCarroll et al., 1993).

Identification or "emotional involvement" with the deceased can be a significant stressor. A common reaction is "It could have been me" (Ursano & McCarroll, 1990). Children's bodies are particularly difficult in this regard. Workers may try to distance themselves psychologically from the bodies by reframing them as "a job" rather than a human being and utilizing an "overintellectualized approach" to maintain their emotional defenses (Wallace, 1956). Avoiding looking at faces can also help in managing the stress of direct exposure (McCarroll et al., 1993).

Timely, skilled intervention can serve to prevent psychological trauma in recovery workers who must handle dead bodies and body parts. As previously noted, prior to exposure, workers should be prepared via practice drills for what they will be encountering, including telling workers what the "worst" might be. During exposure, the risk of "overdedication" is common. Overdedication refers to the tendency to work longer hours than necessary, working under conditions one normally would not tolerate, and guilt over the need for sleep or food (McCarroll et al., 1993). Encouraging or even mandating that workers take breaks is important, along with providing support immediately when the worker wants it and is receptive to the support. Another obstacle to healthy coping is subscribing to a macho attitude. Such subscription undermines permission for workers to express appropriate grief and distress. For example, McCarroll et al. reported that some supervisors laughed at people when they said they "couldn't take it" (p. 212). Another coping mechanism is humor (Jones, 1985). Humor can be helpful in easing stress, although extreme "gallows humor" can be distressing for some. For most professional and nonprofessional volunteers, feeling that they are providing a service and even a tribute to those who died in the disaster gives purpose and meaning to what is very difficult work (McCarroll et al., 1993).

Following exposure to the dead, workers need a postevent debriefing to help make the transition from the mortuary to the "real world." Critical to preventing trauma in the recovery workers is social support from the work group and family members. In McCarroll et al.'s (1993) study, workers reported that caring and sensitivity from their families and primary support group was very important. Almost everyone, however, viewed professional counseling as unacceptable, mostly due to fears of being fired or being ridiculed by fellow workers. Overcoming this obstacle is one of the first tasks for the disaster response social worker.

With their ecological orientation to viewing human problems as interactive phenomena between individuals and their environment, social workers are appropriate professionals to provide support during an event of significant trauma (Aiello, 1999; Hepworth, Rooney & Larsen, 1997). However, to date there is no literature directly addressing the potential role of social workers in this arena. This paper reports on a case study in which a professional social worker provided intervention and support to disaster response workers and volunteers assigned to the morgue following a major air disaster. We argue that much can be learned from this experience for social work education and practice. The unique person-in-environment social work perspective, the network of professional social workers in virtually every community, the availability of professional organizations for a response framework, the emergence of curriculum materials for professional education, the opportunities for social workers to provide local disaster training prior to any disaster, and other strengths and contributions of social work will be discussed along with recommendations for social work education.

A Case in Point

Pittsburgh's new, technologically advanced, international airport is the third largest and sixteenth busiest airport in the nation, with nearly half a million departures and landings each year. In over 50 years of commercial operations, Pittsburgh had never experienced a major crash. Disaster plans in such an environment take on a very abstract, even surreal, character. Disaster preparations tend not to be a high priority sustained by any sense of urgency, especially outside the immediate confines of required airport and airline disaster planning.

On the beautiful, balmy, crystal clear, early evening of September 8, 1994, USAir flight 427 to Pittsburgh from Chicago flipped over and plunged violently into a wooded ravine just six miles from the airport runway (Harr, 1996). The incredible, vertical, 6,000-foot descent at over 300 miles per hour virtually disintegrated the entire plane on impact, along with all its human and other contents. The entire time elapsed between the first hint to the pilots of mechanical trouble and the final flaming wreckage on the ground was a mere 26 seconds.

Rescuers of all descriptions rushed to the crash site hoping to find and save life. What they encountered was a ghastly, grisly sight like nothing any of them, including veterans of war, other air crashes, and other types of disasters had ever seen before. The National Transportation Safety Board's chief investigator legally responsible for every aspect of the investigation and recovery operation, himself a veteran of more than two dozen major plane crash investigations, said he had never seen such carnage. An especially hard-bitten military officer on duty at the scene gasped that he had never experienced such horror, even during his double tour of duty as a medical in Vietnam. Not only were all 132 persons aboard dead, but their bodies had been ripped asunder into tens of thousands of tiny pieces, most entirely unrecognizable. The shreds and shards of human viscera, bone, and flesh were scattered over the wooded hillsides and hung eerily from bushes and trees in chaotic fashion, as though each body had imploded on impact with such force that its fragments were blown outward in every direction for hundreds of yards. There were no faces.

The extreme biohazards at the crash site were palpable to even the most inexperienced observer or volunteer. Fire charred and consumed some body pieces which remained adhered to parts of the wreckage. Investigators were astounded to find the plane shredded into as many small pieces as the human bodies. As overwhelmed rescue workers began to plan and initiate the recovery efforts, night fell, during which a road was cut into the site. By the time morning broke, thousands of official personnel and volunteers had assembled, along with a good contingent of voyeurs, thrill seekers, and an army of news media seeking information and sensational photographs. A light rain began to fall, turning the hillsides to a slippery mud. Biohazard protective clothing was issued to the hundreds of official and volunteer workers who began the 29-day process of picking up the tiny bits of flesh and bone one by one, placing each in a plastic bag, labeling each as to the exact location of retrieval, and seeking scientifically to identify the remains. Aside from the mud, the sight, the rough terrain, and the uncomfortably hot biohazard suits, rescue workers were assaulted by overpowering odors of the fire, aviation fuel, and rotting flesh, which hung over the hillsides like a pall, penetrating every nostril and permeating every thread of clothing.

The Response

Within an hour after the crash, mental health professionals from two counties were on the scene. In all, some 850 mental health professionals volunteered to help. The public mental health agency in the county where the airport was located went directly to the airport to help waiting families and friends, airline and airport personnel, and others directly affected.

At the crash site, which was in an adjoining county, another public mental health agency was setting up one of its command posts on the hillside near the wreckage to serve those working in the immediate recovery. The public mental health agencies, augmented by the services of many other public and private agencies and hundreds of volunteers, fanned out in the days, weeks, and months ahead to serve families, affected corporations, schools, scout troops, sports teams, church groups, workers from the crash and related sites, and countless others. National experts on the scene and investigators afterward repeatedly praised the region's response for several features they identified as remarkable and uncharacteristic in similar situations. One feature was the instant and generous outpouring of every kind of material, technical, and humanitarian assistance. Another was the highly organized manner in which public and private emergency agencies and organizations, the military, police, and professional associations implemented their emergency and disaster plans. The third was the collegial, largely noncompetitive and interdisciplinary manner in which the professional community worked together. A fourth was the compassionate, unified response of the public, who came together like family to support both the survivors of crash victims and those who labored in hundreds of visible and invisible ways to assist in the recovery efforts. Practically everyone in Pittsburgh and the surrounding communities was touched by the crash. Pittsburgh is a relatively small, closely knit community. Many knew someone who lost a loved one, worked at a company affected, had a child who attended school where the family of another child was affected, or belonged to a social group or religious community from which a member was lost.

Back at the crash site, plastic bags with body parts were piling up on a very warm, late summer day. Refrigerated trailer trucks were ordered and the body parts were loaded inside. At a nearby Air Force Reserve base which is adjacent to and shares the property of the international airport which flight 427 was approaching, two hangers were set aside for an emergency morgue and the rest, feeding, and debriefing of morgue workers. Aside from the close proximity of the Air Force base, the security military personnel were able to provide proved highly beneficial in the days ahead as news media and thrill seekers invented numerous ingenious methods for trying to get a look inside the morgue or get photographs from there.

The Morgue

The morgue itself was a maze of aisles, work stations, lights, medical equipment, and people. Radiologists, dentists, forensic anthropologists, pathologists, social workers, psychologists, Federal Bureau of Investigation personnel, Pennsylvania

State Police, nurses, odontologists, coroners, funeral directors, military personnel, hazardous materials workers. USAir employees, and many volunteers filled the area to capacity. In addition to body parts, personal effects of the dead were brought here to be photographed and identified. Without going into great detail about how the work inside the morgue was organized and what was done at each work station, suffice it to say that the primary task was identification. Any clue, from a fingerprint or footprint to a shred of clothing, a piece of jewelry, a tattoo, a small scrap of dental work, a healed fracture, a scar, sternum wires from open-heart surgery, the serial number on an artificial joint, DNA samples, a bone spur, an orthopedic plate, or a tooth fragment might help identify someone or help get a few pieces of the same person together. Every body part had to be X-rayed to look for metal fragments. These had to be removed for examination to confirm or reject the hypothesis that a bomb had caused the crash. This alone took eight days. Every body fragment had to be embalmed for health reasons, to preserve it long enough to complete the initial phase of the investigation, and to have something to return to as many families as possible. As on the hillside, the combined odors of decaying flesh, embalming materials, and the bleach used to decontaminate everything and everyone filled the atmosphere and saturated clothing so that workers could not even escape it after their exhausting 12 to 18 hour days in the morgue.

The hangar was filled with large numbers of the most skilled, specialized, compassionate, dedicated, meticulous, respectful professionals one could imagine, most of them working as volunteers. The hangar was also staffed with large numbers of lay volunteers and some paid laypersons. These were volunteer firefighters, secretaries from the local courthouse, factory workers whose time was donated by the companies for whom hey worked, students, truck drivers, canteen and rest area workers, janitorial staff, electricians, plumbers, equipment operators, and many others. Because of the intensity, duration, and inescapable horror of the environment and tasks, every participant was a candidate for physical and mental stress reactions, and most, if not all, exhibited signs of their distress sooner or later. Provision of the few creature comforts possible, compassionate listening, quiet and unthreatening suggestions of stress management techniques, answering questions, obtaining needed information, debriefing (both Critical Incident Stress Debriefing and Multiple Stress Debriefing),

and massive support in a variety of other forms were made available to everyone.

Some of the professional rescue workers arrived in teams complete with their own mental health and debriefing personnel. These groups usually knew each other personally from previous assignments, tended to work and socialize as much in isolation as possible, and often saw themselves as so experienced in the stress of disaster work that they were immune to it and needed no support. Some within those groups who did experience problems were under considerable peer pressure not to reveal their needs. Others did not respect the debriefing experts who accompanied their team and refused to associate with them or talk to them. At the same time they found it uncomfortable to go outside their closed group and shunned the other mental health personnel available. In short, for some of the professionals, there were aspects of machismo, denial, and isolation evident. They saw themselves as there to do an unpleasant job against which they had steeled themselves and which they hoped to complete as quickly as possible so they could return home, often in another state. Providing support to these workers was more difficult an sometimes impossible. For some personnel, such as the military, debriefing was mandatory after every shift. For others, debriefing was voluntary, though as the days dragged on and the stress began to accumulate, most participated readily and found the sessions helpful.

Morgue Personnel

A large contingent of morgue workers, however, fell into one of the specialist groups. They were the volunteer and paid workers who were not identification, investigation, medical, military, police, or air industry professionals. Nothing in their lives had prepared them for the tasks, stresses, and deprivations they were experiencing. Likewise, nothing in their lives had prepared them to recognize or deal with their reactions, however normal.

To illustrate the situations of these persons, a bit more description may be helpful. In a morgue operation such as this, there are three particular tasks that put workers at the very center of the sights, sounds, touch, and odor of the body parts being retrieved, examined, and identified. The first of these are called trackers. When any professional (pathologist, radiologist, odontologist, for example) is ready to examine the next body part or wishes to retrieve a particular body part for further examination, a tracker is sent to the refrigerated trucks to obtain the body part. This part is carried in a plastic bag (often see-through), usually in the tracker's hands (sometimes on a small tray) to the professional. It is that tracker's assignment never to let that body part out of sight. Each body part is accompanied by a clipboard with identifying data. This identifying information must not only accompany the part constantly, but the route of the body part must be tracked by having every professional in contact with it sign it in and out. One tracker could carry such a body part around for hours, taking it from the radiologist, to the forensic anthropologist, to the pathologist, to the FBI identification team, to the coroner, to the embalmer, and back to the refrigerator truck. During this entire time, every procedure to which the body part is subjected is in the full view of the volunteer tracker, who may not even have a place to sit down. The refrigerator trucks were located about 25 yards outside the hanger/morgue. The same body part could be recalled many times. The tracker's job was to go to the trucks and, with supervision, to sort through the piles of parts and bring the next requested piece.

The second group of workers to be assigned a task for which many of those present were not fully prepared was the scribes. These persons were stationed at the side of each professional to record everything the professional wished to add to the record of that body part. Medical, dental, nursing, and other students from the health professions, along with volunteer licensed medical professionals were assigned to these tasks as frequently as possible because their familiarity with the terminology and spellings used by the professionals examining the body parts contributed to the accuracy of the records and the speed with which the work could be completed. But some scribes were volunteer stenographers, retail sales clerks, homemakers, and others who had no medical experience whatsoever. These persons had responded to requests from their employers, pleas from private organizations, or their own helping instincts to present themselves for assignment if there was anything they could do. They came from every walk of life and sometimes from hundreds of miles away to accept assignments for as long as they could be available. The length of this phase of the work resulted in some turnover and the continual assignment of new volunteers.

The third group was the hazardous materials handlers whose companies had been contracted to collect and dispose of the truckloads of human and medically related waste from the morgue. Unfor-

tunately in this case, many of these workers had no experience with biohazardous waste of this nature. One young father spoke in despair after about a week that his entire previous experience had been cleaning up petroleum and related chemical spills from roadsides following vehicular accidents. He had never seen anything like this; he had never handled materials like these; he had never been trained for this work; he had never before been away from his wife and young children overnight; he had never previously felt endangered by what he had been asked to dispose of; and he had no idea how to explain to his children what he was now doing.

Intervention at the Morgue

One of the authors was assigned to the morgue. He had been trained by the American Red Cross prior to this disaster specifically for intervention in the event of an airport disaster and received a refresher course after the crash before the assignment to the morgue. Perhaps it is self-evident what some of the roles professional mental health volunteers such as social workers have in an environment like this. Providing unthreatening, constant, compassionate availability was perhaps the most important role. The beleaguered morgue workers were reassured by the presence of support, relieved that they could avail themselves of it on their own terms in their own time, and grateful for the resources and help provided. Word spread quietly and quickly. Every mental health worker wore clearly visible identification as a mental health professional, in part to make it easy for other morgue personnel to find them and in part to assure informed consent. No one ever spoke with a mental health worker without knowing the worker's or volunteer's official role. To avoid interfering with the primary work of the morgue, mental health workers remained on the periphery in rest and refreshment areas or near the rest room facilities. Thus, when morgue workers were most likely to have a few minutes and were most likely to evidence signs of stress, mental health workers were usually not more than an arm's length away. A sobbing or vomiting worker did not always want immediate, personal support, but it was present and mental health workers were highly skilled at initiating contact when, in their professional opinion, it was indicated.

A second role was vigilance for signs of stress, fatigue, or illness, which indicated a worker should be relieved from the shift. Of course, volunteer mental health workers had no authority to take such actions, but supervisors who were usually too preoccupied with their work to notice subtle changes in workers assigned to them (most of whom they had never met before) were only too glad to listen to pertinent mental health observations. Almost always it was possible to encourage workers to request relief from the supervisor directly. Permission from the mental health personnel, which acknowledged the reality of the stress and normalized the worker's reactions, made the process easier and minimized guilt.

A third role was the provision of concrete resources. In this case, as in many others, the American Red Cross supplied excellent printed materials for workers on a wide variety of topics, including such things as how to explain death to children, what reactions to expect in themselves after leaving the assignment, and how to explain their experiences to friends and relatives. These materials were never pushed. Piles of copies were made readily available for workers to select what they wanted without having to ask. Of course, mental health workers gave copies of specific items to workers when particular questions arose.

A fourth role was as debriefers. A constant rotation of debriefing groups for workers leaving their shifts was in progress. An attempt was made to debrief every worker at least once every day. American Red Cross and other disaster response professionals and volunteers conducted these sessions and, of course, were themselves debriefed (Jacobs et al., 1990). So much has been written about the debriefing process that more detail is not necessary here (see e.g., Matthews, 1998; Rank, 1997).

One additional element from the 427 crash should be mentioned. It has to do with the matter of handling body parts. Medical personnel such as pathologists are extensively trained to assume these tasks on a continuous basis. Police and firefighters are required to do so on an occasional basis and also receive training to prepare them. But the unprepared hometown volunteer who confronts this task is at extremely high risk. Moreover, in a situation such as this one, these laypersons were required to handle body parts over and over and over for days on end. The longer the process continued, the more fatigued they became, the more deteriorated the body parts became, and the more stressful the conditions became. These are not the kinds of experiences to which one becomes accustomed and immune in a few hours or days, if ever. Rotation of duties, recruitment of new volunteer replacements, massive mental health support, as much attention to creature comfort as possible under the conditions, time at home for as many workers as live nearby, shorter work days as the process continues, provision for long-term follow-up after workers have gone home, and all of the other interventions and supports known to crisis and disaster professionals are essential. In the final analysis, there is no way to identify a small army of lay volunteers and prepare them for handling body parts in every community just in case there might be a disaster in their town one day. Since it can be done for most people only at the time of a crisis, what is required is a core of highly trained mental health professionals in every community who will be able to step in to work with the rescue workers if the need arises.

Handling body parts is extremely stressful for most of those engaged in a disaster recovery and identification effort such as the one described here. The parts have grotesque appearances whether covered with the grit, mud, and other foreign matter from wherever they landed at the crash site to the hoary growths that appeared on them before they were embalmed. As they decomposed, they changed shape, consistency, and appearance. Just one thing was constant and that was that untrained lay volunteers handled them frequently and over extended periods of time. Since very little advanced training or preparation is possible in such disasters, intensive, comprehensive mental health services are absolutely mandatory during the recovery work and in follow-up to the fullest extent possible.

Lessons Learned and Relearned

This case study is intended primarily to raise issues for social workers. Many of the other professional groups responding to this disaster were better prepared to respond on short notice than social workers were. Emergency room personnel of a variety of professional backgrounds respond to crises regularly. Their experiences have been helpful to other groups in designing training. A unique specialization in disaster response is not being suggested for social work. The skills that social workers bring to the interdisciplinary disaster intervention team are based on social work's historic practice in crisis situations (mostly with individuals and families) and are transferable to other settings. In this disaster, social workers were assigned to assist survivors in families, places of employment, schools, churches, and many other contexts. Just one of these was the crash morgue.

As others have noted, social workers are exceptionally well-prepared for disaster intervention because of their person-in-situation orientation (Baker & Zakour, 1996), familiarity with crisis theory, skill in working with people from a strengths perspective, and, perhaps especially, because of their experience and comfort in approaching persons in the field. Anyone who has ever knocked uninvited on a family's door to initiate a child abuse investigation can appreciate the skills needed to engage people under stress. Social workers in oncology, rape centers, shelters for battered women, psychiatric clinics, neighborhood organizing, hospital emergency rooms, teen drug treatment programs, alternative school programs, and many other fields have all developed intervention skills highly transferable to disaster services.

What professional social workers know, however transferable, is only foundational. There is much to learn about the specifics of practice in a disaster setting, just as there would be in any agency. It is unethical to practice outside one's area of competence. Social workers must therefore prepare themselves for practice in such settings purposefully.

Others have spoken about the value of including appropriate material in social work curricula (Baker & Zakour, 1996). While it may be possible to do so in a general way, very few students will ever have the opportunity to make a practice career of disaster response work. That level of specialization is precluded in BASW/BSW curricula by accreditation standards and is probably not warranted in MSW curricula. The basics of crisis theory and crisis intervention, however, should be part of the core curriculum of at least every MSW student. This, along with the standard foundation curriculum areas, will certainly prepare those social workers to pursue the additional training necessary for disaster work if they are interested. Not everyone is cut out for this work, any more than they are suited to hospice, emergency room, child welfare, or other social work.

The faculty at the School of Social Work at the University of Pittsburgh decided in 1985 to provide disaster intervention training for all faculty through an agreement with the American Red Cross. When the training was completed, all were certified and provided identification credentials for immediate assignment in case of an emergency. These could be with a single family who had been burned out of their home or something as momentous as the 427 crash. Over the years, faculty members practiced their skills in a variety of small-scale disasters such as floods and fires, as needed. The irony of the situation was that by the time of the 427 crash, the

School had had so many retirements and new faculty that only a few persons with the original training were available. What had begun as a wise plan had been permitted to fall into the category of "not urgent." Not only is continuous training essential, but rehearsal is a major aspect of any good training (Jacobs et al., 1990). Faculty who are current in their training and well rehearsed are highly likely to weave elements of this information and their experiences into their teaching throughout the curriculum. Continuing education programs can provide introductory training, recertification training, and specific, advanced training for those interested.

Because those in need of follow-up attention scatter so widely and because there can be very large numbers of them, this crucial phase is highly likely to be problematic. Mental health agencies and professionals in the immediate area can provide help for those who identify themselves as having need and who seek help over a long period of time. Despite debriefing, many others experience problems without knowing the nature of their difficulties, are embarrassed to seek help, or are discouraged from seeking help by those well-meaning persons in the community who urge them to "forget it" so they "can put it behind them." Since tracking these volunteers is impractical if not impossible, social workers and other mental health professionals must constantly be alert to the possibility of posttraumatic stress symptoms in every client they meet.

Among those trained to respond should be a group that has been screened, trained, prepared by drills, and, if possible, experienced in at least small-scale disasters to work in morgue settings. Much of the scant literature in this field focuses on the intensive work to be done with surviving families and friends of the dead and injured. This is also exhausting and involves some subspecializations (Jacobs et al., 1990), but it is not the same work as handling body parts. It would be undesirable to create a hierarchy of response workers as though some aspects (e.g., morgue workers, workers giving families death notices, or child therapists) were somehow more important or had more critical assignments. At the time of an actual disaster, the response must be unencumbered by elitism, overspecialization, turf protection, or self-importance. In most disasters, the event itself tends to focus everyone's attention and minimize boundary issues. But there is nothing better than current training and rehearsed drill to assure everyone is at least intellectually prepared for something for which it is, in the final analysis, impossible to be fully prepared.

The National Association of Social Workers, the American Red Cross, the American Psychiatric Association, the American Psychological Association, and other professional groups have agreements and contingency plans and in some places have done joint training. In Pennsylvania, what we learned was that these agreements were primarily paper agreements. There was no concrete implementation plan for social workers. There are divisions of the state chapter in Pennsylvania that have highly mobile teams of social workers ready to respond and who even came to Pittsburgh from the other side of the state. But there was no established mechanism to mobilize social workers regionally or statewide for this crisis. Eventually the School of Social Work in Pittsburgh sent a fax to many of the over 300 agencies that provide field placements for the school, informing people of the need, the training available, and the appropriate way to become a volunteer. Precious time was lost and the response was uneven. It was also discovered that other professional groups did not have this problem. They activated a network of prepared and trained members overnight and had them on the scene by morning of the first day after the crash. Social workers were still being recruited nearly two weeks after the crash. By the time some social workers received the training and were ready to serve, the work was over. This may be our most serious challenge.

Conclusion

Most of the conclusions drawn from this experience may sound self-evident. Were it not for the fact that professionals in most localities are inadequately trained to respond to a large-scale disaster, the conclusions might not bear repeating.

Professional social workers are ideally prepared to provide disaster intervention services and may well be among the last ready to do so if this experience is any indicator. Many disaster relief tasks can be undertaken with minimal, on-the-spot training. However, some of the tasks, such as providing mental health services to volunteers engaged in handling body parts, require not only high skill but specialized training. Social workers providing these services must be able to anticipate the scene in order to prepare volunteers for it, to cope with it themselves, and to be able to support those engaged in the primary identification tasks while at the same time maintaining an objective awareness of their own reactions and needs.

Except in a generic sense, it is not practical to provide the content and skills entailed in a traditional bachelor's or master's social work curriculum. Schools of social work should be on the forefront of interdisciplinary, nondegree training and collaboration for disaster response. The auspices of interdisciplinary organizations like the American Red Cross are ideally suited forums in which to accomplish this. Also needed is an organizational structure for social workers that can be activated instantly to bring those trained to the place of need in the right numbers at the appropriate times. This will in all likelihood have to be done on a state or regional level.

References

Armstrong, K., Lund, P., McWright, L. & Tichenor, V. (1995). Multiple stressor debriefing and the American Red Cross: The East Bay Hills fire experience. *Social Work*, 41(1): 83–90.

Artiss, K. L. (1963). Human behavior under stress: From combat to social psychiatry. *Military Medicine*, 128, 1011–1015.

Baker, L. & Zakour, M. J. (1996). A model of disaster response: A public sector and social work education partnership. Paper presented at the CSWE Annual Program Meeting, Washington, D.C.

Bell, J. (1995). Traumatic stress debriefing: Service delivery designs and the role of social work. *Social Work*, 40, 36–43.

Black, J. W. (1987). The libidinal cocoon: A nurturing retreat for the families of plane crash victims. *Hospital and Community Psychiatry*, 38, 1322–1326.

Butcher, J. N. & Dunn, L. A. (1989). Human responses and treatment needs in airline disasters. In: R. Gist & B. Lubin (Eds.), *Psychosocial Aspects of Disasters* (pp. 86–119). New York: Wiley.

Butcher, J. N. & Hatcher, C. (1988). The neglected entity in air disaster planning. *American Psychologist*, 43, 724–729.

Cervantes, R. A. (1988). Psychological stress of body handling. Part II. In: R.J. Ursano & C.S. Fullerton (Eds.), *Exposure to Death, Disasters and Bodies*. (CTIC No. 203163, pp. 123–149). Bethesda, MD: F. Edward Hebert School of Medicine, Uniformed Services University of the Health Sciences.

Corenblum, B., & Taylor, P. J. (1981). Mechanisms of control of prolactin release in response to apprehension stress and anesthesia-surgery stress. *Fertility and Sterility*, 36, 712–715.

Dalahanty, D. L., Dougall, A. L., Craig, K. J., Jenkins, F. J. & Baum, A. (1997). Chronic stress and natural killer cell activity after exposure to traumatic death. *Psychosomatic Medicine*, 59, 467–476.

Drory, M., Posen, J., Vilner, D. & Ginzburg, K. (1998). Mass casualities: An organizational model of a hospital information center in Tel Aviv. *Social Work in Health Care*, 27, 83–96.

Durkin, M. (1993). Major depression and post-traumatic stress disorder following the Coalinga and Chile earthquakes: A cross-cultural comparison. *Journal of Social Behavior and Personality*, 8, 405–420.

Durkin, M. & Thiel, C. (1993). Earthquakes: A primer for the mental health professions. *Journal of Social Behavior and Personality*, 8, 379–404.

Erikson, K. (1976). *Everything in Its Path: Destruction of Community in the Buffalo Creek Flood*. New York: Simon & Schuster.

Fein, E. & Knaut, S. A. (1986). Crisis intervention and support: Working with the police. *Social Casework*, 276–282.

Fenz, W. D. & Jones, G. B. (1972). Individual differences in physiologic arousal and performance in sport parachutists. *Psychosomatic Medicine*, 34, 1–8.

Freedy, J., Kilpatrick, D. & Resnick, H. (1993). Natural disasters and mental health: Theory, assessment and intervention. *Journal of Social Behavior and Personality*, 8, 49–103.

Groner, E. (1978). Delivery of clinical social work services in the emergency room: A description of an existing program. *Social Work in Health Care*, 4, 19–29.

Green, B., Grace, M. & Gleser, G. (1985). Identifying survivors at risk: Long-term impairment following the Beverly Hills Supper Club fire. *Journal of Counseling and Clinical Psychology*, 53, 672–678.

Harr, J. (1996). The crash detectives. *The New Yorker*, August 5: 34–55.

Hepworth, D. H. & Larsen, J. A. (1993). *Direct Social Work Practice: Theory and Skills (Fourth Edition)*. Pacific Grove: Brooks/Cole.

Hershiser, M. R. & Quarantelli, E. L. (1976). The handling of dead in a disaster. *Omega*, 7, 195–203.

Jacobs, G. A., Quevillon, R. P. & Stricherz, M. (1990). Lessons from the aftermath of flight 232: Practical considerations for the mental health profession's response to air disasters. *American Psychologist*, 45, 1329–1335.

Jones, D. R. (1985). Secondary disaster victims: The emotional effects of recovering and identifying human remains. *American Journal of Psychiatry*, 142, 303–307.

Kliman, A. (1976). The Corning flood project and following natural disaster. In: Parad, H.J. et al. (eds.), *Emergency and Disaster Management: A Mental Health Source Book* (pp. 325–335). Charles, Maryland: The Charles Press.

Laube, J. (1973). Psychological reactions of nurses in disasters. *Nursing Research*, 22, 343–347.

Lindemann, E. (1944). Symptomatology and management of acute grief. *American Journal of Psychiatry*, 101, 141–148.

Lukton, R. (1982). Myths and realities of crisis intervention. *Social Casework*, 63, 275–285.

Matthews, L. R. (1998). Effect of staff debriefing on posttraumatic stress symptoms after assaults by community housing residents. *Psychiatric Services*, 49, 207–212.

McCarroll, J. E., Ursano, R. J., Wright, K. M. & Fullerton, C. S. (1993). Handling bodies after violent death: Strategies for coping. *American Journal of Orthopsychiatry*, 63, 209–214.

Newhill, C. E. (1989). Psychiatric emergencies: Overview of clinical principles and clinical practice. *Clinical Social Work Journal*, 17, 245–258.

Popplow, J. R. (1984). After the fireball. *Aviation, Space and Environmental Medicine*, 55, 337–338.

Rank, M. G. (1997). Critical incident stress debriefing. In: Hutchison, W. S., Emener, W. G. et al. (eds.), *Employee Assistance Programs: A Basic Text (2nd edition)*. Springfield, Ill.: Thomas (pp. 315–329).

Rayner, J. F. (1958). How do nurses behave in disaster? *Nursing Outlook*, 6, 572–576.

Shah, G. (1985). Social work in disaster. *Indian Journal of Social Work*, 45, 463–476.

Slaikeu, K. A. (1984). *Crisis Intervention: A Handbook for Practice and Research*. Boston: Allyn & Bacon.

Spitzer, W. & Neely, K. (1992). Critical incident stress: The role of hospital based social work in developing a statewide intervention system for first-responders delivering emergency services. *Social Work in Health Care*, 18, 39–58.

Talbot, A., Manton, M. & Dunn, P. (1992). Debriefing the debriefers: An intervention strategy to assist psychologists after a crisis. *Journal of Traumatic Stress*, 5, 45–62.

Taylor, A. J. W. & Frazer, A. G. (1982). The stress of post-disaster body handling and victim identification work. *Journal of Human Stress*, 8, 4–12.

Terr, L. C. (1983). Chowchilla revisited: The effects of psychic trauma four years after a school-bus kidnapping. *American Journal of Psychiatry*, 140, 1543–1550.

Ursano, R. J. (1987). Commentary: Posttraumatic stress disorder: The stressor criterion. *Journal of Nervous and Mental Disease*, 175, 273–275.

Ursano, R. J. & McCarroll, J. E. (1990). The nature of a traumatic stressor: Handling dead bodies. *Journal of Nervous and Mental Disease*, 178, 396–398.

Wallace, A. F. C. (1956). *Tornado in Worchester: An Exploratory Study of Individual and Communal Behavior in an Extreme Situation: Report 3*. Washington, D.C.: Committee on Disaster Studies, National Academy of Sciences/National Research Council.

Williams, C. L., Soloman, S. D. & Bartone, P. (1988). Primary prevention in aircraft disasters. *American Psychologist*, 43, 730–739.

Zakour, M. (1996). Disaster research in social work. *Journal of Social Service Research*, 22, 7–25.

70

Long-Distance Psychoanalysis

More and more frequently analysts are conducting treatment on the telephone. It can provide continuity in an increasingly mobile, even nomadic, world. Yet this is ironic, as a more sophisticated awareness of the significance of nonverbal communication is developing in the field. Eliminating the nonverbal dimension of communication creates difficulties for treatment. Reducing the channels available for transmitting and processing affect may impair the expression and detection of dissociated affects, especially with patients who have difficulty integrating affects with verbal expression. The absence of facial expression, eye contact, gesture, and movement interferes with the analyst's ability to attune herself with the patient.

The room's boundary encloses patient and therapist together in a shared space—a metaphor for physical holding. It provides a potential space as well as a real physical space that can contain intense affects. Replacing a shared, enclosed physical space with a telephone line can undermine the safety of a holding environment. Working on the phone may require therapist and patient to create rituals to protect the time and space of the phone session. The textures of tone, sound, and silence may come to replace the room as the physical basis of a holding environment.

Despite the hazards, working on the phone can provide opportunities. The telephone's simultaneous distance and closeness, separateness and connection can create a transitional space in which patients can work on their ambivalence about dependency. For schizoid patients, who long for and fear emotional connection and dependency, working on the phone can serve this therapeutic function.

This paper describes two and a half years of treatment three times a week with a woman in her late twenties. The first nine months were in person and the next 20 were primarily over the telephone. Working on the phone was a shield against fears of intrusion and emotional intensity, but by eliminating nonverbal communication, it created obstacles to meaningful contact that had to be overcome.

Serena

"It is joy to be hidden but disaster not to be found" in Winnicott's words (1963, p. 186). This was true for Serena, an articulate young woman whose words often hid dissociated aspects of herself. Physical expression felt most real to Serena. Yet most of her treatment has been over the phone. Serena was a dancer whose self-consciousness suppressed the passion she yearned to express and who searched for emotional closeness in short-lived sexual relationships. Her need to maintain distance and self-sufficiency disguised her wish to be attached and dependent. The longing for connection and fear of intrusion is the schizoid dilemma. My dilemma was how to make contact with Serena without impinging on her, and how to facilitate the emergence of unarticulated, hidden, dissociated domains (Bromberg, 1994) of her experience.

Our Beginning

We had an easy beginning. She was tall and elegant, with a delicate face, soft brown eyes, and long auburn hair. In the first session she was thoughtful and polite but restrained. I remember wishing there were more emotion for me to connect to her through. Yet my attachment to her developed quickly, and hers to me. By the third week, she said that it felt good to come. She felt insulated and could relax. She cried in a session, something she told me she rarely did. About six weeks into Serena's treatment, I suggested that she come three times a week, and she accepted the idea easily and eagerly. I felt gratified by Serena's involvement and commitment to her treatment. I was comfortable and relaxed with her. We had a natural rhythm together.

Serena eloquently described her profound need to discover a more authentic self, "organic Serena," and her fear of her own emptiness. She said, "It is scary to be alone with someone you don't know" (meaning herself). She was poetic in discussing her painful sense of inner isolation and her yearning for an intimate connection. She spoke of her fears of being alone for the rest of her life, but also her wish to seal herself off, like a hermit. She believed that the only way she could discover her "pure" self was in isolation, so that she would not be contaminated by the needs and responses of others. Lulled by our sessions, it eluded me that her fears of closeness would be as fundamental to our relationship as her longing for closeness.

Serena's Beginning

In contrast, Serena and her mother had a difficult beginning. They had difficulty breastfeeding, which her mother interpreted as Serena not wanting to eat. Her mother was angry and frustrated. After two weeks without Serena eating, her mother took her to the doctor. Her mother recalled that Serena seemed to be slipping out of consciousness. The doctor yelled at her: Didn't she realize that the baby needed to eat even if she as having trouble feeding her? Serena's mother was hurt. The story reveals a paradigm of the way difficulties between Serena and her mother were formulated. Her mother perceived Serena as defective, unwilling, and rejecting. This threat to her self-esteem caused her to withdraw from Serena, canceling her knowledge of Serena's physical and emotional dependence. In telling the story, Serena sympathized with her mother's anger at her, the harmful baby. I thought of a baby who had withdrawn as a form of self-holding in the face of intolerable aloneness and fears of annihilation.

According to Winnicott, "If the first feed is mishandled, then a great deal of trouble may be caused and . . . a lasting pattern of insecurity of relationship may be found to have started at the time of the early failure of management" (1988, p. 100). For Winnicott, the infant is able to experience total dependence because of the mother's sensitive attunement to her needs. Where there is a failure of contact no reliable pathway is forged for contact with external objects. The infant turns inward, meeting needs by passive adaptation to the environment. Withdrawal is employed to maintain a sense of self-continuity, which is easily threatened by absences and the impingements of external objects. Schizoid dynamics can be traced to such failures of contact and the infant's pervasive sense that her love is inadequate and defective. Even more anxiety-provoking, the schizoid "fears that her love is destructive to the object" (Fairbairn, 1940, p. 25).

History

Serena, an only child, believed that her parents had her, not because they genuinely wanted a child, but because normal couples were *supposed* to. Serena described her mother as a tightly wound woman with "rough edges." She has difficulty showing vulnerability, asking for or accepting help, and rejects dependency as "codependency"—a dreaded state of symbiosis and loss of self. When her self-esteem is threatened she responds defensively with angry attack and cold withdrawal. Serena's expressions of unhappiness, frustration, or anger were taken personally and considered "selfish." If Serena expressed hurt, her mother would respond, "I didn't make you feel that way; you made yourself feel that way." She retreated from intense affective states and was unavailable to soothe Serena. Serena remembered herself as an upset young child with her mother seated opposite, leaning over and peering at her, saying, "Can you use your words?" When she craved a hug her mother would say, "Chin up," an admonition to hold yourself together rather than letting yourself be held. She encouraged Serena to "think about" her feelings, to remain "even-keeled," not be "too intense." Serena's reactions were muted because they could hurt or threaten her parents. She described her own psychic interior as having been decorated with "faux feelings."

While Serena's mother withdrew from her dependency on her, she also undermined her autonomy under the guise of protecting her. She needed Serena to be available to *her*. Her mother would express concern just before auditions that Serena was not ready and that she would be disappointed, undermining her confidence. Serena felt that she secretly fed off her depression and even her failures, because they prevented her from becoming independent. When Serena told her mother she was considering auditioning for companies on the West Coast, her mother was concerned that it was too far away. Serena did not audition.

Serena described her father as a mysterious, withdrawn figure who has chronic periods of severe depression. While gentle and sympathetic, she found him inaccessible and felt she did not really know him. While his job demanded that in public he appear happy and well balanced, at home he was usually a quiet figure shut in his study or watching TV. Serena suspects he is an alcoholic. Since Serena left home her parents have lived in separate cities during the week, ostensibly because of their jobs.

Serena's early experience was that even when present, her parents were absent. Her mother told stories, humorously, of forgetting all about Serena for an hour or two, only to discover her playing in her playpen. Serena remembered playing alone for hours once her mother returned to work and she was left with her father, who stayed shut in his study, coming out only to make her a sandwich for lunch. Not confident in her ability to connect with her parents, Serena was threatened by separations and absences. Serena remembered sobbing hysterically when her mother left the house to return to work, when she was 3, protesting and clinging to her mother, who impassively pried her off, mater-of-factly explaining that she had to go to work. What pained Serena the most was that her mother did not seem to experience the same sadness at their separation.

She could not recall her own departure for kindergarten a couple of years later. As the story has been told to her, Serena walked out the door and onto the school bus without even a backward glance. This reveals aspects of Serena's dynamics that I experienced firsthand: her ability to dissociate feelings of dependency and to blank out an ongoing sense of connection to people, especially when there was a separation. As she eventually explained to me, she did not ever want to be the only one to feel pain and distress at separation, so she would feel nothing.

Throughout her childhood, her parents left her to struggle with painful emotions, explaining that they did not want to intrude on her and that they were sure she would prefer to be alone. They projected their own fear of emotion, dependency, and closeness, rationalizing their withdrawal and neglect as Serena's own preference. While Serena longed for more involvement and communication with her parents, she ended up feeling more isolated and defective. For example, Serena fell in love at 16, discovering a new sense of passionate connection with a soul mate. They continued their relationship long distance through letters and phone calls for over a year. When David broke up with her to see someone else, the pain of loss and rejection seemed unbearable. Serena, usually constrained about crying, sobbed loudly in her room for hours, longing for her parents to come in and hold her. They never did. Later, her parents explained that they thought it best to leave Serena alone, that she would want to get through it by herself. This incident came up repeatedly in her therapy as a trauma she dreaded to repeat, that underlay her reluctance to seek comfort when she was emotionally overwhelmed.

Treatment: Inside the Cocoon

In the first stage of treatment, my relationship with Serena provided the insulated "cocoon" (as she put it) of a holding environment. I was inside her psychic space with her, without being acknowledged as a separate outsider (Slochower, 1996). My attentiveness, empathic attunement, and responsiveness was a medium she used to explore and give form to her own psychic reality.

Over time, the holding environment that began so easily and blissfully came under increasing strain. Transference anxieties emerged as her dependence developed. As the months continued, Serena, who had cried in her third session, became more inhibited and apologetic about crying. She said she desperately wanted to cry, yet she was no uncomfortable crying in front of me, while I sat across and watched her. She worried about draining me or evoking a pitying but disgusted response of finding her "pathetic." But she was scared by the sounds of her sobs when alone. She said she would feel safer crying if she knew that I would hug her if she needed me to. I was conflicted. Maybe we were replicating the problem Serena had with her mother in which verbal connection was prematurely valued and deeper contact never established. Maybe Serena would interpret my anxiety about what to do as my wanting to keep a physical distance from her emotions.

Something else then snapped me out of my illusion of our perfect attunement: Serena's wish to leave New York to join a ballet company. She auditioned throughout the spring. She felt vulnerable and was afraid of rejection. Serena never mentioned that leaving New York would mean ending her therapy, let alone discuss her feelings about it. When I tried, gingerly, to broach it, Serena would ignore me or blandly dismiss the subject. Discussing our relationship seemed disruptive to the holding environment and to the productive work going on within it. This holding environment was a transitional space that contained Serena's longing for and her fears of attachment and dependency. Serena's dependency could emerge as long as it was not articulated and the possibility of separation was not introduced. Her unspoken assumption was that her therapy would continue, whatever the outcome of her auditions. In order to preserve this transitional space I had to contain my anxiety about losing her and to wonder on my own how she really felt. Slochower emphasizes that, in a holding environment, the analyst is aware of her separate subjectivity, but brackets it off, not bringing it into the sessions (1996, pp. 24–26).

My approaching summer vacation brought the issue of Serena's dependence on me and her conflicts about it into the foreground of the treatment. Serena alternated between two modes of dealing with her fears about separation. In one mode she was withdrawn and dissociated and tested me to see if I would abandon her. In the other, she talked movingly about her fears and we appeared to be processing them through words. In retrospect it seems clear that although she tried, she was really unable to do this. Instead, she was trying to warn me how hard it was for her to sustain a relationship throughout a separation.

When I told Serena about my August vacation, she seemed indifferent and brought up a recent possibility of a 10-week dance contract in Seattle to begin in September and said, "Maybe if I get a lot done I'll be finished by then." I was disoriented: I never thought that the preemptive flight she had described in her other endeavors and relationships would apply to us. One day, there was an outpouring of emotional material, as if she was trying to finish as soon as possible. The next day, it seemed like an unfamiliar person was inhabiting Serena's body. What she talked about seemed alien and superficial. When I tried to link what was going on with separation, I got nowhere. She thought there was nothing to say about it. I felt very cut off, uncomfortable and sad, and suddenly as if I did not know her at all.

Then she tested me. She called my machine at 10:45 one night, leaving a message that started out sad, tearful, and desperate, saying that the man she was seeing had broken up with her: "Once again it's over before it can start. I'm feeling really really hurt. How can I possibly ever, *ever* see anyone again?" And ending in a contained, matter-of-fact, upbeat tone: "I'll see you Thursday." I called her at 8:30 the next morning. It was too late; the faux feelings had taken over. Everything was fine and she didn't need to talk to me. On Thursday, I asked her about the shift in the message, and then her attitude the next day. She said her tone changed because she was afraid I would think she was going crazy. She did not ask me to call because she was afraid of selfishly using me up. She had waited an hour for me to call, and then given up and gone to bed. Even before then her feelings had transformed from hurt to self-blame to "I'm fine." I said that I imagined that this was like when David broke up with her and she cried but her parents did not respond. She was letting me know how upset she was and I was not responding, leaving her feeling terribly alone. Serena said she was afraid of being too dependent—then if you leaned on someone, if they were not there, you would fall down. I said, "Like with your call to me?" "Yes," she said.

Sometimes Serena was able to talk about her fears that she, and our relationship, would not survive a separation. She worried that during a separation she would be forgotten, discarded, and unable to do anything to take care of herself. Instead, she told me, she does not miss people when they go away; she just does not think about them. She was warning me that with the threat of separation, she cancels relationships. She wanted our relationship to end while it was still good, she said, before I disappointed and hurt her, and before she could sabotage it. This was her attempt to preserve me as the good object and to protect me and herself from what was to come.

In the last sessions before my vacation, I asked if she thought I would think about her. She insisted that she did not want me to because she would be a source of obligation and concern to me. When I said that if just keeping her in my mind was a burden, she must imagine that keeping in mind her deepest needs and feelings was even more so, she cried. She refused to discuss the possibility that she might go to Seattle. I told her that if she did, we could talk on the phone and work out what to do when I returned. She had a fantasy that I would change my plans and stay because I really cared.

She told me that she wanted to make me feel really bad because she did. I felt rotten. I told her that I *would* think about her while I was away and Serena cried.

Rupture and Enactment

When I returned from my vacation, I had a couple of messages from Serena, who had gotten the job in Seattle and had already moved there. In the messages she seemed eager to talk to me and said in an unfamiliar, chirpy voice, "I miss you." That was the last I was to hear of that. When I spoke to her she suggested telephone sessions, but focused on a slew of logistical problems that interfered.

We did begin phone sessions later, but Serena seemed absent and our conversations opaque and flat. Shifting facial expressions and body posture and her evocative hand gestures were now invisible. Until we began phone sessions I had not realized how much I relied on body radar to attune myself to her. Now it was like finding my way in a thick fog. I had trouble remembering what she looked like. Her voice was even, unrevealing. Her analysis of her difficulties seemed logical, even perceptive at times, but I could not feel any affective connection to her. There were moments of accessibility, like when Serena said that she felt more trust and comfort in the "cocoon" of in-person sessions, but those were ephemeral.

If in the first stage of treatment I was inside a psychic cocoon *with* Serena, intimately attuned to her, I now felt excluded. In this phase I became a failing and abandoning person Serena needed to insulate herself from. Now she protected herself from threats of annihilation and abandonment by abolishing our relationship and withdrawing behind an attitude of cheerful self-sufficiency. She wondered if "I'm done for awhile." She did not miss New York; there was nothing there for her, she now said. She decided to remain in Seattle for some months beyond her contract.

I tried to address the huge physical and emotional shifts that had taken place in our relationship. Serena did not acknowledge any change. She acted as if nothing had happened, and she repelled exploration of the issue or fell silent. I felt like the rejected, discarded, dependent one. I felt guilty that I was upset about her being in Seattle rather than pleased and hopeful for her. I thought I was in danger of becoming Serena's mother who did not want her to audition too far away, who did not recognize her autonomy and support her success.

A deeper analysis of the transference-countertransference dynamic explains it differently. In this mode Serena was identified with her mother: the Serena who left for school without a backward glance, like her mother who left her to go to work devoid of any apparent emotion. I was now in Serena's position as the abandoned one. I was hurt that Serena did not seem to share my sense of loss, just as Serena was hurt by her mother. Serena's disavowal of our relationship and of feelings about separation left me feeling ashamed, wrong, inappropriate for missing and wanting her. My dejected, discarded state and my sense of defectiveness was Serena's "dissociated experience that [I was] holding as part of [myself]," as Bromberg describes it (1994, p. 545).

What should I do? Not to address Serena's affective absence and the gulf between us could be an emotional abandonment in the sense Winnicott describes as a "disaster not to be found." But using my countertransference to interpret Serena's dissociation could be experienced as my projecting my own affects into her, like her mother. I could try to introduce my own feelings, but I thought Serena would feel that I needed her to comply with my needs and repair my self-esteem. My feelings felt too precarious to use constructively, but I could not longer contain them.

When Serena wondered, in a detached way, if a long-distance relationship would work as she might not return to New York and reported obstacles to phone sessions when I asked about her feelings, I lurched forward. I said that I felt frustrated because I could not get any sense of how she felt about phone sessions or about continuing at all. Maybe, I said, this was connected to working on the phone instead of in person. Serena said, "Maybe we shouldn't do it, then," Taken aback, I asked what had just happened. Serena said that she was angry, but was not sure why. She said she reacted as though I were someone breaking up with her. Stunned—wasn't *she* breaking up with *me*?—I inquired further. Serena went on to say that she felt "angry, upset, weird. I can't breathe." I was concerned but also relieved by her sudden outbreak of emotion. She felt that I was rejecting her because she had failed to maintain the relationship properly by expressing her feelings. She did not know at some level, she said, that she had "turned her feelings off."

How did Serena believe that I was rejecting her when I felt rejected by her? How did my expression of frustration become a criticism and a rejection rather than something we could share together since, it turned out, Serena felt similarly? We collided in parallel enactments. Serena's experience was that I abandoned and failed her; she withdrew; I was frustrated with her and I rejected her. My experience was that she abandoned me; she refused connection; I felt rejected and when in frustration I tried again to connect, she rejected me. If I had withdrawn like her parents, the enactment would have continued. As it was, my frustration probably contained enough of an edge of criticism for Serena to experience me as an old object, a critical parent withdrawing in frustration because she failed to meet my needs. While my wish to connect with her was indeed frustrated, I was, unlike her parents, lurching *toward* her. For Serena frustration could not be part of an approach, an attempt to reconnect.

It took over six weeks to process this episode. Serena defensively blocked out all memory of it. It took repeated linking it to themes in our sessions to stir a faint recognition that something had happened between us. She suppressed her hurt feelings because she felt like a "big, ugly, crazy person" when she expressed them. She was afraid I would be injured and angry and leave. She felt that she should apologize and take on the blame (as she would do with her mother) in order to maintain our relationship. I discovered that these same fears had prevented her from revealing that *she* had been frustrated with the phone sessions all along. Even though I had asked her what the phone sessions were like for her, she imagined that her frustration would be dismissed or *I* would withdraw, saying "Then let's not do it at all."

I felt guilty about expressing implicit disappointment in her, attacking her defenses, and damaging her trust. I wanted to explain that I really did want to be connected to her and to apologize for hurting her, but in doing so I would be the parent who insists on being the good object, negating the child's experience of failure. Accepting and empathizing with her negative experience of me was a new object experience for her. Her shaken trust in me was developing again, she said, because I did *not* do what she expected me to do: dismiss her feelings or reject her.

At Thanksgiving Serena returned and I saw her in person for the first time since she moved. Serena surprised me by hugging me at the beginning and end of the session. I hugged her back. As if a filter had been removed, her emotional presence was now tangible. Yet as she moved closer, she pulled back. Maybe we should not continue our phone sessions, especially since it was now so clear to her what they lacked. Once again I felt abandoned, but

this time I was able to use what I had learned about my countertransference: that it often reflected Serena's dissociated experience. I told her that even if the phone sessions were not optimal she could continue them until she felt ready to stop. I would not abandon her (while hoping this would not be interpreted as a plea not to abandon me). Serena told me much later that this meant a lot to her, and that she had been testing me, unconsciously, with her dire pronouncements about the impossibility of continuing. If I agreed, I was willing to let her go.

Serena's contract with the ballet company was not renewed as she had hoped, but she remained in Seattle, taking company classes there. At the beginning of the summer she accepted a job teaching in the company's school for children for several months.

Serena in Her Own Cocoon, Connected by a Phone Cord

In the following eight months there was a paradox: the illusion of Serena's self-sufficiency enabled her to be dependent on me. By staying in Seattle, she supported a sense of self-sufficiency while remaining connected to me through the phone. Seattle was now the protective cocoon that insulated her from impinging, disruptive interactions with me, her friends, her parents, and the competitive dance world in New York. It was a cocoon with a very long extension cord. Serena could be dependent on me from a distance as long as she could take it for granted and not be confronted with it. The fact that we continued our sessions whenever she traveled, and that I frequently juggled my schedule to adjust to hers, allowed her to assume that I would be wherever she was—as if I lived in the phone. When I said that maybe the issue was not whether or not Serena was in New York, but that I should be in Seattle, Serena laughed and agreed.

Actual or threatened disruptions cast Serena into a panic of doubt about my ability and willingness to remain engaged with her despite the distance and despite her own unavailability. When there was a twist in her plans she would wonder about ending and then become evasive when I tried to discuss it with her. At times she reacted angrily, as if I were intruding on her by seeking to understand her feelings and wishes. Eventually I understood that she was angry that she depended on me because it made her vulnerable. My increasing recognition that Serena was seeking reassurance from *me* that I was still connected and that she, not I, would choose when to end enabled *her* to begin to process our dynamic. Serena remarked that by threatening to leave she was doing what she hated people doing to her, and that she did not want me to let her end when she had "forgotten all about her other feelings"—feelings of dependency and attachment.

Serena said that these conversations increased her trust in me and our process and enabled her to have a new experience—of talking together about a relationship. Though anxiety-provoking, she found this increasingly valuable. These conversations often led to a more collaborative discussion of the differences between phone and in-person sessions. In person she was more emotionally engaged and felt more connected to me. On the phone it was easier for her to withdraw; her emotions become inaccessible even to her. Serena felt the loss of the physical setting; an enclosed, shared space for verbal and nonverbal communication had been the foundation of the holding environment. Serena said that eye contact and body language made it easier to trust; it was part of "the cocoon." On the phone Serena knew and trusted my voice. I often found myself making sounds to resonate with what Serena was saying. The texture of sounds and silence defined the shape and gave security to the holding environment created over the phone.

The shift to the phone highlighted the inadequacy of words to express Serena's experience fully. With the physical context stripped away, words seemed distant from affect. For Serena, words "anaesthetized" feelings and substituted for them. She felt "dead and empty inside." Complying with her mother's instructions to "put it into words" had linked verbal expression with "false or compliant object-relating," as Winnicott put it (1963, p. 184). Trying to talk one's way out of this was paradoxical. Serena questioned if therapy could help her because she was already too good at talking about her feelings instead of feeling them. She wanted to be able to "bawl," but on the phone the feelings were too distant and she felt too alone. Only in person, with "human contact," would she be able to "break down the wall."

Silences

The unarticulated, dissociated realm of Serena's experience emerged on the phone through a gradual uncovering of the meaning of silences. Serena's silences presented me with a by now familiar dilemma: how to contact her without intruding. Her silences could be a couple of minutes or as long as 10 minutes. Typically the silences felt like a complete blackout in which all emotional transmission

stopped. Occasionally I would have the sense that she was just resting or thinking her own thoughts and would reemerge when she was ready.

Winnicott (1963) distinguishes between "a simple not-communicating" and "a not-communicating that is active or reactive." "Simple not-communicating is like resting. It is a state in its own right and it passes over into communicating, and reappears as naturally" (p. 183). On the other hand, there is "active non-communication because . . . communication so easily becomes linked with some degree of false or compliant object-relating" (p. 184). It is a "protest from the core [against] the frightening fantasy of being infinitely exploited" (p. 179).

Winnicott asks, "Does our technique allow for the patient to communicate that he or she is not communicating? For this to happen we as analysts must be ready for the signal: 'I am not communicating,' and be able to distinguish it from the distress signal associated with a failure of communication" (p. 188). It seemed that if I checked with Serena while she was silent, I could indicate that I expected her to talk. Then communication could become a false production to meet my needs and prevent abandonment. On the other hand, if Serena was withdrawn and dissociated, and I assumed, like her parents, that she would prefer to be alone, I would leave her locked in isolation. I would sometimes make a foray after a while, explaining that I did not want to interrupt her quietude if she was comfortable, but that I was not sure if she was being quiet or if she had disappeared.

I learned about Serena's anxieties about being silent. Her biggest fear was that she would lose me—that I would fall asleep or "go off and do my own thing" and not be available when she needed me. I thought of her mother, who would forget about her baby playing quietly for hours at a time. Serena felt pressure to produce in order to keep me engaged, which made her blank out all the more. She had learned from her mother to connect through "serious conversation" while remaining at a physical distance. She said, "I feel so desperate for connection that I have to say everything that comes into my head." To claim a private self was selfishly to repudiate her mother's need to enter her mind and "share" her thoughts. Yet Serena also knew that not all of herself was acceptable; her emotional needs, her frustration and anger had to be held back. In an impossible bind, Serena would shut down, blank out, dissociate.

The silence began to reveal what was dissociated. Serena would shut down just as she came to the edge of strong affects that she feared would overwhelm her. Consciousness of them would shut down simultaneously, leaving her blank, numb, and unable to explain what had happened. Often, the silences were connected to anger that she told me she was only aware of in retrospect. Serena's dissociation sometimes occurred in response to my lack of attunement with her, especially when she experienced my comments as impinging on her.

There were silences in response to more concrete abandonments as well. Serena often became silent toward the end of a session, especially on Thursday, our last session of the week. She was afraid of being abandoned in the middle of a feeling and suddenly being on her own with it. She withdrew into protective self-holding in anticipation of intervals between sessions. She described it as "hibernating." Sessions after my vacations would often have long silences.

Serena and I were able to discuss together the dilemma of what to do with silences. She could experience my inquiring into silences prematurely as a criticism or a demand, but she was even more concerned about my waiting indefinitely, "leaving her stuck in a cut-off state." She indicated that she was likely to reemerge from shorter silences spontaneously, but once they became longer, she had probably gotten lost in a state "of blank numbness." I should ask her what she is feeling at these times, she said. I became very good at gauging in a silence which kind of noncommunicating was going on. I often found myself resting comfortably, knowing she would speak when ready, or keenly feeling that the emotional radar between us had shut down and that Serena had disappeared. Our conversations also led to a decrease in dissociation and an expansion of the "resting" times.

Hugs

In the in-person sessions that interspersed our work on the phone, dissociated, unarticulated aspects of Serena emerged through physical expression and physical contact. She returned very briefly every few months to see family and friends. At the beginning of each visit she greeted me with a melting hug, and at the end she embraced me as she said good-bye; I always hugged her back, responding with the affection I felt toward Serena. In reacting out physically Serena expressed a wish for closeness and a feeling of connection that was rarely articulated and often dissociated. She needed to reconnect with me physically in order for it to feel real.

Serena created a temporary holding environment in which more intense affects could emerge through actual physical holding. This was comparable to a mother's holding containing the physical sensations of a child's intense affects. But instead of the physical setting being a metaphor for the mother's holding, the hugs are moments of actual physical holding bracketing a protected space in between.

I always had an anxious dialogue with myself afterwards. Was I maintaining appropriate boundaries that would protect the treatment? I did not want to thwart her spontaneous gesture of affection. However, Slochower (1996, pp. 26, 112) talks about the dangers of the therapist enacting the maternal metaphor inherent in holding. If the therapist tries to nurture her patient by becoming a real mother, the transitional space collapses and the treatment can fail. I was concerned about my pull to enactment, of my own wish to adopt Serena and become a nurturing mother to her.

Eventually, I did get Serena to discuss it. The hugs gave her a feeling of closeness that she did not get from talking; "It feels like our relationship," she said. She felt that I had a more maternal role when we hugged, but she, too, wondered about it. She worried about losing me as a therapist if I became too much of a mother. She feared that if it became "too real" I would end up using her for my own needs. Serena also feared, from her early experience, that her genuine way of being loving would be destructive to me and our relationship and cause me to push her away and withdraw. When I tried to sort out this dilemma with her, Serena said she did not want to "plan the moment," she wanted to see what felt right.

Encapsulated Regression

In August Serena came to New York to rehearse a performance and we had five in-person sessions before I took off on vacation. She had a fantasy of nestling into the space between the breasts and stomach of a soft mother—the closest thing to being in the womb, she said. The story of her angular mother's difficulties breastfeeding emerged in contrast. She wondered if she cried as a hungry baby. She felt less of a "freak" for yearning to be held and cared for physically especially in her sexual relationships. I said that what has eluded analysis with words becomes real for her when it is concretely physical. Serena responded that she did not hear my words, but "I felt them in my body—I had a physical reaction." Then she was silent. Then she started crying. Then she started talking. I could *see* the words submerging Serena's feelings. I told her that she did not have to talk. Serena cried and cried. She said, "I feel like I'm crying for my mother, but she won't come. And now I'm here with you, crying for my mother." I said, "I think it's hard for you to know how much you want to get involved with me, because you worry it will take you away from her."

Serena revealed that she has wished for me to be her mother "because you really care and listen and want to know about my feelings." In some ways she felt closer to me than her mother. Then she started to withdraw. It was near the end of the session before my vacation. Serena said she did not want me to go away, but that was selfish. I told her that the way things were now, she got less of me than she could. Serena said it was scary to depend on men, to make our relationship too important—I could abandon and disappoint her. "Somehow I can pick up and leave to go to Seattle without a thought, but talking about coming to New York and seeing you is very hard. But I'd like to try to come more often." At the end of the session, Serena came over to me for a hug. She rested her head on my shoulder and held onto me as if she did not want this to end. As I held her I could feel her crying.

Emerging

When I returned from my three-week vacation, Serena wanted to cut back to once a week. We had been through this so many times. This time, however, Serena was more accessible and I was able to use my past experience to unravel what had happened. Although she felt coerced by my urging discussion of her wanted to cut back, she was aware of pushing me away and of suppressing her emotions: anger and longing.

During these months Serena exposed more of herself and reached out to me more. She verbalized more open ambivalence, frustration, even anger about therapy. She needed something she was not getting. At the same time, she attacked her needs, criticizing herself for not being perfect. To need was to be selfish and greedy, weak and defective. We talked about her hatred of her dependency. She verbalized her longings as well. She allowed herself to express wanting, even when the outcome was uncertain. For a brief time she was in the new situation of wanting sessions three times a week but being unable to schedule them. She cried and said she felt like jumping off a building if changes in her schedule prevented us from talking. This was quite different from the Serena in whom the fantasy of

rejection preempted the expression of a wish for closeness.

As Serena articulated her longing for more contact and connection, she developed more interest in me as a "real" person. She became curious about details of my life and my past, and revealed fantasies about me. She was relieved to discover that I, too, had feelings of anxiety and frustration. This made me more "human" and "real" and made it easier for her to accept her own feelings. With each movement closer to me, Serena expressed anxiety. She was afraid of rejection, abandonment, disappointment, and criticism. She was afraid that her gestures of curiosity and affection and her emotional intensity would make our relationship "too real" and destroy it. She feared that her way of connecting and loving was toxic and destructive.

The closer Serena drew to me, the more she became constrained by her ties to her mother and her residual hopes that her mother would nurture her in the way she always longed for. To act on her wishes to become closer to me made her more aware of her mother's shortcomings and threatened her relationship with her. She sensed that her mother would be jealous if Serena got too close to me. She was working hard to engage her mother in discussions of their interactions, her feelings, and their past, and there was some progress, so she remained hopeful. She was experimenting and taking risks and forging and deepening relationships. For the first time, following confusing, distressing interactions with men, she took the initiative to say, "It's important to talk this through to understand what went on between us and not just pretend nothing happened."

Soon "organic" feelings were breaking through the wall. She started crying on the phone. She spent an entire phone session talking abut what was upsetting her in a way that truly integrated affects into words. I could *hear* how upset she was, instead of decoding it. The experience was new and exciting for Serena, although she imagined that I was annoyed and impatient with her "babbling" and preferred her when she was more thoughtful, organized, and detached (like her mother).

Then in one session, Serena fell into a silence of several minutes in which I rested tranquilly, confident that Serena was connected but in her own reverie. Then she asked, "I wonder what you are feeling right now?" I said, "I feel like you're over there, I'm over here, but we're sharing the silence together." Serena said she had a feeling of just being. "It's really okay to be together . . . and quietly." Winnicott (1958) describes this as being alone in the presence of another. In subsequent sessions Serena told me that it meant so much to her that we both felt connected. She could trust enough to stay open, while feeling that she did not need to say anything.

Serena remarked on our level of attunement: on how we almost always experienced silences the same way, as connected or disconnected. It was that attunement, perhaps, that made her excited and hopeful about communicating. She revealed that she has always wished that people could read her mind, while also being afraid that they can see into her. When it came to seem that I could *almost* read her mind, she realized that *she* could choose what to disclose and express. She did not need to speak to prevent me from abandoning her, nor did she have to hide some of the unacceptable dissociated parts of her self. I could remain connected to her while we were separate; she could remain dependent on me while still autonomous. This dissociated domain of her experience emerged by our living through it together. Bromberg says, "Dissociated states of mind may find access to the analytic relationship and be lived within it. . . . [They] become symbolized not by words themselves but by the new relational context the words come to represent" (1994, p. 535). She began a transition from passive communication, in which unarticulated experience is communicated through dissociative projections, enactments, and physical contact, to more active, verbal, symbolic communication.

At this point I did not miss Serena as much as I had. I felt that we were connected through the phone. There was not such an intense contrast between the dissociated phone sessions and the more intimate, affectively charged encounters bracketed by physical contact. It was this contrast that had made me miss her so much. It began to feel more like one continuous relationship. Then she was preparing to leave Seattle and return to New York. She struggled with this decision and talked at length about the possibilities and losses involved in staying there or returning here, instead of the way she left New York, without a thought.

Bromberg states that "change points occur when . . . enactment is serving its proper function and the patient's dissociated experience that the analyst has been holding as part of himself is sufficiently processed between them for the patient to begin to take it back into his own self experience little by little" (1994, p. 545). Serena became better able to voice her own feelings of connection and her own desire for attachment. Confident that she could be found, Serena was beginning to emerge from hiding and to give voice to a developing self.

While working on the phone presents difficulties because much can be hidden, it can create a unique environment in which meaning can be found. With its intrinsic affirmation of separateness, the phone enables someone struggling with a schizoid dilemma to approach intimacy and to begin to express dependency with less fear of engulfment and less fear of losing a private self. From within this paradox, a pathway can be created for the schizoid patient to begin to emerge from isolation and to discover new ways of relating.

The author gratefully acknowledges comments on this article by Leslie Goldstein, C.S.W., Jay Frankel, Ph.D., Ann Roberts, C.S.W., Kabi Hartman, and Edward Koral.

References

Bromberg, P. M. (1994). "Speak! That I May See You." Some Reflections on Dissociation, Reality and Psychoanalytic Listening. *Psychoanalytic Dialogues*, 4(4): 517–547.

Bromberg, P. M. (1996). Standing in the Spaces. *Contemporary Psychoanalysis*, 32(4): 509–534.

Fairbairn, W. R. D. (1940). Schizoid Factors in the Personality. In: *Studies in Personality*. New York: Routledge, 1952, pp. 3–27.

Guntrip, H. (1969). *Schizoid Phenomena, Object Relations and the Self*. New York: International Universities Press.

Modell, A. (1976). The Holding Environment and the Therapeutic Action of Psychoanalysis. *Journal of the American Psychoanalytic Association*, 24, 285–307.

Slochower, J. (1996). *Holding and Psychoanalysis: A Relational Perspective*. Hillsdale, N.J.: Analytic Press.

Winnicott, D. W. (1958). On the Capacity to Be Alone. In: *The Mutational Processes and the Facilitating Environment*. New York: International Universities Press, 1965, pp. 29–36.

Winnicott, D. W. (1963). Communicating and Not Communicating Leading to a Study of Certain Opposites. In: *The Maturational Processes and the Facilitating Environment*. New York: International Universities Press, 1965, pp. 179–192.

Winnicott, D. W. (1988). *Human Nature*. New York: Schocken Books.

71

Money as a Tool for Negotiating Separateness and Connectedness in the Therapeutic Relationship

Nearly 20 years ago I began working with Lois, a woman just a little younger than myself, who was moving quickly up the all-male corporate ladder of her firm. One of the first women executives in her business, Lois came to therapy because a recent breakup with a boyfriend has been a crushing blow from which she seemed unable to recover. Her sadness was carrying over into her work world, where she would often burst into tears with little provocation. In those early days of women's transition into high-powered careers, it was considered a deadly flaw to cry in front of colleagues, and Lois had been quietly but directly warned that she needed to get control of herself or she would find herself off the fast track. After quickly establishing a positive working relationship, Lois began to make good use of the therapy. Her depression diminished significantly, and she felt hopeful and positive about herself and her future in both her career and her relational worlds.

However, although Louis was bright and eager to learn about herself, she was unable to engage in fruitful exploration of what turned out to be a pattern of negative relationships with men. She began dating again, but each man with whom she became involved was, in one way or another, painfully unavailable to her. For example, she fell in love with a married man, then with a friend's boyfriend. While we attempted to examine some of the issues involved, an interesting, at first unrecognized impasse was developing within the therapeutic relationship: the question of her fee became a silent companion to our work. I initially thought the fee issue was mine alone. Louis was not particularly sophisticated about psychotherapy, and although her salary had doubled and then doubled again during the time we had been working together, it simply might not, I told myself, have occurred to her to suggest raising my salary as well.

This self-deception on my part could not last long. Lois was extremely grateful to me for the help I had given her, and she was an aggressive, successful businesswoman. It was highly unlikely that she had not thought about my fee, and I began to suspect that she had decided, as a good businesswoman, to leave it up to me to bring up the question. Given Lois's tremendous narcissistic vulnerability and concomitant sense of entitlement, I imagined that this attitude would assuage some of the humiliation of paying for the therapeutic concern and caring that, as she had put it on several different occasions, "people should get for free." I wondered how to bring the question into the therapeutic space without putting myself in a one-down position, while at the same time protecting both Lois's self-esteem and the therapeutic relationship. I was also struggling with my own conflicts around money, including my fear of being rejected or dismissed by her if I did raise her fee, and personal and professional issues about how much the work I was doing was worth.

Although I recognized that, despite my misgivings, there were some important therapeutic indications for raising Lois's fee, I did not yet understand that my questions were themselves key to many aspects of Lois's relationships with others. Who owes whom, what and how much, was a basic, unspoken theme not only at her job, but in every relationship in which she had ever been involved. It was not until I actually brought up the money question directly, however, that this material came alive in the therapy. When I told her that I was going to be raising her fee, Lois simply nodded and said, "That makes sense." She asked how much, and when I told her, she smiled, agreed, and went on to speak of other things. Although I asked about her feelings about the increase, she said little about it until the end of the session, when she said, "See, that wasn't so bad. But you should have asked for more." Although there were many dynamics involved, this interaction highlights an often unarticulated and perhaps even unrecognized aspect of what Trachtman (1999) has called "the money taboo," which will be the focus of this article: the use of discussions about money to open up dynamic issues in the world of relationships.

It is, of course, nothing new to suggest that money has meaning. Whether or not one accepts Freud's (1908) linkage of money and feces, in our culture, money is frequently seen as a direct pathway to feelings of power, agency, self-directedness, and personal satisfaction. Trachtman (1999) states, "Money, psychologically speaking, is our projection onto coins, bills, bank accounts, and other financial instruments of our beliefs, hopes, and fears about how those things will affect who we are, what will happen to us, and how we will be treated by others or by ourselves" (p. 283). Phillips (1998) puts it this way: "Because money is the solution to poverty, it can make us believe that we are impoverished only by lack of money. So money becomes a kind of greedy symbol for anything and everything we might want" (p. 82).

In this article we will look at some of the ways money can be utilized to negotiate the ever-changing tensions between self and other, object and subject, intrapsychic and interpersonal, connection and separation that constantly fluctuate in every relationship. In order to get there, however, we must be willing to step into a world not discussed in "polite society": the world of money. With Lois, for example, when I broke the money taboo, I found myself directly involved in one of the complex relational interactions that plagued Lois in "real life." Not only did we suddenly have to face Lois's unspoken feelings about money and power, but we found ourselves deep in the "mire" of Lois's fears about dependency and intimacy. Untangling the multitiered meanings of my request and her reaction to it led us through many painful discussions and gradually into a new and deeper understanding of Lois's conflicts over separateness and connection.

Freud's (1908) suggestion that money represents feces does not do justice to the complexity of the subject or the difficulty inherent in discussing it in analysis. Numerous books and articles have been written on the topic since then, and of course money has taken on new meanings in contemporary society. As Dimen (1994) points out, psychodynamic consideration of money today must take into account not only intrapsychic but also cultural, social, class, and gender meanings, as well as the practicalities of down-to-earth, concrete financial and insurance arrangements. According to Krueger (1986), however, even though therapists today are aware that "treatment can be facilitated or sabotaged by the degree of thoroughness with which money matters are dealt . . . the theory and practice of exchanging money are among the least examined of transactions in psychotherapy and psychoanalysis (p. viii).

Nearly 15 years after Krueger published this comment, and despite a growing body of literature on the topic, however, money is still seldom directly addressed in the formal coursework of analytic institutes. (See Trachtman, 1999, for a further discussion of this problem.) The issue is often only brought into supervision at times of crisis, or when a therapist wants to raise her fees. Obviously, this problem is not one that occurs only for members of our profession. Krueger (1986) wrote that in contemporary Western cultures, "most of us have learned to talk more easily about sex, yet remain seclusive, embarrassed, or conflicted about discussing money. Money may be the last emotional taboo in our society" (p. vii). Further, although Freud (1913) believed that it was possible to separate psychological meanings from the practicalities of running a business, we know now that the two are deeply intertwined.

Therapists' conflicts about running a business and about taking money for our work often intersect with, complement, and/or parallel clients' feelings of entitlement or confusion about wishes to be taken care of in ways reminiscent of the concurrent and complementary interactions described by Racker (1968). Slavin and Kriegman (1998) have described unarticulated conflicts of interest between therapist and client that can also often make it hard to explore openly the meanings of money. For example, it is often difficult for both therapist and client to become comfortable with the business side of the therapeutic relationship, to reconcile the wish to be genuinely caring and/or cared about with the reality of paying for the therapy, and to acknowledge the therapist's financial need.

Some of these issues are particularly salient for social workers. As individuals and as a field of practice, we have a commitment to providing service for those who cannot afford high-priced private practice fees. Because we are often conflicted about what we charge, many of us, even if we offer a sliding scale have difficulty opening up questions about money. Furthermore, since social workers are often women, gender issues, which I will discuss later, influence our attitude toward money and our comfort discussing it. Managed care plays an important but sometimes silent role here as well see, for example, Bornemon, 1976; Krueger, 1986; Klebanow, 1991; Lowenkopf, 1991; Herron and Welt, 1992). Not least important in the managed care muddle is the fact that social workers are reimbursed significantly less for psychotherapy than either psychologists or psychiatrists, thus reinforcing clients' and our own conflicts over our value and expertise.

Because of cultural taboos on discussion of money, as well as intrapsychic conflicts over the multiple meanings of the topic, it is not surprising that even for therapists who recognize many of the psychodynamic meanings, it may not be a simple matter to bring the subject into the therapeutic discussion. Not all clients are as firmly literal as one man who told his therapist, "A check is just a check. Your fee is just your fee. And if I forgot to pay it, it's just because I forgot," but many clients strongly resist their therapists' attempts to open up and explore the more subtle meanings of money negotiations, both in and outside of the therapeutic relationship. Money is, however, always in the room with us. Before the fee is set, before policies about cancellation are ever discussed, they are part of the therapeutic climate. Unexpressed and often even unrecognized issues of self-worth, feelings of deprivation, concerns about envy and competition may be contained in the apparently simple discussion of a therapist's fee, but even the most sophisticated of clients may never be able to open up this material without help.

I have found that recognizing that money is a way of titrating the struggle to balance separateness and connectedness can be a useful and meaningful route into these issues. In this context, therapist and client can develop a "transitional language" (to paraphrase Ogden, 1986) with which to talk about, examine, and explore the many unarticulated, "messy," and confusing aspects of their developing relationship. Lois, for example, understood intrinsically that, as Klebanow (1991) commented, "He or she who possesses money has power as well" (p. 52). This issue, however, was far more complex than it might seem at first glance. For Lois, as we gradually came to understand, the question of power was directly related to what Ghent (1990) has described as a contrast between submission and surrender. Lois could not imagine a relational experience in which there was a genuine give and take of control, power, domination, and dependence.

In her experience, one person always had all of the power and the other none. As we slowly worked on the complicated and often uncomfortable meanings of the exchange of money between us, we were also working, often without realizing it, on the possibilities of a new kind of relationship for her. She began to recognize her own version of Guntrip's (1973) "schizoid dilemma," that is, a struggle to manage the multitiered tension between a wish to be close and a fear of being engulfed, and a wish to be separate and a fear of being alone and isolated. The idea that we could even consider negotiating money issues in a way that took into account both of our needs went a long way toward both ameliorating and opening up these previously unarticulated fears and longings.

I want to reiterate that I believe there is no single meaning for money. It has many different meanings for each individual, whether therapist or client, and I am therefore not suggesting that the tension between separation and connection is the central or the only meaning for money that we can or should explore. Yet looking at money in this light often paves the way to exploration of other aspects of both finances and personal relationships. As clients become comfortable looking at some of these issues in relation to money, they often also become more aware of some of the other, less easily engaged dynamics with which they endow their own or others' money. I have written elsewhere (Barth, 1998, 2000) of the importance of paying attention to apparently insignificant, concrete details in a client's life. These details can take us directly into the specifics of a client's psychodynamics, transference and countertransference issues, and other extremely important therapeutic matters. In matters of money, questions about fees, insurance arrangements, and payment style, for example, can lead to significant information about issues of dependency, deprivation, envy, longing, connecting, and other aspects of relationship—both in and outside of the therapeutic interaction.

The Case of Abby and Jake

Abby was a highly successful businesswoman in her mid-thirties. Jake, her husband of 10 years, had recently lost his own high-paying position in a corporation that had downsized. They sought therapy because their relationship had become increasingly antagonistic since Jake had been out of work. It was difficult for their therapist to know what the relationship had been like before this change, but when they began treatment, they were locked in an ugly, painful to watch, apparently sadomasochistic struggle. In every session, Abby berated and denigrated her husband, who appeared to be settling submissively into a chronic state of depression. Despite the fact that Jake had supported her for most of their relationship, and that now she was earning enough money to support them in relative comfort, Abby was enraged at his failure to continue to bring money into the relationship.

The male therapist felt that he had made some headway with this difficult couple, especially when they began talking about buying a new apartment. He thought at first that this signaled their willingness to make a long-term commitment to the relationship and to recognize that they needed to look for something less expensive than the apartment in which they currently lived. In the course of numerous discussions, however, it became clear that they had significantly more money than they had originally revealed to him and were actually looking for a more expensive apartment. The therapist, who had been seeing them for a reduced fee, was surprised and angered at this revelation. Believing that he had been treated in much the same way that Abby treated Jake, the therapist brought the question of his fee into the therapy. Abby was extremely irritated at the therapist's request to look at this issue and to be paid more, and Jake as mostly silent during the discussion.

The therapist suggested that they needed to talk about the fee. Abby angrily replied that they were paying him to help them with their marital problems, not to talk about his needs. The therapist suggested that the way they had negotiated his initial fee was reflective of the marital problems on which they had been working. Abby snorted angrily and said that sounded like "therapy-ese." The therapist stood his ground, but was unable to get either partner to respond to the possibility that this interaction reflected anything about their relationship or their personalities. In the end, however, after continuing to push the point, the therapist did get them to agree to pay his full fee. He felt that, if nothing else, he had at least modeled to them both that one

could stand up to Abby and negotiate, rather than be mowed down by the woman's angry and condescending manner. The therapy continued with no further reference to the fee. To his surprise, however, some months later he received a phone call from Abby saying that she did not understand something about the bill.

"You seem to have been overcharging us for some months, and you didn't bring it to my attention. What can that mean?" In the following session, the therapist reminded her of the discussion they had had over the fee before he raised it. Neither Jake nor Abby had any recollection of the conversation. Abby said he was unethical and demanded that he refund the money. Jake, perhaps relieved to have the heat off himself for a while, remained passively uninvolved in the discussion. The therapist felt immobilized and enraged. This couple was extremely difficult, and he was resentful of their sense of entitlement and inability to recognize the value of the work he had been doing with them. What he finally said, however, was, "You know, there's no way that I can prove that we had this conversation, and no way that you can prove that we didn't. But what's interesting is that I've entered your system. You and I are having the same kind of difficulty that the two of you have—we each have our own view of what happened, and there seems to be no room for differences of opinion."

Abby became angrier, nastier, and louder, and the therapist told her, "I know you're really furious with me, but I really don't understand why there can't be two different opinions in this room. I have one memory of what we've discussed, and you have another. Why can't we be angry at each other *and* discuss it?" Her response was, "Because you don't know what you're talking about. If you won't pay me back what you owe me, there's no use continuing this conversation. I'll have my lawyer contact you." At which point she stood up and walked out, dragging her husband along with her. Interestingly, they returned for the next session. Nothing was said of the lawyer, and they paid the therapist's full fee. They returned, however, to the idea that there could be more than one point of view in the room. The therapist encouraged them to stop trying to resolve their differences, for the moment, and instead to simply acknowledge that they had conflicting perspectives. Sometimes he would ask Jake to speak first, and then would ask Abby for her version. At other times he would ask Abby to talk about what happened, and then would encourage Jake to tell him all of the details "as you saw them." He found that money was often a useful topic for exploring their different subjectivities.

While the couple remained quite difficult, the therapist felt that by becoming immersed in their system, through the financial negotiations, he had learned something important about what it was like to be inside their relationship. What he began to understand over time was that Jake, in his apparent passivity, was actually actively maintaining a separation from Abby and from the "fray," as he eventually labeled the intense conflict that seem to be part of their daily lives. When the therapist began to understand that Jake's passivity was in fact a silent activity, and that it was specifically directed to managing the tension between separation and connection, he also began to see a different side to Abby's rage. It was surprising to him to see how much of a shift it made in the interactions when he articulated his new understanding that Jake's almost rigid separateness left Abby feeling frightened and alone in the relationship, and that her rage and controlling behavior might well be a reaction to a sense that she had no say in the level of connection and separateness in their marriage.

This new perspective became even more clear around another financial interaction. Jake had begun working again. His mood was better, and the relationship seemed less tense and brittle, although there were clearly still some serious problems. For the first time, the couple failed to pay their therapy bill on time. When the therapist raised the question, Abby turned to Jake and said, "I thought you were taking care of that?" Jake shrugged his shoulders and said nothing. The therapist asked him to try to put his response into words. "She says it's my therapy and I should pay for it now that I'm working again. I told her no way. She's the one who needs help, and she's paying for the therapy." The therapist asked them to tell him about the specifics of their financial arrangements. "You don't have to tell me about the actual amounts," he said, "but let's talk about how you split up your finances." As they slowly, often quite painfully, shared information with him, he learned that they kept their bank accounts separate, that they paid bills separately, and that they each had their own investments. "You keep everything separate?" he asked. They nodded. While reinforcing that this was certainly an acceptable solution, he wondered if it also reflected some of the struggle they had been talking about in their relationship: that is, the tremendous difficulty they had finding a way to be connected, while also maintaining some sense of separateness.

Interestingly, it was Abby who seemed to grasp what he was saying first. She was able to put into words some of her own anxieties about "merging" their accounts, especially her fear of being "eaten up and then spit out" by Jake, who she felt was a better money manager than she was. "But it's more than that," she said. "I worry that I'll really put my faith in him—not just financially, but emotionally—that I'll become dependent on him, and that he'll drop me like a hot potato." It took many months before Jake was willing to admit that he, too, had difficulties trusting, and for the two of them to begin to work to find ways to be connected while maintaining their independence. Money had, however, become a potent symbol for their struggles in this arena, and now became a tool with which they talked about their relationship.

One of the difficulties in any therapeutic exploration of money as a relational tool is that, to borrow from some comments that Simon (1986) made about power, it is not "a unitary concept . . . each person . . . has a particular version and vision of what power [or money] is, wherein it lies, who or what possesses it, and what are the forms of power [or money] that count in life" (p. 127; material in brackets added). Money, of course, does represent power for many people, although even the type of power it symbolizes can differ from one individual to another. Becker wrote, "In its power to manipulate physical and social reality *money* in some ways secures one against contingency and accident" (cited in Olsson, 1986, p. 61; italics in original). While Becker believed that money, because it can be passed on to one's heirs, offers an illusion of immortality and thus a defense against the fear of death, Phillips (1998) has wondered if the fantasy is not even broader. He asks, for example, what we imagine money will do for us. Does it offer protection from

> disappointment, or resentment about the frustration of relationships with other people? The possibility of self-sufficiency, of being exempt from dependent need? The guarantee of safety . . . To be loved forever, never to be left out; to have people sufficiently responsive and attentive to his needs; to be treated affectionately, and with regard for his privacy; to be like the parents; to be free of grief. (p. 82)

Money begins to play a significant part in most therapeutic work from the moment that a prospective client first begins to *think* about going into therapy; yet it is often extremely difficult to find a way to talk about it, and it is almost impossible to take it past the basic and concrete discussion of fees and financial responsibilities. When a client loses his job, or when a therapist raises her fees, some of the unconscious meanings can suddenly explode into the work; but when this occurs the material is often colored and shaped by concrete financial issues that can disguise or screen the multiple, often confusing dynamics that the money has come to represent.

Perhaps because money can make both therapist and client feel inadequate, vulnerable, and/or powerless, while conversely seeming to give the other unfair advantages, both therapist and client may shy away from fully exploring this area of the therapeutic relationship. Money, of course, is one of the things that people in our society covet; relationships are another. Feelings of deprivation and desire can both exacerbate and be fueled by overwhelming or intolerable vulnerability and powerlessness. Greedy demands and stingy withholding are both frequently part of the viscous cycle that Klein (1957/1975) suggested culminates in the inability to take in or enjoy what one does get from the envied other.

Grotstein (1986) suggested that symptoms are "not merely the result of psychodynamic conflict but are also attempts to restore balance to a critically imbalanced psyche" (p. 105). I would add that within each therapeutic dyad, in fact, within every relationship, "symptoms," problems, or apparently maladaptive interactions are also attempts to restore the equilibrium of the relationship. One of the hardest tasks for therapists is to participate simultaneously in and attempt to understand both the intrapsychic and interpersonal systems that a client is trying to balance, both alone and within the therapeutic relationship. Mitchell's (1993) image of analyst and analysand dancing together and gradually beginning to wonder why they are dancing a particular step is extremely useful as a model for this process. Ongoing examination of the choice of "music" and specific dances around money and financial negotiations that we engage in with each client can offer an important key to that client's dynamics.

The Case of Erica

Erica, an extremely bright, sensitive, and likable woman, came to therapy after leaving a cult to which she had belonged for most of her life. She was a fascinating woman who combined qualities of tremendous fragility with surprising strength. From the beginning of our relationship, she occasionally missed sessions, always for what seemed to be good reasons: a sick child, a crisis at work,

a former cult member who needed her help. She paid for these sessions with no question, but when I gently attempted to explore the meanings of the absences, she absolutely denied the possibility of any psychological motive behind them. Erica did well in therapy. The depression and anxiety that had brought her in began to diminish. Her relationships with her children and her own parents and siblings improved significantly, as did some work-related difficulties that she only began to discuss a year or so into the therapy.

I thought that her absences might be her way of titrating the intimacy between us and particularly her dependency on me and, although I occasionally asked about the missed sessions, I did not press the issue. I did, however, wonder if I should stop charging her for the time. Erica was struggling financially, and she generally gave me some advance notice about absences. Furthermore, since it happened so regularly, I had also almost without realizing it set up my schedule to take advantage of the free time when it occurred. This is one of those easy, apparently nonconflicted, nonverbal interactions that occur almost without our notice, which I have found often contain cogent, unarticulated information about the dynamics of the individual and the relationship. One day when I gave Erica her bill, I lightly, almost accidentally remarked that I appreciated that she paid for her missed sessions without ever complaining, but I wondered if she had any feelings or thoughts about it.

"Well," she said hesitantly, in her soft voice, "I hadn't thought about it before. But now that you bring it up, I guess it means I don't owe you anything." She gave me a small, tentative smile. Not immediately, but over a period off time, Erica and I gradually began to explore the issue of "owing." With the help of this "clue," we started the difficult work of teasing out a number of confusing but extremely significant issues in Erica's relationship with her old cult as well as with her family, children, and close friends. A sense of indebtedness to the cult leaders, who had taken her in at a time when her life was in shambles, conflicted with painful feelings of hurt and range that they had controlled her life so completely, and in some ways so destructively. As we discussed her unwillingness to be indebted to me financially, we were also able to open up her fears of feeling gratitude and even love toward anyone.

"I vowed never to let anyone have that kind of power over me again," she told me at one point. Erica almost consciously utilized money as both a symbolic and a concrete means of titrating the tension between connection and separation without losing either herself or the other. Not surprisingly, she broke her vow regularly; but when she felt in danger of being overwhelmed, of losing herself in a relationship, of losing control, she reestablished her separateness by insisting on literally paying her own way, sometimes at great cost to herself and her relationships. Perhaps we would eventually have gotten to these issues even if I had not brought up the question of Erica's willingness to pay for her missed sessions, but the metaphor became an extremely useful one that we used throughout the course of her therapy.

It is my belief that the process of putting into words, out loud, to another person, ideas and feelings that have not been spoken, even if they have been thought, is a key component to what makes psychodynamic psychotherapy work. As Spence (1982), Daniel Stern (1985), Donnell Stern (1997), Bromberg (1998), and many others have noted, experiences change when they are put into words. While it is crucial to the analytic process to respect the importance of *not* articulating everything, of sitting with the unformulated, sometimes for many years, it is also extremely important to recognize that when spoken out loud to another person, experiences can take on new meanings, allow for interesting connections, and provide the possibility of new, often surprising changes of perspective. Given both the cultural taboos and the emotional meanings of money, a therapist's request that an analysand talk about even the smallest elements of his or her use of and relationship to money can arouse feelings of shame, embarrassment, guilt, and fear of rejection in an analysand; and asking for and listening to this information can evoke related responses in the analyst.

I have found, however, that by looking at the small, apparently inconsequential financial matters of everyday life, we make room for dissociated, unformulated, and unarticulated emotions to emerge in small, manageable doses. By focusing on the little details, we help analysands (and ourselves) to build a language for talking about, tolerating, and gradually understanding experience that has never before been put into words and that feels intolerable. In another context, Sullivan (1954/1970) wrote of the importance of detailed inquiry into matters that allowed for anxiety to emerge in tolerable doses for exploration. These ongoing discussions of "insignificant" money issues make it much easier to explore painful, affectively loaded material in those raw and explosive moments that occur in every analysis. Furthermore, because talking about these small details enhances analysands' abilities to discuss more complex and less easily accessible feelings, experiences, and beliefs, this process also leads directly, if gradually, to the examination of the symbolically laden material that is the epicenter of analytic work.

The Case of Jarrod

The process is exactly what did not happen in my work with Jarrod, who began therapy in his late twenties. The middle of five siblings, he was viewed in the family as the "greedy" one. In fact, it seemed to me, he felt deprived and intolerably needy most of the time. Working in a not-for-profit agency at one of their entry-level jobs, he could barely afford his rent and food. He had little money for therapy and less for other luxuries. He had some insurance coverage, and I have a policy of seeing a certain number of low-fee clients and had an opening at the time, so I began to work with him for a substantially reduced fee. The treatment moved slowly, but despite my feeling that we were grinding through each session, over the next few years Jarrod was promoted to a position of leadership in the nonprofit work he had chosen as his profession, and he was living with a woman with whom he was discussing the probability of getting married.

From time to time, I considered raising his fee, but there were always reasons not to: he was moving out of his apartment in a drug-ridden neighborhood to a nicer, but more expensive area of town; his girlfriend lost her job; he wanted desperately to buy some new clothes. We spoke about his family's money troubles, disturbing arguments between his parents over his father's income and his mother's failure to find work. At times we also discussed his wish that his parents could have been more generous with him, his fledgling recognition that they had little to give, either financially or emotionally, and his resentment about the lifestyle decisions they had made that had kept the family from ever being able to feel financially safe (choices that, by the way, were not very different from those Jarrod was making himself). We did not, however, talk about the small details of his daily financial life, nor did I ever share with him my own occasional thoughts about raising his fee and deciding not to. And I never asked him how he felt about paying me what he paid.

Then Jarrod got a new job with a substantial raise, and I told him that I would be increasing his fee. He needed, looked hesitant, and then said, "Okay. My insurance will cover some of it." To my question about how much it would actually cover, he replied that he now had 50% reimbursement for therapy. I was amazed and pleased, and began to try to figure out how much I could raise his fee before it changed what he actually paid me. He looked startled. "But I've been getting 50% insurance for several years; so if you raise it that much, I'll be paying a lot more than before." I was, to say the least, stunned. Hurt, anger, resentment, feelings of betrayal all came later, as did many fruitful but often painful discussions about our relationship and the work we had been doing.

The idea that ours *was* a relationship and that I had needs and expectations in connection to him surprised Jarrod at first, then opened up a new phase of an old issue: the idea that "adults" were neither omniscient nor omnipotent. Although space does not allow me to discuss the experience more fully, it is my belief that if I had been paying attention to and asking Jarrod about the many small details of his financial life, I would have known this was going on long before, and we would have been able to talk about these issues in a less hurtful way. As it was, this episode ushered in some crucial work on what Leowald (1956–57/1980) described as the necessary but mutually painful process of recognizing the flaws and failings of parents and parent figures. Perhaps this "outburst," as Mitchell (1993) has called it, was necessary for the work, but I think we would have been far better prepared if I had been asking about the apparently insignificant financial details that had been hovering on the edges of our interactions throughout the analysis.

Managed Care and Gender Issues

Two final issues that come up in relation to money are managed care and gender issues. We all recognize that managed care has had a tremendous impact on the practice of psychotherapy and psychoanalysis today; but even when clients are paying for their therapy through managed care or other forms of insurance, just as when a parent or spouse takes responsibility for the fee, there are many details regarding financial arrangements and negotiations that can and should be examined in the therapeutic process. Not only the issues of client's daily financial life, but also the many dynamics related to the payment of fees can be discussed directly. How do clients feel about the managed care company, for example, and what sort of service are they getting from it? How do other providers treat them? What are their expectations and concerns, their

worries and their wishes in regard to their medical treatment in general? What about psychotherapy?

An entire generation is growing up without the benefit of what was once a traditional relationship to a family doctor, a change that, like most, has both benefits and flaws; but these clients come into therapy with ideas about treatment and payment that are often significantly different from those of their therapists and that must be discussed and examined as part of the therapeutic work. Many of us hesitate to open these doors, often because of their own feelings about the managed care system; however, we need to find ways to talk among ourselves about not only the irritations of contemporary providership, but also our attempts to survive in this world. This means beginning to talk openly not only about the managed care system, which has been the subject of some recent conferences and much causal discussion, but also about fees, a matter that is still incredibly difficult for analysts to address directly with one another. Only when we are able to bring this material into the class and conference rooms, however, will it regularly make it to the consulting room as well.

The second issue, that of gender and money, has received more attention. According to Donnell Stern (1997), it is time for "the rest of psychoanalysis . . . to catch up with its feminists and theorists of gender . . . who have been arguing for years that power relations, especially those revolving around difference, are central to the constitution of subjectivity and interaction" (p. 10). As therapist and client work to find an optimal balance of connectedness and separateness, preconceived individual and cultural expectations based on gender will color the demands, expectations, and understanding of just how power will be divided in each therapeutic dyad; and money, which has gender-related significance in our culture, may well be one of the tools and the symbols by which this is done. In a fascinating review of the subject Benson (2000) has cited a number of studies that show some of the different ways that men and women relate to money, not only in the ways we earn it, but also in the ways that we spend, invest, and save it.

Burnside and Krueger 1986 and Herron and Welt (1992) report that male therapists frequently charge more than female therapists with the same experience, degrees, and background. There are many different possible explanations for these findings, and I do not have time or space to explore them here; but these issues, like many others, can play a silent, unnoticed role in therapeutic relationships and therefore need to be brought out of the closet, not only in therapy, but also in psychodynamic training. Even when, as is often true, men and women either do not fit or actively renounce cultural stereotypes, talking about these dynamics among ourselves and with clients can open up the dynamics of money and relatedness that inevitably occur in the analytic process and in life.

Conclusion

I am by no means suggesting that all financial issues are about separation and connection. Human dynamics are, as Pine (1985) has suggested, "endlessly complex," and the dynamics that crystallize around money and financial negotiations are equally complex. It has been my experience, however, that the link between money and relatedness is frequently neglected, and since they contain so much of significance, and can also be the cause of major disruptions and failures in therapeutic work, I believe it is worth our while to take some time to focus specifically on them. One area that money frequently highlights is the sphere of power negotiations, including the crucial and sometimes subtle negotiations by which we all attempt to find and maintain an ongoing balance between separateness and intimacy, aloneness and connectedness. Money is a way of titrating and organizing power shifts, and paying attention to the small, manageable details of money in daily life can provide us with language with which to talk about these shifts. Putting into words the many-tiered perspectives on the interplay between therapist's and client's needs, vulnerabilities, and strengths is not always easy, even with insightful, articulate clients. Money negotiations can provide a keyhole through which we can view a multitude of other dynamics—if we can just get our eyes to the opening.

References

Aron, L. (1996). *A Meeting of Minds*. London: Analytic Press.

Barth, D. (1989). Separation-individuation, sense of self and bulimia in college students. In *The Bulimic College Student: Evaluation, Treatment and Prevention*, ed. L. Whitaker. New York: Haworth Press.

Barth, D. (1998). Speaking of feelings: Affects, language and psychoanalysis. *Psychoanalytic Dialogues* 8(5):685–705.

Barth, D. (2000). Eat, shop and be merry. In *I Shop, Therefore I Am: Compulsive Buying and the Search for Self*, ed. A. Benson. New York: Jason Aronson.

Benjamin, J. (1995). *Like Subjects, Love Objects*. New Haven, CT: Yale University Press.

Benson, A. (2000). *I Shop, Therefore I Am: Compulsive Buying and the Search for Self*. New York: Jason Aronson.

Borneman, E. (1976). *The Psychoanalysis of Money*. New York: Urizen Books.

Bromberg, P. (1998). *Standing in the Spaces: Essays on clinical process, trauma, and dissociation*. London: Analytic Press.

Burnside, M., and Krueger, D. (1986). Fee practices of male and female therapists. In *The Last Taboo: Money as symbol and reality in psychotherapy and psychoanalysis*, ed. Krueger, D. New York: Brunner Mazel, pp. 48–54.

Dimen, M. (1994). Money, love and hate: Contradiction and paradox in psychoanalysis. *Psychoanalytic Dialogues* 4(1):69–100.

Freud, S. (1908). Character analysis and anal eroticism. *Standard Edition*, 9:167–175. London: Hagart Press, 1986.

Freud, S. (1913). On beginning treatment. *Standard Edition*, 12:123–144. London: Hogarth Press, 1986.

Ghent, E. (1990). Masochism, submission, surrender: Masochism as a perversion of surrender. *Contemporary Psychoanalysis*, 6:101–130.

Grotstein, J. (1986). The psychology of powerlessness: Disorders of self-regulation and interactional regulation as a newere paradigm for psychopathology. *Psychoanalytic Inquiry* 6(1):93–118.

Guntrip, H. (1973). *Psychoanalytic Theory, Therapy and the Self*. New York: Basic Books.

Herron, W., and Welt, S. (1992). *Money Matters: The Fee in Psychotherapy and Psychoanalysis*. New York: Guilford Press.

Klebanow, S. (1991). Power, gender and money. In *Money and Mind*, eds. Klebanow, S. and Lowenkpf, E. New York: Plenum Press, pp. 51–60.

Klebanow, S., and Lowenkpf, E. (1991). How much is enough? In *Money and Mind*, eds. Klebanow, S. and Lowenkpf, E. New York: Plenum Press, pp. 3–14.

Klein, M. (1957/1975). *Envy and Gratitude and Other Works*. London: Hogarth Press.

Krueger, D. (1986). *The Last Taboo: Money as symbol and reality in psychotherapy and psychoanalysis*. New York: Brunner Mazel.

Loewald, H. (1956–57/1980). The waning of the Oedipus compex. In *Papers on Psychoanalysis*. New Haven, CT: Yale University Press.

Lowenkopf, E. (1991). Poverty and psychopathology. In *Money and Mind*, eds.

Klebanow, S. and Lowenkpf, E. New York: Plenum Press, pp. 41–50.

Mitchell, S. (1993). *Hope and Dread in Psychoanalysis*. New York: Basic Books.

Ogden, T. (1986). *The Matrix of the Mind: Object Relations and the Psychoanalytic Dialogue*. Northvale, NJ: Jason Aronson.

Ogden, T. (1997). Some thoughts on the use of language in psychoanalysis. *Psychoanalytic Dialogues* 7:1–22.

Olsson, P. (1986). Complexities in the psychology and psychotherapy of the phenomenally wealthy. In *The Last Taboo: Money as symbol and reality in psychotherapy and psychoanalysis*, ed. Krueger, D. New York: Brunner Mazel, pp. 55–69.

Phillips, A. (1998). Satisfaction not guaranteed. *New York Times Magazine*, June 7, p. 82.

Pine, F. (1985). *Developmental Theory and Clinical Process*. New Haven, CT: Yale University Press.

Racker, H. (1968). *Transference and Countertransference*. New York: International Universities Press.

Simon, B. (1986). The power of the wish and the wish for power: A discussion of power and psychoanalysis. *Psychoanalytic Injury* 6(1):119–132.

Spence, D. (1982). *Narrative Truth and Historical Truth*. New York: Norton.

Spence, D. (1987). *The Freudian Metaphor*. New York: Norton.

Stern, D. B. (1997). *Unformulated Experience*. London: Analytic Press.

Stern, D. N. (1985). *The Interpersonal World of the Infant*. New York: Basic Books.

Sullivan, H. S. (1954/1970). *The Psychiatric Interview*. New York: Norton.

Trachtman, R. (1999). The money taboo: Its effects in everyday life and in the practice of psychotherapy. *Clinical Social Work Journal* 27(3):275–288.

CIGAL KNEI-PAZ
DAVID S. RIBNER

72

A Narrative Perspective on "Doing" for Multiproblem Families

"Human behavior, unlike that of physical objects, cannot be understood without reference to the meanings and purposes attached by human actors to their activities" (Guba & Lincoln, 1994, p. 106). As helping professionals, we have all too often assumed an understanding of our clients' behaviors, without allowing them sufficient space for the telling of their own attributed meanings and purposes. As Giordano (1977) suggested, "Psychiatry has perpetuated the notion that the patient's point of view toward treatment is likely to be distorted and inaccurate. Because social work agencies have generally maintained a psychological orientation, they, in turn, are able to avoid using the client's viewpoint" (p. 34). Similarly, Mayer and Timms (1969) noted that "the client has rarely been asked what kind of help he wants or what he thinks of the help he has been given" (p. 32).

In this study, clients from multiproblem families in Israel were asked to describe, in their own words and from their own perspectives, a treatment experience that they perceived as having been helpful. The replies were analyzed using narrative research techniques and grouped into conceptual categories with illustrative quotations from the interviews and conclusions then offered regarding client preferences in the areas of technique and outcome of interventions. We see this methodology as contributing a uniquely rich and impactful view of the other side of the client-worker dyad, one that is often lost when employing quantitative procedures: "Those who use narrative methods embrace story methods precisely because they tell us more about the storyteller than about the events that the storyteller is recounting" (Cowan, 1999, p. 166).

We have presented results elsewhere concerning the nature of the treatment relationship desired by these clients (Ribner & Knei-Paz, in press). In this article, we turn to the nature of the assistance seen as constituting a successful helping experience.

Working with Multiproblem Families

The formidable task of helping multiproblem families has long been the subject of social concern. As McNeil and Herschell (1998) noted, "There is no simple, ultimate solution to the challenges they offer" (p. 262). Regarding these clients, the term "inapt" service has been used to describe the "lack of fit between what a family needs and the outside help which is provided" (Rosenfeld & Sykes, 1998, p. 286), setting up all involved parties for inevitable failure. Consistent themes are that conventional methodologies have failed, that new models must be created (Rosenfeld, 1964; Scholsberg & Kagan, 1988; Schorr & Schorr, 1988), that services must be relevant to client needs and wishes (McKinney, 1970), and that the emphasis must be on "doing" as opposed to verbal therapies (Levine, 1964).

One common denominator of innovative approaches reported as successful is that most are based on the perceptions of helping professionals and not on the viewpoint of clients (Rabin, Rosenberg, & Sens, 1982; Schlosberg & Kagan, 1988;

Hines, Richman, Maxim, & Hays, 1989; Reimel & Schindler, 1994; Rosenfeld, Schon, & Sykes, 1995). In recent years, some attention has shifted to research focused on client reports regarding correlations between treatment success and treatment variables. In 1986, for example, in a study done by Benvenisti and Yekel, members of 35 multiproblem families were asked to indicate which behaviors of their student social workers were particularly helpful. Among the responses were willingness to help and be with the family; support, encouragement, and listening; allowing the opportunity for the full expression of feelings; and the provision of concrete services.

Similarly, Krumer-Nevo (1998) looked at the use of support groups for adult female members of multiproblem families. Based on client self-reports of improved self-image and a reduced sense of isolation, she concluded that the reported intervention success was attributable to the group's ability to achieve problem resolution, the three-year length of the project, and the nonjudgmental stance of the social workers. An additional illustration was recently cited by Christoph-Wyler (1998) in her study of a socioeducational day program for multiproblem families in Zurich, Switzerland. As part of the project, parents were asked to describe which interventions helped them and their children with issues such as social behavior and academic performance.

Method

Research Design

In this study, we attempted to further clarify the issues of perceived treatment success with multiproblem families through the use of a narrative research methodology. Clients were invited to participate in a research project that could contribute to the improvement in the provision of social work services. Each was assured that their refusal to participate would not negatively affect them. Interviews were conducted by Knei-Paz in locations other than traditional "work" sites (i.e., either in coffee shops or clients' homes to create a more friendly and less formal or threatening atmosphere.

Each interview was tape-recorded with client permission and lasted approximately one to one and a half hours. Clients were asked to describe a treatment intervention or experience that they viewed as successful, and questions were formulated during the interviews to allow for clarification of words, phrases, and referents (Riessman, 1993; Hartman, 1994). Interviews were then transcribed, mindful that we would be losing the sig-

nificance of body language and facial expressions (Mishler, 1986). Two social workers (the authors) and one sociologist/anthropologist did content analysis for each recorded interview. We stopped the interviews once we reached a count of 11, as we felt we had read narratives rich enough (Patton, 1990) to provide the data for content analysis.

Study Population

Eleven Israeli women were interviewed for this study, referred either by social workers in local welfare offices or by the professional staff at therapeutic residences. At the time of the study, all were clients of social service offices. These offices, under the aegis of the Ministry of Labor and Welfare, provide a broad range of legislatively mandated services and resources to various delineated populations, such as immigrants, the elderly, and the unemployed. While services are provided locally, policy is set by the central government in Jerusalem, with some flexibility for the specific requirements of area populations. The rudiments of this network were established by European immigrants to Israel in the early 1900s and to some extent still reflect a socialist perspective on fulfilling basic human needs.

The women chosen had experienced and were prepared to discuss a positive treatment episode. All lived in households deemed multiproblematic in terms of some or all of the following criteria: low socioeconomic status, lack of permanent residence, unemployment, debt, parent-child and spousal conflicts, social isolation, significant physical illness, and/or substance abuse. We chose female heads of households because, at least in Israel, they represent the population with the greatest direct contact with social service agencies (Jaffe, 1983) and are, therefore, more likely to have experienced, at some point in their client careers, a positive episode of intervention.

All of the women were Jewish and were either Israeli-born or had been residents most of their lives. They ranged in age from 33 to 50 years, seven were single parents, and three were employed out of the home. Presenting problems included dysfunctional, often violent familial relationships; child-rearing issues, particularly in the educational realm; financial and housing instability; and physical and emotional illness.

Content Analysis

Corradi's (1991) hermeneutic framework served as the basis for this study's content analysis. In this approach, the narrative text of the interview is viewed as an attempt, by both the interviewer and the interviewee, to give meaning to an aspect of the latter's social context. The told story provides a mechanism for giving order to past events through providing a connection between what the storyteller was before and is today, allowing for current perspectives to furnish retroactive significance. Analyzing the texts requires cognizance of the impact of the presence of the interviewer in the life of the interviewee, as well as the interviewer's subjective understanding of meanings adjudged accurate and attributed to the interviewee (Bruner, 1990; Rosenthal, 1993).

Themes that emerged from transcripts of the interviewees' success stories were discussed in conferences among the three readers, who reached a consensus regarding the justification of grouping quotations from the narratives into the following categories: (1) description of the client's/family's life before encountering the worker and the specific reason for that meeting: (2) a description of the client's/family's life after encountering the worker; (3) areas in which the client feels she was helped by the worker; and (4) attributions of success of the intervention, such as characteristics of the worker or client's life changes.

Analysis of the client's choice of words was based on the assumption that the language chosen reflected the significance of the event for the client (i.e., these words were understood as representing the experience undergone by each of the women). During the interviews, each participant was asked to indicate what meaning a specific word had for them (e.g., "help"), and, based on their replies, words or phrases were grouped into the data analysis section that follows.

After extracting the elements of success as perceived by the clients, we compared them to the existing literature dealing with multiproblem families. While each narrative was truly unique, it was possible to discern common threads, which we now present.

Findings

All the quotations from the interviewees cited below were translated from their original Hebrew by the authors.

Message of Help

The word "help" appeared in each of the interviewee's descriptions of a successful treatment experience. However, no two women used the term in quite the same way or with the same meaning. Our general impression is that success was linked to both the provision, in whole or in part, of some kind of assistance, as well as the manner in which it was given. It was important to these women that help come *from the heart* and not as the result of a *work* obligation. One woman described the difference between a social worker who did not help and one who did. Regarding the former, she said: "She works, she has to help me, she's obligated to help me, that's what she gets paid for, it's her work." While regarding the latter: "Why does this worker really help me, why does she put in so much effort, does she owe me something? But she loves her work, she gets satisfaction from helping people, so she puts in the effort to help me."

Five of these clients saw a significant difference between help received as the result of professional responsibility as opposed to sincere caring for their welfare. Moreover, they assumed an ability to differentiate between the two: "You can see that someone wants to help you" or "Not because it's work but it's from the heart." One woman observed: "To work with a group like me you need people who enjoy their work, and not where the main thing is to come because the job demands it or for the money or for the sake of the profession." These women needed to feel that the staff members truly wished to help them, even if the efforts bore no real fruit: "At least she tries, she doesn't say 'no' right away."

Nature of Help

Emotional   All of the interviewees cited the significance of emotional assistance, as expressed through sessions and conversations with staff members: "This helped me emotionally, it calmed me down" or "We talked once a week . . . and she helped me a bit to be encouraged about my situation." Sessions were described as a place where the women could feel temporally freed of their burdens, an experience that they defined as being helped: "She allows me to empty out all that I have to tell."

The sessions, and the implied level of emotional support, imparted not only a sense that someone sincerely cared about these clients. They also provided an opportunity for the interviewees to hear themselves and, thus, to more firmly anchor themselves in the context of a supportive relationship: "If there were a worker who would sit with me, who would speak to me so I wouldn't feel alone, like we're talking now, but now I don't have anyone," or "Even a sympathetic ear would be a help," or "I got a lot off my chest, there were days that I would show up crying . . . really . . . but when I left her [the worker] I felt as if I had unloaded a real burden and his helped me a lot." Even the freedom to repeat the same complaint was considered an aspect of a successful experience: "I can say the same thing to her a million times but she doesn't lose hope or tell me to give it up, or that she can't bear to hear these stories another time . . . she's not like that."

The opportunity to easily speak their minds in the presence of an active listener meant a great deal to these clients, and seemed to have a positive impact beyond the immediate moments of the client-worker interactions. As one woman perceptively noted:

> I want more of a sympathetic ear, that they should understand me more, they should understand what I say, that we should try to find help together . . . this helps me so much that it doesn't matter that I don't have something, that things are missing, at that moment I know that there is someone else I can speak to, this gives you such a feeling of relief.

Concrete Services   In the stories of eight of these clients, the provision of financial assistance or other types of concrete services figured prominently as markers of successful treatment: "They gave me a bed, they arranged an afterschool program, that also helped" or "It was a good thing that the welfare office in Tel Aviv gave me a bed, I didn't have a bed." One woman received help from a fund to which the social worker had referred her, another received financial aid to use for house repairs, and seven others used the assistance to purchase household items such as beds and closets.

We note with interest an ambivalent tone in these narratives regarding the interaction between emotional and financial help. On the one hand, interviewees stated that "money isn't the issue," while on the other, they maintained that "to talk and to talk" does not help if there is no concrete assistance. It appears evident from these stories that both kinds of help, emotional and concrete, needed be made available for the experience to be perceived as successful: "Talk as well as help with things . . . from every direction she was okay." One woman, who attempted to explain what kind of help was most important to her, best made this point:

> It's not the money. Even when she doesn't give enough money, when she talks with me, when she laughs with me . . . I don't want money, I don't want anything, I want help, for example,

one time before the holiday season, to give me a check to buy the children clothing.

Marital Counseling   The four women who participated in marital counseling tended to evaluate this treatment experience as successful: "The treatment that she [the social worker] did was successful . . . well, she decided that it was the right thing to do, to have sessions together and that maybe it was possible that in some way it would ease some of the pressure." This client went on to describe that the sessions ended because her husband refused to continue, but she credited the worker with a good idea and remembered the episode positively. Similarly, another interviewee recalled:

> It helped a little bit . . . you can't do everything at once . . . I mean it's impossible in a short time to do something about many years . . . for example, I cooked something, so what happened, I asked during one session that he should at least say thank you, it was good, but he never said anything . . . until one day he finally said it, that changed things a little.

These women were aware that significant dyadic change could take a considerable amount of time and that long-standing behavioral patterns did not shift easily. This perception allowed them to view minimal progress, or indeed the very presence of their husband in marital treatment, and the existence of a positive working relationship as examples of successful intervention. Some saw their husband's consent to marital counseling as the result of the worker's ability to join with these men: "He didn't like any of them [previous therapists], but this one was something else," or "He was very tough with her [the previous worker], but with this social worker he got along, he was with her also, but less," or "He didn't like everyone, but with her it was a little, he was more open, he was ready to cooperate, this helped to change things a little."

Raising Children   Among the most successful aspects of the helping experience for all participants centered on child care issues:

> Now they opened something new . . . they are doing a workshop for parents and children . . . there is one workshop just for parents and one just for children. They keep the kids busy . . . and we parents meet. It's guidance for parents about how to take care of children. Everyone brings up problems and we talk about them . . . I am really pleased with it.

These women did not perceive such efforts as invasive or as designed to monitor their parental functioning. They expressed concern regarding the welfare of their children and a desire to succeed as parents:

> Let's say there's a discipline problem with a child . . . So I really get angry; let's say the child lies to me . . . so I hate it when they lie to me . . . he lies because he's afraid of my reactions. I didn't understand that at first, but after I got some advice . . . I understood.

The interviewees valued the input from the professional staff, but clearly wished to perceive these interventions as advice rather than as directives. As one woman astutely recalled:

> There are workers who first you talk, like, then little by little they say something like another worker would but in a way like you don't feel like you're dumb, or that you don't know what you're doing, or that you're doing like stupid things. You don't get the feeling that you're stupid, like you don't know what to do, she makes it seem like you really decided on your own.

In this example, not only was the result discerned as successful, so was the technique.

Day Care and Placement   Success was also defined by the worker's skill in helping to find suitable child care: "She helped me by getting my child into the afterschool program." The nature of the assistance needed to connect these clients to day care and placement options for their children necessitated a variety of interventions: knowledge of the available alternatives, provision of financing, emotional support, and occasional influence. Somewhat surprisingly, out-of-home placement was also perceived as providing help with child rearing. One woman saw residential placement as an example of treatment success: "She helped me . . . she brought the children to the boarding school [residential facility] . . . she took them so it would be less difficult for me to raise them and all that." Another said: "I wanted him to go to the boarding school, she helped and they took him, I also want him to come back home but he is a tough kid, he doesn't behave, it's hard for me with him, we don't get along."

Group Experiences   In their narratives of successful treatment, six of the women spoke their participation in various kinds of support groups, primarily around women's or parent-child issues. Their positive memories focused on the caring and professionalism of the social workers who had referred them to the group at least as much as the group leaders themselves:

> I just told her that I very much feel that I'm always in the house because the kids are little . . . I invest a lot of time in the house and almost never go out anywhere, so one day she came with a suggestion that there is a group of people where they serve refreshments and everyone can bring up her problems . . . it was her idea, she gets a lot of credit for that.

Discussion

Referring to work with multiproblem families, Rosenfeld and Sykes (1998) have noted: "Only through learning about their experiences, perceptions, and understandings, can researchers learn what they and others like them need and how they can best be helped" (p. 294). In their perceptive and often poignant narratives, these 11 women offer the listener (and reader) a rather cogent evaluation of the help they have received through client-worker contacts. Despite the unique quality of each story, several strands emerge, which should prove valuable for an enhanced understanding of this population.

Interventions were not evaluated from an all-or-nothing vantage point. These women saw various aspects of assistance—from financial support to emotional relief—as constituent parts of the broad range of help. Some women reported coming to see the social workers for concrete services and ending up being helped more by the sessions, while others came for emotional help and, in the process, also required and received concrete services. This confirms research findings by Blumberg, Ely, and Kerbeshian (1975) regarding the needs of parents of hospitalized children:

> Those clients whose initial view of the social worker was as a source for providing concrete services changed their ideas and expressed satisfaction with the fact that the social worker had dealt with their emotional concerns. (p. 47)

Similarly, from the perspective of changes in their lives, there are clear indications of a sophisticated and progressive view of therapeutic success. Thus, the very measures taken by social workers toward engendering change, even when not brought to fruition, were considered as constituting a form of success. The fact that the clients related to the various dimensions of the worker's helping capacity indicates that the words and actions of this specific professional became deeply engraved in the personal experiences of the women.

These clients exhibited sensitivity to the complex character of their presenting problems and a willingness to consider a range of options, as long as they saw themselves as partners in the process. This was starkly illustrated in the understanding several of the women had of their children's need for residential placement and on the effect such a disruption would have on themselves and the children. This is all the more noteworthy when one considers an expressed ongoing desire to see themselves as effective parents.

The women objected strongly to restrictive perceptions and "expert" attitudes on the part of helping professionals, seeing these stances as undermining their trust in the helper and the nature of the help. They desired professionalism and competence, someone who could grasp the problem and find a solution, but not at the expense of a loss of self-respect or freedom of choice. None of the women offered as an example of help a situation adequately dealt with their dictatorial means.

Limitations

We call the reader's attention to three factors that may influence the significance of any data or analyses presented. First, while original content analyses were done in Hebrew, our use of translations in this article may distort meanings and blur nuances. The fact that the authors are English-Hebrew bilingual but with opposite mother tongues has helped sensitize us to the complexity of this task.

Second, we acknowledge the inherent difficulty in extrapolating from 11 personal stories to reach conclusions significant to wider populations. However, in using a narrative research methodology, we have tried to convey the richness and passion of the intervention experiences of "real" clients, a perspective not available in quantitative designs.

Third, we believe that this study fulfills three of Riessman's (1993) criteria for validity: (1) reasonable and convincing interpretations; (2) coherence of specific themes; and (3) pragmatic availability of this study for other researchers.

The fourth criterion, allowing the interviewees to respond to our interpretations, was not done,

and in retrospect should have been. We are comforted, though, by Riessman's (1993) words: "Whether the validity of an investigator's interpretations can be affirmed by member checks is, however, questionable. . . . In the final analysis, the work is ours. We have to take responsibility for its truths" (pp. 66–67).

Conclusion

These stories of success demonstrate that despite life narratives fraught with despair, failure, and disappointment, the women recognized the kind of help they needed in their arduous life situations and were capable of identifying and evaluating specific professional activities. Furthermore, they were able to request and make use of a practical combination of concrete and emotional interventions and to define the most effective style of work.

We see this study as underscoring the principle that as consumers of treatment, clients should be asked what kind of services they wish to receive. Social work assumptions about the manner in which multiproblem families perceive successful treatment could be confirmed or refuted if those seeking help were themselves asked for their views. In 1969, Mayer and Timms wrote, "Clearly treatment effectiveness will increase when casework practitioners, researchers, and mental health personnel in general give more thought and attention to the outlook of clients" (p. 32). Although narrative perspectives are no longer foreign to social work (Sherman & Reid, 1994; Rodwell, 1998), almost 30 years later, our awareness still needs to be sharpened:

> "Good enough" service requires that service providers be oriented towards learning from the families what it is they need and how they can best be helped . . . This type of service provision is in contradistinction to the familiar situation in which providers approach service transactions, armed with a set of relatively standardized, fixed responses. (Rosenfeld & Sykes, 1998, p. 290)

As both practitioners and researchers, we evaluate the narrative approach as particularly effective in understanding and helping families that have myriad problems in various life domains. Such a perspective assists in grasping the totality of their experience and not merely its isolated components. In this vein, we submit the following from Whan (1979):

The move vivid and present the story can become to client and social worker, the more it is possible to understand the narrative context within which predicament and suffering are experienced. The story will begin to show the client's relationship to his troubles, how he comprehends them and wishes others to understand them. (p. 495)

Finally, we remind our colleagues, our students, and ourselves that the provision of concrete services demands the same level of empathy, judgment, and creativity as does the utilization of the most finely crafted therapeutic interventions.

We are grateful to Professor Suzanne Sered for her assistance with narrative research methodologies and to the reviewers for their significant contributions.

References

Benvenisti, R., & Yekel, H. (1986). Family intervention: A description and evaluation. *Society and Welfare, 7*(2), 142–155.

Blumberg, D. D., Ely, A. R., & Kerbeshian, A. (1975). Clients evaluation of medical social services. *Social Work, 20*(1), 45–47.

Bruner, J. (1990). *Acts of meaning.* Cambridge, MA: Harvard University Press.

Christoph-Wyler, Y. (1998). *The contribution of a socio-educational day service to neglected and maltreated children and their families.* Unpublished master's thesis, Paul Baerwald School of Social Work, The Hebrew University of Jerusalem.

Corradi, C. (1991). Text, context and individual meaning: Rethinking life stories in a hermeneutic frame. *Discourse and Society, 2*(1), 105–118.

Cowan, P. A. (1999). What we talk about when we talk about families. *Monographs of the Society for Research in Child Development, 64*(2), 163–176.

Giordano, P. C. (1977). The client's perspective on agency evaluation. *Social Work, 22*(1), 34–39.

Guba, E. G., & Lincoln, Y. S. (1994). Competing paradigms in qualitative research. In Denzin, N. K., & Lincoln, Y. S. (Eds.), *Handbook of qualitative research* (pp. 105–117). Thousand Oaks, CA: Sage.

Hartman, A. (1994). Setting the theme: Many ways of knowing. In E. Sherman & W. J. Reid (Eds.), *Qualitative research in social work* (pp. 459–463). New York: Columbia University Press.

Hines, P. M., Richman, D., Maxim, K., & Hays, H. (1989). Multi-impact family therapy: An approach to working with multiproblem families. *Journal of Psychotherapy and the Family, 6*(1–2), 161–176.

Jaffe, E. D. (1983). Fathers and child welfare services: The forgotten client. *Society and Welfare, 5*(2), 126–133.

Krumer-Nevo, M. (1998). What's your story? Listening to the stories of mothers from multi-problem families. *Clinical Social Work Journal, 26*(2), 177–194.

Levine, R. A. (1964). Treatment in the home. *Social Work, 9*(1), 19–28.

Mayer, J. E., & Timms, N. (1969). Clash in perspective between worker and client. *Social Casework, 50*(1), 32–40.

McKinney, G. E. (1970). Adapting family therapy to multi-deficit families. *Social Casework, 50*(1), 32–40.

McNeil, C. B., & Herschell, A. D. (1998). Treating multi-problem, high stress families: Suggested strategies for practitioners. *Family Relations, 47*(3), 259–262.

Mishler, E. G. (1986). *Research interviewing: Context and narrative.* Cambridge, MA: Harvard University Press.

Patton, M. Q. (1990). *Qualitative evaluation and research methods.* Newbury Park, CA: Sage.

Rabin, C., Rosenberg, H., & Sens, M. (1982). Home based marital therapy for multiproblem families. *Journal of Marital and Family Therapy, 8*(4), 451–460.

Reimal, B., & Schindler, R. (1994). Family-of-origin work with multi-problem families. *Journal of Family Psychotherapy, 5*(1), 61–75.

Ribner, D. S., & Knei-Paz, C. (in press). The client's view of a successful helping relationship. *Social Work.*

Riessman, C. K. (1993). *Narrative analysis.* Newbury Park, CA: Sage.

Rodwell, M. K. (1998). *Social work constructivist research.* New York: Garland Reference Library.

Rosenfeld, J. M. (1964). Strangeness between helper and client: A possible explanation of non-use of available professional help. *Social Service Review, 38*(1), 17–25.

Rosenfeld, J. M., Schon, D. A., & Sykes, I. J. (1995). *Out from under: Lessons from projects for inaptly served children and families.* Jerusalem: JDC-Israel, Children at Risk Area, JDC-Brookdale Institute of Gerontology and Human Development.

Rosenfeld, J. M., & Sykes, I. J. (1998). Toward "good enough" services for inaptly served families and children: Barriers and opportunities. *European Journal of Social Work, 1*(3), 285–300.

Rosenthal, G. (1993). Reconstruction of life stories: Principles of selection in generating stories for narrative biographical interviews. In R. Josselson & A. Lieblich (Eds.), *The narrative study of lives* (Vol. 1) (pp. 59–91). London: Sage.

Schlosberg, B. S., & Kagan, R. M. (1988). Practice strategies for engaging chronic multiproblem families. *Social Casework, 69*(1), 3–9.

Schorr, L. B., & Schorr, D. (1988). *Within our reach: Breaking the cycle of disadvantage.* New York: Anchor Books.

Sherman, E., & Reid, W. J. (1994). *Qualitative research in social work.* New York: Columbia University Press.

Whan, M. W. (1979). Accounts, narrative and case history. *British Journal of Social Work, 9*, 488–499.

HELENE EBENSTEIN
JENNIFER WORTHAM

73

The Value of Pets in Geriatric Practice: A Program Example

Introduction

A program designed to help elderly pet owners is succeeding in reaching people in unexpected ways. Older clients who are willing to accept help for their pets, but not for themselves, at first participate in the program for services such as dog walking and transportation to a veterinarian. In time, they get to know and trust the volunteer and social worker providing the services. The relationships that develop because of a shared concern for the well-being of an animal eventually create an opportunity for wary seniors to begin dealing with other important issues.

The catalyst for change in the PETS Project is the powerful bond between pets and people. When staff and volunteers also feel this profound love of animals, the bond between them and the seniors can encourage the seniors to be receptive to the offer of other sources. For example, the program became the vehicle for staff to identify and discuss with seniors other services they needed and to help them secure the services. This program meets a need so important to one group of the elderly that they are able to overcome their reluctance to participate. The program also acknowledges and pays respect to the central role of a pet in the lives of many elders. Although their importance is routinely overlooked by social work agencies, pets are often considered members of the family and may be the closest or even the only companion of an isolated senior.

This paper will describe the services offered by the PETS Project and the ways they are delivered. It will also highlight how the PETS Project, by viewing a beloved pet as part of a client's support system, offers additional benefits. Participating in the PETS Project benefits clients in four important areas beyond pet-related services by:

1. Establishing an ongoing social work connection which can be tapped in case of an emergency.
2. Increasing social contacts through regular volunteer visits.
3. Reducing the severity of housing problems caused or exacerbated by the pet(s).
4. Creating the opportunity to discuss end-of-life issues.

The intent of this discussion is to demonstrate how a sincere interest by a social work agency in providing services to elder pet owners can have unexpected impact in other significant ways. The PETS Project represents one example of how integral animals are to the lives of many clients. For the elderly, in particular, the relationship with a pet is often especially intimate, anchoring their world. Tapping into the intense feelings that are a part of this relationship helps to establish a bond with a client that may lead to work in other areas. Whether developing a program involving animals or working with an elderly client who has a pet, it is important that social workers be open to the many ways animals are connected to older people.

Program Description

The PETS Project was launched in 1997 by a large urban community-based agency to address the needs of elderly pet owners who are too frail and/or poor to adequately care for their pets. Clients residing in one borough are helped with routine pet care and also in emergency situations such as their hospitalization. Volunteers who live or work nearby are teamed with clients and their pets and provide assistance tailored to the needs of each client. Volunteers also serve as links with seniors who are often isolated and eager for company and conversation. The client-volunteer teams are overseen by the coordinating social worker, who conducts an initial in-home evaluation and is fully involved in the day-to-day activities of each team.

Not all clients seek regular visits from a volunteer. Some are able to handle the routine care of their pet. They worry, however, about what will happen to their pet if they are hospitalized or die. In fact, several clients have firmly rejected treatment requiring hospitalization for this reason. To address the problem, social workers ask clients about plans for their pets in case of an emergency. If no plans are in place, the seniors are encouraged to begin talking to family, neighbors, and friends and, if possible, make arrangements for both short- and long-term care of their pet. For those clients who cannot make arrangements, the PETS Project seeks a volunteer willing to care for the pet temporarily. The volunteer makes a home visit with the social worker to meet the client. They set up an emergency plan and the client reviews the pet care routine, including food, walking, and medication.

The PETS Project has a small relief fund to help clients who cannot afford to pay for needed pet services and/or their own expenses. The fund may cover costs such as veterinary care, emergency dog walking or cat sitting, boarding, and pet food. The fund also helps clients with unexpected expenses such as repair or replacement cost of appliances, unusually high utility bills, and their own medical bills. The aim is to prevent pet owners from having to make dangerous financial sacrifices which might endanger their own health and the health of their animals.

The PETS Project coordinator keeps in touch with ongoing phone calls and holiday cards. When additional social work services may be needed, the coordinator pursues this with the client. The coordinator is also available to provide services to pets in emergencies. When volunteers are involved, the coordinator speaks to them regularly and encourages them to call with any concerns. Volunteers may, for example, have problems dealing with the client or pet. They may also observe a change or decline in the client's situation and want to alert the coordinator. In this way, relationships form and clients receive the assistance that they determine is needed. At the same time, they get to know and trust the program's social workers and volunteers.

The program began in 1997 with seed money of $6,000 from a foundation who funded it for the first year. The agency allowed the social worker to allocate seven hours of a 35-hour week to begin building the PETS Project into a working program. This enabled the agency to invest 28 hours on case management and counseling, supplementing the cost of the worker while avoiding the difficult problem of finding a part-time worker for one day a week. The time was not strictly measured. The PETS Project Coordinator began slowly. As the program grew toward the end of the year, the worker spent more than the seven hours weekly and was given a proportionately reduced caseload for four days.

The second year, the program requested funds from a few foundations and received $35,000 from one organization known for its work with community agencies. As this amount covered the worker's salary as well as partial OTPS expenses, the program expanded to full time. Smaller amounts of $5,000 and $1,000 were received from sources whose focus is the protection of animals. This money went toward the PETS Project relief fund. Over the past two years, the PETS Project has surpassed regular case management and counseling programs in monies spent on pet care and for assistance to pet owners. The agency supplemented with client relief fund of approximately $2,500 for 12 months.

During the past three fiscal years, the PETS Project has served 65 clients with pets, the numbers growing from 33 clients in 1998 to an average of 50 clients served at any given time in 1999. For the current fiscal year (2000–2001), the PETS Project is on target for meeting its goal of 60 clients served. One full-time social worker is responsible for all aspects of the program. Handling the day-to-day operations of client-volunteer teams and the ever-present emergencies is the primary responsibility. Other major tasks include recruiting clients and volunteers, training volunteers, collaborating with social workers both within the agency and from other community-based agencies, collaborating with professionals involved with pet care, compiling a database of pet-related services, educating health care staff and community residents, and raising money for the relief fund.

Volunteer recruitment efforts are ongoing, taking place on many fronts. The PETS Project is included on several Internet sites and databases (national volunteer site, university sites, mayor's office database). Participating in fairs and seminars, publicizing through newspapers, posting flyers in the neighborhood, and working with corporations that learn of the program through an interested volunteer have all been effective. Each volunteer completes an extensive questionnaire and is interviewed personally. Only people who have experience with animals are considered and references are obtained. Currently there are 37 volunteers of all ages. Teaming a volunteer with an appropriate client requires good assessment skills. Training is individualized and focuses mostly on reviewing appropriate volunteer tasks in general and for the particular client, setting realistic expectations and goals, suggesting tips on interacting with many older people (e.g., speak up), handling the initial meeting with the client (meeting both the client and the pet, setting up a schedule, dealing with client's worries), and debriefing after the initial meeting. Volunteers are also given an overview of the agency and its mission and detailed information about the PETS Project and pet-related services that are available. Training is ongoing as the coordinator and volunteer speak regularly and whenever any issues or problems arise. The accessibility of the coordinator is extremely important in retaining volunteers. The PETS Project coordinator encourages volunteers to call, spends time discussing programs, fears, and concerns, advises, volunteers, and brainstorms with them.

Review of the Literature

During the past 25 years, studies have shown repeatedly that people benefit physically and emotionally by associating with animals. Being with an animal appears to correlate with lower blood pressure (Katcher, 1982), greater chance of surviving a heart attack (Friedmann & Thomas, 1995), lower rate of depression and fewer doctor visits (Jessen, Cardiello & Baun, 1996; Siegel, 1990). Caring for a pet also strengthens feelings of usefulness and a sense of responsibility and helps to structure each day (Brickel, 1980; Carmack, 1991). Researchers attempting to confirm these correlations have gotten mixed results. Some found improved health status due to pet ownership and other studies indicated that a more complex relationship exists between pets and health benefits Raina, Woodward & Abernathy, 1999). According to Beck and Meyers (1996), at the very least, interaction with animals resulted in improved morale.

Animal-assisted therapy is increasingly used successfully with both children and adults in a variety of settings (Beck & Katcher, 1996; Sable, 1995). Pet therapy has helped patients suffering from cancer, depression (McCulloch, 1983), and severe mental illness (Corson & Corson, 1980). In a program for cancer patients and their families, animals decreased fears, despair, and loneliness (Muschel, 1984). Elderly people living alone or in nursing homes have responded well to interactions with therapy animals (Brickel, 1980). Serpell (1996) noted that relationships with pets appear able to "break down the barriers of despair and disillusionment" which makes some people less accessible to conventional forms of treatment (p. 97).

When researchers ask pet owners about their animals, the responses reflect intense mutual attachments. Cat owners, asked what they get from their cat that they don't get from people, cited "unconditional love and affection," "undivided loyalty and devotion," and "total acceptance" (Zasloff & Kidd, 1994). Other pet owners said that they talk to their pets as if they were people, and more than 30% of one subject group said that they confide in their pet (Beck & Katcher, 1996).

Beck and Katcher (1996) discuss the special ways pets are important to the elderly. In one study conducted in Sweden, 15% of elderly pet owners considered their pet their most significant social contact, giving their life meaning. Despite the problems of old age, a pet's continuing affection is a sign that the essence of a person remains intact. It does not matter that his owner feels old and unwanted (Levinson, 1972) or fails the tests of beauty and wealth. For an older person who has survived many losses, the constancy of an animal's affection and acceptance are treasures.

Several articles on animal-assisted therapy mention the role of the volunteer who accompanies an animal on visits (Harlock & Sachs-Ericsson, 1998; Savishinsky, 1992). Savishinsky noted that the importance of the social and sensory stimulation provided by animals was often superseded by the relationship developed with the accompanying volunteers. Also mentioned in the literature are the ways volunteers benefit by participating in programs. Volunteers in a home care program reported that their work enhanced their self-esteem and well-being. Luks and Payne (1991) go even further, claiming that volunteering keeps people healthy. More than 90% of the volunteers they studied reported that regular volunteering relieved stress. Volunteering may also alleviate problems such as hypertension, arthritis, and depression.

Benefit's of the Program beyond Animal Care

Although the focus of the PETS Project is assisting seniors in care for their pets, participants have benefited in other important ways. The four major benefits beyond pet care are discussed below and illustrated by examples involving PETS Project participants. The examples are based on the authors' experiences in developing and implementing the PETS Project.

Establishing an Ongoing Social Work Connection

The PETS Project's clients range from those who have extensive experience with social work agencies to people who have never before been involved with an agency. People dealing with a social work agency for the first time may feel uncomfortable speaking to a social worker. Some immediately state that they are managing well and would normally not be contacting an agency. Others go even further by voicing their distrust of social workers and by recounting negative stories. Clients persevere, however, because of concern for a pet.

At times, the social worker senses that there are other serious problems which the client may not be acknowledging. For example, clients may be experiencing deteriorating health, severe financial problems, and increasing inability to care for themselves. At other times, the client's statement about managing well agrees with the social worker's observations. In any event, the client's wishes are respected and only the pet care is initially pursued while the social worker keeps a watchful eye.

Without doubt, the focus on their pets is the only reason some clients will agree to a home visit from a social worker. That an agency realizes how vital their pets are to their clients goes a long way in beginning to forge bonds. Of course, the coordinator's comfort with and love of animals is essential. It demonstrates that the people connected with this program share their views about animals and can be trusted. This approach markedly contrasts with typical agency questions about an animal. Community nursing agencies, for example, ask about pets to identify dangerous dogs that should be avoided when making home visits (Davis & Juhasz, 1984).

Despite their initial distrust, most clients eventually become more comfortable talking to the social worker. Where a volunteer is involved, the client has even more opportunity to develop a relationship and gain trust. The presence of an animal helps a great deal. Pets serve as ice-breakers and facilitate conversation. Brickel (1980) notes that anxious client appear to be soothed by focusing on pets, which can be used as a starting point. A pet's ability to give "tactile reassurance" may also encourage the client to become more communicative.

Brickel's (1980) observations parallel the experiences of those involved with the PETS Project. Visits or phone calls most often center on the client's pet, at least initially. Home visits, especially, provide a great opportunity to overcome barriers. Greeting a pet, enjoying its antics, and encouraging the client to talk about the pet are fun and help a wary client to relax. Often, the client will switch the focus from a pet to other issues during the course of the visit or call. The groundwork has been laid, which makes it more possible to seek help in the future. If the client's situation begins to deteriorate or eventually becomes unacceptable, the lines of communication are open. Problems present at the outset may now be pursued. New problems may be mentioned. A case example from the PETS Project is illustrative.

Christine S., a 79-year-old widow, appeared healthy and vigorous despite a serious heart condition. During the initial home visit, the coordinator noted Ms. S.'s energy, upbeat manner, and spotless apartment. Ms. S. was interested only in making arrangements for her cat, Bella, in case she was hospitalized. She had already arranged in her will for Bella's care after her death but had nothing in place for the short term. Since none of her friends agreed to take on this responsibility, the coordinator located a volunteer who lived in the neighborhood. She visited Ms. S., learned Bella's routine, and agreed to temporarily care for Bella in case of an emergency.

The coordinator kept in touch with Ms. S., who seemed appreciative of the contacts but always stated that things were going well. One call was very different, Ms. S. sounded shaken and worried. During a hastily arranged home visit Ms. S. advised that her heart condition had worsened; it was increasingly difficult for her to cook, clean, and walk and she feared that she would soon have to move to a nursing home. She also acknowledged that her income was so low that she barely made ends meet.

After reviewing various options with Ms. S., the coordinator assisted her in filing for Medicaid, which will help with her medical costs and also provide ongoing home care so that she can continue to live at home. The presence of a positive social worker-client relationship enabled Ms. S. to promptly learn about available options and file for Medicaid so that she could get much needed services.

Increasing Social Contacts through Volunteer Visits

Most PETS Project clients are in their seventies and eighties, have difficulty getting around, and tend to stay at home. Often, they have outlived most family members and friends. Many do not have children or their children have died. Where there are children, they either do not live in the area or the relationships are strained. Even ambulatory clients are not interested in joining programs for seniors. Many feel isolated and lonely, relying on their pet for companionship. Pets usually sleep with clients and stay beside them throughout the day. They are stroked and kissed by seniors who may have no other oulet for touch and affection.

When the PETS Project teams a senior with a program volunteer, the teaming can develop a mutually positive relationship and expand the senior's support system. The coordinator, who has interviewed both, attempts to match compatible people who are also conveniently located. The starting point for the relationship is the focus on the pet tasks that the volunteer will perform. A schedule is negotiated and there are discussions about the volunteer's experience with animals as well as the preferences of clients and pets. Before the volunteer provides any services, the client, volunteer, and pet must feel a certain level of comfort with each other. In effect, they are all getting acquainted. The coordinator will get involved if problems crop up. If, however, the match is not a good one, either party may opt out. Another volunteer is then sought, if appropriate.

Some teams get on well immediately. By the end of the first visit, the senior is going through picture albums with the volunteer. Usually, however, teams progress more slowly and cautiously. Regardless of the rate of progress, most clients come to look forward to visits and phone calls from the volunteer. Sometimes the volunteer is the only caller or visitor for days at a time. The visits become the highlight of a client's week. Volunteers freely acknowledge that they also benefit from teaming with a PETS Project client. Younger volunteers talk about living far from their grandparents or missing grandparents who have died. The seniors whom they visit offer an opportunity to spend time with a person who has years of experience. Some volunteers love animals but cannot have them now, so the PETS Project is a way for them to be with an animal. Volunteers also enjoy the attention they receive from the client and the satisfaction of helping someone who could really use their services. Some lasting friendships are formed. Occasionally, volunteers visit with their own friends or family. A client may invite a volunteer for dinner or they may go to a restaurant together. The following PETS Project case is an example.

Anne G. is a warm and friendly but frail woman in her mid-eighties. She had been caring for her husband for many years with the help of home attendants and spent almost all of her time at home. The couple had no children and all other family members had died. Ms. G. had two cats which she had trouble caring for. One cat, Sammy, had a chronic illness requiring ongoing medication and regular trips to the veterinarian. The PETS Project located a young woman who worked near Ms. G.'s apartment. She began visiting several times a week to help with these tasks.

The visits became important social events for Ms. G. After Sammy was attended to, the volunteer and Ms. G. spent time talking and sometimes went out for a meal together. The volunteer occasionally brought her husband on her visits. When Ms. G. expressed a longing for a computer so that she could begin writing again, the volunteer arranged for her husband to bring over a computer that was being replaced by his company. Both the volunteer and Ms. G. state that they have become good friends and both feel enriched by the relationship. Ms. G. is using the computer to write stories about her life.

Reducing the Severity of Housing Problems

One unexpected benefit of the PETS Project is the chance to work with clients who have serious housing issues. The presence of an animal may cause or at least contribute to unsafe and unhealthy conditions in the home. Some clients are living in apartments reeking of urine and feces. Often, feces are actually present most of the time. The pet owners cannot, for example, walk the dog as needed, so "accidents" happen throughout the day. Cleaning up is sometimes more than the owner can manage. Cat owners cannot bend down to clean out the litter box. Since most cats require a clean litter box, they will find other places to use if that is not provided. Pet food creates additional problems. Food and water kept out for animals attracts insects and vermin. Furniture as well as the client's clothing become covered with animal hair, adding to the disorder. The deterioration of the apartment is usually gradual, and elderly pet owners are less able to see clearly what is happening, smell the stench, and to do something about it.

The end result is an environment that is unsafe and unhealthy for both the owner and the pet. Socialization is also affected as friends and family avoid visiting. Justifiable complaints from the neighbors and landlord compound the situation. Elderly pet owners caught in this dilemma are often paralyzed and/or defensive. Even when faced with potential eviction, the possibility of giving up an animal is unthinkable. There is no way, however, that they can keep their apartments clean.

Several clients living in such situations for years do no seem bothered by the condition of their apartments. They became involved with the PETS Project because a friend, relative, or anther social worker contacts the program, often in desperation. The pet owners do not see what all the fuss is over, but agree that their dog enjoys a brisk walk in the park or their cat loves to be brushed. These clients often distrust outsiders. They have been criticized about the state of their apartment because of their pet and fear that people are trying to take away their animal. The coordinator must be reassuring about the purpose of the PETS Project and clear that the client determines the extent and pace of the Project's involvement. Clients always have the right to think about participation while getting to know a potential volunteer on several visits before making a decision.

The choice of a volunteer in such a situation is crucial. The volunteer must be prepared and willing to spend time in an unclean environment and often interact with a difficult client. Training and ongoing support of the volunteer are essential. If the teaming works well, wary people will respond positively when they see the volunteer's genuine concern and love for their animal. Again, this shared feeling for animals creates a powerful bond. Despite these efforts and the best intentions, the reality of the situation may overwhelm the volunteer, who eventually withdraws from the team (Savishinsky, 1992).

If a client chooses to participate and a volunteer is involved, the animal is better cared for and the condition of the apartment is somewhat improved. The volunteer alone, however, cannot solve the more systemic problem. Usually much

more work is needed to restore and maintain the cleanliness of the apartment. If there is agreement, the social worker will work with the client, involved family, landlord, and others on ways to prevent further deterioration and to begin a cleanup. Even in the most severe situations, the coordinator was surprised at the willingness of landlords to cooperate with clients and not to pursue eviction. This was so despite sometimes strong pressure from angry neighbors. Often, however, the client does not agree to a clean-up. The client and animal still benefit from the volunteer and the link that has been established and can be used if there is an emergency. A PETS Project case example is illustrative.

Frances K.'s social worker contacted the PETS Project in desperation. In addition to many other problems, Ms. K. had received a warning from the Department of Health about the unsafe conditions in her apartment caused by the seven cats she had rescued over the years but was unable to adequately care for. Ms. K.'s neighbors were pressing the landlord for eviction. Her daughters, who lived in the neighborhood, were distraught and angry over her behavior. Ms. K.'s social worker could not convince her to take action to get the apartment in order. She steadfastly refused to place any of the cats but was willing to "talk to an animal lover" from the PETS Project. Although she expressed fear that the project coordinator might forcibly remove her cats and was reluctant to provide much information about them, she did agree to participate in the program.

Working collaboratively with the primary social worker, the coordinator visited and suggested methods for reducing the strong odors in the apartment and also contacted a lawyer specializing in animal rights and housing for advice. Ms. K. was somewhat receptive, and even bought an air purifier, but certainly did not appear to be as concerned about her situation as were her family and social workers. A volunteer who had years of experience with cats offered to visit and help Ms. K. clean her litter boxes. The coordinator prepared the volunteer about what to expect. Ms. K. welcomed the volunteer and seemed to look forward to her visits and the apartment was slightly improved. After one month, however, the volunteer found the condition of the apartment so unbearable that she could not continue visiting. Ms. K. appeared disappointed but not surprised. The family, primary social worker, coordinator, and landlord continue to work together to try to stabilize Ms. K.'s housing. Ms. K. remains peripherally involved. So far, the landlord has not taken action to begin eviction.

Discussing End-of-Life Issues

The question of what will happen to their pets if they die or are suddenly hospitalized is on the minds of many elderly pet owners. Whether or not they express their concerns, the fear remains. Relatively few translate their fear into a plan. One study found about 50% of elderly pet owners said they have plans for their pet if they are no longer able to care for it, but the authors questioned whether the plans were workable (Smith, Seibert, Jackson & Snell, 1992). The PETS Project experience found a much lower percentage of clients had such plans. If there are no clear arrangements in place, often an animal control agency removes a pet and it is euthanized. The owner's worst fear comes to pass.

One of the goals of the PETS Project is to encourage people to talk about and begin making plans for their pet. Several authors, including Davis and Juhasz (1984) and Smith et al. (1992), have noted the importance of this goal. Clients are not pushed to do this, but the issue is routinely raised during the initial visit. An excellent pamphlet on the topic, which recommends providing for a pet in a will, is provided. Reviewing the pamphlet also serves as an avenue for discussing wills. The reaction of clients varies. It ranges from a sense of relief for the chance to discuss the unmentionable, to anger at the social worker for raising an upsetting topic. The coordinator pursues the issue with receptive owners. For those less willing to talk about arrangements, the coordinator suggests that clients look at the pamphlet and leaves the topic for future discussion.

One of the unexpected benefits of raising this topic is the chance for some people to talk about their own death. The two issues are so intertwined that the focus on the client's death is a natural consequence. The opportunity to talk about death also arises when a pet is seriously ill or dies. The connection between human and pet loss is strong and may allow grieving elders to address some of their own fears and hopes. Since many clients own old pets, they often face this situation. The anxiety and grief caused by a pet's illness or death can be overwhelming, as noted by Quackenbush and Glickman (1984) and Sable (1995). For older people the reaction may be especially severe since they have already suffered many losses and rely on their pet for companionship and comfort. Clients may begin to worry that they are overreacting and try suppressing feelings that need to be examined and expressed. Friends and family who do not understand the depth of the loss may exacerbate the situation.

At such times, the involvement of the PETS Project is critical. The volunteer and social worker have an ongoing relationship with the client and understand the impact of the pet's illness or death. They, too, worked with and cared about the animal. The client can express intense feelings confident that the reaction will not be dismissed or viewed as crazy. The social worker might also suggest a bereavement group. During the bereavement process the client may begin talking about his own death or the death of a family member with the social worker, who can provide support and counseling. A PETS Project example illustrates such a situation.

Anna K., an 83-year-old woman, had been devotedly caring for her 93-year-old husband for nearly 10 years. Mr. K. was semicomatose since suffering a stroke and required around-the-clock attendant care. The home attendants were an important part of Ms. K.'s life and served as a surrogate family. Mr. K.'s condition was deteriorating and recently he had been admitted to the hospital to treat recurring infections. Ms. K. was determined to keep Mr. K. alive and could not bear to imagine her life without him. Her social worker was very concerned about Ms. K.'s ability to cope with her husband's impending death.

Ms. K. was referred to the PETS Project for help with her cat, Saralee, who needed medication for a thyroid condition. A volunteer began visiting regularly and giving Saralee her medication. After one year, Saralee's condition worsened. Ms. K. was distraught at the possibility of losing her and her social worker encouraged her to express her feelings and fears and provided supportive counseling. The social worker was sensitive to the connection between the loss of Saralee and Ms. K.'s fear of her husband's death. When Saralee died, the agency's primary social worker and the PETS Project coordinator worked collaboratively to assist Ms. K. They pointed to the strengths she demonstrated in coping with the loss. Two months later Mr. K. died. Ms. K. adjusted well and found she could continue on with her life. She was helped by the need to keep going so that she could take care of the cat she adopted after Saralee's death.

Conclusions

The importance of a pet in the life of an older client cannot be overemphasized. Social workers who recognize the value of pets and aim to preserve the bond between the elderly and their animals increase the probability of working effectively with seniors. One approach is to develop programs similar to the PETS Project model. Programs specifically geared to pet owners meet an urgent need for an unrecognized population. Using volunteers to provide many of the services helps to keep down the costs of the program. Whether or not a program focuses on pets, however, social workers can draw on the human-animal bond to connect with seniors.

Four major benefits beyond pet care are highlighted in this paper: establishing an ongoing social work connection, increasing social contacts through volunteers, reducing the severity of housing problems, and creating the opportunity to discuss end-of-life issues. Although the focus was a program designed to support pet owners, the benefits are applicable to many situations in which social workers are involved with elderly clients who have pets.

1. The presence of a pet helps to overcome barriers to communication and trust. By initially focusing on a pet, wary seniors have a chance to get to know a social worker (and volunteer) in a less threatening way. This process is facilitated by acknowledging the importance of a client's much-loved pet. Should the client's situation deteriorate, the link to the social worker is available.
2. Regular visits from a volunteer who shares with the client a love of animals enrich the lives of both.
3. Frail seniors who can no longer walk a dog or clean a litter box are often living in apartments that are neither clean nor safe. They may be facing possible eviction. Visits from a volunteer and the involvement of a social worker can help to improve conditions in the apartment and avert eviction.
4. Encouraging people to make arrangements for a pet in the event of their illness or death creates an opportunity for a client to discuss end-of-life issues. Concern for an animal may be the catalyst for broaching an uncomfortable topic. The death of a pet may also lead to a discussion of the client's own death or the death of a family member.

Implications for Practice

For social workers to capitalize on the bond between older people and their pets, routinely asking about the presence of pets is an important first step.

Social work assessments are more complete when elderly clients are asked whether or not they have a pet. Affirmative responses allow a social worker to get a fuller picture of the client's living arrangements and social supports. Obtaining information about how the client cares for the pet and observing how the pet is treated offer a window into how the client is functioning. Where there are other family members, by focusing on a pet the social worker can also learn about how the family interacts and functions. Social workers may also get clues that predict how a client will respond to the illness or death of a pet (Carmack, 1991), which may help especially vulnerable clients obtain needed support. The question also demonstrates a concern that is unusual and may help to facilitate a positive relationship. Instead of viewing pets as problems, their role as companions and family members can be considered a resource and included in assessments. Just as Davis and Juhasz (1984) encourage nurses to use pets in clinical practice, social workers can also take advantage of the opportunities they offer.

Many elderly clients receiving home care need assistance not only for themselves but for their pets. Where home care costs are borne by the state, home care agencies advise home attendants that their role is to provide services to the clients but not the pet. Even when the home attendant is willing and able to care for the pet, this is not permitted. The regulation sometimes creates hardship. If the litter box needs to be cleaned or the dog needs to be walked, whom can the pet owner turn to when funds are limited? Of course, if there is a program such as the PETS Project in the area, this would be a valuable resource. Katcher (1982) discusses the dangerous consequences of policies encouraging the elderly to give up commitments such as the commitment to keep a pet. Social workers concerned about the message conveyed by the home care regulation might consider advocating for a change in the policy.

Information about pets is especially valuable when there is a possibility of hospitalization. By including plans for pets in discussions with clients who may need to be hospitalized, the social worker demonstrates an understanding of the pet's importance and also open discussion of a potential barrier to a client accepting treatment. When a client is hospitalized, information about pets is also vital. Patients who are distressed about a pet who is not being properly cared for may compromise their recovery and even leave the hospital prematurely. The information is also necessary when planning for discharge. Will the patient be able to care for a pet upon discharge or are support services necessary either temporarily or permanently?

Social workers might also work with an elderly client who does not own an animal but could benefit from a pet and is able to care for one. Of course, the possibility of adopting a pet should be carefully explored and evaluated with the client before taking action. The type of pet chosen and the size and age of the animal are all critical factors. The client's ability to pay for pet food and veterinary care is also important. Adoption might be especially successful for clients who had pets in the past and are aware of what is involved in caring for one. Where a client cannot make a long-term commitment, there is the option of foster care. Other clients might be receptive to regular visits from a volunteer accompanied by a trained therapy dog. Before discussing these possibilities, social workers should become familiar with community resources and programs involving pets and discuss the pros and cons with the experts who run the programs (Netting, Wilson & New, 1987).

Programs such as the PETS Project rely heavily on volunteers. When matches between volunteers and clients are not successful or volunteers drop out of pet programs, valuable opportunities are lost. More information is needed on volunteer selection, training, and ongoing support and motivation (Savishinsky, 1992). For example, one issue that arises with PETS Project volunteers is a realistic assessment about how much they can accomplish through volunteering. Setting limits with demanding pet owners is another program. Social workers involved with programs such as the PETS Project could benefit from more guidance on assisting volunteers throughout the process.

A social worker who is aware of the strength of the human-animal bond and its impact on the well-being of clients brings a more holistic perspective to practice. Social workers can serve as key professionals in this area by advocating for more programs that directly support pet owners. They can also contribute by using their knowledge of human-animal bonding in ongoing interactions with clients. Preserving and strengthening this vital connection can make the lives of many elderly people more fulfilling.

References

Beck, A. & Katcher, A. (1996). *Between pets and people* (Rev. ed.). West Lafayette, IN: Purdue University Press.

Beck, A. M. & Meyers, N. M. (1996). Health enhancement and companion animal ownership. *Annual Review of Public Health*, 17, 247–257.

Brickel, C. M. (1980). A review of the roles of pet animals in psychotherapy and with the elderly. *International Journal of Aging and Human Development*, 12 (2), 119–128.

Carmack, B. J. (1991). Pet loss and the elderly. *Holistic Nursing Practice*, 5 (2), 80–87.

Corson, S. & Corson, E. (Eds.) (1980). *Ethology and non-verbal communication in mental health*. New York: Pergamon Press.

Davis, J. H. & Juhasz, A. M. (1984). The human/companion animal bond: How nurses can use this therapeutic resource. *Nursing & Health Care* 5 (9), 497–501.

Friedmann, E. A. & Thomas, S. A. (1995). Pet ownership, social support and one-year survival after acute myocardial infarction in the cardiac arrhythmia suppression trial (CAST). *American Journal of Cardiology*, 76, 1213–1217.

Harlock, D. W. & Sachs-Ericsson, N. (1998). Volunteers and animal-assisted activity programs. *Journal of Volunteer Administration*, 7 (1), 22–28.

Jessen J., Cardiello, F. & Baun, M. M. (1996). Avian companionship in alleviation of depression, loneliness and low morale of older adults in skilled rehabilitation units. *Psychological Reports*, 78, 339–348.

Katcher, A. H. (1982). Are companion animals good for your health? *Aging*, (331–332) 2–8.

Levinson, B. (1972). *Pets and Human Development*. Springfield, IL: Charles C. Thomas.

Luks, A. with Payne, P. (1991). *The healing power of doing good: The health and spiritual benefits of helping others*. New York: Fawcett Columbine.

McCullouch, M.J. (1983). Animal-facilitated therapy: Overview and future direction. In H. Katcher & A. M. Beck (Eds.) *New perspectives on our lives with companion animals*. Philadelphia: University of Pennsylvania Press, pp. 410–426.

Muschel, I. (1984). Pet therapy with terminal cancer patients. *Social Casework*, 65 (8), 451–458.

Netting, F. E., Wilson, C. C. & New, J. C. (1987). The human-animal bond: Implications for practice. *Social Work*, Jan.–Feb. 60–64.

Quackenbush, J. E. & Glickman, L. (1984). Helping people adjust to the death of a pet. *Health and Social Work*, 9 (1), 42–48.

Raina, P., Woodward, C. & Abernathy, T. (1999). Influence of companion animals on the physical and psychological health of older people. *Journal of American Geriatric Society*, 47 (3), 323–329.

Sable, P. (1995). Pets, attachment and well-being across the life cycle. *Social Work*, 40 (3) 334–341.

Savishinsky, J. S. (1992). Intimacy, domesticity and pet therapy with the elderly: Expectation and experience among nursing home volunteers. *Social Service Medicine*, 34 (12), 1325–1334.

Serpell, J. (1996). *In the company of animals: A study of human-animal relationships* (Canto Ed.) Cambridge, England. Cambridge University Press.

Siegel, J. M. (1990). Stressful life events and use of physician services among the elderly: The moderating role of pet ownership. *Journal of Personality and Social Psychology*, 58 (6), 1081–1086.

Smith, D. W. E., Seibert, C. S., Jackson, F. W. & Snell, J. (1992). Pet ownership by elderly people: Two new issues. *International Journal of Aging And Human Development*, 34 (3), 175–184.

Zasloff, R. L. & Kidd, A. H. (1994). Attachment to feline companions. *Psychological Reports*, 74, 747–752.

SCOTT E. RUTLEDGE
ROGER A. ROFFMAN
CHRISTINE MAHONEY
JOSEPH F. PICCIANO
JAMES P. BERGHUIS
SETH C. KALICHMAN

74

Motivational Enhancement Counseling Strategies in Delivering a Telephone-Based Brief HIV Prevention Intervention

Introduction

Motivational enhancement treatment (MET) interventions are increasingly being added to the menu of behavioral interventions for reducing risk of HIV transmission among high-risk populations for several reasons. First, although a variety of theory-based HIV transmission risk-reduction interventions have been found effective (for reviews, see Auerbach, Wypijewska, & Brodie, 1994; Centers for Disease Control and Prevention, 1994; Choi & Coates, 1994; Kalichman, Carey, & Johnson, 1996; National Institutes of Health, 1997; Office of Technology Assessment, 1995; Wingood & DiClemente, 1996), a sizable number of individuals at risk of becoming infected, reinfected, or infecting others do not enroll in or drop out of such programs because of logistical and psychological barriers to participation. As many as half of the persons interested and eligible to enroll in HIV prevention interventions drop out, and one in five of those who enroll never shows up (DiFranceisco et al., 1998; Molitor, Bell, Truax, Ruiz, & Sun, 1999; Roffman, Picciano, Bolan, & Kalichman, 1997; Rutledge, Picciano, King, & Roffman, 1999; Rutledge, Roffman, Picciano, Kalichman, & Berghuis, under review). Further, it is likely that many of the highest-risk persons are not reached by traditional risk-reduction counseling (Hoff et al., 1997).

Second, economic burdens, policy constraints, and staffing limitations can restrict or prohibit the use of empirically tested effective interventions in community settings (Kalichman, 1998). While intervention programs demonstrated in research settings to be efficacious hold great potential for risk reduction, mounting them is sometimes not possible given lack of basic infrastructure within community and public health settings, especially in rural areas. Issues related to technology transfer are, of course, not unique to HIV prevention (Beutler, Williams, Wakefield, & Entwistle, 1995; Leviton, 1996).

Third, concerns about AIDS appears to be waning for some populations given recent success in treating HIV/AIDS. HIV prevalence among men who have sex with men (MSM) in the United States is increasing partly because of rising incidence, especially among young men and men of color, and partly because infected persons are living longer as a result of successes in treating HIV disease. Evidence suggests norms supporting safer sex may be slipping for some at-risk populations wherein individuals perceive HIV as less threatening given the well-publicized successes of highly active antiretroviral treatment (HAART) (Vanable, Ostrow, McKirnan, Taywaditep, & Hope, 2000). It also appears some HIV-positive men with undetectable viral loads are having risky sex because they believe they are not infectious (Vanable et al., 2000).

Through reduced intervention duration that lowers barriers to participation and completion, brief MET provides a potential remedy for the problem of attracting and retaining individuals ambivalent about HIV transmission risks in higher dosage interventions. Designed to address directly but nonconfrontationally ambivalence and to stimulate or reinforce risk-reduction attitudes and practices, MET for HIV prevention has been demonstrated to be feasible and holds promise for efficacy among MSM (Picciano, King, & Roffman, 1999; Picciano, Roffman, Kalichman, Rutledge, & Berghuis, in press), including HIV-positive MSM (Ryan, Fisher, Peppert, & Lampinen, 1999), and MSM who are substance abusers (Beadnell et al., 1999). MET has also been found efficacious among injecting drug users (Baker, Kochan, Dixon, Heather, & Wodak, 1994).

In this article, we describe one example of a brief motivational enhancement intervention that was recently pilot-tested for feasibility and promise for efficacy. The Sex Check-Up (SCU) was conceived and designed in response to the need to engage at-risk gay and bisexual men who were ambivalent about safer sex. Results from 89 participants in a pilot trial indicate its potential efficacy for promoting safer sex practices among at-risk MSM (details on outcomes have been reported elsewhere; Picciano et al., 1999; Picciano et al., in press). Following a description of the key concepts of motivational interviewing and elaboration of the structure and delivery of the SCU, we present and discuss a series of cases representing a range of themes to illustrate its practice applications with gay and bisexual men at risk for HIV infection, reinfection, or transmission.

Motivational Enhancement: Theory and Applications

MET is not a bailiwick unique to HIV prevention. Across health and mental health practice domains, programs designed to assist clients achieve behavior changes increasingly have been constructed as brief forms of treatment based on MET principles. A growing literature supports the efficacy of brief interventions in facilitating behavior change in smoking cessation (Bruvold, 1993), cardiovascular risk reduction (Scales, 1998), weight loss and diabetes management (Mullen, Mains, & Velez, 1992; Smith, Heckemeyer, Kratt, & Mason, 1997), adherence to mental health and substance abuse treatments (Daley, Salloum, Zuckoff, Levent, & Thase, 1998), and alcoholism and substance abuse (Anderson & Scott, 1992; Bien, Miller, & Tonigan, 1993; Brown & Miller, 1993; Cisler & Zweben, 1999; Miller & Heather, 1998; Stephens, Roffman, & Curtin, 2000; Wells, Peterson, Calsyn, Perry, & Jackson, 2000; Zweben & Rose, 1998). Among

their advantages, brief interventions decrease treatment burdens for clients and are cost-effective.

As a component of motivational enhancement or in addition to routine services, health and mental health professionals increasingly use motivational interviewing (Miller & Rollnick, 1991; Rollnick, Mason, & Butler, 2000) as a counseling strategy to enhance the likelihood of behavior change for individuals at all stages of readiness for behavior change (Prochaska & DiClemente, 1984). Developed as an alternative to other forms of treatment that may assume clients are ready for change, motivational interviewing is designed to assist individuals identify and explore multiple facets of behavior and cognition that both hinder and spur change.

The Check-Up, specifically structured as a nontreatment opportunity for a low-burden exploration of one's experiences, is an amalgamation of brief interventions and motivational interviewing tailored for use with persons ambivalent about making behavioral changes. Initially designed for use with problem drinkers (the "Drinker's Check-Up"; Miller & Sovereign, 1989), the Check-Up is theorized to be especially helpful for individuals in early stages of readiness for change. Such individuals may be receiving social messages and cues that their behavior is unacceptable, or they themselves may be uncomfortable with their behavior but not be ready to take action steps toward change. These persons often resist enrolling in educational interventions or therapeutic treatment that assumes they are ready to change. The Check-Up can be ideal for individuals in early stages of readiness for change who are experiencing cognitive dissonance about their behavior and present as ambivalent about behavior change. Utilizing the tenets of motivational interviewing, the Check-Up takes place in two steps. First, clients undergo an assessment of a target problem, their attitudes toward change, and self-efficacy. Second, a counselor trained in motivational interviewing provides a counseling session to assist clients in exploring feeling with no pressure to change behavior.

Principles of Motivational Interviewing

To be optimally effective, brief interventions advocate personal responsibility and bolster self-efficacy by providing pertinent feedback, advice as requested about a range of options for behavior change, and encouragement (Miller & Rollnick, 1991). The design of the Check-Up meets such criteria by assessing individuals and providing normative comparisons (e.g., how an individual's frequency of unprotected intercourse compares with peers), working with clients to brainstorm a variety of change strategies, and reinforcing previous success. Engaging and sustaining client participation, however, can be challenging, especially with stigmatized individuals who fear (and may have previously received) judgmental responses about their behavior. Therefore, direct confrontation of denial or resistance is undesirable in motivational enhancement.

Motivational interviewing provides an alternative approach to engaging clients who are resistant to change. Rather than confronting the client's denial that a problem exists, motivational counselors use a variety of counseling approaches based on the five principles of motivational counseling: (1) expressing empathy, (2) developing discrepancies, (3) avoiding argumentation, (4) rolling with resistance, and (5) supporting self-efficacy (Miller & Rollnick, 1991).

Express Empathy Unconditional positive regard for clients includes normalizing ambivalence. The counselor responds with a warm and accepting tone that allows clients to be heard and not pressured. Using reflective listening, counselors echo back clients' cognitions and statements about feelings. The intention is that clients who had expressed ambivalence about change suddenly feel freer to contemplate change.

Develop Discrepancies A discrepancy is a contradiction between present behavior and important personal goals. Many clients realize their behavior may be harmful, but have not adequately assessed the costs and benefits of continuing or stopping. Motivational interviewing seeks to assist such individuals in identifying consequences of their behaviors and changing or not changing. This is in opposition to forced awareness of consequences presented by important persons in a social network, the law, or other threats. The intention is that clients will become more motivated to change when they hear themselves realizing a situation requires change rather than being told they must change. Thus, the counselor optimizes opportunities for clients to express motivation for change.

Avoid Argumentation Direct argumentation likely leads to defensiveness in clients. The counselor uses motivational interviewing skills to support safely the client's self-confrontation about the need to change. This process is intended to help clients discover and illuminate the need for change. The use of labels and direct acknowledgment of resistance are avoided. Client defensiveness is a signal for the counselor to change strategies.

Roll with Resistance Client resistance toward the counselor can take a variety of forms, including challenges, interruptions, denial, and ignoring. Rather than viewing resistance as an obstacle to overcome, motivational counselors use these moments to recognize that clients are feeling misunderstood. A variety of techniques are available for rolling with resistance, including shifting the focus, reframing defensive statements, and simple, amplified, and double-sided reflection. For example, to build momentum toward shifts in perception, counselors use amplified reflections where they exaggerate what the client has just said. Clients often then back down from their statement and express the other side of their ambivalence. Because the spirit of motivational interviewing is one of client self-determinism, a menu of new perspectives is respectfully offered for consideration without expectation they will necessarily be adopted.

Support Self-efficacy Once clients have recognized problematic behavior and begun to generate solutions, self-efficacy is supported. This final principle of motivational interviewing bolsters hope in the process of change for clients. This is accomplished by expressing optimism for and confidence in the client. Additionally, previous success in change for the current issue or related past problems can be emphasized to remind clients that they are self-efficacious and responsible for their own lives.

Rationale and Structure of the Sex Check-Up

The Sex Check-Up (SCU) was conceived and designed following the framework of the Drinker's Check-Up. Postulating that a number of gay and bisexual men experience ambivalence about safer sex and that some shy away from prevention programs with implicit expectations for change, we advertised the SCU as an opportunity for such men to talk with a nonjudgmental counselor about their sexual risk without any expectations for behavior change. Flyers distributed at venues frequented by the target population and paid advertisements in gay and gay-friendly newspapers described the SCU as a research project for men with concerns about their sexual safety. In addition, outreach workers recruited individuals on the street and presented programs to gay/lesbian and AIDS service organizations. To facilitate participation by individuals distrustful of AIDS counseling services or unable to travel to an office setting, the SCU was delivered entirely by telephone with optional anonymity.

From data collected during assessment interviews that lasted about 90 minutes, a personalized feedback report (PFR) was constructed and mailed to the participants. Individuals choosing to enroll anonymously were reimbursed for renting post office boxes to which their materials were mailed. The PFR summarized assessment data in seven sections: recent sexual activity, use of alcohol or drugs, intentions to use condoms, reasons for having sex, consequences of safer sex, benefits and losses of practicing safer sex, and confidence in employing a variety of safer sex strategies. The assessment and counseling staff were racially and sexually diverse and shared sex-positive and gay-affirming value orientations.

The structure of the feedback sessions included a warm-up during which the counselor introduced herself or himself and provided an overview of their time together. At the end of the structured review of the PFR, participants were invited to reflect on where they found themselves in relation to their concerns about safer sex. They were then asked if they wanted to engage in goal setting where cognitive behavioral skills training was employed as needed.

It was important to begin to establish rapport immediately. Because the intervention took place by telephone, facial expressions and body posturing could not be used to assess participant comfort. Instead, counselors gauged client readiness to move forward by vocalizations: we simply asked participants if they were ready to begin or to move on and listened for vocal hesitations. To begin the session, the counselor provided a brief statement about her or his role in the project and experiences working with gay and bisexual men. Then participants were invited to ask additional questions about the counselors and to introduce themselves. Some participants wanted to begin the feedback immediately while others wanted to know more about the counselor or the process before beginning. Next, the process was summarized as an opportunity for participants to reflect on their recent sexual activity and any particular concerns they had through a structured review of the PFR. It was emphasized that the session was not about telling participants what to do. True to the check-up modality, reviewing each section of the PFR and eliciting self-motivational statements constituted the bulk of the session. To maintain research fidelity among participants, it was important to stick to the structure, but not so rigidly as to miss opportunities to reinforce motivation for change. We found it helpful occasionally to note with the participant the significance of a particular concern or theme and plan to return to the issue and discuss it more in detail later in the session.

At the end of the PFR review, we simply asked, "So, where do you find yourself?" This was a pivotal moment wherein clients reflected on their current needs as predicated by their individual readiness for change. Some responded that reviewing their personal information had been helpful, but they were ready to end the call. Some wanted to clarify issues that had arisen. Others were ready to strategize behavioral change. For such participants, the focus shifted from exploring ambivalence to exploring concrete ways of achieving important personal goals. As a variation of the "miracle question" (de Shazer, 1988), we asked participants, "Imagine that a year has gone by and you no longer have these concerns. How did you go about accomplishing this goal?" In this way, we maintained a focus on client self-determinism in building self-efficacy. At this point some individuals accepted our invitation to engage in skills training. While the focus was still on the participant to develop solutions, the counselors now played the role of expert and dispensed advice about cognitive behavioral strategies, including managing risky situations through avoidance or escape, sexual communication skills including assertiveness and negotiation, and other forms of self-regulatory behavior including self-talk, imagery, rewarding, feeling good, and relaxation.

The closing moments of the feedback counseling session were used to say goodbye and to offer referrals for other HIV prevention services or social support. Some participants were interested in referrals for additional therapy, educational or support groups, or substance abuse treatment. Four different handouts had been prepared to send to clients who wanted specific safer sex coping strategies.

Case Presentations

Following are five brief case examples drawn from the Sex Check-Up to illustrate how we applied motivational interviewing principles with a variety of MSM at risk for HIV infection or transmission. To protect confidentiality, names have been changed and identifying information slightly altered in the case descriptions. To be eligible, participants were required to be male and at least 18 years of age, to have had unprotected anal or oral intercourse at least three times with another man in the prior six weeks, and not to be in mutually monogamous or negotiated safety relationships of more than six months' duration. Average age of SCU participants was 36; they ranged from 18 to 70. Mean educational achievement was 15 years. Reflective of Seattle, 24% were men of color. Eighty-three percent identified as gay and 17% as bisexual. Forty-five percent were partnered with another man. Regarding stage of readiness to change, slightly more than half were in precontemplation or contemplation; the rest were in preparation, action, or maintenance. About one-third (36%) of the men reported some concern about their current use of alcohol or drugs. Most (80%) had multiple sexual partners, and 9% reported either paying for or being paid for sex. Although the intervention was directed at HIV transmission risk reduction, related issues arising in the feedback sessions including homophobia, abuse histories, relationship issues, self-esteem, and bereavement.

Milton: Ambivalent about Consistently Using Condoms for Oral Sex

Newly single in the last one and one-half years, 42-year-old Milton called to see if his current practices were in line with current recommendations for safer sex. Milton was somewhat unusual compared to other men in the study: he likes condoms and sometimes uses them for oral sex. His personal feedback report noted he said he had used condoms two of the 10 times he had had oral intercourse in the previous six weeks. Milton was surprised and dismayed by normative data provided in the report that indicated he was having more unprotected oral sex than 35% of his gay male peers. This technique highlighted an important discrepancy. Although Milton had sometimes used condoms for oral sex despite prevailing community norms not to do so, the normative data suggested he still wasn't being as safe as he had thought. During his assessment interview, he said there would be a 50–50 chance that he would consistently use condoms for receptive oral sex. On considering the benefits and losses of practicing safer sex, Milton noted that he often feels guilty after unprotected oral sex. Additionally, he was not confident about negotiating safer sex and was concerned sex partners would reject him for proposing using condoms for oral sex. By the end of the counseling session, Milton had changed

his intention; he wanted always to use condoms for receptive oral sex.

Why the change and what techniques contributed to the motivational enhancement? Three of the five general principles of motivational interviewing were utilized. By simply paraphrasing Milton's statements that he was surprised and unhappy about having had unprotected oral sex despite his affinity for and desire to use condoms, a discrepancy between present behavior and important personal goals was developed. He then asserted that he wanted to recommit to safer oral sex. To support his self-efficacy, the counselor proposed a short role-play wherein Milton asked a sexual partner about using condoms for oral sex. Following this, the counselor expressed optimism and confidence in the participant's abilities. Milton then stated he felt, with practice, he would become more confident in negotiating protected oral sex. Further, he made plans to do additional role-plays with a steady sex partner and his counselor (he was in ongoing individual therapy for family of origin issues).

Graham: Vulnerable to Risky Sex Associated with Drug Use

Like a number of men in the study, Graham grappled with issues of substance use and safer sex. Thirty-one years old and bisexual, Graham was concerned because he had recently had unprotected anal sex with a man even though it was their first sexual encounter. The other man was aggressive and they had smoked pot. He was finding that when he is high, he is more likely to have unsafe sex. A second issue involved recommitting to using condoms for oral sex. A former HIV/AIDS peer educator, Graham insisted on using condoms for oral sex in the past. However, he stopped this practice about one and one-half years previously. A third issue emerged in the Graham was not practicing safer sex with a female partner.

Seemingly, he had all the answers. He thought he should probably limit his use of marijuana, return to using condoms for oral sex with men, and have a lengthy conversation with the woman with whom he had a casual sexual relationship of three months. These discrepancies seemed resolvable. However, Graham's calm and assured voice changed when the discussion shifted to discussing the implications of safer sex. His voice shook and he acknowledged feeling emotional. Expressing empathy became center stage, yet somewhat tricky because the intervention was taking place by phone and not in person. Gentle probes revealed that he found it hard to negotiate boundaries and that he wanted to be more assertive about safer sex. By the end of the counseling session, Graham repeated his commitment to contemplate further his use of marijuana, recommit to using condoms for oral sex, and to negotiate sexual safety with his female partner.

James: Negotiating with Sex Workers

A 50-year-old military nurse who provides care for people living with AIDS, James felt a conflict similar to Graham's: he wants to be safer but is not. Because of his military career, James is very closeted and hires sex workers through classified ads. He reported having had 11 partners and using a condom only once out of nine occasions of anal sex and never for the 25 occasions of oral sex during the six weeks prior to his assessment.

James responded well to the framework of motivational enhancement. He presented as completely baffled and somewhat resistant to the idea that he could make any changes with paid sex partners. He felt he had no control over the situation. The counselor rolled with resistance by turning questions back to the participant. When the counselor cautiously paraphrased reluctance as "hopeless," James heard himself described as feeling he had no control over whether condoms were used because he relied on his sex partners to bring up the topic. Suddenly, consumer rights became the focus of the discussion. James realized "I should get what I pay for!" He then asked the counselor to help him strategize ways to communicate his desire for safer sex with his commercial sex workers. Supporting self-efficacy became important and was accomplished through the use of a role-play wherein James told the sex worker (role-played by the counselor) that he was paying him for anal sex *with* condoms. He recounted a sense of confidence in the interaction. Additionally, James brainstormed other methods of communication and seemed pleased to discover he could communicate his insistence on using condoms by simply leaving condoms in plain sight and by handing a condom to a sex partner while walking down the hallway to his bedroom.

Steve: Sorting through Issues of Responsibility

Steve is HIV-positive and stated he is intellectually tired of taking responsibility for other people's sexual safety. He prefers not to use condoms for anal sex unless his partner asks. He said he feels each man is responsible for his own safety. Steve is a top

(he prefers to penetrate others rather than be penetrated) and assumes if a bottom does not ask him to use a condom that he is also HIV-positive. Empathy was a crucial issue. Steve stated he was not concerned about reinfection or other STDs, but the counselor wanted to further explore—without becoming argumentative—whether Steve was concerned about infecting others. Because he wants to have sex but does not want to disclose his HIV status, Steve goes to bathhouses where he assumes everyone is infected. The counselor identified a discrepancy in the participant's beliefs by paraphrasing his statement that "every man in the baths is HIV-infected." Further exploration of this belief resulted in a statement of guilt. This was painful for Steve; he did not want to think about the possibility that he could be infecting other men. The counselor needed to roll with his resistance to discuss this sense of guilt further. This session was more about consciousness-raising than behavior change.

Rudy: Maintaining Safety through Building Self-Efficacy

On seeing a SCU ad, Rudy thought it might be a good way to take a look at his sex behavior, especially since he "slips up" now and then. He was 23 years old and had been single for the previous year. Rudy said that when he has unprotected anal intercourse, it's because he gets caught up in the heat of the moment. In terms of oral sex, he has never used condoms, but has "heard it's a good idea." His version of safer oral sex is to not swallow ejaculate. Rudy would like ot have more sex and occasionally years for "flesh on flesh" anal intercourse. He has a history of using crystal methadone and cocaine, but stopped about one year ago without clinical support.

An unusual discrepancy arose around self-efficacy. Generally, SCU participants were unsafe and wanted to be safer and hoped they could learn some new safety strategies. Rudy had been safer during anal sex, but he stated there would only be a 50–50 chance that he would consistently use condoms for anal sex in the future. He did not want to set himself up for failure by being "idealist instead of realistic." This elaboration of the nature of his intentions concerning condoms came about as a result of rolling with resistance. His real difficulty appeared to lie in his confidence to employ safer sex strategies such as stopping sex when it started to become unsafe or asking a partner to use condoms. The counselor then asked the participant what techniques he had used to overcome his cocaine and crystal methadone dependence. Rudy suggested that it was due in part to visual imagery. Making a connection, he wondered if he might do the same with safer sex. The call ended with Rudy's conviction to practice visualizing taking charge of sexual situations by putting condoms on himself or his partners.

Summary and Conclusions

The presented cases highlight uses of the five principles of motivational counseling. Assisting participants in identifying discrepancies between behavior and important personal goals is key to the success of this intervention. In the present case of safer sex, education was not the issue; for the most part, gay and bisexual men know they "should" practice safer sex and know how to use condoms. This was certainly the case with Graham. He had already identified his behavioral discrepancy—he wanted to be safe but had recently been unsafe— and his counselor was able to help him further cement his desire to return to safer behavior through paraphrasing and by expressing both empathy and confidence.

Developing discrepancies is not always so straightforward. For example, Steve's discrepancy was not apparent to the counselor at the outset. Steve explained that he was "intellectually tired" of the "positive-negative debate." Being HIV-positive, he did not want to be responsible for others' safety and purposely chose a sex venue—a bathhouse—where he assumes everyone is HIV-positive. Through paraphrasing, it became clear that his decision to avoid safer sex discussions with sex partners still placed him in a bind. The discrepancy became clear when he expressed guilt that he might infect someone who made the opposite assumption about HIV status because the norm of the baths was not to discuss safer sex. Steve was struggling with intellectually rationalizing his decision while being emotionally conflicted over its potential negative outcomes.

As supported by the literature that suggests knowledge and attitudes alone are not sufficient to ensure sexual safety, a common theme for many of the participants centered on self-efficacy. Rudy's case is illuminating: his personal feedback form indicated he had not engaged in unprotected anal sex, his intentions to use condoms for anal sex were only 50–50, and he was not confident in using safer sex strategies. Rudy explained this apparent discrepancy as his need to not set himself up for failure. His ultimate goal was always to be safe, but he said it was more realistic to set

the bar lower to leave room for improvement. As with many of the participants, the counselor needed to sort through issues of confidence and self-efficacy.

Interpreting self-efficacy can be difficult. Some participants said they were not confident utilizing a particular strategy, but in fact they felt the strategy was inappropriate given the context of their sexual experiences. For example, men who frequented bathhouses said venue norms discouraged discussion of safer sex. While they might be comfortable discussing condom use with sex partners in another setting, doing so in a bathhouse was not culturally appropriate. Thus, it is necessary to contextualize self-efficacy.

Avoiding argumentation cannot be overstressed. Because the Check-Up is a one-shot opportunity, confrontation by the counselor is risky. Steve might have engaged in argumentation, but his counselor avoided this. Steve, like a number of HIV-positive men, was defensive about whether he should disclose his serostatus. Rather than directly confronting what seemed to be faulty thinking about "everyone in the baths being negative," Steve's counselor further developed this discrepancy through paraphrasing and gentle probes rather than direct confrontation.

As always, exceptions apply. Graham was initially defensive about gender differences in safer sex; he was safe most of the time with his male partners but not with his female partner. His counselor found it possible to point out this perceived discrepancy and associated rationalizations by first asking permission. Graham was asked, "If it's okay, I'd like to ask you a question that may seem a bit confrontational. Would that be okay?" He consented and the counselor noted that it appeared he might be less concerned about his female partner's safety than that of his male partners. In this way, argumentation was avoided but an important issue was addressed.

Empathy is a requisite skill for most forms of counseling. In the Check-Up, empathy is crucial. Because there is less time to develop a counselor-client relationship, counselors must be able to provide warmth so that clients can voice politically incorrect or socially undesirable responses, such as not wanting to take responsibility for protecting others or for paying or being paid for sex. One participant responded to a probe by asking if he should give "the answer you want to hear" or if he should respond truthfully. A telephone-administered Check-Up provides special challenges in expressing empathy because the counselor and client cannot see one another. Empathy can be expressed through warm vocalizations, but it is more difficult to gauge clients' reactions. For example, it seemed that Graham was quite comfortable in exploring his ambivalence and the counselor might have missed an important moment. Hearing a change in Graham's voice, the counselor simply inquired, "How are you doing?" The participant then acknowledged that he was feeling distressed. The counselor's consistent empathy earlier in the session likely provided Graham comfort to go deeper in exploring his discrepancies.

Resistance took a variety of forms in the Sex Check-Up. Some individuals appeared to be participating only to earn the research incentive payment. This form of resistance requires the counselor to weigh the relative advantages of probing versus using simple empathic paraphrases. In a time-limited intervention, further exploration may not be possible. Another type of resistance is manifested as passivity on the part of the client. For example, one person acknowledged he had participated in intensive therapy for a number of years because he is a registered sex offender. This man appeared to be resistant because his responses were very brief. It was as though he wanted the counselor to tell him what to do. The counselor rolled with this resistance by turning questions back to the participant.

We suggest future work in motivational enhancement should focus on three areas. First, as elaborated in a review of the uses of the transtheoretical model for change with HIV risk reduction (Prochaska, Redding, Harlow, Rossi, & Velicer, 1994), counselors should adopt a variety of strategies for individuals at different stages of change. For example, work could be focused on refining consciousness-raising approaches for gay and bisexual men who are just beginning to contemplate adoption of safer sex practices. Another alternative would be to explore further counseling approaches for men who have initiated change but remain inconsistent in safer sex. Second, in light of successes achieved through Project RESPECT (Kamb et al., 1998) in brief interventions that combine motivational enhancement with skills building, additional work should be dedicated to exploring ways to transition into skills building whenever appropriate. Finally, because the enrollment by some individuals in motivational enhancement might represent either initial contacts or reconnections with help seeking, additional efforts should also be directed to connecting (and tracking for research purposes) individuals to the array of available HIV-prevention programs.

This research was supported by a Centers for Disease Control and Prevention National Center for HIV Prevention grant (R18/CCR015252) awarded to the second author. The first author was supported by the National Institute of Mental Health Pre-Doctoral Research Training Program for Prevention Research in Mental Health Problems and Behavioral Disorders (T32 MH 20010-02).

References

Anderson, P., & Scott, E. (1992). Randomized control trial of general practitioner intervention in men with excessive alcohol consumption. *British Medical Journal, 87,* 891–900.

Auerbach, J. D., Wypijewska, C., & Brodie, H. K. H. (Eds.). (1994). *AIDS and behavior: An integrated approach.* Washington, DC: National Academy Press.

Baker, A., Kochan, N., Dixon, J., Heather, N., & Wodak, A. (1994). Controlled evaluation of a brief intervention for HIV prevention among injecting drug users not in treatment. *AIDS Care, 6,* 559–570.

Beadnell, B., Rosengren, D., Downey, L., Fisher, D., Best, H., & Wickizer, L. (1999, August 31). *Motivational interviewing to facilitate reduced HIV risk among MSM alcohol users.* Paper presented at the National HIV Prevention Conference, Atlanta, GA.

Beutler, L., Williams, R., Wakefield, P., & Entwistle, S. (1995). Bridging scientist and practitioner perspectives in clinical psychology. *American Psychologist, 50,* 984–994.

Bien, T. H., Miller, W. R., & Tonigan, J. S. (1993). Brief interventions for alcohol problems: A review. *Addiction, 88,* 315–336.

Brown, J. M., & Miller, W. R. (1993). Impact of motivational interviewing on participation and outcome in residential alcoholism treatment. *Psychology of Addictive Behaviors, 7,* 211–218.

Bruvold, W. H. (1993). A meta-analysis of adolescent prevention programs. *American Journal of Public Health, 83,* 872–880.

Centers for Disease Control and Prevention. (1994). *HIV counseling, testing and referral: Standards and guidelines.* Atlanta, GA: Author.

Choi, K.-H., & Coates, T. J. (1994). Prevention of HIV infection. *AIDS, 8,* 1371–1389.

Cisler, R. A., & Zweben, A. (1999). Development of a composite measure for assessing alcohol treatment outcome: Operationalization and validation.

Alcoholism, Clinical and Experimental Research, 23(2), 263–271.

Daley, D. C., Salloum, I. M., Zuckoff, A., Levent, K., & Thase, M. E. (1998). Increasing treatment adherence among outpatients with depression and cocaine dependence: Results of a pilot study. *American Journal of Psychiatry, 155*, 1611–1613.

de Shazer, D. (1988). *Clues: Investigating solutions in brief therapy.* New York: Norton.

DiFranceisco, W., Kelly, J., Sikkema, K. J., Somlai, A. M., Murphy, D. A., & Stevenson, L. Y. (1998). Differences between completers and early dropouts from 2 HIV intervention trials: A health belief approach to understanding prevention program attrition. *American Journal of Public Health, 88*(7), 1068–1073.

Hoff, C. C., Kegeles, S., Acree, M., Stall, R., Paul, J., Elkstrand, M., & Coates, T. (1997). Looking for men in all the wrong places: HIV prevention small group programs do not reach high risk gay men. *AIDS, 11*, 829–831.

Kalichman, S. C. (1998). *Preventing AIDS: A sourcebook for behavioral interventions.* Mahwah, NJ: Lawrence Erlbaum.

Kalichman, S. C., Carey, M. P., & Johnson, B. T. (1996). Prevention of sexually transmitted HIV infection: A meta-analytic review of the behavior outcome literature. *Annals of Behavioral Medicine, 18*, 6–15.

Kamb, M. L., Fishbein, M., Douglas Jr., J. M., Rhodes, F., Rogers, J., Bolan, G., Zenilman, J., Hoxworth, T., Malotte, C. K., Iatesta M., Kent, C., Lentz, A., Graziano, S., Byers, R. H., & Peterman, T. A. (1998). Efficacy of risk-reduction counseling to prevent human immunodeficiency virus and sexually transmitted diseases: A randomized controlled trial. *Journal of the American Medical Association, 280*(13), 1161–1167.

Leviton, L. (1996). Integrating psychology and public health: Challenges and opportunities. *American Psychologist, 51*, 42–51.

Miller, W. R., & Heather, N. (1998). *Treating addictive behaviors.* (2nd ed.). New York: Plenum.

Miller, W. R., & Rollnick, S. (1991). *Motivational interviewing: Preparing people to change addictive behavior.* New York: Guilford Press.

Miller, W. R., & Sovereign, R. G. (1989). The check-up: A model for early intervention in addictive behaviors. In T. Loberg, W. R. Miller, P. E. Nathan, & G. A. Marlatt

(Eds.), *Addictive behaviors: Prevention and early intervention.* Amsterdam: Swets and Zeitlinger.

Molitor, F., Bell, R. A., Truax, S., Ruiz, J. D., & Sun, R. K. (1999). Predictors of failure to return for HIV test results and counseling by test site type. *AIDS Education and Prevention, 11*(1), 1–13.

Mullen, P. D., Mains, D. A., & Velez, R. (1992). A meta-analysis of controlled trials of cardiac patient education. *Patient Education and Counseling, 21*, 837–841.

National Institutes of Health. (1997). Interventions to prevent HIV risk behaviors. *NIH Consensus Statement, 15*(2), 1–41.

Office of Technology Assessment. (1995). *The effectiveness of AIDS prevention efforts.* Washington, DC: American Psychological Association Office on AIDS.

Picciano, J. F., King, K. A., & Roffman, R. A. (1999, September 1). *A telephone based brief intervention to motivate safer sex practices among MSM.* Paper presented at the National HIV Prevention Conference, Atlanta, GA.

Picciano, J. F., Roffman, R. A., Kalichman, S. C., Rutledge, S. E., & Berghuis, J. P. (in press). A telephone based brief intervention using motivational enhancement to facilitate HIV risk reduction among MSM: A pilot study. *AIDS and Behavior.*

Prochaska, J. O., & DiClemente, C. C. (1984). *The transtheoretical approach: Crossing traditional boundaries of therapy.* Homewood, IL: Dow Jones-Irwin.

Prochaska, J. O., Redding, C. A., Harlow, L. L., Rossi, J. S., & Velicer, W. F. (1994). The transtheoretical model of change and HIV prevention: A review. *Health Education Quarterly, 21*(4), 471–486.

Roffman, R. A., Picciano, J. F., Bolan, M., & Kalichman, S. C. (1997). Factors associated with attrition from an HIV-prevention program for gay and bisexual males. *AIDS and Behavior, 1*(2), 125–135.

Rollnick, S., Mason, P., & Butler, C. (2000). *Health behavior change: A guide for practitioners.* New York: Churchill Livingstone.

Rutledge, S. E., Picciano, J. F., King, K.-A., & Roffman, R. A. (1999, August 30). *Attrition from a brief motivational intervention to reduce unsafe safe behavior among MSM.* Paper presented at the National HIV Prevention Conference, Atlanta, GA.

Rutledge, S. E., Roffman, R. A., Picciano, J. F., Kalichman, S. C., & Berghuis, J. P. (under review). HIV prevention and attrition: Challenges and opportunities.

Ryan, R., Fisher, D., Peppert, J., & Lampinen, T. (1999, August 31). *Pilot results of a brief intervention to reduce high-risk sex among HIV seropositive gay and bisexual men.* Paper presented at the National HIV Prevention Conference, Atlanta, GA.

Scales, R. (1998). *Motivational interviewing and skill-based counseling in cardiac rehabilitation: The Cardiovascular Health Initiative and Lifestyle Intervention (CHILE) study.* Unpublished dissertation, University of New Mexico, Albuquerque.

Smith, D. E., Heckemeyer, C. M., Kratt, P. P., & Mason, D. A. (1997). Motivational interviewing to improve adherence to a behavioral weight-control program for older obese women with NIDDM: A pilot study. *Diabetes Care, 20,* 53–54

Stephens, R. S., Roffman, R. A., & Curtin, L. (2000). Comparison of extended versus brief treatments for marijuana use. *Journal of Consulting and Clinical Psychology, 68,* 898–908.

Vanable, P. A., Ostrow, D. G., McKirnan, D. J., Taywaditep, K. J., & Hope, B. A. (2000). Impact of combination therapies on HIV risk perceptions and sexual risk among HIV-positive and HIV-negative gay and bisexual men. *Health Psychology, 19*(2), 134–145.

Wells, E. A., Peterson, P. L., Calsyn, D. A., Perry, S. M., & Jackson, T. R. (2000, June). *Motivational enhancement to decrease drug use among cocaine users: A stage II efficacy trial.* Paper presented at the Problems in Drug Dependence Conference, San Juan, Puerto Rico.

Wingood, G. M., & DiClemente, R. J. (1996). HIV sexual risk reduction interventions for women: A review. *American Journal of Preventive Medicine, 12,* 209–217.

Zweben, A., & Rose, S. J. (1998). Innovations in treating alcohol problems. In D. Biegel & A. Blum (Eds.), *Innovations in practice and service delivery with vulnerable populations.* New York: Oxford University Press.

75

Resolving Therapeutic Impasses by Using the Supervisor's Countertransference

A little over four decades ago when I was a supervisor at a treatment institution for emotionally disturbed youngsters, I was summoned one day to the director's office. Without warning I was told that as part of the process of being groomed to be his assistant director, I would be required to fire one of my supervisees. Very anxious, extremely self-conscious, and most uncertain about how I would conduct myself, after much hesitation I arranged an appointment with my supervisee. With enormous trepidation, I initiated the discussion by asking, "How is it going, Melvin?" To my deep consternation, Melvin confidently and enthusiastically responded, "I think you are doing a good job!"

Although Melvin's reply to my query might be considered somewhat unconventional even in the year 2000, it was "out of this world" in 1959. Forty years ago a supervisee was almost always deferential to his supervisor and hardly ever made evaluative remarks about her. He did what he was told without ever questioning the directive, as I behaved when my supervisor told me to fire Melvin.

From the inception of social work practice and through the early 1960s, supervision was essentially "an administrative function" (Richmond, 1917; Williamson, 1965). In essence, the practitioner was directed to fulfill the mission of the agency by practicing what the supervisor preached. The agency prescribed how the social worker should function on the job, and the supervisor tried her best to ensure that the agency's mandates would be executed faithfully by the supervisee. Although the administrative role of the

supervisor had not disappeared and is particularly present in today's mental health centers and other social agencies, many increments have been made to the role-set of the clinical supervisor during the past four decades. By the 1960s the supervisor had "a teaching function" (Feldman, 1950). In addition to ensuring that the supervisee was adapting to the agency's policies, she helped the practitioner learn to make more sophisticated diagnostic assessments, devise more creative treatment plans, and integrate salient practice principles (Bibring, 1950). As notions like transference, countertransference, resistance, and psychogenesis became very much in vogue in mental health parlance, not only was the clinician helped to study the unconscious meaning of his interactions with clients, but this transference reactions and resistances to his mentor were also subjects for study within the supervisory process (Fleming and Benedek, 1966).

Searles (1955, 1962) was one of the first to discuss how supervisory interactions was influenced by transference and countertransference interaction in the treatment relationship. He suggested that clarifying the problems that the practitioner experienced in the supervision would not only diminish the resistances to learning but would also foster change in the therapy. Ekstein and Wallerstein (1972) also discussed this "parallel process" and delineated ways it could be used to understand the therapeutic atmosphere. They focused on the supervisee's inevitable "problems about learning" (interpersonal problems between supervisor and supervisee and the supervisee's resistance to supervision) in order to clarify the transference-countertransference problems between therapist and patient.

In 1966 Fleming and Benedek contributed the concept of the "learning alliance" in supervision. This notion parallels that of the "therapeutic alliance" (Greenson, 1967) and was viewed as the basis of trust, shared learning goals, and mutual involvement on which supervision should be grounded. Doehrman (1976) substantiated empirically the Ekstein and Wallerstein (1972) concept of "parallel process of supervision." She demonstrated that difficulties in the therapeutic relationship were unconsciously communicated to the supervisor by the way the practitioner interacted with his mentor. Unexpectedly, she found that the influence of the supervisor's emotional reactions to the supervisee and to the patient were an outstanding feature of the processes observed.

The Supervisor's Anonymity

Until quite recently, descriptions of supervision that recognize that both supervisor and supervisee mutually influence one another in the supervisory process have only rarely been found in the mental health literature (Lane, 1990; Rock, 1997). As Rock has stated:

> Reports from supervisees about their personal experience in supervision are few and far between, while reports from supervisors about their private experience of the work as opposed to their prescriptions and proscriptions, observations and formulations are even harder to find. Searles' early papers on supervision (1955, 1962), are remarkable exceptions to this observation in that they demonstrate the great value to the student of supervision of disclosure of the inner experience of the supervisor. (p. 4)

For many decades both within social work and among its allied professions, when conflicts developed within the supervisory relationship it was generally believed that they were emanating from the supervisee (Teitelbaum, 1990). The underlying assumption was that the more experienced, better trained (and usually better analyzed) supervisor was less responsible for supervisory problems than washer less experienced and less aware supervisee.

A good example of how supervision was traditionally conducted in the mental health professions was presented by Greenson (1967). He described how a supervisee of his, in order to appear neutral, abstinent, and anonymous, maintained his silence after his patient expressed extreme distress over the sudden and serious illness of her infant son. In response to the supervisee's remarks that the patient's tears and subsequent silence "represented a resistance," Greenson noted, "I shook my head in disbelief and I ended the session by telling him that his emotional unresponsiveness would prevent the formation of a working alliance. . . . I then suggested that he might benefit from some further analysis" (p. 220). Greenson concluded his vignette with an admonition: "These clinical data demonstrate the fact that an objectionable trait in the analyst can produce realistic reactions in the patient which preclude successful psychoanalytic treatment" (p. 221). What Greenson omitted from the aforementioned account were his own countertransference reactions to the patient and his supervisee. It may be hypothesized that Greenson was very identified with the patient's pain and sense of vulnerability and concomitantly felt punitive toward the supervisee who did not overtly empathize with the patient. Not being aware of his countertransference reactions, Greenson helped create a parallel process in the supervision whereby the supervisee's failure to empathize with his patient was recapitulated by the supervisor's failure to empathize with the supervisee.

That the impact of the supervisor's countertransference reactions to her supervisee and his patient was seldom addressed in the mental health literature is not too surprising. It is similar to the history of what has been emphasized and deemphasized in studying the psychotherapeutic relationship. In contrast to his comprehensive and meticulous discussions of transference (1912, 1915, 1926), the founder of modern psychotherapy, Sigmund Freud, wrote very little on the subject of countertransference. He did point out that "the countertransference arises as a result of the patient's influence on [the therapist's] unconscious feelings, and we are almost inclined to insist that he shall recognize his countertransference in himself and overcome it" (1910, pp. 144–145). However, as Abend (1989) in his paper, "Countertransference and Psychoanalytic Technique," pointed out, "Freud's original idea that countertransference means unconscious interference with [a therapist's] ability to understand patients has been broadened during the past forty years: current usage often includes all of the emotional reactions at work" (p. 374).

Rather than viewing countertransference as a periodic unconscious interference, there is now a rather large psychotherapeutic literature on countertransference, with most authors acknowledging that it is as ever present as transference and must be constantly studied by all therapists, from the neophyte to the very experienced (Abend, 1982, 1989; Barchilon, 1958; Brenner, 1985; Fine, 1982; Heimann, 1950; Reich, 1951; Sandler, 1976; Strean, 1988, 1999). Virtually all authors agree that, like transference, countertransference can frequently be subtle but is always very influential on psychotherapeutic outcome. Further, most writers concur that analyzing countertransference is no less difficult for the most experienced therapist than it is for the beginner. Both are too easily satisfied with what Freud called "a part explanation" (1919). Thus, just as the earlier clinicians had little to say about countertransference and did not view the therapist's subjectivity as a central component of the treatment, likewise in supervision. Until recently, only limited consideration has been given to the effects of the supervisor's unresolved conflicts, blind spots, inappropriate expectations, or what Teitelbaum (1990) refers to as the "supertransference."

Similar to the literature on failures in psychotherapy that has focused almost exclusively on the patient's responsibility, with limited attention given to the therapist's contributions (Chessick 1971; Strean, 1986; Wolman, 1972), misalliances in the supervisory relationship have largely been attributed to the supervisee. As a result, the authoritarian atmosphere noted earlier in the Greenson example as for many decades par for the course of supervision. In the available literature on supervision it would appear the rule rather than the exception that the supervisor would take over the case, point out how she would deal with the material, and try to get the supervisee to imitate her (Fleming and Benedek, 1966).

The type of supervision that was practiced for many decades in social work and elsewhere has been aptly termed "superego training" (Balint, 1948; Fine, 1982). It consisted of what Glover (1952) called "authoritarian spoon feeding"—"a mid-Victorian pedagogy." This form of supervision fostered excessive dependency on the supervisor (Arlow, 1963), squelched the supervisee's autonomy, and made it difficult for him to become an autonomous and creative practitioner.

The Supervisor Comes out of the Closet

Although as early as 1954 Benedek called attention to the importance of unresolved problems in the supervisor as a factor contributing to negative therapeutic outcomes, 25 years later Langs (1978) con-

cluded, "There has been a rather striking neglect in the literature of the supervisor's countertransference and . . . it deserves systematic consideration" (p. 333). Later, Schlesinger (1981) echoed the sentiment and suggested that the supervisor may unwittingly contribute to the supervisee's learning problems and the patient's eventual lack of progress in treatment. In 1984 Issacharoff dealt somewhat more directly with the supervisor's countertransference issues, pointing out how the latter may enact a role of either overprotective parent and/or one of overly critical parent. The supervisee, treated like a weak and/or disappointing son or daughter, may then act out with his or her patient in the therapy the anger and discomfort stimulated in supervision.

Just as most therapy patients and their practitioners have the potential to collude with each other to gratify certain illusions of the patient, such as the latter's yearning to be the therapist's favorite child, or to symbiose with the therapist and become omnipotent as the therapist appears to be, similar illusions can be present in the teaching-learning situation in which supervisor and supervisee can also collude. Supervisee and supervisor can share the illusion that the supervisor is omniscient, whereas the supervisee and patient know next to nothing. They can suffer together from the illusion that the supervisor is exempt from pathology, ignorance, and blind spots, whereas the supervisee and his patient are both struggling to maintain their sanity. The learner and his mentor can delude themselves into believing that the supervisor's sexual and aggressive fantasies are in superb control, whereas the patient and the supervisee are either too inhibited by their punitive superegos or too expressive because of their superego lacunae (Strean, 1999; Teitelbaum, 1990).

As Lesser (1984) noted, certain "illusions" may exist in supervision, such as "the supervisor is always objective" or "the supervisor always knows best." She further pointed out that the supervisor's anxieties are "generally unrecognized, perhaps because anxieties are less acceptable to the supervisor than to the supervisee. Yet, awareness of the supervisor's anxieties is essential for fulfilling the supervisory task" (p. 147).

As the aforementioned citations suggest, just as psychotherapeutic interventions by the practitioner are always an expression of his countertransference, even when the technical procedure is considered to be valid and acceptable (Jacobs, 1986), so too can the supervisor's responses be colored by "supertransference" (Teitelbaum, 1990). As more practitioners are shifting their conceptualization of countertransference from the traditional classical model of a one-person psychology nearer to a two-person psychology, it is now a virtual axiom that the therapist's countertransference and the patient's transference are always influencing both parties and, therefore, always affect the therapeutic outcome. Now, the same notion can and is being made about supervision, both parties affect each other and both contribute to the supervisory outcome (Lane, 1990; Rock, 1991; Strean, 1999; Teitelbaum, 1990).

In a previous paper (Strean, 1999), I attempted to demonstrate how certain therapeutic impasses can be resolved when the therapist shares some of his countertransference reactions with the patient. I suggested that the disclosure of the therapist's countertransference frequently tends to clarify the patient's transference. In addition, by appearing less authoritarian and more egalitarian and authentic when the therapist shares his inner processes, it was demonstrated that clients were then more enabled to share their feelings, fantasies, and memories in the treatment. Inasmuch as therapeutic impasses frequently involve a lot of unexpressed hostility, the therapist's disclosing his countertransference responses tended to have the effect of helping the patient discharge her hostility and/or feel safer and less antagonistic in the therapy. As I witnessed the resolution of many treatment impasses both in my own practice and in those of my colleagues and supervisees, I decided to take the use of self-disclosure of the countertransference one step further. In those situations where my supervisee and I were not witnessing much therapeutic movement in the cases on which we working, I have shared certain selected countertransference reactions with the supervisee that I was experiencing toward his patients, toward him, and toward their interaction.

In the remaining part of this article, I would like to discuss several therapeutic impasses that moved toward resolution when I shared some of my countertransference responses with my supervisees. I shall also attempt to explain why disclosure of the supervisor's countertransference can, at crucial times, resolve treatment impasses that other supervisory interventions do not seem to achieve. However, before doing so I would like to offer a few comments on the modern supervisor's complex role-set.

The Complex Role-Set of the Clinical Supervisor

As I have suggested several times in the foregoing pages, the evolution of the role-set of the supervi-

sor has paralleled the professional development of the clinician. Just as many contemporary therapists have moved their conceptualizations of the treatment situation from a one-person psychology to a two-person interaction, the supervisor has reformulated her notion of supervision in a similar manner. And, just as the modern therapist no longer sees himself as a blank screen but is subject to the patient's transference reactions and his own countertransferences and counterresistances, the supervisor has moved from the exclusive position of teacher, administrator, and overseer to being what Marshall (1997) has formulated: "[The modern supervisor] is now an integral part of a system wherein [she] is influenced not only by the therapist, patient and [her] own promptings, but is a prime source of feedback to the patient through the supervisee" (p. 77). The contemporary supervisor sill retains her teaching function, but as she helps her supervisee enhance his diagnostic thinking and refine his therapeutic interventions, she constantly considers how she is being experienced by the supervisee and how his transference reactions toward her stimulate or inhibit his learning. Today, the supervisor makes an educational diagnosis of her supervisee, determines with him what he needs to learn and what his learning capacities and limitations are (Rock, 1997). Just as the therapist has to decide with the client when and how to support her, when and what to clarify or interpret, the supervisor has to determine with the supervisee what will be most beneficial to the supervisee at a particular time with a particular patient (Strean, 1991; Teitelbaum, 1990).

Not only does the supervisor have to deal with her countertransference reactions to the supervisee, but she also has to cope with her countertransference toward the supervisee's client. In some ways, the supervisee's client becomes the supervisor's client! Therefore, the supervisor must consistently be aware of her fantasies, memories, and anxieties that the supervisee's client activates in her. Of enormous importance, the supervisor also has to understand her countertransference responses to the interaction between the supervisee and his client. Does she feel like a competitive lover? An overprotective parent? Or a jealous child? Perhaps all of the above?

Up until now, virtually all of the literature on the supervisor's countertransference reactions has implied that the supervisor understand her responses but keep them to herself. I intend to demonstrate how the supervisor's sharing of certain countertransference responses with the supervisee can resolve therapeutic impasses and strengthen the therapeutic alliance that exists between the supervisee and his client. Just as I believe that the therapist's disclosures of countertransference reactions to the patient can at crucial times strengthen the therapeutic alliance, I also contend that the supervisor's disclosures of her countertransference responses can strengthen the supervisory alliance. In my judgment, when the supervisory alliance is strengthened, the therapeutic alliance between the patient and therapist is strengthened, thereby moving the treatment relationship toward a resolution of the therapeutic impasse.

In the following section, I present several short vignettes that involve therapeutic impasses that supervisees of mine were experiencing with specific clients, and that were not being resolved through supervision. I describe the nature of the impasse, review what transpired in supervision but had not helped resolve the impasse, state the specific content of my countertransference disclosure, and describe the supervisee's response to my disclosure. Finally, I discuss the client's response after the supervisee had integrated my countertransference disclosure. These vignettes will be followed by a summary and analysis of what dynamically transpired in all of the vignettes under examination.

Case Examples

A Therapist's Resistance to a Client's Erotic Transference

Dr. A. was an experienced practitioner in his early forties, married with one child, a director of a large social service department in an industrial setting, and had received his doctorate in clinical social work. He impressed me from the very beginning of our supervisory contact as a very skilled clinician, sharp diagnostician, and an excellent theoretician, who was very dedicated to his clients and achieved good results in his work with them. He was every eager to learn and seemed to enjoy his work with me as he enjoyed his own private practice. I had been seeing Dr. A. on a weekly basis for about three years, working with him on a variety of case situations, when he presented a client that "does not seem to be moving." The client, Beverly, was a single woman in her early thirties whom Dr. A. described as "bright, attractive, and very successful in her work as a publicist" What brought Beverly into therapy was her inability to sustain a relationship with a man. By the time she started treatment with Dr. A. (which was several months before he discussed the case with me), she was moderately de-

pressed, had vague psychosomatic complaints, and her "self-esteem was going downhill."

When Dr. A. initially discussed Beverly with me, he pointed out that at the beginning of treatment, Beverly seemed to look forward to her sessions and enjoyed Dr. A.'s "accepting attitude" and "interested listening." This helped her feel less depressed and more hopeful. She found herself to be less critical of men and though she did not sustain relationships with them, her interactions with them seemed smoother. Despite Beverly's initial progress, Dr. A. pointed out that "lately we seem to be going in circles." When I asked him to describe "the circles," Dr. A. talked about Beverly's "flirtatious attitude," which consisted of her giving him "all kinds of compliments" about his appearance and humane demeanor. When I wondered how Dr. A. felt about Beverly's flattering comments and what he did about them, he became visibly embarrassed and then suggested that Beverly was "idealizing me" and this was "a transference resistance."

As I listened to Dr. A.'s description of his interaction with Beverly, it became quite clear that the client was becoming very enamored with her therapist but that Dr. A. was subtly rejecting her approaches. This seemed even more evident when I learned that Dr. A. was "making genetic interpretations," trying to show Beverly that she was "behaving like a young girl looking for a doting father." Dr. A., who usually welcomed my observations on his clients' transference reactions and his countertransference responses, did not relate too well to my suggestion that Beverly was "falling in love with you, and I think it is making you a bit uncomfortable." Rather, he suggested that he needed some help in formulating "an interpretation to deal with her transference resistance."

As I reflected on my interaction with Dr. A., I began to see a parallel process developing. Like Beverly, I was saying to Dr. A., "Take note of me. I've got something to offer you," and Dr. A. was politely rejecting both of us. Having studied parallel processes previously with Dr. A., I thought he would be receptive to my statement that both Beverly and I were trying to get closer to him but we weren't being very successful. Instead, he changed the subject and, like the therapy he was conducting, in supervision he and I seemed "to be going around in circles." After about four to five weeks of trying in vain to help Dr. A. empathize more with Beverly's longing and show him how to make it safer for her to feel her loving and sexual feelings toward him, I decided to share with Dr. A. my countertransference reactions toward him and Beverly. What I was feeling was very sorry for Beverly, who was being pushed away. Also I was strongly identified with Beverly because I, too, was feeling pushed away by Dr. A. In addition, I felt frustrated with Dr. A. because he was not responding lovingly to a woman who wanted to love him. I said to Dr. A., "You remind me of a time when I was at a college dance. I was watching a good friend of mine dancing with a girl who had 'the hots' for him. My friend kept dancing far apart from the girl and I wanted him to hug and kiss her instead. I felt like yelling to my friend, 'Why the hell are you treating a woman who wants you that way? Make it better for her and for yourself. Dance closer, God damn it!'"

When Dr. A. listened to my story, he responded with a loud giggle. After the giggling subsided, he said, "Herb, I'm really flattered and feel good that I remind you of a friend of yours. So I feel I'm your friend. I also feel that you have my best interests at heart—you want me to enjoy myself with a woman! Thank you!" In the next supervisory session, Dr. A. came in very enthusiastically. Before sitting down, he said, "It really worked. As soon as Beverly came into my office she said, 'You look different. I think you like me today and so I like you.'" Dr. A. went on to mention that "this is just what transpired with us during the last supervisory setting—we both felt closer to each other." When Beverly saw that Dr. A. was more receptive to her loving feelings, she could share some of her sexual fantasies toward him. This helped Dr. A. and Beverly eventually get in touch with a repetition compulsion of hers: seeking out rejecting men like her father, trying to seduce them at first, and then rejecting them before they would reject her. This understanding eventually helped Beverly to form a more sustained relationship with one man.

The Therapist Has Difficulty Beginning Where the Client Is

Ms. C. sought me out for supervision just a few months after beginning her own private practice. In her early thirties, Ms. C. was a single woman and was also employed in a mental health center for about five years as both a practitioner and field work instructor for social work students. In my initial conferences with Ms. C., I experienced her as very outgoing, eager to learn, and with a wealth of warm feelings toward her clients. One of Ms. C.'s major concerns when she started supervision with me was that her clients were leaving her prematurely and she couldn't figure out why. Furthermore, "losing clients" hardly ever occurred when she worked in the mental health center. In addi-

tion, she was able to help her students "keep their clients in treatment almost all of the time."

Ms. C. and I agreed that perhaps we would be able to learn what might be causing her clients to leave treatment prematurely if we reviewed together some of her current private cases. As Ms. C. discussed her clients with me, it became quite clear that she was much too active with them. She asked them loads of questions, made many interpretations, and offered them a great deal of reassurance. Feeling some annoyance with her, my initial reaction to her presentations, which I kept to myself, was, "She's not giving her clients time or room to speak. How can I get her to calm down and be quieter?" When I shared with Ms. C. my impression that she was very active with her clients and wondered if this was her customary way of relating to them at the agency, after seriously thinking about my question she said, "You know, I'm quieter at the center and listen more." Reflecting further on the issue, Ms. C. was able to recognize with just a little help from me that because she was new in private practice and wanted to succeed, she had to work harder for her money or her clients would leave.

Although I thought our discussion would temper Ms. C.'s overactivity with her clients, I was dead wrong! Apparently her anxiety had not abated and she was still unable to listen to her clients. In two or three instances they even implied this themselves. As I began to study further my countertransference reactions to Ms. C., I realized that I was becoming quite frustrated and impatient with her. In addition, I realized that I was becoming too active with her. I tried to get her to "just listen" but to no avail. I tried to discuss her anxiety about being in private practice, and though she thought our discussions were "illuminating," it got us nowhere. I even lent her some literature but that did not help either.

When my "teaching role" was clearly not working, I decided to share some of my countertransference reactions directly with Ms. C. I told her, "You know, I'm feeling very inept with you. I'm working hard to help you relax and it's not helping you. What's wrong with me?" To this Ms. C. said with a twinkle in her eye, "I'm reassured that you can consider yourself a failure. I think I've been working very hard with my clients so that I won't fail with them. Maybe if I could accept the fact that failing isn't so bad, I'd relax more with my clients." Ms. C.'s remarks made me feel a lot warmer and closer to her. As a result I was then able to share with her some of my initial experiences in the army where I was a young social work officer, eager to succeed, but worried I would not. I recalled one time when a G.I. came to the mental hygiene clinic suffering from a severe migraine headache. Instead of letting him talk, I took his history. As a result, his headache got worse. Ms. C. laughed heartily at my story and said, "I've got to bring some of this lightheartedness to my interviews with my clients."

Ms. C.'s overactivity with her clients clearly induced in me a wish to be overactive with her. When my feelings of ineptness that helped create my overactivity were shared with her, Ms. C. could be more relaxed with me and then with her clients. Not to our surprise, the clients we had been discussing remained in treatment.

A Marriage Counselor Takes Sides

Mr. D., a married man in his late forties with two children, was in full-time private practice for about 10 years, specializing in marriage counseling. He had been in supervision about two years, discussing his couple counseling with much animation, confidence, and pleasure. Accomplished in his specialty, he published articles in his field of practice and was well regarded by his colleagues. I felt close to him and enjoyed working with him. Until we began working with the case under discussion, our supervisory work had moved positively and we both felt we were growing professionally from it.

Mr. D., during his third year of supervision, wanted "to spend some time" on a case "that was going nowhere." Eric and Flora had been seeing Mr. D. for close to a year. Flora was feeling very hostile and disappointed with Eric because he "hardly ever wanted to have sex," was "always distant" from her, and made her feel "unappreciated." Eric, on the other hand, felt "nagged," "pressured," and "misunderstood." Dr. D. felt that no matter what he did in the sessions, the couple kept bickering and became even more alienated from each other. As I listened to Mr. D.'s descriptions of his sessions with Eric and Flora, it became quite clear that almost every time Flora talked Mr. D. would emerge as very supportive and empathetic, but almost every time Eric participated Mr. D. said nothing. When I shared my observation with Mr. D., he responded, "The guy doesn't have much to offer, so I don't have much to support." I suggested that this was just what Flora was feeling, so, in effect, he, Mr. D. was more identified with Flora and less with Eric.

Although Mr. D. could acknowledge his countertransference reactions toward Flora and Eric—sympathetic toward Flora and mildly contemptuous toward Eric—it did not alter his way of relating

to them. He continued to favor Flora, and concomitantly the marriage kept floundering. Furthermore, suggestions on my part that Flora unconsciously wanted a withdrawn man and that Eric felt very vulnerable did not modify Mr. D.'s biased treatment. In sharing my countertransference with Mr. D. I said, "You know, as I work with you on this case, I feel very different from the way I do with other marital situations that we've discussed. In virtually every other one, I feel included in the system. In this one, I feel ignored, as if I'm a bump on a log. There's something going on for both of us because you, too, have not been satisfied with the movement in this case."

Mr. D., after a long silence, told me that one word I used brought tears to his eyes. "That is the word 'ignored,'" he said with much emotion. Without prompting, he shared with me how very "ignored" he felt as a child in his own family. Frequently, he felt like a scapegoat in that he experienced his parents and brother as "always ganging up on me." After I commented, "You've had it rough," Mr. D. responded, "I guess I've been wanting to get you and Flora to gang up with me against Eric. Eric kind of reminds me of my older brother, and I'd like to give him a taste of his own medicine. Without realizing it, I'm doing to Eric what was done to me in my own family. I'm identifying with the aggressor."

As Mr. D. could see that he was unconsciously arranging to treat Eric the way he was treated in his own family, he began to listen to him more, empathize with him more, and "try to show him that I understand what an outsider feels like." This modified attitude on Mr. D.'s part helped the marital therapy move a great deal and helped Eric and Flora to communicate with each other in a more mature manner. Their sex life improved and their emotional distance from each other diminished tremendously.

A Fee Problem Goes Unaddressed

Dr. G., a divorced woman in her fifties, was in full-time private practice and had been in supervision with me for close to one year. Although bright, engaging, and very committed to her clients, Dr. G. appeared overinvolved in her clients' lives. She tended to give advice when it was not asked for, intervened in their environments when the clients might have been able to use their own resources, and offered a great deal of reassurance that did not always seem indicated. A case that Dr. G. wanted to discuss with me "in more breadth and depth" involved a client, Mr. H., whom Dr. G. felt was a "psychopath." Mr. H., an accountant, "cheated" his clients, was "unfaithful" to his wife, "neglected" his children, and "gossiped a lot about his friends." He started treatment with Dr. G. about two years prior to her discussion of the case with me, after his physician told him that his psychosomatic problems were caused by "stress."

As I listened to Dr. G.'s description of Mr. H., I was baffled by a number of issues. Although Dr. G. referred to Mr. H. pejoratively as a "psychopath," in the treatment she was warm, tender, and what appeared to me as quite indulgent. I was shocked that she let him owe her well over $2,000 and hadn't explored this resistance in the treatment. Despite his obvious rage at his wife, children, and associates, this too was neglected by Dr. G. When I asked Dr. G. why she let a big debt elapse, she told me that her client "was broke" but that she wanted to help him clear up his debt and this was the only way she knew how to do it. I found Dr. G.'s responses to my other queries quite similar. "The poor guy needs support," "he's never been given to," "I feel sorry for him" were some of her responses.

Inasmuch as I felt that Dr. G.'s treatment of Mr. H. would not get off the ground until she was firmer with him and had him explore his mistreatment of her, I shared this conviction with Dr. G. and said, firmly, "He's taking advantage of you, too. Find out why he's not paying you!" When Dr. G. essentially evaded my suggestion, I felt she was behaving like her client was with her, and not paying attention to my need to be listened to. I then said, "Just as Mr. H. owes you money and should pay you, I think you might consider taking my suggestion seriously," trying to demonstrate to Dr. G. how to be firm. However, Dr. G. responded by saying that I was being "too rough" on her and that I wanted her to be "too rough" on her client. When I observed that all my interventions with Dr. G. were not helpful to her nor to her client, I decided to share some of my countertransference reactions with her. As already implied, I had a load of intense feelings. I was contemptuous and angry toward Mr. H. for exploiting Dr. G. I was irritated with Dr. G. for letting herself be so mistreated. I speculated that just as Dr. G. and Mr. H. were ignoring the fee problem, Dr. G. and I must not be paying attention to something in our relationship because we weren't getting anywhere in our communication.

It seemed to me that the best way to try to reach Dr. G. was to demonstrate the parallel process that I thought was occurring. Therefore, I said, "Just as you and Mr. H. seem to be ignoring the fee and

going on with your work but not getting very far, you and I must be ignoring something in our relationship because we are not getting very far on this case!" As if she had been waiting to tell me for a long time, Dr. G. said, "Yes, we are ignoring the fact that I want to be your friend and colleague and you treat me as if I'm just one of your supervisees. You could be a lot warmer to me, ask me out for lunch occasionally, take a walk with me. What's wrong with you?"

As I reflected on Dr. G's question about what was wrong with me, I came up with the following answers, which I then shared with her. "What's wrong with me is that I haven't been the kind of guy you've wanted me to be. For a year now you have wanted a friendship with me and I've been seeing you only in my office. I didn't realize how much I've been frustrating you!" Dr. G. responded with enormous indignation: "I think your response is full of coldness and hostility. There's no reason why we can't be buddies on the outside and colleagues on the inside. You are much too formal!"

My sharing of my countertransference with Dr. G. was initially more helpful to me than it was to her. By looking at what we were not facing in our work, I not only learned that I was deflecting Dr. G.'s wishes to be a friend, but I saw what I was not attending to in the supervision. Dr. G. wanted me to treat her the way she was treating Mr. H. and instead I was the controlled professional who did not gratify her yearnings for contact and did not discuss this important issue with her.

Once I became sensitized to the fact that Dr. G. wanted to be indulged by me the way she was indulging. Mr. H., I could become more relaxed and therefore more of an enabler. Instead of being irritated with her for not following my supervisory suggestions, I could empathize with her personal loneliness and help her see that she was trying to make her supervisor and her client into boyfriends. Although Dr. G. never entirely gave up her quest to use her professional relationships for personal gain, in time she could be more limiting and more confronting with Mr. H. and with other clients. As she could slowly adapt to my limit-setting (which became warmer and less mechanical), she could eventually set limits for Mr. H. and help him pay his fee. Concomitant with his paying his debt, Mr. H. because more considerate of his family, clients, and friends.

Discussion of Cases

In attempting to assess dynamically the four vignettes that I have presented, it would appear that the material affirms several traditional principles of social work supervision and also generates a few hypotheses that may enable social work supervisors to become more sensitive and competent enablers. Just as every well-motivated client in psychotherapy resists learning about herself, the supervisee who wants to learn more about himself also needs to protect himself from facing vulnerabilities and resists supervision. Furthermore, similar to the patient in psychotherapy who unconsciously arranges to distort the therapist, the supervisee usually has a wide range of transference reactions toward the supervisor. Some of these transference reactions can accelerate learning, whereas others can inhibit it.

None of the four supervisees that I discussed were required to have supervision. Similar to voluntary patients who spend time and money to improve themselves, but also concomitantly have to avoid danger, the supervisees under discussion all resisted my teaching at various points. Dr. A. did not want to face his client's erotic transference; Ms. C. did not want to confront her therapeutic overactivity; Mr. D. was not eager to face the reasons he was biased in the marital counseling; and Dr. G. resisted confronting her indulgence of her client.

In all of the cases "the parallel process" became evident in that the transference-countertransference interaction that took place in the therapy became recapitulated in the transference-countertransference interaction between me and my supervisees. Dr. A. and I could not easily communicate about love and sex, and this was true in his work with Beverly. Ms. C. and I were not able to listen carefully to each other, and this was clearly happening with Ms. C. and her clients. I felt ignored by Mr. D., and this is what he was doing with Eric. Dr. G. wanted me to indulge her as she was indulging her patients, but this was a secret in the supervision as it was in the therapy she was conducting. When I observed that my supervisees did not respond positively to my teaching or my clarifications and interpretations of the parallel process, I decided to disclose some of my countertransference reactions to them. In all four cases, the tension between the supervisee and me then diminished, the supervisory alliance became stronger, and the therapeutic impasse moved toward resolution. Why did this happen?

I believe that just as in psychotherapy, when the therapist relinquishes his traditional role of interpreter and expert and diminishes his omnipotent strivings, the therapeutic impasse frequently can move toward resolution (Strean, 1999); so too in supervision. Dr. A. began to see me more as a colleague and equal rather than as a judge and critic. Ms. C., when she could experience me as fallible and capable of making mistakes, was able to allow herself to feel fallible with her clients and therefore became more self-confident in the treatment situation. Mr. D. could acknowledge his unconscious rejection of Eric when I discussed my feelings of being rejected. Dr. G. could face her wishes to indulge her client when I could more directly discuss my feelings regarding indulging her.

The supervisor's disclosure of her countertransference tends to make her appear much less authoritarian, more egalitarian, less of a wise expert, and more of an authentic human being. This humane attitude of the supervisor helps reduce the supervisee's self-consciousness and need to appear omniscient. As the supervisor relinquishes some of her grandiose wishes to be a "know-it-all," the supervisee tends to do the same. A more relaxed therapist then makes for a more relaxed client and the therapeutic alliance is strengthened. What was most impressive about the cases under review is that the supervisor's disclosing of the countertransference activated a different treatment interaction from the one that contributed toward the therapeutic impasse. Dr. A. and Beverly, from "going around in circles," could more honestly discuss love and sex. Ms. C. could become a better listener and her clients began to stay in treatment. Mr. D. became less hostile and Eric and Flora improved their marital interaction. Dr. G. became less indulgent and Mr. H. evolved into a more decent human being.

As my supervisees observed that I was taking some initiative in disclosing my feelings of anger, hurt, rejection, and so forth, they felt a freedom to identify with me and do the same. And, when I did not reveal very much about myself, they also tended to be withholding. In effect, the supervisor was experienced in all four cases as a role model who set the tone of the interaction. If I was revealing, the supervisee was more including to reveal. And when the supervisee felt less anxiety about revealing himself, he invariably made it safer for his client to face herself. One of the positive effects of disclosing the supervisor's countertransference is that it tends to clarify the supervisee's transference toward her. This was particularly true in the case of Dr. G. who was harboring negative feelings and dependent and sexual yearnings toward me, of which I was unaware and which I tended to deflect.

In reviewing my work with the supervisees under study, I feel quite certain that if I had not disclosed my countertransference reactions, the therapeutic impasses that were resolved would not have been overcome. The supervisor's disclosure of her countertransference seems to strengthen the supervisory alliance, which in turn strengthens the therapeutic alliance.

Conclusion

A common occurrence in most supervisory relationships is that the supervisee resists confronting certain dynamic issues in his client and in him-self. These issues usually become expressed in the transference-countertransference interaction between the supervisee and his supervisor. Mutual examination of this supervisory interaction often clarifies what is transpiring in the therapeutic relationship. When mutual examination bogs down, the supervisor's disclosure of her countertransference appears to strengthen the supervisory alliance. This, in turn, enables the therapist to strengthen the therapeutic alliance with his client, which can then help resolve a therapeutic impasse.

It is hoped that further research on the supervisor's disclosure of her countertransference will be conducted. Is disclosure of the supervisor's countertransference helpful at times other than during a therapeutic impasse? How helpful is the supervisor's disclosure of countertransference in supervisory groups or seminars? When supervisors convene to enhance their skills, would mutual sharing of their countertransference reactions to their supervisees improve their supervisory work? Finally, are there any negative effects of the supervisor disclosing her countertransference responses?

References

Abend, S. (1982). Serious illness in the analyst: Countertransference considerations. *Journal of the American Psychoanalytic Association*, 30: 365–379.

Abend, S. (1989). Countertransference and psychoanalytic technique. *Psychoanalytic Quarterly*, 58: 374–396.

Arlow, J. (1963). The supervisory situation. *Journal of the American Psychoanalytic Association*, 11:576–594.

Balint M. (1948). On the psychoanalytic training system. *International Journal of Psycho-Analysis*, 29:163–173.

Barchilon, J. (1958). On countertransference cures. *Journal of the American Psychoanalytic Association*, 6:222–236.

Benedek, T. (1954). Countertransference in the training analyst. *Bulletin of the Menninger Clinic*, 18:12–16.

Bibring, G. (1950). Psychiatry and social work. In *Principles and Techniques in Social Casework* ed. C. Kasius, pp. 300–313. New York: Family Service Association of America.

Brenner, C. (1985). Countertransference as a compromise formation. *Psychoanalytic Quarterly*, 54:155–163.

Chessick, R. (1971). *Why Psychotherapists Fail*. Northvale, NJ: Jason Aronson.

Doehrman, M. (1976). Parallel processes in supervision and psychotherapy. *Bulletin of the Menninger Clinic*, 40:9–84.

Ekstein, R. and Wallerstein, R. (1972). *The Teaching and Learning of Psychotherapy*. New York: International Universities Press.

Feldman, Y. (1950). The teaching aspect of casework supervision. In *Principles and Techniques in Social Casework* ed. C. Kasius, pp. 222–232. New York: Family Service Association of America.

Fine, R. (1982). *The healing of the mind* (2nd edition). New York: Free Press.

Fleming, J. and Benedek, T. (1966). *Psychoanalytic Supervision*. New York: Grune and Stratton.

Freud, S. (1910). The future prospects of psychoanalytic therapy. *S.E.* (Vol. 11). London: Hogarth Press.

Freud, S. (1912). The dynamics of transference. *S.E.* (Vol. 12). London: Hogarth Press.

Freud, S. (1915). Observations on transference-love. *S.E.* (Vol. 12). London: Hogarth Press.

Freud, S. (1919). Lines of advance in psychoanalytic therapy. *S.E.* (Vol. 17). London: Hogarth Press.

Freud, S. (1926). Inhibitions, symptoms and anxiety. *S.E.* (Vol. 20). London: Hogarth Press.

Glover, E. (1952). Research methods in psychoanalysis. *International Journal of Psycho-Analysis*: 33:403–409.

Greenson, R. (1967). *The Technique and Practice of Psychoanalysis*. New York: International Universities Press.

Heimann, P. (1950). On countertransference. *International Journal of Psychoanalysis*, 31: 81–84.

Issacharoff, A. (1984). Countertransference in supervision: Therapeutic consequences for the supervisee. In *Clinical Perspectives in the Supervision of Psychoanalysis and Psychotherapy* ed. L. Caligor, P. Bromberg and J. Meltzer, pp. 89–105. New York: Plenum.

Jacobs, T. (1986). On countertransference enactments. *Journal of the American Psychoanalytic Association*, 43:289–307.

Lane, R. (1990). *Psychoanalytic Approaches to Supervision*. New York: Brunner/Mazel.

Langs, R. (1978). *The Supervisory Experience.* Northvale, NJ: Jason Aronson.

Lesser, R. (1984). Supervision: Illusions, anxieties, and questions. In *Clinical Perspectives in the Supervision of Psychoanalysis and Psychotherapy* ed. L. Caligor, P. Bromberg and J. Meltzer, pp. 143–152. New York: Plenum.

Marshall, R. (1997). The international triad in supervision. In *Psychodynamic Supervision* ed. M. Rock, pp. 77–106. Northvale, NJ: Jason Aronson.

Reich, A. (1951). On countertransference. In *Psychoanalytic Contributions* ed. A. Reich, pp. 136–154. New York: International Universities Press.

Richmond, M. (1917). *Social Diagnosis.* New York: Russell Sage Foundation.

Rock, M. (1997). *Psychodynamic Supervision,* Northvale, NJ: Jason Aronson.

Sandler, J. (1976). Countertransference and role responsiveness. *International Review of Psychoanalysis,* 3:43–48.

Schlesinger, H. (1981). General principles of psychoanalytic supervision. In *Becoming a Psychoanalyst* ed. R. Wallerstein, pp. 29–38. New York: International Universities Press.

Searles, H. (1955). The informational value of the supervisor's emotional experience. In *Collected Papers on Schizophrenia* ed. H. Searles, pp. 157–176. New York: International Universities Press.

Searles, H. (1962). Problems of psychoanalytic supervision. In *Collected Papers on Schizophrenia* ed. H. Searles, pp. 584–604. New York: International Universities Press.

Strean, H. (1986). *Behind the Couch.* New York: Wiley.

Strean, H. (1988). Colluding illusions among analytic candidates, their supervisors, and their patients: A major factor in some treatment impasses. *Psychoanalytic Psychology* 8:403–414.

Strean, H. (1998). *Don't Lose Your Patients: Responding to Clients Who Want to Quit Treatment.* Northvale, NJ: Jason Aronson.

Strean, H. (1999). Resolving some therapeutic impasses by disclosing countertransference. *Clinical Social Work Journal,* 27:123–140.

Teitelbaum, S. (1990). Supertransference: The role of the supervisor's blind spots. *Psychoanalytic Psychology,* 7:243–258.

Williamson, M. (1965). *Supervision: New Patterns and Processes.* New York: Association Press.

Wolman, B. (1972). *Success and Failure in Psychoanalysis and Psychotherapy.* New York: Macmillan.

DONALD A. GORDON

76

Parent Training via CD-ROM: Using Technology to Disseminate Effective Prevention Practices

The purpose of this paper is to describe how technology can reduce barriers to dissemination and use of parent and family interventions. This technology consists of highly interactive, video-based CD-ROMs and interactive videodisk programming. I begin the paper by presenting the scientific basis for family-based prevention programs, briefly review some effective programs, then describe barriers to their dissemination. I then describe, beginning with the literature on interactive videodisk instruction, the development and research on a parent training CD-ROM, which integrates interactive videodisk methodology with videotaped modeling of parenting skills. I discuss barriers to the technology's dissemination, particularly among mental health professionals, then list gaps in our research knowledge on this technology. Finally, I present steps for overcoming barriers to widespread dissemination.

Family-Related Risk Factors

According to Stewart and Brown (1993), family functioning plays a role not only in the teen's initiation of drug use, but also in its maintenance. Numerous family factors are related to the risk of adolescent substance use. The strongest predictor of adolescent use is parental substance use (D.E. Alexander & Gwyther, 1995; Malkus, 1994; Swaim, 1991; Hundleby & Mercer, 1987; Brook,

Whiteman, Gordon, Nomura, & Brook, 1986; Semlitz & Gold, 1986). When the parent is under the influence of drugs or alcohol, parenting is more likely to be inconsistent (Kumpfer & DeMarsh, 1986) and monitoring of the adolescent tends to be low (Dishion, Reid, & Patterson, 1988; Swaim, 1991). In turn, low parental monitoring increases the risk of substance use because the adolescent may have more opportunities to get involved with drugs and with peers who use drugs (Dishion et al., 1988). Other investigators have found that similar parenting or family management practices (for example, inconsistent parenting practices, poor monitoring, inconsistent punishment) are strong risk factors for teen substance use (Catalano, Haggerty, Gainey, & Hoppe, 1997; St. Pierre & Kaltreider, 1997; Swaim, 1991; Kumpfer & DeMarsh, 1986).

Additional family risk factors include family conflict, conflict with parents (Catalano et al., 1997; Swadi, 1991; Swaim, 1991), parental attitudes favoring substance use (Catalano et al., 1997; St. Pierre & Kaltreider, 1997; Johnson & Pandina, 1991), lack of parental support (Stewart & Brown, 1993; Hundleby & Mercer, 1987), hostility and lack of warmth (Johnson & Pandina, 1991), and poor bonding between child and parent (St. Pierre & Kaltreider, 1997; Santisteban, Coatsworth, Perez-Vidal, Mitrani, Jean-Gilles, & Szapocznik, 1997). Factors such as low parental involvement with children (St. Pierre & Kaltreider, 1992), poor family communication (Glynn & Haenlein, 1988;

Kumpfer & DeMarsh, 1986), and low family cohesion/attachment (Kumpfer & DeMarsh, 1986; McKay, Murphy, Rivinus, & Maisto, 1991; Malkus, 1994) are also related to adolescent substance use. McKay et al. found that higher levels of family dysfunction are associated with higher levels of adolescent substance abuse.

Brown, Mounts, Lamborn, and Steinberg (1993) pointed out that parents have an indirect influence on the peer group with which their adolescents become affiliated. Parent behaviors impact adolescent characteristics, an influence that predicts the type of peer group with which their child associates. If the parent-child relationship is poor, the child is more likely to become involved with deviant peers and consequently to become involved in drug and alcohol use or delinquency (Brown et al., 1993; Patterson, 1986).

Family-Based Prevention Programs

Several studies have illustrated the effectiveness of parenting skills training in reducing such risk factors for substance use as low parental monitoring, family conflict, and child problem behaviors. These parenting programs also strengthen protective factors, such as family cohesion and functioning, positive family communication, and consistent parenting practices. Piercy, Volk, Trepper, Sprenkle, and Lewis (1990, as cited in Malkus, 1994) emphasize the need for programs that improve the quality of the affective level of the parent-child relationship. According to Kumpfer and DeMarsh (1986), effective prevention programs will improve social skills, teach family management skills, increase the time parents spend with children, decrease family conflict, and provide positive role models for children.

Family Therapy

Several models of family therapy have reduced risk factors for and/or levels of adolescent substance abuse. These include Functional Family Therapy, Multisystemic Family Therapy, Brief Structural/ Strategic Family Therapy, Multidimensional Family Therapy, and Purdue Brief Family Therapy. These are labor-intensive interventions that require advanced training and have been reviewed in CSAP's Family and Parent Centered Interventions (Grover, 1998); they will not be reviewed here. Family therapy can be successful at engaging and retaining high-

risk families (Santisteban et al., 1997), particularly when done in the home (Gordon Jurkovic, & Arbuthnot, 1998). For many families not at the highest risk levels, more cost-effective parent education approaches produce outcomes comparable to family therapy (Friedman, 1989).

Parent Training

A well-established family-based approach is parent training, which has been found to decrease family-related risk factors, enhance family-related protective factors, and decrease problem behaviors in children (Catalano et al., 1997). By using more appropriate social skills, teaching these skills to other family members, and strengthening the family in general, parents reduce the risk that their children will experiment with substance use and associate with antisocial peers (Grover, 1998). Approaches to parent skills training typically provide the parent with practice of the newly learned skills as well as feedback on his or her performance. Several parent training programs will be reviewed in the following section.

The Strengthening Families Program (SFP) is a prevention program consisting of three components: parent training, children's skills training, and family skills training (Kumpfer, Molgaard, & Spoth, 1996). The parent training component consists of 14 one-hour sessions that teach parents to increase desired behaviors in their children through use of attention, reinforcement, charts, communication training, limit setting, and so on. Drug education relating to drugs that adolescents use is also included in the parent component. The children's skills component trains children in understanding and sharing feelings and in attending, communicating, problem solving, increasing good behavior, complying with parental rules, dealing with criticism, and handling anger. Children also engage in a discussion session about alcohol and drugs. The family skills component provides additional information about family meetings, as well as a time for the families to practice newly acquired skills while engaging in the Child's Game, a structured play therapy session.

The first study conducted on SFP involved children (ages 6–12) of methadone maintenance parents and substance-abusing outpatients from local mental health centers (DeMarsh & Kumpfer, 1986, as cited in Kumpfer et al., 1996). Subjects were divided into here groups. Group I received only the parent component of the program. Group 2 received both the parent and child components. Group 3 received all three components. Treatment subjects were compared to a matched group of children of non-substance abusers. Outcome studies suggested that subjects in Group 3 (SFP content) showed that most success. SFP improved the children's risk status in three areas: (1) children's problem behaviors, emotional status, and prosocial skills, (2) parent's parenting skills, and (3) family environment and family functioning. Older children (treatment subjects) decreased their use of alcohol and tobacco. Parents reduced their drug use and improved their parenting skills.

In a later study, Aktan, Kumpfer, and Turner (as cited in Kumpfer et al., 1996) investigated the effectiveness of SFP on 88 African American, inner-city, substance-abusing parents. In families of low drug-using parents, family cohesion increased, family conflict decreased, and the families reported spending more time together. In children of high drug-using parents, parents reported that children's internalizing and externalizing problem behaviors decreased (to levels similar to those of children of low drug-using parents) immediately after the 12 weekly sessions. Kumpfer et al. concluded that the SFP does more than merely improve parenting skills. It also decreases children's risk for substance abuse by improving the family environment, strengthening bonds with the school, and decreasing depression and delinquency.

Preparing for the Drug Free Years (Spoth & Redmund, 1993) is a parent skills training program based on Hawkins and Catalano's (1992) social development model. The goal of the program is to increase parenting skills so that parents are able to increase family bonding and reduce family risks for substance use. The program consists of five two-hour sessions. One of these sessions requires the adolescent's attendance. Parents are taught to recognize substance use risk factors and to utilize family management skills for expressing and controlling anger (Spoth & Redmond, 1993). Spoth, Redmond, Haggerty, and Ward (1995) found that randomly assigned parents who completed the treatment group (n = 85) provided reinforcement to their children more often, monitored their children more frequently, and reported being more involved with their children than did control group parents (n = 90). Treatment parents also reported better parent-child relationships and communication and fewer negative interactions with their children than did control parents immediately after the intervention. These studies have made extraordinary efforts to engage parents and reduce attrition once the intervention started. Higher-risk families usually do not initiate or continue participation in parenting programs.

Felner, Brand, Munhall, Counter, Millman, & Fried (1994) evaluated a worksite-based parenting program (n = 191) intended to improve the quality of parent-child interactions by increasing parenting skills. A second goal was to decrease risk factors for adolescent substance abuse while at the same time increasing protective factors. The interventions, which were scheduled twice a week, consisted of 24 one-hour sessions. The program sought to reduce parental stress by increasing the parent's support network. Data were collected at baseline, posttreatment, and at 9-, 18-, and 30-month follow-up. Parents who attended at least 80% of the sessions reported a decrease in both child behavior problems and stress and depression, as well as an increase in positive parenting practice and knowledge of parenting skills. Interestingly, parents reporting higher levels of social isolation and child behavior problems attended a greater number of sessions. There was no control group.

Webster-Stratton (1990) evaluated the effectiveness of a self-help videotaped parent training program. Mothers of 43 3- to 8-year old conduct-disordered children were randomly assigned to one of three groups: videotape with therapist consultation, videotape without therapist consultation, or a wait control. The videotaped program, shown over the course of 10 weeks, sought to improve the mothers' parenting skills and parent-child communication (mean age of child = 5.1 years). Mothers in both treatment groups (there were no differences between treatment groups) reported fewer child problem behaviors, fewer spankings, and less stress than did mothers in the control group at a one-month follow-up. Treatment mothers also showed more positive affect toward their children. As observed during home visits, mothers in the therapist consultation treatment group reported fewer problem behaviors and praised their children more frequently than did either of the other two groups. Webster-Stratton (1992) also found that a videotaped intervention with parents moved the behavior of their conduct-disordered children from the clinical to the normal range, compared to a wait list control group (N = 100, random assignment to groups). O'Dell, Krug, Patterson, & Faustman (1980), O'Dell, O'Quinn, Alford, O'Briant, Bradlyn, and Giebenhain (1982), Nay (1976), and Flanagan, Adams, and Forehand (1979) have also found improvements in child problem behavior using videotaped modeling for parents. Videotaped modeling was superior to written instructions, lectures, live modeling, and role play. These studies, though few in number, illustrate the effectiveness of self-administered videotaped parent training.

The strength of their conclusions is bolstered by the fact that the studies were conducted in four different university settings.

The Coping Power Program (Lochman & Wells, 1996) uses separate parent and child training over 15 months and targets aggressive children during the transition to middle school. Reductions in children's aggressive behavior and parents' physical punishment preceded reductions in substance abuse a year later. The authors found some indications that parenting changes had a preventive effect on early-onset substance use.

When parents meet with a therapist, as in family therapy or parent training, resistance to learning new skills is usually present and may be a function of the therapeutic relationship. Patterson and Chamberlain (1994) found that when therapists increase their efforts to intervene by teaching new skills, resistance increases. The particular therapist behaviors such as "confront" (telling parents directly what they are doing wrong) and "teach" (telling parents what they need to try to improve their parenting) are causally related to greater parental resistance (Patterson & Forgatch, 1985). In order to prevent premature termination, therapists must facilitate and support, effectively retreating from teaching new skills. The relatively high number of sessions necessary to show positive effects may reflect this apparent paradox.

Conclusions from Prevention Literature

Evidence reported to date confirms that it is possible to change risk factors for adolescent substance abuse with prevention programs. Successful school-based prevention programs typically include a normative education program. Other promising approaches consist of a parent education or parenting skills component. Many of these programs, while effective, are time-consuming and costly. With recent cutbacks to social service programs, it is prudent to investigate shorter-term, less intensive prevention programs that can still produce favorable results while minimizing cost. Such programs could be stacked concurrently or offered sequentially to compound their modest benefits. By reducing the length of time that parents need to commit to one program, it is likely that more parents will be willing to participate in substance use and delinquency prevention programs. The brevity of interventions could allow more families access to such programs. Prior use of parenting resources predicts future use of those services (Spoth & Redmond, 1995) so enticing parents with a brief intervention may hook

them into more extended training. The power of having parents view videotapes of parenting skills, which is a brief and self-administered intervention is striking and usually equal in effectiveness to interventions where therapists or parent educators spend more time with parents.

Barriers to Access to Effective Programs

A number of serious obstacles prevent the widespread dissemination of traditional services to families at risk for substance abuse, delinquency, and other problems. For family therapy, parent education, and parent training programs, attrition is often high, especially for the first appointment. When teens are involved, the families with the most difficulties cannot get their teens or their children to the sessions. Barriers such as transportation, costs of treatment, arranging child care, and scheduling around therapists' availability prevent many parents from completing treatment (Webster-Stratton, 1984; Kacir, Gordon, & Kirby, 1999). Another barrier to delivering parent training and parent education has been that most parent training to date has been conducted either in a one-person, face-to-face format with an individual therapist or in a group setting requiring 10 to 12 weeks. Low income parents may be particularly sensitive to the stigma of seeing mental health professionals, and many will not seek treatment unless desperate. For primary or secondary prevention, since parents are unlikely to be very motivated to be proactive if their children's behavior problems are not fairly distressing, moderately lengthy programs (4–10 sessions) fail to attract many parents. Another obstacle is that parent education groups and parent training are not offered continuously and thus serve relatively few parents in a community. There is a need for innovative interventions that do not utilize agency manpower resources, can be offered continuously, and—most important—have undergone careful evaluation. The robust treatment effects for parenting programs that are self-administered videotapes in the work of Webster-Stratton (moderate to large effect sizes), and O'Dell, Nay, and Forehand mentioned above is one solution that has not been used widely.

Another set of barriers, which, I submit, are quite serious, to disseminating effective programs pertains to training service providers. First, we must maintain the therapeutic integrity of the intervention, a task that requires considerable effort and expense. The program's progenitors and experienced associates must be involved in quality control of the training and ongoing supervision of the service providers. If trainees are experienced, it is challenging to persuade them to change their customary practices, as service providers often resist attempts to limit their autonomy. Second, accurate, objective mechanisms to monitor how providers behave are not usually in place, and the consequences for provider change and maintenance of change are inadequate. Bickman and Noser (1999) express concern about therapists' likelihood of following a defined treatment protocol if ongoing close supervision and consequences are not in place. Because they conclude that there is insufficient scientific evidence that treatment for children and adolescents is effective (as it is delivered in community, as opposed to research, settings), we need to implement continuous quality improvement systems to give service providers feedback about their procedures and outcomes. This has been a very difficult challenge because, as Chambless (1999) notes in her discussion of the problems with disseminating empirically validated treatments, practicing clinicians are hampered by time, distance, and money in getting supervised training. Third, it is challenging to recruit and retain providers with those personal attributes and skills necessary to benefit from training (attributes similar to those of highly selected and trained graduate students in clinical psychology, such as receptivity to new methods). Fourth, the anti-empirical bias of those with personal experience (called the common sense revolution by Paul Gendreau) causes administrators, policymakers, politicians, and service providers to discount or ignore empirically based treatments. Such thinking is exemplified by the assumption hat "if I know something about this topic, and the current practice makes sense to me, there is no need to look for corroborating evidence or to evaluate the current practice." Fifth, empirically validated programs are generally poorly packaged and marketed, yet they compete with ineffective or unevaluated programs that are well-packaged and marketed (i.e., DARE, Active Parenting). Finally, service providers often are not trained to evaluate research findings. They have limited access to research and don't subscribe to research journals and they have little time to go to libraries to read the journals. Applied journals that they do read are not research-oriented and they emphasize case studies. Because their access to published research is so limited, they tend to trust the opinions of their peers. Some cause for optimism is the publicizing of evidence-based programs through SAMSHA Web sites (www.strengthening-families.org) and the APA's Division 12 (clinical psychology) Task Force on Intervention's Web site,

which lists manuals and training in empirically validated treatments (www.sscp.psych.nsu.nodak.edu).

Technological Approaches

New opportunities are available today to intervene with parents and families. Given what we know about how people learn and recall new information, the application of this knowledge to the development of interactive CD-ROMs and videodisks has advanced our ability to intervene effectively and efficiently for a variety of problems. Interactive videodisk technology (the parent technology of new interactive CD-ROMs) has been used to provide training to adults in a variety of settings. For example, professionals have taken advantage of interactive training in lieu of attendance at off-site workshops. Interactive videodisk instruction has been provided to professionals for a variety of topics, including emergency medical procedures (Lambert & Sallis, 1987), sales techniques (Goldman, 1988), corporate decision-making processes (Byers & Rhodes, 1989), and divorce mediation training (Gentry, 1992).

In a meta-analysis of 100 studies, McNeil and Nelson (1991) found substantial effects of interactive videodisk instruction on cognitive and performance measures, with a .53 mean effect size across age groups (college students, military personnel, salespeople), instructional content, and environment. These studies were conducted in military, industrial, and higher educational settings, and they have shown that interactive videodisk instruction reduces instruction cost and time (Bosco, 1986; Cohen, 1984; Fletcher, 1990). In addition, this form of instruction has been shown to lead to greater practice time than did other methods; users find the experience very enjoyable. Interactive videodisk instruction has been found to be more effective than traditional lectures, reading, and passive viewing of videotapes, and it produces greater effect sizes than does computer-based instruction (.69 vs. .26) (Fletcher, 1990; Niemiec & Walberg, 1987).

Although the effects of this technology are consistent impressive, it has not been widely adopted outside of private industry. The use of interactive videodisks has been hampered by hardware complexity and costs, since not only a personal computer with monitor, but also a laserdisc player and television monitor are needed. For example, the author used this system when he first implemented the prototype of the parenting CD-ROM. Social service agencies had great difficulty reconnecting the equipment correctly if they moved it, requiring frequent technical support from project staff. None of the agencies was interested in purchasing the program in spite of strong evidence of effectiveness.

Parent Training CD-ROM: Goals, Development, Content, and Evidence

Goals   Seven years ago, the author identified challenges in developing an interactive video program for parents and families. It must be interesting and nonthreatening to parents, be developed with empirically validated content and teaching methods, be applied in a standardized way in a variety of locations, be self-administered, be capable of widespread dissemination, and be affordable to agencies serving families. In order to facilitate dissemination, the program must be capable of being integrated into existing services with no more than minimal staff training in either program delivery or operation. Since the highest-risk families are usually poor, sensitive to implied blame, and difficult to engage, the program had to be brief, easy to operate for those unfamiliar with computers, private, self-paced, and highly engaging, and must meet their own perceived needs.

Development and Content   The author gathered a team of professionals in child and family psychology, film, telecommunications, software development, and multimedia productions to plan and create an interactive videodisk program that would train parents to improve their parenting skills. Research on the impact of videotaped modeling in teaching parenting skills (i.e., Webster-Stratton's work) strongly encouraged the team to adopt a video-based approach.

Parenting Wisely (PW) is a brief (approximately three hours), CD-ROM-based intervention that requires minimal agency resources to operate. All that is needed is a support person to turn on the computer and spend a few minutes teaching the parent how to use a mouse, as pointing and clicking are the only skills needed to operate the program. The program itself teaches the parent how to use it. In order to facilitate its adoption, the ease of agency implementation and parental use was a primary goal for the program's design.

The PW program teaches adaptive parenting skills in the form of using "I" statements, active listening, contracting, monitoring children's behavior, problem solving, assertive discipline, parenting as a team, positive reinforcement, speaking respectfully, and contingency management. The program was developed from both cognitive-behavioral and family systems models. As such, it emphasizes that family members' actions are interdependent and that the thoughts that family members were experiencing with one another prior to interactions with one another are important. The Functional Family Therapy model of James Alexander (J. Alexander & Parsons, 1982; J. Alexander, Pugh, & Parsons, 1998) served as the foundation to the theoretical and functional approach taken in the PW program. I have been teaching this model to graduate students working with families of delinquents for almost two decades and the strong treatment effects from research conducted on this approach at Ohio University (Gordon et al., 1998) convinced me to incorporate essential features of this approach into the CD-ROM.

Parenting skills are presented in a series of videotaped segments showing families attempting to deal with programs, such as children not doing homework or not obeying parental requests, presented in nine case studies. After a case study is presented, the parent is instructed to choose one of three solutions that is most similar to the way he or she would handle that situation. A videotaped portrayal of that solution is then displayed on the computer screen. The program then critiques the chosen solution, providing feedback to the parent on both the positive and negative consequences of dealing with the program in the chosen manner. If the parent chose a solution that was not particularly effective, the computer instructs the parent to choose another solution. Once the most effective solution is selected, an on-screen quiz with feedback provides the parent with an opportunity to see how well he or she learned the techniques taught in the program.

The skills usually emphasized in a behaviorally based approach are discipline, effective communication, monitoring the child's behavior, the use of reinforcement (both tangible and social), contracting, contingency management, facilitating prosocial behavior, and anticipating new conflicts or problems. In a relationship-enhancement approach, the skills typically taught to the parents are mutual play, anticipation of new problem situations, and increased communication through the use of "I" statements and active listening (Ginsberg, 1989; Schaefer & Briesmeister, 1989). The choice of skills to be taught in the PW program was based on those associated with positive outcomes in the literature on parent- and family-centered interventions (Gordon et al., 1998; Grover, 1998). The author's 25 years of experience working with families and supervising graduate students working with families of delinquents also informed the choices of representative problems and effective solutions. For example, the problem of homework noncompliance was chosen because of the high frequency of this problem in families of delinquents. After parents were taught the skills of parental monitoring and parent-teacher communication, academic problems declined.

Evidence   Research conducted on this program has shown PW to be effective at reducing problem behaviors in children, improving family functioning, reducing maternal depression, increasing parenting knowledge, and increasing the use of effective parenting skills (Segal, Gordon, Chen, Kacir, & Gylys, 1999; Kacir & Gordon, 1999; Lagges & Gordon, 1999; Woodruff & Gordon, 2000). In a study using participants referred from outpatient clinics and a residential treatment center for juvenile delinquents, Segal et al. found significant decreases in the number and intensity of child problem behaviors. Parents also reported an increased use of effective parenting skills and showed greater knowledge of parenting skills taught in the program.

Using randomly assigned control and treatment groups, Kacir and Gordon (1999) investigated the effectiveness of the PW program with parents of 38 adolescents recruited through local public schools. At a one-month follow-up, parents in the treatment group demonstrated significantly greater knowledge of parenting skills than did parents in the control group. At one- and four-month follow-ups, parents in the treatment group also reported greater decreases, from 14 to 6, than control subjects in the number and intensity of child problem behav-

iors on the Eyberg Child Behavior Inventory (ECBI, Eyberg & Ross, 1978). Most teens in the treatment group showed clinically elevated scores on the ECBI prior to their mother's using the program. Four months after program use, 50% of the teens were classified as recovered on the ECBI (scoring in the normal range). Average effect sizes for all measures were .46 (see figure 76.1).

While prior research focused on individual administration of the program to parents of adolescents, Lagges and Gordon (1999) investigated the effectiveness of using the PW program with 64 teenage mothers whose children were infants and toddlers. Compared to control subjects, teenage mothers in the treatment group demonstrated greater increases in their knowledge of adaptive parenting skills at a two-month follow-up. Mothers in the treatment group were also more likely than were control subjects to endorse the effectiveness of adaptive parenting practices over coercive practices at follow-up. This study demonstrates the flexibility of the PW program and its potential for use in a variety of contexts. Teachers of high school students in health and home economics classes have their students "fly the parent simulator" when they use the PW program, in an effort to train them before they become parents.

Gordon and Kacir (1998) examined the effectiveness of the PW program when used with 60 court-referred parents of juvenile delinquents. These parents were often resistant to treatment, unmotivated, and had repeatedly demonstrated poor parenting practices in the past. Nevertheless, these parents also showed improvement, in comparison

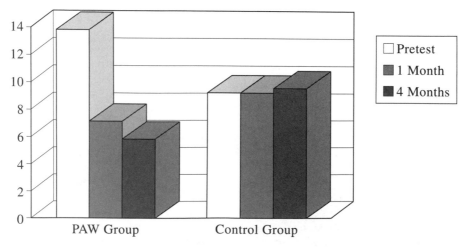

Figure 76.1 Changes in problem child behaviors on Eyberg Child Behavior Inventory.

to a no-treatment control group, on both the ECBI Total Problems scale (Eyberg & Ross, 1978) and on a parenting knowledge test. These improvements were demonstrated at three- and six-months posttreatment (see figure 76.2). Additionally, the children of parents who used the PW program showed decreases in negative behaviors, as reported on the Parent Daily Report (Chamberlain & Reid, 1987) collected one week, one month, three months, and six months following treatment. Effect sizes ranged from .49 to .76, indicating a robust treatment effect. A control group matched on juvenile court involvement, but not on pretest level of behavior problems, did not show changes in either measure of child problem behavior.

A recent study of PW as a strategy for family intervention has found that family functioning, as measured by the Family Assessment Device (Epstein, Baldwin, & Bishop, 1983; Miller, Epstein, Bishop, & Keitner, 1985), improved two months after parents and children used the program (Woodruff & Gordon, 2000). High-risk, disadvantaged families with a fourth- to sixth-grade student were randomly assigned to receive in their homes either the PW program (on a laptop computer) or parent education booklets (*Principles of Parenting*) covering similar content. The PW group showed greater reductions in child problem behavior (on the ECBI), as well as improvement in such aspects of family functioning as role expectations and problem solving. Both interventions produced reductions in material depression. These parents earlier had refused to participate in the same study offered at their children's school, in spite of offers to provide transportation, child care, cash payments, and food. A six-month follow-up showed

that child behavior problems continued to be reduced. Clinically significant behavior change occurred for 42% of the PW group and for 27% of the comparison group. A comparison of studies conducted on PW is presented in Table 76.1.

In all the studies conducted on PW, parents who used the program reported overall satisfaction and found the teaching format easy to follow. They also found the scenarios realistic, the problems depicted to be relevant to their families, and the parenting skills taught reasonable solutions to those problems. The parents felt confident they could apply the skills in their families. These findings may help explain why parents were willing to spend two to three hours in one sitting using the program, and why improvements in child behavior were evident a week after parents used the program.

The size of the treatment effect is highly unusual, given the very brief duration of the treatment. Although effect sizes for other studies using interactive video were also moderately large (McNeil & Nelson, 1991; Niemiec & Walberg, 1987), high-risk families have not, until now, been exposed to this technology, nor has CD-ROM or interactive ideo been applied to parenting and family living skills. These moderately large treatment effects are probably due to a combination of at least three factors: videotaped modeling of excellent and highly relevant content, a very high level of required user interaction, and the private, self-paced, and nonjudgmental format of a computer. Such characteristics should be appealing for primary prevention, where parents are more sensitive to barriers such as inconvenience, stigma, and defensiveness, compared to secondary or tertiary prevention where parents are more motivated to get help for chronic

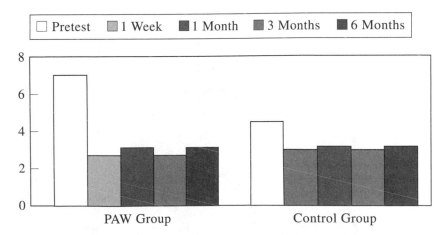

Figure 76.2 Changes in child problem behavior on parent daily report.

Table 76.1 Comparison of Studies of Parenting Wisely

Study	Participants (n)	Site	Design	Follow-up Period	Child Problem Behavior PW Effect Size (Cohen's d)
Segal et al. (1999)	Parents of 11–18-year-olds (42)	Community mental health and juvenile detention	RA[a] to 2 treatment groups	1 month	.78[b], 1.27[c]
Lagges & Gordon (1999)	Teen parents of infants and toddlers (62)	School	RA to treatment and control	2 months	.67[d]
Kacir & Gordon (1999)	Parents of problem adolescents (38)	University	RA to treatment and control	2, 4 months	1.2[b]
Gordon & Kacir (1998)	Parents of delinquents (72)	Community and university	Treatment and matched control	1, 3, 6 months	.59[b], .76[c]
Woodruff & Gordon (1999)	Parents of 9–13-year-olds	Home	RA to 2 treatment groups	2, 6 months	.37[b]

[a] = RA: Random assignment.

[b] = Eyberg Child Behavior Inventory.

[c] Parents Daily Report.

[d] Parental response to hypothetical problem behavior.

child problem behavior. Table 76.2 lists important differences between traditional therapy and CD-ROM approaches, which may explain these treatment effects.

Adolescent problem behaviors and poor family functioning are two main risk factors associated with adolescent substance use (Santisteban et al., 1997). It appears that the PW program is effective in reducing these risk factors. The Kacir and Gordon (1999), Gordon and Kacir (1998), and Segal et al. (1999) studies showed that child problem behaviors decreased while parent knowledge of parenting skills increased. Woodruff and Gordon (2000) found improvements in family functioning as well as reductions in child problem behaviors.

Barriers to Dissemination of CD-ROM Technology

Despite the value of using interactive CD-ROMs for parenting instruction, utilizing modern technology can be daunting for professionals and paraprofessionals. Many barriers block the path of even the most vigilant technology supporter (e.g., the lack of available equipment and funding to purchase, update, and maintain equipment; of technological expertise; and of training on how to implement and use technology within specific fields). However, the use of technology among mental health providers is particularly challenging as the mental health profession holds many views about the nature of change which need to be altered for successful implementation of technological resources.

Many therapists received training influenced by the medical model, which focuses on individual psychopathology. Such professionals believe (1) that psychological services need to be provided in a face-to-face, often one-on-one, presentation in order to be effective; (2) that change can occur only within a confidential, self-disclosing relationship; (3) that services need to be provided by a human being, who can mold the intervention to the individual client; and (4) that meaningful change takes a long time (Kacir et al., 1999). In addition, many therapists are unaware of the literature on the effects of videotaped modeling and interactive videodisk instruction. Thus, they may be skeptical that a computer or videodisk can produce meaningful change in a short period of time. Other professions, however, are more open to this notion. Family life educators are increasingly using technology to reach clients through videos, satellite downlinks, e-mail, the Internet, and interactive CD-ROMs. Judges and children's services personnel have also begun to recognize the ability of technology to reach more families, more often, with less expenditures of time, money, and personnel (Gordon & Kacir, 1998).

Therapists are not the only barriers to implementing technological services. Parents also need to change hard-held opinions. Despite the growth in computer access at work, in local libraries, and in homes, many parents remain computer illiterate. This ignorance of how technology works can lead to fear of the technology itself. In addition to this fear and distrust, many parents do not see the connection between parenting and their children's problem behaviors and thus are resistant to parent training. In fact, many will not attend parent training classes unless mandated by a judge. In a national survey of education programs for divorcing parents, attendance at mandatory classes averaged 110 par-

Table 76.2 Comparison of Therapy and Interactive CD-ROM

Therapy	Interactive CD-ROM
1. Judgment by therapist	No judgment by computer
2. Client defensiveness main obstacle to progress	Minimal client defensiveness
3. Majority of therapy time and cost devoted to resistance	Little of program time devoted to resistance
4. Client discloses parenting errors	Client recognizes parenting errors by actors
5. Feedback on parenting errors infrequent and indirect	Client actively seeks feedback on parenting errors performed by actors in program
6. Verbal descriptions of parenting	Detailed visual and verbal examples of parenting
7. Infrequent reinforcement of good parenting practices	Frequent reinforcement of good parenting practices
8. Client rarely asks for repetition of unclear advice	Client can repeat any part of program any time
9. Pace selected by therapist	Pace selected by client
10. Focus on therapist-client relationship	Exclusive focus on teaching good parenting
11. Difficult to improve therapist skills	Relatively easy to improve program content

ents per month while voluntary attendance averaged about 20 parents monthly (Geasler & Blaisure, 1998). Court-mandated programs have produced positive outcomes, such as improved parental communication and reductions in parental conflict and relitigation (Arbuthnot & Gordon, 1996; Kramer, Arbuthnot, & Gordon, 1998). Therefore, parents whose children are identified by juvenile courts, schools, and child protective services as being at risk for continued problems should be coerced or enticed to attend effective programs.

If parents do attend training, they often are not given the opportunity to actively participate. Only 35% of the programs in Geasler and Blaisure's study (1998) reported using active participant involvement such as role play or skill-building activities despite the evidence that this teaching strategy yields the best outcomes. Parent education for divorcing parents has enjoyed explosive growth, but the growing numbers of court-mandated parents attending these classes has led to larger classes and reduced interaction (Arbuthnot & Gordon, 1996).

Many parents feel uncomfortable in groups or asking their specific questions in front of strangers for fear of being judged, so they prefer small groups or individual parent training. Often, parenting classes are so short that they offer only vague content, and parents do not have their specific problems addressed or do not receive the skill-building practice that change requires. In our experience, most parents who expressed a willingness to receive parent eduction failed to appear for the first session if they were assigned to a group rather than to an individual session. However, those who did attend the first group continued for all three sessions (Ponferrada, Lobo, & Gordon, 2000). Thus, some parents who are contemplating parent education may be more likely to use a CD-ROM program individually than attend group sessions. Perhaps the proactive parents seeking parent education prior to their children developing problems will be open to a private CD-ROM program, and, if that is a successful experience, they will be open to attending parenting classes.

While some clients will have access to computers within their own homes, many will rely on schools, libraries, community centers, and agencies to provide access. In many cases, costs related to equipment purchasing and maintenance would need to be absorbed by someone other than the client (Grover, 1998). The initial costs of implementing technological programs must be considered within the full formula of a cost-benefit analysis. Initial start-up costs, when compared to the price of time, wages, and materials for more traditional programming over time, are minimal.

Therapists must be shown that technology affords the opportunity to provide meaningful, one-on-one, confidential, and individualized interventions for clients in a much shorter period of time. The advantages that interactive CD-ROM technology offers seem significant. Parents can receive immediate, individualized, nonjudgmental feedback in a private setting, proceeding at their own pace. The parents are able to view models of effective parenting, to practice choosing effective strategies for dealing with their child's problem behaviors, and then to incorporate these methods into their repertoire.

Services utilizing technology must strive to make it user-friendly. Programs must be visually appealing and easy to negotiate, and they must offer interactive instruction. Programs must also consider the diversity of users. The content and format should reflect the needs and preferences of the users. Technological programming can more readily accomplish this compared to more traditional programming because it can (1) present a variety of diverse, effective models; (2) provide content that is specific to parents of adolescents; (3) give immediate feedback to parents in a nonthreatening, private setting; (4) offer various levels of accessibility for parents of differing computer literacy; and (5) allow parents to access the program at nontraditional hours to better adapt to busy schedules. When Internet download time is improved through increased bandwidth, these types of programs will be delivered in parents' homes through the Internet. Another advantage of a computer delivering the intervention compared to a person is that the user will not be distracted by characteristics of the person (gender, age, race, social class, marital status, parental status) which are irrelevant to the content.

Gaps in Knowledge of Interactive Video Approaches to Family Interventions

With the exception of the PW CD-ROM, the scientific bases for interactive video approaches to teaching have involved applications unrelated to family or parent interventions. Finding from the handful of studies on the PW program need to be replicated independent of Ohio University faculty and students. Such replication attempts are under way in many locations. This interest in replication has been due to the unusually large effect sizes, ease of implementation, and assurance of treatment integrity. In addition to several university replication attempts, a promising development has been the interest in controlled evaluation studies from social service agencies who have purchased the program. Most of these agencies had to receive grants to fund the program, and evaluation has often been a requirement of the granting agencies.

Although samples in the early studies of PW have included some ethnic diversity, we need to look at larger samples of Hispanic and African American families to learn more about cultural appropriateness and effectiveness. A feasibility study in New York will address this need. Other gaps in our knowledge about the effects of this technology are the relative effectiveness and cost-effectiveness of this approach versus parent eduction, parent training, and family therapy for populations varying in risk. We also need to know the additive effects of this technology when combined with traditional approaches, including the effects on engaging high-risk families. For example, when we offered the PW program (via a laptop computer in their homes) to families of chronic delinquents, several families who had refused traditional services assented and subsequently agreed to participate in family therapy. We also need to know the effects of including other family members in the intervention, such as teens, children, and the father (since all the participants in our studies have been mothers), and we need to determine the maintenance of these effects over time. Can we enhance and extend treatment effects via repetition of the program at certain intervals or by adding brief therapist consultation (either face-to-face or by telephone or via the Internet)? We are looking at this in a large study in Manchester, England. Can this interactive video approach be effective when applied to parents of younger children, as primary or secondary prevention? We are currently developing such a program for parents of 4–10-year-olds.

The gaps in our knowledge between the science base and practice include the issue of understanding the reason for service provider resistance to use of this technology. We have noted that the greatest resistance comes from the mental health profession. Research needs to be done on which activities of therapists, particularly those that cannot be duplicated with multimedia technology, add reliable treatment effects to the technology. We also need to identify the most salient predictors of parental resistance to parent education in general (which may vary by family risk and social class) and develop cost-effective methods of overcoming that resistance (Lagges, 1999). Although we know we can engage high-risk families by providing opportunities for community networking and strong incentives, as well as removing barriers to participation, such labor-intensive approaches limit the widespread application of parent education. Perhaps public service announcements and letters from credible community leaders, aimed at specific beliefs parents hold that prevent them from using parent education, could increase their participation.

Another area for study is reimbursement: What changes in reimbursement for services would be needed to get substantial numbers of service providers to use this technology? Currently, Medicaid, insurance companies, and HMOs require face-to-face contact with a professional or reimbursement. As the number and quality of interactive CD-ROM and Web-based intervention increase, reimbursement policies may include them.

Action Steps for Transfer of CD-ROM Technology from Research to Practice

A variety of steps can facilitate the transfer of our knowledge of technology-based interventions to practice. In addition to the usual route of presenting the program's content and research findings at professional conferences, presenters should demonstrate the technology. Many professionals have never seen a highly interactive (Level III) CD-ROM, interactive video program, or an Internet-based intervention. Seeing it clarifies its advantages immediately. There are many appropriate professional organizations and conferences dealing with the treatment of substance abuse, such as those sponsored by juvenile justice, mental health, child protective services, county extension agents (including certified family life educators), marriage and family educators and therapists, and criminal justice. National conferences permit the widest exposure to those most active in their professions. Presentation at state conferences offers the advantage of increasing the networking and collaboration among a more cohesive group of professionals.

Conferences sponsored by state and federal government agencies are emphasizing "best practices" interventions, which meet varying standards of empirical validation. Governmental agencies also publish and disseminate information on such practices, including Web site listing. This CD-ROM technology can also be demonstrated through a Web site, eliminating the need to mail demonstration versions of the program. The Web site devoted to the CD-ROM can also list all the research on the program, as well as other information important to an agency considering implementation. The PW program has a Web site that exemplifies these suggestions (http://www.familyworksinc.com). Within the next few years, these interactive programs will be available on the Internet and thus will be available worldwide to families who have Internet access (either at home, at work, or through their public library). This development will have truly awesome possibilities for the dissemination of effective interventions.

To maximize access to this technology, as well as to other validated treatment approaches, the program should be packaged where it can be marketed commercially. This is a process for which few academic progenitors of these programs are prepared or supported. Universities can and should assist faculty in these ventures by providing startup help for small businesses, such as the Innovation and Technology Transfer Center at Ohio University. The university provided office space and support in the form of telephone, duplication, faxing, secretarial help, and, most important, consultation with on-site experts in all aspects of developing a small business, including marketing advice and research, copyrighting, patents, and licensing. Universities can offer financial support to bring a program to the market in exchange for royalty-sharing agreements. Family Works Inc. was the company formed at the university's business incubator, whose goal was the marketing of CD-ROM parent and family interventions. Profits from the sale of the CD-ROM are used for developing upgrades based on research and user feedback, as well as for immediate funding for research when unexpected opportunities arise. Such university–private company partnerships offer advantages that neither entity could accomplish alone.

In addition to providing business incubation, universities need to help faculty progenitors of effective programs commit the time needed for the assorted activities mentioned above. The responsibility and opportunity to disseminate programs fall almost exclusively on the progenitor, as he or she is the most (or perhaps only) motivated, knowledgeable, and credible person to do this. Unfortunately, the progenitor's involvement in traditional academic duties precludes serious commitment to dissemination. Academic departments, which tend to be insulated from the community and the applied field, seldom provide rewards for outside ventures (unless tied to grant funding). The typical academic mind-set does not value entrepreneuring. In many locations the progenitor will expose himself or herself to criticism for not sharing the department's workload. To offset such obstacles, university administrations can provide substantial recognition, release time, and financial support. Some progenitors who work at medical schools have far

more flexibility and support for dissemination activities (e.g. Scott Henggeler, who is successfully disseminating Multisystemic Therapy). Some federal grant programs seeking to encourage dissemination of evidence-based programs, such as Karol Kumpfer's Strengthening America's Families grant and Del Elliott's Blueprints for Violence Prevention grant, pay progenitors to provide training and ongoing consultation (essential for maintaining therapeutic integrity) to agencies seeking to implement their programs.

Another step to aid dissemination is media attention. Many universities have media relations departments, which publicize faculty members' work. This can take the form of news releases coinciding with a conference presentation of research findings or making the faculty member available to journalists and radio and TV staff for topics of interest via Profnet. Progenitors who talk to journalists covering professional conferences inform not only other professionals of their work, but the public and policymakers as well. The author's contact with the BBC when they were covering an international conference resulted in a subsequent BBC documentary (*Trouble With Boys*). The documentary showed the changes to a family of a delinquent boy after the family participated in Functional Family Therapy and the PW program. The broadcast facilitated the dissemination of empirically validated parent- and family-focused preventive interventions in the United Kingdom Public policy was also influenced when policymakers attended the same conference and subsequently required "Parenting Orders" to be part of delinquency treatment programs nationwide.

Finally, a step we have taken to foster dissemination is to continue contact with agencies that have purchased the PW program. We make regular calls to encourage them to implement the program as designed, to conduct controlled evaluations on its impact, and to offer consultation on overcoming barriers in their communities. We encourage agencies to collaborate with other agencies to suggest needed areas of research and to submit their evaluations for presentation at their professional conferences. We may also provide a network of other agencies that are conducting evaluations to facilitate information transfer. By staying in contact with a variety of agencies doing this work, we can incorporate their feedback and research results into improvements to the program. This can be done often and inexpensively, via upgrades to the PW program. Changing the CD-ROM is a much less daunting task than that faced by developers of traditional programs when they wish to introduce changes, following initial training, in the practices of service providers.

Conclusion

Professionals who provide services to families at risk for substance abuse and delinquency are very often unaware of evidence-based interventions, and they face serious obstacles to substantially increasing the number of families who can receive effective services. They are also unaware of the literature on the effectiveness of interactive videodisk instruction and on the power of videotaped modeling of parenting skills to produce lasting changes in the children of parents who view the tapes. The author's parenting skill training CD-ROM, which utilized knowledge from those two areas of literature, has shown promise in producing effect sizes comparable to those found with interactive videodisk instruction. Due to the simplicity of implementation, the assurance of treatment integrity, and the low cost, this type of program can facilitate the dissemination of research-based methods among practitioners. Practitioners other than mental health professionals seem to be the most promising audience for technology-based prevention efforts.

I wish to thank Raymond Lorion for his helpful comments on an earlier draft of this paper.

References

Alexander, D. E., & Gwyther, R. E. (1995). Alcoholism in adolescents and their families: Family-focused assessment and management. *Pediatric Clinics of North America, 42*(1), 217–234.

Alexander, J. F., & Parsons, B. V. (1982). *Functional family therapy: Principles and procedures.* Carmel, CA: Brooks/Cole.

Alexander, J. F., Pugh, C., & Parsons, B. V., with Barton, C. Gordon, D., Grotpeter, J. K., Hanson, K., Harrison, R., Mears, S., Mihalic, S. F., Schulman, S., Waldron, H., & Sexton, T. (1998). Functional family therapy. In D. S. Elliott (Series Ed.), *Blueprints for violence prevention (Book 3).* Boulder, CO: Center for the Study and Prevention of Violence, Institute of Behavioral Science, University of Colorado.

Arbuthnot, J., & Gordon, D. A. (1996). Does mandatory divorce education for parent work? A six-month outcome evaluation. *Family and Conciliation Courts Review, 34,* 60–81.

Bickman, L., & Noser, K. (1999). Meeting the challenges in the delivery of child and adolescent mental health services in the next millennium: The continuous quality improvement approach. *Applied & Preventive Psychology, 8,* 247–256.

Bosco, J. (1986). An analysis of evaluations of interactive video. *Educational Technology, 26,* 7–17.

Botvin, G. J. (1996). Substance abuse prevention through life skills training. In R. D. Peters & R. J. McMahon (Eds.). Students and substances: Social power in drug education. *Educational Evaluation and Policy Analysis, 19*(1), 65–82.

Brown, B. B., Mounts, N., Lamborn, S. D., & Steinberg, L. (1993). *Preventing childhood disorders, substance abuse, and delinquency.* Thousand Oaks, CA: Sage Publications.

Brook, J. S., Whiteman, M., Gordon, A. S., Nomura, C., & Brook, D. W. (1986). Onset of adolescent drinking: A longitudinal study of intrapersonal and interpersonal antecedents. *Advances in Alcohol and Substance Abuse, 5*(3), 91–110.

Bry, B., McKeon, P. E., & Pandina, R. J. (1982). Extent of drug use as a function of number of risk factors. *Journal of Abnormal Psychology, 91*(4), 273–279.

Byers, D., & Rhodes, D. M. (1989). Developing sales experience through interactive vide. *Sales and Market Training, 5,* 10–12.

Catalano, R. F., Haggerty, K. P., Gainey, R. R., & Hoppe, M. J. (1997). Reducing parental risk factors for children's substance misuse: Preliminary outcomes with opiate-addicted parents. *Substance Use & Misuse, 32*(6), 699–721.

Chamberlain, P., & Reid, J. B. (1987). Parent observation and report of child symptoms. *Behavioral Assessment, 9,* 97–109.

Chambless, D. L. (1999). Empirically validated treatments—what now? *Applied & Preventive Psychology, 8,* 281–284.

Cohen, V. B. (1984). Interactive features in the design of videodisc materials. *Educational Technology, 24,* 16–20.

Dishion, T. J., Reid, J. B., & Patterson, G. R. (1988). Empirical guidelines for a family intervention for adolescent drug use. *Journal of Chemical Dependency Treatment, 1*(2), 189–224.

Epstein, N. S., Baldwin, L. M., & Bishop, D. S. (1983). The McMaster Family Assessment Device. *Journal of Marital and Family Therapy, 9,* 171–180.

Eyberg, S. M., & Robinson, E. A. (1983). Conduct problem behaviors: Standardization of a behavioral rating scale with adolescents. *Journal of Clinical Child Psychology, 12*(3), 347–354.

Eyberg, S. M., & Ross, A. W. (1978). Assessment of child behavior problems: The validation of a new inventory. *Journal of Clinical Psychology, 16,* 113–116.

Felner, R. D., Brand, S., Munhall, K., Counter, C., Millman, J. B., & Fried, J. (1994). The parenting partnership: The evaluation of a human service/corporate workplace collaboration for the prevention of substance abuse and mental health problems and the promotion of family and work adjustment. *Journal of Primary Prevention, 15*(2), 123–146.

Flanagan, S., Adams, H. E., & Forehand, R. (1979). A comparison of four instructional techniques for teaching parents to use time-out. *Behavior Therapy, 10,* 94–102.

Fletcher, J. D. (1990). Effectiveness and cost of interactive videodisc instruction in defense training and education (Report No. P-2372). Institute for Defense Analysis.

Forehand, R. L., & Long, N. (1988). Outpatient treatment of the acting-out child: Procedures, long-term follow-up data, and clinical problems. *Advances in Behavior Research and Therapy, 10,* 129–177.

Friedman, A. S. (1989). Family therapy vs. parent groups: Effects on adolescent drug users. *American Journal of Family Therapy, 17*(4), 335–347.

Geasler, M. J., & Blaisure, K. R. (1998). A review of divorce education program materials. *Family Relations, 47,* 167–175.

Gentry, D. B. (1992). Using computer aided interactive video technology to provide experiential learning for mediation trainees. *Journal of Divorce and Remarriage, 17*(3/4), 57–74.

Ginsberg, B. G. (1989). Training parents as therapeutic agents with foster/adoptive children using the filial approach. In C. E. Schaefer & J. M. Briesmeister (Eds.), *Handbook of parent training: Parents as co-therapists for children's behavior problems* (pp. 442–478). New York: Wiley.

Glynn, T. J., & Haenlein, M. (1988). Family theory and research on adolescent drug use: A review. *Journal of Chemical Dependency and Treatment, 1*(2), 39–56.

Goldman, B. (1988). Drama on computer screen proves a good teacher. *Canadian Medical Association Journal, 139,* 240.

Gordon, D. A., Jurkovic, G., & Arbuthnot, J. (1998). Treatment of the juvenile offender. In R. Wettstein (Ed.) *Treatment of offenders with mental disorders* (pp. 365–428). New York: Guilford Press.

Gordon, D. A., & Kacir, C. D. (1998). Effectiveness of an interactive parent training program for changing adolescent behavior for court-referred parents. Unpublished manuscript, Ohio University, Athens.

Grover, P. L. (Ed.). (1998). *Preventing substance abuse among children and adolescents— family centered approaches: A reference guide.* Substance Abuse and Mental Health Services Administration, Center for Substance Abuse Prevention, DHHS.

Hawkins, J. D. & Catalano, R. F. (1992). *Communities that care.* San Francisco: Jossey-Bass.

Hundleby, J. D., & Mercer, G. W. (1987). Family and friends as social environments and their relationship to young adolescents' use of alcohol, tobacco, and marijuana. *Journal of Marriage and the Family, 49,* 151–164.

Johnson, V., & Pandina, R. J. (1991). Effects of the family environment on adolescent substance use, delinquency, and coping styles. *American Journal of Drug and Alcohol Abuse, 17*(1), 71–88.

Kacir, C. D., & Gordon, D. A. (1999). Parenting Adolescents Wisely: The effects of an interactive video-based parent training program in Appalachia. *Child and Family Behavior Therapy, 21*(4), 1–22.

Kacir, C., Gordon, D. A., & Kirby, J. (1999). Using technology to change families: Parenting skill training via CD-ROM. Unpublished manuscript, Ohio University, Athens.

Kramer, K., Arbuthnot, J., & Gordon, D. A. (1998). Effects of skill-based versus information-based divorce education programs on domestic violence and parental communication. *Family and Conciliation Courts Review, 36,* 9–31.

Kumpfer, K. L., & DeMarsh, J. (1986). Family environmental and genetic influences on children's future chemical dependency. *Journal of Children in a Contemporary Society, 18*(1–2), 49–91.

Kumpfer, K. L., Molgaard, B., & Spoth, R. (1996). The Strengthening Families Program for the prevention of delinquency and drug use. In R. D. Peters and R. J. McMahon (Eds.). *Preventing childhood disorders, substance abuse, and delinquency* (pp. 241–267). Twin Oaks, CA: Sage Publications.

Lagges, A. (1999). Identifying and overcoming resistance to an interactive CD-ROM parent training program. Unpublished doctoral dissertation, Ohio University, Athens.

Lagges, A., & Gordon, D. A. (1999). Use of an interactive laserdisc parent training program with teenage parents. *Child and Family Behavior Therapy, 21*(1), 19–37.

Lambert, S. & Sallis, J. (Eds.). (1987). *CD-1 and interactive videodisc technology*. Indianapolis, IN: Howard W. Sams.

Lochman, J. E., & Wells, K. C. (1996). A social-cognitive intervention with aggressive children: Preventive effects and contextual implementation issues. In R. Dev. Peters & R. J. McMahon (Eds.), *Prevention and early intervention: Childhood disorders, substance use, and delinquency* (pp. 111–143). Newbury Park, CA: Sage.

Malkus, B. M. (1994). Family dynamic and structural correlates of adolescent substance abuse: A comparison of families of non-substance abusers and substance abusers. *Journal of Child and Adolescent Substance Abuse, 3*(4), 39–52.

McKay, J. R., Murphy, R. T., Rivinus, T. R., & Maisto, S. A. (1991). Family dysfunction and alcohol and drug use in adolescent psychiatric inpatients. *Journal of the American Academy of Child and Adolescent Psychiatry, 30*(6), 967–972.

McConnaughey, J. W., & Lader, W. (1998). Falling through the net: New data on the digital divide. National Telecommunications and Information Administration. U.S. Department of Commerce.

McNeil, B. J., & Nelson, K. R. (1991) Meta-analysis of interactive video instruction: A 10 year review of achievement effects. *Journal of Computer-Based Instruction, 18*(1), 1–6.

Miller, I. W., Epstein, N. B., Bishop, D. S., & Keitner, G. I. (1985). The McMaster Family Assessment Device: Reliability and validity. *Journal of Marital and Family Therapy, 11*(4), 345–356.

Mulvey, E. P., Arthur, M. W., & Reppucci, N. D. (1993). The prevention and treatment of juvenile delinquency: A review of the research. *Clinical Psychology Review, 13*, 133–167.

Nay, R. W. (1976). A systematic comparison of instructional techniques for parents. *Behavior Therapy, 6*, 14–21.

Niemiec, R., & Walberg, H. J. (1987). Comparative effects of computer-assisted instruction: A synthesis of reviews. *Journal of Educational Computing Research, 3*(1), 19–37.

O'Dell, S. L., Krug, W. W., Patterson, J. N., & Faustman, W. O. (1980). An assessment of methods for training parents in the use of time out. *Journal of Behavior Treatment and Experimental Psychiatry, 11*, 21–25.

O'Dell, S. L., O'Quinn, G. A., Alford, B. A., O'Briant, A. L. Bradlyn, A. S., & Giebenhain, J. E. (1982). Predicting the acquisition of parenting skills via four

raining methods. *Behavior Therapy, 13*, 194–208.

Patterson, G. R. (1986). Performance models for antisocial boys. *American Psychologist, 41*, 432–444.

Patterson, G. R., & Chamberlain, P. (1994). A functional analysis of resistance during parent training therapy. *Clinical Psychology: Science and Practice, 1*, 53–70.

Patterson, G. R., & Forgatch, M. S. (1985). Therapist behavior as a determinant for client noncompliance: A paradox for the behavior modifier. *Journal of Consulting and Clinical Psychology, 53*, 846–851.

Ponferrada, E., Lobo, T. L., & Gordon, D. A. (2000). Group vs. individual use of an interactive CD-ROM parent training program. Unpublished manuscript, Ohio University, Athens.

Santisteban, D. A., Coatsworth, J. D., Perez-Vidal, A., Mitrani, V., Jean-Gilles, M., & Szapocznik, J. (1997). Brief structural/strategic family therapy with African American and Hispanic high-risk youth. *Journal of Community Psychology, 25*(5), 453–471.

Schaefer, C. E., & Briesmeister, J. M. (Eds.). (1989). *Handbook of parent training: Parents as co-therapists for children's behavior problems*. New York: Wiley.

Segal, D., Gordon, D. A., Chen, P., Kacir, C., & Gylys, J. (1999). Parenting Adolescents Wisely: Comparing interactive computer-laserdisc and linear-video methods of intervention in a parent-training program. Unpublished manuscript, Ohio University, Athens.

Semlitz, M. D., & Gold, M. S. (1986). Adolescent drug abuse: Diagnosis, treatment, and prevention. *Psychiatric Clinics of North America, 9*(3), 455–473.

Spoth, R., & Redmond, C. (1993). Study of participation barriers in family-focused prevention: Research issues and preliminary results. *International Quarterly of Community Health Eduction, 13*(4), 365–388.

Spoth, R., & Redmond, C. (1995). Parent motivation to enroll in parenting skills programs: A model of family context and health belief predictors. *Journal of Family Psychology, 9*, 294–310.

Spoth, R., Redmond, C., Haggerty, K., & Ward, T. (1995). A controlled parenting skills outcome study examining individual difference and attendance effects. *Journal of Marriage and the Family, 57*, 449–464.

St. Pierre, T. L., & Kaltreider, D. L. (1997). Strategies for involving parents of high-risk youth in drug prevention: A three-year longitudinal study in Boys and Girls Clubs.

Journal of Community Psychology, 25(5), 473–485.

St. Pierre, T. L., Kaltreider, D. L., Mark, M. M., & Aikin, K. J. (1992). Drug prevention in a community setting: A longitudinal study of the relative effectiveness of a three-year primary prevention program in Boys and Girls Clubs across the nation. *American Journal of Community Psychology, 20,* 673–706.

Stewart, M. A., & Brown, S. A. (1993). Family functioning following adolescent substance abuse treatment. *Journal of Substance Abuse, 5,* 327–339.

Swadi, H. (1991). Relative risk factors in detecting adolescent drug abuse. *Drug and Alcohol Dependence, 29,* 253–254.

Swaim, R. C. (1991). Childhood risk factors and adolescent drug abuse. *Educational Psychology Review, 3*(4), 363–397.

Webster-Stratton, C. (1984). Randomized trial of two parent-training programs for families with conduct-disordered children. *Journal of Consulting and Clinical Psychology, 52,* 103–115.

Webster-Stratton, C. (1990). Enhancing the effectiveness of self-administered videotape parent training for families with conduct-problem children. *Journal of Abnormal Child Psychology, 18*(5), 479–492.

Webster-Stratton, C. (1992). Individually administered videotape parent training: Who benefits? *Cognitive Therapy and Research, 16*(1), 31–52.

Webster-Stratton, C., Hollinsworth, T., & Kolpacoff, M. (1989). The long-term effectiveness and clinical significance of three cost-effective training programs for families with conduct-problem children. *Journal of Consulting and Clinical Psychology, 57,* 550–553.

Webster-Stratton, C., Kolpacoff, M., & Hollinsworth, T. (1988). Self-administered videotape therapy for families with conduct-problem children: Comparison with two cost-effective treatments and a control group. *Journal of Consulting and Clinical Psychology, 56,* 558–566.

Woodruff, C., & Gordon, D. A. (2000). Home delivery of parent skills training: A comparison of interactive CD-ROM and booklets for high risk families. Unpublished manuscript, Ohio University, Athens.

DORINDA N. NOBLE
KATHLEEN PERKINS
MARIAN FATOUT

77

On Being a Strength Coach: Child Welfare and the Strengths Model

Athletic teams know the importance of recognizing and developing strengths: large athletic organizations employ strength coaches to do this very thing. Strength coaches assess the individual athlete's physical and emotional capacities and devise programs to strengthen muscles, coordination, skills, and attitude. The analogy between strength coaches and child welfare workers is instructive, for child welfare workers must help families to develop:

- Strong and supple emotional muscles, which give parents skills in nurturing and acceptance
- Coordination between physical and emotional needs, so that parents can set appropriate boundaries, develop self-control, and be flexible in their responses
- Emotional and physical knowledge and skills, which are critical to providing appropriate child care
- Winning attitudes of support, caring, self-confidence, and healthy life habits

These are daunting tasks, since families involved with child welfare often have had a mental and emotional diet deprived of consistent caring and support and have been surrounded by unhealthy lifestyles of poverty, crime, and abuse. This article discusses how child welfare workers can become strength coaches with such families.

The Need for a Change in Perspective in Child Welfare

Most social work theories are replete with the language of pathology and problems, reflecting a social history in which moral character and physical deficits shaped both how people regarded themselves and how social resources were allocated (Saleebey, 1992). Despite changing attitudes and language, social work practice—and particularly child welfare—still emphasizes failure.

As a residual social service system, child welfare deals with involuntary, means-tested clients who are assessed for individual pathology and risk, rather than for the personal strengths they employ to survive life's challenges. From its genesis in juvenile court to its present decided emphasis on serious child abuse, the child welfare movement can be characterized as paternalistic (Hegar & Hunzeker, 1988). Both children and parents feel powerless when the state intervenes to protect children. The client either is ordered by the court to receive services or is coerced by an agency, person, or event to seek services as a "nonvoluntary" client (Rooney, 1992). The poor, minorities, and female single parents, who tend to be overrepresented on public service rolls, feel powerless when they face public service providers who are charged with reporting maltreatment and who may accept the stereotype that poor children are abused, while nonpoor children are accidentally injured (Hegar & Hunzeker, 1988).

Larry was 3 when he was first removed from his mother's custody, because she had been sentenced to prison for robbery and assault. Larry's extended family was chaotic, with a number of his relatives serving prison time, several suffering from serious mental illness, and most of them struggling with physical problems. Poverty and periodic homelessness were staples of the family's existence. Until he was 10, Larry rotated among seven different foster home placements and more relative placements than the agency could track. His schooling was sporadic at best, and his behavior often destructive and violent. At age 10, when the state placed Larry in a residential treatment center, he could not read and had little impulse control. A number of public service and child welfare workers had dealt with the case, and they had little hope of a good outcome for Larry. Reuniting him with his family following his treatment seemed highly suspect, though Larry's mother had recently been paroled.

Clients like Larry's mother feel powerless, and often hopeless, as they view the possible consequences (such as court appearances, juvenile adjudication, substitute placements, or permanent removal of the child from the family) that loom in their futures (Hegar & Hunzeker, 1988). On the other hand, the worker is backed by strong community power. Sue (1981) describes empowerment as the process of moving toward an internal locus of control and an external locus of responsibility. When social control systems, such as the child welfare organization, intervene in family life, the family finds itself living with external locus of control and either internal or external locus of responsibility. If the client perceives the situation as totally out of his or her control, then the situation is no longer one of personal responsibility for the situation and he or she may well struggle against, or sabotage, agency services.

Larry's mother, Estelle, was paroled from prison after six years. She had seen Larry virtually not at all during that time, and, as far as the worker assigned to the case could see, mother and son had almost no relationship on which to build. Estelle said that she hardly knew her son and couldn't think what to do with him now. The worker and Estelle set a goal of Estelle getting to know her child. Fortunately, the treatment center had earmarked some funds to help parents visit, and Estelle and Larry began to have regular visits. The worker encouraged Estelle, explaining that her participation in his treatment was critical.

Moving toward the Strengths Perspective

The child welfare worker, acting as a strength coach, focused on Estelle's human potential and positive client attributes, while encouraging collaboration between worker and client. Though identifying problems is important, identifying client strengths is the goal that guides both assessment and intervention. Once the worker and client have established a viable working relationship, family, friends, and community networks can be included to build on strengths, as the social worker and the client have continuous dialogue and collaboration.

Estelle had no real job skills to market. The worker, however, did learn from the parole officer that Estelle had received her GED while in prison. The worker used achieving the GED as a model with Larry's mother, saying, "Larry's situation is not good. But you've dealt with bad situations before: you ended up in prison and you still worked hard to get your GED. That's something you can really use to start making a life that Larry can come home to." The worker, the parole officer, and Estelle worked together to secure Estelle a job in a mattress factory. Though the worker's time was quite limited, she and Estelle set a priority goal of making Estelle's job work for her, so that she could remain employed and save up money to get her own apartment by the time Larry finished treatment.

Though the worker was fully aware of the problems endemic to this case, she formed a partnership with Estelle aimed at creating a suitable home that Larry could return to after treatment. Intrinsic to ecological theory, which is the heart of the strengths model, is a dual commitment to deliver services in collaboration with clients and to confront dysfunctional service or support systems that thwart client development. Because the strengths model is built around ecological concepts, clients, rather than providers, shape roles, routines, and rules. Consequently, personal dignity transcends the importance of roles (Rose 1992), and diagnosis becomes a descriptive rather than a prescriptive tool.

Several key concepts shape the strengths model. *Empowerment* is the linchpin of the strengths model. The social worker must seek out diverse settings where people are already handling their problems in living, and learn from these examples how to assist others to find their own solutions and gain control over their lives (Rappaport, 1981; Saleeby, 1992). The model's emphasis on collaboration, acknowledging individual realities, and recognizing unique strengths gives voice to people who have been silenced by systems of care. Empowerment underpins the strengths model's view of people as active participants in service delivery, rather than as diagnostic categories, objects to be managed, or passive consumers of service menus.

A close corollary to the concept of empowerment is *suspension of disbelief*, defined as acceptance of the client's "interpretive slant" of given situations (Saleebey, 1992). The worker, once he or she has set aside personal prejudices about the client's situation and possibilities, can clearly hear the client's view (Petr, 1998). Once the worker has accepted the client's view of the situation, the stage is set for *dialogue and collaboration* between clients and social workers as they work toward common goals. Dialogue is possible only when the worker uses language that the client understands. In a collaborative relationship, the social worker and the client achieve his or her wants or goals (Weick, Rapp, Sullivan, & Kisthardt, 1989).

Larry, after a period of initial confusion and turmoil, began to settle down in the residential treatment center. For the first time in his existence, he was exposed to structure and predictability in his life. His behavior and outlook slowly became more functional. Larry's worker at the center was alarmed, however, by the fact that Larry was years behind his age group in schooling. He spent enough time with Larry, however, to see that Larry was always fiddling with people's hair; Larry, in fact, was fairly artistic in styling hair. He often talked about how he would like to be a stylist with his own salon, or maybe he would like to work on movie sets, styling hair. The worker set up a plan with Larry: the worker bought permanent wave solutions and other hair products, and Larry's goal was to learn to read the directions and mix the ingredients properly. Further, the worker secured some books on styling techniques for Larry. The worker also encouraged Estelle, as well as staff members, to let Larry do some simple styling on their hair, and Larry's goal was, not only to style hair, but to develop relationships.

This worker used Larry's natural talent as a vehicle to meet other needs, including relationship building. Collaboration and dialogue enhance the client's sense of *membership* in family, friendship, and community networks. People without membership are extremely vulnerable because they lack supportive networks in caring, interested communities. The strengths model emphasizes connecting clients with supportive networks and contends that the coming together of person and community constitutes *synergy*, the process of creating new energy and resources. New energy and resources lead to capacity for change, which, in the strengths model, is called *regeneration*. Regeneration highlights the fact that the innate abilities of the client can be effective in resolving problems.

After 12 months of residential treatment, Larry showed great strides in self-control. He appeared much more content, and he had gained some reading and math skills. The custodial agency, however, was compelled to move him back home, though workers feared that Larry would not be able to maintain the gains he had made. While Estelle was still employed, she was moving between various relatives' homes, and none of these homes was crime-free or stable. Larry had a rocky transition back to Estelle's supervision. The worker continued to point out to them that they had overcome many difficulties in getting to this point, and that both had talents they could bring to building a good home. Together they decided that Estelle needed her own place away from her relatives, who were frequently in trouble with the law. The worker, who had been closely working with the local housing authority and had forged some good relationships with the agency, was able to help Estelle get a tiny apartment of her own. Larry enrolled in school Ultimately, the child welfare case was closed. Four years later, the worker learned that Larry had killed another teen in a fight and had been sentenced to life in prison. The worker visited Larry in prison, but was careful to avoid blame. Larry was remorseful about the killing; however, he said that his mother was supportive and was visiting him. "At least I have my mother," he said. The worker, though extremely sad about Larry's outcome, was heartened to know that, through all this trouble, this mother and son had forged a lasting relationship which would be a strength to them in the long years to come.

Effects of the Model

The strengths model embodies a holistic respect for the dignity and uniqueness of individuals, and respect builds a stage for extending services beyond the office to the community. Shifting the site of services from the agency to the environment minimizes the isolation of families and children while fostering families' membership in the community, active decision making, and access to services (Tice & Perkins, 1996).

Directly linked to the respect for individual dignity is the importance of self-determination. The strengths model levels the playing field by putting the social worker's power in perspective: the client's needs are more significant than the professional's career or the agency's services. This kind of partnership redefines the roles of client and social worker. Reducing social distance, achieving authenticity, and building mutuality are benefits gained when workers ask clients what they need or want and what works for them (Germain & Gitterman, 1980; Rose 1992).

> Rose, a severely crack-addicted woman with three children, was angry and resentful toward the child welfare system, which had intervened in her life on behalf of her children. The worker, guided by the strengths model, helped Rose to identify some obstacles (being poor, single, female, drug-addicted) that interfered with family success. Once Rose confronted the reality of these obstacles, she acknowledged that they created a great deal of stress. One way Rose had survived and shielded herself from the pain of these stressors was through her anger, and the worker helped Rose translate the anger into an acknowledgment of strength. He also helped Rose to see her addiction as the culprit, rather than seeing herself as the total villain. When the worker visited the children's school, he learned that they were well-behaved and received good grades. Collaboratively, the worker helped Rose see that, in spite of her crack addition, Rose had encouraged the children to do well in school; Rose could then acknowledge her educational support of her children as a family strength and an affirmation that she cared about her children's welfare. The worker also helped Rose to recognize how her anger was now hindering her personal growth and fueling her addiction. Ultimately, Rose admitted herself to a treatment program with the help of the worker, who smoothed the way by taking care of logistics like child care, rent, and utilities. (Callens, 1997)

Focusing on strengths releases clients from the stereotypes associated with labels and categories, such as "bad" mother. Because the system provides social control for those who deviate from community standards, and because child welfare intervention invades the family, the caregiver's autonomy is compromised and his or her personal power is decreased. Centering on strengths allows clients to move beyond labels. If problem solving were placed on a continuum, the medical model, with its emphasis on deficits, pathology, and labeling, would be at one end, while the strengths model, emphasizing empowerment and control, would be at the other end.

The strengths model is also appropriately applied to policy development in child welfare. It shapes the policy to be more responsive to clients' needs and casts policy more in terms of human needs rather than social problems. It further fosters a more humane, client-centered perspective among policymakers and lawmakers (Petr, 1998).

Using a Strengths Model with Families Who Have Experienced Abuse or Neglect

When traumatic events bring a child welfare worker into the home to investigate abuse and neglect, the client who has behaved in socially troublesome ways has little choice but to work with the child welfare worker (Cingoloni, 1984). How does one begin to level this clearly unlevel playing field? Rooney's (1992) perspective can help the practitioner move from a position of authority to one of partner in working with parents whose children have been removed. To begin this process, clients must be very clear about (1) mandates that must be accomplished before the child can be returned home and (2) those goals that would be "nice" to accomplish. Once both worker and client clearly understand this distinction, the real work can begin. Another necessary understanding for both practitioner and client is this: only the client can choose whether or not she or he is going to meet the mandated changes. Further, the client must grasp the consequences of his or her behavior. Giving the client responsibility for making choices and for accepting consequences begins to level the playing field. The worker, as strength coach, helps define these concepts with the client.

Helping the Client to Change

Using the strengths model allows the worker to focus on the strengths, skills, and resources that have allowed the person to cope with difficult life situations in the past, recognizing that some of the client's coping skills—which may be viewed as maladaptive by society—can be turned around and used in positive ways.

Ms. Neal, a client who was always in a financial crisis, either phoned several times a week or came into the office in a panic about some pressing bill, utilities that were about to be disconnected, or necessary food and medicine that she could not afford. Though the agency staff tried to respond helpfully, Ms. Neal finally exhausted both the staff and their resources. When Ms. Neal came in with her newest crisis, staff could offer no assistance, a fact that distressed the practitioner. Ms. Neal left the office stating that she didn't know what she was going to do. The worker was concerned about Ms. Neal's situation all evening, so she was eager to talk to Ms. Neal the next day and hear how things had gone. The client did not even mention the problem of the previous day. When the worker asked how Ms. Neal's financial crisis had been resolved, Ms. Neal off-handedly said she had borrowed money from some friends. She went on to describe how she did this often, and how she loaned others money as they needed it. The worker, who had been wondering what on earth she would do if she were in Ms. Neal's shoes, was amazed at the adroitness with which Ms. Neal had achieved this solution. The client demonstrated skills and resources for solving problems that the worker did not believe she herself could match.

When the worker gains respect for the client's coping skills and resources, both worker and client are able to identify, value, and reinforce those skills. Ms. Neal's abilities to develop and access networks to meet her needs in a crisis can be modified to meet a variety of her needs. As skills are used successfully, clients develop more self-confidence in their strength (or muscle) to repeat and build on those skills. The social worker as the strength coach reminds the person that she or he has this muscle (strength in developing a network), that it has worked before, and that it will become stronger with use.

Valuing and supporting one strength leads the social worker and client to explore other unrecognized skills and abilities. Using a neutral, pleasant environment that is conducive to friendly conversations between equals sets a good stage for collaboratively exploring strengths, defining client needs, and identifying barriers to meeting needs. With clients of child welfare, this process centers on identifying resources needed to adequately care for children.

Applying the Model

A central belief in using the strengths model is that clients are trustworthy—sometimes a very difficult emotional task for the social worker. The investigation worker who discovers a 4-year-old girl and a 3-month-old infant alone in a filthy, unsanitary house at 2:30 A.M. is not inclined to trust the parents. The worker must continue to find and develop a basic belief in the goodwill of parents and the integrity of people. Linked to this basic faith must be a sense of hope in the ability of people to change for the better.

The most pressing task in this situation, however, is to protect the children. Soon thereafter, it is time to listen to the client's story with as much openness as the worker can muster. The client often reveals many barriers and gaps in the eight domains of life which the strengths model identifies as important in the client's efforts to achieve success. These areas are living arrangements, education, social support, leisure/recreation, relationships, health, personal care, and finances.

Because child welfare clients often have grave gaps in all these areas (which are clearly interdependent), it is essential that the worker and client collaborate to prioritize these domains. For the parent who left her young children unattended and neglected, worker and client need to focus on necessary changes to protect the children. Living arrangements, education, relationships, and finances, in that order, may well be the domains that the client and worker agree need attention. Having prioritized her needs, the client and worker can develop a plan that clarifies long-term goals, strategies for accomplishing the goals, the responsibilities of persons in achieving the goals, and time lines for goal attainment. Together, worker and client can prepare a plan for each domain that presents an obstacle to achieving the health and safety of the children. These plans can easily be converted or integrated into the case plan required by the child welfare agency.

Using the Strengths Model in Family Preservation Services

Family preservation services include a broad array of services designed to strengthen families and prevent out-of-home placement (Whittaker & Tracy, 1990). The family preservation or home-based model reflects the belief that a child is best served by remaining in her or his own home, even though the family struggles with major difficulties. As opposed to a pathological view of the family in crisis, family preservation employs a holistic, ecological view which recognizes that family troubles are exacerbated by societal and community issues, such as high unemployment or lack of affordable child care. In this sense, a family preservation approach is quite consistent with the strengths model.

When Family Preservation Works

Beyond this philosophical stance of maintaining children in their home, however, the family preservation movement is also driven by economic and practical motivations: adequate alternatives to family care (such as foster or residential care) are hard to find and expensive to finance. Family preservation programs, through short-term, intensive services, aim to help families improve their functioning and child-caring skills. They offer real therapeutic hope for children in distressed families by acknowledging that children's dependence on parents and family is both real and immense (Gibson & Noble, 1991).

> Patty's mother, Adele, has AIDS, but is very committed to caring for Patty, age 6, and keeping Patty with her as long as possible. Because Adele's physical condition is deteriorating, she can no longer work regularly, and she has had trouble finding shelter. Child welfare authorities became involved with Adele and Patty when Adele was found collapsed and unconscious in the cardboard dwelling they had erected under an overpass. Patty was terrified and hungry. While Adele was hospitalized to stabilize her situation, Patty was placed in emergency foster care. Initially it seemed evident that Patty would need extended substitute care, but a family preservation worker was assigned to deal intensively with the family because Adele was so committed to making a home for Patty, and because Patty was adamant about wanting to be with her. The worker talked with Adele about how to create a home under the circumstances. Adele explained her plan, which was to contact her mother, from whom she had been estranged for some years, and try to mend fences. In order to make a home for Patty, Adele was willing to go back home to Wisconsin and accept family help. The worker assisted Adele in fine-tuning

what was a sound plan, given the circumstances, to provide for Patty in the immediate future and after Adele's impending death. The worker helped Adele role-play the telephone call to her mother and provided the telephone for this all-important call. Getting the invitation home and working out the logistics actually took several calls, but the worker raised money to buy bus tickets for Adele and Patty to Wisconsin and hooked her up with a worker in that state. The worker, in explaining the case to the Wisconsin agency, stated, "Adele really amazes me. She is in bad shape and is dying, but she has developed a plan for her child that makes a lot of sense and shows foresight. She just needed help in making it happen."

Working with these families is fulfilling, though it involves intense labor. There is anecdotal evidence that family preservation workers get more personal and professional satisfaction from their work and tend to remain in family preservation jobs longer than the average child welfare worker (Midgley et al., 1995). This may represent a savings to public child welfare agencies, for which turnover is a major problem (Helfgott, 1991). These facts may demonstrate that workers are more satisfied in working with strengths than in working with deficits. Centering on strengths builds self-confidence in the worker.

> Mike, age 11, came to the attention of child welfare workers through the school, which reported that the child repeatedly suffered from bruises and lacerations. Investigation revealed that his mother's first child had died under suspicious circumstances two years before, though abuse had not been validated. Upon visiting their apartment, workers found the place a disaster: Mike's toddler sister was crawling through dog feces on the floor, and evidence of rodents was abundant. Both Mike and his mother, Latrice, appeared to be battered. Latrice seemed to be at the end of her rope, and without a great deal of prodding, acknowledged that Antwon, her boyfriend, had been drinking heavily and taking it out on Mike and her. He had also been stealing her money, and Latrice felt powerless to send him packing. A family preservation worker began spending several hours per day working with Latrice and Mike, who were clearly devoted to one another and to the baby. Together they assessed the needs they had, which were to get rid of the troublesome Antwon and to improve their physical surroundings. The worker encouraged Latrice to see herself as a woman of some power; she had kept her

little family together despite tragedy and difficulty, and she had a decent job with which to support them. The worker was able to secure legal help for Latrice to get a restraining order against Antwon, and she found funds to fence off the patio to create a pet yard and keep the dog out of the living area. The worker was under no illusions, however; this was an extremely vulnerable family that needed to build great strengths. Much work remained to be done.

One of the most difficult elements of family preservation calls for the worker and the family to be brutally honest: Can this family stay together safely? Not only is this question central to the health and survival of children, but it is also important to the survival of vulnerable adults (the overwhelming number of victims being women) in the family (Grinspoon, 1993). While a worker's belief in a client's innate goodness and optimism for positive change is central to using the strengths model, the worker's trust must be balanced by good sense and realism.

The Strengths Coach

Child welfare and family preservation workers can use the strengths model effectively with their clients by being strengths coaches. Workers who grasp the basic benefits of this model can envision themselves as assisting clients to build emotional muscles, create balance between emotional and physical needs, refine effective parenting skills, and develop winning attitudes. All that is needed to bring strength to its greatest capacity is a coach who believes in the client's ability to cope and change in positive ways and who can identify, value, and develop the client's "muscles."

References

Callens, K. (1997). *Ameliorating risk factors in abusive/neglectful parents through the psychoeducational group process.* Unpublished master's thesis, Louisiana State University, School of Social Work, Baton Rouge.

Cingoloni, J. (1984). Social conflict perspective on work with involuntary clients. *Social Work 29*, 442–446.

Germain, C., & Gitterman, A. (1980). *The life model of social work practice.* New York: Columbia University Press.

Gibson, D. & Noble, D. N. (May/June 1991). Creative permanency planning: Residential services for families. *Child Welfare 70*, 371–382.

Grinspoon, L. (Ed.) (July 1993). Child Abuse—Parts I and II. *Harvard Mental Health Letter.* Cambridge, MA: Harvard University Press.

Hegar, R. L., & Hunzeker, J. M. (1988). Moving toward empowerment-based practice in public child welfare. *Social Work 33* (6), 499–502.

Helfgott, K. (1991). *Staffing the child welfare agency: Recruitment and retention.* Washington, D.C.: Child Welfare League of America.

Midgley, J., Ellett, C. D., Noble, D. N., Bennett, N., Livermore, M., Nauman, S., & Zimmerman, K. (1995). *Statewide personnel needs study for child welfare employees in the Louisiana Office of Community Services.* Baton Rouge: Louisiana State University.

Petr, C. G. (1998). *Social work with children and their families: Pragmatic foundations.* New York: Oxford.

Rappaport, J. (1981). In praise of paradox: A social policy of empowerment over prevention. *American Journal of Community Psychology, 9,* 1–25.

Rooney, R. H. (1992). *Strategies for work with involuntary clients.* New York: Columbia University Press.

Rose, S. M. (1992). Case management: An advocacy/empowerment design. In S. M. Rose (Ed.) *Case management and social work practice* (pp. 271–297). New York: Longman.

Saleeby, D. (Ed.) (1992). *The strengths perspective in social work practice.* White Plains, NY: Longman.

Sue, D. W. (1981). *Counseling the culturally different: Theory and practice.* New York: Wiley.

Tice, C., & Perkins, K. (1996). *Mental health services and aging: Building on strengths.* Pacific Grove, CA: Brooks/Cole.

Weick, A. (November-December 1983). Issues in overturning a medical model of social work practice. *Social Work, 28,* 467–471.

Weick, A., Rapp, C., Sullivan, W. P., & Kisthardt, W. (1989). A strengths perspective for social work practice. *Social Work,* July, 350–354.

Whittaker, J. K., & Tracy, E. M. (1990). Family preservation services and education for social work practice: Stimulus and response. In J.K. Whittaker, J. Kinney, E.M. Tracy, & C. Booth (Eds.) *Reaching high-risk families: Intensive family preservation in human services* (pp. 1–12). New York: Aldine de Gruyter.

78

Evaluation of Yoga and Meditation Trainings with Adolescent Sex Offenders

Literature Review

Adolescent Sex Offenders

Incidence Adolescents commit a sizable number of sex crimes. Estimates of incidence of adolescent sex crimes suggest that the rate of sexual assault per 100,000 male adolescents ranges between 5,000 and 16,000 with the highest rate for 17-year-old teens (Rasmussen, 1995; Davis & Leitenberg, 1987). Adolescents commit about 20% of all rapes in the country (Brown, Flanagan, & McLeod, 1984) and commit up to 50% of all child sexual abuse (Davis & Leitenberg, 1987). Early intervention with adolescent sex offenders is important because they are likely to continue to molest as they age: at least one-half of adult sex offenders began offending in their own adolescence or earlier (Abel, Mittelman, & Becker, 1985).

A sizable national effort is now exerted to deal with adolescent sex offenders, and the potential negative impact of sexual assault on children has been well-established (Becker, 1990). In response to increasing rates of adolescent sex offenders, there are now over 650 inpatient and outpatient treatment centers for adolescent sex offenders in the United States (Lakey, 1993). Little is yet known about the rates of recidivism of adolescents in these programs, but the evidence suggests that community-based treatment programs (in which the teens continue living at home) may be most effective in reducing recidivism (Rasmussen, 1995).

Offender Profile The literature has contributed to an increasingly sophisticated profile of the typical adolescent sex offender. Overall, the sex offender can be described as having a combination of normal and abnormal thinking and behavior patterns. He is typically a male who is unusually self-absorbed and whose sexual interest is "opportunistic and manipulative, laden with inappropriate sexual fantasies which he may scheme to fulfill" (Lakey, 1994, p. 756). Sex offenders usually desire immediate and forbidden sexual gratification and reject building up to a sexual relationship with willing partners (Berenson, 1988). Sex offenders seldom feel guilty about their crimes and in fact tend to minimize or deny their responsibility and the consequences of their actions through their cognitive distortions (Lakey, 1992).

These boys typically have a multitude of problems in the schools and larger community. Adolescent sex offenders often have learning problems, are viewed as having attention deficit disorder by school professionals, and often perform poorly in school (Fehrenbach, Smith, Monastersky, & Deisher, 1986). Their most common diagnoses, however, seem to be antisocial and conduct disorder, which are also often associated with substance abuse, and personality disorder (Kavoussi, Kaplan, & Becker, 1988). Their impulsivity may lead to such additional crimes as stealing, arson, and vandalism (Lakey, 1994).

Additional psychosocial factors have been found to be associated with adolescent sex offenders.

They usually have confusion about their own sexual identity, feel powerless in the world, and have an underdeveloped moral judgment (Knopp, 1986). Many sex offenders have been found to have fear of rejection by and anger toward females, feelings of low self-esteem and inadequacy as males, poor social skills, histories of being sexually abused, and knowledge of violent male role models (Davis & Leitenberg, 1987). They are often socially isolated from peers, prefer spending time with younger children, come from dysfunctional families of origin, and have not been given sex education programs (Fehrenbach et al. 1986).

Treatment of Adolescent Sex Offenders Most treatment programs for adolescent sex offenders focus on the prevention of further offenses rather than on primary prevention (Lakey, 1994). Most programs today are limited to a yet unproven focus on cognitive/behavioral strategies which involve the identification and replacement of thinking errors (Lakey, 1994) and the linkage of events, thoughts, feelings, and behaviors that may lead to sexual misconduct (Kahn & Lafond, 1988). Other currently common strategies include increasing the ability to take responsibility for behaviors, developing empathy for others, managing anger and stress, social skill building, and developing overall impulse control (Kahn & Lafond, 1988).

In most programs, adolescent sex offenders are usually taught to replace their inappropriate sexual fantasies with more acceptable fantasies involving consensual sex between peers (Kahn & Lafond, 1988). The young offenders essentially are encouraged to "feel good about being moral" (Lakey, 1994, p. 755). The offenders are also encouraged to avoid situations that may lead to offending (e.g., visiting a school yard) and to find alternative activities that can be stimulating but do not harm anyone (Berenson, 1988).

Specific interventions used to implement these strategies with adolescent sex offenders are varied. Those reported include exercise assignments, lectures, discussions, films, behavioral assignments, role playing, journal writing, and listening to stories of victims (Lakey, 1994). Whenever possible, peer pressure is employed to encourage change (Berenson, 1988). Probably the most inclusive list of intervention goals in the literature was generated by the National Adolescent Perpetrator Network (1988), and includes the development of self-responsibility, insight into past history, empathy and self-control, healthy thinking patterns, social skills, and healthy relationships.

Research Issues The adolescent sex offender remained relatively neglected by clinical researchers until the past decade (Becker, 1990). Despite the recent interest in adolescent sexual abuse, researchers have still not been able to validate any model that might help explain the development of adolescent sexual deviance (Becker, 1990). What researchers have found is that adolescent sex offenders come from all socioeconomic and racial backgrounds and may have a variety of sexual disorders, such as pedophilia, exhibitionism, and frottage (Becker, Cunningham-Rathner, & Kaplan, 1986).

Studies of Adult Sexual Offenders

Most sexual offender research still focuses on adults. Interestingly, studies suggest that programs for adolescents and adults use similar intervention strategies, except that adult programs use less family therapy and more aversive conditioning and medication (Knopp, Rosenberg, & Stevenson, 1986).

Studies of medical interventions with adult offenders show mixed results. The use of such antiandrogenic (sex-drive reducing) medications as medroxyprogesterone acetate and cyproterone acetate seem to have helped some adult offenders avoid reoffending. Antiandrogenic medications are not used with adolescent males, since they may damage normal sexual development (Lakey, 1994). The use of antipsychotic medications has not yet been well-evaluated (Becker, 1990). Studies suggest that surgical castration of the testicles does not effectively control inappropriate arousal patterns (Heim, 1981).

Studies of psychosocial interventions with adult offenders also show mixed results. Some positive results have been found with behavioral treatments (Abel et al., 1985), psychodynamic interventions (Crawford, 1981), and family therapy (Giarretto, Giarretto, & Sgroi, 1978).

The Use of Yoga and Meditation Training in Professional Helping

Meditation is a self-directed method usually used to help quiet the mind and relax the body. Usually the meditator focuses on a thought, a vision, a sound, or other sensory experience.

There are many types of meditation, but they all have been shown to have similar effects (Chopra, 1991). Although most meditative techniques originated from India, China, and Japan, meditation has also been used by followers of some Western religious traditions. Most research has focused on transcendental meditation and the relaxation response.

Transcendental meditation, essentially a simplified form of yoga, has been shown to help with a variety of issues and problems, including quality of life, chronic pain, anxiety, high blood pressure, cholesterol, and posttraumatic stress (National Institutes of Health, 1992). The relaxation response is the essential body-mind effect that is common to most meditation practices, including those associated with prayer, progressive relaxation, hypnosis, and yoga (Benson, 1974). The relaxation response has also been shown to be associated with changes in many bodily functions (National Institutes of Health, 1992).

In general, researchers have found that meditation can help foster many positive qualities in clients, including mental calmness, a state of relatively low physiological arousal, and reduced mental activity (Dua, 1983; Benson, 1974). Meditation may also help foster creativeness and well-being (Greenspan, 1989). A meditative drumming technique has been used successfully to help adult and adolescent survivors of trauma (Slotoroff, 1994). Meditation ahs been found to be helpful in the reduction of anger (Dua & Swinden, 1992) and anxiety (Kabat-Zinn et al., 1992). Meditative techniques may help psychotherapists themselves be more effective (Dubin, 1991). There is evidence that meditation and therapeutic touch may assist in the education and growth of children (Greenspan, 1994).

During the 1960s and 1970s many studies of Hindu-based and Buddhist-based meditation were performed (Smith, 1975). Research on meditation has tapered off since then. Overall, these studies suggest that religious meditation and relaxation training have essentially equally good results in helping clients relax and focus (Worthington, Karusu, McCullough, & Sandage, 1996). In the United States, about 12% of Christian psychotherapists use religious meditation techniques with their clients (Jones, Watson, & Wolfman, 1992).

Yoga has been practiced in India for thousands of years and includes physical exercise, dietary practices, and a belief system. Although practitioners of yoga believed for millennia that their practices could alter mental and physical processes, researchers in India have applied scientific methods to study yoga only during the past 80 years. Literally thousands of studies in India and other countries have confirmed that yoga practice can help individuals control blood pressure, heart rate, res-

piratory operations, metabolic rate, brain waves, body temperature, skin sweating, and many other bodily functions. Yoga has been shown to help patients deal with a variety of medical problems, including cholesterol, diabetes, substance abuse, asthma, heart disease, headaches, cancer, and arthritis (National Institutes of Health, 1992). Researchers have also established the usefulness of yoga as an adjunct to psychotherapy in some settings and with some problems (Sachdeva, 1978). Yoga and meditation may help relieve symptoms of posttraumatic stress (Marmar, Foy, Kagan, & Pynoos, 1994).

Program and Participants

A group of nine male adolescent sex offenders began the Yoga, Breathing, and Meditation training program. Eight of the teen participants and their parents agreed to volunteer to participate in the evaluation project and the teens were given face-to-face interviews after three months of training. After two more months, eight parents (one for each teen) were interviewed by phone. Nine months after training began, 11 teen participants were interviewed in another face-to-face session. In this second group, five of the 11 were teens who had also been interviewed in the original study group.

Methodology

In this study, in-depth face-to-face interviews were conducted with adolescent perpetrators (n = 14), their parents (n = 8), and their social workers (n = 2). The subjects for these interviews were drawn from a larger study population of perpetrators (n = 18) and parents who were participating in the program at the time. All adolescents who received the training, their parents, and staff were asked to participate in the study through a letter that was distributed by the agency. Only consenting adolescents and adults were interviewed. Of these, all the adolescent perpetrators were European American males and half of the parents were female. One staff trainer was male, one was female.

The open-ended questions utilized in the interviews (see Table 78.1) were formulated by a research team and based on hypotheses developed from the existing literature, which suggested that yoga and meditation trainings would probably give teens skills and resources that would help them avoid further sexual perpetration. Another strategy used to improve instrument validity was to have the instrument drafts reviewed by outside experts. In order to improve instrument reliability, only one

Table 78.1 Sample Questions from Adolescent Interview Instrument

(1) First of all, what did you think overall of the program?

(2) What did you think overall of the Yoga, Breathing, and Meditation trainings you received?

(3) What did you like the best about these trainings?

(4) What did you dislike the most about these trainings?

(5) Did you feel more relaxed after the trainings? Did you feel less anxious?

(6) Do you feel you have more awareness of your thoughts and feelings than you had before you had the trainings?

(7) Do you feel you have more control of your thoughts and feelings than you had before you had the trainings?

(8) Do you feel you could do these techniques on your own now? Why or why not? Have you? Why or why not?

(9) Do you think these techniques would now work better when you do them with a staff person or on your own? Why?

(10) Do you think that these trainings have given you the skills and resources that make it less likely that you will sexually assault someone in the future? Why or Why not?

(11) Do these techniques seem to help you develop the spiritual part of you? If so, is that important in helping you deal with your problems?

(12) Is there anything else that the staff need to know that would help them do a better job working with other adolescents in the future?

---

interviewer was used, and he received instructions and participated in practice role-plays. The participants were told that special care was taken to keep their responses confidential. After the interviews were completed and the responses transcribed, the interviewer identified common themes that emerged in response to each of the research questions. These themes were then quantified in terms of percentage statistics.

Findings and Recommendations

In this section, major themes that emerged in the interviews are discussed. Many of the teen comments were so articulate and helpful that they are quoted in the text (which also further enhances ecological validity). Several teens expressed eagerness to give information (one boy talked for 45 minutes about the class without much prompting from the interviewer).

General Comments

The overall impression was that most of the boys enjoyed the training and all of them reported benefit from using the exercises outside of class to help with their control problems. None of the boys relapsed with sexual offenses during the time of the study. All the teens had something positive to say about the program. For example, even when one teen began by saying that the program was boring and frustrating, he added, "It's doing me good with my anger and urges to offend." The most negative

comment was about the agency staff: "They just sit at their desks; they don't observe us enough and help us." However, most general comments were positive. For example, one student said: "It's been very helpful to me. If I hadn't gotten into the program I would have been very sick or dead, or at least friendless."

What Participants Liked Best

Most respondents especially liked the relaxed feeling they had after the class, although two reported having trouble tolerating the relaxation, especially when the program first began. Several reported that the breathing exercises also helped them get to sleep and control anger. A student said: "It takes hundreds of pounds off my shoulders; it feels good."

Most also liked the time they spent lying down on the floor at the end of each class: "If I am mad or frustrated at the beginning of the session, it just goes away." One student mentioned rocking on the spine as a favorite exercise, and another singled out the music as his favorite. Another respondent said, "It allows me to use stored up energy constructively rather than destructively."

What Participants Disliked

Five boys mentioned that the "goof-offs" in the class were distracting and interfered with their concentration. One said he disliked having the class in the morning. Another boy said he didn't like being so relaxed because he felt more lethargic and depressed when he had to sit still.

Improved Ability to Relax and Reduce Anxiety

Everyone reported feeling more relaxed after class, and two mentioned using the "energy" generated in class for improved concentration in school. All reported feeling less tense, except for one boy who said he didn't feel less anxious, adding, "I always watch my back."

Self-Awareness

All but one participant thought that the training helped them better recognize their thoughts and feelings. Examples of statements included: "I recognize things much easier, like being mad, than before when I was closed up, I think clearer" and "I am more in touch with feelings and thoughts and look at my feelings more than before."

Self-Control

All but one teen felt the program helped them control their thoughts and feelings better. Responses to this question were particularly strong. One boy said, "I can replace unwanted thoughts much more easily now. I try not to control my feelings, just feel them, otherwise they can get stuffed and come out some other way, as abuse." Another stated, "I am more aware now of my anger and how I use it and also how to keep it under control. Concentrating on energy moving through my body helps me to focus inside and track my feelings outside of class."

Additional responses suggested that the self-control generalized to a number of life areas. One boy said, "I can focus on school better and generally choose what I want to focus on. I don't get as upset; I keep it under control and don't yell." Another stated, "Relaxation exercises by themselves release a lot of anger and also free me up to talk about my anger. I can function easier in general and my tone of voice is less tense." A third noted, "I used to swear and blow up a lot but that happens less often now. I feel less stress when I express feelings, so it's easier. Breathing with the diaphragm calms me down right away."

Use of Techniques on Their Own

All the boys reported using yoga techniques on their own. For example, one boy reported, "I use the exercises when my roommate is away, but feel embarrassed to do them around him." Another stated, "I use breathing exercises all the time to

help with anger and getting to sleep at night. My roommate and I go through all the exercises together before we sleep. Sleep is refreshing and I wake up energized, even if I don't get much sleep." A third comment was: "Many times when I get mad, nervous or stressed, I use the breathing exercises to calm me down. I would like to do exercises in my room."

Ability to Do Techniques on Their Own

All but one boy felt that they liked yoga best when the instructor was present with them. One boy stated, "It's better under supervision because I'm afraid I'll do them wrong or hurt myself" and another stated, "My mind wanders if I try to do exercises alone." Another helpful comment was "It takes a lot of concentration to switch from exercise to exercise and it helps to have someone talk it through. Sometimes I forget some of the techniques on my own."

Prevention of Recidivism of Sexual Assault

All the boys stated that the trainings helped them avoid sexually offending again. One teen stated, "Stress is what led up to my offense, so if I have stress I can use the techniques instead of offending." However, another teen cautioned, "The techniques could help prior to victim selection, but not afterwards. Only walking away from situations and doing something else like sports can help me after I have picked out a victim."

Most of the boys identified anger control and reduction as important factors in prevention. One said, "When I get angry, I try to intimidate people or abuse them sexually. Techniques help with anger control." Another added, "If I have a strong urge to reoffend, I can use techniques to get my mind on something else. I have used them successfully once in avoiding sexual acting out with another resident here and innumerable times in helping with my anger." A third concluded, "Controlling my breathing gives me real control over my mind, not superficial control. . . . I am definitely less likely to offend now, as I have more control and less anger than before. I can't believe how angry I was! As I breathe deeper I can see things clearer and clearer. It has opened my mind up. Now I am not as afraid of myself." A teen concluded, "This training should be given in other detention programs where kids have bad tempers; it would help a lot."

Spiritual Development

All but one of the boys felt that the trainings has assisted them in their own spiritual development. For example, one boy said, "I get in touch more with my soul inside. It feels like I am light as a feather." A second said, "I am more comfortable with others and my boundaries are good. Relaxation is something tangible and you can wrap yourself up in it."

When asked about spirituality, half of the boys emphasized caring more about others. One teen stated, "I don't feel closer to God, but I do care more and am more considerate of others." Another said, "I am more self-focused, exploring deeper parts of my mind, helps with my beliefs and abusiveness. I didn't use to care what I said, how I said it, or what I did. Now I care more about others." A third teen concluded, "Now I want to help more than hurt people. I am able to see myself as a person more than just as a sex offender."

However, one of the boys was concerned that too much relaxation could be a problem: "The training has raised my self-esteem. I am less of a jerk now, more concerned with other people's feelings. The problem is I get more aggressive if I get too relaxed in group, like a rebound effect, then I can get abusive."

Additional Recommendations

When asked, the teens made a number of additional recommendations. They wanted the trainings to begin earlier in their treatment and to continue for a longer duration. They also asked to have each class last over an hour so there is time enough to practice all their exercises. Most of the boys actually wanted to continue in the yoga classes after being released from the program. One teen asked the trainer to "bring in new exercises to challenge us, once we are able to do the basic routine. Keep up the variety. As new members come in, review basics; this will help all of us." Another wanted to "kick out the people who are disturbing and noisy."

Follow-up Responses

The responses of the long-term students confirmed that the power of the class builds up over time, in terms of physical flexibility, increased energy, and greater capacity to monitor and control thoughts and feelings. The teens were able to learn concentration and body flexibility and were able to relax during the short silent meditations between the movement exercises.

Several mentioned a growing capacity for moment-to-moment awareness, enabling hem to catch their own emotional reactions earlier. For example, one stated, "I am finding out all kinds of things about myself, knowing what's going on through me as I breathe and do exercises, getting better at untightening my muscles to stop headaches." Another boy has designed his own meditation exercises: "I listen to music and remember something from my life about myself each time." A third boy stated, "The meditations reinforce mental reprogramming learned in the other groups. When I meditate I can zap deviant thoughts the moment they come up." Another theme that showed up for long-term participants was each teen's incorporation of the class skills and self-reliance in using them: "It takes a long time to learn these techniques."

Each boy seemed to be making a gradual progression from practicing yoga for personal abuse prevention to keeping the discipline as a part of a personal identity that included a concern for the well-being of both self and others. One boy summarized the process beautifully: "I want to do these exercises now for their own sake. The exercises themselves are satisfying, whereas before I just did them to improve my coping. Before, I asked how would this help in my treatment. Now I ask how can I make this part of my life . . . as an adult. . . . It hurts to think how many sick people are in pain like I have known."

Only one of the long-term group clients indicated not liking the class as much as at the beginning. He reported feeling more hyper than before and pressured to do exercises he is unable to accomplish. He feels medication he receives for anxiety, paranoia, and depression is helping him, not the classes. He continues to attend only to get credit on his weekly scores.

The boys who discontinued the in-class exercises reported now getting frustrated more easily and having weekly depressions, which never happened while they attended the program: "Things load up and I feel overwhelmed now that I don't have that release of stress anymore. I felt better about myself while I was doing the program. I would do the exercises on my own, but with my other studies there isn't enough time. I didn't realize the stress reduction group was so important to me until we started talking about it." Another boy added, "I miss the way I used to be real calm. The group helped me to step away from situations if I got angry. I feel more positive about the class than when I dropped out and might like to rejoin. I would be more motivated now and wouldn't talk in class."

Trainer Observations

One trainer especially noted an increase in the self-esteem of boys who continued in the program for several months. She observed how these boys improved their posture, held their heads up high, and spontaneously used the breathing exercises outside class to help with stressful situations, such as court appearances. She believed that the program would help the general population of teens in public schools to cope with stress.

Parent Observations

Overall, parents seemed uninvolved with, and uninformed about, the program. Most of the parents did not hear positive comments about the program from their children because there was apparently very little communication at home about these training experiences. Four parents stated that they had not heard anything from their children at all. Only two parents stated that their teens had reported having positive experiences. Two parents reported that their teens were initially nervous but became more comfortable with time. Scheduling and transportation were mentioned as problems by two parents. One mother did say that the program seemed to give her son "other options when he gets mad."

Conclusions and Recommendations

A number of tentative conclusions can be forwarded:

(1) The program was well-liked by the participating adolescents.

(2) The parents of the participating adolescents were supportive of the program but also relatively uninvolved.

(3) The staff who provided the program remained enthusiastic about, and supportive of, the program.

(4) Most of the adolescent participants noted a number of specific results of the program that they particularly valued. These included:

(a) The feeling of being relaxed was immediately reinforcing.

(b) Their ability to focus at school had improved.

(c) They found improvement in their ability to control impulses (e.g., of anger, aggressive sexuality).

(d) They felt that they were treated with caring, respect, and humanness.

(e) They felt that their minds (thoughts) became places of safety and rest rather than the sources of their unwanted impulses.

A number of tentative recommendations can be suggested:

(1) *The program should be duplicated and tested in other sites.* Adolescents, parents, and staff supported the treatment strategy of incorporating yoga and meditation techniques in the program. Since the small sample size of this study limits the generalizability of the findings, similar programs might be duplicated and tested at other sites with larger populations. The following elements seem particularly important to include in such future programs:

(a) *Caring relationships.* The adolescents seemed to know they were respected and cared for by the teachers and seemed to have developed relatively trusting relationships with them. The delivery of the yoga and meditation training seemed to have been always "packaged" in this warm and caring interpersonal environment.

(b) *Empowerment.* The meditation and yoga seemed to empower the adolescents to learn methods of self-control and self-care that they could develop and use independently. Rather than further humiliating the adolescents (who already were likely to have had very low self-esteem), the program seemed to help foster greater self-awareness and self-acceptance.

(c) *Self-mastery.* The adolescents seemed to particularly value their developing ability to calm and direct their own minds. Most of these young men had grown to dislike and actually fear their own minds, because their thinking had often contributed to their sexual assault behaviors. They had not only felt a lack of control in the past, but had also felt an inability to control or impact their own chaotic home and community environments.

(d) *Immediate reinforcement.* The yoga and meditation techniques provided immediate and powerful rewards, in the sense that the teens almost universally experienced relaxed states of consciousness that were quite enjoyable. These young people had not been able in their former lives to develop pleasurable activities that were not destructive to themselves and others.

(2) Some modifications should be incorporated and tested. Evidence emerged that some changes in

the program were needed. The most important modifications suggested are described below:

(a) *Create a flexible program format to meet individual needs.* Although an initial 6–9-month, closed group format may benefit most teen participants, all graduates of the initial training should be able to join an ongoing, open-ended advanced group that helps them continue to maintain and generalize their ongoing development.

(b) *Provide yoga and meditation throughout the program.* The yoga and meditation should be integrated into the program. Initial assessment should include an appraisal of the ability of each teen to begin the trainings.

(c) *Increase parent and community involvement.* With the involvement of parents and other professionals in the community, the teens would have off-site support for the yoga discipline and new behaviors they are developing. Parents and other professionals could also benefit from taking the trainings.

(d) *Individualize yoga and meditation programs.* Every teen has unique needs and learning strengths an limitations that should be addressed. Particularly at risk were the few teens who appeared to experience increased stress in the trainings. Such boys may need a delayed program, extra support, or alternative trainings. As appropriate, participating teens can also be given readings and referrals that further support the trainings. Teens should not be allowed to act out regularly in the trainings, because such behavior is disruptive to others and suggests developmental unreadiness for the training.

(e) *Provide follow-up services.* The teens would be more likely to continue in their disciplines and new behaviors if they had ongoing opportunities to continue their work under supervision.

(f) *Expand prevention services.* A version of these trainings could be incorporated into family life (or other) classes in high schools. Such programs may help reduce the vulnerability of teens to becoming victims or perpetrators of sexual violence and may help increase their overall well-being.

(3) *Include spirituality as a vital component.* The program described in this article appears to foster the spiritual and religious development of most participants. The evidence in the literature strongly suggests that the spiritual dimension of adolescent sexual conduct and misconduct appears to be at least as important as any other developmental dimension (e.g., emotional, cognitive, physical, social) and must be considered in treating the whole person.

References

Abel, G.C., Mittelman, M., & Becker, J.V. (1985). Sex offenders: Results of assessment and recommendations for treatment. In H.H. Ben-Aron, S.I. Hucker, & C.D. Webster (Eds.), *Clinical criminology: Current concepts* (pp. 191–205). Toronto: M & M Graphics.

Becker, J.V. (1990). Treating adolescent and sexual offenders. *Professional Psychology Research and Practice, 21*(5), 362–365.

Becker, J.V., Cunningham-Rathner, J., & Kaplan, M. (1986). Adolescent sexual offenders: Demographics, criminal and sexual histories, and recommendations for reducing future offenses. *Journal of Interpersonal Violence, 1*, 431–445.

Benson, H. (1974). *The relaxation response.* New York: Avon Books.

Berenson, D. (1988). Thinking errors approach to treatment. *Working with the adolescent sex offender, Proceedings of the training intensive for the treatment of adolescent sex offenders workshop* (pp. 65–81). Toronto, Ontario, Canada.

Brown, E., Flanagan, T., & McLeod, M. (1984). Sourcebook of criminal justice statistics. Washington, D.C.: U.S. Department of Justice, Bureau of Justice and Statistics.

Chopra, D. (1991). *Creating health: How to wake up the body's intelligence.* New York: Houghton-Mifflin.

Crawford, D. (1981). Treatment approaches with pedophiles. In. M. Cook and K. Howells, (Eds.), *Adult sexual interest in children* (pp. 181–217). New York: Academic.

Davis, G.E. & Leitenberg, H. (1987). Adolescent sex offenders. *Psychological Bulletin, 101*(3), 417–427.

Dua, J.K. (1983). Meditation: Its effectiveness as a technique of behavior therapy. In J. Hariman (Ed.), *The therapeutic efficacy of the major psycho-therapeutic techniques* (pp. 19–31). Springfield, IL: Charles C. Thomas.

Dua, J.K. & Swinden, M.L. (1992). Effectiveness of negative-thought-reduction, meditation, and placebo training treatment in reducing anger. *Scandinavian Journal of Psychology, 33*, 135–146.

Dubin, W. (1991). *The use of meditative techniques in psychotherapy supervision.* Los Angeles: Transpersonal Institute.

Fehrenbach, P.A., Smith, W., Monastersky, C., & Deisher, R. W. (1986). Adolescent sexual offender: Offender and offense characteristics. *American Journal of Orthopsychiatry, 56*, 225–233.

Giarretto, H., Giarretto, A., & Sgroi, S. (1978). Coordinated community treatment of incest.

In A. Burgess, N. Groth, L. Holmstrom, & S. Sgroi (Eds.), *Sexual assault of children and adolescents* (pp. 231–240). Lexington, MA: Lexington Books.

Greenspan, M. (1994). Therapeutic touch and healing meditation: A threesome with education. *Early Child Development and Care, 98,* 121–129.

Greenspan, M. (1985). Creative meditative workshop: At-one-ment in a dissonant world. *Journal of Professional Counselors, 52*(1/2), 51–55.

Heim, N. (1981). Sexual behavior of castrated sex offenders. *Archives of Sexual Behavior, 10,* 11–19.

Jones, S.L., Watson, E.J., & Wolfman, T.J. (1992). Results of the Rech Conference survey on religious faith and professional psychology. *Journal of Psychology and Theology, 20,* 147–158.

Kabat-Zinn, J., Massion, A.O., Kristeller, J., Peterson, L.G., Fletcher, K.E., Pbert, L., Lenderking, W.R., & Santorelli, S.F. (1992). Effectiveness of a meditation-based stress reduction program in the treatment of anxiety disorders. *American Journal of Psychiatry, 149,* 936–943.

Kahn, T.J. & Lafond, M.A. (1988). Treatment of adolescent sexual offender. *Child and Adolescent Social Work, 5,* 135–148.

Kavoussi, R.J., Kaplan, M., & Becker, J.V. (1988). Psychiatric diagnoses in adolescent sex offenders. *Journal of the American Academy of Child and Adolescent Psychiatry, 27,* 241–243.

Knopp, F., Rosenberg, J., & Stevenson, W. (1986). *Report of nationwide survey of juvenile and adult sex offender treatment programs and providers.* New York: Safer Society Press.

Lakey, J.F. (1994). The profile and treatment of male adolescent sex offenders. *Adolescence, 29*(116), 755–761.

Lakey, J.F. (1993). Protecting our children's childhood. *American Counselor, 2*(1), 40.

Lakey, J.F. (1992). Myth information and bizarre beliefs of male juvenile sex offenders. *Journal of Addictions and Offender Counseling, 13*(1), 2–10.

Marmar, C.R., Foy, D., Kagan, B., Pynoos, R.S. (1994). An integrated approach for treating posttraumatic stress. *Psychiatry, 12*(10), 1–27.

National Institutes of Health (1992). *Alternative medicine: Expanding medical horizons. A report to the National Institutes of Health on alternative medical systems and practices in the United States.* NIH Publication No. 92-066.

Rasmussen, L.A. (1995). Factors related to recidivism among juvenile sexual offenders. Unpublished dissertation, Graduate School of Social Work, University of Utah.

Sachdeva, I.P. (1978). *Yoga and depth psychology.* Delhi, India: Motilal Banaisidass.

Slotoroff, C. (1994). Drumming technique for assertiveness and anger management in the short-term psychiatric setting for adult and adolescent survivors of trauma. *Music Therapy Perspectives, 12,* 25–30.

Smith, J.C. (1975). Meditation as psychotherapy: A review of the literature. *Psychological Bulletin, 82,* 558–564.

Worthington, E.L., Kurusu, T.A., McCullough, M.E., & Sandage, S.J. (1996). Empirical research on religion and psychotherapeutic processes and outcomes: A 10-year review and research prospectus. *Psychological Bulletin, 119*(3), 448–487.

Credits

Chapter 1, "Precursors of Mental Health Problems for Low Birth Weight Children: The Salience of Family Environment during the First Year of Life" (Fall 2002), originally appeared in *Child Psychiatry and Human Development*, 33(1): 327. Used with permission from Kluwer Academic/Plenum Publishers.

Chapter 2, "Resilient Children: What They Tell Us about Coping with Maltreatment" (2001), originally appeared in *Social Work in Health Care*, 34(3/4): 283–298. Used with permission from The Haworth Press, Inc.

Chapter 3, "Five Images of Maturity in Adolescence: What Does "Grown Up" Mean?" (April 2001), originally appeared in *Journal of Adolescence*, 24(2): 143–158. Used with permission from Elsevier.

Chapter 4, "Parent-Child Synchrony and Adolescent Adjustment" (February 2001), originally appeared in *Child and Adolescent Social Work Journal*, 18(1): 51–64. Used with permission from Kluwer Academic/Plenum Publishers.

Chapter 5, "Parenting Expectations and Concerns of Fathers and Mothers of Newborn Infants" (April 2000), originally appeared in *Family Relations*, 49(2): 123–131. Copyright 2000 by the National Council on Family Relations, 3989 Central Ave. NE, Suite 550, Minneapolis, MN 55421. Reprinted by permission.

Chapter 6, "Parenting Stress and Externalizing Child Behavior" (August 2002), originally appeared in *Child and Family Social Work*, 7(3): 219–225.

Chapter 7, "Parental Divorce and Young Adult Children's Romantic Relationships: Resolution of the Divorce Experience" (October 2001), originally appeared in *American Journal of Orthopsychiatry*, 71(4): 473–478. Copyright 2001 by the American Orthopsychiatric Association, Inc. Reproduced by permission.

Chapter 8, "Envisioning Fatherhood: A Social Psychological Perspective on Young Men without

Kids" (April 2000), originally appeared in *Family Relations*, 49(2): 133–142. Copyright 2000 by the National Council on Family Relations, 3989 Central Ave. NE, Suite 550, Minneapolis, MN 55421. Reprinted by permission.

Chapter 9, "The Function of Fathers: What Poor Men Say about Fatherhood" (September/October 2001), originally appeared in *Families in Society*, 82(5): 499–508. Reprinted with permission from *Families in Society* (www.familiesinsociety.org), published by the Alliance for Children and Families.

Chapter 10, "'Undeserving' Mothers? Practitioners' Experiences Working with Young Mothers in/from Care" (August 2002), originally appeared in *Child and Family Social Work*, 7(3): 149–159.

Chapter 11, "Redefining Motherhood: Adatation to Role Change for Women with AIDS" (March/April 2000), originally appeared in *Families in Society*, 81(2): 152–161. Reprinted with permission from *Families in Society* (www.families insociety.org), published by the Alliance for Children and Families.

Chapter 12, "The Long-Term Outcome of Reunions between Adult Adopted People and Their Birth Mothers" (June 2001), originally appeared in *The British Journal of Social Work*, 31(3): 351–368. Used by permission of Oxford University Press.

Chapter 13, "Adoption as a Family Form" (October 2000), originally appeared in *Family Relations*, 49(4): 359–362. Copyright 2000 by the National Council on Family Relations, 3989 Central Ave. NE, Suite 550, Minneapolis, MN 55421. Reprinted by permission.

Chapter 14, "The Trouble with Foster Care: The Impact of Stressful 'Events' on Foster Carers" (April 2000), originally appeared in *The British Journal of Social Work*, 30(2): 193–209. Used by permission of Oxford University Press.

Chapter 15, "The Importance of Partners to Lesbians' Intergenerational Relationships" (March 2001), originally appeared in *Social Work Re-*

search, 25(1): 27–35. Copyright 2001, National Association of Social Workers.

Chapter 16, "The Evolution of Homoerotic Behavior in Humans" (2000), originally appeared in *Journal of Homosexuality*, 40(1): 51–77. Used by permission of The Haworth Press, Inc.

Chapter 17, "Heterosexual Masculinity and Homophobia: A Reaction to the Self?" (September 2002), originally appeared in *Journal of Sociology and Social Welfare*, 29(3): 51–70. Used with permission of The Haworth Press, Inc.

Chapter 18, "From Grandparent to Caregiver: The Stress and Satisfaction of Raising Grandchildren" (September/October 2001), originally appeared in *Families in Society*, 82(5): 461–472. Reprinted with permission from *Families in Society* (www.familiesinsociety.org), published by the Alliance for Children and Families.

Chapter 19, "Grandparents Raising Grandchildren: Families in Transition" (2000), originally appeared in *Journal of Gerontological Social Work*, 33(2): 27–46. Used with permission from The Haworth Press, Inc.

Chapter 20, "Later-Life Transitions into Widowhood" (2001), originally appeared in *Journal of Gerontological Social Work*, 35(3): 51–63. Used with permission of The Haworth Press, Inc.

Chapter 21, "Understanding the Ageing Process: A Developmental Perspective of the Psychosocial and Spiritual Dimensions" (2001), originally appeared in *Journal of Religious Gerontology*, 12(3/4): 111–122. Used with permission of The Haworth Press, Inc.

Chapter 22, "Values Underlying End-of-Life Decisions: A Qualitative Apporach" (August 2001), originally appeared in *Health and Social Work* 26(3): 150–159. Copyright 2001, National Association of Social Workers, Inc., Health and Social Work.

Chapter 23, "A New Understanding of Attention Deficit Hyperactivity Disorder: Alternate Concepts and Interventions" (June 2000), originally appeared in *Child and Adolescent Social Work Journal*, 17(3): 227–245. Used with permission of Kluwer Academic/Plenum Publishers.

Chapter 24, "When She Was Bad: Borderline Personality Disorder in a Posttraumatic Age" (October 2000), originally appeared in *American Journal of Orthopsychiatry*, 70(4): 422–432. Copyright 2000 by the American Orthopsychiatric Association, Inc. Reproduced by permission.

Chapter 25, "Clinical Features of Survivors of Sexual Abuse with Major Depression" (March 2001), originally appeared in *Child Abuse and Neglect*, 25(3): 357–368. Used with permission from Elsevier.

Chapter 26, "Panic Disorder and Self States: Clinical and Research Illustrations" (Summer 2000), originally appeared in *Clinical Social Work Journal*, 28(2): 197–212. Used with permission of Kluwer Academic/Plenum Publishers.

Chapter 27, "Obsessive-Compulsive Symptomatolgy: A Goal-Directed Response to Anticipated Traumatization?" (Winter 2001), originally appeared in *Psychiaty Interpersonal and Biological Processes*, 64(4): 309–318. Reprinted with permission of The Guilford Press.

Chapter 28, "Early-Onset Schizophrenia: A Literature Review of Empirically Based Interventions" (February 2000), originally appeared in *Child and Adolescent Social Work Journal*, 17(1): 55–69. Used with permission of Kluwer Academic/Plenum Publishers.

Chapter 29, "Domestic Violence in Later Life: An Overview for Health Care Providers" (2002), originally appeared in *Women and Health*, 35 (2/3): 41–54. Used with permission of The Haworth Press, Inc.

Chapter 30, "Homeless Persons with Mental Illness and Their Families: Emerging Issues from Clinical Work" (July/August 2000), originally appeared in *Families in Society*, 81(4): 351–359. Reprinted with permission from *Families in Society* (www.familiesinsociety.org), published by the Alliance for Children and Families.

Chapter 31, "Shyness and Social Phobia: A Social Work Perspective on a Problem in Living" (May 2002), originally appeared in *Health and Social Work*, 27(2): 137–144. Copyright 2002, National Association of Social Workers, Inc., Health and Social Work.

Chapter 32, "Smoking Cessation: Increasing Practice Understanding and Time-Limited Intervention Strategy" (May/June 2000), originally appeared in *Families in Society*, 81(3): 246–255. Reprinted with permission from *Families in Society* (www.familiesinsociety.org), published by the Alliance for Children and Families.

Chapter 33, "Stalking: The Constant Threat of Violence" (Spring 2001), originally appeared in Journal of Women and Social Work, 16(1): 46–65. Reprinted by permission of Sage Publications.

Chapter 34, "Social Work with Clients Contemplating Suicide: Complexity and Ambiguity in the Clinical, Ethical, and Legal Considerations" (Fall 2002), originally appeared in *Clinical Social Work Journal*, 30(3): 265 280. Used with permission of Kluwer Academic/Plenum Publishers.

Chapter 35, "Posttrraumatic Stress Symptoms Following Near-Death Experiences" (July 2001), originally appeared in *American Journal of Or-*

thopsychiatry, 71(3): 368–373. Copyright 2001 by the American Orthopsychiatric Association, Inc., reproduced by permission.

Chapter 36, "Lost Boys: Why Our Sons Turn Violent and How We Can Save Them" (March 2001), originally appeared in *Smith College Studies in Social Work*, 71(2): 168–181.

Chapter 37, "A Descriptive Analysis of Older Adults with HIV/AIDS in California" (November 2001), originally appeared in *Health and Social Work*, 26(4): 226–234. Copyright 2001, National Association of Social Workers, Inc., Health and Social Work.

Chapter 38, "Coping Strategies, Lifestyle Changes, and Pessimism after Open-Heart Surgery" (August 2000), originally appeared in *Health and Social Work*, 25(3): 201–209. Copyright 2001, National Association of Social Workers, Inc., Health and Social Work.

Chapter 39, "The Experience of Deafened Adults: Implications for Rehabilitative Services" (November 2001), originally appeared in *Health and Social Work*, 26(4): 269–276. Copyright 2001, National Association of Social Workers, Inc., Health and Social Work.

Chapter 40, "Challenges of Type 2 Diabetes and Role of Health Care Social Work: A Neglected Area of Practice" (February 2001), originally appeared in *Health and Social Work*, 26(1): 26–37. Copyright 2001, National Association of Social Workers, Inc., Health and Social Work.

Chapter 41, "Dialysis Patient Characteristics and Outcomes: The Complexity of Social Work Practice with the End Stage Renal Disease Population" (2001), originally appeared in *Social Work in Health Care*, 33(3/4): 105–128. Used with permission of The Haworth Press, Inc.

Chapter 42, "Senile Dementia of the Alzheimer Type" (Spring 2002), originally appeared in *Clincial Social Work Journal*, 30(1): 95–110. Used with permission of Kluwer Academic/Plenum Publishers.

Chapter 43, "Africans and Racism in the New Millennium" (November 2001), originally appeared in *Journal of Black Studies*, 32(2): 184–211. Reprinted by permission of Sage Publications.

Chapter 44, "Cultural Determinants in the Treatment of Arab Americans: A Primer for Mainstream Therapists" (April 2000), originally appeared in *American Journal of Orthopsychiatry*, 70(2): 182–191. Copyright 2000 by the American Orthopsychiatric Association, Inc. Reproduced by permission.

Chapter 45, "A Body-Mind-Spirit Model in Health: An Eastern Approach" (2001), originally appeared in *Social Work in Health Care*, 34(3/4): 261–282. Used with permission of The Haworth Press, Inc.

Chapter 46, "Does Social Work Oppress Evangelical Christians? A 'New Class' Analysis of Society and Social Work" (October 2002), originally appeared in Social Work, 47(4): 401–414. Copyright 2002, National Association of Social Workers.

Chapter 47, "Depressive Symptoms in Farm Women: Effects of Health Status and Farming Lifestyle Characteristics, Behaviors, and Beliefs" (June 2002), originally appeared in *Journal of Community Health*, 27(3): 213–228.

Chapter 48, "Social Work with Immigrants and Refugees: Developing a Participation-Based Framework for Anti-Oppressive Practice" (December 2001), originally appeared in *The British Journal of Social Work*, 31(6): 955–960. Used by permission of Oxford University Press.

Chapter 49, "Native Hawaiian Traditional Healing: Culturally Based Interventions for Social Work Practice" (April 2002), originally appeared in *Social Work*, 47(2): 183–192. Copyright 2002, National Association of Social Workers.

Chapter 50, "Cultural and Linguistic Considerations in Psychodiagnosis with Hispanics: The Need for an Empirically Informed Process Model" (January 2001), originally appeared in *Social Work*, 46(1): 39–49. Copyright 2001, National Association of Social Workers.

Chapter 51, "Working with Victims of Persecution: Lessons from Holocaust Survivors" (October 2001), originally appeared in *Social Work*, 46(4): 350–351. Copyright 2001, National Association of Social Workers.

Chapter 52, "Migrants and Their Parents: Caregiving from a Distance" (March 2000), originally appeared in *Journal of Family Issues*, 21(2): 205–224. Reprinted by permission of Sage Publications.

Chapter 53, "Biracial Sensitive Practice: Expanding Social Services to an Invisible Population" (June 2001), originally appeared in *Journal of Sociology and Welfare*, 28(2): 23–36. Reprinted with permission from Western Michigan University School of Social Work.

Chapter 54, "Constructing Ethnicity: Culture and Ethnic Conflict in the New World Disorder" (July 2001), originally appeared in *American Journal of Orthopsychiarty*, 71(3): 281–289. Copyright 2001 by the American Orthopsychiatric Association, Inc. Reproduced by permission.

Chapter 55, "Race and Ethnicity, Nativity, and Issues of Healthcare" (January 2001), originally appeared in *Research on Aging*, 23(1): 3–13. Reprinted by permission of Sage Publications.

Chapter 56, "Racism as a Clinical Syndrome" (January 2000), originally appeared in *American Journal of Orthopsychiatry*, 70(1): 14–27. Copyright 2000 by the American Orthopsychiatric Association, Inc. Reproduced by permission.

Chapter 57, "Constructing a Place for Religion and Spirituality in Psychodynamic Practice" (Summer 2000), originally appeared in *Clinical Social Work Journal*, 28(2): 155–169. Used with permission of Kluwer Academic/Plenum Publishers.

Chapter 58, "Mental Health and Social Justice: Gender, Race, and Psychological Consequences of Unfairness" (September 2002), originally appeared in *The British Journal of Social Work*, 32(6): 779–797. By permission of Oxford University Press.

Chapter 59, "Impact of the Threat of War on Children in Military Families" (April 2001), originally appeared in *American Journal of Orthsychiatry*, 71(2): 236–244. Copyright 2001 by the American Orthopsychiatric Association, Inc. Reproduced by permission.

Chapter 60, "The Financial Vulnerability of People with Disabilities: Assessing Poverty Risks" (March 2001), originally appeared in *Journal of Sociology and Social Welfare*, 28(1): 139–162. Reprinted with permission from Western Michigan University School of Social Work.

Chapter 61, "Changing the Rules: A Board Game Lets Homeless Women Tell Their Stories" (2001), originally appeared in *Social Work with Groups*, 23(4): 25–38. Used with permission of The Haworth Press, Inc.

Chapter 62, "The Use of Crisis Teams in Response to Violent or Critical Incidents in Schools" (March 2001), originally appeared in *Smith College Studies in Social Work*, 71(2): 271–278.

Chapter 63, "Nurturing Life with Dreams: Therapeutic Dream Work with Cancer Patients" (Winter 2001), originally appeared in *Clinical Social Work Journal*, 29(4): 375–385. Used with permission of Kluwer Academic/Plenum Publishers.

Chapter 64, "Using Eye Movement Desensitization and Reprocessing to Enhance Treatment of Couples" (April 2001), originally appeared in *Journal of Marital and Family Therapy*, 27(2): 157–164. Reprinted with permission from American Association for Marriage and Family Therapy.

Chapter 65, "Depression, Existential Family Therapy, and Viktor Frankl's Dimensional Ontology" (March 2001), originally appeared in *Contemporary Family Therapy*, 23(1): 19–32. Used with permission of Kluwer Academic/Plenum Publishers.

Chapter 66, "Food for Thought: The Use of Food in Group Therapy with Children and Adolescents" (January 2002), originally appeared in *International Journal of Group Psychotherapy*, 52(1): 27–47. Reprinted with permission of The Guilford Press.

Chapter 67, "Less Is Best": A Group-Based Treatment Program for Persons with Personality Disorders" (2001), originally appeared in *Social Work with Groups*, 23(4): 71–80. Used with permission of The Haworth Press, Inc.

Chapter 68, "The Harm Reduction Approach Revisited: An International Perspective" (April 2000), originally appeared in *International Social Work*, 43(2): 243–251. Reprinted by permission of Sage Publications.

Chapter 69, "Identifying Human Remains Following an Air Disaster: The Role of Social Work" (2000), originally appeared in *Social Work in Health Care*, 31(4): 85–105. Used with permission of The Haworth Press, Inc.

Chapter 70, "Long-Distance Psychoanalysis" (Spring 2001), originally appeared in *Clinical Social Work Journal*, 29(1): 35–64. Used with permission of Kluwer Academic/Plenum Publishers.

Chapter 71, "Money as a Tool for Negotiating Separateness and Connectedness in the Therapeutic Relationship" (Spring 2001), originally published in *Clinical Social Work Journal*, 29(1): 79–94. Used with permission of Kluwer Academic/Plenum Publishers.

Chapter 72, "A Narrative Perspective on "Doing" for Multiproblem Families" (September/October 2000), originally published in *Families in Society*, 81(5): 475–482. Reprinted with permission from *Families in Society* (www.familiesinsociety.org), published by the Alliance for Children and Families.

Chapter 73, "The Value of Pets in Geriatric Practice: A Program Example" (2001), originally appeared in *Journal of Gerontological Social Work*, 35(2): 99–116. Used with permission of The Haworth Press, Inc.

Chapter 74, "Motivational Enhancement Counseling Strategies in Delivering a Telephone-Based Brief HIV Prevention Intervention" (Fall 2001), originally appeared in *Clinical Social Work Journal*, 29(3): 291–306. Used with permission of Kluwer Academic/Plenum Publishers.

Chapter 75, "Resolving Theraputic Impasses by Using the Supervisor's Countertransference" (Fall 2000), originally appeared in *Clinical Social Work Journal*, 28(3): 263–279. Used with permission of Kluwer Academic/Plenum Publishers.

Chapter 76, "Parent Training via CD-ROM: Using Technology to Disseminate Effective Prevention Practices" (Winter 2000), originally appeared in *Journal of Primary Prevention*, 21(2): 227–252. Used with permission of Kluwer Academic/Plenum Publishers.

Chapter 77, "On Being a Strength Coach: Child Welfare and the Strengths Model" (April 2000), originally appeared in *Child and Adolescent Social Work Journal*, 17(2): 141–153. Used with permission of Kluwer Academic/Plenum Publishers.

Chapter 78, "Evaluation of Yoga and Meditation Trainings with Adolescent Sex Offenders" (April 2000), originally appeared in *Child and Adolescent Social Work Journal*, 17(2): 97–113. Used with permission of Kluwer Academic/Plenum Publishers.

Author Index

Subject Index

by children of divorce,
68–69
of children with externalizing
behavior, 61–65
dysfunctional, 63–65
fatherhood envisioning and,
74–86
by grandparent caregivers,
94, 184–94, 196–204
by mothers with HIV/AIDS,
110–18
of newborn infants, 48–58
poor men's view of
fatherhood and, 88–96
programs and services, 90,
101, 103
top-down view of, 46
Parenting Stress Index, 62
Parenting Wisely (CD-ROM),
755–62
parents
with attention deficit
hyperactivity disorder,
240
children's coming out to,
149, 152, 155
depression and, 655–57
empathy and, 46
infant responsiveness to, 5, 6,
40
lesbians' relationship with,
149–56
maltreated children and,
22–26
military, 599–606
noncustodial, 89–90, 94–95
substance abuse by, 750,
751–52
transnational migrant long-
distance caregiving for,
526–35
See also child rearing; fathers;
mothers; parenting
Parent's Fair Share
Demonstration Project, 90
parent training
barriers to access to, 753–54
family-based, 751–53
via CD-ROM technology,
750, 754–63
Parkinson's disease, 420
paroxetine, 319
PARQ. See Parental Acceptance
and Rejection
Questionnaire

Parsonian theory, 526, 548
*Partial View: An Alzheimer's
Journey* (Henderson), 422
Parti Quebecois, 549
partners, of lesbians, 149–56
"passing-for-white," 542, 543
passion, 70, 71, 72
pastoral counselors, 579
paternal identity, 88–90, 91,
95, 96
paternalism, 348–49, 767
paternity
establishment of, 89, 90
young men's views of, 74,
75, 82, 85
peacekeeping operations, 551,
552
peers
ADHD clients and, 237
adolescent importance of, 28,
36, 37–38
adolescent problem behaviors
and, 29, 33, 37, 751
deafened adults support by,
393
widow group networks of,
209, 211
Pennsylvania, 688
Perinatal Complications Scale,
7, 8
perinatal morbidity, 5, 7, 8, 11,
12
peripheralization, 163
adolescents and, 159–60
peritraumatic dissociation, 357,
358
permanency planning, 96
pernicious anemia, 420
persecution victims, Holocaust
survivor lessons of,
516–24
personal accountability, 560
personal assistance services,
disabled people and, 612,
616
Personal Attributes
Questionnaire, 174
personal emergency systems,
304
personal growth, 461, 462, 621
personality
genetic contributory effect on,
129
Holocaust survivor changes
in, 519

racism and politics of, 563
theories of, 1
personality disorders, 249,
252–53
adolescent sex offenders and,
774
group-based treatment and,
669–73
Personal Responsibility and
Work Opportunity
Reconciliation Act of 1996,
90
Person In Environment, 231,
320–21, 331, 682
pervasive developmental
disorder, 289
pessimism, after open-heart
surgery, 378–85
pesticides, 484, 489, 490
pets
elderly owners of, 719–27
as therapy, 721, 727
PETS Project, 719–27
pharmacotherapy. See drug
therapy
phobias, 252, 317, 594
agoraphobia, 271
homophobia, 172–80
xenophobia, 518, 558,
559
See also social phobia
PHSE. See Piedmont Health
Survey of the Elderly
physical abuse
during childhood, 264
elder abuse and, 299–300
posttraumatic stress disorder
and, 248, 250, 253
physical development,
adolescent maturity and,
33, 35–37
physical problems
Alzheimer's disease, 419–27
deafened adults, 387–93
end-stage renal disease,
407–17
HIV/AIDS in older adults,
369–76
open-heart surgery, 378–85
Type 2 diabetes, 395–403
physician-assisted death, 222
Physician Payment Review
Commission on Monitoring
Access of Medicare
Beneficiaries (AMA), 555